# The BeOS BIBLE

**S C O T  H A C K E R**

**WITH HENRY BORTMAN AND CHRIS HERBORTH**

 **Peachpit Press**

# The BeOS Bible

by Scot Hacker

with Henry Bortman and Chris Herborth

**Peachpit Press**
1249 Eighth Street
Berkeley, CA 94710
(800) 283-9444
(510) 524-2178
(510) 524-2221 (fax)

Find us on the World Wide Web at: **www.peachpit.com**

Peachpit Press is a division of Addison Wesley Longman

Copyright © 1999 by Scot Hacker

**Editor:** Simon Hayes
**Technical Editor:** Chris Herborth
**Copy Editor:** Bill Cassel
**Proofreader:** Jimbo Norrena
**Compositor:** David Van Ness
**Production Coordinator:** Mimi Heft
**Interior and Cover Design:** Mimi Heft
**Index:** Karin Arrigoni

### Notice of rights
All rights reserved. No part of this book may be reproduced or transmitted in any form or by any means, electronic, mechanical, photocopying, recording, or otherwise, without prior written permission of the publisher. For more information on getting permission for reprints and excerpts, contact Gary-Paul Prince at Peachpit Press.

### Notice of liability
The information in this book is distributed on an "As is" basis, without warranty. While every precaution has been taken in the preparation of this book, neither the author nor Peachpit Press shall have any liability to any person or entity with respect to any loss or damage caused or alleged to be caused directly or indirectly by the instructions contained in this book or by the computer software and hardware products described herein.

### Trademarks
Be, BeOS, and the Be and BeOS logos are registered trademarks of Be Incorporated in the United States of America and other countries. All other products and company names mentioned in this book may be trademarks of their respective owners.

ISBN: 0-201-35377-6

0 9 8 7 6 5 4 3 2

Printed and bound in the United States of America

*An oracle at Phrygia declared to the people that their next king would arrive by oxcart. As fate would have it, a poor Greek farmer named Gordius arrived and tied the wagon of his oxcart in the temple of the oracle's god just as the Phrygians were selecting their next king. The people, seeing this, selected Gordius as their ruler.*

*King Gordius tied his cart where it stood with a knot so complex and intricate that no soul would be able to untie it. Legend has it that whomsoever could untie the "Gordian knot" would come to rule all of Asia. Many tried, and many failed.*

*One day, Alexander the Great arrived in town, and was taken with the challenge of the Gordian knot. After trying and failing to untie the knot through conventional means, Alexander drew his sword, and with one swift blow, severed the oxcart from its post.*

The best solution to a complex problem may begin by working downward from perfection, rather than upward from chaos and confusion.

# Contents at a Glance

# Table of Contents

# But wait ... there's more!

As this book was going to press, we lamentably discovered that not all of the coverage that had been produced would physically fit between these covers. In order to deliver the most complete package possible, we decided to include here the chapters that *most* users will find *most* important and to publish the remaining content at this book's Web site, **www.beosbible.com**, where you'll find the following "missing" chapters:

**Scripting**—Expertly written by this book's technical editor, Chris Herborth, nearly 100 pages on BeOS scripting concepts, teaching you how to write bash shell scripts step-by-step and how to take advantage of BeOS's built-in scripting architecture to automate your GUI applications.

**Games**—General coverage of the architectural features of BeOS that make it potentially a killer gaming platform, along with synopses and tips on the most popular BeOS games available at this writing. Much of this chapter was written by contributor John Brajkovic.

**Emulation**—A general discussion of runtime environments (virtual machines) and true emulators, all of which allow you to run other operating systems in a BeOS window. Includes detailed coverage of SheepShaver (the MacOS runtime environment) by contributor Henry Bortman.

**Hardware**—General notes on BeOS hardware considerations, covering both x86 and PowerPC sides of the fence.

**The Kits**—Takes a look "behind the scenes" by examining BeOS as the developer sees it. Not a chapter for developers per se, but an introduction to the architecture of the system in general. For geeks only.

**The Future**—A roadmap for R5, along with educated prognostications on what's in store for BeOS in the next couple of years. Includes a discussion of how and why BeOS is so well-tuned for the coming age of "convergence."

# Acknowledgements

*The BeOS Bible* attempts, where possible, to reflect the spirit and atmosphere of the community of BeOS users and developers. Like any large project, this book has drawn upon resources far more diverse than the list of authors named on the cover, and credit is due to the entire BeOS community.

I must begin by thanking my editor, Simon Hayes, who started bugging me to write a book even before we discovered our common BeOS affinity, who worked with me on the book's outline for six weeks before I typed the first word, who helped to shape the book by sharing liberally his wisdom and experience, who injected suggestions and realism throughout, and who tirelessly managed the myriad details required to turn a manuscript into a book.

Chris Herborth is listed as this book's technical editor but contributed in ways that extend far beyond the sphere normally associated with that role. Chris helped to flesh out this book in uncountable ways, caught me when I slipped, and noted dozens of places where more depth was required. Chris is also single-handedly responsible for this book's scripting chapter, which you'll find online at **www.beosbible.com**. Without Chris on board, this book would simply not be as complete as I hope that it is.

Fellow ex-Ziffian Henry Bortman is responsible for conducting and editing the interviews with Be engineers and employees you'll find in these pages. His ability to ask the right questions of the right people rounds out this book and gives it a behind-the-scenes perspective that would not have been possible through reference content alone. Henry was also responsible for most of the Mac-specific coverage you'll find here.

My gratitude is extended to my copy editor, Bill Cassel, whose exacting professionalism helped to put the final polish on the words between these pages, and to Mimi Heft and David Van Ness who did a fantastic job on the design and layout.

BeOS user John Brajkovic wrote most of the *Games* chapter (also online). John produced a lot of excellent copy very quickly, and I am most grateful for his contributions. BeOS developer Tyler Riti generously volunteered his tutorial on using the Japanese Input Method, a field where I lacked personal experience.

Many BeOS software vendors provided information critical to giving their own applications the depth of coverage they deserved, and you'll find their names at the beginning of each application section to which they contributed. I am most grateful to all of them.

As critical as these contributors have been to this book's completion, the project would not have been possible without the attentiveness, patience, and thoroughness of the staff of Be, Inc., who bore with me through ten months of pestering questions. I can't think of another company as receptive to the needs of the journalist/writer as Be has been throughout the course of these email volleys and in-house visits. Special thanks go to Scott Patterson and Michael Alderete for being my contact points and for parsing my questions out to the appropriate engineers.

My thanks go also to the readers of the beusertalk and bedevtalk mailing lists, the `comp.sys.be.*` usenet hierarchy, and all of the contributors to the BeOS Tip Server. Special thanks to the following individuals for their contributions large and small: Osma Ahvenlampi, Christian Bauer, Daniel Berlin, Richard Burgess, Christian Crumlish, Brian Cully, Nils Dahl, Lars Duening, Dave Haynie, Maarten Hekkelman, Mike Knapp, Braden McGrath, Marco Nellisen, Tyler Riti, David Reid, Frank Seesink, Justin Sherrill, Brian Tietz, Matthew Zahorik, and everyone else who shared tidbits, compared notes, and offered suggestions. The community of BeOS users is a bottomless font of information and inspiration.

Thanks to my family for providing an analog upbringing, to Ryck Lent for finally pushing me off the technology cliff, and to Dan Farber for giving me a BeOS corner on ZDNet. Many thanks to antiweb for helping me to remember that technology must always remain in the service of truth and beauty. And of course, thanks to Jean-Louis Gassée for being willing to face the repo-man in order to create an operating system where truth, beauty, and technology come together.

This book is dedicated to Amy Kubes, who supported me morally and emotionally throughout the process, read and commented on manuscripts, rescued me from malnutrition, and soothed my soul.

# Foreword

*Jean-Louis Gassée*

In the domain of descriptive writing, no topic is more seductive—or more dangerous—than a computer operating system. "Seductive" and "dangerous" are bold words for a clean room of cold facts and unsympathetic crashes. But look at it from the writer's point of view: Every operating system is its own world (and the BeOS is richer than most). The system designers spread the seeds (and, some might say, the manure) so that services and applications can grow and cross-pollinate, creating an environment that doesn't have any clearly marked entrances or exits, that has more than one solution for every problem, and that can be molded—or, better yet, that can mold itself—to the tastes and habits of each user. In describing this world, the writer gets to use the entire arsenal of intelligence and imagination in clearing a sensible, well-bounded path for the reader. At the same time, the writer must acknowledge that there are other paths—some equal, some esoteric, some hidden. Moreover, to adequately describe some areas of the environment—areas that can only be understood when the reader has both the big picture and the little details in mind—the writer must walk a tight rope between over-simplification and over-expansion. Walking this tightrope is the author's continual challenge; staying balanced is his continual responsibility.

The challenge becomes even greater for a book such as this one, where the intended audience spans the gamut of computer users, from programming geeks to those who are less familiar with gagging tools such as "awk" and "grep". The problem is this: How do you keep the geeks interested without losing the humans?

When we heard that Scot Hacker was embarking on the *BeOS Bible* project, we recognized him as one of our most well-reasoned champions and gladly opened our doors to his cadre. They have spent an enormous amount of time working and playing with the BeOS and have interviewed a number of the Be engineers in order to understand, to appreciate—to live in the Be world. Indeed, the *BeOS Bible* team found that one of the best ways to express the personality and charm of the BeOS was through the engineer's own words.

I congratulate Scot Hacker and his contributors for meeting the challenges of writing about the BeOS and for exceeding our greatest expectations in producing their *BeOS Bible*.

# Preface

The publication of this book marks just over two and a half years since BeOS first appeared on my horizon. I've watched and participated as the operating system evolved through a series of developer's releases on the BeBox, to its first public introduction on PowerPC hardware, and finally to the Intel Architecture. BeOS is now in its second official revision on the x86 platform, and release 4 (R4) floats yet another raft of functionality and speed improvements our way. Using BeOS day in and day out has spoiled me rotten. I've become intolerant of any and all delays from a computer, have come to revile the very thought of an hourglass (which does not exist in BeOS), and dread the rare remaining occasions to boot into other operating systems.

My editor, the indefatigable Simon Hayes, had cautioned me about the enormity of a Bible-sized project, and I believed him, but there was no way to really know what it would entail without living through it. The /boot/home/ words/bible folder on my machine contains literally thousands of archived email messages from users, developers, and Be engineers. Hundreds of screenshots were thrown away as interfaces changed and evolved. Exciting BeOS projects we just had to cover appeared on the horizon. Even now, as we go to press, the BeOS world remains a moving target, and it's clear that some of the material in this book will be outdated or superceded before it even hits the shelves. Please forgive me if you encounter material here that's not as up-to-date as it could be, and be sure and check this book's companion Web site at **www.beosbible.com** for updates.

The admiration I've come to hold for the engineers and employees of Be, Inc. and their software is both great and genuine. From one perspective, BeOS is just bits, but it's also so much more than that. BeOS as we know it today is the result of the collective brain-power and inspiration of a few visionaries and dozens of the world's best engineers. When working with this operating system, there comes a point at which you realize you're dealing with more than technology. BeOS is both theory and practice. It's an idea as well as an experience. BeOS is an aesthetic, a way of seeing the whole field of computing, of making good on the many unrealized promises of the computer industry. It is my hope that this book will function as more than a technical reference. To live with and comprehend everything that is BeOS is to uncover a richer, more pleasant, and of course, more powerful way of looking at your computing life. It is my hope that *The BeOS Bible* will help you to enjoy this journey of discovery as much as I have.

—**Scot Hacker**
December, 1998

# Using This Book

Because BeOS is in constant development, and was changing beneath our feet even as we went to press, you'll find the expression "at this writing" used liberally throughout this book. This phrase refers generally to the fall and winter of 1998.

You'll also find many references to BeWare and BeDepot throughout this book, with no URL given. BeWare refers to Be's online software library of freeware and shareware, which you'll find at **www.be.com/beware**. BeDepot refers to Be's electronic commerce online software store, which you'll find at **www.bedepot.com**.

You'll find the following icons spread throughout the book, designating specially noteworthy points in the text:

 Designates text not central to an understanding of the current section, but worth reading for additional information or background.

 **Designates non-obvious features, functions, and capabilities that you probably won't find covered in Be's documentation.**

 **Designates tips for advanced users, or that are just really, really good things to know.**

 Designates techniques or behaviors that can lead to BadThings® happening if you're not careful. Always, always, read the warnings carefully before attempting techniques described in these sections.

# 1

# The MediaOS

With the desktop computer industry entering its third decade, the word "entrenched" barely even begins to describe the dominant market position of today's incumbent. If a great technology leader like Apple Computer barely can hold their footing against the Microsoft marketing machine, what makes a startup like Be, Inc. think they can succeed where others have failed? Never mind kicking Redmond butt—that's never been a part of Be's game plan. But just what makes them think they can even make a dent? What could possibly be more economically insane than embarking on a project to launch a new operating system into the world at this point in the game?

Actually, Be isn't as crazy as some people seem to think, and they've got more than a few aces up their sleeve. For one thing, this dinky little operating system vendor has more amazing technology in their collective little finger than the Jolly Green Gates or the intrepid Jobs have in all of their assembled armies. Second, Be has gotten one thing straight with itself: In a market this big and this full of self-avowed geeks, you don't have to win to succeed. You just have to be sexy enough to turn heads. Third, Be seems to know something about evolution that the other guys don't: You can't do the future if you're still trying to do the past.

Be has one huge advantage that the other guys will never have: They're unencumbered by the crippling requirements of backward compatibility; BeOS in 1999 doesn't need to make sure it's capable of running software written for BeOS in 1979. This, in fact, was the entire impetus behind the creation of the company—starting fresh to avoid the legacy problems that hinder other operating systems. Finally, Be has come to the public just in time to shake hands with a steadily growing class of profoundly dissatisfied computer users—those who've lost patience with crappy technology, those who can no longer stand loyally behind the companies they've taken for granted all these years (or who've taken them for granted) and, most importantly, those who can see just how huge the convergence of high-bandwidth multimedia and desktop computing is going to be in the next millennium.

In this chapter, we'll look at the kinds of users who gravitate to BeOS, and why an alternative to the status quo is becoming increasingly attractive to so many. Because so much of the technological underpinning that makes BeOS great involves industry buzzwords that many people aren't familiar with, we'll run through the collection of amazing technologies that form the system's foundation. Finally, we'll take a look at the history of Be and BeOS, starting from the days when it was a sparkle in a crazy Frenchman's eye and seeing how it grew to become the technology darling it is today.

# The Fed-Up, the Disenfranchised, and the Futurists

New users gravitate to BeOS for a variety of reasons, but these can be broken down into three fundamental categories: those who no longer trust unreliable operating systems, those who feel abandoned by their OS companies, and those interested in futurist computing paradigms.

## The Fed-Up

Many people have simply hit the limits of patience with their existing operating systems. Tired of rebooting their machines after random, mysterious lock-ups, tired of waiting 30 seconds or more for applications to launch, tired of cryptic error messages proffering no human-readable assistance, tired of watching MacOS and Windows sink deeper and deeper into the mire of increasing complexity, this group of users is looking for common sense in an operating system. They're trying to find something that isn't saddled with the weight of supporting the bad decisions of the past.

The burden of backward compatibility causes operating systems to bolt on more and more layers of workarounds so that old software continues to work with newer versions of the OS. After 15 or 20 years of this accretion, the silt that's built up in MacOS and Windows has become thick enough to cut with a knife. Today's operating systems are held together with bailing wire, chewing gum, and hunks of twine. When you think about it, it's actually incredible that they work as well as they do. And when they don't … well, you know. You end up staring at "the blue screen of death," or your friendly neighborhood Error 11 bomb.

Users fed up with this pattern of bad operating system design gravitate to BeOS for a chance to see what it's like when an OS is built logically, with one eye firmly trained on the future, unburdened by the mistakes and demands of the past. With 20 years of desktop computing history to study, Be has been able to scrutinize exactly what's been done wrong and what's been done right in the operating system industry, and has built a company around the philosophy that the only way to get maximum yield out of your hardware while simultaneously delivering a pleasant, consistent, and responsive user experience is to throw it all away and start over from scratch.

# The Disenfranchised

Then there's the group of users I refer to as "the disenfranchised," consisting of people who feel they can no longer support—or are not being supported by—the companies to which they've been loyal for years. People who grew up on DOS and Windows see Microsoft going up against the Department of Justice on charges of anti-competitive business practices while Ralph Nader rallies the troops, and it becomes clear that supporting Microsoft with one's wallet can have some rather unsavory implications. On the other side of the fence, no group of computer users is traditionally more loyal than Macintosh users. But over the past few years, this group has had to stand by and endure the torture of watching one of the coolest operating systems ever get stuck in the sand and tossed back and forth from one bumbling executive to the next, while its market share slips lower and lower. While Macintosh love may take on religious dimensions for some, others aren't so pious that they wouldn't drop the platform in a hot second if something better came along that didn't originate in Redmond. Users of IBM's OS/2 have watched for years as their platform of choice lost one battle after another and suffered from an almost nonexistent marketing campaign. OS/2 users typically feel abandoned by the creators of the platform that was supposed to be "a better DOS than DOS, a better Windows than Windows."

In other words, there are profound problems with all of the companies standing behind the world's major operating systems, and many users are casting about for alternatives. Until recently, the only seriously viable alternatives remaining were Linux, the free variant of Unix created collectively by developers all over the world, and FreeBSD, a similar system that's even more finely tuned for networking. Because Linux is not owned by any corporation, it's exempt from the political and managerial downfalls that plague the other major operating systems. However, the Unix family isn't for everyone. While Linux distributions have made great strides forward recently, and have become far easier to install and configure than ever before, many parts of the system still require familiarity with technical arcana that much of the general public would rather not be bothered by. Using Linux still entails a steep learning curve for those not reared in the ways of the command line. Further, the freedom that the Linux community enjoys has a cost: It's extremely difficult to create unified and consistent user and programming interfaces when thousands of developers are working independently (though advances are being made in the consistency department as well). Finally, Unix-based systems share with other operating systems an origin that stretches decades into the past. While Linux and FreeBSD (for example) have accomplished wonders rising to meet modern computing needs, neither is optimized from the ground up to conquer intensive, futuristic multimedia.

For the disenfranchised user, that pretty much leaves BeOS as the only credible alternative. The technology is fresh and intelligently implemented, and the company is still young and politically unassailable. Because BeOS runs on the majority of desktop systems found at your local computer superstore or ma-and-pa corner tweak shop, BeOS appeals to disenfranchised users coming from both the Mac and PC sides of the fence. Users get the advantages of working with a small company committed to listening and responding to its user base, a combination of a graceful, logical GUI with full Unix command-line power, and the ability to milk their hardware for all it's worth rather than having operating system overhead suck half the life out of it.

## The Futurists

Finally, there are the futurist users. By this I don't mean the people who will be coming to the system in the future (though those are the people whose interest will help Be to flourish), but users who know what the computer of the future will be able to do for us, and who recognize that our current operating systems are not going to be up to the task. The future is high bandwidth, and involves shuffling a whole lot of data around in very little time. The future is cable modems or fiber-optic Internet hookups in every home, pumping millions of bits per second into the system. The future is computer games with as much realism as a movie you'd watch at the theater, with you playing the lead role. The future is multiple 1,000 MHz processors in every desktop computer, enabling users to rent movies over the Web and play them in real time, full-screen, on their computers.

For many people, the approach to BeOS begins with disgruntlement over what's out there, while others feel drawn to check it out just because they appreciate groovy technology. Whether you're installing BeOS because you can't stand the thought of wrestling with one more conflicting DLL, or because you can no longer stand the thought of your operating system vacuuming half the life out of your hardware, or because you don't feel you can give one more ruble to a company you feel behaves unconscionably in the marketplace, or because you just can't wait one more day for tomorrow to get here, you're probably going to end up with operating system religion. Where BeOS is concerned, what starts as an experiment often ends up as an obsession.

## Unchain My Hardware

The future is all about media creation and media consumption. Increasingly, the kinds of special effects seen in multimillion-dollar Hollywood movies can be done on the common household PC. Musicians who once had to fork over beaucoup bucks to rent a few hours in a recording studio can now emulate

## BeOS as a General-Purpose System

While BeOS may be designed with the futurist user foremost in mind, and media creation/consumption may be BeOS's true forte, no one can live inside a system devoid of email, spreadsheets, and word processors. Those applications are staples in every user's daily diet, and you can't do media in a vacuum. Just because BeOS is billed as the MediaOS, that doesn't mean it's somehow suboptimal at handling more mundane chores. A subindustry of productivity applications for BeOS is already beginning to thrive, and users already have a choice of multiple high-quality productivity suites, email packages, and desktop utilities.

So is BeOS only of interest to people who want to create the next *Jurassic Park* in their living rooms? Of course not. Can you still write your research papers, cruise the Web, answer email, and squirrel your important stuff away in spreadsheets and databases with BeOS? Of course. If you think about it, working with multimedia is one of the most resource-intensive things you can do with your computer. The vast majority of our daily tasks currently entail little more than launching and closing programs, switching between tasks, and reading and writing text on a screen. Hardly the stuff that makes modern CPUs break a sweat. On the other hand, full-screen video, knuckle-biting games, real-time video capture, and 3D sound spatialization all require tremendous amounts of resources, both from the computer and from the operating system. So if you build an OS that's optimized for media production and consumption, it pretty much follows that that system will automatically be well-suited to handling more pedestrian tasks. Install a media-oriented OS, and Be throws in a high-performance general-purpose operating system as part of the deal.

Just because you're not using your current operating system to do very much with audio and video right now, that doesn't mean that you won't be soon. Hollywood, Silicon Valley, and your VCR, CD player, stereo system, DVD drive, television, and Web site are all beginning to meet at a single point—your PC. The pundits even have a pet name for this ongoing process: "convergence." Whatever you call it, one thing is certain: It's going to be bandwidth-intensive, CPU-intensive, and operating-system-intensive.

The hardware manufacturers of the world can churn out speedy hardware faster than we—or our wallets—can keep up with. But what good is a 1,000 MHz machine if the operating system you run on it keeps crashing because it's so tangled and bloated? Why order a spanking new Porsche only to install Buick seats and a Volkswagen suspension?

most studio conveniences on a $2,000 Mac or PC. Trouble is, all these grand visions of the computer industry are facing some huge bottlenecks, in the form of the operating systems currently available to the public. No matter how fast our processors and video cards become, we still need an operating system capable of handling multiple simultaneous data streams without clogging up. And while current OSs can do that to a certain degree, none of them are *optimized* for it. BeOS is. Every minute aspect of the operating system,

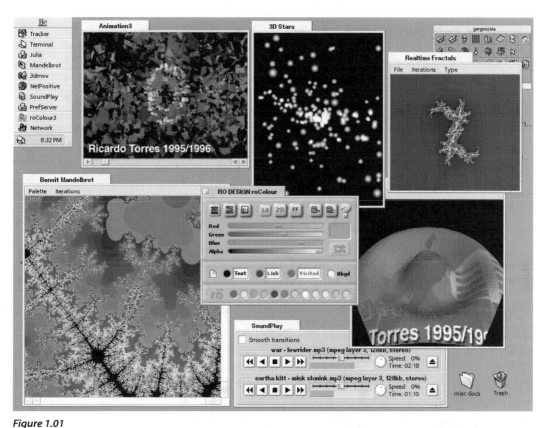

*Figure 1.01*

*BeOS is optimized from the ground up to squeeze every last drop of performance from multimedia applications.*

from the design of the kernel, to the way memory is handled, to the system paths available, to audio and video streams, is fine-tuned to eke out every last drop of performance potential that lurks inside your hardware.

The goal is to create a user experience where the operating system is utterly transparent, so you can concentrate on the media at hand, rather than wrestling with the software and wondering why your sound is all choppy and the video is dropping frames.

To handle media elegantly is the chief design goal that guides all of Be's implementation decisions. In addition to all the buzzwords we'll get to in the next section, this design goal is what really separates BeOS from others in the operating system market. That's why BeOS is often referred to as "the MediaOS."

### *The Rise of the Multi-Boot Environment*

While most of the big hardware manufacturers ship only Windows on every computer they sell, x86 hardware in general is OS-agnostic. Just as you run lots of applications inside one operating system, you can run multiple operating systems on one computer with relative ease, especially with the assistance of boot-management tools like V-Com's System Commander, the freeware LILO, or BeOS's native boot loader, Bootman.

While the idea of reformatting your Windows partitions as BeOS partitions is a noble one, I personally don't think that having BeOS as the only operating system on your hard drive is the right choice for most people. Drive space is cheap, and other OSs have had many, many years in which to build up a library of mature applications. Thanks to a long-forgotten corollary of Murphy's law, it's practically inevitable that the day after you delete your Windows partition you're going to find a reason to wish you still had it.

Fortunately, there's a cottage industry of boot-management and disk-partitioning tool vendors out there that can help you install and run as many operating systems as you like on a single computer (see Chapter 3, *Installation*). Today's partition managers do what once seemed impossible, or at least very difficult or dangerous: resize existing partitions without damaging the data or OSs living on them, so that you can reclaim all that extra space to make way for another operating system. The accomplishments of the boot- and partition-management industry mean there are fewer hurdles than ever for users wanting to experiment.

# The Buzzword-Enabled Operating System

Some operating systems multitask pretty well; others don't. Some implement various degrees of object-oriented design, some are able to take advantage of multiple processors, some have a fully journaled 64-bit filesystem; others … don't. The industry is humming with buzzwords—technical terms that represent the holy grail in certain categories of technology. The problem with adding excellent technology to an existing operating system is that it's exceptionally difficult, if not impossible, to change the fundamental architecture of a system after it's already been constructed and released to the public. Because these technologies lie at the heart of operating systems, rather than being nifty widgets that can be bolted on after the fact, incorporating support for them often means changing the way programs have to be written, or ripping out and replacing the filesystem that governs all of a user's data. Not a trivial matter for systems like MacOS or Windows that were not designed to be fully modular.

Of course, if you build a new operating system from scratch, you have the latitude to do anything you want with it from the outset without shaking things up for your users and developers. This is key to Be's decision to start from scratch and do everything right—no backward compatibility to worry about, and a nice clean slate to work on. With one eye keenly trained on multimedia and futurist computing, Be has done a fantastic job of integrating not just one or two, but pretty much *every* technology considered crucial to modern operating system design. The result is an operating system that stays responsive even under heavy loads, and that seldom makes you wait for *anything* (you'll notice that BeOS has no such concept as the hourglass or ticking watch icons—why should you have to wait?). Because these technologies are implemented and integrated at every level of the system, BeOS is sometimes referred to as "the poor man's SGI"—meaning that ordinary users now have the ability to do the kinds of multimedia computing tricks that a few years ago were only possible on expensive, dedicated, high-end workstations from makers like Silicon Graphics.

Since you'll be hearing a lot of references to these "buzzword" technologies in your dealings with BeOS and the community of BeOS users, let's take a look at each of them and learn how they contribute to the design goals and overall responsiveness of the system. While not everything on this list contributes directly to BeOS's capabilities as a MediaOS, they do all contribute to the system's overall flexibility and power.

## Preemptive Multitasking

It goes without saying that a modern operating system should be capable of doing lots of things at the same time. If you're the only user logged into your machine at a given time, you want to be able to download and decompress files in the background while crunching a database in another workspace and formatting a disk volume or reading and writing your email in the foreground. If your machine is hosting multiple simultaneous users all logged in under different usernames, each user needs to be able to run his or her applications without interference from the others. Whether you've got one CPU or eight of them, your operating system needs a way to share the processor's finite resources fairly and sensibly.

There are two basic models of multitasking: cooperative and preemptive. Cooperative multitasking is found in Windows 3.1 and MacOS, and is handled primarily by the applications; each application needs to be programmed to play nice and give up its access to the processor from time to time to give other tasks a turn. While cooperative multitasking works, it doesn't generally provide the best user experience, since the user can't swap out of a task that's currently hogging the CPU. A familiar example of this is the pre-System 8

MacOS Finder—try copying a 300MB file from one disk to another and then going to use Eudora at the same time. The Finder won't let you switch to another application until it's done with its current operation, and the user doesn't feel in control of the machine.

In preemptive multitasking, all CPU sharing is managed by a component of the operating system called the scheduler, which assigns CPU time to various tasks based on a preestablished set of heuristics (common-sense rules). This way, all applications multitask properly, and neither the programmer nor the user need sweat the details. The result is a system that is far more responsive when multiple tasks are in progress. The drawback is that each time one task relinquishes control to another, the current task must be saved to a known state in memory space so it can pick up again where it left off, and this requires a certain amount of system overhead. However, the advantages gained in a preemptive multitasking system far outweigh the performance cost, and modern CPUs are so fast that the cost is negligible or imperceptible anyway. BeOS and Windows NT are examples of preemptive multitasking systems, and Windows 95 uses a combination of the cooperative and preemptive models (older 16-bit applications are cooperative, while 32-bit applications and DOS applications are preemptive), while the various flavors of Unix have always been preemptive.

Preemptive multitasking in BeOS is implemented automatically and transparently. The only place where the programmer gets involved is in establishing "priorities"—numbers that represent a best guess as to how important the task should be in the overall scheme of things. While defining priorities entails a certain amount of guessing on the programmer's part, common sense prevails pretty well. Developers of programs designed to work in the background will give their applications low priority, so they'll only take up CPU time when the rest of the system is idle. Good examples of low-priority programs are "code crackers" designed to calculate prime numbers or break security codes. These programs don't need to return results immediately; they run for months or years, whenever it's convenient. On the other hand, the last thing you want is for your Web browser to run at a low priority; performance is always of the essence, so relatively high priority numbers are chosen for browsers. Some applications will even let the user establish the priority level.

## Pervasive Multithreading

What's easier—leading a camel through the eye of a needle, or getting a rich man through the gates of heaven? OK, bad analogy, try again. What's easier—pushing grains of sand through the bottleneck of an hourglass, or large rocks?

Most operating systems push a lot of big rocks around, where the rocks are blocks of code on their way to and from the processor. Because of their size, rocks queued up waiting for attention from the processor wait longer for their turn. Wouldn't it be more efficient to use a faster-moving line of really small rocks, or grains of sand, even? The processor wouldn't crunch any faster, but all of your applications would stay more responsive, since all of them would be getting lots of tiny bits of attention all the time.

This is the point of multithreading: Applications' instruction sets are divided up into lots of tiny chunks, or "threads," so that the processor can share her affections among her many suitors more fairly and evenly. The result for the user is that BeOS stays crunchy, even in milk. Or put another way, you can do a whole lot more at the same time with BeOS than you can with other operating systems running on the same hardware. Instead of running instruction sets sequentially, as is the norm, BeOS runs them in parallel. Parallelism is the payoff of multithreading.

Multithreading is at the very heart of BeOS, and is a part of everything it does. Programmers can't write a windowed application that uses less than two threads even if they try; the mere act of creating a window onscreen spawns two threads: one to communicate with the App Server, draw the window and scroll bars, and write to the Deskbar; and one to manage whatever goes on inside that window. In addition, programmers can tell applications to spawn more threads to manage different tasks whenever they like. The threads work together in groups called "teams," and can communicate back and forth with one another, sharing data among themselves via system messages.

 Because multithreading occurs at every level of BeOS, it's said to be "pervasive"—hence the term "pervasive multithreading." Multithreading also works in conjunction with another BeOS buzzword: symmetric multiprocessing. Since applications are broken up into lots of little pieces, the OS can more easily distribute their tasks among multiple processors, if more than one is present. If you've only got one processor, though, don't worry—your threads aren't being wasted. All systems will benefit from multithreading, regardless of the number of processors.

## 64-Bit, Multithreaded, Fully Journaled Filesystem

This buzzword is actually a triple-whammy—you get three buzzwords for the price of one!

**64-Bitness**  If you've been watching the computer industry for more than a few years, you're well aware of the incredibly steep evolutionary curve in the hard-disk price/performance arena. It's hard to imagine that just 10 years ago people were paying major money for 20MB hard drives, and feeling like they had endless acres of space to play in. Ten years before that, mainframe computers with 10MB hard drives cost hundreds of thousands of dollars and were about a meter wide. Today you can pop into your local computer emporium and, for around $250, pick up a 6GB IDE drive that outperforms the most expensive disks available just a few years ago. It just keeps getting better and better for consumers, and there's no end in sight to this pattern. Part of the reason for this cycle is simple supply and demand. Applications and personal data files keep on getting bigger, creating a seemingly endless demand for more storage. This creates an incentive for drive manufacturers to develop more capacity. With bigger hard drives to play on, users think nothing of storing full-length audio and video files, or high-resolution digital images siphoned down from their digital cameras. Pretty soon they need more space again, and so on, and so on …

Trouble is, as home multimedia becomes easier to create and consume, it will very quickly run up against the physical limits of today's filesystems. Even if hard disks are ten times larger two years from now, that won't change the fact that most operating systems use addressing schemes 16 or 32 bits in length, and that address format places limits on the maximum size of files you can store. For instance, FAT32, the filesystem used in Windows 98, cannot store any file larger than 4GB (without resorting to complex technical workarounds). That may sound like a ridiculously large file, but consider this: If you took your average videotape and digitized all 90 minutes of it to your hard disk, you'd end up with a 3GB file. Thus, a 120-minute movie consumes 4GB or more, and may be too large to store on any hard drive attached to a Windows 98 machine, regardless of disk size. To complete the process of blowing your mind, consider that these numbers refer to *compressed* video, such as that stored in MPEG format. Prior to compression, a two-hour movie can consume as much as 300GB of disk space.

### Table 1.1  Data Sizes

| Data | Size |
| --- | --- |
| Average productivity file | .1MB |
| One hour of digital video | 600MB |
| One hour of compressed video | 2,000MB |
| Two hours of high-definition compressed video | 5,000MB |
| Two hours of uncompressed D1 video | 300,000MB |

*Disks are getting larger by the year, partly because the media we're consuming is so data-intensive. However, there's a theoretical limit to the size of files that can be stored with 32-bit filesystems. BeOS's 64-bit filesystem has a maximum file size of 18,000 petabytes. See the sidebar* How Big Was That File Again?

## How Big Was That File Again?

Trying to visualize the size of an 18,000-petabyte file is like trying to wrap your mind around the U.S. national debt—it's almost inconceivably huge. The average hard drive shipping in the average high-end consumer system at the time of this writing was 6GB. If it were 1,000 times larger, it would be 6 terabytes. one thousand times larger than that and it would be 6 petabytes. One thousand times larger than that and it would be 6,000 petabytes. Three times larger than that and it would be 18,000 petabytes, or equal to the maximum size for a file that can stored on a BeOS volume. Thus, BeOS can store a single file that's 1,000 x 1,000 x 1,000 x 3, or 3,000,000,000, or three billion times larger than today's "large" hard drive.

To put it in perspective another way, consider the facts put forth in a rather speculative essay in *Scientific American*, July, 1998. In this piece, the authors attempt to quantify the sum total—in bytes—of humanity's recorded information. It's estimated that the ancient library at Alexandria contained 600,000 scrolls, equal to around 50,000 of today's books. The Library of Congress contains around 20,000,000 books, worth a total of around 20 terabytes in raw data, plus several petabytes of audio data. Humans create around 100 terabytes per year in new books and newspapers, while a century's worth of movies add about a petabyte to the running total. Throw in 50 billion of our family snapshots every year, and you add around 10 more petabytes since the dawn of the camera. Television contributes around 100 petabytes per year, and telephony several thousand petabytes annually. Note here that not everything on this list is recorded in a retrievable form. In fact, subtract the telephony part, and the sum total of humanity's recorded data amounts to around 100 petabytes—a fraction of the data that your BeOS system could store easily in a single file.

These kinds of restraints clearly won't do for an OS calling itself the MediaOS, so Be did the only intelligent thing it could do, and used a 64-bit addressing scheme in the Be Filesystem, or BFS. Result? The maximum file size in BFS is around 18,000 petabytes—probably enough to store the cumulative total of all the data human beings have ever recorded in a single file (see the sidebar *How Big Was That File Again?*). The last time I checked the shelves at ComputerTown, drives this large were either out of stock or had not yet been invented. I'm betting it's the latter. BeOS should be safe from file-size limitations for a long time to come.

**Journaling**    To save on operational overhead, operating systems typically don't commit every little transaction (or read/write operation) to disk immediately. Instead, changes are stored in system memory for a while, and then written to disk periodically, usually when the system is idle. The problem with this method is that if someone walks behind your desk and accidentally kicks the plug out of your computer, it's going to take much longer to boot up again, since the system has to do a lengthy check to get all of its bits back into the right buckets.

BeOS, however, uses a system journal to keep track of all transactions. The journal's job is to keep the filesystem in a "constant state," where all possible variables are known and recorded at all times, including such niceties as the positions of all your windows and Tracker views, so that these things can be easily restored on the next reboot. Since the journal is kept in real time, if your system loses power suddenly or otherwise crashes or locks up, all of the unlogged data simply gets read in from the journal, resulting in boot times after crashes that are almost as fast as rebooting after a normal shutdown—the difference is nearly imperceptible.

Plus, journaling ensures much better data integrity. While non-journaled systems are usually pretty good at recovering uncommitted data, power outages can and do result in data loss for them. In a world where a few bytes can mean that your bank account does or does not record your last deposit, or the difference between a working file and a corrupt one, this kind of reliability is increasingly critical. Journaling thus makes BeOS an even better candidate for high-end implementations where any risk is an unacceptable risk. You can learn more about BeOS's filesystem journal in Chapter 5, *Files and the Tracker*.

**Multithreading**  As described earlier, BeOS is "pervasively multithreaded," meaning that it breaks up large tasks into lots of tiny tasks, thereby increasing the flow rate of data through the system while simultaneously reducing the time that tasks must wait before their requests are handled by the processor. Multithreading applies as much to the way BeOS addresses disk volumes as it does to the rest of the operating system, working to squeeze every last drop of potential out of your hard drive and ensure optimum disk throughput even when running multiple disk-intensive tasks simultaneously.

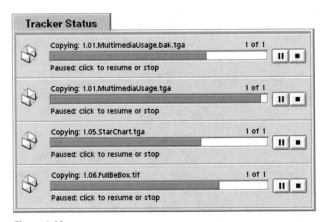

*Figure 1.02*

*BeOS's multithreaded nature is extended to the filesystem, making it possible to throw multiple disk-intensive tasks at the hard disk simultaneously. Pictured are four simultaneous move/copy operations.*

# Client/Server Architecture

"Client/server" is a buzzword that's been floating around for many years, and has as many different meanings as it has contexts. In its broadest definition, client/server refers to situations where you have some kind of master hardware or software located centrally, and lots of "receivers" for the data generated by the master. For example, in a networked office, you might have one big, fast computer storing all of your company's shared files, running the office email system, and keeping traffic logs up to date. That's the server. Each employee has a desktop computer attached to the network, sending and receiving information to and from the central hub. The employees' computers are the clients.

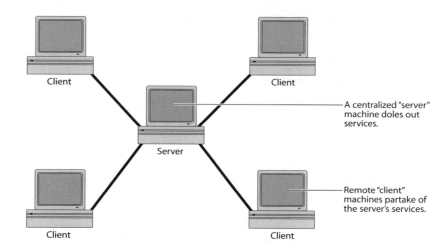

*Figure 1.03*

*In a traditional client/server network situation, a centrally located computer acts as the "hub" of a wheel, doling out data to the (usually smaller) computers attached to it.*

However, that's not the kind of client/server architecture we're referring to in relation to BeOS. When the term is applied in a pure software context, it generally refers to some kind of data service being handled by a "server" program, while lots of "client" programs take advantage of that service. The nice thing about this kind of system is that the clients don't all have to eat up CPU cycles and memory doing redundant work, so they can turn all their attention to doing what they do best.

In the case of BeOS, core functions are broken up into major service categories such as networking, applications, media, storage, the Tracker, and others. Each category has its own server, responsible for handling the core functionality for that category and passing it on to clients that request it. In most cases, the clients are applications. As an example, consider the act of launching a text editor. The editor requires two basic things: 1) a window with scrollbars, pull-down menus, and an entry in the Deskbar, and 2) text-editing functionality. Rather than having the text editor worry about how to draw windows onscreen, BeOS gives that responsibility to the system's "app_server" so the

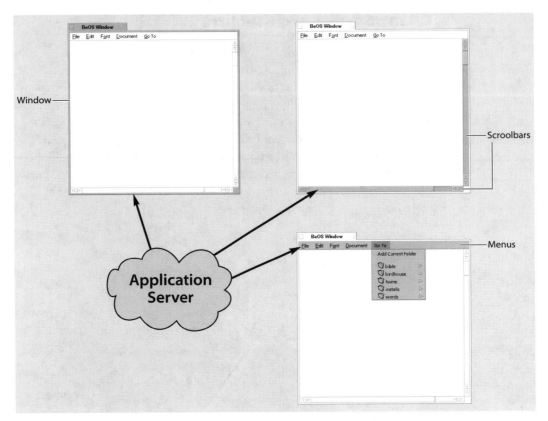

*Figure 1.04*

*In a pure software context, the server is not a machine, but a program or application that doles out services (such as audio or networking) to "client" applications. For example, the BeOS Application Server takes care of the work of drawing windows and menus for programs that need them.*

editor can dedicate itself to the job of editing rather than drawing windows. If you've got 15 applications open at once, all of them are having their windows drawn and managed by the App Server; hence the client/server nomenclature.

Another important thing to note about the system servers is that they're modular. Whereas most operating systems build these kinds of services into the kernel itself, in BeOS the servers exist as separate files. That means that more servers can easily be added to the system in the future, should the need arise. Programmers refer to the general categories of services offered by the servers as "Kits"—the Media Kit, the Networking Kit, etc. You can read more about BeOS's Kits at **http://www.beosbible.com**.

Building an operating system on client/server principles makes it possible to take some of the grunt work out of developers' hands, to ensure consistency throughout the system, and to distribute system resources in the most efficient way.

# Data Interchange and Scripting

Applications in a futuristic operating system need to be able to communicate with one another: to share data, affect each other's behavior, exchange information, and in general operate together smoothly and easily. Without a data-sharing mechanism, it would not be possible to Do The Right Thing™ with bits and pieces dragged out of one application and into another. Nor would it be possible to give scripting systems the ability to automate tasks effectively.

BeOS includes an excellent data-interchange infrastructure based on a programmer's construct called "BMessages." BMessages are discrete packets of information that can be transferred from one application to another. All applications can be built to both transmit and receive BMessages, and applications can decide for themselves what to do with the messages they receive.

For an example of BMessages in action, consider the third-party roColour color manager. Drag the RGB sliders around to create a custom color, then drag that color to your Desktop—the Desktop's color immediately changes to match the one you picked in roColour. Now open up StyledEdit and drag the same color swatch from roColour into StyledEdit—StyledEdit inserts the hexadecimal value of that color, a great boon to people like Web developers, who don't necessarily speak hex. The important thing to note here is that neither the Desktop nor StyledEdit is specifically programmed to accept dropped BMessages from roColour; they simply know how to receive color information from other applications, and they each decide what to do with those messages once

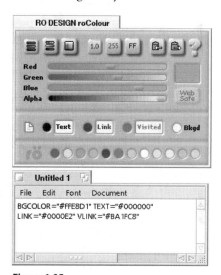

**Figure 1.05**

*Colors dragged out of roColour are encapsulated in BMessages. Applications receiving BMessages respond to them differently: you can change the color of the Desktop or insert a hex value into your editor, for example.*

they've been received. Imagine this kind of interapplication communication extended to every aspect of the operating system and you begin to get an idea of just how powerful this infrastructure can be.

BeOS's data-interchange system becomes even more powerful when coupled with its built-in scripting architecture. No, BeOS doesn't provide a full-blown scripting solution like Apple's AppleScript or OS/2's REXX. Be sees this kind of thing as an excellent opportunity for third parties, and doesn't want to dictate the capabilities or instruction set for such an important feature. Instead, Be has opted to provide an excellent architecture in which third-party developers can build their own scripting solutions. This not only gives the free market the opportunity to sort out a winner for itself, but enables multiple solutions to work in the same operating system so that users can choose the solution that's best for their needs.

 Because BeOS provides a scripting *architecture* rather than a scripting *solution*, you can use any scripting language with any BeOS application. In fact, the scripting language and the applications don't have to know anything about each other, nor do applications have to be written with scripting in mind! Rudimentary scripting is built into *every* BeOS application, courtesy of the BeOS Kits.

What Be *has* done is to incorporate "hooks" into most every aspect of the operating system, and allowed applications to define their own hooks. Think of these hooks as if they were little transmitter/receiver stations with unique names; each one represents an aspect of a program, like the names of the entries on a pulldown menu, or the currently selected cell in a spreadsheet. An application can tell the operating system the names of its available hooks, and scripts can send BMessages to and receive BMessages from the hooks. Because the hooks are independent of all scripting languages, developers can either port existing scripting languages to BeOS or create their own from scratch. The system stays wide open, doesn't endorse any particular scripting solution over any other, and is equally receptive to all of them. You can learn more about scripting on the *BeOS Bible* Web site at **http://www.beosbible.com**.

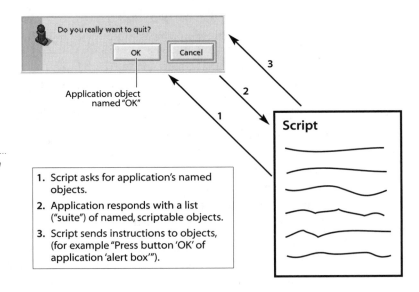

**Figure 1.06**

*Every application in BeOS includes "scripting hooks" attached to its objects. Scripts of any kind can learn the names of these hooks and then send instructions to them.*

1. Script asks for application's named objects.

2. Application responds with a list ("suite") of named, scriptable objects.

3. Script sends instructions to objects, (for example "Press button 'OK' of application 'alert box'").

## Database-Like Filesystem

One of Jean-Louis Gassée's early concepts for a futuristic operating system was to use an actual database for the filesystem (see *The History of Be, Inc.*, later in this chapter). An operating system built on top of a database would be capable of feats undreamed of in existing operating systems. BeOS used a real database as its filesystem until DR8. At that point, however, it became apparent that maintaining a full relational database at the foundation of the OS was a heinously complex task, entailing too many performance compromises. The filesystem was rewritten from the ground up for DR9, and the true database was replaced with a *database-like* filesystem. This resulted in much better performance for the entire system, while sacrificing very little in potential functionality. For most intents and purposes, the filesystem still functions like a database, and the current model can indeed perform many feats undreamed of in other OSs.

Rather than the filesystem being laid out as a complex system of tables and grids, as would be the case in a true database, the hierarchy of folders and files takes a more traditional form. However, every file in the BeOS filesystem can also sport any number of "attributes," which you can envision as being little buckets hanging off of each file, containing any amount or kind of data. Just as you would search through a database using complex combinations of criteria, the system's collection of attributes can be searched and results returned in a user-friendly Tracker display. The advantages here are twofold: The system can be searched much as you would search through a full-blown database, and performance can be maintained because system queries don't have to examine every single file individually, looking instead at a single "pool" of attributes. You can learn more about system queries in Chapter 7, *Working With Queries*.

## Direct Graphics Access

Traditionally, when an operating system is writing video information to the screen, it's capturing every frame of information, preprocessing it, sending it to the video card hardware, and then waiting to receive the final image back from the video card so it can be displayed inside the appropriate window. When you watch a video clip on your computer, this process could be happening 30 times per second, and incurs a whole lot of operating system overhead, which in turn results in a less responsive system. Recent advances in the industry, however, have made it possible to largely bypass the role of the operating system in this process, so video information can be sent directly into the guts of the video card and bounced back to the screen, incurring almost no operating system overhead and offering much higher frame rates on the same hardware. The process of sending data straight to the heart of the video card is

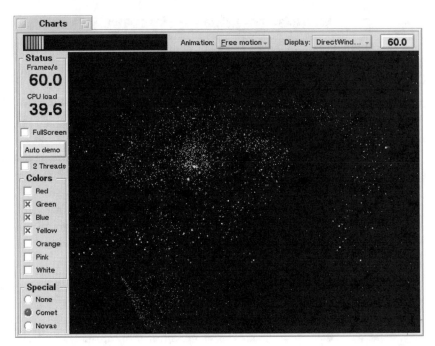

*Figure 1.07*

*For an awesome glimpse of the power of BDirectWindow, check out the Chart demo in your demos folder. Control every parameter of your flight through the galaxies while you compare the performance of standard bitmapped screen-drawing techniques with BDirectWindow techniques. The difference is jaw-dropping.*

called Direct Memory Access, or DMA, and the aspect of the BeOS API that programmers use to access this functionality is called BDirectWindow. While DMA techniques exist in various forms in other operating systems, DMA is far easier for programmers to implement in BeOS, which means that more programmers will avail themselves of it, which means that more of your multimedia software will be running at peak performance.

While programmers do have to take extra steps to avail themselves of BDirectWindow's potential, most find it worth their while, as performance is boosted dramatically while CPU use is correspondingly decreased. The user has a better experience and the system stays more responsive.

## Dynamically Loadable Device Drivers

Chances are you've grown accustomed over the years to rebooting your machine every time you make a major (or even minor) change to your system configuration. Until recently, Windows users had to reboot every time they wanted to make a change to their screen resolution or bit depth (most video drivers can now work around this problem). Setting up a network meant rebooting every time you changed your IP address or DNS settings, or added or removed network protocols. And support for alien filesystems (e.g. a MacOS machine being able to read IBM-formatted floppies) is close to nonexistent in most operating systems.

BeOS, however, incorporates the notion of "dynamically loadable device drivers," which means that the system can be told to load a given driver on the fly and just keep on humming, no reboot required. To give BeOS the ability to read disk drives formatted under other systems, you just drop a driver for that system into the Tracker's add-ons directory and then tell the Tracker to rescan for mountable disks. Bingo—the new filesystem is loaded, no reboot required. Change your IP address or any other parameter in the Network preferences panel and click the Restart Networking button—your changes take effect immediately.

Since every aspect of the operating system can avail itself of these dynamically loadable drivers and modules, downtime is kept to a minimum. In fact, BeOS is so stable, and required reboots are so rare, that you may never have to reboot your system if you don't want to, unless of course you need to open the case to swap I/O cards for some reason. I've personally left my BeOS machine on for weeks at a time without a single reboot, and stability is even more impressive in R4.

The ability to load device drivers dynamically doesn't stop with add-on filesystems or network modules. Adding drivers of all kinds to BeOS is as simple as dropping a file into a directory. Boom—you've got scanner support. Boom—your pen input device is working. Boom—you've got ISDN.

We'll take a closer look at dynamically loadable drivers in action when we look at Tracker add-ons, which make it as easy for developers to extend the capabilities of the Tracker itself as it is to add a plug-in to Photoshop.

## Object Orientation

Here's one you've no doubt heard plenty about. "Object orientation" is a programming concept that enables developers to treat code blocks as reusable, recyclable chunks containing properties and characteristics that can be passed on to or inherited from other objects. Theoretically, object-oriented programming, or OOP, can cut down on development times and result in smaller, faster programs with a cleaner, more scalable architecture.

Suffice it to say that BeOS is object-oriented from the ground up, both in the system code and in the application programming environment. In addition, BeOS's entire API (application programming interface) is clean, well laid out, and mostly free of the kazillion headaches that make programming for MacOS or Windows an unpleasant chore for many. For end-users, all of this means that

### *How OOP Works*

The classic illustration of object-oriented programming concepts uses the architecture of vehicles as an example. "Things with wheels" is a meta-class that encompasses cars, trucks, vans, and motorcycles—all of these vehicles inherit the quality of having wheels from the meta-class. One subclass of "Things with wheels" is "Things with four wheels," or "cars," while another subclass is "Things with two wheels," which includes bikes and motorcycles. The class of cars spawns particular cars—your New Beetle and your neighbor's Vega, for instance.

So let's say you're a developer and you want your program to perform Task B and Task C. Task C is similar to Task B, but has some small differences. Rather than writing separate code for B and C, you would first write Task A, embracing the lowest common denominator of the functions between the two. When it comes time to invoke B or C, you would simply indicate that B and C "inherit" the properties of A, and then specify the areas where they differ. In another OOP scenario, Task C could itself be derived from the properties of Task B, which in turn derives—or inherits—from Task A.

In reality, OOP is a lot more complex than that, but this isn't a programmer's guide, so we'll pass over the details.

applications and upgrades can be developed and moved to market more quickly. A clean OOP model also has the benefit of attracting developers who are fed up with the programming headaches of MacOS, Windows, and the Unix variants, which in turn means more applications—and more creative applications—for you. You can learn more about programming for BeOS in Appendix D.

Object orientation in BeOS doesn't stop at the programmer's desk, however. Recall the discussion earlier in this chapter about BeOS's client/server model, which allows applications to inherit basic system services from servers running in the background. Or consider the file-format Translators (Chapter 9, *Preferences and Customizations*). These allow applications to read certain file formats, such as RTF documents or TIFF images, by looking to a single translation library stored in a central location in the OS. Because of the Translators' object-oriented implementation, you can extend the capabilities of many applications at once by simply downloading extra Translators. You'll find object-oriented design concepts laced through many aspects of BeOS, and in every instance, either you or the developer of your application benefit from increased efficiency, simplicity, and logic.

## POSIX Compliance

Even though BeOS has its own API and requires that programs be compiled specifically for BeOS, it also comes bundled with hundreds of ports of common Unix command-line tools. Compiling command-line Unix tools to run on BeOS is relatively easy to do because the system is "POSIX-compliant," meaning that it conforms to a standard set of commands defined by the Institute of Electrical and Electronics Engineers. The point of the POSIX standard is to make it possible to compile any POSIX-compliant application on any POSIX-compliant operating system. Similarly, shell scripts written on one POSIX-compliant system will able to run on any other POSIX-compliant system (though certain path statements may need to be tweaked somewhat).

 The term "POSIX-compliant" is used liberally here, as POSIX in BeOS is not all the way there yet. While hundreds of POSIX tools have been compiled for BeOS, and POSIX is implemented fairly thoroughly, BeOS itself does not yet pass the suite of compliance tests that would bring it 100% POSIX certification. While certification would be nice, it's not deemed as critical to Be as, say, writing lots of high-quality SCSI and video drivers. First things first.

## BeOS Ain't Unix

Despite rampant misconceptions about what BeOS is and is not, understand this: BeOS is not a Unix-based operating system. If you read something somewhere that says it is—and you probably will eventually—ignore it, or better yet, write to the author and set him or her straight. This common misconception is probably caused by BeOS's Terminal application, which allows users to operate many aspects of the system from a bash shell using common Unix commands. But having a bash shell doesn't make BeOS a Unix-based operating system any more than being able to use a Portuguese-English dictionary makes you Brazilian.

While POSIX derives its commands from Unix, being POSIX-compliant does not make a system a Unix system. BeOS is one of several POSIX-compliant operating systems that are not themselves based in Unix. One of the telltale distinctions is that Unix-based systems can typically boot into command-line mode without ever launching a GUI; BeOS cannot. Most aspects of Unix-based operating systems can also be configured from the command line. While some of BeOS's settings can be tweaked by editing various configuration files via command-line editors, most of them cannot. For instance, there is no way to adjust your screen resolution or bit depth from the command line in BeOS—you have to use the Screen preferences panel.

POSIX compliance does, however, give BeOS a lot of Unix-like functionality. Users migrating from Unix systems can continue to use most of the commands they've used all along. Not only that, but hundreds of command-line tools and utilities can easily be ported to BeOS by simply being recompiled. BeOS comes bundled with a ton of these, and many hundreds more are available in the Geek Gadgets toolkit, available at **ftp://ftp.ninemoons.com/gg/**. Learn more about the BeOS command line in Chapter 6, *The Terminal*.

# Processor Agnosticism and Portability

If you attach a two-button mouse to a PowerMac, install BeOS, and stick the machine out of sight under the table, you'll be pretty hard-pressed to tell whether you're running BeOS on Apple or IBM hardware. Be has tried— successfully—to make BeOS run identically no matter what hardware it's running on. In just a few years, BeOS has been ported to four different hardware platforms: the original Hobbit processor, the BeBox (a custom PowerPC system), the PowerMac (Apple's PowerPC systems), and the Intel Architecture. While Be doesn't have any current plans to port the system to more exotic hardware like the Alpha or Sparc (it's a pretty tough business case to make, in terms of potential market size), doing so would probably not require substantially more work than did the prior ports. The PowerMac port was accomplished in an incredibly short period of time (remember that the BeBox also used PowerPC processors). The Intel port took considerably longer, and Be received technical assistance from Intel engineers, but much of this time was spent figuring out ways to support the incredible array of competing hardware in the Intel world. Regardless, the Intel port took less time than it would take to port other operating systems to alien hardware.

While Be has not yet made any specific announcements about other forthcoming ports, we do know that Be has succeeded in squishing down the OS to its most compact essentials, and has actually been able to store a minimal, bootable version of the system on a single floppy! Whether this experiment was simply a self-challenge or introductory research leading toward grander plans is hard to say at this point, but keep your eye on the horizon for more on minimal versions of BeOS.

Despite their roots in PowerPC-land, Be and BeOS are officially "processor agnostic." They care about delivering an excellent user experience, not about promoting or favoring one hardware configuration or another. Be provides a software-based environment that they'd like to run on as many of the world's desktop computers as possible; the hardware you use is a personal choice. (See the sidebar *PowerPC versus Intel*.)

 While BeOS isn't the first operating system in the world to run on totally different computer architectures, it's been able to do so with less effort and fewer headaches than most others thanks to its extremely clean code foundation. In fact, approximately 95% of BeOS's system code is written in plain old unadulterated C, a platform-neutral programming language. A dash of assembly language is thrown in at the lowest levels for speed.

Your user experience is dictated almost entirely by the operating system and applications you use, not the hardware you're running on (assuming that your hardware isn't old and slow, of course). As Joe Palmer, creator of the BeBox,

## *PowerPC versus Intel*

Some users speak of their hardware in almost religious terms, proclaiming the superiority of either the PowerPC or the Intel Architecture in loud, public, sometimes self-righteous tones.

PowerPC advocates point to superior clock speeds, noting benchmark tests that show PPC winning in pure number-crunching tests again and again. Because of the PPC's emphasis on floating-point operations, this claim is correct—in terms of the chip alone, PowerPC will always deliver more clock cycles, run cooler, occupy less physical space, and shine more brightly in tests like Photoshop filters that involve a lot of pure math.

Intel Architecture advocates point to the fact that x86 chips aren't all that far behind in the speed game, but more importantly, the Intel world is an arena of intense competition, where competing vendors take turns besting each other to win an edge in the market. This competition has resulted in a far more pronounced evolution of the rest of the subsystems that live in the box alongside x86 processors. x86 memory speeds, bus speeds, video speeds, and disk-controller speeds all outstrip their PowerPC counterparts. Because a computer is so much more than a processor, the importance of these subsystems should not be underestimated. Everything in the box contributes to an overall perception of responsiveness, or lack thereof. As a result, equivalently priced Intel-based systems tend to perform better overall than PowerPC machines, and are in general more responsive under stress … as long as you're running BeOS!

Regardless, many people appreciate the consistency, elegance, and simplicity of hardware design in the PowerPC world, and rightly so. When one company controls the specifications for an entire platform, the kind of chaos that rules the Intel hardware world is avoided.

There's another dimension to this puzzle as well. The characteristics that once separated RISC (PPC) and CISC (x86) processors are now showing up on either side of the fence. The PowerPC now utilizes complex addressing modes and multiply/divide instructions like its CISC cousins, and the CISC family of processors has borrowed so many concepts from RISC that some people say there's actually a RISC processor at the heart of every CISC chip. Everything is a hybrid now, and it's no more possible to say that a chip is pure RISC or pure CISC than it is to say that a person is "100% American"—it just doesn't make sense.

However, the entire argument is growing moot as far as BeOS is concerned. In order for BeOS to run on PowerPC machines, Be needs hardware technical specifications from Apple—not for the G3 or G4 chips themselves, which is relatively easy to do, but for the motherboard and onboard chips that ship in these machines. But ever since the release of the G3 Macintosh, Apple has declined to supply these specs to Be. As a result, BeOS won't run on G3 Macs (unless you install a G3 chip on an upgrade card). While Be could technically reverse-engineer the specs, as the Linux community has, that's a hacker's gambit, not the behavior of a company looking for respect in the marketplace. On the other hand, Intel has been more than willing to dance with Be, providing all the support needed to let BeOS add value to their hardware. If something doesn't give soon, BeOS's days on PowerPC hardware are probably numbered.

once said, "It's dark in the box." In other words, people interact with an interface, not a processor. And that interface is provided by the operating system, not by the hardware.

## Protected Memory

If you want to be the Jackie Chan of operating systems, you have to be more than nimble, talented, flexible, and fast; you also have to be able to recover from slip-ups when things go wrong. While BeOS itself is both strong and light on its feet, there's nothing Be can do to stop programmers from releasing unfinished or buggy code into the world, and buggy code crashes, no matter what operating system it's running on. The question is, what happens to the operating system itself when programs go down? If you've been using MacOS or Windows 3.1, the answer is usually the same: The whole system goes down along with the broken app. On the other hand, if you're a user of Linux, you can probably count on one hand the number of times you've seen your system crash completely. NT users see more crashes than do Linux or BSD users, but it's still a pretty rare occurrence for most users. Windows 95/98 users end up somewhere in between, with system crashes being fairly rare, but not unheard of.

The stability difference between these systems involves many factors, from the lowest levels of the system architecture to the kinds of programs being run on them. But one of the most critical aspects of operating system stability is memory protection. When you launch a program, part or all of it is loaded into RAM. When you launch a second program, it's also loaded into RAM. So how does the operating system decide which parts of your system memory are allocated to each application? How is the memory space partitioned? What guarantees are there that no single application is allowed to stomp all over memory space that's supposed to belong to another app?

How the OS handles this situation becomes critical when an application decides to go south. Just as the laws of physics dictate that two cars on the highway cannot occupy the same space at the same time without causing a disaster, operating systems will crash and burn any time two applications try to access the same memory address at the same time. Memory-protected operating systems erect inviolable walls between memory spaces in order to prevent such collisions. As a result, applications in memory-protected operating systems can crash all they want, and the system and other applications will keep on humming along. This protects both your data and your patience.

The implementation of memory protection on BeOS, while not particularly different from those on other true memory-protected OSs, is elegant, simple, and reliable.

# Symmetric Multiprocessing

*"One processor per person is not enough."*
*—Early Be marketing slogan*

If an OS is capable of using multiple processors, operating system tasks can be broken up into pieces and parceled out to the available processors. If one CPU is busy, the current task will be sent to the other(s). This process occurs automatically and continuously, to achieve the best possible perform-ance at any given instant. Since the multiprocessing is distributed evenly and automatically, it's called "symmetric multiprocessing," or SMP for short. These multiple "pieces" are the "threads" discussed earlier.

Only a few of today's operating systems can take advantage of multiple processors. Microsoft's Windows NT and future versions of Apple's MacOS X (as it was called at this writing) can, but applications must be specifically written with more than one processor in mind (or to be multithreaded, in the case of NT)—a drag for developers. Windows 95 and 98 and MacOS 8.x simply ignore any processors beyond the first. Furthermore, Windows NT doesn't take full advantage of extra processors even when applications *are* written to take advantage of them. Only 80% (approximately) of the second CPU is used, with the difference being wasted in the operating system over-head it takes just to control the second chip. This puts a serious crimp in the multiprocessor board market, and leaves many users unconvinced about the advantages of SMP.

## *Sense, Sensibility, and Multiple Processors*

Despite the fact that processors are many times more powerful now than they were when Be first started toying with the multiple-Hobbit concept, the same basic philosophy should still guide your purchasing decision if you're going to buy new hardware just for BeOS: You get a lot more bang for the buck when you go with multiple, slightly slower processors than you do when shelling out big bread for one of the latest and greatest. The chip industry moves at a remarkable clip, introducing its fastest chips at a premium price every few months. And every time it does, the price of the previous fastest chip drops like a rock. At the time of this writing, a machine sporting two 300 MHz Pentium II CPUs cost only $150 more than a nearly identical machine from the same manufacturer with a single 350 MHz chip. You do the math—it's almost always more sensible to buy more of last month's *chip du jour* than fewer of today's hottest … assuming that your operating system can take full advantage of them. BeOS can and does.

Remember too that the thrill of having the fastest chip on the block will never last more than a couple of months—you can't win the clock-speed race indefinitely, so you may as well make the most sensible purchase you can, and drop the money you save into things that will actually make a difference in your daily tasks, like more RAM, a better monitor, an array of 10,000 rpm Ultra3/wide SCSI disks, or a new printer or scanner.

BeOS, on the other hand, had multiple processors in mind from its earliest incarnations. BeOS's very first incarnation was on hand-built, never-released computers equipped with multiple AT&T Hobbit chips. At around $50 each, the Hobbits were incredibly cheap and reasonably powerful (see *The History of Be, Inc.*, below). The thinking here was that if an operating system could take full advantage of all the processors in the system, users would get more bang for the buck by taking lots of very cheap, somewhat slower chips, and using all that power additively. Thus, a machine sporting four 100 MHz chips would have a full 400 MHz of speed for only $200, at a time when 400 MHz chips didn't exist in the consumer markets and multiprocessor motherboards were simply unavailable to the average user.

When AT&T discontinued the Hobbit, Be applied the same logic to their next machine—the BeBox—which used multiple PowerPC 603 chips. The 603s weren't top-of-the-line, but they were quite a bit less expensive than the juicier 604s. The system worked excellently, but a necessary change of company strategy away from proprietary hardware and toward existing desktop machines meant that Be no longer had any guarantee that users would own multiprocessor boxes. In fact, the opposite was most likely to be true, and the "one processor per person is not enough" slogan was put into retirement (for Be at least—some of us still abide by this). Fortunately for Be, their OS ran just as well on single-processor machines as it did on multiprocessor boxes,

## *Why the Upper Limit?*

If you take a close look at Be's documentation, you'll notice that BeOS doesn't currently handle more than eight processors. But if the operating system can theoretically handle *n* processors, what's with this eight nonsense? The fact is, BeOS actually *can* handle *n* processors—any number at all. However, in the current state of motherboard, chipset, and most importantly, system bus design, serious problems start to crop up when you add more than eight CPUs to a single board. Simply managing the tangle of information criss-crossing the bus becomes an overwhelming task, kind of like trying to fold a piece of paper in half more than eight times (go ahead, try it, with any size of paper—bet you can't do it …).

There are such things as computers with hundreds, even thousands of CPUs, but they're built with highly specialized, bizarro designs that bear little resemblance to the computer hardware available to the public today. These beasts are specially built for science and military institutions. Perhaps at some point in the future, 128-processor motherboards will become available for use in home network servers or some such thing, but that point is still a ways off. For now, Be has built the eight-CPU limit into the operating system as a sensible upper limit. When that kind of hardware becomes a feasible option for the public, this limit will change and we'll keep on moving toward the future. So far, though, Be hasn't heard any complaints from their customers. Be sure and let them know if you do install BeOS on a machine with more than eight processors—I bet they'll try to accommodate you … and I'll personally come over to drool on your keyboard.

because the system had been designed to take full advantage of *n* processors (where *n* stands for whatever number of CPUs you might happen to have). Whether you've got one CPU or eight of them (see the sidebar *Why the Upper Limit?*), the operating system is going to milk them for all they're worth, as efficiently as possible.

For more on buzzwords and the technical aspects of BeOS's underpinnings, read Be's white paper on the MediaOS at `http://www.be.com/products/beos/mediaos.html`.

# The History of Be, Inc.

*by Henry Bortman*

*The following recounting of Be's early history is based on interviews conducted with four members of the original Be team: Jean-Louis Gassée, Steve Sakoman, Bob Herold, and Erich Ringewald. The interviews took place in March of 1997, shortly after Apple announced its decision to purchase NeXT Software. Additional interviews with nearly a dozen members of Be's current engineering staff, along with an extensive new interview with Jean-Louis Gassée, can be found throughout* The BeOS Bible.

## The Last Supper: Gassée Exits Apple

The idea for Be germinated in early 1990. It was then that Gassée had what he refers to as his "final night," the beginning of the end of his career at Apple. It was toward the end of January. At the time, Gassée was the president of Apple's products division. His boss John Sculley was the company's CEO. Gassée was unquestionably Apple's most colorful spokesman; unfortunately, Sculley didn't always appreciate what he had to say.

The two executives were dining at one of their favored hangouts, Maddelena's Continental Restaurant in Palo Alto, along with Apple VP of Human Resources Kevin Sullivan. During the course of the dinner conversation, Sculley asked Gassée what he thought of him. This was nothing new; Sculley had popped the question before. But Gassée didn't give his usual answer: He told Sculley the truth. After dinner, as Gassée and Sullivan were waiting for their cars, Sullivan put his arm around Gassée and said, "Jean-Louis, I'm proud of you." Says Gassée, "I knew then that I had done something irreparable."

Sculley was kind enough to allow Gassée to remain in his job at Apple for several months while he pondered his next move. He considered a number of schemes. Among them was the purchase of Compuserve. In retrospect, he's glad the online service had an asking price some half a billion dollars higher than what he could afford. The idea of developing some type of network fax server also occurred to him, but he let that fade into obscurity as well.

Ultimately, Gassée settled on the concept of an inexpensive, multiprocessor, media-savvy computer, "the Amiga done right." The loyal customers of Commodore's Amiga had fascinated Gassée for years. In late 1988, in fact, he had been approached by two programmers from Commodore who had lined up some financing with an eye toward purchasing the company. Feeling that the company's management was squandering its technical assets, they wanted Gassée to be its new CEO. Gassée was interested, but Commodore Chairman Irwin Gould wouldn't sell.

Gassée had a chance to negotiate with Gould again in 1990, during his final months at Apple. Gould offered Gassée a job as the head of Commodore's R&D division. Gassée declined, and made a counter-offer: "I want to run the company. Give me 30 to 36 months, and we'll put the company in shape, and we'll sell it. You give me 20 percent of the difference between the valuation today and the valuation then." There was just one minor problem: Commodore already had a president, who wasn't going anywhere.

But in the course of discussions with Commodore, Gassée began to crystallize his thoughts about building an inexpensive, high-performance multimedia computer. In fact, he decided to start his own company to build it.

## The Early Days: Be Builds a Team

Gassée's last day at Apple was September 30, 1990. On October 1, he and Steve Sakoman took a trip to Fry's Electronics. Sakoman had worked for Gassée at Apple as the head of the Newton group. Sakoman's original concept for the Newton was as a bold new type of computer, rather than as the consumer commodity the Newton was later billed as. Its main feature was active intelligence: It was to be a machine that took 'a more active part in trying to figure out what your intentions were and was able to back out of those assumptions when it didn't guess right.' Handwriting recognition was an aspect of the initial Newton, but not its raison d'être.

It was Gassée who had given the nod to the original Newton project. But with Gassée's departure imminent, Sakoman saw the writing on the wall. He realized that his early vision of the Newton was unlikely to survive the capricious winds of change that blow through Cupertino as executives make their entrances and exits. He began talking to Gassée about life after Apple. And on October 1, Sakoman, the ex-Apple employee, began wire-wrapping together the various parts he and Gassée carted home from Fry's. By the end of the year, he had built the first Be prototype.

It wasn't much to look at. It never even got a name. It was a simple charcoal-colored box containing a logic board, an AT&T Hobbit processor (the same processor used in the early Newton prototype), a hard drive, a floppy drive, serial and parallel ports, and a graphics adapter, which Sakoman also built himself. Its main purpose was to give the software engineers something to write code for.

## The Birth of BeOS

The development of what would emerge five years later as BeOS began in earnest in early 1991, with the hiring of Be's first three software engineers: Erich Ringewald, Bob Herold, and Benoît Schillings.

Erich Ringewald was another Apple refugee. Not coincidentally, he had also been involved in a project at Apple, the Jaguar project, that had been given the nod by Gassée. "Jaguar," recalls Ringewald, "was essentially Be. The Be machine, the BeBox, the BeOS, in a small skunkworks project headed by Hugh Martin." (Martin is now an executive at 3DO.) Jaguar, like Newton, was to be a new type of computer, distinct from the Macintosh. It was to contain dual RISC processors (Motorola 88110s) and to have a lightweight OS, with support for SMP and a focus on multimedia performance. But in June 1990, says Ringewald, "the antibodies at Apple just killed Jaguar. Nobody wanted it." Far from embracing the possibilities of the new technology, Macintosh management saw it as a threat.

Frustrated, Ringewald went on sabbatical. When he returned three months later, he quit, following the trail to Be blazed by Gassée and Sakoman. The following year, Steve Horowitz, another veteran of the Jaguar software team, also came to Be. He brought with him the concepts he had developed at Apple for integrating a database with a filesystem—work that Apple wasn't interested in.

In December 1990, Bob Herold got a call from his former boss at Apple, Steve Sakoman. At the time, Herold was the person responsible for the Newton kernel. But he was no longer enjoying his job. Just as Sakoman had predicted, the Newton project had changed. When Gassée left Apple, management sent Larry Tessler in to shut the Newton project down. Although Tessler, pleasantly surprised by what he saw, decided instead to continue the project, he remolded Newton in a new image that, as Herold puts it, was "not fun to work on any more." Herold signed up to join the Be team, and began working at Be in March 1991.

Among the early employees of Be, Benoît Schillings is unique: He is the only one of the first half-dozen members of the Be team who did not come directly from Apple. Schillings was recruited by Gassée in September 1990 at an Apple Expo in Paris. He was working at the time for Mainstay, where he had written a product called Marco Polo. His work on Marco Polo's storage architecture and search engine fit well with Gassée's desire to have a database fully integrated into BeOS. Schillings and his wife flew out to California to investigate life in Silicon Valley, including lunch at the obligatory sushi bar. Several months later, in the spring of 1991, he began working at Be.

## Offsite on the Cheap: The Hike to the Sea

In June of that year, Gassée decided that his team needed a break. It was time for the company's first offsite. Be's cash flow situation, however, didn't allow for a lavish affair; Gassée chose instead to take his compatriots on a forced march to the sea. The Hike to the Sea took place on the summer solstice, June 21, 1991. It began on the crest of the hills west of Saratoga, California, and ended some 12 hours later on the shore of the Pacific Ocean. Estimates of the length of the now-legendary Hike vary. Some say it was a mere 26 miles, others complain that it was at least 30. Reports of what time the Hike began also vary: Some report getting up at 3 A.M., others at the more sensible hour of 5. But everyone who participated agrees on one thing: It was painful.

Gassée recalls having prepared his troops for the adventure with some cautionary advice: Don't train, don't buy new shoes, and bring some Band-Aids and ibuprofen. The suggestion not to train was unnecessary; everyone was too busy working to have time for it. And there was no shortage of medical supplies.

But several people either never heard or chose not to heed Gassée's admonition against acquiring new footwear. Cyril Meurillon, who had joined Be to work on the BeOS kernel, was among those who purchased new hiking boots for the occasion. His feet were bloody by the end of the day. Bob Herold also sprung for a pair of stiff new shoes. He was fortunate enough to have stashed some sneakers in his backpack for the end of the hike. Within the first mile, his new shoes were jettisoned in favor of the older, more comfortable ones.

Fortune shined less brightly on Erich Ringewald. He also bought new shoes, but didn't carry a spare pair. Still, it isn't blisters from the new shoes that Ringewald remembers most vividly; he credits the Hike to the Sea with permanently ruining his knees. "At about 20 miles, my knees were in such pain. But I kept going and I know I just continued to do more and more damage to them. Now I can't even sit cross-legged on the floor for a half an hour. My knees just freeze up."

Despite their injuries, everyone finished the hike. Be is unlikely to repeat the adventure, though. "It was altogether a fun thing to do," muses Gassée." But now they know."

## Five Chips Are Better than One: The First BeBox

By the fall of 1991 Sakoman had built a second prototype in his garage. (Be couldn't afford an office: Sakoman, Gassée, Herold, and Ringewald all worked from home, communicating by phone and fax.) This model, the first to be dubbed the BeBox, had not two, but five processors, all from AT&T: two general-purpose Hobbit chips—the Hobbit was a RISC-based microprocessor— and three 3210 DSPs. Be used the 3210s for telephony and audio and video processing. Despite this hefty complement of processing power, the total cost of the five chips was only about half of what an Intel 386 cost at the time. 386s, and later 486s when they were introduced, sold for three to four hundred dollars apiece. The Hobbits and 3210s ran around $35 each.

Once Sakoman had finished the design of the BeBox I logic board, Be needed to build units for the company's own software engineers and third-party developers to work with. Although Be sent later designs to an outside assembly house, the first BeBoxen—about 30 units in all—were built by hand in Sakoman's garage. Everyone, including the company's attorney Cory van Arsdale, got in on the act. Sakoman even paid his 12-year-old son to join the soldering party.

Over the course of the next three years, Sakoman crafted a number of add-on cards for the BeBox—a telephony card, a sound card with a built-in music synthesizer, and a succession of graphics adapters. Meanwhile, the software team, which grew incrementally, plugged away at writing BeOS. Bit by bit the new operating system came together. By July 1994, Be's engineers could see the light at the end of the tunnel. They were perhaps six months away from having an OS that they were ready to show publicly.

Then disaster struck.

## The Demise of the Hobbit: Be's Shift to PowerPC

The decision to build the BeBox around the Hobbit processor had been a calculated risk. The Hobbit was never a wildly popular processor. AT&T originally developed it for use in small mobile computing devices, what it called personal communicators. While at Apple, Sakoman had designed the original Newton using the Hobbit chip. But Apple later switched over to the ARM processor, before shipping the first Newton MessagePad in August 1993.

Meanwhile, AT&T had created another home for the Hobbit. In August 1993, AT&T acquired a majority interest in a company called Eo, which had been formed to produce tablet-sized computers that ran Go Corporation's PenPoint operating system. PenPoint was the first commercial OS based around handwriting recognition; Eo was the main supplier of devices that ran PenPoint. Despite aggressive marketing, AT&T was never able to convince customers of the need for Eo's PenPoint-based systems. In July 1994, the telecommunications giant shut the company down.

The Hobbit was homeless. And Be, still months away from having a shipping product, was in no position to guarantee AT&T a market for the chip. With no viable market for its microprocessor, AT&T decided to pull the plug on the Hobbit. And Be was back to square one.

## Starting Over

There was never really a question about whether or not to continue. Be's cadre of engineers had put too much of their lives into the Be effort—and seen too many worthy projects unceremoniously canceled during their years at Apple—to abandon their dream now. Besides, much of the work that had been done on the BeOS was portable to a new processor. The question was, which processor? It came down to a simple choice: Pentium or PowerPC. Pentiums had been introduced the previous year, and had established a reputation for being reasonably fast, reliable (the floating-point bug surfaced later), and expensive.

But there was a great deal of talk, especially among adherents of RISC, that Intel's CISC-based processor line was nearing the end of its road. Apple had begun to sing the praises of the RISC-based PowerPC chips that it had developed jointly with IBM and Motorola. The first Power Macintoshes, based on the PowerPC 601, had shipped in March 1994. Although it would be another 16 months before Apple announced the first 603-based Mac system, the 603 chip was already showing promise as an able challenger to Pentium, in both speed and price.

*Figure 1.08*

*An early BeBox.*

The story of how Be made the decision to use PowerPC over Pentium is a difficult one to nail down. One can only imagine that it was a rather emotional time for the Be team; everyone tells the tale with a slightly different spin. Legend has it that not everyone agreed with the decision, although no one actually claims to be among the ones who disagreed. At any rate, nearly four years after Gassée and Sakoman made the initial trip to Fry's, Be was back to square one, rebuilding the BeBox with an entirely new processor, the PowerPC.

The first version of the PowerPC-based BeBox took multiprocessing to the extreme: It contained seven processors. Not wanting to wait until a new logic board could be built around the PowerPC, Glenn Adler designed PowerPC add-in cards for the Hobbit-based BeBox. Granted, the five processors on the main logic board didn't do much. But this system provided the hardware foundation on which construction of the PPC-based BeOS could begin.

By early 1995, Joe Palmer had finished modifying and building the PPC-based BeBox design initially developed by Adler. It bore little resemblance to the blue tower with flashing running lights that the rest of the world eventually came to know as the BeBox. It was a bare logic board lying on a table, with a bunch of cables connecting it to some peripherals, also lying on the table. But this logic board served as the basis of the BeBox that Be ultimately shipped to customers, and continued shipping through June 1996, when it decided to get out of the hardware business.

## Public Exposure: Agenda 95

Although the PowerPC-based BeBox hardware was finalized early in 1994, it was the better part of another year before Gassée felt BeOS was ready for prime-time viewing. Be offered the first public glimpse of its operating system on October 3, 1995, at Stewart Alsop's Agenda 95.

Gassée was reluctant to unveil BeOS at Agenda. He had always been of the opinion that the natural audience for the first public viewing of BeOS would be a room full of propellerheads who would instinctively understand and appreciate what was going on under the hood. Agenda's audience typically was composed of members of the media and industry analysts. Gassée was concerned that they would be unmoved by his team's efforts. "These are industry insiders," he protested when he was invited to participate in Agenda. "They all hate what we do. I wanted audiences of geeks."

By the fall of 1995, though, Be was in serious debt. It needed a shot in the arm to keep going—not only publicity, but the funding that often comes with publicity. Gassée decided to take the plunge.

Anyone who has attended conferences, trade shows, press conferences, or product rollouts knows that there are, indeed, demo gods. Sometimes they are benign. At other times they are more mischievous. They are not responsive to prayer, or even to ritual sacrifice: They strike capriciously. At Agenda 95, they struck.

Gassée and his engineers arrived a couple of days early. They brought with them everything they needed for the demo—or so they thought. It had all worked flawlessly back at the office. But when they arrived in Scottsdale, Arizona, for the big event, nothing worked. The engineers called back to California, to get people to "bring more stuff," as Bob Herold recalls. "Software, different hard disks, whatever they thought would work. It was a bit of a crapshoot." They finally got it "mostly" working.

The day of Be's presentation also happened to be the day that the O.J. Simpson jury announced its verdict. Be's demo had been timed carefully to be completed before the verdict was read. Although the demo system was still plagued with problems, Steve Horowitz, who was running the demo machine behind the scenes, "got very adept at moving things out of the way," says Herold. "If the debugger would come up, he'd move it away before anyone noticed."

Apparently the ruse worked. Be got a standing ovation, only the second time in the history of Agenda that anyone had received such accolades. Gassée was speechless. Literally. Anyone who knows Gassée knows that this is a rare event. "I wanted to say my thanks to a number of people. And I couldn't do it."

His momentary lapse of eloquence notwithstanding, Gassée's gamble had paid off. "Agenda was the turning point. That got us in the big time. We went from nothing, in terms of VCdom, to the first tier of VCs. Which is very good. Not just the money, but also access." Not that the money was insignificant. While waiting for investors to come through, Gassée remembers, "we had a couple of near-death experiences. I'm not joking when I say that I've seen the whites of the repo man's eyes." Gassée keeps a Xerox copy of the four-million-dollar check from Dave Marquardt, dated April 9, 1996, pinned to the wall of his office. Marquardt had been in the Agenda audience at Be's public unveiling.

## Crossing the Frontier: Be Ports Its OS to the Mac

Buoyed by the public response to its products, and eager to attract application developers to its platform, Be applied for booth space at Apple's 1996 World Wide Developers' Conference. WWDC is held each year in May. At the conference, an area is set aside for a Developer Expo, where companies that produce development tools for the Mac—companies such as Metrowerks and Symantec—display their wares. Initially Be's application was approved without a second thought. Then someone at Apple spent a little too much time thinking, and decided that because Be not only didn't have a Mac development product, but was actually a competitor, it shouldn't be allowed to use the Developers' Conference as an arena for self-promotion. Apple informed Be of its decision just days before the conference.

When he heard the news of their exclusion, Benoît Schillings turned to Bob Herold and said, "Well, let's just port it to the Mac." The idea had come up informally before, but no one had taken a serious interest in it. But it made a lot of sense to port BeOS to Mac hardware. The BeBox and Power Macs had many similar features. In fact, the BeBox logic board was a derivative of PREP, the original PowerPC reference platform design from IBM.

It took Be's engineers about six weeks to get something up and running on a Mac system—or, more accurately, on a MacOS system. The machine that Be first got working was not, properly speaking, a Macintosh, but rather a Mac clone: a Power Computing PowerCenter 132. Power was an early supporter of BeOS.

By the time Boston Macworld Expo rolled around, in August 1996, the BeOS on Mac hardware was ready for public consumption. Ready enough, anyway. There were a few items missing. The floppy drive didn't work. There was no support for PostScript printers. And there was no serial driver, so PPP dial-up access to the Internet wasn't possible. But Expo attendees could view BeOS in all its multithreaded glory, doing what it does best: chugging away at multiple QuickTime movies, sound files, and 3D animations simultaneously. Without crashing. The response was overwhelmingly positive. In addition to being shown in Be's own booth, BeOS was prominently featured in Power Computing's booth.

Of course, there were a couple of behind-the-scenes glitches. At the show, Power Computing announced what at the time was the fastest desktop system available, a PowerTower Pro 225, the first machine ever to contain a 225 MHz 604e PowerPC processor. Both Power and Be were anxious to demo BeOS on the new chip, but the hardware and software didn't get along too well at first. The OS required only a simple change to enable it to support the 604e processor, but that change required modifying source code and recompiling the OS.

After the show closed on the first day, Bob Herold stayed in the Power booth, using its PPP connection to dial back to Be's server in Palo Alto. He downloaded all the kernel sources to a hard disk, borrowed a PowerTower 225 from Power, and went to his hotel room to work.

At 9 P.M., he discovered that one of the files he had downloaded was corrupted. The show floor was locked up. The hotel he was staying in didn't have an Internet connection. And he didn't have a modem. He started calling around Boston to find a Cyber Cafe that was still open. Eventually he found one, inside Fanueil Hall. But first he had to convince the owners of the establishment to let him copy the file he wanted to download onto his own floppy disk. They were afraid of viruses. Eventually, Herold prevailed. By 4:00 A.M. he had made the required change, recompiled, and had BeOS running on the 604e/225.

## Dancing with the Devil: Negotiations with Apple

Meanwhile, quietly, outside the glare of the media spotlight, Be and Apple had begun negotiations. Apple had eventually relented about letting Be into WWDC. But that apparently wasn't the end of the subject. During the conference, Gil Amelio visited the Be booth in person, demanding to know, "What are you trying to accomplish by being here?"

When Gassée got wind of Amelio's inquiry, he sent him an email suggesting that they talk about subjects of possible mutual interest. "Then," says Gassée, "started this eerie six-month period. Believe it or not, from the very beginning I was very frustrated with the way Apple treated us." The two companies managed to keep quiet for the first two months of talks. But Be's success at Macworld Expo had catapulted Be-watching to the top of the list of summer activities for Macophiles.

By the end of August, the cat was out of the bag. On August 29, an article in the *Wall Street Journal* revealed that Apple and Be were negotiating. The news, despite official denials, set off a flurry of rumors that lasted for four months. In early November, just days after Apple issued a press release saying that it was still "in the process of finalizing its long-term operating system strategy and [would] announce this by early 1997," *MacWEEK* boldly declared that "Apple already knows how it wants to deploy the BeOS," and that the company "reportedly has set midsummer 1997 as the earliest time frame for an initial delivery of the hybrid OS."

Popular sentiment was running strongly in favor of BeOS forming the basis of Apple's future system software. But few people—the folks at Be included—thought Apple had any serious alternative. As Gassée recalls, the reaction at Be to the news that Steve Jobs was angling to get Apple to pony up for Nextstep was, "No. It's impossible. NeXT is too big, too heavy. They use Display PostScript in NeXT. It will never work in the home, SOHO, K-12.

"Well," Gassée concedes, "I guess we misread the field." On Friday, December 20, 1996, just hours before Apple shut down for a two-week holiday, Amelio announced his company's decision to purchase NeXT Software and to use Nextstep as the basis of its future OS.

## Flying Solo: Be Returns to Plan A

"For a couple of weeks," says Gassée, I was really depressed." But, he adds, "The good news is that we are doing what we were doing. This hasn't changed." In the weeks after Apple's announcement it was hard to find anyone at Be who was really upset about it. Many of them had previously worked for Apple, and had no particular interest in repeating the experience. As Ringewald put it, "It's better sitting here today than in Cupertino. If in the end application developers can't look at our stuff and understand why their application could be better delivered given the foundation we've provided as opposed to the MacOS, then we just deserve to pack it up and go home."

*Be has clearly not packed up and gone home. Rather, the company has shifted gears—again. Be is now focusing its efforts on yet another new hardware platform, Intel's x86 architecture. Throughout the rest of* The BeOS Bible, *you'll find recent interviews with nearly a dozen Be engineers, filling in more details from Be's early years, and bringing the story of Be's incredible journey up to date.*

## Jean-Louis Gassée
**President and CEO of Be, Inc.**
*Interviewed by Henry Bortman*

**HB:** *It's been nearly two years since we last talked. A lot of things have changed.*

**JLG:** Amen to this.

**HB:** *Back then, you had just learned that Apple had chosen someone else …*

**JLG:** … which turned out to be a good thing for Apple.

**HB:** *Okay, let's start there. Why was that a good thing for Apple?*

**JLG:** Well, I'm a born-again capitalist. I'm this French farmer abducted by aliens and raised in California by VCs. Seriously, we've got to look out for the shareholders, and look at what Steve's coming back as the head of Apple has done for the shareholder, because he has the institutional and historical and charismatic legitimacy and power to change things that we wouldn't have had with the then-management of the company.

Buying Be would have been a very different equation. This might have been a good transaction for the shareholders, although we'll never know. Clearly, the technical choice was not the issue. When Steve came as the interim CEO, he looked at [the OpenStep technology] and said, "Who bought this?" and promptly refocused on the Macintosh, which I think is a good tactical move.

The iMac is an excellent example of Apple promising and—the wise will say, but I would never say it—for once delivering on their promise, which is simplicity and style. The fact that simplicity and style sell seems to surprise people, which in turn surprises me. Look at Chevrolet and BMW. As far as I know, they buy steel, aluminum, and glass from the same vendors, and they transform those commodities into vehicles. It's obvious that simplicity and style on the BMW side allow that company to sell their vehicles for more currency per pound than Chevrolet. Not that I don't like Chevrolet, I have a Chevy Suburban, I love it, especially for Parisians. I was born in Paris, for me a Suburban is the ultimate American vehicle. But then, although I don't drive a BMW, for a lot of European people, the BMW is the ultimate vehicle. So they coexist pretty nicely. And let's say that you want to run Microsoft Office and browse the Web, and that's all you want to do. The iMac is a more expensive solution than a clone, but it's also simpler and better looking, so there's a market for that.

**HB:** *So the decision was good for Apple. Was it good for Be as well?*

**JLG:** Well, we now have a good partner in the [form] of Intel. Ron Whittier, who is the vice president of Intel, came here one day to see yours truly. I explained to him what we are doing. He was a little bit skeptical. We gave him a demo and he said, "We'll be back."

Often people think you're nuts doing another OS. Well, yeah, if we do what OS/2 did—"better DOS than DOS, better Windows than Windows." Look what happened to OS/2, regardless of its merits. It attacked Microsoft, and that was the wrong thing to do. Instead of addressing the mature office-productivity part of the marketplace as OS/2 did, we are trying to position ourselves at the knee of an S-curve, where technology and new trends come out of gestation, and we can ride those trends and technologies in the fast growth part of the S-curve.

On the Intel platform, Microsoft is the de facto standard. It's the weather. And my view is, don't fight the weather, it doesn't work. When you buy a PC, you're on Windows. Let's say for a moment that I'm selling audio and video systems for vehicles and you just bought this new Suburban, and you want an AV system for your Suburban. You come to my shop and I say, "Where did you buy this piece of …?" If I start criticizing your vehicle because you could have bought, maybe, a German sport utility vehicle, which would be more of a connoisseur thing, am I going to make friends with you? Are you going to listen to me?

So, OK, you bought a PC, you have Windows. Allow me to sell you an audio and video system for this vehicle you just bought. And you keep Windows because Windows is the de facto general-purpose standard. And indeed, if you want to run Microsoft Office, Internet Explorer, it does a good job of that. And what we offer is a low-risk proposition, that you supplement/complement your purchase. For a small amount of money you can add the audio and video features that you will not find in a general-purpose system.

The history of any kind of industry, any product category, is that you always have this dichotomy between general purpose and specialized, and that's our life. And it's a good life. Intel likes us for good reasons because of what I call the "silent Cray scandal." Let me explain what I mean by this, if I may. (I have this fondness for the Cray because I was an investor and director of Cray Computer before Seymour passed away.) Today you go to Price Costco. For $2500 you have a Presario system with all the trimmings—17" monitor, 450 MHz Pentium II, 128MB, and so on, including plugs on the front, which I'll mention later. So you buy this, and if you run Word on that, essentially, you have a system which has more power and more storage than an early Cray machine—for $2500. And you use it to run Word and to browse the Web through a very tiny little straw called a 56K connection, if you get 56K. Which is why the $500 PC is becoming such a problem for the $2500 PC, because if all you want to do is run Microsoft Office on the PC, a sub-thousand-dollar PC will do a great job at that. I have a small Hitachi Libretto that has a 133 MHz Pentium. It browses the Web and does Microsoft Office pretty well. You don't have to have a 450 MHz Pentium II for that.

But audio and video applications, which demand more bandwidth, are more naturally coherent with Intel's margin structure. We help create demand. We increase the demand for systems that some people call the poor man's Silicon Graphics. Well, I've heard worse insults. Remember, desktop publishing was considered the poor man's Scitex at one time, but it turned out to be a pretty rich industry. So, if we are the poor man's Silicon Graphics on Intel architecture machines, it's a great life, and we really enjoy it. Developers love it, PC OEMs love it, customers love it, and all we have to do is execute. The door is open.

You know, as we sit here [in October 1998] we are preparing for Comdex. Before going to Comdex, I'm going to Japan to make an announcement with a notable PC vendor and, hopefully, if we continue to do a good job, there'll be more. We've got excellent traction in Japan, which I hate to remind people is the birthplace of many modern media. We think Silicon Valley is everything, but new media is also great for Japanese companies, including software developers, because it's transcultural. A Japanese word processor is not very useful outside of Japan. But a Japanese video editing software product is transcultural. So, this is the sort of thing that is a great opportunity for Japanese partners and European partners, as well as U.S. partners.

## Jean-Louis Gassée (continued)

**HB:** *So you'll be announcing a relationship with a PC vendor in Japan? Is that for the Japanese market only, or for the U.S. market as well?*

**JLG:** I think we'll start with the Japanese market. My view is, "Underpromise." I want to be very careful to do this. I've been accused by one of your brothers [in the media] of under-hyping our product. Thank you. I'd like to keep doing that because I think that we'd like to distinguish ourselves by being consistent and patient and doing a good job for a constituency of software developers, PC OEMs, and direct end users. And if we do a good job there, the rest will follow.

**HB:** *Will you be making any hardware announcements at Comdex?*

**JLG:** I don't think so. Well, there is life after Comdex. I think a lot will happen there in terms of the hardware OEMs.

**HB:** *You don't want to speculate on their behalf?*

**JLG:** No. Seriously, I'm not holding back. My view is, when you deal with large companies, you know, you run the risk of what I call—and forgive me Father for what I'm about to say—politicus interruptus. Things happen in fits and starts until you get going. So you've got to sort of step back. If you're too close, you see all the agitation. If you step back, you see a trend and you get somewhere.

**HB:** *Let me ask it this way: You're saying that the goal for BeOS at this point is to become the … "AV-side OS for Windows" is the term I've heard tossed around.*

**JLG:** That's fine with me.

**HB:** *So let's say a large PC computer maker were to agree to bundle BeOS…*

**JLG:** My dream, which may or may not come to pass is this: You see a great company like Dell. When you buy a computer from them, you have to configure the system. My dream is to have a choice on the configuration that says "Install the BeOS beside Windows for a few dollars."

**HB:** *And then, what would a user's experience be like? They'd have these two operating systems—how smooth would it be going back and forth? What applications would there be?*

**JLG:** Well, let's return to the PC at Price Costco for a moment. You have three plugs on the front of that PC. USB, USB, and FireWire. This is music and video to my ears because this is exactly the sort of media-ready, or media-oriented, hardware system that we can take advantage of. And Windows—it's a great operating system, but it doesn't do such a wonderful job in AV applications. And it's growing in girth. We hear that there will be a consumer version of Windows 2000, which has, at last count, something like 40 million lines of source code. It's getting to a point where the agility required for multiple streams of digital media just isn't there. It does certain things really well, but you cannot do everything. If you tell me that you have a consumer version of a Boeing 747 … Generality has its advantages, but also its limitations.

So, the user experience will be either you pick the system you want to run at boot time, or you use our Be Launcher from Windows, which shuts down Windows and launches the BeOS.

It's fairly smooth. You can read and write files from either system. I don't know if all of that will be in the next version, but the plan is to be able to view the volumes from either system, so it's fairly transparent and safe. And given the boot times involved, it's also very fast. So, if we do a good job with some software developers, or ourselves, we'll make sure that you have a comfortable experience.

I think '99 is going to be the year of digital video. You'll see DV cameras that will cost less than the editing system. But here is the problem with these video cameras—and the opportunity. You go to Greece and you come back with four hours of tape. You know the limit is 10 minutes when you have a social family gathering—the older people start sneaking out of the room. So what do you do? Well, in theory you can edit them, but let's face it—nobody edits their tapes because it's too complicated. With DV, you can take a tape and pump it to your hard disk, because now any PC that has 6GB or more of hard disk space has enough capacity for about an hour of video. So, you can put 30 minutes of tape—3GB, I mean—on your hard disk, then you go snip, snip, snip, and you put the 10 minutes back on tape.

**HB:** *Yeah, but I've yet to see a "snip, snip, snip" video application that normal people can use. Have you got one in the works?*

**JLG:** Yeah, we've got several in the works. They're not shipping today, but when they ship, I'll let the customer be the judge. But, I have great hopes. We'll make an announcement at Comdex with a notable video company: MGI, VideoWave. But there are other nobodies—future notables—who are also working on some, because there are many ways to approach the problem.

I also believe that the thing that people will find retroactively obvious is that audio is important. Now video makes an impression, as it were. But say you go to NAMM, the National Association of Music Merchants trade show, which has three times the real estate of Moscone [Center in San Francisco]. Granted, there are also analog instruments there. Thank God for analog instruments. I'm not all for electronic—I'm for both. I think what you can do with a modern synthesizer you cannot do with a guitar, and what you can do with a guitar, you can't do with a synthesizer. So, why argue? You can afford both now.

I have a great deal of faith in the audio/sound/music/creation/post production. Because today, you and I consume more sound than we consume video. I assume you drove your car coming here. And if you drove your car, or if you listen to your Walkman on the train, the sound you hear more than likely has spent time on a hard disk. Even on the radio, there is a lot of non-live radio. You know, I listen to NPR, and what you hear there spends a lot of time on a hard disk. That's a huge opportunity. And by the way, going back to video, there is no good video without sound. It just doesn't happen.

So I see people using audio and video: editing, creation, rendering, playing—also games. There is no serious computer without games. We see great games coming. We don't ask you to give up Microsoft Office—this would be a losing proposition. We ask you to make a small financial bet to gain access to a growing number of audio and video applications, and games, and maybe also a couple of desktop publishing applications which are a good proof of the general concept that we call real-time WYSIWYG—being able to edit a large amount of data with real-time effects.

## *Jean-Louis Gassée* (continued)

**HB:** *Some people, however, would say that you've been making this argument for a couple of years now, that BeOS is so easy to develop for, but we still don't really see any compelling app. How would you respond to that?*

**JLG:** Well, there is no compelling app today. What's compelling is, BeOS is a compelling app for developers. If we do a good job together, we'll have compelling apps. It takes time. It takes a lot of time. There's no question about this, which is why we raise money to make sure we have the length of runway we require. Because it doesn't happen overnight. You wish it, but look at Java. Java came out with a great deal of fanfare and it's finally finding some traction in enterprise applications for middleware, but there is no compelling desktop application for Java.

**HB:** *You don't consider wiggling icons compelling?*

**JLG:** If wiggling icons are the proof of concept. Because it's OK sometimes to buy a house based on blueprints, because you can see what you have. Sometimes the blueprints can be compelling. But, in our case, yes, it's taking time. It always takes more time. It's like this thing of houses. I've been involved in house remodeling, and it takes a lot more time, a lot more money than you initially thought. But if you do a good job, you are very happy after that, and that's what we are confident is going to happen.

**HB:** *Let me go back to the Apple decision. You said that it was good for Apple, and it turned out to be good for Be. How did it turn out for the relationship between Be and Apple?*

**JLG:** Right now, the last thing I want to do is get in the middle of what Apple is struggling to accomplish. You see from [Apple Senior Vice President of Software Engineering] Avie Tevanian's testimony in the government's suit [against Microsoft] that Apple is engaged in extremely complicated relationships with Microsoft. My view is when you have a messy couple, don't get too close. So, I'd rather stay out their hair.

We think we have ways to make BeOS run on G3 and G4 machines. We are evaluating that as we speak. But right now the focus is to offer ourselves as being of service on the Intel architecture. That's where I think we have a very clear path. We are unencumbered by complicated situations.

**HB:** *But you have a strong base of fans on the Mac who would be very sorry to see support for BeOS on PowerPC eventually go away.*

**JLG:** We have no intention to make that go away. Intel and PC OEMs are extremely pleasant with us because they don't fear anything. We don't disturb the peace, we add value. It's a simple proposition. To paraphrase an ad from a company, "We don't make the PC, we make it better." So, you buy a PC, we make it better. We make it better for applications that people care for. I'm sure in offices, people just doing PowerPoint presentations don't care about us. And they're right. I have no beef with that. But Costco are not philanthropists, so if they sell this system with USB, USB, and FireWire up front, there's got to be customers for that. So, that's what I like.

In the case of Apple, Apple is still fighting for survival. They're trying to see how they can survive with or without Microsoft, because clearly, if you didn't have Office 98 and Internet Explorer on the Macintosh, things would be really different. So, in a sense, the irony is that Microsoft saved Apple but also controls Apple's future. It complicates things. If we can do support independently for PowerPC users without getting entangled in a complicated situation, I'll do it. You didn't ask the question, but I will ask it for you: Do I wish that Apple or Motorola would say, "Yeah, sure, you add value to our system, you're welcome"? Yeah, but that's their decision, not mine.

**HB:** *I want to ask you about something. Your license plate: Is it still AMIGA96?*

**JLG:** No, it's GEEK OS. People say, "Why do you say that?" I think that geeks have now acquired a different connotation. I want to pay homage to the early adopters, basically. But I cannot say "early adopter" on a license plate. So yes, this is an industry that always starts on the wings of geeks because they are the early adopters. They are people who are interested in technology, they are discerning users, and adopters are programmers. You need to take care of your friends first. Which, by the way, is why your question on the PowerPC users is a well-founded question. We need to take care of our friends and we intend to take care of our friends. But how we do that is not clear yet. So, that's why my license plate says GEEK OS. The Suburban says LIMO BE, by the way, which also speaks to the culture of our company. You've seen the furniture here.

**HB:** *Yeah, and I've noticed that you have fancy furniture upstairs now in your reception area.*

**JLG:** Yes, that's correct. But we got it for free from the previous tenant. VeriFone got acquired by HP, so they got very rich. So they graciously abandoned their furniture, which for them was a hand-me-down. And, yep, we do take hand-me-downs.

**HB:** *Speaking of frugality, you also said two years ago that you had created an OS for $20 million. I take it the total has gone up a little.*

**JLG:** Yeah. I think the technical foundation is sound, it has been validated, so that part is done. Now we are getting into the more expensive exercise, which is not the OS itself but the creation of the ecosystem around the BeOS. As it happens, that's a more expensive task than the technical one. Engineering is a lot cheaper than marketing, if that's what you could call it. You know, marketing, evangelizing, sales, OEM relationships—all that stuff—is expensive. Fortunately, we've got good investors who believe in us, and in themselves, in the soundness of their vision. So now it's a more expensive game. That's life.

**HB:** *So, do you have enough funding to keep going for awhile?*

**JLG:** Oh, yeah. Not only that, but let's remind ourselves: A successful OS is an incredible instrument of wealth creation. Just look at Microsoft. Or you can look at the Mac, which created a lot of wealth even with a very small market share. You can look at WindRiver, another example—and it's a good example because they have no applications. So, if you put, as we intend to, the OS and the application business together, you can create a fair amount of wealth. There's a lot of financial incentive for our investors. They're not philanthropists. It's a high-risk, high-reward proposition.

## *Jean-Louis Gassée* (continued)

**HB:** *How do you define success for BeOS?*

**JLG:** Can I try several definitions? We have constituencies, and we work for these constituencies. So, sometimes it's a good idea to look at success through the eye of your key constituencies. Well, we have shareholders. We make shareholders happy—meaning liquid, you know, make a profit on their investment—that's one type of success. It can be an IPO, it can be a transaction. As I said earlier, I'm a born-again capitalist, so I'm here to work for the shareholder and I am one of them.

There is the software developer. We create the next, maybe smaller, John Warnock [co-founder of Adobe Systems] because some guy invents a nice application and we created a nice ecosystem with BeDepot for electronic distribution of software and/or bundles with PC OEMs. And suddenly, you sell a lot of copies of a $49 application, which has zero cost electronically. The money gets pretty good pretty quickly. So, that's success.

You look at Intel, for instance, one of our partners. We create more demand for higher-end processors. Andy Grove demonstrated the BeOS at Agenda. Well, I'm sure this was to be nice to us, but he might have had other aims in mind more aligned with Intel's interests. So we create demand for that, and this would be success as viewed by Intel.

Customers, of course, will declare us successful if they see the kind of applications they want in sufficient number. They don't care if we make money and that's fine—they should care for themselves. So, they see something they like that's inexpensive, that complements or enriches their PC, that's success too. You know it only takes one application. If we have a nice sound-and-video editor that costs you $100 or a couple of hundred dollars on top of the PC, which you bought for $2000—amen. That's success.

So, that's how I look at it. Did I forget any constituencies? I forgot the tax man, but whenever we make a profit, the tax man will be happy. And of course, you know, you could argue about which constituency should take priority. Who takes precedence—the customer or the shareholder? But then we get into debates that I cannot participate in. I'm just a new immigrant.

**HB:** *When do you think you'll be able to say "OK, we've made it"?*

**JLG:** I have no idea. I have no idea because there are too many things brewing here right now for me to understand. We're not used to that, but that's a good sign. We have an unusual amount of activity, from developers to business partners. Talk to me six months from now. You know, if we haven't done a good job, then I might be worried.

**HB:** *What do you worry about?*

**JLG:** Where do I start? I'm the Chief Worrying Officer at Be, I guess. My main worry today is finding enough people because now we are entering a different phase of the game, so we are recruiting. That's my main worry.

My number two worry would be when do we attract torpedoes from a certain company in the northwest of the United States. That's always a worry, because their financial and market power is a concern. If you're not concerned, you're a little cuckoo, in my opinion. It's eerie. We talk to PC OEMs and so we trade stories. I spoke with Joel Klein [assistant attorney general in charge of the DOJ Antitrust Division] at Agenda, and he bemoans the fact that people wouldn't want to testify [against Microsoft] because they are too afraid of testifying. That's his main worry. And that by itself I find very sad. When a company strikes fear in the minds of so many fairly small people, it is sad. I cannot engage in legal discussions because I'm not a lawyer. I'm not competent to do this. But as a businessperson and just as a human being, when an individual or a company strikes fear in the hearts of so many people, well, it strikes fear in me as well. So that's a worry that I have.

And, number three would be just make sure that we execute well. It's an everyday war—details, details, details. The future is in the details. I'm also trying to recruit to strengthen the management team to make sure we do as good a job as possible. One of my role models is Michael Dell. Remember what people thought of him? They dissed him. Sniff. Well, they don't sniff anymore because he was persistent in his goal to do the best possible job. It didn't come easy on the human side, on the technical side, on the financial side in the early days. A lot of experimenting that didn't always pan out well. He looks like a sage in the industry now, but he didn't always look like this. My hope is to remember that you don't become Michael Dell overnight. It takes a lot of persistence. And persistence, I think I can say I have.

**HB:** *Let me switch gears here a little bit. You've talked before about some of the advantages of Intel hardware over PowerPC hardware. Could you go into that a little bit?*

**JLG:** I have two perspectives on this. It's not the instruction set—to me, it's the corporate culture. I think Intel has a very determined, patient approach. Talk about execution—they execute extremely well. It's a pleasure to work with them. You go to meetings, and those are well-run meetings. They are very methodical, they are very well organized, and they've had amazing success in incrementing their architecture and having the kind of reputation and market cap that we see. So, the advantage is they do the processor, and they also do the rest—the chipsets. In some respects, chipsets are more important than the processor, because it does you no good if you have a fast processor but you cannot mediate the interaction with the external world. And so Intel's strength has been that they do the processor, the chipset, the motherboard.

They realize that the BIOS is now obsolete, the EISA bus is now obsolete. So now they have chipsets that do 100 MHz, so you can more profitably use fast memory. There is this scandal of a fast processor and slow memory, so they are removing the bottlenecks. Today, a processor benchmark is not interesting. You want to do system benchmarks. And on system benchmarks, they do well because of the faster chipsets. They introduced USB. They introduced FireWire—which was invented at Apple, if you remember. So there are all of these ironies there because they take a systemic approach. They do a great job of cranking up the clock on processors, but they understand that that's not good enough. So, next year you'll have chipsets with FireWire on the motherboard. You'll have an even faster bus. At some point in time you'll have a faster AGP, faster everything, not just the processor.

Now, let me take the opposite view. Let's say that I am Bill Gates, and Chris Galvin [the head of Motorola] comes to see me. And I say, "You know, Chris, the last time we demanded a couple of hundred million dollars to keep Windows NT on the PowerPC, you turned me down. I was mad, but you know, you were right, because we didn't have Office, and because we didn't have Office, none of the visionary sheep ported their applications to Windows NT on a PowerPC, so all we

## *Jean-Louis Gassée* (continued)

could demonstrate was Solitaire running on a PowerPC Windows system, so it didn't stimulate sales as you expected, and you were right. But we learned a lesson. Now we have an operating system, which is CE, which is like Windows NT Portable, but we also made the key applications, the Office applications, portable to run on a number of processors.

"So, picture this, Chris: Windows 2000 is portable, and Office 2000 will be portable" (I'm speculating). "We now have Office and Windows 2000 running on PowerPC. And of course, as I said, the visionary followers will then follow, so you'll have all the applications you need. So, Chris, how much is it worth to you? The answer is probably a lot because, Chris, I can make Motorola the next Intel and I can make you the next Andy Grove."

By the way, that's a nightmare scenario for Intel because there's a lot of market value stored in a simple fact. If you have two processors with identical figures of merit—cost; MIPS [million instructions per second], according to real benchmarks; power dissipation—technically, they're equivalent, but the processor on the left runs Windows, and the processor on the right doesn't, which one will sell in the highest volumes with the higher margins?

But now, if the processor on the right becomes more equivalent with the processor on the left, its market value goes up. So that's an interesting scenario. I'm not saying it will happen. I don't have any privileged information, but it's an interesting scenario to speculate about.

**HB:** *Last time we talked, you said that you were looking around at some telecommunications things for a while. Do you regret having left that behind?*

**JLG:** Certainly not, because we haven't. It's a little bit early to speculate about what's going to happen, but there are things brewing in the Web appliance space. And there we have a unique position because we have a small core with great media capabilities. The NC with sex.

**HB:** *But you don't have Explorer.*

**JLG:** No, but we have a pretty competent browser. There are things we don't have. But you look at browsers today, these 20MB downloadables. Of course we don't have all that—and you don't need all that to have a reliable Web appliance. I don't know what's going to happen with that space, so I will not speculate at this time, your honor. But we haven't lost sight of that because … you look at IDC, they say that by 2002 there will be 55 million such appliances. The exact number isn't so important, but that is within the same order of magnitude as the PC market. It is within the same multiple of 10. So, it's an interesting market where we have some benefits to offer.

**HB:** *But wouldn't you be going up directly against Windows CE there?*

**JLG:** Well, let's face it, today, the simple fact is if you write a line of C++ code, the chances are, you're competing with Microsoft. I cannot say what Windows CE will be in the future, but I've bought CE devices. As you know, I'm a director of 3Com, and CE has been wonderful for 3Com because it creates a whole lot of interest for the category. People tried, and we are selling a lot of Palm IIIs as result. Windows CE is certainly an excellent operating system, which is getting all the respect it deserves in the marketplace. But it's not a multimedia, singing and dancing OS. I don't know what the strategy is for Windows CE. Certainly in the PAL category, it's not finding traction. Even HP, who is king of small devices because of its glorious history with pocket calculators in the early '70s, they haven't made money there. Everybody's trying, but there's not much traction.

**HB:** *Sometimes I think people believe that Windows will be the dominant operating system eternally.*

**JLG:** I like that belief, personally.

**HB:** *But it's got to wear out at some point.*

**JLG:** Yeah, yeah, but don't fight it. It's a great operating system, and we complement it. Don't tell people it's bad. My view is, customers are smart. You give them a good deal, they'll like it. It's got to be a good deal. It's got to be accessible, it's got to do something real. People say customers are stupid. Well, I don't like that talking down to customers.

**HB:** *So now I'll speculate for a minute. It seems to me that, eventually, Windows has to run out of steam. Microsoft will have to start over. I suppose you could say that NT was starting over, and that's debatable, but at a certain point, they get too big, they get too heavy …*

**JLG:** That's why I started a company.

**HB:** *… and so, someday, people need a new operating system. And BeOS seems to be architected in a way to have the potential to be that operating system, or one of those operating systems. Can you hold on that long?*

**JLG:** Yeah. But that's not the plan. You asked me to define success. The plan is to make the companies I talked about successful on the basis of BeOS being a dedicated media OS. That's the plan.

Look at the advent of Linux. Some people say, Oh yeah, Linux is an overnight success. But it's preceded by 30 years of Unix. So, Linux is a great skirmish in the Unix versus Windows NT battle. Sometimes I say that our goal is to be the audio-and-video Linux—and I'm using Linux as a figure of speech, not literally. Linux has found traction in the enterprise. Now you don't get fired for buying Linux, and I like that. It shows that people are more open minded. Some people say that the thousand-year reich has set in. But look at Linux. Linux is a case where the geeks tried it. Geeks tried it, then their managers said, "What are you running on this?" "It's a version of Unix." "All right." "Well, actually, it's that kind of Unix, Linux." Apache, Linux, Web server—boom. You plug it in and you don't have to worry about it. You don't have to pay tax. It gives better power on the same hardware as Windows NT. It costs less, it does more, it bugs you less.

So, you can translate that in our domain, BeOS, for AV applications. Of course, we have to do a good job. We have to execute a number of parameters. But then overnight people say, "Oh." Who could have put a date on not getting fired for using Linux? Now, the question is, Can we hold on? Well, if we make ourselves financially viable, which is fairly easy on our scale, then it doesn't matter, because we are financially viable. And what will become of us after we become financially viable? I'll be happy to be part of it.

**HB:** *Is the culture changing here as you grow?*

**JLG:** Yeah, a little bit, but it's like as you grow up as an individual—you're still yourself but you are different. So there is the same kind of growth that you experience as an individual. We're

### Jean-Louis Gassée (continued)

becoming a business as opposed to an R&D environment. And that implies changes in behavior and people and structure, and that's my job to put in place. I have done some of that already and I will continue to do that.

Sometimes, you have burnout. You always have a certain amount of it. But we've got a low burnout rate compared to other startups in the Valley. We've got a fairly stable company. The culture is still spartan. I expect it will remain that way. But you'll see more suits, figuratively speaking. And that's OK—it's got to happen. People say, "Oh, we're changing." I don't care either way. To me, changing is not a goal. It's a means toward becoming what our constituencies need us and want us to be. By itself, change has no value. People talk all about change with a capital "C." But it has no value, one way or the other. It's what you do—actually, what you do for whom—that has value.

**HB:** *For what it's worth, I've talked to probably 15 of your engineers in the interviews that I've been doing for the book. You've got a lot of happy people here. That's unusual to find.*

**JLG:** Thank you. But thank them, because they have the job satisfaction of doing work they believe in because they are business people disguised as engineers. They understand the business proposition because I demand that when we do something engineering-wise, it has a business purpose. Why are we doing this? Is it going to sell more? Cost less? Hopefully both, but I'll take either. Will it open new opportunities for developers? Is it a new register on the organ so that we can compose and play better music? It's got to be one of these three—sells more, costs less, or better music. And they understand that.

I started this when I was at Apple and the first reply I got was, "I don't know, it's not my job to know that. That's marketing." I said, "Look, first, you're smarter than marketing. I'm not going to tell them, but you're smarter than marketing, right?" "Yeah." "And when was the last time you listened to marketing? So, stop this. Tell me what you think because you have a point of view. Tell me your point of view. Take time to figure it out because you do it instinctively, that's fine with me. But in the end, tell me your point of view."

Now, if an engineer has a point of view that happens to be congruent with the overall goal and he has the power to go about implementing his point of view, chances are, he'll have some amount of job satisfaction. So, that's what I hope we have. It's not always that pretty. There are lots of frustrations. When somebody leaves, it can be a difficult time. But my job is to make those transitions happen. There is a time when you have a smaller group, focused on R&D, and so you have a certain behavior. Then when you get closer to business activity, as opposed to R&D, you need a different type of a behavior. That's what you need to do. I'm not paid by the shareholders to be nice. Being nice is the ultimate way of destroying a company. Being nasty or mean will destroy it as well. But that has no value. It is what you accomplish for the constituency that has value, and sometimes you've got to do things which are emotionally painful.

**HB:** *Are you having fun?*

**JLG:** Yeah. I have more fun now than when I was raising money last year, that's for sure. But you know, last year, I was amazed at the fact that we maxed out on fundraising, which was a nice vote. When things started coming together, then it became fun. People told me but I didn't believe it, which was in some ways good—when you're an entrepreneur, you've got to be deluded a little bit. To start a family, remodel a house, or start a company, you've got to have some amount of delusion. So, I didn't believe people telling me, Look, most of your time's going to be spent raising money. Yep, that's true, but, that's the lot. Even in dire times, when the company was running out of money three years ago, I was sleeping better than when I was a corprocrat, because instead of political trouble, I had trouble I agreed with. It's difficult to raise money, but I understand why, so it's not stupid trouble. The trouble agreed with me—in some ways. You know what I'm trying to say? You're nervous and all that stuff, but at least you know what you have to do.

And the people here—speaking of your perception—have been amazingly trusting. Two weeks from the last payroll, they had faith, which is touching, also sometimes a heavy burden to carry. But they had faith that things would turn out—blind faith. They believe in what they do. They trust that the management team will do its job. And I discovered once that managing was a service function. When you get that perspective, things get a lot simpler because you have a service to perform, it's pretty clear what the services are, and you get paid for those services. It's been good for me.

# 2

# Meet the System

If you've already got BeOS up and running on your machine, you're no doubt anxious to dive in and start exploring, so this chapter is designed to get you quickly up to speed with BeOS's most important features and applications. If you haven't yet created a new partition and installed the operating system, you can use this chapter to whet your appetite, or skip ahead to Chapter 3, *Installation*.

# User Interface Conventions

An operating system, viewed in its broadest sense, consists of two major categories: its technological infrastructure and its user interface. As with an automobile, you've got a complex, interlinked collection of systems all supporting one another, and you've got a body—a design, a paint job, an interior, an atmosphere. Everybody loves BeOS's technological underpinnings; they're practically unassailable. But the user interface (UI) is experienced at a more subjective level, and thus becomes a topic of much debate. BeOS attracts users migrating from just about every operating system on the planet, but it also borrows UI conventions from just about every operating system. Be has attempted to create a simple, clean, logical, and aesthetically pleasing UI of its own, and it has also honored by imitation some of the best interface concepts the computer industry has come up with over the past two decades.

If you have experience with multiple operating systems, you may notice that certain aspects of all of them are present in BeOS. After all, there are only so many ways to draw windows, menus, and scrollbars. Besides, radical departures from known ways of doing things can do as much to confuse users as they do good. However, don't let this leave you thinking that BeOS is some kind of a "greatest hits" compilation or Frankenstein monster, simply pulling in the best aspects of lots of OSs *a la carte* style. Huge amounts of work went into making the BeOS UI as clean, intuitive, and elegant as possible.

When Be began to pick up steam in the Intel space, many users coming from Windows Land were very vocal about aspects of 95/NT that they found useful and missed. Be has been accommodating to the needs of those users, but they have a policy: *neither imitate nor innovate for its own sake.* In other words, don't copy other operating systems unless it makes sense to do so; likewise, don't be different from other operating systems just to be different. Usability, logic, and elegance are Be's guiding principles in UI design.

Interestingly, by trying to please the greatest number of people and still maintain a distinct identity, Be faces a paradox of human nature. Think for a moment of the stereotypical tourist, packing off to France for a few weeks to experience something new, and then complaining because things aren't like they were back home. Similarly, while some people clamor for BeOS to keep breaking new ground, others complain just as loudly when BeOS doesn't do something the way <insert favorite OS here> does it.

One of the key points of BeOS's UI is that it's *easy*. Things that should be easy to do *are* easy to do. You'll find that you're not thwarted and frustrated by the interface, nor do you have to find workarounds to accomplish things that should be simple. Most people sitting down in front of a BeOS machine for the first time are able to pretty much get straight to work, after a brief orientation. The UI is designed to make sense almost immediately, regardless of the operating system with which you're most familiar. But more than anything, the BeOS UI tends to have a "just right" feeling about it, sort of like arriving at the future and discovering that things turned out like you had always hoped they would.

Of course, there will also be unfamiliar aspects to the UI. Some things will be accomplished differently from what you're used to, and of course BeOS can do some things that no other operating system can do—these things will have to be learned fresh. Rest assured that if BeOS seems unfamiliar at first, it won't for long. Long-standing habits and muscle memory have a funny way of convincing you that "the old way was better," but as the lights begin to blink on, you may wonder how you ever got things done any other way. If you ever feel frustrated that BeOS doesn't work the way your other OSs do, keep in mind that everything in BeOS is designed as it is for a very good and extensively considered reason. You'll be surprised at how quickly you come to feel right at home, and will soon be working as quickly and efficiently as you do elsewhere, if not more so.

## Notes on Keyboard and Mouse Usage

Because BeOS runs on both PowerPC and x86 hardware, and because BeOS users demand customizability, the question of how to refer to things like mouse buttons and keyboard shortcuts in a standardized way becomes difficult in a book like this. We've attempted to refer to all mouse buttons and keyboard modifiers in terms of the largest cross-section of hardware out there.

**On Keyboards**   There are three basic types of keyboards in wide usage today: the standard Apple-issue keyboard that comes with every Macintosh, the classic 101-key PC keyboard, and the newer 104-key "Windows" keyboards (so called because they have extra keys for accessing common functions in Microsoft Windows). It's becoming increasingly difficult to find decent keyboards that *don't* have the extra Windows keys, though plenty of the 101-key variety are still in the field. In addition, there are international versions of all these keyboards with unique keys tailored to languages besides

## Ctrl+C, Alt+Tab, and Other Anomalies

While the team of Be engineers shares an extremely diverse operating system background, a large proportion of them, particularly in Be's early days, were steeped in Macintosh culture (not to mention the fact that Be's CEO spent many years playing a significant role at Apple). As a result, there are certain aspects of BeOS that manifest a MacOS heritage more strongly than that of Windows or other operating systems. Ironically, increasing numbers of BeOS users are also Windows users (or ex-Windows users), who come to the platform with years of muscle memory telling them that certain things are done in certain ways. This fact initially produced a certain amount of discomfort for some users—even those most willing to start from scratch and learn things anew.

Some of the most prominent examples of this "slippage" appeared shortly after the dawn of BeOS for Intel Architecture and had to do with system keyboardability. The universal cut, copy, and paste shortcuts, for example, were mapped to Alt+C, Alt+V, and Alt+X in BeOS, rather than Ctrl+C, Ctrl+V, and Ctrl+X, as they are in Windows. While this may sound like a simple thing to relearn, many Windows users found themselves hitting the wrong keys even a full year into using BeOS. Similarly, users were no longer able to move a file to the Trash, er, Recycle Bin by tapping the Delete key as in Windows—suddenly it was necessary to contort the thumb under the middle of the left hand to make the rather awkward Alt+T gesture.

But to some, BeOS 3.x's greatest "crime" was to offer no mechanism for task-switching via the keyboard. Windows users, who had used the Alt+Tab combination to alternate between running applications since the beginning of history, found themselves punching these keys to no avail and grumbling every time they had to reach for the mouse just to move from text editor to Web browser to mail client and back again.

**Figure 2.01**

*BeOS R4 aims to accommodate a wider array of users coming from other operating systems with tools like the Twitcher, which is similar to—but better than—Windows' Alt+Tab feature.*

While BeOS for Intel Architecture carried these gotchas for Windows users throughout the entire course of R3, R4 made amends … and then some. R4 introduced the Twitcher, which not only emulated the familiar Alt+Tab combination, but put it on steroids, and users finally gained the ability to select which key they wanted to use for which modifiers, so that Ctrl+C, Ctrl+X, and the rest could be mapped as the user preferred them. And lo and behold, that Delete key finally gained the ability to send files to the Trash.

The moral of the story is that, while BeOS's UI may have its origins in a "foreign country," your hosts are most accommodating and are more than willing to be flexible if it means they can better accommodate your needs as a visitor or new resident.

English. The dilemma for this book revolves around the question of modifier keys, which are different on all three major keyboard types. In addition to the Shift key, which is universal,

- The modern Macintosh keyboard has Command (Apple key), Ctrl, and Option as modifiers.
- The 101-key PC keyboard has just Ctrl and Alt keys.
- The 104-key PC keyboard has Ctrl, Alt, Win, and Menu keys.

Be has partially addressed this situation by creating a set of neutral names for modifier keys. However, the neutral name scheme derives directly from Be's PowerPC-only era, which means that the neutral names are more confusing than useful to the majority of BeOS users. Cross-platform issues have also resulted in a "splitting" of the keyboard—for PC owners, the Alt keys on either side function identically, while the left and right Ctrl keys serve separate functions. In general, whenever someone references the Ctrl key without specifying a side of the keyboard, they mean the left side. If the right Ctrl key is needed, it will usually be referred to as Option, even though there is no Option key on x86 keyboards (see Table 2.01).

Confused yet? It gets better. With R4, Be made it possible for users to toggle the function of the Alt and Ctrl keys on PC keyboards. There were some very good reasons for this. First off, it proved more difficult than expected for Windows users to switch from using the Ctrl key for cut, copy, and paste to using the Alt key. Clearly, it's important that new users be able to feel right at home when sitting down in front of BeOS. Second, many users find the Alt key difficult to use regularly due to its position beneath the palm—the Ctrl key modifier lets users keep their hands in a more natural, open position.

This book refers to modifier keys primarily by the key names printed on the labels of the majority of users' keyboards, which is the 104-key Windows keyboard. However, we also translate key combinations for users of other keyboards a certain percentage of the time. Thus, if you're a Mac user, you should find approximately 25% of the keyboard references translated to your keyboard. PC users are free to toggle the function of their Alt and Ctrl keys via the Menu preferences panel, but this book will assume that the user has kept the default settings (where Alt is the shortcut key, rather than Ctrl). If you remap your modifier keys, you'll need to make the translation mentally while reading this book.

If you're a heavy keyboard user, you should be prepared to relearn a few things. While it may feel like the way you learned to do things via the keyboard is the *one true way*, that's irrational. People like their key bindings because they're *used* to them. Muscle memory counts for more than people realize and is often so ingrained that it gets mistaken for righteousness. While some of BeOS's key bindings may seem odd to you at first, you will grow

## Table 2.01   Cross-Platform Keyboard Equivalencies and Functions

| Windows PC Key Label (104 Keys) | Standard PC Key Label (101 Keys) | Macintosh Key Label | BeOS Key Name | BeOS Function |
|---|---|---|---|---|
| Alt (either side) | Alt (either side) | Command (either side), sometimes called the "Apple Key" | Command | Used with other keys as a shortcut to Tracker actions and for selecting application menu shortcuts directly, but not for pulling down menus. Also known as the "trigger" key. |
| Ctrl (left) | Ctrl (left) | Ctrl (left or right) | Ctrl | Used for emacs-style key bindings in Terminal and BeMail (in other words, Left Ctrl+C stops the running Terminal job and Left Ctrl+E jumps to the end of a line in BeMail). |
| Ctrl (right) | Ctrl (right) | Option (left or right) | Option | Used to type special characters such as symbols and accented characters in supporting applications (in other words, Right Ctrl+J in StyledEdit yields the triangular delta symbol: Δ). |
| Menu | No equivalent | Left Command+ Esc | None | Used to pull down application menus (that is, StyledEdit menus can be accessed with Menu+E. Other keyboards must use Alt+Esc to activate the first menu, then arrow keys to navigate). |
| Left Windows key | Ctrl (right) | Option (left or right) | Option | Used for advanced text navigation in some apps (in other words, Win + Left or Right Arrow moves the cursor one word at a time in editors like Eddie and Pe. The right Windows key is inactive in BeOS). |
| Enter | Enter | Return | Enter | Used to "commit" a typed entry or to act on a selected file and as a shortcut for clicking buttons and opening files. Hitting Enter when an item is selected in the Tracker is equivalent to double-clicking it. |
| Esc | Esc | Esc | Escape | Used as an alternative to clicking Cancel in many panels, and to dismiss open pulldown menus. |
| Tab | Tab | Tab | Tab | Used to cycle through multiple fields (that is, to move between fields a in dialog box or between links on a Web page). |
| (arrows) | (arrows) | (arrows) | Arrow keys | Used to scroll through lists and menus and to move the cursor in text documents or wherever vertical and/or horizontal motion is required. |
| Shift | Shift | Shift | Shift | Used to select text in documents (in conjunction with other navigation keys) and to augment other actions (that is, to select multiple files in the Tracker or to cycle backwards in the Twitcher). |

*The keyboard modifiers you'll be using for common tasks depend on the particular keyboard you own, as BeOS maps various classes of keyboard differently. This book refers primarily to the keyboard modifiers listed in the left column of this table.*

accustomed to them in time, just as you grew accustomed to the ones you've been using all these years.

***Switch Your Modifier Keys*** One of the things that Windows migrants have the most trouble with is the fact that, by default, cut, copy, and paste are mapped to the Alt rather than the Ctrl keys. Happily, this key mapping became a user option with BeOS R4. If you'd rather use Ctrl as your main shortcut key, open your Preferences folder from the Be menu and launch the Menu application. At the bottom of the sample menu, you'll see two entries, one marked "Ctrl as Shortcut Key" and the other marked "Alt as Shortcut Key." Select Ctrl as Shortcut Key, close the Menu app, and you're done—the behavior of these two keys will have been swapped, no reboot required. The rest of the Menu preferences are covered in Chapter 9, *Preferences and Customization*.

*Figure 2.02*

*To change your shortcut modifier key from the default of Alt to Ctrl, open the Menu application in your Preferences folder, select Ctrl as Shortcut Key, and close. Changes will take effect immediately. If you do this, remember that you'll have to mentally translate any references in this book to the new key mapping!*

**On Mice** While BeOS can certainly be used with a single-button mouse, you will probably have an easier time accessing many features of the user interface with a two-button mouse. Throughout this book you'll encounter phrases such as "right-click on X and ..." If you own a single-button mouse, be aware that you can duplicate the functionality of just about any right-button feature by holding down your Ctrl key while clicking.

In addition, the BeOS Mouse preferences panel makes it possible to map your mouse buttons any way you see fit. In other words, you're perfectly free to map left button functions to the right button and vice versa. Some mice even ship with three or more buttons, so you may want to map the middle button to right button functions, or whatever suits your work habits. Technically then, it might make logical sense for this book to refer to primary, secondary, and tertiary mouse buttons. However, since the vast majority of users have two-button mice and don't mess with the default button mappings, we have retained the colloquial—and simpler—left and right button terminology. If your mouse usage varies in any of the ways described above, just make the necessary substitution whenever we refer to left or right buttons.

***Macs and Multibutton Mice*** While the Macintosh ships with a one-button mouse by default, there are many multibutton mice available from third parties. Although you'll need special software to use these under MacOS, BeOS handles most of them almost transparently. Kensington mice, in particular, are known to work very well with BeOS. It is possible to emulate any right-button function in BeOS with a one-button mouse by holding down the Ctrl key and clicking, but you'll probably have a better experience by plunking down US $25 or so on a two- or three-button mouse.

# A Tour of BeOS

With that piece of business out of the way, let's dive in and take a look at the key aspects of BeOS, starting with main components of the interface and then digging into the applications and optional files that come bundled with the system.

Note that some of the features touched on in this tour, such as the Terminal and networking, require more coverage than they get in this section. Consider this the executive tour; we'll show you the engine room later on.

## Desktop

As with most operating systems, the desktop is the foundation of BeOS's user interface, and probably needs little introduction. Like most desktops, it comes with a launcher/window manager (the Deskbar) and a Trash can. It also

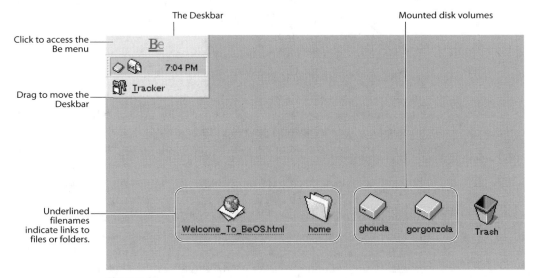

*Figure 2.03*

*The default BeOS desktop includes icons for the Trash, mounted disk volumes, your home folder, and BeOS documentation. The desktop also hosts the Deskbar—yours will probably look quite a bit different after a few days of using and customizing the system.*

includes icons representing your currently mounted disk volumes, a link to your home folder, and a link to the BeOS user documentation. Naturally, the desktop is capable of storing any files, folders or links you care to drop there.

The BeOS desktop is also the "root" (base) of the BeOS filesystem. Any disk volumes currently mounted on your system will appear on the desktop (see later in this chapter for more on mounting and unmounting disk volumes).

**The home Folder**  If you're the sole user of your BeOS machine, you can pretty much store your files wherever you like. But just because you *can* doesn't mean you necessarily *should*. BeOS has a very well-designed and logical directory structure (see Chapter 5, *Files and the Tracker*, for details). Many of the folders in BeOS have system-related purposes so moving, deleting, or renaming them can have potentially harmful consequences. However, your home folder is your sacred territory, and this is where you should keep your personal data. Be promises never to mess with it during upgrades, and only a few applications require the addition of files to your home folder. Even then, added files are stored in well-defined places, away from your personal data.

All of your email, saved system queries, and personal contacts are stored in your home folder. In addition, application customization files are stored in a config subdirectory of your home folder. You'll probably want to create an

## Terminology Used in This Book

Throughout this book, the words folder and directory are used interchangeably and mean exactly the same thing. Paths to files and folders, even when we're talking about the graphical user interface, are specified in standard Unix format (which is also the format used on the Internet), so a brief lesson is in order.

In a pathname, a solitary forward slash (/) represents the root of a disk volume—the top of the directory structure. Moving down the directory tree from there, simply name the folders, separated by slashes, until you reach your destination. Thus, /boot/home/mail refers to a folder called "mail" inside a folder called "home" which is inside a folder called "boot."

The boot folder is the most important directory on your disk and will be referenced constantly. While there are other directories besides boot stemming from the root, you'll rarely need to access them. Again, BeOS's directory structure is explained in detail in Chapter 5.

It's important to observe whether or not a path starts with a forward slash as its first character. If it does, the path starts at the root. This type of path reference is known as an absolute path. If it doesn't, the path starts from where you're currently working—this format is known as a relative path. For example, if you're looking at your home directory and I specify the path mail/in, you should assume that mail is a subdirectory of home. However, if I specified the path /mail/in/, it would mean that the mail folder stems from the root (it doesn't—that's just hypothetical).

array of customized directories inside your home folder as well—you might keep directories here for storing and archiving downloaded files, a mirror of your Web site, graphical works in progress, and the love letter you've been working on for weeks.

Your home folder does not actually live on the desktop. See the gray line beneath its name? Any time you see an underlined filename, you're looking at a link to another location. Your home folder actually lives just off your system's /boot directory—a link to it has been placed on the desktop for your convenience.

Finally, because paths so often begin with /boot/home/, that string is sometimes foreshortened to ~ (the tilde character). Thus, the path ~/mail/in is equivalent to /boot/home/mail/in. This explains why you see the ~ character so often in Internet URLs. Note, however, that the ~ shorthand only works in the shell—you won't see or be able to use this format while using the Tracker.

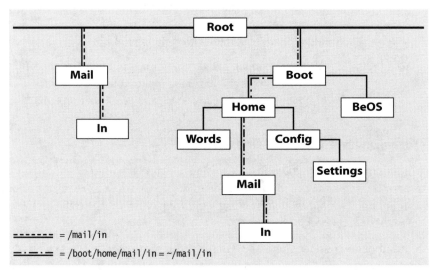

**Figure 2.04**

*If the current directory is /boot/home, then a reference to* mail/in—*which does not start with a preceding /—actually refers to /boot/home/mail/in. However, a reference to /mail/in—which does begin with a preceding /—refers to a hypothetical /mail/in directory stemming from the root. Because /boot/home is referenced so often, it's often abbreviated with a "~" character. Thus, ~config/settings refers to /boot/home/config/settings.*

*These path conventions are used in this book for several reasons. For one, it's the same way that files and folders are referenced from BeOS's command-line program, the Terminal. Second, it's a standard used wherever Unix-compatible systems are found, including on the Internet, and in Be's own documentation. Third, it's an easy shorthand.*

**Documentation**  Naturally, BeOS comes with excellent documentation, and all of it is written in lovely HTML format. Double-clicking the documentation icon on the desktop will launch the documentation home page in NetPositive, BeOS's built-in Web browser.

Because the documentation is all digital, you can't take it to the beach as you can this book, but it does contain answers to many of the questions you might have about your operating system. Be has actually installed entire sections of their own Web site on your hard drive, including the BeOS User's Guide, registration information, configuration details, links to Be's online software libraries, and more. If you ever lose the documentation link, you'll find the actual documents stored on your system at /boot/beos/documentation and its subdirectories. If you're intimately familiar with every aspect of BeOS and you're hurting for disk space, it's safe to delete this documentation ... but not recommended. It only takes up a couple of megabytes total and is exactly the kind of thing you find that you need just a few days after deleting it. If you should ever happen to lose your installed documentation, or would like to make sure you're seeing the latest version, Be stores the most up-to-date copy available at **www.be.com/documentation**.

Note to advanced users: Even if you're familiar with every aspect of BeOS, there are still pages in the user documentation that you may find useful, such as the "man" pages for many of the BeOS shell tools. Since BeOS does not include a man function as of R4, this is your only access to the actual Unix-style documentation for these tools.

**Mounted Volumes**   Every operating system needs a mechanism for file management. In Apple's MacOS it's the Finder, in Microsoft Windows it's Explorer, and in BeOS it's the Tracker. Your desktop represents the root of the Tracker, and displays all of the disk volumes currently mounted on your system. Double-click any volume icon within to start exploring your system's folder hierarchy.

To find out how much space is left on any of your volumes, click on one with your right mouse button (Mac users: Ctrl+click) and choose Get Info from the pop-up menu. You'll be able to see at a glance its capacity, remaining free space, creation/modification dates, and the "kind," or type of drive, BeOS recognizes it as. Note that the "path" field consists of a single "/" character, meaning that this object lives at the root level of the filesystem, or directly on the desktop. Selecting Get Info for any other file or folder in the system will report a full path in this field.

**Figure 2.05**

*Selecting Get Info after right-clicking the drive's icon will display its capacity and remaining free space at a glance. Similar panels are displayed when you choose Get Info for a file rather than a volume.*

If you insert a removable disk such as a CD-ROM, floppy, or Zip or Jaz cartridge, it may or may not appear on the desktop immediately, depending on the drive mechanism and whether or not it's capable of notifying the system of the presence of a new disk. For example, most CD-ROM drives will send a message to BeOS when you insert a disk, but floppy drives will not.

In addition to the disks already mounted on your system, there may also be other mountable disks available to you—volumes

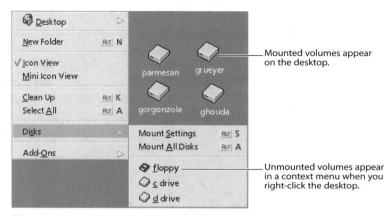

Mounted volumes appear on the desktop.

Unmounted volumes appear in a context menu when you right-click the desktop.

*Figure 2.06*

*Right-click on the desktop, select Disks from the context menu, and you'll see icons for all of the currently unmounted volumes attached to your system. Select one of those icons and that volume will immediately appear on your desktop.*

formatted under other operating systems, for example. To find out which other volumes you can mount, right-click on the desktop and scroll down to the Mount entry in the context menu. Any other mountable drives available to you will appear as entries scrolling from this menu (see Figure 2.06). You can also choose to mount all mountable disks right now by scrolling down to All Disks. To unmount a volume, right-click its icon on the desktop (Mac users: Ctrl+click) and choose Unmount from the context menu.

The last entry in this context menu is labeled Settings. Select it and you'll see a panel like the one in Figure 2.07. The disk volumes that appear on your desktop when you first boot your system are determined by the settings you've established in your Mount Settings panel. For example, if your Mount Settings specify that only BFS-formatted volumes should be mounted automatically, but there are also Windows volumes attached to your system, you

*Figure 2.07*

*Clicking "Mount all disks now" in the Mount Settings panel will cause BeOS to scan all drives attached to your system for mountable volumes. You can also use this panel to specify which kinds of disks BeOS should attempt to automatically mount at boot time and during normal operation.*

might see something similar to Figure 2.07 when right-clicking on the desktop. Click "Mount all disks now" and your new volume(s) should appear on the desktop.

**We'll cover disk mounting in more detail in Chapter 5, but there's one thing you should know: The Tracker sometimes gets confused if you physically remove a removable disk without unmounting it first. While this behavior may be fixed by the time you read this, it's good practice to get in the habit of always unmounting any disk you're about to remove, whether it be a floppy, CD, Zip, Jaz, or anything else.**

***Changing the Behavior of Mounted Disks***  **In BeOS R3, disk volumes were not mounted on the desktop. Instead, they appeared inside a special folder called** `Disks` **that lived on the desktop. In R4, the desktop officially became the root of the filesystem, and the** `Disks` **folder went away ... or so it seemed. Users who had a lot of disks mounted at the same time found that the desktop became cluttered with volume icons too quickly (Mac users will be able to relate to this one), so Be did** *the right thing* **and made the** `Disks` **folder an option. Now you can mount disks on the desktop, or inside the** `Disks` **folder—whichever you prefer.**

**Note: This tip is for intermediate and advanced users. If you're brand new to BeOS, you might want to delay trying this for a while, as it involves some tricky business that we don't cover fully until later in this book.**

**First off, you'll need to know how to kill off and then restart the Tracker. Open a Terminal window where you can access it easily. Then, while holding down Ctrl, Alt, and Shift (Mac users: Shift+Option+Command) on the right side of your keyboard, click the Tracker's entry in the Deskbar. Everything on your desktop will disappear, and all open Tracker windows will close. Now click in the Terminal window and type:**

```
/boot/beos/system/Tracker &
```

**The Tracker will spring back to life and everything will be just as you left it. Now that you've got that trick down, here comes the good part. Open the folder** `/boot/home/config/settings/Tracker`**, and make a duplicate copy of the file** `TrackerSettings` **(so you have an original around as a backup, just in case). Double-click** `TrackerSettings` **and you'll see the following lines:**

```
ShowDisksIcon off
MountVolumesOntoDesktop on
IntegrateNonBootBeOSDesktops on
IntegrateAllNonBootDesktops off
DesktopFilePanelRoot on
```

Each of these lines controls a different aspect of the Tracker's behavior, and you can turn each of them on or off by editing the final word in the line. To make disks in BeOS R4 behave like they did in R3, toggle ShowDisksIcon to on, and MountVolumesOntoDesktop to off. Save the file, then kill and restart the Tracker as described above.

The other lines in this file are a little more obscure, but also potentially useful. As you'll discover in Chapter 9, a desktop folder is automatically created on every BeOS partition. In addition, you can install BeOS on multiple partitions. By default, all desktop folders are merged into a single entity, meaning that you can end up with icons for folders and files you've stored on other partitions' desktops showing up on your current desktop. Toggle the two Integrate lines to their opposite settings to stop this behavior. Finally, you can specify whether or not the desktop appears as the root of the filesystem in all of your applications' file panels by toggling the final line to off.

True to BeOS principles, none of these changes requires a reboot. Just save the TrackerSettings file and restart the Tracker.

**The Trash** You're probably familiar with the Trash can metaphor—every operating system uses a variant of this basic idea. Whenever you delete files from within BeOS's graphical interface, they're actually moved to the Trash for safe keeping. Whether you drag files' icons onto the Trash icon or select files and hit Alt+T (Mac users: Command+T) or tap the Delete key (x86 users only), your files don't disappear into the ether. If you realize five minutes—or five days—later that you needed those files after all, just double-click on the Trash to see all of your "deleted" files. To restore them to where they were, just select them and drag them to wherever you want them. (BeOS R4 is not able to magically restore files to their original locations, though this may change in the future.)

**Figure 2.08**

*To empty your Trash, right-click its icon and choose Empty Trash from the pop-up menu.*

Files are not truly gone until you right-click the Trash icon and choose Empty Trash from the pop-up menu. After you select Empty Trash, the progress indicator displayed includes Pause and Stop buttons in case you feel the need to back out halfway through the job. Pause and Stop will not, however, restore items that have already been emptied from the Trash. If you pause and then want to resume, click the Pause button a second time.

**Deleting Files from the Terminal Is Permanent**  While we won't cover file management from the Terminal until Chapter 6, *The Terminal*, it's worth saying this now, lest you get adventurous: Files are *only* moved to the Trash when deleted from within Tracker. If you use the rm command to delete files or folders while in the Terminal, your files will be deleted instantly, without warning or confirmation. As our technical editor notes, "The command line is a big hammer—watch where you swing it." Well put.

 *Don't Rename the Trash*  You'll notice that the Edit Name option does not appear when you right-click on the Trash icon. But for years, you've always renamed Windows 95's Recycle Bin to "Garbaj," and now you're kind of fond of the name. So you think, "I'm clever—I'll just rename it from the Terminal." You succeed, and everything is peachy, until you try and delete something and find that the Trash—er, Garbaj—doesn't work like it's supposed to. Renaming it back is not as easy as it might seem, either. In short, don't try it—BeOS doesn't like it one bit, and you'll just create headaches for yourself. This, by the way, is not considered a bug; the Trash is a special folder with special properties, and other parts of the system depend on it having the correct name. (If you do get into trouble with the Trash, just reboot your system—a brand new Trash will be created for you, and you can safely delete Garbaj or whatever it was that you tried to create.)

**Deskbar**  The Deskbar is the rectangular block probably hanging out at the top-right corner of your screen, and will likely be the single BeOS feature that you use most often. Its function is to keep tabs on all of your running applications and all of their open windows, giving you instant access to anything you've got open. If it seems familiar in a *dèja vu* kind of way, it's probably because the Deskbar is a perfect example of how Be has looked to existing operating systems for inspiration, paying homage by borrowing from the best, and throwing away the rest.

**Figure 2.09**

The Deskbar keeps tabs on all running applications, offers a link to the Be system menu (the Be menu), and contains a "shelf" that can host special application icons.

When you launch an application, its name and icon are displayed horizontally in the Deskbar. Click and hold on an entry and a pop-out menu will display the names of all the windows currently open under that application. Sliding over to a named window and releasing the mouse will bring that window to the front.

Each entry also has a few extra goodies at the bottom of its window list, giving you even more control. You can bring all of an application's windows forward at once by choosing Show All, or get them all out of the way with Hide All. Choosing Close All will, obviously, close all of that application's windows. In most cases, this will also close the application itself.

**Figure 2.10**

*Sliding through any Deskbar entry displays a list of all open windows for that application. Below the window list you'll find options to Show All, Hide All, or Close All.*

 The Tracker's entry in this menu is an exception to the rule above—even when all Tracker windows are closed, the Tracker will still have an entry in the Deskbar.

 **Use the Vulcan Death Grip**  If an application hangs or refuses to close properly, the easiest way to kill it off completely is to use the Vulcan Death Grip. Hold down the Alt, Ctrl, and Shift keys on the right side of your keyboard (Mac users: Shift+Option+Command on either side) and click that application's entry in the Deskbar. Ninety-nine of the time, that application will blink out of existence. If it doesn't, there are other methods you can use to kill errant applications from the Terminal (see Chapter 6).

**Moving and Configuring the Deskbar**  The Deskbar doesn't have to stay at the top right of your screen—you can move it to any corner or side. Grab the strip of six tiny dots at the edge of the Deskbar's shelf and start dragging. Nothing will happen … until your mouse reaches all the way across the screen, that is. Drag all the way to another corner, and the Deskbar will snap into its new position. You can place it horizontally or vertically across the sides and top, or toss it into any corner.

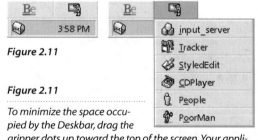

**Figure 2.11**

**Figure 2.11**

*To minimize the space occupied by the Deskbar, drag the gripper dots up toward the top of the screen. Your application entries may seem to have disappeared, but you can still access them by clicking on the chalkboard icon.*

In addition, the Deskbar is "squashable," meaning that you can minimize the amount of screen real estate it takes up. If you move it to one of the bottom corners, this is its only configuration. In one of the upper positions, grab the gripper dots and drag upward until it compresses to a minimal height.

Squashing the Deskbar may save you a little screen real estate, but it also means that all of your applications are now buried one level deeper than before, since you'll have to click on the Be menu's chalkboard icon to get to them.

Running applications

Hash marks
indicate that this
window is in
another workspace.

NetPositive: BeOS vs. Linux Comparison Chart

Arrows indicate that this application
owns more than one window.

*Figure 2.13*

*By holding down your Alt or Ctrl key (depending on your preference settings) and tapping the Tab key, you can wheel visually through all of your running applications. Release the Alt or Ctrl key to bring the selected application to the front.*

**The Twitcher**  If you're not a big mouse fan, you can switch between running applications with the Twitcher (short for Task Switcher), which does everything Windows' Alt+Tab does, but with less clutter and more class. If you haven't changed the default mapping of BeOS's modifier keys, the Twitcher is invoked by holding down the left Ctrl key while tapping the Tab key. If you've chosen to switch your modifier keys in the Menu preferences panel (Chapter 9), you can continue to use the Alt+Tab combination you may have ingrained in your muscle memory from years of Windows use.

Tap Alt+Tab quickly to switch between apps that are not minimized and not in another workspace. Press and hold Ctrl+Tab to invoke Twitcher's interface, which lets you access any open window belonging to any open app.

So how is the Twitcher *better* than Alt+Tab? For many applications (such as Explorer and Netscape), Windows registers every open window as a separate icon in the Alt+Tab wheel, which can get to be rather unwieldy as soon as you've got half a dozen folders and three or four browser windows open simultaneously. The Twitcher, on the other hand, registers one icon per application, period. Regardless, how many Tracker folders you've got open, the Tracker will only appear once in the Twitcher wheel. That's not to say you can't access specific windows from the Twitcher. Anytime an application has more than one open window, you'll see a small pair of arrows pointing up or down on either side of the window name (see Figure 2.13). While paused on a multiwindow entry, use your keyboard's Up and Down Arrows to scroll through that application's windows.

***Moving Backward***  **One significant functional difference between the Twitcher and Alt+Tab is that the Twitcher is truly a "wheel"—tapping Ctrl+Tab once will always take you to the next application, whereas in Windows, a single tap always takes you back to the previous application. While it may take a bit of getting used to, you'll have to learn to augment your keystrokes with the Shift key if you want to move backward on the wheel to the previous application. The Twitcher's use of the Shift key is consistent with the role of Shift as a "reverser" elsewhere in the system and in many applications.**

If you have more applications open than will fit into the Twitcher's window, small arrows also appear at the left and right end to indicate more to come. If a window is open in another workspace, hash marks next to its icon will let you know.

**Click with your mouse on any icon in the Twitcher's interface to jump directly to that app.**

**The Be Menu**   The very top entry in the Deskbar is always the Be Menu, which is marked with Be's logo. Click on the Be logo to access your most-used folders and system-wide controls. Note that this is different from clicking other entries in the Deskbar, which only give you access to a running

*Figure 2.14*

*Click Be's logo on the Deskbar to pull down the Be menu, which gives you quick access to your most-used folders and key system functions.*

application's windows. Accessing the Be menu presents a "compound" menu consisting of system-wide controls at the top and your custom list of favorite folders on the bottom. If you're familiar with MacOS, you'll find that this functions something like the Apple menu. The sections below explain the controls at the top of the Be menu, as well as how to customize the list of favorite folders.

**About BeOS**   While there are more powerful and detailed system profilers available for BeOS (many of them free for the download), this is the official "about box." It tells you what kind of hardware you're running on, which builds of the operating system kernel and Tracker you're running, how long the system has been running without a reboot, and how much RAM is installed in your system. Hold down Ctrl+Alt+Shift while choosing About BeOS to see how much memory is currently in use.

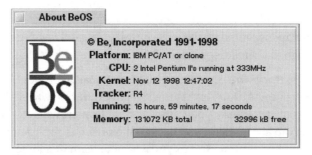

*Figure 2.15*

*Pull up a summary report of your hardware, memory, and kernel and Tracker versions by selecting About BeOS from the Be menu.*

***Resuscitating the Deskbar***  While BeOS gets harder and harder to crash with every subsequent release, it's still mortal, and certain components are still capable of going south when under duress. Of course, if the Tracker or Deskbar crash, you're pretty much sunk, right? Not necessarily. Like all applications in BeOS, you can launch these two critical system services from the Terminal, providing you already have a Terminal window open. If you don't, and have no other way to launch anything, you'll probably have to reboot. Otherwise, open a Terminal window and type:

```
/boot/beos/system/Tracker &
```

**or**

```
/boot/beos/system/Deskbar &
```

In most cases, they'll be restored. In fact, they'll usually jump back in the game right where they left off, with all the same windows open and applications accessible. Sure beats rebooting. The ampersand (&) symbol tells Terminal to run this command in the background. When you add & to the end of a Terminal command, the Terminal returns control to you so you can continue to type other commands. While this technique will still work if you leave off the ampersand, closing that Terminal window would result in that process being killed. In other words, the Tracker or Deskbar would die again as soon as you closed that Terminal window.

**Find**  Sure, MacOS and Windows have Find functions, but they're nothing like BeOS' query mechanism. Because the BeOS filesystem has many database-like characteristics, it's possible to do data mining on your hard drive like you've never dreamed possible. In fact, BeOS queries are so powerful and fast, I've devoted all of Chapter 7, *Working with Queries*, to them. For now, though, why not tease yourself with a taste of Find's speed on a plain vanilla filename hunt?

**Figure 2.20**

*To start a system query, select Find from the Be menu, type in a text string, hit Enter, and watch it cook.*

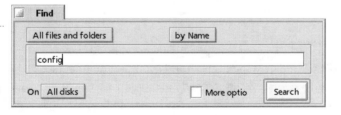

Pull down the Be menu and select Find (you can also get to the Find dialog by hitting Alt+F when any Tracker window is in front). Without using any of the pull-down menus, type in a good, system-y sounding word, like "config" and hit enter. On my BeOS machine, 389 matching files are located on my 1.5GB partition in less than four seconds. Great party trick. Queries can also be run from within the Terminal—you'll find command-line query syntax detailed in Chapter 7.

## The Easter Eggs

Like most operating systems, BeOS has Easter Eggs—jokes hidden in the system code just waiting for nosy or curious users to find them by accident.

Select About BeOS from the Be menu to bring up the simple panel describing your system, then click on the BeOS logo to change the panel to a scrolling list of credits (Be developers and employees). OK—ready to tie your fingers in a knot? All at once, hold down:

- Mac keyboards: Command, Option, Ctrl, Shift

- 101-key PC keyboards: Left Ctrl, Right Ctrl, Alt, Shift

- 104-key PC keyboards, right side: Alt, Menu, Ctrl, Shift

Note that this maneuver will be close to impossible to pull off without assistance from a friend if you have a 101-key keyboard!

Now, while keeping your fingers contorted, use your mouse to click on the very tippy tip of the letter "e" in Be's logo. If you got everything right, the credits will begin to scroll again, but this time they'll be in a red font, rather than yellow, and will begin with the words, "This version of BeOS hacked for you by … " Most of the credits that follow are pretty straightforward, with a few exceptions, but as you get closer to the end, things get a little looser. Without giving too much away, suffice it to say that this is probably the only chance you'll ever get to see an operating system vendor give thanks to Mr. Hanky the Christmas Poo.

*Figure 2.16*

*Does anyone stick around to read credits anymore? You can, if you know the secret handshake.*

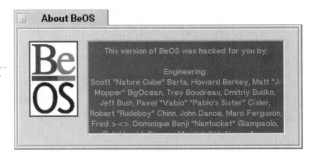

### The Really Hot Easter Egg

What you are about to read may shock and horrify you, as it did that fateful day at Be HQ during this author's first R4 demo. Everything had been going along just peachy, when suddenly I realized that something about the demo was not quite right. R4 was still up and running, but … but … the friendly yellow title tabs on all of the windows were gone. They had been replaced by (are you sitting down?) Windows 95 title tabs, complete with a blue gradient and the three-button array in the upper-right corner. As my face scrunched up in simultaneous disbelief and laughter, Dominic Giampaolo (author of the Be filesystem and tour giver that day) struggled to keep a straight face. "What? What?" he kept asking. After much cajoling and not a little bribery,

I got Dominic to spill the beans. Ready for the cruelest Easter Egg of all time? Here it is:

1. Go to one of your colleagues' BeOS computers while they're on their lunch break.

2. Hold down Ctrl, Alt, and Shift on the left side of the keyboard (Mac users: Shift+Ctrl+Command, either side).

3. Pull down the Be menu and you'll see a new entry labeled "Window Decor."

4. Scroll over to Windows 95/98 and release.

5. Hide behind the water cooler with a periscope until your workmate returns from lunch. Enjoy the show.

**Figure 2.17**

*Painful as it may be for some people to swallow, R4 actually does include an Easter Egg this devilish.*

The fun doesn't stop with Windows 95, though—BeOS can also now emulate the AmigaOS and MacOS window styles from the same menu.

**If you're coming from the Windows world, you're accustomed to being able to resize a window by any border. As a general rule, BeOS does not behave this way. However, when you change the Window Decor to Windows95/98 mode, you'll find that you *can* resize windows by any border!**

**Figure 2.18**

*And for the nostalgic in you, a somewhat more spartan window management scheme—the AmigaOS desktop.*

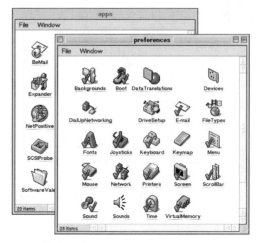

**Figure 2.19**

*Classic beauty—a tip of the hat to the velveteen desktop.*

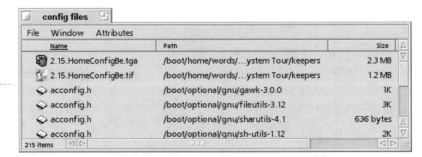

**Figure 2.21**

*Thanks to BeOS's database-like filesystem, finding files is incredibly fast and flexible.*

Query results always show up in a gray Tracker window. You can treat files in this results window just as you would anywhere else in Tracker—copy, move, delete, rename, or anything else. This doesn't scratch the surface of queries, but it's enough to let you find basic files in a hurry.

To fully explore the power of queries, see Chapter 7.

**Show Replicants** Because BeOS's Replicant technology is somewhat abstract, let's jump straight into a concrete example of Replicants in action.

Select Show Replicants from the Be menu (if yours says Hide Replicants, then you've already got them showing). Click on the Be menu again, scroll down to the Applications folder, and release. Launch the Clock application and look for the tiny hand-shaped widget in the Clock application's bottom-right corner (this book will refer to this hand-shaped widget as "the Replicant handle"). With your mouse, grab the handle and drag it to a blank spot on your desktop. A copy of the clock should lift out of its frame and become embedded in your desktop. Now close the Clock application by clicking the small box at the left end of its yellow title bar. At this point, the application has been killed, while the Replicant lives on. In fact, it'll still be going even after you reboot. Now try the same experiment with NetPositive.

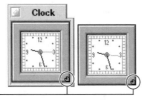

Replicant handle

**Figure 2.22**

*Like weird science, Replicants live on, even after the program that spawned them has been closed.*

The only way to determine whether an application is Replicant-capable is to choose Show Replicants from the Be menu and check to see if a Replicant handle appears in the application's window.

However, the desktop isn't the only place where Replicants can be dropped. The BeOS architecture includes a notion of "containers," or "Replicant shelves," and any BeOS application can theoretically be made into a container by its programmer. In fact, the Container application in your demos folder exists for this purpose alone—to host Replicants.

When you create a Replicant, a copy of the running application is "freeze-dried" and put into storage for safe keeping. Accessing a container—such as the desktop—at a later time "unfreezes" the Replicant and brings it back to life just as it was. Thus, Replicants live on even when their containers are closed, or between boots.

What are some practical applications for Replicant technology? Here's a good one: NetPositive, the BeOS Web browser, is capable of becoming a Replicant. Since the desktop is a container, a copy of the browser can be embedded in the desktop. Make the Replicant browser's home page your favorite search engine, and you've got Web search capabilities embedded right into your desktop. Another extremely cool Replicant is a third-party sound player called SoundPlay. Interestingly, SoundPlay's main window will take on the color of your desktop when it's replicated so that all you have left is a set of controls for playing your favorite MPEG or other sound files embedded in your desktop.

### Dèja Vu?

If the "browser in desktop" trick sounds familiar, it's probably because of all the hoo-haa Microsoft made about this functionality back in 1997 with the advent of ActiveDesktop. But whereas Microsoft required dozens of engineers working for months to embed a browser in the desktop, it took the Be team about nine lines of code to achieve the same effect. Of course, their methods are totally unrelated, even if the end result is similar. Nevertheless, this story still testifies to the simple elegance of BeOS's underlying architecture.

 **Removing Replicants** To remove a Replicant, simply drag it to the Trash. Alternatively, make sure Show Replicants is showing in the Be menu, then *right*-click the Replicant handle (Mac users: Ctrl+click) and choose Delete from the pop-up menu.

**Figure 2.23**

*To remove a Replicant, drag it to the Trash or right-click its handle and choose Delete from the pop-up menu.*

**Reboot and Shutdown** The function of these two Be menu items is pretty obvious. Choosing either of them will initiate a termination sequence for BeOS, shutting down all of your applications and all of the system's servers (see Chapter 1, *The MediaOS,* and Chapter 5, for more on the system servers). A small window will display the icon for each running application (including all running system servers and daemons) as it cycles through the process of killing them off. If any are hung or unresponsive for some reason, you'll get a Kill button you can click to force the issue. On rare occasions, a midbehaved server or application will refuse to die no matter what, and you'll just have to power down your machine. It's nice to know, though, that because BeOS has a fully journaled filesystem, BeOS doesn't even hiccup when rebooting after sudden or ungraceful shutdowns. (More on journaling and the Be file system in Chapter 5.)

**Figure 2.24**

Shutting down BeOS takes just a few seconds. From this screen you can either turn off your computer or reboot with a click.

Most of the time, the shutdown goes by in a flash, and you can turn off your machine in just a few seconds. If you chose Shutdown, BeOS will display a final dialog, giving you the option to reboot in case you've changed your mind. Choosing Restart from the Be menu initiates the same process, but proceeds without displaying the final dialog.

*Graceful Shutdowns* Rebooting a Mac after an ungraceful shutdown requires rebuilding the desktop; rebooting Windows after an ungraceful shutdown sets ScanDisk into motion; rebooting Linux after an ungraceful shutdown requires a lengthy fsck (filesystem check) process. But pull the plug on BeOS and it boots back up just as quickly as if you had shut down normally. So are proper shutdowns a requirement? Well, not a requirement, exactly, but there are some very good reasons to do it right. For one, BeOS actually does use a process analogous to other operating systems, wherein the filesystem journal is compared to the actual state of data on your mounted volumes. Just because this process runs so quickly that you can barely perceive it doesn't mean it isn't happening. By shutting down properly, you ensure that the journal is "synched" to the actual data saved on your hard drive.

Secondly, the nature of BeOS workspaces means that you could have open applications hidden from view (though of course they'll have entries in the Deskbar, even if you can't see the applications themselves). Shutting down properly will cause all running applications to initiate shutdown processes of their own, and this in turn will cause them to prompt you to save any unsaved work.

Don't let the speed of BeOS reboots after ungraceful shutdowns lull you into a false sense of security—the BeOS filesystem is incredibly resilient, but there's no need to tempt fate.

**Be Menu Folder Shortcuts** Since there are some files and folders you need to access continually and others that you almost never touch, it's great to be able to place links to your favorite haunts within easy reach. While you can always access less-essential files and folders from the Disks icon or from any Tracker window, the Be menu doubles as an excellent repository for "quick launch" items. This functions as a fully configurable custom launchpad, much like MacOS's Apple menu or Windows's Start menu.

If you've just installed BeOS, you'll see your Applications, Demos, and Preferences folders listed here by default. It won't be long, however, before you'll want to customize the selection. In order to do this, you first need to know how to make symlinks.

**Creating Links**  Open a Tracker window, any Tracker window. Make sure you can see a bit of blank desktop somewhere. With your right mouse button, grab any file or folder visible in the Tracker and drag it to the desktop. When you release, you'll be asked whether you want to move, copy, or create a link to the file in the new location. Choose Create link, and a copy of the icon will appear on the desktop. It's important to understand that you did not copy the file itself—you just created a pointer, similar to a MacOS alias or a Windows shortcut. Links are distinguished from files by the fact that their names are underlined in light gray. We didn't have to create a link on the desktop, by the way; links can live in any folder. You can learn more about creating and using symlinks in Chapter 5.

To place a link in the Be menu, you'll need to open the folder /boot/home/ config/be in the Tracker. Since your home folder doesn't yet exist in the Be menu, you'll need to do this by starting from your boot disk's icon, which is on your desktop. To make accessing the home folder easier in the future, the home folder itself is probably the first thing you'll want to add to the Be menu.

1. Right-click the icon for your boot volume and scroll up to home, then over to config, then over to be.

2. Release on be and you'll be looking at a Tracker view that mirrors the contents of your Be menu.

3. In this Tracker view, just create symlinks to anything you want to be able to access from the Be menu. we strongly recommend starting by placing a link to your home folder here (if there's still a link to home on your desktop, you could start by making a copy of it here). You can create links to programs or to individual files just as easily as you can to folders.

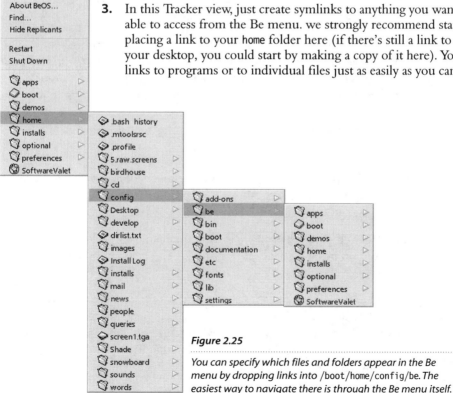

**Figure 2.25**

*You can specify which files and folders appear in the Be menu by dropping links into /boot/home/config/be. The easiest way to navigate there is through the Be menu itself.*

***Mounted Disks in the Be Menu*** **If you'd like to be able to access all of your mounted disks from the Be menu rather than digging around on the desktop, you'll find that you can't do it from Tracker (because you can't exactly drag the whole desktop into the** /boot/home/config/be **menu, now can you?). To get around this quirk, you'll need to use the command line to create a symlink instead. The command for this,** ln, **is covered in Chapter 5, but for now, just open a Terminal window and type this:**

```
ln -s / ~/config/be/Disks
```

**Pay careful attention to the placement of spaces in the command above. Now take another look at your Be menu—instant access to any disk volume!**

**The Deskbar Shelf**  Near the top of the Deskbar is a neat little indented well called the status view, which hosts a digital clock. This area is only semi-configurable by end-users. While the Deskbar shelf is a Replicant container, it won't accept just any Replicant—developers need to create Replicants specifically designed to work in this space. The first Replicant you notice here will probably be the BeMail mailbox icon, which appears as soon as you launch the system's mail daemon (Chapter 4, *Get Online Fast*). The mailbox Replicant lets you check for new messages or write new ones with a quick click, whether BeMail itself is open or not. If you later configure Dial-Up Networking to access the Internet, you'll find another small replicant here as well, which you can right-click to quickly connect and disconnect.

***What's the Date?*** **If you click on the digital clock in the Deskbar shelf, it will toggle to display the current date. Click again to return to the time display. To hide the time/date altogether, right-click in the shelf space and choose Hide Time from the pop-up menu. Right-clicking again will let you turn it back on.**

## User Interface Basics

Chances are, the BeOS user interface will be easy enough to figure out on your own that you won't need to consult documentation. However, there are a few things about the BeOS UI that aren't immediately self-evident. We'll cover those in this section.

**The BeOS Window Format**  Tracker and application windows in BeOS are laid out simply and cleanly, demonstrating Be's penchant for elegant minimalism.

Each window's yellow title tab is always just as long as necessary to accommodate the title words. The square on the left closes the window, the double squares on the right maximizes ("zoom") it to full size, and the title bar itself is used for dragging. Double-clicking on the title tab will minimize the window to the Deskbar, and right-clicking it will send it to the back of the

**Figure 2.26**

*Windows in BeOS are simple, clean, and functional. They also hide a couple of nice usability enhancements. (Hint: Try right-clicking the yellow title tab.)*

window stack. It's worth getting accustomed to this last trick—once you get used to it, it becomes annoying to use an operating system without it.

 ***Move the Title Tab*** **If you hold down the Shift key while dragging the title tab, you can slide it left and right along the top of the window border. This lets you arrange documents as you would the tabs on manila folders.**

If you're coming to BeOS from the Windows world, you may be surprised to find that you can't resize a window by grabbing any border. BeOS borrows from MacOS here, allowing resizing only from the gripper dots in the window's lower-right corner. Dragging a window border will move the window, which can be quite convenient in some circumstances.

 ***Moving Windows without Title Tabs*** **Some windows, like the mail daemon's notification window, do not have title tabs. While it may appear at first that these windows can't be moved by dragging, they actually can—you'll just have to aim a little more accurately with your mouse to grab any border. And if grabbing tiny window borders drives you batty, you can always move them by using the Workspace preferences panel (discussed later in this chapter).**

**BeOS Window Types** There are four different types of windows you may encounter when using BeOS, though some are much more popular than others. The vast majority of windows are drawn in standard format, as described above. Very small windows, for which a normal title tab would be overwhelmingly large, can adopt a smaller title tab and a narrower border, as shown in the second window in Figure 2.27. These windows behave like normal windows; they're just a little more compact. Occasionally, a developer may see the need to either save as much real estate as possible, or to try and discourage users from moving windows around. BeMail's mail daemon window is a good example of this. As long as a window has a border, however,

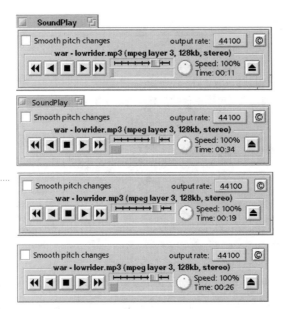

**Figure 2.27**

*The four basic window types in BeOS: standard, compact, tabless, and tabless/ borderless (also known as titled, floating, bordered, and modal).*

you can still drag it around—you just won't have a handy title tab to aim for, and will have to grab the window by its border. In rare instances, you'll encounter a window with neither title tab nor borders. Since the user has no control over the position or size of such a window, they're not too popular, either with users or with developers. They, do, however, make for nice splash screens. In all cases, it is the application developer who determines whether a window will be resizable. And in almost all cases, the developer also chooses which of these window formats to use. Pictured in Figure 2.27 is a rare exception—Marco Nelissen's SoundPlay, which leaves the choice up to users via a preferences panel.

**Scrollbars**  By default, scrollbars get double arrows at both ends, which is a nice way to save mouse miles. Practically every aspect of scrollbar appearance and behavior can be customized from the Scrollbar applet in the Preferences folder (see Chapter 9).

**Figure 2.28**

*Scrollbars in BeOS windows are highly customizable. By default, they include both up and down arrows at either end, which helps you save mouse miles.*

**Meet the Tracker**  There's a lot more to the Tracker than meets the eye. In addition to letting you drag files and folders around, the Tracker's functionality reaches into nearly every aspect of the operating system. When you open, save, or create a file from any application, you're using the Tracker. When you double-click on an icon and it opens in the right application, thank the Tracker. If the Deskbar knows how to take you to the right workspace when you select an application window, the Tracker is involved. Of course it doesn't do all of these things alone, but Tracker code communicates with just about every aspect of the operating system, working in conjunction with components such as the system Registrar (Chapter 5) and the FileTypes database (Chapter 9) to get its work done. You'll find detailed coverage of the Tracker and the Be filesystem in Chapter 5; for now we'll cover the basics.

**Drag and Drop**  Drag-and-drop file management has become pretty much standardized across all operating systems so you won't encounter any big surprises here. Dragging files and folders to other locations on the same volume (disk) moves them; dragging to a different volume initi-ates a copy instead. Dragging with the right mouse button instead of the left will give you the option to copy, move, or create a link to the files in the new destination.

Create Link Here
Move Here
Copy Here
Cancel

*Figure 2.29*

In addition, you can of course drag files onto application icons (or onto links to applications) to open them in that application. When you drag a file over an application icon, BeOS looks at the filetype of the dragged file and compares it against a list of filetypes that that application understands. If it finds a match, the icon will "shadow," or become slightly darker, to indicate that the application understands the dragged file format.

*Dragging with the right mouse button will invoke a pop-up menu that gives you the choice to copy, move, or create a link to the files in the new destination.*

***Override Filetype Matching*** If you want an application to try to open a file even if it doesn't understand its filetype, hold down the Ctrl key and try again—this will force the application in question to try to open the file, regardless. This can be useful when you know that a file is plain text, for instance, but for some reason its filetype isn't correct. See Chapter 5, for more on filetypes.

**File Panels** Because every file panel (known in other operating systems as an Open/Save panel) in BeOS is just a special Tracker window, you can do all the file management you need to while you're right in the middle of opening or saving a file—create a new folder (Alt+N), move up to the parent directory (Alt+Up Arrow), rename files or folders (Alt+E), and so on. I strongly rec-ommend learning the keyboard shortcuts for operations like this, which you'll be performing repeatedly. However, if you're not a big keyboard fan, there are, of course, ways to do the same things with the mouse. You can create a

new folder by select-ing New Folder from the File menu. Files and folders can be renamed by clicking once in their names and then waiting a moment—the file-name will become editable after a very brief delay. You can use the pop-up menu at the top of a file panel to navigate to parent directories.

Navigate to parent directories with the pop-up menu

Right-click in blank space to access a context menu

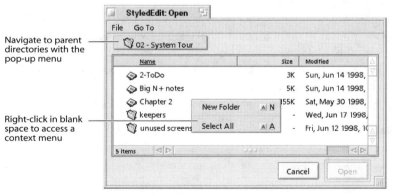

*Figure 2.30*

*Because a file panel is just a special Tracker window, you can do all the file management you need right on the spot. Right-clicking in an open space, for instance, gives you the option to create a new folder or select all files.*

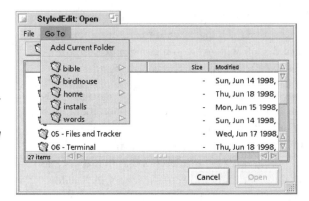

*Figure 2.31*

*You can configure your file panels to jump to customized "bookmarks" in your filesystem by adding folders to the Go To menu.*

In addition, file panels have a few goodies built into their pull-down menus. From the File menu, you can create a new folder, edit a filename, call up the standard info panel, or move files to the Trash. Cooler than that is the Go To menu. Because most of us save a lot of files to a small handful of common places, BeOS lets you to specify your favorite save locations for quick access. To add an item to the Go To menu, navigate to that folder once, and pull down Go To | Add Current Folder. From then on, you'll be able to jump back to the same location in a flash. You can add any number of folders to this menu.

 **Remove Entries from the Go To Menu**  It's a snap to add items to the Go To menu, but it's not quite so obvious how to remove them. In Tracker, open up the `/boot/home/config/settings/Tracker/Go` folder and you'll find links to the folders that show up in the Go To menu. Add or remove as many links as you like, and your changes will take effect immediately.

 **Save to Remote Locations Quickly**  As useful as the Go To menu is, it doesn't help if you need to open or save a file from/to a location that's not already in the Go To menu. If the file you need is buried many folders deep, or on another partition, your only choice is to navigate the entire hierarchy until you get there, right? Wrong. If the folder in question is already open, just drag any file out of that folder into your file panel. This won't move or copy that file to the location of the file panel. Instead, it will change the location of the file panel to equal the location of the dragged file. This is only useful if that remote folder is already open—but when it is, it's an excellent time-saver.

**Context Menus**  BeOS does pop-up context menus right. Right-click on any file or folder and study the menu that appears—unlike the context menus in certain other popular systems, every item on BeOS's menu is genuinely useful.

We'll cover the Tracker's context menus in depth in Chapter 5. For now, go ahead and play with them—you can probably figure out what most of the entries do just by experimenting. Don't forget that the desktop is a part of the Tracker too! Right-clicking on the desktop gets you a context menu almost identical to the one that appears when you right-click in other Tracker views.

**The Terminal** A graceful GUI and a powerful command line—what more could anyone want? With BeOS, you get it both ways, with no compromise on either front. Unix is the granddaddy of all command-line environments, and the most common command shell on Unix is bash (the Bourne Again Shell). If you're already a Unix propeller-head, you know how powerful and flexible this environment is. On the other hand, those coming from other backgrounds may need a little encouragement to get excited about the Terminal. If your command-line experience is limited to the DOS shell in Windows or OS/2, you've got a treat in store—the Unix-style shell in BeOS kicks major booty on those shells, and you may find yourself beginning to use the command-line environment far more than you ever did before. While we'll cover the Terminal in detail in Chapter 6, but it deserves a brief introduction here.

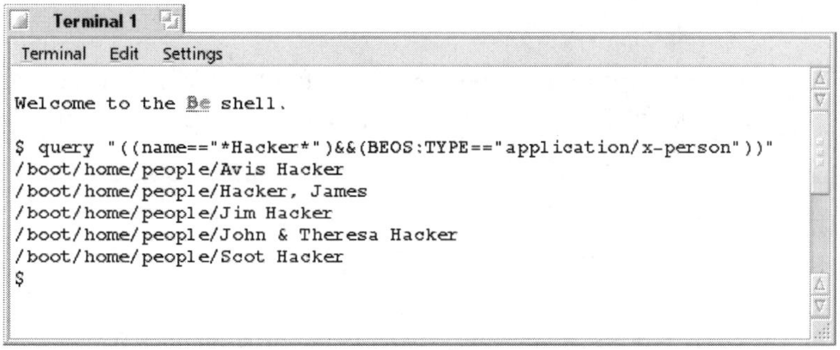

```
  Terminal 1

 Terminal   Edit   Settings

Welcome to the Be shell.

$ query "((name=="*Hacker*")&&(BEOS:TYPE=="application/x-person"))"
/boot/home/people/Avis Hacker
/boot/home/people/Hacker, James
/boot/home/people/Jim Hacker
/boot/home/people/John & Theresa Hacker
/boot/home/people/Scot Hacker
$
```

*Figure 2.32*

*The Terminal is a BeOS implementation of the Unix bash shell, and adds an additional dimension of power to working in BeOS for those unafraid of the command line. What you sacrifice in ease of use you gain back in power and flexibility. Shown: the author queries the system for family members.*

If you've never used a command-line environment before and you've just opened up the Terminal for the first time, you're staring at a "$" prompt and wondering what in the heck to do next. Unlike a graphical environment, which presents all of your current options a mouse click or two away, in a command-line environment you really can't do anything without already knowing your options. At bottom, those options are the same as they are in the GUI: You can launch programs, view and manage your files, use the Internet, edit text documents, and get information about your system. So why would anyone use the Terminal if it isn't as intuitive as the GUI? Three reasons:

- What you sacrifice in intuitiveness and ease of use you gain back in power and flexibility.

- Hundreds—if not thousands—of programs written for Unix-based systems can be recompiled for BeOS's Terminal quite easily, extending the base of available software. BeOS comes bundled with around 200 programs and utilities that run only under the Terminal (you'll find these in /boot/beos/bin/). Some of these are obscure tools that only hardcore hackers will love, while others are easy enough to use that many people will find themselves shelling out to the Terminal frequently, finding that it's simply easier to get certain kinds of things done that way.

- The bash shell supports a native method of scripting that allows you to create automated solutions to simple problems without delving into the world of actual C++ programming. While shell scripts aren't exactly child's play, you'd be surprised by how much you can accomplish with no programming background at all, just by creating a file containing a series of simple shell commands.

On the other hand, if you have a strong aversion to the command line, chances are that you can use BeOS for a long time—maybe forever—without ever launching the Terminal. It's there for those who want or need its power and flexibility, but your BeOS experience will not be compromised (much) if you don't use it.

It's important to understand that BeOS's filesystem is case-sensitive. This means that each of the following three filenames is considered unique, and all three can exist in the same directory:

```
phonelist
PhoneList
PHONELIST
```

Keep this in mind any time you're working with files in BeOS, regardless of whether you're currently in the Tracker or the Terminal. However, it's generally more important to keep in mind from within the Terminal because you're typing filenames directly. Case-sensitivity is a sensitive (sorry) issue for some people—either they love or hate it. However, one thing tends to be true: After getting used to having a case-sensitive filesystem, you'll probably love it, whereas the reverse is not typically true.

**Meet the Shell**  If you're migrating to BeOS from the DOS world, you'll find that the bash shell is both similar to and different from DOS. Everything you can do in DOS, you can do in bash, though you'll have to relearn a thing or two (remember that Unix predates DOS, and that much of DOS's functionality is actually derived from Unix). But since the Terminal is a full bash implementation, it's also capable of a lot more than DOS ever was.

Want a quick taste of the Terminal in action? Try this:

1. Open Terminal and type pwd. This means "print working directory," and the shell should report that the current directory is /boot/home. Now type du and press Enter. The shell will run through your home directory and all of its subdirectories, reporting their names along with the total additive size of the files they contain. Want to keep a copy of this record for posterity? Instead of typing du, type du > /boot/home/DiskUsage.txt. When the command is done, you'll find a new text file in your home directory called DiskUsage.txt, containing the same information.

2. If you want to display this file from within the Terminal, type `cat /boot/home/DiskUsage.txt` and press Enter. Since this text file is probably pretty large, it's going to scroll by way too quickly. To view it one screen at a time, use the `more` command, instead of `cat`:

   `more /boot/home/DiskUsage.txt`

3. Just want to see the first 20 lines? Try this:

   `head -20 /boot/home/DiskUsage.txt`

4. To see the last 20 lines, substitute `tail` for `head`. Pretty cool, huh? You'll find lots more on the Terminal in Chapter 6.

## Workspaces

If you're like most people, the desk in your office or workroom is always a mess. You've got a finite amount of surface area, but a seemingly infinite amount of stuff to organize. You clean up your desktop periodically, but the second law of thermodynamics* inevitably prevails, and you end up staring at the clutter once again. If you had a bigger office—or the budget—you might get a second desk and spread out a little more, maybe even add a second monitor. Be can't help you organize your physical office space or buy you a second monitor, but they've got the problem licked on the virtual front.

One of BeOS's key usability features is its concept of multiple workspaces. Rather than a single computer desktop, you get 32, and you can toggle between them in one of two ways:

- By holding down one of your Alt keys while pressing one of your Function keys (the F1 through F9 keys normally located at the top of the keyboard). This method, however, only gives you access to nine of the workspaces. To access the rest, you'll need to use the next method.

- By clicking panels in the Workspaces preferences applet (open your preferences folder and select Workspaces).

Not only do you get to spread your applications and windows out across as many as 32 separate desktops, but you can run each one of them at a different resolution, bit depth, refresh rate, color, and/or desktop pattern.

If you're worried about losing your applications and windows amidst all of those workspaces, remember that the Deskbar takes care of all of that for you. Since all running applications show up as entries in the Deskbar regardless of your currently active workspace, all you have to do to get back to an application is click its Deskbar entry, and you'll be transported immediately to the

---

* In physics, the second law of thermodynamics states that ordered systems left to their own devices will tend toward decreasing orderliness until, finally, they devolve into pure chaos. Chaos theoreticians, on the other hand, note that there is always some form of order embedded in chaotic systems, but that's another story. For ordered systems to stay ordered requires input from an external force, such as an energy source or organizing principle. In other words, your desk gets messy if you don't clean it. Chalk one up for science.

*Figure 2.33*

*Both the Deskbar and the Twitcher place small horizontal lines next to the icon of any window that's currently in another workspace. This way you aren't whisked off to another workspace unexpectedly. Small visual clues go a long way in BeOS.*

workspace currently hosting that application or window. If you remember that you always keep your word processor in workspace #4, you'll probably be able to get there faster with the keyboard … but it's nice to know that you don't have to memorize anything to use workspaces effectively.

 ***Run Workspaces in Different Colors for Instant Identification*** If you keep all of your workspaces running at the same resolution, you may find it useful to run them all in different colors or with different background patterns. This gives you a solid clue as to where you are as you're cycling through them. "Dark blue is for email, green keeps my Net connection alive, maroon is for programming, and so forth." All screen colors are set from the Screen preferences panel, which is covered in detail in Chapter 9.

 ***Toggle between Recent Workspaces*** Not only can you toggle between your first nine workspaces by using Alt+F*n*, you can also toggle back to whatever the previous workspace was with Alt+~ (that's a tilde—the squiggly character to the left of the 1 key on most keyboards). This gives you functionality somewhat similar to the Twitcher's Alt+Tab, but for workspaces themselves, rather than for open applications.

## Virtual Desktops Done Right

The concept of attaching multiple virtual desktops to a single screen isn't exactly a Be invention—it's existed for years in various incarnations on other OSs. Norton Desktop for Windows used a similar concept years ago, Unix has its multiplicity of X window managers (like fvwm), and MacOS has always had the single giant workspace supporting multiple monitors. BeOS's implementation of the concept is well designed and very easy to use. If you haven't worked with multiple workspaces on other operating systems, it may take a while before their true power really dawns on you. After you've used them for a while, however, you'll begin to arrange your tasks along logical category lines, and to memorize their associated hotkeys. Try opening your email client, word processor, development tool, and time-wasting games in separate workspaces, then toggle between them; this is task-switching on steroids.

**Using Workspace Preferences**   Launch Workspaces (from your preferences folder) and click in a few of the nine squares to jump between your desktops.

Take a look at your current desktop and then look closely at the Workspaces square representing this desktop—those little blobs are thumbnail images of your running applications and open windows. If you've got different-colored desktops, you'll see those represented here as well; this is an entire micro-

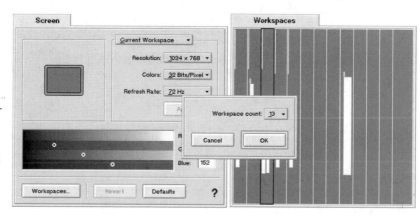

cosm of your current environ-ment. If the thumbnails are too small to make out clearly, resizing the Workspaces window from its lower-right corner will cause all of the thumbnails to scale up accord-ingly—things get very readable at about twice the original size. The name of each application window will become legible in the middle of the thumbnails as the Work-spaces panel becomes larger.

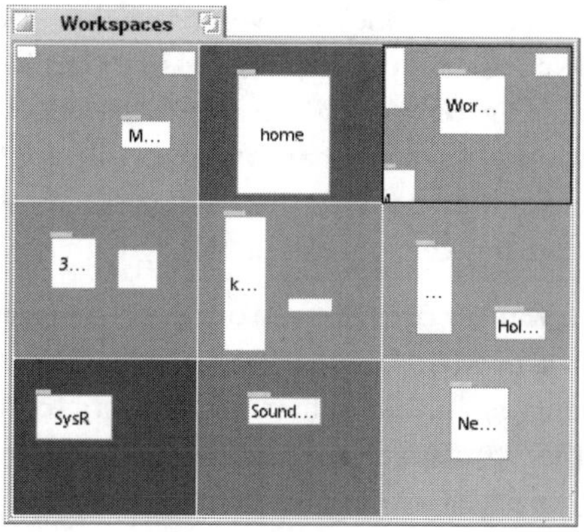

*Figure 2.34*

*Each of your running applications and/or windows is visible in Workspace prefer-ences as a thumb-nail image. Drag a thumbnail into another workspace to move its associ-ated real window.*

Now drag one of your real application windows around, and notice that the thumbnail moves with you, gliding around on its own miniature desktop. Grab one of the thumbnails and do the same thing—your application follows. Drag a thumbnail into another workspace, then release. Whammo—the app slides right offscreen and lands in the next workspace.

The number of workspaces appearing in this grid is an immediate reflection of the number of workspaces you enable from the Screen preferences application. If you open Workspace preferences and Screen preferences at the same time, then change the number of workspaces from within Screen, your workspaces grid will redraw itself instantaneously to reflect the new number. Of course, if you pick a nondivisible number of workspaces, like 23, Workspaces won't be

*Figure 2.35*

*If you choose a non-divisible number of workspaces, they'll be represented as slices rather than as cells in the Work-spaces preferences application.*

able to make a grid out of it, and will represent your workspaces with vertical slices rather than cells.

 ***Smooth Transitions*** While the ability of all your workspaces to run at independent bit depths, refresh rates, and resolutions can be convenient if you have a need for it, it can also be potentially annoying. In order to make these changes as you cycle through workspaces, your video card needs to reset its innards, which causes it to blink off and then on again. To prevent momentary screen blackouts when switching between workspaces, set the workspaces you use the most to identical bit depths, resolutions, and refresh rates. Fortunately, the Screen preferences panel (details are in Chapter 9) includes a setting that can optionally apply the current setting to all workspaces simultaneously. Once they've been set identically, you'll be able to toggle between them seamlessly, with no jarring blackout.

 ***You* Can *Take it with You*** As cool as the Workspace preferences application is, it can also be a little unwieldy, especially if you have tons of workspaces and a lot of documents open. Sometimes, all you want to do is to send a single window to another workspace, without having to open a separate app to do it. R4 introduces an excellent trick for doing just this.

Go to the workspace containing the window in question, click and hold on that window's title tab, and switch to another workspace normally with Alt+F*n*. Rather than being left behind, that document will be carried with you into the new workspace. Unfortunately, there isn't yet a simple mechanism for moving an entire application into another workspace.

 ***Custom Workspace Switching*** Even with all of these cool workspace switching tricks, some developers still aren't satisfied, and want even more flexibility. Some BeOS applications (such as SoundPlay, pictured in Figure 2.27), take advantage of a custom programmer's library called `liblayout`, which lets them add custom layout options to their applications. Any application that uses `liblayout` automatically acquires a hidden pop-up menu that you can

Figure 2.36

Any application that takes advantage of Marco Nelissen's `liblayout` can be sent to another workspace by holding down Ctrl+Alt+Shift and clicking in the application window.

use to send that app to any workspace. Just hold down Alt+Ctrl+Shift and click in the application window to see a menu like the one pictured in Figure 2.36. Select a number from the menu and the application vanishes into that workspace.

***When Nine Isn't Enough***  By default, BeOS is configured to use nine work-spaces, which is more than most people will ever use. If you get really addicted to the feature, however, you can easily turn up the volume and make up to 32 workspaces available. Open up the Screen panel in your preferences folder and you'll see a button labeled "Workspaces." Click it and a pop-up menu will let you select any number from 1 to 32. The Workspaces preferences panel will immediately adjust itself to accommodate the new number of workspaces. Note that only 1 through 9 can be reached via keyboard—you'll have to use the Workspaces preferences panel to access the rest.

# The Bundled Apps

The good folks at Be went to a lot of effort to make sure that you have a good "out-of-the-box experience," meaning that you can install BeOS and start getting work done right away without having to obtain and install third-party applications to start writing email, browsing the Web, editing documents, managing personal and business contacts, hosting Web sites, and the like. That doesn't mean you'll never have to install another piece of software—far from it. The applications Be provides are of the bare-bones variety. You get raw functionality without all the bells and whistles, rather than feature-complete application suites. The reasons for this are threefold:

- Be wants to create a good environment in which third-party developers can make their livings. If the bundled BeMail application, for instance, did everything that Eudora or Claris Emailer did, there would be little incentive for other companies to build BeOS mail clients. Without a rich, thriving, and well-supported community of software developers, Be wouldn't get vary far. On the other hand, the operating system needs to "bootstrap" this process by providing the minimal tools developers and users need to communicate with one another and begin their development work.

- Be's responsibility is the operating system itself, not the applications that run on it. For Be to spend their resources building and maintaining full-blown applications would not only be bad for developers, it would detract from Be's ability to continue improving on the system itself.

- If Be bundles too much, they end up putting themselves in the same position as certain other operating system companies who have come under public and government scrutiny for stifling competition. Be's philosophy is one of openness; they want to create green fields in which competition can flourish.

As a result, you'll find a host of installed applications ready to help you get started in common tasks, but none of them will likely measure up to the more sophisticated offerings in the same categories from commercial BeOS developers. If you're a fan of software minimalism—and there's a lot to be said for that—the bundled apps may suit your needs quite nicely. Otherwise, check out the later chapters of this book for BeOS software.

## BeIDE

Because Be is enthusiastic about helping the developer community get started building applications for BeOS, every copy of the operating system comes bundled with a copy of the BeIDE, an integrated development environment (IDE) you can use to create and compile BeOS applications.

Because this is a book for end-users and not developers, we don't cover BeOS programming in this book. However, you will find more resources for getting started with BeOS programming in Appendix C.

 Every so often, you'll end up downloading an application or tool that ships as source code, rather than as a ready-to-run binary. If you download one of these and want to know how to compile it yourself, you'll also find a crash course on compiling in Appendix C.

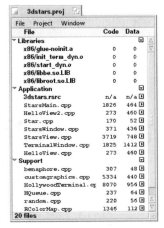

*Figure 2.37*

*You don't have to be a programmer to compile downloaded source code, assuming that all your ducks are in a row. The BeIDE main window displays all of the component files that constitute a program prior to compilation.*

## BeMail

Chances are, one of the first things you're going to want to do is get online and check your email. BeOS includes a simple, utilitarian (but surprisingly powerful) mail client called BeMail. You'll find everything you need to know about configuring and using BeMail in Chapter 4.

## CD Player

BeOS comes with not one, but two built-in CD players. One of them, the MiniPlayer, is truly bare-bones, and does nothing but play audio CDs in the background staying out of your way. CD Player, on the other hand, is a quite handsome application, capable of performing most of the functions you're accustomed to seeing in software-based audio CD applications. You can even save your audio tracks to hard disk from CD Player!

Most of CD Player's controls will be intuitive to anyone who's ever used a CD player. Let's look at some of the goodies that aren't quite so obvious.

**Figure 2.38**

*CD Player not only performs all the functions you'd normally expect from an audio CD player, including track saving, but it remembers CDs' titles and track names for future reference.*

**Customized Track Listings** One of the really cool things about CD Player is its seemingly magical ability to identify a CD you've inserted into the drive and display the name of the disc along with all its track names. No, it doesn't read this information off the CD—you'll have to type it all in the first time, but once you have, that disk will be recognized by the player every time you insert it.

To create your track listings, click the downward arrow at the right of the player and type the track names over the generic entries (you can't edit track lengths). Type the recording's name into the field at the top of the player reading "CD Audio". When you eject the CD or close the player, your listing will be saved to your /boot/home/cd/ folder as simple text file, and automagically retrieved the next time you insert the same disc.

## How CD Player Recognizes Your CDs

Having CD Player automatically recognize the disks you insert is quite a nice little magic trick. Curious how it works? It's pretty simple, actually. The first time you insert a CD the player doesn't recognize, it generates a table of contents for it and writes that table to a text file, as described above. Once this has been written, it uses a special algorithm built into the player's code to generate a unique numerical ID based on the contents of the table. Because of the huge number of variables in the table of contents, the numerical code is virtually guaranteed to be unique, so it can't be mistaken for another CD. It then takes this key and writes it to an attribute associated with the file called CD:key. Every time you insert a CD and launch CD Player, it re-runs the algorithm to obtain the key, then scans the /boot/home/cd directory, examining the CD:key attribute of each file. If it finds a match, it knows you've catalogued this CD before, and brings up the appropriate menu.

 ***Retrieve Playlists from the Web*** So who wants to sit around and type in the playlists of their entire CD collection? Fortunately, you don't have to, since thousands of people around the world have already done the same thing. Instead of using CD Player, download JukeBox from BeWare. Pop in an audio CD; JukeBox will look for an Internet connection, and then reach out to the massive CDDB Internet database, which contains track listings for seemingly 99% of the compact discs ever pressed. A few seconds later, the entire track list for the current CD will become available in JukeBox's drop-down playlist. You'll also see a text document icon in the middle of JukeBox's interface. Drag this to Tracker or to the desktop and double-click it to study or edit the list for yourself. Half the fun of using JukeBox is trying to find a CD that *isn't* already in the CDDB. If you do find one that isn't already databased, do the right thing and log the playlist into the CDDB for other people—you'll find a form on the Web site at www.cddb.com.

**Timing Modes**  Next to the digital track number at the top of the player is a tiny icon containing a clock face. Clicking this button repeatedly will toggle the display between four modes: remaining or elapsed time for either the current track or the entire CD.

**Alternate Play Modes**  In addition to the standard play-through mode, CD Player will also let you toggle into random mode by clicking the "stair-steps" button. Clicking the right-facing arrow button will toggle the player into loop mode, so it will start again at the beginning after playing all tracks once (in either standard or random mode).

**Saving Tracks to Disk**  CD Player has the ability to save entire tracks (or portions thereof) to your hard disk, so you can further manipulate them in other audio software.

To initiate a save, click the floppy disk button and you'll see the Save Preview panel (Figure 2.39). By default, the entire track is selected. If you only want to save a portion of the track, drag the left and right arrows back and forth to precisely define a track segment. The projected file size of the resulting audio file will update itself dynamically as you adjust the segment size. One minute of raw audio will consume about 10MB of disk space, so keep this in mind if you

*Figure 2.39*

*CD Player will let you save any track or track segment to your hard disk for further manipulation. Note that high-resolution audio files consume around 10MB per minute!*

intend on doing a lot of saving. Clicking the Preview button will let you hear the segment you've demarcated, and, of course, clicking Save will bring up a Save panel so you can give your segment a name and disk location.

Note that because data can be retrieved from CD and written to hard disk faster than real time, save operations should take less than half the time it would take to listen to the same segment. When the save operation is complete, navigate the Tracker to the location where the file was saved. Double-clicking it will launch it in PlaySound, unless you've reconfigured your preferred application for this filetype.

***Finer Control over Recording Quality*** **While saving audio tracks via the CD Player application may be the easiest way to do it, CD Player has no controls for settings such as recording levels, signal thresholds, or filters. While it works just fine for most CD-quality audio, there may come times when you want more control over your recording parameters. If so, try downloading and installing one of the more advanced audio manipulation tools for BeOS, such as BamBam (Chapter 15, *Media Applications*). Remember that the quality of the end result is always a function of the quality of the source—strive to get the best recording possible at the outset and everything you do with the recording in the file will be of a higher quality.**

Note also that not all CD players are "frame accurate." This means that it's not always possible for the application to pick up data from an exact location; sometimes it must resort to an approximation instead. If you find that your recordings skip when you use CD Player, you've been bitten by this hardware gotcha. The remedy is to record in real-time with a separate audio application, as described in the tip *Finer Control over Recording Quality*, above.

## Clock

Clock is a simple little tool without menus or controls of any kind. However, clicking its face will allow you to toggle between eight different designs, in separate color schema. If you like Clock and want to keep it running permanently without adding it to your UserBootscript (Chapter 9), try embedding it in your desktop as a Replicant. Pull down the Be menu on the Deskbar and make sure Show Replicants is turned on. Then grab the Replicant handle at the lower-right corner of Clock and drag it to a blank area of your desktop. You can now close the Clock application itself and the Replicant will keep running, even between reboots.

Clock's time is derived directly from the system clock (use the Time panel in your preferences folder to adjust the time—details on using Time are in Chapter 9, *Preferences and Customization*).

# DiskProbe

DiskProbe is very powerful and very flexible. But where there's empowerment, there's responsibility. DiskProbe is not idiot-proof, and it is very much capable of rendering files unreadable, applications unlaunchable, and systems unbootable if you don't pay attention to what you're doing. Don't make changes to file blocks just to see what will happen—you could be very sorry. This is especially true when using DiskProbe to edit entire disks rather than single files—it's all too easy to accidentally kill your filesystem journal or some other equally important component you don't want to live without. When editing applications, create a duplicate of the app first, and run your experiments on the copy. This is not meant to scare you away from using DiskProbe altogether, just to suggest that you proceed with caution. Think of DiskProbe as if it were heavy equipment that should not be operated while under the influence of drugs, alcohol, or extreme exhaustion. Or before your first cup of tea in the morning.

DiskProbe is a powerful system tool with a somewhat misleading name. In fact, our technical editor Chris Herborth thinks DiskProbe should be renamed "The Scary Hex Editor of Doom." If you guessed that DiskProbe could be used to scan your system for connected disks, you guessed wrong—that's what DriveSetup (Chapter 9) and SCSIProbe do. DiskProbe allows you to view and edit actual blocks on your hard drive, whether they relate to individual files or to entire disks. This makes it possible to do things like reaching into applications and tweaking the entries in their pull-down menus, changing parameters in configuration files, and even altering boot flags on your hard disks.

In general, DiskProbe is of interest only to extreme geeks—people intimately familiar with the way their systems operate at the lowest level. However, there are a number of useful things that the average end-user can do with DiskProbe that can't be done any other way (but see warning, above).

*Figure 2.40*

*Launching DiskProbe displays this dialog, asking whether you intend to edit an entire disk or a single file.*

The safest way to launch DiskProbe is to drag a file onto its icon; this minimizes the chances of accidentally opening DiskProbe on an entire disk volume. You can also launch DiskProbe in single-file mode and drag a file from the Tracker into DiskProbe's open window. Alternatively, just launch DiskProbe from its icon and you'll be asked whether you want to edit an entire disk or just a single file. Unless you really know what you're doing, I strongly recommend editing only single files. If you double-click to launch, select the appropriate radio button and use the file panel to navigate to a file or device you wish to view or edit.

You'll be greeted by a display of the file's contents in hexadecimal mode (see the sidebar *Speaking Hex*). The path and icon of the current file or device is displayed at the top of the application, and below it a field displaying your current position in the currently selected block (in hex). The format here is "x of y", where y is the total number of blocks in the file and x is the currently selected block. You can toggle this display from hex to decimal by pulling down Edit | Base and selecting decimal or hex. Move through your file or device by dragging the slider left or right. If you already know the block number you want to edit, type its address into the current block field. Alternatively, you can search for any given string with the standard Alt+F, or move through the file or device one block at a time by using Alt in combination with the Left and Right Arrow keys.

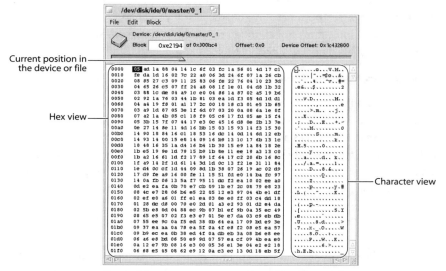

Current position in the device or file

Hex view

Character view

*Figure 2.41*

*Opening a file or device in DiskProbe gives you an editable view of that file or device's filesystem blocks, in addition to several methods for navigating through them. Any string on the device can be edited just as if you were using a plain text editor. Changes are not committed until you choose Write from the dialog that appears after you close the application.*

To edit a given hex block, select it and the equivalent character block on the right side of the window will be highlighted. Type your replacement string over the top of the selection, or paste a new string in from the clipboard. Similarly, you can copy selections from DiskProbe to the clipboard to be used in other applications (this is of interest only to programmers).

## *Uses for DiskProbe*

While engineers and hackers worthy of their moniker will find a million uses for DiskProbe, there isn't a whole lot that the average end-user can do with it safely. Here are a couple of experiments you can try, just to get a taste for what this application is capable of.

### *Change the Text of Application Menu Entries*

In the Tracker, navigate to /boot/beos/apps/. Select StyledEdit and make a duplicate copy of it. Rename the duplicate file FunkyEdit and drag it on top of the DiskProbe icon. Search through the file for the string "Align." When you find it, type the word "Alive" over the selection. Close DiskProbe and click the Write button. Now launch FunkyEdit, pull down the Document menu, and you'll notice that your replacement text has inserted itself into the application binary itself—a customization not possible any other way. It's important that you choose a string of equivalent length ("Align" and "Alive" both have five characters). If you change the number of characters, you risk altering the program's ability to reference things that come after it, as all bytes in the program will be shifted one way or another.

### *Mangle a Sound File into Psychedelic Unrecognizability*

Here's a useless trick. Make a duplicate copy of one of your system's sound files and drag the copy onto DiskProbe. Because a sound file is all binary, you probably won't find much recognizable text inside, if any. Start selecting blocks at random and typing characters over the top of them. Doesn't matter what—just type gibberish, with gusto and wild abandon. Close DiskProbe and launch your sound file normally. You may hear long chunks of silence, but you'll also hear bizarre, psychedelic chirps, moans, buzzes, and all manner of unnatural digital mutations, all resulting from your mangulatory efforts.

All of a file's attributes will be displayed under the Attribute menu; selecting any of these entries will display the values of that attribute in an edit window if an editor capable of handling the data type is available. For example, simple MIME types, which are stored in plain text format, will appear in a small window from which you can manually establish a different MIME string. However, attributes stored as binary information will not be editable (although future versions of DiskProbe may be capable of editing these as well).

Because DiskProbe is capable of making very serious changes, changes are not committed until you choose the Write button in the dialog that appears when you close the application.

## *Speaking Hex*

If we were born with 16 fingers rather than 10, our system of counting would be very different than it is. Everything we do with numbers assumes a base 10 numbering system, but as ingrained as that feels, the base 10 system is no more or less natural than number systems with other bases. For computers, four binary digits (bits) is equal to one hex digit, so a base 16, or hexadecimal system makes sense. Why? Because computers "think" in 1s and 0s, which is a base 2 numbering system. Pack together four of these binary digits (which are also known as bits) and you get a neat little packet that's relatively easy for programmers to read and write—yes, programmers in the Pleistocene era actually had to write this stuff out themselves. These four-bit packets let you count from 0 to 15, for a base 16 numbering system. In other words, the pre-ponderance of base 16 numbering in computers is a little piece of leftover legacy from the days of the very first computers and the programmers who ran them.

Without going into depth on counting systems, here's a simple way to grasp the basics of any-thing you see written in hex. As you know, in base 10, each placeholder represents a factor of 10, so that 348 means you have an eight in the ones place, a four in the tens place, and a three in the hundreds place. In other words, 3 hundreds, 4 tens, and 8 ones. Put another way,

$$
\begin{array}{rcl}
3 \times 10^2 &=& 3 \times 100 \\
4 \times 10^1 &=& 4 \times 10 \\
\underline{8 \times 10^0} &=& \underline{8 \times 1} \\
348 & & 348
\end{array}
$$

Base 16 works in the same way, but we have a dilemma—what happens when you need to rep-resent, say, 13 in the ones place? We don't have a single-digit character for 13, so we use letters, like this: 0 1 2 3 4 5 6 7 8 9 A B C D E F. Thus, the letter "D" is the hex equivalent of the number 13 in decimal. When you string them together, you use the same system as above to translate. For example, look at "3E." We have a three in the sixteens place and a 14 in the ones place. Add them together and you get 48+15=62. Or,

$$
\begin{array}{rcl}
3 \times 16^1 &=& 3 \times 16 \\
\underline{E \times 16^0} &=& \underline{14 \times 1} \\
62 & & 62
\end{array}
$$

There's more to it than that, but this should give you the basic idea of how to translate hex into decimal and vice versa. To learn more, consult any introductory programmer's guide.

# Expander

There are dozens of compression formats out there. Some you're probably familiar with—filename extensions like .zip, .sit, and .hqx are practically household words.

The familiar Macintosh .hqx format isn't technically a compression format, even though it's handled like one. In reality, .hqx uses plain ASCII to encode binary files with a method similar to the UUENCODE/UUDECODE schema. The result of this is that .hqx files are actually *larger* than the binary files they encode.

Others, like .rar, .arj, and .gz, may be familiar only to those coming from Unix or the antique DOS world. While file archivers and decompressors exist for BeOS that handle just about every format ever invented, by far the most common formats you'll encounter are .zip and .gz, and of these, only .zip has Be's official endorsement because only .zip is capable of storing all of the extra attributes that give BeOS some of its extra power—not to mention giving your files the right filetypes and icons.

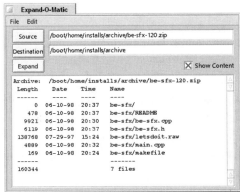

BeOS comes bundled with an archive decompressor called Expander which is capable of handling files compressed or archived in .zip, .tar, and .gz formats. It's important to note that Expander only *unarchives* compressed files—it won't help you to create new ones (see Chapter 5 for details on creating archives).

*Figure 2.42*

*BeOS includes a built-in archive decompressor called Expander, capable of unarchiving .zip, .tar, and .gz files. Its behavior is highly customizable.*

Chances are, the first time you encounter Expander will be the first time you download a compressed file via NetPositive—the moment the download is complete, Expander will pop up automatically and give you the option to decompress the archive on the spot.

Aside from being auto-launched by NetPositive downloads, Expander can be fired up by double-clicking on any file bearing the brown paper bundle icon, or by dragging an archive file onto its icon or into an open Expander window. Clicking the Expand button starts the decompression.

**Expander Settings**  Expander is highly configurable and can be set to decompress your files automatically without clicking the Expand button, to display an "x-ray" of the files contained in the archive, and to decompress files into a custom directory of your choosing.

*Figure 2.43*

*Expander is highly configurable, and can be set to optionally display "x-ray" views of your archives prior to decompression, to use custom directory locations, and more.*

To customize Expander's behavior, pull down Edit | Preferences and you'll see the dialog shown in Figure 2.43. Most of the settings available from this panel are self-explanatory. Click the "Automatically expand files" checkbox if you want decompression to happen without your intervention.

Assuming that you always download .zip files into a preestablished downloads directory, you'll probably want to select the "Same directory as source" radio button for convenience (see the sidebar *Establishing a Download System*). If, on the other hand, you download files to various locations but always want to expand them into a predetermined test folder, you can type that path into the Use: field, or click the Select button to choose that path graphically.

If you want the convenience of checking out your new application or utility immediately after expansion, click the "Open destination folder after extraction" checkbox to cause Tracker to bring the expansion directory window to the front as soon as Expander is done expanding. If you want to see a preview of an archive's contents prior to expansion, click the "Automatically show contents listing" checkbox.

***Automatically Show Contents Listing***  When people create their zip archives, they can choose to format them so that everything is contained inside a new folder, typically named for the archive's contents, or they can zip them up "raw," with no directory names specified. When you decompress an archive including an embedded folder, that folder is re-created on your system, and all of the new files are contained within that folder. This makes it much easier to keep your system organized since the new files don't intermingle with any other files that happen to already be living in the current folder.

While people creating zip archives should have the courtesy to always embed their files in a directory, you can guard against the mess created by those who don't if you leave the "Automatically show contents listing" checkbox on. This way you can see for yourself what's going to happen before you commit to expansion. If an archive's preview doesn't show the included files embedded in their own folder, you can always close Expander, create the folder manually in the Tracker, drag the archive into the new folder, and then let Expander do its thing.

## *Establishing a Download System*

It doesn't take long for hard drives to get cluttered up with bits and pieces of applications and utilities you've downloaded, tested, and decided you don't like. Establishing personal storage systems early on will help you to keep your disk volumes neat and your applications easy to find. I recommend two separate, related systems: one for organizing the applications and utilities you keep, and another for managing your downloads.

### *Organizing Applications*

You could simply place all of your apps in /boot/apps/, but you'll be amazed at how quickly this directory becomes huge and unwieldy. Thus, it's a good idea to create subdirectories of the apps folder for software belonging to various categories. For example, a typical /boot/apps/ directory is subdivided like this:

```
develop/
edit/
games/
graphics/
misc/
multimedia/
net/
office/
sound/
system/
utils/
```

Every single piece of software installed finds its way into one of these subdirectories, even if you have to manually tell the installer programs to put them there. Finding the applications via the Be menu is far easier this way.

### *Organizing Downloads*

Decide early on where you want your downloads to go, and then make sure that all of your downloads actually go there. On my system, all downloads go straight to /boot/home/downloads. Decompressed files automatically create a subdirectory at this location containing the new software. If a downloaded application sucks, both its .zip file and the new folder it created go straight to the Trash. If acceptable, the new folder is dragged into one of the subdirectories named above for permanent storage.

The remaining question then is what to do with the .zip archive that spawned the moved application. For safekeeping, you can hold onto the original archives that contain software you've kept, in a folder under installs called archive. The archive folder, in turn, is subdivided into directories which exactly mirror the directory structure used under /boot/apps. This may sound somewhat anal, but there's a great payoff any time you need to install to a new system or retrieve documentation you may have tossed out.

Theoretically, BeWare and BeDepot check to ensure that archives contain actual directory structures rather than just piles of files before making files available for download. However, experience shows that this doesn't always work, so it can still pay to examine the contents of an archive before decompressing it.

 ***Teach Expander New Tricks*** Expander is really just a window onto decompression commands that take place in the shell. As such, it has a number of common decompression commands built in for handling archives in zip, tar, and gzip formats. However, if you download and install other kinds of command-line decompression tools, you can easily tell Expander how to handle them so that you can start decompressing files in those formats through the graphical Expander, rather than using the shell.

When you launch Expander, it takes a look in your `/boot/home/config/etc` folder for a file called `expander.rules`. If this file is found, it reads rules from the file and adds them to its list of capabilities. As an example, consider the self-expanding archive format for Windows, which creates zip files that don't require unzip on the users system. For example, if you download free fonts for Windows 3.1 from **www.microsoft.com/truetype**, you'll find that you can unzip them from the command line, but that Expander gets confused when you drop them onto its interface. Let's fix that.

In `/boot/home/config/etc`, you'll find a file called `expander.rules.sample`. Make a copy of this and rename it to `expander.rules`. Open it in a text editor and add a line that looks like this:

```
"" .exe "unzip -l %s" "unzip -o %s"
```

Save the file, relaunch Expander, and drag your self-extracting archive onto Expander. This time you won't get an error message—Expander will merrily show you an x-ray view of the archive's contents, and decompress it when you click Expand.

You can see how to format other decompression rules in `expander.rules` by studying the examples in the sample file, but all you need to know is that the first block represents the MIME type of the file (we use blank quotes here because we don't care about the MIME type), the second block is the file extension, the third block is the command you would use to get a listing of the archive's contents without actually decompressing, and the fourth command is what you would use to actually decompress the file. The `%s` characters are used to tell the shell to act on whatever file or files are passed to it, or in this case, dragged onto Expander. You can add lines like this for any decompression format that runs from within the Terminal.

***Store Archives on another Volume*** If disk space is an issue on your boot volume, you probably don't want to store more data there than necessary. One good way to handle this situation is to dedicate a separate partition (or volume) to your software library. After moving your library to a separate partition, create a symlink to it in your downloads directory. Then all you have to do after installing a piece of software is drop its .zip file onto the symlink, and it'll be copied into your library. You can then safely delete the .zip file from your downloads directory. You may also consider using removable storage for your software library—you can fit a whole lot of BeWare onto a single Jaz cartridge, for instance.

As you begin downloading files, it won't be long before you encounter some archives with a .pkg extension, rather than .zip. These are SoftwareValet "package" files, and are part of a complete distribution mechanism for BeOS software. You'll find details on using SoftwareValet and .pkg files in Chapter 10, *System Tools and Utilities*.

**Icon-o-Matic** The icons included with BeOS are quite dashing, but it probably won't be long before you find yourself wanting to either create custom versions of the bundled icons or create your own icons from scratch. BeOS does include an icon editor, but you won't find it in your apps folder—it's kind of hidden. You access Icon-o-Matic by double-clicking in the "icon well" in any filetype panel. As you'll discover in Chapter 5, BeOS has two kinds of filetype panels: one for editing system-wide filetypes, and another for editing individual files. You access the system-wide panel from Preferences | FileTypes and the single-file version by right-clicking on a file and choosing Add-Ons | FileType from the context menu. Every filetype panel includes a square, recessed space into which you can paste or drag icons from other files. Alternatively, double-click one of these wells and you'll end up in Icon-o-Matic.

*Figure 2.44*

*BeOS's built-in icon editor, Icon-o-Matic, offers color and tool palettes you can use to customize existing icons or create new ones from scratch. Since each icon must include both 32x32 and 16x16 versions, Icon-o-Matic lets you preview both versions at once.*

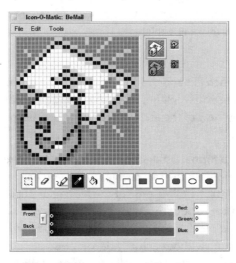

***Icons from Scratch*** You'll notice that Icon-o-Matic doesn't include a New entry under its File menu—it always needs to edit the icon for the current file or filetype. If you want to create an icon from scratch rather than editing an existing one, the best way to do it is to create a new folder, then edit its icon.

If you've ever used a simple paint program on any platform before, you'll find the tool suite here more than familiar. Choosing a color in the Color palette makes that color the active color. Selecting one of the shaded shapes in the Tools palette will allow you to create those shapes pre-filled with the active color. The empty shapes next to them allow you to create the same shapes as outlines.

The width of dragged lines is always dictated by the setting you've chosen in the Pen | Size menu (Alt+[1-6] will let you toggle between pen sizes quickly). Also under the Pen menu you'll find options for pen modes, so you can control whether your strokes overwrite existing pixels, invert them, subtract the current color value from them, and so on. Experimenting with these modes is the best way to get the gist of their functions.

***The Hole in the Middle*** By default, all icon backgrounds are transparent. Of course, transparency is difficult to depict on screen—it has to be represented by *some* color. In Icon-o-Matic, that color is a steely blue. Be careful not to confuse transparent pixels with other blue pixels, and note that transparent pixels will not be clickable once the icon is working on your system. While this doesn't generally pose a problem, you might be in for a surprise if you create an icon with colored areas at the outer perimeter and large transparent regions in the center—users clicking in the center of your icon will complain that the icon won't launch the program or file!

## Build Your Own Icon Library

Windows users will be familiar with the free-standing .ico file format for individual icons, and the common method of distributing icon collections by bundling them into .dll libraries. BeOS has no analogous distribution system for icon collections. In theory, it would be possible to build a BeOS tool that could stuff multiple icons into a resource file and then use a special interface to extract them, though no such tool existed at this writing. The current BeOS method isn't bad, though—it'll feel natural to you soon enough, and even sooner if you come from a background in the Mac, which has an icon storage method similar to the one in BeOS.

To create an icon library for BeOS, simply create a folder containing a collection of other folders (you don't have to use folders, but they're convenient because they take up no disk space) Implant one of your custom icons in each folder's icon well and zip up the entire parent folder. Because the zip format stores all system attributes, your icons will be packaged up along with the files themselves. You can then upload your archive to your Web site or BeWare, or email it to friends.

***Photo-Quality Icons the Easy Way*** Icon-o-Matic is great for getting in close and manipulating icons one pixel at a time, but you'll have to be a pretty skilled artist to create truly stunning icons with it. Fortunately, there's a far easier way. Create an image of any size in any graphics tool. Can't draw your way out of a paper bag? Fine—use a scanned or downloaded photograph or illustration instead. Download and install Thorsten Seitz' excellent ThumbNail tool from BeWare. Run your image through ThumbNail, which will take all of 2.5 seconds. When it's finished, the image file will have a new icon—a tiny version of the same image. Now just use the FileType app as usual to copy the icon to any other file or filetype on your system. Couldn't be easier. It's also possible to create your masterpiece in Photoshop on other platforms and import your creations as BeOS icons. For details on this technique, see Chapter 9.

## Installer

The Installer simply launches the BeOS installation process, which, for the most part, you'll only use when upgrading BeOS to a more recent version. You'll also use Installer if you have a need or desire to have two or more separate bootable BeOS partitions on your system (you might be a developer who needs access to both R4 and betas of R5 on the same machine, for example).

The BeOS installation routine is smart about replacing only the files it knows are safe for replacement—it won't touch your personal data or anything in your home directory unless you choose to do a "clean" install. Since most applications and BeOS preferences keep their settings files in subdirectories of your home directory, the Installer can overwrite BeOS system files like Network safely without messing with your Network settings file.

For complete information on BeOS installation, see Chapter 3.

 The Installer cannot be used to create an emergency boot disk. At this writing, the only way to create an extra boot disk for BeOS is with the dd tool from within BeOS or Linux, or with rawrite.exe from within Windows. See Chapter 16, *Troubleshooting and Maintenance*, for details.

## Magnify

Magnify is a simple little tool that does nothing but give you a worm's-eye view of the pixels that make up your screen, zooming you in to get a closer look, as you would with a jeweler's loupe.

Open up Magnify and slide your mouse around on the screen. By default, the pixels beneath your mouse will be enlarged by a factor of eight, but you're not limited to the default zoom factor—Magnify has tons of options for obtaining

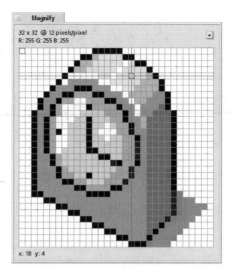

**Figure 2.45**

*Magnify will zoom you in on any area of your screen for a closer look, giving you a worm's-eye view.*

custom close-ups of anything on your screen, at just about any resolution. All of Magnify's options are tucked into a menu that you can access by clicking the downward-pointing arrow at the upper right (Figure 2.46) Try tweaking the Decrease/Increase Window Size options in this menu, then play with the Decrease/Increase Pixel Size options to see for yourself just how tightly you can zoom in on any icon, font, window element, graphic, or other graphical element on your system.

Magnify will also let you determine the RGB value of any pixel. Select Add Crosshair from the options menu, then position your mouse over an area. Hit Alt+F to freeze the current view (so that you can still use your mouse without the view changing), then click any pixel in the view—this causes the crosshair to move to the selected point. The RGB value of that pixel appears in Magnify's status area. Magnify also includes a simple built-in help system. Select Help from the options menu to view detailed descriptions of Magnify's capabilities.

Resolution and color depth of viewed area

RGB value of pixel under crosshair

Click to access options

Simple help system

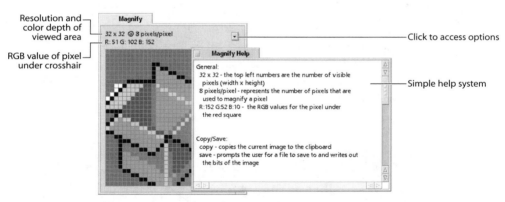

**Figure 2.46**

*Magnify lets you zoom in on any graphical element on your system with highly customizable control over window size, pixel size, and more.*

Aside from playing around, one of the nice things Magnify lets you do is get a sense of exactly how font antialiasing works. Hold it over some screen text and you'll see the gray squares nuzzled up in between the black and white squares that make up your font (read more about antialiasing in Chapter 9).

Designers of icons, game sprites, fonts, and other small graphics may find Magnify useful if the graphics applications they're using don't include a zoom feature of their own. Magnify can also be used for aligning objects and for close-up viewing of the shadings used in buttons, windows, and borders.

 *Custom Magnifications* As if all of that weren't enough, you can also launch Magnify from the command line with a size argument, in other words:

```
Magnify 4
Magnify 64
```

Just make sure that the number you use as an argument is a multiple of four.

# MIDI

There are two kinds of computer sounds in this world: 1) those mapped out bit by bit, sounding as realistic as a compact disc and having absolutely *huge* file sizes, and 2) those created from mathematical instruction sets, sounding sometimes as cheesy as department-store Casio keyboards and having relatively *tiny* file sizes. You probably know sounds of the former type as .WAV or .AIFF files, though there are many more "bitmapped" sound file formats out there. Sound files from the latter class are usually General MIDI files, created by sending a series of on/off signals to a palette of "channels" with predefined instrument sounds.

While BeOS is capable of creating and playing professional-level, non-cheesy MIDI (See the sidebar *MIDI Crash Course*), the two MIDI players that come bundled with your operating system (MIDI and SimpleMIDI) are designed only to handle 16-channel General MIDI files. While both applications are capable of playing the same files identically, the difference is that MIDI gives you an entire keyboard/mixing board interface, while SimpleMIDI offers only an oscilloscope-style viewer.

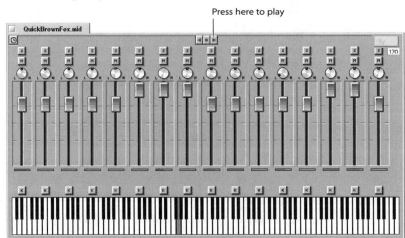

*Figure 2.47*

*The bundled MIDI application is capable of playing any 16-channel General MIDI file, and gives you independent solo, mute, and volume options for each channel.*

## *MIDI Crash Course*

MIDI (Musical Instrument Device Interface) technology was developed by Yamaha and Roland to allow musicians to control electronic devices from other electronic devices—for instance, signals could be sent from the keyboard of one synthesizer to another synthesizer by running the signal through a MIDI interface. Later, it became possible to control electronic devices from analog instruments, as when a musician plays a remote synthesizer by strumming or picking her guitar. Because MIDI signals are just on/off pulses arranged into channels, people even figured out how to use their instruments to trigger light switches, fog machines, and disco balls, running full-on night clubs from the helms of their instruments.

MIDI assumes that the characteristics of various instruments are defined in each channel *on the end-user's equipment*—not in the file itself. Therefore, it's not easy for a musician to simply create a sound file and share it with the rest of the world digitally; the MIDI file contains only the number of tracks and the sequence of pulses within them, not the actual sounds mapped to each channel. Therefore, it was necessary to create the "General MIDI" specification, which declares 16 channels of basic, common instrument sounds, as a lowest-common denominator format. These basic sounds are generally hardcoded into sound cards and MIDI software applications. The existence of this specification makes it possible to assume that people owning even the most basic sound cards are able to hear something resembling what the artist intended. Basic MIDI files thus became shareable, but the limited built-in palette of instruments is why MIDI files downloaded from the Internet usually have such a cheesy quality.

However, the world of professional MIDI is a realm unto itself, and the sounds produced by professional MIDI gear/musicians aren't cheesy at all. Modern MIDI tools are capable of handling hundreds of channels simultaneously, each with precisely defined instruments, and each measuring time in thousandths of a second. Professionally created MIDI can sound truly awesome, but files created this way will only play properly on the same equipment, configured in the same way. Thus, the ultimate destination of files created this way is not the shareable floppy disk or your Web site, but actual recordings—studio tape, game soundtracks, television and movie background music, special audio effects, and the like.

Because BeOS is fine-tuned for multimedia, it makes for an exceptional MIDI-creation environment. See Chapter 14, *Media Applications*, for more on MIDI software.

You can't launch MIDI by clicking its icon—you'll need to drag an existing MIDI file onto its icon. You'll find a sample MIDI file in your home directory by default, under /boot/home/SampleMedia/midi/. If you installed BeOS with all the bells and whistles, you'll find more samples in your /boot/optional/ midi/ folder. Turn down your speakers (so you don't blow an eardrum if they're accidentally set too loud), drag the QuickBrownFox sample file onto the player, and have a look.

The MIDI application is rather wide. You will need to set your screen resolution to a minimum of 800×600 to see all of it onscreen at once.

The file won't begin playing automatically—you'll need to press the forward arrow button at the very top to kick it off. As the file begins to play, you'll start to see some interesting things: the volume sliders for the various channels will adjust themselves automatically, responding to the volume values programmed into the file. The left/right balance knobs will twist of their own accord, and if you press the K button above the keyboard, the keys will glow red as each note is hit. To play any channel solo, click its S button—this will cause all channels but this one to drop out. Conversely, clicking the M button will cause only that channel to drop out.

The MIDI application isn't particularly powerful, and it's designed for people who want to play MIDI files, not create them. For more on MIDI file creation, see Chapter 14.

## MiniPlayer

**Figure 2.48**

*MiniPlayer is a bare-bones audio CD player that offers no advanced controls and won't let you save audio files to your hard disk. If you need more options than this, see the full CD Player application.*

The MiniPlayer is one of two audio CD players that come bundled with BeOS. If you have any desire to customize, tweak, shuffle, record, or do anything else fancy with your audio CDs, use the full CD Player application. If you just want to play audio CDs through with little to no intervention, use MiniPlayer. It's small, it stays out of the way, and it gets the job done.

Use of MiniPlayer is intuitive. Insert an audio CD into your CD-ROM drive, hit the play button, and music comes out. The controls operate just like those on your home CD player.

## NetPositive

BeOS's bundled Web browser may not be as fancy-pants as Netscape Navigator, but it's incredibly lean and efficient, and its capabilities grow with every release of BeOS. In addition, the Be engineers sometimes offer downloadable upgrades that further enrich the feature set between OS releases. NetPositive is covered in depth in Chapter 4.

# People

How many methods have you used over the past few years to database and store information on your personal and business contacts? If you're like many people, you've tried everything from a million yellow sticky notes plastered all over your home or office, to a plain text file you can print out and stick in your wallet, to a variety of commercial PIMs (personal information managers), to home-built experiments with a variety of database products, to the current favorite, the 3Com Palm Pilot. While most of these solutions get the job done, they all share a common problem: they're proprietary. Your home-built database can't read your ACT! contact manager, and the Pilot most certainly doesn't know what to do with your yellow stickies. Every time you give up on one format and try another, you've got to come up with a method of porting the data from one system to another. If you're lucky you can go through a middle-ground file format, like comma- or tab-separated ASCII. If you're not, you've got to open up the old database in a word processor and massage it into a format readable by the new one. In the worst case, you've got to reenter everything by hand. Bleah. Who needs it?

**Figure 2.49**

*Rather than placing all of your contact information into a contact manager's proprietary format, BeOS stores each of your contacts as an independent Person file, created with the People application. PIMs and contact managers simply read these files out of your* /boot/home/people/ *folder.*

The problem here is that each of these systems wants to "own" your data. When a program formats your data so that other programs can't read it, you become locked into that program's system. Knowing that most people are too busy to mess with the details of data-format conversion, the vendors of these products ride a good bet: Once you start using their product, you'll never stop. But hey—it's your data. You created it, so you should be able open it up in any application you want. Text files, HTML documents, and dozens of image file formats can be opened and manipulated by just about any relevant application, on any platform. Why should your contact information be any different?

Good news: BeOS has another excellent solution in store for you, this time in the form of the Person file format. As with the unified email file format (Chapter 4), you get a unique Person file for each of your contacts. And People files live in a central system location so that all of your applications will know where to find them: /boot/home/people/.

*Figure 2.50*

*Opening a Person file lets you enter and edit information related to that contact. You can fill in as many or as few details as you like. You can search your system for People files matching any criteria—everyone you know living in Washington, for instance.*

Thanks to the People system, you can run system queries to find things like all of your business contacts living in California or all of your contacts who don't have Web sites. (See Chapter 7, for details.) You can also do cool things like dragging People files into the To: fields of email messages to create preaddressed starter messages. Finally, you don't have to launch a full-blown contact manager application just to create a new contact. Just launch the People application (or pull down File | New from within an existing Person file), fill in a few fields, and bingo—a new contact has been created in your system, immediately available to any application that cares to avail itself of it.

***Grouping People*** The last item in the People application is a picklist labeled Groups. Groups let you assign each person to one of any number of arbitrary collections, such as "business contacts," "friends," or "surfing buddies." If the group you need doesn't show up in the picklist, just type it in for the current person. That group will now show up as an option in the Groups picklist for *all* Person files, so you can even return to old contacts and assign them to the new group. And of course, you can now perform a system query for all of your surfing buddies.

***Transferring your current contact manager to a collection of Be Person files***
If you've got a ton of contacts stored in a PIM or database that you want to turn into a big pile of BeOS Person files, your best bet would probably be to use the facilities built into one of the commercial or shareware contact managers for BeOS (see Chapter 12, *Productivity Applications*).

You may also want to try the PeoplePorter shell script written by Scot Hacker and available on BeWare. This script accepts a mail-merged version of your PIM or database's contact list and breaks it up into as many individual files as you've got contacts, transforming the data in those files into attributes attached to Person files. However, since there are so many storage formats out there and there's no way for the script to know exactly how your data is currently stored, it will be necessary for you to massage your PIM or contact manager's output into a "lowest common denominator" format prior to running the script. You can do this easily using Word's (or any savvy word processor's) mail merge function.

## PlaySound

PlaySound is another one of those "simple as they come" kind of programs. Drag any .WAV or .AIFF sound file onto PlaySound's icon and you'll see a small window like the one in Figure 2.51, with no controls other than a stop button. Sound will be routed through your system's digital-to-analog converter (DAC) and thus to your sound card and, hopefully, to your speakers.

PlaySound is also set up as the default handler for all audio files on your system. If you find a sound player you'd rather have associated with all of your audio files, see Chapter 9. One such replacement sound player is the shareware SoundPlay (see Chapter 14).

**Figure 2.51**

*Playing system sounds doesn't get much simpler than this. Drop a sound file onto the PlaySound icon and this is what you get.*

## PoorMan

Like the truly modern, Web-enabled operating system it is, BeOS includes its very own Web server. It's no Apache, and you can't exactly run a high-traffic e-commerce site from it. But if your Web-serving needs are moderate, you'll probably find it more than sufficient. While BeOS isn't as fine-tuned as a network server the way, for example, Linux or FreeBSD are, it is capable of handling traffic loads far beyond what most of us receive on our personal and small business sites. Informal interviews with people hosting sites with PoorMan indicate that 100,000–200,000 hits per day is a reasonable load, and the author has sustained 2–3,000 hits per hour over ISDN in one PoorMan test. If your site's traffic requirements extend beyond these estimates, you may want to consider a more high-end solution.

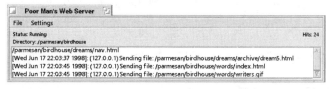

**Figure 2.52**

*BeOS includes a built-in personal Web server called PoorMan. It's nothing fancy, but it's all you need to serve a site for a small workgroup or business, and optionally keeps complete traffic logs as well.*

Learn more about PoorMan and using BeOS as a Web serving platform in Chapter 8, *Networking*.

# Pulse

Wondering just how CPU-intensive your new SuperWhizzy DiskGrinder application really is? There's one good way to find out—open up the Pulse application and watch the blinky lights do their thing while DiskGrinder is running. You'll see as many rows of blinking lights as there are processors in your machine. Each of the rows contains a series of fake LEDs (light-emitting diodes), which rise and fall in accordance with the amount of actual work being done.

Pulse doesn't just monitor CPU activity—it also lets you control it, to a limited degree. If you've got more than one processor in your machine, use the green buttons to toggle your CPUs on or off. Unless you're filled with morbid curiosity over how your system would perform with only half the juice, there are really only a couple of good reasons to turn off processors. First, if you're interested in benchmarking BeOS versus another operating system on the same machine, you may need to turn off one processor in BeOS just to make it a fair test (remember that many operating systems—such as Windows 95/98—can't see more than one CPU). Second, developers interested in performance on a wide array of hardware need to test their applications for single-CPU machines. Even if toggling processors on and off doesn't serve any useful purpose in your situation, you'll still be the envy of all your friends just because you can do it and they can't.

Once upon a time, in the days before R3, the Pulse application had a clever little Easter Egg built into it, in the form of a *developer intelligence test*. It worked like this: if you were clever enough not to try and turn off *both* of your processors at once, you passed the test. If, on the other hand, you wondered how well BeOS could run with zero processors active and thereby succeeded in locking up your machine …

It's rumored that most developers had to try turning off both processors at least once, just because they could. Now that BeOS is an operating system fit for human consumption, however, the intelligence test has been removed— it's no longer possible to turn off all CPUs at once.

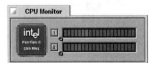

**Figure 2.53**

*Not only does Pulse let you monitor the current load on each of your processors independently, it also lets you toggle them on and off for testing purposes.*

Another cool thing about Pulse is the way it behaves when used as a Replicant. Whereas other Replicant applications we've looked at so far simply let you embed an entire app in the desktop, Pulse lets you "tear off" the green CPU toggle buttons independently of one another. Thus, you can embed one or both switches in the desktop or in any other Replicant-aware shelf space.

If you'd rather be able to tear off the LEDs as Replicants rather than just the switches, download MiniPulse (Figure 2.54) from BeWare and embed that in your desktop instead. This makes for a great Replicant if you'd like to keep tabs on CPU usage on a permanent basis, since you can tuck it out of the way, and it has no window frame or title tab to clutter up your desktop.

For an interesting demo, open up the Mandelbrot application in the demos folder, make sure both Pulse and Mandelbrot are visible simultaneously, and start dragging out areas in Mandelbrot—even and odd Mandelbrot scan lines are drawn by alternate processors (if you have more than one). Now turn off one of the CPUs and try again. Notice how the LED lights jump higher on the Pulse scale, and the drawing of the next fractal slows perceptibly.

**Figure 2.54**

*Unlike Be's built-in Pulse application, MiniPulse lets you embed just the CPU load indicators in your desktop for a clean, unobtrusive window onto your processors' activity.*

## Blinky Lights in Memoriam

The original BeBox (may it rest in peace) had several cool hardware features not available anywhere else. One of these features was the pair of processor load indicator lights running up and down the front bezel of the case. Two towers of phosphorescent green lights, dancing in rhythm with the operating system's every move, keeping the operator in constant touch with the total load being exerted on the dual CPUs inside. While multiproc machines may be more common now, the idea of having two CPUs in one box was something of a rarity at the time, at least in the consumer space. The Blinky Lights, as they were affectionately called by many, capitalized on the coolness factor of symmetric multiprocessing at a time when that kind of technology was in general only available in high-end science and government facilities. And (so I hear) they were a great way to impress dates. Think of Pulse as a vestigial genetic throwback to BeOS's booster rocket, the original BeBox.

Fortunately, all is not lost for Blinky Light lovers. Andreas Kaenner has put together a set of hardware specifications you can use to build a set of external load indicators that plug into

the serial port of any PC. And if you're not good with a soldering iron, an assembled version may become available if interest runs high enough. You can find more information at **www.archi-line.de/ kaenner/Seiten/PulseBox.html**.

**Figure 2.55**

*If you've got more than one CPU, a serial port to spare, and can read electronic diagrams, you can build a set of external Blinky Lights for BeOS for your PC.*

## ROMUpdater—BeBox Owners Only

Chances are likely that you won't find the Updater application on your system—this is a utility seen only by the 2,000 or so BeBox users in the world. Because the BeBox stores its boot code (rather than parts of the OS itself, as is the case with MacOS) in a flash ROM chip soldered to the motherboard, the ROM sometimes needs to be updated when the operating system receives an upgrade. However, this isn't always the case—for instance, R3 ran just fine on BeBoxes still running the PR2 ROM.

If you own a BeBox and undertake a BeOS upgrade, be sure and check out the documentation carefully first, and find out whether the ROM upgrade is necessary or not. Most ROM updates just include support for new video cards, but in the past, indispensable things like the new filesystem were part of this process. If the ROM update is required for your upgrade, drag the ROM image from the installation CD and drop it on top of the Updater icon. It'll chug away for about 30 seconds. When it's finished, install the upgrade and reboot.

 ***Don't Reboot before Upgrading*** If you own a BeBox and need to update your ROM for an OS upgrade, make sure you get the order of operations right:

1. Run ROMUpdater
2. Install the OS
3. Reboot

If you attempt to run the above steps nonsequentially, you may find that you *can't* reboot, as you will have updated the system ROM to an operating system version that isn't yet present. Technically, this shouldn't happen, as BeOS boot ROMs can usually still boot previous versions of the OS. However, some individuals have had problems with this in the past. If this does happen to you, you'll need to get a copy of that boot ROM onto a floppy disk (possibly by using the dd command from another machine) and then boot from the newly created floppy.

## SCSIProbe

If you have SCSI devices (such as external hard disks, Zip or Jaz drives, scanners, or other peripherals) attached to your system, SCSIProbe will display a table similar to the one in Figure 2.56. If no SCSI bus or adapter is found on your system, SCSIProbe won't launch, but will display an error message instead.

The function of SCSIProbe should not be confused with that of the DriveSetup preferences application (Chapter 10, *Preferences*). While DriveSetup

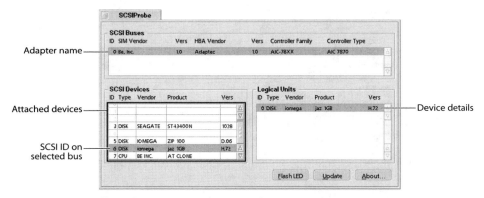

*Figure 2.56*

*SCSIProbe displays any SCSI devices attached to your system in a graphical layout similar to DriveSetup's. Select an entry in the grid to see more information about that device.*

is used for mounting, unmounting, and initializing of SCSI disks as well as IDE, SCSIProbe simply displays the current configuration of SCSI devices on the system (which may just as easily be non-disk devices such as scanners).

Operation is fairly straightforward. All detected SCSI buses—such as adapter cards or SCSI capabilities built into your motherboard—will be displayed in the upper field. Select a SCSI bus to display the devices attached to it in the lower left. Select a device to display more information about it in the Logical Units section at right. Note that a single device can host multiple logical "units," such as virtual drives (not pictured).

If a device has an LED drive activity indicator, select it and click the Flash LED button to confirm that BeOS sees the device. If you've attached or detached a device from the system, click the Update button to make SCSIProbe rescan the SCSI Bus and alert the system of any changes.

## SerialConnect

Don't be fooled for a second (as many people are)—SerialConnect has nothing whatsoever to do with connecting to the Internet, and doesn't speak a word of PPP (for Internet connection instructions, see Chapter 4). So what *does* SerialConnect do? It lets you connect your BeOS machine to text-based terminals such as old-fashioned dial-up bulletin board systems. It's also capable of receiving the "debug output" squirted out of another BeOS machine's serial port, which can be useful for troubleshooting machines that aren't booting properly. Programmers also use this technique to receive machine feedback during driver development, when the machine can't be booted normally.

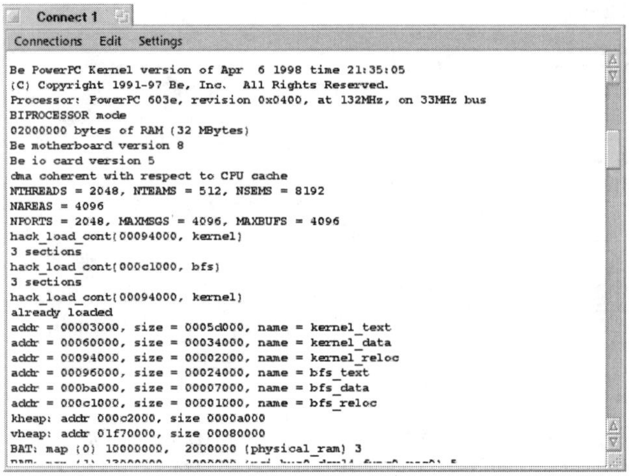

*Figure 2.57*

*SerialConnect is used for dialing into old-style bulletin-board systems and for receiving the "debug output" squirted out of another BeOS machine's serial port. SerialConnect has nothing to do with connecting to the Internet. Pictured: SerialConnect running on the author's x86 machine, in the process of intercepting the bootup sequence from a BeBox across the room.*

Chances are, you'll hardly ever use SerialConnect. The Internet has all but driven bulletin-board systems to extinction, and programmers are generally the only people who care about debug output. Learn more about using SerialConnect to dial into other modems in Chapter 8. Find out how to intercept your debug output in Chapter 16, *Troubleshooting and Maintenance*.

## ShowImage

When you double-click on an image file's icon, BeOS first looks to see what format the image is stored in, then launches the appropriate viewer. If it's a GIF or JPEG file, the image is launched in NetPositive by default. If it's a BMP, TIFF, or TGA file, it will load up in ShowImage (assuming you haven't changed system-wide preference for your image filetypes as described in Chapter 9). ShowImage is just a graphics viewer, not a graphics editor, so don't expect to be able to psychedelicize your cousin's face in it. For that kind of fun, you'll need to download and install one of the many image-editing applications available on BeWare. However, ShowImage does include a few very convenient cropping and format translation features.

One of the interesting things about ShowImage is that it takes advantage of Be's Translators library, meaning that in addition to BMP, TGA, and TIFF, it can display—or save to—any image format for which you've got a Translator installed. Translators are a key part of BeOS's flexibility; for more information on Translators, see Chapter 9.

**Figure 2.58**

*ShowImage is the default image viewer built into BeOS. It's no Photoshop, but it's lightning fast and will display images in any format for which you have a Translator. Drag any selection to the desktop to create a "clipping" file.*

ShowImage makes it extremely easy to crop sections out of your images and save those sections as new image files. Try this:

1. Make a rectangular selection in any open image.
2. Drag the selection to the desktop or into the Tracker.
3. There is no step three.

Your selection is now saved as a separate file on the desktop, with a name like `Bitmap Clip 1`. You can double-click the new file to open it in ShowImage, edit its filename, move it elsewhere on your system, or whatever you like. Of course, you can also copy or paste image data to and from the clipboard by using the Edit menu. For a hidden treat, select About ShowImage from the File menu.

ShowImage is also capable of minimal compositing. You can drag a selection from one image to another, or from one position in an image to another position. Photoshop it ain't, but it's useful if all you need to manipulate are rectangular selections.

***Custom Filetypes on Drag*** This kind of drag-and-drop selection clipping is pretty pervasive throughout BeOS. You'll find that you can do similar things with both text and images in many BeOS applications. In addition, some applications support the process in reverse, letting you drag text or image clippings into existing documents to insert their contents at that point. ShowImage can also take advantage of your system's image format Translators (Chapter 9). Try holding down your left Ctrl key while dragging a selection to the desktop—a context menu will appear asking which image format you want the clipping saved in!

# SimpleMIDI

SimpleMIDI is the little brother of the MIDI application. However, it's more than a simple player and is actually capable of a few cool tricks of its own.

To open a file in SimpleMIDI, either launch SimpleMIDI and click Open File or drag a MIDI sound file onto its icon. The oscilloscope readout will begin to dance, displaying the frequencies of the file as it moves through time. If you want to save a few CPU cycles, you can turn the oscilloscope off by checking the box marked Scope (not that this actually eats up many cycles—open up Pulse while SimpleMIDI is playing and you'll find that your processor is barely even being used at all).

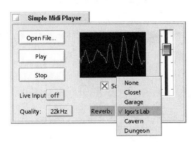

**Figure 2.59**

*Unlike the MIDI application, SimpleMIDI doesn't show you every channel of a playing MIDI file simultaneously. Instead, you get an oscilloscope readout and the ability to add a handful of simple sound effects.*

If you've got an external MIDI device plugged into your sound card and you'd rather run that through SimpleMIDI than a sound file, select your sound card from the Live Input picklist. Changing the quality level from 22kHz to 44kHz will cause the sample rate to be doubled, and you'll hear the sound quality jump appreciably, with more nuances of tone making it into the sound stream. Increasing the sample rate will, however, cause your CPU to work harder.

You can also add one of a handful of built-in sound effects to the output of the playing file by changing the type of reverb. Closet, Garage, Igor's Lab, Cavern, and Dungeon are all available from the Reverb picklist, in addition to the default of None. The slider at the right controls the audio volume being sent to the system's digital-to-analog converter.

# SoftwareValet

From the very start, Be has emphasized the importance of the Internet in its business plan, and has stated its enthusiasm about Internet software distribution in general. While the operating system itself was only distributed over the Internet for a short period of time, Be has diligently maintained BeWare, their comprehensive online software library, since the beginning.

Meanwhile, a company called StarCode was building a comprehensive electronic distribution system for BeOS software. StarCode's system integrated a database-backed Web site—called BeDepot—with a BeOS desktop client

**Figure 2.60**

*SoftwareValet trolls BeDepot for updates to the software installed on your system. It also helps you to manage your software—anything installed via the SoftwareValet interface is logged in a user-friendly database, allowing for easy management and uninstallation.*

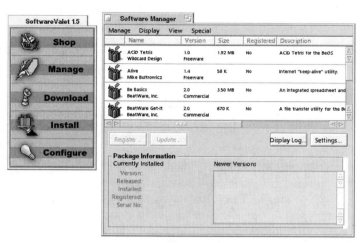

(called SoftwareValet) capable of scanning users' systems for installed applications and comparing version numbers with BeDepot's database. The result was a system that let developers easily peddle their wares online, keep tabs of who their registered users were, and get software updates to users as easily and automatically as possible. In May of 1998, Be acquired the BeDepot system from StarCode and took over development of the SoftwareValet client.

As a result, you've got an excellent system for purchasing, downloading, installing, and managing BeOS software right at your fingertips. Usage of SoftwareValet is covered in detail in Chapter 10.

## StyledEdit

Every operating system has to have a basic text editor—you can't get very far without one. True to form, the text editor included in BeOS goes above and beyond the capabilities of bundled editors on other operating systems (you're probably familiar with Windows's NotePad and MacOS's SimpleText). But StyledEdit doesn't just handle straight text—it also does a bang-up job with fonts, colors, and styles.

If you're thinking that the notion of a plain text editor that also handles fonts and colors is a contradiction in terms, you're not alone. In your experience with other operating systems, you've probably learned that plain text is plain text, and that adorned text is … something else entirely. Typically, attaching fonts and colors to text means creating a new file format and losing the ability to open that file in other plain text editors or on other operating systems. Be, however, has bridged the gap with a truly elegant solution, taking advantage of a unique aspect of the BeOS filesystem called "attributes." We'll explore BeOS attributes in depth in Chapter 5, but for now see the sidebar *A Crash Course in Attributes*.

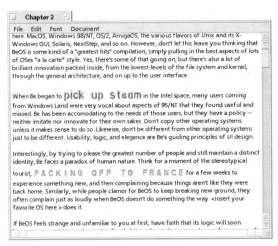

*Figure 2.61*

*Even though StyledEdit is capable of storing as many custom fonts and styles as you like, it still creates plain-vanilla text files that can be opened up in other text editors, even on other platforms. You'll lose your font stylings when viewing StyledEdit files in other editors, but the text itself is unaffected and your documents remain compatible.*

Instead of storing both text and font stylings in the file itself, StyledEdit stores only plain text in the file's body, while all data related to font stylings are stored in the file's attributes. When you move your file over to another operating system (or to another text editor within BeOS), the attributes are lost or ignored, while the data stays intact. SimpleText and NotePad will never even know that the file once contained formatting data. You get the best of both worlds, and BeOS stays cross-platform and cross-editor compatible.

**Using StyledEdit**   For the most part, StyledEdit works just like any plain text editor you've used before. If you can operate NotePad or SimpleText, you can work with StyledEdit. However, it does include a few extra features worth pointing out.

**Revert to Saved**   In most applications, if you've made a bunch of changes and later decide you don't want to keep them, you've got to close the file without saving and then reopen it. StyledEdit includes a Revert to Saved option under the File menu that allows you to throw away all of the changes you've made since the file was last saved. Users of Adobe Photoshop will be familiar with this function.

**Find Selection**   If you want to find more instances of a block of selected text, you don't need to copy it to the clipboard, open the Find dialog, paste in the selection, and hit Return. Instead, just pull down Edit | Find Selection and you're on your way. Alt+G will cycle through all found instances of the text in the selected block.

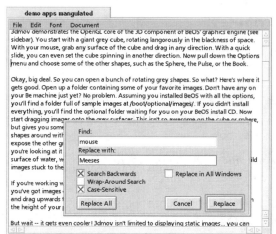

*Figure 2.62*

*StyledEdit's search-and-replace capabilities go beyond those built into most operating systems' default text editors. You can search backward, declare whether you want to search only from the current point on or search the entire file (wrap-around search), and even replace text in multiple documents at once.*

**Replace in All Windows**  It's one thing to be able to search and replace text throughout a document. But what if you're working on a Web site consisting of 100 pages, and you need to change a certain name, date, or block of code in all of them? You could master one of the Unix guru's command-line tools, like sed (Chapter 6), or you could just select all of your files in the Tracker, hit Enter to open them all at once, and pull down Edit | Replace in one of them. Then enter your search/replace text blocks and click the checkbox marked "Replace in all windows." Click Replace All, and your change will be made in every single open StyledEdit window. Note that this will not automatically save every file, so you can back out afterward by closing them without saving. If you need that functionality, you'll need to turn to the command line, or a more high-powered editor such as Pe which will let you run your search-and-replace operations over entire directory structures without having to open your files first.

**Replace same**  If you've just set up and run a search-and-replace operation, made some changes, and now need to run the same operation again, just pull down Edit | Replace Same to repeat it.

**Document menu**  You can control alignment of every line in your document by using the Align | Left, Center, or Right options under the Document menu. Note that this setting affects the entire document; you can't center just a single line. Depending on whether you're writing code or plain text, you may want line wrapping either on or off; this setting can also be found under the Document menu.

## A Crash Course in Attributes

Attributes may well be the single operating system concept in BeOS that is most unlike MacOS, Windows, or other common operating systems. At the same time, attributes are one of BeOS's most powerful built-in technologies. You can learn everything there is to know about filesystem attributes in BeOS in Chapter 5, but here's a brief rundown to help you understand how StyledEdit performs its magic. Here comes the most abstract sentence in this book:

**An attribute is a piece of data stored in the filesystem that is *associated* with a particular file but is *not a part of* the file itself.**

While this idea may seem a little weird at first, it has huge implications for the entire operating system and for the way you will come to store, organize, and mine the data on your hard drive. But rather than talk about what attributes are, let's focus on what you can do with them. Consider again the Person files we discussed earlier in this chapter. Double-click a Person file and you see a collection of data fields.

**Figure 2.63**

*Double-click a Person file and you see a collection of data fields.*

But there's another way to edit and view this same data—via the Tracker:

The Tracker—BeOS' file management system—lets you display and edit the data fields associated with Person files because that data is only *associated* with those files, not contained *inside* them. In fact, Person files don't have any data in them at all! There are several important points to understand about attributes and their relationship to the system:

**Figure 2.64**

*By using the Attributes menu in the Tracker, you can display and edit the data fields associated with Person files.*

- Each file on your system can have any number of attributes associated with it.

- Attributes can contain data of any kind: text, image, audio, binary, and so forth.

- Attributes can be of any size.

- Attributes are always associated with filetypes. For example, the Person filetype has associated attributes for storing addresses and phone numbers, but those same attributes are not associated with your system's plain text filetype.

- You can add attributes to—or remove them from—your filetypes.

- You can search (query) your system for files according to attribute criteria.

- The Tracker can display most text-based attributes as columns (as in Figure 2.64).

- Non-text attributes are not displayed by the Tracker, but are used by the system and by applications in a variety of powerful ways.

Don't worry if some things in this list don't make total sense to you now—we'll get to everything here eventually, primarily in Chapters, 5, 7, and 9.

If you're wondering how we got here from a discussion of StyledEdit's font handling, the last item in the list above is the key—StyledEdit saves font style data to attributes associated with the text file, so that text and font styles can remain joined at the hip, yet totally separable.

See Chapter 5, for more information on attributes in BeOS.

### Table 2.2  A few examples of attribute usage in BeOS

| This Filetype | Uses Attributes to Store |
|---|---|
| All files | MIME type, icon |
| Person files | Everything—name, address, fax number, group, and so on. |
| Bookmark files | Page title, URL, keywords |
| CD Player files | Total playing time, identification key |
| StyledEdit files | Font stylings |

A few of the common filetypes on your system, along with some of their interesting associated attributes.

*Sharing the Wealth*  Ever find yourself working in a particular paragraph and then suddenly wishing you could make that particular section into a separate file? There are two excellent ways to do this with StyledEdit under BeOS.

Window to Window: Drag your selected text from the current window to another open window. Not necessarily just a StyledEdit window, either—you can drag a block of text out of StyledEdit and into Pe, or from Pe to StyledEdit. Basically, any application that can handle BMessage text objects (see Chapter 1) can accept dropped text, regardless of its origin. Try dragging a paragraph out of a BeMail message and into StyledEdit, or out of PoorMan's traffic log and into Pe.

Clippings: Rather than dragging your selection to another edit window, try dragging it to the desktop or into any Tracker window. A new file will be created on the spot with the name Untitled Clipping. You can then rename the file to something more meaningful. Clippings, by the way, don't work just with text—you'll find that many imaging applications will let you drag parts of images out of the application window and into the Tracker, creating a new, cropped image file on the spot.

## The Terminal

One of BeOS's key features is its deep integration of a fine UI with a Unix-style command line. The Terminal is your interface with the command-line side of BeOS. The Terminal was introduced earlier in this chapter and gets Chapter 6 all to itself.

# The Demo Apps

So you've heard all the buzzwords, read the amazing reviews, and witnessed a few jaw-dropping BeOS demos at trade shows. Now you want to make your own machine sit up and do tricks, and bear witness to all of this multimedia glory. Anticipating this desire, the good folks at Be were kind enough to write a handful of applications designed to demonstrate the awesome power now humming through the silicon beast beneath your desk.

Pull down the Be menu and select the demos folder—you'll see a dozen or so icons representing Be's demo apps (if you don't see these in your Be menu, open up the /boot/demos/ folder in the Tracker). So what do these demos do? Well, they won't help you write your book reports any faster, and they won't wire your home for quadrophonic sound. But they will show you exactly what kinds of benefits you can expect to see in applications written expressly for the MediaOS. Each of them exercises one or more aspects of the system directly related to the buzzwords covered in Chapter 1.

 The demo apps are officially unsupported by Be, who make no guarantees about their stability (though we haven't seen any of them crash yet). Just take them for what they are and enjoy the show.

## 3dmov

When Be first started running 3dmov at trade shows in 1997, they set off a buzz. After hearing about it from friends, people who had never heard of BeOS before would navigate through the thronging attendees to catch a glimpse of it, and become instantly hooked on BeOS. Such is the seductive power of a good demo. The 3dmov app demonstrates the 3D Kit in BeOS, which is an API developers can use to work in 3D without getting into OpenGL.

*Figure 2.65*

*Among other wild tricks, 3dmov allows you to drag QuickTime movies onto the pages of a virtual book, then start turning the pages as the movies continue to play. Pages curl naturalistically.*

You start with a giant gray cube, rotating langorously in the blackness of space. With your mouse, grab any surface of the cube and drag in any direction. With a quick slide, you can set the cube spinning in another direction. Now pull down the Options menu and choose some of the other shapes, such as Sphere, Pulse, or Book.

Okay, big deal. So you can open a bunch of rotating gray shapes. So what? Here's where it gets good. Open up a folder containing some of your favorite images. Don't have any on your Be machine yet? No problem. Assuming you installed BeOS with all the options, you'll find a folder containing a few sample images at /boot/optional/images/. If you didn't install everything, you'll find the optional folder on your BeOS installation CD. Start dragging images onto the gray surfaces. This isn't so awesome with the cube or sphere, but gives you some instant cool with the Pulse option. Note that you can still move the shapes around with your mouse. Try grabbing the Pulse shape and turning it over to expose the other gray side, then drop another image onto that. Then move the shape so you're looking at it side-on—almost like wearing a skindiver's mask and looking at the surface of water, with half your mask underwater. Except you've got wild images stuck to the water's surface.

If you're working with the Book option, note that it doesn't get really interesting until you've got images on at least three pages. Grab the lower-right corner of the right page and drag upward to turn the page. Notice how the page curls realistically depending on the height of your page-turning arc.

3dmov isn't limited to displaying static images, though … you can just as easily drop movies onto the same surfaces. You'll find some sample QuickTime movies located in the /boot/optional/movies/ folder. Try the same experiment with those, and prepare to have your neighbors beg you to loan them your BeOS CD. Don't do it! Make 'em buy it, just like anyone else.

So what are you witnessing here? Obviously, you can't do this (or at least not very elegantly) under Windows or MacOS. For one thing, you're seeing the power of the OpenGL library at work, giving your 3D applications all kinds of extra flexibility. Second, you're seeing heavy multithreading going to town. Since each surface is assigned its own thread, it's able to work independently of the others without waiting in bottlenecks for its share of processor time. Lots of threads in one application means that each aspect of the application works smoothly with all the others, neither hogging the CPU nor being ignored. The fact that you can have several 3dmov windows open at once, all doing their rendering simultaneously and independently, is even more testimony to the power of pervasive multithreading.

For more info on Open GL, see *GL Teapot*, below.

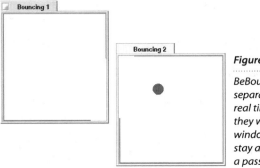

**Figure 2.66**

*BeBounce demonstrates the ability of separate applications to share data in real time, reacting to one another as if they were one. As you drag BeBounce windows around, the gaps in the borders stay aligned with one another to provide a passageway for the ricocheting ball.*

# BeBounce

One of the many technological gems residing in the core of BeOS is an inter-application messaging protocol called BMessages. Without getting too technical, BMessages is a mechanism by which applications can send and receive instructions to and from one another with a minimum amount of hassle on the part of the developer, a minimum amount of overhead from the operating system itself, and therefore a minimum number of CPU cycles consumed. What does this mean for you? Only that your applications can "talk" to one another in ways you never dreamed possible. Take BeBounce for instance.

Fire it up and you get a small window with a small red ball ricocheting off the walls, kind of like a weird Pong variant, but without the paddles. What's so great about that? Nothing, yet. But now, while that first BeBounce window is open, try launching the application again. If necessary, drag the second window out of the way of the first, so that none of the windows' borders is touching. All of a sudden, a gap opens up in the wall of the windows' boundaries. When the ball bounces toward that gap, it passes through open space and enters the second window, where it bounces around for a while, until it finds its own gap and passes back into the first window.

Now try dragging one of the windows around. As you drag a window, note that the position of the gap changes too, always staying aligned with the shortest distance between itself and the other window. Drag the windows to opposite corners of your screen. Drag it around as fast as you can. No matter what you do, you can't confuse the ball or the communication between the two apps. Both of them will always be sending and receiving messages to and from one another and dynamically updating the position of the gaps to allow the ball to pass through.

This may not seem exactly awe-inspiring at first glance, but the important thing to note here is that you launched the application twice—you're running two entirely separate instances of the application, not two windows within one application. It's quite normal for an application to communicate easily with itself, but it's another matter for two applications to communicate so dynamically with each other. You're seeing an example of BMessages in action, not to mention the usual multithreading behavior.

Another great example of BMessages in action is the roColor color picker, which you can download a trial version of from **www.rodesign.com.** Create any color in roColor and drag it onto your desktop—BeOS receives the message and changes to that color instantly. But drag a color into StyledEdit or h.Scribe, and they transform it into its hexadecimal equivalent for use in HTML. The BeOS desktop and h.Scribe weren't designed to receive messages from roColor—they were designed to accept BMessages, which means they have instant communication with any color-management software out there.

## BeLogo

Nothing fancy here... just 120 frames per second of raw 3D rendering power. A 3D version of the Be logo whips around in space as fast as it can, consuming as many CPU cycles as it can get its hands on. If you're running BeOS on an older machine, you may actually feel its impact on the CPU as you try to do other things. More modern machines—like Pentium IIs—won't even have to take a deep breath.

## Calah

Calah neither a CPU hog nor does it demonstrate any amazing multimedia feats. Instead, the program is a sort of elegant proof-of-concept, demonstrating how BeOS's native architecture and the BeOS POSIX layer can work together cooperatively. The Calah "engine," or back-end, is a POSIX program running in the Terminal, while the front-end gameboard is a standard BeOS application. When you launch Calah, you're actually launching a shell script, which originates and coordinates communication between the two layers. Because the two components are distinct, they can even run on separate machines, possibly connected by a serial cable.

This is a rather unusual way to construct a program on any platform, serving as more evidence of BeOS's open and flexible architecture. Calah is the kind of demo only a true geek could love—there's not a whole lot to look at on the outside, but it's pulling off some pretty exotic stuff on the inside. Developers interested in porting existing POSIX applications to BeOS will be especially interested in the Calah demo, which will illustrate to them how they can keep their existing POSIX code base and just write a nice BeOS GUI to ride on top.

# Container

Open up the Container demo, and what do you get? Big fat nothing. Container isn't much in the eye candy department, but it is a nice, clean example of the power of Replicants, which were introduced earlier in this chapter. In a nutshell, Replicants function like carbon copies of applications or application components, and can be embedded into any application that contains a Replicant "shelf." Your desktop is a good example of that, and so is Container.

Pull down your Be menu and select Show Replicants. Now fire up the Clock application (/boot/apps/Clock) and look for the Replicant handle in the lower-right corner. Grab the handle and drag it into Container. Now close the main Clock app—the Clock Replicant keeps on ticking in Container. Now do the same thing with the processor Replicants in the Pulse app (/boot/apps/Pulse). So far so good? Now close Pulse, then close and reopen Container. Notice that your Replicants are still alive, even though the host applications are closed? That's the important bit, because it means that when your BeOS applications share code or data via Replicants, their communications are persistent—when one application functions as a host to another application's Replicant, a semi-permanent bond has been established between them. For example, imagine a word processor that doubles as a Replicant container, and a spreadsheet with replicatable cells. Drag a data cell from the spreadsheet into a word processor document, and the data in the document will always stay up to date with changing data in the spreadsheet.

**Figure 2.67**

*Two instances of NetPositive running inside the Container demo. Container is an example of a Replicant shelf.*

## Dominos

Imagine that, given a pile of around 2,600 dominos and a really big card table, you tried to place as many pieces in legal positions as you could, as fast as you could, using as little space as you could. How long do you think it would take you? A month? You still probably wouldn't have maximized the amount of space and taken all the legal moves. Humans are really slow when it comes to some things.

Dominos demonstrates the BeOS Game Kit, an application interface for game programmers. When you launch Dominos, the application takes over your whole screen. The desktop and Deskbar are gone, and Dominos is the only thing you can see running. Only by using the Game Kit can programmers take over your entire computing environment and make the BeOS user interface go away.

 ***Escaping from the Game Kit*** **Because the BeOS UI goes away any time an application runs in Game Kit mode, you may find it difficult to exit back into BeOS if the running program doesn't provide a quit button of its own. If it doesn't, and you want out now, it's hotkey time. If you want to stop the application, try the standard Alt+W key combination to close the current window. If that doesn't work, there's a chance that Alt+Q will be mapped to the quit function. If you want the application to keep on running while you go do something else, just snap into another workspace with Alt+Fx, where x is the number of one of your workspaces between 1 and 9 (even if you have all 32 workspaces enabled, only 1 through 9 are accessible via hotkeys).**

There's nothing for you to do here but sit and watch as Dominos places tiles at lightning speed, until there are no legal moves left on the entire board. The amount of time required to place around 2,600 tiles is dependent on the speed of your machine—generally 5–10 minutes. It does, however, get slightly more exciting as the game progresses and your screen starts sliding all over the place as the app jumps from one side of the board to the other, trying to eke out the last possible locations. When it's finished, you can use the arrow keys on your number pad (not the normal arrows) to glide around the screen and examine the finished game. Catch any mistakes?

## Flight

If you've played with flight simulators before, you probably won't find BeOS's Flight much to crow about. It's really more of a proof-of-concept than anything. The object is to shoot down enemy helicopters without getting shot down yourself. You can choose to play as either the yellow team or the purple team, and network games are also supported, if you're in the mood to blast some of your workmates out of the sky.

To start a new game, pull down New Game from the Play menu. You can control your flight with the arrow keys on your numeric keypad (not the normal arrow keys), and you can shoot by hitting the Shift key. We'll wait for the dedicated game developers to fill in this niche a little better. Note, however, that games can run excellently inside a window, rather than taking over your whole screen, as they do in Dominos.

If you have a joystick attached to your machine, tell BeOS about it through the Joystick preferences panel (Chapter 9), and select an appropriate gameport from the Control menu.

## Font Demo

What could a new operating system possibly have to offer the world of fonts? Hasn't all of that been done to death? Well, yes and no. One of the nice things about working in BeOS is that all fonts are automatically antialiased—their outlines appear smooth, never ragged.

To understand antialiasing, you first need to understand aliasing, which is a simple side effect of the fact that it's hard to draw rounded edges when your screen has only square pixels. Remember when you were a kid playing with Etch-A-Sketch and you tried to draw circles or curves? The closest you could come was a sort of down-across-down-across approximation. If you look at the edges of a font up close, somewhere along one of its curves, you'll notice the same "stair-stepping" effect. Antialiasing is a trick that operating systems can use to minimize the stair-steps effect. Assuming that your background is white and your fonts are black, and that each pixel can carry only one color, why not make the color of the pixel in between the stair steps gray? When viewed at a micro-level, this can look a little messy, but when seen from a normal viewing distance, antialiased fonts appear curvaceously smooth. To see antialiasing up-close and personal, type something into StyledEdit and then open up the Magnify applet in the demos folder. Hold the mouse pointer over your typed text and Magnify will show you the gray pixels in the corners.

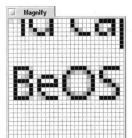

**Figure 2.68**

*Viewing an antialiased font up close (via the Magnify utility), you can see how gray blocks are added into the "stair-steps" of curved lines, producing a smooth, soft effect when viewed from a normal distance.*

This demo, however, isn't so much about the fonts themselves as it is about what can be done to dynamically manipulate objects in the system. It just happens to demonstrate the concept with fonts.

Launch the Font Demo and click the Cycle Fonts button. You'll see two windows, one displaying the words "Be, Inc.," and the other containing a variety of slider controls. Type your name over the top of "Be, Inc." in the control panel and hit Enter. Click the Cycle Fonts button and your name will be displayed in every font in the system, sequentially. Now for the fun part. Start dragging the Size, Shear, Rotation, and Spacing sliders back and forth to change how the fonts are displayed. Notice how the fonts onscreen change their appearance dynamically, not waiting for you to hit OK or Apply, and not waiting for the other controls to update themselves? All of the parameters affect the total appearance of the current font in real time, and all parameters are constantly working together on the total effect. You can, of course, jump instantly to any other available font by selecting it in the list.

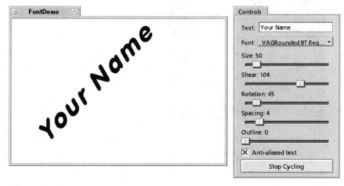

**Figure 2.69**

*Set the Font Demo to cycle through every font on your system, and you can change the fonts' size, shear, rotation, and spacing on the fly. BeOS doesn't even skip a beat—you're seeing pervasive multithreading in action. To compare aliased to antialiased text under real-world conditions, select and deselect the antialiasing checkbox.*

When this demo first appeared on the scene, it existed only as an "imagine what developers could do with this …" sort of example; no shipping software was doing anything similar. But today, several applications do implement real-time font control, in much the same manner as this Font Demo. However, playing with this kind of technology from within a real, shipping application is infinitely more satisfying because it demonstrates that real-time control is not just useful in theory—it's useful in reality.

# GL Teapot

At the core of BeOS's 3D graphics engine is a technology called OpenGL, which is an application programming interface (API), or a sort of syntax for developing sophisticated, fast, 2D and 3D graphics applications. More specifically, OpenGL functions as a standard software interface to high-end geometry and rendering graphics hardware. OpenGL is an industry standard, originally developed by Silicon Graphics in 1992 and currently running in some form or other on most operating systems. Because it's an industry standard, OpenGL libraries are built into many existing video cards and software applications. OpenGL is particularly popular in the CAD (computer assisted design) world, where open, high-performance 3D rendering is essential. The presence of OpenGL on BeOS guarantees excellent 3D performance for users, and many attractive opportunities for developers.

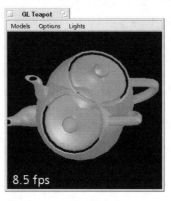

*Figure 2.70*

*The GL Teapot demo shows off the 3D rendering engine at the foundation of BeOS's 3D API. Teapots are mathematically recalculated with every frame, making this demo extremely math-intensive.*

To see OpenGL technology in action, double-click the GL Teapot icon and watch the teapot begin to spin in midair. The important thing to note here is that this is not a bitmapped animation—you're not watching a sequence of pictures of a teapot, you're watching a teapot being calculated from mathematical instructions. As a result, you have total control over parameters like the teapot's color, reflectiveness, and opacity and the shade of the lights falling on the pot. To tweak some of these parameters, start pulling down menu items and experimenting. Under the Options menus you'll find you can control whether the teapot is rendered in full, realistic shading, simple wireframe, or somewhere in between. You can turn the lights on or off, change the perspective, and add fog. Note how each of these effects has a noticeable impact on the speed at which the teapot spins. The more math you make the demo do, the slower it goes. The fewer calculations to be performed, the faster it goes. Under the Lights menu, you'll find that you can add or subtract different-colored lights to various parts of the room, or turn off red, green, yellow, and blue lights independently.

It gets better—try grabbing the teapot with your mouse and dragging it around. You have total control over the pot's orientation and its rate and direction of spin. Try grabbing it and sliding your mouse quickly across the window, then quickly letting go. You can set the teapot spinning wildly in any direction you like. Now, to really give the Teapot demo a run for its money, pull down the Models menu and choose Add a Teapot. Suddenly you've got two teapots occupying the same point in space. The demo will render them so that they pass through each other as they spin, as if they were semi-solid.

Notice that the spin rate decreases dramatically as you increase the amount of calculations that need to be done for every frame.

You can monitor the number of frames per second you're getting by watching the digits flipping in the lower-left corner of the window. This number represents the fps, or frame per second, at which the application is able to render the whole scene. Try resizing the window to see how that affects the overall fps ratio. You'll also find some interesting performance side effects by changing your video bit depth among 32, 24, 16, and 8 bits per pixel while the demo is running (use the Screen panel in your preferences folder).

OpenGL performs at its best when it can take advantage of the hardware acceleration in your graphics card. If your card doesn't support hardware acceleration, or if a driver that takes advantage of hardware acceleration hasn't yet been written for your card, all OpenGL calculations will be performed in software. Things will still work, but you won't get anywhere near the performance you would get with full support for hardware acceleration.

 OpenGL isn't BeOS's only 3D implementation—BeOS also includes its own proprietary graphics language, which is similar in some ways to MacOS's QuickDraw. Some of the 3D calls in BeOS's own Media Kit are, in fact, more efficient for some (usually lighter) kinds of tasks. But for hardcore 3D applications, OpenGL (which Be has licensed from SGI since 1996) is definitely the ticket.

 At this writing, rumors were leaking out of Be that Teapot frame rates are approaching 200 frames per second, thanks to OpenGL hardware acceleration and to improvements in operating system code. Keep your eye on the near horizon for more on this one.

## Kaleidoscope

"One processor per person isn't enough." Or so Be promoted back in the days when BeOS only ran on the BeBox. When the OS graduated to running on PowerMacs and then Intel CPUs, Be stopped using this slogan, probably because they didn't want people to think BeOS would run inadequately on their existing single-processor machines. Of course, BeOS runs just fine on single-proc boxes, but it also *loves* to grab ahold of as many cycles as it can find. If you've got more than one processor in your machine, Kaleidoscope will help you see how clock cycles are distributed.

Open a single Kaleidoscope window and the demo will attempt to throw as many lines—in pretty patterns no less—onto your screen as fast as it can. Now open the Pulse application (/boot/apps/Pulse) so you can monitor CPU usage. Grab the lower-right corner of the window and resize it so you can see both Pulse and Kaleidoscope windows at once. Notice how the demo speeds up when you shrink the window, but your CPU utilization does not go down. This is because the demo is built to run as fast as it possibly can. When running in a smaller window, Kaleidoscope requires less work to draw each frame, so it simply cranks out more lines per second.

If you've got two or more processors, watch the Pulse indicators closely. See how they alternate the workload between them? You're watching symmetric multiprocessing in action, the workload being automatically and evenly distributed between all available processors. Remember that the program's author didn't know how many processors would be in your machine. In contrast to other operating systems, simply writing an application for BeOS automatically makes it multiprocessor-aware.

Still got some juice to spare? Try launching a second instance of Kaleidoscope, then a third, and a fourth. Notice how the responsiveness of your system is affected. Things will slow down at a certain point, but the important thing to note is that the Be menu, the Tracker, and your other applications running in the background continue to stay responsive. BeOS's responsiveness degrades gracefully under extreme workloads. Rather than simply maxing out, grinding away at your disk, and making you wait ten seconds to bring other windows to the front, the rest of the system continues to handle nicely. Of course, even BeOS has its limits, and at a certain point you're going to start detecting delays. Go ahead and push your system till smoke starts coming out of its ears—you won't hurt anything. Notice also that pushing your system isn't going to crash anything. The worst that can happen is that Kaleidoscope will beg for mercy under duress. Either that or your eyeballs will.

## Life

Despite its gentle appearance and pastoral name, Life is one of Be's most grueling benchmarking tools and is heavily multithreaded. In fact, Life was originally used in BeOS demos to show the effectiveness of multiple threads running in a multiprocessor system. The answer to the question, "What Is Life?" is in the sidebar of the same name.

Unlike most applications, Life lets you—the user—choose how many threads will be used. The trick is to keep an eye on the all-important megacells-per-second ratio and note how different levels of threadedness affect overall performance. In addition to the usual two BeApplication threads, one to eight more are used for computation. The screen is divided into eight bands, and each is allocated a thread, which calculates the next generation of Life cells. Not only does Life bang hard on threads, but CPU utilization, memory, and PCI bus speed tests all yield interesting results when you run Life. As of R4, Life was updated to use BDirectWindow, so the powerful graphics optimizations provided there can be monitored as well.

## *What Is Life?*

Life is a port of an ages-old computer simulation that explores the way organisms react with one another under certain conditions. In this case, the conditions are mathematical rules that emulate on a low level the social structures of base organisms. While there are many Life variants floating around out there, they all share a basic tenet: Without living neighbors, you don't live either (or if you do live, you don't prosper). On the other hand, too many neighbors and you die from overpopulation. Thus, a basic rule of Life might be, "If you have between two and six neighbors, you'll get a few offspring and survive this generation. If you have less than two or more than six neighbors, bye bye." The screen is divided into a very fine, invisible grid and a randomly generated "seed" is thrown into the mix—the spark of life. From the point where the seed impacts the grid, the rule is carried out and repeats itself until there are no more "living" cells.

How all of this is mapped varies from one Life emulator to the next, and of course, the rules vary too, with all kinds of caveats and exemptions from game variant to game variant. Luckily for you and your chances of longevity, there are five different Life variants included here. Each of them includes information on the number of generations that have run, the rate of return, and your CPU utiliza-

Because so much is going on onscreen at once, Life is a good opportunity for BeOS to show off its pervasively multithreaded nature. Use your friendly neighborhood search engine to download ports of Life for MacOS, Windows, or Linux and compare their performance on the same machine.

Somewhere in the depths of Be HQ, an engineer was working on a 3D version of Life for BeOS as this was being written. With any luck, you'll be able to download it by the time you read this. Keep your eyes trained on BeWare.

**Getting Out of Full-Screen Mode**   Life is another demonstration of the BeOS Game Kit, and therefore takes over your entire screen. Remember that any time you're in full-screen mode, you can get out by hitting Alt+Q.

## Mandelbrot

Lurking beneath the apparent order of nature is chaos. That's more than a mystical proclamation—it's scientific fact, and you can ask any modern mathematician. Chaos theory has become one of the most interesting pursuits in modern mathematics not only because it raises as many questions as it answers, but because you can make groovy psychedelic pictures by plotting out chaotic equations graphically. One of the underpinnings of chaos theory is the fact that standard mathematics, with their Plain Jane lines and curves, don't take into account the infinitely large surface areas of real objects. For instance, what is the surface area of a pine tree? It all depends on how closely you measure. You could just hold a tape measure around the trunk and boughs, or you could get in there with a micrometer and measure the surface area of the indentations in

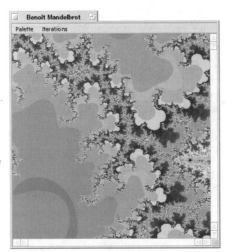

*Figure 2.71*

*If you've got more than one processor, Mandelbrot will send every even scan line to one CPU and every odd scan line to the other as you dig deeper and deeper into the infinite vortex of the fractal universe.*

the bark, or you could use an electron microscope and measure the surface area of every exposed molecule. No matter how deep you look, there's always deeper to go, and more patterns to discover.

A Polish mathematician by the name of Benoit Mandelbrot came up with one of the equations for mathematically describing the infinite spaces of nature, and the graphical representation of his equation is the famous Mandelbrot set. Ready to take a trip into the infinite recesses of mathematical reality? Open up Mandelbrot and study the image. With your mouse, select a square over some part of the pattern. When you release the mouse button, the Mandelbrot window will be redrawn, filling with a detail view of the square you just selected. Do it again. And again. And again. To zoom backward, hold down the Shift key and click once.

Mandelbrot is an excellent demonstration of symmetric multiprocessing and multithreading in action. Every time you drag, the image is divided into even- and odd-numbered scan lines. Each even-numbered line is sent to one processor by one thread, and every odd line is sent by another thread to the other processor. All of the calculation and drawing, of course, happens too quickly for you to see, but it's going on. To control the color palette being used, select one of the four options from the Palette menu. To control the precision of the calculations and screen drawing, select a higher iteration level from the Iterations menu. The higher you go, the more detail you'll get—and the slower the process will become. The effect of choosing a higher level of iterations isn't very noticeable at first, but becomes more important as you dig deeper.

You'll also find a similar demo, called Mandelbrot Zoom, in the same folder. Rather than enlarging the selected area to the window dimensions, Mandelbrot Zoom zeroes in on the selected area automatically. It's as if you had a camera with a super-powerful zoom lens trained on a distant speck in the heart of a fractal.

## MineSweeper

There's not much to say about this one, as anyone who's ever seen a computer has undoubtedly wasted many an evening with this "challenging game of skill and strategy." MineSweeper exists on every operating system known to humanity, so BeOS just wouldn't be complete without it. This isn't so much a demo of BeOS technology as it is a demo of the fact that BeOS can do things other OSs do, in addition to all that wild stuff.

Click on a square to see if there's a mine beneath it. If there is, you lose. If there isn't, you get another turn. If you unveil the number 1, it means there's a mine in one of that square's eight adjacent squares. If you unveil the number 2, there are two adjacent mines, and so on. By studying these numbers and the layout of the remaining squares, you can determine where it's safe to step and where it's not. If you're positive that a square covers a mine, right-click it to mark it with a flag. If you can't be sure, right-click twice to mark it with a question mark. Uncover all of the safe squares without stepping on a mine, and you win. If you want to play again after taking a wrong step, click on the happy face (somehow, the placement of a happy face icon in the midst of a game about treading a field laced with landmines has always perplexed me, but that's another story).

# Optional Media

Early in the BeOS installation process, a checkbox is displayed, asking whether you want to install approximately 200MB of optional goodies. Disk space being the inexpensive commodity it is these days, you of course said yes. If you didn't and want to find out what you missed, you have two options:

- Explore the optional folder on the installation CD without copying it to your hard drive. This will save you a bunch of disk space, but you won't get very good performance, since even the fastest CD-ROM drives don't begin to approach the speed of the slowest hard drives.

- Drag all or part of the optional folder from the installation CD to your own hard drive. The nice thing about this option is that you can pick and choose, leaving the stuff you'll never use on the CD.

Because this is the MediaOS you're dealing with, Be has done the sensible thing and provided you with a ton of sample media, so you can test out your system's capabilities. Not only that, but they've tossed in a healthy collection of miscellaneous programs, scripts, and other stuff that just didn't fit anywhere else. Nothing in the optional folder is necessary to normal operation of BeOS and you can safely delete anything in this hierarchy that you don't want, but there are some nice goodies lurking in here. The contents of the optional folder are described in more detail at **www.beosbible.com**.

# Experimental

Anything that Be labels "experimental" is under development, and not necessarily ready for prime time. If it's here, there's a pretty good chance that it'll make its way into the operating system itself at some point, but for one reason or another, Be didn't feel that it was ready to be part of the official distribution. That said, keep in mind that anything you find here is unsupported by Be—you're on your own.

Because the contents of the experimental folder aren't fully known until just before ship time, it wasn't possible to learn about R4's experimental goodies in time for this book, but everything you find in this folder should be accompanied by its own documentation; read it carefully!

## *Define "Supported"*

Many members of the Be community use the word "supported" to refer to anything they've gotten to work on their BeOS systems. That's a misleading twist of phraseology because the list of hardware and software that works with BeOS is not the same as the list that Be officially supports. For instance, when R3 for Intel hit the streets, Be said they didn't support any internal modems. However, enterprising users discovered that they could make many internal modems work just fine by setting them on COM 2, IRQ 3. That was fine with Be—naturally they don't mind users experimenting with their own systems. However, if users could *not* get internal modems to work with R3, they couldn't go running to Be's technical support staff, because Be hadn't yet determined that the system would work reliably with internal modems.

The equation is simple: If Be lists something as "supported," it'll try to help you out if it doesn't work as advertised. If something is listed as "experimental," or isn't listed at all, you're on your own. Caveat geek.

# GNU

One of the things that makes Unix-based operating systems (BeOS is not Unix-based, by the way—see Chapter 1 for details) is the fact that a wealth of software exists absolutely free of charge. The culture of the Unix community is one of shared resources, and developers spend a lot of time collaborating to perfect their tools and then giving them to the world *gratis*.

Much of the free software out there exists under a license called the GNU General Public License, or GPL, which is administered by a group called the FSF (Free Software Foundation; GNU stands for "GNU's Not Unix"). Not only does the GPL encourage free copying and distribution of software, but it protects the software from exploitation by strictly stating that all distributions *must* include the right for others to request the program's source code, along with the requirement that the code (and any objects linked against it) be handed over on demand. This way, developers can improve and enhance the public software vault and even make a profit doing so, but they cannot stop the buck at themselves; if they distribute software, they have to leave the door open for others to come along and improve on *their* work. This ingenious system goes under the name "copyleft." All GNU software is copylefted.

Which brings us to BeOS and the presence of this folder. BeOS is not Unix, but it is POSIX-compliant (Chapter 1), and its Terminal application is a mostly complete bash shell, capable of running recompiled Unix software. Most of the preinstalled tools that run in the Terminal have been ported to BeOS from the GNU distribution. Their existence greatly enhances the functionality of BeOS, and thus the copyleft requires Be to include the source code for each of the tools they've included in the operating system.

Of course, they don't do it just because they have to—they also do it to encourage the growth of the POSIX application base on BeOS, and because they recognize the inherent value of the free source code economy, even though they don't have plans to make the source code for BeOS itself freely available (see the sidebar *Free Software and BeOS*).

If you're not a programmer and poring over mountains of arcane source code isn't your idea of a good time, this folder won't be of any use to you and can be safely deleted.

## Goodies

Here you'll find a small collection of plain-text data files relating to the English language and to international geography. The dictionary, thesaurus, and words files can all be searched from the command line using the grep utility (Chapter 6), making it easy to look up any word quickly. The maps subdirectory contains data files of interest to cartographers.

Any of the files in this folder can be used by custom applications. For instance, you might want to write a graphical dictionary lookup application or global atlas utility in your spare time. Thanks to these files, you can worry about programming your app, not collecting data.

## Images

A small collection of color and black-and-white images in TIFF format is included here just for the halibut. Double-click an image file to launch it in ShowImage. If you don't have an image library of your own, these samples will come in handy when you start downloading full-featured image-editing applications from BeWare and BeDepot, giving you some material to work with.

Pay close attention to the file named Fearless Leader. That's the one and only Jean-Louis Gassée, whom you have to thank for risking literally everything he had in this world to bring you BeOS. Feel free to tweak, smudge, invert, distort, and otherwise psychedelicize his likeness—he gets a kick out of it.

## MIDI

This pair of MIDI data files will get you started with BeOS's built-in MIDI players, MIDI, and SimpleMIDI. These samples, however, barely scratch the surface of the kind of quality music that can be made with sophisticated MIDI software. BeOS, naturally, makes for a great sound-editing environment, and many MIDI musicians are going nuts with MIDI on BeOS. See Chapter 14 for more information.

## Movies

Ready to buckle your seatbelt and see what kind of media performance your system can deliver? Try selecting four of these QuickTime movies at once and hitting Enter. Watch them all spring to life almost simultaneously, then start dragging the movies around and check to see whether the Be menu is still responsive. If it is, you're not pushing your system hard enough. Close the movies, select six of them, and try again. Is BeOS still barely sweating? Try all eight. Chances are, your system will begin to show noticeable signs of stress at this point. If it doesn't, there ain't nothin' that's going to slow you down. Of course, you'll want to make sure you're running movies from your hard drive, rather than from CD-ROM. Otherwise, expect performance to degrade much more quickly.

## Sample code

If you're anxious to start programming on BeOS, there's no better way to do it than to A) read the BeBook (which you'll find in /boot/beos/documentation/ bebook/) and B) study working BeOS source code written by the experts. Each of these subdirectories contains complete source code for one of the applications preinstalled with BeOS.

Not only do you get to tear apart this source to find out how it works, but Be invites you to improve upon these applications and make your modifications available to the Be user and developer communities. Have at it!

For more information on programming resources, see Appendix C.

# Sound

The sample sounds you'll find in this directory are high-quality, bitmapped recordings in AIFF format. If you're a Windows user unfamiliar with AIFF, think of it as the rest of the world's equivalent to the .WAV format. So where do these songs come from? If you're ever in Silicon Valley on a Friday, stop in to Be HQ for one of their demo days. While you're there in the offices, take a peek into employee cubicles and you'll see an inordinate number of key-boards, guitars, and other instruments. Perhaps it's unsurprising that many of the people behind the MediaOS are also artists, but it's still inspiring to see musical instruments side by side with hundreds of computers running BeOS, and then to suddenly remember that you're seeing all this inside the walls of a corporation, rather than at a mega-rave audio event.

In any case, yes, all of the songs in the optional/sound directory were written and recorded by Be employees. We weren't able to discover the authors of all of them, but we did learn this: The track "virtual(void)" is the creation of none other than the mysterious baron—the same person who appears to own all of your files when you type ls -l into the Terminal.

To experiment with the sample sound files, turn your system's speakers all the way down, then slightly up again (you don't want any nasty surprises). Double-click one of these files and BeOS's built-in PlaySound application will be launched. This lets you test A) whether your sound card is working properly, and B) the quality of the audio throughput in BeOS.

If you don't hear anything, check to make sure your speakers are plugged into the right jack on the back of your sound card. Still nothing? Open up the Sound panel in your preferences folder and check that all outputs are configured correctly. See Chapter 9 for Sound panel instructions.

Of course, you can also open these files up in the far more sophisticated audio applications you'll be downloading from BeWare and BeDepot soon enough.

# xmaps

If you're a programmer, chances are you already know what this collection of optional xmap files is for. If you're not a programmer, you have no use for these and can safely delete the entire folder. In programmer-ese, the xmap files provide symbol information for the shared libraries and the kernel. Developers use them to harvest extra information about mysteriously crashing applications.

## Peter Potrebic
### Director of User Interface and Frameworks
### Interviewed by Henry Bortman

*Peter Potrebic heads the group that works on the Interface Kit, the Application Kit, the Support Kit and parts of the Storage Kit; the Tracker and NetPositive; and the majority of the preference applications that ship with BeOS.*

**HB:** *What was your primary goal in designing the BeOS user experience? Were you trying to come up with something radically new?*

**PB:** We didn't try to reinvent, we didn't try to create a completely different user experience. The premise of the operating system has always been to be very fast and efficient and to take advantage of modern hardware and multiple processors. That was our key differentiation. And we wanted that to come up to the user interface so that it would be a live interface—so that whenever you moved a window around, or resized, or did anything, it would be live, as opposed to some other systems, where something would rubber-band to show you the new size. But it's still a windowing, desktop-oriented user interface.

I've always thought, and most people think, the single most distinctive thing in our user interface is the yellow tabs on our active windows. And when you stand back, if you looked across at a screen and you saw a yellow tab, that would identify it—hey, that's the BeOS. So when some people have wanted to go in other directions for the look of our windows, some of us oldtimers would say, Well, that's the thing. You can't change that, cause that's what makes it BeOS, the little yellow tab.

**HB:** *How is the BeOS experience different from Windows, or Unix, or the MacOS?*

**PB:** There's things you can do on those other systems for liveness—like live window dragging—but it's an extension, or the developer has to work at it to get it to work right. In our system we wanted all that stuff to be the baseline, and you go up from there.

**HB:** *What are some of the ways you've built that liveness into BeOS?*

**PB:** The App Server is one of the key components of the system that delivers that liveness. Also, the BeOS is architected to handle multiple processors transparently, and we take advantage of multiple processors through the design of the App Server and the design of the Interface and App kits. For instance, for every window that you create, there's actually two threads running in the system. One is running in the App Server, and that's the thread that manages input, like the keyboard and mouse events, and it also manages things like when a window moves and part of another window needs to be redrawn. So you have one thread doing that kind of work in the App Server.

And then, on the client side, you also have a thread associated with the window that is running an event loop, similar to the event loop you might have on the Mac or in Windows. That thread basically gets an event, processes it, gets the next event, processes it, and so on. This runs in the application or on what we call the client side. The client-side thread gets these events from the App Server and then processes them. So you have two threads running in parallel, cooperatively.

If you're running on a system that has multiple processors, those two things can literally run in parallel. And even if you have one processor, oftentimes the window thread maybe is blocked waiting to get screen access, but the client side can continue doing something else. So, even on a single-processor system, by having these threads running in parallel, you can get a benefit in terms of performance.

**HB:** *Give me an example of what a BeOS user experiences that, say, a Mac OS user doesn't.*

**PB:** On the Mac, say you're browsing the Internet and you have a slow connection. There'll be times when the system will be waiting for half a second for something to happen over your modem. If you try to click in another window to bring it to the front during that half-second, your system won't respond. Your system will just feel jerkier.

In our system, because of the preemptive multitasking, it's not up to the application to yield and say, "I don't need to do anything now, something else can happen." In the preemptive system, the system just takes control away from one thread and gives it to something else. So when you click, the system can respond to that much more effectively and with much lower latencies than it would on a cooperative multitasking system.

**HB:** *Doesn't Unix have many of the same fundamental capabilities as the BeOS?*

**PB:** Well, it's a multithreaded system, but that's at the kernel level. What we've done is, on top of that we've built an App Server, which we've talked about; a Network Server, which handles all your networking-type facilities; a Print Server… We have a series of servers to actually take advantage of the multithreading. In Unix, if you launch an application, it's still just one thread until you, the programmer, do something to take advantage of it. In BeOS, if you launch an application that has one window, you automatically have four threads working for your benefit.

For example, having the Network Server means that if you establish a connection over PPP, say, sure, you might still be working over that 33.6K modem, but it's only that one thread in the Net Server that's going to be blocked waiting for something to happen half a second later. Your other threads can keep going. So, we automatically take advantage of those things.

**HB:** *The Tracker takes advantage of some innovative features of the BeOS filesystem. Can you talk about that some?*

**PB:** The filesystem is a standard hierarchical filesystem that you find on any OS, but we also support something we call attributes. One way to think about attributes is kind of like on the Mac, where you have the data fork and the resource fork. Well, on BeOS you have the file and then you can have any number of attributes associated with the file, and these attributes can have a name, a string, a type, and data, and that data can be an arbitrary length. And the system can manage an index of each attribute so that you can do queries on that attribute in a very fast manner. What that gives you is kind of a poor man's database facility.

So now we get to the Tracker. We've tried to make the Tracker not just be a tool for browsing a hierarchical filesystem with files and folders, but also be a way to look at this kind of poor man's database of information that might be out there. And we use some of that right off the bat in the system. We have this notion of a Person [file]. So you can create contact-manager-type information and the Tracker allows you to do queries like "I want to see everybody who I know named

## *Peter Potrebic* (continued)

Fred," or "I want to find all the people in the 415 area code so then I can change most of them to 650 when the area code changes." And it allows you to do things like that right from the Tracker.

Our email system also takes advantage of that. Emails are just files that have a whole bunch of attributes: when they were sent, who sent them, what the status is (is it new mail, is it read mail, or is it outgoing mail). And then you can set up queries that look for, say, all emails that came from Henry Bortman. You can have that little query sitting on your desktop and it looks just like a folder and you can open it up. It's not looking at the contents of a folder, but it's looking at the results of a query on this database and what you get is something that looks just like a folder, only it's a query. And these queries can be live as well, so that if all of a sudden you read your incoming mail and you get 12 email messages, two of which are from Henry Bortman, they show up inside this window. So it gives you kind of a different way, a more dynamic way of managing data, all based on our filesystem that supports these attributes, and indexing, and queries, and the Tracker then taking advantage of that. And nothing that the Tracker does with the filesystem is special or is private. Developers can take advantage of that in their own applications as well.

**HB:** *Where were you before you came to Be?*

**PB:** I was at Apple working on the Newton project, and I'd been working on the Newton project for four or five years.

We had like three different resets while I was there. I started there working on wireless communication protocols—radio frequency stuff and infrared. That was for a little while until Steve [Sackoman] and Jean-Louis [Gassée] left. Then there was a big reset.

And then I was working in one of the languages that Apple developed, Dylan, on things like windows and views and controls and how an application would look and feel. I was doing that for awhile until we stopped using Dylan and there was another reset.

And then I worked on printing for awhile. I learned PostScript and I was doing PostScript stuff and I did that up until the alpha/beta release of Newton, the final product.

Then I started working on the development environment, the development tools, which is kind of one of my big loves. I love development tools. I love editors and development environments. The Newton's development environment was very graphical, where you laid out your application and you went into it, graphically, and started writing the code and data. So I worked on that until I left.

**HB:** *Why did you leave?*

**PB:** Because Steve Horowitz called me up one day and I was just kind of tired enough of Apple, or disgruntled enough with some things that I said, "Sure, I'll come over and see what's going on." And I was hooked. Here was an OS that was going to try to take advantage of multiple processors. That was pretty unique back then—having a small, affordable desktop machine that realized there's more to upgrading your computer than sticking in a bigger disk or adding more memory. Why don't you add more CPUs? And that was a great idea in terms of hardware. And then the software just taking advantage of all that, having this idea of a developer creating a window and automatically having multiple threads working for their benefit to take advantage of the hardware. It was just such a nice design and I could see how it would be, how it could be done from the ground up in a very elegant way so that it didn't add complexity to writing applications but you got a lot of benefit from it.

**HB:** *You've got an unusual work arrangement. You're only in the office one day a week. How did you swing that?*

**PB:** A little over two and a half years ago I walked into my boss's office at the time and I told him I was moving to Calistoga. We knew where we were moving, we'd already made an offer on a house, we're on a little piece of land where we're going to have a house built and then right away I told him, "But I still want to work here." And he asked me, "How serious are you?" And I said, "I'm very serious."

That was basically it. Erich [Ringwold] didn't have a problem with me going up there, talked with Jean-Louis a bunch about it and he was OK with it, and throughout the months leading up to when we were moving, I kept them all informed. And I could see that behind closed doors they were saying, well OK, he's going to do it, if it works out great, or if it doesn't, we can fire him, or whatever—that they weren't maybe as sure as I was, which is natural—but I think that Be has been great for me and I think that Be has now no qualms about it and they know that they got a good deal.

# 3

# Installation

. . . . . . . . . . . . . . . . . . . . . . . . . . . . . . . . . . . . . . . . . . . . . . . . . . . .

Even if you've been computing for years, you may never have run more than one operating system on a single computer. Fortunately, Be has made the process of installing a second operating system easier than has any other OS vendor in history. If you've heard stories about the difficulty of maintaining multiple OSs, put your fears aside until after you've installed BeOS. In the vast majority of cases, you'll be done in less than 30 minutes, and in many cases, you could be booting into BeOS for the first time in 15 minutes or less ... and that includes partitioning time!

Most people will be able to get by reading just the first two sections of this chapter: *Pre-Installation Considerations* and *Basic Installation*. Advanced users, or those with unique needs, should also read the sections on dealing with unusual configurations, working with partitions, and working with boot-management software. While most of the basic installation instructions apply equally to Mac and x86 users, Mac users will find PowerPC-specific instructions at the end of this chapter. If your system came with BeOS preinstalled, you're ahead of the game and can probably skip most of this chapter, though you may need to activate your boot management software.

The Installation Guide that comes with BeOS describes the installation process very succinctly in a point-by-point manner, whereas this chapter goes into relative depth on all possible options. If you're a technically savvy user, you may find it easiest to use the BeOS Installation Guide that came with your CD, turning to this chapter only if you have questions you don't find answered there.

# Pre-Installation Considerations

It pays to survey the landscape before jumping into the Installer. Is your machine BeOS-compatible? Do you have the disk space to spare? Is your hard disk ready to be repartitioned?

## Where to Get BeOS

At this writing, Be was just solidifying plans to begin selling BeOS in shrink-wrapped boxes through standard retail channels, and you may be able to find BeOS-in-a-Box at your local computer software retailer (if they don't carry BeOS, ask them to start!). Chances are, though, that the best way to get your hands on a copy of the system is to order it through BeDepot, Be's online software store (**www.bedepot.com**). The BeOS retail package can also be ordered via phone during normal U.S. business hours (Pacific Time) at (800) 491-2818. As of R4.0, BeOS costs US $99.99 through the retail channel, and US $69.99 through BeDepot. These prices may change with future releases.

If you live outside of the United States, you may find that international shipping costs can add greatly to the total cost. Fortunately, there are vendors scattered around the world that may enable you to purchase BeOS domestically without worrying about international shipping, duties, and exchange rates. Visit Be's European (**www.beeurope.com**) and Japanese (**www.be.com/jp**) Web sites for information on international retailers (you'll find links to these sites on Be's home page, **www.be.com**).

## Compatibility

R4 greatly expands the variety of hardware on which BeOS will run (compared to previous releases), but that doesn't mean the system is automatically compatible with every piece of hardware out there. While most unsupported hardware is simply ignored by BeOS, it's absolutely crucial that certain components be supported. Most importantly, BeOS will not boot at all if the BeOS kernel is not familiar with the chipset on your motherboard. Additionally, BeOS must be able to find a driver for the video card installed in your machine if you want to use the system in color and at resolutions greater than 640×480.

**Research before Buying**   Since BeOS won't do you much good if your hardware isn't compatible, it's absolutely essential that you do a little research before attempting to install the system. Be maintains hardware compatibility lists for both PowerPC and x86-based machines at **www.be.com/ products/beosreadylist.html**. In addition to these lists of officially compatible hardware, you'll find a list of "Probably compatible hardware" at **http://www.be.com/support/guides/probably_compatible_intel.html**. This list chronicles hardware that Be hasn't yet officially tested, or hasn't tested thoroughly, but which appears to work fine according to reports from users. Additionally, you'll find a complete database of user-tested (but not Be-tested) hardware at BeFunk (**www.befunk.com**).

 There are known cases in which hardware advertised as supported by BeOS does not in fact work properly in real life. While Be will never, ever advertise as "supported" components that its engineers have not tested extensively, computers are complex beasts, and occasional combinations of specific hardware may present problems. In addition, hardware vendors sometimes make changes to chipsets in the middle of a production run without informing Be that these changes could have an impact on existing drivers. These situations are rare, and Be will do its best to get you up and running with hardware advertised as supported. The authors of this book cannot assist users with hardware configuration, nor can they make guarantees about or officially endorse particular hardware purchases.

As a general guideline, you can expect the motherboard/chipset combinations in the vast majority of x86-based desktop computers purchased since early 1998 to be BeOS-compatible. The likelihood of motherboards purchased in 1997 or before being BeOS-compatible is lower, but some support does exist. 486-class motherboards and chipsets will almost certainly never be supported by Be. Nothing in this section represents a guarantee of support, however; it's still up to you to check the hardware compatibility lists.

Beyond the motherboard, the rest of the hardware in your machine is another question. There are thousands of different video cards, network cards, sound cards, and other I/O devices out there. Be puts a lot of effort into making sure that the most popular hardware on the market gains BeOS support soon after its release, though Be's driver efforts are contingent on either A) direct driver support from the hardware vendor or B) availability of that hardware's technical specifications. You'll find more information on hardware compatibility in Chapter 16, *Troubleshooting and Maintenance*.

**Testing Compatibility with the Demo CD**   The best way to determine whether your hardware is BeOS-compatible is to actually try and boot BeOS on it, and the most inexpensive way to do that is to get your hands on a copy of the current "Demo CD." This is a version of BeOS available on a bootable CD-ROM (meaning that you can run BeOS without actually installing it), complete in every way with one exception: It can only save data to a floppy disk. The Demo CD is available from **www.be.com/demoCD/** for a few bucks plus shipping. To use the Demo CD, you'll need to enter the machine's BIOS (usually by pressing F1 or Delete early in the boot cycle) and tell the machine to look to the CD-ROM device as the first boot device. Alternatively, you can create a BeOS boot floppy using the instructions in Chapter 16, *Troubleshooting and Maintenance*, insert both the boot floppy and the CD, and turn the machine on normally without altering the BIOS. If you can boot BeOS from the Demo CD, you'll be able to install and boot the official version.

 Even if you don't need or want a Demo CD to test the compatibility of your own machine, it can be useful to keep one tucked away in your backpack or bookbag. You never know when you might find yourself engaged in a conversation about BeOS and wish you could offer a demonstration right there on the spot. If you've got a Demo CD handy, just duck into the nearest computer store and hijack a Windows machine for a while. With any luck, you might even attract a crowd.

Needless to say, CD-ROM drives are extremely slow (in comparison to hard drives). While BeOS runs pretty well off a CD, you certainly won't experience the kind of speed and responsiveness for which BeOS is hailed. This is especially true when running applications that require disk access as they're running, as is the case when playing QuickTime movies, for example.

## Hardware Requirements

Once you've determined that your hardware is BeOS-compatible, there are a few other things you'll need to consider.

**Memory**  First of all, you'll need a minimum of 16MB of RAM. In today's computing environment, that's practically a given, and most new machines sold today come with at least 64MB of memory, if not more. While 16MB is the absolute minimum amount of RAM necessary to boot BeOS, you certainly won't get optimum performance without at least doubling that amount. BeOS is an extremely efficient operating system, but it performs best when given a little breathing room. If you're interested in working with high-bandwidth media files, there's no question you'll want to install substantially more memory; I recommend at least 64MB, and double that if you can afford it. Memory has become so inexpensive in recent years that it really makes no sense to skimp in this department; RAM is one of those things from which you'll benefit every moment your computer is turned on, regardless what operating system you're running.

**Disk Space**  By default, the BeOS installation routine lets you create a partition of 500MB, 850MB, or 1.5GB, which means that you must have a minimum of 500MB free on one of your system's disk volumes (advanced users can create arbitrary partition sizes by using third-party partitioning software, or by booting from the CD and launching DriveSetup as described in Chapter 16). If you're just dabbling or experimenting with BeOS, you'll find that 500MB will give you plenty of room to install the system and a wide variety of applications. Because BeOS can read from and write to Windows volumes on the same machine, you don't necessarily need to worry about allocating extra space for storing data files; you can continue to work on data on your Windows volumes normally. As you begin to use BeOS more and more, you'll probably want to reallocate some of that Windows space in order to create dedicated BeOS volumes, so you can take advantage of the superior speed, features, and data protection offered by the Be Filesystem (BFS). You don't need to worry about that for now, however.

BeOS can be installed onto volumes smaller than 500MB, though it is not possible to create such partitions with the limited edition of PartitionMagic bundled with BeOS. You can create smaller partitions with the full and unlimited version of PartitionMagic or with any other sophisticated partitioning utility, such as the DriveSetup application bundled with BeOS. However, partitions smaller than 500MB just aren't very useful. Yes, BeOS and its applications are smaller than their counterparts in other systems, but as you know, applications and data files add up quickly. You're almost certainly better off clearing enough space from your existing drives now, rather than wrestling with a dinky partition later on.

On the other hand, if you've got acres of disk space to spare and you're sure you'll be using BeOS quite a bit, you may as well allocate as much space as possible right now. While there are no performance advantages to doing so, you may find that dedicating an entire physical hard disk to BeOS makes general management easier. Dedicating a complete hard disk to BeOS means that if, in the future, you should decide to do something like reinitialize disks containing your Windows, Linux, OS/2, Solaris, or other operating system, you won't need to disturb your BeOS installation.

Unlike Windows, BeOS does not care whether it's installed on the first drive in the IDE chain or the last. Once BeOS is installed, you can create additional BeOS partitions with the DriveSetup application (see Chapter 9, *Preferences and Customization*). These additional BeOS partitions can be either blank volumes for application and data storage or alternate bootable partitions containing the files necessary to run the system.

Finally, if you have a removable cartridge drive (such as an Iomega Jaz), you can easily install BeOS onto that, leaving the rest of your system as it is. This method gives you an extra degree of portability—you can cart an entire bootable BeOS installation around between work and home, for example. Unlike other operating systems that need to be installed with specific drivers for the hardware they're' running on, BeOS (as of R4) includes all drivers in every installation and detects the drivers it needs at boot time. As a result, a single installation can be booted on any system sporting compatible hardware. Depending on your removable media, however, there may be performance ramifications you'll want to take into consideration, as most removable devices aren't quite as fast as dedicated hard disks. At this writing, only removable devices connected via SCSI or IDE were supported by BeOS. Also at this writing, Zip drives connected via the parallel port were not recognized (though this could change in the future).

**Dedicated Partitions** While BeOS can of course share a hard drive with other operating systems, you can't install BeOS into an existing Windows, Linux, or other filesystem. The BeOS installation process will "rope off" a section of your hard drive called a "partition," and install itself to that.

 BeOS can be installed onto and can boot from either primary or extended partitions. However, be aware that BeOS cannot *create* extended partitions. Thus, if you want to install BeOS to an extended partition, you'll need to perform your partitioning with another tool in another operating system. Once your partition has been created, just insert the BeOS boot floppy and installation CD, boot your computer, and select your target partition in the Installer.

Disk partitioning concepts are discussed in detail later in this chapter (see *Working with Partitions*).

## International Versions

While BeOS was created in the United States and written in English, the architecture of the system makes it theoretically language-neutral. There are two levels at which international OS support can be viewed. At the deepest level, a version of BeOS localized for, say, French users would have all of its dialog boxes, menus, buttons, and other interface elements translated into French. At this writing, there was no version of BeOS localized at this level.

However, BeOS does include an "input method" architecture, which makes it theoretically possible for users to read and write text in any language. The presence of the input method does not automatically give BeOS support for other languages, however; for languages that are read from left to right, a system add-on supporting that language must be installed. At this writing, Japanese was the only language besides English for which an input method add-on existed. Support for languages that are not read from left to right is dependent on future refinements of the system's Application Server (app_server), which may happen in the future depending on demand. As of R4, BeOS offers to install Japanese support during the installation process. If you decline this option and then later decide you'd like to work with BeOS in Japanese, see the section on working with Japanese in Chapter 9, *Preferences and Customization*.

While all versions of BeOS are currently written and distributed in English, you can order BeOS with a User's Guide written in your choice of English, French, German, or Japanese. For updates and more information on localized versions of BeOS, see Be's European and Japanese sites, or visit Be's official Japanese distributor, Plat'home, at **www.plathome.co.jp**.

# Basic Installation

As mentioned earlier, chances are great that, given supported hardware, you'll find BeOS easier to install than any other operating system on the planet. The first part of this section covers the basic BeOS installation procedure, and assumes that you have Windows 95 or 98 installed and that one of the following is true:

- Your primary Windows partition still has at least 500MB to spare.

- You've already set aside an entire partition for BeOS.

- You've set aside an empty hard drive that you wish to dedicate to BeOS.

 We refer to Windows specifically here because the limited version of PartitionMagic that is bundled with BeOS must be installed from within Windows, and is capable of resizing existing Windows (FAT16 or FAT32) partitions without affecting the data they contain. If your machine does not have Windows 95 or 98 installed, or if your primary Windows partition does not have 500MB of free space, you'll need to read the *Other Configurations* section below to prepare your machine, then return to this section to complete the installation procedure. If you don't know what kinds of partitions are currently on your machine, read the section *Discovering Your Partition Types* later in this chapter.

## Basic Installation

As noted, BeOS ships with a limited edition of PartitionMagic, which is capable of resizing existing partitions without damaging the data they contain. This version of PartitionMagic will work *only* if it does not detect an existing BeOS installation. In other words, if you want to create or manage partitions after BeOS is already installed, you'll need to purchase either an unlimited version of PartitionMagic or use another full-featured partition manager. The DriveSetup utility built into BeOS is capable of creating and resizing partitions, but *not without destroying the data they already contain*. More details on the full version of PartitionMagic can be found later in this chapter.

**Preparation**   In order to do its thing, PartitionMagic will need to be able to locate at least 500MB of *contiguous* disk space, meaning that your hard disk may need to be defragmented before you begin your BeOS installation. Even if Explorer says you have 2GB free, that space will not be available to PartitionMagic if the free bits are scattered around at random across the disk. You should find the Microsoft defragmenter in your Windows Accessories program group. If you don't find it there, use the Windows setup utility to add it to your system. Use of Defragmenter is pretty much self-explanatory. See Microsoft's documentation for details if necessary.

**Start from Windows**  Boot into Windows and insert the BeOS installation CD. In most cases, the installer for the PartitionMagic software will be launched automatically. If it isn't, use Explorer to launch setup.exe, which you'll find in the Setup folder on the BeOS CD. Install PartitionMagic just as you would any other Windows software, then launch PartitionMagic itself. Windows will be shut down and your machine will restart in DOS mode, from which the PartitionMagic utility will be run automatically.

**Using PartitionMagic**  You'll find yourself looking at the PartitionMagic setup screen. By default, PartitionMagic will offer to resize the active partition. If the default partition offered is not the one you wish to resize, use the Select Partition picklist to choose a different partition. You'll also be asked whether the new partition size should be 500MB, 850MB, or 1.5 GB. Be sure the appropriate radio button is selected, click OK, then click Yes when asked "Are you sure you want to create a BeOS partition?" A pair of progress indicators will inform you of the progress of the resizing operation, which will probably take ten minutes or more. Be patient, and do not turn off your computer during this process. When the operation is complete, PartitionMagic will tell you to insert the BeOS boot floppy in your machine and reboot. Make it so.

**Using the Installer**  When your machine reboots, the floppy will be detected and the BeOS boot loader on the floppy will take over, launching BeOS from the CD in a special installation mode. When the licensing agreement appears, read it, then click Agree. You'll now be facing the Installer application. Before clicking Begin, note the picklist labeled "Onto:", which will let you establish the partition onto which BeOS should be installed. By default, this should name the partition just created by PartitionMagic. You may want to click and hold this picklist to see the other partitions found on the drive. You probably do *not* want to select any partition listed as containing a DOS filesystem. You probably *do* want to select the partition listed as containing "unknown filesystem" (it's type is unknown at this point because the partition has been created but has not yet been initialized as BFS).

*Figure 3.01*

*The Installer application lets you specify the partition onto which BeOS should be installed.*

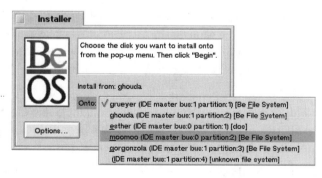

In the highly unlikely event that you have a partition type on your machine that the Installer does not recognize (for example, a partition belonging to some obscure operating system), you may need to pay special attention to the bus and partition numbers also named in the Onto: picklist. As an advanced user, it's your responsibility to know the bus and partition numbers of your installed partitions. You can get this information by clicking the Options button and then clicking "Set Up Additional Partitions." This will launch DriveSetup, which will in turn let you examine your disk's partitions more closely. Alternatively, you can use most any sophisticated disk-management tool in another OS, such as the Unix fdisk or df commands.

**Options** At the bottom left of the Installer tab is an Options button. Click this and you'll see a panel like the one in Figure 3.02. If you select Clean Install, any data on the partition living in a directory with the same name as one of the directories on the installation CD will be wiped out and replaced, *including* data in the /boot/home

directory. If you're installing onto a newly created, blank partition, don't worry about it. If you're upgrading an existing BeOS installation and feel the need to do a clean installation, *make sure you've backed up your personal data and applications first*. If you select Install Optional Items, you'll end up with a collection of media files and other goodies. If you're an advanced user and need to set up additional partitions from this point, click Setup Partitions to launch DriveSetup, which is covered in Chapter 9, *Preferences and Customization*. For the most part, this option should be necessary only if you're installing BeOS onto a blank hard drive (that is, if you were not able to create a partition beforehand with PartitionMagic or another disk-management utility).

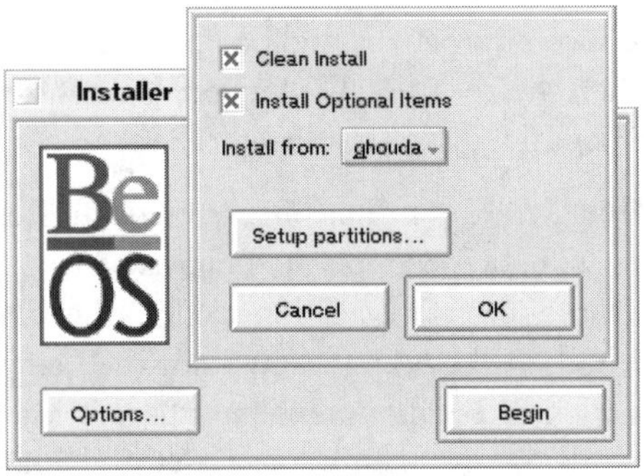

*Figure 3.02*

Click the Options button to specify a Clean Install, set up additional partitions, or install optional items.

This panel also includes an Install From: picklist. For most users, this list should default to the name of the installation CD. If you already have BeOS installed on other partitions, however, you can actually install BeOS to another partition by reading data out of that partition.

Installing BeOS from an existing BeOS partition will simply copy the entire contents of that partition to the new location, including the entire home directory. There is no harm in this, but you could potentially end up duplicating hundreds of megabytes of personal data across multiple partitions.

Most users should simply select Install Optional Items (if they have the space) and click OK. The optional items will require about 100MB of additional disk space.

**Initializing the Partition**  When you click the Begin button, the Installer will tell you that it needs to initialize the partition you selected (in other words, the partition space has already been created, but it does not yet carry the Be Filesystem). This is (almost) your last opportunity to back out and confirm that you are indeed installing to the right location. Click Stop Installation if you need to back out. If you're ready to rock, click Inititialize.

The Installer will ask you for the preferred filesystem block size and a volume name. BeOS lets you select from three different block sizes: 1024K, 2048K, or 4096K. In the vast majority of cases, you should keep the default block size of 1024K, for maximum storage efficiency. See Chapter 9, *Preferences and Customization* (DriveSetup section), for a complete explanation of the relationship between storage efficiency, speed, and block size.

The volume name you assign to the partition here will become the name of this volume when it's mounted on your Desktop later on. Feel free to give it a friendly name, such as Esther or Homer. You can always rename your volume later on, just as you would rename a file.

Click Inititialize, and you'll be given one final warning that you're about to blow away any data that may be living in that partition. Click Cancel if you're unsure, or Initialize if you're ready to go for it.

**Language Selection**  After you initialize the partition as a BeOS volume, a panel will appear asking whether you want to install support for other languages via the input method. English will be installed by default and cannot be deselected. As of R4, the only other language with a supporting BeOS input method was Japanese. If you elect not to install Japanese support now, you can always do it later without running the Installer; the procedure is described in Chapter 9, *Preferences and Customization* (see the *Japanese* section). Note that even if you don't install Japanese support, you'll still be able to read (but not create) Japanese documents and Web pages, as long as you install a Japanese font. Installing Japanese support adds two Japanese fonts to your system in addition to the Japanese input method.

**Installing ...**  The Installer will now begin copying files from the CD to your designated partition, reporting each filename as it does. A progress indicator will show you how far through the process you've come. Even if you selected the Optional Items and the Japanese input method, the entire process will probably take less than ten minutes. If you've recently installed Windows 98 on the same machine, you'll no doubt appreciate this.

**Installing Bootman**  When installation is complete, the Installer will ask you whether you want to install the BeOS boot manager. If your system was already set up for dual-boot capabilities (that is, you already had more than one operating system installed), you no doubt already have a boot manager installed. If you don't want that boot manager to be wiped out and replaced with Bootman, click No, which is the default. If you previously had only one OS installed, you'll need a boot manager of some kind if you don't want to have to use the BeOS boot floppy every time, so you'll probably want to click Yes to install Bootman. However, if you're planning to use a third-party boot manager such as System Commander, you'll want to click No at this screen. You can tell your boot manager about BeOS later. Otherwise, click Yes here, make sure the Install Boot Menu option is selected on the subsequent screen, and click Next.

 **If you've previously installed Bootman and want it removed, select Uninstall Boot Menu to delete it from your boot sector. This option applies only to those who have been through the BeOS installation sequence before.**

The master boot record that currently inhabits your boot sector will be saved to /boot/home/config/settings/bootman/MBR. You can change this path if you like, but you should take care to write down the new path if you use a different location. By saving the contents of the boot record, you can restore your boot record to the way it was before you installed BeOS should you want or need to later on. You should probably accept the default path here and click Next.

**Creating a Rescue Disk**   The BeOS rescue disk is a little different from the rescue disks created by tools such as Norton Utilities. If you create a rescue disk (which is recommended), you can boot from it to automatically restore your master boot record to the way it was before you installed Bootman.

 The rescue disk should not be confused with a standard BeOS boot disk, which simply boots the operating system from floppy, bypassing the boot record stored on hard disk. Booting from the rescue disk will cause actual changes to be made to your system. Be sure to label your rescue disk clearly.

Insert a floppy disk and click OK. Note that creating a rescue disk will completely overwrite the disk's current contents.

**Building the Boot Menu**   The next screen will display a menu of all detected partitions. If any of these partitions include a bootable operating system, check the boxes next to their names. By default, the partitions will be listed in your boot menu by volume name, but you can optionally edit these names if you'd like a boot menu with more descriptive titles. Thus, if your Windows partition is called "esther" and your BeOS partition is called "moomoo," you might want to call them "Windows 98" and "BeOS R4" to make things a little simpler at boot time. Editing these fields only changes the way volume names appear in the boot menu, not the volume names themselves.

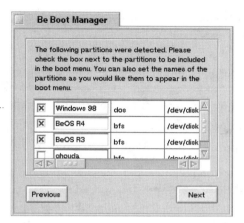

**Figure 3.03**

*Place a checkmark next to each partition you want to appear in your boot menu. Optionally, give your partitions more descriptive names.*

The picklist on the next screen lets you establish which partition should be the default (in other words, if you don't select anything from the boot menu after a specified amount of time passes, that partition will be booted). You can also establish whether Bootman should wait indefinitely or a specified number of seconds before booting to the default volume. If you rarely boot into other operating systems but still need access to them on occasion, you'll probably find that defaulting to BeOS after a five-second delay works nicely.

You'll be asked whether you're certain you want the boot menu to be written to disk. Doing so will replace your existing boot record (which is probably taking you straight into Windows at the moment) with the BeOS boot record, which will give you a choice of operating systems at boot time. Remember that you can always undo this operation later if you created a rescue disk earlier. You can also undo this operation from any DOS prompt by typing `fdisk /mbr`. Other multi-boot management options are discussed later in this chapter (see *"Boot Management"*).

Congratulations—BeOS is now installed on your machine! Remove any floppies or CDs from your machine and click the Quit button to reboot your machine, then turn to Chapter 2, *Meet the System*.

 If you click the Options button on the Installer again, the Quit button will change to Begin. Clicking Begin will start the installation process all over again, which you probably don't want. If this happens, just cancel the installation and press the Reset button on your computer. On the other hand, if you want to install BeOS onto another partition at this point, click Begin to do so.

 If, when you boot into BeOS, the screen appears in grayscale rather than in color, you have installed the system onto a machine with a video card for which BeOS could not find a driver. If a driver for your video card has been released since the copy of BeOS you installed was pressed, you'll be able to download and install it, then reboot to operate BeOS normally. Additionally, you may want to poke around in the /experimental directory on the BeOS CD for drivers that have been created but not yet thoroughly tested. You can read more about video card compatibility in Chapter 16, *Troubleshooting and Maintenance*.

**Using the Boot Menu** If you installed Bootman, the first thing you'll see after your machine exits the POST (power on self-test) will be a menu listing the bootable partitions you just established in the Bootman setup routine. Do nothing and the default operating system will be launched automatically after the number of seconds you specified have elapsed. Otherwise, use the Up and Down Arrow keys on your keyboard to navigate between bootable partitions.

***Dial "M" for Mandelbrot*** **For a good time, call … er, press the M key when the boot menu appears. When the light show is over, tap Esc to return to the boot menu.**

**Reconfiguring the Boot Menu** If you need to add more bootable volumes to the boot menu in the future, there's no need to run the Installer again. Just open a Terminal window and type bootman, then repeat the steps above. You can tell Bootman to boot partitions belonging to any operating system.

Unlike Windows, which absolutely must be set up by running the official installation routine, BeOS can potentially boot from any partition containing appropriate directory structures. You could, for example, simply copy the contents of one bootable volume onto another volume, point your boot loader at the new volume, and boot straight to it. Note, however, that there are some hidden gotchas to this method. Most importantly, the filesystem indexes (see Chapter 5, *Files and the Tracker*) that make sophisticated queries possible, will not be copied over automatically. The Installer is so easy to use, and the process runs so quickly, that using the Installer is highly recommended over simple copying operations.

**Choosing Alternate Boot Volumes** In some instances, it may be desirable to boot a BeOS volume not listed in Bootman's menu. For example, you may want to boot from the BeOS installation CD, from a removable drive, or from a bootable BeOS partition that you didn't add to Bootman's menu for some reason. As BeOS begins to boot, you'll see a message across the bottom of the screen reading "Press Space for Boot Options." Do so, and BeOS will scan your system for bootable partitions (note that you need to press and hold the Spacebar, not just tap it). Use the Up and Down Arrows on your keyboard to navigate among volumes, then hit Enter to boot from the selected volume. If you want to boot from CD and don't find it listed here, you may have to give it a chance to "spin up." Select the option "Re-scan for bootable volumes" and BeOS will make another attempt. Some CD-ROM drives may take two or three rescans before they're detected properly.

**Safe Boot Options** While most people will never need to use them, BeOS can be booted in a number of different "modes," with certain features disabled. Thanks to these "safe boot" options, it may be possible to boot BeOS on a machine that's refusing to boot the system normally. This can be extremely useful if your CD didn't come with a hardware driver that you now have available on floppy or can download from the Internet. To access the safe boot options, press and hold the Spacebar when given the option during the BeOS boot sequence. At the resulting screen, press the S key to see an additional menu with the following options. Navigate between options with your arrow keys, press Enter to select an option, and navigate down to "Continue booting with these options" to start BeOS with various components disabled.

- **Safe mode:** This is the most conservative way to launch BeOS, and starts the system with only the essential servers running. The VGA video driver is used, so your screen will appear in grayscale at 640×480. Sound and network services are disabled. Only the Application Server, Debug Server, Input Server, and Registrar will be running (other servers can be launched manually after booting). This mode gives you the best chance of booting successfully in a worst-case scenario, or with unsupported or problematic hardware.

- **Fail-safe graphics mode:** In this mode the VGA video driver is used rather than the proper driver for your video card. Since the VGA driver is used automatically when a supported card cannot be found, this mode is superfluous in most cases. However, it may be useful if an installed video driver is buggy and programs your video card incorrectly. Booting in this mode will let you into the system to remove or replace the buggy driver.

- **Don't call the BIOS:** This option may be useful in circumventing problems originating from Plug-and-Play settings in your motherboard's BIOS.

- **Disable multi-proc support:** This option should almost never be necessary, but can be useful when attempting to pinpoint the source of a problem that may be related to multiple processor support.

- **Disable IDE DMA:** This circumvents direct memory access to IDE hard drives. Again, this option should almost never be necessary, but may potentially be useful in pinpointing the source of boot problems related to some IDE DMA drives.

- **Disable user add-ons:** Booting in this mode will cause BeOS to ignore any add-ons (such as drivers) found in user-level directories (i.e. those falling under the /boot/home hierarchy). This can be useful if you've added a driver to the system that for some reason caused the system to stop booting normally. In R4.0, this option works only with Media Server add-ons, though it should extend eventually to the entire system.

## Installing BeOS Upgrades

Be has been releasing system updates in the form of full point upgrades approximately twice a year. Whether this pace will continue into the future is not known, but one thing is certain: To date, every BeOS upgrade has been well worth it, adding tons of new features, bug fixes, and performance improvements. Because every update consists of a completely different set of changes, no blanket statements can be made about them, but in general Be offers very fair upgrade pricing to existing users (upgrades are often free, in fact) and users always come out on top.

In all cases, Be posts detailed information about the contents of the upgrade on their Web site (**www.be.com**). Not only does this let you evaluate whether you want to upgrade, but it provides an important opportunity to read any notes or caveats concerning the upgrade. Always, always, read Be's upgrade documentation before undertaking one, and follow any special instructions provided there.

To date, BeOS upgrades have been distributed online in SoftwareValet "package" format. SoftwareValet is covered in detail in Chapter 10, *System Tools and Utilities*, though the process seldom requires more than a couple of mouse clicks and a reboot. Regardless, take care to read any documentation distributed along with the upgrade.

 **After upgrading your BeOS system to another version, remember to take a look in your** /optional **directory (especially in** /optional/experimental**) for goodies—this is where Be places software that will one day make it into the official distribution, but that is still ahead of its time. You never know what you might find in there. Read any documentation accompanying experimental software, and remember that it's not officially supported by Be.**

 While a system upgrade won't touch any of your personal data, it may replace some system files to which you may still want access for some reason. You may find a small collection of "clobbered" files in a directory called /Your_Old_Be_Files_Are_Here. You can almost certainly delete this directory safely after upgrading, but you should probably poke around and make sure nothing you recognize is in this directory before blowing it away for good.

 If you click the Options button in the Installer during a system upgrade and select the Clean Install option, any directory on the installation volume that has the same name as a directory being installed will be replaced. Since a home directory exists on the CD, your home directory will be replaced as well. A clean install really is a clean install, and isn't much different from initializing a partition, unless you have a lot of data in directories at the root level of your boot drive with unique names. Don't accept this option unless you've backed up all of your personal data!

## Other Configurations

All of that is well and good if your machine meets the criteria listed earlier (Windows 95 or 98 installed and at least 500MB free on your primary partition), but what if your machine has only Windows NT, Linux, FreeBSD, or some other operating system(s) installed? What if you want to build a

BeOS-only machine? Most of the basic installation steps above still apply to you, but you may have some additional prep work to do, since the bundled version of PartitionMagic won't work on your system.

**Installing BeOS on a Windows NT Machine**  If your machine has only a Windows NT installation, the procedure will be a little different than described above. Windows NT can be installed onto FAT32 or NTFS volumes. If your NT installation is on an NTFS volume, PartitionMagic will not be able to resize your existing partition. You'll need to use NT's Disk Administrator to prepare a primary partition for use by BeOS (Disk Administrator can't create BeOS volumes, but it can create FAT volumes, which you can reinitialize with the Be Filesystem during the BeOS installation process). Regardless of filesystem, Windows NT includes mechanisms that prevent software from accessing hardware at a low level. In addition, Windows NT does not have a DOS mode like Windows does (NT's "DOS" prompt is just a DOS emulator). For these reasons, you'll need to prepare a pair of special boot floppies. By booting from these with the BeOS CD inserted, you'll be able to bypass NT's protections and install BeOS.

Boot into NT normally, insert the BeOS CD, and run bepm. You'll be prompted to insert two floppy disks. Follow the instructions onscreen, reboot, and follow the normal installation instructions outlined earlier in this chapter.

**Installing BeOS onto a Linux or FreeBSD Machine**  If you're the proud owner of a "Microsoft-free device," you'll need to use a partitioning utility native to your operating system, such as the ubiquitous and powerful fdisk. Create a partition and give it the type "0xeb" (in decimal, 235). Note carefully the exact position of the new partition in your filesystem (for example, /dev/disks/hdb/1/). Next, insert both the BeOS boot floppy and the installation CD (or just insert the CD, and set your BIOS to boot from CD). When the Installer comes up, choose the disk partition you noted down earlier from the picklist as the Install To: volume. Make absolutely, positively sure that this is the correct partition, as the next step will initialize that partition with the Be Filesystem, destroying any data it may contain. Installation will proceed normally.

**Installing BeOS onto an Empty Hard Disk**  If you're one of those hardcore exotic types who's ready to go the distance and dedicate an entire machine to running BeOS and nothing but BeOS, I honor your righteousness. To install BeOS onto a blank hard disk, start your machine with both the boot floppy and the CD inserted. Click "I Agree" when the Agreement screen appears and you'll be facing the Installer. Before clicking anything else, press Ctrl+Alt+D to launch DriveSetup and create a BeOS partition according to the DriveSetup instructions in Chapter 9, *Preferences and Customization*. Let DriveSetup mount the new partition, close DriveSetup, and return to the Installer, from which you can continue to install BeOS normally.

In truth, this final method can be used in place of any of the above methods. However, because it depends on some familiarity with the DriveSetup application and a relatively advanced understanding of partition management in general, it's best reserved for those either very familiar with BeOS and DriveSetup, or very familiar with disk partitioning utilities.

# Working with Partitions

As noted earlier, BeOS can be installed onto either primary or extended partitions. However, BeOS (at this writing) cannot create extended partitions. If you're curious about the difference, or would like to learn more about your partition-management options, this section is for you.

You can use BeOS's DriveSetup application (Chapter 9, *Preferences and Customization*) to format partitions with BFS whether or not they're already formatted with another filesystem, and whether or not they're extended/logical partitions.

## *Partition History*

Back in the old days (OK, five years ago), when a 250MB hard drive seemed like endless acreage, few people were envisioning the possibility that users would one day have a need to subdivide hard drives into smaller pieces. Eventually, however, power users wanted to do just that, so a standard was developed that made it possible to divide a hard drive up into four primary partitions. But hard drives were getting larger, and a few people were starting to install multiple operating systems on a single computer. It wasn't long before four partitions weren't enough. Rather than mess with the existing standard, the industry decided it would be easier to just let users subdivide their primary partitions. It's a shame, too—things would be a lot more flexible now if we could just create as many primary partitions as necessary, but that's not the way it happened (on the x86 side anyway; Macintosh users can create as many as 32 partitions on a single hard drive). This is a perfect example of how standards created and adopted without sufficient foresight can have a negative impact on the future.

Thus was born the extended partition. An extended partition is essentially the same as a primary partition, except that it can also function as a container for further partitions, which are, as you've probably guessed, known as "logical partitions." Since you can have four primary (or extended) partitions and an extended partition can contain four logical partitions, a hard drive can be divided into a maximum of 16 partitions. The sum of the sizes of the logical partitions within an extended partition is always equal to the size of that extended partition. It's also worth noting that an extended partition never appears to DOS or Windows with a drive letter or to BeOS as a volume name (since it's just a container). DOS/Windows drive letters, or BeOS volume names, will always be assigned only to primary partitions or to logical partitions that reside within extended partitions.

## Discovering Your Partition Types

If you're not sure how your hard drive is currently partitioned and want to find out before you begin installing BeOS, you can use either a third-party partitioning and disk-management tool (such as PartitionMagic) or a utility provided by your existing operating system (such as fdisk).

 Be extremely cautious when using any of the three tools described below. All are capable of deleting partitions at the press of a key. Delete a partition and you lose all of the data it contains. Exercise caution, and pay attention!

**Windows 95/98** Boot your machine into DOS mode (this can be done through an option on the Windows shutdown menu or by pressing F8 as soon as Windows starts to boot and choosing "Command prompt only") and type fdisk. Within fdisk, choose "Display partition information." A table will show you exactly how your drive is mapped out. If one of the partitions shown is an extended partition, you'll be asked if you want to view a second table showing the logical partitions it contains. If you have more than one physical hard drive in your machine and are using a later version of Windows (i.e. anything but the very first versions of Windows 95), choose the last menu option in fdisk to select another physical drive.

**Windows NT** Because NT is a fully graphical operating system and cannot be booted to the command line alone, you'll need to use the graphical Disk Administrator tool bundled with NT. Disk Administrator will show you a map of your disks' partitions and partition types.

**Linux/FreeBSD** If you have one of these OSs, you should also have a tool called fdisk on your system, though yours is far more capable than the DOS version. Within Linux's fdisk, press "P" to display your partition information.

**Maximum Partition Management** While the techniques described in this chapter cover everything you need to know to create a new partition for your BeOS installation, power users may want more. The version of PartitionMagic that comes with BeOS gets the job done, but as mentioned several times here, it's a limited version. In fact, "limited" is something of an understatement. The full retail version of Power-Quest's PartitionMagic is an extremely powerful tool, and anyone who's serious about running multiple operating systems on one computer should consider getting it.

*Figure 3.04*

*The full version of PartitionMagic 4.0 lets you manipulate partitions nondestructively, directly from within Windows.*

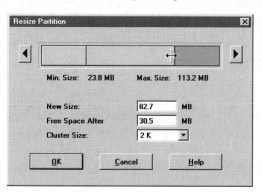

While the limited version will refuse to operate if it finds a preexisting BeOS partition on your machine, the full version of PartitionMagic 4.0 can be used as often as you like, and is not constrained to running in DOS mode. The full version can create, resize, and move FAT, FAT32, NTFS, HPFS, Linux Ext2, and Linux Swap partitions. It can prepare disk space for new operating systems, let you preview partitioning operations before committing them to disk, automatically handle extended partitions when manipulating logical partitions within them, convert filesystems among many common formats without damaging the data they contain, hide and unhide partitions from one another, run extensive diagnostics … the list goes on. The full version also includes its own boot manager called BootMagic, which you can use in place of Bootman for more sophisticated control.

PartitionMagic's documentation is extensive and very readable, so we won't cover its use here. Learn more about PartitionMagic at **www.powerquest.com**. Note that PartitionMagic must be run from within Windows, and is therefore not useful for Microsoft-free computers.

# Other Multi-Boot Options

The Bootman utility bundled with BeOS (covered earlier in this chapter) is a fine boot manager, but it's not the only way to present yourself with a menu of installed operating systems at boot time.

## OS-Provided Boot Managers

Many operating systems include their own multi-boot menuing systems, to which you should easily be able to add your BeOS partitions.

**Linux** The vast majority of Linux users boot their systems with LILO, a boot manager that formed the basis of the old BeOS boot manager, BeLO. Simply edit lilo.conf to include the name and location of your BeOS partition and run the lilo command to update the master boot record. Complete instructions on working with LILO are included in your Linux distribution.

**Windows 95/98** While Windows 95 and 98 do not include their own boot menuing system, it's not difficult to create one, thanks to additional utilities provided by Be, which you'll find on your BeOS installation CD (note that these utilities will only be visible on the CD when it's mounted from within Windows, not BeOS). Insert the CD and use Explorer to navigate to the Win95 directory on the CD. Copy the BeLaunch folder within to your C:\ drive. This folder must be stored in the root of C:\, as this path is hard-coded into the utility.

BeLaunch will not work on multiprocessor machines!

Drag a shortcut from the BeLaunch icon in c:\belaunch to your Windows desktop, then double-click it to close down Windows and launch BeOS. If this process works (and as long as you have a single-processor machine, it should), you'll be able to use the beos.bat batch file from within your Windows boot files. Back in Windows, open a DOS shell, cd to c:\belaunch, and type beos.bat. If BeOS is launched, you're in business. Now you'll need to edit three of your Windows system files to create a boot menu.

To make this work, you'll need to get three DOS files all talking to each other: autoexec.bat, config.sys, and msdos.sys. Because Bootman is a superior solution to this type of makeshift Windows boot menu, there really is no advantage to this method. If you'd like to go for it anyway, you'll find detailed instructions and sample Windows system files on this book's Web site, at **http://www.beosbible.com**.

**Windows NT** Be provides a small utility that will add the name and location of your BeOS partition to the NT Boot Manager. Boot into Windows, insert the BeOS installation CD, find the NT directory on the CD, and double-click addbeos.exe. This will cause a small binary file to be placed in the root of your NT boot drive, and modify the file boot.ini. Note that if you run this utility again in the future, your BeOS partition will be added to the menu a second time. To fix this, you'll need to modify the file boot.ini in the root of your NT boot drive. Because the file is write-protected, you'll need to turn off its protection attributes, which you can access by right-clicking the file and choosing Properties from the context menu.

**The BeOS Boot Floppy** Regardless of how your system is set up, and regardless of whether or not you have a boot manager installed, one of the most fail-safe ways to boot BeOS is to use the boot floppy that came with the BeOS installation CD. When you boot from the floppy, your machine won't even try to find a boot record on the hard disk. Instead, the boot loader will be read from floppy. It will then scan your system for all bootable BeOS partitions. Whichever one is set to be your current drive (from the Boot panel in your Preferences folder) will be booted by default. To boot a different BeOS partition, hold down the Spacebar when you see the words "Press Space for Boot Menu" at the bottom of your screen. You can then use the arrow keys on your keyboard to select from bootable BeOS partitions.

You can also use the BeOS boot floppy in emergency boot procedures, so you can go in and attempt to retrieve data from a crashed or corrupt hard disk. See the section *Disaster Recovery* in Chapter 16, *Troubleshooting and Maintenance*, for details.

Because BeOS R3 and R4 for Intel Architecture are binary-incompatible, you cannot boot an R4 partition with an R3 boot floppy. Because the BeOS boot floppy is backward-compatible with previous versions of the system, however, you can boot an R3 partition from an R4 floppy.

 **Create a Backup Boot Floppy** It's important to have a working boot floppy around. In fact, it's important enough that you should create an extra one, just for good measure. Full instructions on creating BeOS boot floppies can be found in Chapter 16, *Troubleshooting and Maintenance*.

### Boot Glitches

A very small proportion of users may experience boot problems after a successful installation, or after booting back and forth between R3 and R4 partitions. If you see the message "Error loading OS; press any key to reboot," you may be experiencing an incompatibility with the boot sector in R4.0 and certain BIOS implementations that incorrectly implement LBA disk reads. This problem may also crop up if you initialize a BFS partition with block sizes larger than 1024K. If this happens to you, look in the /experimental directory on the CD for a file called makebootable. Copy it to /boot/home/config/bin, open a Terminal window, and type:

```
makebootable -experimental /boot
```

Note, however, that you may need to run this command after each boot into R3. Since makebootable is an R4 binary, it can only be run from within R4. That means that you may need to boot into R4 from the R4 boot floppy in order to run it. Fortunately, by the time you read this, there will be very little (if any) software remaining that hasn't yet been recompiled for R4, which means you'll probably have almost no need to ever boot into R3 again. Users who started running BeOS with R4 or later don't need to worry about this at all.

## Third-Party Boot Managers

If you need more features than those offered by the boot managers typically distributed with operating systems, there are a number of powerful third-party boot managers on the market. Two of the best are described here.

**System Commander Deluxe** My favorite boot loader by far is V Communications' System Commander Deluxe. The fact that System Commander includes native support for BeOS, including built-in BeOS icons, is one of the reasons, but certainly not the only one. Fact is, System Commander simply has more power options than any boot manager I've tried. When you're ready to install another operating system, the OS Wizard will analyze your hard drives and suggest the best location, even modifying drives on the fly as necessary. If you've got a ton of drives connected to your system, all subdivided into logical partitions, System Commander won't bat an eye—it supports up to 100 installed operating systems on a single computer (yeah, dream on). It even saves and maintains multiple copies of critical system files for installed systems and offers boot sector virus protection.

All of that is stuff you'll hardly ever use, though. What you will use on a daily basis is the boot menu, and System Commander offers the most configurable boot menu available. You can set the colors, labels, and sounds associated with every system, and by using a hotkey, you can examine your current partition layouts in a variety of informational tables. Because all of these customizations are saved to an area separate from your boot record, you'll be able to retrieve your settings easily if another operating system installation or upgrade kicks System Commander out of the boot record. Just run the System Commander update utility and it will insert itself right back where it was, settings intact, and even offer to add the new OS to your boot menu automatically, if applicable. Find out more at **www.v-com.com**.

 The one drawback to System Commander is that its setup and configuration software runs only under DOS/Windows, so the product can't be used by owners of Microsoft-free machines.

**PowerBoot**   Somewhat less intense but no less useful is Blue Sky Innovations' PowerBoot, which has the distinct advantage of not requiring a FAT partition (i.e. PowerBoot works fine on non-Microsoft machines). It lacks a few of System Commander's advanced features, but costs around half as much, can work with up to 63 partitions, autodetects operating systems, lets you pretend to "swap" primary and secondary drives (which can be useful if you need to fool Windows into booting off your second hard drive), and lets you hide and unhide partitions on the fly. See **www.blueskyinnovations.com** for more information.

## Install Operating Systems in Optimal Order

If you're building a multi-boot machine from scratch and thus have the luxury of deciding in which order to install your operating systems, always install Microsoft operating systems first. While Microsoft OSs will not overwrite or damage your BeOS installation, they will "steal" the master boot record for themselves, arrogantly assuming a position of primacy on your hard drive. Any boot-management software you've installed, such as BeOS's Bootman, System Commander, System Selector, LILO, or anything else, will be squeezed out of position and replaced with the Microsoft boot loader. The fix for this situation is to simply reinstall your boot-management software. While this is not difficult, life will be simpler if you simply install Microsoft systems first, letting them have their way with the master boot record, then install other systems, and overwrite the MBR later on with whatever boot manager you like.

Note that if you upgrade Windows later on, or convert a Windows FAT16 drive to the FAT32 filesystem, the process will overwrite the master boot record just as if you had installed Windows for the first time.

# Installing BeOS on PowerPC Hardware

*by Henry Bortman*

As is true for installing BeOS on Windows systems, a bit of prep time spent upfront will pay off down the road when you install BeOS on a Mac. You'll want to check to make sure that your CPU model and graphics card are supported, and that you have enough RAM and disk space available for BeOS to give good performance.

## Where to Get BeOS

Since BeOS for PowerPC comes on the same CD as BeOS for Intel, the same guidelines described earlier in this chapter apply for obtaining the operating system. Your best bet is to order it through BeDepot, Be's online software store (**www.bedepot.com**). The BeOS retail package can be ordered via phone during normal U.S. business hours (Pacific Time) at (800) 491-2818. For pricing, and for information on obtaining BeOS outside the U.S., see the previous section entitled *Where to Get BeOS*.

## Mac Hardware Requirements

**CPU** Not all PowerPC-based Macs are supported by BeOS. The first round of Power Macs, which had NuBus rather than PCI expansion buses, can't run BeOS. Likewise, none of Apple's current Power Mac G3 systems can run BeOS (because Apple won't give Be the necessary technical information). Nor are any PowerBooks supported, for the same reason. But all of the PCI-based Power Macs shipped by Apple prior to the Power Mac G3s, and all of the PCI-based machines shipped by clone vendors (Power Computing, Radius/Umax, Motorola, and Daystar) are supported by BeOS, with the exception of a few miscellaneous models from Apple and the earliest models from Power Computing. (If in doubt, check out Be's hardware compatibility lists at **http://www.be.com/support/guides/beosreadylist_ppc.html**.) Particularly interesting are the multiprocessor systems shipped by some of the clone vendors. BeOS takes far greater advantage of the dual- or quad-processor systems than the MacOS ever did.

 The section of this chapter that describes installing BeOS for Intel mentions a BeOS Demo CD that can be used to test hardware compatibility. Because BeOS on the Mac can't start up until the MacOS is at least partially booted, it's not possible to do something similar on the Mac.

**Memory** As with Intel systems, you'll need a minimum of 16MB of RAM for BeOS on the Mac. You'll have a much more pleasant experience, though, if you have 64MB or more.

**Disk Space** Be recommends that you have a minimum of 150MB of hard-disk space available to BeOS. More, of course, is better. It is possible to install BeOS on a 100MB Zip cartridge, but it's not recommended. Although BeOS and its associated applications will fit on a Zip cartridge, running BeOS off a Zip is like asking it to race with two broken legs. Not only are Zip drives notoriously slow, but installation will leave very little room for the operating system's virtual memory swap file (see Chapter 9, *Preferences and Customization*, for more on virtual memory).

One choice you will want to make before beginning is whether to dedicate an entire hard disk to BeOS or to partition a drive and install BeOS on one partition. The basic installation instructions that follow assume that you have taken the plunge and decided to give BeOS its own disk drive. Most of the process will be the same regardless of which approach you choose, but if you plan to carve up a drive into BFS and HFS partitions, make sure to read *Partitioning Your Mac Drive*, below, before starting the installation.

**Graphics** Just about any Mac graphics card will work with BeOS. You'll only get accelerated graphics, though, if you use one of the cards for which Be provides accelerated drivers. These include ATI's Mach 64/XClaim GA (but not the XClaim VR or XClaim 3D); IXmicro's TwinTurbo 128/M2, /M4, and /M8; and Matrox's Millennium and Millennium II. Graphics acceleration is also supported for the built-in graphics adapters on all Mac and Mac clones supported by BeOS. For the latest list of supported graphics cards, check out `http://www.be.com/support/qandas/faqs/faq-0197.html`.

**Monitor** BeOS supports both multiple- and fixed-frequency monitors, but you'll be happier with a multiple-frequency monitor. Regardless of what graphics adapter or card you have, if you use a fixed-frequency monitor, graphics acceleration will be disabled. If you do use a fixed-frequency monitor, make sure to read the note on fixed-frequency monitors below in *Starting the BeOS*.

 **For information on international versions of BeOS for PowerPC, see *International Versions*, in the installation instructions for BeOS for Intel, above. This section applies equally to both platforms.**

# Basic Installation on PowerPC Hardware

 As noted above, before installing BeOS, you need to decide whether you want to dedicate an entire disk drive to BeOS, or to install it in one partition of a partitioned drive. In either case, though, you'll need a minimum of 150MB of available hard-disk space (unless you're willing to settle for lousy performance—and if that's the case, you might as well stick with the MacOS).

 If you plan to install BeOS on a drive partition, you must partition the drive *before* attempting the installation. Partitioning is discussed in the following section. If you plan to dedicate a hard disk to BeOS, you can skip this section and continue with *Easy Install*.

## Partitioning Your Mac Drive

You perform this step on the Mac before you begin BeOS installation. But before you begin partitioning, there's something else you need to do first: Back up your data. If there's no data you care about on the drive you're going to partition, don't worry about it. But data does get destroyed when you partition a drive.

To partition a drive, you'll need a hard-disk-formatting utility like FWB's Hard Disk ToolKit (HDT). This section will briefly describe the partitioning process using HDT 2.5 as an example. For more detailed instructions, consult the documentation for the formatting utility that you use.

When you launch HDT, it will open a window that displays a list of available devices. (If it is not already selected, select Devices from the View By: popup

*Figure 3.05*

*Hard Disk ToolKit is one of many disk-formatting utilities that enable you to partition Mac hard disk drives.*

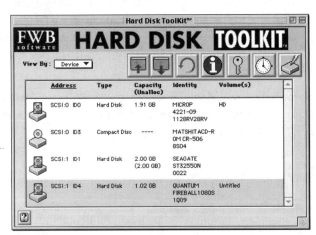

menu.) Select the device that you want to partition and then select View Partitions from the Devices menu.

A Partition List window will open, displaying a list of the drive's existing partitions. We'll assume that you're working with a drive that hasn't previously been partitioned. Even so, the list that appears in this window will contain several partitions. Only one of them, the one whose type is listed as Apple_HFS, concerns you. (When you format a drive for the Mac, you automatically create partitions that you normally don't see, which are used exclusively by the operating system. Although usually invisible, they are listed here. Leave them alone!)

There are several different paths you can take from here. The easiest approach is to delete the existing Apple_HFS partition—you *have* backed up all of your valuable data, right?—and then create two new ones. To do that, select the partition whose type is Apple_HFS and click the Delete button. It will disappear from the list and be replaced by a partition whose title is "Free Space" and whose type is "Apple_Free." Then select the Free Space partition and choose Create New Volume from the Devices menu.

In the Create New Volumes window that appears, set the Number of Volumes to 2, make sure that MacOS is selected in the Volume Type popup, and, optionally, name the volumes. (If you don't name them, they'll be given the default names "Untitled" and "Untitled 2." You can always change them later.) Click the OK button and HDT will create the volumes, which will then appear in the partition list. Close the partition list and quit out of HDT. Your work here is done.

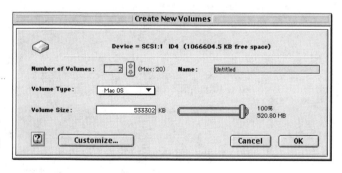

*Figure 3.06*

*In the Create New Volumes window, you tell HDT how many partitions (volumes) you want to create.*

Recent versions of Mac disk-formatting utilities allow you to format volumes with Apple's new disk format, known as MacOS Extended (or HFS+). Don't be tempted. Although HFS+ has certain advantages over HFS when you're running the MacOS, BeOS doesn't support this new format. Make sure that whenever you are given a choice between HFS and HFS+ you choose the former. Otherwise you may have trouble installing BeOS.

# Easy Installation

Once you have checked your hardware for BeOS compatibility and selected a hard disk (or created a drive partition), you're ready to begin the BeOS installation process. The first step is to boot the MacOS.

**Start from the MacOS**    Boot into the MacOS and insert the BeOS installation CD. Double-click on the CD icon. Within the Macintosh folder you will find a folder named BeOS Mac Tools. You'll also find a Release Notes document, which it would be a good idea to peruse. This folder contains three

files: BeOS-Launcher (an application), _OS_Chooser (a Mac OS extension), and Installing_the_BeOS (a text document that it would also be a good idea to peruse).

**Figure 3.07**

The BeOS Mac Tools *folder on the installation CD contains files that you will need to boot BeOS.*

Copy the BeOS Mac Tools folder to your Mac hard disk. Make sure you copy it to a volume (a drive or a partition) on which you *won't* be installing BeOS. You're going to need the files in this folder to boot BeOS after you finish installing it, and if you put them on the volume you're going to use for BeOS, they'll get erased during installation.

**Using the Installer**    To begin installation, double-click on the BeOS_Launcher icon. If your Mac spits out the CD, push it back in. Most likely, your Mac will then figure out that it should run the Installer application from the CD. If, however, you already have BeOS installed on one of your Mac's volumes, BeOS may boot instead of the Installer . If this happens, restart your Mac, double-click the BeOS_Launcher icon again, and this time

**Figure 3.08**

The first step in the Installer is to select the volume onto which BeOS should be installed.

hold down the Shift key until you see an ugly text-only screen. Using the Up and Down Arrow keys, select the installation CD from the list displayed. It will be listed as something like /dev/disk/scsi/0/3/0/2_0 'BeOS' PPC R4', type 'bfs'). Then press the Return key.

When the licensing agreement appears, read it, then click Agree. The Installer application will appear. Now it's time to choose the volume onto which you want to install BeOS. It doesn't matter at this point whether a volume occupies an entire hard disk or was created by partitioning—they all just show up as volumes on this list. Select the volume you want to install the BeOS on. If you're installing onto a disk that formerly contained Mac files, it will appear on the list with "Mac HFS" after the volume name. Don't panic; this is normal. Just make sure you don't choose a Mac volume unless you're willing to erase everything on it. Because that's just what the Installer will do.

Before clicking Begin, you might want to check out the available options.

**Options** At the bottom left of the Installer tab is an Options button. Click this and you'll see a panel like the one in Figure 3.09. Be doesn't recommend using the Clean Install option unless you've been specifically instructed by tech support to do so. If you select Install Optional Items, you'll end up with a collection of media files and other goodies (these are listed in Chapter 2, *Meet the System*).

**Figure 3.09**

*Select Install Optional Items to copy some sample media files and a few other goodies to your BeOS volume. You're best off avoiding the other options on this panel.*

The Setup partitions button will launch DriveSetup, but you'd be well advised to stay away from it. Drive Setup isn't that good at dealing with HFS volumes (that's why you created partitions in the MacOS before you launched the Installer). You're asking for trouble if you mess around here.

This panel also gives you the option to install from an existing BeOS volume instead of from the installation CD. There's no harm in doing this, but you'll end up with copies of all the personal files in your home directory, along with BeOS, on the new volume.

Your best bet is probably to leave all the options except Install Optional Items alone. If you have the disk space (about 100MB is required), select Install Optional Items and click OK.

**Initializing the Partition** When you click the Begin button, the Installer will display an alert asking you if you're sure you want to initialize the chosen volume. Double-check to make sure you've chosen the right volume. As the warning says, if you proceed, all your Mac files will be permanently erased. When you're ready to proceed, click the Initialize button.

The Installer will then display a panel from which you can set a filesystem block size and name your volume. Unless your drive (or partition) contains 15GB or more, stick with the default block size, 1024K. See Chapter 9, *Preferences and Customization* (DriveSetup section), for a complete explanation of the relationship between storage efficiency, speed, and block size.

The volume name you assign to the partition here will become the name of this volume when it appears on your BeOS Desktop. You can always rename it later on, just as you would rename a file.

Click Initialize, and you'll be given one final warning that you're about to blow away any data that may be living in that partition. Click Cancel if you're unsure, or Initialize if you're ready to go for it.

**Language Selection**  Refer to the section of the same name above for information on support for languages other than English. It applies equally to BeOS for PowerPC.

**Installing ...**  The Installer will now begin copying files from the CD to your designated volume, displaying each filename as it does. A progress indicator will show you how far you've come. The entire process shouldn't take more than a few minutes.

If you're installing onto (or upgrading) a volume that already contains BeOS, you may see a message informing you that an application, such as BeMail, already exists on the destination volume. Normally, you'll want to replace any older versions of applications with newer ones. To do this, click the Replace All Older button, and the Installer will automatically replace all such applications without further warning. If you want to decide on a case-by-case basis, use the Keep and Replace buttons instead.

**Figure 3.10**

*If BeOS is already installed, you may see a series of messages like this one. Click Replace All Older unless you have a specific reason to keep an old version of an application.*

When the installation is complete, click the Quit button in the Installer window. Your Mac will reboot. To start BeOS, follow the directions in the next section.

## Booting the BeOS

OK, remember that BeOS Mac Tools folder that you copied to your Mac hard drive earlier in the process? Now you get to find out why you did that.

There are two ways to boot BeOS from a Mac. The first is by using the BeOS Launcher application. You start it like any other Mac application, by double-clicking it. The MacOS shuts down and BeOS starts up. That's all there is to it.

The alternative approach is to use OS Chooser. If you drop this extension into your System folder, when you boot your Mac, you'll be presented with an OS Chooser dialog shortly after the startup process begins. If you click on the Start Mac OS button, the Mac boot process will continue normally. If you click the Start BeOS button, the MacOS boot process will be interrupted and BeOS will boot instead. If you don't click either button within five seconds, whichever OS is set as the default will boot.

Initially, the MacOS is set as the default. Clicking the Start BeOS button, however, not only interrupts the MacOS boot process for that one startup, it also sets the BeOS as the default startup OS. Subsequently, whenever you restart your Mac, unless you click the Start MacOS button, the Mac boot process will be interrupted and BeOS will start up instead.

**If for some reason you don't want to install the OS Chooser extension, you can still boot BeOS on a Mac without having to wait for all your extensions and control panels to load first. Just keep an alias for the BeOS Launcher on your Desktop and hold down the Shift key while starting the MacOS so that it boots with extensions disabled. That gets you quickly to the Finder, from which you can start the BeOS Launcher.**

The OS Chooser dialog also contains a checkbox labeled "Fixed-Frequency Monitor." If you have a fixed-frequency monitor connected to your Mac, you should select this option, or your display may appear degraded. If your monitor is multiple-frequency, don't select this option.

And that's all there is too it. If you have problems, don't forget to read the start of this chapter, which covers installing on Intel hardware, as in many cases processes are identical.

### Bob Herold
*Director of OS Technology*
*Interviewed by Henry Bortman*

**HB:** *Tell me about where you were before you came to Be.*

**BH:** I was at Apple. Immediately before I came to Be I was working on Newton. I joined the Newton team about a year before I came to Be. That was when Steve Sackoman was still running the new group. Soon after I got there, all of a sudden, Jean-Louis Gassée and John Scully had a falling out, and so Jean-Louis resigned from Apple. Although he didn't officially resign until six months down the road, it was official that he was leaving, and all operational responsibility was taken away. And with Jean-Louis's resignation, the sort of protective cover around the Newton group disappeared because it was sort of a special project reporting directly to Jean-Louis instead of through the regular engineering organization.

So, Apple had to figure out what to do with the Newton group. Scully sent Larry Tessler over to sort of try to see if there was any technology worth saving and to see if there were any people worth saving, but otherwise to just sort of take it apart and shut it down. And Larry came over and interviewed everybody, and looked around and said, "Wow, this is is really cool, I want to run this." So he asked Scully to keep it together and if he could take it over.

So I actually was there when Steve left and when Larry came in, and sort of helped them with the whole transition from the Hobbit processor to the ARM processor. And then in December of 1990, Steve called me up, or actually, Corey van Arsdale called me up. Corey was then working with Steve and Jean-Louis at Be; he was our legal counsel. I played frisbee with him a lot, so he called me up and said, "You know, shouldn't you just come over and talk to Steve? There's a lot of interesting things we're going to be doing, maybe you can come over and work for us." So I said, sure, because I had a lot of respect for Steve. I'd worked with him both at Newton and on the Mac II, and so I called him up and said, "Hey, let's get together and talk," and they really sounded intrigued, so I agreed to come.

**HB:** *Before we move forward, let me just go back a bit. What did you do before you worked on the Newton?*

**BH:** I did various stuff in the system software group. I started at Apple in late '86, right at the end of the Mac II project. I came in to work for Eric Harslem, doing just general software engineering. And then pretty quickly I became manager of the ROM team, the team that did all the ROMs. We did the second Mac II ROM. (The first one was buggy, but only a few machines were shipped with that.) Then the Mac IIx, the Mac IIci, the Mac IIfx, the Macintosh portable, the SE/30, and the Macintosh Classic II. I think they were all sort of in that time frame. So, all those ROMs basically came out of my team.

**HB:** *Before that?*

**BH:** I was with Think Technologies for three years. They were a compiler company out of Lexington, Massachusetts. First I worked on Apple II Instant Pascal. You could only write a 600-line program, so you couldn't really do too much with it. But it was this tool designed for schools to teach Pascal, and I worked on the Pascal interpreter. I wrote the whole Pascal interpreter for that.

Then after that I was the product manager for Light Speed Pascal, which was the conversion of the Macintosh interpreter into the Light Speed Pascal compiler, sort of merging some of the Pascal technologies with some of the LightSpeed C technology that had been developed. So, I basically was the project manager for that. The big part of that was the manual, actually.

Then when I finished that, I worked with Mel Conway, who was one of the cofounders of Think. We worked on this database project that actually never saw the light of day, but we did a lot of prototyping of the database and a special interpreted language that I was writing a compiler for. But, at that point I had actually met my future wife, Linda, and she was working for Think. She had gotten recruited by Apple because they were so impressed when she sold them the site license for Inbox, an email package, that they tried to hire her to come into their business marketing group. So we decided to move out together and actually interviewed at NeXt, and at Radius, and at Apple, and ended up going to Apple.

Before Think, I spent a year writing a medical supply company management package and an ambulance company management package in Wang BASIC and installing that at five sites around Massachusetts and Rhode Island. Then I spent three years working for a small company called Aeolian Kinetics. That was in the Jimmy Carter era, when there was money for doing solar and wind research and product development. So, we built anemometers, things that sort of measure how much wind passes a particular place, for scouting out sites for windmills.

We actually made one of the first portable computers. It was really cool. The Rockwell AIM-65 was a single board computer with a 6502 processor, a 20 character display, and a cassette tape storage device, and we packaged it up with a whole bunch of batteries and a Zero [Halliburton] case and attached a data acquisition board to it on the side where you could get 28 channels of digital input and eight channels of digital output, and you could actually run a data collection project for measuring the performance of passive solar homes. And we sold a whole bunch of these things to the Solar Energy Research Institute, and they basically used them to do a big evaluation program for various passive solar home designs. It was fun.

**HB:** *OK, so now let's fast forward to the early days of Be. You were one if its first employees. Who else was there, and what did you work on?*

**BH:** Steve Sackoman was designing a machine in his garage in Scotts Valley, and Erich Ringwold and Benoit and I were writing software for it. With all my EE stuff, I knew lots of things like how to pick up a data book and write device drivers and things like that. So I was doing a lot of the low-level stuff of floppy drivers and serial port interfaces and stuff like that. Erich was working a lot on the kernel, and Benoit was working a lot on the filesystem. So, I came to just basically work on getting that machine going and helping to debug the hardware, helping to get the software written and get started writing an operating system. Although, actually, it wasn't our first intent to write an operating system. Our first intent was actually to go and buy one, because it was like. Operating systems, there are a lot of those—you can just go buy one and save yourself a lot of work.

**HB:** *What made you decide to write one instead?*

### *Bob Herold* (continued)

**BH:** Going out and looking for operating systems to buy and realizing that they didn't really match what we wanted to do. They were really sort of specialized, embedded operating systems. There wasn't a lot there. It might be something very good at running embedded applications, but not scalable to running a computer. We talked to Chorus Microsystems. They made a very portable operating system, very modular—actually, a pretty nice thing. It had a lot of real-time functionality and things like that. But it was expensive. It was sort of an interesting discussion with them, but it just turned out to not be in either company's best interest to do business with the other.

So we decided, all this time we're spending talking about it we could actually be sitting down and writing one, so Erich just cracked open the Xinu book *(Operating System Design, The Xinu Approach*, Douglas Comer, Prentice Hall Inc., 1984) and started typing away. Before you knew it, we had a little kernel going, and we just kept evolving it from there.

**HB:** *And mostly what you did was write drivers?*

**BH:** No, I did a lot of different things. I worked on the debugger, I worked on the kernel, I worked on drivers, I debugged a lot of parts of the system as well, filesystems and things like that.

**HB:** *I have this image of you as being the "making the software talk to the hardware" guy.*

**BH:** Yeah, that was my main role because that's what I was good at, but there were not very many of us and there was a lot of stuff to do, so we all ended up doing a lot of different things— working on the C library, working on parts of the kernel that dealt with launching programs, working on utilities, working on lots of stuff.

**HB:** *Anything that end users see?*

**BH:** Let's see, the debugger. They don't want to see that. When they see that, they're usually upset. Not too much other stuff that end users see.

**HB:** *Does that bother you at all, that you put all this work into something that nobody ever sees except engineers the next level up?*

**BH:** No, not really at all. The thing that's really cool about what I do, what I really like about it, is that I love writing the instruction that's the first one executed when the processor wakes up, and sort of taking it through, building up this logical environment that eventually ends up being a full-fledged operating system. That part of the design is really fun for me. That's one thing that was really cool about working at Apple—working on the ROMs. You knew that that code was going to be run billions of times by people all over the world. So, I didn't really mind having something that users didn't see. I just enjoyed making it go.

**HB:** *What was it like porting BeOS to run on Mac hardware?*

**BH:** I actually knew a lot about the hardware that was in a Macintosh already from having worked on it before, so I knew what data books to go and get for the various chips that were in there. So, I went about basically taking our kernel and porting it over to that hardware platform. I knew how the memory was laid out because I knew on the PowerPC they had tried to keep a similar memory architecture to what they had on the Mac II and there was also a bunch of help in terms of documents that were available. And then eventually, when we actually started developing a close relationship with Apple and they were all excited that we were porting, under our agreement with Apple, we actually got a lot of the ERSs for all the new hardware that they were building.

**HB:** *ERSs?*

**BH:** External reference specifications. It's basically what the engineers write that says "here's what we're going to build"; they write an ERS and they pass it around the company, everybody comments on it and they incorporate revisions, and when it's final, they actually go and build it. It's their way of documenting what they're going to do. From my standpoint, it's an excellent reference on exactly what is going to be in, or what was in all the chips that they had built and what is the overall system design of all the Power Macintoshes that they had built. I took those ERSs and got to understand the whole PowerPC architecture that they had designed.

**HB:** *And this was in the clone era, right?*

**BH:** Yeah, the clone era was starting. Actually, we first worked closely with Power Computing. That's right, we actually first ported to a Power Computing box, not to an Apple box. To the Power Center 120, or something like that. And that was done, probably over the course of about two months—to get the first BeOS booting to the Tracker was the first milestone. And then like another two months to get it ready to show at Boston Macworld in August of '96. People were really puzzled because we were sitting there in the booth and here was the Mac with the MacOS and then here's your Mac running BeOS. They were like, What's going on there?

**HB:** *So, what was easy and what was hard about porting to Apple's PowerPC architecture?*

**BH:** The hard part was the transition in software between shutting down the MacOS and starting up BeOS. The first hack at it was very rude to the MacOS; in the middle of running whatever you're running on the MacOS it sort of just, boom, it took over the machine and started up BeOS. Making that an elegant transition was actually a challenge, figuring out how to go and shut down the MacOS gracefully and at the last minute grab control and start up BeOS.

The other hard part was understanding what state the MacOS left the hardware in and starting up BeOS on top of that hardware state. For instance, how they had set up the processor, whether they had left the cache on, what their virtual memory map was and things like that. So, that was a big challenge, getting started into BeOS, so the first time you actually could spew a line of debugging output out the serial port. That was a big milestone because it meant that I had made the transition from the MacOS into BeOS. Beyond that, it was understanding all the hardware and understanding how the various pieces of hardware that we needed worked. So, understanding the graphics controller, understanding the Ethernet controller, understanding the disk controller, things like that. Writing drivers for all those things.

**HB:** *Be was never able to support the PowerBooks. Why was that?*

**BH:** When it was time to start thinking about supporting those, once we basically had the other three PowerPC architectures covered, that's when Apple decided not to buy us. All of a

## *Bob Herold* (continued)

sudden the ERS spigot turned off. So, we couldn't get information about those designs. Maybe we could have gone and tried to reverse-engineer it by sort of looking at the device tree and things like that, but it was just going to be a lot of work without necessarily a good win in sight, so we decided not to do it. I mean, it certainly would have been cool to have it running on the PowerBook. I think they used the O'Hare I/O chip. And we were running on the O'Hare chip, so it wouldn't have been too much of a leap to actually get running on the PowerBook.

**HB:** *But there was all of the power management stuff that you had never really seen.*

**BH:** We'd never seen and we'd have no idea how to do it if there was anything special you had to know how to do. We still don't know because I haven't seen an ERS for the thing, so I don't know how to power down various parts of the system. It would have been a lot of work, and it would have been a lot of work sort of shooting in the dark too, so we just decided to not do it. And at the time the thinking was, well, if this is going to happen, maybe we should port to Intel. So, the Intel port effort started up soon after that.

**HB:** *I want to get to that in a second, but let me just talk about what's going on in terms of today's Apple designs. The BeOS runs on the second generation of Power Mac systems, and the early PCI-based system, but not on Power Mac G3s, which are all of Apple's current models. So, I assume the spigot turned off and stayed turned off.*

**BH:** Yes. And it's not for lack of asking. We kept asking and we kept getting nos. Before, we were connected right at the highest levels. We were talking directly with the head of hardware engineering and it was sort of by edict of Gil Amelio: let's work with Be, let's make this happen. And then once that got turned off, we were a developer like anybody else. We had to go through the developer evangelism team to go and try to get all the stuff and we kept asking for specs and kept getting turned down.

From their point of view, it makes sense. I mean, here they had made their decision on an operating system, so they want to do everything in their power to make that operating system succeed. We're another operating system on the same platform, so we're viewed as competition, and it doesn't make sense to be giving your competition information to help them succeed. It seemed reasonable to us, but still, on the other hand, we'd hoped that we could help them sell more computers and it might behoove them to be more open about the information that we needed to actually get going…. But I guess they didn't see it that way.

**HB:** *So now the focus is Intel. What's that experience like?*

**BH:** It's been quite a ride. Intel is just … their processor technology is amazing. Both from the point of view of using the logical design of their processors and figuring out ways to take the same instruction set and get more and more performance out of it. And then their process technology, to be able to actually build the things that their logic designers come up with is amazing. The fact that they can crank out these chips with millions and millions of transistors— ever-increasing numbers of transistors—and keep the die size at a point where the price is still competitive and people are still willing to pay for it is just amazing.

**HB:** *Does that make it easier or harder to work with?*

**BH:** Oh, boy. It's both, actually. It's easy because they're everywhere. Intel machines are ubiquitous. In terms of performance, they have amazing performance. Not just at the processor, but also in the total system design. They are leading the charge on upping the memory bus speed—now they're up to 100 MHz, they're talking 120, 130 MHz memory buses. Their PCI implementation actually turns out to be more efficient than Apple's. There were things that we could do over PCI on Intel boxes that we just couldn't do on a PCI bus running at the same speed on Apple hardware just because of the interface between the PCI bus and the memory subsystem. They've really engineered and designed their systems really well.

   The challenge of getting into the Intel architecture is that it's so wide open in terms of hardware that it's a lot of work to get all the drivers. So what we have to do is go and look at the market and say well, what is 80 percent of the market buying? Usually, it's like two or three pieces of hardware in any given six-month period. That's the other problem: It evolves so quickly that you have to keep writing drivers as the new stuff comes out.

**HB:** *So, you're going to be doing that for the rest of your life?*

**BH:** The hard part is when you're a new operating system—we weren't selling anything yet and we didn't have any traction—you go to ATI or somebody who makes a new SCSI controller and you say, Well, we have this new operating system and we want to get a driver for your particular piece of hardware onto it. They say, Well, great—here's a spec book and just don't bother us again, because they don't really want to spend any resources on you. Sometimes they're outright hostile and don't want to give you anything. And some companies are very friendly and give you everything, but they basically want you to do all the work. Our goal is to get to the point where we have enough volume and we have enough market presence that—it's already starting to happen, it's nice—that companies come to us and say, "Oh, we have this piece of hardware and we'd really like to get it running on your operating system. What can we do to write a driver for it?" and offload the work from us to them. That's the only way that long-term we're going to be able to support all this stuff, because we can't possibly support everything and so as these hardware vendors come along, the challenge of actually developing the drivers is something that they hopefully will be taking up themselves.

**HB:** *What keeps you here? It's sort of rare for an engineer of your caliber to stick with one company for this long.*

**BH:** I still believe that something really big is going to happen with Be. This last year has probably been the most excited that I've been about our product. It's basically our prospects that keep me here.

   I tell people I'm in it for the money. Having come in here early I have a sizable chunk of stock options and if something happens, you know Be gets to the point that they actually gain some market attraction and have the ability to go public or merge or be bought by a larger player, there's a chance to make a good chunk of change on it. I could get my family set for life. So the possibility of doing that.

### *Bob Herold (continued)*

Sure, as my wife often reminds me, it's a risky venture and there might have been easier ways, with all the stuff that's happening with networking and the Internet and things like that, to have possibly gone through two startups already in the time that I've been here at Be. Yet startups are an iffy proposition. There's very few that actually make it to the point that we've made it and continue to stay alive.

I've sort of stayed at Be for several reasons. One is just continuing to believe that we really had something that was cool and that would eventually succeed in the marketplace. So one, faith in the technology. Two, faith in Jean-Louis's ability to pull it off, and get us out to market and get us to a point where we have traction, we're actually establishing a platform. And then three, it's also a lot of fun to be working on this stuff. It's what I enjoy doing—what better thing to do in life than to be eager to drive into work knowing that not only are you working on something fun, but there's a chance that you can make some serious money doing it.

# 4

# Get Online Fast

. . . . . . . . . . . . . . . . . . . . . . . . . . . . . . . . . . . . . . . . . . . . .

If only one fax machine existed in the world, it would have no value. As soon as there are two, however, each partakes of the other's value; by forming a network, their owners potentially double their resources. Multiply two fax machines by a few million and you start to see the real power of synergy at work: The whole is greater than the sum of the parts. Because information is quite possibly humanity's greatest resource, the Internet isn't a luxury item or a curiosity anymore—it's central to most people's computing lives.

With the rise of online music and video distribution, wild multimedia plug-ins, and teams of content producers swapping works-in-progress back and forth over the world's Internet backbones, BeOS and the Net have a natural affinity for one another. If you're like most people, one of the first things you're going to want to do after installing BeOS is check your email and hop on the Web.

The networking services built into BeOS cover the needs of all users, whether their needs involve just checking email a few times a day, hosting a small business Web server, or connecting to shared files on the company LAN. Since the needs and requirements of different users vary so widely, this book's coverage of BeOS networking is broken up into two sections. This chapter, will help you get connected to your Internet service provider (ISP) with BeOS's Dial-Up Networking, or to your organization's internal network through the BeOS Network preferences panel. We'll also cover usage of the Internet applications that come bundled with BeOS. Chapter 8, *Networking*, covers the more advanced aspects of networking.

# The BeOS Advantage

Let's go way, way back. In the beginning, there was nothing but swirling gases and dust. No … wait … not that far back. In the beginning there was the mainframe: a big old beast of a computer, occupy an entire room or more and operating at about $1/1000$ the speed of the desktop computer you're using now. Bulky harnesses containing wires leading to terminals and keyboards ran out its backside. The terminals were "dumb," containing no processing power of their own. All of the users in the organization shared the services rendered by the central CPU. Nobody had a hard disk to call their own, and when the mainframe went down, the organization just stopped working.

Fast forward to the mid-80s. Processors live on microchips, hard drives have shrunk to the size of paperback books, and organizations begin to replace all of those dumb terminals with desktop computers. There's still a central machine at the heart of the organization, but its responsibility has shifted primarily to the domain of hosting and serving up shared files, and employees no longer depend on it to get their work done. The hierarchical, "hub and spoke" model of the early mainframe universe has flattened out into more of a heterarchy (a heterarchy is a sort of "squashed hierarchy"), with power points distributed throughout the organization, rather than focusing on a central point.

Meanwhile, something even more exciting was gestating in the background. All of these independent networks began connecting, linking their resources together and sharing information via a meta-network—a network of networks called the Internet. For 20 years, this meta-network grew slowly, establishing protocols, extending its ganglia, linking everyone to everyone else. Every machine in every connected organization gained the potential ability to connect to every other machine. The flow of information was no longer bound by the "top-down" structure of the early networks.

The centralized topology of the mainframe days has given way to the distributed structure of the client/server days, which in turn has given way to the totally open model of the Internet, which has unleashed what is probably the computer industry's largest boom ever. It hasn't let up yet, and there's little sign that it will until the entire world is wired. The interesting thing to note here is that the power base has shifted three times: from the center of the wheel, to the rim, and finally into the spokes themselves. The network itself is where the action is now. As Sun's Scott McNealy is famed for saying, "The network *is* the computer."

Internet access is hardly considered a luxury by computer users anymore, and there aren't many people out there even interested in working with a machine that's *not* connected. In fact, millions of people a year are buying computers just so they can "get the Net." It goes without saying that built-in Internet services are as critical to operating systems now as, say, file management services.

Most operating systems existed long before the Internet became a fact of life, and have had to bolt on their Internet services as an afterthought. Be, however, had excellent timing—the Internet was becoming *de rigeur* just as the company was in the early stages of building BeOS. As a result, TCP/IP (Transfer Control Protocol/Internet Protocol, the networking standard that the Internet runs on) is a fundamental service in BeOS, integrated from the start, rather than as an afterthought.

But BeOS goes a step beyond that. Be knew that users would want to use their machines not only to view the Internet, but to be a part of it. They built in not only the tools you need to browse the Web, read and write email, and download files, but also those you need to host a Web site or FTP server, and even allow others to log in via telnet to run Terminal programs on your machine.

In addition, BeOS includes a number of technologies that give it a leg up on other systems as far as potential functionality for Web serving goes. BeOS attributes, which give the filesystem database-like characteristics, may soon enable enterprising developers to create database-backed Web sites without the need for third-party database tools. Furthermore, the BeOS messaging system in conjunction with the open scriptability of BeOS applications means that we may eventually see intelligent and flexible scripting solutions sitting behind Web sites running on BeOS—solutions that just wouldn't be possible on other platforms.

## *The Three-Minute Web Connection*

If you are intimately familiar with the process of configuring network settings for modems and network cards, feel comfortable entering DNS and IP addresses, and know your PPP from your POP, you may not need the bulk of this chapter. BeOS's settings panels are well-designed and intuitive, and you can probably get online in three minutes or less if you have your service provider's settings handy (or memorized). These steps should be all you need to get online fast—just enter your usual settings into the appropriate preferences panel, restart network services, and you're done; no reboot necessary!

 Throughout this book, the industry-standard abbreviation "DUN" refers to Dial-Up Networking.

### *If You Connect through an ISP*

1.  Open the Dial-Up Networking panel in your Preferences folder (accessible from the Be menu). In the Connect To… picklist, select New and enter a name for your connection, such as "ISP 1" or whatever you like.

2.  Enter the ISP's phone number, along with your username and password. Optionally, select the Save Password checkbox.

3.  Click the Settings… button and enter your DNS servers' addresses. If you've been assigned a static IP address, enter it; otherwise, leave it blank. If your ISP uses a nonstandard login method, select it from the Server Type picklist (most people won't need to do this). Click the Done button.

4.  Back in the main DUN preferences panel, select your modem, port, and speed from the picklists. Select the Pulse Dialing checkbox if you don't have touch-tone phone services. Click Done. When prompted to restart networking, click Restart.

5.  Click the Connect button to establish a connection. You can now use your Web browser and other Internet services normally (see *Email Settings*, below, for instructions on setting up email services). To disconnect, right-click the DUN icon in the Deskbar shelf and choose Disconnect.

If you're using BeOS R3, the descriptions and screenshots in this chapter won't match your computer because the BeOS networking interface changed radically between R3 and R4. You should, however, be able to map the techniques described here to the R3 interface without too much difficulty. In R3, all networking services are managed through a single Network preferences panel. In R4, network preferences are broken out into two separate panels: Dial-Up Networking, for use with modem-based connections; and Network preferences, for use with network interface cards and advanced services. Network services also became faster and more stable between R3 and R4. For this and many other reasons, upgrading to the latest version of BeOS is strongly recommended.

### If You Connect over a Local Network

1. Open the Network preferences panel. On the Identity tab, click Add… and use the Network Interface picklist to tell BeOS about any network interface cards (NICs) installed in your machine. If your organization uses DHCP services (Chapter 8, *Networking*), select the DHCP radio button. Otherwise, select Specify Settings and enter your IP address, subnet mask, and gateway. If you don't know what these things are, see Chapter 8 or ask your network administrator.

2. Click the Add button in this panel, and your card will now appear as an interface in the main Network preferences panel.

3. Enter a domain name, DNS server addresses, and a hostname (the name of your machine, which you can make up if one hasn't been assigned to you).

4. Click Restart Networking and test your connection with any Internet application. If you can't make a connection, see Chapter 8.

### Email Settings

In order to send and receive email, you'll need to enter a few details into the E-mail preferences panel.

1. Open the Email preferences application.

2. Enter the names of your POP and/or SMTP servers.

3. Enter your username and password.

4. Establish a mail-checking schedule.

5. Click Save.

6. In the Network preferences panel, make sure a hostname has been entered. If not, enter one and click Restart Networking.

If none of this makes sense to you or your connection is not happening, read on.

# Configuring Internet Services

Before you can browse the Web or check your email, you've got to tell BeOS how you want to connect. You have your choice of:

- A dial-up connection running through an internal or external modem (PPP).
- A permanent connection running through a NIC.
- A mixed environment using both hard-wired and PPP connections.

In most cases, if your BeOS machine is at home you'll be connecting via PPP, while most machines living in companies and organizations enjoy the convenience and speed of a permanent connection. However, with the rise of xDSL and cable modems, more and more people are able to enjoy permanent connections from home. However you slice it, you need a network interface of *some* kind. We'll cover dial-up services through the BeOS Dial-Up Networking (DUN) preferences panel first, followed by connecting via other interfaces.

 If you connect to the Internet through a cable modem or xDSL hookup, you've got too much bandwidth on your hands for a puny little serial port. Chances are great that your connection interfaces with your computer through a standard Ethernet card. Therefore, this isn't the chapter for you—non-PPP networking is covered in Chapter 8.

## Dial-Up Networking

To access the DUN configuration panel, pull down the Be menu from the Deskbar and scroll down to the preferences folder, then select Dial-Up Networking. You should see the DUN panel, as shown in Figure 4.01.

*Figure 4.01*

*The Dial-Up Networking configuration panel lets you set up a number to dial, enter a username and password, and configure details regarding your modem and connection preferences.*

**Dial-Up Networking**

Connect to: waxwing

Phone number: 15 1085900 10

User name: waxwing

Password: ******

X Save Password

Settings...

**Connection**
Connected at 115200 bps          00:20:32
Local IP address:          207.181.236.24

Modem...     Disconnect     Connect

**Add an ISP** You can set up connections for as many ISPs—or as many different user names and phone numbers at the same ISP—as you like. To begin, pull down the Connect To... picklist and select New. Enter an intuitive name for the connection. For example, if your ISP is called Online.Net and you sometimes need to use various dial-in phone numbers for them, you might call this one "Online 1". To add more ISPs or phone numbers in the future, just run through this process again.

Fill in the phone number, your username, and your password, and make sure the Save Password box is checked if you don't want to end up typing in your password every time you connect.

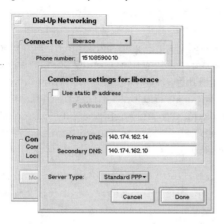

**Figure 4.02**

*Tell BeOS the addresses of your DNS servers, whether or not you'll be using a static IP address, and about the type of server you'll be logging into from the PPP Settings panel.*

**Settings**  Click the Settings button and you'll see a panel like the one in Figure 4.02.

Your IP address is your specific node, or address, on the Internet while you're connected. Most ISPs give you a different IP address every time you log in, so most people should leave the upper portion of this panel blank. Some users, however, are assigned an IP address all their own, which is the same every time they log in. This can be especially useful if you run any kind of server on your machine so you can tell the world where to find your machine on the Internet. If you have a static IP address, click the checkbox and enter it here.

 **Buy a Static Address**  While many ISPs don't advertise the service, most will be happy to sell or lease a static IP address if you want to run low-impact services that won't affect their bandwidth. Contact your service provider for rates and details.

Your ISP's DNSs perform the critical task of translating names like **www.be.com** into machine-readable IP addresses (see the sidebar *DNS Explained*). Your ISP, company, or school should have provided you with the IP address of its primary and secondary DNS servers, and you should enter them here. If you weren't supplied with a secondary DNS, don't worry about it—the second one is just a backup, and is not required.

 In addition to automatically assigning IP addresses during login, some ISPs also assign DNS addresses this way. As of BeOS R4.0, the DUN preferences panel does not include a mechanism for automatically obtaining DNS addresses, though you should see this feature added in the very near future, either as an addition to the DUN panel or as an add-on module. This feature may go by the name LCP (for Link Control Protocol) or something like "Server-assigned DNS" or "DHCP for PPP." Keep your eye on be.com for updates if this affects you.

The final section in the Connection Settings window is Server Type. If you're using standard PPP (which is the connection protocol used by the

## *DNS Explained*

Every computer attached to the Internet has an IP address, a user-unfriendly number like
207.152.25.127. This rule applies to everything from Web servers to your own machine when it's
dialed into your ISP. If something is on the Net, it's got an IP address. But when you connect to
**www.be.com**, you don't have to enter its IP address into your browser—you enter **www.be.com**. If
you've inferred that something out there is translating user-friendly domain names into machine-
friendly IP addresses, you're right. That something is called a domain name server (DNS), and
every ISP has one. A DNS intercepts your requests and looks them up in a massive database
called a domain table. It then sends your request to the appropriate IP address, which returns the
information you requested—such as a Web page—back to you. Without DNS services, you'd have
to memorize (or bookmark) the actual IP addresses. Yuck.

The process is actually somewhat more complex than this, involving a hierarchical system of
DNS table propagation and updates. The important thing to remember is that without a DNS
you won't have much fun online.

You've no doubt seen your browser return messages reading something like "DNS not found."
This means either that the domain you've typed in doesn't exist in the DNS tables on your server,
or that the server itself is down. Since DNS services are so critical, ISPs usually have at least two of
them, with one used for backup. In addition to the DNS services provided by your ISP, it's also possible to use publicly available DNS services, such as those maintained by another ISP, or a corporate or government institution. Not all DNSs can be used by the general public, however; some
deny access to users who aren't connected through the same domain. You may want to ask a
friend to tell you the address of the DNS they use, then test it through your own connection. If it
works, keep the address handy in case all of your ISP's DNS services ever go down.

vast majority of ISPs), you don't need to do anything here. Some ISPs,
however, use other, older protocols. The documentation from your service
provider should be very clear about this. If you have only a shell account,
choose Unix Login from this list.

**Establishing Custom Login Parameters**   In rare cases, ISPs require a
unique login sequence to accept a user's connection. The list of options in
the Server Types picklist in the DUN preferences panel is derived from the
file /boot/beos/etc/servers.ppp. If your ISP requires custom login parameters, just edit the login commands in this file and save. If you've added a new
login type to this file, close and re-open the DUN preferences panel, then
choose your new entry by name. The actual command sequence required
will be provided by your ISP. Note that you'll need to disable this file's write-
protection before you can make changes to it. (See Chapter 6, *The Terminal*,
for chmod instructions.)

**Login Scripts** In /boot/home/config/etc/, you'll find a file called ppp-script.sample. If you rename this file ppp-script, it will be run automatically every time you make a connection. What would you put in such a script? Let's say you want to launch your Web browser and email client every time you establish a connection. Open this file in a text editor and add lines like:

```
NetPositive &
/boot/apps/net/BeatWare/Mail-It &
```

to the end. Save the script, establish a connection, and these applications will be launched automatically, if they're not already.

You can also use this script to log custom connection details into the system's connection log. For example, if you add the line:

```
echo $2 $1 at $3 addr=$4 > ~/ppp-log
```

you'll end up with a line such as:

```
modem0 up at 901200125 addr=10.113.216.32
```

in your ppp-log. This technique may be useful when trying to troubleshoot connection difficulties.

Note that you may need to disable this file's write-protection in order to edit it. See Chapter 6 for chmod instructions.

**Pick a Modem**  Once you've established your settings, click the Modem button on the DUN configuration panel.

Click and hold on the picklist labeled "Your modem is:". The names of all major modem manufacturers will appear, and scrolling over their names will present a sublist of the major models made by that vendor. Pick the modem that most closely matches yours. If you don't find your modem on this list, or if you want to use a different initialization string for some reason, see the sidebar *Adding Modems Manually*. Note also that many of the modems in this list also offer "Generic" options, which may be useful if your modem is similar to but not identical to the modems offered in this list. Just choose the generic option most similar to your modem's actual model.

*Figure 4.03*

*The Modem panel lets you select a modem to be used with Dial-Up Networking, establish a communications port, and specify other connection details.*

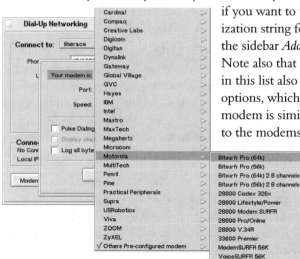

## *Adding Modems Manually*

Be has done a pretty good job of including support for the vast majority of modems out there. However, with the thousands of varieties manufactured over the years, it's impossible to include them all. But just because you don't find your modem on the Be-provided list doesn't mean that your modem won't work with BeOS—all you have to do is add your modem's initialization string to BeOS's modem database.

An "initialization string" is a series of commands that a computer sends to a modem to wake it up, tell it to dial, and establish the details of communication. If you still have the original documentation that came with your modem, it should contain your initialization string. If it doesn't, try the manufacturer's Web site. In most cases, companies post the initialization strings for all the modems they've ever made. If you're running BeOS on a machine that also runs another operating system, the string you need is already somewhere in your other operating system(s).

Once you've tracked down the string you need, open up a Terminal and type:

```
cd /boot/beos/etc
```

and then

```
ls -l modems.ppp
```

In the resulting file listing, notice that the permissions listing to the far left says `-r--r--r--`. That means that this file is marked "read only." In order to edit it, you need give yourself write permissions. Type:

```
chmod 666 modems.ppp
```

Now open up /boot/beos/etc/modems.ppp in StyledEdit. Scroll to the point in the file where your modem should be alphabetically and add its name, followed by its initialization string. Be sure to exactly duplicate the format of the other modems listed there, with underscores taking the place of spaces. Save and close the file, then return to the Terminal and reset its permission status:

```
chmod 444 modems.ppp
```

(You can learn more about chmod and file permissions in Chapter 6.)

This book goes to great pains to emphasize the fact that you should never, ever tamper with any file living anywhere under the /boot/beos hierarchy. This is the sacrosanct user-level/system-level distinction outlined in Chapter 5, *Files and the Tracker*. Consider this case a rare exception to the rule. Theoretically, you should find a user-level version of this file in /boot/home/config/etc, to which you can add your own modifications. Unfortunately, such a file does not exist (and will not be recognized) in BeOS R4.0. If you're reading this after R5 has been released, substitute the path /boot/home/config/etc in the instructions above.

Return to the DUN configuration panel. If it's already open, close and reopen it. Your modem will now show up on the list of available modems and you'll be on your way. There is no technical reason that BeOS wouldn't be able to support a particular modem. If yours is missing, it only means there hasn't been a lot of call for it. After you add your modem's initialization string and confirm that it's working, email the string to **devsupport@be.com** and it'll probably appear in the next BeOS release.

***Don't Use "Virtual" Modems*** There are a few modems on the market that aren't really modems at all, including the GeoPort modem for Macs and the WinModem for Windows. Rather than actual communications chips, these modems simply supply a physical telephone jack and some software. The software emulates the functions of a modem in the operating system, using your computer's CPU. Not only do these modems soak up some of the processing power you could put to better use cracking RC5DES blocks (Chapter 15, *Other Goodies*) or rendering 3D graphics (Chapter 13, *Graphics Applications*), but they depend on the presence of software written expressly for the host operating system. Since no such software yet exists for BeOS, they won't work. Virtual modems are basically just a bad idea and are generally unsuitable for use in multi-boot environments.

 ***The Universal Support String*** Most modems include some kind of flash ROM (programmable memory), which can store a variety of useful and essential data. The documentation that came with your modem should describe how to store initialization strings in the modem itself by sending commands to it from a terminal program such as BeOS's own SerialConnect program (Chapter 8). Once a modem has been programmed in this way, it can be woken up by sending it the ATZ command. In BeOS's Modems picklist, choose Others | Preconfigured Modem, which is just a friendly name for ATZ. Thanks to this option, just about any modem under the sun can be made to work with BeOS.

This option is especially important to those of you with ISDN terminal adapters (TAs) because these "modems" need to be programmed with other parameters besides the initialization string, such as the switch type to which they're connecting. The easiest way to use an ISDN TA under BeOS is to configure it normally under another operating system with the manufacturer's software, then just use it as a "Preconfigured Modem" under BeOS.

**Pick a Port** Next you need to tell BeOS where to find your modem. Mac users will have the option of Modem or Printer ports, while x86 users can choose between serial ports. If you're using an external modem, you can easily see (or may already know) to which port your modem is attached. If you can't tell by looking, you've got a 50% chance of guessing correctly the first time (assuming you have two serial ports on the back of your computer, as most—but not all—do).

If you have an internal modem, it should be residing on either COM3 or COM4 (BeOS does not support modems on COM1 or COM2). If you don't know, you can boot into another OS on the same machine and check its dialer settings, then return here. If your card is jumpered, you can open up the case and look for yourself to see which COM port the modem is set to.

Serial ports are physical, but COM ports are virtual. In general, computers treat COM1 and COM3 the same as Serial1, and COM2 and COM4 as Serial2. Thus, if your modem is set to COM3 or COM4 and BeOS only gives you Serial1 or 2 as options, just choose the serial port that maps accordingly—COM3 users should choose Serial1, while COM4 users should choose Serial2. Who said the x86 architecture isn't intuitive?

**Pick a Speed** In the Modems panel, choose the entry on this list that's just higher than your modem's highest throughput capability. For instance, if you have a 28.8 modem, pick 38,400. If you have a 56K modem, pick 57,600. If you have an ISDN terminal adapter, pick 115,200. Why not just pick the highest speed and let the modem do any necessary throttling, or speed management, in hardware? According one of Be's network engineers, you'll actually waste CPU cycles by choosing a speed higher than necessary. Probably not many, but waste not want not. If you later find that you have difficulty establishing or maintaining a connection, it may mean that your modem is incapable of performing its own throttling. If this happens to you, return to this dialog and try a slower speed (or get a better modem).

**Other Options** In the lower section of the Modems panel, you'll find three checkboxes. Select "Pulse dialing" if you don't have touch-tone services. If your ISP requires you to manually type in a username and password during the connection process (rather than using standard PPP or a connection script as described later in this chapter), select "Display chat when connecting." If you'd like to save a log of the communications sent between your computer and the remote modem during the connection process, select "Log all bytes received." This option may be useful if you have persistent difficulties trying to make a connection—you can share this log with Be customer support or with your ISP for troubleshooting purposes. Since this log isn't quite human-readable, you probably won't find it very interesting reading. (See Chapter 16, *Troubleshooting and Maintenance*, for more information.)

If all goes well (and there's no reason it shouldn't), you'll be able jump online after establishing the basic PPP settings in this section. In order to send and receive email, however, you'll need to skip forward in this chapter to tell BeOS about a few email-specific settings.

**Making the Connection** Once everything has been configured properly and you've clicked "Restart Networking" when prompted after entering your last settings, you'll be able to connect to the Internet in one of two ways. If you're using BeOS R4.0, you'll need to manually establish your connections, either by clicking the Connect button on the front of the DUN preferences panel, or by right-clicking (Mac users: Ctrl+click) the DUN Replicant that should now be in your Deskbar shelf (see Figure 4.04).

*Figure 4.04*

Internet connectivity
can be controlled
and monitored via
the DUN Replicant in
your Deskbar. Its
icon changes to
reflect current status:
online, offline, or
transferring data.

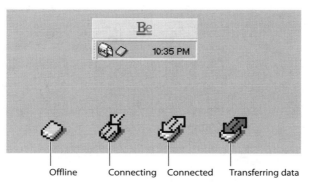

Offline          Connecting   Connected    Transferring data

You can instantly access all of your DUN preferences and alternate ISP configurations by double-clicking the Replicant. If you just want to connect or disconnect quickly, right-click the DUN icon and choose Connect or Disconnect from the context menu.

*Figure 4.05*

Right-click the Dial-Up Networking Replicant in your Deskbar's shelf
and you'll see a pop-up context menu like the one shown here. All
configured ISPs are shown at the bottom of the list, while the
currently selected "default" connection has a checkmark by its name.

 **Command-Line Control** If you're a command-line junkie, you'll be pleased
to learn that BeOS ships with a small tool you can use from the Terminal
to quickly bring your default connection online, or to disconnect. Just type
`dun-control --up` **or** `dun-control --down` **to go online or offline in a flash …
no mouse required.**

As of BeOS R4.1, you don't need to connect manually before accessing Internet services on your machine. Just use your favorite TCP/IP application—such as a Web browser, email client, or ping request—and your default connection will be launched automatically.

**Status Report** Anytime you're online (which is always, for those of you with permanent connections), you can get a mini-report on the status of

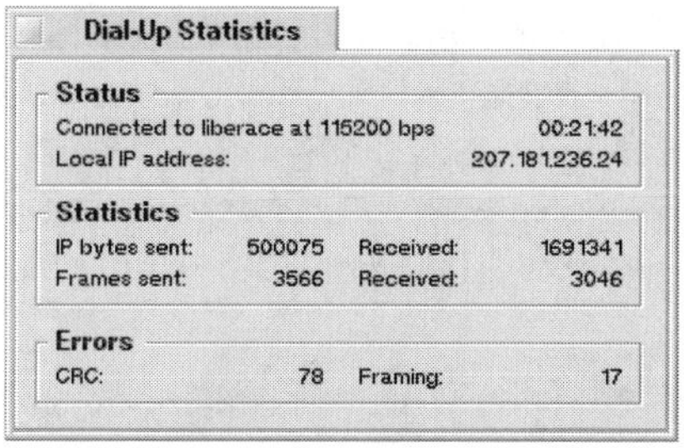

*Figure 4.06*

Choose Dial-Up
Statistics from the
DUN Replicant's
context menu to get
a status report
similar to this one.

your connection by right-clicking the DUN Replicant and choosing Dial-Up Statistics from the context menu. You'll see a panel similar to the one in Figure 4.06.

From here you can find out your current IP address (which will be different each time for most ISP users), which can be useful if you want to run a server of some kind from your machine. This panel will also tell you the maximum negotiation speed between your computer and your modem, the total number of bytes sent and received during this session, and the number of error corrections that have been negotiated between your computer and the host computer (or between modems).

This last bit of information can be useful if you suspect you're getting "noisy" connections when dialing into a particular modem bank or point of presence (POP). Try dialing into alternate POPs and then sending or receiving the same large files—one large text file and one large binary. If possible, always use the POP that results in the lowest number of errors in order to optimize your throughput. Note, however, that conditions on the POTS network (plain old telephone service) can vary from day to day and from moment to moment. If you want a reasonably accurate measurement, you'll have to do a good bit of testing. You may also want to try this test with various modems in your computer.

## *About Framing*

In the Dial-Up Statistics panel, you'll see one entry labeled "Frames Sent" and one in the errors section labeled "Framing." These refer to the status of groups of bits being transferred in the computer-to-modem communications link. Frames are used internally to designate where one group of bits leaves off and the next one begins.

 *Straight from the Horse's Mouth* **If you have any difficulty making a PPP connection with BeOS and aren't able to get it going after reading this chapter, use another operating system or another machine to check out Be's PPP Troubleshooting Guide at www.be.com/support/guides/ppp.html.**

## *About CHAP and PAP*

While most Internet service providers log their users in via the industry-standard PPP protocol, there are two different login procedures possible under PPP: CHAP and PAP. Of the two, PAP is by far the more common. With PAP, you have a password that's the same from one login to the next, and the server keeps that password in a secret database. However, a few servers out there prefer to use the advanced security options of CHAP (Challenge Handshake Authentication Protocol). With CHAP, the user's password is regenerated with every connection and is not completely established until the login procedure is complete. The cost of this advanced security is increased complexity. BeOS R4.0 did not support CHAP, and R4.1 probably will not either, though you should see CHAP support in R5.

It may also be possible to talk your service provider into letting you log in via the more standard PAP protocol—it can't hurt to ask!

# Network Interface Cards

While detailed coverage of installing and configuring network interface cards can be found in Chapter 8, we'll breeze over the basics here in case you only need to configure your machine to work on your organization's internal network.

The Network preferences panel includes two major sections: Identity and Services. Since the Identity tab is about establishing who you are, where you are on the network, and what kind of card is installed in your machine, we'll cover only that section of the panel here. Network Services are covered in Chapter 8.

**Figure 4.07**

The Network preferences panel consists of two sections: Identity and Services. The Identity section lets you specify your host name and DNS addresses, then pick and configure an NIC.

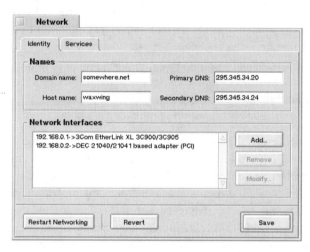

**Names**  If your local network uses a domain (such as **be.com**), enter it into the Domain name field. Do not prefix the domain with "www" or any other machine name—just enter the domain itself. If you are not part of a domain, leave this field blank.

In the Host name field, enter the name by which you want your machine to be identified on your local network. Entering "waxwing" as a hostname with **be.com** as the domain would make your machine **waxwing.be.com**, and if you ran a Web server from your machine, others in your organization would be able to access it as **http://waxwing/**.

 *Always Enter a Host Name*  Even if you're not working on a local network, it's important to enter a hostname here—if you don't, any BeMail messages you create will be queued for delivery, but never sent. This one is important.

Enter your DNS address or addresses into the DNS fields as described earlier in this chapter.

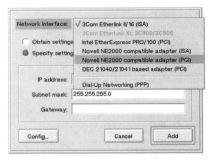

**Figure 4.08**

Select your network card from the picklist at the top of the Add… panel in Network preferences.

**Network Interfaces** If you've got a "nailed down" connection to the Internet or a local area network (LAN) that runs through a network card, click Add in the Network Interfaces section. You'll see a panel like the one in Figure 4.08.

In the picklist at the top of this panel, select your card (one will appear for every NIC driver found on your machine). If your organization assigns IP addresses dynamically via DHCP (Dynamic Host Configuration Protocol), make sure the DHCP radio button is selected. If you want to use a specific address, select Specify Settings and enter them in the fields provided. If you don't know what addresses to enter here, the easiest way to get them may be to copy them from the networking preferences dialog in another operating system running on the same machine. In most cases, you'll want to leave the Subnet mask set to 255.255.255.0. Otherwise, ask your network administrator, or see Chapter 8.

While many (if not most) network cards "just work" in BeOS when an appropriate driver is present, in some cases you may need to manually specify the port, IRQ, and memory address of the card you're using. If BeOS tells you that "A network device failed to initialize" when you try to restart networking later on, it means either that the card you've got installed is not supported by the selected driver, or that the settings are incorrect. You can try other port and IRQ combinations if you like by clicking Config again and changing settings, or see Chapter 8 for more details. If you're able to restart networking without receiving an error message, your card has been properly identified by BeOS.

 If your card is set to use the Plug-and-Play protocol, the Config panel for that card will not let you change any settings. These settings can only be configured manually in BeOS if the card itself is configurable.

## Supported Network Cards

While Be has done a good job of building in support for the most popular network cards, not every network card in existence works with BeOS. Just because BeOS installed properly, it doesn't necessarily mean that all of your hardware is automatically supported (BeOS simply ignores any hardware for which it can't find drivers). If your card doesn't show up in the picklist, read the hardware compatibility pages on Be's Web site and check BeWare for drivers that may have been released since your version of BeOS was released.

## Restart Networking

If you've ever had the pleasure of fiddling around with networking services in other operating systems, you know the pleasure of rebooting your computer about a kajillion times trying to get everything set up right. While most operating systems will let you create or edit dial-up TCP/IP settings without restarting, few will let you change low-level TCP/IP settings (those that are "bound" to a device, such as settings associated with a NIC) without rebooting. Some versions of the MacOS are exceptions to the rule, but all versions of Windows, for example, require a reboot after making changes like this. And of course, most OSs

**Figure 4.09**

*Unlike most operating systems, BeOS doesn't make you reboot your machine every time you tweak your network settings. Just click the Restart Networking button and you're on your way. This is as true for changing NIC addresses and settings as it is for simpler things like changing ISP configurations.*

take 60–120 seconds to boot to readiness; that's a lot of wasted time and needless frustration. It's a perfect example of the kind of legacy baggage that BeOS sidesteps so neatly. Because BeOS uses dynamically loadable device drivers and a system of servers independent of the operating system kernel, restarting network services is a simple matter of killing and restarting the network_server, a process which takes all of a few seconds.

## Network Setup on a Mac
*by Henry Bortman*

Like PC users, Mac users can choose between networked (Ethernet) and dial-up (PPP) connections.

### Networked Connections

Most Power Macintoshes and Mac clones supported by BeOS shipped with built-in 10Base-T Ethernet. If your system has built-in Ethernet, you'll want to choose "PowerMac On-board Networking" from the interfaces list. If your system doesn't have built-in Ethernet, but you have installed a third-party 10Base-T Ethernet card, you'll probably want to choose "DEC 21040/21041 based adapter (PCI)," which is a rather cryptic way of referring to the Ethernet chipset used in nearly all of the popular third-party Mac Ethernet cards, including those from Asante and Farallon. Note that BeOS/PowerPC supports only 10 Mbps Ethernet, not 100 Mbps.

### Dial-Up Connections

If you want to make a dial-up connection to the Internet, launch the Dial-Up Networking panel from your preferences folder and establish a name for your connection, filling in your username and password and the phone number you want to dial into, as described earlier in this chapter. Rather than specifying serial ports by number, however, you'll need to choose "printer" or "modem" from the Port pop-up to indicate which of your Mac's serial ports your modem is connected to. The list of modem supported by Be includes a range of models from the most popular vendors of Mac modems, including Global Village (Teleport), Diamond Multimedia (SupraExpress), Zoom, Best Data, and 3Com (U.S. Robotics). BeOS does not support software-based modems of any kind; this includes the popular GeoPort modem.

**All Set**   That's it! If everything here has gone well, your system is now set up to invoke dial-up connections or use its network card to speak TCP/IP. There's just one more step: the icing on the cake—click the Restart Networking button to reinitialize your network settings, and you'll be on your way. What's so great about that? See the sidebar *Restart Networking* and you'll understand. While your system is now ready to access the Internet in general, using email will require a few tweaks to the E-mail preferences panel.

   The Services component of Network preferences—where you can establish multiple network configurations and run BeOS's built-in servers—is covered in Chapter 8.

# Email

Strictly speaking, email settings aren't part of your system's networking configuration. Nevertheless, BeOS lets you register them in a central location, so that all email applications (including BeMail, the mail client bundled with BeOS) can use the same settings. Pull down the Be menu and scroll to Preferences, then choose the E-mail icon.

## Configuring Email Preferences

The fields in the E-mail preferences panel look much like similar fields you'll find in other email clients such as Eudora, Outlook, Pegasus Mail, or Claris Emailer.

*Figure 4.10*

*If you've ever config-ured the settings in Eudora or Claris Emailer, most of these settings will be familiar to you. How-ever, BeOS's E-mail preferences panel also lets you set up a custom mail-checking schedule and optionally launch a separate mail status window.*

**Account Information**   Your ISP probably maintains two separate mail-handling servers: one for storing your mail (the POP server) and one for sending outgoing mail (the SMTP server).

Type the username you use to check your mail into the topmost field, followed by your password. The POP Host is the name of the server itself. If you don't have this memorized, you can either copy it from a Windows or Mac email program, look for the documentation your ISP supplied when you first signed on, or look it up on their site.

The SMTP (Simple Mail Transfer Protocol) server is the one you use to transfer outgoing mail. Most of the time, this will be `smtp.yourserver.com`. However, there are times when you'll want to use an SMTP server not run by your ISP (see the sidebar *The SMTP Dilemma*).

**Guess Your Server Names**  The majority of service providers (though by no means all) give the machines on their own domains standard names. For example, a provider on the domain `whatis.net` may very likely run these machines:

```
telnet.whatis.net
news.whatis.net
pop.whatis.net (or mail.whatis.net)
smtp.whatis.net
```

and so on. When filling in fields like the ones in the BeOS E-mail preferences panel, you usually stand a pretty good chance of guessing the names of your mail servers, if you don't want to go hunting around for the documentation.

## The SMTP Dilemma

Thanks to the rise of spam, many ISPs have cracked down on the free use of their SMTP servers. Once upon a time, you could pretty much use any SMTP server, whether it was your own ISP's or someone else's. However, this flexibility made it very easy for spammers to hijack other providers' servers to send unsolicited messages to unsuspecting netizens. As a result, many ISPs now require you to be directly connected to the server hosting the SMTP service. The downside to this is that if you are, for instance, checking your personal email from the LAN at work, your ISP won't recognize you as a customer because you'll have an alien IP address. You'll be able to check your mail, but you won't be able to send. In this case, you might have to use your company's SMTP server to handle your outgoing mail. Separating incoming from outgoing mail functions gives ISPs an important measure of protection against potential abusers.

**User Settings**  Real name is the name that will appear as the sender of each message, and Reply to is the address to which messages will be sent when people respond to your mail. This is especially handy if you use multiple machines but want all of your mail to be routed to the same address.

If you fill in the Default domain field, you'll be able to send mail to users on that domain by addressing messages to just their usernames. For example, let's say you write to a lot of people at **whatis.net**. If you enter **whatis.net** in this field, you'll be able to send messages to **simon@whatis.net** by addressing them simply as **simon**.

**Mail Schedule** The right side of the E-mail preferences panel includes options for scheduled mail checking, which should be pretty self-explanatory. Use the drop-down lists to configure your system to check for new mail at regularly scheduled intervals, from continuously to never (and everything in between). Keep in mind that if you use a dial-up account and aren't permanently connected to a network, mail scheduling will cause the PPP dialer to pop up when you don't necessarily want it to. Note that automatic mail checking can have a detrimental effect on your personal productivity.

In the Unix world, automatic mail checking is often accomplished with a command-line utility called biff. According to legend, the original programmer had a dog named Biff who barked whenever someone came to the door. By extension, email schedules such as this one are sometimes called "biff schedules." While BeOS doesn't explicitly refer to this functionality as "biffing," you may occasionally hear it referred to this way. The terminology has probably stuck around just because it's so fun to say. Biff. Biff. Biff. Biff. Biff.

*Figure 4.11*

*Keeping the mail status window turned on not only gives you easy access to one-click mail checking, but also displays a progress indicator showing the status of message transfers.*

**Mail Notification** The Mail Notification options let you specify what should happen when you check for new mail. If you check Show Status Window, a progress indicator will appear any time messages are being sent or received. This window will tell you how many messages are being transferred or how far you've made it through the transfer of a large attachment. The status window will also let you know how many messages are being downloaded or sent and how many unread messages are on your system. The status window also provides a Check Now button you can use to check your mail at any time.

If you'd rather not have a status window taking up screen real estate, you don't have to enable this option—if you select the "Autolaunch mail_daemon" option, you'll be able to check for new messages by right-clicking the mailbox Replicant in your Deskbar's shelf.

You can also tell BeOS whether or not it should launch the mail_daemon automatically at startup. If you've decided not to use BeMail and to work exclusively with a third-party email client instead, you may want to deselect this option—though you'll probably still find it useful to be able to fire off quick messages with a click on the Deskbar, so I recommend leaving this option checked regardless.

Select the "Beep when new mail arrives" checkbox if you want audible alerts to let you know when new mail has arrived (and don't worry—it doesn't talk, it just beeps).

***Don't Skip the Hostname***  It's important that you remember to include something in the Hostname field of the Network preferences panel; otherwise your mail will never be sent, no matter what you do in the E-mail preferences panel. It doesn't matter what you enter—your login name will work great—as long as it's not blank. Why is this? Because when the `mail_daemon` connects to your SMTP (outgoing) mail server, it needs to identify itself—there's no way to send mail out to the Internet without a host identification. So why don't you have to do this in MacOS or Windows? Because those systems fake it on your behalf, using your IP address or another unique identifier as a hostname. That's fine—it doesn't really matter, but Be likes to do things *the right way*, and letting you control this parameter is the right thing to do.

Once preferences have been set, click the Save button to commit your settings.

*C'est tout!* Those are all the system-wide settings you could possibly need to browse the Web, download files, and read and write email. Let's dig into BeOS's bundled Internet applications and tools.

 Any time your computer is connected to the Internet (on any operating system), you are potentially vulnerable to intrusions by malicious hackers and crackers. You'll find a short list of Internet security suggestions in Chapter 8.

# Bundled Internet Apps

BeOS comes bundled with two graphical Internet applications (a Web browser and an email client) and a handful of common command-line tools.

## NetPositive

NetPositive (a.k.a. "Net+") may not be loaded down with all the bells and whistles you're accustomed to using in Netscape Navigator or Internet Explorer, but it still has some pretty cool things going for it … starting with raw speed. Chances are you've never used a browser this fast in your life. NetPositive launches in well under one second on most machines, pulls pages and images out of its cache like lightning, and starts rendering most pages almost immediately.

 To head objections off at the pass, it's true that Internet Explorer launches in under one second on most Windows machines as well. But there's a critical difference: Explorer is part of the operating system, so all of its code is preloaded. Launching Internet Explorer is just a matter of opening a window. Not so for NetPositive—it's a complete application, not preloaded by the operating system in any way, and it really *does* launch in under a second!

## NetPositive's Secret Past

Once upon a time, when BeOS was still under construction and available only to developers, Be cobbled together a browser called Orb so that programmers could at least read documentation in HTML format. Orb had a cool name and a cool icon, but beyond that it was nothing to write home about. As BeOS headed closer to public release, a better browser was needed. Work on Orb picked up again eventually becoming the NetPositive you know and love today. You can read a little more about Orb at **www.be.com/users/iconworld/icon12.html**.

### Table 4.01 NetPositive Hotkeys

| Hotkey | Action |
| --- | --- |
| Alt+N | Open new browser window |
| Alt+L | Open location (type a URL) |
| Alt+H | Go home |
| Alt+I | Load images |
| Alt+B | Bookmark current page |
| Alt+Shift+H | View HTML |
| Alt+R | Reload page |
| Alt+Left Arrow | Go back |
| Alt+Right Arrow | Go forward |
| Spacebar | Page down |

*NetPositive has a good collection of hotkeys to help you minimize mouse usage.*

NetPositive's basic interface needs no explanation—it works pretty much like every browser you've ever used. You'll find your familiar Back, Forward, Reload, Stop, and Home buttons, plus a location field (URL window) for typing addresses. Even the hotkeys will be familiar to most users (see Table 4.01).

**Hotkeys** While all of NetPositive's hotkeys are plainly marked in its menus, you may find the quick reference chart in Table 4.01 useful.

Of course, NetPositive also supports the full range of standard BeOS hotkeys for Cut, Copy, Paste, Select All, Print, Close, and Quit (see Appendix B).

**Figure 4.12**

*NetPositive's toolbar includes the usual collection of controls.*

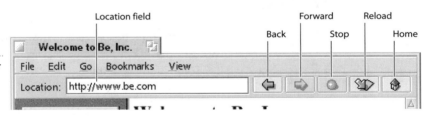

Rather than dwell on the obvious, let's dig into NetPositive's preferences and options, and then check out some of the cool things you can do with NetPositive bookmarks that you can't do on other operating systems. To access NetPositive's Preferences panel, pull down Edit | Preferences and you'll be looking at a five-tabbed panel similar to the one in Figure 4.13. These tabs are covered in the following sections.

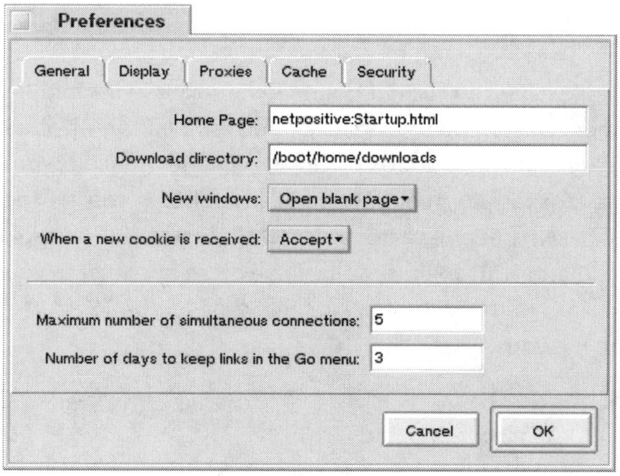

*Figure 4.13*

*NetPositive's Preferences panel is subdivided into five major sections.*

**General**  The default NetPositive home page, which is actually built into the browser itself, is loaded with links to BeOS resources, both on your hard drive and on the Web. If there's another Web page on your system or elsewhere that you'd like to start with, paste its URL into the Home Page field. If you want to use a page living on your own hard drive, the easiest way is to double-click its icon and copy its location from NetPositive to this field.

The Download directory field isn't filled in by default, so if you enter a path here, your downloads will be automatic: Click on a link to a zip file or other binary and it will start streaming straight into your chosen download directory—no navigating file panels or clicking confirmation dialogs necessary. If you also set Expander (Chapter 2, *Meet the System*) to decompress files for you automatically, the entire process will be hands-free, start to finish.

Since opinions differ over what exactly should happen when you open a new browser window, NetPositive gives you the choice. If you'd like Alt+N to create an exact copy of the current Web page in a new window, choose the "Clone current window" option. If you'd rather have new browser windows launch with your home page preloaded, choose door #2. If you'd prefer to launch blank browser windows this way, pick door #3.

If you have privacy issues with Internet cookies, use the Cookies drop-down box to tell NetPositive whether to reject them categorically, to warn you first, or to accept them unconditionally. Cookies have become so prevalent, however, that the warning option will cause your patience to wear thin quickly on some sites—you could end up clicking confirmation boxes as often as hyperlinks, depending on where you surf.

NetPositive, true to its heritage, is heavily multithreaded. This lets you keep lots of browser windows open simultaneously, each of them downloading separate pages if necessary. Unfortunately, all the speed in NetPositive and BeOS

## Error Message Haiku

How many times in your life have you clicked boring OK buttons in boring dialog boxes feeding you boring messages about busted DNS whatsits and 404 something-or-others? Hang around with NetPositive for a while and your outlook on error messages may be permanently affected. If you're familiar with the Japanese form of poetry known as haiku, you'll recognize the 5-7-5 syllabic structure in most of NetPositive's error messages. These haiku started appearing in beta versions of NetPositive 2.0, and with any luck will still be there by the time you read this. These dialogs are a perfect example of the kind of personality that sets BeOS apart—other operating systems don't dare to be hilarious.

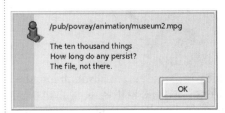

**Figure 4.14**

Better than any 404

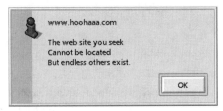

**Figure 4.15**

The Tao of the Web

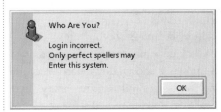

**Figure 4.16**

Can't get into a secure site? The problem could be a typo on your part.

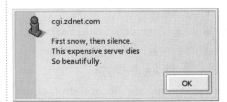

**Figure 4.18**

Brings tears to the eyes.

**Figure 4.17**

How many clicks in the About box does it take to get to the Easter egg that doesn't exist?

**Figure 4.19**

OK, so this one is a little annoying. Rumor has it, this message arose from an inside joke at Be HQ.

combined can't help you if you get stuck with a slow Internet connection and a Web site with a ton of graphics. If you limit the number of simultaneous connections under low-bandwidth conditions, your pages won't get all choked up by limited resources spread across tons of connections (remember that every image or other element on a Web page requires a separate connection).

Finally, you can control the number of days' worth of surfing history logged in NetPositive's Go menu. If you visit hundreds of sites per day, you may not want to store more than a couple of days' worth of history, just so you can navigate the menu easily when necessary.

*Figure 4.20*

*Control every aspect of the way HTML documents are rendered in NetPositive from the Display preferences tab.*

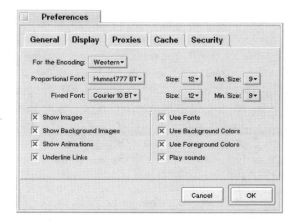

**Display** Preferences relating to the visual appearance of Web pages in NetPositive can be controlled from the Display tab.

The proportional font option refers to the font NetPositive should use anytime:

- The Web page designer did not specify a font for the page, or
- They did, but neither that font nor any of the specified alternates were found on your system, or
- The Web designer hasn't called for a monospaced font by using <PRE> or <TT> tags.

In other words, this is the font you'll be seeing most of the time. Personally, I find that Humnst Regular, which ships with every copy of BeOS, makes for an exceptionally clear Web font that can be read for hours without fatigue.

 **Common Web Fonts for Free** Web browsers have been font-savvy for several years now, and Web designers now specify fonts on their pages with some regularity. For better or for worse, it's a Windows world out there, meaning fonts like Arial, Verdana, and Trebuchet are being invoked regularly. If you don't already have these fonts on your system, Microsoft offers them free for the download, and it's worth it to be able to see pages as their designers intended. Before you squinch up your nose at the prospect, you should know that Microsoft's free TrueType Web fonts were designed by master fontographer Matthew Carter specifically for onscreen use (rather than for paper). These fonts can be downloaded from `www.microsoft.com/typography/fontpack/`, but you'll need to take care to grab the Windows 3.1 version, since the 95/NT version uses a Windows installer, whereas the 3.1 version is just a `.zip` file disguised as an `.exe`. You can unzip the font executable from the Terminal (or see *Expanding Expander's Horizons* in Chapter 2). Note that you'll also get monotype.com, which makes for an excellent Terminal font, in the MS font pack.

*Change Your Font Mappings* Not only can you download and install common TrueType fonts for use in NetPositive but you can also tell NetPositive to use "closest fit" fonts, translating from the designer-specified font to the most similar font in BeOS. For example, BeOS doesn't ship with the common Windows font Lucida Console, but it does ship with the similar Swis721. To see how this translation table is working on your system, use the Tracker to open up `/boot/home/config/settings/NetPositive/FontMappings`, then pull down the Attributes menu and select Original Font and Maps to from the submenu. Drag these two columns all the way to the left of your Tracker window for optimal viewing.

If you'd like to make changes to these mappings, just edit the attributes themselves (see Chapter 5). If you want to add new translations, duplicate one of the existing files and edit that.

Conveniently, you can specify minimum sizes for both your proportional and nonproportional fonts so you won't go blind on pages where designers have carelessly specified tiny fonts. The rest of the options on this tab are self-explanatory, letting you selectively enable or disable images, background images, animations, underlining, font specifications, colors, and sounds.

*Figure 4.21*

*Open the folder /boot/home/config/settings/
NetPositive/FontMappings in the Tracker and
adjust the Attributes menu to show these
columns. You can then control how NetPositive
translates common Web fonts into common
BeOS fonts.*

## *Displaying Non-English Web Sites*

If you read a non-English alphabet such as Japanese, you can take advantage of the Unicode system built into BeOS in conjunction with fonts specific to your language. There are two steps to enabling support for non-English pages in NetPositive.

First of all, you must have a font or set of fonts installed on your system that supports the character set of the language you want to use. Chances are, if you need non-English support, you already own or know where to get such fonts. In NetPositive's Display preferences panel, use the Encoding picklist to select Japanese, Cyrillic, Greek, or another character set, then tell NetPositive which fonts to use when visiting pages written in those character sets. Note that this option doesn't tell the browser to start displaying pages in those languages immediately—it just establishes preferences that will go into effect when those encodings are enabled.

To actually enable an alternate encoding, use the View | Document Encoding menu to toggle to an alternate encoding. See Chapter 9, *Preferences and Customization,* for a demonstration of using NetPositive with sites written in Japanese.

**Proxies**  If your BeOS machine borrows its connectivity from another machine on your local network (in other words, doesn't have a modem or direct connection of its own), you'll need to tell NetPositive the hostnames of the Web and FTP proxy servers (along with their port numbers). Your network administrator will have these details if you don't know them already.

**Cache**  As you visit Web pages, NetPositive stores copies of cached files (and their images) in a special directory in your settings folder. When you return to a page later, any content that hasn't changed can be read from your hard disk rather than over the Internet. The result is much faster performance for frequently visited sites. If you almost never visit the same sites twice, no amount of browser cache will do you any good. But because most of us at least read all of the BeOS-related news sites daily, it makes sense to keep at least a 10MB cache going (older cached files are pushed out so that newer ones can take their places). If you're low on drive space but have a free partition elsewhere, you may want to store your cache on another partition, though you probably don't need to worry about this.

The most important option on this tab is the Refresh cached pages picklist, which lets you choose once per session, once per day, every time you access each page, or never. In other words, you get to tell NetPositive whether to pull pages out of the cache automatically (for optimum performance), or if it should compare their creation datestamps and sizes against files on the live server to determine whether there might be fresher content on the server than in your cache. Of course, you can always click NetPositive's Reload button when you're in doubt; this option restores the browser's automatic

## *Accessing Super-Secret Settings*

With all of these preferences and settings options, you'd think that was the extent of NetPositive's settings. Not so, grasshopper—but you'll have to dig in pretty deep to tweak the settings not provided on the surface. NetPositive stores all of its settings in the file /boot/home/config/settings/NetPositive/settings. But before you go trying to open this file in a text editor, don't bother—it's a zero-byte file, and everything it stores lives in that file's attributes. Thus, changing settings beyond the ones provided in the GUI means you'll need to find some way of changing these attribute values.

There are two ways to do this using BeOS's bundled tools. You can either 1) remove attributes with the rmattr command and then restore them with the addattr command (as described in Chapter 5), or 2) use the attribute editor built into the DiskProbe application (Chapter 2). You would do well to read those sections before attempting this trick. And just to be safe, always make a backup copy of any settings file before you attempt to edit it.

### *The Terminal Method*

To see all the settings stored in this file, open a Terminal window, change directories to /boot/home/config/settings/NetPositive, and type listattr settings | more. You'll see a very long list of attributes. To see the current value of any of these attributes, type catattr AttributeName settings, replacing AttributeName with the real name of the attribute. Most of the values in these attributes are stored as Boolean 1s (for "on") or 0s (for "off"), or as arbitrary digits. As an example, let's turn off the haiku error messages described earlier in this chapter, to see standard error messages instead. Type these two lines:

```
rmattr HaikuErrorMessages settings
addattr -t bool HaikuErrorMessages settings
```

It's important to specify the datatype of the attribute correctly—since the listattr command told us that this attribute's value was Boolean, we need to specify the same when adding the attribute back in. This is what the -t bool part of the second command does. NetPositive will now display bland, corporate error messages, rather than the groovy haiku versions.

### *The GUI Method*

You can also use DiskProbe to change settings in NetPositive. (As noted in Chapter 2, DiskProbe can be dangerous to your system if used improperly—never use it to change anything you don't understand intimately.) Drag NetPositive's settings file onto DiskProbe's icon. Pull down the Attributes menu and you'll see a long menu containing all of the same entries you saw with the listattr command above. Select one of them to bring it up in a small edit window and change it to another value. Close DiskProbe, relaunch NetPositive, and your changes will have taken hold.

If anything goes wrong in your experiments, just delete the settings file and rename the backup you made back to settings—you'll be right back where you were before you began.

behavior. In general, the sites that change the most frequently are news and auction sites. If you visit sites like these often, set the option to once per session. Otherwise, you'll probably find once per day to be more than plenty.

If you ever feel like doing some spring cleaning, the Clear now button will delete your entire cache at once. Click this button any time you're sure that the content on a Web site has changed, but NetPositive isn't seeing it. This isn't likely, but can happen in rare instances.

**Figure 4.22**

*The padlock icon in NetPositive's status bar reflects the security status of the current Web page, and will change to a closed padlock whenever you enter a secure site.*

**Security**  With electronic banking and online shopping becoming more popular each day, more and more Web sites are providing secure services to their customers. NetPositive lets you know whenever you enter a secure site by changing the padlock icon in the lower left of the status bar from open to locked.

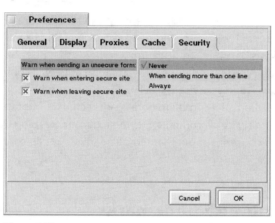

**Figure 4.23**

*NetPositive can warn you as you enter or exit secure sites and when you click the Submit button on Web forms.*

NetPositive will optionally warn you as you enter or exit a secure site, and can also alert you if you click the Submit button on an unsecure form (you could potentially have typed personal or financial data into the form). Since this alert could be a pain in the neck if it popped up every time you typed a few words into a search engine, NetPositive includes the option to only post an alert when you're about to submit more than one line.

**Figure 4.24**

*Check the Remember password box and you won't have to retype it the next time you visit. Password-protected sites are not the same as secure sites; the latter actually encrypt your communications.*

## *On Strong Encryption*

In addition to simple security as described here, some Web sites require actual encryption of all data transmitted. Probably the most prominent example of this is online banking, where it's absolutely critical that data be indecipherable if it should fall into the wrong hands. Unfortunately, national governments around the world have very different (and ever-changing) positions on the matter of encryption, which puts browser vendors in an awkward position. At this writing, the U.S. government defined any tool with greater than 56-bit encryption to be classified as a "munition," requiring the person possessing it to register with the U.S. government. Penalties for exporting "strong" encryption to other countries are stiff, but since the Internet has no concept of national borders, things get tricky.

The version of NetPositive that ships in BeOS comes with 40-bit "lite" encryption guaranteed not to offend governments or to put Be or their customers at risk. However, a separate version of NetPositive including stronger, bank-quality, 128-bit encryption is also available for download to U.S. residents who can prove that they're registered as legal recipients of a munition. This situation is unfortunate for residents of other countries, but it appears that Be's hands are tied for now. Keep your eye on **www.be.com** for updates to this situation as Be will continue to do whatever they reasonably can to make this service is available to all users who require it. Keep in mind, though, that the biggest logistical problem here is not technical, but rather the lack of uniformity in views held by the world's governments. Staying legal and keeping up to date with current encryption laws in all countries at once would be nearly impossible for a company with the limited resources Be has at its disposal.

## Working with Bookmarks

Netscape Navigator gives you a single text file to organize your bookmarks in, while Microsoft Internet Explorer gives you a loose pile of individual files. NetPositive, on the other hand, gives you a virtual bookmark database. By taking full advantage of BeOS filesystem attributes, NetPositive lets you organize your bookmarks in a multitude of ways not possible on other platforms. You can search on bookmarks by keyword across thousands of folders in an instant, or use the Tracker to sort, manage, and filter them every which way to Sunday.

**How Bookmarks Are Stored**   There's an important aspect of BeOS bookmarks that you'll want to get a handle on: Rather than giving bookmarks a filename based on the <TITLE> tag of each page, BeOS names bookmarks with a timestamp generated at the time the bookmark is created, using the Unix-style method of counting time in terms of the number of seconds that have passed since New Year's Eve 1970. As a result, your bookmarks end up with filenames like 906239588 (see Chapter 6, for more on this convention). There are several good reasons why this technique is used. As you know, no two files in any directory can have identical filenames, but many pages have identical <TITLE> tags. How many pages out there are simply titled "Welcome," for example? If bookmarks were named by title, you'd run into frequent overwrite problems.

Fortunately, the Tracker makes it easy to work around this problem through creative use of attributes. The Bookmark filetype uses three of them: Title, URL, and Keywords. The URL attribute, obviously, is hoovered from the page's address, while the Title attribute is extracted from the site's <TITLE> tag. There's no problem with identical attributes existing in the same directory, so you can bookmark a million pages named "Welcome" with no overwrite problems—as long as you don't bookmark more than one page per second, you'll never run into naming conflicts. To make bookmark display user-friendly, use the Tracker's Attributes pull-down menu to hide the filenames and drag the Title column to the far left. When you create new folders in the Tracker, they always inherit the properties of the parent folder, so all of the bookmark folders you create will be organized just like the main bookmark folder.

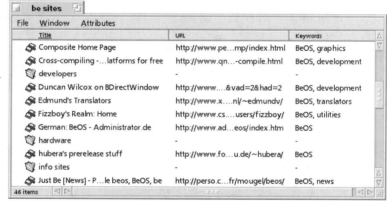

**Figure 4.25**

*Use the Tracker like a database to organize and manage your NetPositive bookmarks. The Keywords attribute is free-form, and can contain anything you like.*

 **Fish out of Water**  There is one disadvantage to NetPositive's method of naming bookmarks based on timestamps. While you can easily organize the Tracker to display the Title attribute prominently, the actual filename remains a number. This makes things a bit awkward when you drag bookmarks out of their main folder and onto your desktop, since you can't view attributes on the desktop. However, just because NetPositive names bookmark files with numbers, that doesn't mean they have to stay that way! Just right-click a bookmark file on your desktop and choose Edit Name to give it any name you like. This applies to BeMail messages as well!

**Keyword Searches**   The Keywords attribute associated with bookmark files is completely free-form. You can enter as many keywords as you like for any bookmark and create custom queries for any predefined collection of book-marks (see Chapter 7, *Working with Queries*, for more). For example, let's say you assign the keyword "BeOS" to all of your BeOS-related bookmarks, and add some more specific keywords to specific sites, as shown in Figure 4.25. You would then be able to perform queries that represent highly specific bookmark collections like the one shown in Figure 4.26. Save the query for later use and you'll be able to view your collections in real-time without ever having to hunt through your bookmark hierarchies.

However, before you attempt to create queries based on your Keywords attributes, remember an important aspect of queries discussed in Chapter 7: All attribute queries must include at least one indexed attribute. This means one of three things in this case. You must:

**A.**   Include a filename in the query, or

**B.**   Include an attribute such as the URL or the Title in your query, or

**C.**   Add the Keywords attribute to your system index manually

In the case of Keywords searches, option A is almost impossible due to the cryptic filenames given to bookmarks. Option B is suboptimal because you probably don't know what URLs or Titles will be associated with the book-marks you want to appear in your query results. Therefore, I strongly recom-mend adding the Keywords attribute to your system index. A complete description of this process can be found in Chapter 5, but in summary, all you have to do is open a Terminal and type lsindex. Study the resulting list and look for an entry called META:keyw. If it does not appear, type mkindex META:keyw. After this point, any keywords you add to your bookmarks will be indexed by the filesystem, and thus be queryable without being combined with other preindexed attributes (keywords added previously, however, will not become immediately queryable).

*Figure: 4.26*

*After adding the Keywords attribute to your system index and setting keywords for your bookmarks, you can find all bookmarks on your system that match detailed criteria. Shown here is a search for all bookmarks that contain the keyword "beos" and also contain either the keywords "graphics" or "development."*

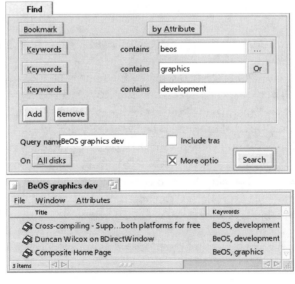

***Create a Query for Frequently Visited Sites*** You may find it extremely useful to add a keyword such as "daily" to the Keywords attributes of sites you like to visit every day. This lets you generate a quick list of sites to check out with your morning coffee, even if they have nothing to do with one another topically. The other nice thing about this method is that it lets you jump directly to the sites in question without having to launch your browser first. After creating the query, store the query file on your desktop for instant access.

**Changing Associated Applications** While NetPositive can handle a wide variety of filetypes, it also relies on other applications installed on your system to handle certain kinds of media and links. For example, consider the common `mailto:` link, which launches a new BeMail message with the address field already filled in. This works well and is very fast, but what if you're using one of the third-party email clients available for BeOS and want one of those to be launched instead? You won't find any entries in NetPositive's Preferences panel for configuring this, because the browser simply relies on the application you've established as the preferred handler for that filetype system-wide in the FileTypes preferences panel (Chapter 5). Thus, to change the application invoked by `mailto:` links, you'll need to make that application your preferred email handler (see Figure 4.27).

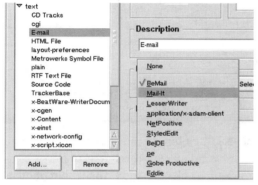

*Figure 4.27*

*To make NetPositive use a different application for handling a given filetype, just change your system-wide preference for that filetype. Here BeatWare Mail-It is made the preferred email handler, rather than BeMail.*

**Context Menus** Right-click on images or links in NetPositive and you'll get a context menu similar to those found in Netscape Navigator and Microsoft Internet Explorer. Unlike context menus found elsewhere in BeOS, these menus provide access to shortcuts and options not available from the standard pull-down menus. This is true because their options relate to specific elements of the page, rather than to the page itself. Among the most useful of these is the New Window With This Link option, which will load the page into a new browser window. This makes it very easy to check out various links on, say, a search engine results page without having to use the Back and Forward buttons, or to retrieve the page from cache every time you move backward.

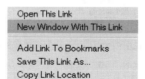

*Figure 4.28*

*Right-click any text link in a NetPositive window and you'll get a context menu like this one, giving you the option to open the link in a new window, make a bookmark of it, or copy its URL to the clipboard.*

The Save This Link As option is useful when you attempt to download a file of a type unfamiliar to NetPositive. For example, in early versions of NetPositive, clicking a link to an MPEG video file confused the browser because it was not yet trained to deal with that file format. By right-clicking one of these links and choosing Save This Link As you could force downloading the file. While you won't encounter this situation very often, keep it in mind for any kind of "alien" filetype that gives you guff.

You'll also appreciate the abilities to add the current page to your list of bookmarks with a right-click anywhere in the page and to access your entire bookmarks menu in the same way.

| Open This Link |
|---|
| New Window With This Link |
| |
| Add Link To Bookmarks |
| Save This Link As... |
| Copy Link Location |
| |
| New Window With This Image |
| Save This Image As... |

**Figure 4.29**

*Right-click any image and you get a similar-but-different context menu, letting you save the image.*

***Three-Button Shortcuts*** If you have a three-button mouse, you can use that third button as a shortcut to the New Window With This Image or New Window With This Link options. Clicking a link or image with the third mouse button is equivalent to right-clicking and choosing one of those items from the context menu (whichever is appropriate to the item being clicked on). There is no equivalent to this tip for one- or two-button meeses.

**The Go Menu** As you surf, NetPositive keeps track of the sites you visit, making it easy to return to a site you happened upon yesterday, or a week ago. After surfing for a couple of days, pull down the Go menu and you'll notice that all of the pages you've visited today are listed on the main menu. You'll also see yesterday's date at the bottom of the menu—scroll over it to view a list of all the sites you viewed yesterday. You can change the number of days stored in the Go menu from the General tab in NetPositive's preferences.

**The View Menu** If you ever find yourself viewing a humongous Web page and want to try and fit as much of it as possible onscreen, try pulling down View | Full Screen. This mode can also be pleasant when viewing arts sites, where you want to minimize the intrusion of the computer's interface on the artwork.

Also under this menu, you'll find the option to Show HTML, which is useful when studying other sites for HTML code techniques. If you've been surfing with images off and want to turn them on for just this page, choose Load Images from this menu (or tap Alt+I). Finally, the international document encodings described earlier in this chapter are available here.

## What about Navigator?

Soon after the release of BeOS R3, Netscape Communications Inc. announced their "open source" program, not only making Navigator free but giving developers the opportunity to rebuild it, improving it in whatever ways they saw fit. Independent developer Richard Hess quickly assembled a team to tackle the port of Navigator to BeOS, and while the task has been monumental, it should be just about complete by the time you read this.

Will the presence of Navigator on the scene make NetPositive irrelevant? I don't think so. There's a lot to be said for simplicity, especially when your Web browser launches in less than one second. While Navigator's got all the bells and whistles, NetPositive has the ability to pull pages out of cache like lightning, not to mention a refreshingly uncomplicated interface. OK, so NetPositive doesn't do JavaScript, cascading style sheets, or dynamic HTML (yet), but it's got the comforting feel of a well-designed tool—balanced, functional, and efficient.

Depending on just how well Navigator performs under BeOS, I suspect that many users will leave NetPositive configured as their default browser, only pulling out the "big guns" when encountering pages that NetPositive can't handle. However, if Hess's team finds a way to make the far more monolithic Navigator as lean and efficient as NetPositive, it may become the browser of choice for BeOS users.

# BeMail

BeMail, the email client that ships with BeOS, isn't anything fancy. It gets the job done and not much more. For advanced features like filters, multiple mail accounts, and address books, check out one of the commercial clients discussed in Chapter 11, *Network Applications*. If you like it simple, though (and there's a lot to be said for that), BeMail is both fast and pleasant to use.

**A Different Approach**  Using BeMail is different than using traditional email clients in several important ways. BeMail isn't a self-contained application that lets you set, configure, and read and write mail from a single location; instead, these functions are somewhat spread out:

- Your login, password, and automatic mail-checking schedules are set from the E-mail preferences panel, not from BeMail itself.

- Rather than launching a separate application to read your mail, you use the Tracker—each BeMail message is a separate file, and you can manage your mail messages just as you would manage any other collection of files.

- You check for new mail manually via the mailbox icon in the Deskbar, not from the BeMail window itself.

- New messages can be created via the Deskbar icon, or by pulling down File | New (hotkey: Alt+N) while viewing an existing message.

These quirks may seem a little strange at first, but they result from the fact that BeMail is constructed modularly, so that other applications can take advantage of mail services built into the system itself. As unfamiliar as this approach may be, it has some distinct advantages over the usual method, where the mail client "owns" your mail. We'll have more on that later, in Chapter 7, but let's get the little sucker set up and running first. Naturally, before you can use BeMail or any Internet services, you'll need to have configured your BeOS machine to dial out or use your company network for connectivity. If you haven't yet established an Internet connection, see the first part of this chapter, then return here.

Keep in mind that, in addition to establishing connectivity and setting up the E-mail preferences panel, you'll have to enter a hostname in the Network preferences panel in order to send your outgoing mail. It doesn't matter what you enter, so long as it's not blank.

 Before checking your mail, there's one thing you should know about BeMail: It won't let you specify that messages should be kept on the server after downloading. That means that your messages will be deleted from the server as they're downloaded. If you had intended to retrieve the same messages again later through another email program or on another operating system, you won't be able to. That's one of the things that makes BeMail simple. However, Be intends to add this feature to BeMail in a future version of the system, probably R5.

**Checking Mail**   Ready, Freddie? Let's check mail. First, open up your inbox by double-clicking the mailbox icon in the Deskbar. If necessary, establish an Internet connection with the Dial-Up Networking panel, then right-click on the mailbox icon in the Deskbar and select Check Now. If the Mail Status window is open, you can click its Check Now button instead of using the Deskbar. The Mail Status window will start churning as it logs into your POP server and starts retrieving your mail—you'll see your /boot/home/mail/in/ directory start to fill up with your messages.

If the connection attempt is unsuccessful, check the following:

- Are you connected to the Internet at all? If you can use NetPositive to browse the Web, you are. If you have an external modem, are its lights blinking? If not, go back over the steps outlined at the beginning of this chapter.

- Are all the fields in the E-mail preferences panel filled in correctly? If necessary, you can copy these from a working email client on another operating system.

***Launch Anything from the Mailbox Icon*** By default, clicking the mailbox icon in the Deskbar will launch your /boot/home/mail/in folder in the Tracker. However, that icon is *actually* connected to /boot/home/mail/mailbox, which is simply a symlink to /boot/home/mail/in. That means you can optionally have something besides your default inbox launched when clicking this icon, just by making that symlink point to something else. For example, you might want to create a system query that searches for unread messages (see Chapter 7). Rename the query to mailbox, move it to your /boot/home/mail folder, and the next time you click that icon, your query will be launched instead! Alternatively, create a link to your favorite third-party email client and do the same thing. Now the mailbox icon will launch Mail-It, Postmaster, Adam, or anything you like.

**Reading Mail** One of the refreshing things about BeMail is its multithreaded-ness—you don't have to wait for all of your messages to come in before you can start reading the ones that have already arrived. Double-click any message's icon from the Tracker to open it up in a BeMail window. Take a look under the Message menu from within any email and you'll find familiar options for replying, forwarding, and deleting messages. Table 4.02 shows BeMail's most important hotkeys.

## Table 4.02  BeMail Hotkeys

| Hotkey | Action |
| --- | --- |
| Alt+N | Create new message |
| Alt+R | Reply |
| Alt+Shift+R | Reply to all |
| Alt+J | Forward |
| Alt+T | Move to Trash |
| Alt+H | Show header |
| Alt+P | Print |
| Alt+E | Add attachment |
| Alt+Shift+M | Send now |
| Alt+M | Send later |
| Alt+W | Close and leave status as is |
| Shift+Alt+W | If message is new, keep as new |
| Ctrl+Alt+W | Close and set status to Saved |
| Alt+1 | Insert signature #1 (Alt+2 inserts #2, and so forth) |
| Alt+Up Arrow | Open previous message |
| Alt+Down Arrow | Open next message |

*In addition to the usual system-wide hotkeys, BeMail has a good collection of its own for message management.*

Pay special attention to the last two rows in Table 4.02—they're key to one of the coolest things BeMail can do, and let you navigate through a folder full of mail faster than a greased pig. Rather than closing the current message and opening the next, BeMail keeps its main window open, while the message contents appear and disappear. If this is difficult to visualize, just try it—you'll like it.

That's great for working with messages, but what about shortcut keys to be used in the message body itself? If you've ever been frustrated by the fact that the Home and End keys in BeMail go to the top and bottom of the document rather than to the beginning and end of the line, don't fret—BeMail uses a few of the more popular emacs key bindings (emacs is a high-powered text editor from the Unix world). These are listed in Table 4.03.

### Table 4.03  Undocumented BeMail Hotkeys

| Hotkey | Action |
| --- | --- |
| Ctrl+E | Jump to end of line |
| Ctrl+A | Jump to start of line |
| Ctrl+B | Go back one character |
| Ctrl+F | Go forward one character |
| Ctrl+O | Open new line |
| Ctrl+N | Go to next line |
| Ctrl+P | Go to previous line |
| Ctrl+K | Delete (kill) to end of line |
| Ctrl+Y | Paste from kill buffer |

These undocumented hotkeys (which are borrowed from the emacs editor) can be used in the BeMail message body itself.

 **Fix It Yourself!**  Still not happy with the hotkeys provided in BeMail? Want to add some extra functionality not provided by Be? Go right ahead—Be provides the source code for BeMail, right there in the optional/sample-code directory on your installation CD. Of course, you'll need to know something about C++ programming and the BeOS API to get anywhere with it, but it's great to know that this is an open application, and that Be wholeheartedly encourages you to hack it, improve it, and share your modifications with the rest of the community. BeMail isn't the only bundled application that Be provides the source code for—you'll find source for several other applications in the same directory.

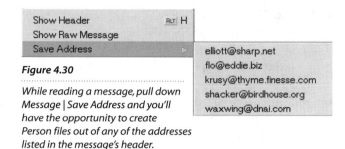

**Figure 4.30**

*While reading a message, pull down
Message | Save Address and you'll
have the opportunity to create
Person files out of any of the addresses
listed in the message's header.*

**Saving Addresses** Another handy feature built into BeMail is its ability
to create Be People files out of addresses buried in email headers. If you're
reading a message from someone whose address you'd like to keep, pull down
Message | Save Address and you'll see a sublist of all the email addresses
contained in the header, including your own. Selecting one of these will bring
up the People application with that address already filled in. You can fill in
any other fields you like at this point and save the Person file to your
/boot/home/people/ folder.

***Quick Access to Addresses*** When creating a new BeMail message, click
on the To: or cc: buttons and you'll see a quick list of all the People files on
your system. Selecting one inserts that email address into the appropriate
field. Alternatively, you can drag People files out of their home folder and
into this field.

***Query for Pending Messages*** When you create new messages, they're
stored in your /boot/mail/out/ folder, and you can tell whether or not
they've been successfully sent by checking their Status attribute. There are
two ways to do this.

Since the status marker is saved as an attribute, you can run a lightning-fast
system query. Pull down the Be menu and select Find (or hit Alt+F from any
Tracker window). Click "By Attribute" on the picklist, select E-mail | Status, and
type pending into the text field. To save time down the road, click the small
triangle to see more options and name the query something intuitive, like
"outgoing mail." Click Search to examine your system for unsent mail. If you'll
be doing this often, navigate Tracker to /boot/home/queries/ and find the
query you just named "outgoing mail." Drag it to the desktop, and you'll be
able to run it any time in the future with a double-click.

If you just want to examine the Status field for all of your email, pull down
the Attributes menu and scroll to E-mail while in your /boot/home/mail/
folder (or any of its subdirectories). Make sure Status is selected. Widen your
Tracker window if necessary so you can see the values in the Status column.

**Setting Up Signatures** Before you start sending new messages, you'll probably want to make sure they contain a signature bragging to the world about how you're now surfing from BeOS. Or something. Pull down Edit | Signatures and you'll be able to create a new `.sig` file. If you've already established one or more `.sig` files, you can pull down Signature | Open from this window to edit them. You can set the default `.sig` from BeMail's Preferences menu. Once created, signatures can then be inserted into the current message by pulling down Edit | Add Signature and scrolling over to the `.sig` you want to use.

 Remember: email signatures should be no wider than 78 characters and no longer than four lines. This guarantees A) that your `.sig` won't get wrapped improperly onto the next line, and B) that your recipients won't complain that you're hogging bandwidth with endless signatures.

*Figure 4.31*

*Signatures are text blocks that get automatically appended to the end of your email messages. BeMail lets you set up as many signatures as you like with its built-in `.sig` editor.*

 **Instant Access to Signatures** If you keep a small library of signatures on hand and use them for different types of correspondence, you'll love not having to navigate through menus to get to them—just tap Alt+1 to insert signature #1, Alt+2 to insert signature #2, and so on.

**Fonts** Depending on your screen resolution settings, your mail may be appearing in a dinky little font, requiring you to squint and strain to read and write messages. Pull down Edit | Preferences to change the font size or select another font altogether. Click OK to see your font in action. From this dialog, you can also turn text wrapping off, set your preferred `.sig` file, and change the user level from Beginner to Expert.

 **Expert Mode** Toggling to Expert mode from within BeMail's Preferences panel means that you'll no longer be asked for confirmation when deleting your messages. Hitting Alt+T will now send messages directly to the Trash.

**Making Sense of the Mail Folder** At this point, you've probably noticed that the layout of your `inbox` folder is a little less than informative. You can see the senders' names, but where are the subject lines? The default settings here may not be optimal, but you can easily customize the view to suit your needs. Because BeMail messages are stored as individual files in standard Tracker windows, you can customize your view the same way you would customize any Tracker window.

With your mail folder open in the Tracker, pull down the Attributes menu, slide down to E-mail, and select Subject. Release the mouse button, and a Subject column will appear in the Tracker window. You may have to stretch the window horizontally and scroll horizontally to see it. You may also want to do the same for Status, so you can see at a glance which messages have been read.

Don't like the order of the columns? Maybe you prefer to see the sender's name in the left column and the subject line right next to it. To do this, look at the gray column headers at the top of the Tracker window. Grab the header of your Subject column and drag it to the left until it's next to the Name column, then release. Bingo!

You can rearrange Tracker columns however you like, whether you're in an email folder or anything else. Clicking on a column header will sort your files by that criterion. For instance, to sort your mail alphabetically by sender's name, just click once on the Name column header. To reverse-alphabetize, click again. To sort by arrival time, click the header labeled Modified, and

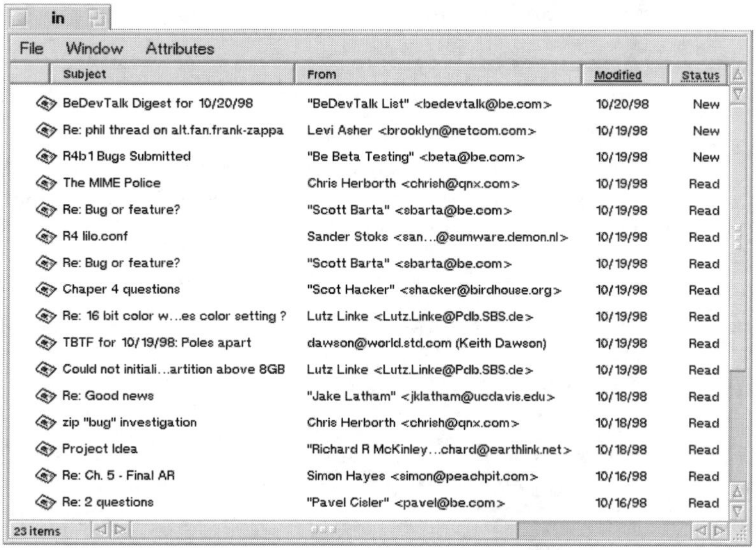

| Subject | From | Modified | Status |
|---------|------|----------|--------|
| BeDevTalk Digest for 10/20/98 | "BeDevTalk List" <bedevtalk@be.com> | 10/20/98 | New |
| Re: phil thread on alt.fan.frank-zappa | Levi Asher <brooklyn@netcom.com> | 10/19/98 | New |
| R4b1 Bugs Submitted | "Be Beta Testing" <beta@be.com> | 10/19/98 | New |
| The MIME Police | Chris Herborth <chrish@qnx.com> | 10/19/98 | Read |
| Re: Bug or feature? | "Scott Barta" <sbarta@be.com> | 10/19/98 | Read |
| R4 lilo.conf | Sander Stoks <san...@sumware.demon.nl> | 10/19/98 | Read |
| Re: Bug or feature? | "Scott Barta" <sbarta@be.com> | 10/19/98 | Read |
| Chaper 4 questions | "Scot Hacker" <shacker@birdhouse.org> | 10/19/98 | Read |
| Re: 16 bit color w...es color setting ? | Lutz Linke <Lutz.Linke@Pdb.SBS.de> | 10/19/98 | Read |
| TBTF for 10/19/98: Poles apart | dawson@world.std.com (Keith Dawson) | 10/19/98 | Read |
| Could not initiali...artition above 8GB | Lutz Linke <Lutz.Linke@Pdb.SBS.de> | 10/19/98 | Read |
| Re: Good news | "Jake Latham" <jklatham@ucdavis.edu> | 10/18/98 | Read |
| zip "bug" investigation | Chris Herborth <chrish@qnx.com> | 10/18/98 | Read |
| Project Idea | "Richard R McKinley...chard@earthlink.net> | 10/18/98 | Read |
| Re: Ch. 5 - Final AR | Simon Hayes <simon@peachpit.com> | 10/16/98 | Read |
| Re: 2 questions | "Pavel Cisler" <pavel@be.com> | 10/16/98 | Read |

23 items

*Figure 4.32*

*Because every Tracker window in BeOS can be customized, you can view and sort your BeMail messages however you like. Here the defaults have been altered to display the subject line first, then the sender's name, date, and status. Messages have been sorted with the newest on top—the opposite of the default. All customized Tracker settings throughout BeOS are automatically retained (in the folder's attributes) until you change them.*

## BeMail and Filters

You've probably noticed that BeMail has no concept of anything like the filters you may be using in other email clients to auto-sort your messages as they roll in. As mentioned earlier, BeMail isn't meant to be a full-featured mail client—just a serviceable one. If you'd like to run filters on your BeMail messages, look into one of the commercial products covered in Chapter 11.

so on. If you have a lot of messages in a given folder and want to sort them with tighter control, the Tracker will let you create sorts within your sorts. See Chapter 5, for details.

Feel free to create more folders inside your inbox and to drag messages into them for increased organization. In fact, one of the great things about BeMail messages is that you can put them anywhere on your system. If a message comes in that relates to Chapter 9 of a report you're writing, just drag it into the Chapter 9 folder! However, email organization and sorting doesn't stop with folders. There's much, much more you can do by tapping the power of BeOS queries. In fact, BeMail sorting is one of the key examples in Chapter 7.

 **Folder Properties Are Inherited** Whenever you create new folders in the Tracker, they inherit the properties of the parent folder. Thus, if you sort your inbox to display the subject line as the leftmost column, any new folders you create will have the subject on the left as well. If you're going to be creating a bunch of subdirectories to categorize your mail, perfect the layout of your main inbox folder first.

**Attachments** It's easy to attach files to your BeMail messages, and just as easy to receive incoming attachments. To attach files to a message, pull down the Enclosures menu and choose Add; then use the File panel to navigate to the files you want to attach. Even easier, just drag any document into the upper portion of the Message window. Your Message window will change format, and a new Attachments field will appear.

*Figure 4.33*

*The BeMail Message window gains an Attachments field as soon as you add an attachment. Double-click any file to launch it; select it and choose Enclosures | Remove to delete it.*

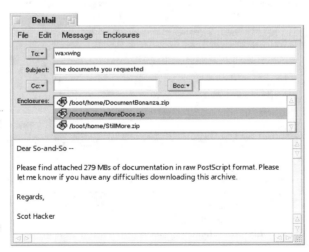

***Drag-and-Drop Technicalities*** Files dropped into the BeMail window do
different things depending on their type. If you drag any kind of binary file,
such as an image or a zip file, to anywhere on the BeMail window, it will
become an attachment. But if you drag any kind of text file into the message
field, its text is inserted at that point. If you want to attach (not embed) any
kind of text document to your message, be sure to drag it to the top of the
window, over the To: field, for instance. Alternatively, use the Enclosures
menu to add your text attachment manually.

When you receive a BeMail message with attachments, they're displayed as
blue hyperlinks. There are three ways to extract or view your attachments.
Probably the easiest is to simply drag the blue link out of the message and into
the Tracker—couldn't be easier. Second, try right-clicking on an attachment
link and choosing Save… from the context menu. This will detach the file,
giving you a standard File panel that you can navigate to save it anywhere.

Or, click once on a link and BeMail will attempt to launch the file in an
appropriate application. For example, text files will be launched in StyledEdit

(or your preferred plain text handler), JPEGs will be
launched in ShowImage, zip files in Expander, and so
on. If BeMail can't determine an appropriate handler,
you'll see a dialog like the one in Figure 4.34. At this
point, you can change the filetype of the attachment
so that it *does* match the right handler, or you can save
the file out of the message and into a folder, to be
dealt with later.

**Figure 4.34**

*BeOS's standard way of telling you it couldn't
find a preferred application for a given filetype.*

To change the file's type, click the Find button in the panel shown in Figure
4.34 and select the FileTypes application. When FileTypes appears, enter
an appropriate MIME string into the field, or use the Same As… or Select…
buttons to find another file whose MIME type you want to mimic (see
Chapter 5 for more on MIME and BeOS filetypes).

 ***Where Do Attachments Live?*** In most mail clients, downloaded attachments
are stored as individual files in a separate "attachments" directory. Since BeMail
messages are already individual files, though, there's no point in storing attachments elsewhere. By default, any BeMail message with an attachment is a compound file consisting of both the message text and the attached data. The nice
thing about this system is that it makes your messages with attachments more
portable and frees you and BeOS from having to keep track of the location of
both the message file and its attachment. If you want to store the attached file
elsewhere, use the instructions above to detach it. Otherwise, feel free to move
BeMail messages anywhere you like—their attachments will come along for
the ride automatically. Note that if you're using BeOS R3, BeMail attachments
are separate files, living in /boot/var/tmp/.

# Using FTP

BeOS's implementation of FTP (File Transfer Protocol) is a port of the standard Unix version, and thus uses several standard Unix commands for manipulating files and directories. If you've already got a little experience working in the Terminal, you've got a head start. By the way, the FTP tool built into Windows 95/98 and NT is an identical port of standard FTP; if you've used command-line FTP in Windows, you already know how to use it in BeOS.

---

## Real Men Use the Terminal

Before the Web came along, before it was possible to download a file by clicking on a link, Internet users transferred files from hard drive to server and back again by using FTP from the command line. While the rise of the Web and of graphical FTP clients has resulted in fewer command-line FTP users, it's still good to know how the system works, so that if you're ever caught on a machine without a graphical client, you can still log into remote servers and grab the files you need. BeOS is just such an animal—an Internet-enabled operating system without a graphical FTP client (NetPositive will allow you to download from—but not upload to—FTP sites).

---

**Uploads and Downloads**   For this example, we'll assume that you need to download a file called ToolSet.zip from BeWare's utilities directory and upload a file called MyApp.zip to its incoming directory.

Let's say someone has emailed you the address **ftp://ftp.be.com/pub/ contrib/util/ToolSet.zip** and you want to grab it without using NetPositive or a graphical FTP client. Open a Terminal window and type:

```
ftp ftp.be.com
```

You'll be prompted for a login and password. Many FTP sites are anonymous, meaning that you don't have to have an account on the server to use them. In these cases, always log in as either "anonymous" or "ftp" and enter your email address as a password. If your connection attempt is rejected, the site isn't anonymous, and you'll need to get an account from the administrator. BeWare is anonymous. Once you've logged in, you'll find yourself staring at a prompt like this:

```
ftp>
```

At this point, you can issue a couple of standard bash commands, such as pwd, which prints the current working directory to the screen, or ls, which prints a listing of the files and folders in the current directory.

At BeWare, you find that / is the current directory, meaning that you're sitting at the root. Typing ls produces:

```
ftp> ls
200 PORT command successful.
150 Opening ASCII mode data connection for /bin/ls.
total 14
drwx--x--x    2 root   wheel    512 Aug 19  1997 bin
drwx--x--x    3 root   wheel    512 Oct 23  1997 etc
drwx-wx-wx    6 1001   wheel   2560 May 29 22:51 incoming
drwxr-x--x    7 1001   wheel    512 May 29 08:22 outgoing
drwxr-xr-x   10 root   wheel    512 May  5 02:02 pub
226 Transfer complete.
ftp>
```

Note that each line here starts with a "d", meaning that these are all directory names. Since you know that the file you want is stored in /pub/contrib/util, change to that directory:

```
cd pub/contrib/util
```

Type pwd to make sure that you have indeed landed in the right spot, and then ls to get a file listing of everything living in that directory. Chances are, the listing was too long for one screen and scrolled right by. You could use Terminal's vertical scrollbar to scroll up, but you might want to get a more refined listing. Since you're looking for ToolSet.zip, type:

```
ls T*
```

Since Unix is case-sensitive, the uppercase "T" is important. However, if you don't see ToolSet.zip in the resulting file list, try ls t* as well, just in case someone messed up the filename at some point. Now you're looking at a listing of all the files in the directory starting with a "T", and you're almost ready to download. Before you do, however, there are a few parameters you'll need to set.

For starters, where are you going to download to? By default, FTP will download files to the shell's current directory. If you began your FTP session from /boot/home/downloads and this is where you want your files to go, do nothing. If you want to change the download directory to another location, type (for example):

```
lcd /boot/home/installs
```

Typing lcd by itself will always report the local current directory. Secondly, is the file you want to download a binary file, like a zip archive or image, or is it an ASCII file, like a text or HTML document? By default, FTP uses binary mode. To switch to ASCII mode, type ascii.

Never switch to ASCII mode unless you're absolutely sure you're downloading a text file. Binary files downloaded in ASCII mode will be unusable. To switch back to binary mode, type `bin`.

Finally, if the file you intend to download is larger than a few kilobytes, you're going to want some kind of progress indicator. Type `hash` to turn the download progress indicator on. Now you're ready to download. Transfers in FTP are accomplished via the `get` and `put` commands. To grab your file now, type

```
get ToolSet.zip
```

A moment after you hit Return, a series of hash marks (#)will start appearing in Terminal, one for every kilobyte transferred. The hash marks won't tell you how far through the current download you've come, but at least you'll know it's still chugging away, so you won't think your connection has hung. Feedback is good, especially when you've got a slow connection or are connected to a sluggish server.

 ***Multi-File Transfers*** **To upload or download multiple files at once, use the** `mget` **and** `mput` **commands in combination with Unix wildcards. For instance, to download every file in the current directory, type** `mget *`**. To upload every file starting with "T" and ending with "zip," type** `mput T*zip`**. By default,** `mget` **and** `mput` **are pretty brain-dead and ask for confirmation for every matching file, meaning you can't go out to the laundromat during one of these sessions. To make these commands work without confirmation between files, type** `prompt` **before running them to turn prompt mode off.**

When the download is complete, you'll be returned to the `ftp>` prompt. You might want to take a look in the Tracker to make sure your new file is there, and that it opens properly.

Now it's time to upload `MyApp.zip` to BeWare's incoming directory. Since the incoming directory is right off the root, type:

```
cd /incoming
```

Use the `lcd` command to change local directories to the location of `MyApp.zip`, then use the `put` command with the filename to upload it; for example:

```
lcd /boot/home/projects
```

```
put MyApp.zip
```

 The `bin`, `ascii`, `hash`, and `prompt` commands all function as toggles. If you've already set them once in this session, don't set them again—that will reverse their behavior.

That's it! When you've completed your session, type `bye` to log out.

There are quite a few more FTP commands not covered here. Type help at any FTP prompt to view a list of all possible commands, then type help and a command name for brief instructions on that particular command.

***Going Graphical*** If all of this command-line stuff seems like nothing but a big pain in the neck and you'd rather do all of this via drag-and-drop, you'll find several excellent graphical FTP clients on BeWare. Not only do these clients make most of these procedures much easier, but many of them let you pull off tricks that can't be done from the command line, like transferring an entire, multilevel directory structure with a single drag operation—excellent if you need to download or upload your entire Web site at once.

I particularly recommend BeatWare's Get-It and Zeid Derhally's NetPenguin. Both take full advantage of BeOS's multithreadedness, so you can download and upload multiple files at multiple locations simultaneously. Both offer excellent bookmarking facilities and other advanced functions.

***FTP on Steroids*** Standard FTP is limited in quite a few ways. For instance, it's not able to bookmark your favorite FTP sites, so you have to remember all of their addresses every time you start a new session. It's also not able to do a lot of the fancier shell tricks you may be accustomed to from using the Terminal on your own machine—it can't do Tab completion (Chapter 6), for instance, so you have to type files' entire names (although you can always copy and paste text into and out of Terminal sessions). If you're a fan of command-line FTP but are looking for some more advanced features, download the port of NCFTP from BeWare. You can use NCFTP as a replacement for standard FTP and enjoy much more advanced functionality.

## Using Telnet

The nice thing about the command line is its lightweight versatility. Because text mode requires little overhead from the operating system and bypasses the graphical interface, it's inherently cross-platform and flexible. For decades, Unix users and administrators have controlled their systems from remote terminals via telnet. Whether they're in the next room or halfway around the world, they can log into their machines via telnet and control every aspect of the system for which they're authorized.

Because most Internet service providers run on Unix, many people telnet into their Internet accounts over PPP connections to read their mail, administer their Web servers, and run programs on the remote host. Some Unix hosts keep programs running continuously in the background as a public service— anonymous users can telnet into libraries to search through the card catalogs, have interactive chats with artificial intelligence programs, and participate in text-based group games, called MUDs or MOOs.

BeOS includes a telnet client as part of its bash shell. To use it, you'll need the telnet address of the machine you're connecting to. If there are no machines to which you normally telnet, you might want to find an anonymous telnet server just for the experience. Search the Internet for keywords "+telnet +library +games," or the like, to find good listings.

To initiate a telnet session to your own ISP (assuming they allow telnet sessions; check their Web pages or write to their support staff to find out), for instance, open up a Terminal window and type:

```
telnet shell.mysite.com
```

replacing shell.mysite.com with your server's address. Once you've logged in, you'll be sitting at a shell prompt on the remote machine and you should be able to run a wide variety of standard Unix commands (see Chapter 6, for an introduction to bash, which is the shell included with BeOS). Note that some ISPs allow only a limited subset of Unix commands to be run by their users. These limitations are in place for security reasons to prevent users from compromising the system or chewing up clock cycles needlessly. At the very least, you should be able to manipulate your own files and directories, edit files with vi, and create .tar and .gz archives.

***Terminal Emulation*** When you connect from your Terminal window to a terminal running on another machine, probably a non-BeOS machine, you're connecting one terminal type to another. In the Unix world, there are a variety of basic terminal types, and in order for one machine to connect with another, a process called "terminal emulation" must occur. Without digging into all the hairy details of terminal emulation, you should know that BeOS's Terminal identifies itself as "beterm," which may or may not be compatible with other terminal emulators running on other machines.

If your telnet sessions are working just fine, you're all set. If, however, you're not able to log into remote servers successfully, or you get unreadable screens full of garbage when you do, the problem is most likely that the remote terminal doesn't like beterm. In this case, all you have to do is tell BeOS to identify itself to the remote servers with a different terminal emulator. From a Terminal prompt (not a telnet prompt), type:

```
export TERM=ansi
```

**or**

```
export TERM=vt102
```

**or**

```
export TERM=vt100
```

and try your session again. These are by far the most popular terminal emulators, and should clear up your problem. If they don't, ask the system administrator which terminal emulator you should use, and use that instead.

If you're connecting to an anonymous server to run a specific program, as you might do to search a card catalog or chat with a "bot," you'll usually need to type a login and/or password. If you don't have one, try guest as your login. Sometimes instructions onscreen will tell you how to log in anonymously. After that, you're on your own—since all remote programs operate differently, use the onscreen menus and prompts. Once you're logged into a remote program, you're using that program—not telnet; telnet is just the protocol that encapsulates your communications.

 **_Telnet into Your BeOS Machine_**  **Because you may want to control your BeOS machine from a remote location, BeOS includes a telnet server built right into the system's network services. Full details on using BeOS as a telnet server are covered in Chapter 8, but in a nutshell, all you have to do is open the Services tab in the Networking preferences panel, check the box marked "Telnet server," enter a username and password into the Login Info fields, and then obtain your current IP address, either from the Network preferences panel or from the Dial-Up Networking statistics panel. Give this IP address, along with the appropriate login information, to anyone you trust to log into your BeOS machine, and they'll be able to run command-line programs on your machine from anywhere in the world (so long as they can find a networked machine with a telnet client of some kind).**

## Using ping

The most elemental of all Internet connections is the simple ping, which has one use and one use only: to test whether the route between you and another machine is open and if the remote machine is alive and kicking. When you ping another machine, a series of packets is sent from your computer across the network and received by the remote machine. If the remote machine is turned on and connected to the Internet, it sends back a pong saying, "I'm alive!" As simple as it sounds, ping can be your best friend when troubleshooting network connections.

Let's say that Dial-Up Networking shows that you're currently connected to the Net, but you can't bring up **www.be.com** in NetPositive. Has **www.be.com** crashed? Is there a router blockage somewhere between you and Menlo Park? Has your TCP/IP connection been dropped by your ISP even though the modem is still connected? A quick way to find out is to open up a Terminal and type"

```
ping -c 5 www.be.com
```

The -c 5 argument tells ping to make five attempts before quitting. If you run the ping command without the -c flag, it will go on forever, until you stop it manually by hitting Ctrl+C (which is the universal "stop this process now" hotkey in the Terminal).

If the route is open and Be's server is turned on and connected to the Internet (highly likely), you'll get a report that looks something like this:

```
/boot/home>ping -c 5 ftp.be.com
32 bytes from 207.126.103.9    sequence  1 round-trip-time 64.0 msecs
32 bytes from 207.126.103.9    sequence  2 round-trip-time 58.5 msecs
32 bytes from 207.126.103.9    sequence  3 round-trip-time 75.2 msecs
32 bytes from 207.126.103.9    sequence  4 round-trip-time 59.2 msecs
32 bytes from 207.126.103.9    sequence  5 round-trip-time 74.3 msecs
```

What you're seeing is a report from the ping/pong sequences' round trip. The server name is translated into its real IP address, and the total round-trip time is reported in milliseconds. If **www.be.com** responded to a ping request but wouldn't open in NetPositive, you know that you've got a valid Internet connection, and something else is wrong (in this case, probably a faulty DNS server entry in your DUN configuration panel, or perhaps Be's server software has crashed even though the machine is still alive). If you get no response, or the phrase `ping timed out`, then no connection is being made. You could try disconnecting (if using PPP), checking all of your network settings and connections, restarting networking, and redialing.

## *Interpreting Round-Trip Times*

A ping report is all well and good until you realize that you have no standard of reference against which to measure the round-trip times. Is 113 milliseconds good or bad? The answer to that depends on many factors, such as knowing from experience how solid your own Net connection generally is and how likely you are to be seeing router blockages. Trip times will also vary widely at different times of day, so if you're trying to get an overall measurement, you should establish a series of sites to ping, located in different parts of the world, and try them at three different times in the day. Save the reports to a file or files, and compare them at the end of a few days of testing.

In any case, for informal pings, here's a *very* general guideline to acceptable ping times, based only on my own experience:

- Sites in your region of the country: 50–100 ms
- Sites on the opposite end of the country: 150–250 ms
- Sites based in Europe (from the U.S.): 200–350 ms
- Sites based in other parts of the world (Russia, China): 250–700 ms

Note the greater the distance from the pinger to the remote location, the greater the number of possible blockages that can get in your way, and the higher the latency and acceptable variance in ping times.

If you're occasionally getting higher numbers than these, don't worry about it—the Internet's performance fluctuates wherever you are. But if you're getting consistently higher numbers, you probably have a router blockage upstream from your ISP. That's not your ISP's problem, but they might like to know that their customers are noticing.

## *Stay Awake*

One particularly handy use for ping is in dealing with a flaky PPP connection. Some ISPs will drop your connection a little too frequently if you're not moving constant wake-up calls through the system, regardless of what timeout value you've set. If you've got a chronic problem with this, you might want to keep a Terminal window open, running a "keepalive" script, which will ping a variety of sites in an order and frequency you determine. If you'd like to use a simple version of this, type this into a Terminal window:

```
while true ; do
ping -c 1 your.isp.com ;
sleep 60 ;
done
```

This will create an endless loop that sends out a ping request every 60 seconds. To end the sequence, hit Ctrl+C. If you'd like more control over the sequence than what's shown here, download the author's KeepAlive shell script from **www.beosbible.com**

To avoid hogging bandwidth as much as possible, be courteous and point the ping sequence at your own site, not someone else's. Set it to send tiny packets—like eight bytes—and space them out every 30 seconds or so (see the Power Tip *Fine-Tuning Ping*, on the next page). All you need in most cases is a trickle signal … just enough to remind your ISP that you haven't gone to sleep.

Note, however, that if you depend on timeout values to disconnect you, this method will prevent you from ever timing out, unless you very carefully adjust the number of round trips and their frequency.

**Check Out Traceroute**  If ping doesn't provide enough information, you may want to take it to the next level and use a traceroute program. Traceroute programs work a little like ping, but report back with detailed information on the names and response times of every single router lying between your machine and the destination. Even if you're not troubleshooting, experimenting with traceroute can give you a fascinating picture of the Internet's topology. Traceroute for BeOS should be available by R5.

***Fine-Tuning Ping***   The `ping` command is capable of accepting a number of arguments, so you can fine-tune its behavior. If you want to send smaller or larger packets, adjust their size with the -s flag. While the default is 32-byte packets, you can use, for instance, 8-byte packets by typing:

```
ping -s 8  ftp.be.com
```

To adjust the interval length, use the -i argument. For example:

```
ping -i 10 ftp.be.com
```

will place your pings 10 seconds apart. If you want control over the number of round trips, use the -c flag. For example:

```
ping -c 20 ftp.be.com
```

will send 20 pings and then quit. Of course, you can use these arguments singly or all together:

```
ftp -s 8 -i 10 -c 20 ftp.be.com
```

# 5

# Files and the Tracker

. . . . . . . . . . . . . . . . . . . . . . . . . . . . . . . . . . . . . . . . . . .

When you get down to the nitty-gritty, an operating system is all about data: storing it, moving it, processing it, reading it, creating it, compiling it, analyzing it, manipulating it … and hopefully not losing it. For data to be meaningful or useful, it needs to somehow become manifest—to exist in a nontransient state that persists between boots. It needs to be stored in a known format and accessible in a known manner. Data may always be ones and zeros at some fundamental level, but that's not what you see when you open up a folder full of movies, games, or political manifestos.

Files appear as discrete units of meaningful data, parsed out of the sea of ones and zeros as if they were freestanding entities. Accomplishing this convincing magical act are two things: a storage system and an interface to that system. In BeOS, the storage system is known as BFS (Be filesystem), and the interface is known as the Tracker. As an interface onto the filesystem, the Tracker serves a role similar to that of the MacOS Finder or Windows Explorer, while BFS is analogous to HFS or FAT. The only difference is that the Tracker and BFS are way more powerful and flexible than their legacy cousins. But you already knew that.

The roles of the Tracker and BFS necessarily pervade every aspect of BeOS, from the lowest levels to the highest. We took a brief look at BFS in Chapter 1, *The Media OS*, and caught a glimpse of the Tracker in Chapter 2, *Meet the System*. Now we're going to get in deep with both of them.

# A Closer Look at the Tracker

As discussed in Chapter 2, there's more to the Tracker than dragging around files and folders—the Tracker is involved in literally every operation you do that involves file management from the GUI, from obvious tasks like creating a new folder in an open Tracker window to less obvious things like keeping the query engine from searching through the Trash while you're running a system search. Of course, the Tracker seldom acts alone—it's in constant communication with other subsystems like the FileTypes database, the Registrar, the query engine, the application server, the messaging and scripting infrastructure, and more. But the Tracker does act as a sort of umbrella object to all of these subsystems, presenting a constant, accurate view of the state of your filesystem, and intercepting interactions like double-clicks and hotkeys, then sending them along to the appropriate subsystems. But while the Tracker's influence and control is utterly pervasive, it's also a free-standing application like any other; you can kill it off and restart it without locking up your entire system.

Let's look at Tracker-based file management a little more closely than we did in the System Tour, and then dig into the Tracker's relationship with some of these other subsystems.

 Many of the concepts and techniques described in this chapter may sound somewhat abstract on paper. The best way to get a good handle on them is to actually work with them. Study the figures and screenshots and work along with the provided examples to get the most from this chapter.

## Working with Files and Folders

Some of the most common operations you'll be performing from within the Tracker will be second nature to anyone who's ever used a graphical file management system, but the Tracker also has quite a few tricks up its sleeve that give it additional powers you probably won't discover by accident. It's worth spending a little time familiarizing yourself with some of the Tracker's advanced features, though we cover the basics in this section as well.

**Drag Operations**    Operating systems have pretty much standardized on a handful of behaviors associated with dragging files and folders around, and BeOS follows these standards fairly closely—you won't find any great surprises in this department.

- Dragging a file or folder to another Tracker location (including the desktop) on the *same* disk volume will *move* the file or folder to that location.

- Dragging a file or folder to another Tracker location (including the desktop) on a *different* disk volume will *copy* the file or folder to that location.

- Dragging a file or folder onto an icon causes the Tracker to inquire whether the target accepts dragged files. If it does, the target will become shaded in gray. What happens next is up to the target: If the target is a folder, the dragged object will be transferred to it. If the target is an application, it will launch and try to open the object.

- Dragging a file or folder with the *right* mouse button (Mac users: Ctrl+drag) will cause a context menu to appear when the mouse button is released, asking whether you want to move, copy, or create a link to the file. As is standard, the right mouse button lets you override the default behavior. If you're dragging to a location on the same volume, the right mouse button lets you copy the file or folder rather than moving it. The Create Link option is covered in detail below.

 *Take Care When Replacing Folders*    If you've been using Microsoft Windows or Apple's MacOS, you know that when you drag or paste a folder to a location where a folder with the same name already exists, you're asked whether you want to replace items in the existing folder if they have the same name. When you do the same thing in BeOS, you also get a dialog asking whether you want to replace, but there's a big (and very important) difference—you're being asked whether you want to replace the *entire folder*. If you say yes to the

Replace dialog, the contents of the existing folder will be *completely* replaced by the contents of the new folder. For example, if you drag a folder called config into your home directory and say yes to the Replace dialog, you'll inadvertently blow away all of the settings for all of your applications and for much of the system itself—not good. Although the situation arises infrequently, it's worth paying close attention if you ever find yourself needing to do this. At this writing, Be is working on an improved copy dialog for R5 that will give you the option to Cancel, Skip, Replace, Replace All, Merge, or Merge All.

As described in Chapter 2, this book uses the convention of referring to the right mouse button, even though you can easily remap your mouse buttons to function like other buttons. See Chapter 9, *Preferences and Customization*, for more on that.

***Using Clippings*** Dragging data such as a block of text or the selected area of an image out of many applications and into any Tracker view will turn the dragged selection into a free-standing file called a Clipping. Clippings don't work with all applications—the developer must specifically code in Clipping support. Many do.

Conversely, dragging a text or image file into an open document will insert the entire contents of the file at the insertion point in many, but not all, applications, so long as the dragged content is in a compatible format. Again, applications must provide this support themselves, and many do.

*Figure 5.01*

Drag a text or graphic selection from a text or image editor and into the Tracker. A Clipping, a new, free-standing file consisting of the selected area only, will be created. On the other hand, dragging a file into an editor will often insert that file's contents at that point in the document. Try this with StyledEdit, BeMail, Pe, and most of the products from BeatWare, Gobe, Adamation, and others. Experiment! If one of your favorite apps doesn't support Clippings, send email to the developer and ask for it in the next version.

**Hierarchical Folder Menus** One of the biggest problems with drag-and-drop *anything* is the requirement to have both the source and target windows open and visible before anything useful can be done. Being able to drag a file onto a folder in order to move it there is no big time-saver if you have to dig and click all over the place first just to make the destination folder visible. Similarly, one of the biggest problems with nonhierarchical file management tools is that they require lots of clicking and digging, and can leave behind a mess of open windows.

BeOS includes a solution to these problems that's so elegant you'll wonder how you ever lived without it. Anytime you see a folder icon, whether it's on

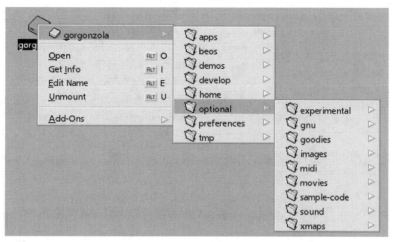

*Figure 5.02*

*The easiest, fastest way to navigate to a file or folder elsewhere on your system is almost always to use the Tracker's "hierarchical folder menus" feature. Click on a folder icon with your right mouse button, then just keep sliding through subdirectories until you reach your destination. You don't even have to hold the mouse button down—just right-click once and start gliding. Clicking on any folder or file in the hierarchy will open or launch that location. No more opening tons of windows or struggling to find your drag-and-drop targets!*

the desktop, in a Tracker window, in a context menu, or in a file panel, try *right*-clicking on it (one-button mouse users: Ctrl+click). When the pop-up context menu appears, slide your mouse over the top entry, which is the folder's name. All of the files and folders contained within will appear. You can then slide over any file or folder and release your mouse button to open or launch it, or slide over a subdirectory to keep drilling down. Thanks to this ingenious solution, you can open any folder on any drive on your system with the absolute minimum amount of effort and the absolute minimum number of open Tracker windows. Live with this feature for a day and you'll grumble the next time you have to use an operating system without it.

**Alternate Tracker Views**  There are three ways to view the files in a folder—Icon View, Mini Icon View, and List View—and you can cycle the view of any folder among the three by using the Tracker's Window menu. Icon view displays your files as large (32-by-32 pixel) icons on a "free-form field" that lets you drag your icons around inside the window to any position; dragged icons stay where you put them. Mini Icon View also operates in free-form mode, but uses a small (16-by-16 pixel) icon for each file, so you can fit more files into a given window at once.

If you need to do any kind of advanced file management, sorting, or viewing, you'll want to be in List View, where the real power is. See the next section for more on List View.

There are a few other interesting options under the Window menu: Resize to Fit and Clean Up. The Resize to Fit option (hotkey: Alt+Y) will bring the boundaries of the Tracker window in as close as possible to the edges of your icons, while the Clean Up option (Alt+K) will snap each icon to the nearest point on an invisible grid. However, Clean Up will not "squish out the white space" between your icons, so a cleaned-up Tracker view can still look pretty messy. Your best bet is to manually drag icons into tight formation, then use Clean Up and Resize to Fit in succession.

**Customizing Tracker List Views**  When the Tracker is in List View mode, all files in the current folder are automatically sorted. By default, the sort order is alphabetical by filename. However, you can sort your list views by all kinds of advanced criteria—you can even perform sorts within sorts.

All settings for Tracker views are remembered on a folder-by-folder basis and will still be there the next time that folder is opened, including the position and size of the window, its current hidden and displayed attributes, column width and order, and all of your sort criteria.

***Inheriting Tracker Views***  Chances are, if you've organized the Tracker view of a particular folder in a particular way, you're going to want its subdirectories organized similarly. For example, if you've organized your email inbox so that the Subject attribute is leftmost and then you create subdirectories in your inbox, you'll probably want those subdirectories to be organized the same way. Fortunately, the Tracker is smart—any time you create a subdirectory, it inherits the properties of the folder it lives in (that is, of its parent folder). This makes it easy to create an entire hierarchy of folders within folders, all with exactly the same layout.

**Hiding/Displaying Columns**  To control which columns are displayed in List View, use the Attributes menu. Any entry with a checkmark next to it will be displayed in the view; those without will be hidden. Checkmarks are toggled by selecting them (release the mouse button on a checked item and it will become unchecked, and vice versa). By default, the only attributes displayed are Name, Size, and Modification Date, but depending on the purpose of the folder, or your needs at the time, you may find it useful to add Kind (filetype) and Created (original file date) to the view.

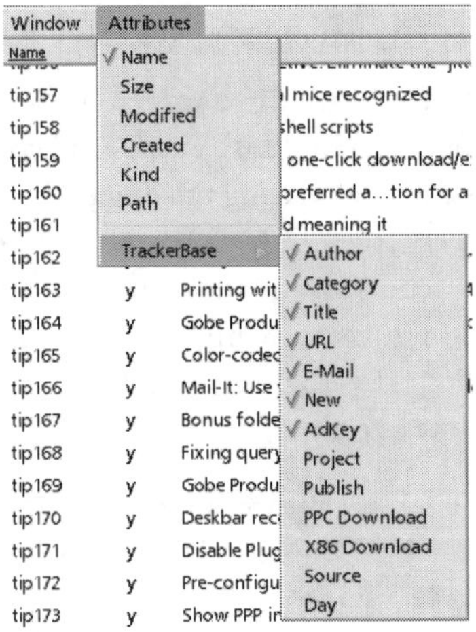

*Figure 5.03*

Show or hide the columns displayed by the Tracker by selecting their names in the Attributes menu.

**Extra Columns**  If the current folder contains any files with extra attributes, as is the case by default with E-Mail and Person files, look at the bottom of the

*Figure 5.04*

*If any of the files in the current folder have extra attributes, you can make the Tracker display them by pulling down the Attributes menu and selecting the filetype in question. The filetype's extra attributes will scroll out from its name. The folder shown contains two filetypes with extra attributes, so column options for both types are shown in the Attributes menu.*

Attributes menu—you'll find one entry for every such filetype in the current folder. For example, if your folder contains a mix of email messages and Person files, you'll see E-Mail and Person entries as the last items on this menu. Cascading down from them, you'll find a list of attributes associated with each type. You can display and hide any combination of these filetype-specific attributes just as you would with standard attributes. See the BeMail section of Chapter 4, *Get Online Fast*, and the attributes discussion later in this chapter for examples of custom columns in action.

If a folder contains no files with extra attributes, this entry will not be present on the Attributes menu.

**Change Column Width and Order**  At the top of every Tracker window in List View mode, you'll find a row of column headers bearing the column names. The names are separated by vertical bars. To change the width of a column, drag the vertical bars left or right. Your cursor will change as you hover over the column separator to indicate that it's moveable. To change the order of the columns, drag a column header left or right into the preferred position. As you drag a header, its outline will appear to float above the other headers. The header you're currently hovering over will become highlighted, indicating that if you drop the column you're moving, it will take the place of the highlighted column in the sort order. Dropped column headers will occupy the space to the left of the displaced column.

**Column Sorting**  The default sort order for the files and folders in a Tracker window is alphabetical by name, but you can change this by clicking once on a column header. For example, clicking once on the Size column header will sort the view by file size, from smallest to largest. To reverse the order of a sort, click the column header a second time. This will cause files starting with letters to be reverse-alphabetized, and files starting with numbers to be ordered backward.

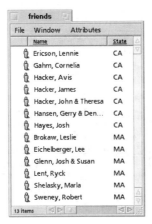

**Figure 5.05**

*If the Tracker's default sorting options don't give you enough control, try creating subsorts by holding down the Shift key and sorting again. Identical entries in the first sort will be grouped and sorted by the criterion of the second sort. Sorting these Person files by state only does so much good because so many of them live in the same state. Subsorting them by name gives us alphabetical name listings, grouped by state.*

 ***Sorts within Sorts*** Need more control than that? The Tracker will actually let you create subsorts within your sorts. To do this, create your sort normally, then hold down a Shift key and click another column header. Any items that are identical when sorted by the first criterion will be subsorted by the second criterion. For example, let's say you've done a sort by size, but in this particular folder, dozens or hundreds of your files have identical sizes. In that case, Shift-click the Name column header. All of your 2K files will be grouped alphabetically by name, then all of your 4K files will be listed, again sorted by name.

Because this technique depends on the fact that there are identical entries in the first sort, there are many situations where it's not useful. It can never be used when filename is the first sort, for instance, because filenames within a folder can never be identical. However, the subsort can be a real boon in other situations. For example, let's say you've got hundreds of Person files in your /boot/home/people/ folder, and you want to view them state by state. You do this, only to discover that you've got two dozen friends living in Oregon, and they're displayed in no particular order. Shift-click the Name column and you'll have a view of your contacts ordered by state, and subsorted within states by their names.

 ***What about a Hierarchical View?*** Chances are, you're accustomed to managing your files from a hierarchical tool, like Explorer or Finder. But you won't find one in R4 of BeOS (though there should be one by R5). The Tracker's chief engineer has some strong notions about why existing hierarchical file managers are less than adequate. If BeOS is going to have a hierarchical file manager, it's going to have an exceptional one. Meanwhile, if you simply must have hierarchical file management, try downloading a shareware file manager called BeTree from BeWare.

**Finding Your Path** Tracker windows have a wonderfully uncluttered interface, but one of the things you may miss from Windows Explorer's clutter is the ability to see at a glance (without having to dig around) the complete path from the root to the current folder, as well as the additive size of all files in the current folder and the total space remaining on the disk. While Tracker windows won't give you all of that at once, it will give up some of this info with a couple of quick clicks.

To find the complete path of the current folder, look at the lower-left corner of any Tracker window, where you'll see a small status area reporting the number of files and folders in the current view. Click in this area, and a pop-up window will display the directory structure leading all the way back up to the root. Even cooler, releasing the mouse while over any folder along the chain will open that folder in a Tracker view.

**Figure 5.06**

*Click in the lower-left corner of any Tracker view and you'll see the complete path from the root to the current folder. Release the mouse on any entry to open that folder.*

Alternatively, right-click on any file or folder in the current directory and choose Get Info from the context menu. The Get Info panel will display the current path, along with other details on that file or folder.

**Finding Directory Sizes** Getting the additive size of the files contained in the current directory isn't quite as direct as it could be, but once you've got the right hotkeys, you can do this almost instantaneously. All you have to do is navigate up one directory so you can see the icon for the current folder, then do a Get Info on this folder. Alt+Up Arrow will always open the current folder's parent, and Alt+I is the hotkey for Get Info. Thus, just tap Alt+Up Arrow, Alt+I in quick succession and you'll have your answer in a hot second.

As for the total space remaining on disk, there's only one way you can find that out easily from the BeOS GUI, and that's by choosing Get Info on a disk volume. Disk volumes are mounted on the desktop.

**Hotkeys** The Tracker provides a ton of hotkeys that let you easily manipulate and manage files and folders without reaching for the mouse. While the Tracker's hotkeys may differ from the keys you're accustomed to using on other systems, learning them will save you hours of needless mousing. Some of the hotkeys you may be addicted to, like the ability to cut, copy, and paste files and folders, are not available in BeOS, though the Tracker's chief engineer has hinted that he has even cooler tricks in store. Then again, the Tracker includes many hotkeys your other OSs may not have. Spend some time studying Table 5.01 and practicing these shortcuts—it's time well-spent.

### Table 5.01  Hotkeys available in any Tracker view

| Hotkey | Function |
| --- | --- |
| Alt+A | Select All |
| Alt+E | Edit Name (rename a file or folder) |
| Alt+F | Start a system query |
| Alt+D | Duplicate the selected file or folder |
| Alt+I | Get Info on the selected item |
| Alt+N | Create a new folder |
| Alt+O | Open the selected item |
| Alt+T (or Delete) | Move the selected item to the Trash |
| Alt+W | Close this window |
| Alt+Y | Shrink the Tracker view to current icon layout |
| Alt+Up Arrow | Open the parent folder |
| Alt+Down Arrow | Launch the selected item |
| Alt+Right Ctrl+Up Arrow (Mac: Opt+Command+Up) | Close the original window and open the parent |
| Alt+Right Ctrl+Down Arrow (Mac: Opt+Command+Down) | Close the parent window and open the child |
| Menu Key+W, I (Mac: no equivalent) | Icon View |
| Menu Key+W, M (Mac: no equivalent) | Mini-icon View |
| Menu Key+W, L (Mac: no equivalent) | List View |
| Right Ctrl+double-click file or folder (Mac: Opt+double-click) | Close the Tracker window and launch a file or folder |
| Any letter | Jump to the first file beginning with that letter, or come as close as possible |
| Tab | Jump to the next file or folder in the current sort order |
| Esc | Stop renaming an item and restore name; pressing Esc twice deselects a selected block of files or folders |
| Shift+click | Select multiple nonadjacent items |
| Shift+drag | Select multiple adjacent items (note that you can select multiple blocks of nonadjacent items this way as well) |

**Symlinks** Most operating systems have some mechanism for hyperlinking files to each other: aliases in MacOS, shortcuts in Windows, and symbolic links (or symlinks) in Unix. BeOS uses Unix-style symlinks, which are essentially nothing but a dummy file containing a pointer to the original file and bearing the original file's icon so it appears normally in Tracker windows.

 If you have a Unix background, you may be wondering about hard links. These are an entirely different animal from symlinks and aren't really links at all (a pair of hard links are nothing but entries in the filesystem pointing at exactly the same data). BeOS does not support hard links, even though it may appear that they do when you run the `ls -l` command from the Terminal—that's just a `bash` relic in BeOS.

**Figure 5.07**

*You can tell a symlink at a glance by the light gray underline beneath its name (we've used the Magnify application to zoom in on one here).*

Symlinks are an excellent example of the tight integration between BeOS's unique GUI and its Unix-style `bash` shell. Whether you create a symlink via the Tracker or from the Terminal, identical linking files are created. And whether you access a symlink by double-clicking or by typing its name into the Terminal, you get identical results.

So why might you want to do this? Here are a few ideas and common implementations:

- To provide a shortcut on the desktop or in your home directory linking to a file with a long pathname. This could save you repeated typing of lengthy path names, or deep folder digging.

- To keep multiple versions of the same program on your machine for testing purposes, using the symlink as a constant access point, always linking to the current working version.

- To satisfy badly written programs with pathnames hard-coded into them. By placing strategic links, you can fool the program into thinking that it's installed somewhere it's not. For example, if you're using a quick-n-dirty port of someone's homemade Linux program that has the path `/users/john/home` hard-coded into it, you could create a link to `/boot/home` in that location. When the program runs, it will find the symlink and follow it to your actual home directory.

- If you run a Web server such as PoorMan on your BeOS machine, you can create redirects just by placing symlinks in strategic locations (though there are some issues associated with this technique—see Chapter 8, *Networking*).

**Creating Symlinks** To create a symlink from the Tracker, drag any destination file with your right mouse button to the folder where you want the link to appear. Release the mouse button and choose Create Link Here from the pop-up menu.

To create a symlink from the Terminal, type `ln -s TargetPathName LinkPathName`. Let's say there's a calculator you like to use stored at `/boot/apps/research/utils/DeskCalc` and you want to create a link to it in your home directory, where you are now. You also want to give it a nice short name. You would type:

```
ln -s /boot/apps/research/utils/DeskCalc /boot/home/dc
```

From then on, typing dc from your home directory would launch the calculator. If you wanted to be able to launch it from anywhere, you'd create the link in /boot/home/config/bin instead.

***Symlinks Are Fragile*** If you're coming from the Mac world, you're accustomed to the intelligence with which the Finder handles aliases—if you move the target to which an alias points, your alias continues to work normally. While this is convenient for the user, the complexity of the Finder and the tangled mess of "cowpaths" it maintains behind the scenes is one of the reasons why MacOS is so slow.

If you're coming from the Windows world, you know that moving the target will cause Explorer to scan your system for it next time you click the link, and give you the option to hunt it down manually. The system is dumb as an ox, but it gets the job done fairly well through brute force.

BeOS, unfortunately, employs neither technique as of R4. Click a broken link and you'll just get an error message: "There was an error resolving the link."

The reason for the absence of smart links on BeOS is that it's very difficult (if not impossible) to make them work well with other filesystems, while BeOS needs to be able to work gracefully in a world full of other operating systems and networked filesystems. There may be a fix for this situation in the future, but for now, simply take care if you're using symlinks as a means to make anything mission-critical run properly. If possible, rewrite or reconfigure the application so that it's not dependent on symlinks to get its job done.

***Building Tunnels with Symlinks*** Not only can symlinks launch documents and applications elsewhere on your system, but if you create a symlink to a folder, it will function as a "drag-and-drop tunnel"—any items dropped on the link will be magically transported to the destination folder. Let's say you're working on a project that lives in /boot/home/projects/reports/school/bebox/ and you're taking a lot of BeOS screenshots for it. Every time you take a screen, a targa

*Figure 5.08*

*To build a symlink "tunnel," create a link to a remote folder wherever it's convenient. Dragging files onto this link will cause them to be "teleported" to the remote location.*

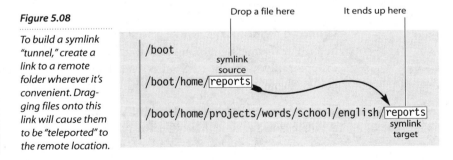

image file appears in your home directory, and you've got to move it to its destination later on. By creating a link in your home directory to the remote directory, you can "teleport" them through the directory structure by dragging them onto the symlink.

Every now and then, you'll download a .zip file from BeWare and find that it contains files with names like "Drag me …" and "… onto me." Since the "… onto me" folder is really just a symlink to the intended install destination, all you have to do is follow the instructions embedded in the filenames and you're done.

# Context Menus

Right-click on just about anything in BeOS, and a pop-up menu will appear. Because the exact contents of this menu differ depending on what's just been clicked, these menus are said to be context-sensitive, and the menus themselves are called context menus. For the most part, the biggest differences you'll encounter from one menu to the next are A) the top item in the menu and B) what appears on the Open With submenu. However, a few items (such as the Trash icon) have entirely different context menus, and of course, context menus found within applications relate specifically to those programs and include options not related to BeOS itself.

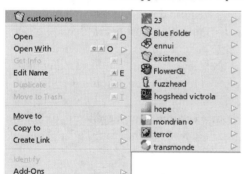

**Figure 5.09**

*Context menus appear when you right-click on various items in BeOS, particularly in the Tracker. Right-click a folder and scroll up to the folder name at the top of the context menu—the contents of that folder will appear, and you can use the standard hierarchical menu folder operations described earlier.*

**Right-Clicking Queries**  If you right-click a query icon and select its name from the top of the context menu, the query will be executed in real time. This means you can access query results on your system without launching the gray query results window. Learn all about BeOS queries in Chapter 7, *Working with Queries*.

**Figure 5.10**

*Right-click a file, and the top entries will always be Open and "Open With" (described below).*

**Figure 5.11**

*Right-click a query and it will be executed in real time.*

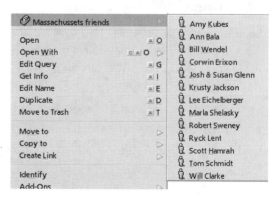

**Open and Open With** The technique BeOS uses for determining which application should be used to open a file once it's been double-clicked is ingenious—we'll look at that in detail in the next section. For now, suffice it to say that BeOS not only knows which application is your preferred plain text handler (for instance), but it also keeps track of *all* editors on your system capable of opening plain text files. When you double-click a text file, it's launched into your favorite editor. If you'd rather open it in something else, right-click the file's name, choose Open With, and you'll see a list of all applications registered on your system as being capable of handling that filetype. These are called candidate applications.

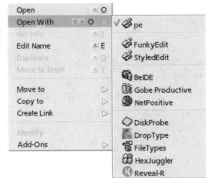

*Figure 5.12*

*The Open With entry on the Tracker's context menus gives you the option of opening a file not only in its preferred application, but in any application on your system capable of handling that filetype.*

Study Figure 5.12 and you'll notice something else interesting: The candidate applications are grouped according to relevance. In the top group is my favorite text editor, Pe, all alone. Just below that are two more dedicated text editors, StyledEdit and FunkyEdit. Just below that is a group of apps that happen to be able to handle plain text files, but aren't dedicated to the task. Finally, at the bottom, there are a few apps that can handle any filetype at all. These are interesting programs for other reasons, but *not* what I want to open my plain text file in. BeOS has not only found all my text-capable apps, but it's successfully grouped them according to how well-suited they are to the task at hand. Of course, you'll see totally different groups of applications when you right-click on other kinds of files.

There's a second way to access Open With applications that gives you a little more information than what you see on the standard context menu. Click and release on the Open With entry itself, and you'll see a panel like the one in Figure 5.13, on the next page.

## The "Open With" Relationship

So how does BeOS determine how to group the candidate applications in the Open With menu? A set of built-in rules are run against the FileTypes database to determine their "relationship" to the file in question. The context menu is constructed from the results of this query. There are four possible relationships:

- The app is the declared "Preferred App" for that file.
- The app can handle the file's full type (e.g. text/plain).
- The app can handle the file's supertype (text/...).
- The app can handle any filetype (.../...).

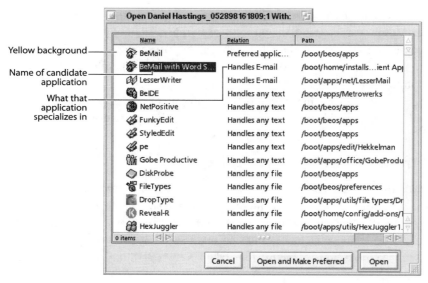

Yellow background —

Name of candidate — application

What that — application specializes in

*Figure 5.13*

*By selecting the Open With menu entry itself, you can bring the same candidate applications into a special panel, distinguished by a yellow background. This panel will actually tell you what each of your candidate applications specializes in. This panel also gives you the option to establish one of the candidate applications as the new preferred application for that file.*

The rules used for determining how candidate applications are grouped in this panel are identical to the rules used to build the Open With… context menu, described above.

**Get Info** You met the august Info panel earlier, when we first looked at disk mounting (Chapter 2). The same panel can be accessed by right-clicking on any file or folder anywhere in the Tracker, and will always give a quick synopsis of the item's exact size, location, filetype, modification date, and, if you've clicked on a link, the path to which the link points.

*Figure 5.14*

*Right-click any file, folder, or disk in your system and Get Info will report back on its size (accurate down to the last byte), creation and modification dates, filetype, and absolute path from the root.*

**Edit Name, Duplicate, and Move to Trash** The purpose and operation of this trio should be self-explanatory. You'll probably use these frequently enough that you'll want to use their direct keyboard shortcuts (Alt+E, Alt+D, and Alt+T, respectively) rather than accessing them from the context menu.

***Another Way to Rename*** In addition to renaming files by choosing Edit Name or Alt+E on a selected file, you can also simply click once on the filename, pause for a moment, and the filename will become editable. If you're coming to BeOS from the Mac world, you'll find this behavior familiar. But if you're coming to BeOS from other operating systems, be careful! It's all too easy to accidentally rename files if you're not paying attention and use the keyboard a lot, though you'll become accustomed to this behavior quickly.

## Desktop and Trash: More than Meets the Eye

In Chapter 2, I told you that the desktop and the Trash were just special folders with a few unusual properties. To be truthful, the desktop and the Trash are *really* strange folders, with some *really* strange properties. In fact, Pavel Cisler, father of the Tracker, refers to them as "the Tracker's abstractions." Every time you initialize a BFS partition, whether on a floppy disk or three-petabyte SCSI RAID array, a home directory is installed on that partition, complete with its own desktop and Trash folders.

The paradox facing Be engineers was the fact that the desktop represented a central and solitary system object. To have two desktops would make no sense. Yet every mountable volume had to have one in order to function as a BeOS volume. To guard against entanglements of logic and impossible Tracker situations (like dragging one desktop folder into another one), the Tracker simply reads the desktop and Trash folders of every mounted volume and joins them into a single virtual entity. The illusion is executed so transparently that you may never even realize it's happening.

**Move To, Copy To, and Create Link** If hierarchical folder menus are a brilliant innovation, then these three context menu entries represent brilliance within brilliance. They operate in an identical way, but allow you to move or copy the selected item or items to the destination folder. Create Link places a symlink to the selected item at the destination.

If you've been missing Windows's ability to cut, copy, and paste files and folders in Explorer, you'll find that this feature easily compensates for its absence in the Tracker (although, unfortunately, this function is not keyboardable in the Tracker).

**Identify** The purpose of the Identify entry eludes many new users. They select a file, click Identify… and nothing happens. The point of the Identify entry will make more sense after you've read about the system Registrar later in this chapter. In a nutshell, Identify forces the system to try to assign the right type to the file immediately. If you have a file with a generic icon (a plain blue square), try the Identify option on it. This may or may not result in the file acquiring the correct icon and filetype; if it doesn't, see the *Changing Icons* sidebar later in this chapter and fix it manually.

*Terminal Tip* When you're in the Terminal, you can use the "old" form of Identify, `mimeset`. Type `mimeset filename` and the same process will be run as the Registrar attempts to identify a correct MIME type for the file in question. One thing you can do with `mimeset` that you can't do with Identify in the Tracker is to run the process over your entire hard drive in a single swoop. Just type `mimeset -all`. Allow up to several minutes for the process to run, depending on the size of your hard drive, the number of files it contains, and your system's speed. Remember that you can set any Terminal job to run in the background by succeeding it with an ampersand symbol, like `mimeset -all &`.

 *Batch Identify* You're not restricted to using Identify on one file at a time—you can easily do it for an entire directory of files at once. Let's say you copied a directory full of TIFF images from Windows to your BeOS machine. Once they're on BeOS, they show up in the Tracker with the generic file icon rather than the TIFF icon. Why? Because the files have never lived on BeOS they don't yet have any attributes. Yet when you double-click one of them, it opens just fine. In the absence of attributes, the Tracker applies a set of rules to determine the filetype, and the last-resort rule is to look at the three-letter extension and see if it finds a match in the FileTypes database.

This process works just fine, but it would be nice to get those icons right away so you can tell the TIFFs from the BMPs from the HTML documents at a glance. To force the system (actually, to force the Registrar) to attempt to identify the type of a bunch of files at once, select them all, right-click on the selection, and choose Identify from the context menu. They should acquire appropriate filetypes and corresponding icons in a hot second.

## Add-Ons

Most people are familiar with the concept of plug-ins. The makers of programs like Netscape Navigator and Adobe Photoshop use this concept to allow third-party developers to extend the functionality of their applications. The companies publish plug-in specifications—sets of "hooks" that can be used to communicate with the programs—and developers write their add-in programs in conformance with these hooks. BeOS takes the concept of the plug-in and extends it to the entire operating system—these BeOS plug-ins are called add-ons.

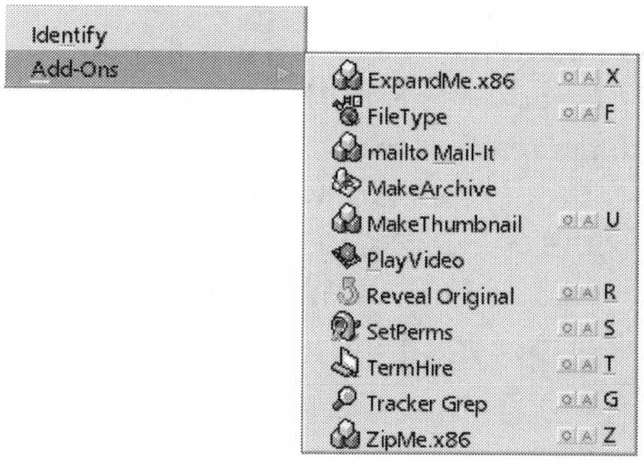

*Figure 5.15*

*Users can install third-party enhancements to the operating system by simply dropping add-on files into ~/config/add-ons. Because add-ons are dynamically loadable, they go to work immediately; no reboot necessary. Access Tracker add-ons by right-clicking any file or folder (or in the blank space in any Tracker view) and choosing Add-Ons from the context menu. Most of the add-ons pictured here do not ship with BeOS.*

Be thus benefits by having its OS enhanced, and developers benefit by being able to sell extended BeOS functionality to users.

Add-ons to the BeOS filesystem allow users to read and write to disks formatted on lots of other operating systems. Add-ons to the Translator system allow any application to support any filetype for which a Translator is installed (Chapter 9).

 When add-ons function as device drivers, as they do in the case of filesystem or network protocol drivers, they're sometimes referred to as "dynamically loadable device modules," though you'll usually only see this terminology used in whitesheets and other technical documentation.

The Tracker accepts add-ons too, and there are many available for download from BeWare. A couple of add-ons are installed automatically, and users can install downloaded add-ons by dropping them into the appropriate directory. Be puts Tracker add-ons that ship with the system into /boot/beos/ system/add-ons/Tracker/. If you download your own Tracker add-ons, you should store them in /boot/home/config/add-ons/Tracker. When you right-click any file in the Tracker and choose Add-Ons from the context menu, the contents of these two directories will be merged into a single list.

 As mentioned at several points in this book, it's important to maintain the distinction between user-level and system-level directories. The /boot/home hierarchy is yours to do with as you please, and should be used for any changes you make to system behavior, such as the addition of new add-ons. The /boot/beos hierarchy belongs to Be. With the appropriate permissions you *can* put add-ons here, but be prepared to have them wiped out or overwritten next time you upgrade BeOS.

We'll be exploring the FileType add-on in some depth later in this chapter; essentially, this add-on makes it possible to change the preferred application for a single file, as opposed to making changes to filetypes on a system-wide basis. The MakeArchive add-on will make a Unix-style .tar file out of any selected file or folder, the Reveal add-on lets you find the original file pointed to by any symlink, and the TermHire add-on (my favorite) will open up a Terminal window with its path set to the current Tracker window.

 **Fast Access to Add-Ons**   You may have noticed that add-ons usually end with "-X", where X is the first letter of the add-on's name. These letters determine the hotkey associated with that add-on, which are invoked by pressing Ctrl+Alt+X (on the *right* side of your keyboard; Mac users: Option+Command+X). Thus, in Figure 5.15 (above), TermHire can be invoked from any Terminal window by simply pressing Ctrl+Alt+T, no mousing around required (if you're a big Terminal user, you'll end up using this hotkey *constantly*).

# Attributes

As described in Chapter 2, any file stored on a BeOS machine can also have related data stored along with it in the filesystem. The collection of extra data related to a given file is referred to as that file's attributes. Attributes can be of any size or type, and each file can have an unlimited number of attributes associated with it.

## What's in a File's Attributes?

So what exactly is in a file's attributes? While it's impossible to give a blanket answer to that question since attributes are not absolutely required, a typical file will store at least its filetype in an attribute. If that file has a custom icon attached to it (rather than inheriting the icon for its filetype from the FileTypes database), it will gain two more attributes: one each for the small and large versions of that icon.

So how are attributes used? What are they good for? What kinds of things are stored in them? The use of attributes is unrestricted, and is as broad as the practical imagination of the user, or of the developer of an application that uses attributes to do something cool. Let's look at some of the best examples of attribute usage built into BeOS by looking at two special filetypes: the Person file and the email file.

If you haven't yet created any Person files, launch the People application in your apps folder, fill in some or all of the blanks with information about yourself, and save the file. Now open up your /boot/home/people folder, pull down the Window menu, and choose List View. Do you have a column marked Size? If not, pull down the Attributes menu and select Size. Note that your new Person file has a size of zero bytes. How can a file that you know very well contains real data have no size? Because all of that data was written into the file's attributes. There is no data in a Person file *per se*—everything is stored in meta-data.

**How Are Attribute Sizes Accounted For?**  Astute readers will have noticed an interesting side effect of BeOS attributes: While files are allowed to have as many attributes as they like, and while each of those attributes can store any amount or kind of data, the size of a file's attributes is not reported by the Tracker. So where is this data stored and how much of your hard disk is it eating up?

A very good question, the answer to which comes in two parts:

- While attributes *can* store as much data as they like, in reality the vast majority of files store only minute amounts of data in their attributes; usually little more than the filetype and possibly a custom icon. The total amount of data stored in all the attributes on your system typically amounts to a hill of beans.

- That fact notwithstanding, it is at least *theoretically* possible for attributes to consume huge chunks of disk space. For example, there's nothing standing in the way of you or one of your applications creating a zero-byte file with a single 2GB attribute. Or of an application creating files that store almost all of their data in attributes, so that the Tracker would tell you that only small amounts of data are being used, when in reality substantial portions of your disk are being consumed by attributes. The key word in this scenario is "theoretically." In reality, almost no one is using attributes like this, and it's hard to think of a reason why someone would feel tempted to. One notable exception at this writing is the most excellent Thumbnail add-on, which stores miniature versions of images in image file attributes—these can certainly add up if you have hundreds or thousands of images. In general, though, it's just not a problem, and disk space is cheap enough these days that the small amounts of space that go uncounted are a non-issue.

## Attributes and the Tracker

Since attributes become part of your search criteria when you run a query, you can search your system for all people living in Texas, or all people whose names begin with M and who also have phone numbers in the 617 area code, excluding those who are members of your bowling club (more on queries in Chapter 7).

In addition, you can create customized Tracker views showing just the data you want, ordered and sorted the way you want it. With your People folder open in List View mode, pull down the Attributes menu and scroll down to Person. From this entry you'll find options for displaying all known attributes for that filetype. Select E-mail and Home Phone, then use the List View customization techniques described earlier in this chapter to display just the Name, E-mail, and Home Phone columns. By combining the power of attributes with the

Tracker's precision display and sorting options, you've just transformed your file manager into a customized Rolodex.

*Figure 5.16*

*Because the display of attributes in Tracker List Views can be toggled on and off, and because you can order Tracker columns in any order you like, you can create customized Tracker views specific to your needs. Custom settings like this one are stored (guess where?) in the attributes of the folder itself, so when you next open the folder, it will look the way you left it.*

***Edit Attributes from within the Tracker***  Most attributes that can be viewed in Tracker columns can also be edited there. Just select the attribute in question, click once in the selection to enter edit mode, then type normally. For example, if Krusty Jackson in Figure 5.16 above were to change his email address, you wouldn't even have to open his Person file to update your records—you could just open your People folder, select his email address, click to edit, and type or paste his new address over the top of the old one. Hitting Enter commits the change.

There is an exception to the rule: Attributes can be set to be uneditable. For example, you'll find that you can't change the To: attribute of a BeMail message. To change the editable status of an attribute, use the FileTypes panel in your preferences folder. But remember—uneditable attributes are usually uneditable for a good reason! See next section (*Creating Custom Attributes*) for details.

## Creating Custom Attributes

If you're not getting what you need out of the attributes already associated with a given filetype, you're free to add your own, or to change certain qualities of the existing attributes.

Let's say you maintain a monthly newsletter that runs contributions from dozens of writers, who send you their submissions as plain text files. You store all of these files in a folder called submissions, and use the Tracker to sort them by date. Your system is good, but imagine how much better it would be if you could also use the Tracker to sort the submissions by the author's name, the month the piece is scheduled to run, and the section of your newsletter you intend to run it in. In essence, you're really going to start using BFS's database-like qualities to organize your hard drive as if it were a true database. In order to pull this off, you're going to need to add a few new attributes to your system's text/plain filetype.

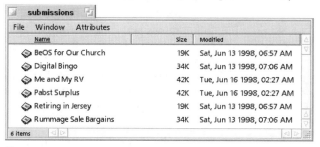

*Figure 5.17*

*By default, your newsletter's text submissions show up in the Tracker showing only the filename, size, and modification date. You'd like to be able to see at a glance who wrote each piece, along with the section of the newsletter and month in which the piece is intended to run. You'll need to add a few new attributes to your text/plain filetype.*

While we're going to look at the FileTypes dialog in detail in the next section, we'll work with its attribute editor now. Open the FileTypes panel in your preferences folder and you'll see a list of all the supertypes known to your system: application, audio, image, text, video, and possibly more. Click the triangular latch next to the text supertype and scroll down to the entry marked

. . . . . . . . . . . . .

*Figure 5.18*

To add an attribute to a filetype, locate it in the FileTypes panel, click the Add button in the Extra Attributes section, and fill in the appropriate details.

Text File. Farther down in the dialog, you'll see a section labeled Extra Attributes. Click the Add button and you'll be faced with a blank dialog similar to the one in Figure 5.18.

There are two name fields here. The "Attribute name" field will become the name of the column header we're trying to create and will show up as a searchable attribute in the Query tool. The "Internal name" field is used by BeOS itself to keep everything unique. The first section should be related to the filetype, and the second part should reflect the attribute name from the top field. If your attribute name had spaces, remove them for this field. Most of the entries in the "Attribute type" pop-up are of concern only to programmers. You should choose String for user in Tracker views. Of course you want to be able to edit and view this attribute from the Tracker, so check those boxes. The "Display width" field will determine the default column width of this attribute's column—150 is a comfortable, average column width. Choose Left alignment, click OK, and close the FileTypes panel (there is no Save option here).

 ***Don't Alter Existing Attributes*** While adding new attributes to existing filetypes is completely safe, it's impossible to categorically say the same for changing or removing existing attributes. When developers create an application, they often create a new filetype that goes along with it so they can store specific kinds of meta-data. The application is built to look for and work with specific attributes, so if the attributes are missing or changed, bad things can happen. For example, if you change the name of the State attribute for People files to "Province," you'll still see a State field in the People application, and be able to use it normally. However, when you go to run a query on all people living in California, you'll find that the Query window won't let you search by state. At the same time, a search by Province for all people in California will yield no search results. In other words, things get all bunged up, so don't do it.

| Name | Author | Section | Month |
|------|--------|---------|-------|
| Digital Bingo | Alfred Dominischnikov | ChurchTech | August |
| BeOS for Our Church | Krusty Jackson | ChurchTech | July |
| Rummage Sale Bargains | Homer | Cruise Control | August |
| Retiring in Jersey | Jean-Paul Sartre | Cruise Control | May |
| Me and My RV | Edsel Eddie | RV Life | June |
| Pabst Surplus | Simone Du Beauvoir | RV Life | June |

6 items

*Figure 5.19*

By adding Author, Month, and Section attributes to the FileTypes panel, we were able to extend the file sorting and sifting abilities of the Tracker. Now we can see at a glance an array of meta-data related to our files, and sort our files on these criteria. Here we've sorted submissions by section name and subsorted within section name by month name.

To test your work, return to your submissions folder. If it's open, close and then reopen it. Pull down the Attributes menu and choose Text File | Author to display your new column. You can now edit any Author field by clicking once to select, then pausing for a moment to enter edit mode. It's a little tricky at first since you're clicking in a single-character field (which uses a hyphen as a placeholder), but you'll get the hang of it. Once you've entered a few author names, you can test their sortability by clicking on the Author column header, and dragging the Author column to a better position, if you like. If everything worked out, you can return to the FileTypes dialog and enter extra attributes for month and section.

## Searching on Custom Attributes

If you've created custom attributes for any of your filetypes (as in the example above) and gotten them to display properly in the Tracker, you probably want to do the next logical thing: use the query engine to search on them. Hit Alt+F, select Text File as the filetype, change the query type to By Attribute, select Author as the attribute, type in one of your authors' names, and … nothing. Zero results. Why?

**Working with the Index** When you run a search, BeOS doesn't examine every file on your system. It only searches through an index that it maintains for just this purpose. Certain attributes, such as filename, filetype, size, and modification date, are added automatically to the index every time a new file is created. If you want BeOS to index other attributes, you have to tell it to do so. Once the index knows to watch for a given attribute, it will be indexed automatically every time a new file with that attribute is created.

Open a Terminal and type `lsindex`. A list of the internal names of all currently indexed attributes will fly by. Note that `Text:Author` (the internal name we added in the example above) is not on the list. To add it, type:

```
mkindex -t string Text:Author
```

Hit Enter, and type `lsindex` again (note that `-t string` denotes the datatype of the index—all entries for this attribute will be added as text strings). You should see the author entry now. Do the same for `Text:Section` and `Text:Month` and you're all set. However, there's a catch: Indexing has only been enabled for files created from now on; any files created before the index was looking for them were not indexed, so don't bother trying to search for your sample files just yet. Return to the Tracker view, select one of your files, and hit Alt+D to make a copy of it. *Now* you can run a successful attribute query for that file.

***Batch-Indexing New Attributes*** As described above, attributes attached to files created before that attribute's index was created are not searchable. If you have a lot of files with new attributes that you want indexed, the easiest way to go about it is to create a temp folder and use the Tracker to copy (not move) the files into the temp folder. The act of writing those files to a new location on disk will cause the new index to pick up on your attributes. After confirming this and checking to make sure you copied all of the right files, you can delete the originals.

***Don't Go Nuts with Custom Indexes*** BeOS has a good reason for not automatically indexing every single little attribute: performance. The more indexes that are being created and stored, the more work the system has to do with every query. If you want to create custom attributes for a specific purpose, you should do so by all means, without hesitation. The functionality is there to make your life easier. However, you should be mindful of the fact that if you go hog-wild with the indexing, you could impact your system's query speed. Note that performance is affected not by the *size* of your indexes, but by the *number* of them.

To remove an index, type rmindex TEXT:section into the Terminal, replacing TEXT:section with the internal name you want to remove. If you've followed along with this example but don't intend to use the author, month, and section indexes, remember to remove them! You may also want to remove the extra text attributes we created from the FileTypes dialog, though there's no harm in leaving those in place.

**Searching on New Filetypes**  Separate from the issue of attributes is the question of the types of files the query interface lets you search on by default. You'll note that there are many more filetypes in your system's FileTypes database than there are searchable types in the query tool. That's because the query tool only picks up types that have a "friendly name" associated with them. If you create an entirely new filetype, be sure to give it a friendly name in addition to an internal name, or it won't appear in the query tool's picklist. See Chapter 7 for more information.

## Viewing Extra Attributes

The Tracker is a great way to view and edit attributes, but it also shields you from a certain amount of hidden attribute data. Most files have more attributes than are generally useful to display. If you're working with extra attributes, remember that many of them are set to be uneditable and/or unviewable. If you're feeling geeky, however, there are a number of ways to view or edit *all* of a file's attributes.

**FileType**  If all you want to access is the file's MIME type, right-click on the file and select Add-Ons | FileType. The resulting panel will display the file's MIME type and let you edit it manually.

**DiskProbe**  Remember all the warnings earlier about the dangers of using DiskProbe injudiciously? Well, they're still true. However, DiskProbe is the only graphical application included with your system that will show you all of a file's attributes at once. Right-click on a file, select Open With..., and scroll down to DiskProbe (or drag the file onto the DiskProbe icon if it's already visible). DiskProbe's Attributes menu will include one entry for every attribute associated with the file—select one, and one of two things will happen. If the attribute is stored in plain text, DiskProbe will open it in a small text editor, which you can use to change it manually. (Test this on one of the files we created in the example above.) If the attribute is storing binary information, DiskProbe will probably tell you, "Sorry, no editor available for this attribute type."

**The Terminal**  BeOS includes a handful of command-line attribute manipulation utilities that will let you view and make changes to attributes that can't be accessed in any other way. Open a Terminal and type cd /boot/beos/bin/, and then ls *attr*. You should get a listing of four files: addattr, catattr, listattr, and rmattr.

The command listattr filename will show the type, size (in bytes), and name of each attribute associated with that file. Chances are, unless you're a programmer, much of what you see here will look like garbage. However, if you run listattr on a file with custom attributes, you should be able to recognize their names. Here's the listattr output for one of our files from the example above:

```
file Rummage Sale Bargains
    Type          Size                    Name
 ----------    ---------      ------------------------------
0x696e666f        328                          pe-info
    Int-32          4                             wrap
    Int-32          4                        alignment
0x52415754        160                           styles
   MIME str        28                    BEOS:PREF_APP
   MIME str        11                        BEOS:TYPE
     Text           6                      TEXT:author
     Text           7                       TEXT:month
     Text          15                     TEXT:section
```

All of the file's attributes are listed in the right-hand column. Now that we know what attributes are associated with the file, we want to be able to see their contents. That's what catattr is for; its usage is catattr attributename filename. Let's go from bottom to top. The last three entries are the easiest— obviously, they represent our custom attributes. Typing catattr TEXT:author RummageSale yields this report:

```
RummageSale : string : Homer
```

Now we know that Homer is the author of the newsletter article on rummage sales, just as we would expect. The next entry is particularly interesting and is one of the only attributes you'll find attached to practically every single file on your system. Typing catattr BEOS:TYPE RummageSale yields:

```
RummageSale : string : text/plain
```

Ah—now we know the filetype, without even looking at the Tracker. Typing `catattr BEOS:PREF_APP RummageSale` yields:

`RummageSale : string : application/x-vnd.Hekkel-Pe`

This is telling us the signature of the application specified as the system's preferred plain text handler (in this case, it's Pe, the Programmer's Editor, by Maarten Hekkelman). The three entries above this—wrap, alignment, and styles—represent Pe-specific settings used to specify how this particular text file should be displayed. Running `catattr` on alignment and wrap will return just a 0 or 1, for on or off; while running `catattr` on styles returns jumbled garbage, meaning that this information is stored in binary mode and can't be displayed by the Terminal. Running `catattr` on pe-info returns another incomprehensible list of data—this time readable, though—that apparently contains specifics about window position, tab stops, and other miscellany.

To change the contents of an attribute, you'll need to delete the entire attribute and then replace it. To remove an attribute, use `rmattr ATTRIBUTE:name FileName` (replacing these with the real names of the attribute and the file). To add an attribute, complete with content, use `addattr ATTRIBUTE:name "my content here" FileName`. Note that if your content includes any spaces, it should be enclosed in quotes, as it is here.

 **If all you want to change from the command line is the filetype (rather than any other attribute), you can use the settype command, like this:**

`settype -t text/html filename(s)`

**This lets you change a filetype directly, without having to remove the existing type first.**

**There are also a few third-party attribute editors available as add-ons or standalone applications. Keep your eye on BeWare for existing tools such as NodeInspector or Attribute Viewer, as well as other tools likely to show up in the future.**

# The Filetyping Problem

If you've been poking around in BeOS's nooks and crannies, you've probably noticed two rather similar applications with almost identical names. One is called FileTypes (plural) and lives in your Preferences folder. The other is called FileType (singular) and is accessed as a Tracker add-on (right-click any file and select Add-Ons | FileType from the context menu). It's important to understand the difference between these two, and to learn to use them both. Mastering this pair can help you to better understand how BeOS works internally, and will simultaneously give you more latitude and control in your daily work. Before diving in, though, I'm going to branch off on a detour and take a look at the big picture so you know exactly why BeOS filetyping works the way it does, and what problems it's meant to solve. We'll return to the FileType panel after this brief message.

## Guilt by Association

What happens when you double-click on a file in other operating systems, like MacOS or Windows? A file is launched in an application, sure. But how does the system know what application to launch? What criteria does it use? Are they good criteria, or are you stuck with a set of 15-year-old rules for defining preferred applications?

Let's say you're in Microsoft Windows (any version) and you double-click a file called readme.txt. It pops up in Microsoft Notepad because Notepad is set up to be your preferred application for all files ending in .txt. Files ending in .doc open up in Microsoft Word, files ending in .psd open in Adobe Photoshop, and so on. If you want a file to open up in another application, you just rename it with a different extension. It's fast, easy, filesystem-independent, and … stupid. Really, really brain-dead.

For one thing, the three-letter extension is an inelegant requirement and makes your directory listings look as complicated as the NASDAQ. Second, it's a lot to ask of new users, who are having enough trouble finding their way around the system without having to memorize a huge list of extensions. But finally, and most profoundly, it's too easy to screw things up. If you rename a text file to readme.doc, no problem—Word can open up a text file just fine. But if, on the other hand, you rename a Word document with a .txt extension, Notepad is going to try and open it, and choke badly. Rename an Adobe Acrobat file with a .jpg extension, and your image viewer is going to get very confused. What's more, you now have no easy way of determining what the actual filetype is, aside from making educated guesses until you get it right. Tagging a few letters onto a filename only *appears* to change the type of the file because it changes the icon. In reality, the actual document type is untouched, and you end up with icons that lie to you, masquerading as something they're not.

Granted, this scenario doesn't happen too often, and most people get used to using extensions early in their Windows careers and never think about it again. The nice thing is that you can change the preferred app for an entire directory of files just by typing something like ren *.txt *.html from a DOS prompt, which can come in pretty handy. The other nice thing about using extensions for filetype identification is that files coming from the Internet or other operating systems are handled quite easily as long as the extension is in place. Finally, and perhaps most importantly, Microsoft Windows users can make a single tweak and change the preferred application for every .txt file on their system, instantly. But woe be unto the poor user who finds herself with a file called J8tee7x with no extension and no clue whether it's supposed to be a text document or a bitmap image.

On the other side of the fence is the Mac way of doing things. Under MacOS, every file stores extra data in the filesystem, containing information on things like the preferred application for that file. As a result, Mac users can call their files anything they like and the files will still open up correctly in the preferred application. In addition, their files can take any icon, giving them a higher degree of customizability. But there are big problems with the Mac way as well. For one thing, MacOS makes one big assumption: that the application that created a file is the one you'll prefer to view it in. As a result, if you make a JPEG file in Photoshop and then later double-click its icon, you're going to have sit around and file your nails while you wait for Photoshop to load just so you can view your image. Yes, you can change the preferred application so that this particular file launches in a snappy little app like JPEGview, but there's no way to do it for all of your JPEGs system-wide. Third-party utilities help some, but this really shouldn't be the domain of third parties. Even worse is the inconsistency. Let's say you have a folder containing 100 HTML files. Some of them were created in SimpleText, some were saved down from the Web via Netscape, some were made by a co-worker using BBEdit, and a few were written in Microsoft Word. All of the files are pure HTML, but MacOS displays them with four different icons and opens them with four different applications. Again—brain-dead.

But one of the most problematic things about filetyping on the Apple Macintosh is the fact that it only works as long as you're exchanging files with other Mac users. Because Mac users aren't in the habit of using extensions on their filenames, and because the extra filesystem data isn't understood by or transferred to other operating systems, Mac files just get blank, generic icons when copied to a Windows system. And try teaching a MacOS newbie learning to build his first Web site why it's important that he end all of his documents with ".html". The Internet (which runs mostly on Unix) uses extensions for file identification too.

Both of these systems have their strengths and weaknesses. The Windows way is fast and efficient as long as everyone follows the rules. But the rules really suck, allowing for mismatched filetypes. The Mac way is more elegant for the newbie, but it makes terrible assumptions about which application should be the preferred one. It also has serious limitations for the power user, who can't change the association for a given filetype system-wide. Third-party utilities help in this domain, but this really should be considered the province of the operating system itself. There's got to be a better way. Which brings us to BeOS.

# The Filetyping Solution: MIME

When MacOS and Windows were developed, hardly anyone knew the Internet even existed. But BeOS had the advantage of evolving while the Internet was in heavy growth mode, and Be was paying attention. One of the Internet's great strengths is the fact that it's inherently cross-platform. Theoretically, documents made on any operating system can be viewed on any other operating system. While that may seem obvious and old-hat to you by now, this was pretty exciting stuff to geeks the world over once upon a time. In fact, it's one of the many reasons for the Web's rapid rise to mass popularity. And how did the Web break the cross-platform boundary? By adopting an intelligent, platform-neutral system for identifying filetypes.

Rather than worrying too much about how to handle proprietary file formats like Word and Photoshop documents, the Internet depends on a system called MIME, or Multipurpose Internet Mail Extensions (the "mail" bit arises from the fact that MIME grew out of solutions originally built for handling email attachments). The MIME system looks at filetypes in terms of their overall class (image, text, audio, and so forth). Every file, without exception, belongs to one of these meta-classes, or "supertypes." Then the exact type of file within that class is specified. For instance, images can be JPEGs or bitmaps, text files can be plain text or HTML, and so on. There are hundreds of MIME types registered by an international standards organization called the Internet Assigned Numbers Authority (IANA, **www.iana.org**), and developers of new file formats are free to register them in this central MIME database. Filetypes are thus assigned in "supertype/type pairs" with the following format:

```
CLASS/TYPE
image/jpeg
text/html
audio/wav
application/exe
```

and so on.

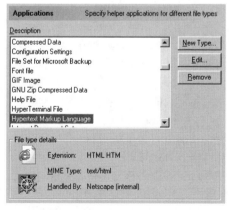

**Figure 5.20**

*You may be familiar with the Internet's MIME schema if you've ever poked around in Netscape Navigator's MIME database, which lets you establish preferred applications for files accessed online. BeOS takes the same MIME concept and extends it to the entire operating system.*

Whenever a file is transferred from a Web server to your browser, its MIME type is sent along with it. Neither the server nor the Web page dictates which application should handle any given MIME type— that's up to the recipient's browser or operating system, and is configurable by the end-user. Thus, say your copy of Netscape is configured to launch the RealAudio player whenever it receives a file with the MIME type of audio/x-realaudio, and to display documents of type text/html within its own window. If you'd rather have your favorite audio application play downloaded .wav files rather than your browser's built-in player, all you have to do is tweak the MIME type in your browser preferences. In this way, the MIME system serves as a sort of abstraction layer, doling out just enough information about a file's type to get the job done, but leaving plenty of room for every user to configure their preferred application for each filetype.

What happens when the server doesn't send a MIME type along with a file? That's when Plan B kicks in. The browser examines the file's extension and runs a lookup in its database of known types. If your browser already knows that files ending in .wav are almost always of the type audio/wav, then it can still figure out which application gets to handle the file in question. The system is fast, logical, inherently compatible with any operating system, and, thanks to its simplicity, reliable.

By now you're probably wondering what all of this has to do with BeOS (or maybe it's obvious by now). Rather than repeat the sins of systems past, Be took the well-established MIME system and fused it into their operating system. All application associations in BeOS are handled by MIME types—the same kind of type/creator pairs used on the Internet.

 Be's adoption of the MIME standard is a fine example of the company responding to the wishes of the developer community. Chris Herborth, this book's technical editor, spearheaded a movement to get the original Mac-style type/creator system replaced by the superior MIME scheme.

Of course, the MIME standard was never designed to support an entire operating system, so Be has added a lot of extra functionality and intelligence to the basic idea, adapting the concept to suit their needs. For instance, the MIME system already handles classes and types of documents very nicely. But what about the program files themselves? In BeOS, most of your applications have both a standard MIME type (application/x-vnd.Be-elfexecutable for x86 or application/x-be-executable for PPC), as well as a unique "signature" that looks much like a MIME type, but is not.

### Table 5.02  Signatures of some common applications

| Application | Signature |
|---|---|
| StyledEdit | application/x-vnd.Be-STEE |
| Tracker | application/x-vnd.Be-TRAK |
| CDPlayer | application/x-vnd.Be-CDP! |
| Pulse | application/x-vnd.Be-PULS |
| BeMail | application/x-vnd.Be-MAIL |

For the sake of illustration, we'll use the CDPlayer application that comes with your system. Its MIME type (on R4/x86) is application/x-vnd.Be-elfexecutable, while its signature is application/x-vnd.Be-CDP! (I'll show you how to discover these later), and this is the *only* application on your system with this signature. As you can see, the format of the signature is similar to the MIME-typing convention, but you should not confuse application signatures with MIME types, which are functionally different.

Because every application has a unique signature, the system can communicate with it (or launch it) without having to know where on the user's hard drive the program lives. This lets you do things like launch applications from scripts without having to know where on the system the application is located.

 The somewhat confusing distinction between MIME types and signatures will probably never affect your daily work, as it applies only to applications, not to your data files. Remember: All files have a MIME type, but only applications have a signature as well.

 Not *every* executable application on your system has a unique signature. For many smaller applications, especially command-line-only apps, there's just no reason to establish a signature. For example, the small binaries that live in /boot/beos/bin/ all share the same MIME type—application/x-vnd.Be-elfexecutable (on R4/x86) but none of them has signatures. While this is not universally true, in general you can expect that GUI applications will have signatures, while command-line programs will not.

The "vnd" in the signature, by the way, is short for "vendor." Commercial BeOS application vendors will include some part of their company name, whereas these signatures say "Be" since that's who provided them.

## The Format of a MIME Type

When a developer is creating a new application or filetype, she has to assign it a MIME type. But she can't just make it up from scratch—BeOS respects international MIME type standards, along with all of their formatting rules. The MIME type must consist of printable, seven-bit ASCII characters, and must not use any of the following reserved characters:

/<> @,;:\"()[]?

BeOS limits MIME type lengths to 240 characters, but does not enforce any other rules on top of these. Since the list of valid types is dynamic, Be can't be in the position of policing every new type that gets created—it's up to the developer to use proper types. However, illegal MIME types will generally be brought to the developer's attention by the mysterious "MIME Police" (a pseudonym for a loose band of techno-terrorists dedicated to stamping out evil, invalid MIME types).

Even though BeOS itself does not enforce additional rules for MIME types, it's a good idea to get in the habit of following the international MIME standards if you intend to create your own filetypes. If you create a new type for your personal use or for use by your own application, you should precede the type with x- to indicate that this type has not yet been accepted into the official, published database of known MIME types. For example, if you want to create a new type of text document for your own use, you'll want to give it a type something like text/x-funky, not text/funky. Nothing in BeOS will prevent you from doing anything you like, but you probably don't want to risk a visit from the MIME police.

*Revenge!* **Want to find out if there are any invalid MIME types lurking on your system? Download Rainer Reidl's Revenge of the Mutant MIME Types from BeWare—it'll scour your volumes for nefarious, naughty MIME types and give you the option to automatically correct them.**

For more information on the MIME standard, see
`http://www.qnx.com/~chrish/Be/info/mime-references.html`.

## Meet the Registrar

A brand-new, fresh BeOS installation already registers more than a hundred MIME types. As time goes on and you install more software that creates more types of files, that list will grow. If you guessed that someone—or something—must be keeping track of all these MIME types, you win a cigar. Just as your browser keeps a running database of known MIME types as you surf, BeOS also has a central MIME registry, and it's administered by something called the Registrar. You'll never see the Registrar onscreen, but it's chugging away tirelessly in the background, making sure your files are launched into the right applications, remembering which signatures belong to what, and checking to see that all of your files have associated MIME types.

You don't have to do anything special to put the Registrar to work; each time you launch an application, the Registrar checks the program's signature to see whether it's already in the database. If it isn't, it gets added. If it is but the user has moved the program, the entry is updated. The Registrar then announces to the rest of the system that the app is running so that scripts and other programs can interact with it by its signature.

So how does all of this work again? You double-click an icon and the Registrar takes a look at the file's MIME type. If the file has the MIME type of an application, the app is launched. If it has another MIME type, the Registrar looks in the FileTypes database to learn the preferred application for handling files of that type and launches your document in that application.

If the file you selected doesn't have a signature, as would be the case with files arriving via floppy (a.k.a. "sneakernet") from another operating system, or in some cases with files downloaded from the Internet, the system has a backup plan. Each filetype is allowed to have extensions associated with it in the FileTypes database, so that if the MIME signature is missing, BeOS can do its best to assign it one. For instance, if you get a floppy full of HTML files from a Windows friend, the Tracker will display them with generic icons, since it can't find a MIME type in their attributes. But if FileTypes has been told that files ending with an `.htm` or `.html` extension are almost certainly HTML files, the Tracker will associate the files with the application specified under `text/html` in FileTypes (which is most likely NetPositive).

From where you sit, though, it's all very simple. You double-click on an icon, and BeOS does *the right thing*.

Thanks to the MIME system and the tireless efforts of the Registrar, BeOS effectively solves the filetyping problem that plagues most operating systems. With BeOS, you get the best of all worlds:

- No arbitrary restrictions on filenames.
- System-wide control over preferred applications for given filetypes.
- Localized control so that you can change the preferred app or icon for a single file or an entire directory of files (although you'll need to use the Terminal to change types for all files in a directory, or use a tool like DropType, which is discussed in Chapter 10, *System Tools and Utilities*).
- Control over the list of filetypes that an application handles by default.

In the next section you'll learn how to change the preferred application for a given filetype, alter or repair MIME types when necessary, and make changes to the list of filetypes that an application can handle.

## Assigning MIME Types: The Rules of Engagement

There are two major points at which BeOS must address how to handle your files: deciding what to do when you double-click a file's icon, and assigning MIME types when none are present. Each of these tasks involves stepping through a series of conditionals: if/then statements that lead to *the right thing* taking place.

**Deciding What to Do when an Icon Is Clicked**  When you double-click an icon, the Tracker and the Registrar work together to determine the proper course of action. They go through the following steps, which sound simpler than they actually are:

1. The Registrar looks for a MIME type in the file's attributes. If none is found, branch to "Assigning a MIME Type," below.

2. If the MIME type is that of an application, launch the application.

**Figure 5.21**

*When BeOS runs out of tricks to determine a suitable application to launch a file in, this dialog is displayed. Clicking the Find button launches the Open With panel, shown in Figure 5.22.*

3. If this file has its own preferred application, launch this file into that application.

4. If not, then look up this MIME type in the FileTypes database. Does this MIME type have a preferred application? If so, launch this file in that application.

5. If not, does this MIME supertype (that is, "text") have a preferred application? If so, launch this file in that application.

6. If not, announce to the user that no suitable application could be found (Figure 5.21).

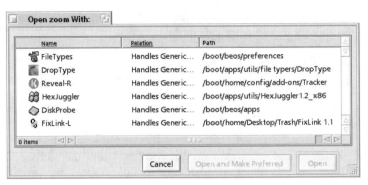

Figure 5.22

Clicking Find will display the Tracker's last resort: the Open With panel, which displays all of the applications on your system registered to handle all types of files (these applications are also known as "superhandlers"). While there are quite a few choices pictured here, in reality most of these applications won't do you much good. Ninety-nine percent of the time you'll want to choose the FileTypes panel, which you can use to manually specify an appropriate filetype.

**Assigning a MIME Type Where There Is None**  When a new file arrives on your system without a MIME type (as happens when bringing files over to BeOS from other operating systems), the Tracker and the Registrar work together to assign it one.

The Registrar's first recourse is to look for an extension on the end of the filename, like .jpg, .txt, or .html. If it finds one, it checks the FileTypes database to see whether you've connected that extension with any particular filetype. For example, you may have used the Extensions section of FileTypes to declare that files ending in .html were likely to be HTML documents, and that they should inherit the text/html filetype.

If no extension is found, the Tracker will actually read a small portion of the file with a "sniffer." If it encounters plain text, it will assume that this is a text document and give it the appropriate MIME type. A similar process occurs with GIFs, WAVs, and other common filetypes. Because the extensions technique is more likely to be accurate, it's run first. Assuming you've set up a few common extensions in your FileTypes database, BeOS can guess a file's type accurately the vast majority of the time, with the vast majority of files.

 To put this process to the test, try this: Make sure you've added the .html extension to your text/html filetype in the FileTypes database. Close it and find a plain text document on your system. If its name has an extension, rename it so it doesn't. Open a Terminal and use the rmattr commands described in the previous section to remove the attributes BEOS:TYPE and BEOS:PREF_APP (if there is one). Back in the Tracker, your file should have the blue generic icon. Double-click it, and it comes right up in StyledEdit. Remove its attributes once more, then rename it with an html extension. Double-click it, and it comes up in NetPositive. From this you can see that a filename extension is respected first if one is present. In its absence, the file data itself is sniffed.

If all of this sounds like a lot of work, remember that the whole process is transparent to the user. In addition, the vast majority of the time a valid MIME type is found immediately and BeOS doesn't have to complete more than a couple of these steps. Even when it does go through them all, however, there's no perceptible performance hit. In exchange, you get maximum flexibility and intelligence from the design and construction of this system.

### *The Rules of Inheritance*

On occasion, you may end up with files on your system with MIME types that are only partially understood, or partially present. For instance, let's say you created your own filetype with a MIME type of text/x-funky. It will work fine on our system because you're installing it in your own FileTypes database. But what would happen if you zipped up an archive including some of those files and sent it to another BeOS user? Amazingly, they would open up just fine on his system. His Registrar would encounter the MIME type text/x-funky and say, "Well, I don't know from funky, but I know text," and would promptly send the file to the app associated with the text supertype. Because x-funky is a child of the parent group text, it inherits text's properties if it can't find anything more specific to go on. As in any object-oriented system, BeOS always starts with the most specific rules, only resorting to more general rules when specific ones fail. Remember the discussion about icon inheritance earlier in this chapter? The exact same kind of specific-to-general rule ordering is taking place there. This system of object-oriented inheritance pervades BeOS, from the lowest levels of its programming API to its highest levels of interface design.

# Changing FileTypes— Think Globally ...

In the last section, I mentioned that it's possible to either change the preferred application for a given filetype system-wide or change filetypes on a case-by-case basis. The need for both generalized and localized control is the reason why the FileTypes application can be accessed from two different places—one in a central system control panel, and the other at your fingertips while you're there in the Tracker. Let's tackle the Big Kahuna, the system-wide control panel, first. Keep in mind as we muck about in FileTypes that any changes you make will be committed when you close the application—there is no Save menu, so make sure you understand this section before making any changes.

# Meet the FileTypes Database

Pull down the Be menu, scroll to Preferences, and select FileTypes. The first thing you'll see is an expandable menu, with the five major MIME classes (application, audio, image, text, and video) listed. Click on the triangle next to text to display the various kinds of system-recognized text files, which include E-mail, HTML, Metrowerks Symbol File, Text File, x-Content, and x-source-code.

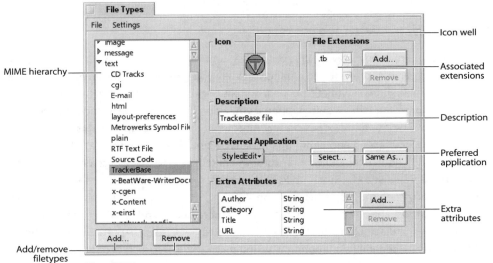

**Figure 5.23**

*To make changes to your system-wide filetypes, open the FileTypes panel in your preferences folder. Select a filetype and you'll be able to customize many aspects of the behavior or appearance of all files carrying that type, such as icon, preferred application, associated extensions, and extra attributes.*

Double-click an entry, such as Text File, and you'll get an exact breakdown of the MIME-naming scheme at work. To be more user-friendly, BeOS offers an alternative name for MIME types, called "type name," written in plain English. Below that, you'll see an uneditable reference to "internal name," which represents the real MIME type used by BeOS itself—in this case, text/plain. Since the type name is just an alias to the internal name, feel free to edit this if you like.

**Figure 5.24**

*To rename any entry in the FileTypes database, double-click its entry in the hierarchy and replace the contents of the Type Name field with a description of your choosing. Note that the group and internal names are not editable unless you're creating an entirely new filetype.*

## Changing Icons

Most of the panels shown in this section display either a prominent icon or one well off to the side, to be associated with the file or filetype in question. What may appear confusing, however, is the fact that all files have icons that show up in the Tracker, but not all icons are displayed in the FileTypes panel. Here's how it works: Anytime an icon well is blank, you know that the icon for that file is being "inherited." For example, plain text files inherit their icons from the text supertype in the FileTypes database unless you override them by specifically giving them icons of your own. There are three ways to change icons in BeOS:

• Open a second FileType panel containing the icon you want to use and drag the icon from that panel's well into this one's. Alternatively, select an icon anywhere in the system by clicking it once (a blue border will indicate that it's been selected), and copy it to the clipboard with Alt+C. Paste it into the destination well with Alt+V.

• Double-click the icon to open it in BeOS's icon editor. Perform your artistry, then close the editor to save your changes back into the current icon well.

• Create your icons in Adobe Photoshop (or another imaging application that supports the RAW image file format) as 32-by-32 and 16-by-16 squares. Save them in .raw format, copy them to your BeOS machine, and drag them into an icon well. Drag the large one first, then the smaller one. You won't get any feedback to confirm that the second drag was successful, but you can trust it (if you don't, double-click on it to open up the icon editor; it should display both of your dragged icons). Close the FileType panel in question and your changes will take effect. On occasion, you may need to toggle a Tracker window from Icon View to List View and back again to see your changes, or even close and reopen the folder.

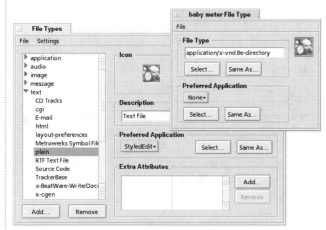

*Figure 5.25*

*To change icons for a single file or an entire filetype, either drag and drop or copy and paste icons from one icon well to another. In this figure, a custom icon was created in Photoshop and attached to an empty folder for storage. It's just been dragged from that folder's icon well into the system's* text/plain *filetype.*

## Changing the Preferred Application

In the FileTypes preferences panel, select each of the filetypes in the text group in sequence (by single-clicking their names), watching as the contents of the preferences panel change. Note that each entry includes at the very least a preferred application for that filetype. When you click and hold in the Preferred Application list box, you'll see a list of all the applications on your system capable of handling that type of file.

How does this list box know which applications can handle that particular filetype? Simple: The authors of those applications programmed their software to announce to the Registrar that the application was capable of handling certain filetypes. For example, the author of NetPositive knows that his program is capable of displaying all types of plain text files in addition to HTML, so he programmed NetPositive to announce this capability to your system. When NetPositive first ran, the Registrar hoovered that information into the FileTypes database. As a result, you'll notice that NetPositive appears as an option under all entries in the Text group.

Let's change one of your preferred apps as a test. First, find a plain text file somewhere on your system—anything that launches in StyledEdit when double-clicked will do. Next, use FileTypes to change the preferred application for the Text File entry from StyledEdit to NetPositive. You'll need to close the FileTypes dialog to make your changes take effect, since FileTypes has no Save option. Back in the Tracker, double-click your test file's icon and watch it pop up in NetPositive rather than in StyledEdit. Of course it's not too likely that you'll want to start displaying your text files in a browser win-

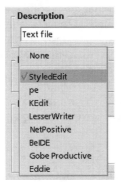

dow, but it's nice to know you have the option. If, at some point in the future, you discover the text editor of your dreams, you can return to this spot and switch your preferred plain text handler for good. For now, just change it back to the way it was (StyledEdit is the default association).

**Figure 5.26**

*To associate a filetype with a different application, open the FileTypes panel in your* Preferences *folder, find the filetype, and select an app from the file panel. Only applications registered as being capable of handling that type will appear here.*

***Forcing an Association*** If the application you want to create an association with doesn't show up on the drop-down list, it's because FileTypes doesn't know that the application you have in mind can handle this type of file. That's what the Select and Same As buttons are for. If you already know where on your system the desired application lives, click Select and navigate to it. On the other hand, let's say you don't know the name or location of the application you want to associate, but you know of another file that already has the desired association. Click Same As, navigate to that file, and click Open. The currently selected filetype will inherit its preferred application from the one you choose here.

However, if an application isn't on the pop-up list, there's a good chance that it's because that application *can't handle* this filetype. If you choose an alien application anyway (by using the Select or Same As buttons), then try to double-click the icon for a file of that type in the Tracker, you'll get a warning dialog telling you that this application isn't registered to handle files of that type. Not to worry—there may be hope yet. Find the actual application in the Tracker, right-click its icon, and select Add-Ons | FileType from the context menu. In the ensuing dialog, tell the application that it knows how to handle the filetype. Close the FileType dialog and try double-clicking a file of this

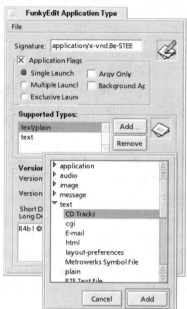

type. At this point, your preferred application should at least *try* to open the file. If it succeeds, you're golden. If it doesn't, there's no hope—this application is simply incapable of handling that kind of file. Give up.

*Figure 5.27*

*If an application claims that it can't recognize how to handle the kind of file you've just associated with it, chances are it can't. Sometimes, though, you're smarter than it is, and have to force the issue. You may happen to know that the CD Tracks filetype created by the system CD player is just plain text. But when you make FunkyEdit the preferred application for CD Track files, FunkyEdit cannot read the type. To remedy the situation, open the FileType dialog for FunkyEdit itself, click Add, and designate that it supports CD Track files.*

***Drag Files into FileTypes*** If you drag a file out of the Tracker or off the desktop and into the FileTypes dialog, the FileType options for *that file* will appear. This is the same dialog you would get if you had right-clicked the file and chosen Add-On/FileType from its context menu.

## Adding New Filetypes

At the lower left of the FileTypes dialog, you'll see a pair of buttons labeled "Add …" and "Remove." The Add… button, obviously, allows you create entirely new filetypes. Why would you want to create a new type? Let's say you're a writer, and you want the text documents you've written to have their own icons, separate from the default text icon. You could easily create a filetype identical to the type already existing for plain text, but with a different MIME type (for example, you might give your new text file variant the type text/x-funky) and icon. Since you're not creating a new application, you can still associate files of this type with StyledEdit. You will, in essence, have two nearly identical plain text entries in the FileTypes database, but the Tracker will display them differently so you can tell them apart at a glance.

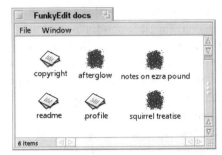

**Figure 5.28**

*While the creation of new filetypes is generally the domain of programmers, there are a few creative kludges that end-users can pull off by adding a new type to the FileTypes database. Pictured are six plain text documents, all associated with StyledEdit. However, three of them have the MIME type* text/plain, *while the other three are* text/funky. *The user can tell his personal documents apart from downloaded and system-provided documents at a glance.*

The only problem with this scheme is that the FunkyEdit application may only be capable of saving the files it creates with the type text/plain. As a result, your new FunkyEdit files will always get the default StyledEdit icon and MIME type. The best workaround is to duplicate an existing FunkyEdit document (Alt+D) every time you want to start a new document. Rename it with Alt+E and hit Enter to open it. Delete the old contents with Alt+A then Backspace, and you're on you way. A suboptimal solution, but not a terribly onerous one.

 **Use Pe to Create Files with Alien Types**  A great alternative to the method described above (duplicating existing files from the Tracker rather than with File | New in your text editor) is to use an editor like Pe, which has the most excellent capability to save files in any type registered on your system. See the full details on creating files with alien types in Pe in Chapter 12, *Productivity Applications.*

## Removing FileTypes

It's pretty clear *how* you would go about removing a filetype from your system: just click the Remove button in the FileTypes panel. The question is, why would you want to? Well, you may have removed an application a while ago, and just discovered that its MIME type is still living on your system. A badly programmed application may have created an invalid MIME type, which you want to eradicate. You may have been creating dummy MIME types as you experimented with some of the ideas in this chapter. Or you may have noticed a near-redundancy and just want to tidy up.

 *Take Care when Removing Filetypes*  A word to the wise: don't remove filetypes unless you're absolutely sure you don't need them. If you accidentally remove a filetype you later find out you needed, re-establishing the right associations can take some sleuthing, so tread lightly, especially if you're not entirely comfortable in these waters. If you do happen to remove a filetype and can't remember enough details about it to restore it manually, read the sidebar *Invasion of the Meta-MIME* to learn how to replace filetypes from your installation CD.

### *Invasion of the Meta-MIME*

So where does FileTypes store all of this information? In
/boot/home/config/settings/beos_mime/ and all of its subdirectories. Navigate to this folder in
the Tracker and you'll find hundreds of individual files arranged into subdirectories, exactly mirroring the hierarchy found in the FileTypes panel. The name of each file is equivalent to one
MIME type—in other words, the files in these directories have names like x-email and rtf. While
each of these files is iconless and does nothing when double-clicked, its attributes are stuffed
with the same information you find in the FileTypes panel. If you check the filetype of these files
themselves, you'll find that they're all of the type application/x-vnd.Be-meta-mime, indicating
that these are files that govern your MIME types.

When you open FileTypes, it simply reads this directory structure and displays these files' information in a compact, hierarchical viewer. When you make alterations to a filetype, you're changing attributes in one of these meta-MIME files. When you use the FileTypes panel to create a new
filetype, it creates a corresponding file in this directory structure. Delete a filetype, and its corresponding meta-MIME file vanishes instantly.

 **Restoring Lost or Damaged Filetypes**  If you're going to make changes to
your filetypes, do it through the FileTypes panel, not by visiting the meta-
MIME directory. However, there's one exception to this rule: If one of your filetypes ever becomes corrupted, or if you lose a system icon by accidentally
pasting over it, open up the /boot/home/config/settings/beos_mime/ directory structure on your hard drive, then the identical structure on your BeOS
installation CD. Drag the meta-MIME file for the type in question from the CD
to your hard drive, say yes to the Replace? dialog, and the type will be
restored to its factory state. If you purchase BeOS applications on CD, you
may also be able to do the same trick with third-party applications.
Reinstalling an application will do the same thing behind the scenes.

## Attributes

All extra attributes (those added to a file by the user and not present originally) are added to and removed from your filetypes in the global FileTypes
dialog. Everything you need to know about adding and editing attributes is
covered in the previous section.

## Extensions

The last item in the FileTypes dialog is the small field labeled File Extensions,
and it's there so you can set up a Plan B for any files that end up on your
machine without a MIME type to call their own (see the sidebar *Assigning a
MIME Type*). If you plan on exchanging files with users of other platforms

with any regularity (or accessing filesystems from other operating systems also living on your BeOS machine), it's not a bad idea to go through the FileTypes database now and add extensions for filetypes you expect to see regularly. For example, if people will be sending you JPEG images on a regular basis and you want BeOS to handle them perfectly every time, navigate through FileTypes to image/jpeg and add the extensions .jpeg and .jpg. You'll enjoy smooth sailing from there on.

# Act Locally

So that takes care of your global preferences, but what if you just want to change the association for a single file? That's what the FileType app is for (note that we're now talking about FileType singular, not FileTypes plural—these refer to two separate but related panels in BeOS). FileType is a Tracker add-on, so it doesn't appear in your Preferences folder. Instead, it's accessed by right-clicking a file, then sliding down to Add-Ons and selecting FileType.

## The FileType Panel for Individual Files

The FileType panel used for changing the type, preferred application, and other details related to a single file is a smart little sucker, and appears differently depending on the kind of file from which it's accessed. Let's start again with a plain text document.

Because its principles are so similar to the global FileTypes panel, operation of this panel should be pretty much self-explanatory if you've read the above section on working with global types. To change the type of a single file, either enter a known MIME type or use the Same As or Select buttons to choose a preferred application manually (or to inherit the properties of another file that's already set up properly). When you click the Select... button, a miniature version of your system's hierarchy of filetypes will be displayed so you can expand and collapse supertypes as well as find subtypes easily. The Preferred Application section of the dialog works identically to the one in FileTypes, as does the icon well. Unlike FileTypes, however, you'll have to save your changes before closing this panel (use Alt+S, Alt+W to save and close).

*Figure 5.29*

*The FileType panel for a single file is considerably simpler than the global version, as your configurable options are whittled down to just the MIME type, icon, and preferred application.*

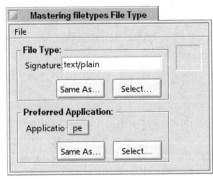

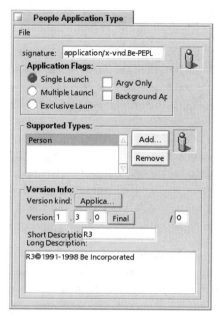

*Figure 5.30*

*The FileType dialog for an application file is completely different than that for a document file. Instead of a MIME type, the application's signature is displayed. In addition, a list of supported types replaces the list of candidate applications, and fields for application flags and version info appear.*

# FileType Settings for Applications

The standard FileType dialog is used to set the preferred application for a given filetype so it wouldn't make sense to let you set the preferred application for a file that is itself an application. Thus, the FileType dialog for an application looks quite a bit different than does the same dialog for a document.

 While it's easy and safe to change the MIME type of a document or a global filetype, changing the signature of an application could result in wacky (read: weird) behavior. Don't do it.

While it's not advisable for end-users to make changes to an application's signature, it can sometimes be useful to adjust the Application Flags and Supported Types fields.

**Application Flags**   The section labeled Application Flags lets you specify certain aspects of the application's launch behavior. You've got three radio buttons (choose just one) and two checkboxes (choose any number). By default, the Single Launch radio button is selected. When this button is on, only one instance of the application can be launched in BeOS at a time. For instance, if you have a StyledEdit document open and then double-click StyledEdit's icon again, you'll get a second StyledEdit window, but the application will appear only once in the Deskbar. However, if you made two copies of the StyledEdit application and stored them in different locations with different names, you could launch each of them once and get two StyledEdit entries in the Deskbar.

## *Change Batches of Files*

We said earlier that Be's filetyping solution would allow you to change the filetype of batches of files at once, or of entire directory trees. While BeOS's MIME system does make this possible, BeOS does not come with a built-in tool for accomplishing this task. However, you can make batch changes to entire directories at once either by using the shell or with third-party tools.

### *Via the Shell*

While using the Terminal isn't fully covered until the next chapter, we'll toss this goodie in right here. BeOS ships with a handy little tool called `settype` that lets you establish filetypes from the command line. Its usage is simple: `settype -t MIMEtype filename`. For example, to change the type of a file called `home.html` from `text/html` to `text/plain`, you would use:

```
settype -t text/plain home.html
```

After you type this command into the Terminal and press Enter, the icon of `home.html` will change to a plain text icon, indicating that its type has indeed changed. Because the shell can always take "wildcards" (Chapter 6, *The Terminal*), you can run this command on every HTML file in the current directory, like this:

```
settype -t text/plain *.html
```

The `-t` flag tells `settype` to work with filetypes. If you use the `-s` flag, `settype` will work with application signatures instead. However, note that this command only works on the files in the current directory. If you want it to burrow down through subdirectories of the current directory, things get a little more complicated, as you'll need to first use a shell tool capable of doing this, let it build a list of files for you, then pass that list on to the `settype` command. You can use the `find` command to build the file list:

```
find .-name \*.html | xargs settype -t text/plain
```

This command introduces a number of tools and constructs not covered until Chapter 6, but for now, it'll get the job done.

### *Via the FileTypes Database*

Suppose you've got 100 files in a directory, they're all of type `text/plain`, and you want to change them all to `text/html`. Open the FileTypes panel in your Preferences folder, then select the files whose type you want to change in the Tracker. Drag the files from the Tracker and drop them *en masse* onto the FileTypes database. A special dialog will appear, from which you can choose a new filetype. Do so, click Save when the confirmation dialog appears, and all of your selected files will be changed to the new type simultaneously.

*Figure 5.31*

*Drag a collection of selected files onto the FileTypes panel and you'll have the opportunity to change all of their types to a new type simultaneously.*

With rare exceptions (noted below), you won't find many reasons to make changes to the application flags. Experiment if you like—you won't hurt anything—but you'll probably want to leave these at their default settings most of the time.

**Multiple Launch**  When Multiple Launch is selected, a new instance of the application is opened every time you double-click its icon. The Terminal application is a good example of a BeOS application set to Multiple Launch by default. The distinction is somewhat subtle: Open multiple documents in StyledEdit, and the system only launches StyledEdit once, while allowing it to have multiple windows. Open multiple Terminal sessions, and you've actually launched multiple instances of the Terminal application. From your point of view, however, there's no difference, since in both cases, you get only one entry in the Deskbar and in the Twitcher, and the multiple instances appear as if they were multiple windows.

**Exclusive Launch**  If Exclusive Launch is selected, it doesn't matter how many copies of the application you have—only one of them may be running at any one time. Thus, if you duplicate the StyledEdit application as FunkyEdit and set both of them to Exclusive Launch, you won't be able to run both applications at the same time. In this case, the system examines the application signature and prevents multiple instances of the same signature from running at the same time. The net effect is that if an app is already running and you double-click a data file, the system will launch the data file into another window of the currently running instance of the application, rather than having to load another instance into RAM. Note that you can fool this feature by changing the application signature of one copy—the system will see them as two separate applications.

**Argv Only**  This is an odd one. By enabling Argv mode, you're telling the application to refuse to deal with BeOS's messaging world—the app will not be scriptable and won't respond to anything dragged onto it or its icon. The most common usage of this option is with ported Unix tools because their non-BeOS heritage can make them ill-suited to BeOS messaging.

**Background App**  By selecting Background App, you tell an application to run without appearing in the Deskbar. This comes in very handy with launchers like DeposIt (Chapter 10), which you want open all the time, but never want to switch to and therefore don't want appearing in your Deskbar.

**Supported Types**  Think of the Supported Types section as though it were the inverse of the Preferred Application field in other filetype dialogs. By entering a filetype into this field, you're declaring that this application should be registered as a candidate app for that filetype. For example, if you were to add the type CD Track to StyledEdit's list of supported types, then went and right-clicked on a CD Track file and chose Open With from the context menu, Styled Edit would appear as one of apps capable of opening it.

The rest of the panel is of interest only to programmers, though its purpose is evident—it's used for registering information and notes about this particular version of the program.

# Dealing with Archives

Every operating system has its favorite compression tool. MacOS has StuffIt, Unix has gzip, old hands and software pirates use .rar and .arj, Microsoft Windows and IBM OS/2 have zip, and BeOS ... also has zip. Zip, in fact, is the world's most popular compression technology, meaning that archives you create on BeOS can be decompressed on just about any computer. There's another very important reason to use the zip format on BeOS—for more on that, see the sidebar *Stick with Zip*.

## Decompressing Archives

Most of the files you download to your BeOS machine, whether they come from BeWare or anywhere else, will arrive in .zip format, and should show up in the Tracker with an icon depicting a package wrapped in brown paper and twine—quaint and rugged.

Double-clicking a zip file will launch Expander, a file unzipping utility that comes bundled with BeOS. When you click the Expand button, the files in the archive will be decompressed to the path named in the Destination field. By default, this path is simply the location of the zip file you've just launched, although you can change this by naming a permanent destination in Expander's Preferences panel. You can also use Expander's preferences to automatically close the Expander window when you're finished, to bring a Tracker window containing your new files immediately to the front, or to get Expander to close upon completion.

 Expander isn't just an unzipper—it provides an interface to any decompression utility available in the BeOS shell. By default, it's also capable of expanding .tar and .gz files, but you can easily extend its capabilities to work with *any* command-line decompression utility. See Chapter 2 for details.

## Compression Basics

Ever notice that copying a single, 1MB file onto a floppy is much faster than copying 100 files of 10K each onto the same floppy? Reading multiple files from and writing them to disk requires a lot of overhead. The same phenomenon applies when transferring files over the Internet—one large file is much more efficient to transfer than 100 small ones. Any time you need to handle lots of files, whether on disk or online, it makes sense to concatenate them into a single package.

In addition, most files are highly compressible. You can squeeze the air out of them by eliminating redundant information. Without getting into the inner workings of file compression technology, suffice it to say that most files can be compressed to an average of 50% of their original size. This is an average, of course, with lots of variance on either end of the spectrum. Some files, like images containing big fields of contiguous color (like the deep blue sky) will compress to as little as 5% of their original size. On the other hand, some files, like WAV sounds, barely compress at all. Other file formats, such as JPEG and GIF images, have compression technology already built in so compressing them further may not make them much smaller.

### Table 5.03  Common compression formats and their extensions

| Format | Extension |
|--------|-----------|
| Zip | .zip |
| Gzip | .gz |
| StuffIt | .sit |
| Arj | .arj |
| Rar | .rar |
| Cab | .cab |

By compressing lots of files and storing them in a single archive file, you can create complete backups of your entire system, make directory structures portable, and reclaim disk space currently being wasted by the air in files you seldom use. Table 5.03 lists the most commonly used compression formats and their corresponding file extensions.

### What about tar?

In Table 5.03, you may have noticed the absence of the tar format common in the Unix world, and seen occasionally on BeOS. That's because tar (Tape ARchive) isn't a compression format—it's only a concatentation scheme. All files in a .tar archive have been written end-to-end into a single file, with no compression. However, a .tar file can easily be compressed after the fact by using any of the tools above. The compression scheme most commonly used with tar is gzip, which is why you often find files—especially in the Unix world—with names like filename.tar.gz (you'll also occasionally encounter files with a .Z extension, indicating that they've gone through the now-outmoded Unix "compress" utility).

***X-ray Your Archives*** Most people who create zip files compress an entire directory, starting from one level *above* that directory. As a result, when you decompress their archives, all of the new files are expanded into a single new folder on your system, which helps you keep things organized. Occasionally, however, people create archives from *within* the directory in question. As a result, when you decompress their archive, all of the new files expand into the current directory. If you've already got lots of personal files, other down-loaded zip files, or anything else there, the new files are going to get all mixed up with the existing ones.

To sidestep this occasional annoyance, open up Expander's preferences and select the checkbox labeled "Automatically show contents listing." With this enabled, you'll get an "x-ray view" of the contents of the archive before click-ing Expand. Get in the habit of always glancing at the paths listed in the x-ray view. If everything isn't under one directory, close Expander and create a new folder manually with the Tracker. Move your archive into that folder, then try again. This could save you from having to clean up a mess you never made.

Likewise, when creating archives for distribution to others, please be courte-ous and remember to zip the entire folder, not just its contents. To do this from the command line, use the -r flag, as in `zip -r archivename foldername`. More details on command-line zipping below.

## Unzipping from the Terminal

If Expander gives you any guff, or if you simply prefer the command line, you can unzip your files from the Terminal just as easily. In fact, there are some things you can do with zip more easily from the Terminal than from Expander, such as decompressing batches of zip files at once.

Start by navigating to the directory that contains the zip file you want to decompress, then type `ls -l *.zip`. If the file you're looking for isn't listed, you're in the wrong directory.

***Easy Terminal Access to the Current Directory*** The easiest way to get from the Tracker to the Terminal and stay in the same directory is to use the TermHire Tracker add-on, downloadable from BeWare. Once TermHire is installed, just right-click in some of the Tracker's white space and choose Add-Ons | TermHire from the context menu. You'll be transported to a Terminal window in the current directory. Even easier, use the keyboard shortcut: Ctrl+Alt+T on the right side of your keyboard. Note that to use this, you can't have any files currently selected. If you do, you'll need to click once in some white space to deselect all files, then hit the keyboard shortcut.

Unzipping the archive is as simple as typing:

```
unzip filename.zip
```

If you'd like to preview the contents of the archive before actually expanding it, use the -v flag:

```
unzip -v filename.zip
```

This will give you the same kind of x-ray view of the file's contents that Expander gives you, so you can decide whether or not to decompress it in this location. To force the archive to expand into a directory of your choosing, use the -d flag along with a directory name (for example, unzip foo.zip -d bar will expand the contents of the archive foo.zip into a directory called bar). To make sure that decompressed files don't overwrite existing files with the same name, use the -n flag. To force overwrites without prompting, try it with -o. You can see unzip's complete list of arguments by typing:

```
unzip
```

### Table 5.04  unzip's most commonly used flags

| This unzip Flag | Does This |
| --- | --- |
| No arguments | Displays brief zip documentation. |
| -v | Shows archive contents without actually decompressing. |
| -d | Used in combination with a directory name, decompresses in that directory. |
| -n | Won't overwrite files with the same name. |
| -o | Overwrites existing files without prompting. |
| -f | Only decompresses files that are newer than existing ones. |
| -t | Tests an archive's integrity (in case of possible download errors). |
| -a | Converts text files from DOS format to Unix/BeOS format. |
| -L | Lowercases filenames (in other words, changes FILENAME.TXT to filename.txt); useful for working with DOS zip files. |

To use multiple flags in combination with one another, just stack them up. For example:

```
unzip -naL archive.zip
```

will decompress archive.zip but won't overwrite any existing files with the same names, will convert DOS text files to BeOS format, and will change any uppercase filenames to lowercase.

## Compressing Files with zip

So much for unpacking other people's archives; what if you want to make your own? BeOS does not include a graphical zipping tool, and Expander can't be made to work in reverse. One of the easiest ways to create a zip archive on BeOS is to download and install the ZipMe add-on from BeWare. Once ZipMe is installed in /boot/home/config/add-ons/Tracker, you'll be able to right-click on any file or folder and create an archive almost instantly. This is one tool well worth keeping around.

However, ZipMe has some limitations. For example, if you select multiple files in the same directory and choose the ZipMe add-on, you'll end up with multiple zip files, rather than all of them together in a single archive. In addition, ZipMe won't take advantage of zip's many advanced options. Thus, for anything but the most basic zip operations, you'll need to turn to the shell. Fortunately, zip is as easy to use from the command line as unzip.

Whereas unzip is installed on your system by default, zip is not. Download the latest version of zip from BeWare and decompress it with Expander. Take a look at the accompanying documentation, then move the four included binaries—zip, zipnote, zipsplit, and zipcloak—to/boot/home/config/bin.

 The port of zip to BeOS was initially undertaken—and is still maintained—by this book's technical editor, Chris Herborth. You can follow the status of zip for BeOS and download the very latest updates at **www.beosbible.com**.

Once zip is installed, open up a Terminal window and pick a file—any file. Let's assume it's called foo. The basic format of the zip command is:

```
zip DestinationFile SourceFile(s)
```

On top of this basic syntax, there are many optional arguments you can use to fine-tune the way archives are created. We'll go over a few of those arguments later in this section, but to see a complete list of zip's arguments now, type zip -h. For much more detailed explanations, read the MANUAL file that comes in the zip distribution.

**Sample zip Sessions**    Let's create a temporary directory and some dummy files we can practice on. Type these commands, hitting Enter after each one:

```
mkdir temp
cd temp
touch foo boo bloo loo
```

Now zip one of the files:

```
zip bar foo
```

Type ls -l to get a directory listing, and you'll see that a new file has been created called bar.zip. Notice that you didn't have to type "bar.zip" in your zip command—the .zip extension was added for you. If you double-click bar.zip in the Tracker, it'll open up in Expander and you'll be able to see foo inside. Now make an archive of our four test files:

```
zip bar2 foo loo boo bloo
```

Note that you can specify as many source files as you like. Of course, there are easier ways to accomplish this by using wildcards:

```
zip bar3 *oo
```

will search the current directory for files ending in "oo" and use them as the source files. To be more selective,

```
zip bar4 *l*
```

will compress only bloo and loo, since they're the only files with the letter "l" in their names. See Chapter 6, for more on wildcards.

That's all well and good, but most of the time you're going to want to compress entire directory structures. To do this, use the -r flag, which tells zip to walk recursively down the directory tree. If you've got a directory named foo and it has dozens of deeply nested subdirectories contained within, you can easily stuff them all into a single archive. Start by navigating the Terminal to the point right in front of (above) the directory you want to compress. For instance, if you want to compress the directory /boot/home/foo/, your current directory should be /boot/home/. Then all you need to type is:

```
zip -r foo foo
```

This will create an archive called foo.zip, containing the folder called foo and all of its contents, including subdirectories. If you move foo.zip to another temporary folder and decompress it with Expander, you'll see the entire directory structure under foo magically reappear. All of your icons and file-types should stay intact. This file, moved to another person's machine, would create the foo directory and subdirectory structure at whatever point the user unzips it. In other words, if the other user downloads foo.zip to her /boot/home/Downloads directory and decompresses it there, she'll end up with a /boot/home/Downloads/foo/ structure on her hard drive. If you like, you can create your zip file so that it replicates the directory structure not just starting from the current point, but going all the way back to the root. Rather than using the command above, try it like this:

```
zip -r foo /boot/home/foo
```

Now when you unzip foo.zip, it will create the entire /boot/home directory structure. It won't include all the files in that path, just the directory structure.

This can be useful if you want to give a clue to your users about where they should put your files. For instance, if you've created a file that has to live on the end-user's system at /boot/home/config/bin, you can use this trick to replicate this structure when your archive is decompressed. Users who refuse to read the documentation you so painstakingly wrote would at least see this structure and know that they'd better move the file to the same location on their system.

 As useful as this technique can occasionally be, it also has the potential for unfortunate consequences. A nefarious rapscallion could, for example, zip up a bogus /boot/home/config/settings directory and embed it in an archive. Unwitting users decompressing this archive without checking its contents first or using the -n flag could end up having important system settings over-written. Always exercise caution when decompressing archives downloaded from sources other than BeWare or BeDepot.

**Advanced zip Options**    So what if you've got a *huge* directory structure, and a lot of the files it contains are gigantic? Can you skip just these files to save on compression time and final file size? Of course. You can specify files either by inclusion or exclusion. Inclusion grabs files only of a certain kind or kinds, and exclusion grabs everything but. For the sake of argument, let's say you want to archive only files starting with the word "The" or the letter "d" that live any-where in the foo directory structure. You can do it with this command:

```
zip -r foo /boot/home/foo -i */d* */The*
```

The -i flag simply says "include only these files," and is followed by its argu-ments—the wildcard identifiers you would use anywhere in the Terminal to locate the same files. To archive everything but these files, just replace the -i flag with an -x flag, for "exclude."

Let's say you want to zip up the files that result from another command that creates a list of files. This is a good opportunity to link up two shell com-mands via a "pipe" (details are in Chapter 6); this command will use the Unix find command to find all files ending in .html, then pass that list as an argu-ment to zip:

```
find *.html -print | zip html -@
```

(Yes, you could have just used zip html *.html to get the same effect, but it's an illustration, OK?) The first part of the command finds all files ending in .html. The results of the find are then passed off to zip to create the new file html.zip (note that the .zip extension is added automatically; you don't have to specify it). The zip command knows that when it sees the -@ flag it should use the list of files coming from the previous command (in Unix terminology, find's standard output is piped to zip's standards input—see Chapter 6, for more on stdin and stdout).

**Zipping Up Query Results**   There's another creative way to use the pipe in conjunction with zip's ability to accept input from other commands. Because you can run BeOS queries from the command line almost as easily as from the Tracker, you can build a query as fancy as you like, run it in the Terminal, and have the resulting files compressed into an archive for posterity. You can learn more about queries from the command line in Chapter 7, but here's the nutshell version:

1. Create a standard or attribute-based query using the normal Tracker Find dialog. Use as many criteria as you want to fine-tune your search.

2. Once you've seen the query's results and are satisfied, pull down File | /Edit Query (or hit Alt+G) to return to the query constructor. Use the picklist to switch from attribute mode to formula mode. The dialog will change to show you the text version of your query, written in BeOS's internal query syntax, which is also used for command-line queries. Select it with your mouse and copy it to the clipboard.

3. Back in the Terminal, type:

   ```
   query '<now paste from the clipboard with Alt+V>'
   ```

   Be sure you get the quote marks in there. Hit Return—the Terminal should spit back the same list of files that the Tracker did earlier. Did it work? Excellent. Now, to send that same output to a zip file, tap your Up Arrow to return the last command to the prompt, but before hitting Enter, append | zip foo -@ to the end. For example, if you wanted to zip up an archive of all the Californian Person files on your system, your command line would look like this:

   ```
   query '((META:state=="[cC][aA]")&&(BEOS:
   TYPE=="application/x-person"))' | zip californians -@
   ```

   (This line has been broken for readability, and must be a single line in the Terminal.)

By welding together various command-line programs with zip, you can create archives containing anything at all.

## Growing a zip Archive

Sometimes you want to add more files to an existing archive, rather than creating a new one. This is easy to do, thanks to the -g flag. Assume you already have an archive called html.zip, and now you want to add to it files in the current directory starting with the letter "d". Here's all you need to do:

```
zip -g html.zip d*
```

If you want to make sure that any files in the archive that have since changed on disk are updated, use the -u option. If you want to make sure that zip doesn't follow symlinks (which can end up consuming huge amounts of space in your archives if you're not careful), use the -y flag. You can also change the level of compression used by zip (at the expense of a little speed) by using a numerical flag. Try adding -9 to your command and see if the resulting archive is any smaller.

## tar and gzip

Support for the Unix tar and gzip formats is built into BeOS. You'll find binaries for each of them in /boot/beos/bin/, and Expander is capable of handling both tarred and gzipped archives. The tar and gzip combination differs from zip in several ways. As described in the sidebar *What about tar?* a few pages ago, tar doesn't compress files—it just concatenates them end-to-end. You can then compress a tar archive with any compression tool you like, though gzip is the most common. Because compressing a single archive is slightly more efficient than resetting the compression algorithm for every file, a tarred and compressed archive is sometimes a little smaller than a normal zip archive. However, with tar plus compression, you lose a few advanced features, like the ability to selectively add or remove files without unpacking the whole archive. More importantly, tar can't handle BeOS attributes, making this combination close to useless on BeOS. However, since you will from time to time end up downloading tar.gz files and may want to know how to handle them from the command line, here's how.

Unarchiving a file called foo.tar.gz (also sometimes foo.tgz) is a two-step process: decompress the gzip file, then de-concatenate the resulting tar file. Note also that gzip has one significant behavioral difference from zip: When you create a gzip file, the source files are transformed into an archive (as opposed to zip, which makes an archive but leaves the source files untouched). Likewise, when you decompress a gzipped file, the gzip archive is transformed into the source .tar file, so that the .tgz file no longer exists. Neither of these things will happen unless the entire operation is successful, but this quirk still requires that the user pay a little more attention than with zip. Don't delete the source files thinking you're safe becuase you still have the archive—you don't.

To decompress a gzipped file named foo.tar.gz, type gzip -d foo.tar.gz (the -d flag means decompress). The .gz file will disappear, and you'll find a new file: foo.tar.

 Alternatively, you can always use the command gunzip in place of gzip -d. In reality, the gunzip entry in /boot/beos/bin is just a symlink to gzip.

To de-concatenate foo.tar, type tar -xvf foo.tar and its contents will come spilling out, hopefully into a new directory tree. The -xvf flags represent extract, verbose, and file, respectively. In other words, you're telling tar that it should extract files from an archive (rather than creating or testing an

### *Stick with zip*

The zip format may be popular, but it isn't the only compression format in the world. In fact, it isn't the only archive format on BeOS, either. Many of the archive formats listed in Table 5.02 can be created and decompressed with freely downloadable tools, and support for both tar and gzip comes bundled with BeOS. But while other archiving formats may have small advantages here and there, they're definitely not worth the price of admission: Neither tar nor gzip, nor anything else, will respect your files' attributes. And without attributes, your files have no MIME types, no special icons, no fancy fonts in StyledEdit, nothing in People files, and so on.

Decompress an archive made with anything other than zip on BeOS and you'll end up with directories full of generic icons. Double-clicking those icons may or not launch the file in the appropriate viewer. And because many BeOS applications store some or all of their data in attributes, losing attributes is not acceptable. For instance, if you use tar to compress your email directory, you'll end up with a bunch of plain text files—you will have lost the sender's name and return address, the subject line, the date ... everything but the message itself. That's how important attributes are to BeOS.

Stick to zip—it works on just about every operating system in the world, the compression is very good, and you get to take full advantage of your filesystem's unique qualities. The tar and gzip formats are on your system to make it possible for you to download and use files created on Unix platforms, but offer little benefit beyond that. On the other hand, your zipped files can be unzipped on Unix, and the recipient won't miss anything (remember that he won't be able to take advantage of your attributes anyway).

archive), that it should give you a full report while it's working, and that you're about to give it a filename as an argument (foo.tar).

To create a new .tar file, type tar -cvf newfile.tar sourcefileorfoldername. Note that you need to specify .tar in the new filename if you want it to appear—it's not automatic as it is with zip. The -c flag means "create." Like zip, tar can also take the -9 flag to work at maximum compression, with only a slight performance hit.

To gzip your new .tar file, type gzip filename.tar. You don't need to specify the new filename—it will be created automatically as filename.tar.gz.

For more details on gzip or tar , type gzip -h or tar --help into the Terminal, or consult a Unix manual. For a great tip on using tar and gzip for uploading large sites to Web servers, see Chapter 8.

# SoftwareValet Package Files

Zip may be popular, but it's not the only archive game in town. Many of the files you download from BeWare, BeDepot, and elsewhere will have a .pkg ("package") extension, rather than .zip. Rather than the brown paper bundle icon, these files will bear the icon of a satellite transceiver. Double-clicking these files will launch an application called SoftwareValet, which is included on your system. SoftwareValet package files are similar to zip files in the sense that they contain nested directory structures packed with compressed files, but differ in several important respects:

- SoftwareValet performs logged system installations rather than simply decompressing to a given directory.

- SoftwareValet can be seamlessly tied in to an online commerce system so that applications can be purchased on the spot, or registered with the software developer.

## Zipping Files on the Mac
by Henry Bortmann

While zip may be the preferred compression/archive format on most operating systems, the Mac world has standardized on Aladdin Systems' StuffIt, which creates .sit (StuffIt) or .sea (self-extracting archive) files. But it can't create .zip files, and BeOS' zip-centric utilities don't know what to do with a .sit or .sea file. If you want to move compressed archives between MacOS and BeOS, you need to stan-

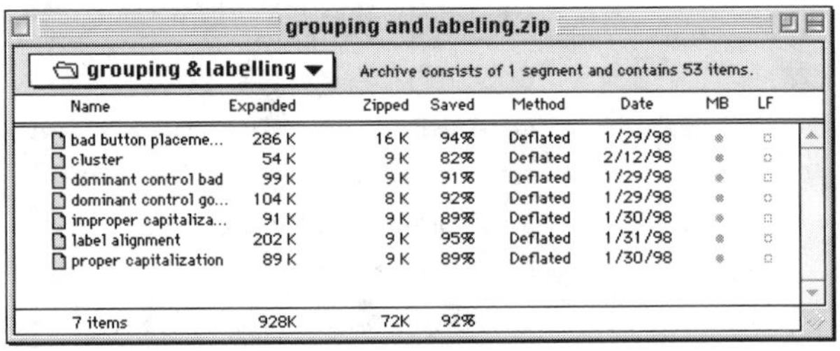

**Figure 5.32**

One of the best utilities available for creating and decompressing .zip archives on the Macintosh is the ZipIt shareware utility.

dardize on one format or the other. The decision is a simple one. There is no utility available for the BeOS to handle StuffIt files, and none is planned. Zip is your only choice.

There are a number of shareware zip utilities available for MacOS. The two best are ZipIt ($15, available from **www.macdownload.com**) and PK ZIP Mac from Ascent Solutions ($19.95, **www.asizip.com/products/pkzipmac.htm**). PK ZIP is from an established company that also sells zip utilities for a number of other platforms. ZipIt, however, fully supports Macintosh drag-and-drop interaction with the Finder for selecting files to be compressed or decompressed, which PK ZIP doesn't. Both of these utilities can zip and unzip files.

If all you need to do is unzip files on the Mac, you might want to consider Aladdin's DropStuff with Expander Enhancer, available as a $30 shareware download (**www.aladdinsys.com/dropstuff/**). Aladdin's commercial StuffIt Deluxe product ($75) will also unzip .zip archives. You'll need version 3.5 or later of either utility. Neither of these products can create zip files, however. And don't bother trying the zip thing with Aladdin's free StuffIt Expander. It doesn't do zip.

- SoftwareValet cannot be operated from the command line.

- SoftwareValet displays an expand-able/collapsible preview of the directory structure(s) about to be installed.

- SofwareValet files are specific to BeOS and cannot be opened on any other operating system.

**Figure 5.33**

*SoftwareValet and its* .pkg *files aren't so much a file archiving system as they are a software distribution and installation mechanism.*

But what really sets SoftwareValet apart from zip and the others is that it's really more of an installation assistant than an archiver. Yes, SoftwareValet does compress your files, though not as effectively as zip. But SoftwareValet is custom-tailored to make BeOS software installation smooth and painless, and it adds many options for application installation that aren't available with any of the standard formats. Usage of SoftwareValet is covered in depth in Chapter 10.

# BFS: The Be Filesystem

The information in this section explains the fundamental principles of the remarkable Be filesystem. Reading this will help you to better understand how BeOS operates at a low level, but it doesn't contain information critical to the average end-user.

The filesystem of any operating system defines how the data on the raw disk platter is mapped out, how it's accessed by your programs, and how it's used by the operating system. While the filesystem is never seen by the user, she is constantly affected by its overall responsiveness, its throughput capabilities, its integrity and stability, and any special capabilities it has to offer.

When defining and engineering the filesystem to be used in The MediaOS, Be had specific goals in mind. To excel at handing futuristic multimedia, the filesystem had to be capable of handling files of an almost unlimited size, and of sustaining very high disk throughput rates without skipping a beat (which is critical to tasks like multitrack audio mixing and digital video editing). In addition, Be had intended to build an operating system on top of a database from the very beginning. While BFS stopped being a true database with DR9 because of the complexity and performance penalty it incurred, it still retains much of the functionality of a database (you'll find examples scattered throughout this book of things you can do on BeOS because of its database-like filesystem that you can't do on any other operating system).

The maximum allowable file size in BFS is now 18 petabytes (equivalent to 18 *billion* megabytes), so that question is safely out of the way—BeOS will be able to store digital representations of all the atoms in the human body and perform other late-21st-century computing tasks. And disk throughput in BFS is right up there with the media world's best, getting 95% of some hard drives' top rated speed (in ideal conditions). All of this in a world where 80–85% of maximum throughput would be considered blazing. In other words, BFS met its goals … and then some.

BFS does what it does so well because it incorporates not just one or two, but all of the industry's hottest storage technology concepts, and adds a few of its own to boot.

## Journaling

The notion of the journaled filesystem was introduced in Chapter 1. Let's zoom in for a closer look.

In any operating system, there are essentially two kinds of data being stored: raw data belonging to you, the operating system, and your applications; and meta-data, which describes how the raw data is laid out on the disk (don't confuse this meta-data with the meta-data belonging to individual files in the form of attributes, as discussed earier). Filesystem meta-data is a sort of table of contents, keeping track of the location of every file and folder on your system, along with filenames, modification and creation dates, and start and end points. You may know this meta-data table from the DOS world as FAT, or the file allocation table. On other systems, this area is called the disk catalog. While you never access it directly, the integrity of your meta-data is actually more important than your actual data. If it's lost or damaged, your entire disk will probably become unreadable, and you'll find yourself reaching with crossed fingers for your trusty copy of Norton Utilities or another low-level filesystem tool.

The BFS filesystem uses a journal to keep track of all changes made to your disk. If you pull down File | Save in StyledEdit, the change of data represented by that save is logged in the journal. The structure of data on the disk (the meta-data) is, in turn, written out to disk in specific "chunks." This system guarantees that the data on disk is always kept in a consistent state, never in an in-between, half-written limbo. The result is that if someone walks behind your desk and accidentally kicks the plug out of the wall, there's a pretty good chance that when you reboot, your system isn't going to go into shock because it can't find a good copy of the meta-data. On most Unix systems, rebooting after any kind of abnormal shutdown means waiting many minutes while the system attempts to reconstruct the meta-data from the structure of the raw data found on disk (some Unix systems are journaled, however). While Be didn't invent the notion of a filesystem journal, the BFS journal is exceptionally high-performance. If your BeOS machine boots in a fraction of the time your other operating systems require, you have the journal to thank in large part.

So the journal is keeping your meta-data in a constant state, but what about your actual, raw data? How safe is that? BeOS prioritizes the integrity of the journal—and thus your meta-data—over the actual data, meaning that while kicking the plug out of the wall is never going to cause damage to or confuse the state of the filesystem, it is conceivable that the portion of the file you were working with at the time of the crash may not be recoverable (as is true with other operating systems). However, even though your data itself is not journaled, you're virtually guaranteed that your journal will not be damaged or out of sync. The integrity of your entire disk is retained, and your reboot is still speedy. You may lose whatever you were working on before your last save, but the rest of the data on your disk won't be harmed. No operating system can protect you against losing data you haven't yet saved, but BeOS guards against catastrophes better than most.

**The journal syncs itself against your raw data almost continuously, so you should never have to think about it. However, if you're ever doing some kind of testing that you fear could potentially lock up or bring down your system, it's possible to force a sync at any time by typing** sync **into the Terminal.**

**Under normal circumstances, there is no good reason to ever do this manually—BFS will take good care of you behind the scenes.**

The journal contributes to BeOS's amazingly fast boot speed by restoring an image of the state of the disk. No painfully slow inspection of the disk structure is required. For comparison's sake, try hitting the power switch on your Windows NT machine while the system is running and get out your timer to see how long it takes to boot back up (the author assumes no responsibility for data damaged in this test). Then try the same thing on your BeOS machine.

This becomes incredibly important when you start attaching multiple 9-GB drives to your system for mass digital video storage. Regardless of the amount of attached storage, BeOS won't take more than 30 seconds to read the journal back into memory.

If that seems like a ridiculous amount of storage, consider this: 47-GB disks have been selling for under US $2500 at the time of this writing. Two years ago, the cost of this much storage would have been astronomical. And the prices keep falling. Don't underestimate the power of the computer industry to make what seems impossible this year affordable next year.

As a result of BFS's journaled filesystem, BeOS offers much better native disk protection under any circumstances than do, say, MacOS or Windows 95/98. While all filesystems are susceptible to data loss to the file or files you're working on at the moment a system goes down (the journal can't protect you against that, even theoretically), BeOS is far, far less likely to endure disk damage resulting from abnormal circumstances and unrecoverable disk catalogs. Damage will be limited to individual files rather than affecting the entire filesystem. Your prophylactic against losing data you're working with when the power cuts out? Buy yourself a high-quality uninterruptible power supply, and save early and often.

## Multithreading

Like the rest of BeOS, BFS is heavily multithreaded. Disk read and write operations are broken up into minute tasks that all run simultaneously, rather than queueing up behind one another. The result is that BFS can read and write multiple streams of data at once. Of course, the actual disk head can only be in one place at a time, but that's not Be's fault. The important thing is that BFS is actually aware of these multiple simultaneous tasks and can handle them as concurrent processes. This is obviously important during any kind of multitasking, but it becomes even more important when BeOS is in multiuser mode and four or five users are logged into the system at once, each doing their own thing. On other filesystems, this situation would be handled by doing something called blocking, or freezing pending requests until the current one is complete. That's a major bottleneck from which BFS is largely exempt.

 The solution to the speed dilemma posed by the disk head's inability to be in more than one place at a time is to use a "redundant array of independent disks," or RAID, system. In RAID, multiple disks can be treated as a single volume, effectively giving you multiple read/write heads that can work simultaneously (in some configurations, RAID is also used to provide redundant data security). Be is working on RAID support behind the scenes, so you can expect to see it in place in a future release.

## Attributes

Earlier in this chapter, we covered BeOS attributes in depth from the user's point of view. By allowing every file to store any kind of data in any number of extra fields associated with that file, BeOS attributes allow for complex queries on just about any criteria, enabling you to find arbitrary collections of files stored on any BFS-formatted drive attached to your system.

What makes attribute queries so fast is the presence of an attribute index that functions as a single file, eliminating the need to examine every file on the system for matched criteria. For example, you may have 500 Person files but when you want to find only the Person files that are a part of the group "bowling club," only a single file needs to be searched.

 The index lives in the filesystem, of course, but it's not a file in the standard sense. Don't bother looking for the index—you won't be able to find it, either with the Tracker or from the Terminal.

As you've already discovered (and will continue to discover throughout this book), attributes add a lot of value to BeOS. However, there is a downside to heavy attribute usage, as well as to the indexes maintained by the filesystem. Because attributes are stored outside of the file itself, they appear to the hard disk (not to BeOS) as separate files, as far as read/write operations go. Thus, a file with a bunch of large attributes can take longer to write to or read from disk than it would if it were a simple, unadorned text file (the same is not necessarily true when you have just a few small attributes—if they can fit into the file's entry in the filesystem, there will be no performance penalty).

To see an example of this in action, let your Trash fill up with 1,000 or more files, then empty the Trash. The emptying operation will actually take quite a bit longer on BeOS than it would under Microsoft Windows because so many attributes need to be deleted from the filesystem, and their associated indexes need to be updated. From the perspective of the hard disk, many more read/write operations are required. BFS is simply not optimized for extremely rapid file creation/deletion operations in general—it shines most brightly when moving large files around quickly, not when juggling zillions of small data files. Most of the time, however, you're not going to notice this difference, and most files on your system don't have very many attributes anyway.

Note, however, that this does *not* affect Be's MediaOS goals. Media files are large—huge even. The speed of reading or writing a sound or video file to disk is a question of throughput, not a question of manipulating attributes, maintaining indexes, or reading and writing lots of small files. According to BFS's creator Dominic Giampolo, there is actually an undocumented method of creating a BFS partition without keeping an index (therefore making it impossible to perform queries), and the speed of such a partition is breathtaking. However, indexed attributes bring so much value to BeOS that Be decided it was well worth the performance penalty, which is unnoticeable under most circumstances anyway.

## Node Monitors

Unbeknownst to the end-user, BeOS queries actually have a mutant cousin, in the form of an API feature called node monitors. These allow programmers to build applications that have the ability to "watch" files and folders, reporting back when they've been altered in any way (deleted, moved, or added to). For instance, a programmer can theoretically build a graphics utility that converts JPEGs to GIFs by allowing the user to drop files into a special folder (which, by the way, can have a customized icon thanks to the folder's manipulable attributes). When a file drop is detected at that node, the program would be alerted and would snap into action, converting the file to another format and alerting the user.

One good place to see node monitors in action is the Trash, which changes icons depending on the number of files it contains. If the Trash contains zero files, it gets an empty trash can icon. If it contains one or more files, the icon changes instantly to that of a full trash can.

## Disk Utilities for BeOS

Thanks to years of training on inferior operating systems, many users assume that all hard disks need to be defragmented from time to time to maximize performance. Many operating systems allow the data that comprise files to be split up in pieces across the disk surface. If the user wants to write a 60K file but only 30K is available in the current platter location, the filesystem will store the rest of the file somewhere else, and record the difference in the journal or allocation table. But if files can be stored in contiguous blocks on the disk surface, the disk head has to do less dancing around to retrieve all the data that make up that file, so companies like Norton have made a mint selling tools that accomplish just that.

While in theory it is possible for BFS to become fragmented, in practice it's another story altogether. According to Dominic Giampolo, "In practice BFS seems quite resilient against fragmentation. I recently ran some diagnostics on some systems around here that have been in constant use for six months or more … over 98% of the files on all three machines were stored in one or two contiguous runs of disk blocks."

There's another dimension to the fragmentation question as well: BFS's multithreadedness makes it a bit of a moot point. If the system is doing several things at once, the disk head is going to be dancing all over the place anyway, and accessing blocks in a noncontiguous order whether the disk is fragmented or not.

Between BFS's fragmentation resistance and its constant-state journaling, old Peter Norton is going to have a tough time finding a market for BeOS disk utilities. In fact, at this writing, not a single developer has released, or made any mention of working on, hard disk utility software for BeOS—it just isn't needed.

## Sixty-Four Bit Storage System

As described in Chapter 1, Be was adamant that there not be arbitrary limitations on the size of files users could store in BFS, and thus moved to a 64-bit storage system for DR9. While 32-bit filesystems have a maximum file size of around four gigabytes, BFS can store files as large as 18 petabytes. Just how big is a petabyte?

1,000 kilobytes   = 1 megabyte
1,000 megabytes  = 1 gigabyte
1,000 gigabytes  = 1 terabyte
1,000 terabytes  = 1 petabyte

In other words, 1 petabyte is equivalent to 1,000,000,000 megabytes, so BFS's maximum file size is 18 million gigabytes. That's one big honkin' hard drive. Of course, the way software is bloating these days ... nah, it'll never happen.

To get a good mental picture of the amount of data you can store in 18 petabytes, see Chapter 1.

## Speed

Because the "speed" of a filesystem is completely dependent on the speed of the disk it's running on and the cumulative bandwidth of the drive controller, quality of connecting cables, and many other factors that are impossible to normalize, there is no meaningful way to measure it. However, BFS competes extremely well when reading and writing large blocks of data to and from disk. In fact, Be has been able to achieve 95% of some hard disks' maximum rated throughput in laboratory conditions (lab conditions in this case mean a newly formatted disk and large buffers).

As a general rule, big reads and writes mean big performance, while small reads and writes mean the disk head spends more time seeking and less time transmitting data.

If you feel the need to compare your hard disk's speed with those of other BeOS users, download BeRometer from BeWare and run the disk tests. When they're complete, you'll have the opportunity to compare your results with those sent in by owners of many different machines, both Intel and Macintosh together in a single bar chart.

# Working with Other Filesystems

Popular operating systems get to call the shots, while the underdogs have to learn to play nice with others or risk being swept under the rug for being incompatible with the standard. That's why MacOS learned to read DOS-formatted disks years ago, while Windows—with all of the money and marketing expertise at Microsoft's disposal—has not deemed it worthy to spend the time learning to read disks formatted under other operating systems. Sure, there are third-party utilities that will allow you to read Apple Macintosh disks from within Windows, but getting along with other systems should be considered a fundamental part of making the customer's life easier. Not supporting other filesystems is indicative of Microsoft's desire to build a closed loop, with their customers trapped inside.

BeOS, on the other hand, has already learned how to talk to a multitude of different filesystems even though the system is still young. This is partially out of necessity, partially because Be appreciates open playing fields and customer choice, and partially because Be built technology into their operating system that would make it as easy as possible to do so.

The notion of dynamically loadable device modules comes up in several places in this book because the same basic notion applies to so many aspects of the operating system. Rather than hard-code everything into the kernel, Tracker, or filesystem, Be builds these core units as lightweight and bare as possible, streamlining for efficiency as they go. To hard-code alternate filesystems into the kernel would add a huge amount of bloat to it that few people would actually use. If added functionality is needed, the user just drops an add-on into the appropriate folder. The system is designed to look for files living in particular folders. When it finds one, it checks to make sure that the file is indeed a legitimate add-on, and then bolts it on to its own structure. As long as the module remains present, BeOS will treat it as a part of the system.

Note that the paragraph above doesn't include the word "reboot"—that's what earns these drivers the adjective "dynamic." With the sole exception of graphics drivers, which are add-ons to the app_server and thus wedded to the current video card driver, the system can load and unload modules in real time, while it's up and running. Add-ons to various parts of the system are covered in their respective chapters; here we'll look at filesystem add-ons, which enable BeOS to read from and write to filesystems created by other operating systems.

A certain amount of alien filesystem support is included with every installation of BeOS, so you can access your Macintosh and DOS/Windows partitions automatically, without doing anything special at all.

# Mounting Alien Filesystems

Any disk volume appearing on your desktop is fully readable by BeOS. Whether you're also able to write to the volume depends on the particular filesystem and the current state of driver development for that filesystem (details below). In addition, there may be other mountable disk volumes available to you; right-click on your desktop and choose Mount from the context menu to find out whether BeOS has detected other mountable partitions.

In order for BeOS to "see" a drive, an add-on (driver) for its filesystem will need to be present in one of two directories:

`/boot/beos/system/add-ons/kernel/file_systems`

or

`/boot/home/config/add-ons/kernel/file_systems`

The first directory is where Be stores the filesystem add-ons that shipped with your system. The second is where you can place previously downloaded drivers.

Whether or not you see alien volumes on your desktop or in the Disks window depends on how your mount settings are currently configured. Right-click on the desktop and choose Mount | Settings from the context menu. You'll see a dialog like the one in Figure 5.34.

*Figure 5.34*

*The Mount Settings panel is accessed by right-clicking on your desktop and scrolling to the Mount entry in the context menu. Two sets of controls let you configure mounting behavior during system operation and during the boot sequence.*

If you don't want alien filesystems mounted automatically but want to access them right now, click the "Mount all disks now" button. Any volumes attached to your system for which add-ons exist will appear on the desktop (or in the Disks window), and be ready to use. Access them from the Tracker or the Terminal just as you would a BeOS partition. Note that some filesystem add-ons don't offer write support. If you find that you can copy files from but not to your alien volumes, check BeWare for updated drivers.

The first section of the Mount Settings panel lets you control whether and how disks are automounted during normal operation. When automount is turned on and you insert a new CD-ROM or removable cartridge, BeOS will make the disk immediately accessible. If Don't Automount is selected, you'll need to mount additional partitions manually. All BeOS Disks, obviously, will only automount BFS-formatted partitions.

Floppy drives do not automount in any circumstance—you'll always need to mount them manually.

The second section of Mount Settings offers similar options, but replaces the Don't Automount option with Only the Boot Disk. Thanks, Be, for not letting us try to boot our systems without mounting the boot disk!

Click Done or close the Mount Settings panel to commit your changes.

## Custom Mount Control

The Mount Settings window may offer a nice, simple set of options and easy access, but if you have three DOS partitions and two Mac partitions attached to your system and you only want to mount a few of them, just right-click anywhere on the desktop and scroll to the Mount entry on the context menu. Currently unmounted drives will be displayed in a submenu—select one to mount it and it will appear on your desktop instantly.

**Figure 5.35**

*With Mount Settings configured to mount only BeOS disks at boot time, partitions belonging to alien filesystems are ignored at boot time. With Mount Settings configured to mount all disks, both Windows partitions would have been mounted automatically.*

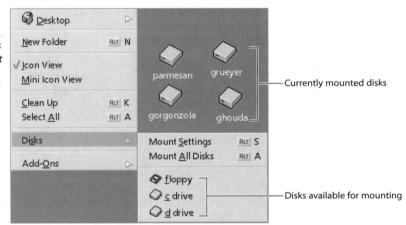

While this option may not sound all that necessary to the average home user, it becomes increasingly important as the number of available partitions on your system increases. In a networked environment, for instance, there may be dozens of drives potentially available, when you only really need one or two.

## Unmounting Partitions

When you no longer want a volume to be visible to you in the Tracker and Terminal, right-click its icon on the desktop (or in the Disks window, if you've fiddled with the TrackerSettings file as described in Chapter 2). If the volume is a removable disk, it will disappear immediately. If the volume is a fixed (hard) disk, the operating system will prompt you for confirmation.

*Figure 5.36*

*Unmounting a hard disk will bring up
this dialog asking for confirmation, while
unmounting a CD, floppy, or other
removable disk will not.*

You can also unmount removable disks by simply removing them. However, it's good housekeeping to always use the Unmount command. This ensures that the journal on the disk has been fully synced with its actual data.

## Natively Supported Filesystems

Table 5.05 lists the filesystems that BeOS R4 supports out of the box. Because Be strives to keep the PowerPC and Intel releases of BeOS as indistinguishable from one another as possible, it shouldn't matter whether you're running the OS on an Intel machine, a BeBox, or a PowerMac. Yes, this does mean that BeOS for Intel can read Mac floppies effortlessly, and vice versa!

This book was written for BeOS R4. If you're using a later version of the operating system, Table 5.05 may not be complete. Look for filesystem modules in the directory /boot/beos/system/add-ons/kernel/file_systems/. You'll find exactly one module for every supported filesystem.

### Table 5.05  Supported File Systems

| Filesystem | Native OS | Notes |
|---|---|---|
| BFS | BeOS | Reads and writes Be's own high-performance native filesystem. |
| DOS | DOS, Windows 95/98 | Reads and writes FAT 16 and FAT 32 partitions for all versions of DOS and Windows except NT. Includes long filename support. |
| HFS | MacOS | Reads and writes all MacOS partitions with the exception of HFS+. Reads MacOS icons too! |
| ISO9660 | All platforms | Reads data from CD-ROMs burned with the industry-standard cross-platform CD format. |
| OFS | BeOS | Reads and writes to disks formatted with the old (pre-DR9) BeOS filesystem. Obsolete but present for backward compatibility. |

*BeOS ships with a handful of drivers that let your system read from and write to a variety of common filesystems. In addition to the filesystems shown here, third parties can create drivers for less common filesystems. Adding support for a new system is as easy as dropping the new driver into the appropriate folder.*

**Coming Soon** In a future version of BeOS, probably either R5 or R6, you can expect to see read/write support for NTFS (Microsoft Windows NT's native filesystem) bundled with the system as well. And if demand is sufficiently high, don't be surprised to see some of the drivers listed in Table 5.06 making their way into the official distribution.

In addition, future versions of BeOS will ship with tools to let you access your BeOS volumes from within Microsoft Windows or Apple's MacOS, so that you'll finally have true two-way read/write capabilities between BeOS and your other operating systems.

## Optional Filesystem Support

While having native support for the filesystems in Table 5.05 should cover 99% of users' needs 99% of the time, there *are* other filesystems in this world. While Be may not write the add-ons for these themselves, the system can handle filesystem add-ons written by third parties. If you're working with BeOS in a media shop where, say, Irix or Solaris machines are prevalent, your company may find it to be worthwhile to undertake driver development themselves. On the other hand, someone might have already done this work. Check BeWare for filesystem add-ons not included with BeOS.

### Table 5.06 Alien File Systems

| Filesystem | Native OS | Notes |
|---|---|---|
| NFS | Multiple | Reads and writes to Network File Systems (requires you to have access to an NFS server machine or to run an NFS server on your BeOS machine—NFS is somewhere between a filesystem and a network protocol). |
| EXT2 | Linux | Reads the native Linux filesystem (should support write access by the time you read this). |

*Drivers for some less common filesystems are downloadable from BeWare, but do not ship with BeOS.*

### CD-ROM Formats

ISO9660 is an industry standard used to create CD-ROM sessions that can be read by a wide variety of platforms, and it is the ISO9660 driver on your BeOS system that lets you easily read most CDs in circulation. ISO9660 has gone through a number of iterations throughout its history, including level 1, level 2, Rock Ridge, and Joliet. Without going into details on differences between the specs, you should know that the ISO9660 driver in BeOS R4 supports everything but the latest iteration, Joliet. This means that you should be able to handle CDs pressed with long filenames and deeply nested subdirectories without difficulty, but you won't get the Unicode internationalization support that is part of the Joliet spec. You may also experience some bugginess with very old CD-ROMs, but this is unlikely to affect the vast majority of CDs. Expect Joliet support in a future release of BeOS.

# The Directory Structure

By now you've likely spent a good bit of time just wandering around in BeOS, using the Tracker to navigate through the directory structure and poking your nose into folders. Unless you've come to BeOS from the Unix world, BeOS's directory structure may seem somewhat alien at first. But the amazing thing is that even if you've never browsed a Unix-style directory tree in your life, it's not difficult to at least get a sense of what things do and why they're placed where they are. That's because the BeOS directory structure is supremely logical, and almost explains itself—unlike some operating systems, which dump hundreds of obscurely named files into giant holding bins willy-nilly. BeOS directory paths and file names almost always describe their own purpose, which in turn makes it much easier to decipher some of the operating system's internal logic.

If you've restricted your wandering to the Tracker's graphical view, you may be surprised to learn that there's more to your directory structure than meets the eye—the Tracker doesn't show you the whole story, and hides a few directories from view permanently. Don't feel too cheated, though; most of the hidden directories are just links to system directories, and the few remaining ones don't contain much of interest to end-users anyway (we'll describe these hidden directories at the end of this section). However, any time you get to feeling adventurous, you can drop into the Terminal and take a gander at the Hidden Directories of Montezuma. Just be careful if you do—they're hidden for a reason.

## User-Level and System-Level Directories

There are two basic classes of directories in BeOS: those meant to be touched only by BeOS, and those meant for you and your data. It's not hard to remember which is which: The system gets the entire /boot/beos/ directory structure and the handful of hidden directories, while you have safe access to everything else. While nothing is going to stop you from messing with things in the /boot/beos/ hierarchy, it really isn't advisable, since Be reserves the right to do whatever it likes with this branch of the tree at upgrade time—any changes you make now could very well be overwritten later. That doesn't mean any loss of control for you, though, because the system knows to look in certain user-level directories for all of your hacks, tweaks, and additions. For instance, take a look at these two paths:

```
/boot/beos/system/add-ons/Tracker
/boot/home/config/add-ons/Tracker
```

If it seems like these two directories must serve similar purposes, it's because they do. One is for Tracker add-ons installed and maintained by BeOS, and the other is for Tracker add-ons installed and maintained by you. When you access the Tracker's add-ons menu, the Tracker reads the contents of the two directories and merges them into a single display, as if they had always been a single unit. This way, Be is able to protect and preserve the things that are essential to the system's operation, and simultaneously honor and serve the user's needs.

When BeOS gains multiuser capabilities, this system will become even more important, as each user will be able to have their own add-ons, configuration files, and other custom tweaks, while BeOS will be able to provide the same system services to each user without having to duplicate files. Note also that everything under /boot/beos/ becomes write-protected under multiuser conditions, and you'll need god-like privileges to edit, add, or delete anything in the entire system-level directory.

### Keeping the System Safe and Sane

Another important ramification of the user-level/system-level dichotomy is the fact that in several key locations you'll find links in the user-level directories pointing to actual files living in the system-level tree. For example, all of the icons in your preferences and apps folders are links to applications living somewhere in the /boot/beos tree. This is done for a couple of reasons. First, this protects the user from accidents. Because accidentally deleting something like the Network preferences panel could have devastating effects for the entire networking subsystem, it's tucked safely away in a system-level directory. A user can delete the link to it without causing any real harm; links can always be re-created. Second, this system anticipates BeOS running in multiuser mode. Rather than duplicating the Web browser for every user, all of them can share a single copy of NetPositive living in a system directory, accessed from the link in their personal directories. Each user is still able to use their own bookmarks and browser settings because those things live in a subdirectory of /boot/home.

## What Lives Where on Your Boot Drive

Unlike some other operating systems, it's very easy to boot BeOS from any partition containing an appropriate directory structure and startup files. Some users like to install multiple copies of BeOS (for example, during the R3 to R4 transition, some users kept both systems installed, since programs built for one version would not run on the other). In addition, BeOS lets you name your disk volumes or partitions anything you like. But at the same time, BeOS needs to recognize where certain important files and folders reside, independent of what you've named your disk volumes. To reconcile these two facts, the operating system uses a clever trick: Regardless of how you've named your partitions, BeOS always regards the partition you booted from as the boot partition. For example, even if you have only one partition on your system, named Sir Gallahad, you can open a Terminal window and type cd /boot—you'll see that the /boot directory is just another name for your Sir Gallahad partition. If you boot from the BeOS Installation CD and do the same thing, you'll find that the CD itself is now recognized as /boot. And if you have multiple bootable partitions and switch between them with the Boot preferences panel (see Chapter 9), you'll see that the system gives the name /boot to whatever volume you just booted from.

By default, you'll find the following directories stemming from the root (top-level directory) of your boot drive:

```
/boot/apps
/boot/beos
/boot/demos
/boot/develop
/boot/home
/boot/optional
/boot/preferences
/boot/tmp
```

Of course, you're free to create your own directories in the root as well, though in general it's good housekeeping to store as much as you can in subdirectories of these directories—especially in /boot/home/.

## User-Level Directories

As described elsewhere in this book, you're allowed to mess with (add to, delete from, or modify) just about any directory on your hard drive(s), with the important exception of the /boot/beos hierarchy. That, however, does not mean that it's a good idea to go deleting things willy-nilly. Not only will Murphy's law probably apply later (you'll find yourself wanting access to something tomorrow that you deleted today), but many components depend on other components. One of the great things about BeOS, though, is that the installation CD is an exact mirror of the directory structure it installs on your hard drive, meaning that if you delete or modify something you later wish you hadn't, all you have to do is insert the BeOS CD and copy the file or files back into place. The /boot/beos hierarchy is an exception to this rule because if you delete something there, you could easily end up with an unbootable system.

That said, let's dig in to the user-level directory structures, and then look at the hidden and system-level directories later.

### /boot/apps

On a fresh system, the user will find here a collection of links to built-in applications living in /boot/beos/apps. Users may store their own applications in this directory as well, or optionally create an apps subdirectory inside of /boot/home. Because a list of applications can grow quite long rather quickly, it's a good idea to subdivide the apps directory into logical categories, such as:

```
/boot/apps/develop
/boot/apps/edit
/boot/apps/games
/boot/apps/multimedia
/boot/apps/net
/boot/apps/productivity
/boot/apps/utils
```

### /boot/demos

This is a collection of attention-grabbing applications created by Be engineers to demonstrate special properties of BeOS. They serve no purpose other than to impress your friends and slack-jawed crowds at trade shows and conventions. You can remove the demo applications without harming your system, though you won't save more than 5MB.

### /boot/develop

Header files and libraries used in software development are stored in this directory. Of interest to programmers only, these files ensure a common codebase for the most basic functions. For example, if a programmer needs a slider bar in her application, she'll obtain the baseline code for a slider by invoking the header Slider.h in her code. Libraries exist to invoke the system Kits to achieve basic modalities such as gaming, networking, or multimedia. The tools subdirectory in this folder contains the egcs toolchain of compilers and debuggers used to actually create applications from source code. Since you'll occasionally download tools or applications that you'll need to compile yourself (see Appendix D), deleting anything in this directory is not recommended.

### /boot/home

This is your home base—your living room, a place to hang your hat. The /boot/home directory is "sacred," and will never by touched by Be during system upgrades. While you can certainly create new directories in the root, add new applications to /boot/apps, and in general add new files or make changes to any directory besides /boot/beos, /boot/home is your default "nest." In addition to the preinstalled subdirectories of /boot/home listed below, you'll probably want to create subdirectories here to store your images, sounds, projects, writings, and other personal data. If you store these things on a separate partition, you may want to create symlinks in this directory pointing to those locations. Some users even store their applications in /boot/home/apps. Aside from the special subdirectories of the home folder noted below (which must be present to make certain things work properly), "anything goes" in /boot/home.

 Do not remove /boot/home! Your system will not operate properly (possibly not at all) if the /boot/home directory is not found at boot time. Nor can you fool the system by moving your home directory to another partition and creating a link to it here (because the other partition might not be mounted early enough in the boot process to be found). Just leave it where it is and you'll be fine.

### /boot/home/cd

If you use the CDPlayer application and create track lists of your favorite CDs, they'll be stored here. When you later insert the same CD again, the original track list will be invoked automatically. See Chapter 2, for details.

### /boot/home/config

The subdirectories of /boot/home/config serve almost as a mirror of many of those under /boot/beos/. This is where the vast majority of user-level customizations and behind-the-scenes additions to the operating system live. By providing this directory tree and marrying it to parallel trees under /boot/beos/, BeOS allows users to hack to their heart's content without disturbing the sacrosanct system-level directory.

### /boot/home/config/add-ons

Contents of the subdirectories of ~/config/add-ons serve to extend the functionality of the operating system and are conjoined with the globally applied add-ons in the system-level directory. Some of the add-ons folders listed below may not be installed on your system by default—you may end up creating them yourself when installing certain kinds of add-ons to the system. If you do, create subdirectory structures here as exact mirrors of those in /boot/beos/system/add-ons.

### /boot/home/config/add-ons/app_server

Users can add test or beta video drivers to this directory without disturbing the official drivers at the system level. If a driver is found here at boot time, it will be used instead of the system-level driver if it identifies the video hardware properly. If it fails, it can be removed through an emergency boot (see Chapter 16, *Troubleshooting and Maintenance*) and the system will resume functioning normally.

### /boot/home/config/add-ons/kernel

Experimental I/O (input/output) drivers not distributed by Be can be placed here (these may include things like SCSI adapter drivers and alien filesystem support). This would also be a good place to store drivers for proprietary or test hardware that will never have broad support. At some point in the future, all of the system-level directories will become write-protected, so these directories will become the *only* place where users can place their own drivers, add-ons, and so forth.

### /boot/home/config/add-ons/Print

Any printer drivers that weren't initially supplied with your BeOS installation (in other words, those you download later) should be placed here.

### /boot/home/config/add-ons/Screen Savers

Not present by default, this directory will be created as soon as you install Blanket or other screen saver engines willing to share a common data pool. Screen saver modules are placed here.

### /boot/home/config/add-ons/Tracker

Any Tracker add-ons downloaded and installed by the user will live here, and be merged in the Add-Ons context menu with add-ons living in /boot/beos/system/add-ons/Tracker. See Chapter 10, for documentation on Tracker add-ons.

### /boot/home/config/add-ons/Translators

This is where you'll install data format Translators not in official distribution by Be (such as those downloaded from developer's sites or those that you've written yourself, if you're a programmer). See Chapter 9 for more on Translators.

### /boot/home/config/be

This subdirectory stores links to files and folders that you want to appear on the Be menu in the Deskbar. See Chapter 2 for details.

### /boot/home/config/bin

You should use this directory, empty by default, to store command-line tools (either binaries or shell scripts) that you want to be available from any Terminal session. This is the user-level version of /boot/beos/bin.

### /boot/home/config/boot

Initially, this directory contains four scripts: UserBootscript.sample, UserSetupEnvironment.sample, UserShutdownScript.sample, and UserShutdownFinish.sample. If you rename (or copy) any of them without the .sample extension, the system will find and run them at boot time or during the shutdown process. UserBootscript is used to automatically launch applications and background processes (daemons), while UserSetupEnvironment is used to establish "environmental" parameters, such as global variables you might need to access from the shell at any given moment. Both scripts are run *after* the system-level boot scripts. Conversely, the shutdown scripts let you play sound files as the machine is shutting down, kill running processes, or do anything else that can be done from the command line. Each of the sample files includes a note in the header, which you should read. As is always the case when there are both user-level and system-level versions of the same files, any settings declared in these scripts will override those declared in the system-level scripts.

### /boot/home/config/documentation
Applications can optionally install documentation in this subdirectory, which is not present by default, rather than in their own directories. Users can optionally move application documentation from its original location to this directory, which lets you keep all of your documentation together in one place (though this practice isn't really as useful as it might sound).

### /boot/home/config/etc/
This subdirectory contains extra configuration data for BeOS system services that can be controlled at the user level. By default, it contains dummy scripts for expander.rules (see Chapter 2) and ppp-script (see Chapter 8).

### /boot/home/config/fonts
Like its mirror directory in /boot/beos/etc/fonts, this directory can contain subdirectories for different classes of fonts (though only TrueType and some PostScript fonts work with BeOS at this writing). Any fonts added to this directory will appear in the font lists of the user's applications. If your fonts folder is empty and you want to add to it, first create a ttfonts folder inside this folder, drop your fonts into ttfonts, then open the Fonts preferences panel and click the Rescan button. You'll need to restart a running application in order for the new fonts to appear in its fonts menu.

 Before your applications will "see" newly added fonts, you must click the Rescan button in the Fonts preferences panel. Note also that if you create further subdirectories under this directory, any fonts inside them will not be recognized.

### /boot/home/config/lib
This is a cousin of the system-level libraries directory. Any libraries required by user-installed applications can be placed here.

### /boot/home/config/settings
This directory is packed with files and folders containing settings and customizations for dozens of applications and system services (and will grow steadily as you install and use more applications). Some settings files are stored in text format and can be edited by the user, while others are in binary format and are only editable by applications. You can tell at a glance which are which since text-based configuration files will appear with a text icon in the Tracker, whereas binary files will have the generic blue square icon. More details on this directory can be found in Chapter 9.

### /boot/home/mail

This directory will be created as soon as you set up mail services on BeOS, and is used for storing email messages. It can optionally be subdivided into more directories for customized mail categorization. BeMail considers /boot/home/mail/in the home base for all incoming messages, while outgoing messages are stored in /boot/home/mail/out. See Chapter 4 for details.

### /boot/home/news

This directory will not appear by default, but will function similarly to /boot/home/mail if the user installs a Usenet reader such as BeInformed, which creates a standard news directory and news message format.

### /boot/home/people

This is a central location for the storage of Person files, created as soon as you create your first Person file. By customizing the layout of this folder, you can build an effective contact database.

### /boot/home/queries

All BeOS system queries are automatically saved to this folder (though there's no reason they have to stay here—you can drag queries from here to anywhere you like). See Chapter 7 for details.

### /boot/home/SampleMedia

If you elected to install BeOS without the optional files, the small collection of images, sounds, and MIDI files in this folder will still give you a few media files to play with. This being the MediaOS, you'll probably be storing volumes of this kind of stuff before long—you might even want to dedicate an entire partition to storing media files.

### /boot/optional

If you choose the "optional" install option, a collection of sample media and data files such as movies and MIDI files are installed here. Complete descriptions of the contents of the optional subdirectories can be found in Chapter 2.

### /boot/preferences

Links to the preference applications in /boot/beos/preferences are stored here. Like the application links to in /boot/apps, these links provide user-level access to system-level applications. This folder is mirrored as the Preferences entry in the Be menu, and should be your main access point to all BeOS preferences. Occasionally, application vendors will install interfaces to their own applications' preferences here—the Blanket screen saver is one example of this. If you accidentally delete a link in this folder, just open up /boot/beos/preferences and drag links from there into this folder.

**/boot/tmp**

This directory is not present by default, but is likely to be created soon by applications looking to create temporary files at the user level, in contrast to the default temporary location, which is /var/tmp. This temp location is visible to the Tracker, while /var/tmp is not.

## Hidden Directories

The Tracker may be a great file manager, but there are some things that can only be done—or can be done best—from the command line. Viewing BeOS's hidden directories is one of those things. You should understand that when things in BeOS are hidden, they're hidden for a reason. Either they're not useful to end-users or they're dangerous to fiddle with. The hidden directories fall more into the former category than the latter, though you certainly could cause problems if you did something really drastic, like deleting or renaming them. Simply poking around and viewing their contents, however, is perfectly safe.

Finally, most of the hidden directories are virtual, rather than actual. You'll notice in the directory listing below that they exist at the same level as—not inside of—your mounted disk volumes. From this, you can infer that these files and folders do not exist on any physical disk media. Instead, they're loaded into the filesystem's image of itself at boot time and treated *as if* they were real.

Take a look at the disk volumes mounted on your desktop. At the very least, you'll see your boot drive and likely a few other partitions as well. You're looking at the root of the filesystem. Figure 5.37 shows a Tracker view of the root of the author's filesystem.

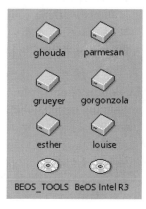

**Figure 5.37**

The root of the filesystem, as seen from the Tracker (in other words, the desktop). In this case, there are four BeOS partitions (named after the author's favorite cheeses), two partitions on the BeOS installation CD (the BeOS entries), and two DOS partitions (Louise and Esther). Interestingly, the two partitions on the CD are formatted in different filesystems: one is a BeOS partition, while the other is a DOS partition. The same CD viewed in Windows shows only a single partition.

Now let's take a look at the same location in the filesystem from the perspective of the command line. Open up a Terminal and change to the root directory (cd /), then get a directory listing (ls -l or dir). You should see something like this, which is the Terminal equivalent of the Tracker view in Figure 5.37:

```
/boot/home>cd /
/>dir
total 8
dr-xr-xr-x   0 users    baron     2048 Mar  9 09:24 BEOS_TOOLS/
drwx------   1 users    baron     2048 Mar  3 13:16 BeOS Intel R3/
l---------   1 users    baron        0 Jun 19 12:51 bin -> /boot/beos/bin/
drwx------   1 users    baron     2048 Jun 18 13:19 boot/
drwxr-x---   1 users    baron        0 Jun 19 12:51 dev/
drw-rw-rw-   1 users    baron        0 Dec 31  1969 esther/
l---------   1 users    baron        0 Jun 19 12:51 etc -> /boot/beos/etc/
l---------   1 users    baron        0 Jun 19 12:51 gorgonzola -> /boot/
drw-rw-rw-   1 users    baron        0 Dec 31  1969 louise/
drwx------   1 users    baron     2048 Jun 16 05:46 parmesan/
drwxrwxrwx   1 users    baron        0 Jun 19 12:51 pipe/
drwxrwxrwx   1 users    baron        0 Dec 31  1969 pnp/
l---------   1 users    baron        0 Jun 19 12:51 system -> /boot/beos/system/
l---------   1 users    baron        0 Jun 19 12:51 tmp -> /boot/var/tmp/
l---------   1 users    baron        0 Jun 19 12:51 var -> /boot/var/
```

 See Chapter 6 for details on interpreting bash file entries. You can also learn how to change baron's name to your own in the same chapter.

There are several interesting things to note about this listing, not least of which is the fact that there are many more entries than are visible from the Tracker. Five of the six drive entries are obvious, and correspond to the same names in the Tracker. The partition gorgonzola, however, appears somewhat differently—as a symlink to boot. As described earlier in this chapter, that's because you're allowed to call your partitions anything you want, but the partition you boot from will always be called "boot" to guarantee the sanity of programs, scripts, and operating system code that need to know where to find important files.

Note also that from this view, each of your mounted volumes appears to be a directory (as indicated by the "d" entry in the far-left column). This is because you're seeing mount points, rather than actual drive entries (mount points are described in Chapter 9). Though a mount point is not a directory in the standard sense of the word, it functions like one for all intents and purposes. Accessing a drive from the Terminal is always as simple as changing directories up to the root and then down to the partition's name, as if it were a regular directory (in other words, cd /esther will allow me to start navigating one of my DOS partitions from within the Terminal). This is why almost every pathname specified in this book begins with /boot/.

**Other Symlinks in the Root**  Also notice that five of the entries in the root listing are actually symlinks, as indicated by the horizontal arrows toward the right:

```
l--------- 1 users   baron      0 Jun 19 12:51 bin -> /boot/beos/bin/
l--------- 1 users   baron      0 Jun 19 12:51 etc -> /boot/beos/etc/
l--------- 1 users   baron      0 Jun 19 12:51 system -> /boot/beos/system/
l--------- 1 users   baron      0 Jun 19 12:51 tmp -> /boot/var/tmp/
l--------- 1 users   baron      0 Jun 19 12:51 var -> /boot/var/
```

Thus, any access to /var will actually resolve into a link to /boot/var, and any access to /bin will resolve to /boot/beos/bin. The reason for this has to do with BeOS's POSIX compliance (see Chapter 6), and the vast number of command-line tools that have been ported to BeOS as a result of it. Because many Unix systems have such directories in the root while BeOS keeps them in subdirectories of the boot drive, placing links to the real locations in the root enables these programs to run normally—hard-coded paths in Unix tools are simply rerouted to the appropriate locations. These links also make it a little easier to access certain directories while working in the shell. Interestingly, if you type cd /bin and then pwd, the shell will report that you actually *are* currently in /bin. The shell maintains the illusion that the symlink is an actual directory.

**More Strange Directories**  Finally, three directories can be found in the root which are neither symlinks nor drive mount points:

```
drwxr-x--- 1 users   baron      0 Jun 19 12:51 dev/
drwxrwxrwx 1 users   baron      0 Jun 19 12:51 pipe/
drwxrwxrwx 1 users   baron      0 Dec 31  1969 pnp/
```

### /dev

The /dev directory and all of its subdirectories function as pointers to the physical and virtual devices attached to your machine. While it may seem strange to users of other operating systems to list physical devices like printers and modems as if they were part of the filesystem, this is the way Unix systems have always worked, and the technique actually has some very interesting benefits, such as enabling you to send commands to and receive output from your devices from within shell scripts, or while working in the Terminal. For example, if you have a printer connected to your parallel port, try this:

```
cat /boot/home/filename.txt >  /dev/parallel/parallel1
```

With any luck, your printer will spring to life and spit out the contents of the file filename.txt (though it won't look too pretty).

While other devices in this hierarchy can be written to in this way, results can be unpredictable and Be doesn't recommend it. Don't think of these directory entries as general shortcuts to your system devices; they're required by the system, but not very useful to the user. Results can be unpredictable.

## *Digging into /dev/disk*

The /dev/disk directory structure is of little concern to end-users. This section is presented as optional reading for those interested in learning how BeOS maps partition device points to volume names. The contents of this section are fairly technical, and presume some understanding of the bus system in x86 computers. Note that your machine may show different things when you dig into this directory.

### /dev/disk

The subdirectories of /dev/disk represent the real locations (device pointers) of your disks in the filesystem. While your disk volumes are mounted in the root with user-friendly names like /boot and /Galileo, the operating system really sees them as being attached in this directory tree. To translate from the real device locations to the user-friendly device locations, BeOS places mount points in the root. It may seem like a strange system at first, but there's also a simple logic to it. Disks need to be attached alongside all the other devices referenced by the filesystem because they are, after all, devices. At the same time, the device points in the /dev tree aren't files or folders in the traditional sense, and you can't view or edit them like regular files and folders. So a hard disk needs to be treated as both a device and a directory at the same time.

Confused yet? Try this: cd to /dev/disk and get a directory listing. You should see something similar to:

```
drw-r--r--  1 coyote  milkbone         0 Jun 20 00:39 floppy/
drw-r--r--  1 coyote  milkbone         0 Jun 20 00:39 ide/
drw-r--r--  1 coyote  milkbone         0 Jun 20 00:39 scsi/
```

These are the three major classes of drives attached to the author's system. Tunneling down through the IDE chain, we see:

```
drw-r--r--  1 coyote  milkbone         0 Jun 20 00:39 0/
crw-r--r--  1 coyote  milkbone    0,   0 Jun 20 00:39 rescan
```

The first is a directory called 0, and the other is a virtual device (as denoted by the "c" as the first letter in its entry). The directory is displaying the contents of the IDE bus in the current system. There are always two IDE buses: 0 and 1. Apparently we don't have anything connected to the second bus interface, so it doesn't appear here. rescan is a virtual device used at boot time (or when you run DriveSetup or mountvolume) to try and force the CD-ROM to spin up and is of no interest to us here. Drilling down the 0 chain, we see:

```
drw-r--r--  1 coyote  milkbone         0 Jun 20 09:52 master/
drw-r--r--  1 coyote  milkbone         0 Jun 20 09:52 slave/
```

Ah—this makes perfect sense. Every IDE interface, as we know from Chapter 3, *Installation*, can host two devices, with one configured as master and another as slave. Now let's drill down once more, into master:

```
total 0
crw-r--r--  1 coyote   milkbone   0,   0 Jun 20 08:33 0_0
crw-r-----  1 coyote   milkbone   0,   0 Jun 20 00:39 0_1
crw-r--r--  1 coyote   milkbone   0,   0 Jun 20 07:39 0_3
crw-r--r--  1 coyote   milkbone   0,   0 Jun 20 09:52 0_4
crw-r--r--  1 coyote   milkbone   0,   0 Jun 20 00:39 raw
```

This is the place—ground zero for partitions seen by the system on the first IDE bus, master channel (see Chapter 3), mounted or not. Note that the letters in the left column have changed from d's to c's—these are the real devices, not directories, and we can't drill down any farther. Any time you see "raw" when looking at drive listings in the Terminal, you're looking at the representation of the actual, physical disk—that's my 6GB hard drive represented in the filesystem as a little zero. Kind of pathetic, huh? The other four entries are the partitions on the raw disk. Only two of them are BeOS partitions, but partition types aren't distinguished from one another at this low level; if it's seen by a device driver, it's reported to the system.

This leaves you with a dilemma—how can you tell from here which of your actual volumes these device points point to? Here's the trick: use the Terminal's df command, which reports on available disk space. The cool thing about df is that it gives you more details than you might expect. Check it out:

```
/boot/home>df
Mount               Type      Total       Free    Flags Device
----------------    --------  ---------   -------- ----- ----------------------------
/                   rootfs          0          0     0
/dev                devfs           0          0     0
/pipe               pipefs          0          0     0
/pnp                pnpfs           0          0     0
/boot               bfs       1574370     360348 70004 /dev/disk/ide/0/master/0_1
/parmesan           bfs       1333395    1225611 70004 /dev/disk/ide/0/master/0_3
/BeOS Intel R3      bfs        532464     234894 70005 /dev/disk/ide/0/slave/1_0
/louise             dos       2096448          0 30005 /dev/disk/ide/0/master/0_0
/esther             dos       1285152          0 30005 /dev/disk/ide/0/master/0_4
/BEOS TOOLS         iso9660      5120          0     5 /dev/disk/ide/0/slave/0_0
```

This listing is similar in ways to the plain directory listings we were studying earlier, but now we get a one-to-one correspondence between volume names and device points.

So … now that we've ferreted out all these great details, what do we do with them? Well, not a whole lot, unless you're working with low-level command-line disk utilities. For instance, you may want to use fdisk from within Linux, but you want to be damn sure you don't mess up the wrong partition. By booting into BeOS and printing out this listing, you can have it at your side while working in another operating system where you'll be able to see the same device points, but not the volume names. You'll also see these device points referred to in a few of the BeOS installation and setup dialogs. Finally, if you experiment with mtools (see Chapter 16), you'll need to know exactly which volume maps to which device point.

### /pipe

This virtual directory serves a critical, low-level function internally any time you use the pipe (|) character in a shell command.

### /pnp

Present on x86 systems only, this virtual directory helps to route communications between plug-and-play devices and the rest of the operating system.

### /boot/var

Unlike the other hidden directories, /boot/var is not located in the root. This is because it serves a function related only to the boot drive, not to the entire filesystem. In addition, the virtual directories in the root do not exist on disk, and thus cannot store actual files. In contrast, /boot/var *does* store actual files, so it cannot exist in the root. In the Unix world, the /var directory contains administrative and log files. Under BeOS, its function is similar. Its contents are detailed below.

### /boot/var/swap

The swap file is a critical component of your system's operations and is created at boot time by BeOS after it determines how much physical memory is in your machine. You can come here to see the actual size of your swap file if you don't trust the Virtual Memory preferences panel, but you cannot delete, view, rename, or otherwise alter the swap file from the command line. It's write-protected, and even though you can change its file permissions if you know how, it's highly inadvisable and the results could be unpredictable.

### /boot/var/log

This subdirectory contains the syslog, a file written to at boot time by the syslog_daemon. When the log gets too full, a new one is created, so depending on the history of your machine, you might find a file called old-syslog as well. Keep these around—you may need to send one to Be's technical support team if you ever get in a jam.

In addition, applications can write their own log files to this directory if they wish, though it's not a great idea since this directory is invisible to the Tracker.

### /boot/var/tmp

This contains temporary files created by the operating system during the performance of certain boot and maintenance tasks. These files are overwritten with each boot, so their timestamps will always reflect the current date.

## System-Level Directories

As described earlier, there's a line in the sand in the BeOS directory structure. You're free to add, delete, and modify files and folders anywhere you like on your disk, but you should leave everything that falls under the /boot/beos tree alone. The following section is here to give you a sense of what does what in the system-level directories, not as a hacker's guide. You have been warned.

### /boot/beos

This is the prime system-level directory, containing all of the files required for BeOS to boot and run properly. Users should never need to alter anything under the entire /boot/beos/ directory structure, and are strongly discouraged from doing so.

### /boot/beos/apps

The links in /boot/apps point to this directory, which contains the real applications installed with BeOS. See Chapter 2 for details on these applications. You should install your own applications in /boot/apps or /boot/home/apps, but never in /boot/beos/apps.

### /boot/beos/bin

By default, around 200 command-line tools are provided here for use in the Terminal. The vast majority of these have been ported from open-source Unix utilities. Even if you never intend to use the Terminal, don't delete this directory or any of its files—BeOS uses many of these files internally, as do many installation scripts. See Chapter 6 for details. If you download other command-line tools, always install them in /boot/home/config/bin, never here.

### /boot/beos/documentation

In this subdirectory you'll find electronic documentation on many aspects of using, installing, and developing for BeOS. You'll also find press materials, screen shots, and, perhaps most informative of all, a vast collection of frequently asked questions, or FAQs. The "Welcome to BeOS" link that appears on your desktop with a fresh installation serves as a home page to the entire collection—double-click it to launch the user documentation in NetPositive. If you can't find the answer you're looking for in this book, it's highly recommended that you peruse this collection before writing to Be customer support or posting questions to BeOS mailing lists or newsgroups.

 **Unix** man **Pages**  If you're a Terminal junkie and you've noticed the absence of the Unix man **command, note that you'll find man pages for many of the bundled shell tools in HTML format, in the** Shell Tools **subdirectory of the** Documentation **folder.**

### /boot/beos/etc

Some BeOS tools and applications require external configuration and data files to function properly. The function of this directory is similar to, but not quite the same as, the user-level /boot/home/config/settings directory tree.

### boot/beos/etc/bebox_bootmain.image

This raw data file is a mirror of data that gets loaded into system memory as the BeBox begins its boot process. It's not present on Intel machines, though users of both Macs and BeBoxes will find this file here.

### /boot/beos/etc/bison.hairy, /bison.simple

These are support files for bison, which is a tool that developers can use to add text parsers to their applications. The bison file is of no use to the end-user.

### /boot/beos/etc/calah

The "engine" for the game of Calah, which you'll find in your demos folder, resides here. Calah is covered in Chapter 2.

### /boot/beos/etc/connect

This subdirectory contains support files and scripts for the SerialConnect program, which is not related to PPP (see Chapter 8 for details on SerialConnect).

### /boot/beos/etc/fonts

Fonts provided with your BeOS installation live here, subdivided into directories named after font types. At this writing, the only supported font type is TrueType, so the only subdirectory here is called ttfonts. However, BeOS will soon support some PostScript fonts as well, so you may soon see a parallel directory at /boot/beos/etc/fonts/psfonts. Never add your own fonts to this directory—place those in /boot/home/config/fonts/ttfonts. or in ~/config/fonts/psfonts.

### /boot/beos/etc/fortunes

Messages used by the fortune shell command (see Chapter 6) are stored here.

### /boot/beos/etc/hosts-sample

This is a sample hosts file used by the networking subsystem to locate hosts on the network if you've checked "Disable DNS" in the Network preferences panel (see Chapter 8), often used when setting up BeOS to use external proxy servers.

### /boot/beos/etc/joystick-README

This README provides documentation on using joystick configuration files in the joysticks folder (below)

### /boot/beos/etc/joysticks

This directory contains a collection of configuration files for the most popular joysticks in circulation. To use one, create a link to the config file in your settings directory as described in the README, then edit to suit. Make sure that the number in the filename (such as Analog_3_Axes) matches the port to which your joystick is connected. See Chapter 9 for more details.

### /boot/beos/etc/Keymap

The data files here are used by the Keymap preferences panel (see Chapter 9) to set up the keyboard for use in different languages.

### /boot/beos/etc/less.hlp

This is a help file for the less command line tool (Chapter 6).

### /boot/beos/etc/libexec/

Support executables used by several of the GNU command-line utilities can be found here.

### /boot/beos/etc/lilo

Contains files used during the boot process on x86 machines—not present on Macs or BeBoxen. See Chapter 3 for details.

### /boot/beos/etc/modems.ppp

PPP configurations for the computer industry's most popular modems, including modem model names and initialization strings, are here. See Chapter 8 for details.

### /boot/beos/etc/ppd

Printer description files—one for every printer supported by BeOS—are in this directory. Major classes of printers are defined by the presence of printer drivers loaded as kernel add-ons, while individual printer model parameters are contained in these files.

### /boot/beos/etc/profile

This is similar to the .profile you may have in your home directory. It sets up environment variables and default configuration for the Terminal, which gives you a workable default bash shell. Make all shell profile changes to /boot/home/.profile, not this file.

### /boot/beos/etc/ROMUpdater

Only present on BeBoxes, this contains a program and disk image (bebox_bootmain.image) used to update the boot ROM of a BeBox when the operating system is upgraded. See Chapter 2 for details.

### /boot/beos/etc/servers.ppp
Some Internet service providers require special login scripts to launch a successful connection. Chances are slim that you will need to use these; consult with your ISP if you think you might, and see Chapter 8 for details.

### /boot/beos/etc/services
This is a table of standard Internet port addresses. A port is a numbered address through which certain kinds of TCP/IP communications flow, and is often used in setting up firewalls, proxies, and third-party Internet applications that rely on port-mapping capabilities. See Chapter 8 for more.

### /boot/beos/etc/synth
This data is used by BeOS's built-in software-based synthesizer.

### /boot/beos/etc/teapot.data
This is data read by the OpenGL Teapot demo.

### /boot/beos/etc/termcap
The list of all known terminal types found here is used in the shell.

### /boot/beos/etc/timezones
Data on all known time zones, for use by BeOS's Time application, is stored here.

### /boot/beos/etc/vattr, vattr.src
These are config and data files used by the command-line editor ve.

### /boot/beos/etc/vconv
This converter is used by the command-line editor ve to generate configuration files.

### /boot/beos/etc/vim/
Help files for the vi-like editor vim are located here. For more details, vi is covered in Chapter 6.

### /boot/beos/preferences
This directory contains the real preferences panels installed with BeOS, to which the links in /boot/preferences point. See Chapter 9 for details.

### /boot/beos/system
This is perhaps the single most critical directory structure in all of BeOS, and you should exercise extreme caution when poking around in the system folder or any of its subdirectories. You're in the engine room now, and insurance is extended only to engineers.

### /boot/beos/system/Deskbar
This is the Deskbar application itself. See Chapter 2 for details.

*Figure 5.38*

*You're in the engine room now: operating system kernel, Deskbar, and Tracker—heart, brain, and lungs. The rest of the body's organs are buried one directory lower, in /boot/beos/system/servers.*

### /boot/beos/system/Tracker

The Tracker is ground zero for file management and application launching. Without the Tracker, the BeOS desktop is Nowheresville. The Tracker, by the way, is the most complex application in BeOS. NetPositive runs a close second.

***Resuscitating the Deskbar and Tracker*** **While it happens very rarely, it is possible for the Deskbar or Tracker to crash. In many instances, if you already have a Terminal window open you can restart them by typing** /boot/beos/system/Tracker **&** or /boot/beos/system/Deskbar **&. In order to do this, you may have to kill off their stray threads first. See Chapter 6.**

### /boot/beos/system/kernel_intel
### /boot/beos/system/kernel_mac
### /boot/beos/system/kernel_joe

This is it—the kernel, the true heart of the system. The kernel is the first thing loaded into memory as the system boots (well, practically), and the last thing to die when you shut down. Your system will have one of the kernels above, depending on which version of BeOS you're running. In case you're wondering, kernel_joe is the BeBox kernel, and is named after Joe Palmer, who designed and built the original BeBox.

### /boot/beos/system/zbeos

This is the Intel bootloader, and is not present on PowerPC systems. It helps bring the system from a state of nothingness into a state of somethingness by reading the first stepping stones of the OS off the disk media and into memory. Soon after starting, zbeos quits, having successfully done its job, and passes the torch on to the kernel. zbeos includes a section of GNU code—the same code that boots Linux! Note that you can create a BeOS boot floppy by writing this file to a disk with the dd command (Chapter 3).

### /boot/beos/system/add-ons

Chapter 1 introduced the concept of BeOS's "dynamically loadable device modules." On some operating systems, adding support for new printers, network cards, video cards, and alien filesystems requires complex changes to configuration files, registries, and the like. Adding these things to BeOS is much simpler. Need to add a new printer? Drop its driver into /boot/home/config/add-ons/Print, select it in the Printer preferences panel, and you're done. Need to be able to read the filesystem of an old SparcStation? Assuming you could find a driver, all you would need to do is drop it in /boot/home/config/add-ons/kernel/file_systems and mount the drive.

This directory is parent to a sprawling network of subdirectories containing system-provided add-ons. We'll just cover the most important subdirectories here, though you should be able to determine the function of just about anything under this tree by studying folder names.

 This section chronicles the add-ons that ship with R4. To install your own downloaded add-ons, *do not* add them to these directories. Instead, drop them into the same directory structures under /boot/home/config/add-ons. In some cases, you may have to create new directories there—see the documentation that comes with the new add-on for details.

### /boot/beos/system/add-ons/accelerants
Most modern video cards have acceleration features built into their chipsets. Taking advantage of these features requires a driver separate from the one used to operate the card in its normal mode. This directory contains accelerating drivers for many of the video drivers that ship with BeOS.

### /boot/beos/system/add-ons/app_server
This directory stores add-ons that let BeOS talk to your video card. Because this list is always changing, we won't list them here, as they're likely to be different by the time you read this. In addition, a supervga driver allows users of just about any x86-compatible video card to at least boot BeOS into "safe boot" mode (see Chapter 16 for details), though it isn't pretty. Search Be's Web site for your video card's name to learn about updated drivers.

### /boot/beos/system/add-ons/drive_setup
The modules in this folder's three subdirectories are used by the DriveSetup application (see Chapter 9) to create partitions, filesystems, and CD-ROM sessions of various flavors. Note that DriveSetup's ability to create these filesystems is not equivalent to the system's ability to read from and write to them. That functionality is handled by kernel add-ons, which are discussed below.

### /boot/beos/system/add-ons/input_server
As of R4, BeOS handled all input, such as that coming from keyboards, mice, and pen tablets, through its new input server architecture. Drivers for common hardware input types are found in a subdirectory of this folder called devices. In addition, you may find other folders here. If you have a filters subdirectory in this location, it's being used to store "input filters" that developers can use to

pre-massage data in the system's stream even before it arrives at their applications. If you're using an internationalized version of BeOS, you'll also find a methods subdirectory here, which is currently used for the Japanese input method, but can easily be extended to work with other languages, such as Chinese, Korean, or Hebrew.

### /boot/beos/system/add-ons/kernel

You'll find five folders inside the kernel directory: bus_managers, busses, drivers, file_systems, and media. Since these are kernel add-ons, anything that falls under this directory structure is a driver that allows devices to speak directly to the kernel. There are too many subdirectories in this hierarchy to list them all, but you'll find drivers here for a broad array of input/output devices such as system buses, sound and network cards, SCSI devices, keyboards and mice, infrared, parallel, serial and MIDI ports, video capture cards, and more. BeBoxes, Macintoshes, and Intel machines all have different—and changing—lists. In many cases, it will be possible to determine what a driver does by its name alone. If you're curious about driver names you don't recognize, look at the documentation that came with your input/output cards, or pull the cards out of your case and examine the names and numbers printed on the chipsets—these should provide sufficient clues. Remember, though, that just because a driver is present here, it does not mean that you necessarily have that hardware installed—the fact that popular drivers are preinstalled is part of what makes it so easy to add new hardware to your BeOS system.

The kernel uses this directory structure to find out which drivers will publish names in which directories in the /dev hierarchy. Subdividing this directory into multiple folders makes it much easier for BeOS to scale—in other words, as the number of drivers available for BeOS increases, the operating system won't have to do a corresponding amount of work to keep up with them all or find out which ones are actually communicating with your hardware.

As of R4, the exact method of storing and loading drivers is this:

1. Actual drivers are stored in
   /boot/beos/system/add-ons/kernel/drivers/bin

2. If the driver finds a corresponding device on the system, it will "publish" a device point somewhere under the /dev hierarchy (such as /dev/foo). If this happens, a corresponding folder will be created at
   /boot/beos/system/add-ons/kernel/drivers/dev/foo.

3. Within foo, a symlink will be created pointing to the actual driver binary living in /boot/beos/system/add-ons/kernel/drivers/bin.

Note that all of this happens automatically, and users never need to think about it. Just install your driver in the right folder (as described in its documentation) and the process above should be taken care of automatically.

### /boot/beos/system/add-ons/net_server

The chipsets found on the industry's most common network interface cards (NICs) are supported by drivers found in this folder or in its parallel folder, ~/config/add-ons/net_server. See Chapter 8 for details on installing and configuring NICs.

### /boot/beos/system/add-ons/Print

Major classes of printers (such as Apple Laserwriter or HPCL3 LaserJet and compatible printers) are recognized by BeOS by virtue of these add-on modules. However, your specific printer model still needs to be added and selected in the Printer preferences panel in order for you to use it. In the case of PostScript printers, this panel reads the list of model names from /boot/beos/etc/ppd.

### /boot/beos/system/add-ons/Tracker

Of all BeOS add-ons, the Tracker's are the most visible to the user. Because it's easier to write a Tracker add-on than, say, a SCSI driver, there are more of them. And because they're always a right-click away, you encounter them often. The three Tracker add-ons in this folder, FileType, Backgrounds, and MakeArchive, show up side by side with any add-ons you've added to /boot/home/config/Add-Ons/Tracker, as if they were all together in one directory. System-level and user-level directories come together as a single merged entity.

Using MakeArchive couldn't be easier. Select a file or folder, choose MakeArchive from the Add-Ons menu, and a file called archive.tar will appear in the same directory. FileType is covered in detail in this chapter. The Backgrounds add-on is covered in Chapter 9—this add-on makes it easy to make any image into a desktop background with a right-click.

 If a Tracker add-on's name ends with a dash and a letter, this means that it can be invoked with that hotkey, in combination with right-Ctrl and Alt. For example, the FileType add-on is named FileType-F, and can be invoked by selecting a file or folder and tapping right-Ctrl+Alt+F.

### /boot/beos/system/add-ons/Translators

One of BeOS's many ingenious implementations of add-ons extends the notion to dealing with datatypes (a.k.a. file formats). You've got dozens of applications that handle the same filetypes (such as TIFF images, for instance), so why should each application developer have to build their own TIFF engine? By offering a central repository of modules that know how to read and write certain datatypes, Be frees developers up to spend their time working on the aspects of their programs that will really make them stand out. The presence of a given module in this folder means that any application on your system that cares to can read and write that file format. If you download

Translators of your own from BeWare or from vendors, place them in /boot/home/config/add-ons/Translators, not here. See Chapter 9 for more on Translators.

BeOS R4 comes bundled with Translators for the BMP, PPM, TGA, and TIFF image formats, in addition to a StyledText Translator that can help other applications use fonts and colors similar to those used in StyledEdit in plain text.

## Add-Ons versus Drivers

At this point, you may have noticed that there appears to be little difference between an add-on and a driver, at least as far as directory names are concerned. Actually, that's pretty close to correct. In BeOS's system of dynamically loadable device modules, the mechanism by which the Tracker extends its functionality with right-click Tracker add-ons is not fundamentally different than the mechanism by which the kernel incorporates support for alien filesystems or new sound cards.

The difference in terminology is accounted for by the privilege level accorded to each. A driver is simply an add-on with privileges to access the kernel. User-level add-ons can access the filesystem, the sound stream, and so forth, but can't touch kernel functions.

### /boot/beos/system/boot

This directory contains a handful of shell scripts used by the system during various stages and flavors of the boot process. Bootscript, SetupEnvironment, and Netscript are run automatically during normal boots, Bootscript.cd is run when you boot from the CD or when there isn't enough space to create a swap file. The Shutdown scripts, obviously, run as you're shutting down your system, and the Installer scripts are used to start and finish system upgrades. Do not edit these files—any changes you want to make to the boot process should be made to equivalent scripts in the /boot/home/config/boot hierarchy.

### /boot/beos/system/lib

This is a collection of libraries, or system code shared by multiple applications and system components.

### /boot/beos/system/servers

As described in Chapter 1, BeOS is based on a client/server architecture. Core system services run continuously in the background, listening for requests from applications to carry out certain mundane chores, like drawing windows or piping audio through the system. This directory contains the actual servers themselves—the programs that dole out critical services to the rest of the system. Again, this modular approach frees developers from the need to code more of the grunt work than necessary.

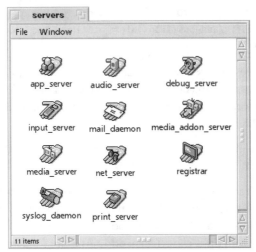

*Figure 5.39*

*Many of BeOS's critical system services are handled by servers running in the background. The* net_server, *for instance, handles all incoming and outgoing network services on behalf of your applications. The system also allows multiple client applications to partake of the services of a single server, keeping resource consumption to a minimum.*

### /boot/beos/system/servers/app_server

The app_server takes care of basic window management services on behalf of applications. It draws menus, scrollbars, and title tabs, keeps track of which windows are at the front, and more. It also communicates directly with video card drivers. BeOS won't function without it.

### /boot/beos/system/servers/audio_server

This server manages throughput of DAC (digital-to-analog conversion) and ADC (analog-to-digital conversion) audio streams running into and out of the system, and connects applications with system-wide audio services. Learn more about the ADC and DAC streams in Chapter 9.

 The role of the audio_server is officially deprecated as of R4. Its duties are now optimally handled by the media_server. The audio_server is present for backward compatibility, but it may disappear entirely in a future version of the system.

### /boot/beos/system/servers/debug_server

The debug_server traps errors in system or application code and routes them to output such as Terminal debug windows or the serial port for troubleshooting (see Chapter 16 for details). Its meatgrinder icon used to be the coolest in the system, but it's unfortunately too small to see clearly in R4.

### /boot/beos/system/servers/input_server

New in R4, this server manages input queues such as those from keyboards, mice, and pen tablets. It also manages alternative input methods such as those used to input Japanese kanji characters.

### /boot/beos/system/servers/mail_daemon

The mail_daemon trolls the network for new email messages at user-defined intervals, interfaces with the E-mail preferences panel and mail log window, and routes outgoing mail to the pending queue and then out the door. This makes it easy for developers to email-enable applications.

### /boot/beos/system/servers/media_addon_server

This server manages system add-ons interfacing with the media_server.

### /boot/beos/system/servers/media_server

New in R4, this server manages requests from applications wanting to use services provided by the Media Kit, including audio/visual streams.

### /boot/beos/system/servers/net_server

The net_server oversees all incoming and outgoing network requests, manages PPP and Ethernet connections, interfaces with the Network preferences panel, and manages the TCP/IP layer, making it easier for developers to build network-aware applications.

### /boot/beos/system/servers/print_server

This server manages the printer queue and interfaces with printer drivers, printing applications, and printer ports.

### /boot/beos/system/servers/registrar

The Registrar monitors system filetypes, registers new filetypes in the system's MIME database, identifies the MIME types of alien documents, and manages inter-application communication. When the system is idle, it searches the hard disk for files missing their MIME types and attempts to assign MIME types to them.

### /boot/beos/system/servers/syslog_daemon

The syslog_daemon writes system events to a log file and takes note of hardware configuration, memory status, and system messages. The log file is created at /var/log/syslog. Since this directory is not visible to the Tracker, the easiest way to study it may be to open a Terminal and type cp /var/log/ syslog /boot/home. You can then open it in StyledEdit or another editor for study. Note that not a great deal of useful information is stored here now; you may see a more detailed syslog in the future, as well as applications capable of displaying this information hierarchically or graphically.

A complete chronicle of all hidden and system-level directories can be found at this book's website: **www.beosbible.com**.

## Pavel Cisler
### Software Engineer, responsible for the Tracker
*Interviewed by Henry Bortman*

**HB:** *What is it that appeals to you about working on the Tracker?*

**PC:** I really like to work on stuff that I can at least imagine how people will use. But what totally gets me excited about programming is writing developer tools. The Tracker is somewhere in the middle. It's something that I use every day, but it also has a wide audience, which developer tools don't have, so it's the best of both worlds.

I think it's a great project also because Windows and Mac have an equivalent app that's been around forever, and yet every day you feel there's so much more that a program like Tracker or Finder, or whatever, could do for you because it's the first thing you start using when you turn on your computer.

I have a feeling that software today is inferior. I have the feeling that it's totally driven by marketing decisions, that it's a race for more features that nobody cares about. Bloat to sell bigger hardware, bigger hard disks. And somewhere along the line people forgot that computers are about helping you, about giving you tools that let you be productive.

Maybe you don't care about a word processor that has 20 million new features that are whatever. How about if it didn't crash, how about if it was smaller, if it launched faster? How about if it was more intuitive, how about if it tried to be user-friendly and didn't require me to be a computer geek to use? That's why I like the Mac, because it tried to address that. I feel like BeOS learned a lot from the Mac. Every time I use Windows I get annoyed with stupid little things Windows users don't have any problems putting up with. And as a programmer, I really see it as a challenge to write software that kind of goes against this tendency—that's intuitive, user-friendly, that my grandma can use.

**HB:** *What kind of changes can people expect to see in the Tracker in R4?*

**PC:** A lot of code needed to be rewritten for performance optimization. You do a rewrite like that at the beginning of the release so that whatever bugs you introduce with the new code, you'll have time to fix. Then you do the medium-sized features. So we did more liveness, we did better integration of Find. There's more features in the Find panel. We made querying work a little better. If you query for email now, the query result will come up configured for mail because it noticed you queried for mail. If you query for People files, it will come preconfigured for that. It won't show the size of a Person because that's not interesting at all. It will show their home number or whatever you want. So developers can preconfigure queries to come up different ways for different filetypes.

We did a lot more scripting, which is interesting for developers so that they can integrate apps. Actually, BeMail now integrates much better with the Tracker. You can iterate your mailbox really quickly without closing a BeMail window—you can go to the next message or the previous message—so you can zip through your emails real quick. That's all done by scripting, and any developer can take advantage of that and do the same with their email app if they want.

Let's see, what else? Background images. That's a big one, everybody wanted that so you can have background images in every workspace. You can have background images in any window if you feel like it. We have a translucent drag now, like on the Mac and under Windows. We do it a little better because on the Mac and under Windows you can only translucently drag one icon; in the Tracker you can drag six or so.

**HB:** *What features are people still clamoring for that you weren't able to get in?*

**PC:** Well, the big one is hierarchical list view. I was planning on doing it right after the performance update because it's a lot of code and you want to do it early on so you have time to fix the bugs, but since our release time got slashed by almost half, it would have been a big gamble, so I decided not to do it. So we'll do it in the next release.

**HB:** *Where do you see the Tracker heading in the future?*

**PC:** We want to do a new view in the Tracker. I call it the media view—I don't know if we'll end up calling it that—for displaying media-rich files, like images or videos or sounds. Kind of like what we have now with attributes that let you show information in a folder differently for different filetypes, but just at a different level. For instance, for a movie you could have a button where you could ask to play a thumbnail or a preview of a movie. Same for sound, same for images.

Also, I'd like more of the Tracker's functionality to be open to applications and third-party developers. For instance, every app now can have a piece of the Tracker in itself, which is the File panel. It would be really nice if every app could have any kind of Tracker window in it. Let's say you're writing a printer spooler and you want to have a list view that shows spool files in a certain way that is specific to printer spooling, but it uses a Tracker view to do that, and it overrides it a little bit and it's in a separate application. That would be a nice thing to have for developers so they could focus more on whatever the printer spooler does and not "How am I going to draw this file here and show its size and date?" The Tracker already does that for you. So, if you could package up the code and make it available like that, that's one of the things we're looking into.

I have more ideas about File panels. I think we shouldn't even have them. One of the things I want to do eventually with File panels is have a nice drag-and-drop interface where, besides the stuff you have now with a list of files, you could have an icon representing the file you want to save and you could grab it and drag it into a Tracker window. That way, you would say, "Here's where it goes," and you could maybe name it in the window or name it later or name it from the panel itself, but you wouldn't have to browse through layers of hierarchies when you already see the folder right there in your Tracker.

**HB:** *Are there features of either the Windows Explorer or the Macintosh Finder that the Tracker doesn't have that you wish it did have?*

**PC:** Yeah. Outline list views is the most notable one. Explorer has this nice thing in Windows 98 where the Get Info is kind of integrated in the window so you can select individual files and the Get Info panel shows the information right there in the window. You don't have to bring up a separate panel. That functionality would kind of be in the media view spirit, where you have

### *Pavel Cisler* (continued)

more ways of showing information about a file and more fine-tuned for a particular filetype. If we end up doing something like that, we'll probably do it with the media view.

**HB:** *What were you doing before you came to Be?*

**PC:** I worked at General Magic for three years. I was responsible for the object run time. General Magic was doing Magic Cap, an operating system fine-tuned for a handheld, pen-driven device. I came at the end of the release of the first device, where there was still a lot of enthusiasm. They had really heavyweight developers there. They had Andy Hertzfeld and Bill Atkinson, Phil Goldman (he's at Web TV now), Darrin Adler. It was fun working with all of them, getting to know them. But I also experienced a time when a lot of them left, disillusione, because their dream didn't happen. Then I was there when the remainder regrouped and worked on a second-generation version of the operating system, and I was heavily involved in that. Magic Cap 2.0, or whatever they ended up calling it, was pretty good. I think they're still trying to position it as a vertical market solution.

**HB:** *So how did you end up at Be?*

**PC:** When I was ready to quit Magic I was looking around and the CD came out and I tried it out. I tried writing an app. I wrote my weekend app, Eddie, which I still work on. In two weeks I got it working, I felt, well, there's no MPW [Macintosh Programmer's Workshop, a Mac OS development environment] on here. There's CodeWarrior, but I don't like that so much. What would it take to write an MPW? I had an editor in a week, but then the linker wouldn't start working because it was the demo linker and had a 64K limit. So I decided that I would have a plug-in architecture, and I put all the extra functionality into plug-ins and it just got me so excited about it. I still have Eddie now.

**HB:** *And what is Eddie?*

**PC:** Eddie? Eddie is like Pe; it's a programmer's editor. It's on BeWare. A lot of people use it, actually. It's kind of more of a hardcore editor than Pe is. Pe is sort of mainstream, you can use it for HTML editing. Eddie is really just for developers, see, because I only add stuff that I care about, whereas Martin has to add stuff that will make his thing [Pe] sell.

**HB:** *Let me go back a little bit. Before General Magic, what were you doing?*

**PC:** I came from the Czech Republic. I had a Mac software company there. I was one of the founders and I had a small software team of 10 people. We did a lot of Mac programming, but the kind that made money was a little boring because it was mostly language-solution oriented. It was localizations for Apple first; then we actually picked up Microsoft, too. Things like hyphenation, spell checking, Czech fonts—which is fun, but becomes repetitive. We wanted to do some real mainstream development, but we didn't have the financing to get any critical mass, so it never happened. Then I came here, and General Magic was my first U.S. company.

**HB:** *Back to the present: How do you feel about Be's switch to Intel?*

**PC:** That's a really interesting question. At home, on my work desk, I have a Mac and an Intel box, and the Intel box is faster just because I bought it recently, and the Mac, I've had forever. There's like no difference between the two. They run BeOS exactly the same, the Intel box, a little faster. That to me is like, I don't care about Mac, I can do all this on cheaper, faster hardware, so I still use my Mac for running Photoshop or running Deck II that I don't have on BeOS. Eventually, if stuff goes well with us, we'll have that sort of stuff on BeOS, too, especially the sound recording applications. So, I was really surprised how easy it was for me. I have Windows 98 installed on my Intel box and I run it like every once in three months. I sometimes run the Mac, but pretty much it's BeOS, and it doesn't make a difference whether it's PowerPC or Intel.

**HB:** *Are you a workaholic?*

**PC:** I think unfortunately I am, and I try not to be. You know, I don't work, I play, right? I play with programming and I can't get enough of it. Sometimes you do so much you get burned out and your brain just stops. And it has a bad effect on your family life and everything, so I'm trying to learn how to do my work, still enjoy it, do it in normal hours, get more work done in a short time. Sometimes when you just work on and on and on, you don't get more work done, you just goof off in between doing the work, or you slow down because you're tired. I've seen colleagues that could do a lot of work, but just in normal working hours and they just had it in them. I'd like to learn that. If I didn't have a wife and a family, I would work all the time. I work on weekends sometimes.

**HB:** *Do you do anything besides write code?*

**PC:** I play guitar. I like doing woodworking.

**HB:** *Woodworking?*

**PC:** Yeah, yeah. I like anything that's creative. When I was a kid I was building airplane models, then I switched to electronics because I wanted a remote-control for my plane and I was doing electronics for 10 years. I studied, I have an EE degree from Czech Polytechnic.

And then halfway through school, I noticed computers and I totally got immersed in computers. After school I did hardware for a living, but I realized that software lets you be creative so much faster. So, whatever is creative, I like. Woodworking is creative, but it's messy. It makes a lot of dust, and you can cut your fingers off.

# 6

# The Terminal

Ask anyone who's spent any time working with a Unix-based computer, and they'll tell you the same thing: The Unix command line can't be beat when it comes to power and flexibility. BeOS integrates its futuristic technology with the Terminal, a full implementation of Unix's most popular command-line environment, bash (the Bourne Again SHell). While it's theoretically possible to operate BeOS without ever firing up the Terminal, the more you allow yourself to explore the command-line side of the operating system, the richer and broader your BeOS experience will be. Yes, there is a greater learning curve associated with shell operations, but there's also a huge reward: Once you've honed your chops in the Terminal, you'll be able to build customized solutions to just about any problem the day may throw at you.

This chapter isn't for everyone. Those who have absolutely no interest in learning to use the shell can pass it over, referring to it only if necessary. On the other hand, those who have prior experience with Unix shells—such as Linux users—probably won't find much here that they don't already know. This chapter is written for the typical Windows or MacOS user who has little or no experience working with the command line. Those with a DOS background but no Unix exposure will be right at home in this chapter, which covers the basics of bash, the operation of common command-line programs and tools, and the art of assembling these tools into customized solutions.

# Critical bash for BeOS

Because BeOS attracts as many users from the desktop publishing and digital video crowds as it does from the geeky Unix universe, BeOS users tend to fall on all points of the spectrum when it comes to how they perceive the Terminal. On one end of the spectrum are users who tend to think visually, and interact with computers best when its options are laid out in a clean, visual interface. For some of these users, the command line represents a hell they had hoped to escape decades ago, and may in fact be the very reason they ditched their IBM PCs at the dawn of the Macintosh. Others who have come to computing in the past decade have been born and raised on the GUI, and have never had much cause to deal with the command line at all.

On the other end of the spectrum are longtime Unix jocks (and a few DOS-heads looking to take their command-line skills to the next level) who twiddled enough cryptic commands to become hooked for life. Some of these users probably would never have become interested in BeOS to begin with if it hadn't included the deeply integrated Terminal environment.

One of the amazing things about BeOS is the graceful way in which it legit-imizes both of these perspectives by integrating a graceful GUI with a com-plete command-line interface (CLI). While some systems feel like their GUIs were slapped on top of the command shell as an afterthought (because they were), BeOS was born with two faces: The graphical and command-line interfaces are welded together seamlessly. Unlike Unix-based systems, you cannot boot BeOS into command-line-only mode. Nor can the graphical interface be booted without the assistance of the shell, as BeOS's startup sequence is governed by a series of bash shell scripts.

Why does the shell offer power that the GUI can't match? Because of the "atomic" nature of a shell. Commands (atoms) can be strung together into customized "molecules." Think for a moment of the English language (or any language, for that matter). Every word represents a fraction of the world, and by virtue of grammar and syntax, we can string them together into sentences that have meaning: ideas, proclamations, questions, poems. To paraphrase the philosopher Wittgenstein, with language it is possible to express anything that lies within the bounds of language. Beyond that is the inexpressible, and whereof one cannot speak … ah, let's not go there.

Unix-ese isn't quite as philosophical as all that, but the idea here is the same. By employing a large collection of small, discrete commands and by stringing them together with a consistent and known syntax, you can make your com-puter sit up and do tricks the GUI can only dream about (of course, the GUI can also do things the CLI can't, like advanced image editing). Enough spiel, let's dig in.

There are two things that come together when you use the Terminal:

- Unix-based command-line programs and tools.
- The shell, which provides the environment in which these tools operate. bash is the name of the particular flavor of shell that runs in a windowed BeOS application called the Terminal.

The Terminal and bash don't have any kind of necessary connection—the Terminal is capable of running any kind of text-based application, even other shells ported from the Unix world, such as tcsh or zsh. However, bash is the shell that ships with BeOS and it's unlikely that you'll find a need to run an alternative shell, so we'll only cover bash here.

While the command-line tools provided with BeOS live in /boot/beos/bin, you may also access them from /bin—a symlink in the root of your filesystem makes these two paths equivalent for purposes of compatibility with hard-coded paths built into some tools.

### *About Open-Source Tools*

The Terminal is not Unix. Unix is an operating system, and BeOS is an operating system, but BeOS is not a Unix-based operating system. BeOS is, however, POSIX-compliant, just like Unix. That means that BeOS has built into it a core set of command structures that are agreed upon by international committee as a standard to provide a degree of interoperability between disparate operating systems. What this means to users is that if they've used one POSIX-compliant operating system, they can probably use another without much difficulty (at least the command-line part). It also means that programs can be ported from one platform to the other with minimal changes.

Interestingly, Unix culture is heavily rooted in a tradition of free, open-source, POSIX-compliant software. Rather than trying to profit from every hour of coding time, Unix developers often build programs and then give them back to the community along with the source code. Under an agreement called the GNU (Gnu's Not Unix) general public license, users are free to use the program and redistribute it to others, as long as the source code and the GNU license travel along with it (or are provided on demand). The user can modify the source code and try to make the program better if they like, or even try to profit by selling the program along with their modifications—so long as they in turn distribute their modifications along with the code. In other words, no one can stop the buck at their own desk if they want to play in the open-source software community.

This unique arrangement has a great name, too: copylefting. Most of the commands that run in BeOS's shell have been ported from Unix to BeOS under the GNU public license, and are copylefted. That's why you'll find the source code for most of the CLI programs on your system in an /optional directory when you install BeOS. There are some exceptions: A number of programs specific to BeOS are mixed in with the command binaries in /boot/beos/bin—these are not GNU or copylefted.

## The Purpose of This Chapter

While you can start doing cool things in the Terminal almost immediately, learning bash inside-out can take years. It can go as deep as you want to go with it, and just when you think you've got it mastered, you'll probably uncover yet another unexplored dimension. I'm not going to pretend to teach you bash. What I am going to do is to show you the very basics and share what I think it means to have just enough to get by. If you finish this chapter and are able to open a Terminal window without scratching your head and wondering what to do next, we'll be in good shape. I'm also going to intermix a discussion of general bash concepts with basic descriptions of the most common command-line tools.

If after reading this chapter you feel you want to learn more about bash, the best way to proceed is to beg a shell junkie to teach you—there's no substitute for a human mentor. The second best way is to purchase a book on bash, and possibly a second on common command-line tools. You'll find a short list of recommended resources at the end of this chapter. Once you've got a handle on basic shell operations, you may want to take your skills to the next level by diving into BeOS shell scripting. Extensive information on BeOS scripting is available to you at **http://www.beosbible.com**.

# Using the Terminal Application

Because bash on BeOS runs inside a window of the Terminal application, we'll cover use of the Terminal application before digging into bash proper.

## The Terminal Application Window

Launch the Terminal from your /apps folder and you'll be greeted with a message from Be: "Welcome to the Be shell." You'll see a few pull-down menus on the menu bar, but that's it for the GUI. Let's get those menus out of the way first.

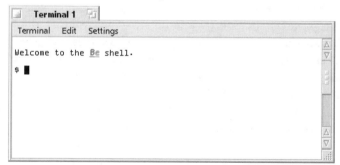

*Figure: 6.01*

*The Terminal application is nothing but a window hosting Be's implementation of the* bash *shell. It offers a few menus for configuring preferences, but that's about it. By default, the prompt is a useless "$"— we'll change that soon enough.*

Under the Terminal menu you'll find two entries: New Terminal (Alt+N) and Switch Terminals (Alt+G). Learn these hotkeys—you'll be using them often. You can open as many Terminal windows as you like, and each of them can be busy running separate tasks, benefiting from BeOS's excellent multitasking capabilities. Alt+G cycles through open Terminals in the current workspace in the opposite order from that in which they were opened.

 ***Quick Logout***  Though you won't find it aliased under any of the Terminal's pulldown menus, you can close any Terminal session by tapping Ctrl+D. Since the standard Alt+W works in the Terminal just as it does in any other application, this isn't hugely helpful; but if you're coming to BeOS from the Unix world, you'll find Ctrl+D familiar, since it's the standard logout shortcut on most Unix systems. In fact, if you watch the command line real closely while hitting Ctrl+D, you'll actually see the word "logout" printed just before the window closes.

You'll find standard fare under the Edit menu, as the Terminal is fully copy/paste aware. You can use the clipboard to move text or data to and from the Terminal just as you would with any other application. Interestingly, the Terminal is also drag-and-drop-aware. There are many things that can be dragged into a Terminal window—more on that later.

The options available under the Settings menu are, for the most part, self-explanatory, and allow you to specify the font, font size, window size, and foreground/background colors of your Terminal window.

 ***Save Your Terminal Settings*** If you spend any energy configuring the Terminal with custom settings, don't forget to select Save as Defaults before you close the window, or your changes will be lost. Note that this rule also applies to the Terminal's window size—whereas most applications remember window size and position automatically every time you close them, the Terminal's window size must be manually stored via the Save as Defaults menu entry. The Terminal window is fully resizable, and text in long listings will reflow dynamically, accommodating new window sizes.

 ***Manage Multiple Terminal Settings Files*** While the Terminal makes it easy for you to save its current configuration as a settings file, it provides no simple mechanism for retrieving saved settings files. However, you can launch Terminal windows in different fonts, colors, and sizes by double-clicking their settings files. Once you've got the Terminal configured as you like it, pull down Settings | Save as Settings File and save it to a location. I recommend a subdirectory of /boot/home/config/settings called termset. Now you can create a symlink to this folder on your desktop and have instant access to a library of different Terminal configurations. If you want to get really fancy, use the system's FileTypes preferences panel to assign a custom icon to the filetype application/x-vnd.Be-pref.

If you want to manage settings files manually, you need to know that the current settings file is always /boot/home/config/settings/Terminal. To use others, you'll need to go through the process of manually renaming this file to another name, then renaming one of your custom files with this name.

To make this process painless and smooth, download the author's TermSet script from BeWare. TermSet lets you save as many settings files as you want, and then retrieve them by typing their names. TermSet also makes it easy to launch multiple Terminal windows in different colors for easy identification.

***Title the Terminal*** **If the Terminal is already open, you can always launch a new Terminal window with Alt+N, or by typing** `Terminal` **into the currently open Terminal. By default, your Terminal windows will get names like "Terminal 1," "Terminal 2," and so on (these names appear in the Terminal window's title tab and in the Deskbar). If you'd like to dedicate a Terminal to a specific task and give it a descriptive name, launch your new window with the** `-t` **flag, followed by a descriptive label. For example, if you've got one Terminal window dedicated to displaying the output of your** `rc5des` **code-cracking efforts (Chapter 15,** *Other Goodies***), you might launch its session like this:**

```
Terminal -t "Code Cracker" &
```

**Remember to finish the command with an ampersand (&) so that the prompt in the current Terminal window is returned to you!**

*Figure 6.02*

*Launch new Terminal windows with the* `-t` *flag and they'll get a descriptive title, rather than the boring default.*

Alright, let's dig into bash itself. We'll take it from the top.

# Basic bash

Before you can begin using the shell to create custom command structures, you need to get a firm handle on shell-based file management. Creating, copying, moving, and deleting files and folders from the command line is Shell 101.

## Navigation and File Management

When it comes to managing the organization of files and folders on your system, just about anything you can do from the Tracker can also be done from the Terminal. In addition, there are many things you can do from the Terminal that can't be done from the Tracker, and vice versa. Savvy users will split their file management time between the two, using the best tool for the job at any given moment.

 As mentioned in Chapter 2, *Meet the System*, the BeOS filesystem is case-sensitive. In other words, you can have the following three files in the same directory:

```
BeOSBible.txt
beosbible.txt
BEOSBIBLE.TXT
```

## Change Your Prompt

Because it's almost always useful to know your current path, it should be the shell's responsibility to inform you of the current path after every command. Unfortunately, this is not the default behavior of the bash shell, so it's worth taking a moment out to enable this reportage.

Use the Be menu to open up the file /boot/home/.profile in StyledEdit (if it doesn't exist, you can create this file—be sure it starts with a period). Somewhere in this file, add the following line:

PS1='$PWD>'

Save .profile, then close and restart the Terminal. Your prompt will now always report the current directory, like this:

/boot/home>

> You don't *have* to close and restart the Terminal to make these changes take effect. You can also type ~/.profile, which essentially causes .profile to run as a script, and thus resets the variables it contains. Alternatively, use the source command to perform a similar function, as in source ~/.profile.

It's important to use single quotes rather than double in the command above. If you use double quotes, the path will be evaluated literally when the command is first run, and will thus report "boot/home" for the entire time the current Terminal window is open. Single quotes, on the other hand, cause the command to be reevaluated every time the path changes; in other words, the prompt will change every time you change directories. See the next sidebar *Quoting and Escaping* for more.

Prompt customization doesn't stop here—you can make your prompt display practically any kind of information you like by using any of the prompt variables built into bash. For example,

PS1='\t>'

will cause your prompt to consist of the current time, in HH:MM:SS format, since \t means "print time" to the prompt. Some people like to display the hostname of their machine as their prompt, or the history number for future reference, or both! Set your prompt in .profile as:

PS1='u@\h [\!]:'

*(continued)*

This is just as true in the Tracker as it is in the Terminal, but it can be more important to remember from within the Terminal, since you're going to be typing filenames directly. If you try a command and it doesn't work, case problems are often the culprit, and are worth checking before anything else.

**The Current Directory** Just as the selected folder in any Tracker view will always be the target of the next action, there's always a currently selected directory in the Terminal. To learn the current directory, type pwd (for "print working directory") and hit Enter. The shell will spit back a directory path, most likely /boot/home, the default launch location for the Terminal.

and your prompts will look like:

```
coyote@waxwing [991]:
```

This, however, assumes that you've set your user and group names to something other than the BeOS defaults. See page 381 in this chapter for details on that.

To find a complete list of the prompt variables built into bash, open the folder /boot/beos/documentation/shell tools and launch the HTML file index.html. Click the link to bash for cryptic but detailed information on the bash shell. Search for the term "PROMPTING" and you'll find a list of allowable prompt variables.

For more details on changing the default behavior of the Terminal via .profile, see Chapter 9, *Preferences and Customization*.

## Quoting and Escaping

Throughout this chapter, you'll notice that there are three different kinds of quote marks used in the examples, as shown in Table 6.01. It's important to understand the difference between these three quoting mechanisms because even though they appear to be similar, each can have very different effects on the output of your shell commands. In order to illustrate the difference, it will be necessary to refer to a few commands that aren't explained fully until later in this chapter, but I'll try to keep things clear.

 Technically speaking, backticks are not quotes, either in the English language or in bash. However, their placement and appearance in bash shell commands gives them certain functional similarities to quotes. I include them here to illustrate how they compare and contrast.

### Escaping Special Characters

As you'll discover, many keyboard symbols have special meanings to the shell. For example, the > character tells the shell to redirect the output of a command into a file. But what if you want to refer to the > character itself, rather than having the shell act on it? You might be using the echo command to create HTML files, for instance. The echo command simply spits back plain text, the value of a variable, or both. Meanwhile, HTML files are full of < and > angle brackets. So, a command like

```
echo title
```

causes the shell to return the word "title." But the command:

```
echo <title>
```

will generate an error message. Why? Because the shell sees the angle brackets and assumes you want to redirect something, without knowing what. There are two possible solutions

### Table 6.01

| | |
|---|---|
| ' | Single quotes, also known as "strong quotes" |
| " | Double quotes, also known as "weak quotes" |
| ` | Backticks |

*The three types of quote marks used in* bash

*(continued)*

## *Quoting and Escaping* (continued)

to this situation. The first is known as "escaping," and you'll probably end up doing a lot of it pretty soon (the other is "quoting," which is explained below). To escape a special character, just precede it with a backslash (\) and the shell will know that you want that character to be treated as plain text:

```
echo \<title\>
```

The shell now returns "<title>," which is what you want.

### *Quoting Strings*

In some situations, you'll wind up with lots of special characters to escape. Inserting a ton of backslashes can become tedious, and can make your command difficult to read. In that case, you'll be better off "quoting" the string that you would otherwise escape. This command achieves the same effect as the one above:

```
echo '<title>'
```

and so does this one:

```
echo "<title>"
```

As you can see, there are two forms of quoting, and so far they seem indistinguishable. That's not always true, however. As seen in Table 6.01, single quotes are referred to as "strong quotes," while double quotes are referred to as "weak quotes." The difference lies in how *literally* the shell treats the contents of the quoted string. With strong quotes, all special characters will be treated literally, no matter what. With weak quotes, most special characters are treated literally, but some are not. This difference really only comes into play when you delve deeper into bash than this chapter dares to tread, but it typically involves the nesting of variables within quoted strings. In the sidebar *Change Your Prompt*, I noted that it's important to use strong quotes rather than weak to ensure that the shell reevaluates the PS1 variable every time a condition (your current directory) changes, rather than just the first time it's called.

Confused yet? Don't worry about it. For the purposes of this chapter and all of your initial bash explorations, you'll want to use strong quotes 99% of the time. When in doubt, stick with strong (single) quotes and you'll be fine.

Here's the complete list of characters that have special meaning to the shell (i.e. that need to be escaped or quoted if you want them interpreted literally):

```
{ } ( ) ! # $ % ^ & * ? / <> ~
```

and the space character.

### *Backticks*

So what about those backticks? First of all, you'll need to locate this key on your keyboard. On most keyboards, it shares the ~ key, just to the left of the 1 key. Backticks are used to force the shell to evaluate the contents of the string they contain so that you can do something else with it. This concept may be best explained by example; but first, a short preface.

Later on, you'll be working with "variables." Variables are nothing more than tokens, or place-holders for values which are subject to change. For instance, if you're working with a list of employee salaries and each employee makes a different wage, you might create a variable called Salary, the value of which is different for each employee. A variable's value can always be invoked by putting a $ symbol in front of it (for instance, the current value of Salary is invoked as $Salary).

Now, instead of working with a list of predefined salaries, what if you need a variable that stands in for the result of a shell command? For example, you might want a variable called TimeStamp that represents the system's date and time at the moment the variable is created. This is where those backticks come in. The shell has a command called date that will report the current date and time. So, try this:

```
TimeStamp=`date`
```

When you type this command, it will appear as though nothing happened. But if you now type echo $TimeStamp, you'll see the system's timestamp from a few moments ago. Echoing your TimeStamp variable displays the value of a "marker in time" that you established in memory a little while ago. While your system's notion of the current time changes from moment to moment, the value of TimeStamp won't change until you run the command again.

Creating variables from the output of shell commands can be very useful, especially when you start scripting the shell. Remember that the command contained in the backticks can be as simple or as complex as you need it to be!

There is yet another technique you can use to assign the results of a command to a variable. The backtick trick works fine, but is officially "deprecated" (or demoted) in favor of the new format, which uses parentheses:

```
TimeStamp=$(date)
```

This serves exactly the same purpose as the backtick method above, but is now considered The Standard (we had to cover the backtick method here because it still appears frequently in shell documentation and scripts floating around out there, and because both methods are used in examples throughout this book).

Again, for all intents and purposes, and especially while you're starting out in the shell, don't worry about this stuff too much. Stick with simple escapes (\) and strong (single) quotes, and you'll be fine.

**Changing Directories** To change to a different directory, type cd followed by the destination path. While you can always type the full path if you want to (for example, cd /boot/home/people), there are a number of shortcuts you can use, depending on your current location. If the destination is a child of the current directory (a subdirectory of the current directory), the current path is assumed in the cd command. So to get from /boot/home to /boot/home/people, all you have to do is type cd people.

To go up to the parent directory, type:

cd ..

To go up three directories, just repeat the pattern:

cd ../../..

You can also use this construction to change to a parallel directory by going up and then back down in the same command. To get from /boot/home/people to /boot/home/mail type:

cd ../mail

You can always foreshorten the path to your home directory by using the tilde character (~). For instance, say you're in /boot/beos/system and you want to get to /boot/home/mail—the shortest command would thus be cd ~/mail .

***Drag-and-Drop Directory Changes*** What's the sense in typing out a long directory path when the destination folder is visible in a Tracker window right in front of your eyes? Type cd and then drag a folder (or file) out of the Tracker and into the Terminal. The complete path to the file will be appended to the end of your cd command, and all you'll have to do is hit Enter to jump to the new location.

There is one caveat, however. When paths include spaces and you want to access them from the Terminal, you need to surround the block containing the spaces with single quotes, like:

'/boot/home/New Projects/July Research/'

Unfortunately, these quote marks aren't inserted for you when you drag a file or folder into the Terminal, so you'll have to use the Left Arrow to scroll back and insert them manually. To avoid this necessity, do this instead: Type cd, then a single quote, then drag and drop your file or folder, then type another single quote, then hit Enter.

***Edit Commands Quickly*** If you find yourself needing to repeat your previous command, or to run a variation of it, you can always hit your Up Arrow key to place the last-run command back on the command line (more on this in the sidebar *History Lesson* in this chapter). Once the previous command is on the command line, but before you press Enter again, you can use Ctrl+A to jump to the beginning of the line or Ctrl+E to jump to the end of the line. This is often much faster than simply using the Left and Right Arrow keys to scroll all the way through the command. These key bindings, by the way, are borrowed from the famous emacs editor, and also work in BeMail!

**File Listings**  To see the names of the files in the current directory, type ls. This, however, doesn't give you a whole lot of information to go on. For more details, try ls -l (that's a lowercase L, for "long" format).

Whoa! More information than you wanted to know? Here's how it breaks down for a sample listing (yours will have different contents, but the structure is always the same).

File permissions

| Entry type | Number of hard links to entry | | Modification date | |
|---|---|---|---|---|
| | Owner | Group | Size | File or folder name |

```
drwxr-xr-x  1 baron    users        2048 Sep 26 12:46 log/
drwxr-xr-x  1 baron    users        2048 Sep 29 02:45 mail/
drwxr-xr-x  1 baron    users        2048 Sep 12 11:50 misc/
drwxr-xr-x  1 baron    users      208896 Sep 23 18:44 news/
-rw-r--r--  1 baron    users        1040 Sep 18 13:52 pavel qs
drwxr-xr-x  1 baron    users       14336 Sep 29 14:09 people/
drwxr-xr-x  1 baron    users        2048 Sep 22 13:18 public_html/
drwxr-xr-x  1 baron    users       17408 Oct  1 20:39 queries/
-rw-r--r--  1 baron    users     2359314 Oct  1 23:57 screen1.tga
lrwxrwxrwx  1 baron    users           0 Sep  7 23:30 sounds -> /grueyer/sounds/
drwxr-xr-x  1 baron    users        2048 Sep 30 08:48 switch/
-rw-r--r--  1 baron    users       13624 Oct  1 09:51 switch.zip
-rw-r--r--  1 baron    users       33791 Oct  1 18:29 talkin.tga.zip
drwxr-xr-x  1 baron    users        2048 Sep 25 14:03 words/
```

*Figure 6.03*

*File and directory listings in the Terminal appear similar to this one, with loads of detail.*

The first character on the left will always give you an indication as to the type of entry. All directories begin with a "d", all files begin with a "-", and virtual devices begin with a "c" or a "b". The next block of nine characters describes the file's permission settings—we'll cover those later in this chapter. The number 1 is a holdover from true Unix, and represents the number of hard links to the file. BeOS does not support hard links, so you can ignore that (it's present because you're looking at a port of Unix bash, warts and all). Next you'll see two strings naming the owner of the file. In this example, a user named "baron" (that's you) owns all three files and belongs to a group called "users."

This book was written for BeOS R4, when the system was not yet fully "multiuser." In true Unix-based operating systems, multiple users can log into a single machine from multiple locations, sharing the same filesystem and applications. To protect users' data from tampering, a system of "file permissions" ensures that the user who creates a file gets to decide who can read, edit, or execute that file. In the future (possibly R5, but more likely R6), BeOS will become fully multiuser. In order to prepare thoroughly for that future, the BeOS filesystem already includes the basic architecture for setting file permissions. Even though they don't do much just yet, they *are* used in some cases to keep you from editing important system files. The name "baron" is used by default in BeOS to represent you, the current owner of all the files on your system. You can change "baron" to any other text string with the instructions in this chapter.

The next entry is the size of the file measured in bytes. Finally, the file and directory names are listed on the right.

The ls command has a number of interesting "flags" you can use to view your files and folders in various ways. Try ls --help to see a complete list of all possible flags (the most common ones are shown in Table 6.02). Flags can also be coupled with one another for finer listings. For example, the -a flag means that hidden files should be displayed (filenames that begin with a period are hidden to the shell by default, though they appear normally in the Tracker), while the -G flag suppresses the group information. So to show all

### Table 6.02  ls Flags

| Flag | Stands for ... | Description |
| --- | --- | --- |
| -a | All | Do not hide entries starting with ".". |
| -c | Sort by change time | Use in conjunction with -1 to sort by last modification time. |
| -F | Classify | Display directory entries with a trailing slash and executables with an asterisk (*). |
| -G | No group | Suppress group information |
| -i | Inode | Display the file's "address" in the filesystem. |
| -1 | Long | Long listing format—all details. |
| -m | Comma delimited | Short listing, no columns, entries separated by commas. |
| -n | Numeric-uid-gid | Gives numbers rather than names to users and groups; will be more interesting when BeOS is multiuser. |
| -o | Long without groups | Long listing format without group info; same as -1G. |
| -Q | Quote-name | Enclose entry names in double quotes, insert escape characters for spaces in filenames. Useful in some scripts. |
| -r | Reverse | Sort in reverse order. |
| -R | Recursive | List subdirectories recursively—directory crawl down from current location. |
| -s | Size | Print size of each file, in blocks (for example a 2048-byte file prints as two blocks if the partition is initialized at 1024 bytes per block). |
| -S | Sort by size | Sort by file size. |
| -t | Sort by time | Use with -1 flag to show modification time. |
| -X | Sort by extension | Sort alphabetically by extension (file.txt comes before file.zip). |
| --help | Help | Show everything in this table and more. |

*The ls command can take many additional options, or "flags," in order to generate customized file listings. Many of those shown here work best in conjunction with the -1 flag.*

files including the hidden ones, in long format, while suppressing the group entries, you'd type ls -laG. Another goodie you may find useful is the -F flag, which causes all directory names to end with a slash and all executable files to be followed by an asterisk. This lets you see a little more easily which entries in your file listing can be run by typing their names, and which represent deeper file hierarchies.

**Customize Directory Listings with Wildcards**   Let's say you're looking for a particular file in a directory containing two or three hundred files. No way are they going to all fit on screen at once, no matter what you do with ls flags. If you have an inkling of what the file might be called, you can start applying "filters" to your listings with the assistance of bash wildcards. A wildcard is like a placeholder that can stand in for any number of other characters. Imagine you at least know that the file you're looking for is a .zip file. Try typing ls -l *.zip and see how much more focused your list becomes. Now you remember that the files started with a "j", but you can't remember whether it was an uppercase or lowercase "j"—bash is case-sensitive! You could do two listings in a row, such as ls -l j*.zip and then ls -l J*.zip, but there's a better trick to use when you're not sure of the case—enclose both the uppercase and lowercase letters in brackets, like this:

ls -l [Jj]*.zip

This will find JuJu.zip, julio.final.zip, and jack_straw.zip. It will not, however, find proj.zip. Because the J and the period are next to each other, there's nothing in the expression to match the initial "pro". If you want your wildcard to stand in for a single character only, not any number of them, use a ? instead of a *.

By the way, this case-insensitivity trick will come into heavy play later on when we look at running BeOS queries from the command line.

*Bracket Expansion*   **You can make the shell look for multiple wildcard strings at once by surrounding them with brackets. For example, if you want to find all of the .zip and .pkg files in a directory, use:**

ls -l *.{pkg,zip}

**Take care not to insert a space after the comma!**

**Viewing Files**   There are a number of ways to view files from the command line without actually opening them in an editor. One of the simplest is to use the cat command:

cat filename.txt

If `filename.txt` is longer than a page, though, it's going to go whipping through the Terminal so fast you won't have a chance to see anything but the last 20 lines or so. You could use the Terminal's vertical scrollbar to catch some of what you missed, but the Terminal's buffer isn't large enough to hold everything that moves through it, so you may miss some. Besides—why use a mouse when you don't have to? After all, you could more or less just use *more* ... or *less*!

 ***PageUp in the Terminal*** **Even though the Terminal window has vertical scrollbars, you'll find that you can't use the PageUp or PageDown keys normally to move up or down. However, if you hold down the Shift key, then PageUp and PageDown will work normally.**

The old Unix command *more* is designed to give you one screenful of information at a time. You use it like this:

```
more filename.txt
```

It even lets you search through files while you're viewing them (type / followed by your search string while viewing a file, and the resulting line will appear at the top of the Terminal window). To search for the next instance of the same string, just type / on a line by itself and hit Enter.

Later in the evolution of Unix tools, an alternative to *more*—called *less*—came to popularity. *less* was similar to *more*, but had more features. For instance, you could scroll backward in a file by hitting the B key). On BeOS, *more* is really just a symlink to *less*, so either command gets you identical results. Hit the Spacebar while viewing a file to page through it; hit Enter to scroll down one line a time. To get out of the *more* program, type q, then hit Enter.

If you want to get really fancy, you can jump ahead in the Terminal lesson and make `cat` and `more` work together by piping the output of `cat` into the input of `more`, like this:

```
cat filename.txt | more
```

Same result, more typing, no net benefit. But you did just succeed in turning two atoms into your first primitive molecule! More on piping later.

**Heads or Tails**  Sometimes you don't need to view an entire file—you just need to see enough of it to remind yourself of what it contains. The `head` and `tail` commands take care of that need quite nicely, by giving you just the first or last 10 lines of your file. Of course, you can easily change this default if you need to see more or less of the file in question.

```
head -25 dirlist.txt
```

will give you the first 25 lines of `dirlist.txt`. `tail` works exactly the same way, but displays the specified number of lines at the end of the file instead.

## Standard In, Standard Out

The vast majority of CLI tools are built to spit their output into—or get their input from—a function of the shell called "channels" or "streams." These channels are sort of like conduits that carry your data while it's being processed, and you can weld these conduits end-to-end. The default output location for any channel is your screen, meaning that the results of your shell commands will appear in the Terminal window. Because these data channels are standardized, there's a high likelihood that two or more commands will interoperate with one another seamlessly.

When reading Unix-related documentation, you'll often come across the terms "stdin" and "stdout." These terms simply refer to the fact that the program in question is interoperable with other standard shell tools. If a program's documentation says something like "WidgetX accepts parameters from stdin and returns results to stdout," it simply means that WidgetX can accept the output of most other shell commands as its input, and that it prints its results as plain text either to the screen or into the "input jack" of another command, depending on whether redirect operators have been used.

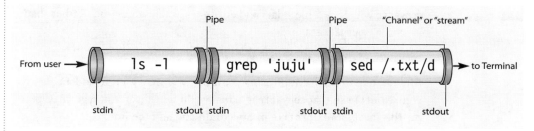

**Figure 6.04**

*The shell's "channels" or "streams" can be glued end-to-end to form command chains. Each accepts standard input (stdin) and emits standard output (stdout). Shown here is a visualization with channels and pipes of the command* `ls -l | grep 'juju' | sed /.txt/d`, *which will find all files in the current directory with "juju" in their names, except for those that contain ".txt".*

**Making Copies** To copy a file, use the `cp` command:

```
cp source destination
```

For example, assuming there's already a file called `foo` in the current directory, issuing the command `cp foo bar` will result in the creation of an exact copy of `foo`, called `bar`. But the shell does a few tricky things with its file management commands. Let's say your current directory already has a child directory called `bar`. In that case, if you typed the exact same command, the shell would assume that you wanted to put a copy of `foo`, also called `foo`, inside of `bar`. In other words, if the named destination already exists as a directory, it will treat your command more intelligently. But if `bar` exists as a file instead of as a directory, something nasty is going to happen: `bar` will be overwritten with the contents of `foo`! Unlike the Tracker, the Terminal doesn't prompt you for confirmation when potentially bad things are about to happen. It assumes that you know what you're doing.

For this reason, commands such as cp have an -i flag, for interactive mode. If you use the -i flag, the Terminal will prompt you before overwriting existing files and folders. If you want this to be the default behavior, I'll show you how to set that up on the next page.

 *Use* copyattr *Instead of* cp    The cp command comes to BeOS straight from Unix, and thus doesn't know anything about one of BeOS's most powerful features—attributes. As a result, copying files from the command line copies the data in your files, but doesn't copy their associated attributes—not good. While some of your files will do just fine without attributes, you definitely don't want to lose them for things like Person or BeMail files, which depend heavily on attributes.

Fortunately, BeOS provides a special tool for dealing with this situation, in the form of the copyattr command. Used in conjunction with the -d flag, copyattr will copy a file's data and attributes at the same time. Rather than using cp source data, use:

```
copyattr -d source destination.
```

After getting in the habit of using copyattr, you may want to add an alias to your .profile so that copyattr is actually run whenever you type cp. Open the file /boot/home/.profile in StyledEdit and add the line:

```
alias cp="copyattr -d"
```

There is, however, another gotcha if you do this: You won't be able to use some of cp's flags, such as the -R flag, which moves recursively through subdirectories. This is because the cp command will now call the copyattr command, which does not recognize the -R flag. To avoid this, you can either create the alias under a name other than cp, or just get in the habit of using the Tracker to copy or move files that need their attributes preserved.

**Moving Things**    mv is the move command, and has the same syntax and habits as cp. Interestingly, mv doubles as a file renamer. For instance, mv foo bar will move the file foo to a new location, and that location is a file called bar in the current directory. This is exactly the same as renaming, and means you have one less command to remember. Of course, if bar already exists, it will be overwritten unless you use the -i flag.

Both cp and mv can be used on entire directories in addition to single files. However, you'll need to add the -R flag (for recursive) to get this to work—all directories are considered recursive, even if they don't include subdirectories. Thus, cp -R ~/mail ~/shemail will make a copy of the entire mail directory structure as shemail in the home directory.

**Making Directories**   This one is cake: `mkdir Sartre` makes a directory called Sartre in the current location. `mkdir` is capable of a few other tricks, too. For example, you can create multiple directories at once. To create four different subdirectories of the current directory at the same time, try:

```
mkdir Sartre Camus Heidegger Springer
```

You can also create *nested* directory structures (directories inside one another) all at once by simply using the `-p` flag (for "create parents") and typing their paths:

```
mkdir -p books/authors/philosophers/Camus
```

Even if the `books` directory doesn't yet exist, this command will create the entire directory tree, a task that would take considerably more handwork from the Tracker!

**Deleting Files and Folders**   Fortunately, the `bash` deletion commands (`rm` to remove files and `rmdir` to remove directories) aren't *quite* as reckless as `cp` and `mv`. `rm *.txt` which will delete every file ending with `.txt` in the current directory without asking for confirmation, but `rmdir ~/mail` will (thankfully) refuse, on the grounds that it still contains files. You have three options: 1) `cd` to the `mail` directory and delete every file in it, then go back up to the parent directory and try `rmdir`—it'll work this time; 2) decide you want to keep all of your accumulated email after all; or 3) use `rm` instead of `rmdir`. How's that? Oddly enough, `rmdir` doesn't offer a way to remove directories that still contain files. Thus, if you get in the habit of using it, you'll never be sorry (though you may get annoyed). Remember—these aren't pretend commands, and files deleted from the Terminal *aren't* sent to the Trash, as are those deleted from the Tracker. If you actually do want to delete an entire directory tree, do so by appending the `-r` (recursive) flag to `rm`, as in `rm -r ~/foo`.

 *Safeguard against Accidental Overwrites and Deletions*   `rm` is not a tool to experiment with idly. Simply "testing" `rm`'s various flags can get you into one of those "I was just cleaning it and it went off!" situations. How bad can it be? Consider this: If you were sitting in the root and tried `rm -Rf *` out of simple curiosity, you could end up with a blank partition. Exercise caution, and add this line to your `.profile`:

```
alias rm="rm -i"
```

to make `rm` always behave interactively, giving you at least a bit of warning and an opportunity to back out if your data is about to be reduced to digital dust.

If you do set aliases for commands like this, however, you'll need to pay special attention any time you sit down at someone else's machine, since you'll have gotten in the habit of being asked for confirmation, while the new machine may not have the same aliases installed!

**Archiving Files** It's worth learning at least the basics of creating and decompressing archives from the Terminal—you'd be surprised how handy that knowledge can be in a pinch. Complete coverage of archiving from the Terminal can be found in Chapter 5, *Files and the Tracker*.

**Symlinks** As easily as you can link up documents on the Web, you can create hyperlinks within your own filesystem, so that by accessing one file (either from the Tracker or from the Terminal) you actually end up accessing another. This is a great way to link up disparate parts of your system when you find yourself commonly needing access to some/remote/directory/with/a/hella/long/path, when you need to satisfy the needs of some cranky program with pathnames hard-coded into it, or when you want to create a drag-and-drop "tunnel" so that files dropped on a folder actually end up elsewhere on the system. You can read all about symlinks in Chapter 5, *Files and the Tracker*, but here's the quick-n-dirty on creating them from the Terminal:

```
ln -s TargetPathName LinkPathName
```

Let's say you're currently in your home directory, and you find yourself needing constant access to your NetPositive bookmarks folder for a special project you're working on. Type:

```
ln -s /boot/home/config/settings/NetPositive/Bookmarks bookmarks
```

From now on, all you have to do to get to your bookmarks from the Terminal is type cd ~/bookmarks. Interestingly, pwd will report that bookmarks actually *is* a subdirectory of home, even though you know it's just a link. In other words, the illusion of the symlink is real as far as the shell is concerned, so any programs or scripts you create that access ~/bookmarks will actually have access to the remote directory. BeOS itself uses this technique liberally, especially in the root directory, to maintain compatibility with programs ported from the Unix world that expect to find certain directories in certain places.

When viewing Terminal directory listings, you can always tell a symlink at a glance by the presence of an arrow pointing from the source to the destination:

```
l---------   1 baron    users        0 Jun 23 11:37 bin -> /boot/beos/bin/
```

Back in the Tracker, the icons for the symlinks you create from the Terminal will always inherit the icon of the target.

 The ln command won't prevent you from creating a link to a target that doesn't exist, so if you make a mistake, you could end up with an unresolved link! It's a good idea to test your links before depending on them.

## Terminal/Tracker Integration

If you want to see for yourself just how tightly the Terminal is tied to the Tracker, try this test on your BeOS machine, then boot into Windows, Linux, or another operating system and try an equivalent experiment.

1. Create a new folder and open its window in the Tracker.

2. Open a Terminal session and change directories to the same path as the Tracker view (the easiest way is to install the TermHire Add-On so you can press Ctrl+Alt+T to bring up a Terminal session in the current directory).

3. Arrange your Terminal and Tracker windows so they're both visible onscreen simultaneously.

4. Create a new file in the current directory from the Terminal by typing touch test.

5. How long did it take from the time you pressed Enter until the test file appeared in the Tracker? On most systems, you'll barely be able to detect a delay.

6. Delete the file by typing rm test. Again, the Tracker's reaction to changes made from the Terminal is virtually instantaneous.

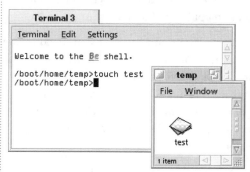

**Figure 6.05**

*To see for yourself how closely the Tracker and the Terminal are tied to one another, try making changes to your filesystem from the Terminal while the equivalent files and folders are visible in the Tracker. Changes are reflected in the GUI view so quickly it's almost like you're using it directly. Try an equivalent experiment in Windows 95 or Linux to see the difference.*

You're witnessing BeOS multithreading in action. Because every Tracker window keeps a node monitor trained on its directory, it's able to report changes at that point in the filesystem with almost zero lag time, even if resource-intensive tasks are going on elsewhere in the system. Launch a few of your most CPU-intensive demos and try the same experiment while they're running. The Tracker stays sensitive and responsive no matter what's going on in the rest of the system (within reason). How far can you push it before the response times slow down noticeably?

# Basic Shell Syntax

So much for working with files and folders. What about the hundreds of command-line programs you've been hearing about? cd over to /boot/beos/bin (or its symlink equivalent, /bin) and start getting some directory listings. You'll find so many files here that you may want to view them one letter at a time: ls a*, then ls b*, etc. While most of what you see here will be of immediate interest only to extreme geeks, there are plenty of cool toys floating around for first-time shell users as well.

Running programs from the command line is a bit of an art and a bit of a science. There are often dozens of different ways to accomplish a single task, and it's up to you to learn the most effective way of doing any single thing. Another tricky aspect to starting from ground zero as a new shell user is that you often find yourself needing to use standard bash syntax and the specific syntax of a CLI program at the same time. A certain amount of trial and error can be expected as you work through this process. With practice, however, you'll soon find that you're able to successfully run command-line programs correctly the first time. A feeling of tremendous empowerment will wash over your soul, and you'll lean back in your chair, bathed in golden light, and vow to conquer the bash beast for good. Little do you know, you've barely scratched the surface. Bwah-hah-hah-hah-hah!

**Rather than copying bash syntax blindly from manuals and books, try to understand what you're doing at every step along the way. Knowing "how to work it" and "how it works" are two completely different things. Remember the old saying, "Give a man a fish and he eats for a day; teach him how to fish and he eats forever." Learn to fish and you're set for life.**

**Running CLI Programs**  You can run a program from the command line by typing its name along with any extra information the program needs to do its job. For example, a program that reformats text documents can't operate unless you tell it which documents need formatting and how you want the documents modified. This kind of extra information is known as a command's "arguments." Some commands, such as ls, can be run without arguments. Others are useless without them.

Let's say you've got a small program called lines that will tell you the number of lines in any text file. Usage of the program might work like this:

```
lines filename.txt
```

The lines program referenced here is imaginary, and used for illustration purposes only—it does not exist on your system.

The shell will report back to you the results of the command, which may consist of nothing more than the number "32." Many programs also take extra options, or flags, which let you refine the way they do their job. For instance, our lines program might be able to tell the difference between lines that begin with numbers and lines that begin with letters, and the documentation might tell us that in order to make it only count lines beginning with numbers, we use the -c option:

```
lines -c filename.txt
```

In some programs, the options themselves can take arguments. Perhaps the number counting option has the ability to count only even numbers. The syntax might be:

```
lines -c even filename.txt
```

Some programs accept multiple files as their input. For instance, if you wanted to count the even lines in three files, your command might look like this:

```
lines -c even filename.txt file2.txt file3.txt
```

However, a much easier way to do something like this would be to use your friendly neighborhood wildcards. The above command would be easier to issue by typing:

```
lines -c even file*.txt
```

This would cause the program to operate on all three of these files, plus any others that start with "file", end with ".txt", and live in the current directory.

While there are many general guidelines and rules of thumb for command-line syntax, and most of the syntax habits you pick up with one program will translate pretty well to the next, remember that most shell programs are written by independent individuals—not Be employees—who sometimes insist on making up their own rules as they go along. As a result, you will encounter occasional inconsistencies. For example, most commands that take one file as input and create another as output have the syntax:

```
commandname input.txt output.txt
```

But on occasion, you'll encounter a program that reverses this order:

```
commandname output.txt input.txt
```

bash syntax will be better illuminated through the examples below.

**Syntax Help** To learn the exact syntax of any command, you can usually type its name into the Terminal with no arguments. Doing this may spit back a set of usage guidelines, typically in a rather cryptic format. If that doesn't work (or if the program is designed to be run without arguments), try commandname -h or commandname --help.

In addition, you'll often find very detailed (but still frustratingly cryptic) instructions for program usage in the program's "man" (short for "manual") pages. Unfortunately, BeOS does not yet include the Unix man command. Be has, however, ported most of the man pages for the programs it bundles to HTML format and included them in the user documentation. Take a look in /boot/beos/documentation/Shell Tools/. If you're just starting out with bash, though, you'll probably find a user-friendly book more helpful than the man pages.

In addition, bash has a delightful little help command that offers short, not quite pithy blurbs on the essential functions of many shell commands. Like most Unix-oriented documentation, help has a tendency to assume that you already know more than you actually do—in other words, it's seldom any help at all unless you already have a solid handle on bash.

Often, your best learning bet is to experiment by trying the command in a variety of configurations and contexts; you'll be surprised how often you're able to get it to work properly by trial and error, or to extend your knowledge of the shell by examining the results of Terminal experiments.

## Redirection

I've been harping on this "atomicity" metaphor, but it really is true: Every command in the bash environment is just a tiny piece of the big picture. The real power of the shell begins to emerge when you start gluing commands together to make strings—command-line creations that are bigger than the sum of their parts. Like Legos with their standard plugs and sockets, you can assemble any combination of these commands into custom tools that do specific jobs. By taking the output of one job and jacking it into the input of another, you have the opportunity to create a virtual application from a pile of parts. There are two basic mechanisms for gluing together commands. One is called the "pipe" and the other is called "redirection."

The simplest form of redirection is taking the output of a job and writing it to a file. Take a simple file listing command from one of the earlier examples:

```
ls -lGa [Jj]*.zip
```

This means "find all the files in the current directory starting with a J (upper- or lowercase) and ending with ".zip", and display them in long format, suppressing the group names to which the files belong." But say that now you want to mail the results of this command to a colleague in Australia who's working on the project with you. To store the results of this listing as a file on your hard drive, just redirect the output to a file:

```
ls -l [Jj]*.zip > ~/JZips.txt
```

Now scoot over to your home directory, and sure enough, you'll find the newly created file. Double-click the file from within the Tracker, and the same listing pops up in StyledEdit. So far so good, but what if the listing is huge? It sure could benefit from being compressed before it hits the Net. At first glance, it may seem that it would be possible to generate the new file and send it to the zip program all at once. When you think about it, though, you're actually requesting that the output of the first ls command be sent to two different destinations (the text file and the zip program). What's actually necessary is to run two commands in sequence—one to get the custom listing into a text file, and the second to zip up the newly created text file. You can run sequential commands from the same command line by separating them with semicolons:

```
ls -l [Jj]*.zip > ~/JZips.txt ; zip ~/JZips ~/JZips.txt
```

Instead of redirecting your output to a file, however, you may want to send it to another command for further processing. In that case, use the vertical bar, or pipe (|) character on your keyboard. Whenever it encounters a vertical bar, the shell redirects the output of the first command (stdout) straight into the input jack of the subsequent command (stdin). For this example, we'll use a CLI tool we haven't yet covered in depth: grep. All grep does is search through input (from a file or from another program) for a string that you feed it. I'm going to tell grep to look for the string "JuJu" in the output of the file listing:

```
ls -l [Jj]*.zip | grep JuJu
```

In other words, rather than redirecting the output of ls into a file, we've "piped" that output into another command. To have grep send its output to a text file instead of to the screen, use the standard redirect operator described earlier.

```
ls -l [Jj]*.zip | grep JuJu > ~/JZips.txt
```

 ***Redirect and Append*** **When you use the single redirect operator > to output the results of a command to a file, you clobber (overwrite) any file with the same name that may already exist. In many instances, this may be what you want to happen. If you'd rather have the results of your command appended to an existing file rather than overwriting it, use double redirect operators (>>), like this:**

```
ls -l >> ever.growing.file.list.txt
```

The input redirect operator, <, behaves as you would expect, moving data in the standard input stream to the command, rather than the other way around. Guess what this does:

```
cat < filename.txt
```

If you can't guess, try it out!

By now you're starting to see how CLI programs can be welded together in sequences to tackle any situation. There are hundreds of command-line tools to play with, and far more depth to the shell.

## Tab Completion

Getting tired of typing the same thing over and over again? If you're not by now, you will be soon. Experimenting with the shell typically means a certain amount of trial and error, and repeating long commands with slight variations as you fine-tune your command constructs. The next time you're typing a filename, stop halfway through and hit the Tab key. With any luck, the filename will complete itself before your eyes! If the file had a similar name to another file in the same path, the completion will stop at the point where the shell can no longer guess which file you mean. An audible beep will remind you when this happens. Hit Tab again and the shell will display a list of all files that match the string you've typed so far.

Tab completion isn't limited to the files in the current directory, either. If your current directory is home and you're typing the name of a command you know is located over in /boot/beos/bin by invoking its full path, try typing the first few letters of the command name, then pressing Tab. You can save yourself quite a bit of typing this way. Become accustomed to Tab completion, and you'll almost *never* end up typing complete filenames or paths.

## History Lesson

The shell has an amazing memory—it keeps a log of everything you do in the Terminal in a text file located at /boot/home/.bash_history, and can replay even your longest, hairiest, multiline shell constructs. The easiest and most common way to replay previously entered commands is to use the Up Arrow and Down Arrow keys on your keyboard to cycle through your most recent commands. The Up Arrow key alone will save you countless keystrokes.

There's more to bash history than tapping arrow keys, though. Try typing history into the Terminal and you'll get back a numbered list of the last 500 shell commands you've issued. To repeat your last command, type ! and press Enter. To repeat any command in the list, type ! followed by the command's number. For example:

!134

Finally, you can specify that history only give you the last *n* commands. To see a list of your last 25 commands, try history 25. If you find yourself accessing history functions frequently, you may want to create an alias in your .profile as described earlier in this chapter. The single letter "h" could stand in for history 20, for example.

***Find History Commands Fast*** If you're working with a series of complex commands from several days or weeks ago, it's great to be able to retrieve them on the spur of the moment, even between reboots. Of course, the list of commands you've entered in the last few weeks is pretty long, so if you can remember some part of the command you're trying to retrieve, you'll probably want to couple the history command with grep to narrow down the possibilities. Let's say you ran a neat little awk command the other day and you're trying to find it in your history list. Type:

```
history | grep awk
```

If you've been working through examples found later in this chapter, your results may look something like this:

```
history | grep awk
  3581  awk '{ print $3 }' oldphone
  3582  awk '{ print $4 }' oldphone
  3583  awk '{ print $1 $2 }' oldphone
  3584  awk '{ print $1 " " $2 }' oldphone
  3585  awk '{ print $1 " " $2 "--" $7 }' oldphone
  3586  awk '{ print $1 " " $2 " -- " $8 }' oldphone
  3587  awk '{ print $1 " " $2 " -- " $8 $9 }' oldphone
  3588  awk '{ print $1 " " $2 " - long distance - " $8 $9 }' oldphone
```

Assuming that the last one you used was the one that did the trick, all you have to do to repeat it is type !3588.

 ***Change the Size of Your History File*** Your history list may seem endless, but in fact only the last 500 commands you've issued are remembered by default. If you'd like the history function to remember a smaller or larger number of commands, open up /boot/home/config/boot/UserSetupEnvironment (or create this file if it doesn't exist) and add a line reading:

```
export HISTSIZE=100,
```

replacing "100" with the number of commands you want remembered. The next time you access the history command, your bash_history file will be truncated to the new size.

 ***Instant Replay*** Rather than viewing or grepping through your history file for a previous command, try tapping Ctrl+R. The shell will prompt you to type in a string, at which point you can type in the first few letters of a previous command. Enter a couple of characters and the shell will show you the first command it finds in your history that match that string. If the command displayed is close-but-no-cigar, type a few more characters to fine-tune the search. When the correct command is displayed, hit Enter to execute it.

# Finding Stuff

While BeOS queries can be run from the shell, there are other tricks to finding data from the command line that you should know about—especially considering the fact that you can find some things from the Terminal that you can't from the GUI, like text strings buried in your files (queries search only on attributes, filenames, and modification times). That functionality is covered by grep, an old Unix favorite.

In addition to command-line queries, the traditional Unix find command is alive and well in the BeOS shell. Queries may be more powerful than find, but find doesn't need any fancy query syntax to work. If you already know all or part of the filenames you're seeking, find may be just the ticket. We'll check out grep and find here, but leave query coverage for Chapter 7, *Working with Queries*.

**Finding Buried Text with grep**  grep (get regular expression and print) is a card-carrying member of the Unix canon, having been around forever, and never having lost favor to newer tools. Regular expressions are another topic worthy of a book unto themselves (see the *Learning More* section at the end of this chapter). In essence, regular expressions are a system that takes the notion of the wildcard (*) that we met earlier to a much higher level, allowing you to uncover patterns and strings of almost unlimited complexity by intermixing special symbols (see Table 6.03) with regular text characters. Regular expressions are used in text editors, in database query tools, and as part of the syntax of many command-line tools. grep lets you use this advanced querying syntax to dig needles out of haystacks.

Fortunately, you don't have to learn all there is to know about regular expessions to get good mileage out of grep. In fact, you don't have to learn anything—you can simply type grep string filecollection. grep will scan the contents of the files specified in filecollection for that string, and report back to you with a list of all matching files. Use grep -n to include line numbers with the matching files.

Let's say you vaguely remember a piece of email about oyster ranching that floated over your transom months ago. At the time it barely seemed worth keeping; now you desperately need to find that message. Trouble is, you've accumulated thousands of messages spread over various mail folders over the past year. Since BeOS queries won't find text embedded in files, grep is your best bet. Try this:

```
cd ~/mail
grep "oyster ranching" */*
```

Since grep has to actually read through the contents of each file, it won't be as fast as a BeOS query would be, but if the string "oyster ranching" exists in any of the thousands of messages buried in ~mail/ and its subdirectories, grep will find it. Unfortunately, BeMail messages have very long filenames, including numerical identification strings to guarantee uniqueness, so grep's results are going to look kind of messy for this particular search. But you will discover the exact folder and filename you're after. You can then use less, cat, or anything else you like to view the contents of the message.

Let's try another grep example, this time conjoining it with another Terminal command. Let's say you've got a directory containing hundreds of files and you want to get a listing of just the ones that were modified today, September 26. When you run the ls -l command, you can see that each file reports its modification date along with the rest of the file details:

```
drwxr-xr-x    1 baron      users          2048 Sep 26 12:46 log
-rw-r--r--    1 baron      users          3268 Sep 23 19:15 ls.txt
```

If you treated the entire output of ls -l as if it were a text file, you would be able to scan through it for lines containing the string "Sep 26." Thus, the simplest way to get such a listing would be to conjoin the ls and grep commands with a pipe:

```
ls -l | grep "Sep 26"
```

 Remember the discussion on escaping or quoting special characters from earlier in this chapter? You'll find that it comes into heavy play when working with grep. As soon as you begin to use search strings that contain two or more words, your search string will include a space, which is a special character to the shell and must be escaped. If your grep commands give you errors, take another look at the escaping and quoting sidebar earlier in this chapter.

 It's important to remember that grep is case-sensitive, just like the BeOS filesystem. Whether you're searching for files or for text inside of files, remember that "sep 26" is not the same as "Sep 26." The same rules described earlier in this chapter apply—if you don't know the case before beginning your search, you can bracket the letters you're searching on like this: [Ss]ep 26. Alternatively, use the -i flag to tell grep to ignore cases in the search string (e.g. grep -i "sep 26").

**Exploring Regular Expressions**  grep isn't the only shell tool that uses regular expressions—you'll find their syntax (often collectively referred to as "regex") used by most CLI tools that deal with text. In fact, you'll even find a few GUI applications capable of taking regex syntax. For example, the Pe editor (Chapter 12, *Productivity Applications*) lets you run multifile search-and-replace operations with regular expressions if you like. The power of regular expressions comes at a price, however: They can quickly grow very complex, and there are entire books dedicated to milking regex for all it's

## Table 6.03 Regular Expression Syntax

| This Expression | Means | Example | Finds This | But Not This |
|---|---|---|---|---|
| . (period) | Any single character | a.c | "abc" | "abbc" |
| [x-y] | Range of characters | a[b-d]e | "ace" | "age" |
| [0-9] | Range of numbers | waxwing[0-9] | "waxwing3" | "waxwingz" |
| ^ (when used in a range) | Don't find the specified range | waxwing[^0-9] | "waxwingz" | "waxwing3" |
| ^ (when used outside a range) | Beginning of line | ^Waxwing | "Waxwing" only when it appears at the start of a line | "Waxwing" in the middle of a line |
| $ | End of line | Waxwing$ | "Waxwing" only when it appears at the end of a line | "Waxwing" in the middle of a line |
| * | Match preceding expression zero or more times | ab*c | "abc" or "abbbbbc" or "ac" | "bce" |
| + | Match preceding expression one or more times | ab+d | "abd" or "abbbbd" | "ad" |
| ? | Match preceding expression zero or one time | ab?d | "abd" or "ad" | "abbbbd" |
| \ | Interpret the next character literally | ab\*c | "ab*c" | "abbbc" |
| \\ | Escape the back-slash character | ab\\c | "ab\c" | "ab/c" |
| \| | One of a choice of regexes | ab\|cd | "ab" | "bc" |
| ()\|() | One of a choice of groups of regexes | (a.c)\|(a[b-d]e) | "abc" or "ace" | "abbc" or "age" |

*These are the most common special characters used in constructing regular expressions. Mix and match them to create custom expressions.*

worth (see the *Learning More* section at the end of this chapter). If you're ready to go a bit beyond straight text searching, however, a few of the juicy bits of regex are outlined in Table 6.03. Any and all of the examples in the table can be combined to create custom search strings.

## *Tracker Grep*

If you think it should be possible to search *through* (rather than for) text files from BeOS's query interface, you're not alone. After all, Windows can do this, why can't BeOS? The primary reason is that the BeOS query engine is a unique part of the operating system, while grep is just a port of a Unix shell tool.

Until BeOS does provide this functionality, there's an excellent workaround in the form of a Tracker add-on you can download from BeWare, called Tracker Grep. Once the add-on has been copied to /boot/home/config/add-ons, all you have to do is right-click on any file or folder and choose Add-ons | TrackerGrep. A dialog box into which you can type your search string will appear. Hit Enter, and TrackerGrep will search through all of the selected files. Each searched file will be listed in the output window, and any file that includes the string you're after will get a line of text beneath it showing you where in the file the string appears. Remember that you'll still need to escape any characters that have special meaning to the shell, such as spaces and slashes.

**find**   Even though the Unix find command doesn't take advantage of BeOS query power, it's still a lean, mean searching machine that can help you find specific files in a hurry. Because it doesn't require you to learn any of queries' more complex syntax, it's sometimes easier to use than queries are. However, its results aren't normally returned as quickly because find has to examine every file, rather than relying on BeOS's filesystem indexes (Chapter 5, *Files and the Tracker*). On the other hand, it lets you do one thing that queries don't: specify a starting path to limit the search to a specific subdirectory. Want to find all files that exist somewhere under the /boot/home hierarchy and begin with the string "alpha"? Type in:

```
find ~ -name alpha\*
```

 There are two noteworthy peculiarities here. First, we use ~ rather than ~/ to indicate that we're starting from home. The shell's filename completion feature knows to fill in the slash for us since it's going to be digging down through subdirectories. Second, we need to escape the * by preceding it with a backslash so it isn't interpreted by the shell.

To use find, you must always begin by specifying a starting path. Here we use the ~ shortcut to specify the home directory. Because we're searching on filenames, we use the -name flag, with a string and wildcard as qualifier. Find doesn't *have* to look only for filenames—it can take a variety of arguments. To find files with a specific modification date, use the -mtime flag:

```
find ~/ -mtime -30
```

will find all files under your home directory that have been touched in more than 30 days. To take it a step further and make it really useful, we can pipe the results through the xargs command, which passes the list of found files to another command for further processing. Let's say you're trying to track down all of your NetPositive cache files that haven't been used for more than a month and delete them, all in one command. You might try:

```
find $HOME/config/settings/NetPositive/NetCache -type f  \! -mtime -30 | xargs  rm
```

A couple of new bash elements come into play here. The {HOME} environment variable inserts the path of your home directory automatically, as specified in the system's SetupEnvironment script. This accounts for the possibility that BeOS could be running in multiuser mode. The! symbol negates the command that follows it—in other words, it tells find to look for files that were *not* created within the last 30 days.

## Setting Permissions

One key element of all Unix-based filesystems is the notion of file ownership and permissions, which determine which users can do what with files. While BeOS is not Unix-based, its filesystem does share the same protection scheme, and future versions of BeOS will be fully multiuser. Until then, a Unix-style permissions scheme is in place, but only partially active. You can, for example, control whether a given text file is editable or not, but you cannot yet specify that certain users can edit the file while others can't. Until further notice, BeOS is effectively a single-user OS.

There are, however, a few good reasons to know how permissions operate even when BeOS is used in single-user mode. For example, you'll find that when you copy files from a read-only disk (like a CD-ROM) to a BeOS volume, those files will retain their read-only permissions. If you want to edit them, you'll have to make them writeable as well. Of course, in order to do this, you'll have to have the appropriate level of permissions yourself, which you necessarily do as long as BeOS remains a single-user system.

To learn the current permission settings for any file, take a look at its long-format directory listing:

```
-rw-r--r--   1 users baron   2608 Jun 17 01:49 dirlist.txt
```

As discussed earlier, long-format file listings (those generated by ls -l) always include a block of ten characters at their left. The first of the ten characters indicates whether the entry is a file or a folder. In this case it's a file. The remaining nine characters represent the file's permissions, expressed as "r" for read permissions, "w" for write permissions, and "x" for execute permissions. Now break the nine characters into three groups of three. The first group of three represents permissions pertaining to the owner of the file, which is the person who created it (we'll assume that's you). The second block of three characters expresses permissions bestowed on the rest of the members of the group to which you belong (users on a multiuser system can break themselves into "groups," so they can give certain permissions to their trusted colleagues, but not to the rest of the world). The final block represents permissions granted to "the world"—anyone who happens to be accessing the system who is neither you nor a member of your group. Thus, the example file above is set to allow its owner (baron) to read the file and to make changes to it, but not to execute the file if it contains bash commands (e.g. if the file is a shell script). Baron is allowing his group to read the file, but not to make changes to it or to execute it. The same permissions are granted to the world. So how do you make changes to these settings?

**chmod**  To change the permissions associated with a file, directory, or group of files, use the chmod (change mode) command to specify whether you're changing permissions for the user (u), group (g), or other (o). Then specify whether you're adding permissions (+), subtracting them (-), or making them equal to the next argument (=). For example, consider this file:

```
-rw-r--r--    1 users baron    2608 Jun 17 01:49 dirlist.txt
```

To make dirlist.txt writable and executable by the rest of your group, you could type:

```
chmod g+wx dirlist.txt
```

To safeguard the file from your own accidental edits, you could try:

```
chmod u-w dirlist.txt
```

By using the = operator, you specify that all existing settings for that group will be overwritten with the new ones. chmod g=rwx dirlist.txt will bestow all permissions for that file on your group, regardless of what they were before.

As long as BeOS is a single-user system, you have "god" privileges and can change the permissions of any file on your system at will. Note, however, that when BeOS is fully multiuser, you will only be able to change permissions for the files you already own.

Just because you *can* change permissions on any file on your system doesn't mean you *should*. Many of the files that make up your BeOS installation are write-protected for a reason. These are primarily the files that exist under the /boot/beos hierarchy, and editing them can potentially render your system unbootable or otherwise screwy.

### *The Rule of Sevens*

If you want to be a real geek about it, you can change permission settings with the Rule of Sevens, by means of the Sacred Algorithm. You don't have to sacrifice a goat or anything weird like that—just remember that each of the three letters used to represent types of permission— "r", "w", and "x" is equivalent to a number:

```
r = 4
w = 2
x = 1
```

To assign a permission status to owner, group, or world, simply add up the appropriate numbers. If you want the owner to be able to read, write, and execute the file, add up 4, 2, and 1 to get 7. If you want the group to be able to read and execute but not write to the file, add up 4 and 1 to get 5. If you want the world to be able execute but not read or write to the file, they get a 1. Thus, the new permission status for this file will be 751. To apply the new status, use the chmod command:

```
chmod 751 dirlist.txt
```

Get yourself a new long-format directory listing, and the block of characters in the left column has changed appropriately:

```
-rwxr-x--x   1 users baron   2608 Jun 17 01:49 dirlist.txt*
```

Note also that an asterisk now follows the filename, indicating that it has execute permissions and is probably either a script or a binary program.

The advantage of the Rule of Sevens is that it lets you set permissions for user, group, and world all at once, without having to go through multiple steps. Its cryptic nature, however, means it can take you as much time to calculate the algorithm in your head as it would have taken to just type out three separate commands.

**chown and chgrp**   These two commands are similar to chmod, but are used to transfer the ownership of a file to another user or group. Because BeOS is not yet a multiuser operating system, it's logically impossible for these commands to work properly. You can issue chown and chgrp commands, but they will fail. For future reference, the syntax is pretty much what you would expect:

```
chown username filename
chgrp groupname filename
```

# Text Processing

The bash environment provides a seemingly infinite number of ways to process and manipulate text files from the command line, in a myriad of ways not possible with even the most sophisticated GUI word processors. The teases here serve only as the barest introduction to the possibilities of bash-based text processing. For complete documentation, consult a Unix manual or the output of each command's --help option.

**cat**   Ever wish there were an easy way to join a bunch of files end to end as a single file? In bash there is, and believe it or not, it's the same command you used a few pages ago to view a text file—cat is short (sort of) for concatenate (to link together), and that's exactly what it does. In order for it to be useful, you have to use it in conjunction with a redirect operator, like this:

```
cat file1 file2 file3 file4 > foobar
```

This simply creates a new file called foobar consisting of files 1 through 4, glued together end to end.

**csplit**   That explains how to fuse many files into one, but what if you want to go the other way 'round? Maybe you've already got a big file, and you want to make a bunch of smaller files out of it. That's exactly what csplit does. csplit is capable of very complex splitting operations, but in its most basic form it works by scanning through a text file for regular, repeating strings, and creating new files out of the text that comes between the found strings. You can tell it to do this a specific number of times, or to continue until it reaches the end of the file.

Let's say you've trained your database to export one giant text file consisting of the totality of all records in a found set, and you now want to split them into separate files—one file for each record (this is a great way to hack Web pages out of a database, by the way). Assume that you've rigged your database so that each new record in the exported file is demarcated by the string "NewRecord," that the exported file is called export, and that you want each of your new files to start with "tip." This command:

```
csplit -f tip export /'NewRecord'/ {*}
```

will open up the file called "export," scan it for instances of the string "NewRecord," and output files called tip01, tip02, tip03, and so on until it runs out of instances of "NewRecord." The -f flag means that the next string will be the prefix for the new filenames, while the {*} at the end is what tells csplit to keep going until all instances of "NewRecord" are exhausted. If, on the other hand, you only want the first 25 instances of "NewRecord" to be used, replace {*} with {25}.

**split**   Of course, you don't always necessarily want to split your file on the basis of text strings—sometimes you want to break it up in evenly sized chunks. split will do that for you with this simple syntax:

```
split -b 1000 export tip
```

This will take the same file we used in the csplit example and break it up into 1,000-byte pieces, each beginning with the prefix "tip."

 **_Stuffing Huge Files onto Floppies_**   split isn't limited to splitting text files—it can be used on any kind of file, which comes in handy when you're trying to fit large files onto floppies. Try this:

1. **Copy the** zip **file containing one of your downloaded pieces of BeOS soft- ware into a temp directory. Say it's called** hooey.zip.

2. **Type** split -b 1000 hooey.zip hooey.

3. **The temp directory will fill up with tons of 1,000-byte files with names like** hooeyaa, hooeyab, **etc.**

4. **Delete** hooey.zip.

5. **Reassemble your files with the** cat **command:** cat hooey* > newhooey.zip.

6. **Double-click** newhooey.zip **to bring it up in Expander. You should see an x-ray view of the archive's contents, and you can even decompress it if you want, confirming that it's possible to rip any binary file to shreds and reassemble it later with no damage to the file. It is, of course, important that the pieces be reconstructed in the same order in which they were decon- structed. This will happen automatically if you follow these steps.**

**vi**   vi is a full-fledged text editor that works from the Terminal, rather than through the GUI. While its operation is somewhat cryptic, it's not all that diffi- cult to learn. Thousands of Unix devotees swear by vi, using it for everything from writing research papers to building Web pages. While its interface is so simple that it's almost nonexistent, the vi editor is packed with power. However, only real shell junkies and Unix veterans will reap vi's benefits. For the vast majority of your needs, you may be as well served by StyledEdit or a more complete GUI text editor like Pe or Eddie. In fact, it's incredibly easy to launch a file into StyledEdit from the command line—just type StyledEdit filename. On the other hand, becoming adept at using vi means you have one less reason to jump out to the GUI when you're busy working in the Terminal, and vi gurus claim to be able to work more quickly and fluidly in vi than in just about any GUI editor. Of course, people who claim that often have a third cranial lobe not found in the brains of mere mortals like you and me.

If you're interested in learning vi, perhaps the best way is to use its built-in help file. To access vi's help, type vi into the Terminal. Once it's open, type :h and then press Enter (F1 will also take you straight to help at any time;

## *Crunching Numbers*

Having the power to crunch mountains of text is great, but from time to time you may find your-self with the need to crunch a few numbers as well. No problem—just pull up the shell's trusty calculator, expr. It works with standard mathematical notation, just like the kind you learned in high school. If you type in:

```
expr 455 + 88
```

the shell returns 543.

Spaces are very important when using expr—make sure all of your digits and operators are sep-arated by spaces or you'll receive error messages. Say you type in:

```
expr ( 89 - 78 ) * 3
```

Oops! The shell returns an error. Why? Because the parentheses and the * wildcard are special characters as far as bash is concerned, and need to be escaped. Try this instead:

```
expr \( 89 - 78 \) \* 3
```

 ***Advanced Calculations*** **Unfortunately, expr is only capable of returning results in pure integer values. That means, for instance, that you can divide 4 by 2, but you'll get incor-rect results if you try to divide 4 by 3. If you need more calculating power at the com-mand line, download the tiny becalc program from BeWare. Install the becalc binary in ~/config/bin, and you'll get correct results from commands like:**

```
becalc 4/3
```

**becalc is capable of handling very sophisticated mathematical and scientific expres-sions, in case you want to use BeOS for your trigonometry homework.**

If you've got variables stored in the shell, you can insert them at any point in your calculations. Let's say you're looping through a script and one of your variables (we'll call it $n) is increment-ing by 1 with each pass through the loop. In the script, you might use a statement like:

```
n=`expr $n +1`
```

to increment the value of n (there are easier ways to increment values in scripts, but this is how you would do it with expr). Later on, you can stuff whatever the current value of n is into an equation:

```
expr \( $n - 78 \) \* 3
```

type :q to leave help). Use your arrow keys to scroll around among the pre-sented topics and Ctrl+] to select one. Here's a rundown of a few of the most basic vi operations.

vi operates in three modes: command mode, edit mode, and ex mode. When you're in command mode, you can press a number of (typically) one-letter commands to manipulate text under the cursor. When in edit mode, you can enter new text. In ex mode, you can type commands into the bottom line of the editor to perform sophisticated text manipulations, open, close, and save files, and the like.

Launch a file into vi by typing vi filename. You will be in command mode. To begin editing the file, hit the I key (for insert) or the A key (for append). You'll be in edit mode, and can now type normally or use the arrow keys to navigate up and down or side to side. Ctrl+F and Ctrl+B will move you forward and backward through the file one screen at a time. To exit edit mode and enter ex mode, hit the Esc key and then the : (colon) key. Your cursor will appear at the bottom of the editor, awaiting your command. Let's try some ex commands.

To find a text string, type a slash (/) followed by your search string and another slash into vi's command line and hit Enter. Your cursor will jump to the first instance of that string and place you back in command mode. To find the next instance, hit the N key. To search and replace on a particular string, return to ex mode by hitting Esc again, and use the syntax:

```
:s/SearchString/ReplaceString
```

## GeekGadgets

What? The huge collection of command-line tools bundled with BeOS isn't enough for you? Take heart—there are many more ports of common Unix-based tools and utilities available than what shows up on your BeOS installation CD. A community of hardcore users headed up by Be shell guru Fred Fish maintains an ever-growing archive of such tools under the name GeekGadgets, available for free download from **ftp.ninemoons.com/pub/geekgadgets**.

There you'll find tons of slightly more esoteric, high-powered tools such as the Tcl scripting language, the most recent version of perl, indent, flex, and dozens more. You'll also find updates of many of the tools already bundled with BeOS, in case you find yourself in need of the latest version of something.

The GeekGadgets tools can be downloaded as source code or as compiled binaries for both PowerPC and x86 platforms. If you're new to bash, chances are pretty slim that you'll find anything here of interest, but shell junkies will revel in the GeekGadgets gold mine.

At this writing, the documentation that accompanied GeekGadgets referred to installation on the Amiga platform, and was less than clear on how to go about installing them on BeOS. By the time you read this, Fish intends to have worked out a user-friendly BeOS installation method that will make installation of GeekGadgets a breeze. But just in case, here's a crash course on adding GeekGadgets tools to your system manually.

1. Create a GeekGadgets subdirectory in /boot/apps.

To globalize your search-and-replace operation, follow it with the g flag:

```
:s/SearchString/ReplaceString/g
```

All search-and-replace operations are based on regular expressions, so they can be as simple or as complex as you require.

To delete the line you're on, press dd while in command mode. Deleted text is actually placed on the clipboard-like "buffer" (not to be confused with the BeOS clipboard), so you can now navigate to another location in the document and use P to paste the line back in. To delete 12 lines at a time, use 12dd instead.

To save the current file, enter ex mode and type w. To quit, type q. To quit without saving, follow the q with an exclamation point: q!

This brief introduction doesn't even scratch vi's surface; there's almost nothing you can't do with vi, though it may take a little practice and an hour or two spent with vi's built-in documentation. If you want my opinion, though, this is a role better served by the available GUI editors.

2. Save the code below as a text file located at /boot/apps/GeekGadgets/etc/gg-startup.sh:

```
#! /bin/sh
### GeekGadgets  ###
export GG=/boot/apps/GeekGadgets
export PATH=$GG/bin:$GG/X11R6.3/bin:$PATH
export LIBRARY_PATH=$GG/X11R6.3/lib:$LIBRARY_PATH
export C_INCLUDE_PATH=$GG/include
export SHELL=$GG/bin/bash
export CONFIG_SHELL=$GG/bin/bash
export BELIBRARIES=$BELIBRARIES:$GG/lib
```

3. Open your ~/.profile or ~/config/boot/UserSetupEnvironment and add the following line:

```
source /boot/apps/GeekGadgets/etc/gg-startup.sh
```

Save and close these files, then type source .profile into the shell to make the new environment variables take hold. Essentially, what you've done here is to create a new file containing environment variables specific to GeekGadgets, and invoked that file from .profile. By doing it this way, you decouple GG variables from the rest of your system variables, so you can remove them from your path and system memory at any time by removing the source line from .profile.

To install individual GeekGadgets programs, download them from **ftp.ninemoons.com** directly into /boot/apps/GeekGadgets (or move them there after downloading to your usual location), then double-click to let Expander decompress them. It's important that they live in this location, and that you decompress all GG tools from your GG root. You can install as little or as much of GeekGadgets as you like.

vi may be among the most popular command-line text editors, but it isn't the only one; nor is it the easiest to learn. For alternatives, search around on BeWare for editors with names like pico, joe, and jove. Each of them has its own set of strengths and weaknesses, and may prove easier to learn and use than vi. However, vi is "grandfathered in"—it's an entrenched standard that you'll find common references to (and documentation for) in just about every Unix-related book ever published.

**emacs** Another extremely popular command-line editor is the infamous emacs—one of the most bloated applications ever developed for use in the shell. emacs has been extended with so many advanced capabilities over the years that some people almost treat it as if it were the shell itself. People have found ways to use emacs as an email client, a Web browser, and a high-powered turnip grater. Because emacs is not preinstalled with BeOS, we won't cover it here. It is, however, available as part of the GeekGadgets toolset (see the sidebar *GeekGadgets*), though the BeOS implementation of emacs was not 100% stable as of this writing.

If you have an existing relationship with emacs hotkeys, remember that some of the more advanced GUI editors (such as Pe) employ emacs key bindings so you can continue working as if you were in emacs, but with the added advantages the GUI environment provides.

**sed** sed (short for "stream editor") is unique among text editors because it has no interface whatsoever. It performs its operations by "streaming" through text files, running a series of commands on them and saving the altered files, all without ever displaying a single line of text or hint of an interface. If you've ever done hours of tedious handwork on a text file (or group of files), wished there were a way to search and replace the task to completion, tried in vain, given up, and returned to hand-massaging, it might be time to take a look at sed. Like most command-line tools that deal with text, sed uses regular expressions to get its work done. sed commands can be run one a time, or added to a text file to create a script. This command:

```
sed s/pattern/string/g < file1 > file2
```

will hand the contents of file1 to sed as standard input, replace every instance of "pattern" with "string," and output the results to file2. The s at the start of the command tells sed it's going to be running a substitution, while the g at the end of the command specifies that the substitution will be run globally (for every found instance in the referenced files). sed can also be useful when you need to delete specific lines from your output. For example, when you use the BeOS query engine from the command line (see Chapter 7, *Working with Queries*), files that are in the Trash are returned as part of the query results (even though the GUI query tool ignores the Trash by default). If you want to make sure that trashed files don't appear in your results, you can filter a query through sed with the /d (for delete) option:

```
query [your query here] | sed /Trash/d
```

 ***Remember to Escape!*** **As described earlier in this chapter, you must always take care to escape characters that have special meaning to the shell if you want them to be interpreted literally. You'll probably end up doing quite a bit of escaping in your sed commands. If sed commands don't work at first, take a second look at the string you're searching on and ask yourself whether it contains any of the following characters:**

**{} ( ) ! # $ % ^ & * ? / < > ~**

**or the space character. If so, remember to precede them with a backslash (\\).**

**Match Letters and Numbers Only**  Here are a few examples of techniques you can use to search on arbitrary strings of numbers and letters, with fine-grained control over exactly which characters get included in the search pattern.

```
sed s/[a-f]/z/g < oldphone > newphone
```

replaces all lowercase letters between "a" and "f" with the letter "z".

```
sed s/[a-f3-7]/z/g < oldphone > newphone
```

replaces all lowercase letters between "a" and "f" and all numbers between 3 and 7 with the letter "z".

```
sed s/[a-zA-Z]/z/g < oldphone > newphone
```

replaces all letters (both lowercase and uppercase) with the letter "z".

Let's say you've got a file full of phone numbers that looks like this:

```
<file 1>
Name -- Nickname -- # is 555.555.555
Larry Smith -- Toad -- # is 510.555.0498
Annie Stevens -- Diva -- # is 314.555.9283
etc.
```

and you want it to look like this:

```
<file 2>
Name - 555.555.555
Larry Smith - 510.555.0498
Annie Stevens - 314.555.9283
etc.
```

There are several things to take into consideration here. For one, you're going to have to escape all of those spaces and # signs. Second, the names you're searching on aren't known strings—they're collections of letters of indeterminate length and mixed case. To trap those, you'll need to use the bracketed syntax [a-zA-Z] to trap all letters regardless of case and follow it with a ★ wildcard to make sure you get as many letters in a row as apply on each line of the file. Finally, you'll need to make sure those letters fall between two sets of double-dashes and a space. All those escape sequences can make the command look a little hairy, but once it's constructed properly, you'll be able to get your job done in a flash, saving yourself minutes or hours of handwork. Here's the complete command:

```
sed s/--\ [a-zA-Z]*\ --\ \#\ is/-/g < oldphone > newphone
```

And remember—you can get around all of that escaping by surrounding entire strings in strong quotes, as shown below.

```
sed s/'-- [a-zA-Z]* -- # is'/-/g < oldphone > newphone
```

Try that in Microsoft Word! And don't forget, you can do this on hundreds of files at once if you like by using appropriate wildcard filters as input rather than a single filename. Embedding multiple sed commands in a script isn't as simple as creating a bunch of lines like the examples above; sed scripts have their own syntax. We won't cover that syntax here, but suffice it to say that you can do some pretty incredible text processing with sed scripts. If you want to learn more about sed, see the *Learning More* section at the end of this chapter.

## Quick Access to Long Commands

Let's say that something about the project you're working on requires you to run the sed command above several times a day. You could go digging through your history list for it every time, but this one is used frequently enough to deserve its own hotkey.

We've touched on the convenience of using aliases elsewhere in this book, but here you can really see how an alias would make your life much easier. Try this:

```
alias phone="sed s/--\ [a-zA-Z]*\ --\ \#\ is/-/g < oldphone > newphone"
```

Now all you have to do to run your sed command is type phone into the Terminal. If you want this to be available to you at all times, just add the line above to your /boot/home/.profile. Of course, you can set up aliases for anything you do frequently, from logging into your FTP site to compiling programs.

Here's another good one. The cp and mv commands (for copying and moving files) are a little dangerous. By default, they'll overwrite any files with the same name as the one you specify as part of the command, without prompting you for confirmation first. If you'd like a little more insurance against slip-ups, set up these aliases permanently in your .profile:

```
alias cp="cp -i"
alias mv="mv -i"
alias rm="rm -i"
```

From now on, the shell will prompt you before rm, cp, or mv go bulldozing your existing files.

**sort**   One of the simplest text-manipulation utilities on your system is the sort command, which is capable of reading the lines of an input file and arranging them alphabetically or numerically, in either ascending or descending order. Using our phone list example again, typing sort oldphone > newphone would generate a file called newphone with Annie's name listed before Larry's. To go the other direction (i.e. to sort in reverse order), use the -r flag. Remember that you can combine commands with other commands to get customized results. If you had a giant unsorted phone list and just wanted to see the 25 entries that came first alphabetically, you could use the pipe to join your sort with the head command:

```
sort oldphone | head -25
```

**awk**   A tool with certain parallels to sed, but important differences, is called awk (some people say that "awk!" is the sound you make when you see its syntax, but it's really not all that bad). awk lets you treat any text file as if it were a database, and to refer to its fields by column. Like sed, awk can be run either as a command from the shell prompt or as a sequence of commands embedded in an awk script. Scripts can have conditionals, loops, and other common programming structures that can be strung together to transform text files into all kinds of custom, field-based output formats. Let's look at our phone file example again, but from the awk perspective.

In awk, each field is numbered from 1 to however many fields occur before the end of a line. To refer to a field, just use $n, where n is the field's number. Since awk can print directly to standard output, we can get a list of, say, just the nicknames in our phone book by using something like this:

```
awk '{ print $4 }' oldphone
```

This command goes through the file and prints the fourth field on every line, spitting out a list of nicknames.

By default, awk assumes that the fields of your text-file-cum-database are separated by spaces. If you want to use a different field delimiter, use the -F flag, followed by the delimiting character. The following command specifies that fields are delimited by colons:

```
awk -F: '{ print $4 }' oldphone
```

To trap the output to a file, use the > redirect operator:

```
awk '{ print $4 }' oldphone > newphone
```

To get the same exact output we got from our sed command, we would just name the desired field numbers in order:

```
awk '{ print $1 " " $2 " - " $8 " " $9 }' oldphone > newphone
```

Interestingly, we can easily interpolate any extra text we like into the print string by surrounding it with quotes. Content contained within quotes, by the way, is always escaped automatically in awk. In other words, any of the special characters noted in the sidebar *Escaping Special Characters* do not need to be escaped with backslashes when they appear inside of quotes. The command

```
awk '{ print $1 " " $2 " - long distance - " $8 " " $9 }' oldphone > newphone
```

will give us output that looks like this:

```
Larry Smith - long distance - (510) 555-0498
Annie Stevens - long distance - (314) 555-9283
```

 Even when surrounding text in quotes, you'll still need to watch for certain characters to prevent the shell from treating them as commands. For instance, if your quoted string includes any ! characters, use \! instead.

awk is a deep and powerful language, and when used in its script mode is capable of solving huge text- and data-manipulation problems. Consult a Unix tools manual for more information.

**cut** Sometimes your problem is more pedestrian, and all you need to do is extract a single field from the columns of a text file. The cut command exists to do just that: count in x number of fields from the beginning of each line and extract the data from there until the next field. An obvious question here is how to define the delimiter between fields. By default the delimiter is a tab, but if your file doesn't include tabs, you can define any *single-character* delimiter you want by using the -d flag. In our sample file, the only thing we have to go on is the space character. Therefore,

```
cut -d" " -f4 oldphone > newphone
```

will parse the input file as though every space character represented a new field, and then return the fourth field in each line. In other words, we get a list of nicknames. It's important that you leave no space between the -d flag and the delimiter.

**Word Counting with wc** If you're a writer or reporter dealing with strict word counts, you need to monitor your word count constantly as you work. The wc command will do this for you, and has three simple options: -w for word count, -l for line count, and -c for byte count. To count the number of words in oldphone, simply use wc -w oldphone.

The -l option has the excellent side effect of letting you count all kinds of elements. For example, to learn the number of files in the current directory, try this:

```
ls | wc -l
```

Note that if you use ls -l instead of just ls here, your count will be one too high, since the shell includes a summary report when you use the -l flag. If you want to count the number of files in the current directory and all of its subdirectories, use the find command instead:

```
find . -type f | wc -l
```

***Parsing Web Logs with wc*** By combining wc with grep, you can easily find the number of instances of a given string in any text file. One really useful application of this capability is to quickly find out how many times a particular Web page was accessed over the period covered by one of your Web logs. Let's say you have a BeOS-related page on your site, and every reference to it in your logs contains the string "/beos/about.html." Assuming the log file is called weblog.log, you can count the number of "hits" on that page by typing:

```
grep "/beos/about.html" weblog.log | wc -l
```

If you'd like to keep track of multiple Web pages, add several such commands to a text file and save it as a shell script. Talk about the power of the command line! Try and get similar information out of a text file from within MacOS or Windows without importing your logs into a database first!

**Formatting with fmt** In most word processors, the text you type "wraps" down to the next line as soon as your cursor hits the right margin. As far as the computer is concerned, a paragraph is just one long line, even though it's displayed with virtual breaks at the right margin. When you resize the window, the wrapping changes to accommodate the new width. This is known as "soft wrapping." Any time you hit Enter, though, an actual hard return is inserted into the file, and will be preserved even when you open the same file in another editor. This is known as "hard wrapping." In some cases, it's helpful to be able to create documents with lines that hard-wrap at certain line lengths, rather than soft wrapping. Rather than insert hundreds or thousands of hard returns automatically, you can hard-wrap a file from the command line with the fmt command:

```
fmt -w 50 file1 > file2
```

This command will hard-wrap every line in file1 at 50 characters and create a new file from the standard output as file2. fmt will also let you create files where each line is indented from the left margin the same amount as the first word in that paragraph. For instance, if the first word of this paragraph were indented one tab stop and I ran this command on it:

```
fmt -c -w 50 file1
```

## *Using Shell Commands from the GUI*

If you use a programmer's editor such as Pe or Eddie, you can execute many shell commands directly from inside your documents. This lets you do things like launch applications, get directory listings, control threads and processes, find out how much disk space is remaining on your volumes, or anything else you can do from the command line. In Pe, type any shell command and hit Alt+Enter. In Eddie, type a command and press Enter.

The nice thing about this method is that it keeps all of your recent commands stored right there at the top of the document so you can go back and edit them easily without having to use the shell's history function. Both editors also include "worksheets" for just this purpose. The worksheet pops up automatically when you launch the editor, and retains your commands from the last session so you can easily pick up where you left off. You can also use this feature to eliminate the need to redirect the output of commands into text documents. Since the output spills automatically into the current document, all you have to do is issue the command directly. If you're happy with the results, just pull down File | Save and you're done.

One of the ways I used this functionality in Pe while writing this book was to include the following line at the top of each chapter:

```
wc -w /boot/home/words/bible/'Chapter xx'/ChapterName
```

That way, anytime I needed a word count I could hit Ctrl+Home to jump to the top of the document, then Alt+Enter to get a word count. Note that when you're in the GUI, the shell doesn't know the full path of your current document. Therefore, you'll need to include fully qualified paths in all filename invocations when using this method.

In Pe, you can do this from within any document; but in Eddie, this technique only works in "Worksheet" documents by default. To enable this for other Eddie documents, pull down Settings | Shell Window, or click the second blank square on the toolbar. A seashell icon will appear to indicate that the document is shell-mode enabled.

my output would look like this:

```
This command will hard-wrap every line in file 1
at 50 characters and create a new file from the
standard output as file2. fmt will also let you
create files where each line is indented from
the left margin the same amount as the
first word in that paragraph. For instance, if
the first word of this paragraph were indented
one tab stop and I ran this command on it:
```

Note that no lines in this example are longer than 50 characters.

On the other hand, you can turn this "column narrowing" technique inside out, to undo pre-wrapped files. When you receive a document that already has line feeds placed every 72 characters (or whatever) and want to bring it into your text editor, you're likely to find the pre-coded line widths a nuisance, and either remove them all by hand or devise some kind of macro to do it for you. This situation, by the way, happens any time you want to make a document out of an email message, since most mail clients hard-wrap lines at a preestablished width. To unwrap such a document, all you need to do is run it through fmt with an impossibly wide line length. For example:

```
fmt -w 10000 BigHonkinDocWithHardWraps > NewlyManageableDoc
```

By setting the margins to 10,000 characters, you essentially make every paragraph into a single line, which allows your word processor or text editor's own soft-wrapping feature to take over. Another common GUI problem solved with a few keystrokes to the Terminal.

## Communing with the Shell

The power of the shell doesn't stop with the execution of straight commands; it's also able to accept user input, run "subshells," process variables imported from elsewhere in the system, and more. Here we dip very close to the territory of scripting, which is covered in depth online at **http://www.beosbible .com**. However, a few of the basic notions of extended shell control are worth covering here, as they have uses apart from scripts.

**Environment Variables**   The shell stores a handful of permanent variables that define the parameters of your working environment. For example, you've noticed that when you run the ls -l command, it appears that all of your files are owned by a mysterious user named "baron." This username is established in the /boot/beos/system/boot/SetupEnvironment file, which is read into system memory at boot time.

*Dissing Baron*  **If you'd rather have your own name appear as the owner of your files rather than Baron's, open the file** /boot/home/config/boot/ UserSetupEnvironment **and add a line reading:**

export USER=myname

**replacing "myname" with any name you like. Save the file, type** source ~/ config/boot/UserSetupEnvironment, **and try** ls -l **again—you'll now be the rightful owner of your own files. You can also change the group name associated with your files by adding:**

export GROUP=mygroupname

**By adding these entries to the user-level** SetupEnvironment **file in the** home **hierarchy, you will override the entries defining Baron's name in the system-level version of this file. See the warning below: Don't edit the system-level** SetupEnvironment **script.**

## Who the Hell Is Baron, and Why Does He Own My Files?

*Someone* had to own your files! Baron Arnold is Be's main QA engineer, and he gets the honor because Dominic Giampaolo (author of the BFS filesystem) "gave" the files to Baron as a birthday present one year. Baron is also the author of the virtual(void) audio clip you'll find in the optional sounds folder on your BeOS installation CD. Check out more of Baron's audio explorations at: **www.catastropherecords.com**.

Until BeOS is a multiuser system, it may seem like a bit of an oxymoron that users and groups even exist in BeOS. However, BeOS's bash is a port of Unix's bash, so file ownership pretty much had to come along for the ride. Plus, by instituting users and groups now, BeOS becomes forward-compatible with future versions of the operating system, which *will* be multiuser.

A similar thing happens with commonly used directory paths on the system. Every time you type a command, the shell needs to find the file that makes that command run. If you're currently in your home directory and the ls command lives in /boot/beos/bin, the system can't very well go running all over your hard drive looking for the file that makes ls command do its stuff. Instead, BeOS will look in a series of directories specified in the $PATH environment variable. Since one of the directories stored in the $PATH variable is /boot/beos/bin, the ls command is found and runs properly. If BeOS looks in all directories specified in $PATH and still doesn't find a file with that name, it will return a "command not found" error. For more on making changes to your path, see the sidebar *Tweaking Your Path*.

Environment variables are available to the shell at all times, and are initially established during the boot process when the /boot/beos/system/boot/ SetupEnvironment script is run, and augmented when ~/config/boot/ UserSetupEnvirnoment is run (if it exists).

To see all of your currently established environment variables, type set | more.

 ***Don't Edit the System-Level SetupEnvironment Script*** If you want to make changes to your environment variables, don't edit the system-level SetupEnvironment script. Instead, take a look in /boot/home/config/boot and you'll find a file called UserSetupEnvironment.sample. Copy this file as UserSetupEnvironment in the same directory and make your changes to this file. Any parameters you establish here that do not appear in the system-level file will be added to the system's collection of environment variables. Note that any parameters you set up that conflict with the system's collection will override them. In other words, the proper way to override the system's default variables is not to edit the system-level script, but to provide replacements for those variables in your user-level script, which is loaded *after* the system's script. Editing the system-level SetupEnvironment script in /boot/beos/system/boot can cause unpredictable results.

## Tweaking Your Path

Whenever you type a command into the shell, the shell looks for a program or script of the same name in the current directory. If it doesn't find one, it begins to scan the directories listed in its current path statement, which is an amalgamation of the path statements found in `/boot/beos/system/boot/SetupEnvironment` and `/boot/home/config/boot/UserSetupEnvironment`.

It's very important that if you go to edit your path, you don't accidentally overwrite it in the process. If you want to add the directory /boot/home/projects to your current path, do it by appending that directory to the current path statement, like this:

export PATH=$PATH:/boot/home/projects

By including $PATH:, you are first copying the entire contents of the current path, and *then* adding your modifications to it. If you leave out $PATH, you will *replace* the current path with the addition, and will no longer be able to use any of the shell commands lying in the now wiped-out path.

By prefacing the new path statement with the export command, you are saying to the shell that this variable should be available to anything that occurs in the current instance of the shell. It does not, however, make these variables available to other open Terminal windows. If you want the new variables to be stored in global memory, available to all Terminal sessions, all scripts, and all commands, you'll need to add the new export command to your UserSetupEnvironment (or .profile), as described above.

Why would you want to make changes to your path statement? You might be storing programs or scripts in a test directory that you want to be accessible from any point in the filesystem, but not want to place your test programs in one of the usual permanent storage locations until they've been perfected. Similarly, you may have some data files that you want to be accessible to your programs and scripts. By adding the path to the directory where your data files are stored, you ensure that your programs and scripts will be able to find them even if the programs don't have the data paths hard-coded into them.

### Directories in the Default Path

The following directories are in BeOS's default path:

*   /boot/home/config/bin
*   /bin (a.k.a. /boot/beos/bin via the symlink in the root directory)
*   /boot/apps
*   /boot/preferences
*   /boot/apps/Metrowerks/tools
*   /boot/beos/apps
*   /boot/beos/preferences

Note that /boot/home/config/bin is the best place to store scripts and binaries that you've downloaded or created yourself—always keep user-level and system-level directories separate when possible!

### UserSetupEnvironment versus .profile

By now you will have noticed that some Terminal customizations are accomplished by editing /boot/home/.profile, while others are accomplished by editing /boot/home/config/boot/UserSetupEnvironment. So what's the diff? Good question. In fact, most options can be set in either file. The key difference is that UserSetupEnvironment is read into system memory while your system is booting and the parameters it establishes are available system-wide, while .profile is read into memory only when a Terminal window is opened. Think of UserSetupEnvironment as working at a "deeper" level, and being used to store variables that affect the system globally. Since .profile lives in your home directory, it's a little easier to access, but the bottom line is that it ultimately doesn't matter much which file you use to establish customizations. Personally, I like to keep all environment variables in UserSetupEnvironment, while all of my aliases and prompt customizations go into .profile. If you come from the DOS world, you can sort of compare .profile to autoexec.bat, and UserSetupEnvironment to config.sys, though the analogy breaks when pressed too hard.

**echo**   Any time you want the shell to report the value of a variable back to standard out, you can use the echo command to request it. To learn your current path, type:

echo $PATH

Similarly, if you've set up a custom, or localized, variable for use in this session only, type:

echo $MyVariableName

The $ symbol always means "the value of whatever comes next."

 If you use echo to get the value of any nonexistent variable, the shell returns a blank line rather than an error message. For example, echo $FOOBAR will return a blank line, even if you've never declared a value for FOOBAR. Don't be misled by typos!

**Localized Variables**   In addition to globally available environment variables, it's also possible to create variables that are available only to the current Terminal session. While localized variables are of the most importance when you're working with scripts, there are a few occasions when they can be useful in a nonscripting context. For example, let's say you need to quickly determine the Unix date/time format number for a date one year in the past (see the date section below). You only need this number one time, so there's no point in writing a script to do the job. You'll need to take the following steps:

1. Determine the Unix date right now and save it as a variable called Now.

2. Determine how many seconds are in a Unix year and save it as a second variable called YearAgo.

3. Subtract YearAgo from Now.

Before you can run this series of commands, you need to know how to store and retrieve variables in the shell. In order to define a new variable, simply type its name and assign it a default value via the = operator, like so:

```
MyTemp=hello
```

You can test that your new variable has been accepted by typing echo $MyTemp (note that your new variable applies only to the current Terminal window— open a new Terminal session, and you'll find that echo $MyTemp will return nothing).

## Assign the Results of a Command to a Variable

As described earlier in this chapter, it can be convenient to work with variables that represent the outcome of some command. For example, you might want to create a variable called Dir that equals the name of the current working directory. Since the command pwd prints the working directory, you could use:

```
Dir=$(pwd)
```

From then on, $Dir would stand in for a text string reflecting the current working directory, at the time the variable was set.

So to store the current date/time as a variable called Now, you'd use:

```
Now=$(date +%s)
```

To retrieve the value of Now, you use echo $Now. Thus, your Terminal session might look something like this:

```
Now=$(date +%s)
YearAgo=$(expr 60 \* 60 \* 24 \* 365)
echo "One year ago today the Unix time was " $(expr $Now - $YearAgo)
```

Note that in the second command, each of the * symbols here are escaped with backslashes so that bash doesn't mistake them for wildcards. In the third command, we enclose our mathematical expression in parentheses and preface it with $ in order to evaluate the whole thing as a single entity.

**read**    The shell can also read in variables "on the fly," by accepting strings typed into the shell after the read command. Type in:

```
read MyTemp
```

After you hit Enter, the shell will pause until you type something and press Enter again. echo $MyTemp will report back the string the user typed in response to the read command. read is primarily of use in building interactive scripts.

**sleep**    The standard output of some commands produces huge amounts of text, which of course flies by on the screen far too quickly to be read. You can intentionally slow down the flow of commands by using the sleep command to tell the shell to "go to sleep" for a specified number of seconds, minutes, hours, or days after each line of output. The syntax of sleep is simply sleep followed by the number and type of units. For example:

```
sleep 10s (10 seconds)
sleep 22m (22 minutes)
sleep 7h (7 hours)
sleep 31d (31 days)
```

## Miscellany

There are many ways to control your system, gather critical data, and otherwise interact with the BeOS environment from the command line. A few important commands that don't fit into the categories above are touched upon briefly here.

**date**    Simply typing date into the Terminal will generate a line of text reporting the exact date and time. There are actually quite a few parameters you can use with the date command to control the exact output format. For example:

- date +%e tells you the day of the month
- date +%b reports the abbreviated month name
- date +%W returns the week number in the year (1–52)
- date +%A tells you the day of the week
- date +%H gives you the hour in 24-hour format
- date +%s returns the number of seconds since 1/1/1970

You can, of course, string these together however you like. By using these options in combination with %n and %t for newlines and tabs, you can create a handsome, customized date display. For instance, try putting this in your .profile:

```
date +"Holy cow! Today is %t %A %b %e %Y %n and it's already %t %R"
```

Every time you launch a new Terminal you'll be reminded how late it is. You can find the complete list of % arguments accepted by date by typing date --help.

To set the date use this exact format:

date 062307301998

in which the first two digits are the month, the second two are the date, the next four are the time in 24-hour format, and the last four are the year. The example above translates to 7:30 A.M. on June 23, 1998. Of course, you can set your system's date and time much more easily from the Time preferences applet, but you may find precise control over time and date formats useful in home-brewed shell scripts (scripting is covered in depth online at **www.beosbible.com**).

**du** If you need to find out how much disk space is being occupied by all the files in a directory structure, the du (disk usage) command is your ticket. While you can get this kind of information from the Tracker by right-clicking a folder and choosing Get Info from the context menu, this is the only way to get a fully detailed report of the cumulative totals for every subdirectory in a given hierarchy. Not only that, but by monitoring disk usage from the Terminal, you can easily redirect your reports to text files for archiving, monitoring, emailing, etc. Or if your ISP allows you only a limited amount of disk space on their Web server and you keep your site mirrored on a BeOS partition, you can use du to monitor the site's total size.

By default, du crawls the directory tree from the current point down as far as it can go, and reports the number of filesystem blocks being used. Note that if your partition was initialized using the default of 1,024 bytes per block, a block reading is equivalent to a reading of the number of kilobytes. To force du to report back in kilobytes, use the -k flag. If you'd rather have an exact byte count, use du -b instead. To have du count individual file sizes, not just directory totals, use the -a flag. If the directory tree contains any symlinks, make sure du doesn't follow them with -D (dereference). Thus, to get a report of all file sizes and directory totals in the hierarchy of your Web site mirror directory MySite, and make sure that du doesn't follow your symlinks, you'd use:

du —b —a —D /boot/home/MySite

If you can do without the detailed reporting and just want a simple total, use the -s flag to "summarize."

***Stopping Processes in the Terminal*** If you run du from the root, it's going to take a while to run—probably too long. While it's running, you're going to lose control of the Terminal until the process is complete and the Terminal returns you to a shell prompt. Any time you want to halt a process that's apparently going to take longer than you want to wait, just hit Ctrl+C and the task should come to an immediate halt.

If you know beforehand that the process is going to take a while, place an ampersand after your command, like this: du & . The process will go ahead and do its thing, but it will do it in the background, out of your way, and you can continue to work normally on other projects. Of course, you wouldn't want to run a job in the background if you were counting on seeing the screen output of something like a directory listing. In that case, it's best to redirect the output to a new file so you can study the results later, at your leisure.

If you prefer to get this information graphically, there are several utilities available on BeWare that serve as graphical interfaces for du, with fancy bar charts and other bells and whistles.

**df** You've already met the df (disk free) command in Chapter 5, *Files and the Tracker*. This invaluable tool will let you know at a glance exactly how much space is available on every volume attached to your system. At the same time, it's the easiest way to quickly discover where on your IDE or SCSI chains each of your volumes is mounted.

**shutdown** Did you know that you can actually shut down your system from the command line? Simply typing shutdown will initiate a normal system shutdown. If you have unsaved data in any open applications, you will be prompted to save your documents before proceeding with the shutdown. If you'd like a little grace period before the shutdown begins, use the -d flag, specifying the number of seconds to wait:

```
shutdown -d 120
```

will wait two minutes, then begin the shutdown process. If you'd like your system to reboot after shutting down, use the -r flag. If you want to be ornery about it, use the -q flag to shut down immediately, without being prompted to save work in your open applications.

**uptime** While you won't find an uptime binary on your system by default, it's a good one to download from BeWare. Type uptime at any Terminal prompt find out how long your system's been alive without rebooting. You can use this number to win system stability arguments with your MacOS and Windows friends. And remember—as of R4, uptime information is also displayed in the About BeOS panel accessed from the Be menu.

**/dev/null** This directory, which exists only in memory (not on your hard disk), is also known by such endearing appellations as The Great Bit Bucket and The Black Hole. Why? Because anything you send to it disappears into the void forever. For example:

```
ls -l > /dev/null
```

does absolutely nothing whatsoever. The output of the command is eaten up, destroyed, nullified. How could this possibly be useful? Beats me. Seriously, though, you may come across a tool or utility that spits out voluminous amounts of useless data that you'd rather it just kept to itself. Redirecting its output to /dev/null will make sure you don't see a single byte.

**ps** Technically speaking, BeOS does not run processes in the same sense that Unix machines do (a group of BeOS threads working together as a "team" is equivalent to a Unix process). However, BeOS does use the Unix ps command to generate a listing of all currently running threads. The last lines of the ps report will tell you how much physical memory is installed in your machine and how much of that memory is currently in use.

## Why Is So Much Memory Being Used?

People are often surprised when they see how much memory is being used just by the system alone, before applications have even been opened. How can such a lean operating system consume so much memory? This initial shock is understandable, considering what a critical measure of system efficiency available memory is on most operating systems.

However, BeOS uses a very different memory model than do other systems. Because virtual memory usage is treated by the system as a part of main memory, it's almost impossible to distinguish how much of the memory reported as being in use is actually residing in a chunk of your swap file. Therefore, this number does not really provide any useful information, and is in fact quite misleading. That's why Be removed memory reportage from early versions of the Pulse application.

In addition, because of the way in which BeOS uses memory, the system is working at peak efficiency when it's using as much RAM as it can. A high number doesn't mean the system "needs" all of that RAM to get its work done, but rather that it knows how to avail itself most efficiently of the resources at its disposal. Your RAM is there to be used, and that's exactly what BeOS is doing with it—loading as much code as possible into memory so it can perform optimally no matter what you request from it next, without having to scoop more code off your hard disk first. And just because memory is reported as being "in use" doesn't mean that it's unavailable to applications that need it. For example, when you shut down an application, the memory it was using becomes available to other applications, even though an image of that app remains in memory. In other words, reports of available memory in BeOS are misleading by definition, and therefore practically useless.

**sysinfo** Type sysinfo into the Terminal and you'll get back a brief summary of the current state of your system, including the number of processors, amount of installed RAM, and a bunch of technical mumbo jumbo on available semaphores, threads, and teams that only a programmer could love. If you just want to find out whether you're using an x86 or a PPC machine, type sysinfo -platform instead. The shell will report the just the platform, without all the extra details. Of course, that's really only useful when you're telnetting into another BeOS machine, since you can usually see the machine sitting right there in front of you.

**kill** As noted earlier, you can easily winnow down the list of threads to just those in which you're interested at the moment. For instance, if your net-server has been acting up and you want to kill it off completely in order to restart it, you might want to combine the ps command with a grep operation:

```
ps | grep net
```

will return a list of just the threads running on your system that contain the string "net" in their names. Of course, this is not a 100% guarantee that you've caught them all, since it's possible that some Net-related threads might not have the string "net" in their names, but it's a pretty good bet. A typical return from this command might look like this:

```
/boot/home>ps | grep net
/boot/beos/system/servers/netserver (team 42)
   110          netserver  sem  10    2      6 AppLooperPort(1877)
   117           net main  sem  10    5    118 timeout-cancel(1948)
/bin/grep net (team 74)
```

While it may look at first like there are four Net-related threads running, note that the last thread is actually assigned to the grep operation you just ran, so that one doesn't count. Left over are two semaphores and one team (a team is a set of threads associated with one another by the application developer, while a semaphore is a token used to synchronize multiple threads). To kill them off, all you have to do is type:

```
kill 42
kill 110
kill 117
```

At this point, the chances are very slim that anything is left of the ornery net-server, and you should be able to restart it easily.

Alternatively, you can often kill entire teams at once just by typing their names:

```
kill net_server
```

**strings**  If you've ever opened up binary files or applications themselves in DiskProbe (Chapter 2, *Meet the System*), you know that they contain tons of buried text strings. The text inside an application binary, for example, includes the names of the entries in the application's pull-down menus, as well as text that appears in the program's various dialog boxes. It also includes the names of any external libraries (code depositories) that the application requires in order to run. If you type `strings filename` into the Terminal, you'll get back a (typically quite long) list of all text strings consisting of four or more characters found within the file.

Why is this useful? Because every now and then you'll encounter a file that doesn't run when double-clicked. As described in Chapter 16, *Troubleshooting and Maintenance*, this will be either because the file was compiled for a different version of BeOS (remember that R3 binaries won't run under R4!), or because the program is missing a required library. To find out whether the program is missing a library, try this (we'll assume the program in question is called FooBar):

```
strings FooBar | grep lib
```

The shell will return a list of all strings buried in the application binary that include "lib". Now all you have to do is run a few BeOS queries to determine whether those libraries exist on your system. If you find some that don't, you have your answer. Search the developer's Web site or BeWare for missing libraries, install them in `/boot/home/config/lib`, and your app should now run.

***Graphical Thread Management***  If you'd prefer to view and manage your system's threads from the GUI, there are bunches of applications you can download from the Utilities section of BeWare to do just that. Programs such as TManager, ISIS, SysR, and SystemStatus all do basically the same thing, but with slightly different interfaces.

***Restart Networking from the Terminal***  If you're like most people, when it comes time to restart the netserver, you'll do what you always do: open up the Network preferences application and click Restart. But this is a Terminal chapter, and we're not going to leave the command line. Here's how true Unix-hairy guys do it—type:

```
/boot/beos/system/boot/Netscript &
```

This will run a system script that reinitializes everything related to BeOS networking, putting you right back where you were when you booted, network-wise.

***A Better Way to Kill Threads***  Poke around on BeWare for a file called `killteam`. Unpack the archive and drop the `killteam` **binary into** `/boot/home/config/bin`. From now on, you can reduce all of the above steps to a single command:

## *Fun with Alert Boxes*

BeOS includes an "alert" function that can be used to send small dialog boxes to the screen with multiple-choice buttons. Each button can be labeled with a couple of words of plain text. The text on the clicked button is sent back to the Terminal as a response. Try this—type:

*Figure 6.06*

*A simple Terminal command will send a custom alert box to the BeOS GUI. The text on the clicked button is returned to the shell.*

```
alert "Are you sure about that?" "Yes" "No"
```

As you'll see online, these alerts can be extremely useful when used in interactive shell scripts. You can also use alerts to display reminders or other goodies at boot time. Add this line to /boot/home/config/boot/UserBootScript and you'll be greeted with a graphical fortune cookie each time you boot:

```
alert "`fortune`"
```

Note that those are backticks inside the quotes, not apostrophes! Excellently, you can also use the alert function to display dialog boxes on remote BeOS machines—to be seen by a friend, colleague, or loved one—by telnetting into the remote machine and using the alert command as described above.

So, for example, let's say you had a fight with your girlfriend last night. She's going to be home before you, and you know she always leaves her BeOS machine turned on (hey, a feller can dream …). From your machine at work, telnet into her BeOS machine and type this:

```
alert "Louise -- I'm really sorry I was such a dork last night. Will you forgive me?
If so, I'll pick up a pizza on the way home and we can watch ER." "Get stuffed" "Of
course" "Anchovies"
```

Then when she returns home, she'll see the message shown in Figure 6.07.

While the introductory statement can be as long as you like, the button choices have to be quite short to fit on a button, and unfortunately, there's an upper limit of three choices. But hey, at least you'll know whether she still loves you or not!

*Figure: 6.07*

*You can invoke BeOS alert boxes remotely, via telnet.*

killteam -s net **(replacing "net" with any appropriate string for the team you're trying to off). This will, in effect,** grep **the running processes, identify all relevant threads, and kill them for you, all in one fell swoop.** killteam **also knows how to kill teams by their application signature if you prefer (use the** -r **flag), or to limit its thread-hunts to exact matches only.** killteam **is well worth the download if you find yourself doing this often.**

***Extra Info on GUI Apps*** You've already seen how you can launch GUI applications from the command line just by typing their pathnames. Not only is this convenient if you're already in the Terminal, but many applications (not all) will spit out extra "debug" or "status" information to the Terminal when launched this way. If a GUI application is giving you problems for some reason, try launching it from the Terminal and then using it normally. You may find information waiting for you in the Terminal that will help you or the application developer determine why the app is malfunctioning.

# Learning More

If any of this is beginning to click for you, you may be eager to dig in a little deeper and start building your own custom tools. There are heaps of books on bash out there, but you can't go too far wrong with a double-header from the king of Unix documentation, O'Reilly and Associates. With one of these covering general bash concepts and procedures and the other covering the ins and outs of using Unix command-line tools, the pair of these working as a team will take you much farther down Terminal Road than has this chapter. If you want to go deeper into specific tools provided by the bash shell, you'll also find plenty of books dedicated to topics like Regular Expressions, sed and awk, and more. Remember, however, that there are a few differences between the BeOS implementation of bash and the version of bash found on traditional Unix systems, for which these books have been written. Don't be surprised if a few things don't work as advertised.

*Learning the Bash Shell*, 2nd Edition. Cameron Newham and Bill Rosenblatt
1998, 1995, O'Reilly and Associates.

*Unix in a Nutshell*. Daniel Gilly
1986, 1992, O'Reilly and Associates.

*Mastering Regular Expressions*. Jeffrey Friedl
1997, O'Reilly and Associates.

*sed & awk*, 2nd Edition. Dale Dougherty and Arnold Robbins
1997, O'Reilly and Associates.

Peachpit also has an excellent introductory reference guide, titled *Unix Visual QuickStart Guide*, by Deborah S. Ray and Eric J. Ray. Learn more about this at
`http://www.peachpit.com`

Just because I like these books, doesn't mean that others won't serve you well. Spend some time in a bookstore browsing the shelves of the Unix department. Read a little of some books, absorb, and ask yourself how easily you digested the information they contained. The Unix world has a tendency to make new users struggle far too hard to get from zero to 60.

In addition, few things you can read will be as educational as studying actual, working code. Search the Web (BeWare especially!) for bash scripts—they're nothing but a sequence of bash commands arranged in a programmatic fashion, and you should be able to at least divine the author's intentions by chewing on them one line at a time. Spend time lurking in Usenet groups such as **comp.unix.shell** or **gnu.bash.bug**, and of course you can always ask questions in **comp.sys.be.help**. Above all, experiment!

### Cyril Meurillon
#### Senior Kernel Engineer
#### Interviewed by Henry Bortman

**HB:** *Perhaps you should start by explaining what a kernel is.*

**CM:** You can look at an OS like an onion. It's made of layers, and the kernel would be the inner layers of the OS. It's the part that talks to the hardware. It's the part that provides low-level services to higher-level software, like libraries or applications. You don't want applications to deal with low-level concepts—you want to put some lipstick on that.

**HB:** *Why don't you want applications to deal with low-level concepts?*

**CM:** For a number of reasons. Because you don't want to force every developer to have knowledge of the inner implementation of the hardware—because it's not practical. You cannot force everybody to read a 2,000-page book. You want your system to be hardware-independent, more or less platform-independent. Of course, at some levels, there are dependencies. But this way, for example, we could easily port BeOS from PowerPC to Intel. It required an application recompile, but no application source had to be modified. Actually, very little had to be modified.

**HB:** *Did you have to rewrite the kernel for Intel?*

**CM:** Yes. That's the part that suffers in the port. Hopefully, the kernel is organized nicely enough so that only certain layers have to be rewritten and, actually, that was the case. But only the parts at the lowest level, deeper in the onion, have to be rewritten—the ones that talk directly to the hardware.

**HB:** *So, you've written the kernel twice then—or three times, actually?*

**CM:** It's not only me. I'm part of the kernel team. But, some parts of the kernel had to be written a number of times. Remember that initially we were on the Hobbit. So, going from the Hobbit to PowerPC, it had to be ported, and going from PowerPC to the x86 architecture, it had to be ported again.

**HB:** *Were you involved in writing the kernel for the Hobbit as well?*

**CM:** Yes. I've been involved with Be for … well, essentially since it started in '91. It was created in '90, but things really started in '91. I worked as an intern first. I was doing foreign study. I knew Jean-Louis, I knew Erich Ringwold. That's how I was introduced to the project.

Initially we were playing, experimenting, having crazy dreams about how things should be. We played a little while, and then some of things got more mature, so I had the opportunity to take part in the early days of the adventure.

**HB:** *Tell me about some of the crazy things.*

**CM:** For example, we wanted a flat filesystem, where you wouldn't put your files in directories, but you would tag them with keywords, and instead of saying, "Open this directory," you'd say, "Open all my email and send it to this person." In the end we realized that directories are nice

## *Cyril Meurillon (continued)*

and the industry has been using directories for a long time, so it's almost intuitive. We do have database features in the filesystem, but they're not as extreme as we first thought.

For the graphics system, we had crazy ideas of the sort where the drawing should be completely device-independent and Benoît, who wrote the App Server, realized that perhaps we should be more practical. We've matured a little. This is not a completely conventional OS, but we're more conventional than we intended to be.

**HB:** *What were your goals for the kernel?*

**CM:** Simplicity. In general, if a system is too complex, over-engineered, it will be very slow to boot. Things will be slow because it's being too general. That means more code, more data and more things to load, more dispatching. A simple system is lightweight and fast and responds quickly. That's why the BeOS is so fast to boot, for example. That's why launching apps is very fast.

**HB:** *How is that different than, say, Windows or the MacOS?*

**CM:** Well, first of all, there are many things that we have not implemented in the OS yet. Printing, for example, is quite minimal at this stage, so we have a very small print server and we don't have to look at 2,000 printer drivers. A lot of steps are simplified, partially because they are not implemented yet.

But also we have adopted a more practical approach, like the App Server. The App Server is modular, but doesn't need to go and look for 100 different modules. We tried at all stages of development to keep things very simple. So, when the window server loads, it's almost immediately ready for services. It doesn't need to go and look for 47 different keyboard maps because we know we only need the one you're using.

We try to remain very practical, very simple in what we do. It's unlike, for example, at Apple. When Apple designed QuickDraw 3D, they tried to do a lot. In my opinion, they tried to do too much. It's a huge API with many calls, and that means a lot of code, and of course it means it's slower. Pierre [Raynaud-Richard] designed our 3D Kit to be very result-oriented. It's simpler, you can do less, but it's much quicker; it's smaller. It's more efficient. You don't have all the features you have in QuickDraw 3D, but for that we have OpenGL. It's important that we have simple and fast APIs for the simple things.

**HB:** *When things like printing are fully implemented, will the BeOS take as long to boot as any other operating system?*

**CM:** Things will be slower than now, necessarily, but I think that we can manage not to over-engineer things. To go back to QuickDraw 3D, a lot, perhaps 50 percent of the features will never be used by anybody because it's been over-engineered. We implement things on an as-needed basis. If it's needed, we implement it. So that way we can keep the system small as opposed to other software companies that try to do everything and end up with more than they need.

**HB:** *You've worked on the BeOS scheduler. Can you explain what that is?*

**CM:** A scheduler is the central task dispatcher of the system. It's the part of the kernel that decides which thread to run and that operates the context switch from one thread to the other. When designing the kernel it was a very important constraint that the system be very responsive. In the older versions of Unix, for example, if one thread is busy in the kernel reading from a slow device, another thread cannot get in the kernel and do something unrelated.

BeOS on the other hand has been designed with the goal of being preemptive at all times. That means when a thread is in the kernel doing something, it can be interrupted and another thread can be scheduled and do something completely unrelated. As a result, when a thread is reading from File A, another thread can go and read from File B at the same time. That means your system will be more responsive.

Our scheduler is very simple compared to the Unix scheduler. The Unix scheduler is, I won't say fancy, but it's more fancy than what we have. Some people complain about the way our scheduler behaves, because … well, scheduling is something that students write whole theses about. And people have been talking for decades about what the proper scheduling algorithm is. But nobody really agrees. It's a highly controversial issue. I try to retain only the very simple ideas. I understand exactly how my scheduler works as opposed to some very fancy scheduler that's behaving in a very stochastic manner and you can't really understand it because it's too complex.

**HB:** *For the end user, what kind of experience would that translate to?*

**CM:** Responsiveness of the interface. You can click on a window while it's being refreshed. There is no blocking there. Even though the same data structures are being updated, internally, they are managed in such a way that moving the window still allows refreshing to take place. And that means things feel more responsive. I don't get this empty window outline when I'm moving a window because it continues to get refreshed. It's more live, it's more pleasant to use. Not only more pleasant—for a lot applications, it's critical. For example, you don't want the sound to stop while you're moving a window or opening a file.

**HB:** *What's the most interesting thing you've done here?*

**CM:** I very much liked rewriting the filesystem because it was a long project, very risky. This one is perhaps the most spectacular challenge that I have taken on here. But overall, I love to work here. We don't have huge challenges every day, otherwise life would be impossible. But work is not only taking on big challenges, it's also solving simple problems every day. Helping to make the system more stable. Even that is very exciting because you have so much impact on the whole system.

It's not a huge company with a team of 200 engineers. I can fix bugs, I can make the system more robust. I understand most parts of the system. It fits in my mind. And to have this much impact on the end product is very exciting.

And things are very straightforward, too. When you want to make a change, you do it. You talk with your co-workers, but you just go do it. You don't first have to write tons of documentation about what you want to do. That's the upside. The downside is that when someone leaves, he's leaving with the documentation, because it's in his mind. So then you have to figure out what he's

## Cyril Meurillon *(continued)*

done. I guess that we're trying to formalize a little bit the way code is designed and written. But for now, it's still a very young, very fresh company. We don't have to encumber ourselves with rules.

**HB:** *So you're telling me that BeOS isn't properly commented?*

**CM:** Not all parts are properly commented, no. It depends on who's writing the code. Some people are very greedy about comments. I think I'm in between. Some people don't write a single line of comment. Others write more comments than code.

**HB:** *Let's take a step back. What were you doing before you came to Be?*

**CM:** I was a student in France. I was studying information technology at an engineering school in Paris. Actually, Jean-Louis Gassée and I went to the same school.

**HB:** *Did you know him there?*

**CM:** No, I met Jean-Louis here. I was visiting the Bay Area as a tourist and I stopped by Apple with a few floppy disks with my programs on them to show what I had been doing. At the time I was an enthusiastic teenager, a hacker as some call it, and so that's how I met Jean-Louis.

**HB:** *He was at Apple?*

**CM:** Yes. I met some other people there, too. I met Erich [Ringwold]. I met Phil Goodman, who was my other manager. I had Erich and Phil Goodman as managers then. You know, when you're 17, 18, you need heroes and they were my heroes. Interestingly enough I did—are you familiar with MultiFinder?—I did something very similar to MultiFinder. That's how I got Phil's and Erich's attention. Then I talked to Jean-Louis. So, that's how I met Jean-Louis and some people at Apple and we kept in touch. But I had to go back to school in Paris.

**HB:** *So, you didn't go to work at Apple?*

**CM:** No. They offered me a job, but my parents convinced me to go back. I was 17. I think that was the right thing because I was a little too young. I'm glad I studied a little more in France. That gave me more perspective on things. I didn't specialize too early.

So, I kept in touch with my friends, my contacts here, and I was visiting here during the summers, working. I worked for Apple and then Jean-Louis left Apple. I was a little anxious when he left. My whole world collapsed. At the same time, Erich left Apple, Phil left Apple. It was a big diaspora at the time. The good engineers left Apple. It was an uneasy time for me. My values were a little shuffled.

**HB:** *I take it that's where you were expecting to end up working?*

**CM:** Yes. I was very naïve, in a way. But then Jean-Louis told me about Be. At the same time Phil worked for General Magic, he was one of the founders of General Magic and he tried to hire me, so—remember that internship?—I had the choice of either going to work at Be and working with Erich and Jean-Louis or with Phil at GM, and I decided to work for Jean-Louis.

It was a tough decision. Both were working on operating systems for radically different products. One was a small product and the other was a real computer. It was almost like flipping a coin because I knew a little about the project but most of it was confidential. It was a tough decision. So I did an internship, and then I went back to France.

**HB:** *This was in what year?*

**CM:** That was in '91. The company was just Jean-Louis, Erich, Bob Herold (actually Bob had just started), Benoît [Schillings], and me as an intern.

**HB:** *And you were working on the kernel?*

**CM:** Yes. At the time the kernel was a bootstrap piece of code. We had a motherboard that had no disk, no nothing, so it loaded code through a serial port that was connected to a PC. We had a ROM on the motherboard uploading the code from the PC. We needed some bring-up code. We were just testing the hardware. I wouldn't call that a kernel, really.

So, that was my first internship. Then I moved back to France and I took a BeBox with me and I worked at a distance. Then I came back the year after for some more time. By that point, my relationship to Be was very tight. I was a telecommuter, essentially. Then in '94, I came here for good.

**HB:** *What do you do with the rest of your time? I see you've got piloting charts on your wall. Do you fly?*

**CM:** No, I don't fly. I love to travel and for those areas you see on the map, these are the only maps you can get.

**HB:** *So, where is this?*

**CM:** Central Asia. This the ex-Soviet Union, republics of the Soviet Union. I've been there, I've been to Pakistan, Iran, India. I've been to other Middle Eastern countries like Syria. I went to Turkey. I like Asia. I have this affinity for Moslem countries, too. I like the culture. Many things I disagree with, of course. But I like the mystery that is around many of those countries. It's very hard to understand.

They still have values we have forgotten, like hospitality. In many of those countries I didn't go to a single hotel, first of all because there was no hotel where I was going, but also because people invited me to stay at their homes. You know, you'd take a bus ride or a jeep ride and the person invites you. That's something that doesn't happen here anymore. But in Moslem countries there is still this strong belief that perhaps a god is hiding behind a stranger and you need to be nice to them. Perhaps he's sent by Allah.

I remember I was in Turkey in a bus, actually at the border of Kurdistan and Armenia. I was sitting next to a man who was a shepherd and he was obviously very poor and I started to talk with him. I know perhaps 15 words of Russian, some of Armenian, some of Kurdish. But it's amazing how far you can go with only a few words. And at the end of our conversation, the man wanted to give me his shirt. It's a very strong memory. Then he wanted to kill a goat for me. Things like that are hard to experience here.

# 7

# Working with Queries

BeOS may be the "MediaOS," but you're about to meet some powerful Be technology with a considerably lower fireworks factor. Queries aren't glitzy, and they don't typically bowl over crowds at industry trade shows. But they do represent a fundamental shift in the way users organize and retrieve information on their hard drives, and understanding queries will help you come to a deeper appreciation of an important aspect of Be's reconsideration of operating system design.

In addition to its many technical advantages discussed in Chapter 5, *Files and the Tracker*, the Be filesystem also stores lots of extra information about your files in special fields called "attributes." These attributes can be indexed by the filesystem and used in combination with other criteria to perform powerful system-wide searches at lightning speed. System searches, called "queries," are automatically saved to a special folder and can be rerun with a simple click at any point in the future. Queries are as easy to use as the Find function in your current operating system, but return much more detailed cross-sections of your personal data.

# Data Mining Your Hard Drive

This chapter will show you how to find information stored on your disk volumes in ways you've probably never dreamed possible. But in order to talk meaningfully about queries, it's useful to first come to a better understanding of three things:

- The basic concept of the database and how piles of data can be turned into useful information
- The "common data pool" model often used in BeOS
- The concept and structure of the Be filesystem

Once we get those things out of the way, we'll be ready to extract some needles out of the haystack that is your hard drive. If you just want to learn about using queries without learning how they work, skip to the section *Constructing Queries*, later in this chapter.

## Database 101

In its simplest form, a database is nothing but a plain text file containing rows and columns. The columns (or fields) represent categories of information such as names, addresses, and phone numbers, while the rows represent "records," or individual database entries. One column, one category, one row, one record. A good analogy is the classic Rolodex: Each card—or record—represents a single person, and each card contains fields for address, phone number, company, and the like. What's so special about looking up phone numbers? Nothing. The real power of a database begins to emerge when you stop looking at individual Rolodex cards and consider instead what can be learned when you look "down" through the fields with your X-ray vision, or with a database query tool.

Let's say you've got 1,000 cards (friends) in your Rolodex, and you want to learn how many of them live in California. A database query will look down through the stack of cards along the State field, counting instances of the string "California" as it goes. It then returns the answer to your question in the form of what's known as the "found set"—a subset of only those records belonging to your Californian friends.

Things get much more interesting when you combine several kinds of search criteria with "and/or" operators to answer harder questions. For example, if your Rolodex had a field for income, you would be able to determine statistical correlations between home state and income level by constructing a query of the form: "For each state listed in the database that includes at least one person who makes more than $50,000 a year, determine median income. Then list the names of the found states in order from highest median income to lowest." Your resulting list would tell you which states have the highest geography-to-income ratio and return a list of your rich friends at the same time. All of that from a simple table of columns and fields.

Crank this concept up to the $n$th level, and you get a powerful online database like your favorite Internet search engine. Now imagine having that kind of speedy, ultra-detailed search and retrieval capability built into your operating system. And imagine that you have a much better collection of file details to search on than you do on the Mac or in Windows. And that search results are returned faster. Way faster.

## The Open-Minded Data Format

On Macintosh and Windows systems, many kinds of data can be used only in particular applications. For instance, if you use Eudora for reading and writing your email, you can't turn around and open up that same mailbox or message in Claris Emailer. Some filetypes—like plain text and many common image formats—can be shared between applications. But you can't make monthly calendars in Schedule+ and open them up in Now! Contact; that's just an unfortunate fact of life. When you think about it, though, it's ridiculous that any particular application should "own" your personal data and thereby make it difficult for you to try competing products.

In response to this situation, BeOS defines a small collection of new filetypes to be shared between all applications and the OS itself: Bookmark, Person, and E-mail. Rather than all of your browsers maintaining separate bookmark collections, you simply organize bookmark files on your hard drive as you would organize any other collection of personal files, either through an interface provided by the browser or via the Tracker. Web browsers built for BeOS can simply read from and write to the central bookmarks folder, bringing an elegant end to the bookmark synchronization problem.

Similarly, all BeOS email programs can simply read from and write to the Be mail format (note that they don't necessarily have to do this, but they can if they want to). As a result, you can switch email programs every day if you're so inclined. The formatting and storage of your personal data is no longer in the hands of a single company. Developers can write special scripts and programs for email processing without having to bother creating yet another mail format. Applications you've never associated with email—like word processors and image editors—suddenly gain the ability to participate in a broader array of system-wide and personal messaging, or the ability to handle URLs. But best of all, this approach opens up the entire operating system to centralized queries. For example, even if you could run a MacOS or Windows search on "email messages from JLG which I still haven't read after 22 days," those operating systems wouldn't be able to figure out which files were email messages and which ones weren't, as each email client would be producing a separate file format for email messages. Not to mention the fact that many existing email applications store all of your email in one giant, concatenated file per mail folder, which makes it impossible to search on individual mail messages from outside of the mail application itself.

In addition, the field is wide open for other new types of "open" file formats to be created and implemented by third parties. For example, developers could create a new scheduling file format in which each "event" was represented by a single file with queryable attributes. When you wanted to learn which birthdays you need to plan for in July, you could simply run a query on July birthdays. Such files could also be connected to "event triggers," backing up your hard drive every two weeks, for example. Personal information managers and other organizers (such as Palm Pilot databases) could read from and write to this centralized format, so that all of your organizers could stay in sync with one another and other applications could be integrated with your personal schedule. The possibilities are endless, and await only the perfect implementation by developers.

 While such a universal scheduling file format does not (as of this writing) exist for BeOS, you can get much of the functionality described above with an excellent system tool called Scheduler, which is discussed in Chapter 10, *System Tools and Utilities*.

Let's take a closer look at what makes this open data system tick.

## Attributes and MIME Types

In addition to their actual contents, files in BeOS always have the option of storing an associated collection of "attributes" in the filesystem (not in the file header, and not in a separate file). Attributes and MIME types were covered in depth in Chapter 5, *Files and the Tracker*, but let's recap quickly.

Just as every card in a Rolodex system has a collection of fields associated with it, every file in BeOS can have an associated collection of fields, in the form of attributes. Each of these associated fields can contain any amount or kind of extra data. At the very least, each file gets an attribute in which to store its file-type. If the file has a custom icon, that icon will live in another attribute. Beyond that, the possibilities are open. Attributes in BeOS files contain information as divergent as email headers, color correction data, window size and positioning information, special instructions to host applications, and so on. While the attributes already associated with your files on a fresh BeOS installation are great, you're free to create new and additional attributes for existing filetypes, or to create entirely new filetypes with custom attribute collections. See Chapter 5, *Files and the Tracker* for details.

Each attribute has a name, and these names can be the same from file to file. Thus, you may define all of your text files to have Author, Issue, and Month attributes. Just as the most interesting things happen with a Rolodex when you look "down" through the fields, interesting things also happen on BeOS when you select subsets of groups of files with the same attributes (e.g. when you search for all of your Person files that include the string "California" in the State field).

So we've got a database-like filesystem made possible by attribute collections attached to each file, coupled with a large array of concrete, known filetypes (the collection of all known MIME types on your system).

We've also got a few new open file formats that make it possible to do things like find all email messages that fit certain criteria regardless of the application that created them (just as you might do with text files, which we never think of as being "owned" by certain applications).

## Digging for Gold

So what can you get out of a BeOS system query that you can't get from a Mac or Windows Find dialog? Let's look at a few examples, starting with queries you can run on BeOS in its default configuration, with the filetypes and attributes that ship with the system. Afterward, we'll look at some hypothetical queries you *could* run if you added new attributes to your existing filetypes or created/installed new filetypes with custom attribute collections.

**Queries You Can Run Right Now**   Here are some examples of queries you can run on BeOS "out of the box," with the filetypes and attributes provided by the system.

- Show me all the email on my system that's more than a week old and that I still haven't read.

- Find all BeMail messages currently queued for delivery to "krusty". Make sure to pick up both krusty@site.net and krusty@jackson.org, even if those messages are in the trash. Delete the query file after seven days.

- Dig up all of the Bookmark files on my system, scattered across multiple partitions, with "beos" somewhere in their URLs and using "news" as a keyword.

- Show me all of the Person files on my system for friends who live in Oregon and who belong to my bowling club.

- Find all of the Be employees who work on the Web team but who are not part of BeEurope.

- Find all of the folders on my system created within the last 30 days that contain the word "submissions" in their names, but exclude those named submissions from scot and submissions from simon.

- Find all SoftwareValet package files on a partition called gorgonzola that are larger than 200K and that I've last accessed within the last six months.

- Find all of the saved queries on my system with "Be" in their names.

- Find all of the mail I've sent to Be employees (this one is trickier than it sounds!).

You'll find out how to create each of these queries later in this chapter.

**Hypothetical Queries**   Here are some examples of queries that *could* be run if you added new attributes to your filetypes, created new filetypes, or installed as-yet-uninvented applications supporting new filetype/attribute combinations.

- Find all of the GIF images on my system with a width greater than 200 pixels and a file size smaller than 25K (requires installation of Thorsten Seitz's Thumbnail, described in Chapter 13, *Graphics Applications*).

- Show me all of the birthdays coming up this month that I have to buy presents for (would require a new filetype dedicated to scheduling).

- Show me all the meetings in Conference Room B today (again, would require a new filetype dedicated to scheduling).

- Show me all of the video files on the company network (both QuickTime and MPEG) that are slated for deletion next month. Skip the ones smaller than 300K (would require the addition of a Deletion Date attribute to your QuickTime and MPEG filetypes).

- Show me all of the BeatWare Writer documents that were written before last month and were also edited by Louise this month (would require the addition of Author and Editor attributes to the Writer filetype—which you could easily do).

- Show me Person files, text files, and email messages that include information about friends of mine who live in Oregon (this could be done by learning the name of the Person filetype's State attribute and adding it to your existing text/plain and text/x-email filetypes).

- Collect all the spam mail from Sanford Wallace and trash it without showing me first, unless it has the word "monkey" somewhere in the subject line (contingent on an as-yet-nonexistent Event file type to trigger the trashing).

# Constructing Queries

Enough talk—let's get hands-on with this stuff. There are several ways to begin a query:

- Pull down Find from the Be menu on the Deskbar.

- Hit Alt+F any time a Tracker or Tracker-related window has the focus (is the frontmost window). If another application has the focus, Alt+F will probably invoke the find function for that application, rather than a system query.

- Pull down File | Find from any Tracker window.

- Click once on a bare spot on the desktop and hit Alt+F.

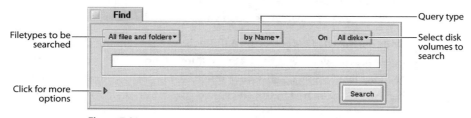

*Figure 7.01*

*The Find window looks like this in its bare minimum state. The default search looks for files or folders on all drives with a name equal to or containing whatever string you type next. Enter a string, click Search, and watch it go. D'ja blink? Yes, you just searched your entire drive in a couple of seconds.*

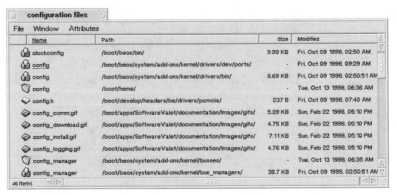

*Figure 7.02*

*The results window is identical to a standard Tracker window, with the exception of its gray background and a few different entries in the pull-down menus. Naturally, you can double-click files appearing in this window, drag them to the Trash, rename or move them, drag them onto applications, or anything else you can do from a normal Tracker window.*

**Instant Updates** Query results windows are a good place to see some of BeOS's instant update functionality in action. Here's an interesting real-time OS trick you can try:

Rename a file in the resulting set to something else so that it no longer meets the search criteria. For instance, if you searched for all files that start with "tr", rename one of the files to start with "sr". The second you hit Enter, the file disappears from the results window because it no longer qualifies against your criteria. Likewise, if you delete a file from the Tracker that happens to be shown in a query results window, it will disappear from the results window instantly, because queries don't "see" the Trash by default (though you can optionally select the Include Trash checkbox in the Query dialog).

**Opening Parent Folders** Just to the right of the filename column in any query results window is the path column, telling you where on your system each file lives. If you double-click one of these paths, the parent folder of that item will be launched in the Tracker so you can zoom in for a closer look.

**Saved Queries** As if it wasn't great enough that you can dig up file collections like this, there's a bonus feature. Every time you run a query, its parameters are automatically saved as a query file in your /boot/home/queries folder. By default, queries are saved with slightly cryptic, slightly informative names, such as name=flow - Oct. 11, 12_02_56 PM. While you can always dig around in your queries folder, try to figure out which queries are which by studying their filenames, and then rename them, there's an easier way. If you come up with a query structure you think you'll find useful again at some point in the future, give it a descriptive name before you close the Query dialog by clicking the triangular latch and typing the name into the Query Name field.

The name you give the query will appear as the filename in your `queries` folder instead of the cryptic name.

You can drag any saved query to the desktop or to another folder. From then on, double-clicking the query file will yield an up-to-the-second collection of files on your system matching those criteria. And if you'd like to fine-tune the query later, just pull down File | Edit Query (hotkey: Alt+G) to find your search terms just as you left them, waiting to be tweaked to further perfection.

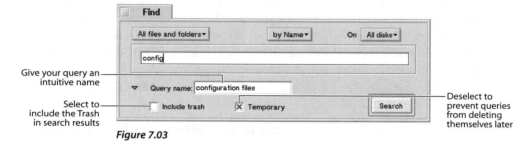

Give your query an intuitive name

Select to include the Trash in search results

Deselect to prevent queries from deleting themselves later

*Figure 7.03*

*Click the triangular latch at the left of the Query dialog and enter a descriptive name to have your query saved with an intuitive filename, rather than the default cryptic name.*

 **Preventing Query Overload** If you use queries frequently, your `~/queries` folder can fill up pretty fast. Even though it's great that queries are automatically saved for you, in reality you're not going to need to revisit most of the queries you create. For this reason, queries will self-destruct in seven days by default. If you plan on using a query again in the future, be sure to uncheck the Temporary checkbox in the extra options section of the Query dialog.

 **Search the Trash** By default, queries won't find files that have been moved to the Trash. If you do want trashed files to show up in the query results window, click the Include Trash checkbox. Note that the Trash is *not* excluded by default when you run queries from the command line.

## All Files and Folders versus Individual Filetypes

The default query is indiscriminate of filetypes; it will seek out every file that meets your criteria, regardless of its type. But you can narrow your search immensely—and get much tighter results—if you know before you begin that, for instance, you're looking for an image file or a text document. When you click the All Files and Folders button to see its sub-options, you're confronted with a list of all MIME types registered on your system that also have "friendly" names. Try a query on all files, then try the same query again, but this time pick a specific filetype. Note how much tighter your results are (you may even end up with none).

## *Unlisted Filetypes*

The filetype picklist in the Query dialog doesn't list every type of file known to your system—only those that also have "friendly names." If you want a given filetype to be searchable from the query interface without your having to create a formula query, all you have to do is go to your system's FileTypes preferences panel and give that MIME type a friendly name, then restart the Tracker (or reboot).

Let's say you want to be able to search on AIFF audio files. By default, these are not searchable from the query interface. Launch FileTypes from your preferences folder, open the audio category, and double-click on the type aiff. The resulting dialog will tell you that both the type name and the internal name are aiff. Any time the type name (or friendly name) equals the internal name, that filetype is considered to be obscure enough that users probably don't need to access it. To change this behavior, give the type a friendly name, such as AIFF Audio File. Click the Done button and close the FileTypes panel.

You're not quite done, though—you'll still need to kill and restart the Tracker to make the new friendly name available. You can do this either by restarting your system, or by taking these steps:

1. Open a Terminal window.
2. Hold down Ctrl, Alt, and Shift on the right side of your keyboard, then click the Tracker's entry in the Deskbar.
3. Type /boot/beos/system/Tracker & into the Terminal.

Reopen the query panel and you'll now be able to search on AIFF files. You can, of course, use this technique for any filetype currently lacking a friendly name.

**Query by Attribute**  Here's where things start to get really interesting. When you switch to searching by attribute, the Attribute drop-down becomes linked to the selected filetype. For instance, if you've chosen to search on the E-mail filetype, the attribute options will be From:, To:, Subject:, etc. If you search on the Person filetype, the attribute options will be phone number, address, and so on. In all cases, however, you'll also get the standard options, such as Starts With, size, modification date, and the other standard options you already get in Mac and Windows finds.

**Limiting Searches to Specific Volumes**  To further narrow your search, choose a specific disk volume to query from the picklist at the top right of the Find window. If you already know that the files you seek aren't on your Jaz or Zip disks, for instance, there's no reason to search All Drives. You can select any number of volumes to search from this list by selecting volumes successively. Let's say you have disk volumes named gorgonzola, ghouda, grueyer, and parmesan, and you only want to search on gorgonzola and grueyer. Select one and then the other from this list, and the list's label will change from "All Disks" to "Multiple Disks." The selected volumes will

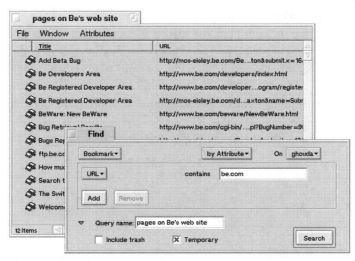

**Figure 7.04**

*To switch to attribute mode, use the picklist at the top of the Query window. By changing your search from a filename query to an attribute query, you can eliminate the vast majority of uninteresting search results. In addition, attribute searches are much faster than filename searches. Even if you are searching for files by name, specifying a filetype in conjunction with the file's name allows the query engine to skip right over thousands of irrelevant files, drastically improving search times.*

appear with checkmarks by their names so you can see exactly which of your multiple disks are about to be queried.

 ***CD-ROMs Slow Down Searches*** **CD-ROMs are second only to floppy disks when it comes to slowness, but the default query mode is to search all mounted BeOS volumes. To improve query speeds, use the Volume picklist in the top right of the Query window to eliminate your CD-ROM from the query process. If you run a lot of queries and don't use your CD-ROM drive very often, don't leave CDs sitting around in your CD-ROM drive.**

**Adding Criteria**   The more details you can provide, the "cleaner" your search results will be. A search on all Person files living in Kentucky doesn't do a ton of good if you have hundreds of them and all you want to find are people who live in Kentucky and also have 1-800 numbers that you can call for free. To further narrow your search, add a second set of criteria by clicking the Add button. There are two modes of adding criteria: "and" and "or". The default mode is "and", which finds only files that meet *both* of the specified criteria. By changing to "or" mode, you'll find files that meet *either* the first or second set of criteria. In other words, if you search on people who live in Minnesota and add "starts with "W"," you'll get back only the Person files that match both of these criteria, whereas running the same query in "or" mode will find all files for people who *either* live in Minnesota or have names that start with "W".

**Available Criteria** When you search by attribute, your search options change depending on the type of file you're looking for. If you're searching for Person files, you'll be able to construct queries such as "state contains 'CA' & name begins with 'R' or name begins with 'S' & zip code begins with '934'." Similarly, if you're searching on email messages, you'll be able to construct queries such as "sender contains 'Tom' or sender contains 'Louise' & modification date is older than 15 days & status equals 'read'." As shown in Figure 7.05, all attributes registered to a given filetype will automatically appear in the attributes picklist.

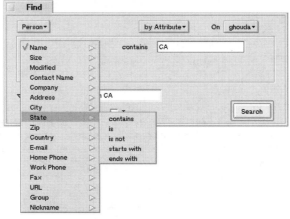

*Figure 7.05*

*When you're searching on a particular filetype and switch to attribute mode, all known attributes associated with that filetype appear as queryable options. These options change automatically whenever you change the filetype. Shown here are the options available when searching on Person files.*

 ***Edit Queries Quickly*** When you're running a query repeatedly and modifying it slightly each time, trying to dial it in to perfection, you don't have to start the query over from scratch each time. Instead, pull down File | Edit Query to pick up where you left off, or use the hotkey Alt+G.

 ***Queries Are Case-Insensitive*** Queries run from the Find interface are always case-insensitive, even though BFS itself is case-sensitive. In other words, the Tracker will allow you to store files called Williams, williams, and WILLIAMS all in the same folder, as three distinct file names. But when you're looking for a file, there's a good chance you won't remember exactly how its cases are rendered. The query engine does a nice bit of footwork behind the scenes on your behalf so that all instances of your chosen filename are found, regardless of case. If you want to specify case-sensitive queries, use the Find by Formula option described at the end of this chapter.

### *Use Plain English*

The BeOS query engine is capable of a few seemingly magical feats when it comes to comprehending your intentions, especially when it comes to modification dates. First of all, it's able to interpret dates written in just about any format. For example, if you want to find files modified after June 7, 1998, you can express that date in any of these ways:

```
June 7, 1998
06/07/98
7 June '98
06071998
6-7-98
7 Jun. 1998
```

See Appendix C for a complete list of date and time formats recognized by the BeOS query engine.

But that's not the really cool bit. The query engine is also able to translate dates and times relative to the current time as easily as if you were talking about these times to another human. For instance, all of the following expressions will be interpreted correctly by the query engine:

```
yesterday
last Friday
last June
day before yesterday
9 days before yesterday
last month
13 days after last month
```

**Query by Formula**     The third option on the Query types drop-down—query by formula—is considerably more complex (and correspondingly more powerful) than are standard name and attribute queries. Don't let that stop you from digging into formula queries; they can do some pretty amazing stuff, and they're not that hard to learn. Formula queries are covered at the end of this chapter.

### Querying Custom Attributes

Remember that it's possible to create custom attributes for your BeOS files, and to run queries on them later. However, the attributes you create aren't automatically searchable—you'll need to make sure they make it into the system index first. Complete instructions on adding attributes to the system index can be found in Chapter 5, *Files and the Tracker*, but to recap, the basic commands are:

* `lsindex`, which displays a list of all attributes currently being indexed.
* `mkindex -t string indexname`, which adds a new attribute name to the system index with the type `string`.
* `rmindex attribname`, which removes an attribute name from the system index.

So to make sure that your text files' Author attributes are searchable, you'd use:

```
mkindex -t string TEXT:author
```

Remember that existing files aren't automatically added to the index—only files created after the index is created will be searchable.

**The New Index Workaround** If you create a new attribute for an existing file-type and you've already got lots of those files, you don't want your searches to be limited by the fact that your new indexes don't log your old files. To get around this quirk, create a temp folder and copy (don't move) all of your old files into it. The act of writing copies to the filesystem will cause their attributes to be added to the index. Once you're sure all your files have actually been copied correctly, you can delete the originals and move the new copies back to the original folder.

# Using Saved Queries

As noted earlier, every query you create is automatically saved for you. If you create a complex query today and want to use it again tomorrow, you don't have to go through the hassle of creating it again from scratch—just double-click the query file and it will be run. Every time a query is run, it matches criteria on your system *now*, not when the query was first created. The results of the same query run yesterday and today may be entirely different. If you created a query to find all bookmark files to .edu domains and you've added a few .edu bookmarks since yesterday, today's list of results will be larger than yesterday's.

There's nothing that says your queries have to remain in your /boot/home/queries folder—you can drag them to any location on your

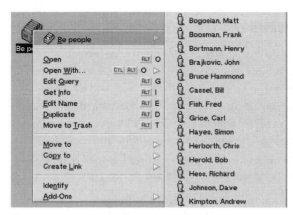

**Figure 7.06**

*Query results are resolved by the Tracker in real time when you right-click a query file icon and select its name from the top of the context menu. Pictured is a query constructed to find Be employees. Rather than digging around in the People folder (or folders), the query roots them out regardless of their location on the system. Release the mouse over any Person to launch it in the People application.*

system you like. The desktop is a good place to store queries you run on a regular basis. You may also want to create a subdirectory system under /boot/home/queries so you can arrange and store your queries using any system that makes sense to you.

One of the really cool aspects of query files is the way the Tracker is able to resolve them on the fly. Instead of double-clicking a query file, try right-clicking its icon and selecting its name from the top of the context menu. The query's real-time results will cascade off the context menu as if you were looking into a directory.

## Do "Real" File Locations Matter Anymore?

An interesting side effect arises when you start to base a lot of your work on live system queries: The actual location of files on your system becomes less important. For example, if you always look up Person files via query, it suddenly ceases to matter whether you've stored them all in /boot/home/people, in another directory, or scattered all over your system. If the filesystem functions like a database, why bother organizing anything, since queries will pull up the files you want regardless where they live?

While this is theoretically true, and is certainly a nice side effect of query technology, in practice things don't work out that way. For one thing, as discussed in Chapter 5, Tracker views can be customized on a folder-by-folder basis so you can view arrays of attributes in a manner most appropriate to any given directory, and that's not a feature you're liable to be willing to give up. Second, it's just plain old poor housekeeping. Rather than having your person files in all sorts of random locations, it makes sense to store them together in one place so that scripts and other applications can find them easily, and so that you can create clean, uncluttered views of them as a group.

Consider the fact that queries don't care where files live to be a bonus feature, not an excuse to keep a messy hard drive.

### *Is the Be Filesystem a "True" Database?*

If you're at all familiar with databases or database management systems, you've probably noticed many similarities between the capabilities of BFS and those of some common database functions. Queries and found sets, in fact, are central functions of all databases and database management systems. However, BFS isn't built to operate like a high-end relational database, and there is (currently) no way to extract and view the collection of all attributes of all files in tabular format, as you would in a relational database management system. Neither does BFS incorporate any kind of high-end query language like SQL (though Find by Formula is capable of accomplishing most of what SQL's SELECT statement does). There are several reasons for this.

For one thing, the attributes given to your thousands of files are dissimilar from one filetype to the next (Person file attributes share only a single common field with StyledEdit's file attributes, for instance). Therefore, keeping everything "connected" would require the maintenance of an insanely complex relational system, incurring overhead that's better kept out of the operating system itself (this is part of the reason why the true database foundation of the early Be filesystem was abandoned in favor of the current "database-like" filesystem). Second, Be's usual M.O. is to provide an elegant infrastructure in which third parties can develop high-end applications, rather than to provide so much native functionality that some third-party tools are simply unnecessary. For Be to provide that kind of functionality within the operating system itself could curtail demand for development of high-end database products by third parties. Finally, any data collection large and important enough to benefit from the advantages of a real database system would be better stored in a format completely controlled by dedicated applications.

### *The Same, Only Different*

Like a database, the Be filesystem includes collections of named fields containing discrete values. And as with a database, you can mine the system by running powerful queries against attribute fields to extract meaningful information from your file collection. However, BeOS returns its query results in the form of file collections in Tracker windows, rather than as data collections in tables (although with the Tracker's customizability, it comes pretty darn close). Unlike a database, BFS won't let you establish lookup systems or other complex relations between tables. Finally, BFS doesn't do SQL.

# Case Study: Queries and BeMail

If you took one look at BeMail and found it a little too simplistic for your needs, it might be worth taking a second look. Only this time, add your knowledge of BeOS query power to what you already know about customizing Tracker views. For instance, if you thought you couldn't work with BeMail because it doesn't provide a function equivalent to Eudora's filters, you'll be amazed how much similar functionality you can achieve with BeOS system queries. In fact, because BeMail messages exist as independent files and use BFS attributes so liberally, there are many things you can do by combining the power of customizable Tracker views and BeOS queries. Let's take a look at a few of the possibilities.

Before you begin, you might want to create a special folder on your desktop where you can store your named queries for safekeeping. Call it something like `mail queries`. Remember that you can pre-name your queries by clicking the More Options button in the Find dialog, then drag the newly created query file out of `/boot/home/queries` and into your new folder.

Remember also that any queries you run are completely independent of any custom directory structures you've already established for organizing your email. In other words, if you've created subdirectories of your inbox called `beusertalk`, `Aunt Mary`, and `HugeProject`, a query for all email messages older than 15 days will find relevant messages in all of these folders at once. Queries don't care where your files are, only whether they meet your search criteria.

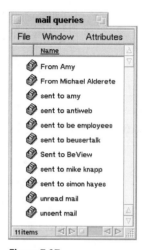

*Figure 7.07*

*BeMail may be simple, but by creating a collection of customized queries associated with your BeMail messages, you can maintain an array of "views" of your personal messages. Pictured is a whole collection of BeMail queries, conveniently stored in a folder on the desktop.*

 Making the query engine capable of limiting its search to particular directories (or ignoring certain directories) is a common request of BeOS users and developers. Don't be surprised if this feature shows up in a future release!

 Just because you can do a lot of cool tricks with BeMail messages and queries, that doesn't mean that the commercially available mail clients for BeOS aren't even better—they are! BeMail's functionality is intentionally limited in order to leave the road open for third-party developers. See Chapter 11, *Network Applications*, for details.

## Quick Glimpses

When you're in a rush to check your mail and get out of the house (or office), the last thing you need is to sit around sifting through your inbox to find messages with a certain status—you want to be able to see your new messages immediately. Create and run a query for all email messages with a status of "New," then drag the newly created query file to your `mail queries` folder. From now on, double-clicking this icon will bring up every email message on your system that has never been read.

*Figure 7.08*

*Creating an attri-
bute query that
scans for all email
messages with a
status of "New"
will let you see at
a glance the mes-
sages on your
system that have
never been read.*

You could create a similar query that finds all messages with a status of
"Pending" to see which messages are currently queued for delivery. Got a
favorite correspondent? Try creating a query that searches for all mail from
"JLG" if you want to gather up all of the messages Jean-Louis has ever sent
you, regardless of whether they're currently living in your beusertalk folder,
your inbox, or anywhere else (for the purposes of this exercise, you'll have to
pretend that you and the CEO of Be, Inc. are on a first-name basis).

Want to find all the messages you've ever sent to beusertalk? Adjust your
query to scan on the To: field and enter beusertalk@be.com. This will find
messages to beusertalk whether they're sitting in your pending mail folder or
were sent a year ago. Want to limit the scan to the past 30 days? Narrow the
criteria by adding a second attribute to the Find dialog and setting the modification date to 30 days. While this technique doesn't move any files from one
folder to another like, say, Eudora's filters would, you can use a BeMail interface application such as Postmaster and configure it to move BeMail messages
to other folders for you based on any criteria you like.

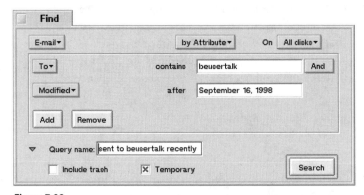

*Figure 7.09*

*By combining criteria in the BeMail To: field and the file modification date, you can bring up all
the mail you've sent to beusertalk after a certain date, whether it's in your pending mail folder,
hidden away in your outbox, or living on another disk volume.*

## *Scripting BeMail Queries*

If you really want to get fancy, you can create shell scripts that run BeMail queries like the ones described here and then perform operations on the query results. This will let you do things like deleting mail older than a certain date, or moving BeMail messages from one folder to another. After reading the *Query by Formula* section later in this chapter and the extensive information on BeOS Scripting online, you'll be well-equipped to create your own BeOS version of Eudora's filters. You can even associate your scripts with x-icon so you can run them by double-clicking icons.

However, there are a few gotchas to watch out for when doing things like this. Most importantly, you'll need to be very careful about how you move BeMail messages from one folder to another. Since the shell's mv command doesn't respect BeOS attributes, you could end up stripping the attributes from huge batches of messages at once, and as you know, a BeMail message without any attributes isn't worth its weight in bytes. One possible solution to this dilemma would be to use the copyattr command (Chapter 6, *The Terminal*), followed by the rm command—in other words, instead of just moving files, copy them with attributes, then remove them from the original location.

Second, command-line queries include the Trash, so you'll need to use the sed command (Chapter 6, *The Terminal*) to filter anything living in the Trash out of your search results, or you'll end up moving deleted messages right back into your mail hierarchy. Third, shell scripts don't offer much in the way of a user interface, and every time you want to make a change or create a new filter, you'll have to go mucking about in code that you wrote months ago.

If you're up for it, it is possible, but personally, I think it's much easier and cleaner to use one of the several commercially available email clients out there (see Chapter 12, *Network Applications*)—they do it all with a lot less hassle.

Of course, all of these examples can be more finely tuned by adding more specific criteria. For example, you may not want to see all of the new mail that's come in since you last checked—maybe you only want to see your new beusertalk mail. By now it should be obvious how to create such a filter. This is a great way to sift quickly through high-traffic lists.

Notice that all queries are truly live: If you're reading mail by double-clicking entries in the results window for a query that included Status=New as part of its criteria, messages will disappear from the results window the moment you open and then close them, since their status will no longer be new (unless you use the Message | Close | "Leave as New" option). In addition, new messages arriving from your ISP will appear immediately as they roll in.

**Batch Operations** You're not limited to simply viewing a list of files in the query results window. On occasion, you may find it useful to be able to drag the results of a query into another program. For example, if you've set up custom PubDate attributes for your text files and it's now time to prepare the July issue of your newsletter, why dig around for all of those files? Just run a query on all text files with a PubDate of July, then hit Alt+A in the results window and drag the whole mess into StyledEdit, Pe, BeatWare Writer, or any other text editor.

Here's another good example. Let's say you find the need to change all files bearing a certain filetype to another filetype. For example, you may have discovered that you've got a bunch of a illegal MIME types on your system (Chapter 5, *Files and the Tracker*), and you want to change them all to a legal type. The simplest way to do this is with an application like Francis Bogasyani's DropType (Chapter 10, *System Tools and Utilities*), which will instantly change the MIME type for any file or files dropped on its interface to the currently selected type. Just set DropType to the right type, run a query on the illegal type, and drag all files from the query results window onto DropType's interface.

# Sample Queries

In order to help you get as much mileage as possible out of system queries, I've lined up a handful of sample queries designed to help you realize your full potential as a transcendental query master. Figures 7.10–16 show you exactly how to set up some of the query possibilities outlined earlier in this chapter.

*Figure 7.10*

*Show me all the email on my system that's more than a week old and that I still haven't read.*

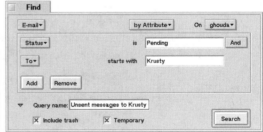

*Figure 7.11*

*Find all BeMail messages currently queued for delivery to "krusty." Make sure it picks up both* **krusty@site.net** *and* **krusty@jackson.org***, even if those messages are in the Trash. Delete the query file after seven days.*

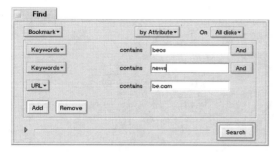

**Figure 7.12**

*This query almost gets us to where we're going, but not quite. We want to dig up all of the bookmark files, scattered across multiple partitions, using both of the keywords "beos" and "news" but excluding any URLs from* **be.com** *(we only want to see BeOS news not written by Be itself). We'll need to edit the query formula slightly to make this query work properly.*

Figure 7.12 includes a little gotcha. We want to find all bookmarks that include both of the keywords "beos" and "news," but exclude any that are on Be's own Web site. Problem is, the query interface has an "is not" option, but not a "does not include" option. Therefore, we create this as an attribute query, coming as close as possible to our goal, then toggle to formula mode and edit the formula just slightly. To reach our goal, all we have to do is change the part of the formula that says META:url== to read META:url!=. In other words, we have to manually invert the equality in the search expression.

The example in Figure 7.13 makes use of the "and" and "or" operators together in one query. We want to find people who live in Oregon, but we can't run a query on "state contains OR", because that would find people in CalifORnia as well. We can't just run a query on "state is OR", because we may have entered both "OR" and "Oregon" into the state field when creating Person files. The solution is to use "is" statements, but join them with an "or" operator: Find "state is OR or state is Oregon", Finally, we want to restrict the search to members of our bowling club, so we use an "and" operator to query on the Group field of Person files.

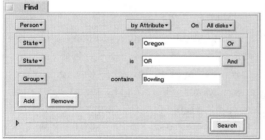

**Figure 7.13**

*Show me all of the Person files on my system for friends who live in Oregon and belong to my bowling club.*

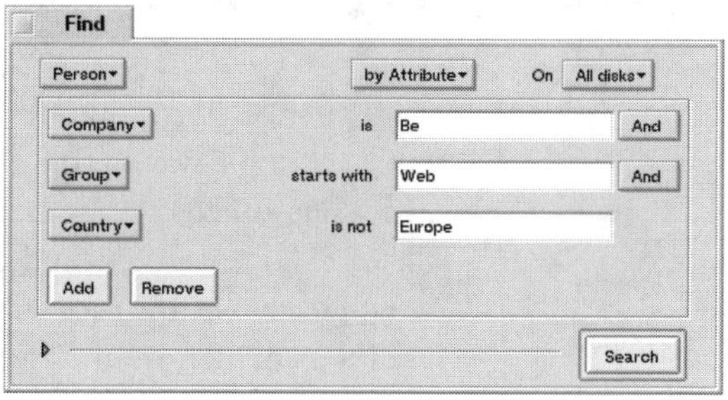

**Figure 7.14**

*Find all Person files for Be employees who are on the Web team but who are not based in Europe (this assumes that you've logged all European Be employees with Europe as their country—not technically correct of course, but useful for our purposes).*

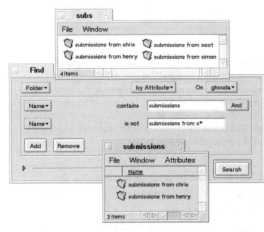

*Figure 7.15*

*Find all of the folders on my system that contain the word "submissions" in their names, but exclude those named "submissions from (anyone whose name begins with 's')".*

*Figure 7.16*

*Find all SoftwareValet package files on partition grueyer that are larger than 200K and that were downloaded more than one month ago. (Installing a SoftwareValet package does not affect its modification date, so we can't use a query to find old installations, but this query could give us a useful starter list of applications to consider weeding out.)*

The ability of queries to filter out certain kinds of results is as powerful as its ability to include them. In the example in Figure 7.15, you can see that there are at least four folders on the system starting with "submissions from." If we run a query on all folders that contain the string "submissions", but exclude those called "submissions from s★", only Chris and Henry's folders appear in the results, while Simon's and Scot's are excluded. Note that wildcards are allowed in GUI queries, just as they are in formula queries.

# Query by Formula

The query engine's Find by Formula option is far and away the most powerful and flexible way to find files on your system, and enables you to perform many fine-tuned queries that are impossible to do any other way. As is often the case, however, this kind of power comes at a price. The Find by Formula option lets you construct queries with the same powerful but complex syntax used to run queries from the Terminal. While the formulas you'll see here may appear a little intimidating if you're not already comfortable working with command lines, it's not as difficult as it may appear at first glance.

 The query syntax is Be's own invention, though it is derived from C and bash constructs. That doesn't mean you have to learn bash and C to use it, just that some of the common syntax structures used in C and in the bash shell are also used in the query syntax.

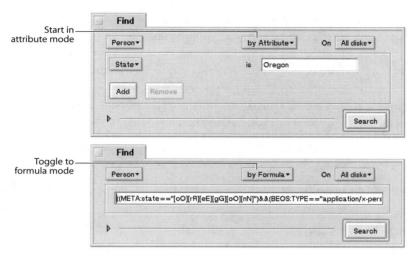

Start in attribute mode

Toggle to formula mode

**Figure 7.17**

*To get started with formula-mode queries, construct your query normally in attribute mode, then use the mode picklist to toggle to Find by Formula mode. Your attribute query will be automatically translated into BeOS's native query syntax, saving you the trouble of constructing formula queries from scratch.*

## Starter Formulas

Formulas may appear somewhat cryptic, but fortunately, it's almost never necessary to create them from scratch. Instead of starting your queries in formula mode, create them normally in attribute mode. Once you've got them as close to what you want as possible, switch from attribute mode to formula mode and you'll find a formula already filled in for you. All you need to do then is edit your formula to perfection.

The basic structure of a formula query takes the form:

`<attr-name> [logical-op] <value>`

where `[logical-op]` is one of the operators in Table 7.01.

In actual operation, a formula query looks like this:

`(ThisAttribute=="ThisValue")`

In other words, you can search on any attribute known to the system, and you can specify that that attribute is or is not equal to, or is less than or greater than, a value that you specify. The value is always

### Table 7.01  Query Operators

| Operator | Meaning |
| --- | --- |
| == | Equal to. |
| != | Not equal to. |
| < | Less than. |
| > | Greater than. |
| >= | Greater than or equal to. |
| <= | Less than or equal to. |
| ! | Negates whatever it precedes. |

*You can specify relationships between named attributes and their values by using the operators in this chart.*

contained within quotation marks, and the equation is always enclosed in a set of parentheses. Remember that many more things than you may expect are attributes. Email subject lines are attributes, Person files' nicknames are attributes, and all filetypes are attributes. And even though filenames, modification times, and sizes are not officially attributes, they behave like them as far as queries are concerned. Thus, the values expressed in a query can be MIME types, file sizes, modification dates, or arbitrary strings.

Let's look at a few examples. To find all of the files on your system containing the string "config" in their names, you'd use this formula query:

```
(name=="*config*")
```

## Why the Double Equal Signs?

In the C language syntax, you'll often find two equal signs next to one another, (e.g. a==b). Whenever you see equality expressed this way, you're dealing with a test of existing conditions, as opposed to making a declaration. In other words, the statement a=b means "set variable a to the value b", but a==b means "check to see if a is equal to the value b." Since we're running queries and not writing a program, we always use the double equal signs to test for the existence of certain conditions in our filesystem.

The problem with this sample query is that BeOS is case-sensitive, but you may want to find files with names like TermConfig, ConFigThis, and CONFIG.TXT. That's why when you switch from attribute mode to formula mode, you'll see all names expanded out with a lowercase and uppercase option for each letter, using the same bash mechanism you learned about in Chapter 6, *The Terminal*:

```
(name=="*[cC][oO][nN][fF][iI][gG]*")
```

So any time you want to search on particular cases in filenames, just edit the formula to fit your needs, stripping out the case options for any letters that matter. For example, this query

```
(name=="*Config*")
```

will find files named Configurator and SomConfig, but not config.txt. Right off the bat, you've already accomplished something you can't do with standard attribute queries.

**Boolean Operators** A string like the one above can easily be combined with a second set of criteria by joining the two statements with an "and" (&&) or "or" (||) operator, then surrounding the whole mess in a new set of parentheses. If you want to find all filenames containing either "config" or "tweak", your query string will look like this:

```
((name=="*config*")||(name=="*tweak*"))
```

Of course, you can combine any type of criteria with any other type of criteria. In the next example, we're searching for all Person files that include the letters "CA" in their state field by combining a MIME type search with an attribute search.

```
((BEOS:TYPE=="application/x-person")&&(META:state=="[cC][aA]*"))
```

Note that we've used a * wildcard *after* [cC][aA], but not before. This ensures that we'll only catch state names that start with "CA", and that we won't accidentally catch "North Carolina", for instance. This example raises an interesting dilemma: How do you discover the attribute names so you can use them in queries? You'll find a detailed explanation of how to root out attribute names in Chapter 5, *Files and the Tracker*, but the short version is this: To learn the names of the attributes associated with any file on your system, open a Terminal window, cd to the directory containing that file, and type listattr filename.

**Logical Grouping**  Sometimes you'll need to create queries where sets of parameters are grouped together logically into larger groups. Because the GUI Query dialog only lets you create sequential lists of parameters, you'll need to jump into formula mode to change the way groups of parameters relate to each other.

Here's a problem that seems like a simple query on the surface, but that actually takes a little juggling: find all email you've ever sent to Be employees. If it were as simple as querying for "be.com" in the To: field, it would be a piece of cake. But what if you're subscribed to the beusertalk and bedevtalk mailing lists? Everything going to those lists is addressed to be.com. And what if you've written to gobe.com at some point? Those messages need to be filtered out as well.

What you need to do is satisfy two major groups of criteria:

- The file must be an email message and must include "be.com" in the To: field.

AND

- The To: field must not contain any of the strings "beusertalk", bedevtalk", or "gobe.com".

So you'll need a query structured like this:

((A and B) AND (not C and not D and not E))

Pay attention to where the parentheses are situated—they're used to separate logical groups from one another. Since each of A, B, C, D, and E is a clause unto itself, each will need to be enclosed in parentheses as well.

(((A) and (B)) AND ((not C) and (not D) and (not E)))

When trying to make query formulas work, pay careful attention to placement of your parentheses as they relate to logical groupings—one misplaced parenthetical will break the query.

As of R4, a broken query does not return any kind of error message, it just yields zero results. There's no easy way to determine whether you're getting zero results because there are no matching files or because your syntax is wrong.

In the end, the working query looks like this (we've wrapped it here—you'll have to imagine it all on one line):

```
(((BEOS:TYPE=="text/x-email")&&(MAIL:to=="*be.com*"))&&
(MAIL:to!="*beusertalk*")&&(MAIL:to!="*gobe*")&&(MAIL:to!="*devtalk*"))
```

Note the != characters used to negate equalities. Note also that we've stripped out the case-insensitivity syntax to make this formula easier to read.

**Multiple Filetypes**   Once you've got grouping down, you can do another trick not possible from the GUI query interface: searching on multiple filetypes at once. Let's say you want to find all sound files of the type MPEG or AIFF whose names start with "burnside":

```
(((BEOS:TYPE=="audio/mpeg")||(BEOS:TYPE=="audio/aiff"))&&
(name=="burnside*"))
```

Since you need to find *either* MPEG *or* AIFF files, they're contained within a set of parentheses all their own, and are separated by the || ("or") operator. You could easily extend this formula to search on four or five audio filetypes at once.

***Legal Queries***   When you're using the GUI front end to the BeOS query engine, it's impossible to create an illegal query, but once you're in formula mode, it's your responsibility to make sure your queries are actually working with searchable criteria. And just how do you determine this? With this simple rule: All queries *must* include at least one indexed attribute. As described in Chapter 5, *Files and the Tracker*, BeOS maintains indexes in the filesystem to keep logs of certain attributes attached to your files. BeOS doesn't index *all* of your attributes, because that would result in a performance impact on the filesystem. In order for you to run a query, at least one of your search terms must be one that's logged in the index. If you want to search on an attribute you've added to your text files called "PubDate", and PubDate isn't being indexed by the system, you'll need to construct your query so that it also looks at filenames, sizes, modification dates, or types. This needn't limit the scope of your search at all—if you want to find all text files with a PubDate of November, just make sure that the query also specifies the text/plain filetype; otherwise you'll find yourself frustrated because the query will return no results at all.

**Special Query Characters**    The example above makes use of the friendly neighborhood * wildcard (to match any number or kind of characters). Other examples in this section use the [] bracket set to group ranges of characters. In addition to these, formula queries can also take advantage of the ? symbol for matching any single character, and the ^ symbol for negating the contents of characters specified within brackets.

 While these characters may remind you a bit of the regular expression syntax described in Chapter 6, *The Terminal*, regular expressions are not part of the formula query syntax. Why not? Because regular expressions are used for digging strings out of text files, but that's not what we're doing here—we're just searching on criteria associated with entries in the filesystem, which is a very different task.

The ^ negator inverts the meaning of the contents of a bracketed expression. For example, [^0-9] finds everything that is not a number (in other words, finds all letters and punctuation marks).

### Table 7.02  Query Special Characters

| Symbol | Matches |
|--------|---------|
| * | Any number of characters (including none) |
| ? | Any single character |
| [] | The range/class of characters inside the [] |
| [^] | The negated range/class of characters inside the [] |

*A small handful of special characters can be used in the formula query syntax.*

**Working with Dates and Sizes**    While the GUI version of the Query dialog is quite forgiving and allows you to enter dates in any of the formats listed in Appendix C, and file sizes in bytes, kilobytes, or megabytes, formula queries require more specific date and file-size formats.

All dates are expressed in elapsed seconds since New Year's Eve, 1970, which is the POSIX date format described in Chapter 6. Since there's no way to calculate this without shelling out to the Terminal, the easiest way to get this number is, once again, to begin your query in attribute mode and then switch to formula mode. If you do need to enter this number directly, open a Terminal window and type:

```
date +%s
```

The shell will report back with the nine-digit Unix-style date, which you can copy and paste back into your formula.

File sizes always need to be entered as bytes; when converting from megabytes or kilobytes to bytes, just add the appropriate number of zeros. For example, 2MB equals 2,000,000 bytes, 2K equals 2,000 bytes (yes, technically there are 1024 bytes in a kilobyte, but it's hard to imagine a scenario where you would need to specify that much detail in file sizes—make it easy on yourself and just add the zeros).

**Querying for Blanks**   There may come a time when you want to search for attribute fields that are empty. For example, what if you want to find the collection of all Person files for whom you still have not collected an email address? That means you need to query for all Person files where the email field is empty. You can't use a *, because that will find anything (even if that anything is nothing), and you can't negate the *, because the opposite of something is not necessarily nothing. What a dilemma. Fortunately, a construction like this will solve the problem:

```
((META:email!=?*)&&(BEOS:TYPE=="application/x-person"))
```

By using != we say "not equal to." Since ? means "single character" and is modified by *, we're saying "any single character." In other words, "find all Person files where the contents of the email attribute are not equal to any single character."

Now what if you want to invert the operation and find instead all Person files for which you *do* have an email address? Just change != to == , so that you match all email attributes that do include any single character. Of course, this presumes that anything entered in the email attribute is necessarily a real email address. If you suspect that you might have some bogus entries in those fields, you could easily modify this to make sure that the string contains an "@" character. Grasp the logic of these basic constructs, and there's practically no limit to what you can dig up on a BeOS volume.

## Running Queries from the Terminal

Because the formula query syntax is identical to the syntax used to run queries from within the Terminal, you can easily construct queries in formula mode and then paste them into the Terminal. However, there's a small extra step involved. To run a query from the Terminal, do this:

1.   Construct your query by attribute, switch to formula mode, and copy the query to the clipboard.

2.   In the Terminal, type query, then a space, then a single quote mark ('), then paste your query from the clipboard with Alt+V, then type another single quote. A Terminal query looks like this:

```
query '(name=="*config*")'
```

Even though the results aren't as pretty (and aren't clickable), running queries from the command line has a few advantages over running them from the GUI. By obtaining file listings from the Terminal rather than the Tracker, you can print them out or parse them any which way to Sunday using bash tools like awk and sed (Chapter 6, *The Terminal*). Secondly, you can combine a Terminal query with other shell commands to perform further operations on your query results. For example, let's say you keep all of your business contacts in BeOS Person files, and you need a printout of just the names of your American partners—something neither the People application nor the Tracker will let you do (though the Tracker will gain the ability to print in a future release of BeOS). This Terminal command will redirect its output to a single text file in your home directory, which you can then print out or email to someone else:

```
query '((META:country=="*[uU][sS][aA]")&&
(BEOS:TYPE=="application/x-person"))' > /boot/home/contacts.txt
```

 We had to wrap this command onto two lines in this book, but you'll need to enter it all on one line.

The query results will be sent to standard output (see Chapter 6, *The Terminal*) and redirected into a text file living in your home directory. You can then open that file in any text editor and print it out.

Here's another good one. Let's say you want to delete all MPEG files starting with "burnside", regardless where they live on your system. This command:

```
rm `query '((BEOS:TYPE=="audio/mpeg")&&(name=="burnside*"))'`
```

simply applies the rm command to the results of the content appearing within the backticks. Thus you end up running a query and a batch delete operation simultaneously. As is true with any kind of batch operation, handle with care!

 Due to the way the shell works internally, a command like the one above will fail to operate on any files with spaces in their names. There is no easy solution to this dilemma, besides not storing your files with spaces in their names to begin with. This is one reason some Unix jocks use underscores in place of spaces in filenames—it makes some shell operations more trouble-free.

### George Hoffman
***Uppity Bit Flinger***
*Interviewed by Henry Bortman*

**HB:** *When did you start at Be?*

**GH:** I first got here at the end of fall of '96 and I was interning then. During my internship, I ported OpenGL and wrote/adapted the HFS filesystem. I was a student at Cornell at the time, so I went back to Cornell for a semester, came back for the summer, did a lot of work on the 3D Kit (before we changed the focus to concentrate pretty much exclusively for the time being on OpenGL). Then I pretty much started working on the App Server full time. Since then I've been doing a lot of work on the App Server, rearchitecting, rewriting, adding features.

**HB:** *Let us go through these one at a time. What is OpenGL and what did you have to port it from?*

**GH:** The GL implementation that we have now was given to us as part of the license agreement with SGI. We gave them much money and they gave us the ability to use the OpenGL logo and a simple reference implementation of the OpenGL library. It's a bad implementation.

**HB:** *Theirs, or yours?*

**GH:** Theirs. It's slow and it had some bugs in it, so I ended up fixing a number of bugs and speeding it up a little bit. It's all in software, and it's very general-use and all the code is meant to be clear rather than fast. In any case, I ended up porting that and doing some small optimizations, and now Jason Sams is taking the code that I ported and did some work on and actually making it into a full-fledged, hardware-accelerated GL.

OpenGL is a 3D graphics API and it's almost exclusively meant as a software interface to 3D hardware. It's meant for very fast access to high-performance hardware and it is the de facto industry standard. Much as Microsoft would like to make Direct 3D the standard, the big game makers and other companies pretty much universally support OpenGL as the better API. OpenGL is a clean, well-thought-out interface to that hardware. Direct 3D is arguably very clunky: It has these parallel modes, has a retained mode and a direct access mode, whereas GL is very straightforward. There's pretty much the right way to do things and that's about it.

Low-end cards usually only support rasterization at a very low level of primitives—drawing triangles and drawing them with shading and texturing and so on. But high-level cards actually implement the entire OpenGL pipeline in hardware, and that's what SGI machines do. They have hardware that, so Dominic says, gets each OpenGL function call to hardware within seven clocks, which is quite impressive. We haven't quite gotten there yet on PCs, but within probably two or three years you'll see cards that upload the whole GL platform, which will be pretty fantastic.

**HB:** *What's the relationship between OpenGL and the 3D Kit?*

**GH:** The 3D Kit is a much different kind of concept. It would be possible, for instance, to put the 3D Kit on top of GL because GL is a low-level API. It deals with triangles, basically, triangles and quads and lines and points. It doesn't have any kind of object model. You can't say, "Create a sphere and put it here." You have to say, "Draw a triangle, draw another triangle, draw another triangle," because it's supposed to be an interface to hardware. So, the advantage of GL is that it's so general-purpose you can draw anything with it and pretty much do anything you want. The purpose of the 3D Kit would be to make it very simple to do things like create 3D controls, put a sphere here, put a line coming off of it, make it able to be rotated in any direction with the mouse. Put a little arrow on the end and you have something that indicates direction that you can play with and use as a control in your UI.

**HB:** *You mentioned that you came here right out of school.*

**GH:** I'm still in school. I'm still attending Stanford. I'm still an undergraduate.

**HB:** *In computer science?*

**GH:** Unfortunately, yes.

**HB:** *Unfortunately?*

**GH:** Well, I do enough of it, right. They're not teaching me a whole lot more. Actually, this quarter I'm a little more hopeful because I'm taking some networking-hardware-physical-layer-kind of classes. That's one class. Then I think I'm taking knowledge representation, an AI kind of class. Then I'm taking "The Craft of Comedy" and private voice lessons.

**HB:** *Voice as in singing?*

**GH:** Oh, yeah. I sing a lot. I was lead in Ram's Head Theatrical Society's production of Chess, a musical by John Watte's favorite group, Abba. We were the two male members last year at Stanford. I sing in an a cappella group, you know, did the collegiate thing, sang in an a cappella group at Stanford, called Harmonics, and that's a lot of fun. We do pretty much everything. Pop, jazz, grunge, industrial. It's very eclectic. I mean all the groups have their own little niches. The Harmonics have less of a niche than anyone else. It's very eclectic. Sort of the antithesis of Be.

**HB:** *So, how'd you hear about Be?*

**GH:** I think I found it on the Web. I was interning at Intel as part of a program with Cornell, and I had heard about Be I think about half a year earlier and thought it was pretty interesting. Then while I was at Intel, I got really bored because they gave me so little to do.

So, during the summer of '96, I ordered a BeBox and started playing with the BeBox and had it in my cube at Intel, and they were all like, "There's a PowerPC chip in there." So, I started playing with that and I wrote a little newsreader called NBTN and I wrote a multitrack audio recording thing that I used to make an eight-track of me. I was like, This is really cool stuff.

But there were a lot of things about the BeOS that really sucked, and I thought I could help. So, I wrote and said, You guys are creating something really cool here, and I'm really bored at Intel, and I'm supposed to return in the fall, but I'd much rather intern with you guys. Melissa Rogers wrote back about two days before I had to go down to Santa Clara and said, We'd like you to come and work doing QA. I said, I don't want to do QA. As part of the development cycle, I'll do it, but I don't want to do QA, I want to develop. So, they flew me down for an interview, at the end of the day they offered me a position, and I interned.

*(continued)*

## George Hoffman (continued)

**HB:** *Are you planning to stick around for awhile?*

**GH:** Yeah, I'll be here for awhile. It's very different from working at Intel. In the Intel software division they come up with some cool stuff, but it's a hardware company—they're not required to be profitable. They just sort of come up with things that are kind of cool and make people say, "Wow, I'd like an Intel box." Then they actually go and give money to the people who make them. The fact that it's not required to be profitable is much like our government. It makes it somewhat slow and kind of boring.

They do some interesting things. For instance, when I was there, I was working on the Internet phone thing. Forty or 45 people total were working on the Intel Internet phone, and there were about 35 to 40 people here at Be at that time writing an operating system. I was like, I want to be down with these guys because there's a high level of competency here and I love working with competent people. It's very satisfying. It's more than a job for almost everyone here. People really enjoy what they're doing and they really care about the product. It's very satisfying to create something of the magnitude that we're creating with a small team of very competent people. That's what employment should be like.

**HB:** *If you could work on anything you wanted to here, what would it be?*

**GH:** Well, I think the App Server is one of the most interesting pieces, which I already work on, because it's very complex. There's so much going on. I like the fact that it's big. Basically, I'm interested in large-scale architecture. I like architectures, and the App Server definitely needed one when I got here, and I think I've done a good job putting one in place and working with Pierre to come up with a real solid architecture. I don't know what the time schedule is, but we have a lot of plans for what we want to do with it in terms of how we split up the client/server interaction.

**HB:** *Can you explain that at all?*

**GH:** No. Because we're not sure exactly how it's going to work and we haven't actually gone through any of the design phases. We've just informally talked about it. We want to basically put as much as possible on the client side and keep the system as tight and fault-proof as possible while keeping only the information that's necessary and that really needs to be shared in a server.

**HB:** *When you say client/server, you're talking about a single machine, right?*

**GH:** Yes. The App Server and the Kits work as a client/server within a single machine. The way the App Server works now, all the drawing is done on the server side. We basically want to move all drawing to the client side, because when you get to the point of dealing with hardware, if I say, Draw a line and the line gets drawn by hardware, that's like a couple of clocks. Whereas with the way the App Server works now, you have to send the message through a port and so on, and it's cached, and there are things that we do to speed that up a lot, but there's only so far you can go with that. It's an inherently somewhat inefficient architecture.

The way NT has solved it with 4.0 from 3.51 is they put the entire windowing system in the Win 32 API in the kernel, which is not something that you want to do. The evidence is there: It's increased the instability of the system. NT 4.0 is arguably not nearly as stable as 3.51 and I think a lot of that is because they put so much in their kernel. How do you solve these problems of sharing data? Well, how they've done it is just give everyone access to everything. Printer drivers are in the kernel in NT 4.0, which is ridiculous. I don't think it's necessary to have that kind of abandonment of security and fault tolerance in order to get performance. So, we're going to be trying to go through the same growing pains that NT 3.51 went through, but hopefully we'll come out on the other side with a better product, a better architecture for the windowing system.

**HB:** *The benefit to the end user will be performance?*

**GH:** Performance and stability. The way we want it to work is if the client crashed, there would be so little going on in the server—it would be such a small piece of code, really—that we could probably make it bug-free. And if the server is bug-free, then clients crashing won't make any difference. There's no way it could bring down the system.

**HB:** *Legend has it that you're a workaholic. How many hours a week do you spend here?*

**GH:** Well, during the summer, I usually don't leave. Yeah. When I was an intern, I didn't have an apartment. I just slept in my cube—when I slept. During this past summer, I very rarely went home. I'd go home to shower.

**HB:** *Ever take a vacation?*

**GH:** Sure. I took a vacation this summer. I went with a friend of mine to England and Germany and bummed around there.

**HB:** *When you go home, do you have a computer there?*

**GH:** No. I have nothing at my apartment. I have a futon. I just don't go there. It's nice to go there sometimes and sleep because I have sheets and a comforter and a pillow. Shower, mattress.

**HB:** *So, you figure on living like this for how much longer?*

**GH:** As opposed to having like what in my apartment? I mean, what would I do there?

**HB:** *Read a book? Listen to music, play cards.*

**GH:** Oh, my god. Man. I read books while I'm compiling, which is good because now with the whole compiler switch it's a lot longer time. I listen to music while I'm printing. I'm very much about creation, so I have a lot of … I don't know, it never really occurs to me to go and like sit and listen to music or watch television, or something like that. Definitely not watch television. I haven't watched television in years and years.

# 8

# Networking

As you discovered in Chapter 4, BeOS makes getting online a piece of cake. Users armed with their ISP's network settings information can usually establish a simple dial-up Internet connection in three minutes or less. But networking on BeOS doesn't stop at dialing into your ISP—many users also employ their systems as Web or FTP servers, operate their machines by remote control, and share disk volumes with corporate or academic LANs. This chapter takes you beyond the PPP basics. You'll learn to network your BeOS machine with other operating systems, get a Web server up and running, share your Internet connection with multiple machines, and more.

# Networking Concepts—Beyond PPP

While establishing a dial-up connection may be the first thing most people want to do after installing BeOS, it's certainly not the end of the networking road. Networking is a two-way street, as much about what you and your machine can provide to the rest of the connected world as it is about what you get back. And of course, if you've got more than one computer in your home or office, you'll want to get them talking to each other. After all, what's a home office without shared printers and network Quake?

## Networking from 20,000 Feet

As with any operating system, networking BeOS requires the presence of several cooperating factors.

- The connected machines must be capable of speaking the same language—that is, they must share at least one network protocol in common. It doesn't matter whether they're all running different operating systems or all the same; a common network protocol guarantees that each machine is at least theoretically capable of receiving intelligible data from the others.

- Each machine must have some kind of physical "interface" to the network. This usually takes the form of an installed network interface card (or NIC), though some machines have network-savvy chips soldered directly to the motherboard. A network interface can also be a modem or an ISDN terminal adapter.

- Each machine must be physically connected to the others, either directly or through an intermediate device such as a hub. Of course, if you're lucky enough to have a wireless infrared LAN in your home, you can scratch this point. Needless to say, wireless networking is going to be very big in the future.

- Finally, each machine must have a unique identity on the network—a name or numerical address that enables others computers to figure out whom the heck they're talking to.

Let's look at each of these components individually before attempting to build our own BeOS network. For the most part, the information in the remainder of this section is not specific to BeOS. Rather, this is an overview of the baseline concepts that cover all TCP/IP-based networks.

**TCP/IP—The Mother Tongue** While BeOS is capable of speaking other common network protocols, it's TCP/IP (Transfer Control Protocol/Internet Protocol) that was BeOS's first true love. Unlike most operating systems, BeOS has spoken TCP/IP for most of its born days. Because BeOS doesn't have the large installed base of some other OSs, it's critical that BeOS be able to communicate easily with others, and TCP/IP is the lowest common denominator of network protocols. Because of the Internet's immense popularity, there's hardly a machine left in the Western hemisphere that doesn't already have a TCP/IP "stack" installed. And that means you shouldn't have much difficulty connecting your BeOS machine to just about any other networkable machine, regardless of operating system. In fact, because most network protocols are specific to the operating systems that gave rise to them, TCP/IP is almost always your easiest bet in successfully wiring together otherwise incompatible computers.

One of the most elegant aspects of TCP/IP is the fact that it can just as easily be deployed on a two-machine network that stretches from one side of your den to the other as it can be to connect to the rest of the Internet. Barring the presence of security firewalls sealing a small internal network off from the rest of the world, distinctions between a personal TCP/IP-based network and the Internet at large can be hard to draw; connecting your BeOS machine with your hubbie's Windows NT box and using one of them to dial your ISP can potentially put both of you in contact with millions of machines in an instant. It's this seamlessness, in part, that makes TCP/IP such a popular protocol.

BeOS isn't limited to TCP/IP networking, however. Because of the system's modular design, support for other network protocols—such as older corporate standards like NetBEUI or IPX—works in much the same way as support for new filesystems. Drag an appropriate driver into /boot/home/config/add-ons/net_server, restart networking, and bingo—you're on the LAN. (Note that NetBEUI and IPX drivers do not exist at this writing and Be doesn't plan to provide them, but there's nothing stopping third parties from developing them on their own.) Similarly, protocols riding on top of TCP/IP, such as NFS, can be supported with the addition of a single driver. In addition, we've heard early indications of a driver for Novell networks over TCP/IP being in development by a third party.

### *BeOS's Home-Brewed TCP/IP Stack*

TCP/IP may be pretty easy to use, but it isn't an easy thing to implement. In fact, neither Sun nor Apple use their own TCP/IP stack—both companies license a stack from Mentat called Streams. Not Be, though. Almost all of the TCP/IP in BeOS is home-brewed, for that rich aroma and down-home chocolaty goodness. In fact, the bulk of the TCP/IP work in BeOS was done by a single engineer, Brad Taylor. Taylor began his work with source code from another stack, but did almost all of the heavy lifting (porting) himself. This fact is testament to both the uncluttered ease of BeOS development and the skill of Be's engineers. Through successive generations of the operating system, the quality of the BeOS TCP/IP stack has been enhanced. The difference in network speed and reliability between R3 and R4, for example, was stunning, and we've heard reports of even more emphasis going into robust, speedy TCP/IP for R5.

## How TCP/IP Works

While the exact details of TCP/IP's implementation fills many books, here's the nutshell version. Every chunk of data that needs to transferred from one machine to another (like, say, Be's home page en route from the Web server at **www.be.com** to your computer) is broken into a collection of packets. Each of these packets reserves a few bytes for its destination address and an identifying label (like an envelope entering the snail mail system, properly bearing the addresses of both its sender and its destination). Interestingly, the packets that comprise a given transfer don't necessarily travel together. Each packet heads off into the ether alone, seeking the shortest path to its destination. Of course, the path it ends up taking is not necessarily the shortest route possible. Instead, reality intervenes. Routers get backed up, causing traffic jams which cause packets to head off in other directions, seeking a clear route. Networks that operate in this manner are referred to as being "packet-switched." The pieces that make up Be's home page may travel dozens of different routes before arriving at your machine. On the way, a few packets become irretrievably lost.

As the packets begin to roll in to the recipient machine, it starts a head count. When it learns that a packet hasn't made it or is hung up somewhere, the packet is re-requested from the sender in a process called "error correction." When all packets have arrived and been accounted for, the recipient machine reassembles them into their original state and passes the completed work on to the user. There are other Internet transfer protocols (such as UDP) that don't perform this kind of error correction. As a result, they're somewhat faster, but only appropriate for certain kinds of traffic. Streaming audio, for example, needs as much speed as it can get, and it doesn't matter if a packet is lost here and there—you'll never notice the difference. However, drop a single packet from a zip file transfer and the file will be corrupted.

Of course, TCP/IP-based personal networks don't subject their packets to the same kind of harrowing journey as does the Internet, but the basic principles remain the same.

**Cards and Cables**  The physical part of your network—your actual hardware—can take many forms, but a few ingredients are essential. At the very least, you'll need a network interface card, or NIC. Just as your video card serves as intermediary between your monitor and graphics instructions in system or application code, the NIC takes a bus slot in your computer and sits between your operating system and the network (some computers have networking functions built into the motherboard, but the principle is the same). By far, the most common networking architecture in use is a standard called Ethernet (originally developed by Xerox, DEC, and Intel in 1976). Network cards are often generically called "Ethernet cards," and they come in two basic flavors: 10Base-T and 10Base-2. These cards can be distinguished by their connectors—10Base-T cards have an RJ-45 socket on the back, which looks just like a phone jack, only larger. On the other hand, 10Base-2 cards have what is known as a BNC connector, a small silver post that works similarly to a coaxial cable TV hookup. The advantages of the 10Base-T format are that A) it doesn't require termination, and B) it's "hot-pluggable"—you can connect a cable to a card in a running machine without interrupting the network.

In addition, these cards come in two speeds: 10 Mbps (megabits per second) and 100 Mbps. While 100 Mbps Ethernet is not *technically* Ethernet, the name seems to have stuck, and these cards can be made to coexist with their 10 Mbps cousins in a mixed environment. Prices are dropping quickly these days on cards of both flavors, and you can find mixed 100/10 cards for under $50 at some locations, though high-quality 100 Mbps cards run upward of $200. Finally, a new standard called Gigabit Ethernet is gaining currency, though that kind of bandwidth is far more than the average user can use. In order to get significant speed boosts from the faster Ethernet flavors, you'll need a hub capable of performing the translation between the two speeds (more on hubs later in this chapter).

Don't confuse a megabit with a megabyte. In fact, don't confuse the two meanings of megabit. When applied to disk storage, a megabit is 1,024 kilobits (remember, there are eight bits in a byte). When used to describe network throughput, a megabit is one million bits. To confuse matters even more, some disk manufacturers call a "megabyte" an even 1,000,000 bytes, so their drives will appear to be larger than they actually are; read the fine print.

Some NICs have sockets for both BNC and RJ-45 cables; these are known as "hybrid" or "combo" cards since they can do both 10Base-T and 10Base-2 networking. The latter is on its way out, and the vast majority of cards and cables sold today are 10Base-T. Thank God.

Unsurprisingly, the cable used to connect NICs to their networks is often called "Ethernet cable." Network cables terminate with one of two kinds of connectors, BNC or RJ-45, depending on whether they're meant to connect to 10Base-T or 10Base-2 cards. Functionally, the two cable types are roughly equivalent, but BNC cables have an extra inconvenience: You have to remember to terminate the last one on a chain, much as you would with SCSI. A missing fifty-cent BNC terminator can prevent an entire network from functioning.

**Hubs and Routers** The layout of a network is referred to as its "topology," of which there are three basic types. "Ring" networks are shaped exactly as they sound: Machines are connected in a circle. This topology is difficult to configure—experts only—but is very fast because data doesn't get bottlenecked at a central point. "Bus" networks have a central cable functioning as a spine, with each machine tapping into the spine. Many small networks are configured bus-style because it's easy to install and manage. Finally, there's the most common small office/home office topology, the "star" network. Star networks include a central device called a hub. Hubs simply act as traffic cops, juggling data as it moves from one machine to the next and making sure packets don't trip all over themselves on the way. Star systems are the easiest topology to install and manage, because the hub takes care of the traffic problems for you. Some organizations mix and match topologies as necessary, hanging stars off a spine, for example.

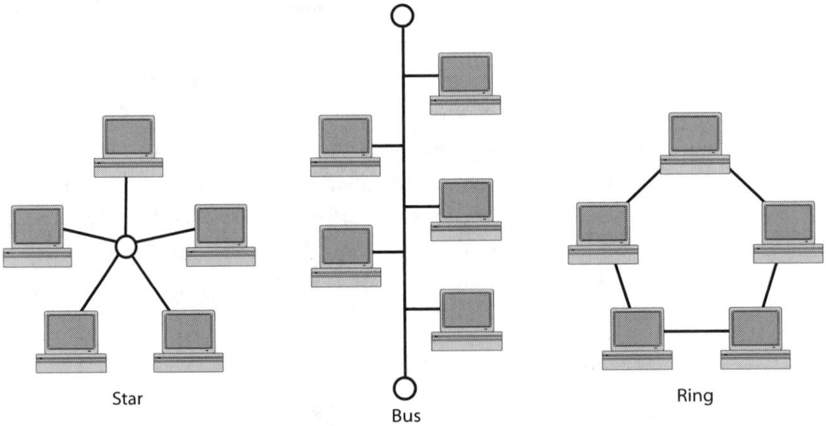

*Figure 8.01*

*Star, bus, and ring are the three most common network topologies. The vast majority of home and small office networks use the star layout for its ease of installation and management.*

Star

Bus

Ring

If you're going to build a small network, even if you have only two machines, you'll almost certainly want to spring for a hub. Inexpensive five-port hubs can be purchased for as little as $30 at most computer stores. Because they sit between machines and are not a direct part of your system, they require no drivers or installation routine. Most hubs have blinky lights for each port, letting you monitor at a glance which of the cards on your network are powered on or currently transferring data; these indicator lights can be invaluable when troubleshooting or setting up networks.

As you know, the Internet is a network of networks. Your company and your brother's university both have their own networks, each of which is connected to the Internet via routers (or gateways), which sit just outside the local network and "sniff" the destination addresses of packets as they flow by.

## LANs versus WANs

You may often hear the terms "large area network" (LAN) and "wide area network" (WAN). These are functionally similar; the difference usually boils down to geography. A LAN typically occupies a single building or a few buildings side by side, while a WAN typically connects multiple offices spread geographically around the country, or even around the world.

If a packet is destined for that router's home network, it grabs it out of the stream and ushers it inside. If not, the router compares the destination address to a stored lookup table and determines the best possible route to get the packet closer to its destination.

Internet service providers or network administrators manage the routers most of us use—you may never even know they exist. However, some small organizations—those who want to run their own Web, email, or other servers on the premises—also maintain their own routers, though these are smaller and less complex than the expensive routers that keep the Internet humming. The most low-profile form of router is the software-based "proxy server" (see "Proxies, IP Forwarding, and Masquerades," this chapter), which simply allows a small group of machines to share a single Internet connection or modem. While they are very different from routers per se, proxy servers are still essentially performing routing functions, sniffing packets and sending them to appropriate destinations.

**IP Addresses** Earlier, I mentioned that every machine logged into a network needs to have a unique identifier—a name or number that marks that machine as a unique participant on the network. Without this, we would lose all ability to transfer anything from anywhere to anywhere, and the network would become meaningless.

 The exception to this rule is the case of the proxy server, where multiple machines share a single connection. In this case, the machines on the internal network have "fake" IP addresses. But as far as the Internet is concerned, the proxy server is just one very busy user. More on that later.

On a corporate or institutional file-sharing network, users are typically assigned a username, often of the format first initial, last name (e.g. shacker). Clearly, a scheme like that doesn't guarantee uniqueness on the Internet, where millions of machines are connected at once, rather than dozens or hundreds. Instead, the TCP/IP protocol utilizes a hierarchical numeric scheme for identification. IP addresses take the form of four blocks of up to three digits each (e.g. 207.43.145.210). Because blocks of IP addresses are methodically doled out to institutions and companies, and these organizations then dole out individual addresses to each machine, unique addresses are virtually guaranteed.

There is, however, a slight problem with the IP address scheme: There are too many of us and not enough addresses to go around. A few years ago, it was common practice to assign every one of an ISP's subscribers an IP address to call their very own. Now, most ISPs assign an available IP address to your machine dynamically each time you log on, then throw it back into the pool when you log off (though some ISPs will sell you a permanent address for a small ransom). Similarly, most institutions assign addresses dynamically when users boot their machines, using a DHCP (Dynamic Host Configuration Protocol) client (more on DHCP later).

With new users jumping online every day and the fixed collection of available addresses not getting any larger, the Internet will one day face a serious address shortage. This problem is addressed in the next revision of the TCP/IP protocol, called IPv6. But if history is any teacher, the industry won't be bothered to migrate to IPv6 until circumstances become dire.

There's another reason why we need a jillion times more IP addresses than we've got, too: As the world becomes more wired, it's not just computers attaching to the Net. We (and I use the term "we" loosely) are someday going to want separate IP addresses for our refrigerators, toasters, Cuisinarts, carburetors, and sandals. We won't rest until we can ping our coffee makers and run traceroutes on our egg timers. But I digress.

**My Own Private Internet**   All of this raises the question of how IP addresses are assigned on a "private" TCP/IP-based network (such as one you might set up between your BeOS and Linux machines at home). Here it's a different story. If you're not connecting to the Internet, uniqueness is not an issue, and theoretically, you could give your machines any IP address you like. But what if one of the machines on your private intranet also uses PPP to connect to the real Internet? If you had assigned your internal IP addresses randomly, then one of your addresses could conflict with an existing address "out there" when you connected to the Internet.

For this reason, there are special blocks of addresses that are reserved for internal TCP/IP networking, such as the entire block starting with 192.168. Thus, you can be connected to 192.168.0.3 across the room, then simultaneously dial into your ISP and get online with a dynamically assigned "real" IP address. Since the 192.168 block is never assigned to anyone "for real," you won't run into conflicts. In a pinch, you can also use the easy-to-remember 10.x.x.x address, though we'll use the 192.168.x.x format for the examples in this chapter.

Another special, reserved address is the "loopback IP" of 127.0.0.1, which is every machine's way of referring to itself. Try pinging that number; if you get a normal ping response, you'll know that your network card is installed and at least able to talk to itself properly. This loopback IP is valid on every operating system—it's part of the TCP/IP spec, not any particular OS. The loopback address can also come in handy when you work with a personal Web server running on the same machine you're sitting at. More on that later.

## Kernel Space versus User Space

In Linux, FreeBSD, and other high-powered networking platforms, all network services are part of the operating system's kernel—compiled right into the heart of the beast. In BeOS, however, networking runs in "user space," where normal applications run. And like a normal application, BeOS networking can be stopped and started, reconfigured, jimmied, and restarted on the fly. For example, click that Restart Networking button and your network springs back to life with a new IP address associated with your network card. Make a similar change to a Windows NT machine, and you'll have to reboot before your changes take effect.

There is, however, a side effect to BeOS's dynamic network handling. Because networking isn't living in the kernel, overall network performance is not as awesome as Linux's is. Not that you'll ever notice a difference as an end user—the performance hit is too miniscule for that. But put a BeOS machine under an extremely heavy network load, as you would if you ran a very high-traffic Web site from a BeOS Web server, and you'll find that BeOS doesn't stack up to Linux.

Be had a choice: make things as easy and pleasant as possible for the average multimedia prosumer using the BeOS for what it does best, or optimize it for heavy-duty networking loads, a job that doesn't fit the MediaOS description. Remember: Be is not competing with Linux, which has a well-established foothold in a very different corner of the market.

By the way, don't let this scare you away from considering BeOS as a Web serving platform. The traffic levels we're talking about here are very high—far higher than those of most end users' sites. For traffic specifics, see *Performance Issues* this chapter.

### Epilogue

The user space versus kernel space distinction may not be the end of the story for BeOS networking performance after all. In the R3-to-R4 transition, network speed improved dramatically, even though the basic model of implementation did not change. And at least one other OS vendor (Canada's QNX) implements TCP/IP networking with a similar user space/kernel space separation, while still managing to get nearly 100% of theoretical maximum performance from Ethernet. Clearly, there's room for improvement in this department, but if anyone can figure out a way to let us have our cake and eat it too, it's Be. More fine-tuning and another major BeOS release will tell us more.

# Building a Network

OK. Let's turn theory into praxis and actually get your BeOS machine talking to other machines. It doesn't matter whether your other computer(s) are running BeOS, Linux, Microsoft Windows, or Apple's MacOS. As long as the other machines speak TCP/IP (all of the above do) and have a network interface card installed and working, you'll be all set. You may, however, need to obtain FTP and/or telnet software for some of the above operating systems. Note that this section is about TCP/IP-based networks only. Other kinds of networking are covered in the next section.

In addition, if you connect to the Internet through a cable modem or xDSL connection, it almost certainly happens through a NIC installed in your computer. Even if it also uses an external device, it probably does so by interfacing with a standard NIC. If your service provider refused to help you get things set up on the grounds that you weren't using Windows, raise hell. If they refuse, this section is for you as well. We won't reference those devices specifically, but all of the same concepts and principles apply.

## Making the Connection

Getting two computers to shake hands across a thin stretch of Ethernet cable for the first time can be extremely satisfying. Sometimes it works right off the bat, and sometimes you get to wrestle with the connectivity gremlins for a while. Keep in mind as you read this that some of this information is covered in other guises in Chapter 4, *Get Online Fast*, and you'll also find a section on Network Problems in Chapter 16, *Troubleshooting and Maintenance*.

**Hardware Considerations and Setup**   Your networking hardware needs, of course, depend a good deal on your existing setup. If your BeOS machine already has an NIC installed and working under another OS, or if Ethernet is built-in on your computer's logic board, you're ahead of the game. If you're trying to attach your BeOS machine to an existing network rather than creating a network from scratch, then you, too, are ahead of the game. Take a look at the checklist below to see if you have everything you need, and prepare to take a trip to Elwood's Computer Discount Mart for some parts if you don't.

*Network Hardware Checklist*

- One BeOS-compatible network interface card in each BeOS machine, configured as per instructions in the next section. Check for BeOS compatibility before making any purchases. Mac users: The networking hardware built into all BeOS-supported Macs is automatically supported, as are the standard DEC-based PCI Ethernet cards.

- A network hub ($30–$60 at most computer stores). Your basic hub is a pretty generic device with no moving parts, and no software or drivers to worry about. Most are trouble-free. The author has had excellent success with MaxTech hubs (not to be taken as an endorsement), and one bad experience with a LanPro device (not to be taken as a warning). Of course, those of you attaching your machine to a preexisting network don't need to worry about this—just make sure there's a port free for your machine.

- Ethernet cable compatible with your NIC (10Base-T or 10Base-2) and hub—one length of cable for each machine.

- BNC cable terminators if you're using 10Base-2 NICs and cables. These usually come with the Ethernet card, but can be purchased for pennies if not. Just make sure you have them before you begin.

 **If your hub has blinky lights, try to set it where it will be visible while you're attempting to make a connection for the first time. If you have problems, you may be able to determine where in the loop things are going wrong by carefully watching the send and receive lights for each port. For example, if you send out a ping to another machine and the light connected to your computer's port on the hub doesn't blink, then you know the signal isn't even leaving your computer, and the problem must lie with card configuration in your machine, not in the network itself or the other machine.**

**Network Card Installation**   If you haven't yet physically installed the NIC in your machine, consult the documentation that came with the card for complete instructions. Always press I/O cards into their slots gently so you don't damage the contacts. A gentle lengthwise rocking motion is often helpful in getting stubborn cards in without damaging them.

 Always remember to turn your computer's power off and unplug its power cord before removing the case. After removing the case, always touch one hand to a piece of bare chassis before touching any of your I/O cards or silicon chips—static electricity from your hands can permanently damage sensitive hardware components.

 **If you have an old ISA network card with jumpers (rather than the card being software-settable), leave the case off as you begin to test. If it doesn't work the first time, you don't want to have to remove the case again just to move a jumper around.**

**Power On**   After connecting cables from each machine to the hub, make sure the hub has power, then power on your computers. Watch the lights on the hub as your machines power on—these should glow almost immediately as soon as the NIC gets power from the motherboard. If the hub doesn't register that you've turned on your machine, you should suspect bad cables, a totally dead NIC, or a weird hub that doesn't include port power indicators—

check your hub's documentation to make sure. Check all cable connections to make sure they're secure.

**Tell BeOS About Your NIC**  Now that your card is installed and you've verified the network hub can "see" your NIC (as indicated by its blinky lights), you need to tell BeOS a few things about the card you're using and the network you'll be attaching to.

1.  Pull down the Be menu, scroll to Preferences, and choose Network.

2.  Click the Add... button and choose your NIC from the list. If it doesn't appear on the list, Be doesn't officially support your card, though it may work anyway. Check the listings at **www.befunk.com** to see if others have gotten your card to work with BeOS.

3.  You'll see a dialog similar to the one in Figure 8.02. If your network assigns addresses automatically every time you boot up, keep the DHCP checkbox selected (you will need to be attached to a DHCP server for this to work). Otherwise, enter an IP address, subnet mask, and gateway. If you have no idea what to add here, see *Choosing an IP Address and Netmask* below.

4.  Click the Config... button. You'll be presented with one of two types of dialogs depending on your card. If you just get a panel naming your card and two buttons labeled Cancel and Set, there's nothing you can do to configure your card from within BeOS because it's a Plug-and-Play or PCI card. If you get the option to set port and IRQ addresses, your best bet is to try and click Set, then restart networking. If, after a few seconds, BeOS has not complained, your card is probably set properly. If you see a dialog saying "Device failed to initialize," then that IRQ is probably occupied. Return to the dialog and try another setting. Note that these issues should only crop up with ISA network cards—BeOS is able to work with PCI devices much more elegantly.

 Setting IRQs from within Network preferences does *not* affect the settings of the card itself. It merely tells BeOS how it should try to "see" the card. In other words, this process is about reconciling BeOS's notion of how the card is configured with reality. To actually change these settings, you'll need to either move jumpers around on the card or use the configuration utility that came with it. If, on the other hand, your card is Plug-and-Play, you'll need to either use the card's configuration software to disable PNP or remove the card's jumper to do the same thing. Finally, setting the wrong port address will always result in an error message from BeOS, but setting the wrong IRQ may or may not generate an error message, and could give you the false impression that the card is configured correctly. Whenever possible, avoid these kinds of hassles by purchasing PCI Ethernet cards rather than ISA, which rely on legacy protocols for address assignment.

***A Note on Card Configuration Utilities***  If you have a jumperless NIC and need to reset its IRQ address or other settings, you'll need to use the software-based configuration utility that came with the card. But because Windows rules the world (economically speaking), these configuration utilities typically run only under DOS/Windows. If your machine doesn't have a Windows partition, you face a bit of a dilemma.

Fortunately, you don't have to compromise your machine by installing a DOS/Windows partition just to configure your card. The easiest way to get around this is to keep a DOS boot floppy around (of course, you need to have purchased a copy of DOS or Windows at some point in your life in order to legally own a DOS boot floppy). Boot from the floppy to load DOS into RAM, then insert the floppy containing the configuration utility and run it from there. Eject the floppy, reboot into BeOS, and your card will be configured with the new settings.

A considerably less convenient method is to remove the card from your machine and stick it in a DOS/Windows machine temporarily, configure it, then reinsert it in your BeOS machine.

The best solution, though, is probably to replace the NIC with a PCI-based card, which shouldn't give you any trouble at all in BeOS.

***Use Device Preferences to Divine Settings***  If for some reason you need to know how BeOS is "seeing" your NIC, use the Device preferences panel (Chapter 9), which provides reports on resource allocations for every piece of hardware in your machine. If you're having trouble getting things up and running, this panel can provide important clues as to why.

***Disable Plug-and-Play***  It's been mentioned elsewhere in this book, but it bears repeating since it's the source of so many hardware-related bugaboos: If you have a Plug-and-Play NIC and are having trouble getting BeOS to see it, disable the card's PnP functionality altogether and set your IRQs manually. If your motherboard allows it, you might want to disable the "Plug and Play OS" function in your motherboard's BIOS (if it has one) as well.

You'll find additional tips on dealing with problematic network card installations in Chapter 16, *Troubleshooting and Maintenance*.

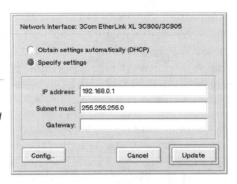

*Figure 8.02*

*Enter an IP address
and netmask for
your NIC. If you need
more information,
see* Choosing an IP
Address and
Netmask, *below.*

**Choosing an IP Address and Netmask** What you should enter into these two fields depends on whether your machine will have a "real" address on the Internet, or will be used only to connect to machines on your internal network.

**Dedicated Connection through This NIC** If your BeOS machine is in an office or academic setting where your organization has a dedicated Internet connection, it's likely that each desk or cubicle has a dedicated IP address. In other words, this is any situation where the NIC will be your primary or only interface to the Internet. If you don't know your IP address, you'll need to obtain it from your network administrator. Alternatively, you can write down the IP address of an already-networked machine (any operating system), unplug that machine from the network, and plug your BeOS machine in its place, using its IP address. (Of course, you'll probably have to give the port back to its rightful owner, but at least you can test your connectivity this way.)

Ideally, you'll have installed BeOS on a partition of a system that's already net-worked, in which case you won't have to unplug anything—just use the same IP address in both OSs. After all, you can only have one of them booted at a time. Set the Netmask field to be the same as the netmask for other machines in your workgroup. Ask your network administrator if you're uncertain. It's likely that you'll be able to leave this set to the default value of 255.255.255.0.

**NIC Connecting Only to Others in a Workgroup** If you're in a home or small business environment where your Internet access is via dial-up and you'll be using your NIC to connect only with a local group of machines (or even a single other machine), you should use an IP address selected from the reserved block of addresses described earlier in this chapter. Give your first machine the address 192.168.0.1, the second 192.168.0.2, and so on. Accept the default netmask of 255.255.255.0.

**Other Network Settings** If your primary Internet access is via PPP and you've already established domain, DNS, and hostname settings in Dial-Up Networking, you won't need to touch those settings. The network-ing you'll be doing via your NIC is unrelated to your PPP settings, which apply only to communications with the Internet at large, not those within your local network.

On the other hand, if this NIC will be your primary access point to the Internet, you'll need to complete these fields as described in Chapter 4, *Get Online Fast*. To summarize, make the DNS (domain name server) fields identical to similar fields on other machines in your group, then enter the name of the domain from which you're connecting. For example, if you work at Be, you would enter **be.com** here, not **www.be.com**. Enter a hostname by which you'd like to be identified (see the *Setting a Hostname* tip below) and a router address if your network requires one (ask your administrator, or try it with the default setting of 0.0.0.0, which means "no router").

***Setting a Hostname***  **Some local networks run a "nameserver," which lets computers on the internal network be identified by name rather than by IP address. Thus, if you're running a Web server on such a machine and you want to give its URL to co-workers, you can tell them either http:// 192.168.0.3/test.html or http://louise/test.html, for example. Note that hostnames are only usable in this manner from within your internal network and when a nameserver is also on the same network. Outsiders would not be able to access your Web site with either of these URLs—to do that, they'd need your "real," or non-reserved, IP address.**

**Even if you don't have a nameserver on your internal network, it's a good idea to enter something friendly here, like "esther" or "bebox." Note that you must enter something here if you want BeMail to be able to actually send any messages you've queued for delivery (see Chapter 4, *Get Online Fast*, for an explanation).**

**What about the Other Machines?**  So far we've focused entirely on your BeOS machine. But a network of one isn't much of a network. If you're connecting to an existing network, you obviously don't have to worry about anything but getting your machine configured. If your other machine(s) are also running BeOS, you'll want to apply these same instructions to them, remembering to give each of them a unique IP address within the reserved block.

If your other machine(s) are running other operating systems, I can't offer instructions for configuring them here, though the general principles and parameters will be identical, even if the interface used to configure them is different. If you run into difficulty networking other operating systems, consult your local guru or reference manual. (Remember: Peachpit also publishes the *Macintosh* and *Windows 95/98 Bibles*!)

In any case, you'll need to take note of the IP addresses assigned to each machine. If you're dealing with a lot of them, it may be helpful to write them on slips of paper and leave these next to the machines, so you can methodically test connectivity to them all.

**Wrapping Up**   If all has gone well, you'll be able to click the Restart
Networking button in Network preferences without BeOS returning an error
message. If you can get that far, the chances are very likely that the next steps
are going to go well too!

## Test Your Connection

Okay, here we go—the moment of truth. Since we're building a private network without a domain name server, we'll be using IP addresses to try and
"see" other machines on the network. Of course, you want to make sure that
any machine you're going to try to reach is actually powered and fully booted.
Remember to try to do this with your hub's indicator lights in plain view, so
you'll have a chance at seeing where communications break down, just in case.

Assuming that you're on a machine with an address of 192.168.0.1 and
another machine is at 192.168.0.2, open a Terminal window and type `ping`
`192.168.0.2`. With any luck, the shell will respond with a series of reports as
the ping bounces off the other machine's NIC and is returned to you. You
should see something like this:

```
32 bytes from 192.168.0.2     sequence  1 round-trip-time  1.3 msecs
32 bytes from 192.168.0.2     sequence  2 round-trip-time  0.5 msecs
32 bytes from 192.168.0.2     sequence  3 round-trip-time  0.5 msecs
32 bytes from 192.168.0.2     sequence  4 round-trip-time  0.5 msecs
```

You can stop the sequence (and just about any shell process, for that matter)
by pressing Ctrl+C. Congratulations—you're connected! Because ping is a
TCP/IP-based tool, you've just guaranteed that any TCP/IP application or
tool will be able to interact with that machine from this one. You can learn
more about using ping in Chapter 4, *Get Online Fast*.

If, on the other hand, the shell returns the message `ping timed out`, then your
network isn't quite there yet, and you should read the NIC problems section
of Chapter 16, *Troubleshooting and Maintenance*. Here are the most likely things
that could have gone wrong:

- Your hub is not working or not connected properly. This is unlikely—
  there's not too much that can go wrong at the hub. Watch its indicator
  lights carefully to try and determine whether your ping made it as far as
  the hub, then try and determine whether it was passed from the hub out
  to the other machine.

- Ethernet cables are not secured properly or are damaged. Inspect carefully
  and press connections in firmly.

- Your NIC either is not supported or is misconfigured. Does the same
  card work in the same machine under another operating system? Search
  BeWare for a driver for your NIC, and/or read the IRQ and PnP sections
  of Chapter 16, *Troubleshooting and Maintenance*.

- Network parameters are incorrect on the other machine, or its card is misconfigured. If the other machine is not running BeOS, consult documentation for its operating system.

- You didn't use the actual IP address of the machine you're trying to reach. Take a look at its network settings to confirm the address, and make sure that all machines on your network have unique IP addresses.

- Try cold-rebooting both machines (in other words, don't just press the reset button, but turn the machine all the way off and then on again), just to make sure that any new settings have taken, flush memory, and make sacrifice to the gods of network vexation.

# Moving Files via FTP

Now that you've established a baseline connection, you no doubt want to put it to good use, and file transfer is about as fundamental as "useful" gets. FTP, or File Transfer Protocol, is the Internet-standard method for flinging files around. And since it's TCP/IP-based, you're virtually guaranteed to be able to share directory structures with any other machine you should happen to encounter.

BeOS is fully FTP-enabled right out of the box, including a command-line FTP client that lets you log into other FTP sites, as well as an FTP server, so that other people can log into yours. This is yet another of those cool things that BeOS has that MacOS and Windows don't. While Windows comes with a command-line FTP client, and both platforms can download and install any of several FTP client and/or server packages, only BeOS comes with an FTP server built in so you can start sharing files with other operating systems the minute you establish your first connection.

## GUI versus CLI

There are two basic ways to use FTP on BeOS: in command-line mode from the Terminal, or in graphical mode via third-party software. Both methods have their advantages, but the majority of users may prefer the intuitive nature of graphical FTP clients over the clunky command mode. Graphical FTP clients display the filesystem on the remote machine in a window similar to standard file managers such as the Tracker, Explorer, or Finder. Downloading files to your machine is often as simple as navigating to the files you want and dragging them to your own machine; uploading is also typically a simple drag-and-drop operation. Some FTP clients, however, display a two-paned window, with your filesystem on the left and the remote system on the right.

A decent GUI FTP client also excels at batch processes, like transferring deeply nested subdirectory structures. Many of them also have the ability to automatically decompress your files upon arrival.

However, there are some notable advantages to command-line FTP as well. For one thing, it's guaranteed to be there. If you need to use someone else's machine, for instance, they may not have a graphical client installed. But you know they'll have the Terminal, and where there's a Terminal, there's FTP. Many people also find command-line FTP handier to use—there's no need to launch a client application and click around; just type an address into any Terminal window. Because both FTP and BeOS use Unix-style navigational commands, many people also find it more "transparent." In any case, even if you hate command-line FTP, it's worth spending a little time practicing with it so you'll be ready should you ever need it.

## Setting Up the Server

For you to FTP into another machine, that machine needs to have an FTP server installed and running. Such a machine is known as a "host," and you'll see this term in FTP client dialog boxes. To turn your BeOS machine into an FTP host so that other machines can access your filesystem, open the Network preferences panel and select the Services tab. Check the FTP Server box, then click Login Info… and enter a username and password. Be sure to choose a suitably cryptic password! (See the section *Is BeOS Secure?* in this chapter for more on choosing secure passwords.) Restart networking services, and you're done.

 ***Don't Leave Yourself Vulnerable***  Be's FTP server is rather primitive. A full-featured FTP server would have much more advanced options, starting with the ability to register more than a single username, as well as the important ability to restrict access to specific subdirectories. If you're using the built-in FTP server and are in a networked environment where hackers or crackers could make an attempt on your machine, keep in mind that should they be successful, they'll have free reign over your entire system—every single mounted partition on your machine is accessible to incoming visitors. Be careful when giving out your password, and if you have reason to be wary, don't leave your FTP server running unnecessarily. You may want to check out a more sophisticated FTP server, such as Campus (Chapter 11, *Network Applications*).

You don't have to start the FTP server every time you need it. Like every aspect of your networking configuration, it will remain as you set it, even between boots. This can be very convenient in a small, secure environment, but heed the warnings above.

# Logging In

Once the FTP server has been started, go to another machine and point its FTP client at your IP address.

***Easy Two-Way Access*** **BeOS makes it easy to get at files on your BeOS machine from other operating systems, but to get to other operating systems from BeOS, the other machines have to be running FTP servers as well, right? Well, yes, but only if the machines are physically separated. If the machine running the other operating system is in the same room or building as you are, you can walk over to it, FTP into your BeOS machine from there, and transfer files back to the BeOS machine. This is convenient when the two machines are physically near each other and you don't want to install an FTP server on the other machine.**

**If you do need an FTP server running on a non-BeOS machine, there are plenty of them out there. Check software libraries such as `www.hotfiles.com` or `www.download.com`.**

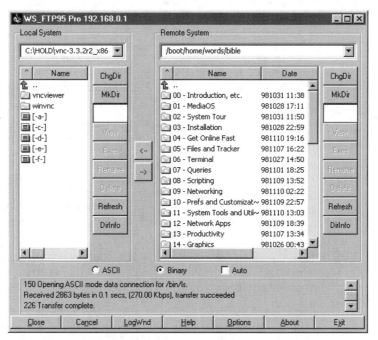

***Figure 8.03***

*If you've entered everything correctly, you should see directory listings for the machine you're currently at on one side, and for the remote machine on the other. Transferring files is as simple as selecting them and clicking the left or right arrow buttons. Many clients also support drag-and-drop operations.*

***Remember to Zip Up!*** If you plan to move files from BeOS to another operating system, don't forget to zip them up first! If you don't, all of their attributes will be irretrievably lost, which may or may not have devastating side effects. For example, if you move a bunch of StyledEdit documents that included font formatting, all of that formatting will be lost for good, since the formatting is contained in attributes and no other operating system understands BeOS attributes. The text they contain, however, will be preserved since that constitutes the actual data of the file. On the other hand, People files consist of nothing *but* attributes. Move them to another OS without zipping them and you'll end up with a pile of zero-byte files.

## Command-Line FTP

A complete description of command-line FTP usage can be found in Chapter 4, *Get Online Fast*. In addition, knowing how to navigate around in BeOS's own Terminal (Chapter 6, *The Terminal*) will help to make you a confident command-line FTP user, since most navigational commands are the same. Here's a summary:

- Log into an FTP server by typing ftp `ftp.sitename.com` or ftp `192.168.0.7` (substituting appropriate domain names or IP addresses, of course). When prompted for a username, if you've been assigned one, enter it. If not, enter anonymous or ftp, then enter your email address as a password.

- The server will report the current directory. You can always learn the current directory by typing pwd (for print working directory).

- Once logged in, navigate to your destination directory just as you would in BeOS's Terminal. For example, if you know the file you want is in `/pub/software/utilities` and you found yourself logged automatically into /pub, you would type cd `software/utilities` to get there.

- Browse file listings on the server by using the ls and ls -l commands. Remember that you can filter long listings by using wildcards (see Chapter 6). For example, to see all zip files starting with either an upper or lowercase S, type ls -l `[sS]*.zip.`

- To switch to binary mode prior to transferring images, sounds, programs, or archives, type bin. While binary mode is the default on Unix and BeOS FTP servers, some platforms default to ASCII mode, which will corrupt any binary files you download.

- To transfer a file to your computer, use the get command; for example, get `Samba.zip.` To transfer a file to the remote computer, use the put command: put `share.txt.`

- To enable a progress indicator prior to long downloads, turn hashmarks on by typing hash. These won't tell you how far through a download you are, but you'll at least know your connection hasn't been dropped.

- To see a summary of other available commands, type help by itself or with a command name (as in help `commandname`).

- To exit an FTP session, type bye or quit.

# Other File-Sharing and Transfer Methods

FTP is all well and good, and its ubiquitousness makes it a good fallback in open environments, but it's certainly not the most elegant way to sling files back and forth. Furthermore, FTP is restricted to file transfer, not true networking. In other words, I can't open up a BeatWare Writer document while it's still on your machine—I have to move it to my machine first, and then work on it. Fortunately, there are other Be-supported networking protocols out there that *do* support true networking, some via TCP/IP, and some via proprietary protocols.

## Common Internet Filesystem (CIFS)

FTP gets the job done, but wouldn't life be easier if you could just make your BeOS machine show up in Windows' Network Neighborhood on a machine across the hall, or mount shared Windows volumes right in the Tracker? You can. CIFS (Common Internet Filesystem) is an extension of the ubiquitous SMB (Server Message Block, or "Samba") protocol, which was originally developed by Microsoft, Intel, and IBM in the early 1980s. Samba provides resources (such as disk volumes and printers) over networks shared by machines running multiple operating systems. If you've been using just about any flavor of Windows over the years, you may not have realized it, but you've had a Samba server right there at your fingertips. Unlike FTP, which requires that you transfer a file from the host machine to your own machine before working on it, CIFS lets you work on remote files directly, without downloading them first.

 If you're having trouble sorting out the difference between CIFS and Samba, don't worry about it. You'll hear the protocol referred to as Samba most often in "the real world," while BeOS refers to it by its fancier, more inclusive name. Technically, CIFS is a superset of SMB.

**CIFS and BeOS**   As of R4.1, BeOS ships with a CIFS client, making it easy to connect to and use shared disk volumes and printers spread across an organization. Soon, BeOS will also include a CIFS server, so you can participate in a CIFS network in one of two ways:

- Running the CIFS client on your machine and mounting shared volumes from other operating systems directly in the Tracker.

- Running the CIFS server on your machine and defining a directory structure to be shared. That directory structure will appear as mountable volume to Windows, Linux, and other types of machines on the same network.

At this writing, the bits and pieces that make up CIFS for BeOS were just beginning to take shape, and its full implementation could not be tested. Depending on when you read this, the CIFS landscape could appear very differently, and these instructions may be outdated. Read the Be-provided documentation for updates.

The CIFS filesystem add-on (probably to be called cifsmount) may be found in the /experimental directory on your installation CD. If necessary, move cifsmount to /boot/home/config/add-ons/kernel/filesystems. You should also find a remote filesystem mounting tool, probably to be called easymount. Move this to /boot/home/config/bin and type easymount into a Terminal window, followed by the name of the mount point at which you want the remote system to appear in the Tracker. For example, you can tell easymount to mount a remote volume called Fred at /boot/home/network/Fred. At this point, you'll be prompted to enter the name of a shared volume somewhere on the CIFS network. If the volume name you enter is found, you'll be prompted for a password (if connecting to a Windows 95 machine) or a username and password (if connecting to a Windows 98 or Windows NT machine). If all has gone well, you should now see a new folder in the Tracker at the path you specified earlier. The contents of that folder will appear as if they were on your own machine, even though you know they actually live on a colleague's hard drive on the third floor.

If all of this seems like a bit too much futzing around, you might want to wait a few months—CIFS is going to get much friendlier very quickly. The CIFS tools should soon move out of the /experimental folder and become integrated into the system. A CIFS "browser" will also become available, which will tell you the names of all of the available shared volumes on your network, so you don't have to enter them from memory. By R5 (and possibly sooner in experimental form), a CIFS server component will become available as well, and all CIFS services will be folded into the Network preferences panel, alongside IP Forwarding and AppleTalk.

Updated CIFS instructions will be posted at **www.beosbible.com** as they become relevant. If you can't wait for R5 to get your hands on a Samba server for BeOS, visit **www.lightlink.com/landrum**, where you'll find a port of a GPL Samba package built by the same engineer who brought CIFS to BeOS.

**What about Other Operating Systems?**  CIFS clients and servers exist in some form for most operating systems, and should be downloadable from your favorite software archive. You should be able to find Unix/Linux/FreeBSD clients and servers as free software at the usual haunts. If you'd like to tie MacOS machines into your CIFS network, you'll want to check out a utility called simply Dave ($149), from Thursby Systems (**www.thursby.com**). Rather than AppleTalk, Dave uses standard Microsoft networking protocols (read: SMB/CIFS) to connect MacOS machines to a CIFS network.

# NFS

If any filesystem could be said to be both a floor wax *and* a dessert topping, it would have to be NFS, or the Network File System. NFS, developed originally by Sun Microsystems, is an open protocol, meaning that it isn't tied to any particular operating system. In fact, the main purpose of NFS is to allow diverse groups of computers running various operating systems to share files and directories transparently. In other words, whether you're running Solaris or VMS, BeOS or NetWare, you'll be able to mount shared volumes elsewhere on the network from within your own file management system, whatever that may be. Although NFS servers and clients are available for just about every operating system under the sun, it is most popular in the Unix/Linux world.

So what's that about a dessert topping? Because NFS provides a layer of "abstraction" between the native filesystem and the way it manifests in each file management system, it's also possible to use NFS to mount alien filesystems on one's own machine. For example, providing you have the appropriate drivers, it's possible to mount a Unix hard disk attached to a Windows machine by using NFS's abstraction abilities. It really isn't important whether the alien filesystem is being accessed over a network or not.

**NFS and BeOS**   Thanks to the presence of freely available NFS source code, a number of ports of NFS servers and clients began to appear for BeOS as early as PR2, and you can find the most up-to-date NFS client on BeWare today. As of this writing, only the NFS client was available, not the server. This means that you can install an NFS driver and gain access to mounted, shared volumes on other machines running other operating systems when an NFS server is present on your local network. You will not, however, be able to give other users access to your filesystem via NFS until an NFS server is available for BeOS. Don't be surprised if one is available by the time you read this.

# AppleTalk

Although AppleTalk appears in the Network preferences panel, don't be fooled into thinking you'll be able to mount volumes on your local network. Enabling this option does indeed let your machine "see" an AppleTalk network, but as of R4, the Tracker has no mechanism for mounting or displaying shared disks and folders on an AppleTalk network. What you *can* do with AppleTalk, however, is send documents to AppleTalk-connected printers.

Select the AppleTalk radio button, restart networking, then launch the Printers preferences panel. Click the Add... button and choose Apple LaserWriter Compatible. The ensuing dialog will display an upper and a lower pane. If there are any AppleTalk-connected printers on your local network, you'll see their names listed in the upper pane. Select one, give it a name, click OK, and print to it! This works as easily from BeOS/Intel machines as it does from BeOS/PowerPC. Note that AppleTalk printing works only over Ethernet, and not over LocalTalk (due to the lack of BeOS synchronous serial port drivers for Macintosh hardware).

If you want a printer connected to your BeOS computer to appear on MacOS machines (via the Chooser), things get a little trickier. You'll need to have an AFP (AppleTalk Filing Protocol) server running somewhere on your network, and register a file server name using the Name Binding Protocol.

# The Five-Minute Web Server

What would an Internet-ready operating system be without a Web server to call its own? As you learned in Chapter 2, BeOS includes a bundled Web server with every installation. If you thought that only extreme techno-weenies were allowed to be Webmasters, you might be surprised to learn how easy it is to publish your own site. And by the way, you don't necessarily have to publish a site to the world at large—there are many good reasons to run a small server for your private or internal network.

## Who Needs a Personal Server?

Web server software comes in a wide array of types. Some, like Apache, are so complex and finely tuned that people make their careers just maintaining them. Others, like PoorMan, have just a few controls, are not optimized to work under heavy stress loads, and may not offer the customizability that power users need. On the other hand, small personal servers can be set up and launched in a matter of minutes, and suit the needs of individuals, work-groups, and low-to-medium-traffic sites just fine. Remember—you don't need a giant printing press to put out your own newsletter. Let's look at a few of the reasons why people find personal Web servers useful.

**Mirror Sites**  If you have a site on the Web—even if it's just a few pages—you probably have an exact replica of it on your hard drive somewhere, with all directory structures mirroring those on the live server (if you're not doing this, you probably should). When you go to test your pages before uploading them, however, a few things may work differently than you expect them to, or than you wish they would. A personal server fixes several vexing problems with local site mirrors.

The biggest problem has to do with pathnames in your documents that reference other pages and embedded images. A Web server always has a root directory. Just like your BeOS system, the root of a Web server is represented by a

## *What Do You Mean, "Web Server"?*

Some people get confused about the meaning of the term "Web server," since the term means two different things.

In hardware circles, "Web server" often refers to the physical machine that dishes up pages to the world. Web server hardware on the very high end, such as that which runs major corporate sites and ISPs, still tends to comprise a lot of very expensive equipment—striped SCSI RAIDs, big fat T3 cables jacked into Gigabyte Ethernet cards and ATMs, beautiful purple boxes with names like "Onyx," and so on. But with the rapid rise in the quality and speed of consumer-level hardware, many professional Web servers are little more than stock machines with plenty of RAM and a nice, fast hard disk. It takes a heck of a lot of pounding to max out a P300 with 64MB of RAM, and a standard 2GB hard disk is hundreds of times larger than most Web sites.

But "Web server" also refers to the software running on these machines—the software that intercepts incoming HTTP requests, figures out where on the system the requested files live, and doles them out through the network card or cards. With software, unlike hardware Web servers, expense is not an accurate measure of quality—the majority of the world's Web sites run a software package called Apache, which is absolutely free of charge (Apache runs on Linux, Solaris, Windows NT, and, yes, BeOS).

Of course, the most accurate use of the term "Web server" is when it refers to the whole she-bang—hardware and software. Fire up PoorMan and your ordinary computer becomes a Web server instantly.

single "/" character. This makes constructing paths very easy. For example, let's say you keep all of your site's images in a directory called /images, and you're currently working on a document that's going to live at /projects/articles/june/drafts/test.html. To insert an image into this document, you could reference ../../../../images/logo.gif, or you could reference /images/logo.gif. It doesn't make much difference, except that A) the first version is more difficult to figure out, and B) will stop working if you move it to a different directory depth! If, on the other hand, all of your links and image callouts start with /, then any document can live in any directory and be guaranteed to work properly. But when you use the more elegant second method, your mirror site is not properly viewable on your hard drive, because the browser alone doesn't know where the root is supposed to be. This is the single largest functional problem solved by having a personal Web server: Because you can tell your server which directory is the root, all of those paths will resolve properly, and your site will behave on your hard drive just as it does on the live site.

In addition, you'll be able to link to directory names instead of index.html. In other words, if you put a file called index.html in a directory called /words, the

URL to that file should be **www.yoursite.com/words/**—the user should never see the index.html filename; it exists for the express purpose of being hidden. Unfortunately, a link to /words/ will not work as long as the site is on your hard drive, making testing very difficult. Again, a personal server fixes this problem.

Finally, if your site uses CGI scripts such as those written in Perl, those parts of your site are going to be completely broken on your local mirror. By installing a personal Web server and a copy of Perl, you can work on your CGI projects offline, then upload them when they're perfect.

***Personal Servers and Workgroups*** **If you work on a Web site as part of a team, you probably keep your mirror on a shared network volume, and you probably deal with some or all of the problems mentioned above on a daily basis. To solve these problems for everybody on your team at once, all you have to do is use CIFS or NFS to mount the network drive, then run PoorMan on one of the machines in-house. Tell PoorMan that the root of the server is on the network volume. Then, everyone in the workgroup can access the site in all its glory by typing the IP address or hostname of the PoorMan machine into their browsers. They can also edit documents on the server and have changes take effect immediately on the mirror site, no upload required.**

**Intranet Use**  You may not be a professional or even semi-professional coder. That's OK—you can learn enough HTML to fake it in about two hours. It really is that easy. Which is good, because your boss wants to see a graphical presentation of the documents you've been working on lately. Wouldn't she be impressed if you built a little Web site on your hard drive and made it available on the company network? PoorMan makes the publishing side of this a cinch.

If the idea catches on, you're in good stead, because PoorMan is more than capable of dishing up enough documents to keep a 50-person team all clicking away from their respective cubicles all day long. It won't even miss a heartbeat.

**Internet Publishing**  Earlier in this chapter I described how every computer attached to the Internet has a unique IP address. Some machines have a static address, which is always the same. Most people with dial-up PPP accounts have dynamic IP addresses, which are different every time they connect. Either way, all you need to host a Web site is an IP address, a few HTML documents, and a Web server. With PoorMan's help, you can have people accessing a site hosted on your BeOS machine from anywhere in the world within minutes (more on that below). However, there's a slight catch to hosting a site this way: You'll have to give out your IP address as your URL, rather than a domain name. Not only is that unintuitive and difficult to remember, but if you have a dynamically assigned IP, you'll have to give out a different address every time you connect—there will be no way for others to bookmark your site, since it might have a different address tomorrow (see the sidebar *Hosting an Actual Domain* for the solution to this).

However, this can still be an effective (and fun!) solution for certain situations. For example, you may be in a situation where you don't have permission to post pages on an actual Web server, but you need to present some HTML documents for someone's review. All you have to do is create them on your hard drive, point PoorMan to that location, and email your IP address to a few people.

## Hosting an Actual Domain

If you want to host a site on your BeOS machine that's accessible to the outside world, all you have to do is give out your IP address instead of the usual URL. That means you have to tell people your site is at **http://139.49.44.58/** rather than at **http://www.mysite.com/**. Why? Because using an actual domain name for a Web site depends on the cooperation of the Internet's DNSs, or domain name servers, which maintain tables that draw correspondences between IP addresses and the domains mapped to them.

If you want to host an actual domain name on your home or office BeOS machine, you'll have to go the extra mile and take care of some business. First, you'll need to work with your ISP to secure a static IP address—one that will always be assigned to your machine, no matter what. Second, it goes without saying that you'll need to leave your machine turned on all the time, and have someone around who can reboot it if it should ever crash or hang while you're on vacation or something. Of course, you'll also need to maintain a connection to the Internet 24 hours a day. I don't recommend attempting this unless you have at least an ISDN connection or faster, though newer home and office connectivity options like xDSL and cable modems make this part much easier. Also, remember that if your BeOS machine multi-boots with other operating systems, you'll never be able to boot into them without taking down your server for a while, so you should be prepared to commit that machine to BeOS alone. Third, you'll need to work again with your ISP to have them map your domain name to the IP address assigned to your machine. They, in turn, will coordinate with InterNIC (the Internet's domain registration organization) to make sure that all of the DNS tables out there reflect this information. In a few days, the world's DNS tables will be updated and people will actually be able to access the site PoorMan is hosting on your machine by typing in your chosen domain name (assuming someone else doesn't already have it).

You can expect there to be some cost associated with this—consult with your ISP to find out how much. Your 24-hour Internet connection and phone bills will probably add up to something substantial as well. Not many people go this route, for obvious reasons. For $25 a month, you can get a big chunk of real estate on a professional Web server with massive speed and bandwidth, never have to worry about the server going down while you're not home, and basically save yourself a lot of hassle. In fact, the only compelling reason to want to go deep with home/office Web hosting is if you need control over the server environment that your ISP doesn't give you. For example, you may want to run BeOS-only CGI software, or script portions of your site with BeOS-only scripting solutions. Or you may want up-to-the-minute access to your traffic logs, while your ISP may offer them only once a week. Or you may just be a control freak, like our technical editor, Chris.

You will, however, win major, major geek points for hosting a domain on a BeOS server.

***Locating Your IP Address*** Once you've established a PPP connection, right-click the Dial-Up Networking Replicant in the Deskbar and choose Statistics. Your current IP address, along with a bunch of other potentially interesting information, will be displayed in the PPP window. If you need more detailed information, type netstat into the Terminal. netstat will report your current PPP IP address, as well as the address assigned to your network interface card (if you have one), and your loopback address. If you want to get really clever about it, read the scripting information that's available free at http://www.beosbible.com and use the hey utility to create a script that mails out your current IP address every time you connect. By using this in conjunction with xicon, you could just click an icon on your Desktop every time you connect to accomplish this for you!

## Publishing with PoorMan

Alright. Enough introduction—let's serve up some Web pages. In a nutshell, the process boils down to this:

1. Establish a directory for your mirror site.

2. Point PoorMan to that directory.

3. Enter your IP address and any necessary paths into a Web browser.

4. Establish a logging system, if desired.

5. Make sure PoorMan is always running (optional).

**Prepare Your Site** As described earlier, every Web server has a "root." This is not the same thing as the root of your filesystem (though it could be). Rather, it's an arbitrary directory that represents the base of your site, at "/". The end user typing a URL into their browser will never see the name of the root directory. In other words, if you store your mirror site at /boot/home/web_sites/be_site/ and a user types your domain or IP address into a browser, the browser's location field will display only the IP address or domain name, not the directory path above. A common directory name for Web sites is public_html, but this is not necessary. If you run more than one site, you may want to store them as subdirectories of a single directory dedicated to mirror sites. Thus, you might have /boot/home/public_html/be_site and /boot/home/public_html/other_site.

If you are using PoorMan as a Web server, this is the *only* way you can serve both sites at once, since PoorMan is only capable of recognizing a single root directory. In the example above, assuming your IP address is 205.195.212.14, the URLs given to users would be:

**http://205.195.212.14/be_site/**

and

**http://205.195.212.14/other_site/**

## *Case-Sensitivity Issues*

If you're migrating to BeOS from the DOS/Windows world and copying a mirror site over from a DOS partition, there's a small issue you're going to have to deal with: DOS and Windows are pretty much brain-dead when it comes to filename case. When viewed under Windows Explorer, a file may be called `Test.html`, whereas the same file viewed from a DOS shell could be called `TEST.HTML`. As you already know, you need to take care when uploading your mirror site to a live Web server, since most Web servers are Unix-based (and thus case-sensitive), and you need to make sure the cases of all of your names are consistent. Many people simply use the "force lower-case" option in their FTP client, if available, to take care of everything upon upload. However, BeOS is also case-sensitive. Since the Tracker can mount FAT16 and FAT32 volumes transparently, copying your mirror over to a BFS partition won't be a problem, but the case of names most likely will be. There are a couple of possible solutions.

If your mirror is on another machine and you can FTP it to your BeOS machine, you can use the same "force lowercase" option you do when uploading to a live server. Of course, if there are any mixed-case filenames or link references anywhere in your site, those references will be broken by this technique, so you'll want to use it only if you've been doing so all along.

If the mirror is on a DOS partition on the same machine, FTP is not an option, and you'll need to change the case of all files after they've been copied over. If your site is small, you can do this manually. If not, you may find a couple of small shell scripts called UPPERCASE and `lowercase` useful—these can be found on BeWare, and will change the name of every file in the current directory to upper- or lowercase. Again, if you have a mixed-case site, this will not be a complete solution.

The most accurate and complete way to handle the situation is to copy your mirror down from your ISP's server, rather than from your DOS partition. The easiest way to do this is to telnet into your ISP, tar and gzip your site into a single file, FTP it down to your BeOS machine, and decompress it there. If your ISP's shell supports zip, you can use that, but most don't, so do it this way:

1.  Telnet in and `cd` to the directory just above your site's root. For example, if your site is stored at your ISP at `~/yourname/public_html`, then you'll want to `cd` to `~/yourname`.

2.  Type `tar -cvf mirror.tar public_html`.

3.  When this operation is finished, you'll find a file in the current directory called `mirror.tar`. Now type `gzip mirror.tar`. You should end up with a file called `mirror.tgz` or `mirror.tar.gz`. Log out of the telnet session.

4.  FTP into your ISP and download `mirror.tgz` to BeOS, then delete that file from your ISP's server.

5.  In the Terminal, `cd` to the location of `mirror.tgz` and type `gunzip mirror.tgz`. When finished, you'll have a file called `mirror.tar`.

6.  Make sure that `mirror.tar` is located one directory above where you want your mirror, then untar it by typing `tar -xvf mirror.tar`. The entire `public_html` directory and all of its subdirectories will decompress into the desired location, with all case names identical to the ones on the live server. Your site will work perfectly under BeOS!

If you already have a mirror site, copy or move it into the folder you've established. If you don't have a mirror site and are just experimenting, create a simple HTML document and place it there (if you don't speak HTML, you can always save an existing Web page down from NetPositive into this location, but it's up to you to respect all copyrighted material).

**Do It with Symlinks**  Of course, there's no reason why you should feel compelled to keep your site on your boot drive. If you have multiple mounted BFS partitions and your site is large, you may want to keep your mirror on a separate partition. If, as recommended elsewhere in this book, you keep your applications on your boot volume and your data on a dedicated data volume, this approach makes logical sense, since a Web site is just a pile of data. Since you'll generally spend most of your Tracker time on your boot volume, however, it can be nice to have easy access to your site from there. Just create a symlink in your home directory from the root of your site (see Chapter 5, *Files and the Tracker*, for more on symlinks). You can add this link to your Be menu, and even point PoorMan to the link if you like. Interestingly, if you do this, PoorMan's traffic logs will make it appear as though the site really is located on your boot volume.

**Launch It**  This is the easy part. Launch PoorMan, pull down Edit | Preferences, and click the Select Web Directory button (or type in a path). Navigate to the root of your mirror site, and click Select. If you want to specify a default file in your directory to be served when only the directory name is accessed, enter that here—most sites use index.html. If you want users to be able to see the contents of your directories when no filename is specified, click the Send Directory List checkbox. Click Done, and the status line at the top of the PoorMan window should say Status: running. If it doesn't, pull down the Controls menu and choose Run Server. Now to give it a whirl...

*Figure 8.04*

*Configure PoorMan for the first time by telling it where your server should find its root, its default filename, and whether users should be able to see directory listings.*

From the same machine, launch a browser (such as NetPositive) and enter your loopback IP into the location (URL) field, along with any pathname necessary. Remember: your loopback IP is *always* 127.0.0.1, regardless of whether you have an NIC installed, regardless of your PPP configuration, and regardless of operating system.

When entering the location into your browser, you must pay attention to the relationship between your mirror location and the site root you've told PoorMan to use. Table 8.01 shows some sample situations.

### Table 8.01

| Mirror Location | Home Page name | PoorMan Root | URL |
|---|---|---|---|
| /boot/home/mysite | index.html | /boot/home/mysite | `http://127.0.0.1` |
| /drive2/public_html | index.html | /drive2 | `http://127.0.0.1/public_html/` |
| ~/public_html/sites/mysite | default.htm | ~/public_html | `http://127.0.0.1/sites/mysite/` |

*When entering a URL into your browser for the site you're serving, correlate between your mirror location and the site root you've told PoorMan to use.*

If you can't get your site to work, there are only a few possible problems:

- PoorMan is not actually running. Check its status, and close and restart it if necessary (it shouldn't be).

- There's a mistake in your path. Check Table 8.01 to understand the correlation between PoorMan's root and your mirror site.

- There's a mistake in the loopback address. Make sure you're using 127.0.0.1.

- NetPositive has become confused. While later versions of NetPositive have gotten much better about this, early versions could get confused if a mistake was entered initially and then corrected—error messages could be false. Close and restart NetPositive.

 Remember, your loopback IP will *only* work as long as you're on your own machine. If someone types 127.0.0.1 into their browser, they're going to be contacting their own machine, not yours!

Once you've got your site working from your loopback IP, try it from one of your other addresses. For example, if you're on an internal network, you've associated an IP address, likely something in the 192.168.xxx.xxx range, with your NIC. Read this address from the Network preferences panel, and type that in instead of your loopback address. If that works, you can give that URL to others connected to your internal network, but remember that addresses in this range will not be accessible to people in the outside world. If your internal network is permanently connected to the Internet, you probably have a "real" IP address, outside of the 192.168.xxx.xxx range. If so, your site will be accessible by anyone in the world, with any browser, so long as there isn't a firewall in place at your organization. If there is (and for security reasons, your organization probably should have one), you'll have to ask your network administrator if they can "punch a hole" in the firewall on port 80 to your address. This will give the world HTTP access only to your machine.

Different organizations have different policies on this practice, so you may or may not be successful in getting this to happen.

If you use PPP for dial-up, grab your current IP address from the Dial-Up Networking Statistics window and enter that address into the browser instead. If this works, the whole world can now access your site at that address for as long as you maintain your connection. Again, remember that most PPP accounts assign addresses dynamically, and it will probably be different next time you log on.

 If you do give out your IP address as a URL, don't leave your telnet server running at the same time (turn it off via the checkbox in Network preferences). Even though telnet access is password-protected, the nonconfigurability of the telnet implementation and BeOS filesystem permissions add up to a pretty poor security situation. By broadcasting your IP address and running the telnet server at the same time, you're inviting trouble. If you absolutely must run both simultaneously, choose the most complex telnet password you can, to minimize the possibility of its being cracked by algorithms.

 Even if NetPositive isn't capable of displaying all of the technological wizardry on your site, don't let that stop you from serving it from PoorMan. Happily, any Java, JavaScript, CSS, DHTML, or anything else coded into your pages will work normally when other browsers on other platforms access your PoorMan-hosted site. PoorMan is just dishing up files over HTTP, not processing them. However, there may be some limitations if your site depends on any kind of CGI processing, such as embedded Perl scripts. While Perl for BeOS is available, PoorMan did not know how to work with CGI directives as of R4.0.

 **Autostart PoorMan** If you want your machine to function as a Web host whenever it's turned on, all you have to do is add the following line to /boot/home/config/boot/UserBootscript:

/boot/beos/apps/PoorMan &

If you've moved PoorMan to another location, of course, you'll need to use a path equal to its new location. PoorMan remembers all of its settings, including whether or not it was currently running when you last shut off your machine. If it was running when you last shut down, it will be running next time you boot.

**Redirecting with PoorMan** In some instances, you might want to funnel all accesses to a given directory on your site to a new page. This is often the case when you move pages or directories around on your site (a bad idea, in general, and a practice that can usually be avoided by planning ahead carefully when building your site). While professional Web servers have sophisticated mechanisms for handling redirects, PoorMan does not. However, you can always resort to the "poor man's redirect" (pun intended) by using symlinks.

Create a link to the new location in the old location, and make sure the link has the same filename as the old page. This will effectively send users to the new location, but has an unintentional side effect: As you know from previous chapters, the operating system's notion of the current directory after following a symlink is a complete illusion. Unfortunately, this illusion can create havoc with certain forms of relative links. For example, let's say you use a symlink to redirect users from /words/index.html to /images/index.html. After arriving at /images/index.html, the location (URL) field of the user's browser is going to say that they're still looking at the words directory. Not a big deal, unless there are any links on the page that don't use the "/" format to start from the server's root. If there are, links on that page that are supposed to dig deeper into the images directory are going to try to dig deeper into the words directory, which will, of course, result in errors.

Symlinks can be used as redirects, but you'll need to make sure that links on the destination page are formatted fully, or the user is going to run into problems.

 Of course, you could get around this by simply moving the entire directory structure to the new location, but it's rare that you'll want to rearrange your site's directory structure after it's been created. If you need to do tricks like this, the best solution is to use a Web server that handles redirects natively.

**Log It** If you're interested in keeping track of who's visiting your site, which pages or images are the most popular, and when your traffic spikes occur, PoorMan is capable of keeping detailed traffic logs on your behalf. However, at this writing, PoorMan logged to a nonstandard format. While perfectly informative, the nonstandard format makes it a little tough to analyze traffic patterns with most out-of-the-box log-parsing tools. Depending on your needs, this probably isn't that big of a deal. If you're really serious about tracking traffic, you probably aren't serving your site with PoorMan (not because it isn't robust enough, but because it doesn't offer much in the way of configurability). And there are plenty of command-line tools, such as grep and wc, that make it easy to whip up your own log-parsing scripts. Since PoorMan probably will generate standard log format before long, we'll use sample lines from a standard log below to get acquainted with the typical Web log.

Regardless of what server creates them or what format they take, Web logs always record one line in a text file for every file requested. Since most Web pages consist of an HTML document and several images or other types of files, every page request will typically generate multiple "hits" on your server. A typical line in a Web log looks like this (though you'll have to imagine it all on one line, rather than wrapped as it is here):

```
www.birdhouse.org 209.142.19.73 - - [25/Jul/1998:05:39:12 -0700]
"GET /beos/tips/ HTTP/1.0" 200 15177
```

The fields, in order from left to right, are:

- **Domain being accessed:** Since a single Web server can dish up multiple domains, this knowledge can be critical in analyzing your logs later, enabling each domain to be separated out into a separate report.

- **Requesting address:** The IP address of the machine requesting the file.

- **Date/time stamp:** This appears in a variety of formats, depending on the server.

- **Request header:** In quotes, this is the full text of the HTTP request made upon the server. It includes the action (which is almost always GET), the path, and the HTTP level, or protocol, that should be used for transfer.

- **Server code:** One of a list of numbers representing the status of the transfer: 200 indicates a successful transfer; 300 indicates that the requesting browser found the file in its cache so file transfer was not necessary; and 404, as you well know, means "file not found."

- **Size:** Size of the file, in bytes.

Turning your Web logs into meaningful data is a matter of running them through a program or script that looks for patterns determined by you, then generates reports in plain English, in text or HTML format. There are literally hundreds of log parsers available, and they're different for every operating system. Search BeWare for "web log" or "log parser" to find tools that work on BeOS (the freeware Analog tool is covered in Chapter 15, *Other Goodies*). Alternatively, see if you can build a log parsing script of your own from the command-line tools bundled with BeOS. It's not that hard. Many people also import logs directly into their database applications and use custom-built systems of macros or scripts to generate reports.

In PoorMan's preferences panel you'll find a Logging tab, which includes options to log to the "console" (PoorMan's main window), or to a file, the location of which you can specify. Note also the hit counter in the upper-right

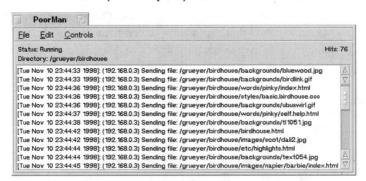

*Figure 8.05*

*PoorMan logs every incoming file request to a text file, to its own console, or both. In the upper-right corner you'll find a hit counter for the current session, while the upper left displays the server's status as either Running or Stopped.*

corner of PoorMan's main window, which reports the total number of requests for the current session. You can turn logging on or off "on the fly" from the Controls menu.

**Performance Issues**  As described elsewhere in this book, BeOS is not the finely tuned network server that Linux or FreeBSD are. It doesn't suck, but neither does it excel. You'll find it approximately as effective as Windows 98— adequate for most people's needs, but not for high-end Web sites that serve hundreds of thousands of files per day. Should you let this stop you from running your site on BeOS? The answer to this depends entirely on your needs and the amount of traffic your site receives. On one hand, BeOS's advanced capabilities mean that there will probably be quite a few very handsome scripting and CGI solutions for BeOS that aren't available on other platforms. On the other hand, if your site gets more than, say, 100,000 hits per day, you should probably consider a more network-specialized operating system. This number, by the way, is based on informal estimates made by people using PoorMan regularly, in heavy testing. It does not reflect any hard numbers or benchmark testing. Suffice it to say that that leaves more than enough overhead for the vast majority of us. However, PoorMan is not a full-featured server, and lacks many features associated with professional Web-serving. You may want to explore some of the other servers available for BeOS, discussed in Chapter 11. In addition, keep in mind that Be's current priorities (as of R4) are in the area of optimizing multimedia performance to the fullest—that has always been the company's #1 priority. That doesn't mean, however, that networking performance is unimportant to Be, and you can probably look for more improvements to the BeOS TCP/IP stack in future releases.

 Want some real-world numbers? One Be employee reports that for a while he was running BeWare highlights with PoorMan on a BeBox and registering 20–30 hits every few seconds. He further went on to note that the BeBox's CPU load indicators were not stressing out in the least. It's also worth pointing out that—no matter how cool they are—BeBoxen are *slow* compared to today's commonly available hardware. Let's interpret "20–30 hits every few seconds" as "25 hits every ten seconds." That's 150 hits per minute, or 9,000 hits per hour, or 216,000 hits per day. Of course, traffic doesn't move that way—it comes in lulls and spikes. Nevertheless, that kind of traffic is nothing to poo-poo, and it should give you some indication of what's possible. So unless you're running **cnn.com** and dishing up copies of the Starr report (CNN was serving up around 5,600 pages per second for a while there), you probably don't need to take all of these caveats *too* seriously (and remember— a site with that kind of traffic is going to seriously stress any system short of the expensive big iron discussed earlier).

## *Got Bandwidth?*

BeOS networking performance issues aside, you also need to consider the width of the pipe leading out the back of your computer and onto the Net before making your site publicly accessible. A well-designed site that doesn't overdo it on the graphics can actually be served quite efficiently over a 56K modem or ISDN line; I don't recommend it with anything slower unless your site is extremely low-traffic. Of course, the only way to know for sure is to test it for yourself, but if you want to do a rough estimate, here's how.

Modem speed is measured in kilobits per second. To translate that into kilobytes per second, divide by eight. For example, a 56K modem is capable of transmitting 56/8 kilobytes per second, or 7K. Now calculate the weight of an average page on your site, measured as the total size of your HTML and all of the images it references. Let's say it comes to 35K, meaning it will take five seconds to transmit the whole page. Now figure that multiple people will be visiting your site at once. If only 10 people are visiting your site at once, that speed could instantly rise to 50 seconds! Finally, remember that 56K is only a theoretical maximum, and a standard modem connections is almost never as fast as its theoretical maximum. Clearly, sites should be served over normal modems only in very low-traffic conditions.

**PoorMan and MIME Issues**  By now, you're well familiar with the way the Internet's MIME typing scheme is integrated into BeOS for filetyping needs. When BeOS files are served through PoorMan, Internet MIME and BeOS MIME come together. When Web servers—on any platform—send a file to a browser, they send the file's MIME type along with it. Of course, on Unix, Windows, and MacOS systems, the MIME type isn't encoded in each file, and must be derived by other means. This is typically done via an extensions table. The extensions table tells the Web server, "Any time you serve a file ending in .html, send it as type text/html. Any time you send a file ending in .gif, send it as image/gif." Since BeOS already has MIME types attached to all of its files, you'll notice that PoorMan does not have an extensions table like most Web servers do. This can be really convenient for Webmasters, but there can also be some gotchas associated with the system.

For example, the text editor you use to create HTML documents probably saves the files it creates with a type of text/plain. PoorMan does The Right Thing with plain text files, and displays them as plain text, rather than making assumptions and interpreting them as HTML. That, however, means that when you access such a file from a PoorMan-hosted site, it's displayed in "raw" format, with all of its tags and none of its formatting. Changing that file's type to text/html will solve the problem, but you probably don't want to have to do that for every file you create. You basically have two options here. One solution is to continue creating your files as text/plain so that they're easily editable when double-clicked. Then, later on, you can change their types individually, or batch change them with a tool like DropType (Chapter 10, *System Tools and Utilities*). The other solution is to leave them all as text/html documents, then just use the Open With option that appears on the context menu when you right-click the file in the Tracker. Alternatively, you can use the File | Open option in your text editor, rather than double-clicking the files. Finally, if you use an editor like Pe (Chapter 12, *Productivity Applications*), you can tell it to use an alternate filetype when saving, which is really an ideal solution to all of this.

 ***Professional Web Servers***  PoorMan is great, but its capabilities are limited (intentionally). If you need advanced features like the ability to interact with CGI scripts, host multiple sites from the same machine, or password-protect certain directories, you'll want to check out the descriptions of some of the third-party Web servers available for BeOS in Chapter 11, *Network Applications*.

# Remote Control

You don't have to be sitting in front of your BeOS machine to operate it. If you have the telnet daemon enabled and an Internet connection of some kind, you can log in from any machine in the world that also has an Internet connection. Or, you can operate your BeOS machine from across the room, over your internal network. You'll only have access to the shell, but that's enough to view and edit text files, get directory listings, start and stop programs (even GUI programs, though you won't be able to see them), or do anything else you normally do from the Terminal.

There are also limited possibilities for controlling other operating systems from your BeOS machine.

## Telnet to Your BeOS Machine

While the future may hold a greater array of remote access possibilities for BeOS, telnet is currently the only remote control option available for BeOS users.

**Enable Telnet Daemon**  In order for you to log into your BeOS machine from a remote location, BeOS must be "listening" for telnet requests. All you have to do is open the Network preferences panel and click the "Enable telnet server" box in the Network Services group, then assign a username and password. If you enabled the FTP server earlier in this chapter, you've already established a username and password, and don't need to do so again. Restart networking, and you're done. Now take note of your IP address, make sure your machine is currently connected to the Internet or to your local network, and go to another machine.

 As discussed in the FTP section above, there are security issues associated with running a telnet daemon. If unsavory persons should obtain or hack your password, they'll have free reign over your machine, at least until BeOS has a real security model in place. Nothing will stop them from running any piece of installed software or from deleting all of your files. As always, choose a secure password, exercise caution when distributing your password, and change it on a regular basis.

**Operate Your BeOS Machine from Anywhere**  The only software you need on the remote machine is a telnet client. Since these are built into (or easily available for) nearly every operating system, this should not be an obstacle. From another BeOS machine or any Unix-based operating system, just open a Terminal and type telnet <ip address>.

## Telnetting from Other Operating Systems

If you need to access your BeOS machine from a Windows or MacOS machine, you have a number of options.

### Telnetting into BeOS from Windows

From any Windows machine, click the Start button, then Run. In the run field, type telnet 192.168.0.1 (replacing this IP address with the address of the machine you want to access). You can also type the same command at any DOS prompt. Alternatively, you can create a shortcut on your desktop to the telnet client by opening c:\windows in Explorer, finding telnet.exe, right-dragging it to the desktop and selecting "Create Shortcut here" from the context menu. If you use telnet frequently, you may want to look into more advanced telnet clients available for download from any software library, such as **hotfiles.com** or **download.com**. These may offer features such as customizable ANSI coloring or file download capabilities.

### Telnetting into BeOS from MacOS

Telnet is not built into the Macintosh operating system, but it is easy to download a free telnet client for MacOS. The most popular client is NCSA Telnet, free software developed at the National Center for Supercomputer Applications at the University of Illinois at Urbana-Champaign. Don't let the advanced parentage fool you, though—NCSA Telnet is easy to install and operate. Simply download the latest package from ftp.ncsa.uiuc.edu if you haven't already, and use a compression utility to expand it. Make sure you have a connection to the Internet, and double-click the NCSA Telnet client from the Finder. Choose New Connection from the file menu, or use the command key shortcut Command+O. In the Open connection dialog box type the hostname or IP address of your BeOS machine, and give the session window a name, if you would like. You can also define a terminal type here, but it's OK to use the default. Hit Return and telnet will make the connection and throw a terminal window on the screen so you can log in. Some versions of MacOS come with NCSA Telnet already installed. Before going to the trouble of downloading the package, search for telnet using Fast Find to see if it is already available.

**Apple has in the past made available the Apple Internet Connection Kit (AICK), which included the NCSA Telnet client. Prior to System 7.6, the AICK was available as an additional package. As of MacOS 7.6, the AICK was bundled with the system. However, it is no longer included as of MacOS 8.5. You can, of course, still download NCSA Telnet (or any other telnet client) from your favorite MacOS shareware library. You'll find a variety of clients from which to choose at www.hotfiles.com.**

When your BeOS machine responds, you'll be prompted for a username and password. Enter the combination you entered into the Network preferences panel and you'll be sitting at a Terminal prompt on the remote machine. You can now do anything you can do from a "native" Terminal (see Chapter 6, *The Terminal*, for a refresher course). Some examples:

- Get file listings.
- Copy, move, create, or delete files and directories.
- Find the mount points of mounted volumes with the df command.
- Find out how much space a directory hierarchy is taking up with the du command.
- Get your fortune told with the fortune command.
- Zip and unzip files and folders with the zip and unzip commands, or use tar and gzip.
- Make the machine go "ping" by typing beep.
- Make alert boxes pop up onscreen with messages in them (see Chapter 6, *The Terminal*, for details).
- Manipulate text with the sed, awk, sort, and fmt tools.
- Run system queries with the query command.
- Find text in files with grep.
- Run mathematical calculations with the expr tool.
- Change file permissions with the chmod command.
- Kill a running process by using the ps, grep, and kill commands.
- Create a new document with the touch command. Edit it with the built-in vi editor.
- Create or run shell scripts.
- If the machine has the uptime tool installed (available on BeWare), find out how long the machine has gone since its last reboot.
- Reboot the machine by using the shutdown -r command (note that this will disconnect your current telnet session, as well as terminating any PPP connection the remote machine might be connected with, so you may not be able to get back in after the machine reboots, unless it's set up to dial in automatically).
- Launch GUI software. Of course, you won't be able to see what that software is doing, but it may be useful, for example, to be able to launch the

remote machine's copy of PoorMan so that you can access its Web serving capabilities. To launch anything from the Terminal (or telnet), just type the path to its executable. If the application is already in your path statement, you can skip the path and just type the executable's filename. For example, to launch StyledEdit, just type StyledEdit into the Terminal (since StyledEdit is in your path). But to launch an editor called XYZ that you've got living in /boot/home/apps/edit, you'll need to type /boot/home/apps/edit/XYZ &. Remember, too, that most applications can take document names as arguments when launched from the Terminal. To open a document called test.html in StyledEdit, type StyledEdit test.html. If you add the & character to end of these commands, the prompt will be returned to you immediately. For example, type PoorMan & to launch the Web server and continue with your telnet session.

## Accessing Other Operating Systems Remotely

It's a two-way street: Not only do you want to access your BeOS machine from afar, but sometimes you want to be able to access programs running on other operating systems from within BeOS. Amazingly, you can do this right now, with a freely available client called the VNC (Virtual Network Client) viewer.

**Using VNC** VNC is an amazingly open and flexible little tool. Any machine running the VNC server, which is nothing but a small daemon lurking in the background, can make its desktop and all running applications available to anyone with an Internet connection and the VNC viewer software, which itself runs on a number of platforms. Since the viewer software isn't tied to any particular OS, you can install the tiny (75K) VNC client on your BeOS machine and then access MacOS, Windows 95, 98, NT, Solaris, or Linux desktops. You can launch and run any application on those machines for which you have permission (relative to the username and password you enter when logging in), and basically pretend that you're there at the remote site, operating the machine directly. Interestingly, VNC does not save a "state" while you're working. This means that you can log into, say, a Macintosh from your BeOS machine, type half a sentence into SimpleText, then go log in again from another machine and finish that sentence where you left off.

Don't confuse the VNC system with an emulator—the machine running the VNC client doesn't emulate any code from the remote operating system. Rather, it simply passes a picture of the remote desktop into the client's window, then allows you to interact with that picture. Sound too good to be true? Well, there is a catch: The client is slow. There's no way to pass all of that information through any size network cable and get the same kind of screen update frequency you're accustomed to seeing when working on a machine directly. As a result, you'll notice significant lag times in all operations. Not enough to prevent you from getting your work done, but enough to make it somewhat annoying. You'll probably want to reserve your VNC use for times of real need, and for low-impact activities. Nonetheless, if your work or play requires this kind of access, you'll find VNC a godsend.

To get started with VNC, go to **www.cam-orl.co.uk/vnc/** and download a VNC server for the platform you want to access. Install it on that platform according to the manufacturer's instructions (which is no more difficult than installing any standard application). Launch the server, and establish any special properties you'd like to apply to connected sessions, such as the polling rate (this will affect the performance of the viewer, and may take some tweaking to optimize).

Download the BeOS VNC client from BeWare, launch it, and type in the IP address of the machine you want to access. Although the VNC login screen doesn't say it, you'll get an error message if you don't follow the remote machine's IP address with a colon and a port number. Unless your network administrator tells you otherwise, the port number you want to use is zero. In other words, you'll need to enter something like 192.168.0.3:0. Click the OK button, and a few seconds later the remote desktop will take over your BeOS Desktop.

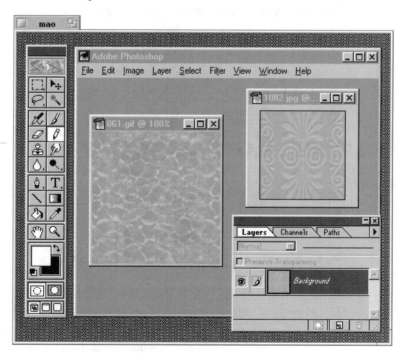

***Figure 8.06***

*Here ORL's Virtual Network Client for BeOS is being used to access a Windows 95 machine running Adobe Photoshop. The client is operating-system agnostic—this same client can access MacOS, Linux, any flavor of Windows, and other OSs as well.*

While it's possible to run VNC in a window, as shown in Figure 8.06, you probably won't want to if the remote desktop is running at the same resolution as your BeOS Desktop, since this will make it difficult to access important system functions, such as Windows 95's TaskBar. You'll probably have a better experience by dedicating one of your workspaces to VNC, allowing the remote desktop to take over an entire BeOS workspace. This way you can easily toggle between BeOS and the other operating system by tapping your Alt+F*x* keys (where *x* is a number between 1 and 9).

If you do want to run VNC in a window, it may not be immediately obvious how to do this, since all window borders and the application's title tab will be offscreen if the two systems' resolutions are set identically. You can, however, move your mouse pointer down to the extreme lower-right of the desktop and drag upward and in toward the center, pretending that you're resizing a normal window. After the window borders become visible, you can use them to move the window to a more normal location.

 **As of this writing, a few standard system calls were not transferred to the remote client properly. For example, right-clicks on a Windows desktop as seen through BeOS do not bring up a Windows context menu. Similarly, it is not possible to copy data to the clipboard with either standard BeOS or Windows hotkeys. You'll have to use the pulldown menu equivalents of these functions (e.g. to copy text to the clipboard, then pull down Edit | Copy). And yes, you can then paste that data into any other BeOS window.**

 The version of the VNC Viewer we tested was a little buggy, and we experienced occasional crashes, both on the server and client sides. If you plan to use it for mission-critical work, we recommend testing thoroughly beforehand, and saving your work frequently.

# Advanced Connectivity

While all of the above networking goodies may seem like a lot, network gurus will want more … and there is more. This section covers BeOS networking possibilities "beyond the norm."

## Multiple Network Configurations

Imagine this scenario: You've fine-tuned the Network preferences panel to work perfectly with your network interface card, and your local, internal network. Now you find out that your housemate wants to use your BeOS machine to access his dormitory's network during the day, while you're away at work. Unfortunately, his network requires a different IP and DNS settings. Or here's another scenario: Let's say you're running BeOS on a laptop, and most of the time that laptop is plugged into the company network via its built-in network card. Sometimes, however, you're on the road and using your dial-up ISP account from hotel rooms as you travel. Since your organization and your ISP use separate DNS servers, you need to be able to switch back and forth between them whenever the need arises.

For your convenience, BeOS will let you set up as many network configurations as you like, so you can switch between them with the click of a button, rather than resetting all of your parameters by hand every time. For dial-up networking, all you have to do is create alternate ISP configurations with the interface described in Chapter 4, *Get Online Fast*. For other types of networking, you'll be using the Configurations section of the Services tab in the Network preferences panel.

**Establishing Configurations**  Once you've got your networking set up and working the way you like it, click the Backup button and give the configuration a name. Then return to the Identity tab, enter another set of networking parameters, come back to the Services tab, and click Backup again. The Configurations window will display one entry for every configuration you've backed up. To remove a configuration, select it and click Delete.

**Restoring Configurations**  To enable a particular configuration, click the Restore button, restart networking, and you're in business.

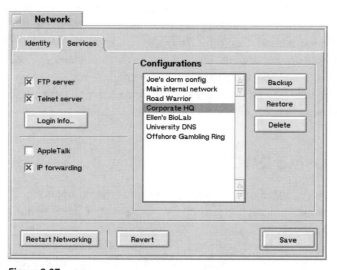

*Figure 8.07*

*The Network preferences panel will let you create as many alternate networking configurations as you like, to be restored or deleted as you see fit. Select any entry, click Restore, and restart networking to make that configuration active.*

### *Editing Network Preferences Manually*

Ninety-nine percent of the time, when you want to add functionality to your system, including network functionality, it can be done with the simple addition of a new driver or the installation of a new application. Occasionally, however, you'll encounter a network utility that requires a little additional hacking. This is the case when you extend the system in ways that Be hasn't foreseen.

The Network preferences panel is, in fact, nothing but a front end to a standard, text-based configuration file, located at `/boot/home/config/settings/network`. Since editing of this file is not officially encouraged, its filetype is not set to `text/plain`, so double-clicking on it will not launch it in your text editor. Instead, you'll have to use the File | Open panel from within your editor.

Within this file you'll find several major sections, the purposes of which are pretty much self-explanatory. For example, you'll find your current system mail settings at the top of the file, complete with username, encrypted password, SMTP server, mail-checking schedule, and the rest of the options found in the E-mail preferences panel. Lower down in the file you'll find the global settings for your router, DNS servers, hostname, and the like. In addition, if you've saved multiple network configurations as described above, you'll find separate files, with names like `Network.Main` and `network.Joe's Dorm`, reflecting those settings.

It's not often that you'll find cause to hand-edit this file, if ever. In R3, adding the third-party DHCP client to the system required adding DHCP-specific settings to this file, while in DR8, adding the ability to use internal modems to BeOS meant hand-tweaking this file. With R4, it's hard to imagine finding a need to edit this file at all. You'll know that you need to if the instructions accompanying a downloaded file instruct you to. The only thing you need to remember is that if you do edit this file, you'll need to commit your changes to the system by saving your changes, reopening the Network preferences panel, and restarting network services. If you're not sure whether you need to edit this file, then *don't*.

## Using DHCP

As discussed earlier, some networking environments (such as those in a corporate or academic setting) may use a central server to automatically assign IP addresses to machines as they log onto the network. This helps the organization to conserve resources if the block of available IP addresses is limited. This service, known as Dynamic Host Configuration Protocol (DHCP), was available only as a third-party solution with BeOS release 3.x, and required hand-editing of the Network preferences file. However, DHCP was made a standard part of BeOS networking with R4, and can be enabled easily, allowing BeOS machines to be configured automatically alongside machines running other operating systems in any DHCP environment.

In the Network preferences panel, double-click the name of your network card, and make sure the "Obtain settings automatically (DHCP)" radio button is selected. Click the Update button, restart networking, and you're done. All necessary network addresses should be assigned automatically every time you boot your machine.

## Proxies, IP Forwarding, and Masquerades

In many environments, it's convenient to let multiple machines share a single Internet connection, rather than having each machine maintain its own connection. For example, your home office may have four machines, but only a single ISDN terminal adapter. It's possible to maintain a network interface (such as cable modem or ISDN device) on only one of your machines, and then tell all of your other machines to use that machine as a virtual router, directing all of their TCP/IP requests to it for processing. While this kind of functionality may be achieved most efficiently by a dedicated hardware router, emulating routing functions in software can be a more cost-effective solution, and can provide plenty of connectivity for a small network. If the connected machine has a fast connection to the Internet, it can even serve medium- and large-sized organizations effectively.

**Sharing the Load**   In reality, there are several flavors of software routing, and they run in both directions, either allowing BeOS to direct its requests to other machines running other operating systems, or using the BeOS machine itself as a routing machine. These solutions are known as proxy servers, IP forwarding, and network address translation (also known as "IP Masquerading").

**BeOS Using a Proxy Server**   When digging around in the preferences and options panels in most of your TCP/IP-based software (on any platform), you may have noticed options to use a "proxy server." For example, NetPositive, Internet Explorer, and Netscape Navigator all give you an option to "Use Proxy Server," then offer fields for entering the address of the proxy server. If you fill in these fields, those browsers will stop looking to the current operating system for network services, and instead forward all requests to the specified machine for processing. Thus, there are two catches to using proxy servers: A) you have to reconfigure every TCP/IP application on every machine on your network to take advantage of them, and B) if a certain piece of software doesn't know how to talk to proxy servers, it's not going to be easy to use it through one (though there's usually a way to hack your way around this limitation).

There are many proxy server solutions available for other operating systems. Some of the most popular are WinGate for Windows 95, 98, and NT (**www.wingate.net**), CSM Proxy for Linux (**alibaba.csm.co.at/proxy**), and SurfDoubler for MacOS (**www.vicomtech.com**). Each proxy has its own set of configuration instructions, but one thing they all have in common is that they use TCP/IP's standard port mapping scheme to assign specific kinds of communications to specific "channels" on the TCP/IP pathway (MacOS implementations of the scheme differ a little, though the principle is the same). For example, Web servers almost always "listen" on port 80, while mail servers usually pay attention to port 25. Typically, you'll need to enable each Internet service you want handled by the proxy to use a separate port.

 As of R4, BeOS includes a complete port mapping table, which you'll find on your system at /boot/beos/etc/services. In some cases, TCP/IP applications such as proxy servers will interact with this file. Because this file is located centrally in the operating system, any applications that need it can share a common table, eliminating possible conflicts. Note that this file currently lives in the system-level hierarchy, so any edits you make to it could be overwritten next time you upgrade BeOS. If you edit this file, make a copy of the modified version somewhere under your home folder for safekeeping.

After your proxy server has been installed and configured, you need to tell BeOS how to redirect its TCP/IP needs to the new server. Start by opening /boot/beos/etc in the Tracker and finding a file called hosts.sample. Make a copy of it as hosts (without .sample) and open it in a text editor. You'll find lines that look like this:

```
192.168.0.2          bebox.mycompany.com          bebox
```

 Theoretically, you should never, ever tamper with any file living anywhere under the /boot/beos hierarchy. This is the sacrosanct user-level/system-level distinction outlined in Chapter 5, *Files and the Tracker*. Ideally, you should find a user-level version of this file in /boot/home/config/etc, to which you would be free to add your own modifications. Unfortunately, such a file does not exist (and will not be recognized) in BeOS R4.0. Consider this case a rare exception to the rule. If you're reading this after R5 has been released, you should be able to substitute the path /boot/home/config/etc in the instructions above.

The first entry on this line, obviously, is the IP address of the host machine you want to commune with. The second entry is the fully qualified domain name that the host machine is living on. Since you're most likely working on a private (or internal) network, you can just enter a single-word hostname here, such as ntbox—whatever the hostname is of the machine that will be acting as the proxy. The third entry is an "alias" for that machine—you can either ignore it or enter a descriptive name for your machine. Save and close the file, then launch NetPositive and pull down Edit | Preferences. Click the Proxies tab, and select Enable Proxies. In the first field, enter the hostname of the proxy server (the same name you entered in the hosts file above), then enter the port assignment for all HTTP requests (most likely this will be port 80, but check with your network administrator if that doesn't work properly). If you want to be able to click on FTP links from within NetPositive and have

## *DNS versus the hosts File*

Any time an address needs to be "resolved" (i.e. the computer needs to turn your request for a URL like **www.be.com** into an actual IP address), BeOS follows a series of steps. First, it looks for the presence of a /boot/home/config/etc/hosts file. If it finds one, it turns its attentions to the host or hosts listed in that file. If that file does not exist or does not contain a valid host, it turns to the first DNS server you've entered into Network preferences, and then to the second DNS server if the first does not respond. Only if all three of these methods fail will BeOS post an error message. Since the hosts file is the first thing to be checked, it's not necessary to click the "Disable DNS" checkbox. The only instances in which this could be useful are those that occur when your proxy server is down and you don't want network requests to result in your local machine's PPP (dial-up) services being launched. In normal usage, it should be possible to have both a hosts file and a pair of DNS servers registered without them stepping on one another's toes.

them run through the proxy server as well, enter similar information on the second line, but use an appropriate FTP port, as described in the proxy's documentation (most likely this will be port 21). You can use the hosts file to name any IP address to which you're connected, and your TCP/IP requests will be automatically routed to that machine.

Now all that remains is to open a URL or click on a Web link. If you've configured everything properly, the modem on the host machine should spring to life, request the page you want, and send it back to your browser, just as if you were using a modem on your own machine. If the proxy server has a permanent connection, you should get your requested page immediately.

Any TCP/IP software you want to use over a proxy server will need to be configured similarly. However, not all Internet software has a proxies dialog, so you may need to hack your way around this limitation. For example, consider the telnet client built into BeOS's Terminal. Obviously, this client has no Preferences panel, and thus no way to tell it to use a proxy server. To get around this limitation, most proxy server software has a built-in workaround. For example, if your proxy server is running WinGate and the hostname is "ntbox", you can simply type telnet ntbox into the Terminal, then issue a username and password assigned by your WinGate administrator. When faced with

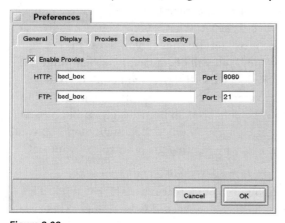

**Figure 8.08**

*To tell NetPositive to use a proxy server instead of your normal networking preferences, pull down Edit | Preferences and click the Proxies tab, then enter the hostname and port address for HTTP and FTP services. Port addresses have standard assignments, and should be documented along with your proxy software—HTTP proxies typically run on port 8080.*

the WinGate> prompt, you can enter your telnet command normally. Consult your proxy server's documentation for exact instructions, which may differ.

Similarly, BeMail does not include a proxy server preferences option. You may want to consider a more advanced mail client, such as BeatWare's Mail-It, which does speak proxy. Otherwise, you can cheat a little by entering your E-mail preferences somewhat differently. Again, these instructions may differ depending on the particular proxy server software you're using. Essentially, you need to tell the proxy server the name of the POP and SMTP servers to be used, then tell your email client to combine your username with your proxy's hostname. For example, if you're using WinGate, you might enter beos#peachpit.com@ntbox. Consult your proxy documentation for details.

**BeOS as a Proxy Server**  Looking at the situation the other way around, you may want to give your BeOS machine the role of proxy server, and configure your other operating systems to redirect their network requests through the BeOS gateway. At this writing, proxy servers for BeOS are not as fully evolved as those available on some other platforms, but there is one available that gets the job done quite nicely: Joe Kloss's HTTP Proxy. The principle here is identical. Download HTTP Proxy from BeWare (or get the latest version from **users.deltanet.com/users/axly/proxy.html**), and read its documentation thoroughly. All configuration of HTTP Proxy happens through a Web-based interface, which has the added advantage of making it configurable through any Web browser on your system, or from a remote location, letting you add and remove proxy services on the fly, if necessary.

Start HTTP Proxy from the command line, then launch NetPositive and open this URL: **http://127.0.0.1:25000**. That is your loopback address at port 25000, which is where the proxy service runs (if you access the configuration panel from another machine, you will of course have to substitute the machine's real IP address for the loopback IP above). You don't need to be running a Web server for this to work, as the proxy is self-contained. You'll find HTTP services enabled by default. You can immediately enable Netscape Navigator or Microsoft Internet Explorer on other operating systems on your private network to use HTTP Proxy by entering the hostname of your BeOS machine on port 8080.

At the time of this writing, configuring other services to work with HTTP Proxy was slightly more difficult, since they needed to be configured as "generic" proxies. At the bottom of the proxy administration screen you'll find an HTML form. To enable HTTP Proxy to handle POP (mail-checking) services, enter POP (or a similarly descriptive title) in the first field, port 110 in the Local Port field, a number such as 5 in the Max Connections field (this is your means of keeping the proxy server from becoming overloaded in case you have a lot of machines on your internal network), the server name

| Proxy Name | Local Port | Hits | Connections | Remote Host | |
|---|---|---|---|---|---|
| HTTP Proxy | 8080 | 174 | 0 / 32 | N/A | delete |
| POP3 | 110 | 0 | 0 / 5 | pop.dnai.com:110 | delete |
| SMTP | 25 | 1 | 0 / 5 | smtp.dnai.com:25 | delete |
| NEWS | 119 | 0 | 0 / 5 | news.dnai.com:119 | delete |

**Figure 8.09**

*HTTP Proxy's administration functions are Web-based, so you can configure them from any Web browser. Add the service name, the server name to which it should connect, and the port address through which that service connects, then click the Add Service button. Here, HTTP Proxy for BeOS is dishing up Web, Usenet, and mail checking and sending services to modem-less machines on the author's home network.*

of the remote service (in this case, your ISP's POP server), and again the port number 110.

The second port field should be used only when the client software you intend to route does not have a dialog dedicated to configuring proxies. For example, if you use Eudora for email on your other machines, you'll have to enter 110 in HTTP Proxy's Remote Port field so the proxy will know how to map these requests.

Do the same for every service you want routed, clicking the Add Service button after entering each one.

**Configuring Software on Other OSs**   Once HTTP Proxy is up and running, first verify that it's working properly by configuring a browser on another machine on your network to retrieve pages by means of your BeOS machine. Once you can do this successfully, tackle your other software. Any software that does not have a proxy services dialog will need to be manually configured. For example, if you use Eudora for MacOS or Windows, pull down Tools | Options, navigate to the Hosts dialog, and change the settings there. Your POP account should read:

`youraccountname@IPAddress`

In other words, if the IP address of the BeOS proxy host was 192.168.0.1 and your account name with your ISP was kernel_joe, then you would enter:

`kernel_joe@192.168.0.1`

Note that you don't specify the name of your real POP server here, since HTTP Proxy is going to take care of mapping that for you. In the SMTP field, simply enter the IP address of the BeOS host.

Similarly, tell your news client to stop using your normal news server, and to use the BeOS machine's IP address instead. HTTP Proxy will take care of the necessary remapping.

Once you've got everything working properly, you'll probably want to make sure HTTP Proxy is running whenever your BeOS machine is turned on. As usual, simply add its path, followed by an ampersand, to your `UserBootscript` file. For example, add

```
#### HTTP PROXY
/boot/home/config/bin/httpproxy &
```

Remember to adjust the path statement in this example if yours is different, though ~/config/bin is a good place for it if you don't want to run it all the time, but do want to be able run it on a whim without having to remember its path.

**IP Forwarding** If you're like many BeOS users, you've probably been tempted by that little IP Forwarding checkbox in the Network preferences panel. IP Forwarding, however, may not be what you think it is. Yes, it will turn your BeOS machine into a software router. No, it doesn't do this without a bit of effort on your part. First of all, you're going to need to contract with your ISP or upstream provider to lease a small block of IP addresses. Technically, you'll only need as many addresses as you have machines on your network, but they'll probably only lease them to you in blocks of five or ten at a time. You'll need to inform your provider that you intend to do IP forwarding with these addresses. Second, you'll need to install two network interfaces in your machine: one to communicate with your upstream provider, and the other to jack into your hub and communicate with the rest of your network (note that this doesn't necessarily mean you need two network cards—one of the interfaces can be a modem or terminal adapter). Each of your other machines will need to be assigned one of the IP addresses in the block you've leased.

Once these steps are out of the way, just check the IP Forwarding box in Network preferences, restart networking, and your BeOS machine should begin functioning as a software router. Note that this is different from proxy serving—the BeOS machine is not handling requests on behalf of your "fake" IP addresses. Instead, you've got a collection of real IP addresses, and the BeOS machine is just acting as a traffic cop for them. This is a great solution for small- to medium-sized organizations with heavy network needs, as they'll be able to save hundreds of dollars over the cost of a real hardware router. For most of us, however, the IP Forwarding checkbox is pretty much useless.

IP forwarding is a processor-intensive task. If your IP Forwarding machine has limited resources or is sharing time with other computing tasks, or if your network is very busy, you'll probably feel the hit. Your best bet may be to make this into a dedicated machine and not try to get normal work done on it while it's also busy forwarding.

**Network Address Translation**   The final flavor of software routing is known by names such as "IP masquerading," "network address translation," or simply "NAT." You'll typically hear this referred to as masquerading in the Linux world, and as NAT in the FreeBSD world. The idea here is that rather than each piece of client software being configured to use a proxy server, the central machine "masquerades" as a real router. In this case, all the client machines have to do is set their router addresses to equal the IP address of the NAT server. While IP forwarding depends on each networked machine having a "real" IP address, a masquerading environment allows you to continue using your "fake" private addresses, with the only real address being assigned to the network interface (whether that be an NIC or a PPP connection) in the server machine. This solution is easier to implement than a proxy server, but has a minor drawback: Protocols that use port numbers outside of the TCP/IP headers (notable examples being active-mode FTP and ping) are more difficult to implement.

A NAT solution is available for BeOS in the form of a network add-on created by Richard Burgess and available on BeWare. At this writing, the exact installation procedure for the NAT add-on was in flux, but it should be well documented in its accompanying README. In any case, you'll need to move the nat binary to /boot/home/config/add-ons/net_server/, select the IP Forwarding checkbox in Network preferences (because you're essentially using BeOS's IP forwarding features, but without its "real" IP address requirements), and make a couple of edits to ~/config/settings/network. Restart networking, and you can go tell your client machines (running any operating system) to use the NAT machine as a router through their own network control panels. Do not set individual applications to use a proxy server—that's a whole different kettle of packets.

You can now use Internet applications from other machines on your local network—they'll utilize the BeOS machine's Internet connection automatically. If that connection is via PPP, there may be a brief delay as the NAT machine fires up its connection.

# Serial/Terminal Communications

As noted elsewhere in this book, BeOS ships with a program called SerialConnect, which has nothing to do with PPP (and may, in fact, cause conflicts with PPP networking attempts). SerialConnect is, however, quite useful for a variety of other, non-PPP-related tasks.

## What Is SerialConnect?

If it's not for PPP, then what is SerialConnect for? The purpose of this tool will be more clear to old-timers, who cut their online teeth with bulletin board systems (BBSs). In fact, SerialConnect is capable of conducting several kinds of communication over the serial port (labeled as the modem and printer ports on the Macintosh), whether that port is connected to an external modem or to another computer.

**Connecting to Bulletin Board Systems**   If you go back far enough to remember a time before being online meant having a Web browser, you know how important the BBS scene was. Just as everyone can have their own Web site now, once upon a time, the truly wired would set up a dedicated machine in the basement with a couple of modems. Other users in the community would dial into these BBSs and trade files, use message boards, and engage in live chat. Of course, the Internet has put a huge dent in the BBS scene, but it does still exist. In fact, there's been a recent resurgence of interest in home-brewed BBSs as TCP/IP-based bulletin-board software gains currency.

To experience for yourself the excellent community atmosphere of your local BBS, search the Web for +"BBS" and +"YourCity". Find a BBS within your area code, then disconnect and launch the SerialConnect application.

 If you use an ISDN terminal adapter, you won't be able to use SerialConnect with it. Even if you could get it to dial, which is tricky, the vast majority of BBSs run on analog modems. However, if you have an old external modem sitting around, it's easy enough to jack that into your serial port instead of the ISDN connection—you don't even have to turn your machine off to do this. If you've got a free serial port (i.e. the other one isn't occupied by your mouse or another device), you can easily connect one modem to each serial port and have it both ways.

The first thing you'll need to do is make sure that the communications settings in SerialConnect are set properly. The vast majority of BBSs operate at no parity, eight data bits, one stop bit; this is also known as 8N1 (you can look up the meaning of these terms in any general computing reference if you're terminally curious). These are SerialConnect's default settings, but you can easily

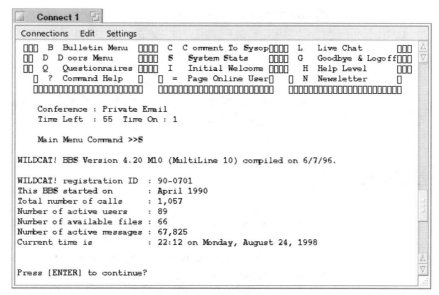

*Figure 8.10*

*Enter the phone number of the BBS to which you want to connect into SerialConnect's Connection dialog. If you already have an account on the system, enter your username and password. You can probably leave the Modem Init. String alone, unless you aren't able to make a connection with the default, which is unlikely. Take care to select the correct serial port from the dropdown at the bottom of the dialog.*

change them by using the options on the Settings menu, which will also let you configure other parameters, such as your fonts and colors, modem speeds, and other details with which you probably don't need to be concerned.

Next, pull down the Connections menu and select Connect via Modem. You'll be facing a dialog similar to the one in Figure 8.10.

After filling in the Connection dialog, click the Connect button. Your modem will dial the bulletin board, and onscreen prompts specific to that board will take it from there. You're in!

## Customizing Connections with Dial-o-Rama

If you find yourself using SerialConnect frequently and want to automate your login sessions to various bulletin board systems, check out the Dial-O-Rama scripts in /boot/beos/etc/connect. Copy one of these to a user-level subdirectory (out of the /boot/beos hierarchy), and open it in a text editor. Uncomment the line beginning dial-o-rama and replace its contents with a phone number, username, and password specific to a favorite BBS. In the SerialConnect application, enter the path to this script in the Script field and your login details will be taken care of for you. If your BBS requires an alternative login procedure, use one of the .ali scripts in the same folder, customizing its contents according to instructions provided by that particular BBS.

**Connecting to Other Machines**  In addition to using an external modem connected to a serial port, it's also possible to establish direct communications between two computers over their serial ports. The most likely use you'll have for this technique is trapping debug output from a problematic machine so you can send a complete log of the machine's internal state during the boot process to Be for analyzing. This technique is fully covered in Chapter 16, *Troubleshooting and Maintenance*.

# Security

No chapter on networking would be complete without covering the important question of network security. After all, any time you're connected to the Internet, your machine is theoretically available to the world. While there are plenty of mechanisms around to keep your data safe from prying eyes, there are also plenty of dedicated hackers and crackers out there. It's worthwhile to be wary.

## Is BeOS Secure?

BeOS has the foundations for security in place, in the form of file permissions (see Chapter 5, *Files and the Tracker*). However, BeOS 3.x and 4.x do not yet enjoy a full, system-wide implementation of file permissions (technically, R4 does honor permissions established on files and directories, though there's no easy way to see this for yourself while the system is still single-user). In other words, anyone who sits down at—or hacks into—your machine has full, unadulterated "god" privileges. They can view, rename, or delete any file on your system. While this isn't much of an issue for standalone machines in home and small office environments, it can be in open environments such as the Internet.

Does this mean that every time you use BeOS to log onto the Net someone could be tapping into your life's work? Extremely unlikely. For one thing, most of us have dynamic IP addresses, so it's difficult to monitor and identify our login habits long enough to create a breach. Secondly, Internet hack attacks are almost always targeted at organizations, not individual users. Third, if you're using BeOS in a corporate or academic environment, you're almost certainly sitting behind some form of firewall, and aren't any more vulnerable than MacOS or Windows 95/98 machines on the same network (since those operating systems also lack any kind of file-based security).

The caveats here are nothing more than basic, common-sense prophylactics that apply equally to any operating system. This section is paranoid in tone, and it's meant to be.

**Choose Secure Passwords** Whether you're choosing a password for your online bank account or your ISP's logon sequence, it's important that passwords never be easy to guess, either by humans or by cracking programs. Tempting thought it may be, don't use plain old words from the dictionary when setting passwords. Don't use your Social Security number, your phone number, or your girlfriend's birthday, either. The best way to create a secure password is to use a combination of uppercase and lowercase letters, at least one numeral, and at least one punctuation mark. Make sure your passwords are at least eight characters long. You can then use these rules to create a mnemonic device so that your passwords will still be relatively easy to remember. For example, let's say you were tempted to use your dog's name as your password, and your dog's name is Charlie. A good, difficult-to-crack password based on Charlie might be cH*rl1e23 . One of the vowels has been changed to a numeral that resembles the letter it replaced. Another vowel has been replaced with a punctuation mark. An uppercase letter has been used, but not in the obvious first position. Finally, two extra digits have been added to make the name longer, and therefore harder to crack.

**Be Cautious with BeOS's Built-In Servers** As mentioned earlier in this chapter, the FTP and telnet servers built into BeOS networking include no options for restricting incoming users to specific directories. This is a potentially serious security hole. It's up to you to do any or all of the following:

- Don't leave your servers enabled at all times—turn them on only when needed.
- Change their passwords on a regular basis, and take care whom you inform about your machine's availability.
- Instead of using the built-in servers, use third-party solutions (such as Campus for FTP) that allow you to establish tighter access restrictions.

**Be Cautious When Downloading Software** As of this writing, there are no known cases of software viruses that affect BeOS. However, BeOS virii are not outside the realm of possibility, and damage can be done by non-virus software as well—it wouldn't be difficult to create a downloadable shell script that wipes out all the data on an unsuspecting user's hard drive. We're extremely fortunate that this kind of maliciousness is as yet unknown in the BeOS world, but it's probably an inevitability at some point in the future.

Both BeWare and BeDepot are secure locations—Be tests every piece of software they distribute, so you have reasonable assurance that anything you download from one of these locations is safe and sane. If you come across software that's only available on the author's site and not on BeWare or BeDepot, be wary. I'm not saying that that's necessarily a suspicious thing to do, but just be cautious. If it's a shell script, open it in a text editor and search for the strings rm or mv before running it. If you find these, study them closely to see what they do. You may also want to ask the author to upload their program to a Be-sanctioned software library. Of course, you'll need to add common sense to the mix as well. It's extremely unlikely, for example, that a Be developer with a stake and reputation in the community would endanger their reputation by releasing potentially dangerous software.

**Use Encryption**    If you need to be absolutely certain that your data is secure if it should happen to fall into the wrong hands, you'll want to download and install a copy of PGP, or Pretty Good Privacy, for BeOS. PGP is covered in Chapter 15, *Other Goodies*.

*Boot-Time Security*  Even though BeOS currently lacks its own login authentication feature, you can add one to your system easily enough by downloading and installing BeCheckPoint from BeWare. Once it's installed and configured, add it to your UserBootScript. Every time your machine starts up, the Tracker and Deskbar will be killed immediately, and you'll be prompted for a username and password—without supplying the correct pair, you won't be able to access any of the machine's functions. This will prevent all untrusted parties from accessing your machine directly, which could be useful if your BeOS machine is in a public space such as an office cubicle, where you won't be around to watch over it at all times.

Additionally, a new user-authentication scheme called BHand was just entering beta at this writing. If successful, BHand will be capable of recognizing users by evaluating their typing style—no passwords required. Keep an eye on BeWare for developments.

## Russ McMahon
### Director of Networking
### Interviewed by Henry Bortman

**HB:** *I've heard it said that BeOS is "network-aware." What does that mean?*

**RM:** It means that out of the box, it's ready to be plugged into the network. That kind of leads into what I do. Because the underlying services ship with the OS and are ready to go, my job is to make that really easy. Ideally what I would like to see is [that you'd] just drop it in, plug it in, and you're on the Net. TCP/IP has a lot of configuration.

   I think some of my goals are to abstract that a little bit, make it easier, while still maintaining the productivity needed. It's just too hard to get on the Net right now. There's a lot of praying that it works once you're plugged in. I think BeOS, like a lot of the OS's, Microsoft included, has the underlying engines and everything that work fairly well, but it's kind of hit and miss to get all that working together—getting the correct drivers, getting the network cards, getting good feedback in case something doesn't go right.

**HB:** *When do you think users will see some of these changes?*

**RM:** Well, they'll definitely see changes in the next release, R4. They will see a new preference panel that is easier to use, doesn't go through as many steps, still some typing. But I think the most noticeable thing in the preference panel will be support of DHCP, the Dynamic Host Configuration Protocol, which will ship out of the box as checked. And so, under ideal circumstances, if you've got your hardware set up and it's plugged in, you should be able to just boot up BeOS and have it go right online. So, that's going to be shipping in R4.

   There will be some intervention, mostly getting the hardware set up. Say you just got a machine. It's brand new, never been installed. You have a network card. You will drop the network card in, you will go to the Network preferences panel and you will have to type in a couple of things, but the main thing is you will configure the interface, hit Add, and you will be given a choice: Specify Settings—which is subnet mask, the typical things that you're often asked about—or just choose DHCP. If you choose the dynamic host resolution stuff, then you'll get an address automatically. Now, in that case, there needs to be a server in the LAN that will serve that information up to you. And in a LAN environment, there's a good chance there will be a DHCP server out there giving you the information.

   So in the home, you will still probably need to type in your things. But to help that a little bit, we have actually separated dial-up networking completely out of the LAN-based networking. So you'll go to a separate menu choice called Dial-up Networking. And from Dial-up Networking, it's really easy. You'll type in some phone numbers, and that's it. You won't have to worry about dropping in a card, or configuring interfaces, or any of that stuff.

**HB:** *What about modem drivers?*

**RM:** If you're on a serial port, or something like that, should be taken care of for you. You'll select a modem, of course; it's a pretty good list. But, modems are a little easier to hook up because

## *Russ McMahon* (continued)

they just talk a modem protocol. So, if you have US Robotics or something else that's fairly common, you'll just stick that on and say, "Use this serial port, this is my modem, connect."

So we're trying to make it easier. There are still a few steps necessary, and as I see us going further I'll try to eliminate more and more of that. Ideally, I'd just love for the user to not have to do anything, but there still is some information that needs to be typed in. But we're trying to focus on keeping that to a minimum, and that'll continue.

**HB:** *BeOS networking is TCP/IP based. You support FTP, but you don't have any kind of file sharing integrated into the Tracker. Do you see FTP being integrated in that way?*

**RM:** I don't think so. I think any integration into the Tracker will be as a Microsoft client. FTP typically has been used as a command line–based tool. People use FTP to get and put files. They don't typically share volumes using FTP. It's not something it was really designed to do, so it's kind of a hack to make that all work.

However, there are protocols out there that are fairly good at doing volume-type stuff. Something that's coming up very quickly is Windows 95 connectivity and NT connectivity. To do that, you become a Microsoft client, and it's then very easy in a Microsoft network to drop your machine in there and just share files, volumes, printers—there's a lot of benefits to being a Microsoft client.

Being a Microsoft client is one thing. It means that you will talk a protocol called SMB. It's just Microsoft's way of hooking their machines together, and it just allows us to get the file list, move files, put files, and that sort of thing.

Now, there's another thing that you can do, which is be a server. And to be a server, you really need to support the entire protocol—it's relatively complex. However, there is available through the GNU license, like on Linux, the code that will do that. Essentially, it does the sharing parts of NT. Someone has written that and made it publicly available. So if you have the client and have the server, Be can share up files to itself, mount volumes, and all that from the server to the client. And then, if you drop it into an NT network, or you have NT printers, those will just connect seamlessly. And then NT can get files from the Be server.

**HB:** *So rather than try to make FTP perform a function it was never designed for, the direction will be to integrate into Microsoft networks?*

**RM:** Yes.

**HB:** *Will that be in R4?*

**RM:** Yes, hopefully. I wouldn't want to be held totally accountable to that, but our goal is to put that into R4. We have it working here, but it needs some testing.

**HB:** *Both sides, client and server?*

**RM:** The server has some issues of licensing that I would probably have to deal with a little bit. The client is a lot easier for me. On the server side, although the GNU is publicly available, we have to be very careful of what we do, how we use it, and then we notify the correct people and give credit due, and that sort of thing. So that sometimes takes a little longer, because I have to wait for people to get back to me and that sort of thing. But, we do have it working. We have Be being the server, and I can go to my NT box and grab Be files. So I think what the user will have is a nice ability to create multimedia apps and sound, and grab it from one place, edit it, and grab it from another. With better support built into the apps for conversion of those formats, everything will be very, very seamless and nice.

When all that is in place, you won't have to worry about any of the attributes or any of that. You'll simply take a file, it'll show up in the Tracker, and you will just go over to an NT (or vice versa), you'll take the NT, drop it onto Be, and all the attributes and all that will be saved. That's some of the harder work that has to be done, because then you do have to encapsulate that, put it in the file, move it over. But we should be able to handle that.

**HB:** *Printing. It's not exactly BeOS's strong suit.*

**RM:** We are looking at printing. R4 was a tough thing because it wasn't totally on the task list to get in. We were looking more at printing for R4.1, or later, maybe even R5, because we really want to do it right. It's been kind of muddled for a while, and we just want to sit down, look at what we have available to us. Like this Microsoft client and server—it's a new thing, so we wanted to take all the stuff that we know we have, the abilities we have, and sit down and architect it.

We have gone through that phase. We pretty much know what we want printing to look like and how it will feel. We've got the spec, we've got the developers. We had all the developers that are interested put in their pieces. We all agreed on a solution that would be good. Some developers have gone off and started working on their particular part. Whether we can get all of the pieces from all of the developers in the R4 time frame is kind of tricky, so we're just on a wait-and-see. If not R4, then R4.1, which will follow probably first quarter next year.

So, printing is a very high priority. Really high, there's just no doubt about it. We don't ignore printing. I know it might look from the outside like we do, but printing has been kind of a beast with us because it's this always-changing thing. Network printing, local printing, are you printing to AppleTalk directly, are you printing to an NT server that's doing AppleTalk? There's so much stuff going on there, and I think we've always had kind of little pieces, but we've never taken this approach—Well, let's grab everything we know and look at how we're going to do it from here, rather than each of the different teams or each of the different developers kind of doing their own thing and having varying degrees of support.

So, that's where we are with printing. I think the news is good. When we pull this all off it's going to look really nice. And back into your thing with the Tracker, the idea is to integrate it much closer to the Tracker, put it right in, so your printers will just show up as devices inside a list. And hopefully, at the end, you'll be able to just drop documents on the printer and that sort of thing, and get status right back from the Tracker. So, that'd be nice.

**HB:** *How did you hear of Be?*

**RM:** I had heard of Be for a long time. I've always been into different ways of doing things, particularly OS's. I think my interest in the bigger picture came from probably the workgroup stuff. You really start seeing that the problem with any workgroup solution is handling the multiple OS's, and so I think from there I developed a sensitivity to what OS's are out there, what they're doing,

## *Russ McMahon* (continued)

how open they are, what kind of networking they are doing. Early on I developed this interest, and so I followed OS's, staying pretty neutral. I liked Apple for many things, I liked Windows for many things. I don't think I ever really said, This one's the best; they each were good. So I stayed fairly neutral. And when Be came along, I saw that as one more OS. I think with Be probably I felt a bit more feeling of Wow, finally, someone did it right. I didn't really know the OS. It was mostly from the outside, from what I'd heard about its multithreading.

The whole thing was, Well, why does the world need another OS? You wouldn't really ask that question if you really knew what the OS's were—because of the legacy they were pulling forward. The answer was that the world really does need a new OS. And there was Be. So, I had an interest in it, saying that if they do the right things, they learn from all this legacy that has been developed—Apple, Windows, all that stuff—they can really do it right. But NetManage was totally successful, so I didn't have an opportunity to pursue it more than just kind of following up, listening. If somebody had worked on it, I'd always ask them and kind of follow it that way.

So, I'd heard about it, and toward the end when I was thinking about leaving NetManage, I was kind of asking myself what I'd really like to do. I'd never really worked on an OS, so I thought it would be great to get involved with. It was kind of a coincidence that Brad had hired one of the guys who had worked for me for years, and he brought me here. So, I was pretty fortunate. It's like the dream job.

**HB:** *How so?*

**RM:** I wanted to get involved with an OS. A lot of people criticize OS's—Windows this, Windows that. For me, I never really liked to talk too much, or get too vocal. As I said, I was fairly neutral. So, I wouldn't just rave about something because I always felt there was good and bad in both. I think for me it was the dream job because if I really did want to get vocal, I felt I had a right. So now I think I've earned my right to say, "This sucks," but the interesting thing is, I still haven't changed. I'm still fairly neutral. I see really good things on NT; I think Apple really hurt themselves by staying with OS 8, by not joining the modern world for years, but I think they're changing that. I can see them being a player again. I've been an application writer, I've developed, even when NetManage was doing the [TCP/IP] stack, it was added as an outside part to Windows not integrated into the OS. When we were working on it, we said it would be better in the OS. And once I got here and started working, I found out the BeOS really is a good OS.

**HB:** *What's good about it?*

**RM:** The integration. In some ways, the simplicity. It doesn't have the legacy. It's everything I thought would be good if you came later and decided to build this thing: You would limit how much assembly and how much C and how much Pascal and how much God knows what would be in this thing.… You'd say, OK, well, we'll put some C here to make it fast, and we'll do everything else in C++ to make it easy for developers. We'll expose this in a fairly clear, concise class library to get at the OS services. We will make networking, TCP/IP a part of it, we'll have a nice usable UI, just that sort of thing. I think the simplicity of it. The fact that it's not burdened with these years of crap that it's got to support. It's kind of refreshing.

**HB:** *But five years from now isn't it going to be burdened with its own legacy?*

**RM:** Yeah, it probably will. If it goes with the Microsoft mentality or the Apple mentality that prevails right now still: the monolithic OS taking care of everything and just growing to be huge and the best OS with everything in it. But there seems to be starting—and it's being forced by the Compaqs or Gateways—the idea of maybe not having such a huge OS, but smaller, more focused OS's for specific tasks. In some ways we're already doing that with our multimedia. Saying we don't want to be everything. Saying we'll let Windows do that, we'll let Apple be everything to everybody.

So, maybe I'll take that back a little bit. No. At least we'll try not to be. There's a fine line in having enough of the drivers so people aren't frustrated because your stuff doesn't work. So you get enough of the drivers in there to make sure that people can do their jobs and maybe you don't put everything in there, but you get enough, staying focused. It's not real easy to do, because everybody wants you to be everything. They're calling you for this, they're calling saying they want that. The example may be AppleShare, maybe we don't want to support AppleShare, yeah, but there are a few people out there that we'll piss off and that really want AppleShare. But is it in the best interest to load everybody up with AppleShare just to make a few people happy? Those decisions are kind of hard to make, but I think Be is pretty good about making those. Be really has a vision of being a snappy, lightweight OS.

**HB:** *I've noticed there a lot of musicians here at Be. Do you play an instrument?*

**RM:** I do have a guitar at home, I try and play. I am very much into audio. I am not really a musician, but I am a big fan of stereo. I'm very interested in tube electronics, which is another reason I come back to why I like working here. You'll find a lot of the guys have these kind of funky tastes like that. Pavel, one of our developers, is very much into tube amplifiers for his guitar. I'm very much into tube audio equipment. So you get this kind of interesting people, that have eclectic tastes outside of work.

**HB:** *What kind of music do you listen to?*

**RM:** Kind of a mix of jazz—Miles and some Coltrane. But I also listen to a lot of older Pink Floyd. Pink Floyd actually sounds really good on tube. Although it's electronic music, somehow it just really sounds good on a nice gear turntable.

# 9

# Preferences and Customization

Trying to decide where preferences stop and customizations begin can be tricky work for an operating system vendor. If there's little that's configurable about a system, it will never feel like home to anyone. On the other hand, customizations can go too far. If you could reverse the order of all your menus, rearrange your close and zoom buttons, and use round windows instead of rectangular, other users sitting down at your machine might have a tough time operating your system. Not only that, but endless technical support headaches could be introduced, applications and the operating system could come into conflict with one another, and the system's visual and functional identity could be compromised.

While it's sometimes difficult to draw a distinct line between preferences and customizations, for the purposes of this chapter we'll say that preferences pertain to the configuration of system functions provided by Be and are accessible by way of the applications found in your Preferences folder. We'll define customizations, on the other hand, as resulting from solutions that you or others in the Be community have come up with; home-brewed tools that give you customizability Be never intended, replacement font choosers, and third-party hotkey utilities are all examples of what we'll call "customizations" in this chapter. However, in the real world, there's quite a bit of crossover. It's not as cut-and-dried as saying that preferences relate to raw functionality while customizations affect only the chrome—some preference settings are merely cosmetic, and many customizations are capable of enhancing your system's functionality.

 **Note:** All of the applications found in your Preferences folder will be referred to in this chapter as "panels."

# Preferences

Like most operating systems, many aspects of BeOS are configurable, and can be adjusted to suit your aesthetic preferences, working habits, or specific hardware configuration. You'll find links to a healthy handful of panels that let you tweak BeOS's default settings by pulling down the Be menu and selecting the Preferences folder. Some of these are simple, obvious, and intuitive, like the Printers panel. Others are more complex and technically oriented, like the Network and FileType preferences. These more involved panels get entire sections all to themselves elsewhere in this book, but we'll introduce you to them here and tell you where to turn for more information.

## *Preferences—or Links to Preferences?*

If you open your Preferences folder from the Be menu, you'll notice that the icons have underscores beneath them, indicating that they're just links to the actual preferences panels, not the
programs themselves. The actual preferences panels live in the /boot/beos/preferences/ folder.
This is a safety mechanism intended to save us from ourselves. Because the preferences panels
are crucial to system operation, Be doesn't want new users accidentally deleting them. By
default, the /boot/beos hierarchy isn't available from the Be menu. Therefore, it's far less likely
that new users will accidentally delete these important programs—they would only delete the
links to them. Of course, it's still possible to get into the /boot/beos/preferences folder, but the
user has to be more proactive to do that. There are actually a number of places in BeOS where
users are presented with links rather than actual files, and in all cases, it's for the same reason:
accident-proofing.

 While most of the preferences are innocuous enough, there are a few places
here where choosing the wrong setting could be a Bad Thing. Watch for warning markers in the margins—these flag places where you need to be careful.

# Audio

If the MediaOS were a living thing (and who's to say it isn't?), the Audio
preferences panel would be one of its kidneys. While many of your audio-
related applications will have their own sliders and knobs for fine-grained signal control, the Audio preferences panel lets you adjust the levels of all audio
coming into, being generated within, or going out of your system. It's worth
studying the relationships between the tabs and controls in the Audio preferences, just to get a handle on how sound moves through BeOS. In a way, this
panel functions like a visual flowchart of your audio subsystems.

You've seen mixing panels before, but this one comes with a BeOS twist—the
groups of controls on the Mixer tab directly represent the number of currently running audio streams. Start a new audio application, and you immediately get a new set of controls. Stop it, and they disappear. In other words, this
panel represents both the static (hardware) and dynamic (software) states of
your audio environment. More on that later.

 You'll see the acronym ADC (and possibly DAC) in this and other audio
applications. ADC stands for analog to digital converter. Since your ears are
analog while your computer is digital, this bridge must be crossed any time
you transform something you can hear into a digital audio file, and crossed in
the other direction whenever you want to get an audio file out of your system
and into your ears.

**Input** The entries at the top of the Input tab represent all possible points of incoming audio signal, and will reflect the input jacks on the back of your sound card. If you have more than one sound card, you'll see more than one control group here. Due to the nature of most consumer-level audio hardware, it's not always possible for BeOS to process incoming signal from more than one source at once; you'll usually need to pick a source from the picklist on this tab (if you have a high-end audio card, you may see a different interface here). Your options will most likely be CD, Line, Mic, and Mic+20db. CD refers to your machine's internal CD player, Line is present so you can hook up standard audio equipment like a tape deck or keyboard, Mic is for microphones, and Mic+20db is for unpowered microphones, which have a very low gain.

**Dragging any slider in the Audio preferences panel with the left mouse button will alter the level of both left and right channels simultaneously, while dragging with the right mouse button will let you control left and right channels independently.**

It's important to note that the Input control group is not *necessarily* tied to the sound you hear coming out of your speakers. You're only controlling the internal levels of these sources on their way to digital conversion. If you're recording to hard disk from an external input, for example, this is where you would come to set your recording levels.

We were only able to test an early version of Audio preferences; the interface shown here could change significantly by the time you read this, though the basic concept and functionality of the panel should remain the same.

**Output** The Output tab lets you control the master volume for each of the primary audio channels in your system before they head for the output jack(s) on the back of your sound card. As shown in the diagram at the bottom of this control, however, signal must pass through the system's mixer before being funneled through the master volume control. This is why one of the sliders is named, simply, "BeOS"—it represents the collection of all audio signals generated from within the system itself (rather than externally) after they've been mixed down on the Mixer tab. Note that signal coming from the CD Player application gets a control all to itself; that's because it's an actual device. Even though you can control it through BeOS software, it still represents a physical input point much like a microphone or tape deck.

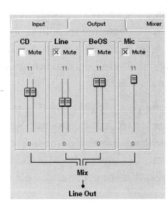

*Figure 9.01*

The Output tab in the Audio preferences panel lets you control the master volume for a signal that's already passed through the system mixer.

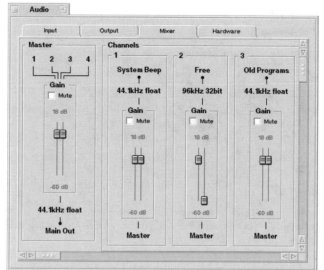

**Figure 9.02**

All software-generated signals "publish" themselves automatically to the Mixer tab, where you can control their levels independently.

**Mixer**  Now for the fun part. Most operating systems include an audio mixer like the one on the Output tab, but they don't let you mix down signals being generated by every audio application currently running. That's because most operating systems don't have a messaging architecture as thorough as the one in BeOS. Nor are those systems so deeply optimized for handling media in all its forms.

The Mixer tab is divided into two fields: Master and Channels. Channels represent streams of audio being generated internally. Examples of BeOS-generated sound would be software synthesizers, wave generators, or music recorded in, say, MP3 format and played through SoundPlay. Every time you launch an instance of a sound-generating application that takes advantage of the Media Kit, it's automatically "published" to this panel as an independently controllable channel. Old audio applications, which do not use the Media Kit, register in the Old Programs channel. After mixing your collection of currently running audio signals to perfection, you can control their signal level collectively via the Master channel, which in turn is passed on to the Output tab discussed earlier, where it's mixed against signals coming from actual devices. This panel can expand indefinitely, accommodating as many channels as are currently running. You may have to do a bit of horizontal and vertical scrolling to locate an individual channel if you're running a lot of them.

**Hardware**  At this writing, the Hardware tab lets you see, but not choose between, multiple sound cards (if you have more than one, as audio professionals are likely to). This function should become fully selectable in a future release (perhaps by the time you read this).

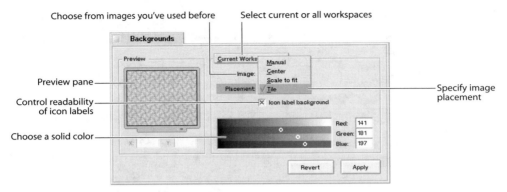

Choose from images you've used before    Select current or all workspaces

Preview pane

Control readability of icon labels

Choose a solid color

Specify image placement

*Figure 9.03*

*The Background preferences panel lets you establish a solid color or image to be used as the background of your Desktop in the current workspace, in all workspaces, in a specific folder, or in all folders.*

# Backgrounds

Way back when, in the halcyon days of yore (or around DR7, anyway), BeOS let you use images as your Desktop background. The method for doing so was quite arcane, but since BeOS was still in developers-only mode, nobody cared. With R3, the first version of the system offered to the public, this capability disappeared, leaving only the option for solid colors on the Desktop. Needless to say, this resulted in much gnashing of teeth from users, and the capability returned in R4. Only now, the method is no longer arcane, and is in fact easier to use and more flexible than similar tools in other operating systems.

The Background preferences panel lets you establish either an image or a solid color to be used as a Desktop pattern for the current workspace or all workspaces. Additionally, you can use this panel to specify that images be used as backgrounds in any folder on your system, or in all folders.

**Preview** The Preview window lets you see how your Desktop will look before you commit to any changes. If you're working with image backgrounds that are smaller than your screen's resolution, you can also use the Preview window to drag the image around, so you can place it anywhere you like rather than being constrained to centering or tiling it, as other OSs require. If you need precise control over its placement, you can also type X and Y coordinates into the provided fields.

 If you've done a lot of customization to individual workspaces and then apply your changes in this session to all workspaces, you'll lose all of those customizations irretrievably. A warning dialog will alert you about this, but keep in mind that if you've got 32 workspaces enabled and apply changes to all, you're going to lose the changes you made to the other 31.

**Workspace**  From the topmost picklist, tell Backgrounds whether the changes you're about to make should apply only to the current workspace or to all workspaces. Additionally, you'll find two entries marked Default Folder and Other Folder. The Default option applies the currently selected background to all Tracker windows, but *not* to all Tracker views. Background images are only available in folders when viewed in Icon View or Mini Icon View. Because of the level of detail provided, and the high likelihood of having the data become difficult to read, List View will not display backgrounds. Choosing Other Folder launches a File panel, from which you can choose any folder on your system. If you've used this option to select other folders in the past, their names will appear at the bottom of the list so you can reset their backgrounds again easily in the future.

**Figure 9.04**

*The Background preferences panel lets you establish background images for Tracker views (except when the Tracker is in List View mode).*

**Image**  The Background preferences panel works in conjunction with your system's installed Translators (see *Data Translations*, this chapter) to determine what image formats can be used as backgrounds. You can use any file format for which you have an image Translator installed. The easiest way to get images onto your Desktop is to drag them out of the Tracker and onto the Preview window. If you'd rather navigate a File panel, choose Other… from the Image picklist. Any images you've used in the past will also appear on this menu, so you can easily access them again. This makes it easy to make the current workspace's background equal to that of another workspace, for example.

**Placement**  The Placement picklist lets you specify how your image will appear. Its options are fairly intuitive. The Manual option lets you drag your image around in the Preview window (or enter exact X and Y coordinates). Center, obviously, centers your image. "Scale to fit" will stretch or shrink your image horizontally and/or vertically to match the resolution of the current workspace. Depending on what you're after, this can either make a beautiful image hideous or create very intriguing effects (pixelation, anyone?). The Tile option will cause your image to be repeated as many times as necessary to fill the entire screen. This generally looks terrible with standard images, but can create awesome effects with images specially designed to work as tiles. Search the Web for "background tiles" and you'll find vast repositories of just such images.

 If you want to make your own tiles, both Gobe Productive and BeatWare's e-Picture include tile-preparation tools.

**Icon Label Background**  Because it's easy to read text over the top of some images but not over others, Backgrounds lets you control whether or not the text in icon labels is rendered in a small, solid-color rectangle. The rectangle color will always be equal to the screen color behind the current image.

**Color Picker**  As in any standard color chooser in BeOS, drag the RGB color sliders to any value you like to establish solid Desktop colors. Alternatively, type RGB values directly into their fields. This can make it easy to match your Desktop color to a color you've chosen in another application's color chooser.

 If you're running at 8 bits per pixel, color choosers in BeOS will appear with a grid of squares representing the 256 colors in the BeOS palette, rather than the color sliders mentioned above. See the *Screen settings* section in this chapter for more information on resolution settings.

 **Move Your Title Tabs**  You can use the title tabs on any collection of BeOS windows just as if they were tabs on folders in your office filing cabinet. Just hold down the Shift key and drag the title tab left or right. You can now toggle between open windows belonging to any application as if you were using a tabbed dialog box.

## ScreenSaver

Remember when your mother told you that if you didn't get that grin off your face it would freeze that way? To my knowledge, this has never actually happened to anyone, but long ago, this *could* actually happen to computer monitors. Back when monitors where monochromatic and people ran the same program all day long, screens would be bombarded with the same pattern—the light areas of the screen light and the dark areas dark—day in and day out. After a while, monitors could develop a phosphor burn pattern, their frequently used screen layouts etched into place forever. Screen savers were invented to give screens a bit of a relief, deferring the effects of phosphor burn.

It's been a long time since monitors suffered from this problem, and screen savers don't actually save your screen anymore. Today's screen savers are little more than eye candy—something cool to gaze at while you lean back in your chair and talk on the phone or contemplate how to code a three-dimensional chess game.

 Aside from "burn" issues, some screen savers are capable of putting your monitor to sleep for a while to save energy (and money). At this writing, there were no BeOS screen savers capable of using built-in sleep functions, though you could choose to use ScreenSaver's plain black screen saver.

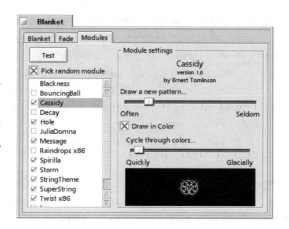

Figure 9.05

*Drop a Screen-Saver module into the left pane of the Modules tab, and you're all set. Many ScreenSaver modules include their own panels of specific settings and controls.*

Note: ScreenSaver was previously known by the name "Blenket" and was not included with BeOS.

ScreenSaver consists of three major components: The ScreenSaverServer, the ScreenSaver preferences panel, and the actual screen saver modules. The ScreenSaverServer sits in the background minding its business, waiting for a signal to "wake up and go to sleep." That signal can be either a period of inactivity specified by you, or the placement of your mouse in a particular corner of the screen. The ScreenSaver preferences panel lets you configure these parameters and decide which screen saver module will be launched.

Usage of ScreenSaver is pretty intuitive. On the Modules tab of the ScreenSaver panel, select your favorite screen saver. Note that some saver modules are configurable. If the selected module is one of these, ScreenSaver's right pane will contain the configuration controls. In other cases the right pane will include a mini-preview of the module. To get a preview of the selected module in action without waiting around, click the Test button. Can't decide which module to set as the default? Check the "Pick random module" box, then check all the saver modules you want to see in the random rotation.

On the Fade tab, specify how many minutes of inactivity should pass before a module is launched. If you want the ScreenSaverServer to be running in the background every time you boot, check the "Autolaunch on restart" box. Otherwise you'll have to start the ScreenSaverServer manually with every boot. When you're done configuring, close the ScreenSaver panel to commit your changes.

If you download new modules, you don't have to worry about deciding where to store them, since ScreenSaver works by availing itself of BeOS's add-on architecture—all screen saver modules are stored in /boot/home/config/add-ons/Screen Savers/.

**_The Easy Way to Install ScreenSaver Modules_** If you read the documentation accompanying the screen savers you download, many of them will tell you to drop the modules into `/boot/home/config/add-ons/Screen Savers/`. While this is where they end up, you usually don't have to navigate the Tracker to get your modules in the right place—ScreenSaver is smart. Just drag new saver modules onto the Modules pane and ScreenSaver will ask whether you want to move, copy, or create a link to the new module in the destination directory. It's easiest to keep your system free of redundancies if you move the modules here rather than copying them.

Alternatively, many downloaded ScreenSaver modules create a symlink to the correct destination in the folder you unzipped them in. Drop a module on one of these links and it will be magically "teleported" to the right place. See Chapter 5, _Files and the Tracker_, for more on symlinks.

## Boot

If you have more than one bootable BeOS partition, this panel lets you specify which partition should be used on the next reboot.

When you launch the Boot preferences panel, BeOS scans your system for all bootable BeOS partitions attached to your system. If you select a different volume than the one that's currently selected, BeOS will attempt to boot from that volume the next time you start your computer.

So why might you have more than one bootable partition? Why not just create multiple BFS partitions but just boot from one of them? In the transition between R3 and R4, it was useful to keep both versions of the operating system available, since applications written for one version wouldn't run on the other. Registered developers often have access to beta versions of the system that aren't yet available to the public. Or you might want to install a second version of BeOS on a removable disk, such as a Jaz or Sparq, which you can then cart around between work and home in your backpack. For the majority of users, however, installing BeOS on multiple partitions does nothing but waste disk space.

_Figure 9.06_

_If you've got more than one bootable BFS partition on your system, Boot will give you the opportunity to boot from something other than your current drive. The large red checkmark indicates the currently selected boot drive._

Installation is covered in depth in Chapter 3, but a quick note is in order here: If you do decide to install BeOS onto a second partition, pay close attention when the Installer comes up and asks which drive you want to install onto—the first one listed will probably be your normal boot drive, rather than an alternative partition. While a standard installation won't damage your data or your custom settings directories, a clean installation will overwrite everything but your personal data. Always pay close attention when working with the Installer, and see Chapter 3 for more details on the difference between standard and "clean" installations.

**Expert Mode**  If you run BeOS on a PowerPC machine, your version of the Boot preferences panel will have an additional option. Use the picklist labeled "Easy" to toggle to Expert mode. From the resulting panel, you'll be able to designate a boot drive by specifying its SCSI or IDE bus number, rather than its volume name. You'll need to be well familiar with your device's ID, LUN, and partition number. If you don't know what these things are, then you probably don't need them; stick to the volume name mode, which is much easier to use. If you do choose to use Expert mode and you'll be booting from a SCSI hard disk, leave the LUN (logical unit number) set to zero.

## Data Translations

As described elsewhere in this book, BeOS is "object-oriented" through-and-through. While that term is typically only of interest to programmers, there are a few places where the concept bubbles up to the user level, and the concept of Translators is one of them. Any time an application has a Save As... option, you're being given the option to translate the data format of the current file into another format. For example, an imaging program might let you save TARGA images as TIFFs. In other operating systems, the code that handles this translation has to be built into each and every application, which means several things: The developer has more work to do, the program becomes more bloated, and if you need access to a file format that isn't built into the application, you're out of luck. Know what Be has to say to that? Hooey.

In BeOS, data translation engines are "objects" called Translators that live in a central location in the operating system. Any application can take advantage of format translation services by simply taking a look at the list of installed translation objects. Programs stay smaller, developers don't waste time duplicating each other's work, and you can extend the capabilities of many applications at once by adding a single file to your system. Just the way it should be.

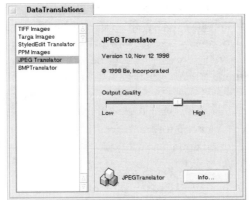

*Figure 9.07*

*Data Translators found in the system-level and user-level* Translators *directories are combined into a single list in the Data Translators preferences panel, which you can use to fine-tune Translator settings.*

Translators can exist in one of two places:

/boot/beos/system/add-ons/Translators

or

/boot/home/config/add-ons/Translators

As always, the first location contains files provided by Be with your BeOS installation, and the second location is the one you should use to add new Translators to your system. If you add Translators to the user-level folder that have the same names as files in the system-level folder, they will be used instead of the system-provided versions.

As you know, some file formats also have optional settings. For example, the JPEG file format in imaging applications always gives you the option to specify the degree of "lossiness" with which images should be compressed. Specifying those kinds of preferences is the purpose of this panel.

Not all Translators have configurable settings, though. When you select non-configurable Translators in this panel, you'll just see a few details about it in the right-hand pane. Clicking the Info… button may give you additional information, if it's been provided by the developer.

As of R4, the majority of Translators that come with BeOS deal with image formats. However, you'll eventually begin to see a larger number of filetypes with applicable Translators as well. For example, if a developer creates an appropriate Translator, all of your word processing applications could suddenly gain the ability to read and/or write common word processing formats popular on other operating systems. As of R4, the only non-image format available was the StyledEdit Text translator, which gives plain text editors the ability to use fonts and colors and still retain the plain text file format, just as StyledEdit does now.

In order for an application to take advantage of translation services, the developer must program it to do so. Most do, but you can't assume that all applications automatically use the translations system. If your favorite application doesn't, write a polite note to the developer requesting the feature.

# Devices

Present only in x86 machines, the Devices panel provides an interface onto every piece of hardware built into or attached to your motherboard. For the most part, this panel is purely informational in nature; it's not going to let you just jump in and start reconfiguring your hardware with wild abandon. However, there are a few editable components here that may, in certain specific cases, help you to get supported hardware working with BeOS. Note the word "supported" there. If a driver for a specific piece of hardware is not present on your system, no amount of twiddling with Devices will get it working.

If it ain't broke, don't fix it. If everything attached to your system (for which you have drivers installed) is working fine, there's no reason to fiddle with settings in this panel. Injudicious tampering with resource settings can yield unpredictable results. Change only the settings you understand, and change only one thing at a time, testing after each change.

**What This Panel *Isn't*** If you've used Windows's Device Manager before, this panel may look somewhat familiar. On closer inspection, however, you'll notice some important differences. For one thing, Windows's Device Manager is aware of devices beyond your motherboard. It knows not only that you have a video card installed, but what brand of monitor is on the other end of the video cable. It's able to do this because Windows's Device Manager is also an interface onto the drivers installed in your system, not just the physical hardware. In contrast, the Devices preferences panel in BeOS works at a very low level, and does not tell you anything about drivers that are available or in use. Second, Windows's Device Manager lets you configure—or even remove—just about anything in your system. Users can get pretty tangled up in Windows's Device Manager, and can end up spending hours reinstalling drivers and juggling resources to make everything right. BeOS takes a different approach. It says, "Look. This is a list of all of the hardware that has been clearly and unambiguously identified by the operating system. If you have a driver for it, or if it's supported by the kernel, it will work."

The vast majority of the time, everything does work. However, there are variables out there in hardware land that can make things very difficult for BeOS. It all boils down to resources: IRQs (interrupt request queues), DMAs (direct memory addresses), and IO Port Ranges. We don't need to get in too deep with those terms (and they're covered in more depth in Chapter 16,

*Troubleshooting and Maintenance*), but it's useful to understand the difference between the major categories of devices listed in this panel.

**x86 History** In the past, most x86 hardware was incapable of sharing most resources with other hardware in the same machine. This limitation was built into the ISA bus, which once prevailed in x86 computers. Since the early 90s, however, several other pieces have been added to the puzzle: First, Microsoft's Plug-and-Play specification was designed to manage resource conflicts at the operating system level. As you've no doubt heard (and possibly experienced for yourself), PnP is not always successful in its mission. Next, the PCI bus was introduced, improving the situation greatly by simply allowing many resources to be shared between devices without complaint. Plug-and-Play devices exist for both ISA and PCI buses, but the nature of the PCI bus actually makes the PnP mechanism unnecessary in a well-designed operating system. Finally, the USB and FireWire buses were introduced to put an end to this nonsense for good. You can read about those buses online in *The Future* (**www.beosbible.com**).

At this point in history, most x86 machines include both ISA and PCI buses, and many users out there own both ISA and PCI devices. That means we have to mix shareable and non-shareable resources in the same machine, and to make them all behave under a single operating system. The most important consideration for the operating system is this fact: Most modern devices can have resources assigned to them by the operating system at boot time, while most older devices cannot. Therefore, the OS needs to accommodate the inflexible devices first, and give them the resources they demand. After those devices have been satisfied, whatever resources are left over can be divvied up among the rest of the devices. The moral of the story is this: The fewer legacy ISA devices you have in your machine, the better off you'll be, and the smaller your prospects of experiencing resource conflicts.

**When to Use Device Preferences** Despite all of this, you may very well own perfectly good legacy devices such as modems, network cards, or sound cards. These devices' resources are set in one of two ways: by moving physical jumpers around on the card itself or through a software-based configuration utility provided by the manufacturer. In either case, the resources are "locked in" as far as the OS is concerned, and cannot be set by the system at boot time. Thus, the primary purpose of the Device preferences panel is to let you tell BeOS that a certain collection of resources is reserved for a specific device at a specific address, and must not be offered to other devices.

If you have such a device, you know it is supported by BeOS with appropriate drivers, and yet you cannot get it to work, then the Devices panel is for you. Let's take a look at the panel's layout, then talk about what you can do with it.

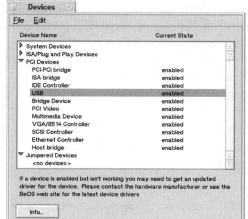

*Figure 9.08*

*The Device preferences panel is broken down into four categories. Devices are assigned to a category depending on how the system allocates resources to them.*

**Meet the Panel** The Devices panel breaks down your hardware into four categories, each of which can be expanded or collapsed to show the devices in that category. The four categories are:

- **System Devices:** These devices are embedded in the circuit logic of your machine's motherboard. You'll find entries such as serial controllers, RAM, system timer, and keyboard and mouse ports.

- **ISA/Plug-and-Play Devices:** These devices live on the ISA bus, but are Plug-and-Play enabled. The most common devices you'll find in this category are the less expensive sound and network cards.

- **PCI Devices:** This category hosts a mixture of I/O cards and motherboard components, all living on the PCI bus. In newer motherboards, you're likely to find your hard drive controllers, bridge devices that let the two buses cooperate in the same system, newer SCSI adapters, video cards, TV tuners, and the like. Your system may differ.

- **Jumpered Devices:** This category is reserved for any device that cannot have its resources set by the operating system, such as legacy ISA modems, network cards, and sound cards. This is the only category to which you can manually add entries.

Double-click any device entry to see its Info panel, which has two tabs. The Info tab offers a few low-level stats of interest mainly to developers writing drivers. It also includes an "Enabled" checkbox, which is probably grayed out. Very few devices can be disabled by the user. The Editor tab includes checkboxes and fields reporting on the device's IRQ, DMA, IO port address, and memory range. In most cases, every entry in the Editor panel will be grayed out and uneditable.

 As of R4, it was not possible to see a listing of all IRQ assignments at once. This feature will be added to the Devices panel in a future release.

**Disabling Devices** In contrast to Windows's Device Manager, you cannot arbitrarily tell BeOS to stop "seeing" devices. You can't physically remove your hard drive controller if it's built into your motherboard, so BeOS doesn't let you remove it from the preferences panel either. The exception to this rule is with Plug-and-Play devices. Because the PnP mechanism can cause headaches for users of alternative operating systems, you'll find that the "Enabled" check-box in a device's Info panel is not grayed out, and can be deselected, thus disabling that device. The only reason to do this is if you suspect a resource conflict between two devices that BeOS was not able to resolve. If this is happening, you should see an entry in the main device list reading "Disabled by system."

Let's say you find that neither your network card nor your sound card works, and they're both ISA/PnP devices. You may be able to get one of them work-ing by disabling the other. Not much of a solution, I know, but better than nothing. The real solution, of course, is to replace one or both of these cards with equivalent PCI cards. A PCI NE2000 network card can be had for $35 or less, and is virtually guaranteed to work perfectly.

*Disable Plug-and-Play OS* **The first thing you should always try when expe-riencing hardware conflicts in BeOS is to enter your system's BIOS (usually by pressing F1 or Del immediately upon boot) and look for an option reading "Plug-and-Play OS." Disable this option and BeOS should be much happier, though you may have to manually reconfigure some resources in Windows later on.**

**Adding Jumpered Devices** Finally, we come to the real power of the Devices preferences panel. If you have a legacy modem, network card, or other device that is not Plug-and-Play and not PCI, and that is supported by BeOS, but that you can't get working, there's hope yet. Pull down File | New Jumpered Device and you'll find an empty template similar to the Editor tab for existing devices. Give the device a name, choose its type from the picklist, and enter as many relevant details as you have on hand. At the very least, you must enter an IRQ and in most cases, a DMA as well. It's not usually neces-sary to enter a memory range, since the chances of these causing conflicts is slim. If you're working with a network card, do enter an IO port address. You should be able to determine these settings by studying the card's documenta-tion, the arrangement of jumpers on the card, or by using a software configu-ration utility that came with the card. Close the template to save your changes, and reboot to see if your changes enabled the device.

Unfortunately, this technique will *not* help you to get jumpered sound cards working in BeOS. Jumpered sound cards are simply unsupported, period.

What you have done is to "rope off" a set of resources, telling the system to leave them alone at boot time. The device that demands dedicated resources

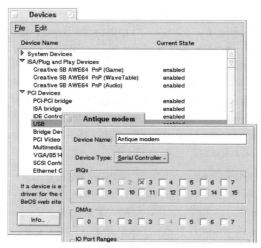

**Figure 9.09**

*To reserve a collection of resources for a legacy device, use the New Jumpered Device template. You'll usually want to choose Communications Device | Serial Controller as the device type.*

will get what it needs. Interestingly, this type of resource blocking can be useful even if you're not trying to add an older device to your system. For example, some PS/2 mouse ports have been known to prevent PnP modems from using a valid IRQ (modems should be on IRQ 3 or 4). By creating a new template that reserves IRQ12 for the mouse, you can force the modem back to a valid IRQ. Isn't Plug-and-Play wonderful?

**Modem Notes**  Probably the most common use of the New Jumpered Device template will be to reserve resources for older modems. When adding a modem, use the Device Type picklist in the template to scroll to Communications Device | Serial Controller.

If your modem is on COM3, use IRQ4 and set the I/O range to 3E8–3EF.

If your modem is on COM4, use IRQ3 and set the I/O range to 2E8–2EF.

## Dial-Up Networking

Use this panel to configure your machine to communicate with your Internet service provider. Detailed instructions can be found in Chapter 4, *Get Online Fast*.

## DriveSetup

DriveSetup is an all-purpose utility used for mounting and unmounting, formatting, partitioning, and initializing all kinds of drives, from floppy disks to removable cartridges to monster SCSI drives. When DriveSetup is launched, your system is scanned for all readable drives and partitions, regardless of filesystem, partition type, or mount status. If it stores data and is physically attached to your system, DriveSetup will see it.

DriveSetup is a powerful application. Like fire or water, it can be your best friend or your worst enemy. While DriveSetup is well-designed and does what it does very well, misuse can potentially destroy your data or render your system unbootable. Because it sees and can operate on your entire hard disk (not just your BeOS partitions), it can even potentially damage other OS installations. Proceed with caution, don't click any buttons marked "Yes" without thinking twice, and don't operate after trigger-happy gaming sessions. If an alert box pops up, read the information it contains twice to make sure you understand what it's telling you.

**About the DriveSetup Table**    The DriveSetup window consists of a table listing your physical drives on the vertical, with their individual statistics on the horizontal. If any of your drives have multiple partitions, the disk's icon will have a small arrow (a "latch") next to it. Click the latch once to expand the view and display individual partitions for that physical drive. Note the conceptual difference here: The Tracker displays each of your mounted partitions as root objects (i.e. as "volumes"), whereas DriveSetup displays physical disks at the root, with your various partitions listed as their children. This makes sense because DriveSetup is capable of operating on entire hard disks at once, whereas the Tracker only sees individual partitions. Let's take a look at each of the columns in DriveSetup's table.

| Device | | Type | File System | Volume Name | Mounted At | Size |
|---|---|---|---|---|---|---|
| /dev/disk/floppy | Format | | | | | 1.4 MB |
| /dev/disk/ide/ata | Partition ▷ | apple... | esther | | | 6.0 GB |
| /dev/disk/ide/ata/1... | Initialize ▷ intel | intel... BeOS | Be File System | grueyer | /grueyer | 1.3 GB |
| | | BeOS | Be File System | ghouda | /boot | 1.3 GB |
| | | BeOS | Be File System | gorgonzola | /gorgonzola | 1.3 GB |
| | | Linux | unknown | | | 1.3 GB |
| /dev/disk/ide/atapi... | multisession | | audio, audio, ... | | | 430.4 MB |
| /dev/disk/scsi/0/5/0 | no media | | | | | |
| /dev/disk/scsi/0/6/0 | intel | | Be File System | tink | /tink | 1021.0 MB |

Figure 9.10

*Rather than displaying your partitions as root objects as the Tracker does, DriveSetup offers a view based on physical drives, with all attached disk drives at the root and their partitions branching from each device.*

**Device**    The paths listed in the left column of DriveSetup are the "real" names of your storage devices, as known to the system internally. BeOS typically hides these paths from the end-user, though you can navigate to them (but not through them) via the Terminal (see Chapter 5, *Files and the Tracker*, for details). Since all BeOS system devices are mounted under /dev (for device), all storage device paths start with /dev/disk. From there, they branch into the disk type, such as floppy, IDE, or SCSI, then on down the chain to the exact bus and partition (in the case of IDE drives) or to the exact bus, ID, and LUN (in the case of SCSI drives).

**Map Style**  While there are many types of partitions out there (such as BFS, HFS, and NTFS), each of these filesystems needs to be established within a basic "map style," which is like a level of disk formatting that lies beneath what you normally think of as a disk's format. There are very few valid map styles; Apple and Intel are obviously the big ones, though there are a few relatively rare ones around, such as those used with Solaris and FreeBSD. Apple and Intel are currently the only map styles supported in BeOS. As an end-user, chances are almost nonexistent that you'll ever need to think about map styles, and if you do, you don't need this book.

**Partition Type**  It's very easy to confuse this column with the next one over, File System. Drives can be chopped up into many combinations of primary, extended, and logical partitions, but you can install various filesystems onto any of these partition types. A FAT32 filesystem, for instance, could live on any of these partition types.

DriveSetup will do its best to recognize all partition types and filesystems, but that doesn't necessarily mean you'll be able to mount them in BeOS. For example, Figure 9.10 shows DriveSetup reporting an NT installation as living on an "unknown" filesystem (although BeOS will learn how to recognize and communicate with NTFS filesystems in the future).

**File System**  The computer industry has chewed up and spat out dozens, if not hundreds, of different filesystems over the past half a century. While Be promises no support for most of the older, less popular file systems, it has supported reading and writing to the HFS (MacOS) filesystem since early on, and can now read and write to FAT16 and FAT32 (Windows) volumes. Because it's relatively easy to write filesystem add-ons for BeOS (easy compared to other operating systems, that is), DriveSetup does its best to recognize them all, even if the Tracker can't mount them.

**Volume Name**  This is the "friendly name" for a given volume. In almost all cases, the volume name is equal to the volume's name at the root of the filesystem. For example, if you call a partition Galileo, then open a Terminal window and get a directory listing from the root of the filesystem, you'll see an entry at /Galileo. However, there is an exception to this rule: If Galileo is your boot drive, it will appear as /boot in the root of the system, with a symlink to /Galileo. For this reason, not all entries in the Volume Name column will match those in the next column over, Mounted At.

Why is this so? Because it's essential that the system be able to count on the presence of a volume named /boot. Just about every script, installation package, and instruction manual out there depends on the existence of the /boot volume. Therefore, no matter what names you give to your volumes, BeOS will always mount the partition from which it boots, "/boot", even though /boot is just the name of the mount point, not the actual volume name. The system reconciles the two names through clever use of symlinks. Take a look at the root of your filesystem from the Terminal, and you'll see that both /boot and /Galileo are listed, but that /Galileo is in fact just a symlink to /boot.

**Mounted At** The Mounted At column shows you how actual volume names are reconciled with the filesystem's view of them. Remember the "real" system paths to your devices described earlier? Nobody wants to type the full /dev/disk/ide/0/master/blahblahblah path to access their disks. Thus, when disks are mounted in BeOS, a virtual directory is created in the root of the filesystem for each attached device. Once mounted, your disk can be accessed as if it were a standard directory with a standard name—your traveling hard drive thus becomes accessible as /Galileo (or whatever name you've given it).

**Rename Your Volumes** Tired of your default volume names? Right-click a volume's icon, and choose Edit Name, just as you would do with a standard file. The new name will be visible in the Terminal (at /newname), in DriveSetup, and in all Tracker views. Renaming a volume from the Terminal is just as easy:

mv oldname newname

Note that you're also free to attach any icon to any volume, just as you would to any file (see the Icon-o-Matic section in Chapter2 for details).

**Size** The size of the disk, as measured in kilobytes, megabytes, or gigabytes, depending on the medium.

**Mounting and Unmounting** DriveSetup can be used to mount and unmount drives in much in the same way that you do so from the Desktop. To make a disk visible to the Tracker, select it in DriveSetup and pull down Mount. Each entry on the resulting menu will represent a partition on that disk. Any partitions that are not in a format recognizable by BeOS will be grayed out and therefore inaccessible. Select a partition that isn't grayed out and DriveSetup will mount it on the Desktop. The Unmount menu works the same way, but has the reverse effect. You can also mount and unmount partitions by right-clicking drive entries and sliding through the relevant menus.

## MacOS Trying to Mount BeOS Partitions

In rare cases, Mac users have found that MacOS insists on trying to mount their BeOS partitions. Of course, MacOS doesn't read BFS, so the attempt fails. If this is happening on your Mac, it's because your BeOS partition has its automount flag set, and MacOS responds to anything waving that flag. The fix is to fire up your Macintosh partitioning software and turn off the automount setting. Apple's Drive Setup has options for customizing your volume parameters, and you'll find the automount flag there. Similarly, if you use Silverlining for MacOS, look for the Mounting checkbox.

## *Disk Mount Settings*

In Windows, Explorer shows you all the drives connected to your system, regardless of whether there's currently a disk in the drive or not. If you have removable drives connected to your system (and everyone has at least a floppy drive), you often don't find out until you click on the disk's icon that "Drive G: is not ready." In MacOS, the Finder only displays currently mounted volumes—when a new disk is inserted, its volume(s) appear automatically. This is partially a result of the way Macintosh hardware is built and partially a factor of OS design philosophy. (Mac floppy drives are specifically built to communicate with MacOS, whereas PC floppy drives are operating-system agnostic, and lack any kind of "wake up" mechanism.)

Since BeOS straddles these worlds but needs to keep the OS consistent regardless of the hardware on which it's running, a compromise was required when establishing automounting rules. The Tracker won't display any disk drives that aren't currently mounted, and automounting behavior is the user's choice. You won't find a Disk Mount Settings panel in the preferences folder, and you won't find these settings anywhere in the DriveSetup interface either. The only way to access automount settings is to right-click on the Desktop and scroll to Mount | Settings in the context menu.

 Floppy drives are in a category all by themselves, and behave a little differently. Floppies will not automount in any circumstance, but the floppy mechanism is always visible in the Mount menu, even when there is no disk in the drive.

If your hardware has some kind of built-in notification mechanism, it'll "wake up" whenever you insert a disk. When it does, it sends a signal to the operating system that there's a new volume asking for attention; all BeOS has to do is listen in the background for the wake-up call. This is the case with Zip and Jaz drives, for example. On the other hand, PC floppy drives don't have any such mechanism. The only way BeOS would be able to determine if a new floppy volume had appeared on the scene would be to "poll" the mechanism by sending out a signal of its own every few seconds. Unfortunately, this not only makes a nasty grinding sound, but it's not a very good use of system resources, either—especially given how seldom people use floppies. As a result, the Tracker will never display icons for newly inserted floppies automatically, and you'll always need to mount them manually.

**Working with Partitions**  Any disk can be divided into multiple sections called "partitions." Partitions can contain more partitions, different filesystems, different operating systems, or multiple, separate "volumes" of the same filesystem. Regardless of operating system, each volume appears as a separate disk with a unique name. DriveSetup is capable of creating partitions on all of your disk drives except for CD-ROMs (which are read-only) and floppy disks (which are too small). You can create partitions in blank, unused space or by overwriting existing partitions (which, of course, erases all existing data on that partition).

While some modern partitioning software is seemingly capable of magic—resizing and reshuffling existing partitions without damaging a byte of data—you can't partition a drive that's already mounted and in use. That means that if you have multiple operating systems sharing your only disk and you're currently booted into BeOS, you won't be able to change partition information on the same disk from within DriveSetup. DriveSetup's partition mapping tool will, however, let you examine existing partitions on a mounted drive, though all options will be grayed out. Thus, the partition mapping tool remains a good informational tool even when you can't use it to make changes.

The only way to make changes to partitions in a case like this is to use a low-level partitioning tool available from a third party, such as PowerQuest's PartitionMagic. Since these tools can be run after booting from a floppy rather than from the hard disk, they can work on any disk or volume. Learn more about partition types in Chapter 3, *Installation*.

**Creating New Partitions**  To create a new partition on an unmounted drive, select that drive in DriveSetup, pull down Setup | Partition, and choose either Apple or Intel, depending on your machine. If you try this while the disk is mounted, you'll be able to view but not edit the resulting partition table. When the partition table pops up, study it carefully before doing anything.

The partition table will display the number of partitions found on the currently selected drive. If you're working with a fresh, unformatted drive, click the Layout pop-up to establish the number of partitions you want to create (x86 users will be limited to four partitions per disk here). Choosing an option from the Layout pop-up will display partition sizes with the assumption that the drive is to be sliced up into partitions of equal size. For example, if you have a 2GB drive and choose "4 25% partitions," you'll see four 500MB partitions displayed in the map. You can then fine-tune the partition sizes by

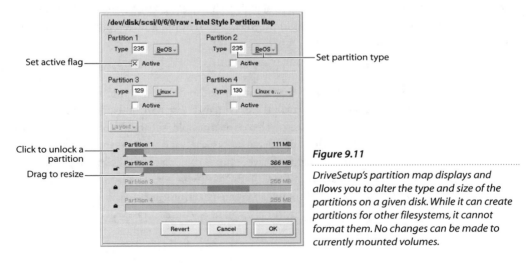

Set active flag

Set partition type

Click to unlock a partition

Drag to resize

**Figure 9.11**

*DriveSetup's partition map displays and allows you to alter the type and size of the partitions on a given disk. While it can create partitions for other filesystems, it cannot format them. No changes can be made to currently mounted volumes.*

dragging the triangular sliders left and right. Because no changes are made to your drive's partition table until you click OK, you have the option to revert to the layout as it was before you began by clicking the Revert button. You will be warned repeatedly that resizing partitions will destroy all data in that partition. Any partitions you create will still need to be initialized prior to use (see below). Partitions created for non-BeOS filesystems will need to be initialized from within their native operating systems.

If the drive has both free space and preestablished partitions, the Layout pop-up will be grayed out and the existing partitions will be "locked." See *Resizing Partitions*, below.

Each partition includes options for setting its type and bootable flag—the blue checkbox labeled "Active" denotes the currently set partition as bootable.

Even though BeOS recognizes the Active flag, it's actually ignored at boot time. Instead, BeOS seeks out a special "flag file," which is created by the Boot preferences panel. The boot loader just tracks down this flag file to discover which of your BeOS partitions it's supposed to boot.

Each type of partition has an associated type number, which is recognized across various operating systems so that they can identify one another (being able to identify a partition type, however, does not imply the ability to use another OS's filesystem). Choosing a partition type from the pop-up will display its type number in the editable field to its left. If you want to create a partition type for a filesystem not listed in the pop-up, type its number into the field and press Enter. Since you would need to know the number in question beforehand, this is really an option for expert users only—the most common types are included in the pop-up.

Intel-mapped drives are limited to four primary partitions. Primary partitions can in turn host extended partitions, which can in turn host logical partitions. BeOS is capable of recognizing extended partitions, but DriveSetup will not help you to create them—you'll need to use a third-party utility (such as DOS or Linux fdisk) to do that. Apple-mapped drives are not subject to this limitation, and can have as many as 32 partitions per drive. The partition map in Figure 9.11 will grow scrollbars in such a case, letting you view and/or work with any number of partitions on an Apple-mapped drive.

**Resizing Partitions**    DriveSetup will let you resize partitions, but be aware that all data will be destroyed on the partitions you resize. If there are preexisting partitions on a given drive, the Layout pop-up will not be available to you, and an icon displaying a closed lock will appear to the left of each partition.

If you are absolutely positively sure you know what you're doing and want to resize a partition even if that means destroying the data it contains, you can unlock a partition slider by clicking on the padlock icon. A warning dialog will appear, and the color of the partition bar will change from blue to red. If you unlock all partitions, the Layout pop-up described above will become enabled. It is not possible to create overlapping partitions.

Remember that DriveSetup is *not* a non-destructive partitioning tool. Use these features entirely at your own risk. See the section on Partition Magic in Chapter 3 for more information.

**Initializing and Formatting Drives** Because a partition does not necessarily contain an actual filesystem, it's not enough to simply create one—you must initialize a volume before it can be used.

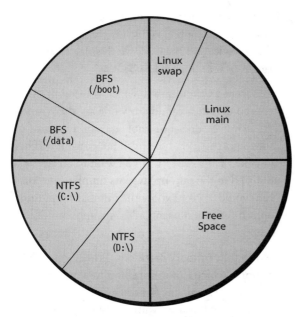

**Figure 9.12**

*The terms "disk," "partition," and "volume" are not interchangeable. "Disk" refers to the physical unit. A disk can be divided into multiple sections, called partitions. Partitions can host one or more volumes. Volumes are the only units visible from the Tracker.*

You'll notice that DriveSetup gives you options both to Initialize and to Format volumes. While most operating systems require volumes to be formatted prior to use, BeOS requires them only to be initialized. What's the difference? Do you need to do both? No. In the vast majority of cases, simply initializing a volume will install the Be filesystem, and you'll be ready to rock. In some cases, however, initialization can fail (this usually indicates that your drive is going south anyway, and you should consider investing in some new storage). In these cases, you'll need to format your drive after initializing it. Always try initializing first—formatting is slow and usually unnecessary.

Select the partition and pull down Setup | Initialize. You'll be given a choice between the Be filesystem, Mac HFS, ISO 9660, and the old Be filesystem. Mac HFS partitions are probably more effectively managed from within MacOS, ISO 9660 is for CD-ROMs, and I can't think of a reason why anyone would choose the old Be filesystem, which was phased out with DR9 (it's present only for backward compatibility). A dialog will appear asking you what block size you want to use, and will prompt you for a volume name. When the operation is complete (normally just a few seconds), you'll be given the option to mount the drive. Do so, and your new volume will appear on the Desktop.

**Choosing Block Sizes**   If you chose the Advanced button when you first installed BeOS, you probably saw the small dialog asking whether you wanted to initialize your new partition with a block size of 1024, 2048, or 4096. In all likelihood, you left it alone and kept the default of 1024—a wise choice. When you initialize a disk with DriveSetup, you see the same dialog. What's this about?

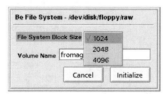

**Figure 9.13**

*When you initialize a new device, choose one of three possible block sizes. Unless you're storing a lot of large files on the partition, the default of 1024 will be your best bet.*

Hard disks, regardless of the filesystem(s) installed on them, store information in pre-allocated "blocks" of a certain size. Think of blocks as if they were tiny boxes in which you're going to store your data, and each file you store occupied a minimum of one box. However, the average user's files are of many different sizes, ranging from a few K to (potentially) many terabytes. Large files can be split across thousands of blocks, but small files occupy one block at the very minimum. If your minimum block size is 16K, then every 8K file you store is going to leave 8K of wasted space in its box. Storing lots of small files on a filesystem initialized with large blocks is a very wasteful way to store data.

On the other hand, if you typically store a smaller number of larger files, block size isn't nearly as important. You will, however, gain a little efficiency in disk read/write operations with larger blocks, so if all of your files are large, you'll enjoy a small performance boost by using larger block sizes.

Filesystems in the DOS, Windows, and Mac worlds have traditionally been pretty wasteful, forcing you to use 16K or even 32K block sizes. Later versions of FAT32, NTFS, and HFS+ use smaller block sizes for more efficient storage, but none of them comes close to the tiny, 1K block sizes used by BFS. Not only that, but BFS allows you to select alternate block sizes when a disk is first initialized. This way, if you know for a fact that a given partition will be dedicated to storing large files, you can choose the slightly faster 2048 or 4096 block sizes. BFS, however, is a highly efficient filesystem, and most people will get the most bang for their buck by accepting the default size of 1024.

To illustrate this concept, we'll use a story. Dan and Zoe have each been asked to pour a total of 25 gallons of water into a row of five 10-gallon barrels. The rules are that they can make as many or as few trips as they want, and if they

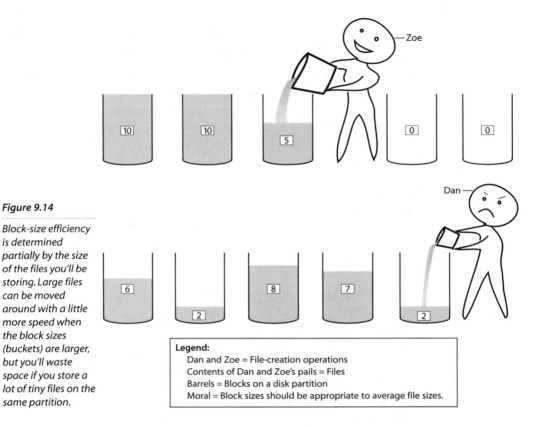

**Figure 9.14**

*Block-size efficiency is determined partially by the size of the files you'll be storing. Large files can be moved around with a little more speed when the block sizes (buckets) are larger, but you'll waste space if you store a lot of tiny files on the same partition.*

**Legend:**
Dan and Zoe = File-creation operations
Contents of Dan and Zoe's pails = Files
Barrels = Blocks on a disk partition
Moral = Block sizes should be appropriate to average file sizes.

carry more water on one trip than will fit in a barrel, the remainder can spill over into the next empty barrel. But every time they make another trip, they have to start filling a fresh barrel—they can't use leftover space in partially filled barrels.

Dan has been making lots of small trips: six gallons here, two gallons there, etc. He finished the job, but is out of empty barrels. Zoe brought all 25 gallons at once, and still has two empty barrels to spare—she could keep on working if she wanted to. Since Dan was carrying lots of small pails around, he would have benefited by being able to fill lots of one-gallon barrels and not wasting all that space. Smaller barrels wouldn't affect Zoe's space efficiency, but it would have taken a little extra time for her to spread her big load among a lot of small barrels.

Moral of the story: When initializing a new partition, ask yourself whether you think you'll be creating lots of small files or a smaller number of large ones. The default block size of 1024K turns out to be an optimal size for general usage. 4096K will give you slightly better performance on large files, but will waste space with smaller files. Even at 4096, you're still using *far* smaller blocks than you do with other operating systems; BFS hates wasted space.

***Create a "Media" Partition***  Because sound, video, and other sorts of multi-media files are typically very large, and because those are exactly the kinds of files that benefit the most from maximum disk performance, it makes sense to store your media files in a partition with a larger block size. If you work with a lot of media, consider creating a separate, dedicated partition formatted with 4096K blocks. You won't waste much, and you'll win a few points in throughput rates.

 ***Mastering CDs***  If you intend to use BeOS to create disk images that will later be burned onto CD-ROMs, create a partition no larger than 650MB, and initialize it with 2048-byte block sizes. Otherwise, no CD-ROM drive in existence will be capable of reading the CDs you create!

**More DriveSetup Options**  In addition to the primary functions described above, DriveSetup has a variety of additional options available from its pulldown and context menus.

**Eject**  If your drive sports its own eject mechanism, as is the case with Mac floppies and all Zip and Jaz drives, you can unmount and eject a disk by pulling down Options | Eject.

**Surface Test**  As hard drives age, blocks sometimes start refusing to accept data, resulting in all kinds of flaky behavior. While a number of tools are available for various operating systems that specialize in moving data out of bad clusters and into good ones (and marking the bad clusters as unusable), most hard disks perform this kind of management behind the scenes automatically, without you ever even noticing. Thus, if you're actually noticing flaky behavior from your hard drive, the problem has already gotten bad. It's probably time to go buy a new drive; storage is cheap, and your data is valuable. In the meantime, DriveSetup's Surface Test may be able to save your data from disaster—run it at the first sign of strange disk behavior.

To run a surface test, select a drive and pull down Options | Surface Test. DriveSetup will take a close look at every single block on your drive, examining the storage integrity of each one. If it finds any errors, it will attempt to remap data found in those blocks to known good blocks. The process can take half an hour or more, depending on the size of your disk.

**Rescan**  The final menu option in DriveSetup is Rescan, which simply repeats the process that took place when you first launched DriveSetup, scoping out your system for newly attached devices. This is useful if you need to swap removable disks in and out and don't want to quit and restart DriveSetup. Just pull down Rescan and select the IDE or SCSI bus you need examined.

**Formatting Floppies with DriveSetup**  Floppy disks are small. They're fragile, they decay with time, and they barely hold enough data to be useful. For the most part, floppies have been relegated to the role of the sneakernet transfer, and will be most useful to BeOS as a means of carrying the occasional file between your Windows, Linux, OS/2, or Mac machines and your BeOS machine when the network is down. Because the lowest common denominator here is the DOS filesystem (all of these operating systems have mechanisms for reading DOS disks), you'll find the greatest amount of flexibility by keeping floppies destined for cross-platform transfers formatted in FAT.

On the other hand, BeOS supports the Mac filesystem (HFS) natively *on both Intel and PowerMac versions of BeOS*. If you don't need floppy compatibility between anything but MacOS and BeOS, you'll probably benefit the most by sticking to Mac-formatted floppies.

If you do want to create BFS-based floppy disks, there are a couple of important things to note.

For one, all BFS volumes—no matter what their size—come with at least 500K of mostly invisible filesystem-related data, including the journal (see Chapter 5, *Files and the Tracker*), and a home directory complete with Desktop. On most disks, you'll never notice the missing space (2MB on hard disks). On floppies, however, you lose 500K, almost a third of your storage capacity. This isn't a bug, and Be isn't going to fix the situation—it's a side effect of the structure of BFS itself. The floppy disk is regarded by Be and just about everyone else as a medium on its way out, and it wasn't worth compromising the benefits of BFS just so you could fill your dinky little floppy disks all the way up. If you need more than 900K of space on your floppies, you're probably better off leaving them formatted as FAT.

If you do want to format a floppy with BFS, insert a floppy disk and launch DriveSetup. Your floppy should appear at the top of the list, above other drives found during the initial scan.

# E-mail

Because Be built an email-capable infrastructure into the operating system itself, the E-mail preferences panel is separate from the BeMail application. This way you can establish your email preferences once, and other applications can reach out and read them from this central location (similar to MacOS's InternetConfig feature). You'll find everything you need to know about configuring and using E-Mail preferences and BeMail in Chapter 4, *Get Online Fast*.

# FileTypes

The seemingly simple question of how to associate your files with particular applications is actually much thornier than it sounds. The difficulty lies in finding a reliable system that always does the right thing by default, yet gives users the ability to override the default settings either globally or on a file-by-file basis. While various operating systems handle various aspects of the filetyping problem better than others, all of them involve some kind of unfortunate compromise for the user—making terrible assumptions like "The application you created the file with is the best one to open it with," or "files without a three-letter extension won't get an association at all." For a complete discussion of the filetyping problem, see Chapter 5, *Files and the Tracker*.

Be has developed an elegant, no-compromise solution to the filetyping problem by adopting the Internet's MIME standard and extending its capabilities to take advantage of BeOS's unique capabilities. Because the MIME arrangement is pervasive throughout BeOS and comes up just about everywhere you look in the system, this book covers FileTypes in depth in Chapter 5, *Files and the Tracker*. Here's the bullet-point summary:

- There are two levels of filetype control in BeOS: global and local.

- To change the system-wide association between any type of file and its preferred application, use the FileTypes panel in your preferences folder.

- To make preference changes to a single file, right-click its name in the Tracker, choose Add-Ons, and select FileType (or select the file and press Ctrl+Alt+F).

- The dialogs you'll see in either case are similar in important ways, but serve different functions.

- The MIME classification system works by way of a collection of "super-type/type pairs," such as image/jpeg, text/html, application/zip, or audio/wav. Hundreds of MIME types are preregistered on a fresh BeOS installation, and you'll end up with additional MIME types as you experiment with new applications. Users can keep the defaults, add new types, or modify existing types. MIME types are stored in each file's attributes along with other metadata and icons.

- There are only a few supertypes, but lots of types within those; check **www.qnx.com/~chrish/Be/info/** for useful MIME information.

- Most applications have special MIME types called "signatures," which are unique throughout your system. While you may have thousands of documents of the type text/plain, only one application, StyledEdit, should be signed application/x-vnd.Be-STEE. (There are some exceptions to this rule, notably with Terminal programs that can't be launched from the Tracker.)

When you double-click an icon, the system uses an algorithm to determine which application should be launched, asking a series of questions in a fixed order:

1. Is this file an application or a document?
2. If a document, does it have a specific preferred application?
3. If not, does it belong to a MIME type that has a preferred application?
4. If not, does it belong to a supertype with a preferred application?
5. If not, does it have an extension (like .txt) that can be used to guess the supertype?

If the answer to the last question is no, the system sends up a dialog and gives the user the opportunity to either change its MIME type or choose an application. It sounds complex, but for the vast majority of files it all happens instantaneously and transparently.

Usage of the FileTypes preferences panel is covered in depth in Chapter 5, *Files and the Tracker*.

***Drag Multiple Files onto FileTypes*** As of R4, you can drag multiple files at once onto the FileTypes application, so you can change the types of dozens or hundreds of files at once. Try it!

If you're a developer, or are considering developing applications for BeOS, be sure to check out the New Resource File entry in the FileTypes File menu. From this panel you can give your new application a signature and icon, associate it with filetypes, establish version information, and set other details. The resulting resource file can then be compiled into your application.

## Fonts

The Font preferences panel performs two important system functions. First, it works in conjunction with the Menu preferences panel to let you customize the appearance of Be's system fonts—the fonts that appear in your pulldown menus, on your windows' title tabs, and in your dialog boxes. Second, it allows you to customize the amount of font-related information that stays cached in system RAM, as opposed to staying on your hard disk.

**Font Settings** The first tab in the Fonts panel is used to declare your system-wide font preferences. You'll see three fields here: Plain, Bold, and Fixed, corresponding to three font display protocols in BeOS. The Plain field controls the majority of onscreen text provided by the operating system itself (as opposed to text in word processors or applications like browsers where you have independent settings for displaying Web pages). The plain font is seen in the Deskbar, on buttons, and in dialog boxes. Note that fonts on pulldown menus are configured through the Menu preferences panel, not here. The

Bold font is used most notably on your windows' title tabs, while the Fixed font is displayed only rarely. The default Terminal font and X-ray views of your zip files in Expander are a good example of fixed fonts in action. Note that the fixed font field is smart—when you click its pop-up button, the list of available fonts will include only your monospaced fonts, rather than your entire collection. By definition, each character in a fixed font occupies exactly one space. Dialogs and panels that use fixed fonts use them for a reason, generally to display tabular data where it's important that characters line up from row to row.

Note that if you pick a font that's too large, you'll find that bits of text are "clipped" in many of your dialogs and menus. As of R4, BeOS lacked the native ability to adjust dialog layouts to accommodate unusually large fonts, though this bug should be resolved in a future version of the operating system.

***Liblayout*** Thanks to Liblayout, a programmer's "library" created by an independent developer, some third-party applications are able to resize themselves as necessary to accommodate extra-large fonts. Liblayout is covered in Chapter 15, *Other Goodies.* In addition, the BeatWare family of productivity applications solves this dilemma with their FreeStyle UI. See Chapter 13, *Graphics Applications* for more on FreeStyle.

Closing the Font preferences panel puts your changes into effect system-wide. However, you will need to close and restart any currently running applications to see the new settings. If you want to restore your font settings to the way they were when you first installed BeOS, clicking the Defaults button will return them to the original factory configuration. Clicking the Revert button restores things to the way they were before you launched the Fonts preferences panel.

**Cache Settings**   Every time you pull down an application's Font menu, a list of all the available fonts on your system needs to be displayed. If you have hundreds of fonts, this can obviously be a CPU- and memory-consumptive task. Same goes for the display of fonts in your documents—if you're using many of them simultaneously, BeOS has to store all the font information it needs in order to paint the screen properly. Since RAM is hundreds of times faster than even the fastest hard disks, it makes sense to store some of this font information in RAM, rather than leaving it on disk.

BeOS gives you the option to decide exactly how much RAM should be dedicated to storing font information. If you've got a lot of fonts and a lot of RAM, you should definitely consider going higher than the 64K

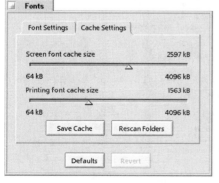

*Figure 9.15*

*Use the pair of sliders in the Fonts preferences panel to allocate more RAM to storing font information for use onscreen, by your printer, or both. Keep in mind that any extra RAM you give to your fonts is subtracted from available system memory.*

default—you can assign as much as 4MB of system RAM to your font cache, and font performance will increase dramatically. What's the catch? Obviously, the RAM dedicated to fonts is no longer available to your applications or for general operating system use. While 64K is small enough that you'll never feel it, 4MB on a 32MB system would probably cause a perceptible difference in general performance. If you have a bunch of RAM, like 128MB, you might want to set the font cache size to its maximum. While there are no hard-and-fast rules here, balance the amount of font cache against the number and variety of fonts on your system and the amount of installed RAM.

The printer cache slider on this tab works in an almost identical manner, except that it determines the amount of RAM cache dedicated to fonts headed for your printer. Adding more printing font cache will speed up print jobs that use multiple fonts. If you don't print very often, and if your print jobs generally use only one or two fonts, you're best off leaving well enough alone here, and keeping that extra memory available to the rest of the system.

## *Fontology*

Most everyone has heard of PostScript fonts, but most of us use TrueType. Go to any of the Web's font archives, and you'll find that the vast majority of downloadable fonts are TrueType. But talk to an old-school print professional and they might tell you that PostScript is the only way to fly. So what's the diff, and where have all the PostScripts gone?

Before the Macintosh, both computer screens and printers were restricted to displaying arrangements of largish dots. The Mac changed all of that by introducing bitmapped fonts, which offered an onscreen clarity that helped spark the computer publishing revolution. Bitmapped fonts, however, were difficult to work with, since they required that the user have an actual picture of each character—in each point size—stored on their machine. It was also impossible to send these fonts to any printer besides the Apple ImageWriter. A year after the Mac's introduction came the LaserWriter, which was capable of printing at resolutions of 300 dpi and higher. Around the same time, Adobe introduced PostScript, which was a technology for describing fonts, images, and entire documents mathematically. Because PostScript fonts weren't bitmapped, they could be scaled to any size with no loss of resolution. With PostScript, an outline of the font was sent to the printer, which filled in the outline in a process called "rasterization."

Despite the improvements offered by PostScript fonts, they also had a few limitations. For one thing, you had to have a PostScript printer to print them. Secondly, high-quality output relied on a process called "hinting," which compensates for any inabilities the printer might have in perfectly filling in the font outlines. Finally, PostScript fonts had to be delivered in pairs: Versions of the same font for use onscreen and in the printer both had to be installed. Eventually, PostScript fonts were divided into two branches: Type 1, which included hinting information, and Type 2, which did not (don't confuse PostScript types with PostScript "levels"—level 3 PostScript, for example, refers to a specific version of the PostScript interpreter living in the

When you've dialed in your cache preferences, click the Save Cache button to commit a memory block to font storage. The cache contents will be written to disk, and will be loaded into memory on the next reboot.

**Adding Fonts**  BeOS comes bundled with a nice collection of both mono-spaced and variable-width fonts, ready to use. Need more? If you're coming from the Windows world and you've amassed a large collection of TrueType fonts, you're in luck, since BeOS will use your old fonts without any modification. Copy your TrueType fonts from a Windows system to your BeOS partition and move them into /boot/home/config/fonts/ttfonts/.

Open up the Fonts preferences panel, click on the Cache Settings tab, and hit Rescan Folders. Your applications will now display your old Windows fonts along with the fonts that came preinstalled. No reboot necessary.

As of R4, BeOS is able to utilize PostScript fonts as well as TrueType, albeit with some limitations. BeOS is capable of recognizing only PostScript fonts

---

printer itself). Adobe Type Manager (ATM) was later introduced to create screen fonts on the fly by examining information in the printer font.

Because of its high output quality and early appearance on the scene, PostScript gained a well-entrenched position in the market. Because of their unique position as owners of the world's best font technology, Adobe was able to charge hefty licensing fees for use of the PostScript system. To deflect Adobe's hegemony, Apple and Microsoft put their heads together in 1991 and created a direct PostScript competitor called TrueType. While both PostScript and TrueType work on the outline principle, TrueType puts the scaling technology in the operating system, rather than in the printer.

Apple and Microsoft's new ability to embed quality font technology in the OS resulted in PostScript being marginalized at the high end, where it remains the choice of many graphics professionals. However, this does not necessarily mean that PostScript always produces a higher-quality output. In fact, TrueType output is indistinguishable from PostScript output in almost all applications and uses. These days, pretty much the only place you'll find PostScript in use is at high-end print shops. That doesn't mean, however, that if you want to create high-quality output at a service bureau you'll need to use PostScript fonts. Most modern print shops can handle either format with equally good results.

Finally, Microsoft and Adobe hammered out a new "OpenType" font technology toward the end of 1997 in an attempt to "end the font wars" once and for all, and to solve lingering cross-platform issues while introducing advanced typographic features and international character support. The OpenType spec also aims to bridge the gap between screen, print, Web, and other publishing media by using a single technology that "just works" no matter where it appears. OpenType, however, has not gained a whole lot of traction since its introduction. There is no word at this time on OpenType technology in BeOS.

created with standard Macintosh Roman encoding (these are the most common type available). If you need to use other PostScript fonts, you'll need to represent them with the "Standard Macintosh Roman" code with the same index values as the characters you want to use. In other words, BeOS will not properly translate from UTF-8 into whatever font encoding you happen to have enabled, so you'll need to perform the translation manually. To add PostScript fonts to your system, drop them in /boot/home/config/fonts/psfonts and use the Fonts preferences panel to rescan the font cache.

If you're not sure whether you need PostScript fonts, then you almost certainly don't. Read the sidebar *Fontology* for more information.

 ***Don't Store Fonts Twice*** **If you already have a font collection on a Windows volume on the same system and you've got the Tracker set up to automatically mount non-BeOS volumes at startup (see the DriveSetup section in this chapter), you can just create a symlink from your** C:\WINDOWS\FONTS **directory to** ~/config/etc/fonts/ttfonts **and have instant access to your complete font collection, regardless of whether you install fonts from within Windows or BeOS. There are a few drawbacks to this technique, though. If you delete Windows from your system, you'll lose those extra fonts from within BeOS, and if you unmount your FAT volumes, you'll temporarily lose access to them.**

Mac users: Your collection of TrueType fonts will work in BeOS as well, but only after being run through a converter. You'll find just such a converter on your MacOS volume, after you install BeOS. Look for a utility called TTConverter which converts your TrueType fonts to Microsoft Windows TrueType format, which works on the BeOS. You can convert any font this way, except for the system fonts which come with your Macintosh: Chicago, Courier, Geneva, Helvetica, Monaco, New York, Palatino, Symbol, and Times.

## Bitstream and Be

One of the first comments many new BeOS users make is how smooth all of the onscreen fonts appear. That kind of visual quality doesn't happen by accident—Be knew that a platform designed for creative multimedia professionals and "prosumers" wouldn't get far without excellent font technology. Rather than inventing it themselves, they partnered with Bitstream, one of the publishing industry's most respected font technology vendors. Because Bitstream's excellent font-rendering engine is built into BeOS, you don't need to purchase expensive add-on packages to enjoy high-end font capabilities. Be sure and check out the FontDemo application in your /boot/demos folder for a taste of the kinds of things you can do with fonts on BeOS that can't be done on other operating systems.

Fonts are so smooth because everything in the system—not just special fonts in particular documents—is antialiased. See Chapter 2, *Meet the System*, for more on antialiasing.

# Japanese

As of R4, BeOS includes a complete input method architecture, making it possible for users to create documents in non-Roman character sets such as Japanese or Cyrillic. However, the mere presence of the input method does not automatically make it possible to work in any language under the sun; you must still install an input method add-on specific to each language, and (obviously) a font or collection of fonts supporting that character set. In addition, languages that are read right-to-left are not yet possible, as this requires updates to the app_server as well.

Most users will not find the Japanese preferences panel installed on their systems by default. Japanese support is available as an option during the installation process, or can easily be added to your system in the future if necessary. This section covers more than just the Japanese preferences panel; we'll take a look at installation and usage of the Japanese input method as well, then finish up with a guest tutorial for those interested in getting their feet wet with hiragana.

**Installing Support for Japanese Input**   If you'd like to work in Japanese but didn't choose the option during the BeOS installation process, insert the BeOS CD and navigate to beos/etc/install/_japanese_install_. Within this folder you'll find subdirectories labeled home, preferences, and beos. You'll need to navigate through each of these folders and place their contents in the equivalent locations on your boot drive, then restart your machine.

 As noted in Chapter 5, *Files and the Tracker*, BeOS's behavior when copying folders to a location that *already contains a folder of the same name* has very different results than it does under some operating systems. If you simply drag these home, preferences, and beos folders into equivalent locations on your boot drive and click the Replace button, you will *overwrite the contents* of the existing folders. If you come to BeOS from Windows, this is not the behavior you will have come to expect, so be very cautious. The Tracker will offer improved handling for this situation with R5.

**Using the Input Method**   Once you've rebooted, you'll find a new Replicant in the Deskbar and a Japanese panel in your Preferences folder. You will also have installed two Japanese fonts: Haru and Haru Tohaba. These two fonts are designed to look similar to Swis721 BT and Courier10 BT (the Japanese fonts can display Roman characters as well as Japanese). Thus, if you use the Fonts preferences panel to change your system-wide plain, bold, and fixed fonts to Haru and Haru Tohaba, you won't notice any difference in the Tracker or other applications, and you'll be able to display and create Japanese characters anywhere in the system, including in the Tracker.

An easy way to test your new Japanese fonts is to launch NetPositive, pull down Edit | Preferences, set the Encoding picklist to Japanese, and choose

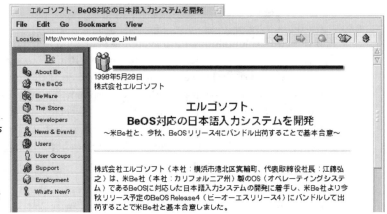

**Figure 9.16**

*Once Japanese fonts have been installed on your system, pay a visit to Be's Japanese site with Japanese document encoding enabled.*

**Figure 9.17**

*After installing the Japanese input method and rebooting, you'll find a new Replicant in your Deskbar. Click and hold on the input method icon to toggle between Roman and Japanese input methods.*

your new Japanese fonts. Next, pull down View | Document Encoding | Japanese and point your browser to **www.be.com/jp**. If the page displays kanji characters rather than unprintable characters, you're in business.

The Japanese input method can be toggled on and off system-wide in one of two ways: Use the Deskbar Replicant to switch back and forth between Roman and Japanese, or use the keyboard shortcut Alt+Spacebar to do the same thing. Whenever you're in Japanese mode, a floating Input Palette will appear in all workspaces. You will, of course, need to tell applications you're working in to use one of the bundled Japanese fonts. Launch StyledEdit and try it!

If you're familiar with the Japanese Language Kit in MacOS, you'll find that the BeOS input method works similarly. Simply key in the hiragana and press the Spacebar to convert it into kanji. If you're not familiar with these terms or the process involved, see the sidebar *Japanese Input Method Tutorial*. Use your Up and Down Arrow keys or press the Spacebar repeatedly to flip through the kanji until you've located the character appropriate for the context. Press Enter to confirm your selection. If you want to type in katakana, hold down Shift or press your CapsLock key (uppercase Roman characters result in katakana).

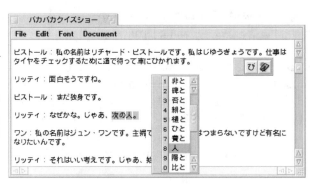

**Figure 9.18**

*Launch StyledEdit, set it to use one of your Japanese fonts, tap Alt+Spacebar, and start typing. Use your arrow keys and the Spacebar to flip through possible equivalents.*

### *Baka Baka Quiz Show*

Figure 9.18 demonstrates the work of a sophomore *gaijin* (Tyler Riti) and his college buddies, as rendered through BeOS's Japanese input method. "Baka Baka" means "Really Stupid."

**Pistole:** My name is Richard Pistole. I'm self-employed. My job is to check tires by lying in the middle of the street and getting run over by cars.

**Riti:** Sounds interesting.

**Pistole:** I'm still single.

**Riti:** I wonder why. So, next person.

**Wang:** My name is June Wang. I'm a housewife. My life has been pretty boring and I wanted it to be more exciting so I came on this game show.

**Riti:** That's a good idea. Well, let's start the show!

**Beyond StyledEdit**  If you want to type kanji into an application that doesn't explicitly support the input method, no problem—BeOS provides a workaround by overlaying the application with a slim input window. For example, launch a Terminal session, toggle to Japanese mode, and start typing. Your characters will appear in a small, floating text window above the Terminal. When you press Enter, your text will be transferred to the command line. That doesn't necessarily mean that the application will be able to display your characters properly, but their character values will indeed be there. Thus, you can theoretically create folders in the Tracker with kanji names and then cd to these folders from the Terminal, even though the Terminal can't display the kanji characters properly.

I say "theoretically" because this technique doesn't always work as it should; as of R4, Terminal and other command-line tools are not yet UTF-8-aware, so they get somewhat confused with languages such as Japanese. This should be cleared up in a future release.

**Mode Selection**  Take another look at the Input Palette mentioned above, and you'll notice that it has two buttons. The right button will launch the Japanese preferences panel, which is described below. The left button lets you choose which writing system you want to use: hiragana (which is the default), full-width katakana, full-width Roman, half-width katakana, half-width Roman, or "Direct," which is plain Roman. Again, the CapsLock key will let you switch quickly between hiragana and katakana.

### *Using the Japanese Input Method: A Brief Tutorial*
*with Tyler Riti*

*If you already speak Japanese and use a computer, you're probably very familiar with using input methods. Consider this a primer for those who have never spoken Japanese or used an input method, but who are interested in getting their feet wet.*

Let's assume you have the Japanese input method (JIM) installed, including at least the Haru font. These simple exercises will show you how to use the JIM to type a very simple phrase.

Today, we will write the following:

# 今日は。ポテトが大好きです。

It is pronounced, "Konnichiwa. Potato ga dai suki desu," which means, "Good day. I really like potatoes." If you want to try and pronounce this, say your vowels just like you would in Spanish.

Let's start with the first sentence. Launch StyledEdit and:

1. Make sure the current font is Haru.

2. Invoke the JIM by tapping Alt+Spacebar.

3. Type exactly the following: konnnichiha.

   You should see the following highlighted in blue: "こんにちは。" This is the word "konnichiwa" written in phonetic hiragana. The characters are "ko-n-ni-chi-ha" followed by a period. For some reason, "ha" is pronounced "wa" when it is used as a topic marker. Isn't Japanese fun? You probably recognize this as the Japanese way to say "hello." See, Japanese isn't all that hard.

4. Press the Spacebar once. The first four hiragana will (hopefully) be converted into two kanji, "kon" and "nichi", which mean "now" and "day/sun" respectively. This is what you should see now: "今日は。" The character "ha" will stay in hiragana since it is a "particle word," and has no meaning. If you got something different, press Backspace to turn the kanji back into hiragana and make sure you typed in the right kana. When everything is correct, press Enter.

So far so good? Great! Now, let's try the next, slightly harder sentence.

1. Potato is a "loan word" (borrowed from English), so we'll need to type it out phonetically in katakana, as opposed to hiragana. To do that, either choose the second menu command (the one that says "全角カタカナ") from the first button in the floating window (it has the び symbol on it), or the third menu item from the Japanese submenu of the Deskbar Replicant. Alternatively, you can just press the CapsLock key. I prefer the latter. If you used one of the menus, the び character in the floating window will change to a ビ, which is the same syllable

("bi," which is pronounced just like "Be"), only written in katakana. If you use the CapsLock key, the symbol will not change. (Note: The CapsLock key is actually used as a toggle between hiragana and katakana. If you choose katakana mode from one of the menus, CapsLock will take you into hiragana. If you are in hiragana mode, CapsLock takes you into katakana mode. Get it?)

2.  Type exactly the following: poteto. You should now see the following highlighted in blue: "ポテト". This is the English word "potato," phonetically spelled in Japanese syllables: po-te-to.

3.  Press Enter. Loan words do not get converted into kanji, so we can move on.

4.  Type dai, and you should get "だい". This is pronounced just like "die," as in "Die, you silly fool!"

5.  Press the Spacebar once to convert "dai" into kanji. Most likely, it will not be converted into the correct kanji, as many kanji have the same pronunciation, even though they have different meanings. The trick now is to select the kanji with the correct meaning from all of the available choices. We're specifically looking for this kanji: "大". If a different kanji is being shown, try pressing the Spacebar again and a new kanji will appear. (Actually, even if the right one is being shown, press the Spacebar just to humor me.) Press the Spacebar a third and fourth time. On the fourth press, a floating window will appear listing all of the possible kanji that fit that pronunciation (there should be about 29). When you consider that there are over fifteen thousand kanji and countless combinations, the fact that your computer just found in the span of a few microseconds the 29 that match that pronunciation is quite amazing! Use the Up and Down Arrow keys to find the character we need, which looks like a stick figure without a head (poor guy), then press Enter. This kanji means "big/greatly," and it kind of looks like a person with his hands and legs spread out. I'd do the same thing if I were missing my head, too.

6.  No time to waste now, this explanation is already taking too long. Type exactly the following: sukidesu. (including the period). You should get "すきです。". These two words are pronounced "Sue key dess," even though nobody actually pronounces it that way. Isn't Japanese fun?

7.  Press the Spacebar to convert the text into kanji. You should get "好きです。". (Only the first character should be converted; the rest remain in hiragana. Well, technically, not all are hiragana since one of them is now called okurigana. Did I mention that Japanese is fun?) Once again, if you do not get the correct kanji right away, keep pressing the Spacebar until it appears. The meaning of "suki" is "like" and "desu" means "stupid Japanese word that appears at the end of a sentence."

Now you know how to tell all of your Japanese friends how much you really like potatoes. Just don't blame me when they look at you weird.

### *About Japanese Writing Systems*

Written Japanese spans three different writing systems, which are separate but interrelated. You'll need to understand the difference in order to use the Japanese input method. Hiragana and katakana, which are collectively known as "kanas," are phonetic systems. The actual writing system, called kanji, was brought to Japan from ancient China, and consists of ideograms, or "picture words." Kanji is unique in that each character not only contains a pronunciation, but also conveys a meaning. The Chinese language uses nothing but kanji, and is possibly the hardest language to learn. That methodology didn't quite fit in with the preexisting Japanese language, so the Japanese derived the two phonetic systems, hiragana and katakana, from certain kanji characters. The kanas are pretty easy to learn and use, and most take just two or three strokes to write. Since kanas carry with them only pronunciations but no meanings, it became necessary for Japanese to learn kanji in order to have any proficiency in reading.

**Preferences** The Japanese preferences panel itself includes settings for the type of punctuation, width of spaces, and the number of times you must press the Spacebar before the kanji selection window appears. The second tab in the panel includes fields that let you enter new words into your dictionary, including their plain pronunciation and grammatical meaning (or "part of speech").

*Figure 9.19*

*The Japanese preferences panel lets you specify dictionaries, parts of speech, and the behavior of the input method itself.*

*Many thanks to BeOS developer Tyler Riti for his assistance in preparing this section, and to Be's Hiroshi Lockheimer for bringing the Japanese input method to BeOS.*

## Joysticks

Because BeOS is so heavily performance-optimized, its potential as a gaming platform is great. Needless to say, gamers take their joysticks seriously, and so does BeOS. The Joystick preferences panel, new with R4, lets you install and calibrate a number of the most popular joysticks available in the gaming market. In addition, most any no-name, generic joystick you find at your local computer mart can likely be configured to work perfectly through the multiple "Analog" options.

After connecting a joystick to your gameport (the spare port on the back of your sound card), launch the Joystick preferences panel, which is divided into two panels. If you'd like BeOS to try to auto-detect your joystick, click the Probe button. You'll be presented with an alert box warning that in rare instances, the probing process can run into an interrupt conflict and hang your machine. Probe didn't lock up our test machine with a generic joystick, but if it does happen to you, just reboot your machine and assign the port and joystick model manually.

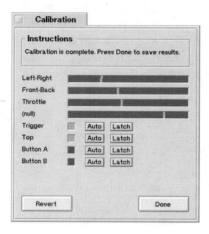

After selecting a port and joystick model, click the Calibrate button to make sure that the behavioral nuances of your particular joystick are recognized properly by the system.

**Figure 9.20**

*Click the Calibrate button and you'll see a panel similar to this one. Follow the instructions onscreen to have BeOS recognize all of your joystick's controls properly.*

The Calibration panel will ask you to operate each of your joystick's controls in sequence. Push your joystick all the way to the left, then to the right, then all the way forward, then all the way backward. Click each of its buttons to see which control is which—a light will flash on the calibration panel corresponding to the button you've just pressed. Once you've gone through the entire sequence, click Done and your settings will be written to disk, and will work properly in any joystick-enabled game or application in BeOS.

***Custom Joystick Control*** If you need more control than the Joystick calibration panel offers, or if you need to configure a joystick for which BeOS has no built-in configuration options, take a look in /boot/beos/etc for a file called joystick-README and read it carefully. Also in this folder is a subdirectory called joysticks, which contains text-based joystick description files. Rather than editing any of these files directly, find the one most similar to your current joystick and make a copy of it. Now navigate to the ~/config/settings/joystick directory and create a subdirectory named after the port you're using—for example, ~/config/settings/joystick/gameport. Now rename the copy of the configuration file you saved after the port number it will be connected to (e.g. "201") and drop the file into this directory. Any file found in this folder will appear as an option in the Joystick preferences panel. You can now edit this file to your heart's content, though you'll need to be a hardcore gamer, familiar with tweaking individual parameters for hats, axes, buttons, and other gadgets. You should find full configuration options in the BeOS release notes, or on www.be.com (search on "joystick"). After installing the file, select its name in the Joystick preferences panel and everything should work properly.

## Keyboard

Open up StyledEdit and hold your finger down on a key, such as B. Notice that holding down a key is the same as punching it over and over again. While it's not often that you need 723 copies of the letter B, you often do want to quickly backspace or delete the last few letters or words you've written. Problem is, if your key repeat rate is too fast, it's too easy to delete stuff you meant to keep. Too slow and it can test your patience.

You can customize the repeat rate by using the slider in the Keyboard preferences panel—Slow will make your backspace operations crawl safely along, while Fast will cause it to zip backward through sentences like a greased pig. Season to taste. Similarly, you can adjust the amount of time you need to hold down a key before repeat mode kicks in. Use the blank field in the Keyboard preferences panel to test the settings until you get it right. In general, new users prefer slower settings, while power users crank them way up. Keep this in mind when setting up a machine for your mother.

## Keymap

Different languages have different alphabets, and use different characters and symbols to create words. Keyboards purchased in Norway have different character sets than keyboards purchased in Minnesota. Macintosh and IBM keyboards all come in a growing array of layouts and special keys, not to mention their few inherent incompatibilities. While the first BeBoxes used Intel-style keyboards, much of BeOS's early evolution took place on PowerMacs, with Apple keyboards. Finally, 104-key keyboards have become very common in the Intel world, and include three more keys than the long-standing 101-key standard. Maintaining some consistency of behavior across these points of slippage is a challenge for all hardware and software vendors interested in internationalizing their products.

BeOS takes advantage of the industry standard "keymap" scheme to compensate for these differences. The keyboard industry defines a standard set of all possible keypresses along with the signals sent by those keys. The operating system vendor creates translation tables to function as go-betweens between the hardware and the operating system. Once loaded, keymaps can also be customized by individual users and saved in settings files for later use.

Because BeOS will soon be a multiuser operating system, the Keymap panel is capable of establishing custom keyboard settings for all the users who will be using the machine. This way, a Japanese user can go to lunch, and a Norwegian user can log into the same machine and work comfortably with his own familiar keymap. Because Keymap preference files will be stored in each user's home directory, BeOS will automatically switch keymaps when a new user logs in.

Of course, the labels on the keyboard won't change accordingly, so each user will have to be capable of translating non-corresponding keys on their own.

Keymap comes with dozens of preconfigured maps corresponding to the world's major keyboard layouts. You can also find some less common keymaps on BeWare, free for the download in most cases. Each map file stores nine separate tables, including the unmodified keys plus all possible combinations of Alt, Ctrl, Shift (Intel), or Option, Command, Control, and Apple (Mac).

The mapping tables are:

- Control
- Option-Caps-Shift
- Option-Caps
- Option-Shift
- Option
- Caps-Shift
- Caps
- Shift
- No modifier

If you open the Keymap preferences panel and start typing normally, you'll see that each of your keypresses is instantly reflected by a virtual press on the keyboard diagram. Clicking a key with your mouse will print the output of that key to the field at the top of the keymap window. Note especially what happens as you press your various modifier keys—both left and right Ctrl, Alt, and Shift. If you're having any difficulty migrating to BeOS keyboard shortcuts, studying the behavior of the modifier keys while in Keymap could prove useful.

**Special Characters**   Just because your Plain Jane text editor doesn't include a menu option for inserting special characters such as the ones for Yen (¥), microns ($\mu$), the Euro (€), or British pounds (£), that doesn't mean you can't use those symbols without a full-featured word processor. Hold down your modifier keys in various combinations and Keymap will show you the special characters associated with those keypresses.

To get a character out of Keymap and into your text editor, select it in the upper field and drag it into your document. You can even drag special characters directly into the Terminal. The Terminal is not, however, capable of rendering all of the characters that can be dragged out of Keymap. For example, it'll complain with a beep if you try to feed it something like "√". Note, however, that just because special characters can't be displayed in the Terminal, it doesn't mean they're not there. Throughout BeOS, unprintable characters are represented by a small square. The actual ASCII value of the character is still preserved by the system—you just can't see it because the font or application doesn't support it.

***Working with Unprintable Characters in the Terminal*** To get a handle on how this works, create a new folder in the Tracker called thΔt. To get the triangular delta symbol, use Right-Ctrl+J. Notice that this extended character displays just fine in the Tracker. Now open a Terminal window, type cd ' and then drag that folder into the Terminal. Follow it with another ' and hit Enter. Even though the folder name appeared with a square in its name instead of the delta character, the cd operation worked properly, proving that the Terminal properly understood it, even if it couldn't display it.

As if all of this weren't complicated enough, different fonts produce different characters (though the core alphabet generally remains identical). Choosing a different font from Keymap's Fonts menu will let you see the characters that that font will produce in given combinations.

**Dead Keys** You may have noticed that there are many characters that Keymap is incapable of generating from the standard American map, such as many of the more common German and French accented characters. That's no one's fault; even with nine key tables, there are simply too many special characters to map them all to standard keypresses. To get around this problem, we use what are known as "dead keys"—key combinations that display nothing until you press another key, which then adds a modifier to that letter and inserts a corresponding character.

The standard BeOS text-rendering engine supports dead keys, so any application built around the standard text engine (which is pretty much every editor and email client available) gains dead key support automatically. You can see which keys are modified by dead keys by holding down Right-Ctrl (or the left Win key) in Keymap. The keys highlighted with a yellow box are the dead keys for the currently selected keymap. Wherever possible, dead keys are mapped to keys labeled with similar characters. For example, the colon is mapped to the German umlaut, since they look somewhat similar. So let's say you need the ü symbol (a "u" with an umlaut). You'll need to activate the umlaut dead key and press the U key. Open up a StyledEdit or BeMail window, press Right-Ctrl+: (the colon key), release, then press U. A ü will be inserted. If you know the right shortcuts, you can insert special characters into your documents without using the Keymaps panel at all. Note that this method is far easier than the Windows method, which requires you to select characters from a floating palette built into individual applications such as Word. In BeOS, all applications using the standard text view automatically support dead keys. Table 9.01 shows some common dead key mappings.

The special key modifiers in Keymap preferences don't stop at vowel modification. While only the dead keys are highlighted in yellow when you press Right-Ctrl or the Win key, you'll notice that almost all of the keys in Keymap change to another character, even though they're not highlighted. For example,

## *Table 9.01  BeOS Special Characters*

| This dead key, followed by a vowel... | Yields this character in any BeOS text view | | | | |
|---|---|---|---|---|---|
| Right Ctrl+` | à | è | ì | ò | ù |
| Right Ctrl+6 | â | ê | î | ô | û |
| Right Ctrl+e | á | é | í | ó | ú |
| Right Ctrl+: | ä | ë | ï | ö | ü |
| Right Ctrl+' | ã | õ | ñ | | |

*The five dead keys in the American keymap (other keymaps use different dead keys). Press a dead key combination, release, then press a vowel key to get common special characters in almost any BeOS application.*

the J key turns into a Δ symbol when you press Right-Ctrl. Thus, to get this symbol into any document without launching Keymap preferences, just press Right+Ctrl+J. There are dozens of special characters available; if you don't see the one you need, try a different font, or invoke the keymap from another language. Most of the time, however, it will be possible to find the character you need without switching to another keymap.

**Switching Keymaps**  Take a look at the System Maps listing on the left side of the Keymap panel, which shows all countries with supported keyboard mappings. To try out an alternate keymap, select it from the list and start typing normally. To switch your default keymap, click the Use button at the lower right. Your changes will remain between boots. The Revert button will erase changes made during this session only. If you'll be switching keymaps with any frequency, use the File | Save As option to create a quick list of custom maps, which will appear in the User field (Figure 9.21). To use a downloaded keymap, use the File | Open menu, then Save As to make the new map a permanent part of your list. Alternatively, place newly downloaded keymap files in /boot/home/config/settings/keymaps and they'll appear in the Users list next time you launch Keymap.

**Figure 9.21**

*Keymap lets you switch between built-in international mappings, install other keymaps you may have downloaded, customize your current map one key at a time, and retrieve special characters for use in your applications.*

**Removing Custom Maps**  If you started experimenting with new Users maps and ended up with a bunch of maps you don't want to keep, you may have trouble finding out how to delete entries from the list. As of R4, there is no way to do this from within the Keymap GUI interface. All you have to do is delete your excess keymaps from /boot/home/config/settings/keymap and they'll disappear from Keymap application next time it's launched. Hopefully this will be rectified in a future release.

**Customizing Keymaps**  If one of the built-in maps suits your needs with the exception of just a few keys, you can tweak your keys' functions one at a time. Before starting, you'll have to make a copy of a working map, since BeOS will (wisely) not allow you to edit the originals (since making an error or receiving a visit from a prankster could make your system unusable). Pull down File | Save As, give your new map a memorable name, and it will appear in the User panel. Select it, and you can begin.

To customize keys, right-drag the character you want onto the key you want. For instance, to make your A key display the character "D," drag the D key onto the A key with your right mouse button. Note that doing this will give you two D keys and no A key. You may have some difficulty with this feature if you have a one-button mouse. Try various command key combinations in the event this has been rectified in a later version of BeOS, or better yet, buy a two-button mouse. If you have a third mouse button, dragging a character with the third button will actually drag all nine possibilities for that character into the space for the new key.

Note that you cannot change the mappings of your modifier keys with Keymap.

**Keymap from the Terminal**  If you switch maps often, or simply prefer to work from the command line, you can load and replace keymaps from the Terminal. The map currently in use is always located at /boot/home/config/settings/Key_map, and the alternate maps saved by the Keymap application are in a subdirectory called Keymap.

Type keymap -d to dump the entire contents of the current map to stdout (Terminal output). To store the output as a new keymap file, redirect it to a new file (e.g. keymap -d > MyMapName). To load a new keymap, type

keymap -l < MyMapName

This will read MyMapName into memory, then replace the current map with itself. You can also restore the default system keymap from the Terminal by typing keymap -r. Note that keymap -l only works with keymaps that have been dumped to output via keymap -d, so you won't be able to use this trick with freshly downloaded map files. Keymaps are not plain text files; keymap -d will only let you view, not edit, your maps.

### *About the Dvorak Keymap*

If you were scrolling through the language list out of curiosity, you may have been surprised to see a little country called Dvorak among the entries. Actually, Dvorak isn't a country, but an alternative keyboard layout for people interested in typing 50% faster. Select Dvorak in the list, and study the map. Notice that the letters now on the home row (where your fingers sit when at rest) are the most commonly used letters in the English language. The rest of the keys are placed according to the frequency of their appearance in English, and relative to the ease with which your fingers can reach their positions. Users report huge increases in words-per-minute rates with the Dvorak layout once they've accustomed themselves to it. Dvorak keyboards are available in some stores and by mail order, but you can just as easily remap a standard keyboard to the Dvorak layout, if you can deal with having the wrong letters printed on every key. Or you can spend an hour or two with White-Out and a black marker.

During the 1930s, an early human-factors specialist named Dr. August Dvorak observed that the arrangement of keys on typewriters was a barrier to efficient typing, partially because then-current typewriters were so slow and clunky that the key hammers would slam together and get jammed, but also because the standard keyboard layout didn't correspond to any logic of common usage. He embarked on a rigorously scientific experimentation binge, building, testing, and gathering mountains of data. Unfortunately, it was too late for the august researcher to have a hope of making a dent in the typewriter market. Typewriters had been in production for decades by the time his layout was perfected, and the market was too entrenched.

While there are about as many people in the world using the Dvorak keymapping as there are people speaking Esperanto (in fact, there are allegedly more fluent speakers of Klingon than there are of Esperanto!), those who do are passionate—almost cultish—about it. They run a lonely and mostly ignored crusade to turn the world on to a better system. If you're willing to put in the time to unlearn years of typing and start all over, you may want to give Dvorak a try. However, it may be a confusing process with your current keyboard, since everything will be labeled wrong. You may want to look for a genuine Dvorak keyboard, with the keys labeled properly.

By the way—having a Dvorak keyboard on your desk is allegedly better than any password at keeping unwelcome guests from using your machine.

## Menu

The Menu preferences panel lets you control the appearance and behavior of all pulldown menus throughout BeOS, both in your applications and in the operating system itself. It's also used to control the fonts used in your menus, a setting not covered by the standard Font preferences panel.

Menu displays a small mock menu, which reflects your changes in real time. Closing the panel will propagate your changes to all menus in the system, although you'll need to close and restart any running applications to see the changes take hold in them.

**Font and Font Size** These probably require no explanation. Note that you can't choose a font larger than 18 points, as this would cause menus to be too wide, or would cut off the ends of longer words in your menus. BeOS should become more font-sensitive in the future.

**Click to Open** Click to Open is another name for the behavior more commonly referred to as "sticky menus." When Click to Open is enabled, menus stay visible after you click once on the menu header—you don't have to hold the mouse button down while reading through the menu. It's hard to imagine why anyone would want to turn this off, but it's nice to know you have the freedom to do so just in case you get the urge to test your own patience. The mouse, by the way, is a major culprit in repetitive stress injuries. Your wrists would do well to avail themselves of anything that can minimize mouse usage.

**Always Show Triggers** Menu triggers are the underlined letters in your pulldown menus that let you operate menu functions from the keyboard. However, if you use the mouse exclusively to access your menus, there's no point in cluttering them up with all those underscores, right? Not quite—on occasion, you may want to activate a menu via the mouse, and then hit a key to trigger one of the items on that menu, thus combining mouse and keyboard in the process of making your menu selections. At the point of clicking the menu header with the mouse, you would not want the triggers to be visible. But at the moment of releasing the mouse and moving to keyboard control, triggers should become visible.

BeOS includes a very smart feature for dealing with this situation—a subtle option for a difficult problem. If Always Show Triggers is turned on, triggers are visible no matter what. But if Always Show Triggers is turned off and you access a menu via mouse, triggers will be off until you release the mouse button (prior to accessing a menu entry). Release the mouse button, the menu stays put, and the triggers blink on. *Muy elegante.*

**Color Scheme** Color Scheme lets you set the background color of your menus by using an interactive RGB slider. When you open the slider window, reposition your windows so that both the slider and the Menu panel are visible simultaneously. This way you'll be able to see the effects of your changes in real time; the sample menu will change colors as you drag. Note that if you have a particular RGB value handy, you can type the values directly into the small boxes to the right of the sliders (you might want to use this if you've found a great color combination in the color panel of another application, for instance—typing in its RGB values will be more accurate than trying to replicate the color by dragging sliders).

***Drag-and-Drop Menu Colors*** If you have a copy of RoColor (Chapter 13, *Graphics Applications*), you can ignore the Color Scheme option and just drag any color swatch out of RoColor and onto the Menu preferences panel for instant gratification. This should also work with any other color-mixing application that works with BMessages; you should find a couple of others on BeWare.

**Separator Style** This entry in the Menu preferences panel lets you set the appearance of the lines that separate groups of menu items. You can choose a fine line running all the way across the menu, a fine partial-width line, or a fat partial-width line.

*Figure 9.22*

*The Menu preferences panel gives you a "live model" on which to practice. Configure the separator style, trigger behavior, and font and color, then commit your changes throughout the system by closing the panel. Most such changes in BeOS don't take place until affected applications have been closed and then reopened.*

**Shortcut Key** New in R4, the last two entries in this panel let you tell the system whether Alt or Ctrl should be the primary shortcut key throughout BeOS. As described in Chapter 2, *Meet the System*, the default shortcut key is Alt, which may or may not be what you're accustomed to, depending on whether you come to BeOS from Apple's MacOS or from other operating systems. With this entry set to Alt, you rename a file with Alt+E and copy items to the clipboard with Alt+C. Ctrl+C is then used to stop running jobs in the Terminal. If you select "Ctrl as Shortcut Key," these roles are reversed.

Note that changing the behavior of the shortcut key will also impact usage of the Twitcher (the "keyboardable Deskbar" described in Chapter 2, *Meet the System*).

## Mouse

The simple act of double-clicking an icon or folder requires your computer to monitor your actions closely and apply your click pattern against a set of rules. For instance, if you click once, move your mouse a few pixels, and then click again, does that count as one click or two? How much distance is the mouse allowed to travel between the first and second clicks before the operating system assumes you're starting a new click, rather than registering the second as part of the first? How much time is allowed to pass between clicks one and two? While the Mouse preferences panel won't let you configure all of these settings, it will let you set the double-click speed, mouse pointer travel speed, and button layout.

**Double-Click Speed**  If files and folders don't always react to your double-clicks, the problem could be that you're simply not clicking quickly enough to register a double-click. This situation is both common and easy to rectify—just drag the slider towards "Slow" and use the "Click test" area to check it out. You'll know you've successfully double-clicked when one of the words in the test area becomes selected. If the whole phrase is selected, you've triple-clicked.

**Mouse Speed**  The Mouse Speed slider controls the ratio of the distance your mouse travels on its surface to the distance your cursor travels across the screen. Setting this to Fast will cause your cursor to zip across the screen with only short mouse movements; Slow will require you to move your mouse a long way to move your cursor a small distance.

 ***Accommodating Special Needs*  Turning down the double-click and mouse speed settings can come in handy when making your computer comfortable to use for children, people with arthritis, or the disabled.**

**Mouse Type**  Pointing devices come in a million flavors. If you're on a PowerMac, chances are you have a single-button mouse (though you should probably consider investing in a multibutton mouse if you'll be using BeOS frequently). x86 users will have either a two- or three-button mouse. Devices such as trackballs and built-in laptop pointers also may have from one to three buttons. If for some reason you don't like the default button mapping on your pointing device, you can use the Mouse preferences panel to change it.

Select one, two, or three buttons from the picklist above the mouse diagram, then right-click on each button in the diagram and use the pop-up picklist to select the button you want to emulate. The default layout (see Figure 9.23) for a three-button mouse is button one on the left, two on the right, and three in the middle.

*Figure 9.23*

*From the Mouse preferences panel, you can remap the function of your mouse buttons, establish mouse travel speed, or toggle into Focus Follows Mouse mode.*

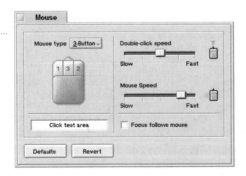

**Focus Follows Mouse**  In order to type in a window that's not currently at the front, you have to click in it to give it focus, right? That's how most operating systems work, but it's not the only way to do things. Many X Window managers from the Unix world—and BeOS— include a feature called Focus Follows Mouse (FFM). When this option is enabled, the window with focus is defined as being whichever one lies under the pointer, regardless of whether that window is "in front." You can thus type into windows that are almost entirely hidden. Depending on your point of view, this can either be the greatest boon ever bestowed on operating systems, or a royal pain in the butt.

The nice thing about FFM is that it lets you keep the window you're *really* working in on top and up front, while still letting you work in background applications. It also means that every time you bump the mouse, it could end up bringing another window into focus, and your typed characters could suddenly be piped into an unrelated application or window. When FFM is turned on, the only clue you'll have as to which window has the current focus is the fact that its title tab will glow the brightest. Depending on your work habits, this may or may not be enough feedback for you. My thinking is that if you have to bother to reach out and grab the mouse to activate another window anyway, you may as well click once (big deal!) to bring it forward. Not everyone agrees, and even power users (including this book's various editors) squabble over the utility of FFM.

## Network

The Network preferences panel is your central interface with BeOS's built-in networking capabilities. It does not, however, let you configure Dial-Up Networking (DUN) preferences. Use of this panel is covered in depth in Chapter 8, *Networking*, while DUN is covered in Chapter 4, *Get Online Fast*.

## Printers

If you're using a version of BeOS prior to R4, you'll find two separate panels: AddPrinter and SelectPrinter. As of R4, these two are merged into a single panel called simply Printers. This panel is used to tell BeOS about any printers attached to your system or network for which you have installed drivers. Since you can only print to one printer at a time, this panel also has a secondary function: telling BeOS which of your printers should be considered the default by your applications.

**Add...**  When you click the Add... button, a list of files is read from two directories: the system-level /boot/beos/system/add-ons/Print and the user-level /boot/home/config/add-ons/Print. The contents of these two folders is

*Figure 9.24*

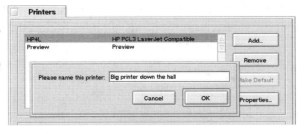

*If you're adding a printer from the HP LaserJet family, you'll be given the chance to give your printer a friendly name after clicking Add.*

combined into a single list, which is displayed in a window like the one in Figure 9.24. This dialog doesn't list every printer that BeOS supports; it lists major *classes* of printers. For instance, as of R3, BeOS supported 27 different printers, but only Apple LaserWriter-compatible and HP PCL3 LaserJet-compatible show up in the Add… dialog. Each of the 27 supported printers belongs to one of these two classes.

When you select a printer class and click the Add button, you'll see one of two things. In some cases, as with the HP LaserJet class, you'll have the opportunity to type in a name for your printer. You can call it Main LaserJet, HP4L, Henry, Pearl, Jonas, or anything else that will be easy to remember. In other cases, as with the Apple LaserWriter family, you'll see a dialog listing all of the supported printers in that class. Select your exact printer from the list, give it a name, and click OK.

 ***Adding New Printer Drivers*** **If a new printer was added to Be's family of supported devices after your version of the operating system shipped, it won't show up in this list, and you'll need to download it from BeWare or obtain the driver from the manufacturer. If the driver doesn't come with its own installation routine, just copy it to the** /boot/home/config/add-ons/Print **folder, then close and reopen the Printers panel.**

**At this point in the game, not all hardware vendors write their own drivers for BeOS, but this situation is slowly changing. If you'd like to see your hardware supported in BeOS and Be hasn't gotten to it yet, write a polite note to the vendor requesting BeOS drivers. You can help make vendors aware that there is a viable BeOS market that they need to support!**

 If you'd like to see how your documents will look before you send them to the printer, be sure to enable the Print Preview driver from this panel. Thereafter, printing to Print Preview will cause your document to be rendered exactly as it will be sent to the printer, then displayed in the Print Preview window.

**Make Default** It's possible that you or your office may have several printers installed on your network, and BeOS needs to know about each of them. Then again, you can only use one printer at a time, so BeOS needs to tell your applications which of your installed printers it should be using at the moment. Click this button to make it so.

### Who's That in the Print Setup Dialog?

You've probably noticed that when you initiate a new print job, the Print Setup dialog box includes a sample image you can use to visualize your page orientation and scaling options before committing to paper. But where most OS's use a boring line drawing to represent your document here, BeOS includes the image of a jovial fellow kicking back with a martini after what appears to have been a fine meal. Classy guy that he is, his pinky juts out from the glass's stem *just so*, as if welcoming you to the party. What a cool operating system, huh?

In case you're wondering who that is, I have it on good word that it's kernel engineer Cyril Meurillon, relaxing after Be's big coming out at MacWorld Boston in 1996.

**Remove**  Clicking the Remove button doesn't remove the actual printer driver from your system—it just removes the printer from Printer panel's list of available printers. Therefore, the only reason to do this is to clean up the list in case it becomes cluttered, or if you want to rename one of your printers (by removing it and then adding it back in with a new name). If you do want to remove an actual printer driver, delete it from /boot/home/config/add-ons/Print.

**Properties**  Depending on the capabilities of each printer driver, the panel that appears when you select a printer and click the Properties button will differ. By default, you'll see a small window containing a few technical details on the current printer. If the driver is capable of sending additional information to the printer, such as resolution or color parameters, you'll be able to use this panel to establish further preferences.

## Screen

The Screen preferences panel does exactly what it sounds like it should do—it lets you configure the color, resolution, bit depth, and refresh rate of your screen. In addition, if you find that you need more workspaces than the default of nine, you can add more in an instant from this panel. Not only do you not have to reboot your system after making changes to the Screen preferences, but you can apply your changes either to the current workspace only, or to all of them at once (by using the picklist at the top of the panel, seen in Figure 9.25). After making changes to most of these settings, you'll have a few seconds to click OK and confirm that you

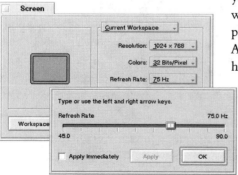

**Figure 9.25**

*Launching the Screen preferences panel will let you configure the resolution, bit depth, and screen colors for the workspace in which the control panel was launched. There's no safety on the refresh rate chooser, so make sure you know what your monitor is capable of before pushing it too hard.*

want to keep them. Otherwise your previous setting will be automatically restored. This can be especially handy if your monitor can't handle the resolution or refresh rate you just picked.

**Resolution** One thing that new users often have trouble understanding is the fact that the mesh of a monitor screen doesn't map one-to-one with the number of pixels being displayed. The size of your screen never changes, of course, and the monitor mesh diameter (the "dot pitch") never changes either. However, you can use your monitor's finite number of dots to display a few big pixels, or lots of tiny ones. When you crank up your resolution, you're throwing more pixels at a screen that stays the same size, so onscreen objects get smaller, and you're able to fit more objects onscreen at once. While resolution isn't necessarily tied to screen size, people tend to find that the following resolutions work best:

### Table 9.02 Monitor Resolutions

| Monitor size | Resolution |
| --- | --- |
| 14" or less | 640x480 |
| 15" | 800x600 |
| 17" | 1024x768 |
| 19" | 1152x900 |
| 21" | 1280x1024 |

*While you can run your monitor at pretty much any resolution that suits you, certain resolutions seem to just "feel right" for most users, and are generally considered optimum for a given monitor size.*

These resolutions aren't rules—just happy mediums for most users. However, since BeOS lets you keep your workspaces set at independent resolutions, some people (especially Web designers and programmers) like to keep a variety of resolutions running so they can see instantly how their work would appear on someone else's monitor. If you don't have a need to check out other resolutions frequently, I recommend setting all of your workspaces to the same resolution— switching between them will be much smoother, since your video card won't need to black out momentarily as it resets itself.

**Colors** The number of colors being thrown at a computer screen is measured in "bit depth," referring to the number of bits of color information attached to each dot of color. Each color dot, in turn, is composed of four pixel values: red, green, blue, and alpha (transparency). Therefore, the number of colors that it's possible to display on your screen is equal to the number of bits raised to the fourth power. Setting your display to eight bits will get you around 4,000 distinct colors, 16 bits brings it up to 65,500 colors, and 24- and 32-bit color (a.k.a. "high color" and "true color") border on photographic (though monitors will never appear truly photographic as long as they're composed of tiny dots). Note however that BeOS doesn't support 24-bit color, since 24-bit is just 32-bit minus that alpha layer. In other words, with BeOS you get true color, plus all kinds of room for transparency effects, a fact which makes graphics dweebs very happy.

In general, you'll want to set your color depth as high as you can, but you should know about the inverse relationship between resolution and color depth: Given a fixed amount of video RAM, one setting will go down as the other goes up (see the sidebar *Why Some Settings Are Grayed Out*).

You should also know that some graphics-intensive applications, multimedia presentations, and games perform better at lower color depths. Each pixel in 32-bit mode carries four times as much data as each pixel in 8-bit mode. More bits means more data needs to be shoved around, which means more strain on the system. This is a limitation of contemporary machine architecture, not of BeOS itself. Turning down the bit depth can mean you've got more memory bandwidth left over to shoot aliens with.

**Refresh Rate**   This picklist lets you change the number of times per second the electron gun in your monitor shoots waves of pixels at the screen. The higher the refresh rate, the more "rock solid" your screen will appear. Higher refresh rates also produce less eye strain; lower refresh rates can give some people headaches and even seizures. Interestingly, it can sometimes be difficult to see monitor flicker when you're looking straight toward the screen (until the refresh rate gets really low). Try looking at your screen sidelong (using only your peripheral vision) for a while and you may notice a flickering you hadn't seen before (alternatively, look at your monitor, keep your head steady, and raise your eyes toward the ceiling).

This flicker may be affecting you in ways you aren't even conscious of. You should set your refresh rate to at least 72 MHz or higher, if your monitor supports it. Read that last bit again: *if your monitor supports it.* Note that some people are simply more sensitive to refresh rates than others, and that some contemporary ophthalmologists are now recommending refresh rates of 85 MHz and higher. However, even if you can't consciously detect any visible flicker, it may still be impacting your nervous system, resulting in brain and eye fatigue. Cranking up your refresh rate can actually result in you being able to work longer hours with less fatigue (though that's no excuse for not hopping on your bicycle for the body's sake from time to time).

***Custom Control over Refresh Rates***   **If you need more control over the refresh rate than is offered by the options on the picklist, choose Other... from the bottom of the list, or tap Alt+C to launch a custom refresh rate slider.**

Many monitors—especially older ones—can't handle refresh rates as high as some video cards can deliver, and the results can be disastrous. This is one of very few places where adjusting a software control can cause physical damage to your hardware. For this reason, MacOS and Windows build in all kinds of safety mechanisms, hiding the refresh controls in hard-to-find dialogs, or disallowing adjustments altogether. Be trusts that you're sharp enough to read the manual that came with your monitor before cranking this sucker way up. Your manual contains exact specs on how much refresh your monitor can handle at various resolutions—it's your responsibility to read up. And, no, stories of older monitors actually going up in a puff of smoke are not merely apocryphal—it used to happen with some frequency (though it's much more rare now).

Keep in mind that you may have to adjust the height and width of your screen after making changes to the refresh rate.

**Fine-Tuning Image Placement**   In addition to your monitor's controls for adjusting the height, width, and placement of the screen relative to the bezel (the frame of your monitor), BeOS also lets you adjust these settings internally. The nice thing about this is that if you use a monitor switchbox to share one monitor between multiple computers, you're probably well aware of the annoyance caused by having to readjust these settings every time you switch back and forth. By compensating with BeOS's internal controls, you can put an end to that nonsense.

With the Screen preferences panel open, hold down the Ctrl key and use your arrow keys to move the screen image up, down, or side to side. Use Shift in conjunction with the arrow keys to resize the image in various directions. Your screen will flicker somewhat since you're actually making alterations to the frequency and timing of your video card. If nothing happens, or if your screen blacks out for a moment and then returns with no visible changes, your video card does not support this particular adjustment.

**Power Controls**   If you click on the large question mark icon in the Screen preferences panel, a small window will appear, informing you of the availability of a ton of hidden controls and options. These are shown in Table 9.03.

### Table 9.03  Screen preferences hot keys

| This Hotkey | Does This |
| --- | --- |
| Alt+D | Sets workspace to default resolution |
| Alt+R | Sets workspace to default refresh rate |
| Alt+P | Sets workspace to default position |
| Alt+X | Shows workspace configuration dialog |
| Alt+C | Shows custom refresh rate dialog |
| Alt+Shift+D | Sets workspace to system defaults |
| Alt+Shift+R | Reverts workspace to initial settings |
| Alt+S | Saves current settings |
| Alt+U | Reverts workspace to previously saved settings |
| Alt+Shift+U | Sets all workspaces to previously saved settings |
| Ctrl+Alt+Shift+F12 | Emergency revert to system defaults (does not require Screen preferences panel to be open) |

*The Screen preferences panel boasts a ton of hotkeys, which are important to have handy in case it becomes impossible to use onscreen controls due to mucked-up settings.*

***Restore Your Screen Settings*** If you should happen to hit on a combination of resolution, color depth, and refresh rate that doesn't work on your card, if a buggy game or demo crashes without resetting your resolution properly, or if your card's drivers are buggy for some reason, it's possible that your screen could become unreadable. This, of course, would make it extremely difficult to reestablish comfortable settings. If this happens to you, remember your Boy Scout training: Ctrl+Alt+Shift+F12 will restore your screen to 640×480, 8-bit color. By the way, this works whether or not you've got the Screen preferences panel open.

## Why Some Settings Are Grayed Out

If you've been playing with the Screen controls for a while, you may have noticed an inverse relationship between resolution and color depth. If you max out one, you have to compromise on the other. The reason for this is simple math. If you've got a 2MB video card, you've only got about two million bytes of storage for screen information. Let's say you want to run your screen at a 32-bit color depth and a resolution of 1024×768. The equation is this:

(bits per pixel/bits per byte) * width * height = (bytes required)

so:

(32/8) * 1024 * 768 = (3,145,728)

Oops! Your 2MB video card only has 2,048,000 bytes. Let's cut the bit depth down to 16:

(16/8) * 1024 * 768 = (1,572,864)

Bingo—that's the sweet spot. Conversely, we could keep the 32-bit color and lower the resolution to 800×600. We'd still come in under the memory limit, but 800×600 sucks on a 17" monitor, whereas 16-bit color is perfectly acceptable to most people. The important thing to note is that with a finite amount of video RAM, you either get more bit depth or more resolution, but not both. This is why consumer machines are finally beginning to ship with 4MB of video RAM—more video RAM doesn't necessarily give you better performance (unless you get interleaved video memory, but that's another story), but it allows you to enjoy no-compromise resolution and color depth.

**Workspaces** As described in Chapter 2, *Meet the System*, BeOS lets you spread your work out over multiple virtual Desktops. Rather than crowding yourself out with tons of little windows cluttering everything up, you may find it easier to switch to a new workspace before launching your next application (or you can use the Workspace preferences panel to move already open windows to other workspaces, or you can click and hold on a title tab then use Alt+F*n* to move a window to another workspace).

By default, you get nine workspaces to work with, and you can switch between them quickly by holding down an Alt key and pressing your F1–F9 function keys (at the top of your keyboard). And what if nine isn't enough? No problem. Launch the Screen preferences panel, click the Workspaces… button, and use the picklist to select anywhere between one and 32 workspaces. The Workspace preferences panel will immediately adjust itself to display an equal number of workspaces. Note that you won't be able to use the keyboard to access any more than the original nine—you'll have to use Workspace preferences to do that.

 Remember: Anything you do in the Screen preferences panel can be made to apply only to the current workspace or to all workspaces at once, by using the picklist at the very top of the panel.

## ScrollBar

Scrollbar customization is one of the little niceties Be throws in just because they're good folks with excellent taste. Use of this panel is fairly obvious— you have your choice of either single or double arrows at the ends of your scrollbars. You can choose between two decorative and one plain "knob" style, and you can opt for either knobs that are always the same size or knobs that grow and shrink in proportion to the current document. Finally, you can specify that knobs never get any smaller than the size you choose by dragging the small green arrow left and right. I highly recommend using double arrows on your scrollbars—it's one of those things you'll grow to love very quickly,

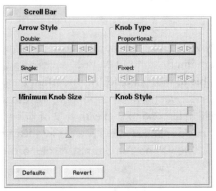

and curse the absence of when you find yourself back in some other operating systems.

Clicking the Defaults button will restore your scrollbars to their factory settings.

*Figure 9.26*

*You can customize the appearance and behavior of your system's scrollbars by changing their gripper knob style, arrow configuration, and proportions.*

## Sounds

New in R4, the Sounds preferences panel lets you associate sounds with system-wide events. The panel is yet young, and doesn't offer a whole lot of choices. In fact, at this writing, the only two system sounds configurable from here were System Startup, which is played right after the Desktop appears at boot time, and Beep, which is played any time you try to do something that's not allowed, such as scrolling past the end of a document or trying to select a

**Figure 9.27**

Associate system events with sound files from the Sounds preferences panel.

dialog option that's currently grayed out. The system beep is also played when the Terminal completes a process, which can be handy if you've got a long render or other task running in the background. Other system events will likely appear in this dialog in future releases.

Use of the Sounds preferences panel should be fairly obvious. Select one of the system events listed, then click on the Sound File picklist to choose a sound. Preview (or "prehear") your sound by clicking Play. To choose a sound other than the ones provided by default in the picklist, choose Other… from the bottom of the list and navigate the File panel to a sound file of your choice. Alternatively, you can drop your favorite system sounds into /boot/home/config/sounds and they'll appear in the picklist automatically. You can use sound files in AIFF, WAV, or RAW format.

 **If you chose to install the optional extras during installation, you'll find a pair of folders living under** /boot/optional/sound, **labeled** Startup Sounds **and** System Beeps. **Each of these contains a pile of funky options, most of them created at Be HQ by resident musician/engineers. If you didn't install the optional extras, you can still copy a few of the sounds you like from the CD to your hard drive. Better yet, create some of your own sounds with one of the many audio tools listed in Chapter 14,** *Media Applications.*

## Time

Have you ever removed the case of your computer and gazed in wonder at the marvelous complexity of your motherboard? While lost in your reverie, you may have spotted a circular, shiny thing roughly the size of a quarter. That's your CMOS battery, and it powers a miniscule crystal embedded in a chip somewhere else on the board. When charged, the crystal vibrates at an extremely precise frequency. Its vibrational cycles are counted and translated into seconds, and the result is sent to your computer's clock. BeOS intercepts the clock's signal and throws the current time into the Deskbar's shelf.

If your time settings ever start to behave unpredictably, it's likely time for a new CMOS battery. But before you spring for a new nickel cadmium, open

## *Is BeOS Year 2000-Compliant?*

As the industry scrambles to prepare for the long-feared Y2K disaster, BeOS users can rest easy. It almost goes without saying that BeOS was built to be Y2K-compliant nearly from the start.

up the Time preferences panel and have a look. From here you can specify the month, date, or year by clicking in the date field and using the up or down arrows, or select a date by clicking directly in the calendar. Even more fun can be had by grabbing the hands of the clock face and dragging them around the dial. As always, BeOS reacts in real time; keep your eye on the clock in the Deskbar shelf—it resets itself the moment you release one of the clock's hands. You don't need to click OK or Apply, or even close the Time panel. Alternatively, click in the digits above the clock and use their corresponding up and down arrows to set your clock with more precision.

BeOS is also fully aware of international time zones. Click on the Time Zone tab and select your continent from the picklist. The lower pane will fill with a list of regions on that continent. Choose the region nearest you, and BeOS will always be able to reconcile international time differences, update your system for Daylight Savings Time, and work with Internet-based atomic time clocks.

## *Atomic Time*

If you're a stickler for time, you probably want the most accurate kind of time there is—the kind you get when you count the electromagnetic emanations of a decaying atom. That's how spacemen, the gub'mint, and pencil-necked engineers around the world measure time, and your BeOS machine can too.

Go to BeWare and search on NTP, which stands for Network Time Protocol. After you've got it installed, search the Internet for NTP servers. Locate the one geographically closest to you (to reduce time discrepancies caused by network latency), and enter its address into your NTP client. Be sure to read the server's Terms of Service, and make sure the server is meant to be publicly accessible—you don't want to be tapping into a server meant for private or institutional use only. You shouldn't need to worry about whether the server is in your own time zone, as all atomic clocks should deliver time signals in Greenwich Mean Time, and the translation to your own time zone will be taken care of automatically. Your system clock will now be automatically synchronized with the most accurate clocks on earth.

# Video

Like its cousin the Audio preferences panel, Video preferences represents a set of controls and setup defaults for your installed video hardware. Note that the the category of "video hardware" does not include standard video cards, but rather devices such as TV tuner and video capture boards.

The Video preferences panel consists of three tabbed sections, representing Input, Output, and Hardware. When the Input tab is selected, three additional tabs appear, representing Controls, Defaults, and Setup options available for the default video input device. Because different devices have different capabilities, these tab titles may differ depending on your installed hardware.

**Input/Setup**  Use this tab to tell BeOS about the video devices attached to your machine. Up to four inputs are available, and each input can be set to one of Composite 1-4, Tuner, SVideo, or none. The same is true for audio inputs, but note that these are not the same as the audio inputs established in the Audio preferences panel; these are audio inputs related or connected to your video signal, such as a microphone jack on your video capture board. The options you establish on this panel will become available as choices on the Controls tab.

**Input/Defaults**  This tab lets you configure settings specific to the default video input device. This way, you can select the "preferred" format for a given node. In some cases, as with the node for the popular bt848 video chipset, you'll also be able to specify the default video format (e.g. NTSC, PAL, or SECAM), locale (because different video transmission standards are used in different countries), and tuner brand (such as Philips, Samsung, Alps, or Temic) from here.

By choosing defaults from this tab, you're specifying which parameters should be tried first by any application making use of that node, though you'll probably be able to override these settings from separate controls in the application itself.

 It may not be immediately clear which tuner brand to choose from this last picklist, as there is no necessary equation between the brand of the video capture/playback hardware in your machine and the brand of the chips on these boards that perform the actual encoding and decoding of video signal. It may be easiest to simply try them all until you find one that works (there aren't many), but if you really want to know, carefully remove the video capture card from your machine and examine the fine print on the flat metal box soldered to the printed circuit board, where you should find a reference to one of these brand names.

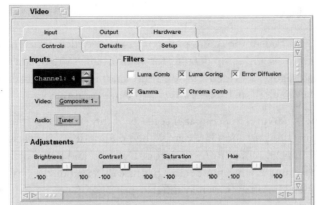

**Figure 9.28**

*The Video Preferences panel lets you monitor controls for video hardware attached to your machine, such as capture boards, TV tuners, and video cameras.*

**Input/Controls** The Controls panel (Figure 9.28) is analogous to the audio input source selector and gain control in the Audio Preferences panel, and lets you select from a number of available inputs, and then to alter that input in some fashion. However, many more modifications are possible from this panel than from the corresponding panel in Audio preferences.

If the chosen input is capable of selecting from among TV channels, a channel chooser will appear here as well. Use the Adjustments sliders to control brightness, contrast, saturation, and hue, just as you would with the controls on your television. If you'd like to fine-tune the appearance of the incoming video signal, you can optionally enable or disable various luminosity, chromatics, and error diffusion filters.

**Output** In most cases, the Input and Output nodes will represent different devices. The bt848 node, for example, is input only, as it sends output to a window screen. As a result, you'll probably see a blank panel here, with the words "This hardware has no controls." If you have an NTSC output card or other device with hardware output capabilities, the output controls for that device will appear on the Output tab.

**Hardware** If you have more than one video capture / playback device installed on your system, the Hardware tab will let you select from amongst them. All options available in the other panels of the Video preferences panel will relate only to the input and output devices currently selected in this panel. If you have only one video device installed, this panel will report its name, but will not offer any user-settable options.

In R4.0, this tab simply reports the first devices found by BeOS, and does not let you change the default device. In R4.1, this will be enhanced to let you select from amongst multiple video devices.

# Virtual Memory

RAM keeps getting cheaper every day, though it's still not as cheap as disk space. However, it *is* a lot faster. When BeOS wants more RAM than your machine has to give, it starts removing less-used data from memory and writing it to a "swap file"—a portion of your disk dedicated to extending the reach of your computer's physical memory. But if the data is going back to the (much slower) hard disk anyway, why bother putting it in a special file? The data in a swap file is a mirror image of the data that was in RAM, as opposed to the format of raw files on disk. For example, the contents of your system memory right now are some combination of the byte-code comprising your open applications and the documents you've currently got open. Being able to retrieve that "state" directly is much faster than reconstructing it from the original files (though it's not as fast as real RAM, of course). Virtual memory is a physical extension of electronic memory. It may live on your disk, but it functions like RAM.

**Figure 9.29**

*The Virtual Memory slider lets you increase the amount of disk space you want to commit to handling temporary swap data. BeOS uses fixed algorithms for determining the minimum size of this space—you can go higher but not lower than BeOS's guidelines permit.*

Technically, it's possible to run BeOS without a swap file—after all, that's what happens any time you boot from the installation CD. However, performance can be so seriously compromised by the absence of a swap file that it's not an option; you can't set your swap space to zero. In fact, BeOS requires that the swap file be at least a particular size, as determined by the rules in Table 9.04.

In most cases, the swap file size BeOS establishes for you works just fine. If, however, you're working with a lot of really large files, running many programs at once, or simply don't have a lot of memory installed in your system, you might consider allocating a larger chunk of disk to virtual memory. Drag the slider to the desired size, and … reboot your computer. Yes, this is one the very few places in BeOS where a reboot is required after making changes, but there are good reasons for it (mostly revolving around the fact that the swap file is established as a special, internal section of the Be filesystem, rather than as a simple, free-standing file as it is in Windows). In addition, the swap file is in use as soon as the boot process begins, and the virtual memory subsystem won't be happy without it.

By the way, the Virtual Memory panel is fully keyboardable—try using the Tab key to navigate between fields, and the arrow keys to adjust the slider.

### Table 9.04  Swap Sizes

| Physical Memory (MB) (Virtual Memory) | Swap File Size |
| --- | --- |
| 16–31 | 3.0 × RAM size |
| 32–63 | 2.5 × RAM size |
| 64–127 | 2.0 × RAM size |
| 128–511 | 1.5 × RAM size |
| 512–4095 | 1.25 × RAM size |
| 4096+ | RAM size |

*Virtual memory default sizes are based on expected usage patterns, and are the result of extensive testing at Be headquarters to determine optimum settings for a variety of machines.*

The swap file's size is also limited by how much free disk space is available on your boot volume. If you're extremely low on disk space, BeOS will never use your last 16MB of free space for the swap file. For example, if you have 64MB of memory, the swap file size is computed at boot time to be 128MB. But if you only have 100MB of free space on your boot volume, the swap file will be set to 84MB instead. In other words, the maximum size of the swap file is the minimum size computed using the table above plus the amount of free disk space, minus 16MB. It's even theoretically possible for the system to decide not to create a swap file at all. This can happen if, for example, you have more memory than free disk space.

## Workspaces

You've already encountered BeOS's multiple workspaces feature, and hopefully discovered by now just how much this tool can improve your sex life. OK, it's not quite that good, but it still rocks.

Usage of the Workspaces panel is covered in detail in Chapter 2, *Meet the System*.

# Customization

Customization picks up where preferences leave off. When you tweak system preferences, all of your options are laid out in front of you; but customizations let you to go beyond the obvious and make appearance and behavior changes that even Be may never have envisioned, through the use of scripts, hacks, and third-party applications.

 Note that some of the customizations covered in this section involve techniques that aren't officially supported by Be. While most of this is pretty innocuous stuff and I won't recommend anything that I haven't tested myself, or that I suspect may be flaky or lead to other problems, you still must proceed at your own risk.

## Scripts

While scripting in general is a deep enough topic to deserve its own section, BeOS itself uses a handful of built-in scripts at boot time and when calling certain OS functions. Some of these scripts are safe and easy to customize, while others are highly sensitive and should only be edited by those who consider themselves bash shell experts.

A script is simply a text file containing a sequence of shell commands—anything you find in a shell script can also be typed into the Terminal. A shell

## Table 9.05  BeOS User Scripts

| Script | Function |
| --- | --- |
| `/boot/home/config/boot/UserBootscript` | Automatically launches custom programs and services at boot time. |
| `/boot/home/config/boot/UserSetupEnvironment` | Establishes the value of user-configurable system variables; mostly of interest to programmers. |
| `/boot/home/.profile` | Configures aspects of Terminal behavior; run every time the Terminal is launched. |
| `/boot/home/config/boot/UserShutdownScript` | Automatically launches custom programs and services at the beginning of the shutdown process. |
| `/boot/home/config/boot/UserShutdownFinishScript` | Performs tasks at the very last instant before the system is shut all the way down. |

*A few of BeOS's system scripts are safe for users to edit.* UserBootscript *and* UserSetupEnvironment *are both run automatically as the system is booting, while* .profile *is run every time you launch the Terminal. The two shutdown scripts are run at different points in the shutdown process.*

## Table 9.06   BeOS System Scripts

| Script | Function |
| --- | --- |
| `/boot/beos/system/boot/Bootscript` | The big daddy. If this script is missing or damaged, your system will not boot. (See *Disaster Recovery* in Chapter 16, *Troubleshooting and Maintenance* to learn how you can boot from CD, then replace this file with an original copy from the CD). Launches critical system services, such as the Tracker and Deskbar, app_server, print_server, audio_server, Registrar, and system debugger. It then invokes other scripts, such as the SetupEnvironment, the Netscript, and, finally, your customized UserBootscript. |
| `/boot/beos/system/boot/SetupEnvironment` | Establishes the value of important system variables, such as where the home directory lives, the path to the shell, the hardware architecture in use, the location of programmer's services, and where the system should look for add-ons. |
| `/boot/beos/system/boot/Netscript` | Launches the net_server and, if you've chosen them in the Network preferences panel, the FTP and telnet servers, and finally the mail_daemon. |
| `/boot/beos/system/boot/{ShutdownScript, ShutdowFinishScript}` | Potentially used to perform final cleanup activities, and to launch the user-level shutdown scripts. |
| `/boot/beos/system/boot/{Bootscript.cd, Installer.init, Installer.finish}` | Scripts used only to establish and finish the installation procedure, and to boot from the CD. Because you *need* these scripts to function if you should ever have to reinstall or emergency boot, it's highly inadvisable to mess with these. |

*Scripts run automatically by the system should only be edited by expert users fully prepared to hack their way out of trouble if things go wrong.*

script can be run just like a program, by typing its name at the command line, or it can be invoked in other ways. BeOS automatically runs several such scripts at boot time. In the tables above, note that the first batch (Table 9.05) lives in subdirectories of your home directory, indicating that you're free to alter them without risk to your system. The second group (Table 9.06) lives in a subdirectory of /boot/beos/system, indicating that they're for internal consumption only. These scripts are run automatically by the operating system and are not officially customizable by the user. Each of these files contains a comment in the header reading:

```
# Do not edit or change this file.
```

That's good advice for the vast majority of us, and you would do well to heed Be's warning. Table 9.06 is included for your informational purposes only, so caveat emptor if you decide to modify any of these. And if you do decide to take the risk, be aware that any changes you make could be overwritten next time you upgrade BeOS.

**Customizing UserBootscript**    The fact that UserBootscript and UserSetupEnvironment live within your home directory tree is a good indication that you're free to customize them. By default, these files don't exist. Instead, you'll find UserBootscript.sample and UserSetupEnvironment.sample. In order to have them invoked at boot time, you'll need to make copies of them (select them in the Tracker and press Alt+D), and rename the copies without .sample on the end.

In shell scripts, lines beginning with a "#" are comments, and are always ignored by the system. Use comments liberally to annotate your scripts for clarity—you'll be glad you did when you come back for a second look someday. Your new UserBootscript includes a block of comments from Be about the file's purpose; you can delete these comments or leave them in—it doesn't matter.

To launch any program from the command line (or from within a script), just type its path. If the program is already in your path statement (see Chapter 6, *The Terminal*), you don't need to specify the full path, and can just use the program's name. For example, all of the applications bundled with the system and living in /boot/beos/bin and in /boot/beos/apps are already in your path, and can be invoked by typing their names alone. A path invocation might look like this:

```
"/boot/apps/SoftwareValet/SoftwareValet Transceiver" &
```

The quotation marks are included only because the filename includes spaces. If your path has no spaces, you don't need the quotes.

If you read Chapter 6, *The Terminal*, you know that the "&" (ampersand) character at the end of the line is important. It means that the program should be launched in the background and that the shell should return control to the user and keep on going. If you launch a program from the shell without the ampersand, the program will be launched but you'll no longer be able to type into the shell. Similarly, if you fail to include this character at the end of a command in a startup or shutdown script, nothing in the script after that point will be executed until after that command has finished or the application it represents has been closed.

**Launching Documents and Files**  You're not constrained to launching executable programs from `UserBootscript`—you can also launch commonly used files, like particular documents you work on every day, or a sound to be played automatically at startup. To do this, you'll need to specify both a program and a filename in the same command. To do this from the command line, you can usually just type

```
path_to_program  path_to_file
```

For instance, if you're in the `home` directory in the Terminal and a file called `todo.txt` is in the same directory, you can type

```
StyledEdit todo.txt
```

to launch them together. Note that this works only because StyledEdit is in your path. If you want to launch something that's not already in your path, you'll need to use its absolute path. For example:

```
/boot/apps/audio/soundplay/SoundPlay  /boot/home/sounds/plasma.wav &
```

will launch the `plasma.wav` sound file into the SoundPlay application.

## The Launch Alternative

Launching programs, documents, and utilities by invoking their paths isn't the only way. A command-line utility called "Launch" is capable of hunting down an application by its signature regardless where it lives on disk. The system Registrar keeps track of the location of program executables according to their signatures, so that you can move programs around without breaking references to them from other places, as seen in the line below. Launching a program by its signature is simple:

```
Launch application/x-vnd.VendorName-ProgramName &
```

You can learn the signature of any program by right-clicking its icon and choosing Add-Ons | FileType from the context menu (don't confuse signatures with filetypes though!). Application signatures are discussed in detail in Chapter 5, *Files and the Tracker*.

This method has the advantage that it enables you to move applications and tools anywhere on disk, and your startup or shutdown scripts will never fail as a result.

**Testing from the Terminal**  You don't have to reboot every time you want to test a modification to UserBootscript; you can simply test your commands from the Terminal to make sure they work. If it works in the Terminal, it'll work in UserBootscript. This applies equally to launching via signature or via absolute path. Keep testing in the Terminal until you've gotten your application to launch from the command line, then paste the working command string into UserBootscript.

**You can also run your entire UserBootscript from the Terminal to test that it's working start to finish. Type**

```
sh -x ~/config/boot/UserBootscript
```

**The shell will run all of the commands in your boot script, reporting back as each line is executed.**

**What to Launch?**  So now you know how; the question is, what? Since you can launch any file or application you like, there's no limit to what you can include here, but keep in mind that the more you add, the more you'll slow down the boot process. I prefer to keep autolaunched items to a minimum; a good launcher on the Desktop (see Chapter 10, *System Tools and Utilities*) obviates the need to autolaunch the kitchen sink. In addition, I prefer to put only small, fast-loading programs here, not full-blown productivity suites. Here's a copy of my current UserBootscript, with comments:

```
### TURN ON THE SCREEN SAVER ###
Launch application/x-vnd.wilcox-blanketserver &

#### INFORM ME OF SOFTWARE UPDATES AUTOMATICALLY ###
"/boot/apps/SoftwareValet/SoftwareValet Transceiver" &

### START MY APP LAUNCHER ###
Launch application/x-vnd.lcook-DeposIt &

### LAUNCH THE WORKSPACES PANEL ###
Launch application/x-vnd.Be-WORK &

### HIT AND RUN (FOR HOTKEYS) ###
Launch application/x-vnd.kaktus-hitrun &

### START CRACKING BLOCKS FOR THE RC5DES EFFORT ###
/boot/home/config/bin/rc5des &
```

## *About the Shutdown Scripts*

As of R4, BeOS started shipping with two additional scripts in the ~/config/boot directory: UserShutdownScript and UserShutdownFinishScript. Obviously, these two scripts (if found) are run by the system as it's being shut down, and complement the system-level versions of the same scripts. But what's the difference between the two? Nothing but the order in which they're run. However, this order is important, because as the system is shutting down, its servers are going down with it. UserShutdownScript runs at the beginning of the shutdown process, while UserShutdownFinishScript is run as the very last item before the system really goes to bed. Therefore, you can't add anything to the UserShutdownFinishScript that will depend on the presence of system servers. For example, you can easily have your system play a sound file as it goes down by tweaking UserShutdownScript, but if you add the same line to UserShutdownFinishScript, the media_server will not be around to handle your request.

So what can you put in that final script? Not much, really. If you keep an uptime log, you might want to update its statistics as the very last thing you do. You could eject your Zip disk from the command line, or run a sync on a particular disk, just to be sure to the point of paranoia (disks are automatically synced at shutdown by the system-level script, so this really won't do you much good). The vast majority of time, you'll want to add any shutdown commands to the standard UserShutdownScript, not UserShutdownFinishScript.

### Customizing UserSetupEnvironment
The user-level UserSetupEnvironment script works in conjunction with the system-level SetupEnvironment, adding optional environment variables to the system-defined variables. For most users, environment variables are of little concern. These variables specify the values of things like how debugging and the freeing of memory should be handled when applications misbehave—in other words, things only a programmer would care about.

There are, however, a couple of things that end-users might want to change, if only for cosmetic reasons. In the Terminal, when you do a file listing with ls -l, it will appear that your files were created by a user named "baron," who belongs to a group called "users." As long as BeOS is single-user, this is of no consequence. However, in a multiuser BeOS, it will become important to keep track of who owns which files, so that permissions can be applied appropriately.

If you'd like your Terminal file listings to display another user or group name, uncomment the lines in UserSetupEnvironment which look similar to the following example by removing the # symbols at the front of them, and enter your custom replacements, such as:

```
export USER=coyote
export GROUP=milkbone
```

or whatever you like. To make changes appear to all new Terminal sessions, reboot your system. To see them taking effect in the current Terminal, run UserSetupEnvironment from the shell:

```
source ~/config/boot/UserSetupEnvironment
```

Some modifications to this file depend on offerings from program vendors. For example, if you install Pe, the Programmers Editor, it comes bundled with a small command-line program called lpe, which lets you send files straight into Pe from the command line. Once lpe has been added to UserSetupEnvironment, you can be sitting at any Terminal prompt and type

```
lpe filename.txt
```

to launch that file in Pe, which is a heck of a lot more convenient (in my view) than using a Terminal editor like vi. The environment variable set in UserSetupEnvironment is, intuitively, the EDITOR variable, so you'll need to add something like:

```
export EDITOR=/boot/home/config/bin/lpe
```

The export command lets all applications started from that shell "see" the variables it sets. In this case, it lets Pe receive filenames as variables passed to it from the shell.

**Customizing .profile** In the root of your home directory, you'll find a file called .profile. If this file doesn't exist, create it with any text editor (it's important that the filename begin with a period!). .profile is read into memory every time you launch the Terminal, and specifies aspects of Terminal behavior such as keyboard shortcuts and the configuration of the Terminal prompt. Note that any changes you make will only take effect after you close all Terminal windows and then relaunch the Terminal.

**Customize Your Terminal Prompt** I dislike the default Unix prompt, which is simply the $ symbol. It tells me nothing. Those of you who are old DOS hands have probably come to count on the command line always reporting the current directory at the prompt. To duplicate this behavior in the Terminal add this line to your .profile:

```
export PS1='$PWD>'
```

PS1 is the environment variable referring to the prompt. "$" in Unix-ese refers to "the value of whatever comes next." Since pwd means "print working Directory," the value of the working directory is always written into this location. The angle bracket separates the end of the prompt from what comes next, so it won't look like you're typing into the end of the working directory's name. Now when you launch the Terminal, you'll be greeted with the prompt:

```
/boot/home>
```

instead of the $, and the prompt will change every time you change directories. The only disadvantage to this configuration is that when paths become very long, as they sometimes do, the prompt can reach halfway across the Terminal window, which can in turn cause longer commands to wrap down to the next line. This, however, is purely an aesthetic, not a functional, hindrance. If you want the prompt to report the name of the current directory without displaying the entire path (to avoid this path length issue, use bash's built-in \W flag, like so:

```
PS1='\W>'
```

Using this method, if your current directory is /boot/home/projects/research, your prompt will appear as simply:

```
research>
```

Note that you must use an uppercase "W" in the command above. A lowercase "w" will report the complete path in the prompt, putting you right back where you were with the PWD technique.

There are many more ways to customize your Terminal prompt. See Chapter 6, *The Terminal*, for details.

**Custom Keyboard Shortcuts**    Another good use of .profile is to store your favorite Terminal aliases. An alias is just what it sounds like: a command that "stands in" for another command. Aliases can be defined on the fly every time you use the Terminal, but why bother? If you find yourself typing ls -l -a continually, you might find it easier to create an alias, so you can get the same listing by typing two characters, rather than eight. At a Terminal prompt, type

```
alias ll="ls -l -a"
```

Then you can just type ll (that's two lowercase "L"s) to get a long-format directory listing. Like it? Paste the above command into your .profile, then close and restart the Terminal. Of course, the longer your commands, the more useful aliases become. For instance, if you find yourself frequently FTPing into your Web server, you may want to set up a three-letter alias to get you in quickly:

```
alias fts="ftp ftp.mysite.com"
```

If you find yourself wanting to browse through your recent Terminal history frequently, you might want to try something like:

```
alias h="history 20 "
```

You need to be careful that your aliases don't preempt existing commands. There are a ton of little programs hanging out in /boot/beos/bin and in other locations with short names like ci, bc, co, rcs, sed, and so on. You may seldom use these, and therefore may not even know they exist. But if you create permanent aliases with these same names, you not only make it difficult to use these programs in the future (without changing those aliases), but you could also potentially screw up other scripts that invoke those commands. Before establishing an alias, type

```
which xyz
```

where xyz is replaced by the letters you plan to use as an alias in the Terminal. If the shell reports back with a pathname, then don't use those letters—they equal the name of a preexisting command. If the shell reports back with nothing, you're clear to use those letters.

**Other Uses for .profile**  You'll also find that various programs and utilities use .profile for more esoteric purposes. For example, if you install the TermHire Tracker add-on, you're instructed to paste half a dozen lines of shell script into your .profile. This script lets the Terminal accept a message passed to it from the GUI, so that it can change directories to the same location you were browsing in the Tracker.

For more ideas on .profile customization, consult any bash manual (see Chapter 6, *The Terminal*).

## Miscellaneous Settings Files

Most BeOS applications—both bundled and third-party apps—are customizable in some way or another. But exactly how are your preferences stored between reboots? Take a look at your /boot/home/config/settings directory in the Tracker. You'll find a laundry list of files and folders, most of them with familiar names, and each of them storing parameters and configurations set by you and currently in use by various applications. Some of the files found here are stored in binary format, and can't be edited. However, many of them are plain text files, and can be opened in StyledEdit, Pe, vi, or any other text editor. However, if you try to double-click a file and are told it can't be opened, don't automatically assume that it's a binary. Try using File | Open from within a text editor. If it comes up as garbage, it's a binary file and shouldn't be touched—close without saving. If it comes up readable, feel free to edit its contents (carefully, of course).

**beos_mime**  This folder contains an entire hierarchy of files and folders that mirror the hierarchy of MIME types registered on your system. For instance, you'll find folders named image, audio, text, video, message, and application. Within the image folder, you'll find individual files for each image type known to the system's FileTypes database, such as gif, tiff, and jpeg. In addition to describing the MIME hierarchy to the system database, each of these files also contains the icon used to depict that filetype (icons are stuffed into these files' attributes; you won't be able to see them from here).

While you can pretty much control everything you need to from the FileTypes application itself, from time to time you may find the need or desire to remove or replace certain filetypes in this hierarchy. See *Restoring System Filetypes and Icons*, later in this chapter.

**network**  While it's not likely that you'll find anything in here that you can't configure from within the Network preferences panel, there are rare instances when you may need to edit Network's config file manually. For example, in DR8, the standard preferences panel provided only for modems attached to external serial ports. If you wanted to install an internal modem, the only way to make it work was to open this file, change the DEVICELINK entry to reflect a COM port, save, and restart networking. It's possible (though unlikely) that you may run into a similar situation if you experiment with hardware not supported by Be. Similarly, if you want to add network address translation services to BeOS (Chapter 8, *Networking*), you'll have to add a couple of lines to this file.

There are too many entries in this file to recount them all, but their names should make their functions self-explanatory. If you make any changes to this file, you'll still have to restart networking in the usual way in order for your changes to take effect.

If you use the Backup and Restore functions in the Network preferences panel, you'll find separate files in your ~/config/settings directory, one for each configuration you've backed up.

**Terminal**  You've probably noticed the option under the Terminal Settings menus labeled "Save As Settings File." This option lets you establish a different combination of background/foreground colors, font, and font size. So you tweak out the perfect Terminal configuration and save it as a custom settings file, only to discover later that there's no menu option for retrieving your previously saved settings files. Hopefully a future release of BeOS will rectify the situation, but for now, here's a way to set up multiple Terminal configurations.

Let's say you saved your settings file to /boot/home/SkyTerminal_23. Open up the /boot/home/config/settings folder and find the file called Terminal. Rename it to Terminal.old. Then move /boot/home/SkyTerminal23 to /boot/home/config/settings/Terminal. Close and restart the Terminal and your settings file will be retrieved. This way you can create and save as many Terminal configuration files as you like, and toggle between them at will.

Even better, download the author's shell script, TermSet, from BeWare. TermSet does essentially the same thing, but has the advantage of letting you store an unlimited number of different Terminal configuration files and retrieve them instantly. Type termset at any prompt and you'll see a list of all your configurations. The bonus here is that if you launch new Terminals by using the termset command, you can have multiple Terminals running in different colors and fonts for easy identification.

 As of R4/Intel, you can launch new Terminal sessions by simply double-clicking on their settings files (this was always possible on BeOS/PowerPC). Thus, you might want to store a library of Terminal settings files in a folder on your Desktop for easy access to different-colored Terminal sessions. If you want to get really fancy, open your system's FileTypes preferences panel, navigate to application/x-vnd.Be-pref, and drop a custom icon into the icon well. This way your Terminal settings files won't have those plain gray "generic file" icons.

**Tracker**    There are a few useful things to find in the Tracker subdirectory.

**Go**    The Go folder contains links to other folders on your system. Any link found in this folder will appear in the Go To menu of all of your File panels. Because the File panels let you add new folders but not remove them, you'll need to come here if you ever find that you want to remove links from that menu.

**tracker_shelf**    Every so often, a Replicant can go bad and mess up your Desktop. In the worst cases, a corrupt Replicant can make your system unusable (although this is very unusual). Deleting the file tracker_shelf from this directory will delete all Replicants embedded in the Tracker, which includes those on your Desktop, thereby clearing up any problems you may have been having with them. You may want to send a note to the author of the software you were running as a Replicant when things went bad.

**DefaultFolderTemplate**    DefaultFolderTemplate serves as a model on which the layout of new folders is determined, including dimensions, view (Icon View, Mini Icon View, or List View), and column order. As described in Chapter 5, *Files and the Tracker*, new Tracker windows always inherit their layout from the parent folder. However, if no "state" can be determined for the parent folder, this folder is used as a layout template. The most common case of a parent folder state not being found is when you create a new folder on the Desktop.

**DefaultQueryTemplates**    The subdirectories of this folder work similarly, but let you completely customize the way query results will be returned for certain types of files. Take a look inside this folder and you'll find, by default, four other folders named after common MIME types on your system (but with the forward slash in the MIME type replaced by an underscore). Try customizing the default query results layout for a search on Person files. Open the folder application_x-person and copy one of your Person files into it.

Close and reopen the folder so that Person file attributes will become available from the Attributes menu. Rearrange and show or hide columns as necessary to create what you consider to be the perfect layout for viewing Person files in the Tracker. Close this folder, then run a query on Person files, noting that the results precisely mimic the layout you created with the query template folder.

You can, of course, repeat this process for any filetype on your system—just create a new subdirectory of this folder named after that filetype, drop a sample file into it, and customize to your heart's content.

 The folder and query customization process will reportedly become much easier in a future release; these instructions could change by R5.

**FilePanelSettings**  As of R4, the Tracker will remember the height, width, and layout of your Open/Save File panels—a true blessing. This file simply stores those settings in its attributes. There's nothing to edit here, folks. Move along.

**TrackerSettings**  As of R4, the Desktop became the root of the filesystem. Because some people don't like to have a zillion disk volumes arranged on the Desktop, this option is user-configurable. If you'd rather have your volumes appear within a Disks window than on the Desktop, see Chapter 2, *Meet the System*, for details.

## Customizing Icons

BeOS borrows more of its icon-customization behavior from MacOS than from Windows, so if you're coming from the Windows world, you'll find things a little odd at first. Rather than using a free-standing icon file format, BeOS icons are stored in files' attributes, and are accessed differently depending on whether you want to change the icon of a single file or make a system-wide change. Single-file changes are made by right-clicking the file in question and choosing Add-Ons | FileType from the pop-up menu. System-wide changes are made by choosing the appropriate filetype in the FileTypes preferences panel. (See Figure 5.25 in Chapter 5.)

Once the appropriate filetype's dialog is open, you have three choices:

- Double-click the icon to send it to Icon-o-Matic, where you can repaint it to your heart's content. Closing Icon-o-Matic will commit your changes back into the FileType panel.

- Single-click the icon well (a blue outline will appear around the icon to show that it's been selected) and paste in a new icon from the clipboard. Icons can be placed onto the clipboard by selecting them and hitting Alt+C, then pasted by selecting and hitting Alt+V.

- Drag a raw image file from the Tracker into the icon well (see the sidebar *Creating BeOS Icons in Photoshop*).

## *Creating BeOS Icons in Photoshop and Other Imaging Applications*

Not satisfied with the icon selection available to you on BeOS? You can easily paint your master-piece in Photoshop on the Mac or PC and then use it as a BeOS icon. Here's how:

1. In Photoshop, create your image at exactly 32×32 pixels and save it in .RAW format.

2. Resize the image to 16×16 pixels and save it under a different name, again in .RAW format. The small version is needed for Tracker list views.

3. Move both raw files to your BeOS machine via FTP or floppy, or by copying it over across partitions from within BeOS.

4. In BeOS, create a new file or folder (any type—it doesn't matter), right-click, and choose Add-Ons | FileType. When the dialog appears, drag the larger of your two images into the icon well. The new icon should appear immediately.

5. Now drag the small version to the same location. Oddly, this dialog won't give you any feed-back to let you know that the second one was imported successfully, but you can trust it. If you want to be sure, double-click to see your new icon in Icon-o-Matic, which will show you both icons.

6. Save and close the FileType dialog and you're all set.

Of course, this only changes the icon for a single file. If you want to use this icon system-wide, you'll need to repeat the steps above, but instead of using the FileType dialog for this particular file, use the global, system-wide FileTypes panel found in your preferences folder. Just navigate to the filetype you want to change and drag your icon into its icon well instead.

As of R4, Icon-o-Matic is capable of performing a similar function. Just drag any image file for which you have an installed Translator into Icon-o-Matic's main image area and it will be scaled appropriately. Touch up if necessary, save, close, and you're done!

If you obliterate one of your system icons and want it back again, see the sidebar *Restoring System Filetypes and Icons* in this chapter.

## *Why Some FileType Dialogs Have Blank Icon Wells*

There are actually some pretty tricky rules that establish which icons get displayed where, and the rules are based on a system of inheritance. If a file has a custom icon attached to it, that icon will be displayed. If not, the system looks to see if the file has a preferred application. If so, that applications's icon is used. If not, the system checks to see whether the file's filetype (e.g. text/plain) has a preferred application. If so, that application's icon is used. If not, the system checks to see if that file's supertype (e.g. text) has a preferred application. If so, that application's icon is used. If not, the generic icon is used.

Any time you see a blank icon well in a FileType dialog, it means only that no custom icon has been attached to this file or filetype. Of course, the rules of inheritance outlined above still guar-antee that an appropriate icon will be displayed in Tracker views.

## *Restoring System Filetypes and Icons*

Because of the way BeOS stores system icons, there may come a time when you find yourself unable to restore one of your system icons to its original state. This could happen if you've edited it into oblivion or accidentally pasted over it with another icon, or if a badly behaved application has co-opted it. In any case, the fix is simple.

1.  First, you'll need to determine the MIME type of the file in question. Right-click on the file and choose Add-Ons | FileType. Look for the MIME type in the main field. If there's something there, skip to step 3.

2.  If the field is blank, you need to do some extra footwork. Open up the Terminal and cd to the file's directory. Now type

    ```
    catattr BEOS:TYPE filename
    ```

    Your output will look something like:

    ```
    sysinfo : string : application/x-vnd.Be-elfexecutable
    ```

    The last bit is the MIME type of the file. In this example, application/x-vnd.Be-elfexecutable is the MIME type. In many cases, you can just right-click a file and select Get Info from the context menu. This, however, does not work with some files, such as generic executables.

3.  The next step is to find the file on your original installation CD bearing the same name as the MIME string. Open your installation CD and navigate with the Tracker to /boot/home/config/settings/beos_mime/supertype, where supertype is the first part of the MIME string. In other words, in this example you'd look for the subdirectory called application. Within that subdirectory you'll find files with names that look like MIME strings. Find the one corresponding to the file you want fixed.

4.  Since the directory structure on the CD mirrors the directory structure on your hard drive, you now need to find the same file on your hard drive and replace it with the good one from the CD. Your original filetype—along with its icon—will be restored and you'll be back in business.

## Hiroshi Lockheimer
*Software Engineer*
*Wrote StyledEdit; currently working on an Input Server for R4,*
*which includes a Japanese input method.*
*Interviewed by Henry Bortman*

**HB:** *Let's start at the beginning. Where'd you go to school?*

**HL:** Well, I grew up in Japan. I was born there, grew up there, in Tokyo. And I went to school, finished high school there. Went to Rice University for three months, then I dropped out. Then I went back to Japan and started doing some contract work. I learned to program after I left college.

**HB:** *What kind of stuff were you working on?*

**HL:** Mostly CD-ROM titles ranging from Macromedia Director-ish stuff, to actually writing a C++ PowerPlant-based applications for the Mac. It's specialized for the medical-educational market— one was especially for heart surgeons.

And then in my free time I bought a BeBox.

**HB:** *How did you hear about Be?*

**HL:** I was working, just looking around. I was in `comp.sys.mac.programmer.codewarrior`, or something, looking at the news. And someone had posted, "Check out www.be.com." This was right after the October announcement, you know in '95. So, I went to the site and I was very impressed.

**HB:** *What impressed you?*

**HL:** Well, a number of things. I think I was already starting to get a little bit bored with the MacOS, as a user as well as a developer. It seemed like there was already tons of stuff out there. I was a newcomer and I wanted to sort of do a new thing. And also the whole dual processor thing. I didn't know anything about SMP or multithreaded issues, or preemptive multitasking. I didn't know really what that meant, technically speaking, but I thought that was very intriguing. So, eventually, after looking at Web pages and drooling over it for about four months, I finally decided to buy a BeBox.

The first thing I did to sort of accustom myself to the Be API was I wrote a modular screen saver, which had this plug-in architecture where people could write plug-ins, sort of like After Dark where you have these files which are the modules. So, I wrote something like that.

And I had always wanted to write a text engine, so I figured, hey, you know, try writing one for BeOS.

**HB:** *It didn't have one?*

**HL:** No, it had one built into BeOS itself called BTextView, but it was rough. It couldn't handle multiple styles, for example, so you couldn't change the style or the font or the size of it in the middle of the sentence. I wanted to write a stylable text engine. So, I did that and released the source code and everything.

**HB:** *And this was all still when you were not working here?*

**HL:** This is before. It was just in my free time during the summer of '96, or whenever it was. And, Brian Stern and Jon Watt were actually looking for a style text engine so that they could do syntax styling in the IDE. Of course, BTextView couldn't do that, so they were holding off on that feature, which everybody wants. So they decided they would use my thing, which people heard about.

Eventually, someone from Be contacted me and said, "Maybe we can introduce you to some publishers out there and you could write something." And I said, "Well, why don't you introduce me to yourself? I want to work at Be." So I came here for an interview and that was that, pretty much.

**HB:** *So, they got your text engine for free?*

**HL:** No, I actually got 10 bucks. I licensed it to Be for 10 bucks and I still have that check, I haven't cashed it yet. It was supposed to be a buck, apparently.

**HB:** *Oh, they made a mistake?*

**HL:** No, but Mel Rogers felt sorry for me or something. She just wanted to be nice, so she gave me 10 bucks instead. I heard a rumor that Jean-Louis was complaining about that.

**HB:** *You also worked on NetPositive for a while. How did you get that assignment?*

**HL:** The reason why I ended up with it was that we got NetPositive from this contractor, Peter Barrett, who apparently is a very famous Mac developer. For example, I heard he wrote the Cinepak codec for QuickTime. Once we received final shipment from Peter, someone needed to maintain it. I wasn't really interested in that, to be honest with you, but I was interested in getting NetPositive to handle Japanese because I wanted to surf Japanese Web pages. We were just in the process of adding UDF8 support.

If you don't support UDF8, basically you just see the encoded text, which just looks like ASCII garbage. It looks like noise. What I did was, I added conversion routines to detect what sort of encoding it was in, and convert it to UDF8 so that you could display the Japanese text.

**HB:** *What about Japanese fonts?*

**HL:** Starting with DR9, our font engine supported Unicode format—Windows format TrueType fonts with a Unicode character map—which is basically most of the fonts out there. So, if you bought a font, you could just drop it into the BeOS and it would work.

My primary goal for R4 was to get Japanese working or to be able to release a Japanese version of BeOS. So everything that entails: getting a Japanese font, getting an input method, and incorporating those things into the whole OS and making sure everything interacts well.

**HB:** *And translating all the menus and all that?*

**HL:** No, the localization part we decided we weren't going to do for R4 because that's primarily just translation work. It's not a technically difficult problem, it's just a lot of brute force. Currently, our strings are all embedded in the source code, which is sort of not a good thing. We want to

## Hiroshi Lockheimer *(continued)*

switch over to resource-based strings pretty soon, but we don't have that mechanism right now. So, once we have that we will switch. Then we have to go through the brute force thing of looking through all the strings in the system, moving them out into resources, and then translating them. So, we decided we weren't going to do that for R4, but we did want to be able to input the Japanese because, usually, Japanese users are very savvy. And as long as they can type in their own language and do email and all that in their own language, they're OK. Especially for the target market for us.

**HB:** *Part of your work now is writing a Japanese input method. How do you think your method compares to other input methods?*

**HL:** It's like many things in BeOS, it's very minimalist. It's not the smartest of the input methods out there. But on the other hand, it's very fast. It's sort of a tradeoff. I don't think we can be experts on everything out there.

We actually licensed the core kanji-conversion engine from this Japanese company called ErgoSoft. ErgoSoft was, I think, the first input method vendor for the Mac OS. This was before System 7. Way before WorldScript or any of that. They were the first to do that. We asked them to do our own, just a library, to convert Japanese Kiragana strings into kanji, and we licensed that from them.

So, I wrote the wrapper, the basic architecture for input methods so that it's not just for Japanese, and I also wrote the Japanese wrapper that wraps around ErgoSoft's library. But we didn't try to get the Swiss Army Knife of input methods because it's just heavy, it takes up a lot of hard disk space, it slows everything down. So we just want to have the minimal implementation that other people can then improve. It's a third-party opportunity.

**HB:** *What do you like most about working at Be?*

**HL:** Well, you know, it's a small company. I have a lot of responsibility. Like I said, I haven't been programming for years and years. I'm still somewhat of a newcomer, but I still get to do these very exciting things. So, I like that a lot. It's sort of a no-nonsense kind of place. I mean, you don't really spend years researching something. You look for the right answer, and sometimes you go by your gut feeling and you just do it. I think that translates into quicker releases and being flexible. When you notice that something's wrong, you fix it.

# 10

# System Tools and Utilities

Take a stroll through the software archives of BeWare or BeDepot, or spend some time surfing around at any of the hundreds of sites run by independent BeOS developers, and you'll find a seemingly bottomless cornucopia of tools and utilities you can add to your system to extend its functionality. Some of these tools are ports of preexisting Unix applications, while others have been written natively for BeOS. Some work from the command line, while others are graphical. In this chapter, we'll cover software installation mechanisms, backup utilities, application launchers, Tracker add-ons, performance monitors, and more. We will not, however, even begin to scratch the surface of what's available out there.

# Installers

It's great to be able to unzip an archive and run the enclosed program immediately, but things aren't always so simple. The more complex and full-featured an application, the greater the chance that it will require additional libraries, filetypes, or settings files to run properly. Developers can (and sometimes do) tell users to move peripheral files around manually, or they can create their own installation scripts, but the ideal solution is a system-standard, application-agnostic, dedicated installation package. At this writing, Be's SoftwareValet is the de facto standard in the installation department, but it isn't the only kid on the block.

## SoftwareValet
**www.bedepot.com**

Be sees Internet software distribution both as an important part of their business model and as a means to keep developers and users in close contact. The BeDepot Web site provides a centralized and secure download/purchase point for commercial BeOS software. The SoftwareValet client software (which you'll find in your Demos folder) communicates with BeDepot's back-end database to make sure you always have the most recent BeOS software available. Meanwhile, developers are able to tap into a globally accessible electronic commerce database, custom-tailored for BeOS and its users.

pov-ray.pkg     datum.zip

**Figure 10.01**

*Unlike* .zip *archives, SoftwareValet packages end with the* .pkg *extension and sport this dashing "butler" icon.*

**Meet the "Package" File**  While you can use many of BeDepot's services through browsers on other operating systems if you like, BeDepot is specially built to communicate with SoftwareValet, and transfers files in a BeOS-specific format: the .pkg or "package" file. On the surface, it may appear that package files are similar to other standard file archives such as zip. There are some important distinctions between the two, however. The package format is not intended to replace zip or other standard archivers on BeOS. Rather, it's one-third of a system (consisting of BeDepot, SoftwareValet, and Package files) intended to make application installation and management easy and pleasant for users. The package format has a couple of shortcomings: Its compression algorithm isn't as good as zip's and package files can't be decompressed from the command line. SoftwareValet does do a bang-up job at application installation, though it currently lacks an uninstallation mechanism.

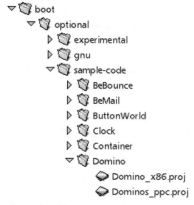

The package format lets developers ensure that settings files and libraries are placed in the right locations during application installation. Developers can insert customized splash screens, instructions, and scripts into the installation process if necessary, and users can selectively choose which files to overwrite and which ones to preserve. By itself, the package format is not useful. But by using it in conjunction with SoftwareValet, you get an attribute-savvy archive format and user-friendly installation routine all at once.

**Figure 10.02**

*SoftwareValet lets you study the file/folder hierarchy that's about to be installed on your system.*

Because of these capabilities of the package format, creating a package archive is not quite as simple as creating a zip archive. Fortunately, you don't have to worry about that. Since package files are intended primarily for application installation, only developers need to create them. Users only need to know how to run them.

Double-clicking a package file should launch it in SoftwareValet. If it doesn't, see the sidebar *Fixing Corrupt Package Files*.

 **If you'd like to experiment with creating package files, download PackageBuilder from BeDepot and read through its documentation. Building packages isn't a difficult process, but there's no real reason to do so unless you intend to distribute a BeOS application.**

**Getting Started**  The first time you launch SoftwareValet, you'll be asked to enter your name, address, email address, and other details. Most of the requested information is optional, but at the very least you'll need supply your name and email address if you want SoftwareValet and BeDepot to keep you abreast of OS and application updates. Note that Be keeps all of your personal data to itself—your name and address will not be sold to marketing firms. They will, however, be shared with the companies who provide any applications you purchase from BeDepot. After filling in the form and clicking Register, proceed to the Configure panel. Let's look at each tab in turn.

## *Fixing Corrupt Package Files*

In order for package files to launch in SoftwareValet as they should, they must have the correct MIME type. In the past, it wasn't unusual for these files to land on users' systems with incorrect types, a situation caused primarily by Web servers that weren't configured to dish up the correct MIME type along with the file. If you encounter a file with the `.pkg` extension that won't open in SoftwareValet, here are a few things you can try.

- Some improperly configured Web servers serve up package files with a MIME type of `application/octet-stream`. In addition, early versions of NetPositive incorrectly gave this type to package files. To set the type correctly, right-click on the file, choose Add-Ons | FileType from the context menu, and change the type to `application/x-scode-UPkg` (or use the Same As... button to locate a known working package file on your system). Save and close the FileType panel, then try again.

- Rather than double-clicking the file, launch SoftwareValet, click the Install button, and navigate to the file manually. Alternatively, hold down your Ctrl key as you drag a package file onto SoftwareValet's icon.

- If SoftwareValet tells you the package is corrupt, it may have been downloaded in ASCII mode rather than binary. On the chance that your browser is doing this automatically (this has been known to happen with the Macintosh version of Netscape Navigator), try to obtain the file with a standard FTP client, making sure that it's set to download in binary mode.

- As a last resort, ask the site's Webmaster to zip the package file for you. If it's working on her system and she zips it for you, the file is practically guaranteed to work on your system (since zip will preserve the file's correct type, and won't be assigned a funky filetype by unsavvy Web servers or browsers).

**Download**  This tab lets you establish a download directory where all package files will be placed. You'll probably want to keep the default of /boot/home/downloads. Detailed logs are kept of each SoftwareValet installation you perform. To view these logs, click the Display Log button and select an application from the list.

**Communication**  If your organization (or home LAN) connects via a proxy server, you'll need to tell SoftwareValet about it (proxy servers are covered in Chapter 8, *Networking*). This tab also lets you control whether SoftwareValet should communicate the version numbers of your installed applications back to BeDepot. This process, run by a "Transceiver," is harmless and runs invisibly in the background. Clicking the "Launch automatically at boot" option will add a line launching SoftwareValet to your UserBootscript, so you'll always be in touch with the mothership.

**Install** If you have no interest in seeing the installation logs referred to above, you can tell SoftwareValet to stop creating them. If you've decided to install your applications somewhere other than in /boot/apps, you can specify an alternate installation location from this tab.

 Choosing a new default folder does not guarantee that all applications will be installed in your chosen location. Developers creating package files have the option to use the user's default location or to force a location—this option only pertains to applications that use your defaults. If you encounter an application that forces itself into a specific location, you can always move it later via the Tracker, but you should read the program notes before you do—there may be a good reason why it's installed where it is.

**Register** This tab will contain the same information you entered when you first launched SoftwareValet. Each time you register a downloaded application, a panel will appear containing this data prior to its being sent back to BeDepot. If you move or change email addresses, make the change here so you won't have to reenter your contact information each time.

**Update** Use this tab to specify a schedule for SoftwareValet to check for new versions of your installed software. If you don't want it to do this, choose Never from the pop-up list.

 Because BeOS establishes PPP connections automatically when network requests are made, your machine could end up dialing your ISP when you're not around. This may or may not be want you want ... especially if your modem is loud and SoftwareValet is scheduled to do its business in the middle of the night.

**Logging** SoftwareValet is both honest and meticulous. It logs every move it makes so you know it's never sneaking around behind your back. You can't turn logging off for the four behaviors on this tab, but you can control whether or not they're displayed in SoftwareValet's "Manage" section.

**Shop** Returning to the main SoftwareValet selection panel, click the top button to launch your browser and traipse over to **www.bedepot.com** to have a look at the latest BeOS software offerings. BeDepot functions like any other "shopping cart" site—you can add items to download or purchase to a list as you surf, then click any Check Out button when you're finished. Your order will be totaled for you automatically. At this writing, BeDepot's shopping cart feature is not "persistent"; it won't save items in your cart between separate visits, for instance.

 Take care to select your platform from any pop-up lists that appear before downloading, since you don't want to accidentally purchase x86 software for your PowerPC BeOS installation (or vice versa) by accident. If you do download the wrong version of an application by accident, your registration number should let you return to the site to download the correct version, though you may need to send email to BeDepot so they can grant you access.

 **If you're shopping at BeDepot from within BeOS, be sure to click the "Download with SoftwareValet" option when given a choice. This will both give you resumable download capabilities and make sure your system logs the download properly.**

*Figure 10.03*

*If you clicked "Download with SoftwareValet," you'll see a download window similar to this one. If your download is slow for some reason (due to excessive Internet traffic, for instance), just click the Defer button to pause the transfer indefinitely. Clicking Activate later will resume the download where you left off.*

When your download is complete, click the Install button to try out your new software.

 If BeDepot or the application developer sends you a message including a registration or serial number, don't delete it! You may be entitled to future updates of that application, and you'll need this number to download them without having to enter your credit card number again. This is a very important point—this email and your SoftwareValet logs are your only proof of purchase. That means that if, for example, your hard disk bites the dust and you haven't backed up your system, it may be difficult to prove that you actually purchased your software. It's not a bad idea to copy your registration and serial numbers to paper, store them in another computer, or do whatever it takes to protect your right to the software you've purchased. In addition to your regular system backups, use SoftwareValet's built-in backup feature to make a copy of your transaction logs. Of course, BeDepot will have a record of your purchase as well, but they're not set up to verify that you are who you say you are, so there are no guarantees here. Just play it safe now and you'll be all set in the event of data loss.

**Install**  When you double-click a package file you'll be launched into the SoftwareValet installation routine automatically. Alternatively, click the Install button to open a package file from a standard BeOS File panel. You should see a screen similar to the one in Figure 10.04.

Descriptive notes from the application developer occupy the upper part of the window, while the panel on the left lets you opt to install all or just part of an application. Details on the selected element appear on the right. In most cases,

Notes from the developer

Click for SoftwareValet assistance

Click to install just part of an application

Click to change installation folder

Click to change installation volume

**Figure 10.04**

*Opening a package file launches the SoftwareValet installer.*

the default installation location will be the folder you specified in SoftwareValet's Configure panel. Click on the folder pop-up to change the destination if you like, keeping in mind the applications hierarchy you may have established in Chapter 2, *Meet the System*.

Click the Begin button once you've set your preferences.

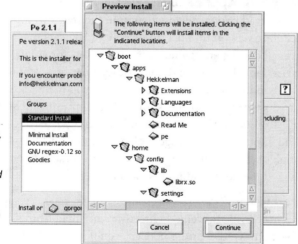

**Figure 10.05**

*After you click Begin, SoftwareValet will show you the entire hierarchy of files and folders it intends to install. Click the triangular latches to open and close folders.*

As SoftwareValet does its thing, it will check to make sure it's not overwriting any of your important files. If you're reinstalling or upgrading an application, you probably *do* want all of the existing files overwritten—with the Replace Existing radio button selected, check the "Don't ask again, use this setting" box and your old application will be overwritten with the new one. If you fear that an important file is about to be overwritten, select Rename Existing and your old file will be saved with a .bak extension so you can check it out later on.

**Manage** SoftwareValet maintains a complete record of every package file you've installed. This management panel cannot be used to add or remove software from your system. Instead, this window lets you do things like register your software or check for updates without waiting for your scheduled session to roll around

*Figure 10.06*

*Use the Manage panel to register your software, troll for updates, or remove items from SoftwareValet's application log.*

**Updating Your Applications** Select any application in your Manage list and you'll see additional details about it in the status window at the lower left, including version number, software build date, and your last installation date. Not all developers enable their applications for automated updating, but if you select one that does and SoftwareValet has been trolling for updates, the status window at the lower right will tell you if any are available. You can force SoftwareValet to check for updates immediately by pulling down Special | Troll Now. If an application has been updated and you want to download it, pull down Manage | Update. SoftwareValet will ask you for the application's serial number (you did save your serial number, didn't you?). Enter it, and the download process will begin.

**Registering Applications** In some cases, you may be supplied with a serial number by the developer directly, rather than from BeDepot. In order to be able to download future updates, you'll need to let BeDepot know that you've registered. Select the application in the Manage list, pull down Manage | Register, enter your serial number, and you're all set.

**Other Options** SoftwareValet maintains a database of all transactions and installations. It's not a bad idea to create a backup copy of this database from time to time, especially if you're not in the habit of backing up your entire system anyway. Pull down Special | Backup and choose a location (preferably on another disk volume), and your entire logged history will be duplicated for safekeeping.

***Restoring the SoftwareValet Database***  As described earlier in this section, you have two "proofs of purchase" after purchasing an application from BeDepot: the registration or serial number you receive via email, and the logs created by SoftwareValet and stored on your system. This is why it's important to use the backup feature offered by SoftwareValet, especially if you don't run regular system backups. If you should ever happen to suffer a catastrophic disk failure and need to restore your SoftwareValet logs on a fresh BeOS installation, just place them in /boot/home/config/settings/StarCode. Restart SoftwareValet, and it will be aware of all transactions made before your disk failure. Note that this directory could be renamed to /boot/home/config/settings/SoftwareValet **in the future.**

The purpose of the Reset Services button may not be immediately clear. In some instances, you may have installed an application via SoftwareValet before that application was offered on BeDepot, so BeDepot-related services may not be available in the menus. If the developer later hooks up with BeDepot, select the application and pull down Special | Reset Services to enable these options. Finally, if you installed an application with SoftwareValet and then removed it later on, there's no reason to keep it around in the SoftwareValet database. In this case, select the application in the Manage list and pull down Special | Remove. Note that this does *not* remove the application itself— you'll still need to do that through the Tracker if you haven't already.

**Download**  The Download window will appear automatically any time you begin a SoftwareValet download, but you can also access it manually by clicking the Download button on the main SoftwareValet menu. If you've previously deferred any SoftwareValet downloads due to a poor Internet connection or some other reason, you'll see them listed here along with a progress indicator showing the proportion of the transfer that was completed. The Download feature has the added advantage of letting you queue up multiple downloads simultaneously when shopping at BeDepot.

## OmicronSoft's EasyInstall/EasyDeinstall
www.omicronsoft.com

SoftwareValet isn't the only installation game in town. OmicronSoft (makers of BeRometer, below) make a competing solution, called the EasyInstall Family. Like SoftwareValet, EasyInstall consists of an archive creation tool for developers and an installation tool for users. However, OmicronSoft adds a third component to the mix: EasyDeinstall, which could finally make it possible for users to remove an application in the confidence that all ancillary files are being removed as well. At this writing, however, EasyInstall archives were not commonplace at the usual BeOS software download locations.

**Figure 10.07**

*The EasyInstall panel functions similarly to SoftwareValet's. The difference is that applications installed with EasyInstall can be completely removed from your hard drive in the future by using EasyDeInstall.*

You'll know you've encountered an EasyInstall distribution if you find an Installer icon in the application's folder after unzipping the archive. Usage is pretty intuitive. As with SoftwareValet, you can preview the files that are about to be installed, then choose a disk volume and destination folder. Once installation is complete, the newly created application folder will be opened in the Tracker, where you'll find an installation log file as well as the application files themselves. Additionally, you'll find an icon labeled EasyDeinstall. To

## What about Orphans?

When more than one application wants to share the same block of code, they draw on a shared "library," stored either in /boot/beos/system/lib (in the case of BeOS-provided libraries) or in /boot/home/config/lib (in the case of libraries added to your system by applications you've installed). But this kind of code sharing raises a small problem (not unique to BeOS): When an application is uninstalled, does it have the right to remove any libraries it may have installed? What if some other application is also using that library? Removing it would cause the other app to stop functioning. On the other hand, if you leave it on the system and no other application is using it, you become a litterbug. Over time, hard drives can get cluttered with unused (or "orphaned") libraries left behind by long-gone applications. Fortunately, the impact is minimized on BeOS by the fact that third-party libraries are always stored in the same location, rather than being scattered all over your disk.

While no perfect solution existed at this writing, BeOS's attribute-based filesystem could potentially provide a neat solution. If every application that used a given library attached its name to an attribute of that library, you'd know exactly which applications depended on it. During the uninstallation process, the list of attributes attached to a library could be checked. If the application being uninstalled was the only one on the system using that library, the library could be safely deleted.

On the surface, this scheme (which has been floating around for quite a while) sounds like a panacea. However, there are some problems with it, starting with the fact that you would need a guarantee that the user would *always* use an uninstallation utility capable of doing this (or be savvy enough to check the attributes manually, which would be asking a lot). Secondly, if the user remove the application at any point in the future, launch EasyDeinstall to scan your system's disk volumes for occurrences of the files named in the installation log. You can then review the list of found files and decide whether to move them to a new location or to the Trash.

# Tracker Add-Ons

We've talked about various kinds of add-ons quite a bit in this book. To refresh your mental cache, add-ons are modules (files) that can extend the functionality of the system. Add-ons can give BeOS the ability to read and write to alien filesystems, make the system recognize a new network, video, or sound card, or give the Tracker superpowers. Tracker add-ons are the most visible of all BeOS add-ons, as they're used directly, rather than lurking behind the scenes. Essentially, a Tracker add-on is just a BeOS application written in such a way that it can communicate with the Tracker and do interesting things with files and folders.

just dragged an application's folder to the Trash, the attribute would remain with the library, falsely reporting that the library was in use. What BeOS really needs is a utility that would crawl around on your hard disk while your system is idle, keeping a roster of which applications are using which libraries, determining which libraries are unused, and offering to delete them for you. The problem is tricky and remains unresolved.

As of this writing, there's nothing you can do to ensure you don't have any orphaned libraries on your system, but you don't have to worry. You're not going to end up with hundreds of libraries lying around (as you might in Windows), and those libraries that are on your system are well-contained in a single directory and don't take up much space.

However, libraries aren't the only thing that can get left behind when you send an app to the Trash. Poke around in your ~/config/settings directory after you've been using BeOS for a while and you're likely to find quite a few old settings files and directories named after applications you know are no longer installed on your system. If you're absolutely positive you don't need these, it is safe to delete them, but *don't* delete any settings files or folders if you're not sure what they're for—BeOS adds its own settings files to this directory structure too, and things could get pretty mucked up if you delete stuff willy-nilly. Finally, many applications create new filetypes on your system, and these filetypes can become orphaned if you delete the application that created them. It's worthwhile sifting through your FileTypes preferences panel on occasion looking for filetypes you know you no longer need, but the same warning applies: Delete only the filetypes you're sure no longer have a purpose.

It probably won't be long before an enterprising BeOS developer creates a tool that will help scout out and remove orphaned libraries, settings, and filetypes. Keep your eye on BeWare!

# System-Provided Add-Ons

Three Tracker add-ons come installed on your system, and live in
/boot/beos/system/add-ons/Tracker. All Tracker add-ons can be accessed in
two ways:

- By right-clicking in a Tracker view or on any selection of files and folders,
  then choosing Add-Ons from the context menu.

- By tapping Alt+Right Ctrl+X, where X is the last letter of the add-on's
  name. For example, the system-provided FileType add-on is actually
  named FileType-F, so you can invoke it by selecting any file and tapping
  Alt+Right Ctrl+F. To customize the hotkey associated with any add-on,
  just rename the add-on itself. Of course, technically, you're not supposed
  to be touching anything that falls under the /boot/beos hierarchy, but
  renaming these files is harmless. Just make sure that all of your Tracker
  add-ons end with a unique letter, or your hotkeys may not work as
  you expect!

**Backgrounds**   As discussed in Chapter 9, *Preferences and Customization*, you
can use any image on your system as the background for your desktop or for
your folders (though you must have a Translator installed on your system for
that image format, and folders only get backgrounds in Icon or Mini Icon
view). If you're browsing through lists of images and want to try one out on
your desktop, choose the Backgrounds add-on to pass the selected image to
the Backgrounds preferences panel.

**FileType**   If you've read Chapter 5, *Files and the Tracker*, this add-on should
need no introduction. Use it to establish the MIME type and preferred application for any single file on your system. Remember: This dialog is functionally similar to the system's FileTypes database (found in your Preferences
folder), but whereas FileTypes is used for making system-wide changes, the
FileType add-on changes only a single file at a time.

**MakeArchive**   If you traffic in .tar files (see Chapter 5), you'll appreciate
this add-on, which will create an instant .tar archive out of any selected collection of files or folders. After the add-on hums away for a few seconds,
you'll find a new file in the same directory called archive.tar, which you can
then rename to anything you wish. MakeArchive really comes in handy when
you need to make a tarball out of a large, discontiguous selection of files, since
it's much easier to select arbitrary files from within the Tracker than it is to
specify all of their names from the command line. Of course, you'll probably
want to compress your archive after it's been created, because .tar files are
only concatenated, not compressed. Fortunately, there are other add-ons available to take care of that…

# Third-Party Add-Ons

In addition to the Be-provided add-ons, you'll find a bunch of Tracker extenders written by independent developers and companies on BeWare, which has an entire category devoted to them. Store all of the add-ons you download in /boot/home/config/add-ons/Tracker.

**ZipMe**  This one does exactly what you would expect: creates a .zip archive from any selected file or folder. However, be aware that it works differently from the MakeArchive add-on described above. If you select a group of scattered files and choose the ZipMe add-on, you'll end up with just as many separate .zip files, which is probably not what you want. ZipMe is, however, extremely handy if you need to zip a single file or an entire directory. And whereas MakeArchive always names its output archive.tar, ZipMe will create archives named after the selected files. In other words, if you select your mail folder and choose the ZipMe add-on, you'll end up with an archive called mail.zip in the current directory.

**ExpandMe**  ZipMe's sister, ExpandMe, does just the opposite: decompressing .zip, .tar, or .gz archives instantly. Though not much easier than double-clicking an archive and letting Expander do its thing, you may appreciate being able to decompress files with an add-on hotkey.

**TermHire and ShellMe**  If you use the Terminal often, TermHire could quickly become one of your most-used add-ons. When you launch the Terminal normally, the current directory defaults to /boot/home. When you launch the Terminal via the TermHire add-on, however, the current directory will be the same as the folder you were just viewing in the Tracker. If you just need to drop into the shell to take care of some quick business, this can save you from having to cd to a new location. Just tap those hotkeys and you're in.

If you'd like to get a little fancier, download ShellMe, which lets you run any Terminal command using the selected file(s) or directory(s) as arguments. For example, you might want to view a text file with the shell's more command, rather than with StyledEdit. When you invoke ShellMe, it checks in a special configuration file to see which Terminal commands you've established as your favorites. Any commands you've placed in the configuration file then show up on a floating context menu. Select a command from the menu, and the files you selected in the Tracker will be passed to that command. At the time, many of ShellMe's functions weren't enabled in the version we tested, but theoretically, you should be able to invoke customized shell commands of almost unlimited complexity directly from the Tracker.

**Reveal Original**  Every so often you'll find yourself looking at a symlink and needing to find where its target lives. Clicking a symlink launches the program or file it points to, so that doesn't do you any good. Right-click a symlink and choose the Reveal Original add-on, however, and the folder hosting the target file will be opened in the Tracker.

**MakeThumbnail**   As described in Chapter 13, *Graphics Applications*, MakeThumbnail will examine any image file for which you have a Translator installed and make two tiny versions of it. These thumbnail-sized images will then be stuffed into the file's large and small icon attributes, so that your image files' icons will appear as tiny versions of the actual image. Make-Thumbnail also grabs each image's height and width, so you can determine its dimensions directly from the Tracker without even launching the image. This add-on simply invokes the MakeThumbnail application and passes on the selected file names.

**TrackerGrep**   BeOS queries are amazing, but they lack one important function: the ability to scan through your files for a given text string. You can, of course, do that from the command line with the Unix grep tool, but if that's not your cup of tea, the TrackerGrep add-on provides a graphical interface with grep. Right-click any text file or folder containing text files, choose the TrackerGrep add-on, and a window will appear into which you can enter your search string. You will, however, still have to escape your special characters. grep usage is covered in more depth in Chapter 6, *The Terminal*.

**SetPerms**   As discussed in Chapter 5, BeOS will one day be a multiuser operating system and will use Unix-style file permissions to guarantee that the creator of a given file has control over who gets to view, edit, or execute that file. In preparation for that great day, BeOS already lets you set permis-

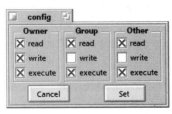

**Figure 10.08**

No need to open a Terminal window or bother with chmod; SetPerms lets you establish file permissions directly from the Tracker.

sions on files. In fact, some files that ship with the system are already write-protected, to prevent users from accidentally editing them. If you'd prefer not to use the chmod command to edit file permissions when you need to do so, Chris Herborth's SetPerms will let you establish them by simply checking or unchecking boxes in a small window. Select a file and choose the SetPerms add-on and you'll get a dialog like the one in Figure 10.08.

**Mailto**   There are actually two Mailto add-ons available: one for BeatWare's Mail-It and one for Adamation's Adam (both are covered in Chapter 11, *Network Applications*). Both add-ons serve the same function: select a file, choose the Mailto add-on, and the appropriate email client will be launched with a new open message that has your selected file already attached as an enclosure. You won't find these add-ons on BeWare; they're installed automatically when you install Adam or Mail-It.

# Backup Tools

Nothing can ruin your day like losing years' worth of precious data. Even a robust filesystem like BFS can't save you if your physical disk mechanism decides to head south at the worst possible moment. And then there are accidents—just about everyone has at one time or another sent the wrong file to the Trash in a moment of inattention, then emptied the Trash before realizing their mistake. Stuff happens. Your best hedge against data disaster is, as always, a good backup plan. While the zip archiving utility that ships with BeOS is fully capable of reliably creating and storing exact images of your filesystem (or any subsection thereof), many people will appreciate the advanced, backup-specific features offered by third-party tools. These BeOS backup applications give you a graphical application in which to work, make it easy to base your backups on queries, and offer point-and-click restoration options.

## Bald Mountain's BeB  *with Geoffrey Clements*
**www.bald-mountain.com**

Whereas backup systems on other operating systems typically restrict you to either backing up entire directory structures or hand-picking all of your files, the BeOS query engine lets applications transcend directory structures, and think about data in terms of its role instead (for example, "Don't show me the text files sitting in /boot/home—I want to see all of the Person files for people living in Kentucky, regardless where they're stored."). This capability lends amazing powers to BeOS applications that choose to take advantage of it. BeB lets you select files for backup by creating queries.

BeB can store backup data in a specific file, on a device like a Zip or Jaz drive, or on tape. BeB can be configured to back up your file selections automatically at preestablished times, can run verification passes to guarantee data integrity,

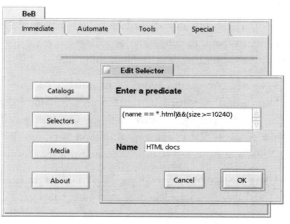

*Figure 10.09*

*BeB's four-tabbed interface lets you move easily between the program's functions. Establish selectors (queries), media types, and catalog names from the Special tab, then switch to the Immediate tab to begin your backup. Pictured: setting up a system backup of all HTML documents larger than 10K.*

and can of course compress your files, either with zlib or with native methods on supporting media.

**Getting Started with BeB**  To start a backup, you need to specify three things: a selector, media to back up to, and a catalog. We'll look at each of these in turn.

Selector is the term BeB uses to refer to BeOS queries, since in this context they're used not just to find files, but to select them for backup. A predicate is a part of a selector, such as the bit specifying a particular attribute field. BeB selectors are created with the formula query syntax covered in Chapter 7, *Working with Queries*. Select the Special tab and click the Selectors button. From this panel, you can either edit an existing Selector or create a new one. The default selector, "all files", contains the predicate "name == **", which will back up all files on a given volume.

 Selector predicates can be very powerful—take another look at Chapter 7, *Working with Queries* (especially the section on formula queries) to get some idea of the kinds of file collections you can gather up with carefully crafted queries. Remember that every query must include at least one indexed attribute, so if you're using very basic predicates, the attributes they refer to must be in your system's index. Again, see Chapter 7 for more on the system index. Keep in mind that a newly formatted BFS volume is indexed only on filename and modification date.

Next, click the Media button to tell BeB whether you'll be backing up to a file, to a device, or to tape. You'll also need to specify a destination for the backup. If you're backing up to a file, click the Location button and use the File panel to create a filename for your backup. If you're backing up to a device or tape drive, use the provided menus to select a storage unit.

Finally, you'll need to create a catalog, which is a combined selector, media type, and destination volume. Choose one of each and give your catalog a name.

 Actual backup events are stored with filenames that combine the date and the catalog name, so they can get pretty long. Keep your catalog names on the short side, if possible (less than 10 characters).

Once you've created a catalog, you can initiate the backup by clicking the Backup button on the Immediate tab. Choose a catalog from the list and click OK. If you want to change options, click the Options button. The backup will begin and a progress dialog will appear. If necessary, use the Pause or Cancel buttons. Paused or canceled backups can be resumed by clicking Restart.

**Automating Backups**  If you'd like BeB to do its thing in the middle of the night, establish a backup schedule from the Automate tab. Simply associate existing catalogs with timed events and you'll be able go on vacation without any lingering anxiety about the security of your data. Don't forget to enable the "Perform backups automatically" checkbox, or your scheduled backups will never happen!

Conveniently, BeB doesn't need to be running for automatic backups to occur. BeB includes a small daemon called BeBDaemon, which will automatically launch BeB if it's not running when it's time to do a backup. You may want to launch the BeBDaemon from your UserBootScript. You can also start or restart the BeBDaemon from the Tools tab.

**Incremental Backups**   Once you've created a full backup, there's no need to back up the same files every time—you only want to back up new or modified files. To create incremental backups, just modify your selector predicate like this:

```
((predicate) && (last_modified > "date of last backup"))
```

where "predicate" is your usual selector predicate. Aren't queries awesome?

**Restoring Backups**   If you accidentally delete a critical folder from your machine and need to bring it back from beyond the grave, you've got no reason to worry. If you've been using BeB all along, just launch it, click the Immediate tab, and then click Restore. From there you'll be able to choose a catalog and a particular backup event (remember: a catalog is a combined selector, media type, and destination volume; a backup event is an actual instance of a particular catalog having been run). If you've been making incremental backups, you may need to restore multiple events in order to get back all of your data. Note that you can select individual files from the file list for each event. If for some reason you don't want to replace everything, you can control exactly what gets replaced and what gets left behind. Finally, use the BeOS File panel to select a destination to which you want to restore. Naturally, you can choose to restore to a location other than the original source.

**Recovering from Disasters**   The restoration instructions above assume that BeB's database files are still intact on the boot volume. If something bad has happened and this is not the case, you'll need to rebuild them. Begin by creating a media item describing the location of the backup information. There is enough information in the backup data to rebuild the Catalog databases. Now go to the Tools tab and click Repair. You'll be presented with a list of media items; choose the item that describes the location of the backup data for which you need a new catalog. A progress dialog will indicate that file information and backup events have been found, including events that are in the process of being turned into catalog databases. Once the repair is complete, you should have backup databases capable of generating complete restorations.

## OmicronSoft Restorer *with John Tegen*

**www.omicronsoft.com**

OmicronSoft's Restorer gives you seemingly unlimited flexibility in establishing the parameters of both automated and manual backup and restoration procedures. Restorer is based on the concept of SaveSets, which are collections of files that match custom criteria and can be associated with a backup schedule. You can, for example, tell Restorer to back up all files once a month with a type of `text/plain` that don't reside within your `~/config/settings` directory. Or you can build a SaveSet to back up files ending in ".h" and living under the `/boot/develop/projects` folder, excluding those found in a folder named `OLD`, every other Friday. You can create as many SaveSets as you like and schedule your sets to run whenever you please.

Restorer provides two primary services: backing up files to a designated volume, and restoring selected files to a designated folder. Accordingly, Restorer's interface includes Backup and Restore tabs—the "meat" of the program. In addition, a Log tab lets you control whether Restorer keeps detailed reports on its activity. The Backup tab displays each of your named SaveSets alongside its next scheduled backup run. The third tab in the Restorer window lets you view a log of all Restorer transactions. The transaction log lists when a SaveSet was run, any problems that may have occurred, and any files that have been restored.

**Creating SaveSets** Restorer ships with several sample SaveSets that you can use directly or edit to suit your needs.

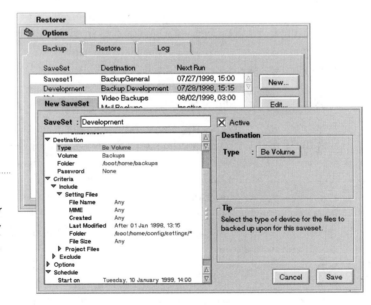

*Figure 10.10*

*Restorer's Backup tab serves as an interface with your library of SaveSets, and lets you see at a glance when the next backup run is scheduled to take place.*

Click the New button and the SaveSet editor window will appear. From here you can give the set a name, establish the destination of the archived files, and define a backup schedule for this SaveSet. You might, for example, tell Restorer to back up all of the HTML and JPEG documents on your system next Thursday at 1:00 P.M., and to repeat that backup every week thereafter.

SaveSets let you build both *inclusive* and *exclusive* filters. In a nutshell, inclusive filters specify which files will be archived and exclusive filters subtract from that set files that match certain criteria. For example, you could build a filter to find all Person files (inclusive) except those that start with the letter "J" (exclusive).

**Restorer lets you specify how many different versions of the same file will be maintained in an archive. If you tell a SaveSet to back up your docs directory every day for five days, you can restore a document to the way it was, say, three days ago, before you introduced that horrendous math or spelling error, for instance.**

If you can't wait for a particular SaveSet's scheduled run to roll around, just select its name and press Run.

**Restoring from Backups** Let's say a few days have gone by since your last backup, and you've just discovered that you accidentally deleted an essential file. No need to panic—you've got Restorer! Click the Restore tab and you'll be looking at a list of all of your SaveSets. If you think you know which SaveSet contains the file you need, you can go straight to it and locate your file manually. Alternatively, you can run a Find that traverses the SaveSet collection. Once you've located your file, select it and click Restore. You'll be prompted to select a destination, and your file will be returned to its rightful home. You may now return to your normally scheduled daily activities. Your day wasn't ruined after all!

*Figure 10.11*

*Browse through individual SaveSets for needed files or search the entire collection. Either way, you're going to get your file back. Don't panic!*

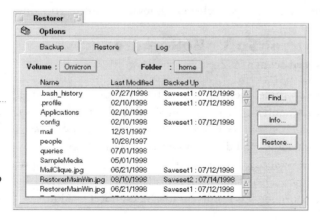

# Benchmarking

So you've got this ultra-high-performance operating system loaded onto your machine. You know it's fast because you can feel it trembling beneath your fingertips. But if you're looking for real numbers (i.e. bragging rights), then you need to be able to quantify your machine's performance. Benchmarking tools use a standard (well, sort of) set of tests that can be run on various machines to find out exactly how well those machines' subsystems stack up against one another. This, in turn, can potentially help you determine how much you stand to gain by doubling your RAM, buying a faster video card, or opting for a motherboard with a faster frontside bus.

 All benchmarking tools come with big caveats. Every system is a collection of variables, and even though benchmark tests try to isolate those variables, subsystems still affect one another. But more importantly, no benchmark result can tell you how a machine *feels*. It's all about responsiveness. In addition, many differences that are measurable in raw numbers are nevertheless imperceptible to humans. Don't let benchmarks fool you into thinking that you *need* some piece of new hardware. The only time you need new hardware is when you can detect a perceptible slowdown in some task, or overall system sluggishness.

The point is, benchmarks strive for objectivity, while your relationship with your computer is subjective. The exception to this rule is when you need your machine to perform extremely computation-intensive tasks, like raytracing or applying effects to digital video footage. Two machines that feel equally responsive under a normal workday load may perform very differently when asked to generate a zillion polygons in two minutes. Speed in cases like that can mean the difference between continuing to work or having to go to lunch while waiting for your chrome dinosaur to finish rendering.

## OmicronSoft's BeRometer
**www.omicronsoft.com**

At this writing, the only full-featured benchmarking suite for BeOS was OmicronSoft's BeRometer, which is a collection of tests that stress your machine's graphics and memory-management capabilities, floating-point computations, and disk input/output speeds. After running the test suite, you can compare your machine's accomplishments to those of other BeOS machines. This comparison is made possible by the fact that BeRometer offers to ship your results off to OmicronSoft headquarters, which in turn

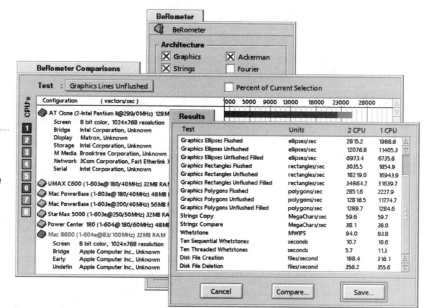

*Figure 10.12*

*BeRometer runs a suite of resource-intensive tests on your machine, then lets you see how your computer stacks up against other machines running the same tests on the same operating system.*

bundles unique results into the mini-database that ships with future versions of the program. Interestingly, you can even compare how PowerPC machines fare against Intel machines on identical tasks on an identical operating system, which may amount to one of the fairest PowerPC-versus-Intel contests available anywhere. Download a copy and check it out for yourself.

Read BeRometer's documentation to learn more about its test suite, then select the particular tests you want to run. Before you begin the test, make sure your Screen preferences are set to 1024×768, 8-bit, so that all graphics measurements can be equalized against other machines. Naturally, you'll want to turn off any CPU- or disk-consumptive applications or background processes so as to not cripple yourself unnecessarily. Pull down BeRometer | Test and sit back—you'll see some pretty psychedelic stuff as the graphics tests are run, and some pretty boring stuff as the disk tests execute. When the tests have been completed, click the Compare button to start wading through charts. Use the picklist at the top of the Charts window to navigate through the various tests. Note that you can click on any machine's icon to get more details on its hardware.

When you're done studying, click the Save button to have your results zipped up and emailed to OmicronSoft HQ.

# Launchers

The Be menu provides an excellent mechanism for organizing and accessing your most-used applications and keeping piles of icons off your desktop, but it has one disadvantage: you have to scroll down through menus to get to your applications. Not a big deal, but sometimes it's nice to have instant access to your favorite apps without having to go hunting for their icons. Application and document launchers take two forms: floating palettes that let you store symlinks to your most frequently accessed files, and hotkey managers that let you assign system-wide keyboard shortcuts to any application or document.

## DepositIt

`wwwusers.imaginet.tr/~1cook`

Laurent Cook's DepositIt is just one of many "launchpad" utilities available for BeOS designed to address just this need, but while each of the BeOS launchers has its advantages, DepositIt is by far the most customizable and configurable of the lot. DepositIt works by storing symlinks to your favorite applications or documents in a compact, multilayered interface (which it calls a "document"). You can have as many documents open as you like, though chances are one will be plenty. Within each document, you can gather groups of icons into layers.

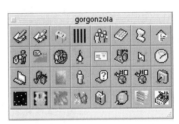

**Figure 10.13**

*In one of its most basic and compact configurations, DepositIt provides a simple grid of mini-icons. A single click launches the associated application.*

 **To get DepositIt out of the way quickly, double-click its title tab to reduce it to a thin strip. MacOS users will find this behavior familiar.**

To begin configuring DepositIt, drag application icons or symlinks onto cells in DepositIt's default grid. Even though you won't find a File menu in the interface, you'll still need to save your work, either by right-clicking on the grid and choosing DepositIt | Save Now, or by closing DepositIt and clicking Save.

For maximum flexibility when storing dozens of links, DepositIt lets you either resize the grid to any dimensions or create additional "layers," which work like folder tabs. You might create one layer for each of several main application categories—one for network applications, another for productivity tools, and a third for system preferences, for example. Icons can be dragged from one cell to another—or even between layers—by holding down the left Win key (Mac users: Option key) while dragging.

There's no reason to limit yourself to storing application links in DeposIt— you can just as easily drag documents, images, sounds, or any other file to a DeposIt cell, rather than crowding your desktop with files and symlinks. If you run out of space on a DeposIt grid or find it too large, it can be resized by dragging the tiny (almost invisible) gripper dots at its lower-right corner. Note that you must have the footer bar enabled through the global preferences panel in order to do this.

If you move the target of a symlink in BeOS, the link will break. The fragility of symlinks affects DeposIt just as it does the Tracker. If you move an application from its original location, its icon in DeposIt will appear with a red slash through it, indicating that the link no longer works. To fix a broken link, right-click the icon and choose Remove, then replace the link normally.

**Figure 10.14**

Another of DepositIt's practically unlimited number of configurations

**Customizations**   There's virtually no aspect of DepositIt that isn't customizable. Icon cells can be displayed in any of four sizes; header and footer tabs can be turned on and off; grid layers can be any color; grid tabs can be situated on any of DepositIt's four sides (and can have either text or icon labels); and the list goes on. Study DepositIt's documentation for examples of the many configuration possibilities. Customizations are accessed from two separate control panels: one for DepositIt's appearance and behavior in general; and one specific to the currently selected layer. To access the customization panels, right-click anywhere in DepositIt's interface and a context menu will appear. Select Layer | Preferences to make changes to the current layer, or DepositIt | Preferences to make global changes.

**Preferences**   You can specify from the Document field whether your DepositIt document appears with or without title and footer bars, and with or without a customized title in the title bar. Remember to press Enter after typing in a title, or your changes won't stick. In the Layer field, choose Multiple only if you need more than one category—layer tabs take up space needlessly if you use only one layer, and the interface appears cleaner without them. The Workspaces field provides an option that more BeOS applications should consider implementing: the ability to appear in all workspaces, so DepositIt is always there when you need it.

**Layer Preferences**   The Index Position field refers to the position of the title tab for the current layer—select one of the radio buttons to send the tab to the top, bottom, left, or right side of DepositIt's interface. From the Index Type field you can control whether the current tab uses text for a label or an icon. Drag any icon onto the tab to set its picture. Choosing Adaptable in the Index Behavior section will let the tab's width automatically adjust to fit with the other tabs. The Cell Type field lets you establish the cell size for your icons, which means you can use different cell sizes on different layers if you like! The Color Background field is self-explanatory, but the Comment Type field is not.

This refers to the message that will be displayed in DeposIt's footer bar as you roll over your icons—you have the option to display the application's actual name, the path to which the symlink points, or nothing at all. You'll probably find Name the most useful choice here.

**All of your customizations are written to preferences files in your** /boot/home/ config/settings/DeposIt **folder. If you ever want an easy way to start over from scratch, just delete this file and relaunch DeposIt—you'll be back to square one. If you'd like to have more than one DeposIt window open at once, create multiple document configurations by right-clicking a grid and choosing DeposIt | New Document from the pop-up menu. The next time it launches, DeposIt will launch one window for each configuration file found.**

## Hit&Run
`www.algonet.se/~taiken/kaktus`

Since your hands are almost always on the keyboard, the fastest way to launch any application or document is by punching a quick key combination. Hit&Run runs in the background as a daemon, waiting to intercept keystrokes you've associated with applications or documents. Set up your system to launch Hit&Run daemon at boot time so it'll always be there, lurking in the background.

**Configuration** The Hit&Run Preferences panel is launched in a slightly unorthodox way. Because the application normally runs in the background, double-clicking the Hit&Run icon appears to do nothing at all. However, if you double-click the icon a second time, a Preferences panel will be launched from which you can establish your hotkeys. Once the daemon is running, you can always invoke the Preferences panel by tapping Ctrl+F12.

*Figure 10.15*

*Establish a hotkey combination and drag any application, symlink, or document into Hit&Run's Preferences panel.*

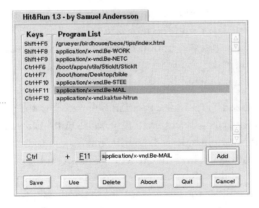

Configuring Hit&Run is pretty intuitive. Use the modifier and hotkey picklists at the bottom of the panel to choose a unique key combination, then drag any application, symlink, or document into the text field. If you've dragged an application or a link to an application, its signature will appear in this field (see Chapter 5 for more on app_sigs). Since signatures are being used rather than paths, you can move applications around on your hard drive later without breaking your Hit&Run associations. If you drag a file or folder into the panel, its path will be displayed instead (remember: only applications have signatures). You can, of course, type a path directly into the field. Click the Save button and the Preferences panel will disappear. You can then test your new hotkey. Note that Hit&Run hotkeys are truly system-wide—regardless of the application or workspace.

**What to Launch?**  So what kinds of things make for good Hit&Run hotkeys? The sky's the limit, but you may find it handy to be able to start a new BeMail message from anywhere with a quick keypress, or to launch a new StyledEdit document for quick note-taking, or to launch the folder where you store a current project. The Workspaces preferences panel is also nice to have within close reach.

After you've got Hit&Run configured to suit your needs, you'll want to start launching it from ~/config/boot/UserBootScript, so it'll always be there when you need it. Something like:

```
/boot/apps/utils/HitRun/HitRun &
```

would work nicely. You'll probably find that the hardest thing about using Hit&Run is trying to remember all of your new hotkeys.

Note: For another excellent system-wide hotkey management option, download SpicyKeys from BeWare.

# System Monitors

If you like to keep a close eye on every last aspect of your system, you'll find dozens of tools on BeWare that let you put your machine under the microscope. There are utilities to help you monitor your available memory, control all running threads, keep an eye on remaining disk space, watch your processor(s) toiling, and so on. Here are a few exemplary tools that you can use to monitor your system's status.

## SysR

If you're a detail-oriented person for whom too much information is never enough, you'll want to download one of the combination system-probe/thread-management tools, such as Roberto Attias's SysR (previously known as SysInfo). While some of SysR's functionality is now subsumed by the

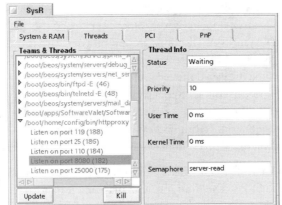

**Figure 10.16**

*SysR packs a system and memory monitor, thread-management tool, and hardware probe into a four-tabbed interface.*

Devices preferences panel in R4, it still packs a ton of data into a compact interface. In fact, you really get three applications in one.

The first tab lets you know what platform you're running on (in case you somehow forgot), the speed of your system bus, the build date of your BeOS kernel, and the amount of memory installed and currently in use.

There is simply no such thing as an accurate measurement of free versus used memory in BeOS. Because of the way the BeOS memory model is architected, the system will take gobs of memory for itself, which tends to make some people wonder why this modern, unbloated system should be such a memory hog. In fact, BeOS is using memory to do just what it's supposed to do—minimize the necessity of scooping data off your disk, which is an inherently slow task. There are several other reasons why memory readings in BeOS are misleading as well. You can read all about those in Chapter 6, but for now, just keep in mind that you'll never get useful information out of tools claiming to be BeOS memory monitors.

SysR's second tab provides a full-featured thread- and team-management system. Thread management is discussed in detail in Chapter 16, *Troubleshooting and Maintenance*, but the short version is this: If an application appears to crash—that is, if an application dies but still hangs on in the Deskbar—you may have to manually kill off remaining threads in its team, either from the Terminal or with a tool like SysR. Select the problem team's name from the hierarchical list and press the Kill button. If that doesn't do it, you're probably going to have to reboot—a clinging ghost thread can impact your machine's performance, leave half-drawn windows hanging in your face, and have other unpleasant side effects. If it happens frequently with the same application, write to the developer and let him or her know.

### *What's Your Uptime?*

Many people take great pride in the number of days, weeks, or months since their computer was last rebooted. The stability of an operating system is a badge of pride for its owner. However, if you're running a multi-boot system, there's a good chance that you'll need to restart your machine long before it crashes, just to get to that old DOS app from which you still haven't weaned yourself. Regardless, there's something satisfying about discovering that your BeOS machine has been running nonstop for three and a half months. There are two ways to discover your uptime in BeOS. One is to download the uptime command-line utility from BeWare. Drop it in /boot/home/config/bin and type uptime at the command line for a report. The other way is even easier: Pull down the Be menu and select About BeOS. The system information panel will tell you what hardware you're running on, the kernel and operating system versions, and your uptime.

The PCI and PnP tabs simply display details about hardware devices attached to your system. Interesting, but you'll get even more data from the Devices preferences panel.

 **For a system monitor with a twist, give Attila Lendvai's SyX a try. Primarily a CPU and memory usage monitor, SyX takes a different approach by representing this data graphically and mapping it over time, so you can see how your resource usage dips and falls as you put your machine through its paces. You might say that SyX is sort of a cross between Be's Pulse application and SysR, but way more configurable than either.**

## freeSpace

You don't need a third-party utility to find out how much space is left on a given disk volume; you can always right-click a volume icon and choose Get Info, or type df into any Terminal window. But if you'd like to see a handsome, resizable representation of the free and remaining space on all of your mounted volumes at once, grab a copy of Bob Maple's freeSpace from BeWare. Each mounted BeOS volume gets a histogram (bar chart) all to itself. Each bar is colored to indicate how close to capacity it is at any given moment:

- **Green:** Volume is less than 60% full.
- **Blue:** Volume is 60–80% full.
- **Yellow:** Volume is 80–95% full.
- **Red:** Volume is more than 95% full.

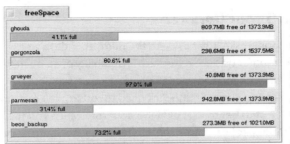

**Figure 10.17**

*freeSpace represents the amount of space remaining on each of your mounted volumes with color-coded bars. Drag some huge files around and watch the bars update themselves in real time.*

If you find yourself copying huge files around frequently, you might want to keep freeSpace open in the background so you can see whether you're pushing your disk volumes' limits. I like to run it when creating backups—those 200MB archives can chew up a volume pretty fast.

If you like freeSpace but are looking for something a little *less* colorful, check out Scott Tadman's Drive Watcher, a similar utility with a more compact, businesslike interface.

## *Dominic Giampaolo*
*Software Engineer / Kernel Engineer*
*Responsible for the BeOS file system and disk cache*
*Interviewed by Henry Bortman*

**HB:** *Tell me about the filesystem. What were your goals in writing it?*

**DG:** The original goals were to make it fast, because everything about BeOS is about performance, and to make it 64-bit capable, and to have journaling as well as to support attributes and indexing.

**HB:** *Let's go through those. For a user, what difference does a 64-bit filesystem make?*

**DG:** 64-bit is interesting for a filesystem because it allows you to have very large file sizes and very large disks. So there is no limitation on whether or not your disk is over 2 gigabytes or 4 gigabytes or, these days, 18 or 36 gig. You know you just can use it. Because $2^{64}$ is such a large number—it's enough to hold 900 years of uncompressed video at 30 frames a second. So it's pretty big, not something that we are going to run into a limit there anytime soon. So that's the idea, that people who are doing video and audio editing can run into very large files—two minutes of uncompressed video is already over 4 gig—and you don't want to be hampered by the OS.

**HB:** *And what's journaling?*

**DG:** Journaling is a way to protect the disk data structure. So there is user data—you know, the files and the things that you have written to them—and then there is the structure that the filesystem keeps on the disk to allow it to find things and to know where the data is for a file and to know what files are in what directory. That's known as the meta data, the information about the files on the disk.

Journaling protects that data so that even if you crash, you don't have a corrupt data structure on disk. So there is no rebuilding the desktop database, there is no FSCK that has to be run when you reboot—that's a Unix File System Check program—you know Windows has Scan Disk, whatever—none of that stuff is really necessary.

Journaling is a technique that was borrowed from the database community that made its way into a few filesystems. A number of advanced versions of Unix have journaling filesystems, and NTFS has journaling as well. The biggest thing about it is that it can actually improve performance over non-journaling file systems. It allows you to boot very quickly because you don't have to sit there and scan the disk to make sure that it is OK, you can just assume that it is correct.

**HB:** *How does it work?*

**DG:** It sounds like magic but is not really. Basically you commit the changes to one area of the disk first, and then you allow them to be written to their normal place on disk. By having committed them first to this one location, if anything happens and all the changes haven't been written to the real location you can just play back the journal entry. So, let's say you create a file that creates a journal entry. Until that journal entry is written, the file is not considered to be added to the directory. Once that's written to disk safely, then if you crash and the other disk data structures haven't been updated properly, you simply replay that journal entry, which tells you go modify this piece, this piece, and this piece and the file will be created.

## Dominic Giampaolo (continued)

**HB:** *How does that improve performance?*

**DG:** The reason that it can improve performance is because you can batch changes and write them once to the journal. A traditional filesystem has to write things synchronously. So it says, "I'm going to change this directory block," and has to write it and wait for it to complete and then it says, "I'm going to add this piece over here," and has to write it and wait for it to complete, and that can be very slow because disks are not particularly fast relative to the speed of the computer. What disks are good at is writing big chunks of data. There is really almost no difference between writing out 100K and 1K—well, a little bit, but not very much. So that's the idea, to take advantage of bulk transfers.

**HB:** *You also mentioned attributes and indexing as things that are unique to the BeOS filesystem.*

**DG:** Well, the combination is unique. Attributes on files have sort of existed in various forms on different systems. An attribute on a file is like a name, you can have a file that represents an image, you can have a GIF image in it or a JPEG image in it, and you can have an attribute about it that has, for example, the dimensions of the image. Or who the photographer was. And that's information that may not have a mechanism to be stored in the file but you can attach it to the file.

So these attributes are just information about the file. Now the unique thing about the BeOS is that we also index them. Other systems support attributes: HPSS on OS/2 and NTFS, although they are not heavily used. But we also index them so you can say, "Show me all the photos taken by Galen Rowell or Ansel Adams."

Email has attributes such as who it's from, the subject, when it was received, and when it was sent. So you can say, "Show me all mail from Jean-Louis Gassée received in the last week." So that is an example of combining attributes and indexing. The filesystem maintains these things automatically so the programmer doesn't have to do very much to take advantage of them.

Then, in addition, we index three integral attributes for all files: name, size, and last modified time. So the query "Show me all files whose name is 'main.c'" is extremely fast to answer no matter how many files are on the disk; it is a very directed search.

**HB:** *What are some of the other interesting ways you've seen attributes used?*

**DG:** People are associating things like a last backup time with a file, so that way you can have a backup program which can tag a file that has been archived or something like that. There is the People database that we ship. People files are just files in parentheses. It is more just an entity, a named entity, and then you can have attributes for their email address, their phone number, their Web address. And different programs in the BeOS take advantage of that. If you drag a Person onto an email program it will know that you are attempting to send something to their email address. If you have a fax program and you drag a Person to it you will send a fax to their fax number. So it is kinda this nice system with wide integration of a lot of features that otherwise would be put in separate programs and have duplicated functionality.

**HB:** *Are you still working on the filesystem now, or are you doing something else?*

**DG:** There is always maintenance and bug fixes and certain corner cases that didn't work so well. The testing group is fairly devious and comes up with good test cases. You know one time they came to me and said, "Well, I added three million attributes to a file, and when I deleted it the system hung." Well, OK, sure, that is a problem. So you have to look at things like that.

**HB:** *Keep it under three million?*

**DG:** Yeah, put it in the docs.

**HB:** *A lot of what you do is stuff that users never see directly. Does that bother you at all? Do you wish that you could point to the screen and say, "I did that"?*

**DG:** I guess that I make up for that in other ways. Like the directory structure of the BeOS, where everything is laid out. I was a motivating force behind that layout. There was quite a bit of discussion behind that the scenes with quite a number of people. But I really pushed for a lot of things. There is also some gratification in knowing that every time you do anything there is some piece of your code that is being executed. When you work on the depths of stuff, you know that whenever the mouse moves it goes through some piece of code that I've touched, whenever you type a key it goes through something that I've done or worked on. I think in general kernel people feel that way. If it wasn't for the kernel people nothing else would take place. Not that it is better than anything else, it's just that your satisfaction comes from different things.

**HB:** *What were you doing before you came to Be?*

**DG:** I worked at Silicon Graphics in the Advanced Systems Division. I was there for just over two years. It was my first job just out of college. I worked on the Reality Engine and Infinite Reality products, which are their top-end graphics systems. I did the bring-up of the Reality Engine on the R8000 processor.

**HB:** *Was that 3D stuff?*

**DG:** Oh yeah! This is monster 3D stuff. It was stuff that would cost in the $100K to million-dollar range, depending on how you configure it. It was big iron, and it was pretty fun, I mean I liked working with high-end computer systems. There was something pleasing about booting up a machine with 16 processors and 16 gigabytes of memory—not disk space, memory! That's kinda fun stuff to work on. And you know, making all of that work.

It was also the first 64-bit implementation of IRIX, and so there was a lot of work that had to be done there. I didn't work directly on the kernel so much, but there were a lot of bugs and processor bugs and chip bugs that had to be tracked down. That it was part of a bring-up was kind of fun too. That was more immediate feedback too, because when you work on a graphics system you get to see cool stuff in the end. And when you are done, you've got all kinds of millions of polygons, texture maps flying around on the screen.

**HB:** *So there you are at Silicon Graphics. How did you hear about Be and how did you end up coming here?*

**DG:** At poker one night. I play poker with a bunch of guys on Thursday nights. And one of them showed up, and he had these printouts from the Web, and he said, "Oh you have to see this.

### Dominic Giampaolo *(continued)*

There is this cool company called Be, and they have this box that is dual processor." And, you know, just poring over the data sheets and looking over the Web site I was just sold instantly. I mean it was like—this is cool.

**HB:** *But that was just two processors when you were working on 16. What was the draw?*

**DG:** The draw was that it was something that your friends might actually buy. Nobody that I know is going to be buying a 16-processor box anytime soon. It was kind of neat being at Silicon Graphics, and I could say that I helped fix bugs so they could get movie *Speed* done, but who really cares?

**HB:** *Did you help fix bugs so they could get movie* Speed *done?*

**DG:** Yeah, there was this one time, that was sort of where I got a feather in my cap at SGI. Because there is a company called Discrete Logic that has a video production system called "Flame," which is used in all of the post-production houses in L.A. And the systems were crashing every two or three hours. They didn't have a journaled filesystem and they had huge amounts of disk and it was taking them an hour to come back up. So it was like you would work for two hours and then rest for an hour while it came back up.

That was unacceptable to them. So the Discrete Logic people came and said, We need to get this bug fixed. And I made the mistake of saying I won't leave until it's fixed. And three days later I went home. But the systems were a lot more stable and they were able to get their work done. And everyone was a lot happier.

When I interviewed at SGI I interviewed with a guy, Mark Stadler, and when I was brought into his office the guy who was hosting me for the interview said, "This is Mark, he's the guy that we take problems to when the machine runs seven hours and then crashes." In my mind I said that is what I want to do—I want to be that guy.

Mark was more than happy to let me take over that stuff, and so I got a reputation for being able to fix the really hard bugs. The difficult MP-related issues where you have race conditions measured in nanoseconds. There was one that was like something bad would happen but there was only like a 12-nanosecond window of time when it could happen, and you had to be on an 8-processor system. Those are juicy problems and it takes a lot of time to figure them out and it really takes a lot of thinking. It's like a puzzle and you figure it out and you make sense of it. And you understand what's going on and you make it better, so that's pretty fun.

**HB:** *Okay, then what was it about Be that was even more appealing?*

**DG:** You could actually change more about the system. Sure, while it is interesting to fix bugs and all that, it's also kind of fun to have an influence over the direction of the system. There is a phase that every computer science student goes through where you say, "I'm going to write an OS."

You sit down, you get out the low-level data books and you start trying to muck about with it, and at some point into it you realize, Wow, this is really hard. And it is, to do it completely from scratch. I mean in grad school I thought I was going to do the whole OS from scratch in like six months and have a window system and everything.

It's not quite that easy. At some point you scale back. I mean, sure a lot of people write their own little kernel that has some amount of functionality. And I had done that on my Amiga just as a side project and it was sort of fun—you could context-switch and you had two little threads printing things to the screen and it was cool—but it takes a lot more than that to do a real system.

And so it's fun to work on something that is nascent, you know, that's just emerging, and to have an influence over the direction of it. And that was really the draw to come and do real kernel work. You get tired of just reading OS papers about other people doing it. You want do some of your own.

**HB:** *So actually you didn't write a paper, you wrote a book?*

**DG:** I did write a book about the Be filesystem. *Practical File System Design With The Be File System* [Morgan Kaufman Publishers, 1998] I think is what we settled on and that will be out this November. That was a big project, but it was a lot of fun basically documenting the design decisions that were made, the choices that people have, what the issues are that you have when building a filesystem. There is no right way. It's not like I could say BFS is the ideal file system, because it depends on the problem that you are trying to solve.

You know, people have to write filesystems for the Nintendo 64—well, I don't know about the Nintendo 64, but for a plug-in flash ROM cartridge that is rewriteable. In fact the 3DO box actually has a journaled filesystem that works on the user card that can be put in, because it can be ejected at any time, and we have the same problem. But of course they don't have attributes or indexing because that is not interesting to them. So it's sort of like, what is the problem that you are trying to solve. If you have a mainframe database system, I should say a mainframe transaction-oriented system, you are real interested in high throughput, and you don't care about other things that make it easy for users to find files and things like that.

**HB:** *You care about journaling though.*

**DG:** Yes, definitely, there are mixes of features you need. And actually you may even argue that you are not interested in journaling because it can actually be a bit of a hit, compared to not doing any consistency checking at all. It depends on the environment. Linux has extremely fast filesystem, but they don't do any consistency checking. They depend on not rebooting very often and having a really good check program. And with the stability of the system, that works out for them in their environment. But if you do go down and you lose data, well, that sucks and you're out of luck.

It is a book about design issues, because it really isn't a book describing how you would write a filesystem. I really had to hunt hard to find a lot of the information that I needed to do it.

**HB:** *So how does writing a book about writing a filesystem compare to writing a filesystem?*

**DG:** It's way easier to write the code—of course I'm still writing the code and once the book is done it's done and I won't have to touch it. Yeah, it was interesting, because it was really arduous to get pages out sometimes. Especially first starting. When I reread some of the first stuff I wrote it was really poor. Because I hadn't done much prose writing in a long time and I didn't know where to begin, and there were so many things that you would have to understand. Interdependent things so that to understand A you had to understand B, but to understand B you have to know A.

### *Dominic Giampaolo* (continued)

So how do you describe that to someone? There were days where you'd get like five pages done and be happy because that was like a lot. Toward the end I started to ramp up and some of it got easier to write. But yeah, it was a hard project. It was fun, I enjoyed it.

**HB:** *Did you learn more about writing filesystems from writing this book?*

**DG:** Oh yeah, cause when you would be writing things you would be scratch your head, you'd go, "Why did I do that again?" and you would think, but couldn't come up with a really good reason. Or you would be writing "This is how it is …" and you would think, Oh gee, that could be a lot better … if I just did this or that and changed it around, I could have improved things. That is some of what came out of … boy I'd like to redo things, came out of writing the book. Which is good—I mean it shows that you are still learning. If I came out and said that everything was perfect, I think I'd be full of shit there.

**HB:** *So let's go back a little bit. … Where did you go to college?*

**DG:** I went to Worcester Polytechnic Institute. Well, undergraduate I went to American University in Washington, D.C. Sort of funny—Boston University was too expensive and I don't think I got in anywhere else. My mother kept telling me that you did better on verbals so you could be a political science major and with a political science degree you could do anything and so I went to American University and after the first semester decided that political science was not for me and that computers were the way to go. And that was about all she wrote.

**HB:** *What was the allure of computer science?*

**DG:** Um, I don't know, it just was fun … it was fun just to hack on computers and write programs that did stuff. I took this computer programming class and all the programs, it was like how cool can I make this and what features can I do? Because I had just gotten an Amiga and so I was into all this neat stuff that you could download. And it was really a lot of fun to know people and you'd download programs and they would be really cool and you would try to figure out how they work. I don't know, it just kind of sucked me in. It was just sort of a personality thing, I think, where you know obsessive-compulsive people get into it because it's like this big puzzle. It's this big thing in front of you.

Yeah, I learned a lot on the Amiga, I really cut my teeth on that. And then I wouldn't say graduated to, but also started using Unix at the time. I remember walking by the lab and there was this wild-hairdo professor, MIT-graduate-in-math kind of guy just hacking away furiously on this big Sun workstation—big 19-inch monitors, and you know that's really sexy stuff and I was just pulled right into figuring it out. And just, you know, working a lot. Then he left and he was like, "This is how you do a backup and this is how you recompile the kernel—see ya!" And then so here I was in charge of these Sun workstations. They were down more than they were up for the first few months. But I learned a lot. It was more of this trying to understand the whole thing sort of mentality.

**HB:** *So let me just get a few facts straight. You graduated American University in computer science, then went to…?*

**DG:** Worcester Polytechnic Institute, which is a little technical university in Worcester Massachusetts, outside of Boston. Spent two years there doing graduate school. Got a master's degree in computer science and did some work on filesystems, content addressable filesystems and typed filesystems, something like that. It was OK work but it never got published. Taught that summer and then drove west and ended up at Silicon Graphics. Literally, I got in the car and started driving west and wound up at SGI.

**HB:** *So what is it about being at Be that appeals to you the most?*

**DG:** Well, originally it was a systems company, because we were making the BeBox. And it's fun to work when you have control over the hardware and software because you can make the two work well together and I liked that. I mean, that is why I liked SGI, because they are building kick-ass hardware, and you make the software go on top of it. At Be it seemed to be the same thing. Presumably we were going to do new computers, and it's fun to build computers, that's a cool thing. But the hardware business got dropped because it wasn't cost-effective. And that was sort of sad, but you could still have influence over the software. It was still OS work, which is what I like to do.

So it is fun work, it is what I want to be doing. You know, having an influence on and building something that I use day to day. Every morning I come in and I see my email with those attributes, and if the system crashes and it sucks, it's my fault and I can go look at it and fix it. If it doesn't work the way that I think it should and/or it's buggy, I can go fix it or I can talk to the person who wrote it to get it fixed. I like having that ability. To really build and mold the system that you use.

**HB:** *So I'm going to switch gears here a little bit. You said you play poker on Thursday nights. Any other recreational activities, or do you like to go home and code more when you leave here?*

**DG:** I'm actually rather low-tech at home—I don't have a television, I don't have a computer at home. I get my fill here because usually I'm here ten or twelve hours a day. So in terms of other recreational activities, I like to ride my bike a fair bit. I have both a road bike and a BMX bike that I had in high school. And despite the fact that I'm almost 30 years old, I still do that—it's kind of fun. Outdoor hiking sort of stuff, traveling is fun—although I don't get to do much of it. You know, going places and seeing things, basically being outdoors is fun.

**HB:** *So ten to twelve hours a day … Do you work weekends?*

**DG:** That depends. This time of year, with a release coming up, yeah, I've pretty much written off all of the time between now and November. That's fine, I don't mind. You take little breaks and you back off a bit now and then. Yeah, it's heavy work but I enjoy it. My girlfriend doesn't live here, she lives in Davis, so I don't have much to do in the evenings. She's not around so I'd rather not sit at home and watch TV, especially because I don't have one. So work is fine.

# 11

# Network Applications

Just because BeOS comes bundled with its own Web browser and email client, that doesn't mean there isn't plenty of room for third-party developers to create more sophisticated Internet tools. In fact, you'll find dozens of network applications available for download from BeWare and BeDepot. Some of them improve on the Be-provided tools by offering advanced features that go beyond those found in Be's apps, while others do things BeOS doesn't do at all, like letting you participate in IRC (Internet Relay Chat) and Usenet discussions or graphically transfer files between FTP servers and your machine. This chapter is all about extending the networking capabilities of BeOS with third-party applications.

# Email Clients

Nothing is more fundamental to being well-wired than email. Most of us spend a good portion of every day reading and writing electronic messages, so a good mail client is a necessity, not a luxury. BeMail (see Chapter 4, *Get Online Fast*) is a pretty groovy little mail client, but if your needs go beyond email basics, it can't hold a candle to the features offered by other vendors' products.

## Adamation's Adam

www.adamation.com

Email is email, right? You need to be able to read, write, and organize your messages, and that's it, no? Well, if that's all you need, you may be perfectly satisfied with BeMail. However, BeOS offers services like a built-in query system and contact database (via Person files) that are a perfect fit for email clients that take messaging to the next level. Adam not only makes good on some of the promises of BeOS's database-like filesystem, it offers a few features that are (at this writing) simply not available anywhere else, like graphical game play by email and mail-based "forms" technology. Thanks to these advanced features and its super-elegant interface, Adam has become the mail client of choice for many BeOS users.

 Adam's documentation is detailed and easy to read, so we'll just brush on the basic features here, and focus instead on some of Adam's more unique capabilities.

**Setup**   Start by using Adam Setup to configure at least one email account. Adam differs from other BeOS mail clients in that it ignores the usual /boot/home/mail/in directory (it won't hurt to have one, but it will be ignored). Instead, each of your POP accounts gets its own mail hierarchy under ~/mail/mailboxes. For example, if you have two POP accounts, with usernames of "waxwing" and "liberace," you'll end up with directories called ~/mail/mailboxes/waxwing and ~/mail/mailboxes/liberace. These directories will be created for you automatically when you establish accounts with Adam Setup, and represent the root mail level for each account.

 **If you're just experimenting with Adam, you can safely use the Tracker to move or copy your existing mail hierarchy into the folder representing one of your POP accounts. You can always move it back later on if you elect to use a different mail client.**

When you first install Adam, it will ask whether you want your mail messages and Person files reindexed. The reason for this is that Adam makes use of queries on some mail attributes that are not indexed by default. Allowing Adam to reindex your files may take a few minutes, but is harmless and will not cause problems for other applications making use of the same attributes. The indexing process runs in the background for a few minutes, and you can safely do other things while it's running (though the heavy disk access involved may slow your machine down a bit until it's finished).

You'll find that most of the third-party mail clients available for BeOS offer a three-paned user interface. A mailbox view lets you organize and navigate through your collection of accounts or mailboxes, a list view displays the subject lines of all messages in the selected mailbox, and a preview panel lets you take a look inside the selected message without actually opening it. Double-clicking an individual message opens that message in a separate "reader" window.

**Browser and Reader** The Adam Browser is the primary interface onto your collection of mail messages, and is organized through a tabbed interface. The first tab, labeled "Mail Folders," offers a hierarchical view of each of your POP accounts living at the root level, with mail folders relevant to those accounts beneath them. You can organize and sort your messages just as you would if you were using the Tracker, by clicking and/or dragging column headers.

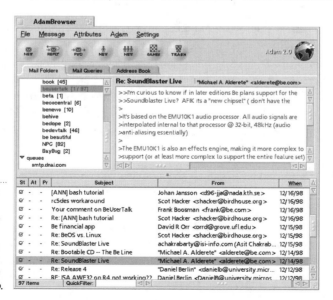

*Figure 11.01*

*Unlike other BeOS mail clients, Adam maintains separate folders for each of your POP accounts. Navigate amongst your accounts from the Mail Folders tab.*

If you work with a lot of mail, you'll appreciate the QuickFilter feature when you need to find a message or two in a hurry. Look for the small QuickFilter input box at the bottom of the list view and type the first few letters of the name of someone whose messages you're trying to find. Your message list will immediately be pared down to just the messages matching that string. You can do the same for subject lines. To restore the original message list, just tap Backspace a couple of times to undo the QuickFilter.

 Adam has the unique ability to "iconify" itself. While minimizing most BeOS windows sends them to the Deskbar, iconified Adam windows shrink to a tiny window on the Desktop. To iconify any Adam window, just click the Adam logo (the "Spinner") at the upper right. Restore an iconified window to its previous size and location by clicking once in the iconified window.

 After double-clicking a message to bring it up in the Adam Reader, you can navigate to the previous or next message without closing the current window. Just click the Prev or Next buttons on the toolbar, or press Alt+Left Arrow or Alt+Right Arrow.

**Working with Queries**  In Chapter 7, *Working with Queries*, we took a look at the amazing ways you can use the power of BeOS attributes attached to BeMail messages to search, sort, and filter your mail collection. Adam lets you use these queries as if they were virtual mailboxes so that you can, for example, display a folder of all unread messages, regardless which physical directory they're currently stored in. To use this feature, just create an email query of any complexity as described in Chapter 7, then move the saved query from its default location of ~/queries to ~/mail/Queries. The query will appear under Adam's Mail Queries tab as a virtual folder, and selecting it will cause it to be executed in real time. Try *that* in Eudora!

In a similar fashion, Adam takes advantage of your built-in BeOS address book, in the form of your collection of People files. When you select the Address Book tab, you'll find two entries labeled "People" and "Groups." Select the People entry and you'll be able to edit data related to your existing collection of People files. When you enter the name of an existing person file into the To: line of a new message, Adam will try to locate a Person file of the same name. If it finds one, that person's email address will be inserted for you automatically.

**Working with Filters**  Like any mail client worth its salt, Adam lets you create sophisticated filters that grab incoming mail matching some set of criteria and then perform some action on it. For example, you can have mail from known spammers automatically deleted, or have mail from Aunt Phoebe automatically moved to your family folder. To access Adam's filter creation tool, pull down Settings | Filtering, and click the Add button to begin. In the right pane of the Filter Settings panel, establish a set of criteria to be run against incoming messages, and the lower pane to establish the actions that will be performed when those criteria are met.

 **If there's a particular person who sends you extremely important mail and you want to make sure you respond to their messages quickly, use the Actions pane to specify that a certain sound file be played automatically whenever a message from that person arrives. This way you'll know you've got urgent business to attend to even if you're in the next room.**

**Working with Groups**   A Group is defined as a collection of Person files gathered together under a single name. If you've been using the Group field in the People application to organize and sort your contacts, you'll find that Adam will have created a collection of groups for you, based on these criteria. For example, if you've been setting all of your BeOS contacts to belong to a group called "Be People," you'll find a new ~/home/groups folder in the Tracker, and within that, a group called "Be People."

Double-click any Group file to edit its member list. Add a person by dragging one in from the Tracker, or select a name in the list and pull down People | Remove to remove it. Note that removing a person from a group will actually change the Group attribute for that Person file. Launch the Groups application from the Adam folder to create a fresh group. Once Groups have been established, you can send a single message to every person in the group by simply entering the Group name into the To: field of a new Adam message.

**Working with Forms**   One of Adam's most unique features is its ability to work with "forms." Imagine that you're an application developer looking for feedback and bug reports on your new product. Or that you're starting an online custom T-shirt ordering business. Or that you want to conduct a survey to find out what kind of hardware your users are running. In any of these you could gather information via email by creating a form in Adam. Double-click the AdamForm application in the Adam program directory and you'll be able to drag and drop text boxes, checkboxes, radio buttons, popup lists; establish names and values for all of your form elements; set background and foreground colors; and do everything else you would do with a Web-based form. After saving your form, begin a new message and pull down Views | Add Form. Pick your form from the list, and it will appear on a second tab in the new message exactly as it appeared when you created it. Users receiving the form will be able to fill it out and send it back to you for processing. Note, however, that these forms will only appear correctly to users who view their mail with Adam.

 **If you're receiving filled-out forms from users and want to extract their data programmatically, pull down Message | Show Original MIME for a text equivalent of the form's contents, which you can then further process with** grep **or other power tools.**

**Playing Games** For centuries, chess masters separated by thousands of miles have played games of chess by mail, sending their moves to one another and then waiting days or weeks for a response. Adam takes the old chess by mail concept to the next logical step, bringing it into line with the email age. You don't have to master chess notation to play chess by email, either, since Adam gives you a full graphical game board on which to play.

Of course, your Soviet chess partner may not have a copy of Adam with which to play email chess, but that doesn't mean he's out of the picture—all he has to do is enter his moves in text mode from his own mail client, and Adam will display the updated chess board graphically when it's your turn again. In other words, you can play chess with anyone in the world, using any operating system or email client (but when you send them the screenshots of how the game appears to you, they'll probably get jealous and want to install BeOS...).

*Figure 11.02*

Adam brings the concept of chess by mail into the digital age.

 Adam's gaming capabilities don't stop with chess—it lets you play the ancient Chinese game of Go or the Japanese game of Shogi in the same way. Adamation also makes the add-on API available to developers, so other games may appear in the future. Select any of these games from the submenu that appears when you click the Games button on the toolbar.

 You don't *have* to play games by email. If you just want to play a game of chess, Go, or Shogi with someone else in the same room, you can just take turns with the mouse.

Want to hook up with other gamers with similar skill levels? Adamation hosts a Web site that will help you to meet other gamers. See `www.adamation.com` for details.

## BeatWare Mail-It  *with Karen Cassel*
`www.beatware.com`

If you're serious about email, you need a mail client that can reliably send, receive, and manage hundreds of email messages and contacts. BeatWare's Mail-It is just the application to do this. Because Mail-It is efficiently multi-threaded, you can send, receive, and compose email simultaneously. If you've got multiple email accounts, Mail-It lets you receive from them all at once or choose amongst them. Mail-It's sophisticated filtering capabilities let you sort and organize large volumes of incoming or existing email. You can have Mail-It automatically file, delete, color-code, forward, or reply to any email matching custom criteria. And its preview feature lets you get a glimpse of a message's contents without having to open it first.

Mail-It has an integrated address book that stores complete contact information and enables one-click email addressing. You can even have multiple address books—one for personal contacts, another for business contacts, and yet another for customers. You can also create address lists or groups within each address book, so you can quickly send a message to all the members of your Canasta Club, for instance. Mail-It's address books use your existing database of BeOS People files, so you can access contact information entered in another BeOS application from Mail-It, or vice versa.

**Figure 11.03**

*Use Mail-It's Accounts panel to enter your name and email address, POP and SMTP server addresses, and other details. Click the Advanced tab to specify custom settings, such as timeout values and maximum number of messages to download.*

## Getting Started with Mail-It

To start sending and receiving email with Mail-It, you first need to give the program a few details about your mail account or accounts. Pull down View | Accounts to access a dialog functionally similar to BeOS's E-mail preferences panel, and enter your real name, email address, account name, password, and POP and SMTP server addresses (see Chapter 4, *Get Online Fast*, for details). To work with multiple accounts, just click the Add button and enter the same information for another account. Be sure to give each account a meaningful name, such as Karen's home, Karen's work, Jeff's work, etc. You'll need to refer to these names later if you want to receive email from some of your accounts but not others.

 **If you only have one account but want to be known by multiple identities, you can create multiple mail accounts that are identical except for the name. This way you can write to your friends under your real name, and to customers under your business name, for example.**

Be sure to specify whether you want messages to be deleted from the server after downloading. If messages are not deleted, you'll be able to download them again later from another email application, machine, or operating system. BeatWare recommends leaving your mail on the server for at least 30 days, or at least until you're comfortable with Mail-It's features and have decided you want to use the program permanently.

**Digging In**    Now you're ready to use Mail-It for all your personal and professional email. The quickest and easiest way to get your mail is to tap Alt+M or click the icon with the red and green arrows at the far right of the

**Figure 11.04**

*By default, the main Mail-It window displays your message folders on the left, subject headers in the upper right, and a preview of the currently selected message in the lower left. Click the triangular latch in the status bar to hide the preview and provide maximum viewing space for message headers.*

Mail-It toolbar. Since Mail-It can send and receive email simultaneously, this icon (or its hotkey equivalent) initiates both your send and receive connections. Mail-It will deposit all your new mail in your in folder and send any messages flagged to go from your out folder. A status bar indicates how many new messages you have in total and how many of those have already been downloaded. If you want to stop your mail from downloading at any time, click the Stop button on the status bar.

 Context menus let you quickly change the status, priority, or label of any message by right-clicking on the message (Mac users: Ctrl+Command+click).

The New Message window includes built-in shortcuts that make it easy to send both personal and professional email. You can address the email either by typing in the recipient's address or by choosing a Person file from your address book (by typing in a person's nickname or dragging the name from the address book into the New Message window).

 If you want to add a sender's name and email address to your address book, you can do so quickly by right-clicking on the sender's email address, which appears in red in the message header.

If you've been storing your People files with commas in their names—as in Lastname, Firstname—you'll need to replace those commas with underscores, as in Lastname_ Firstname. If you choose People from Mail-It's address book, the program will take care of this conversion for you.

 **Mail-It makes it easy to import your address book from Eudora, Microsoft Mail and News, Claris Emailer, or any tab-delimited text file. Simply export your address book from within your other email application, then open your Mail-It Address Book (View | Contact Manager | Main Address Book) and select File | Import. In the resulting File panel, choose the file to be imported and set the file format field to match the name of the email program that originally created the Address Book.**

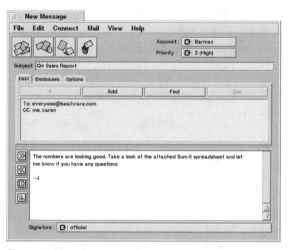

**Figure 11.05**

*Tap Alt+N or click the New Message icon on the toolbar to create a new message. Drag files out of the Tracker and into the message body to create attachments (enclosures). If you have multiple mail accounts, tell Mail-It which account you'd like to send this message from by using the picklist at the upper right. Set a signature by clicking the picklist at the bottom of the message.*

If you who don't want your boss to get a message from couchpotato@mailnet.com a pop-up button at the top of the window lets you choose to send from any of your other mail accounts. Mail-It also gives you easy access to any number of user-defined signatures, so you have the option of signing messages to friends differently than messages to business associates. To create and manage your signatures, select View | Settings | Signatures from the main menu. Stamp your signature anywhere within the body of the message by clicking the Stamp icon to the left of the Message Body field.

Sending attachments (or "enclosures") is as easy as dragging a file from the Tracker or the Desktop and dropping it into the New Message window. The reverse is also true: You can save attachments back to the Tracker by dragging and dropping. You can quickly turn any file in the Tracker into a Mail-It attachment by using the Tracker add-on. Right-click any file and select Add-Ons | mailto Mail-It from the context menu. This will launch Mail-It and create a new message with the selected file included as an attachment.

**Managing Your Mail**  Since the flood of email in most of our lives is so unrelenting, it makes sense to keep your messages well-organized. Mail-It reads the structure of mail folders under /boot/home/mail just as if you were using the Tracker to organize your mail. You can create new mail directories from within Mail-It's interface by clicking the New Folder icon on the toolbar. Select a folder and click the subdirectory icon to create a folder within that folder. You might, for example, want to subdivide your Be folder into subdirectories called `beusertalk`, `bedevtalk`, `Yak Facts`, and `misc`. Depending on the contents of each folder, you may want the mail sorted by date, by subject, or by sender. To do this, just click on the appropriate column heading in the Main Mail window for each folder.

**You can move messages from one folder to another by dragging. To select multiple messages at once, Shift+click (to select a block of messages) or Ctrl+click (to select messages that aren't next to each other). You can then drag your entire selection into another folder.**

**Power users will want to make Mail-It their default email application. This will cause BeOS to open Mail-It whenever an email application is called by another application (e.g. when you click on an email address from within your Web browser). To make Mail-It your default email application, open the FileTypes application in your** Preferences **folder. Select and expand the "text" field from the list of filetypes located just below the File menu. Select "E-mail" from the list of items listed under "text." Under "Preferred Application:" select "Mail-It" in the drop-down list.**

**Navigating through Mail** You can move quickly through Mail-It messages just as you would through BeMail messages, by holding down Alt and pressing the Up or Down Arrows on your keyboard. To delete the currently displayed message, press Alt+T. To delete the current message and display the next message in the same window, hold down the Option and Alt keys and press the Up or Down Arrows. To select multiple contiguous messages or addresses, hold down the Shift key and click on the first and last item in the group to be selected. To select a noncontiguous group of messages or addresses, hold down the Option key and click on each of the messages you wish to select.

**Mailbox Caching** In order to remain responsive even when mailboxes are stuffed with thousands of messages per folder, Mail-It maintains a cached listing of the items in each folder. Normally, Mail-It updates this cache automatically. However, under certain circumstances, the cache for a given folder may become corrupted, making it necessary to rebuild the cache. These are some typical circumstances that might cause the cache to be corrupted:

- You lose power to your machine while running Mail-It.
- You add or remove files in your ~/mail folder from outside of Mail-It.
- You temporarily use another email application (like BeMail) to send or receive messages.

To rebuild the cache for a given folder, hold down the Ctrl key and click on the folder for which you wish to re-create the cache. In order for Mail-It to recognize that you want to rebuild the cache, a different folder must be selected when you Ctrl-click on the folder in question.

For similar reasons, it might also be necessary to rebuild the cache for the Folders List itself. To do this, hold down the left Ctrl key while starting Mail-It. This will cause the caches for all of your mail folders and message headers to be rebuilt at once.

**Finding Messages**  Still can't find that email you received six months ago with your best friend's new address in it? Lucky for you, Mail-It has a search engine that will let you search by field through any or all of your folders. To find Jeff, I would just tell Mail-It to search all email in my Golf folder for the word "Jeff". When the search is complete, I'll have a list of all email containing the word "Jeff", the date it was sent, and the folder where it resides. To read any found message, click on it from the Find window.

**Figure 11.06**

*The Mail-It Find function lets you search through messages for content embedded within the body text, something you can't do with BeMail queries. Alternatively, use the picklist to search on any header field, or limit your search by constraining it to a single folder.*

Folders and the Find function ensure that you don't lose or misplace an important message, but sometimes it's nice to have a reminder that a message contains particularly important information, requires follow-up action, or warrants a detailed reply. Mail-It's priority settings and labels are perfect for creating these kinds of reminders. You can attach a priority from very low to very high to any email, or create a color-coded labeling scheme to create a To-Do list. Nothing says "urgent" quite like a fiery red message among a sea of black type.

**Filtering Messages**  Mail-It's powerful filtering capabilities take filing, labeling, and prioritizing a giant step forward. Let's say, for example, that you get hundreds of messages a day and want to be sure that the ones from your boss don't get overlooked. You can set up a filter that basically says, "If an email is from 'boss', then change the color to red and mark it highest priority." Or, if you can't seem to get yourself off of an annoying mailing list, set up a filter that will automatically move email from a particular sender to the Trash. In addition to filing, labeling, and prioritizing, you can set up filters to send an automatic reply or automatically route certain email messages to a predefined group. You can have Mail-It react to the arrival of messages by alerting you of their arrival with sound or pictures, printing, or executing another application on your computer. And of course, you'll probably want to create filters to immediately move all incoming messages from mailing lists into dedicated folders.

 **Automatically create a filter to remove recurring junk mail by highlighting the mail in the main window and selecting Mail | Create Filter from the main menu.**

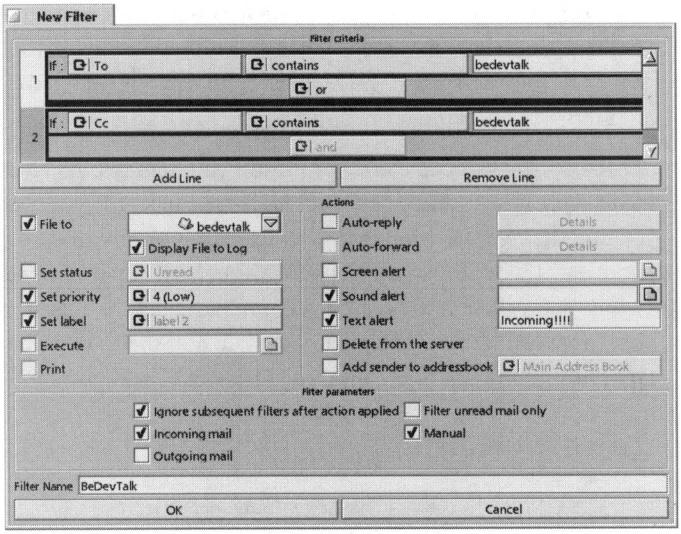

**Figure 11.07**

*There's practically no limit to what you can do with Mail-It's filters. You can establish multiple interrelated criteria and set any of a zillion parameters to control what happens to particular messages as they roll in.*

Filter actions aren't limited to new messages, though—they can also be useful for cleaning out overcrowded folders. Perhaps you've requested that computer tip newsletters be pushed to you daily. Some days you read them, other days you don't, but you want to save them all, just in case. Set up a folder to house the newsletters, then create a manual filter that says, "If computer tips have been read, move them to the newsletter folder." Select all the email in your In folder by using the Alt+A shortcut, then select Mail | Filter Mail. Mail-It will move all the read newsletters into the folder for you.

***Outgoing Filters*** **You may have dozens of folders for organizing your incoming mail, but you've probably only got one Out folder. Everything you've written over the past 79 years is stacked up in there, with no hope of ever being organized the way you'd like it. Fortunately, Mail-It lets you establish filters for outgoing mail as well as incoming. Create some subdirectories in your Out folder to categorize your mail logically, check the Outgoing checkbox at the bottom of the Filters panel, and you'll be able to finally add some order to the bottomless chaos of your outbox.**

**Using Templates**    So far, we've focused on ways to manage volumes of incoming mail. But if you use email to communicate with customers, you may send more email than you receive. Mail-It can save you time with its drafts, stationery, and integrated address book features.

A "draft" is merely an unfinished email message. If you are interrupted in the middle of composing a message for some reason, Mail-It will hold a draft for you in your Out folder until you have time to finish it. This prevents you from losing the work you've already done.

If you've ever provided customer support via email or sent regular mailings to a customer base, you know how tedious it can be to type the same information time and time again. Cutting and pasting from previously sent messages helps a little, but there are still preferences and formatting to tweak each time. Mail-It's stationery saves you time and frees you from the boredom by letting you create email templates where you preset all of your email options, such as account, priority, subject line, and signature, as well as the full message body. Give each template a meaningful name, and when the time comes to send one off, all you have to do is select the template, enter the recipient's address, and click Send.

## OmicronSoft Mail Clique   *with John Tegen*
**www.omicronsoft.com**

Standard email applications are great for sending a message to one or two people, but what if you need to send the same message to a whole group of people? You could use carbon copy (cc:) or blind carbon copy (bcc:), but manually figuring out which people should receive your message takes a lot of work. If you have a frequent need to send out press releases, product change announcements, or meeting notices to large groups of people, Mail Clique can make your life much easier. And unlike the simple groups features available in other mail clients, Mail Clique lets you automatically personalize the messages in your batch mailings. You can even schedule your messages to be sent at a future date and time so you don't have to be there when the messages go out. This way you can do things like dispatch press releases from your office while you're on the other side of the country attending a trade show.

**Getting Started with Mail Clique**  Mail Clique uses the BeOS People application for its address book, which eliminates the need to import address books or contact databases. Mail Clique will only display Person files that have a name, email address, and at least one group defined in the People application. All others are ignored. If you need to enter a new contact while using Mail Clique, select New from the File menu to launch the People application.

As its name implies, Mail Clique groups recipients together in "cliques," which can be formed on any basis you find useful. For example, you might create one clique consisting of people who should receive your company's press releases, and another clique consisting of people who get your company's

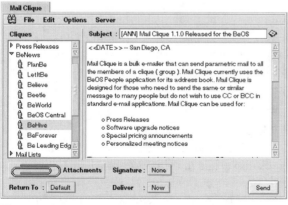

*Figure 11.08*

*Use Mail Clique to manage "cliques" and send messages from a single application window.*

technical bulletins. Of course, each person can belong to more than one clique, but Mail Clique is smart enough to make sure that no single person will receive duplicate messages even if they do. You're not constrained to sending messages only to your cliques, either—you can just as easily select a few arbitrary people from your address book and send a message to them alone. Since Mail Clique is fully integrated with the People application, you can edit anyone's contact information by double-clicking their name, which will launch that person in the People application. Similarly, additions to the People database will automatically update the clique list even if they are performed outside of Mail Clique.

**Personalizing Messages**  One of Mail Clique's strengths is its ability to personalize messages to each clique member, which it does by means of a few standard tags that can be inserted into the body of any message. Because these tags are evaluated individually for each message, they're called "parametric" tags (from the mathematical term "parametric equation," which functions similarly). Right-click in the body of your message to display a context menu of the available parametric tags.

Select NAME from the context menu and the tag <<NAME>> will be inserted at the current cursor location. When the message is sent, the <<NAME>> tag will be replaced with the person's actual name, making it easy to personalize each message as it goes out. You can see how the final message will look before sending it by selecting Preview from the menu bar.

**Defining Additional Tags**  If there are phrases or slogans you need to use frequently, you can define them as custom tags, which you can then reuse in any future message or template. In Mail Clique's Preferences panel, enter a name and value for your custom tag. You'll then be able to insert your custom tag into outgoing messages by using the context menu as described above.

You may want to create custom tags containing such information as your company's slogan or URL. You can then insert these tags into your collection of message templates, and if your company's slogan or URL changes, you won't have to manually update all of your templates—you can just edit the custom tags and all templates invoking them will be up to date the next time they're used.

**Scheduling Deliveries**  While you can always send a message immediately by clicking Send, Mail Clique also lets you set the date and time for delivery, so you can have your messages dispatched in the middle of the night, or while you're out on the road. Select Later from the Delivery menu, and an additional field will be displayed, showing the current date and time. Change these to the date and time at which you'd like the message to be sent, and press Send. Your messages will not be sent until the time you entered rolls around. The date/time entry also accepts entries relative to the current date like "Next Tuesday," "Tomorrow," or "3 days." Since Mail Clique uses BeOS's built-in mail_daemon, you can optionally tell the program to use the mail-checking schedule you've established in the system's E-Mail preferences panel. When BeOS logs in to check for incoming mail, Mail Clique will send your outgoing messages. Use the Options menu to enable this behavior.

**Foreign Dates**   Mail Clique provides the unique capability to format dates in any number of languages, including English, French, German, and Spanish. The <<DATE>> and <<DATE_SENT>> tags will be resolved in the language chosen in the Preferences panel.

**Message Templates**   You can save messages as templates for future reuse, thus reducing the time it takes to create and transmit announcements. Simply

**Figure 11.09**

Messages can be saved as templates and resent or edited later.

create a new message, enter whatever you like into the Subject line and message body, and select Save. To display a saved template, select the icon to the left of the subject and a list of all of your saved templates will be displayed. You might want to create one template for press releases, another for corporate announcements, and so on. In the future, all you'll have to do is enter new content into an existing template, pick a clique, and shoot your message off into the ether.

# Postmaster
`cs.ubishops.ca/Postmaster`

In addition to being a great (and inexpensive!) all-around mail client, Kenny Carruthers' Postmaster takes excellent advantage of the BeOS query engine to let you create "virtual" folders and groups. You get the convenience of a full-featured mail client and the power of BeOS queries within the same interface.

**Working with Panes**   All of Postmaster's panes are fully resizable. Grab the border between the list view and the message view and drag left/right/up/down to change the amount of space allocated to any one view. You'll find small, triangular latches at the upper-left corner of the main tool and status bars. Clicking either of these expands or collapses that region. This way you can reduce the standard toolbar icons to simple text labels, or expand the status view to display more details than are shown by default.

In addition to providing a preview of the contents of the currently selected message, the bottom pane has two optional functions. If you'd like to be able to see list views for two folders at once, pull down Views | Mail Folder, then drag any folder from the folder view into either of the two main views. If there's a groovy Replicant you'd like to have available only when reading mail messages, pull down Views | Shelf and drag the Replicant into this space.

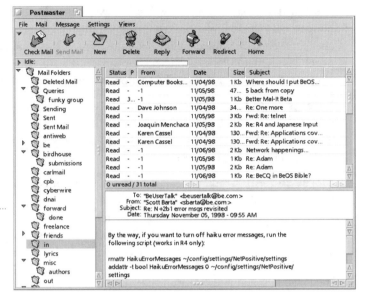

**Figure 11.10**

*Postmaster lets you create mail queries in "virtual" folders that appear along- side your standard mail folders.*

Future versions of Postmaster may gain the ability to display Usenet news- groups and/or FTP sites in the left-hand folder collection. Carruthers is also talking about adding the ability to play media attachments (such as sounds or movies) directly from within Postmaster message views. Some of these fea- tures may appear only in a "Deluxe" version.

 You can navigate through messages just as you do in BeMail, by pressing Alt+Up Arrow and Alt+Down Arrow. Right-click in the body of any message and you'll get a context menu from which you can turn text coloring on and off; establish font and font size; "freeflow" the text; reply to, delete, forward the message; and more.

**People** Like Adam and Mail-It, Postmaster doesn't create a proprietary address book (as most mail clients on other operating systems do). Instead, it provides its own interface onto your existing collection of People files. There's no need to use the People application to create new contacts, either— you can add, remove, and edit People files directly from within Postmaster.

As long as you've been storing email addresses in your People files all along, you won't have to remember anyone's email address when creating messages in Postmaster. After beginning a new message, just click the To: button near the top of the window and you'll see a scrolling list of your contacts. Selecting a person inserts their email address into the To: field.

 If there are a handful of individuals to whom you write frequently, check the Favorites boxes next to their entries in the People tab. From the New Message window, click the To: button and those people's names will come up immediately, saving you from having to scroll through hundreds of entries.

**Groups** If you frequently send messages to many people at once, Postmaster groups will let you gather multiple people under a single name, which makes batch-sending easier (although if you have a frequent need to send batch mailings, you'll want to check out Mail Clique, discussed earlier in this chapter). To create a new group, enter a new group name in the text field near the bottom of this panel and click Save Changes. A list of all the People files on your system will appear in the right-hand panel. Select a person and click Add to make them part of this group. Lather, rinse, repeat. When you're finished, click Save Changes again.

To send a message to a group, click the To: button in a new message window, scroll over to Groups, and select the group name. Bingo—instant mailing list (sort of).

 **If you're sending messages to groups, you might want to respect the privacy of the recipients by not broadcasting their email addresses to everyone on the list. This is what the bcc: option is for—"bcc" always stands for blind carbon copy, and any time you use this option (in any mail client), no recipient will be able to see the other recipients' names or addresses. Of course, you'll still need to enter a regular address on the To: line to make the message sendable; just enter your own address and you're good to go. The bcc: field, however, is not immediately apparent. To display it, click the triangular latch in the New Message window. This will display the cc:, bcc:, and Attachments fields.**

**Virtual Folders** Remember all of the BeMail queries we ran in Chapter 7? Those are great, but you still end up having to read your mail out of a query results window, rather than from a dedicated email application. With Postmaster, all you have to do is define a virtual folder with the same parameters as your BeMail queries, and that folder will appear alongside all of your existing folders as if it were a standard folder. This way, you can have your cake and eat it too. For example, you might have a regular mail folder dedicated to one of your mailing lists. At the same time, you might want a separate folder that only displays all of the messages your friend Krusty has posted to that mailing list. No problem. Just create a virtual folder and establish its query parameters as:

```
To: bejunkies@listbox.com
```
and
```
From: krusty@jackson.net
```

Your new virtual folder will appear to contain only the messages that Krusty has sent to the bejunkies mailing list. This "virtual folder" functionality is similar to Adam's; Mail-It did not offer virtual folder capability at this writing. To create a virtual folder, pull down Settings | Virtual Folders and enter a name for the folder in the text field at the bottom of the panel, then click Save Changes. The new name will appear in the Virtual Folders panel at the left of the dialog. Select your new entry on the left and click the Add button; you'll find an interface that works just like the standard BeOS query mechanism. You can build your virtual folder query with any of the standard BeMail attributes, such as Name, Size, Status, To, From, and so on. The second button gives you access to the usual Contains, Is, Is Not, Starts With, and Ends With options. See Chapter 7 for more on query building.

The important thing to keep in mind when dealing with mail appearing in virtual folders is that it doesn't "live" there. In other words, you may see the exact same message in a real folder dedicated to a mailing list and also in a virtual folder. This doesn't mean that you have two copies of the message. Deleting the message from either view will remove the original message from your system, causing the message to disappear from both views. A future version of Postmaster may display virtual folders with a different background color so you have some visual feedback indicating that your current mail view is virtual, not real.

**In some cases, seeing all of the messages that relate to a given set of criteria may be enough, but more often than not, you'll find that what you really want is to just see the *new* messages that also satisfy that folder's criteria. Experiment with adding a "status is new" line to your virtual folder queries, and you'll be able to see just the beusertalk messages that you haven't yet read, for example, rather than all messages to beusertalk. You might want to think of real folders as a good place for permanent storage, and virtual folders as a good place to view messages that just interest you today. Then again, you might not. Virtual folders have no "true" purpose—they can be whatever you need them to be. In any case, remember that if a virtual folder uses "Status is New" as a criterion, messages will disappear from this folder as soon as you read them, since their status will no longer be New (the exact same thing happens with regular BeOS queries on new mail). A future version of Postmaster may have interface options to give you tighter control over this behavior.**

**Virtual Groups**  Here's another one of those areas where Postmaster takes excellent advantage of technology built into BeOS. Rather than creating groups by manually adding users one at a time, you can create groups based on specific criteria, using the BeOS query engine. If you want to send a message to everyone you know who lives in Japan, just build a query for all Person files where the Country attribute is equal to "Japan". Give the new virtual group a name like "Japanese friends" and you'll never have to modify the group again, as long as you're rigorous about always filling in the Country field of your new Person files. Similarly, you can create a virtual group for the members of your bowling club or all of your clown friends working at Barnum and Bailey (by using the Company and/or Group attributes in combination), or everyone with names starting with Q, X, or Z. By including

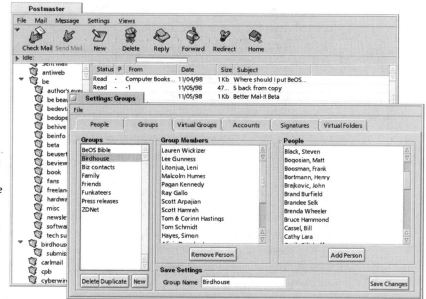

**Figure 11.11**

*Postmaster's Groups and Virtual Groups features let you write to dozens—or hundreds—of people at once. Groups can be created either manually (as shown) or by creating system queries on specific criteria.*

additional attributes and taking advantage of the Boolean AND/OR options, you can make your groups as specific as you want them to be.

Once your query has been created, its results appear immediately in the Members panel at the right of the dialog, so you can make sure your query is picking up the right people.

 If you're sending a message with sensitive or private information, exercise particular caution when working with virtual groups, perhaps returning to the Virtual Groups panel before sending your message to reexamine the list of recipients the query is picking up. One mistake in a Person file attribute could end up sending your message to the last person in the world you would want to see it.

**Mail Accounts**   Like all of the third-party mail clients covered here, Postmaster lets you establish and check multiple mail accounts on multiple mail servers. If Postmaster's Mail Accounts panel looks familiar, that's because it's almost identical to the BeMail preferences panel. In fact, the first time you launch Postmaster, you'll find all of your mail preferences already filled in for you, since Postmaster simply reads them from your system settings. If you change something here and click the Save Changes button, then launch the system's E-Mail preferences panel, you'll find that you've actually changed your system preferences from within Postmaster's interface. Change them from the system panel and reopen Postmaster's panel, and they will have changed back. However, this exchange only occurs with the default account, which is labeled "System Account." If you add additional accounts to Postmaster, your system's settings won't be affected.

Additionally, Postmaster lets you establish whether or not messages should be deleted from the server after download. You can also choose to skip messages larger than a certain size, so you don't get bogged down waiting for huge attachments when you're not ready for them. To control whether any given account is checked every time you check your mail, toggle the box labeled "Check Mail on Manual Checks."

 Enabling "Check Mail on Manual Checks" does not necessarily mean you have to check every account every time you check your mail. If you just want to check for new mail on a single account, pull down the Mail menu in Postmaster's main interface and you'll see all of your accounts listed. Select any one of them to check only that account.

**Filters** Postmaster's filters function just like filters in other popular mail clients, but are constructed through an interface similar to that used to create virtual groups and folders. The difference is that a filter's actions are real, not virtual. That is to say, filter operations will actually move a message to another folder, rather than just making it appear that way. You can, for example, cause an incoming message with the string "beusertalk" in the To: field to be physically transferred to your beusertalk mail folder. You can also set filters to play a sound whenever new mail arrives, display an alert box, or even launch another application.

 **Not only is Postmaster competitively priced, but your registration entitles you to upgrades for life! Pay for the program once, and you'll still be fully paid up with version 23 a century from now. You can't beat that deal with a stick.**

# FTP Clients

If the command-line FTP program built into BeOS (see Chapter 4, *Get Online Fast*) proves inadequate for your needs, you'll be happy to learn that you've got other options. Full-featured graphical FTP clients available from third parties make the upload and download of files—or even entire directory structures—to and from the Internet a piece of cake.

## BeatWare's Get-It *with Karen Cassel*
www.beatware.com

BeatWare's Get-It is the most full-featured FTP client available for BeOS, featuring a ton of power options and an intuitive interface. If you've used four-paned FTP clients like WS_FTP for Windows, you'll find Get-It's interface fairly familiar. Whether you use FTP to download games, publish a Web site, or move files and folders around between BeOS and other machines on a local network, Get-It will give you the ability to manage multiple simultaneous connections, transfer files via drag-and-drop, and establish connections through firewalls and proxy servers.

Get-It also includes several one-click features that make managing file transfers faster and easier. For example, if you aren't sure exactly which of the files named Photo1, Photo2, etc. you're interested in downloading, click the View button and get a close look before committing to the download—clicking View will cause that file to be launched directly into the preferred application for that filetype. Afterward, you can use one of Get-It's Uncompress options to open the latest version of *Doom* that you just grabbed from BeWare.

**Getting Started with Get-It**  To establish a connection to another computer, you need three pieces of information:

- Hostname (the name of the machine to which you want to connect)
- Username (the name of an account on the host machine)
- Password (the password for the above account)

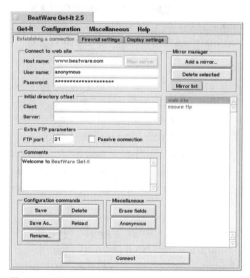

**Figure 11.12**

*Get-It's Connection window lets you establish and manage the FTP equivalent of bookmarks, so you can completely customize parameters related to each server you log into frequently. If you often log into different directories on the same server, you may appreciate the Save As feature, which lets you create and then edit a clone of the current configuration.*

Enter this information into the appropriate fields in the "Establishing a connection" panel in the main Get-It window.

In many cases, the host machine to which you want to connect will offer a guest account for you to use. Guest accounts generally have a username of "anonymous" or "ftp" and accept any valid email address as a password. You can have Get-It enter this information for you automatically by clicking the button labeled "Anonymous."

Select any of the FTP sites for which you've established connection details and click the Connect button to initiate a live connection with the host machine. Once the connection has been established, a new File Transfer window will overlay the main window.

The File Transfer window, which is divided vertically and horizontally, is where you'll do all of the real work in Get-It. The left side of the window displays the filesystem on your machine, while the right side pertains to the host or server machine. All of the folders in the current directory are displayed in the top half of each machine's window, while the lower half displays all of the files in the same directory. Buttons down the center of the window let you navigate up to the parent directory or create, delete, or rename directories.

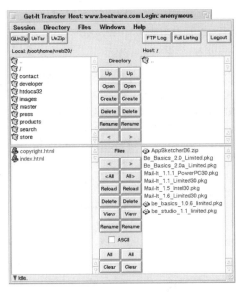

*Figure 11.13*

*The four-paned Get-It interface displays your machine on the left and the host machine on the right. The upper and lower halves display folders and files in the current directory. Buttons running up and down the middle give you file-management options on both machines.*

To download a file, locate and highlight the file to be transferred on the right side of the window. Indicate the directory to which you want the file transferred by selecting it from the list on the left side. When both have been selected, click the < button to initiate the transfer. A status bar will open, showing you the transfer's progress and giving you the opportunity to cancel the transfer midstream or to kill a slow or unresponsive connection. To upload a file, just reverse the process.

 Get-It is fully drag-and-drop aware. If you'd like to upload or download a file directly to or from any Tracker location, just go for it—no need to navigate through directories in Get-It if the file you need to transfer is already right there in front of you!

You can using the same method to transfer multiple files or entire directory structures at once. To transfer an entire directory, including all files and subdirectories, highlight the directory in the top directory panel and click either the < or > button in that panel to initiate transfer. If you'd rather transfer only the files in a given directory, use the All button in the files panel. To transfer multiple specified files, hold down the Shift key and select multiple filenames. Once the files are selected, the < and > buttons in the files panel will move the selected files simultaneously.

Like the excellent BeOS citizen it is, Get-It is fully multithreaded, meaning that it's capable of logging into and transferring files back and forth between multiple servers at once. The Get-It File Transfer window will display transfer statistics for each file in progress. The number of simultaneous transfers possible is limited only by your available bandwidth.

**Transfer Options** You can select multiple contiguous files for transfer by first selecting a single file, then holding down the Shift key while clicking on the last file you wish to transfer. To select multiple noncontiguous files for transfer, hold down the Ctrl key while selecting subsequent files. Once the complete selection is made, press the < or > button to start the transfer.

You can stop an active or idle file transfer from the Transfer Status window. To do so, select the file transfer you wish to stop from those listed and pull down Session | Stop. Get-It will notify you that the download has been terminated.

Get-It supports resumable downloads. If your connection is interrupted for any reason, just return to the site and reinitiate the transfer; Get-It will detect that a partial file by that name already exists on your machine. You'll be asked whether you want to "re-get" (append) or overwrite the file. Select re-get and the file transfer will pick up where it left off.

Not all directories on a given server machine are necessarily visible. This is especially true when you log in as a guest user. However, if you know the name of an invisible subdirectory, you can open it by pressing the Open button with no directory selected. Just enter the name or path to this directory when prompted. The same holds true for invisible files. If you know the name of an invisible file, you can download that file by pressing the Open button with no file selected. Enter the name of the file when prompted. Assuming the file exists, the download will proceed as if the file were visible to you.

If you log out of a server via the menu options, Get-It will prompt you for confirmation. If you just want to get out quickly, tap Alt+X to log out without seeing the confirmation dialog. You'll find several other convenient hotkeys in Get-It's pulldown menus as well.

 **Get-It displays appropriate icons for each of the files and folders on both the client and host systems. If these icons appear too large or too small, select the Display Settings tab and change the font size. Because icons in Get-It are sized in accordance with the font currently in use, your icons will be resized accordingly.**

 **File management in Get-It is not limited to file transfers. You can also create, rename, delete, or view files on the local or host computer. The File Transfer window contains one-click buttons for each of these operations.**

**Uncompressing Files**   Many files on publicly accessible servers are stored as compressed files to save on both storage space and download time. After you download one of these files, Get-It makes it easy for you to decompress it without task-switching out to the Tracker or the Terminal. At this writing, Get-It can uncompress the following file formats:

- **gzip:** Files that have been compressed using the GNU file compression utility. These files will have a `.gz` or `.tgz` extension.

- **tar:** Archived files created using the `tar` utility. Uncompressing these will restore them to their original file or directory hierarchy form. These files usually use the `.tar` extension.

- **zip:** Files that have been compressed using the zip file compression utility. These files usually use the `.zip` extension.

Future versions of Get-It will support additional compression schemes.

# NetPenguin

`http://www.desertnights.com/netpenguin.html`

Graphical FTP clients typically use one of two basic visual schemes. In clients like BeatWare's Get-It (described above), you get a two- or four-paned view, with your local filesystem displayed on one side and the remote filesystem on the other. Other clients, such as Zeid Derhally's NetPenguin, display only the remote filesystem, depending on the operating system's file manager to provide the local view. With this type of client, all file transfers are handled via drag-and-drop; you either drag files from the Tracker onto the FTP server, or from the server directly into the Tracker. There are no real functional advantages to either approach; the difference is one of personal preference.

The NetPenguin interface consists of three windows: the Login and Shortcut window, the File Transfer window, and the Remote Server window. Because NetPenguin is fully multithreaded and can be logged into multiple servers at once, you may end up seeing more than one Remote Server window onscreen.

**The Login Window**    The options here are pretty simple: Enter the FTP server's hostname in the upper field, followed by your username and password. If desired, enter a starting path on the remote machine. NetPenguin's shortcuts work much like bookmarks in your favorite browser. If you've previously stored shortcuts to particular FTP servers (see below), you can select them from the Shortcuts pick-list. In the vast majority of cases, you'll want to leave the port ID set to 21, which is the Internet-standard port mapping for FTP connections. Change this to another port only if the server's administrator tells you to.

## Passive Connections

FTP connections are established in one of two ways: The FTP server can actively establish the details of communication between client and server or it can passively sit back and let the client establish these details. There's no easy way to determine beforehand whether the server you're logging into expects an active or a passive connection, so the best way to find out is to try and log into the server with the Passive Connection radio button unchecked. If NetPenguin gets part of the way into the login process but won't show a directory listing, close the Remote Server window, select the Passive Connection radio button, and try again.

 To log into anonymous FTP sites, use either "anonymous" or "FTP" as a login, and your email address as a password. Pull down Edit | Preferences in the main NetPenguin window to establish your default password, upload and download directories, and window layout. You can even tell NetPenguin to play audio files when files are successfully transferred!

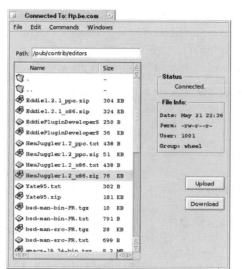

*Figure 11.14*

*NetPenguin displays the directory structure on the remote server graphically. Change to a new directory by double-clicking folders. Change to a parent directory by double-clicking the two dots (..) near the top of the window.*

Once everything is filled in properly, click Connect and the Remote Server window will appear.

Copying files back and forth between your machine and the remote server requires no explanation. Just drag and drop to or from the Tracker. You can even copy entire directory structures if you like, which makes it extremely easy to upload an entire copy of your Web site from your local site mirror, for example.

**Log Window** Whenever you communicate with an FTP server, a series of commands and detailed status reports are tossed back and forth between the client and the server. While these commands aren't displayed by default, you can display them by pulling down Windows | Log Window. This can be useful in troubleshooting if you're having trouble establishing a connection or uploading or downloading files. Also, many FTP servers display a welcome message when you first establish a connection. Since this message is the administrator's only chance to communicate with users, it can be worthwhile reading it to find out if there's anything you should know about the server that might not be immediately obvious. Check the Log window immediately after logging in to see if it reports anything interesting. Note that additional messages are sometimes displayed after you change to a new directory. You might want to check the Log window again if, for example, you switch to an uploads directory.

**Commands** Provided you have appropriate permissions, you can rename and delete files and folders on the remote server by using the same shortcut keys you would use in the Tracker (Alt+E, Alt+T, etc.). If you'd rather use a standard BeOS File panel to upload and download files (rather than drag-and-drop), pull down the Commands menu or click the Upload and Download buttons in the main window.

If you'd like to view a file without saving it to the Tracker first, select it and pull down Commands | View File. This will cause the file to be displayed in a small text viewer, which can be handy for reading the description files that often accompany binary downloads. Note that this viewer is (at this writing) only useful for viewing text-based files.

If your Internet connection gets broken right in the middle of a transfer, you don't have to start download the file again from scratch. Just begin the transfer again and NetPenguin will ask whether you want to continue transferring the original file. Say yes and you'll pick up right where you left off.

**File Transfer Window**   Because NetPenguin can support as many simultaneous uploads and downloads as your bandwidth will accommodate, and because your remote server windows may all be logged into different sites, the Transfer window provides a convenient central location from which you can monitor and control multiple transfers. When transferring multiple files at once, NetPenguin will do its best to balance the load fairly between them. To cancel any transfer currently in progress, select its progress bar and press the Cancel Transfer button.

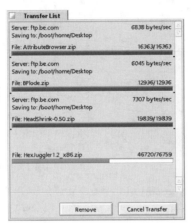

*Figure 11.15*

*The Transfer window displays all files that have been or are in the process of being transferred. Even if you're logged into multiple servers, all file transfers will be logged in the same Transfer window.*

**Shortcuts**   If there are locations that you're going to be visiting often, you may want to save them as shortcuts for future reference. Once you've successfully logged in and found your way to the right directory, pull down File | Add Shortcut (or tap Alt+S). The next time you launch NetPenguin, you'll be able to jump directly to your favorite directories on your favorite sites.

# Usenet News Clients

Usenet news may be one of the Internet's most underrated resources, and is without question the world's largest and most active gathering place for discussions on every topic imaginable (and many topics you can't imagine as well).

## BeInformed
http://home.beoscentral.com/beinformed/

At this writing, there was only one graphical news client for BeOS. Dick Oberlitz's BeInformed is an offline reader, meaning that it downloads all available new messages from your subscribed groups every time you log into your Usenet server. After everything has been downloaded, you can disconnect from the Internet to save on connection fees. Any responses you create will be stored in a special folder labeled "Outgoing articles" and posted back to the server next time you log in.

## *Usenet in a Nutshell*

If you're not familiar with Usenet, the basic idea is simple. Unlike the Web, where each site lives on a single server, Usenet servers around the world are in constant communication with one another, in a state of more or less continual update. To participate, you log into a Usenet server (most likely one run by your ISP or organization), which mirrors the contents of threaded discussions taking place on the rest of the world's Usenet servers. Because the volume of Usenet content is so huge, each server's administrator decides how much content will be available at any one time (seldom more than a week's worth).

When you log into a Usenet server, your client software tells it which discussions you want to follow (you specify this by "subscribing" to certain groups). The client then requests all new discussion topics posted or responded to in those groups since the last time you logged in (some clients will let you download both the topics and the message bodies). Each post has a unique identification number, which your Usenet reader uses to re-create the branching-tree nature of a threaded discussion. Some clients require you to stay logged into the server while you're reading, while others let you grab messages, log off, and read everything offline. After reading a given message, you have the option to respond to its author via email or to post a public reply back to the group. Thus, Usenet functions a little bit like email, offering text-based communications between individuals, and a little bit like the Web, offering a universal public access medium to anyone who cares to check in.

Usenet predates the Web by a good two decades, but has become polluted by exploitative advertisers in recent years. Some Usenet groups are now so clogged by spam that they've become nearly unusable. Fortunately, the `comp.sys.be.*` newsgroups are still mercifully readable, though not 100% spam-free.

Regardless of the type of Usenet client you use, you'll have to tell it which server to connect to (ask your administrator or search your ISP's Web site for this information), your name and email address, and the names of the newsgroups to which you want to subscribe. Many clients will optionally download a complete list of newsgroups from the server, which you can then search through for keywords prior to subscribing. Note, however, that at this writing there were more than 30,000 newsgroups from which to choose.

**Getting Started**  To tell BeInformed about your Usenet server, pull down File | Add Host and enter its address, which will likely be something like `news.myisp.com` or `nntp.myisp.com`. If you'd like to check up on multiple servers, repeat the process. To manage your list of hosts, pull down Window | List of All Hosts, then right-click a hostname to edit it or remove it from the list. In general, the only reason to check multiple hosts is if a specific server hosts a newsgroup that isn't mirrored automatically to your standard server. Note that this is common for "private" newsgroups, which are becoming increasingly popular for product support and highly specialized topics.

Pull down Window | Settings to enter other important details, including your name, email address, and signature.

 Many unscrupulous spammers use "bots," or automated software agents, to comb through Usenet and harvest email addresses. To protect yourself from being flooded by spam, alter your email address so that it will be readable by humans but technically non-functional. For example, if your address is krusty@jackson.net, you might want to enter krustyATjacksonDOTnet here instead. If anyone wants to get in touch with you, they'll be able to manually edit your address so that it will work again.

Use the Header tab of the Settings panel to tell BeInformed how much detail you'd like to see on each message. For example, you can tell it to show you only the Subject line and the Sender's name, or you can specify that every little detail, including the message's ID number, be displayed.

From the Connections tab you can specify how and when BeInformed should connect with your server: continuously, incrementally, or only when you specify. This determines whether you'll see any new messages that are posted to a group while you're online. However, regardless of which option you choose, BeInformed is still an offline reader—you'll have to download all of the headers and messages in all of your subscribed groups every time you connect.

Now that you're all set up, you can dig in.

**Using BeInformed** The BeInformed interface consists of three panes. The upper-left pane contains two hierarchies: Filters and Newsgroups. Accordingly, there are two ways to read your messages: by navigating through newsgroups themselves, or by using built-in queries to view only new, unread, marked, or outgoing articles (we'll get to those in a moment). The upper-right pane displays all of the message headers available in that view, and the lower pane displays message bodies themselves. In the message header view, click on any latch to expand or collapse the hierarchy of messages below it.

 **When participating in threads, always take care to respond to the right message. After reading through an entire thread and then deciding you want to participate, don't just hit Reply immediately—navigate back to the message most relevant to what you have to say. Threads can be chaotic enough as is, and the entire Internet will appreciate your doing your part to help keep discussions cogent and organized.**

**Filters** Much like Postmaster, BeInformed uses the power of BeOS queries to let you view your news in ways not possible on other operating systems. Usenet news messages are downloaded to your system at /boot/home/news, and carry with them a collection of attributes, including Subject, Date, From, and Newsgroup. At this writing, however, BeInformed did not include a graphical query creation tool, meaning that you'll have to create your filters

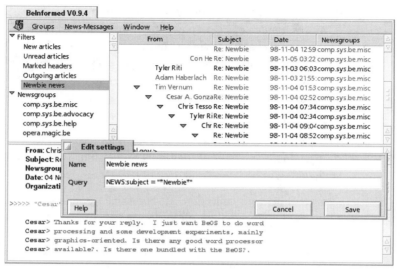

*Figure 11.16*

*BeInformed news queries are capable of extracting any type of data out of your news collection, and are constructed with the BeOS formula query syntax.*

using the more cryptic "formula query" method. Formula queries are covered in depth in Chapter 7, *Working with Queries*, but you should be able to create simple queries without studying too hard. The easiest way to create a news query is to right-click on one of the existing queries and choose Edit Query from the context menu. Copy that query to the clipboard, then pull down Groups | Create Filter. Give your new filter a name, paste the query formula from the clipboard, and modify it to suit your needs.

In Figure 11.16, we've used this formula:

```
NEWS:subject = "*Newbie*"
```

to create a filter that will comb through all of our subscribed groups (which is the default behavior if you don't specify a group) and pull up any article with a subject line that contains the string "Newbie". If we wanted to find only messages from a certain person, we would have used NEWS:from instead, and substituted all or part of that person's email address or name in place of "Newbie". Note also that this query is case-sensitive, and won't find "newbie". To find both "Newbie" and "newbie", we would have used [Nn]ewbie instead. Of course, you can also use any of the AND/OR operators described in Chapter 7 to further narrow your search and retrieve tighter results.

 Remember that the queries you're running here are against your own hard drive, not the news server itself. Thus, BeInformed filters can only find messages you've already downloaded, not messages that are still "out there" somewhere.

Unread messages are always displayed in blue, rather than in black. This makes it much easier to navigate through groups without rereading messages you've already seen. Using the built-in filter for New Messages, however, makes this part even easier. Right-click in any message for a context menu that will let you quickly reply back to the newsgroup or to the original poster via email, or delete just that message.

**Other Options** If you come across a Usenet post that looks like gibberish, it may be encoded in ROT13, which is a very primitive encryption scheme that simply moves all of the letters of the alphabet over by 13 places. Select the message body and pull down News-Messages | ROT13 to decode it.

Over time, your collection of news articles is going to grow huge and unwieldy, which will result in slower access to all of your news views and filters, not to mention making it harder to navigate through them. To delete older messages, pull down News-Messages | Remove and enter a number of days into the small resulting dialog. Click OK and all messages older than that number of days will be deleted or moved to the Trash, your choice.

BeInformed includes its own help system in lovely HTML format. This is definitely worth a read if you intend to spend much time on Usenet; it includes many more details than are covered here.

### Usenet Access from the Terminal

If you're hooked on the shell, or simply prefer older-style, text-based Usenet readers, you'll find a port of the popular Unix slrn newsreader on BeWare. slrn for BeOS works just fine, but lacks the ability to sort messages through the query engine. If you do attempt to get slrn up and running, the one configuration requirement you may not find immediately apparent from reading the documentation is that you must place a file called .slrnc in your home directory, containing the following line:

```
hostname "mysite.com"
```

replacing mysite.com, of course, with your own domain, or that of your ISP. Follow the rest of the instructions in slrn's included readme files and everything will work hunky-dory.

You may also want to check out Chris Herborth's port of trn, which some people prefer. It's also available on BeWare.

# IRC Clients

Despite the rise in popularity of proprietary Internet chat services such as Mirabilis's ICQ or AOL's InstantMessages, Internet Relay Chat (IRC) is still the most-used means of chatting in real time with other Internet users. What do I mean by "real time"? Simply that all users engaged in a conversation are online at the same time and can see each other's words almost as soon as they're typed, which is different from the "asynchronous" Usenet and email models, where users' messages are posted so they can be read and responded to later on.

At this writing, the only IRC client available for BeOS was Xavier Ducrochet's Felix, which is a clever pun. Ducrochet is French, and "chat" in French is the equivalent of "cat" in English. Felix the Cat, get it?

## IRC 101

Unlike a Web site, which typically resides on a single server and hosts the only copy of its contents, IRC servers—of which there are thousands—work in collaboration with one another like Usenet servers, updating one another's contents on a more or less continual basis. Each server can play host to any number of "channels," which are like chat or conference rooms. In addition, users can create new channels if none of the existing ones suit their needs, or if they need to create a private place to "meet" with colleagues. In addition, IRC servers participate in one or more IRC networks, each of which may contain thousands of channels. So let's say you log into your ISP's IRC server, which participates in the EFNet IRC network. By participating in EFNet, you have access to all of the channels being hosted by other servers participating in EFNet, but not to channels that are part of other IRC networks.

Accessing an IRC channel thus requires several steps:

1.  Find out which network hosts the channel you want to join.
2.  Find a server participating in that network.
3.  Choose a "nick" or nickname for yourself.
4.  Log into that server and join the channel.
5.  Once you're in, you'll see a list of the channel's participants. Words they type will show up on your screen, regardless which server they're logged into, just as your words will show up on their screens.

All IRC clients (programs) are different—some require you to know a handful of IRC commands in order to join or leave channels, or to express yourself in various ways. Others have completely graphical and menu-driven interfaces, allowing you to do the same things without learning the commands.

To get a better handle on the machinations of the IRC system, take a look at **www.irchelp.org**, which includes every scrap of information you could possibly need on using IRC, including links to lists of servers. For best results, always try to find an IRC server geographically close to your location.

# Felix

www.mygale.org/10/ducrohet/

**Getting Started** Before logging into an IRC server, use Felix's Preferences panel (Figure 11.17) to enter your name and nickname (or "nick"). Since most networks require that every nick be unique, Felix lets you enter alternate nicks; if your first choice is already in use, your second will be used automatically, and so on. Enter the name of the server you want to use in the Server field, followed by the port number (in the vast majority of cases, the default of port 6667 will work—only edit this if you've been told to do so). If you've never tested this server, don't click the Add to List button just yet, since there's no point in bookmarking a server that's difficult to access. Later on, you can edit your list of saved server "bookmarks" by clicking the IRC Prefs tab and then the Servers tab. If you always want to join a particular channel directly after login, enter # followed by the channel name in the Start in Channel field (IRC channel names are always specified with a "#" character in front of them).

**Figure 11.17**

*Before you try to do anything on IRC, use Felix's Preferences panel to enter your name, nicknames, and server name.*

While this is probably all you'll need to do to jump into IRC, there are many more tabs and options in Felix's Preferences panel, most of which should be self-explanatory (see Figures 12.18 and 12.19).

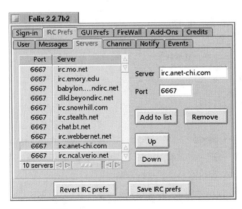

**Figure 11.18**

*Felix uses a multilevel tab system—the lower row of tabs changes depending on which tab is selected in the upper row. For example, selecting the IRC Prefs tab in the upper row gives you a lower row of tabs with options specific to server and channel behavior. Pictured is Felix's server bookmark manager.*

**Figure 11.19**

*If you start spending a good amount of time with Felix, you'll probably want to configure your Font & Color preferences to something a little more aesthetically pleasing than the defaults. Click the GUI Prefs tab in the upper row, then Font & Color in the lower row.*

Once you've got everything configured, click any Save buttons you see on the current tab of the Preferences panel and return to the Sign-in tab, where you can click the Start the Connection button. A window will pop up, and if the IRC server responds, you'll see the main screen fill up with "welcome" information as well as any rules that apply on that network. In the lower portion of the window, type

```
/join #beos
```

Direct commands to the server are always prefaced with a "/" character. If the channel #beos exists on that server, you will be entered into that channel, and other users will see your presence announced by a brief onscreen message. If #beos doesn't exist, you will have just created it, and will be all alone there. You can sit around and wait until someone else finds you, but you'll probably find it more fruitful to check and make sure you joined the right network. Because BeOS users are spread all over the world, it's extremely unlikely that you'll ever end up alone in a preexisting #beos channel.

 #beos is just used as an example here—you can, of course, use Felix to join any IRC channel.

Time            Sender                   Message text                    Ban list

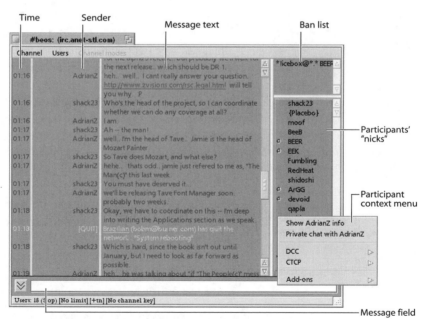

**Figure: 12.20**

*This window shows an IRC chat in progress on channel #beos using Felix. Messages from the system, such as the QUIT message, appear in different colors.*

Participants' "nicks"

Participant context menu

Message field

Most elements of the Felix window can be optionally displayed or hidden by selecting and deselecting items in the Channel menu. If you're hurting for screen space, you may want to turn off the Time column. If there are a lot of users on the channel, you may want to hide the Ban List. Some (but not all) of Felix's window panes can also be resized by dragging.

Once you've successfully joined an IRC channel, basic usage is pretty intuitive. Any messages you type into the Message field are sent to the screens of all participants as soon as you hit Enter. To find out more information about one of the other participants, select their nick in the right-hand column and pull down Users | Show User Info. To invite them into a private chat, select their name and choose Users | Private chat with user. Doing this will cause a smaller Felix window to open. If the other user accepts your invitation, you'll be chatting with that person just as you were in the main window, but no one else will be able to see your conversation. You can also send files to another user directly through IRC by selecting that user and choosing Users | DCC | Send. This will cause a BeOS File panel to open. Select a file and it'll be on its way as soon as the other user accepts the invitation to have a file sent to them. Even though other users can refuse incoming files, it's good netiquette to ask permission before attempting to send a file.

 **All of the user actions discussed in the paragraph above can also be accessed by *right*-clicking on nicknames and choosing the appropriate action from the context menu (see Figure 11.20). Mac users: The right-click equivalent in Felix is Ctrl-Command, rather than just Ctrl.**

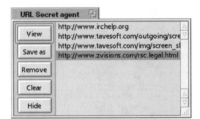

**Figure: 12.21**

*One of Felix's bonus features is its URL Secret Agent. Any time a user enters a URL into the discussion, it shows up here for future reference. Clicking the Save As button will generate a plain-vanilla HTML document consisting of links to all the sites mentioned in the current session, which can be very useful after a fast-paced chat where you didn't have time to visit and bookmark all the sites you wanted to.*

There are a number of ways to change the way your messages are presented to the rest of the channel. People sometimes describe their "virtual actions" in IRC by referring to themselves in the third person. For example, before leaving the channel a user named "Joe" may send a message to the channel reading "Joe takes a bow, then exits," with these words displayed in a different color than the default. Joe accomplishes this by prefacing his message with /me. In other words, Joe would type:

```
/me takes a bow, then exits
```

When you use somebody's nick in the body of your message, your message will show up in a different color on that person's screen, even though it shows up in the normal color for everyone else. This is a convenience that makes it easier to find the messages that are directed at you in a fast-moving conversation where lots of people are talking at once.

There's a lot more to IRC and Felix than what's covered here, but this should be more than enough to get you chatting. To learn more, dig around in Felix's many preference menus, or spend some time at **www.irchelp.org**.

# Web Servers

BeOS Web serving doesn't stop with PoorMan (which is covered in Chapter 8, *Networking*). If you're interested in serving up a world-class Web site from your BeOS machine, there are several high-quality options out there, with others likely available by the time you read this. What can these servers do that PoorMan can't? Plenty. But whether you need them or not depends on your needs as Webmaster. Do you need the ability to host multiple sites from a single server? Do you need to be able to password-protect certain directories beneath the root, or close them off entirely? Do you need CGI capabilities? Do you need assurance that you're getting the maximum possible performance? All of these are potential reasons you may want to check out some of the third-party Web servers available for BeOS. Otherwise, you may want to stick with PoorMan, which you'll probably find easier to set up, configure, and manage.

## What about Web Browsers?

As described in Chapter 4, *Get Online Fast*, NetPositive is a super-snappy, effective little browser. It doesn't offer the level of advanced features you'll find in a browser like Netscape Navigator, but it gets the job done, and many people appreciate its simplicity.

At this writing, NetPositive was the only Web browser available for BeOS, but that situation may have changed by the time you read this, as there are two important browser development projects in the works.

### BeZilla

Netscape's decision to release its browser to the world as open-source software meant that the Navigator codebase became available to programmers, which in turn meant that BeOS developers could port Navigator to BeOS themselves, rather than waiting for Netscape to do it. A team led by BeOS developer Richard Hess has spent many long months on this effort, and has been making steady progress. If BeZilla (so called because Navigator was called Mozilla once upon a time) isn't available by the time you read this, you can track the project's status at `reality.sgi.com/rhess/beos/bezilla`.

### Opera

Over the past couple of years, Opera, an alternative to Netscape Navigator and Internet Explorer, has been growing in popularity. Sporting a tiny footprint and excellent multitasking capabilities, Opera has gained currency among power users for being incredibly fast and compact. Opera's decision to port the browser from Windows to a variety of alternative operating systems excited many BeOS fans, and the development project has been making great strides. With any luck, you'll have your choice between NetPositive, BeZilla, and Opera sometime in 1999. Keep your eye on `www.operasoft.com/alt_os.html` for project updates.

# Apache

Of all the world's Web servers, perhaps none has quite the legendary status of Apache, a piece of exceptional freeware that powers the majority of all Web sites. While Apache's original home is Unix, it has been ported to a variety of other platforms, not the least of which is BeOS. Up until recently, one of Apache's biggest shortcomings was that it was "old Unix"—single-threaded— and therefore not capable of taking advantage of pervasive multithreading, one of BeOS's more significant trump cards. However, a fully multithreaded version of Apache is in development as Apache 2.0, and will be available only for operating systems that support true multithreading. Naturally, BeOS is on the list, developers are hard at work, and you can download and install early builds of Apache 2.0 for BeOS now (or possibly final builds by the time you read this). Once the Apache 2.0 codebase solidifies, the BeOS version will be merged into the standard distribution channels, and will be offered through **apache.org** alongside Solaris and Linux versions.

It's worth noting that even with the juicy new multithreading in Apache 2.0, it may not be easy for it to take advantage of other unique BeOS technologies, such as the attribute-based filesystem and the sophisticated messaging infrastructure. This is the tradeoff we make with ports on BeOS: They bring important software to the platform, but have difficulty milking the platform for all it's worth. Nevertheless, Apache is extremely fine-tuned, and has a leg up in the evolution department compared to other BeOS Web servers. As of this writing, Apache was by far the most configurable and customizable of all BeOS Web servers. Even though it had just been ported, early indications were that it was already slightly faster than PoorMan when serving small files, and far faster when serving large files.

So what's the catch? Well, setting up and configuring Apache isn't the intuitive, three-minute joyride that setting up PoorMan is. First of all, Apache for BeOS is distributed as source code, rather than as a ready-to-run binary. That means that you'll have to compile it yourself with the tools provided in your BeOS installation. Second, Apache has no interface—all customizations are accomplished by editing text configuration files. Figuring out which files to tweak and what to enter into them will take a bit of getting used to and some time spent with your nose in the documentation. If you're already comfortable compiling your own software, using command-line tools, and editing configuration files, you'll get amazing performance out of Apache. Otherwise, you'll probably want to stick with PoorMan or Zorro (discussed later in this chapter) for now.

The BeOS community has two people to thank for getting the Apache port off the ground and to where it is now. David Reid initiated the port and spent the time digging around in the codebase and making the technical adjustments necessary to get Apache compiling on BeOS. Matt Zahorik did exceptional work on the Netscape Portable Runtime Library (NSPR), which is a networking layer developed by Netscape, made available through Netscape's open-source software distribution agreement, and ported to BeOS as part of the BeZilla (Navigator for BeOS) effort. Apache for BeOS would not have been possible without NSPR.

**Getting Started** The steps involved in getting Apache running on your system are roughly as follows (note that these instructions may change somewhat by the time you read this—read the included documentation carefully, especially the file readme.beos).

1. Download the Apache 2.0 source code from **dspace.dial.pipex.com/ dreid/apache_beos.html**, and the rest of the Apache distribution from **www.apache.org**. The source code package includes everything you need to create the httpd (daemon) binary, and the rest of the Apache distribution gives you the configuration files and related documentation you'll need to get everything running properly. At some point in the future, everything you need will be bundled together as a single download, probably available from **www.apache.org** as well as from the usual BeOS software haunts.

2. You'll need to specify the root directory of the Apache server in one of three ways. For the best possible performance, you'll want to hard-code the root into the server binary itself, so you'll need to edit one of the header files before beginning. In the directory where you decompressed the Apache/BeOS "tarball" (the tar.gz file), open the file apache-nspr/include/httpd.h and find the line "Set default for BeOS". Beneath that, you'll see that the root is set to /boot/home/apache. Edit this to equal the actual root of your server. Farther down in this file, you'll find a section called "Document Location," which defaults to /htdocs. This will become the subdirectory of your site's root containing the actual HTML files and images you want to serve. This may be different from other servers you've tried, in which the server root is where you store your documents. By storing your files one directory down from the actual server root, you prevent your /conf, /logs, and other administrative directories from being mixed in with your actual data. This is useful for two reasons. One is that it's just plain good housekeeping. The other is that if your administrative directories were mixed up with your data directories, the public would potentially be able to access and read them (unless you were careful with your access permissions settings). In any case, you get more security storing your files in subdirectories. If you'd like to use a different directory name for your data files, edit the "Document Location" line. You could make this line equal to your actual server root if you were so inclined; however, Apache pros avoid this, and it is generally considered unwise for the reasons outlined above. Alternatively, you can specify a server root path in a configuration file (see below), or you can feed the server a root path as a command-line argument. Still, if you'll be serving your site from a single root, you may as well hard-code it into the binary now.

3. Open the folder called apache-nspr and rename the file called Configuration.beos to Configuration. Launch this file in a text editor, and you'll find four lines starting with EXTRA_LDFLAGS and EXTRA_INCLUDES—one set each for PowerPC and x86. Uncomment the two that apply to your platform, and edit them to reflect the directory in which you're currently working. Save and close.

4. Open a Terminal window and cd to the directory nsprpub, then type make. During this and the next two steps, you may see a number of error messages, but as long as the compiler doesn't say "halted," you can safely ignore them.

5. Change to the directory apache-nspr (where your Configuration file lives) and type ./Configure. Let it do its thing.

6. Type make. This is the final build process, and will take longer than the previous two steps. When it's finished, you'll have a shiny new binary file called httpd. Again, note that these steps may not be exactly the same by the time you read this.

7. From the official distribution package, copy the conf and logs directories to your server's root. In the directory containing the httpd binary, type httpd & to launch the server daemon itself.

8. Open a browser and enter your loopback address (**http://127.0.0.1/**) into the URL field. If everything has been built and placed properly, you should see your site's home page. Congratulations—you're running Apache on BeOS!

## Troubleshooting Apache

If you were able to build the binary but can't bring up your site, the problem is almost certainly with an incorrectly specified path or missing directory somewhere. You must place both the conf and logs directories in your server's root, or httpd will give you an error message. Once the logs directory is in place, you can look inside for a file called error_log. Opening this file can give you important clues about paths that have been requested but don't exist as far as Apache is concerned. You may find that the server root you compiled into the binary is not equal to your actual server root, or that it's looking for an htdocs directory when you haven't actually placed your site inside that directory. If, as described here, you end up working with the Apache 2.0 binary but the Apache 1.3 configuration files, you may run into occasional snags. For example, Apache won't like the MaxRequestsPerChild line in your httpd.conf file, so you'll need to comment it out to get things humming. Watch carefully for any error messages returned to the Terminal when you start the server. If the server is running properly, you should see no error messages, and the prompt should not be returned to you (assuming you didn't start it with httpd &).

From this point, it's only a matter of fine-tuning the behavior of your Web server.

In the `conf` directory in your server's root, look for the file called `httpd.conf-dist` and make a copy of it as `httpd.conf`. This file lets you specify parameters for all kinds of server options, such as the server's root, the administrator's email address, the maximum number of connections, and so on. This file contains detailed descriptions of all allowable settings, and should be relatively self-explanatory. You'll also find two other configuration files in the same directory: `access.conf` (for specifying who can access which kinds of services) and `srm.conf` (for configuring the "namespace" of your server, which controls settings such as the paths to document directories stemming from the server's root). All three of these configuration files work in exactly the same way, and each can contain settings initially described in the others. For simplicity's sake, you can optionally use a single settings file (probably `httpd.conf`) and manage all of your settings from there.

`httpd` can also be launched with a number of command-line arguments. For example, to specify a server root other than the one hard-coded into the binary or specified in `httpd.conf`, try this:

```
httpd -d /gorgonzola/mysite
```

(substituting your actual root path for `/gorgonzola/mysite`, of course). You can also specify alternative configuration files by using the `-f` flag, followed by a path.

 ***Apache and MIME Types*** Unlike other BeOS Web servers, Apache does not use the MIME types built into the BeOS filesystem. Instead, it uses a standard extensions table, which you'll find in `conf/mime.types`. Edit this file as necessary to serve nonstandard filetypes with Apache.

You'll find the complete manual that covers configuring and using Apache in a subdirectory of the `htdocs` directory called `manual`. In addition, you'll find tons of useful information and Apache tips floating around at **www.apache.org** and **www.apacheweek.com**.

## diner
**www.stegemann.net/Incorporated**

The first BeOS Web server to be released onto the scene that wasn't developed by Be itself was a tiny, highly efficient server developed by Stegemann & Stegemann called POW, which was later renamed "diner". diner isn't quite as easy to set up or configure as PoorMan, but it's definitely easier to get up and running than Apache, since you don't have to compile anything first. And since diner is BeOS-native, it can take advantage of special BeOS features that may be more difficult for Apache to incorporate. In any case, diner does quite a few nifty tricks that PoorMan does not. For instance, diner will let you map multiple root directories so you can serve up multiple sites simultaneously, even if they don't share a single parent directory. Also unlike PoorMan, diner supports redirects, so that you can have all accesses to one file point instead to another file, which is very useful if you need to move things around and don't want everyone's bookmarks to break. Finally, diner supports CGI, so you can back your Web pages with Perl scripts, for instance.

**Figure 11.22**

*Diner doesn't have much of a GUI, and all configuration takes place via a text-based configuration file. The small diner window displays only the cumulative number of requests and a row of indicator lights telling you what the server is doing at any given moment.*

As of this writing, diner had no configuration GUI (though one was rumored to be in development and may be available by the time you read this). The small graphical applet (Figure 11.22) simply displays a set of blinky lights to indicate the presence of incoming requests, successful accesses to files on your server, and the like. All configuration is accomplished by editing a text file, which you may find similar to configuring Unix-based Web servers. After downloading diner from BeWare and decompressing its archive, move the file diner_settings to /boot/home/config/settings. You may want to create a symlink to that file in your diner directory for easy access.

While most personal Web servers allow (or require) you to set up a root directory, you won't find anything called "root" in the diner_settings file. Since diner is capable of serving multiple sites from multiple directories, this makes sense, since the concept of a single root is gone. You want to look instead for entries in the configuration file called remap. These work pretty much as you'd expect. If you store your site at /boot/home/public_html/mysite, then you'll want to make the very first remap line read like this:

```
Remap   /   /boot/home/public_html/mysite
```

This, in essence, says that every access to the root of the server (e.g. to **http://127.0.0.1**) should pull up the default file in your site's folder, which you can specify by tweaking the IndexFile line in the settings file.

diner also has customizable error messages. Don't like the standard 404 (file not found) error? Just create a custom HTML document containing your error message and edit the line at the end of the configuration file to reflect a path of your choosing:

```
OnError404   /boot/apps/net/diner/errors/error_404.html
```

As of this writing, diner's CGI implementation was somewhat limited (due to BeOS limitations that may be fixed by the time you read this), meaning that your existing CGI scripts may or may not work with diner. We were not able to confirm future plans for advanced CGI support in diner, but if you want to give it a shot, try this: Open up Preferences | FileTypes in BeOS and add the type data/x-pst-CGI to your system's database (diner, like PoorMan, depends on your system's MIME types, rather than having a MIME extensions table of its own). Then make sure that the CGI scripts in your site mirror have the same type and try to access a page that invokes one of your scripts. With any luck, the page will have the same functionality that it does on your live server … assuming, of course, that you've got Perl, Tcl, or whatever other language the script is written in installed and working on your system, and that the path to that language is properly referenced at the head of your script file.

Future versions of diner will use an add-ons architecture to extend CGI and SSI capabilities and make it easy to tell diner to work with, say, Java Servlets.

 In our testing of diner 1.1, we found that NetPositive became confused when reading pages containing images served up by diner, even when the same pages could be served properly by PoorMan. While this bug should be cleared up by the time you read this, check your pages in Internet Explorer or Netscape Navigator on another platform; we found that these browsers were able to read the same pages served up by diner just fine.

# Zorro
`littlebig.rsn.hk-r.se`

Every bit as easy to set up and maintain as PoorMan, LittleBig Software Engineering's Zorro has several advantages over the Web server bundled with BeOS. First of all, Zorro gives you real-time traffic reporting like no other BeOS Web server. Not only can you see the total number of requests in the current session, you can also see individual hits on every single directory and file in your site as they roll in. You also get live updating of the number of users who have visited your site, the number of 404 errors

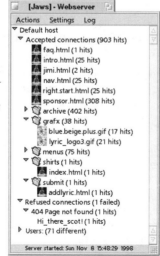

**Figure 11.23**

*Thanks to BeOS's real-time live update capabilities, Zorro maintains independent traffic reports for every single directory and file in your site as it's being served, potentially saving you the trouble of parsing logs with other tools later on.*

encountered, and other details. Serving multiple Web sites simultaneously from the same server is a piece of cake, and SSI (server-side includes) and CGI (Common Gateway Interface) capabilities are built-in and ready to use. Zorro has a full graphical interface, which means no messing around in configuration files and no compiling binaries by hand.

Zorro displays a hierarchical view of your entire server environment, with collapsible views of your server roots and the directories and files they host. As you can see in Figure 11.23, the default server always occupies the top level of the hierarchy. As soon as the first file is requested from that root, the directory it lives under appears as a folder in Zorro's interface, and the requested file itself appears beneath that folder.

The process of setting your server root in Zorro is pretty simple. Select the Default Host entry in the hierarchy and pull down Settings | Set WWW Root. Navigate to your site's root and you're done. To serve multiple sites, pull down Actions | Add Virtual Host, give the server a name, and go through the same process of establishing a root. You can serve as many sites simultaneously as your bandwidth will permit. You'll probably also want to establish separate log file directories for storage of Zorro's text-based access logs.

CGI and SSI functionality are enabled by default, but you can disable them if necessary by deselecting their entries in Zorro's settings menu. See Zorro's documentation for details on using these features. Future versions of Zorro will gain security and authorization functionality, as well as the ability to make administrative changes remotely via Web browser.

In our testing with an early beta, Zorro withstood more than 1,000 requests per hour without flinching. With the beefed-up networking code in BeOS R4 and further improvements to Zorro itself, we can see no reason why this server shouldn't hold up with the best of them in any traffic conditions that BeOS itself is capable of withstanding.

 It is possible that Zorro's name may change by the time you read this. Keep your eye on `littlebig.rsn.hk-r.se` for information and updates. Zorro itself is available on BeWare.

# FTP Servers

The FTP server built into BeOS's Network preferences panel is convenient, but as described in Chapter 8, *Networking*, it doesn't offer the advanced functionality that many people will want. You can't, for example, limit your FTP access to certain directories. Nor can you establish multiple username/password combinations or log hits to your FTP server. Fortunately, a third-party alternative called campus is available.

## campus
**www.stegemann.net/Incorporated**

The only third-party FTP server available for BeOS at this writing was campus, from Stegemann & Stegemann. Like its big brother diner (discussed earlier in this chapter), campus is configured entirely via text files, which you should find pretty intuitive, save for a couple of important notes.

First, unless you intend to run campus on a port other than the default of 21, you'll need to make sure you've disabled BeOS's built-in FTP daemon before starting campus. Uncheck the FTP Server box in Network preferences and restart networking before launching campus. If you fail to do this, campus won't start properly, nor will it inform you why it isn't working.

Begin configuring campus by moving its configuration file to your ~/config/ settings directory, then opening it in any text editor.

**Setting Up Directories** The first thing you'll want to do is determine which of your directories visitors will be able to access and which ones will be off-limits. This is a three-step process that involves establishing users, groups, and corresponding allow/deny statements. You must establish all users above all groups in the configuration file, and you must establish all groups above all allow/deny statements, or the results could be unpredictable.

Let's say you want to grant access to your /boot/home/ftp directory to the entire world. In addition, let's say you have a trusted friend who logs in as JLG, and you want to give him access to your home directory as well. Finally, there's you—you want to give yourself permission to access your entire system. Start by creating appropriate user entries in the config file. User lines always start with "user" and are followed by the username and, optionally, a password:

```
user anonymous homedir /boot/home/ftp
user JLG zo0mer homedir /boot/home
user root abracad*bra homedir /
```

Note that JLG and root have passwords specified, whereas the anonymous user's password is not specified—those users can use any password. Now that you've got multiple users, you may want to place them into different groups:

```
group public anonymous JLG root
group friends JLG root
group private root
```

In other words, you've created three groups, called public, friends, and private. All users are now members of the public group, only you and JLG are members of the friends group, and only you belong to the private group. Finally, you need to establish allow/deny privileges for each group. These lines take this form:

```
allow/deny    path        groupname    permissions
```

Thus, your entries might look like this

```
deny / public     all
allow /boot/home/ftp    public    cd, list, put, get
allow /boot/home friends    all
allow / private    all
```

You can probably infer from this that the public group only gets access to your /boot/home/ftp directory, and even then, they only get to run a few commands. Meanwhile, you're letting your friends do anything they want to in your home directory, and giving yourself full permissions throughout your entire system. The most important thing to note here, however, is the *order* in which the two statements directed at the public group are entered. We start by denying them access to everything, then granting limited access to just one directory. Each statement augments or modifies the one that comes before it. Therefore, if you reversed the order of these two directories, you would be allowing access to one directory, and then reversing that decision by denying access to everything. The order in which you install your allow/deny statements is critical!

All of the configuration settings described above have more options than are described here. See campus's documentation for more details.

## Email Servers

For those looking to use their BeOS machines as mail servers, developer Wes Peters is producing a POP3 and SMTP server for BeOS called BePost. Developed from the ground up to take full advantage of BeOS's multithreadedness, BePost should be an excellent performer, and will use BFS attributes to store the parameters of each user's account. It will intercept and spool outbound mail in its own SMTP server, and will make incoming messages available to users through its own POP server, which will be accessible by any standard POP mail client, such as BeMail, Mail-It, or other clients available on other operating systems. If work proceeds apace, BePost may be available on BeWare by the time you read this.

While BeOS may not be the ideal operating system for Internet service providers (for reasons outlined in Chapter 8, *Networking*), it will serve just fine on smaller networks. For example, an organization of a couple hundred employees (or even a simple home network!) running its own domain on its own servers will be able to manage mail spools on its own internal network, rather than relying on external providers for this service.

# Miscellaneous Tools and Utilities

In addition to the major categories of Internet applications touched on in this chapter, there are dozens of smaller, dedicated tools available on BeWare that may prove useful. A couple of good ones are covered here.

## ANewsWire

If you're a news junkie, you'll appreciate the fact that a desktop "push" client already exists for BeOS, in the form of AbiSoft's ANewsWire. This little gem reaches out to Yahoo!'s online news service and retrieves headlines and brief

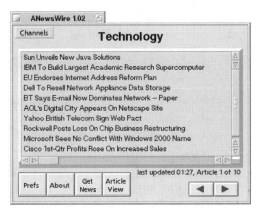

*Figure 11.24*

*AbiSoft's ANewsWire is a "push" client for BeOS, grabbing up-to-the-minute headlines from Yahoo!'s news service and delivering them to your Desktop.*

stories in your choice of nine "channels," such as Technology, Sports, Health, Business, and so on. Jump online, select a channel, and up-to-the-minute headlines related to that topic will fill the main view. Click any headline to read a brief synopsis of the story. If you want to learn more, click the link in the story to launch its full text in your Web browser.

You can customize just about every single aspect of ANewsWire's appearance and behavior by clicking the Preferences button—you can even make every button in the interface a different color if you like. Oh, and don't be shocked the first time ANewsWire starts talking to you in a freaky robot voice … it does that quite a bit, though you can easily turn this feature off from the Preferences panel.

## Stamina & Charisma

If you pay dearly for your online connection time, or if you run BeOS on a laptop and wish you could read today's Web-based news on the train on the way home, then you need an offline reader for the Web. Fortunately, just such a tool exists for BeOS. Sylvain Demongeot's Stamina & Charisma is a two-part utility. Stamina reaches out to the Web and grabs your favorite site (or portion thereof) and saves it to your hard disk at /boot/home/theWWW/www.mysite.org. You can tell Stamina to what depth level it should dig and how often it should refresh its cache (so you can make sure you get the latest news without wasting time downloading pages that haven't changed since your last visit).

Charisma is a cleverly designed proxy server that feeds Stamina's saved sites back to NetPositive. To use it, pull down Settings | Select Web Directory and point it to the site you want to view. Then pull down the Settings menu again and select Net+ Autosettings. (This will change NetPositive's proxy server settings, so be sure and disable this option when you're done, or change them back manually from NetPositive's Preferences panel.) You can now enter the URL of the site you want to view and browse it normally, even if you're completely disconnected from the Internet!

## BeCQ

One of the most explosive software hits on the Internet over the past couple of years has been a chat client called ICQ, from Mirabilis, Ltd. While Internet users had long enjoyed the IRC network, it had always been difficult to send AOL-style "instant messages" to friends, to learn if your friends were online at any given time, or to connect up with colleagues in a particular IRC channel. ICQ changed all of that, rocketed to popularity, and was eventually acquired by America Online, which is now Mirabilis's parent company. You'll find a version of the ICQ client for BeOS on BeWare, under the name BeCQ. At this writing, BeCQ was able to reproduce most (but not all) of ICQ's features, but was avidly being upgraded for a new version to be released shortly after R4. The most recent version should be a nearly complete ICQ client for BeOS.

# 12

# Productivity Applications

Despite all of the big words about BeOS being "The MediaOS," sometimes you just need to sit down and count your beans. In fact, many of us spend a great percentage of our computing time with our noses buried in spreadsheets and word processors. Officially, Be is not trying to create "a better DOS than DOS, a better Windows than Windows" (which was IBM's OS/2 marketing slogan for a while). And that's a good thing—the general-purpose operating system market is well-served by MacOS and Windows, and indeed, Be would be foolish to venture into that territory. No doubt about it, BeOS is optimized from the ground up as a multimedia operating system. But that marketing strategy doesn't take into account a few important points:

- Many people *are* dissatisfied with the existing general-purpose operating systems, and they *are* looking for a superior alternative.

- Booting back and forth between one operating system and another is an inconvenience, no matter how easy multi-boot managers make it.

- Nobody likes having half of their data stored in one OS and half of it in another; people appreciate having choice, but the laws of convenience dictate that life is simpler when you can spend as much of your time as possible in one OS, not two or three.

- When you optimize an OS for highly taxing media jobs, you end up with an OS that's efficient for *all* kinds of tasks.

In addition to the many features of the MediaOS that make it inherently good at handling your daily, possibly mundane, computing tasks, there's also a wide array of general productivity applications available for BeOS—applications that do the same things you already do in MacOS or Windows, but that, thanks to features like real-time live updating and pervasive multithreading, also offer capabilities you won't find in their counterparts on other OS's. This chapter takes a close look at some of the general-purpose productivity applications available for BeOS, such as those from BeatWare, Gobe, AbiSoft, Hekkelman Programmateur, and others.

# AbiSoft's BePlan

*with Kenneth Flaxman*

www.abisoft.com

BePlan by AbiSoft is a datebook for BeOS that synchronizes with 3Com's PalmPilot connected organizers.

If you have a life, you have a datebook. BePlan won't help you get a life, but it's more than happy to be your datebook. And if you store part of your brain in a PalmPilot (as so many of us do), BePlan will synchronize the datebook on your PalmPilot with your BeOS machine.

A demo version of BePlan is available at www.abisoft.com. If you decide you like it, you can purchase the full-featured version through BeDepot.

## Using BePlan

Launch BePlan and you'll see a calendar for the current month, similar to the one in Figure 12.01.

**Figure 12.01**

*The current day is designated with a dark outline. Any day with scheduled events will appear in the user-settable "emphasis" color. The background picture is set by dragging an image file onto the calendar.*

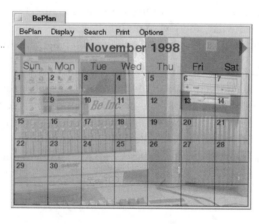

The controls for the calendar fall easily to hand:

- Click on the arrows to the left or right of the month title to make the calendar display the following or previous month.
- Click in the month title itself to select a different month.
- Click in the year title to select a different year.
- Click on the title bar between the month and year and use the right or left arrows to return the calendar to the current month.
- Click any day in the month to launch the "day view."

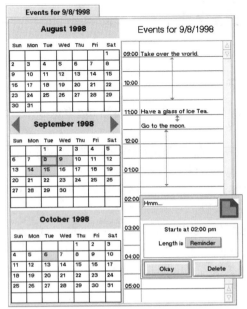

**Figure 12.02**

*Click on the time of an appointment to add, change, or delete an event. A note can be attached to an event with the appointment editor. Click and drag an appointment to change its time. Drag an event onto a calendar to change an appointment's date.*

**Working with Appointments** Double-click on any day in the current month view and you'll get a form like the one in Figure 12.02, which lets you enter events for the day, and gives you quick access to calendars for past, present, and future months. An arrow represents the length of the appointment.

**Syncing with the PalmPilot** Syncing BePlan with your PalmPilot is a two-step process. Launch the included BeHotSync module and press the HotSync button on your Pilot. Your calendar will be synchronized, so that anything you've entered into your Pilot while on the road will now be in your computer, and all of the events you've entered into BePlan will now be in your Pilot. And you didn't have to boot into MacOS or Windows to do it, either. Life is sweet.

## Features

Need a hard copy of today's events to store in your briefcase or backpack? A menu on the main window lets you print all events for the current day or week.

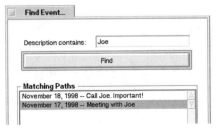

Does your week start on Monday? No problem—a menu on the main window lets you set the week to start on either Sunday or Monday.

**Figure 12.03**

*Since every event can contain a description, you can search for upcoming events by looking for keywords.*

Need to search for an appointment? BePlan takes full advantage of the BeOS filesystem to allow near-instantaneous searching for events by keyword.

 BePlan's chief developer is Seth Flaxman, who happens to have been 12 years old at the time he wrote it. You can read an interview with Seth at `www.bedope.com/int/int06sf.html`.

# BeatWare's Be Basics

*with Karen Cassel*

`www.beatware.com`

BeatWare was the first company out of the gate to establish a niche in the BeOS productivity market, and their suite of applications for getting everyday work done within the context of the MediaOS remains among the strongest and most popular available.

## The Two Applications You Need Every Day

What's a computer worth without a word processor and a spreadsheet program? To most people, not much. BeatWare calls its productivity suite Be Basics because it includes the two of the most essential BeOS applications. But don't let the name fool you—no BeOS application can really be considered basic.

Be Basics includes BeatWare Writer (a word processing and page-layout application) and BeatWare Sum-It (a full-featured spreadsheet application for creating worksheets, tables, and charts). The two are separate applications, so you're free to install and use just one or the other, but together they give you all you need to create really compelling documents.

Both Writer and Sum-It are capable of importing and exporting documents to and from other word processing and spreadsheet applications, so you can continue working with the library of, for example, Microsoft Office documents you've built up over the years. Writer will import and export plain text, RTF, and HTML files, so you have several ways of sharing your work with users of other platforms. Alternatively, since BeOS supports reading and writing to Windows and MacOS disk volumes, you can leave all of your data right where it is and keep working normally. Similarly, Sum-It will import and export comma- or tab-delimited text (`.CSV` files), SYLK, and Microsoft Excel files.

 **Be Basics is suitable for use both in the U.S. and in Europe. It supports international character sets, and international currency, date, and time notations. Foreign language dictionaries are planned for release in early 1999, though that does not represent a commitment to ship.**

# Getting Started with Writer

BeatWare Writer is a "frame-based" word processor, which means that all your text, images, tables, and charts are stored in onscreen containers called frames. You can move, resize, add, and delete frames at will, so you have total control over the layout of your document.

When you launch Writer, you'll notice a dotted blue border around the page—this is the frame. Inactive frames are blue, while active frames are red. To move, resize, or delete a frame, you must first make it active by clicking on it.

By default, each page of a Writer document has one frame that contains the full contents of the page. If you want to create a basic letter or document, ignore the frame, or lock it by selecting View | Lock Frame, and begin typing. In this mode, Writer acts just like a souped-up word processor.

 **To highlight a word in Writer, place your cursor anywhere within the word and double-click. Triple-click to highlight an entire paragraph.**

Because BeOS supports live updating, changes such as font size and shear are made without the need for dialog boxes or pulldown menus. There's no more guessing—just select your text, then click and hold on the toolbar's font-selection arrows. The text will grow or shrink before your eyes.

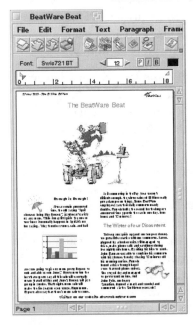

**Figure 12.04**

*Sometimes it's hard to tell whether Writer is a word processor or a page layout program. In reality, it's a little bit of both.*

**Word Processor or Page Layout Application?** The real fun begins when you use Writer's page layout capabilities to create a newsletter, user's manual, or flyer. Start by visualizing the overall layout of your document. Will the page have evenly spaced columns? Will it be divided into quadrants? Where will you put your pictures? Is there a chart or table that you want to embed within the text? Because Writer can do all of these things within its own interface, it's sometimes hard to tell whether you're working with a word processor or a page-layout program like QuarkXPress.

Once you have a clear idea of how you want your page to look, you can begin drawing the layout with your mouse. In reality, you'll be positioning a collection of frames in your document, but you can think of it as simply sketching an outline onto the page. To add a frame, make sure that Lock Layout is not selected in the View menu, then hold down the Ctrl key and use your mouse to draw a rectangle where you'd like a block of text or an image to appear. You can move frames around by grabbing any side with the mouse and dragging. To resize a frame, grab one of its handles and drag inward or outward. To get rid of an unwanted frame, activate it with a click and hit the Delete key.

Now you'll want to start adding some content to your page. Text can be added in one of two ways: You can either type it directly into the frame, or grab a text file from the Tracker and drag it into the frame. Images are inserted the same way: Grab an image file from the Tracker and drop it anywhere within the frame. Ready to see something cool? Drag an image into a frame that already contains text, and that text will automatically flow around the image. Once the image has been placed, you can resize it or move it just as you would a frame. Use the arrow keys on your keyboard to move a selected image one pixel in any direction. Hold down Shift while pressing an arrow key to move the image 10 pixels at a time. As you move images around, Writer automatically adjusts your text so you don't have to!

 **If you have BeatWare's e-Picture installed and want to edit an image in a Writer document, just double-click it to launch it in e-Picture, a full-featured image editor. After you make and save your changes in e-Picture, Writer will update the embedded image instantaneously.**

Writer offers a number of additional options for controlling the pattern and direction of your text flow. You can specify that text be situated to the left, to the right, or straight through an image. For front-page newsletter articles that you'd like to continue on another page, you can direct the flow of text from the first page to a later one by using your mouse to draw an arrow from the original frame to one a few pages later. If you want to get really fancy, try right-clicking in a frame and choosing Shape from the context menu—you'll have the option to automatically reshape your text into a pyramid, oval, or other geometric pattern.

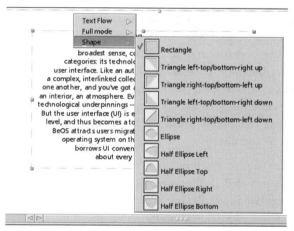

**Figure 12.05**

*Right-click in any Writer text block and choose Shape from the context menu to automatically reshape your text flow. Pictured is a paragraph from this book reshaped as an oval.*

## Getting Started with Sum-It

In the process of using the MediaOS to edit digital video or mix audio sound-tracks, you may find yourself with the need to keep track of all your multimedia resources, and BeatWare's Sum-It spreadsheet may be just the ticket. Its numbered rows and lettered columns are universally familiar and convenient for setting up budgets, check registers, sales logs, and portfolio models.

In addition to the tabular layout, you'll also find that Sum-It's look and feel are very similar to your current spreadsheet's. BeatWare has maintained common keyboard navigation and menu command shortcuts to make your transition to Sum-It virtually seamless.

 **Sum-It's context-sensitive menus provide a number of cell pasting and linking options. To access context-sensitive cut-and-paste options, use Ctrl+Alt+click. For quick access to a context menu relating to the moving, copying, or linking of cells, just Ctrl+click over any cell.**

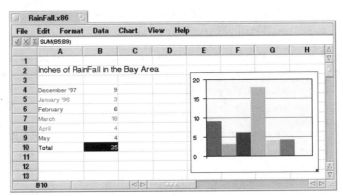

**Figure 12.06**

*After a long day of digital video editing, it's time to sit down and count the beans. BeatWare's Sum-It may be just the ticket.*

About the only significant difference between Sum-It and other spreadsheet applications is its speed. Because Sum-It was written natively for BeOS, it's fully multithreaded. What does pervasive multithreading mean for a spreadsheet? It means that every formula in a spreadsheet can be calculated simultaneously, each in its own thread. In contrast, spreadsheets on other platforms have to calculate functions sequentially, in a single thread. By processing calculations in parallel, Sum-It can save you a lot of waiting time, especially on large spreadsheets with lots of functions.

Sum-It ships with more than 80 predefined mathematical, statistical, logical, and financial functions. Also included are a number of charting functions for automatic creation of line and bar charts. Ambitious users and developers are free to define additional functions and plug them into Sum-It's interface.

## Getting the Most out of Be Basics

Real-time updating of data within a single file or spread across multiple files is one of BeOS's many real-world benefits, and Be Basics takes full advantage of this capability. By viewing multiple copies of the same file simultaneously, you can see in an instant how edits made to page one of your document affect pagination and text flow on page six. To do this in Writer, open another view of your document by selecting View | New Viewer from the main menu. Then hold down the Alt key and press the + and – keys on your numeric keypad. This will cause the current view to zoom in and out, so you can go in for a close-up or zoom back for the bird's-eye view. When you zoom out far enough, you'll be able to see multiple pages of your document in a single window at the same time, which can be very useful when preparing to print layouts that need to be carefully paginated. Try minimizing the second document view to the point where the text is unreadable and you can view all six pages. Use the mouse to reduce the size of the window, and move this "page layout" view over to the right side of your screen.

As you make changes to your document in the main window, notice the immediate updating that takes place in your page layout view. Enlarge the font size and see the length of your document increase in both windows. Add an image and the text in both windows will reflow to accommodate it instantly. Use the mouse to move or shrink the picture, and the text in both windows will automatically move to fill in the space left empty by the picture.

**Figure 12.07**

*In addition to images and pictures, you can add charts and tables created in Sum-It to your Writer documents. Simply highlight the cells behind the chart or table in Sum-It, hold the Ctrl key, and drag it into Writer. You can move or resize it just as you would any other frame.*

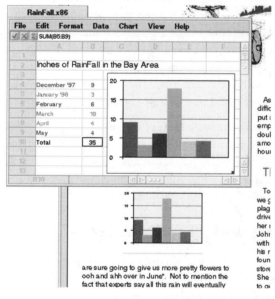

Two remaining features worth mentioning are Be Basics' "unlimited undo" capabilities and its comprehensive online HTML documentation. You also may find it useful to work with some of the sample documents created at BeatWare headquarters and find out how the pros do it. You'll find a collection of sample Be Basics documents at **www.beatware.com/press/scripts/basics.html**.

Other excellent applications from BeatWare are covered in Chapter 11, *Network Applications*, and Chapter 13, *Graphics Applications*.

# Gobe Productive

www.gobe.com

Gobe's all-in-one productivity suite combines word processing, spreadsheet, graphics, illustration, presentation, and charting functions into a single application with a single document format. Gobe Productive is the brainchild and creation of a team of ex-ClarisWorks engineers now dedicated to BeOS application development.

## Integrated Productivity

Unlike other integrated productivity suites like, say, Microsoft Works, Productive isn't just a collection of related applications—it really is one application. This makes linking different kinds of information together in one document a piece of cake. For example, you can embed a spreadsheet inside a word processing frame inside a graphics frame. In turn, the data in the spreadsheet can be inherited from another, larger spreadsheet elsewhere in the document. Need to fine-tune your graphics? You can do basic image editing from within the same document. And when you've got it all nailed down, you can transform all of your content into a business presentation.

Gobe Productive comes with very extensive and well-organized documentation in HTML format (which you can access by pulling down File | Help), so you can find answers to just about any question pretty easily. We'll cover the basics, then dig into a few advanced features to give you an idea of what Gobe Productive can do.

## Working with "Environments"

Productive consists of five major "environments": Word Processing, Graphics, Spreadsheet, Image Processing, and Presentation. Even though there's only a single document format, you will always be working in one of these environments at any given time. Thus, when you first launch Productive, you'll be asked about the primary function of your document, as seen in Figure 12.08.

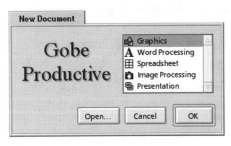

To insert an element from one environment into another environment, pull down Frame | Insert Frame and choose another environment. For example, if you begin with a word processing document and

**Figure 12.08**

*When you launch Gobe Productive, you'll be asked in which of the five primary "environments" you want to work.*

then insert a spreadsheet frame at some point, you will have switched to the spreadsheet environment, even though you're still in the same document. The only difference that you'll notice is that the toolbars will have changed to reflect the currently active environment—it's as if you're changing from one application to another, but your document remains the same. The objects you insert into your documents are called "parts," and you can have as many types of parts in a single document as necessary. Toggling between environments is a matter of selecting any part that belongs to another environment. Doing this does not change the environment of the entire document; it just changes the options available to you at any given time, which is always a function of the type of part currently selected.

While this may sound a little confusing on paper, it's quite intuitive in actual practice. If you have word processing and spreadsheet parts in the same document, try clicking in one and then in the other, and watch your toolbars reconfigure themselves to reflect the changing environment.

 **You don't always have to use the Frame menu to insert new parts in your documents, as Productive is fully drag-and-drop aware. You can insert a graphic or text file at any point by dragging it out of the Tracker and into your document. Drag in a graphic, click on it once, and you'll find yourself in image processing mode. In order to insert a graphic in a Productive document, you must have a Translator for that image format installed on your system (see Chapter 9, *Preferences and Customization*, for more on Translators).**

 **The capability to embed elements from one environment in another has great implications for people who often need to work with text and graphics at the same time. Rather than bitmapping your text and having it become uneditable, you can "float" your text above your graphics in word processing**

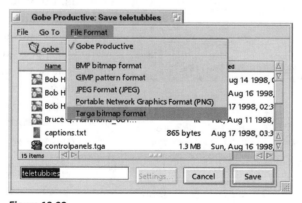

*Figure 12.09*

*If you intend to save your creation as a graphic later on, start your work in graphics mode. When you go to save your document, you'll be able to choose from among the image Translators installed on your system, even if you've got free-floating text or spreadsheet parts embedded in the document.*

frames and edit or alter the appearance of that text to your heart's content later on. The thing to keep in mind here, however, is that if you want to save your image out in a standard image file format, you should start your piece in the graphics environment. If you start out in another environment, your Save As file format options (which you'll find at the top of Productive's File panels) will only offer you text formats and the native Productive format as options.

## Digging into the Interface

Gobe has obviously gone to a lot of trouble to bring as much consistency as possible to Productive's user interface. You'll notice that as you switch from one environment to another, menu and icon options remain similar. You format text and numbers in spreadsheet and word processing parts identically, for example. Of course, it isn't always possible for the interface to be exactly the same—it wouldn't make sense, for example, to give you text-justification options when you're working in image-processing mode.

Most of Productive's toolbar icons and picklists conceal a lot more functionality than is evident at first glance. For instance, consider the paint bucket icon that appears in most environments. It doesn't represent simple color fills as you might imagine—instead, clicking this icon causes a color-picker palette to appear beneath it, and four more icons to appear beside it. Slide your mouse sideways over the other icons (color, pattern, gradient, and opacity), and the palette beneath them will change to reflect fill options for that category. Roll over the gradients icon, and a palette of prefab gradients appears, and so on. But it gets better. Slide your mouse a little farther, all the way off the palette, and an outline of the palette will appear around your mouse cursor. Release the mouse button, and the palette will become a free-floating window, now separated from the toolbar so you can work with it more closely. And why would you need to? Because it goes even deeper still! Double-click a color, and you'll find yourself in a full-spectrum color picker, so you have more control over fine shades. Double-click on a pattern, and you'll find yourself in a pattern editor. Double-click a gradient, and

**Figure 12.10**

*One of Productive's distinguishing characteristics is its "tear-off" menus. Drag sideways off any options palette and release to turn that palette into a free-floating window.*

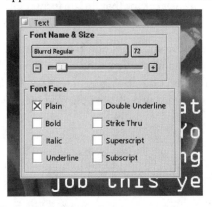

**Figure 12.11**

*Double-click in any of the prefab colors, patterns, or gradients to access a hidden editor that lets you fine-tune the current fill to perfection. Shown here is the gradient editor, which lets you customize the spectrum, direction, and type of gradient to be used in the fill.*

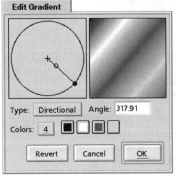

you'll find the hidden gradient editor; each of these mini-editors is like a little application unto itself.

 **Before you worry about messing up the prefab colors and gradients that appear by default, remember that you can save your customized palettes as "Sets" by using the File menu in the palette itself (not in the main application). This way you can create complete, custom libraries of fills; one for every project you maintain, for instance.**

The fill tools can be used with any selected object—you can apply your gradients, colors, and patterns to blocks of text, free-form selections, or entire graphics.

**Text Options** On the surface, the font and font size menus work just as they do in any word processor (but notice the groovy way the font menu renders all of your fonts in real time, so you see what you're getting before selecting a font). Tear off a font menu, however, and you get something extra: a floating text palette that does something you can't do on other platforms—true real-time interaction. With some text selected, drag the slider on the Text palette left and right to change its size. Whereas many applications on other operating systems make you click Apply or OK to preview or commit your changes, Productive's text palette applies your changes as you make them—you'll never need to make more than a single trip to this dialog to get your fonts just right.

**Working with Styles** If you use Microsoft Word very much, you may be familiar with its Styles function, which lets you specify, for example, that 24-point bold blue Bodoni can be applied in an instant to any selected text by choosing it from a pulldown menu. Nice, but Word styles are unnecessarily

*Figure 12.12*

*Select some text and turn it into a new style—you can then apply that style to any other selected text you like. Pictured: A block of text is filled with a grayscale gradient, a style is created from it, and the new style is applied to other selections.*

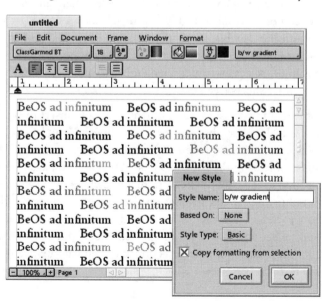

complex to create and store. Not so with Gobe Productive. Format some text the way you like it, click the Styles button, and choose New Style. In the resulting dialog, give your style a name and check the "Copy style from selection" button. Click OK, and your new style will now appear in the Styles picklist, and can be applied to any other selection by choosing it from that list. You can even store styles complete with built-in color gradients!

Productive's styles aren't just limited to word processing, either—they'll work in spreadsheets as well.

**Advanced Selections**   As in any application, selections in Productive define the content to which the next thing you do will apply. For example, select some text and change its font, and the font is only changed for the selected text, not for the whole document. Standard fare there, no big deal. But Productive also offers two additional selection features designed to make your life easier. First of all, selections don't have to be contiguous—you can select bits and pieces of text all over your document at the same time, and operate on them simultaneously. Just hold down your Alt key and select whatever you like (see Figure 12.13).

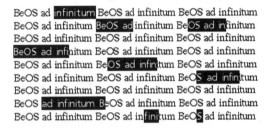

**Figure 12.13**

*Hold down the Alt key and make multiple selections anywhere in your document. Make a change (such as the font change pictured) and it will apply to all selected areas simultaneously.*

Second, Productive lets you name your selections, similar to the way you name styles. These selections can then be invoked by referring to them by name. Try this: In a spreadsheet environment, create a column of numbers, select them all, then click on the paper clip icon on the toolbar and give your selection a name (let's call it Fred). Now click in any blank cell in your spreadsheet and type in =SUM(Fred). When you hit Enter, the value in that cell will equal the total of the values in the cells in the selection named Fred. You can, of course, invoke named selections from other sheets (see below).

In the word processing environment, you can't insert the contents of a named selection elsewhere, but you can create hugely complex discontiguous selections, name them, and then reselect them in an instant by choosing the selection's name from the paperclip icon. Then all you have to do is copy the selection to the clipboard and paste it elsewhere. You can use exactly the same procedure in graphics and imaging modes. Note, however, that if you make changes to text that falls within a named selection, it may not appear as you expect when invoked later on. For example, if you insert new text into a sentence that's part of a saved selection and then later invoke that selection, your new text will be selected as well.

**Working with Sheets** If you don't want to float text over your images, or embed spreadsheets into word processing documents, you don't have to—you can just as easily maintain related works separately within the same file, thanks to a Productive feature called "sheets," which work similarly to Microsoft Excel sheets. Thus, you can have all five Productive environments in the same document even if they're not simultaneously visible. This can be a great way to organize and sort related information. You could, for example, work on the design draft of a Web site by creating your page layout in graphics or illustration mode with word processing parts laid on top of it, keep the site's proposal in a separate word processing sheet in the same document, keep tabs of your billable hours and resources on a spreadsheet sheet, and then tie everything together into a business presentation that draws on content created in the other sheets.

Pull down the Window menu and select Show Sheetbar. A new toolbar with folder-like tabs will appear. Double-click a tab to give the sheet a descriptive name. To create another sheet, click and hold on the icon at the left of the sheetbar, choose New Sheet, and choose an environment for it. You can create as many sheets as you need, and copy and paste data between them as necessary. In some cases, you can also link live data between different sheets (see the next section).

**Connecting Your Content** In many cases, you can cause data living in one frame to flow or be copied into another frame. There are two separate methods for doing this. In the first, known as "cloning" frames, you create an exact copy of the frame and place it elsewhere in your document. Because both frames are exact copies of one another, any content entered into one frame will also appear in the other. This can be very useful if, for example, you're creating a multipage newsletter and want a common header on all of them— you'll be able to change the header content in one place and have the headers on all pages be updated in real time. To do this, insert a frame, enter some content into it, select it, and pull down Frame | Clone Frame.

 **Selecting frames can be tricky sometimes. If you've been working on content inside a frame, you'll usually need to click outside of it, then click back inside of it once. You'll know a frame is selected when its bounding box has small black squares at its corners. If you double-click in a frame, you'll be in edit mode for that frame, working on its actual contents. You can't make changes to the frame itself while you're in edit mode. It's worth practicing this a bit and getting a handle on the difference between these two modes.**

In the second method, a new frame is created as an adjunct to the first. When content in the first frame overflows its bounding box, it simply flows down into the linked frame, wherever it may happen to be. To do this, create your first frame, enter some content into it, select the frame (not the content) and pull down Frame | Linked Frame. This will insert a new, linked frame into your document. You can then move your linked frame anywhere you like.

## Spreadsheets

At bottom, the Productive spreadsheet environment is pretty much like any spreadsheet you've ever used. You've got rows, columns, and cells, and you can define certain cells to display a mathematical or text-based "function" that results from the analysis of some other collection of cells. For example, you could specify that cell B13 be equal to the average of all the values in cells B1 through B12. To insert a function, click in a cell, then click the "ƒ%" button on the toolbar. A dialog will display a hierarchical menu of function categories, such as Date and Time or Trigonometry. Expand any branch of the hierarchy to see all of the allowable functions in that category.

You'll find complete documentation on the included functions in Productive's help system. Their syntax follows the same standards used in other spreadsheets on other platforms, so if you're familiar with using functions or formulas in another spreadsheet, they'll work as expected in Productive.

You can also create charts from the data in your spreadsheets, so that you can more easily visualize any data collection. By default, charts are always created in a new frame in the current sheet, but you can easily move the chart to another sheet in the same document, or to another document altogether. Note, however, that if you move your chart to a separate document, the data connection will be lost, and your chart won't update itself dynamically when the data in the spreadsheet changes.

To create a chart, select the part of the spreadsheet you want to display, making sure to include the leftmost column and topmost row (since the labels in these cells will become the chart's labels). Pull down Frame | Insert Frame and choose Chart from the menu. After the chart has been created, you can right-click in it and choose Chart Type or Axis from the context menu to customize the type of chart being created—you'll be able to rearrange your display as a pie chart, line chart, or histogram, and control whether the display is 2D or 3D.

 **Gobe Productive includes an extensive and very educational tutorial, which you'll find as a menu item in the help system. If you're going to be spending much time with Productive, running through this tutorial is highly recommended. You'll also find a subdirectory containing a variety of sample documents that show off Productive's basic and advanced capabilities and their potential uses.**

## Graphics

You'll be amazed at the flexibility of Productive's graphics environment, which supports layering, combined bitmap and vector graphics, infinite ability to reshape lines and curves, and of course, editable text objects.

Create a new document, sheet, or frame in graphics mode, and you'll be able to create free-form shapes from scratch, or drag images in from the Tracker. On the left side of the Productive window, you'll see a vertical column of graphics-specific tools. Take a look at the "pointing finger" icon at the top of this column—as with all Productive icons, the small arrow at its lower right indicates that if you press and hold, you'll see more options. By default, this tool is set to select or move a given frame (note that you can also move selected objects around by using the arrow keys on your keyboard). By scrolling over to the second finger icon and then moving your mouse to the edge of a frame, you'll be able to rotate that frame freely to any orientation. Select the third finger icon and you'll be able to use the frame's "handles" to resize the frame to any dimensions.

In graphics mode, the top of the working window also displays a row of "position fields." While they may not look editable, try clicking in one—you'll find that you can type in exact values to precisely specify the distance of the selected frame from the top, bottom, left, or right of the working window. In addition, a rotational field lets you specify the exact number of degrees to rotate your object.

One of the most fascinating possibilities in the graphics environment is the ability to deform your object in just about any way you can imagine. Try this: Create a simple free-form shape (by choosing one of the lower icons on the left-hand toolbar), and fill it with an ink (such as a solid color, a pattern, or a gradient). With the object selected, pull down Arrange | Reshape (or select the reshape finger icon). The object will acquire small dragger handles around its outline. Use your mouse to drag these handles anywhere you like. If you hold down the Shift key, you'll be able to select multiple handles for dragging at once.

As you drag handles around, the object's ink will refill to accommodate the new shape. You'll also notice that small lines with extra "vertex control" handles will protrude perpendicularly to the current handle—slide these around to change the orientation of the area you're reshaping. If you have a need to

*Figure 12.14*

*Select an object and pull down Arrange | Reshape to see an object's reshaping handles. Drag one anywhere to distort the object, or use the vertex control handles to re-orient it.*

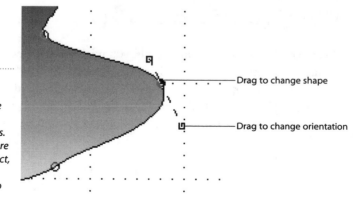

Drag to change shape

Drag to change orientation

create smooth curves out of clunky corners, right-click on any handle and choose Smooth Handle from the context menu. These techniques may take a little practice to get right, but you'll find them more intuitive in practice than they may sound on paper.

## Image Processing

At this writing, Productive's image processing environment wasn't anything to write home about. It's no Photoshop replacement, but it does include a nice array of cropping and selection tools, plus a very healthy handful of image processing plug-ins. If you're familiar with the GIMP application popular on many Unix platforms, you'll recognize many of the plug-ins here, as they've been recompiled from GIMP to work with Productive. Select any area in a bitmapped graphic and pull down the Plug-ins menu to see your choices.

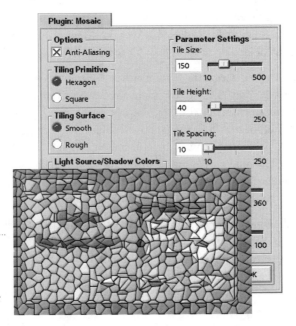

**Figure 12.15**

A screenshot of the Gobe Productive launch menu after having been run through the Mosaic plug-in.

If you have heavy-duty graphics needs, you might want to look at a more full-featured application such as BeatWare's e-Picture or Sander Stok's Becasso (see Chapter 13, *Graphics Applications*). Otherwise, consider this environment a great way to make quick nips, tucks, and modifications to existing graphics prior to importing them into other areas of your Productive documents.

# Presentations

After you've created a pile of related data in various formats in a single document, why not tie it all together into a full-screen presentation you can give to your potential clients? Like most Productive environments, presentations can use "layers," which work much like the clear plastic sheets used by non-digital cartoon animators. You can establish that one or two backgrounds are always present, then place other sheets (layers) over the top of your backgrounds. Each layer can store as many or as few frames as necessary. When the presentation is displayed, tapping the Spacebar moves you through the layers one at a time.

 Before you begin creating your presentation, establish the screen size, or the resolution of the monitor on which you intend to run your presentation. This is especially important if you intend on using quality resolution graphics and don't want them rescaled. Also keep in mind that many presentations are given on laptop displays, typically running at resolutions of 640×480 or 800×600, which is probably smaller than the resolution you run BeOS at.

*Figure 12.16*

Use the Edit menu on the Presentations palette to create, rename, or delete slides, and to arrange the layers that constitute each slide.

The presentation environment is very similar to the graphics environment, and you can do anything in a presentation that you can do in graphics mode. Before beginning, it's a good idea to get a handle on the difference between slides and layers. Each slide in your presentation comprises one screenful of information and must include at least one layer. Slides are not, however, limited to one layer, and can contain as many as necessary to achieve a particular effect. The Presentation palette will appear as soon as you enter presentation mode. Always make sure that the appropriate point in the presentation is selected in this palette before placing content. New content can be placed in any of the standard ways: by pasting it in from other sheets in the same document or by inserting new frames and entering your content fresh. To test your presentation at any point, just click the Start button on the Presentation palette.

 **Bitchin' Transitions**   Rather than jump-cutting from one slide to the next, you can use any of the three prefab "transitions": Wipe, Venetian Blinds, or Elevator Doors. To set a transition, click and hold on the small gray icon in the Presentation palette at the point denoting the beginning of the next slide. If you want to further customize the behavior of that transition, click this button again and choose Settings… from the context menu. You'll be able to control things like whether the transition effects are applied horizontally or vertically, or whether your "Elevator Doors" are opening or closing.

# Maarten Hekkelman's Pe

`www.hekkelman.com/pe.html`

Don't let the name of this first-class editor scare you—just because Pe stands for "Programmer's Editor," that doesn't mean you have to be a programmer to use it. In fact, this book was written almost entirely in Pe!

## The Programmer's Editor

Since BeOS already comes bundled with StyledEdit, you may be wondering why you would need a second text editor. The answer is simple: Pe has tons of functions that StyledEdit doesn't. If you've ever used BBEdit on the Macintosh, then you've got a good sense for the kind of extra functions I'm talking about: a zillion hotkeys, integration with programming environments like the BeIDE, more sophisticated search-and-replace capabilities, built-in tools to change word cases, floating customized tool palettes for inserting pre-defined blocks of text … the list goes on. In fact, some users who've used both Pe and BBEdit claim that Pe is even better than BBEdit. We'll leave that judgement up to you.

### Word Processors versus Text Editors

Pe is a full-featured text editor, not a word processor, and it's important to understand the difference. Word processors are geared toward advanced formatting of your text. They support bold and italic text, for instance, and let you use multiple fonts, embedded images, frames, and other goodies. In order to support these features, word processors need to save their work in (usually proprietary) binary formats, which means you often can't open your files in other word processors or on other operating systems. Text editors, on the other hand, deal only in plain-vanilla ASCII (well, technically, UTF-8 on BeOS, which is ASCII-compatible). You can *view* your text in other fonts, but you can't save it that way (StyledEdit being the lone exception here). Text editors have the advantage of reading and writing universally accessible plain text. In addition, advanced text editors often have features not found in word processors, like search and replace that burrows down through multiple subdirectories, line numbering, and tool palettes optimized for working with HTML or programming code.

## Using Pe

If you've ever used a plain text editor like StyledEdit, NotePad, or SimpleText, you'll find basic usage of Pe pretty much self-explanatory, so we'll skip the fundamentals and jump straight into the funkier features. Note that we won't cover every single one of Pe's menu options here—there are just too many!

***Launch Documents in Pe from the Terminal*** When Pe is installed, it adds a small utility to ~/config/bin **called** lpe.

**If you're working in the Terminal, just type** lpe filename.txt **to toss** filename.txt **into Pe for editing. Beats the heck out of using** vi!

**Using "Groups"** Pe has the ability to create loose "associations" of related files. If you have files scattered all over your hard drive that all relate to the same project, you can pull down File | New Group in Pe and drag your files into the resulting window. This neither moves nor copies files anywhere; a Group window is just a list of links to other locations you can use for convenience. You might, for example, want to create a group containing the index.html files that live in each of your Web site's directories, or all research papers relating to a given topic. This lets you store your files one way but group them logically in another, if the situation warrants. The Groups preferences panel lets you establish whether your group listings are sorted, and whether the symlinks they contain are stored with relative paths (this option is only useful if you think you'll be moving your projects to other disk volumes).

**If you double-click a Groups file and it comes up as a plain text file rather than in a Group window, the file has lost its MIME type. To repair it, use the FileTypes add-on to change its type to** text/x-vnd.Hekkel-Pe-Group.

**Open Files on Web Servers** Webmasters will love this one. If you'd rather edit documents directly from your Web server rather than from a local site mirror, choosing this option will open a dialog prompting you for the server's address, along with your username and password. In other words, Pe essentially has a built-in FTP interface, though it's no replacement for a full-featured FTP client. After logging in and receiving your document, choose File | Save to send it back to your Web site. If you want to create a new document on the server, use the Save to Server option.

**Recent Documents** This submenu remembers the last ten or so documents you've worked on, making it much easier to retrieve a specific document-in-progress than it is with standard File panels. You can change the number of entries stored here from the Preferences | Files dialog.

***Drag-and-Drop Options*** **Drag any text file from the Tracker into an open Pe window to insert that file at the current point. If you'd rather open that file in a new window than insert it, hold down the Alt key while dragging.**

**Undo/Redo** Pe is able to undo or redo any changes you've made, even between saves (that is to say, Pe supports unlimited undo). However, it does not keep track of changes after you close a document. The standard Alt+Z hotkey is used for undo; add Shift to the mix to redo (which makes for a great shortcut when you need to repeat advanced functions, as opposed to just pasting in text repeatedly).

**Figure 12.17**

*Click anywhere in your document and you'll see a context menu similar to this one. Select a block of text first, then right-click outside the selected area before clicking to make sure that all of the menu's options are available.*

Many of Pe's File, Edit, and other features can be accessed by right-clicking in the document window. This can be very useful for quickly showing and then hiding invisible characters, for turning syntax highlighting on and off, and for commenting out blocks of text.

**The Text Menu** Pe includes a handy collection of built-in text manipulation tools, most of which are self-explanatory. For instance, you can cause a word or sentence to be spelled backward by choosing Text | Twiddle, or change the case of a selection to uppercase, lowercase, or any of several variants.

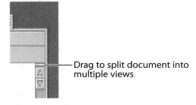
———Drag to split document into multiple views

**Figure 12.18**

*If you'd like to be able to see both the top and the bottom of a long document simultaneously, grab the small horizontal line above the upper scroll arrows and drag downward. This will split your document into two panes, or views.*

If you're coding HTML or using Pe for programming, you'll use the indentation feature frequently (Text | Shift Text Left/Right), though you'll probably want to use the Alt+ hotkeys instead. You can also comment out selected areas with the Text | Comment/Uncomment options. The type of comment is determined by the programming language in which the current document is written (which you can control from the Languages preferences panel, described below).

 When creating HTML documents in Pe, get friendly with the Alt+Shift+B hotkey, which is a shortcut to Text | Show in Browser. This makes it incredibly easy to preview your work in your system's preferred browser, which is probably NetPositive.

**Searching** Pe has tons of powerful search capabilities, some of which will be familiar, and some of which will not. One of the coolest (and most useful) is the Incremental Search option, which you can also access by clicking the second magnifying glass icon on the toolbar or by hitting Alt+I. No dialog is presented when you enter Incremental Search mode, though you will see the toolbar icon become depressed.

To give you an idea of how incremental search works, let's say the following words are scattered throughout your 100-page document:

do
doctor
document
DocuTech

After entering Incremental Search mode, press D, and the cursor will jump to the first "d" found. Now press O, and the cursor will jump to the first

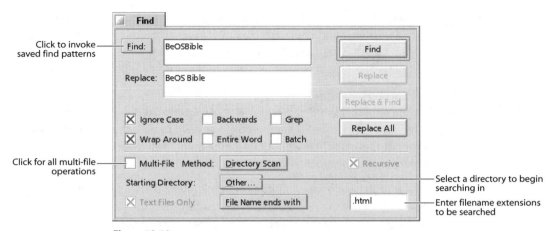

Click to invoke saved find patterns

Click for all multi-file operations

Select a directory to begin searching in

Enter filename extensions to be searched

*Figure 12.19*

*Pe's find-and-replace features are many and powerful. You can search in any direction, across multiple open files, down through subdirectories, or only on files with a given extension. Regular expressions can be used just as if you were in the shell.*

instance of "do". By the time you've typed "docut", you've probably reached the first instance of "DocuTech" (incremental search is case-insensitive by default, though this can be changed in the Searching section of Pe's preferences). This method of searching takes a bit of getting used to, but once you do, you'll probably want to use it more often than standard search.

The standard Find dialog (Alt+F) doubles as the Find and Replace dialog, and has many powerful options. As in most BeOS applications, Alt+G will always find the next instance of a string in any find pattern. By default, find-and-replace operations work only on the current document, but you can tell Pe to look for your string in all the files in a directory and all of its subdirectories, or to limit its search to all open windows, by selecting the Multi-File checkbox and tweaking the various picklists found there. Remember to select the Recursive checkbox if you want Pe to look in subdirectories!

### Table 12.01  Pe grep

| These Characters | Are Replaced by |
| --- | --- |
| \n | Linefeed |
| \r | Carriage return |
| \t | Tab |
| \\ | Single backslash (\) |

*Pe augments the usual* grep *standard with these options, which are especially useful in text processing.*

If your search-and-replace needs go beyond simple text strings, Pe is fully grep-capable. You can enter any regular expression you like into the Find field to perform find-and-replace operations possible nowhere else in the BeOS GUI (although the TrackerGrep add-on, discussed in Chapter 10, *System Tools and Utilities*, will let you find—but not replace—text strings in documents). Pe offers some additional options not found in grep, as shown in Table 12.01.

If you aren't intimately familiar with using regular expressions, be exceedingly careful when using them in search-and-replace operations, especially when coupling them with subdirectory crawling. One misplaced character in a regex string and you can mess up your Web site beyond the point of repair. Test your strings on single documents before applying them to your whole site!

 **If there are search-and-replace strings you find yourself having to run repeatedly, Pe can remember them so you never have to type them in again. Pull down Window | Preferences | Grep Patterns and add a new search-and-replace operation (with or without regular expressions).**

**Give your pattern a memorable name, click Apply, then reopen the Find dialog. To the left of the Find field is a Find button. Click the Find button, and all of your named patterns will appear in a context menu. Select one, and the pattern you just entered in Preferences will pre-fill the Find and Replace fields.**

**Extensions** Pe is capable of using add-on modules written by third parties (or you). Any modules stored in the Extensions subdirectory of Pe's installed location will appear on the Extensions menu. Some of these are useful, some just for fun. One of the more useful extensions is Copy/Cut Lines Containing. Open this dialog, enter a text string or regular expression, and Pe will either delete all matching lines from your document, or copy them all to the clipboard. Just for fun, you can create a "ransom note" effect by selecting some text and choosing Extensions | drieuxCaps. And if you ever encounter text on Usenet that appears scrambled, try pasting it into a Pe document and running the ROT13 extension over it (ROT13 is an extremely simple form of encryption that simply displaces each letter of the alphabet by 13 characters).

## Preferences

One of the easiest ways to get familiar with Pe's features (aside from reading the excellent documentation in HTML format, available from the Help menu) is to start poking around in the many settings and preferences dialogs. Pe has two different preferences panels: one for controlling global preferences that apply to all documents (pull down Window | Preferences), and another that applies only to the current document (pull down Window | File Options). There are far too many options to cover them all here, but let's look at some of the most important, starting with the global settings.

**Colors** If you aren't particularly fond of black text on a white background, you can customize Pe's coloring any which way to Sunday—just click once on any colored square and use the resulting color picker to choose an alternate.

 **If you have a copy of RoColour (see Chapter 13, *Graphics Applications*) you can drag colors out of RoColour and onto the color squares to make the process even easier. You can also use this technique to match your document colors to other colors, such as that of the Desktop, for example.**

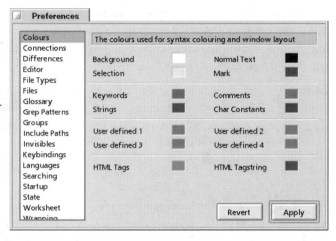

*Figure 12.20*

*Pe is so customiz-
able it's not even
funny. Click a cate-
gory on the left and
available options for
that category will
appear on the right.
Click Apply to set
your changes in
motion, or Revert to
return your settings
to the state they
were in before the
panel was opened.*

Pe supports "syntax highlighting," which means that it can display parts of
your document in different colors depending on their roles. For example, if
you use Pe for writing HTML, you can have it display your HTML tags in a separate color from your plain text, your comment tags in another color, and
your tags' arguments in another color still. The same principle applies if you
use Pe for writing C++ code. Syntax highlighting can be tremendously helpful when scanning through documents quickly—for example, it makes it
much easier for the eye to skip quickly to comment tags you've embedded
for future reference. All colors for Pe's syntax highlighting are established
from the Colors preferences panel.

**FileTypes**   By default, new documents created in Pe get the text/plain
MIME type, while the filetypes of existing files will be preserved. However,
when you save a document from within Pe, take a look at the bottom of the
File panel, where you'll find a drop-down picklist. You can add to the filetypes
displayed in this list by adding them in the FileTypes section of Pe's preferences panel. The new filetypes won't appear in the picklist until after you've
closed and restarted Pe. In addition to the obvious convenience provided here,
this feature gives Pe the ability to work around a limitation encountered when
you establish a new filetype on your system but don't have an editor capable
of generating that filetype. For example, if you install TrackerBase (downloadable from BeWare), you'll find that it wants to work with files of the type
text/x-vnd.shacker-trackerbase. But when you create a new file with
StyledEdit, it ends up with the type text/plain. One solution to this problem
is to simply duplicate existing TrackerBase files, but if you work a lot with Pe,
you can simply tell it about the text/x-vnd.shacker-trackerbase filetype, and
then save files directly into that format.

Rather than using Save As to change the filetype of the current document, pull down Window | File Options and choose Statistics. From there, you can use the drop-down picklist to choose an alternate filetype. Clicking Apply will set the new type—no save required.

**Glossary** While it may not be very aptly named, the Glossary is one of Pe's most useful features, and is something I wish every text editor had. Essentially, it's a palette of customizable buttons associated with blocks of text you define in a configuration file (see Figure 12.21). Click one of the buttons to insert a chunk of text of any length.

*Figure 12.21*

*The author used the Glossary above to write this book. Each button inserted specially formatted blocks of text with special strings, such as rows of +++s or ^^^s. Later, Microsoft Word macros were used to find those strings and format the sections according to Peachpit style guidelines.*

To customize your glossary, open the file /boot/home/config/settings/ pe/settings and add strings that look like this:

```
## option-y ## My Address
Jean-Louis Gassee'
123 TechnoGeek Blvd.
Menlo Park, CA 99999

## option-z ## My Signature
[your signoff here]
```

The first bit after the "##" represents the hotkey that will insert the text if you'd rather not reach for the mouse. The string after the second "##" will show up on the Glossary palette (if you leave this string out, your Glossary entry will still work via the hotkey, but will not appear in the palette). Everything below the first line is the text block to be inserted. The block ends with the beginning of the next glossary entry.

After customizing the Glossary settings file, save it, return to the Glossary preferences panel, and click Reload Glossary. You can also select whether the Glossary is automatically displayed at startup and whether buttons receive your first click (rather than your having to click in the Glossary window to give it focus before choosing a button; in other words, selecting this option makes the Glossary behave like standard windows in Microsoft Windows).

**Keybindings**  For many power users, Pe's Keybindings feature is one of its most-loved capabilities. Not only does Pe ship with hotkeys for most of the actions it's capable of performing, but you can change every single one of them to suit your own preferences, add hotkeys for actions that aren't yet assigned, and even assign multiple hotkeys to the same action, which is especially useful if you share your computer with multiple users.

If you have experience with the Unix emacs editor, you'll find that Pe recognizes several emacs commands, including the powerful Mark and Point feature. See Pe's documentation for details.

**Languages**  As discussed in the *Colors* section above, Pe uses "syntax highlighting" to set certain kinds of text apart from others—a feature especially useful to programmers and HTML coders. Every programming language has its own syntax, so Pe needs to be able to tell which language it's dealing with before it can highlight any syntax. The Languages preferences panel lets you establish a default language. If you use Pe mostly for coding Web pages, you'll want to choose HTML here. If you use Pe for just plain writing, you'll probably want to choose None from the pop-up. To help Pe determine which files are written in which language, you can associate extensions with certain languages. For example, Pe assumes by default that only files ending in .pl are written in Perl. If you store your Perl files with a .cgi extension, you can add the new suffix here.

**State**  Pe makes great use of BeOS filesystem attributes to store particular details about your files, so that when you open them up later they look exactly like they did when you left them. Beyond the usual BeOS behavior of remembering the size and position of windows, Pe can remember where the cursor was in the document when you last closed it and return you to that location when you open it again. It will also remember a document's display font, the directory you were last working in, and whether any text was selected when you last closed. You can alter each of these behaviors individually from the State preferences panel.

 If you attempt to edit a document and Pe tells you, "Sorry, this document is read-only," then the file's permissions (Chapter 6, *The Terminal*) don't have the proper write bits set. While you can always close the file, change its permissions, and reopen it, Pe gives you an easier way—look for the pencil icon on the toolbar. Non-writability is indicated when the icon has a red slash through it. Click once on this icon and, if possible, Pe will make the file writable for you (though of course it won't be able to if the file is on a CD-ROM or other non-writable medium).

**Worksheet** If you're a shell junkie, you'll love this: type any shell command into a Pe document, then hit Alt+Enter (alternatively, click the checkmark icon on the toolbar, use the Enter key on your numeric keypad). The command will be sent to the shell for processing, and the results (stdout) will be returned back into the current window.

 The shell processing your commands behind the scenes is unaware of the current directory, so you'll need to be specific about paths if your commands require them. For example, if you're working on a document that lives in /boot/home and you type ls -l into a Pe document, you'll get back a file listing from the root of the filesystem. Instead, use ls -l /boot/home. Another way to achieve the same effect is to group commands together in parentheses and execute them sequentially: ( cd /path/to/dir ; the-command ).

For convenience, Pe will optionally open a special document called a Worksheet, which you can use to store your most-used shell commands. This way you don't have to think about using the shell's normal history functions—just find the relevant line in your Worksheet, click in it, and hit Alt+Enter. If you don't want to keep a Worksheet open in the background at all times, use the checkbox in the Worksheet preferences panel. If you're a programmer, you can also tell Pe to redirect error messages from a shell stream called stderr to a separate window.

**Wrapping** As discussed in Chapter 6, *The Terminal*, lines in editors can be wrapped in two ways: "hard wrapped," with hard returns placed every so many characters, or "soft wrapped" at the edge of your window, wherever that may be. After establishing your preferences here, you can turn soft wrapping on or off for each document individually either by clicking the soft wrap toolbar icon, or by right-clicking in your document and selecting the Soft Wrap entry from the context menu.

## File Options

In addition to all of these global preferences, other options can be set on a file-by-file basis, including font, statistics, and wrapping.

**Font** If you want to override the default document fonts specified in the global preferences, this dialog lets you establish whether invisible characters such as tabs and hard returns are represented by symbols (Show Tab Stops and Show Invisibles), the number of spaces to be occupied by each tab stop, the display font and font size, and whether to use BeOS/Unix, Mac, or Windows-style line breaks. This dialog also lets you specify the character encoding to be used in the current document. You can also change the encoding of the current document by pulling down the Text menu and choosing Encoding.

### *About Document Encoding*

The eight bits that are used to create any given character are not necessarily locked to that particular character. The "translation table" that turns a collection of bits into a character onscreen is known as that document's "encoding." There are quite a few document encoding schemas floating around, though most people will never need to worry about anything other than the default UTF-8.

If you do receive (or need to create) a document in a different encoding (which is most likely to happen if you're working in languages other than English), use the picklist in the File Options | Font preferences panel to specify which one you want to use. Note also that this list includes the Macintosh Roman encoding, which will let you properly view documents created under MacOS that include "special" characters not included in the 7-bit ASCII character set.

**Statistics**   There isn't much of anything to choose in the Statistics section, aside from the filetype of the current document, which can be changed by choosing an alternative from the picklist. The Statistics panel will, however, give you a wealth of information on the current document, including path, modification date, size, and number of lines.

*Figure 12.22*

*Pe's floating HTML tool palettes make it easy to insert commonly used tags into your documents, or to access dialogs with further HTML-related options.*

## Building Web Sites with Pe

While Pe is built to work with plain-vanilla text or any programming language, one of its strongest suits is its adeptness as an HTML editor, thanks mainly to the floating HTML tool palette.

**The HTML Tools Palette**   If the HTML tool palette is not showing, access it from the Window menu. To begin a new document, click New. Don't like the default HTML template? You can easily customize this by editing ~/config/settings/pe/Template.html.

The HTML palette includes three types of buttons:

- Plain buttons, such as the Paragraph and Linebreak buttons, simply insert a tag at the cursor's insertion point.

- Buttons with downward arrows indicate that those buttons hide further options. For example, click Font to see a submenu of choices like Italic, Bold, etc.

- Buttons with ellipses (three dots ...) will launch a dialog box offering more options. For example, click the Image button and you'll get a dialog into which you can type the path and dimensions of the image you want to insert.

As you know, Web pages load much faster when you include HEIGHT and WIDTH arguments on all of your IMAGE tags. There are two ultra-easy ways to get these dimensions in BeOS. One is to use Thumbnail (Chapter 13, *Graphics Applications*) to write image dimensions to attributes you can display in the Tracker. The other is to drag your images onto Pe's Image dialog box. Pe will try to read the dimensions out of the image itself, then insert them for you. Remember to use ALT arguments for the benefit of those surfing with images turned off!

**Using the Update Feature**  One of Pe's coolest HTML features, though, is its Update feature. If you've ever worked with server-side includes, you know how powerful it can be to treat blocks of HTML as independent objects. Just as you can include a single image on every page of your site by simply invoking it with the IMG tag, includes let you do the same thing with blocks of code. This way, you can do things like store page headers, footers, or navigation elements in a single file and invoke them from all of your pages. When you need to make changes to these elements, all you have to do is change a single page, rather than every page on your site. Unfortunately, many (most) ISPs don't allow server-side includes, which is a drag for users, but prevents server overload for the ISP.

The next best thing, then, is to place similar functionality in your HTML editor. Let's say you've got a block of code defining your site's left-hand navigation stored in a file at /boot/home/public_html/objects/leftnav.html. Insert the following code in one of your HTML documents, save, click the Update button on the HTML palette, and the entire contents of the include file will be inserted at that point.

```
<!-- #include "/boot/home/public_html/objects/leftnav.html" -->

<!-- end include -->
```

Any time you make changes to leftnav.html, you'll have to open each document that invokes it and click Update. It's not quite as easy as working with SSI, but much easier than making the changes manually to every page on your site.

The HTML palette's Preview button will launch the current document in your default Web browser, but you'll probably prefer the hotkey Alt+Shift+B.

***Another Killer Text Editor***  Pe isn't the only programmer's editor in town. Be's own Pavel Cisler (father of the Tracker) has written his own high-powered editor called Eddie. Eddie is both similar to and different from Pe, but on the whole, is geared more toward hardcore programmers, while Pe is geared more toward power users. Eddie, for example, does not have a mechanism for soft-wrapping text, making it unsuitable for general writing jobs (this may change by the time you read this, however). Eddie is available on BeWare.

# Brian Tietz's Scheduler

`www-biology.ucsd.edu/~btietz/Scheduler.html`

Computers are supposed to make your life easier. They're supposed to do things *for* you, to extend the reach of your memory, and to get real work done while you're out playing. Clearly, it doesn't turn out that way for most of us. Part of the problem lies in the fact that with many mainstream operating systems, it's not easy to schedule our machines to be takin' care of bidnis in the middle of the night, or to remind us when to go to the dentist or to buy a birthday gift for Aunt Lulu. Fortunately, there's a tool for BeOS called Scheduler that *does* do all these things, and it is as easy to use as it is reliable.

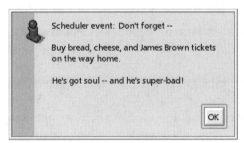

*Figure 12.23*

*Scheduler's simplest function is to throw alert boxes onto your screen. These are like sticky notes with a built-in clock.*

## Creating Events

Scheduler lets you set up "events," which can be scheduled on a one-time basis or to repeat every Tuesday at 3:00 A.M., every year on your sister's birthday, or in any arbitrary time frame that suits you. The program keeps an eye on your database of scheduled events, and when an event time matches the time on your system clock, it springs into action. The exact action it takes, of course, is entirely up to you, but they always fall into one of three broad categories, also known as "handlers": displaying a message, acting on a file, or running a command.

**Display a Message in an Alert Box**  An alert message can be anything you like, of course. Some examples: "Buy opera tickets on the way home or face a weekend of wrath." (Set this one to go off five minutes before you leave work.) Or this, set to go off every hour until you finally get up the nerve: "Talk to boss about raise. Don't mention his dandruff." Or this one, set to appear every morning when you boot your machine: "Enter last night's totals into database—FIRST THING!" You get the picture.

**Act on a File**  The Act on File and Run Command handlers, however, are where Scheduler really starts to get work done. Think of Act on File as being like double-clicking a file by remote control. If you invoke an application file, that application will be launched. Reference a text document and it will be launched in your preferred text editor, or specify an image or sound file to spring multimedia surprises on yourself. Or let's say that part of your job involves combing the company network for files larger than 2MB every day. Just create and save a query that runs this search, then point Scheduler at that query file and tell it to run every day at 1:00 P.M.

**Run a Command**   If you want more power than that (and who could blame you?), try integrating some of the techniques you learned in Chapter 6, *The Terminal*, with Scheduler's temporal awareness. For example, you could run a Terminal query for all unread mail, then pipe the results of that through grep to find, say, only unread messages from your spelunking partner. Or if you want to get really fancy, you can combine a bunch of commands into a script, save it to /boot/home/config/bin, and reference the script's filename as a command.

One of the more powerful and useful tricks you can do with the command-line mode is to establish a regular backup system for all or selected portions of your disk volumes. Remember that zip has a ton of options, so you can easily update existing archives with just the files that are new or that have changed, so that you have an incremental backup plan in place. You can also tell zip to include only—or exclude only—files with certain extensions. That means you can create backup commands or scripts that back up just the HTML files in the mirror of your Web site, while excluding all of its multimedia components, for example. More on zip in Chapter 5, *Files and the Tracker*.

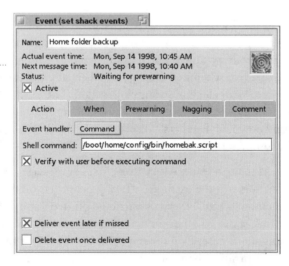

*Figure 12.24*

*One great way to use the Run a Command handler is to create a shell script that backs up all or part of your system, and places the generated archive on a separate volume, where it will be safe in the event of a disk emergency.*

If it's important that the event not be skipped, even if the computer isn't turned on when the scheduled time comes, remember to check the "Deliver even later if missed" checkbox. This way it will run the next time you boot into BeOS. Better late than never, right?

**Setting Schedules**  Scheduler has a clean and simple interface—you probably won't need to consult the documentation much (if you do, you'll find it thorough and intelligible as well). The main Scheduler window shows all of the events you've got lined up in the current event set. Double-click an event to edit it, or pull down Event | New Event to create a new one. After entering a name for the event in the upper field, select a handler from the drop-down list on the Action tab. This tab's interface will change depending on which handler is currently selected.

## What About Cron?

Scheduler is incredibly useful, but true Weenix Unies may prefer to use its command-line equivalent, cron, which works similarly but must be configured by editing a text file. After downloading cron from BeWare, you'll need to compile it for your platform (compilation instructions can be found in Appendix D). After compilation, the cron and crontab binaries will have been placed in your /boot/home/config/bin directory. Create a text file (also known as a "crontab" file, though this should not be confused with the crontab binary) listing the jobs you want to schedule, as described below. Save the file anywhere you like and call it whatever you want. You might want to create a ~/cronjobs directory just for good housekeeping. Now launch a Terminal window and type:

```
crontab <path to schedule file>
```

This sets cron running as a background process, simultaneously telling it where to look for a schedule. Once you've tested cron, you'll probably want to add the command above to your UserBootScript so it will always be running.

### Creating the Schedule File

Dates and times in schedule files are specified as a string of five numbers, ranges, or wildcards, then followed by the path to the command you want to run. The date/time options are:

Minute: 0–59
Hour: 0–23
Day of month: 1–31
Month: 1–12
Day of week: 0–6 (where 0=Sunday)

Use * characters to stand in for all possible values (i.e. any time you don't want to specify).

Thus, to run a program called HelloWorld at 2:23 PM every Tuesday, you might use:

```
23 14 * * 3 /boot/home/config/bin/HelloWorld
```

You can list as many commands in a crontab file as useful (but don't follow them with an & character, at least in the current version). cron will check its database once per minute and run the specified command if the date/time specifications match the current time. If you'd like a quick look at your current crontab file, type crontab -l at any prompt. To edit your crontab in Terminal's vi editor, type crontab -e.

If you want your event to run when you're not physically at the machine, pay close attention to the checkboxes on some of these tabs. If you click the "Verify with user before running" box, Scheduler will sit around and wait for you to return to the machine before executing.

The When tab is where you enter the actual schedule to be followed for this event. Click on the dropdown list to change the interval to any of a dozen presets, or type a date and time into the field provided. The time field here is smart—if you change a date and hit Enter, the day will be updated automatically, which saves on both typing and errors.

The Prewarning tab is your hedge against the frailty of human memory—you can use it to have messages pop up every few minutes, hours, days, or whatever prior to an actual event. Unfortunately, it also makes it impossible to use excuses like "I forgot you had a birthday coming up" ever again. The Nagging tab does the same as the Prewarning, but operates after the event has passed, so you can send a belated birthday card if all of those Prewarnings didn't work. Finally, the Comment tab is available for you to enter notes related to the event (your niece's birthday wish list, for instance).

**Making Sure Scheduler Is Running**  Of course, all of Scheduler's cleverness won't do you a damn bit of good if it isn't running. Fortunately, you don't have to actually launch the application to have it monitor your event list. Just invoke Scheduler's background daemon from your `/boot/home/config/boot/UserBootscript` like this:

`/boot/apps/utils/Scheduler/Scheduler -background`

(Customize this path to match your actual installation location.) Next time you boot, Scheduler will be there, humming away in the background either ready to stop you from slacking off, or doing your work for you so you *can* slack off.

# Working Software's Spellswell and QLAB

`www.working.com`

Some of the most basic services your computer has to offer are also some of the most important. The name of this Santa Cruz, CA software firm is fitting—Working Software produces BeOS software designed to help you accomplish basic tasks (like looking up business contacts and spell-checking documents), but with a twist: Working Software titles take excellent advantage of internal BeOS technologies like BMessages and software modularity to make your applications work with, rather than against, each other.

# Spellswell

You write an email message, you want to spell-check it. Write a word processing document, you want to spell-check it. Create a Web page, you want to spell-check it. Chances are, the spell-checkers built into most of your applications are very close to identical. So why should each developer spend time and energy building spell-checkers into their applications? They shouldn't. Why should you have multiple dictionaries laying around on your hard drive? You shouldn't. True to the modular design of BeOS, Working Software's Spellswell lets you store a single spell-checking module on your system and tell all of your text-savvy applications to use it as their spell-checker. Developers benefit by saving their energies for more important efforts, and you get to use and customize a single dictionary, not a bunch of them.

Developers who want to use Spellswell as their application's spell-checker purchase a license for the "hooks" needed to tie into the program, and users who want to be able to use Spellswell with their applications purchase the "client." To get a taste for how Spellswell integrates with other applications, download the latest version of Spellswell from BeWare and you'll find that it comes with a slightly modified version of BeMail. Launch this version of BeMail and notice the new menu entry, reading "Services." Paste a few paragraphs into the body of a test message, pull down Services | Check Spelling, and you'll see a panel like the one in Figure 12.25.

**Figure 12.25**

*The Spellswell interface and dictionary is the same for all of your Word Services-enabled applications. Shown here is Spellswell working with a modified version of BeMail.*

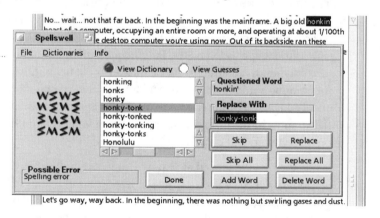

Spellswell is capable of flagging down more than just spelling errors, though. It also catches:

- Common typos
- Extra spaces between words
- The letter "a" before words starting with vowels
- Repeated words
- Spaces before punctuation

- Two spaces after periods
- Capitalization at the start of sentences
- Mixed numbers and letters
- Uncapitalized proper nouns
- Improperly hyphenated words like "back-up"

If you're a Web page author, you'll find that Spellswell is able to check your Web documents while ignoring anything coming between <angle brackets>. If you write in multiple languages or need multiple custom dictionaries, you can toggle between the dictionaries installed on your system on the fly (just pull down Dictionary | Open Dictionary from within Spellswell).

 **If you're about to paste in a big block of text, you can spell-check it** *before* **pasting it in by pulling down File | Check Clipboard.**

## QuickLetter Address Book (QLAB)

BeOS People files are a unique and useful aspect of the operating system, but they don't do all of the things you might expect from a full-fledged contact manager. That leaves the field wide open for developers of more sophisticated tools, and Working Software has stepped up to the plate with QuickLetter Address Book, or QLAB.

The first time you launch QLAB, you'll be asked to create a new address book. Give your new database any name you like, and you can begin adding records by pulling down Records | Make New Record. You'll see an interface similar to that provided by the People application, but offering quite a few new goodies. In addition to the standard People fields, QLAB gives you fields for entering a middle name, two address lines, a cell phone number, two email addresses (because all of your friends are so wired), two comment fields, and a birthday. Enter any information you like (you don't have to fill out everything) and click Done.

While the beta we looked at required addresses to be entered manually, future versions of QLAB will be capable of importing addresses from your collection of People files, and possibly from databases created in personal information managers (PIMs) on other platforms as well (though you'll probably have to export those to standard tab- or comma-delimited text files first). To edit a record again at any point in the future, just double-click its entry and you'll get the same dialog. Any changes you make will be updated instantly in the main address book window.

To search through your database of contacts, use the standard Alt+F hotkey to bring up the Find panel and enter a string. Your search will scour every field

**Figure 12.26**

*To demonstrate its ability to integrate its functionality with existing applications, QLAB ships with a specially modified version of BeMail, sporting a new Services menu.*

in every record, so you don't have to worry about specifying only the last name, or just the address field, for example.

QLAB's View menu lets you manipulate the layout of your address book much as you would with the Attributes menu in a standard Tracker view. Select any field to display it in the database window, and deselect to hide it again. It should be possible to rearrange the order of columns in the near future.

So much for the utilitarian stuff. The real fun starts when QLAB starts talking to other BeOS applications. Take a look under the Action menu and you'll find the following possibilities:

- Send E-mail
- Address an Envelope
- Make a Letter
- Mail Merge
- Send a Fax
- Open Web page

QLAB itself doesn't fax, handle email, or print labels, but it does make heavy use of BMessages (Chapter 1, *The MediaOS*) to communicate with other software installed on your machine. While most of these features weren't yet enabled in the version we tested, you'll soon begin to see a wider array of BeOS software designed to intercommunicate effectively, and QLAB hopes to be a "home base" for many of these interactions ... or at least those that involve your personal and business contacts.

As an example of the way these interactions can work, QLAB comes with a specially modified version of BeMail, which is identical to the version shipping with BeOS except for the addition of a new pulldown menu labeled Services. This menu lets BeMail interact both with Spellswell, so you can spell-check your messages before sending them off into the aether, and with QLAB, so you can address your messages without having to remember actual email addresses. For example, if you've entered a record into QLAB for your friend Krusty Jackson but can't remember his email address off the top of your head, just type his name into the To: field of the special version of BeMail, then pull down Services | Look Up E-Mail Address. If Krusty's name is found in your QLAB address book, BeMail will change the name you typed to Krusty's actual email address. Similarly, if you need to get Krusty's street address into the body of your message, just put your cursor inside his name and pull down Services | Look Up Street Address.

Theoretically, there's no end to the number or type of services that can be provided to your existing software by integrated tools like those produced by Working Software. This kind of tight-knit cooperation between applications makes your life easier and lets developers concentrate on their own specialties. If you're using two applications that you wish could cooperate better, why not write to their developers and ask? You're the customer, their motivation should always be to give you what you want, and BeOS makes this kind of interapplication cooperation much easier than it would be on other operating systems. It can't hurt to ask!

 Both Spellswell and QLAB take advantage of the Word Services Suite, a protocol that allows any application to link to a spell-checker, encryptor, or other text service as if it were a built-in menu item. See **www.wordservices.org** for more information.

# 13

# Graphics
# Applications

2D graphics may not move or make sound, but graphics are still media, and BeOS still offers distinct advantages to 2D artists, such as native transparency built into the OS itself via the alpha channel, speed advantages and real-time preview options made possible by pervasive multithreading, and the ability to test graphics at multiple resolutions simultaneously via workspaces.

This chapter divides graphics applications into three basic categories: image manipulation and paint programs, modeling and raytracing, and graphics utilities.

# Image Manipulation and Paint Programs

Historically, imaging applications have tended to fall into one of two categories: those designed to edit and alter existing graphics and those designed to create new graphics from scratch. Image manipulation applications offered tools for resizing, cropping, inverting, and applying filters to images or parts of images, while paint-oriented applications specialized in digitally recreating brushes, paints, pencils, and canvas and/or paper textures. Over time, graphics applications on both sides of the fence increasingly came to cover both territories within a single application. While modern graphics programs still tend to specialize on one side or the other, most graphics applications these days let you do some of both. This is as true on BeOS as it is on other platforms.

## ArtPaint
**www.helsinki.fi/~hsuhonen/artpaint/**

Heikki Suhonen's BeOS Masters Award-winning ArtPaint is a paint and image-processing app with some wonderful and surprising twists. While much of its toolset will be instantly familiar to anyone who's spent time with similar programs on other platforms, some aspects of ArtPaint represent a rethinking of the standard approach to image manipulation.

 **ArtPaint has many small floating control panels and tool palettes, some of which you may need frequent access to. To prevent a given panel from getting lost behind other windows, pull down Window | Settings and put a checkmark next to that panel's name. You can also control whether undo privileges are unlimited, disabled, or constrained to a specific number of undo operations.**

## *What about Photoshop?*

One of the questions frequently asked by skeptics and people being introduced to the platform for the first time is, "Where can I get Photoshop for
BeOS?" The answer to this question comes in several parts:

- Photoshop for BeOS does not exist. Or, at least, not officially. Rumors have
  long circulated that Adobe did port Photoshop to BeOS once upon a
  time, but wants to wait for the platform to really take off in a big way
  before releasing the port to the public. If the rumors are true, this stance
  would make a certain amount of sense for a company the size of Adobe,
  which would need to put in place a full BeOS department, complete with
  engineers and support staff, which would in turn require a very large,
  guaranteed revenue stream. Still, if you want to see Photoshop for BeOS,
  it can't hurt to write a polite request to Adobe.

- Ports, by their very nature, do not provide a compelling reason for users to
  migrate to a new platform. Why would someone install a new operating
  system just to run the same software they're already running elsewhere?
  For the most part, they wouldn't. BeOS gains many of its speed and technical advantages from its unique architecture, its fine-grained multithreadedness in particular. An application ported from MacOS or Windows is
  probably not going to shine on BeOS as would an application written
  from scratch with BeOS's unique features in mind. Nor is it easy to simply
  take a single-threaded application and make it multithreaded. Photoshop
  is an awesome application, but it's not exactly modern. Photoshop was
  developed originally for a very different operating environment—early
  versions of MacOS. Photoshop isn't optimized for a modern operating system like Be's, and simply porting it to BeOS would not make it so.

- BeOS offers "green fields" in which new developers, with new ways of thinking about application programming, hope to flourish. The presence of
  Photoshop on BeOS would all but close the doors for developers of next-
  generation imaging software, simply because Photoshop is the "default
  product." Let's give companies like Táve and BeatWare a chance to excel in
  this environment. If you're willing to learn a few new tricks, chances are
  you'll find you can do nearly everything in these applications that you can
  in Photoshop, and then some. Just because Photoshop was one of the killer
  apps for MacOS, doesn't mean it should be for BeOS as well.

So, all of that said, sure, Photoshop for BeOS would be great in many ways,
and the big-name support of a company like Adobe would be a nice feather
for BeOS's cap. But don't be surprised if you find that neither Be, Inc. nor most
veteran users don't stay awake at night dreaming of a Photoshop port.

The same arguments, by the way, apply equally to potential ports of all big-
name software products.

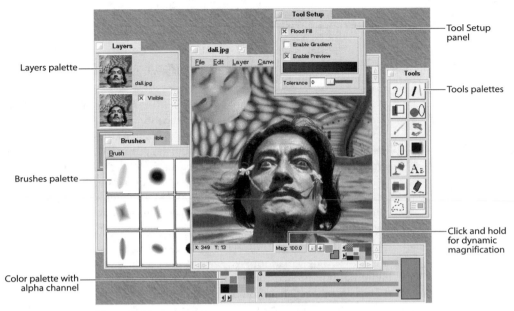

Tool Setup panel

Layers palette

Tools palettes

Brushes palette

Click and hold for dynamic magnification

Color palette with alpha channel

Layers palette

*Figure 13.01*

*ArtPaint's interface is clean and logical, though some tools may behave differently than you expect.*

 ArtPaint lets you open and save "projects" as well as files. An ArtPaint project is capable of storing extra data that standard image file formats don't recognize, such as layers, canvas sizes, and floating text.

**Working with Layers**  ArtPaint uses the same concept of layers that you'll find in most imaging applications; think of layers as if they were sheets of clear plastic stacked on top of one another. By hiding and showing various layers, you can experiment without fear of ruining your image—just delete a layer if you don't like it. You can create layers by tapping Alt+. (period) or by using the Layer menu. After creating two or more layers, be sure to try out the Layer Transparency slider, which lets you specify whether the current layer is completely transparent, completely opaque, or somewhere in between. You can achieve beautiful blends by placing different images on separate layers and setting each of them to a percentage of the total transparency.

Each layer is represented in the Layers palette by a thumbnail-sized version of the image it contains. You can hide an individual layer by unchecking its Visible checkbox. Right-click in the Layers palette to access a context menu that will let you selectively merge, add, duplicate, or delete layers.

 **Every action you take in ArtPaint affects *only* the layer currently selected in the Layers palette. If you try something and it doesn't have the intended effect, tap Alt+L to bring the Layers palette forward, then click in the corresponding layer and try again.**

**The Color Palette** ArtPaint's color palette is basically similar to those in other graphics programs, but has a few unusual options. Use its Mode menu to choose palettes other than RGBA (such as the CMYK palette, or the standard BeOS color picker). From the Set menu, you can load and save custom color collections for later use. If the color palette is hidden, invoke it by double-clicking the foreground/background color icons in the lower right of the status area. As with many BeOS color pickers, you can drag color swatches to the Desktop to change its color instantly.

## About the Alpha Channel

Naturally you've seen RGB (red, green, blue) color sliders before—they appear wherever colors need to be chosen. What you may not have encountered before, however, is anything like the fourth slider, labeled "Alpha" in the color pickers belonging to many of the graphics applications covered in this chapter.

One of the coolest features BeOS offers to imaging jocks is its alpha channel, which augments the usual red, green and blue color channels by adding transparency to the color's description so you can establish whether the current color is visible, invisible, or see-through (note that this is not the same as a transparency "mask," which is used in other operating systems to hide parts of icons, for instance). Each of these four channels can have one of 256 values, numbered from zero to 255. If you study a four-channel color picker, however, you'll notice something slightly counterintuitive. The red, green, and blue values are darkest when set to low values and brightest when set to high values. Set the red slider to 0 and you've chosen the absence of red (which appears black) for that channel. While the same is true for green and blue, the alpha channel registers faint when set to zero and bright when set to 255. When you look at the color picker, the order seems to have been reversed. The trick to keeping this straight in your head is to think of the alpha level as an opacity level, rather than as a transparency level. Zero alpha gives you zero opacity for the current color, so it's totally transparent; 255 alpha gives you full opacity. Behind the scenes, it's a more complex game of filters and color theory, but this makes it easy to remember.

To see a quick demonstration of the alpha channel in action, take a screenshot of your Desktop by hitting the PrintScreen key on your keyboard. Double-click the file screen1.tga in your home directory, and it will be opened in ShowImage. Now drag out an area an inch or two square (this won't work with large selections) and start dragging it around. Note that you can see right through your moving selection as if it were printed with light ink on clear plastic. When you drag icons around in the Tracker, the same effect is used to provide user feedback, so you always know exactly what's being moved.

While you will, of course, find transparency sliders in some graphics applications on other operating systems, BeOS is unique in that it supports the alpha channel natively. Recall the Screen preferences section in Chapter 9. When your resolution is set to 32-bit mode, 24 bits of data are used to store red, green, and blue values, leaving eight bits left over to handle transparency values. But hang on! Notice that if you reset your resolution to a value less than 32 bits, transparent icon dragging still works. How is this possible?

*(continued)*

### *About the Alpha Channel (continued)*

First of all, the transparency is an illusion; you're still just seeing a mixture of colors from the available palette. Painting the colors on your screen is no big deal. What's tricky here is how BeOS determines what those colors will be. For this it uses one of several algorithms, depending on whether the pixel is part of a bitmap or is being drawn to the screen (as is the case with, say, title tabs or window borders), along with data about the current bit depth. BeOS is doing magic behind the scenes so you can enjoy alpha channels in the OS even when you're running at less than 32-bit resolution.

The presence of the alpha channel in the operating system itself does not benefit the user directly. Rather, it makes it very easy for developers to add alpha channel support to their applications. As a result, the end-user benefits indirectly because just about every single BeOS graphics application includes RGBA color sliders, rather than just RGB sliders, which means you can control transparency levels in even the simplest BeOS graphics tools.

**Working with Brushes**   Most of ArtPaint's brushes are described by two sets of parameters: controls that apply equally to all brushes (brush shape, width, height, and degree of fade), and controls that apply only to that brush (for example, the airbrush has a flow control, while the hairy brush lets you set the number of hairs). You can build a library of general brush styles by clicking the standard brush icon, selecting one of the preexisting brushes, and manipulating its parameters in the Tool Setup panel. Fiddle with the width, height, and fade controls, then save your configuration for later use by clicking the Store Brush button. Your brush variant will be added to the Brushes panel, rather than replacing the selected brush.

The Tool Setup panel is context-sensitive, and changes depending on the currently selected brush. So let's say you want to customize the way your airbrush is applied. Start by selecting the standard brush icon and selecting a brush type (or creating a new one). Then select the airbrush icon and the Tool Setup panel's contents will change to let you customize parameters that are specific to the airbrush.

 **If you hold your mouse over the brush preview icon in the Tool Setup panel, a pair of crosshairs will appear. Drag the crosshairs in a circular motion to change the orientation of the brush. You'll notice this effect most acutely when there's a wide variance between the width and the height of a given brush. Drag the preview icon to the Brushes panel with the right mouse button as an alternative to clicking the Store Brush button.**

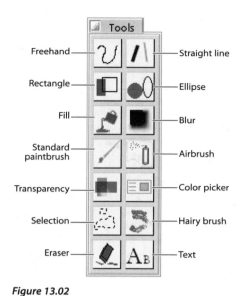

**Figure 13.02**

The ArtPaint tools palette

**The Tools**  ArtPaint's main tools palette is similar to those found in most imaging applications, but the tools it contains have some important differences. To learn any tool's purpose, select the tool and hold your mouse over the canvas; a description will appear in the status area at the bottom of the image window.

Essential to the use of each tool is the Tool Setup panel, which changes depending on which tool is currently selected, offering options specific to that tool. The function of each tool in the ArtPaint palette is described below.

 **Right-click anywhere in the canvas to access any of these tools from a context menu.**

- **Freehand line:** Draw simple lines in the currently selected color without any brush effects. Change the diameter of the line with the size slider in the Tool Setup panel.

- **Rectangle:** Not your ordinary Rectangle tool. From the Tool Setup panel, you can enable rotation. When this is selected, drag out your rectangle normally, release the mouse button, and the rectangle's outline will spin as you move your mouse. Click again to "nail it down." Since this means you can set your rectangle at an angle, you could end up with jaggies. To avoid this, select the tool's antialiasing checkbox. You can also choose whether or not the rectangle will be filled with the current color.

- **Standard paintbrush:** Configure general parameters for the current brush, or build a library of brush styles for later use. See *Working with Brushes*, above.

- **Airbrush:** Works like a real airbrush, inheriting properties of the standard paintbrush and augmenting them with its own Size and Flow controls. The slower you drag the Airbrush tool, the more paint will be applied to that area, which lets you create very realistic airbrush effects.

- **Fill:** With the Flood Fill option checked, works like a standard paint bucket tool. With Enable Gradients checked, offers amazing real-time gradient manipulation. See *Creating Gradients*, below.

- **Transparency:** Brush-on transparency lets you make an area more opaque or more transparent by hand, rather than via selections, as you would with other imaging applications. Works in conjunction with the alpha channel setting in the color picker. With the alpha value set to full opacity (which is the default), this tool will have no effect. Drag the Alpha slider down halfway, though, and this tool will make the area under your brush more see-through. This tool is like a standard eraser tool with superpowers.

- **Selections:** Selection methods in ArtPaint are similar to those you've encountered in other imaging applications but make some tasks much easier. See *Working with Selections*, below.

- **Straight Lines:** These work in the standard manner, with the convenient addition of an antialiasing option that lets you draw straight angled lines free of jaggies.

- **Ellipses:** These work in the standard manner but let you decide whether you want to pull the ellipse out from its corner or drag it out from top to bottom, side to side. Hold down the left Ctrl key as you drag to constrain your ellipse to a perfect circle.

- **Hairy Brush:** Perhaps the most painterly of ArtPaint's tools, the Hairy Brush lets you simulate an actual artist's brush, complete with traces left in the paint by the individual hairs. Since a real brush lays paint down unevenly and stirs up layers of paint beneath the current layer, real brush strokes appear multicolored. You can control the nuances of this amazingly realistic effect by adjusting the Color Variance and Color Amount sliders, in addition to the exact number of hairs you want on your brush and the brush's size.

- **Blur:** Functions like a standard blur tool so you can paint in your blurs if the occasion calls for it, rather than applying blur effects to selections.

- **Text:** ArtPaint's Text tool functions a little differently than the others. When you select it, the Tool Setup panel will become empty. The moment you click in your canvas, however, a text options panel will appear. In addition to the standard font, font size, and font style options, this panel gives you full control over font size, shear, and rotation before the text even hits the canvas. The beta we tested was able to create only black text, regardless of the currently selected color; hopefully that will change soon.

Text created in ArtPaint is laid down as a bitmap and thus isn't fully editable. You might want to place your text elements on separate layers so you can easily remove and replace text blocks later if necessary.

- **Eraser:** Standard fare here. Note that you won't find a pressure option associated with ArtPaint's Eraser tool—it completely erases everything to which it's applied. Fortunately, you have the far more sensitive Transparency tool at your disposal. In fact, by setting your alpha channel all the way down to zero and erasing with the Transparency tool, you can get exactly the same effect as the Eraser, which renders this tool somewhat superfluous. Consider the Eraser a shortcut to achieving transparency with a 100% alpha setting.

Looking for the Move tool? ArtPaint doesn't exactly have one, but you will find a Translate option under the Layer menu. Choose Translate and drag in the canvas to move its entire contents to a new location. To accept or reject your move, use the X and ✔ buttons at the right of the status window.

- **Color picker:** Similar to your standard eyedropper tool. As you drag your mouse over the canvas, the color beneath it will appear in a floating info panel, along with the exact RGB and alpha values for that color. This makes it easy not only to reselect colors you've used before, but also to determine numeric color values, should you need them in another program.

**Working with Selections**  ArtPaint's selection tools offer a couple of interesting usability enhancements over those in Photoshop. For example, to add to or remove from a selection in Photoshop, you need to hold down a modifier key while you're working. Let up on that finger, click in the canvas, and you could lose your selection in an instant (unless you've saved your selection). In ArtPaint, just select the Add or Subtract radio button and you won't have to worry about it; since selecting one of these radio buttons is equivalent to holding down a modifier key in other apps, they make it impossible to accidentally deselect your work.

The Intelligent Scissors option is also unusual. It operates basically like the freehand selection mode, but with a twist: As you drag, your selection lines will automatically seek out areas of high contrast (as defined by the Tolerance slider) and cause the selection line to "snap" to the contour of the nearest area with high contrast. This makes it much easier to accurately select the contours of irregular objects.

In Figure 13.03 we used the Magic Wand tool (which selects areas of contiguous color as determined by the Tolerance setting) to make a selection, then painted some more, then used the same tool to subtract from the selection, then used the Edit menu to invert the selection (turn it inside out), then used the Intelligent Scissors mode to select along contours, then applied the Negative add-on, and kept right on going, never worrying that we might accidentally disable the entire selection.

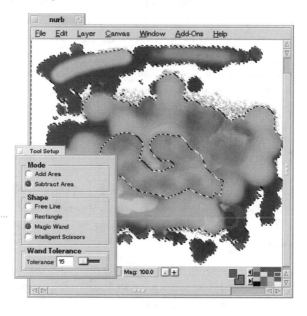

*Figure 13.03*

*ArtPaint's radio buttons and Intelligent Scissors make complex selections easier to create.*

One of the most effective ways to get good mileage out of selections is by applying some of the effects available under the Add-Ons menu, which let you adjust brightness and color balance, add oil-painting effects, and blur, twirl, and otherwise manipulate or enhance the selected area.

**Zoom Levels**  If you need to zoom in for a closer look at something, or zoom back for a bird's-eye view of a larger image, you have a number of options. You can hold down the Alt key and press the + and – buttons on your numeric keypad, pull down the Window menu and choose Zoom In or Zoom Out, or use the + and – buttons in the status area at the bottom of your image. Coolest of all though is the real-time zoomer, which is slightly hidden. Next to the + and – buttons in the status area is a small box labeled "Mag." Click and hold in this box and a slider will appear. With the mouse button still depressed, drag left or right to zoom in or out in real time. If your image grows larger or smaller than the window it's in, tap Alt+Y (resize to fit) to make the window size equal to the image size. To quickly reset the zoom level, pull down Window | Set Zoom Level and choose a preset magnification ratio.

**Creating Gradients**  ArtPaint uses BeOS's real-time processing capabilities to take gradient creation to the next level. Rather than making you create a gradient, see how it looks, and if you don't like it, undo and redo it, ArtPaint lets you deal with gradients almost as if they were live. Create a new canvas, select the Fill tool (paint bucket), and in its Tool Setup panel, select Enable Gradient and deselect Flood Fill. Now use the Colors panel to select a starting color. Drag your color from the Colors panel to the left edge of the spectrum in Tool Setup, then do the same for the ending color. Now you're ready to play. Click and hold anywhere in the canvas and start dragging. The canvas immediately fills with the starting color, but as you drag your mouse, more and more of the ending color will fill the space. As you drag, the gradient changes in real time, reflecting the distance and direction from the first place you clicked. Your screen will almost dance as washes of the spectrum flow across it! It may take some practice to get used to this gradient-creation method, but you'll find it offers much more flexibility than traditional methods.

## Sum Software's Becasso  *with Sander Stoks*
`www.sumware.demon.nl`

Sum Software's Becasso is a combined paint and image-editing application featuring alpha channel support, layering, multilevel undo/redo, an add-on architecture for third-party filters, transformers, and generators, and an orthogonal user interface.

You can launch Becasso by double-clicking its icon, by dropping one or more files of a supported type onto its icon, or by double-clicking an image file (provided you've associated that image's filetype with Becasso; see Chapter 5,

*Files and the Tracker*). You can make Becasso the preferred handler for any image type for which you have an installed Translator. Becasso includes all the tools you're used to finding in graphics manipulation and paint programs: Eraser, Fill, Text, Spray Can, Freehand, Line, Free Shape, Polygon, Rectangle, Oval, Circle, and Ellipse.

## Orthogonal?

Becasso refers to its interface as being "orthogonal." In its strictly mathematical sense, orthogonal means "mutually perpendicular." But in the context of Becasso, it means that everything you can do with paint, you can do with selections, and vice versa. This means you're never limited to creating selections with the standard collection of selection tools. To create selections, just enter selection mode by clicking the main toolbar's leftmost button and choosing the hand icon, then start working with *any* tool (even the Text tool). Rather than laying down paint, you'll be laying down selection areas. Accordingly, the Fill tool will act as a magic wand, selecting areas of contiguous color. In other words, if you can paint it in Becasso, you can select it just as easily.

 **Save As... versus Export** When you chose Save As... from Becasso's File menu, your image will automatically be saved in Becasso's native file format, with a filetype of `image/x-becasso`. To save images in standard file formats, use the File | Export option instead. You'll be presented with a menu of file formats representing all of the image Translators installed on your system.

**Deceptive Simplicity** Becasso's interface is specifically designed to minimize the amount of clutter floating around on your screen. Upon launch, all you'll see is a tiny window with five buttons.

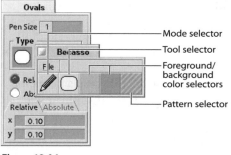

**Figure 13.04**

*Becasso's interface is designed to prevent your screen from becoming cluttered with tons of minor panels and toolboxes. Right-click any tool's icon to launch a settings window specific to that tool.*

Don't be fooled by the deceptive simplicity of the main toolbar, though. These buttons harbor quite a bit of hidden functionality. For example, click and hold on the paintbrush icon, and more than a dozen other tools will appear in a pop-up panel. Select any tool from this panel, then right-click its icon (Mac users: double-click). A new settings panel will appear, letting you adjust the properties of that tool. Becasso packs a lot of interface into a very small space!

As you scroll down through the list of tools, try sliding sideways from a tool rather than releasing the mouse button over it. The palette will tear off, letting you work with an easy-access palette rather than the standard, compact interface.

**Working with Selections**  To create selections, click and hold the first button in the main toolbar; its icon should depict a hand, rather than a pencil. Alternately, you can use the Tab key to switch quickly between Selection and Draw modes. Once in Selection mode, you can draw, paint, or edit normally, but whatever you draw or paint will appear on the canvas in negative (each pixel's complementary color will be used). One thing that sets Becasso apart from other paint programs is the fact that its selections are not simply binary. Whereas most graphics applications require that a pixel be either selected or not selected, Becasso supports 256 levels of "selectedness." To see this effect in action, try painting with a largish, "fuzzy" brush, first in normal mode, then in Selection mode. In Draw mode, less paint is deposited at the edges of the brush; in Selection mode, those same pixels end up "less selected." Try copying and then pasting such a selection, and you'll see that the pixels at the edges of the selection blend in with the background.

While Becasso selections can be copied, pasted, and moved around normally, the version we tested did not support selections being used as blocking masks. For example, painting back and forth across a selection edge does not limit the application of paint to the boundaries of the selection. A future version of Becasso should support this feature.

**Working with Text**  While most of Becasso's tools work much as they do in other imaging applications, the Text tool uses a different metaphor. Rather than typing your text into a preview panel, you set your font and font size from the Text options panel, click in the canvas, and start typing directly in the image, as if you were using a word processor. Pressing Return will "fix" the text onto the canvas. The color of the text is determined by Becasso's current foreground color.

**Working with Layers**  Like most modern paint applications, Becasso supports the notion of layers. Think of them as transparent sheets placed on top of each other. You can add new layers to any image via the Layer menu, or access the Layers palette from the Window menu. The transparency of each sheet can be modified independently.

In addition to providing a mechanism for altering parts of an image without affecting the rest of it, layers make it easy to achieve effects like drop shadows. If you store your background, text, and shadows on independent layers, you can quickly change the darkness of the shadow, for instance, by adjusting the transparency of its layer.

**Colors and Patterns** The three buttons at the right of the main toolbar let you select, from left to right, the foreground color, background color, and fill pattern. There are two ways to select a color. To access a simple color palette, click and hold on the foreground or background color buttons, then choose a color from the resulting grid. To access a complete color-selection spectrum, double-click one of the color buttons.

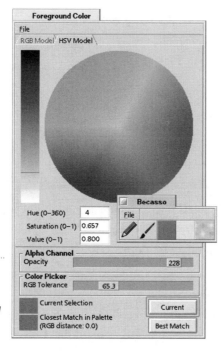

*Figure 13.05*

*The toolbar's color-selection buttons hide an extensive color editor, offering RGB and HSV color pickers.*

The color editor window (and the color buttons themselves) accept "color drops" from external color pickers such as roDesign's roColour. Becasso can also *initiate* such color drops. Try dragging a color from the Current Selection and Closest Match color patches at the bottom left of the color editor to the Desktop, or into a StyledEdit or Pe window (to get hexadecimal equivalents of those colors). Of course, you can always drag colors from these swatches onto a Becasso canvas to initiate a flood fill.

Click and hold the main toolbar's rightmost button to access the pattern picker (a future version of Becasso will include a full pattern editor). Initiate a flood fill or use one of the shape tools, and the area will be filled with the chosen pattern, rendered in the current foreground color.

**Scripting Support** Becasso includes full support for BeOS's native scripting architecture. Let's say you have a bunch of PNG files you want to convert to JPEG format. The following hey script should do the trick:

```
Becasso &
hey Becasso set ExportFormat to image/jpeg
for x in *.png
do
    y=$(basename $x .png)
    hey Becasso load file[$x]
    hey Becasso 'expt' with name=$y.jpg
done
hey Becasso quit
```

You can also set the current tool or mode via scripts:

```
hey Becasso set Tool to Brush
```

or set colors (by name or by RGB value):

```
hey Becasso set Foreground to rgb_color(100,50,30,255)
hey Becasso set Background to DarkOliveGreen
```

As an aside: All the options for all the tools are also adjustable via scripts, so you can say:

```
hey Becasso set Width of Tool Brush to 20
```

# Boo
## w3.datanet.hu/~amazei/Boo

Despite the many amazing things you can do with the image manipulation tools covered in this chapter, most of them restrict you to working on standard drawing and painting surfaces, like paper and canvas. Wouldn't it be excellent if you could work on an elastic surface such as rubber or clay instead? And what if, rather than making changes to the paint or image, you could alter the shape and texture of the surface itself, letting the image warp and morph sympathetically to reflect the changing surface beneath it?

Boo is an image-morphing and texture-generating tool written by a pair of Hungarian programmers, Levente Levai and Attila Mezei.

 If Boo seems somehow familiar, it may be because you've seen a similar application with a similar name from MetaCreations that runs on other platforms.

The beta version we tested supported only the provided demonstration images in Targa format, though future, registered versions should support any file format for which you have a Translator installed.

**The Interface from Mars** Rather than using standard BeOS buttons and sliders, Boo takes advantage of the BeOS programmer's ability to replace standard UI elements with uniquely designed interactive bitmaps. The vertical stack of buttons at the right of the Boo window is divided into two sections: clay tools (which are reddish in color) and rubber tools (which are purplish). Each of the rubber tools hides additional options; click the raised dot at the button's right edge to launch a preferences panel for that tool.

Usage of the individual tools is, for the most part, self-explanatory, though some work in ways you may not expect. For example, the Twirl and Zoom tools are operated by dragging your mouse over the canvas in circles. Whereas the Twirl tool in, say, Adobe Photoshop requires you to set a Twirl level in a separate panel and then apply it to the image with a button, Twirl effects in Boo are created additively. The more you move your mouse around in circles,

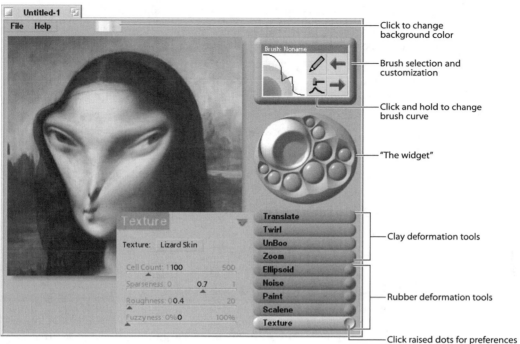

Click to change
background color

Brush selection and
customization

Click and hold to change
brush curve

"The widget"

Clay deformation tools

Rubber deformation tools

Click raised dots for preferences

*Figure 13.06*

*Reddish buttons control clay deformations, while purplish buttons are for tweaking rubber surfaces.*

the twirlier the image becomes. Likewise, the size of your circles defines the size of the twirl. To undo the amount of twirliness, just circle your mouse in the opposite direction.

**"The Widget"**  When any rubber deformation tool is selected, an additional toolset appears above the stack, looking like some kind of weird lunar landscape (see Figure 13.06). For lack of a better term, I call this the widget. The best way to learn how to use this unusual interface element may be to simply play with it. Each of the dots and wells in the widget can be operated by clicking and dragging up and down or side to side to adjust numerical parameters. For example, to change the red, green, or blue levels in your image, grab one of the colored dots and drag to the left or right. A numeric indicator will appear next to the widget, indicating the current level of that color value; when you release the mouse, the color balance of the image will change accordingly. Some of the dots and wells can also be clicked to toggle various effects. For example, you can toggle between various lighting effects by clicking repeatedly on the largest raised dot, and change the degree to which they take effect by dragging the smaller gray dots.

 **To undo any effect, select the UnBoo button and point to the effect you want to undo.**

**The Brushes** Boo comes with a set of four brushes, some defined by mathematical precepts such as Linear, Sine, and Exponential. Click the pencil icon to choose a basic brush type. Below the pencil icon you'll find the image of a hammer poised above a curve. Click and hold on the hammer to gradually smooth out the drawing curve of the currently selected brush. To change the breadth of coverage, click and drag the brush's curve diagram. Click and hold at the top of the brush window to give the brush you've just created a descriptive name. Move between named brushes by using the left and right arrow icons.

**A few of Boo's less-used options do not appear as options in the interface. For example:**

- **Ctrl+drag = Scroll image**
- **Alt+drag = Scale image**
- **Shift+drag = Move light source**

## BeatWare's e-Picture  *with Karen Cassel*
www.beatware.com

This discussion of BeatWare's e-Picture was prior to the product's actual release, so some features in the final version may be implemented differently than described here. If e-Picture isn't available by the time you read this, it should be soon—stay tuned to www.beatware.com for updates.

If you've ever created graphics for the Web, you know firsthand how surprisingly labor-intensive it can be to create a simple 10K banner or button. Take a Web button, for example. You probably started by designing your button in one of those expensive, professional-strength, does-more-than-you-need-but-not-what-you-want vector applications. Next, you may have imported it into another expensive, professional-strength, does-more-than-you-need-but-not-what-you-want application to convert it into a bitmap. Maybe you applied a filter for a special effect. If you wanted your button to look "active" when a mouse passed over it, you might have duplicated the image and added a drop shadow or a lighting effect.

And then you worried, "What if the images are too big and take too long to download?" You saved the images as GIFs to minimize file size, but just as you suspected, it was too big. So you went back and eliminated colors, one by one. You resaved the file and rechecked the file size and returned to eliminate another level of detail. Once the image was sufficiently small, you began the nail-biting process of viewing it from within a number of the more popular browsers. Ugh! the color was awful under Net Positive, and oops! you found a typo. Back you went to your vector program to start over again. And you *still* hadn't begun coding JavaScript for the mouse-overs!

**Figure 13.07**

BeatWare's e-Picture
is custom-tailored
for optimizing Web
graphics.

BeatWare's e-Picture is designed to take the repetition and guesswork out of creating graphics for the Web. e-Picture includes both the drawing tools you'd expect to find in an expensive vector application and a full range of bitmap brushes and filters. You get all the control and special effects you need in one neat package. e-Picture also give you real-time file compression, a JavaScript generator for creating mouse-over buttons, and an innovative, time-saving means of generating fluid animation.

**Getting Started**  e-Picture supports most common image file formats, including GIF, TIFF, JPEG, BMP, PNG, PNM, and Targa. You can open an existing picture by selecting File | Open from the main menu, or by simply dragging the file onto a blank canvas. Alternatively, create a new picture by pulling down File | New, then specify your canvas size by choosing one of the standard Web banner or button sizes, or by entering your own dimensions.

**Real-Time Feedback**  One of the biggest challenges in creating Web graphics is optimizing—balancing image quality and color depth against file size (which directly affects download time). Ironically, optimization is too often the final step. e-Picture saves you time and spares you agony by offering real-time feedback on the size and quality of the final, compressed image.

e-Picture lets you open a second view of your file and specify that you want this view to optimize and display the graphic as though it were being viewed through any one of a number of popular browsers. As you draw, paint, or apply filters in the original view, you'll get instantaneous feedback on the size and appearance of the graphic bound for the Web. Does a particular filter appear grainy when viewed through Netscape Navigator? Then undo it now, not later. Does NetPositive make your rich gold lettering look like rust? Change it before you go any further. Does that drop shadow put your file over the size limit? Maybe one of e-Picture's built-in glow effects would accomplish the same thing and save you a few precious kilobytes.

 **e-Picture's effects palette doesn't stop with the glow filter. You can easily apply built-in filters like blur, brighten, contrast, convolution, facet, oilify, and many more to your work-in-progress at any time. And of course, e-Picture also includes the usual collection of classic drawing tools, including lines, polygons, ellipses and Bézier curves.**

Speaking of unlimited flexibility, with BeatWare's LiveEdit technology, every line you draw, every bit of text you place, and every object you paste will remain 100% editable. You can even apply filters to your drawings while still retaining the ability to move, reshape, or recolor text and lines. Combine this with e-Picture's unlimited undo and redo capabilities, and it's never too late to try something new!

**Visual Image Slicing**   If, despite all efforts, your image is still bigger than you'd like, don't despair. Slicing up a large image into smaller pieces can reduce the apparent download time, since the user can see something onscreen almost immediately. Oddly enough, image editors like Adobe Photoshop don't make cutting large images into smaller pieces as easy as it should be. With e-Picture, all you have to do is invoke the slicing tool and draw a pattern of rectangles on the image. e-Picture will not only cut the image into pieces for you, it will also generate the HTML table code needed to reassemble the image on your Web page.

**Embedding URLs**   If you'd rather keep your image intact and link various parts of it to different URLs, e-Picture makes image-map creation a piece of cake. Select an area of your image and pull down File | Embed URL. Do this as many times as necessary, and e-Picture will generate image-map code on your behalf. You can edit embedded URLs at any time, or even create multiple maps from the same image.

**Mouse-Overs Made Easy**  Web buttons that light up as the mouse passes over them can make your site feel more dynamic, and give your site's visitors navigational guidance. To create a mouse-over button without e-Picture, you'd need to create two or three distinct buttons, each with distinctive shadows or light sources to indicate active and selected states. And once they were created, you'd still have to hack out the JavaScript code necessary to make them work properly.

e-Picture automates the whole process, so all you have to do is create a single button, then sit back and let e-Picture do the rest. Choose and define active and selected states from a list of options including drop shadows, lighting effects, beveled edges, and more. e-Picture automatically creates the additional buttons for you, then generates accompanying JavaScript to your specifications. Of course, you always have the ability to manually edit all effects later on.

**Animating GIFs**  Most GIF animation software requires you to create and edit each individual frame of an animation. Shortcuts and features like onion-skinning abound, but the fact remains that you have to create and tinker with each cell. e-Picture handles animation in a whole new way, generating smoother animations faster.

Let's say you want to create an animation of a dog wagging its tail. Traditionally, you'd create two or three images, with the tail at a different angle in each one. With only three frames, the effect will be somewhat choppy, but more frames take time, and you don't have all day. With e-Picture, just create the first frame with the tail out to the right, and the last frame with the tail out to the left. Select the number of frames you want, remembering the tradeoff between file size and quality. e-Picture uses animation paths to generate all the frames in between the first and the last. Once the images have been generated, you have the option of tweaking each frame or adding and deleting frames, as necessary.

**Gradient Fills**  If you've seen what happens when a gradient is produced in 32-bit color and then viewed through a browser in 8-bit color, you know the results can be a streaky mess. e-Picture uses intelligent algorithms written specifically to minimize the degradation that can occur in 8-bit color. Select a gradient pattern from a list that includes linear, radial, conic and others, then simply drag and drop any two colors from the color palette into the gradient panel. You can preview the optimized results in real time. Rather than just looking good on your monitor, your gradient should appear with the highest possible quality at all color depths.

### *About BeatWare's FreeStyle UI*

Each member of the family of BeatWare applications offers a highly customizable working environment, made possible by the company's FreeStyle User Interface Technology. Whether you're working in e-Picture, Writer, or Sum-It (see Chapter 12, *Productivity Applications*, for more), launch the FreeStyle utility (which you'll find in the BeatWare application directory) and you'll find that you can easily customize that application's look and feel. For example, you'll find options that let you:

- Customize the color of your background, text, and cursor

- Select the font, style, and size of your text

- Add pop-up labels to your icons

- Use patterns or pictures to decorate any background

- Control the click and hold speed of your mouse

- Display menu commands in any one of a number of supported languages

Because the FreeStyle configuration utility lets you use bitmap images as well as solid colors for interface elements, you can customize the look and feel of your BeatWare applications practically into infinity. For example, you might want to make all of the application backgrounds take

on the appearance of water, and all of your buttons and sliders appear with a light green ripple effect, for a maritime theme. Of course, this capability can easily lead to the process of infinite revision, or tweakaholism—it can be tough to know when to stop.

It's also worth noting that when you change your application font sizes with FreeStyle, all buttons, labels, and interface elements will expand accordingly, circumventing a bug in the BeOS Interface Kit that causes some words to be clipped when the font exceeds a certain size.

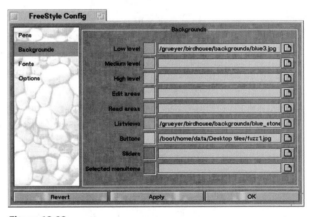

**Figure 13.08**

*The FreeStyle configuration utility lets you customize every tiny aspect of the UI in BeatWare apps.*

## Other Image Editors

By no means is this list of image editors for BeOS complete or definitive. Plenty of others are bound to be released after this book goes to press. At the time of this writing, for instance, the mysterious Táve Software (www.tave.com) had been toiling away behind the scenes for quite some time on an imaging and paint application code-named Mozart, though Táve wasn't handing out any prerelease details. And don't forget that Gobe Productive, which is covered in Chapter 12, *Productivity Applications*, includes its own built-in image editor. Keep an eye on BeWare and BeDepot for more.

# Modeling and Raytracing

The world of 3D modeling and raytracing is completely different from that of two-dimensional graphics. Rather than having you create images by hand, modeling programs typically work by generating images mathematically. Most modeling programs present the artist with a two-dimensional representation (computer monitors are flat, after all) of a three-dimensional space. Within this space, the artist defines the shape, size, and coloration of objects by constructing wireframe models, usually based on variations of simple primitives such as spheres, cubes, cylinders, and cones. Objects are bound together and moved into various positions. The wireframe models are covered with surfaces such as texture maps, colorations, and reflectivity quotients. Lights are placed in the space, and cameras from which to view the scene are put in position.

Finally, the scene is rendered. The modeling application calculates where and how light will fall on the predefined objects, bending it if it moves through glass, or bouncing it back if hits a reflective surface. Ideally, the end result is some approximation of a believable 3D environment. A huge amount of math is required to generate a 3D scene from simple descriptions, and so rendering is one of the most CPU-intensive things you can do with your computer. The fact that BeOS takes full advantage of multiple processors, in addition to its other performance advantages, means the platform is a great candidate for artists serious about 3D work.

## MAXON's CINEMA 4D XL V5.25
**www.maxon.de**

This discussion of MAXON's CINEMA 4D was written prior to the product's actual release and may not represent actual shipping features. If CINEMA 4D isn't available by the time you read this, it should be soon—stay tuned to www.maxon.de for updates.

MAXON has repeatedly impressed the 3D modeling and raytracing industry with the blazingly fast speeds of its rendering engine. Meanwhile, CINEMA 4D XL takes maximum advantage of up to 16 processors, making it a perfect 3D modeling and raytracing complement to BeOS.

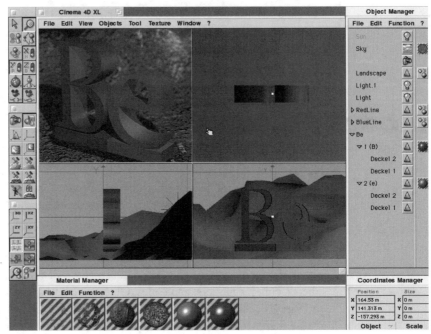

*Figure 13.09*

*CINEMA 4D XL's many tool and configuration panels augment the primary workspace.*

**Getting Started** While it's not difficult to create scenes from scratch in CINEMA 4D XL, you may want to start by opening some of the sample scenes bundled with the product and distributed free at MAXON's Web site. When you open a scene, you'll be presented with a collection of windows and panels. The tool palettes let you position and manipulate geometric primitives, bind multiple objects together into single units, rotate, skew, and deform objects, and zoom in and out within your scene.

The Object Manager provides a logical view of the hierarchy of assembled objects in your environment. While most objects you create will consist of multiple smaller objects, the Object Manager will remember all of their relationships, so you can see at a glance how complex scenes have been constructed. Expand or collapse any branch of the tree to study groupings more carefully. Another important aspect of the Object Manager is its ability to let you select any object out of the maze quickly, a task that can be difficult from within the main workspace when a scene becomes complex. Double-click any object to access its properties panel.

The Material Manager stores libraries of texture maps, which you can use to make your objects appear as realistic as possible. Drag any texture from this panel onto any object. A properties panel will appear from which you can specify parameters such as the method of wrapping or tiling to be used.

**Previewing and Rendering** Because rendering is mathematically intensive, modeling applications typically offer multiple shading options for use while building your scene. By displaying objects only as wireframe models, you can navigate your scene without delay, even on slower machines. If a scene isn't too complex, or if you have a faster machine, you can opt to cover the wireframes with Gouraud shading, which is a simple method of stretching a quick skin over the wireframe. This gives you a much better sense for how the final scene will come together, but definitely requires more processing power. Because CINEMA 4D XL has such speedy rendering capabilities, however, it's able to actually give objects textures, highlights, bump maps, and transparencies while in Gouraud mode. MAXON calls this technique real-time texture mapping, and it really does provide an excellent compromise between the blockiness of general Gouraud shading and the quality of the final rendered image, without sacrificing responsiveness as you work.

 **To move between CINEMA 4D XL's many preview modes, pull down View | Display Mode and choose among Gouraud, Quick Shading, Wireframe, Bounding Box, or Skeleton. Each option also has an associated hotkey, so you can bounce between preview modes quickly.**

When you're ready to see how your scene will appear as a fully rendered environment, pull down View | Render Picture | All (or tap Alt+R). If you're viewing one of the included demo scenes, the entire render will probably take less than a minute, which may or may not amaze you, depending on whether you've used other raytracers with slower rendering engines. If you have a slower machine or a very complex scene, you can optionally choose from the same menu to render just the selected object.

*Figure 13.10*

*Work in one of CINEMA 4D XL's many preview modes while building your world (behind). Tap Alt+R to generate your final scene (in front).*

 **If you have a ton of scenes to render and want to take a lunch break, pull down View | Render Picture | Batch Render and enter the paths to the files you need rendered. Click OK and go munch a hoagie.**

**Features** CINEMA 4D XL includes tons of options we don't have time to get into here. You can work with an unlimited number of light sources, each with dozens of individual parameters. You can use the built-in particle system to recreate natural elements such as flickering fire, flowing water, drifting fog, or impenetrable smoke, or to generate artificial snowfall or dust in the sunlight by creating a "particle swarm." In addition to the standard collection of materials, you can work with shaders, which are defined mathematically and are therefore immune from the distortions and tiling effects of bitmapped textures. You can base objects on NURBS (non-uniform rational B-splines), which make it easy to change the shape of objects in real time, or to animate them via spline morphing. Nearly all editable properties in CINEMA 4D XL can be animated via keyframes, inverse kinematics, "bones," or freeform deformations (which let you reshape objects by dragging control points around). If you get to be a real pro, you can take your modeling to the next level with C.O.F.F.E.E., an integrated programming language similar to Java or C++ that lets you create effects not implemented in the program itself. Because C.O.F.F.E.E. modules are platform-independent, you can download examples created by other developers and use them as plug-ins.

## Persistence of Vision (POV-Ray)

www2.dynamite.com.au/pedro/BeOS/

Far from the point-and-click, drag-and-drop world of GUI modelers like Cinema4D lies the old school—the world of the command-line raytracer, where scenes are defined via text-based configuration files. The Persistence of Vision raytracer, or POV-Ray, is a near-legendary piece of open-source software with a long history and thousands of devotees. POV-Ray has been ported to nearly every OS under the sun, including BeOS. But let's get one thing straight right away: POV-Ray probably isn't what you or I would call intuitive. The images it creates can be as stunningly gorgeous as those produced by raytracers costing thousands of dollars, but its interface is pretty much nonexistent. While there are some ports of POV-Ray for other platforms that include a windowed environment in which to work, you're still not going to get a full drag-and-drop GUI environment, and you're still going to be hand-editing a description language.

That said, POV-Ray is an extremely powerful and flexible raytracer. If you're willing to put the time into learning it, you'll be rewarded both in personal satisfaction and in amazing images. Fortunately, POV-Ray comes with more than 300 pages of documentation. That documentation doesn't exactly hold your hand, but the distribution does come with dozens of sample scenes and objects ready to be pasted into your own scenes, used as tutorials, or hacked into something else altogether. You should be able to create some pretty cool scenes in just a few hours of practice. This book can help you get started, but to dig in deep, you'll need to get your nose into the documentation.

**Figure 13.11**

*A scene created and rendered completely in POV-Ray for BeOS.*

If you'd like to see a few exemplary POV-Ray images in full color, head over to www.povray.org.

**Installation and Setup** Because it has customizable configuration files and many command-line options, there are many possible ways to set up POV-Ray. Here's a method that's worked well for me:

1. Move the povray binary to /boot/home/config/bin.

2. Move the povray3 directory wherever you like. For this example, let's say it's /boot/apps/graphics/povray3. The povray3 directory may contain many files and subdirectories, and you may want to clean house a bit. Just make sure that the include directory and the files res120.ini through res1024.ini are in the root of your povray3 directory.

3. Find the file .povrayrc and move it to your home directory. Open it in a text editor and scroll to the bottom, where you'll find two lines that look like this:

```
Library_Path=/boot/apps/graphics/povray3/
Library_Path=/boot/apps/graphics/povray3/include/
```

Sticking with our example install path, make sure these lines read as above. Otherwise, edit them to match the actual path on your machine. That's it—you're ready to start raytracing.

**Getting Started** While there are tons of command-line arguments you can feed the renderer, two are essential. You'll need to specify which .ini file to use and which scene file to render. The .ini file will establish some basics; the default .ini files provided just specify the resolution at which to render, such as 640×480 or 800×1024.

**The higher the resolution of your rendered scene, the longer the rendering will take. By using these external .ini files, you can change rendering resolutions quickly without editing your actual scene file. When practicing, or if you have a slower machine, always render your scenes at low resolutions. When you're sure you've got the scene set up just the way you want it, go out for a burrito while you render the big one.**

To specify a scene, use the +I argument followed by the scene's filename, with no space separating the two. For example, if you had a scene file called scene.pov in the current directory that you wanted to render at 640×480, you would issue this command:

```
povray res640.ini +Iscene.pov
```

Note that you don't have to specify a path to the .ini file—your .povrayrc file takes care of that for you.

Your povray3 folder contains a couple of directories full of demo scenes. Plumb these directories to find interesting-sounding filenames, and try some test renders. Note that subdirectories of povscn are named level1 through level4; level 1 scenes will take the shortest time to render. For starters, let's try the tasty little cantaloupe scene in the directory povscn/level1:

```
povray res320.ini +Ipovscn/level1/cantelop.pov
```

The rendering engine will chug along merrily for a little while, and the command prompt will be returned to you. You should now have a new Targa file in the current directory called cantelop.tga. Double-click it to bring it up in ShowImage. Juicy, eh? Well, maybe not. Kind of plastic-looking, actually. But it's still pretty cool that you can create fruit from a mathematical description.

**If you don't want to set your resolution from .ini files, you can optionally do it by adding more arguments to the command line. For example, instead of**

```
povray res640.ini +Iscene.pov
```

**you could use**

```
povray +w640 +h480 +Iscene.pov
```

**However, .ini files also let you establish many additional parameters, which you may want to use as your skills advance.**

If the renderer gave you error messages instead of a cantaloupe, check all of your paths. Make sure your current directory is /boot/apps/graphics/povray3, that this same directory is specified in your .povrayrc file (which lives in /boot/home), and that your .ini files are in your povray3 directory.

As your scenes become larger and more complex, you're going to want some feedback from the program as it's working so you know what's going on. In the future, POV-Ray for BeOS should be able to render directly into a real-time preview window. This early port, however, is only capable of drawing an ASCII likeness of your image in the Terminal (which is actually pretty cool, in a retro sort of way). Just add the +D flag to your command and tell it to use display type 1:

```
povray res320.ini +D1 +Ipovscn/level1/cantelop.pov
```

**What's in a Scene File?** At the very minimum, every scene needs to include a camera, so there's something present to capture the view; a light source, so the camera will actually be able see something; and an object, so there's actually something to see. Each of these things is placed in a virtual 3D universe, in positions designated by a simple coordinate system. An X axis runs horizontally through the universe, a Y axis vertically, and a Z axis through the scene from front to back. The three axes meet at a point, designated as <0, 0, 0>, which is the center of the universe. You can refer to any point in this coordinate system by specifying a distance and direction from the center. For example, if you want to place an object to the left of center and raised up a bit, you might specify coordinates <-2, 1, 0>.

And what kind of units do these numbers represent? None—they're just units, totally arbitrary. Everything is relative to everything else in the raytraced universe. Size is only an illusion created by the distance of the camera from the object. You could just as easily use <-200, 100, 0> and end up with an identical result, as long as all of your other coordinates are specified in large numbers as well.

The best way to begin placing objects is to use some of the built-in primitives, such as spheres, cubes, and planes. To place a sphere at coordinates <-2, 1, 0>, try something like this:

```
sphere { <-2, 1, 0>, 1.5
  pigment {Orange}
  }
```

The 1.5 argument specifies the radius of the sphere, while the pigment gives it a color (everything must have either a pigment or a finish in order to be visible). The POV-Ray documentation includes lists of all possible geometric primitives, along with the arguments they can take.

In order to see the scene with our camera, we're going to need to step back from the origin a few paces, just as we would in real life. Of course, we'll also have to tell the camera in which direction to point:

```
camera {
   location <0, 2, -3>
   look_at  <-2, 1, 0>
}
```

So we've pulled back three units and up two to get a good view, and pointed the camera at the exact center of the sphere, which is our subject matter. Finally, we need to shed some light on the scene. We'll pull the light way back and up high, so everything is evenly illuminated:

```
light_source {<10, 20, -30> color White}
```

Before we can render the scene, we have to take care of a little business. Put these lines at the top of the file:

```
#version 3.0
global_settings { assumed_gamma 2.2 }
#include "colors.inc"
```

This will tell the renderer which version of POV-Ray we're designing for, establish a gamma value (don't worry about understanding gamma right now; it's in the documentation), and, importantly, tell the renderer where to find the file that defines colors, since we invoked the color Orange. Dig around in your include subdirectory and you'll find dozens of prefab textures and colors, complete with reflectivity and opacity options. Pretty much any surface found in the real world has been encoded as a POV-Ray pigment or texture by somebody at some point. If you can't find what you're looking for in your POV-Ray installation, you can probably find it on the Internet somewhere. Start at www.povray.org.

Your finished scene file should look something like this:

```
#version 3.0
global_settings { assumed_gamma 2.2 }
#include "colors.inc"

light_source {<10, 20, -30> color White}

  camera {
    location <0, 2, -3>
    look_at  <-2, 1, 0>
  }
```

```
sphere { <-2, 1, 0>, 1.5
  pigment {Orange}
  }
```

Save the file with a .pov extension and use the instructions above to render it. You'll end up with a dull orange ball on a black background. A far cry from the delicate pocket watches and glamorous Trekkie-mobiles you've seen rendered elsewhere, but it's a start!

 Once you've got the hang of rendering with POV-Ray, you can easily create animations by batch-rendering the same scene over and over, moving the objects and/or camera slightly each time. You can then use software like Adamation's personalStudio (Chapter 14, *Media Applications*) to sew your sequence of Targa files together into an MPEG movie. Command-line tools that accomplish the same task are also available, though at this writing, none had been ported to BeOS.

# Graphics Utilities

Beyond all the high-falutin', industrial-strength image creation applications available for BeOS, there are quite a few smaller, more task-specific graphics tools and utilities out there as well. These utilities will help you convert between image file formats, select color values with precision, use the Tracker for enhanced graphics file management, and automate complex image manipulation routines.

## Adamation's ImageElements
www.adamation.com

Most graphics applications offer features like the ability to crop, resize, invert, blur, emboss, or otherwise manipulate an image. Trouble is, sometimes you need to perform a bunch of these operations in sequence, over and over again. While a few imaging applications, such as Adobe Photoshop (with its built-in actions), will let you create macros to script these operations, most do not, and Photoshop actions have their limitations. People serious about automating complex image manipulation sequences usually turn to a program like Equilibrium's DeBabelizer. So what's the BeOS version of DeBabelizer?

Adamation's ImageElements takes an approach to programmatic image manipulation that is probably unlike anything you've ever worked with. ImageElements provides a palette of elements, each of which represents a particular imaging operation. For example, one element knows how to pixelize an image, another knows how to change brightness, another is capable of

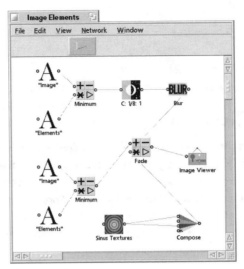

**Figure 13.12**

An ImageElements "network" consists of a collection of elements, joined together in what amounts to an image-processing flowchart.

tiling an image across a canvas, and another converts to grayscale. Rather than operating on images in an editing window, you use the ImageElements workspace to arrange the elements you need in a sequence, then glue them together with connectors, much as you would assemble a dragster from the pile of parts in an Erector Set (or, to use a metaphor closer to home, much as you would assemble a complex shell command from the pile of tools in /boot/beos/bin). Assembled configurations of elements are called "networks," and can be saved for reuse.

**The Elements**  The main ImageElements palette is divided into five categories:

- **Inputs:** contains various mechanisms for getting image data into the network. The most commonly used method will probably be File Input, but images can also be hoovered out of the system clipboard, or you can begin with image data generated within ImageElements itself, such as text or math-based textures.

- **Outputs:** contains mechanisms for getting the processed image out of ImageElements and into another format. For the most part, you'll want to use the built-in Image Viewer for testing and the File Output element for real work. You can also output to the clipboard.

- **Channel Operations:** provides mechanisms for separating an image into its constituent red, green, blue, and alpha channels, or for reconstituting images from previously separated channels.

- **Filters:** includes analogs to some of the most familiar image filters found in other imaging applications, such as blur, convolution, edge detection, emboss, sharpen, and grayscale conversion.

- **Miscellaneous:** provides extra goodies that don't qualify as filters, such as brightness and color balancing, pixelization, posterization, scaling, and automatic cropping.

**Getting Started**  Before building networks from scratch, you'll probably find it useful to check out some of the prebuilt networks bundled with ImageElements (our demo version came with 20 of them). Open any sample

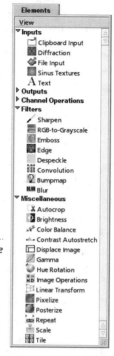

*Figure 13.13*

The Elements palette lets you select from among dozens of basic imaging operations. Drag elements from here into the workspace to build networks.

network and you'll notice that each element includes a number of connection points. Elements that can both accept input and generate output have connectors on both sides. Elements that can accept or generate multiple inputs or outputs will have correspondingly different numbers of connectors. Create a connection by dragging from one connector to another; break a connection by right-clicking a connector and choosing Disconnect. If you attempt to make an illegal connection (such as trying to connect two outputs together), no connection line will be drawn. Rearrange elements in the workspace by dragging; their connection lines will be redrawn in real time. To view the results of a network in operation, press the Play button in the upper part of the window, or tap the Spacebar. Note that the network must have a valid input before it will play—if the network is using File Input as its starting point, drag an image from the Tracker onto that icon. Zoom in on or out from the network with Alt++ (Alt and the plus key) or Alt+− (use your numeric keypad).

 There is no requirement that a network consist of a single chain of events. In fact, you can create as many event sequences as you like in a single network, even if they're not connected to each other and have nothing to do with one another. Playing the network will execute all event chains simultaneously. To experiment, pull down File | Merge and choose another of the prebuilt networks. Both networks will now appear in a single network window, and can be run in parallel or joined together by drawing appropriate connections.

Try double-clicking any element in an open network—you'll find that nearly every element has an options panel specific to its duties. For example, the Text Input element wants to know what to write, which font, font size, and font color to use, and so on. The Color Balance element needs to know exactly how much cyan you want to add and whether it should apply that color change to shadows, midtones, or highlights. The Edge Detector wants to know how sensitive it should be, and so on.

**Roll Your Own**    Now that you've explored some of the prefab networks, try building one of your own. The simplest network you can build consists of two elements: File Input and Image Viewer. Drag these two elements onto a new network, connect them by dragging your mouse between connectors, and drag an image from the Tracker onto the File Input element. Press Play, and your image will be displayed in a new window. Now right-click a connector and break the connection. Drag the blur element into the workspace, and connect the three elements in sequence. Got the hang of it? Experiment with as many elements as you can, and try to imagine the kinds of repetitive image manipulation chores you could automate with ImageElements.

 **Nothing constrains you to using a single image as input—you can create collages and blends by feeding multiple file inputs into the same network.**

**Compositing Channels** As you know, every image is composed of red, green, blue, and alpha channels. ImageElements is capable of stripping these channels from images, or using a preexisting image as one channel in another image. The purpose of the Channel Operations elements may not appear obvious at first, but they can yield some interesting effects. A good way to get familiar with them is to start with some grayscale patterns generated from within ImageElements itself and fuse them together into a new RGB image. The Sinus Texture element offers a wild array of mathematical texture-generation options. Drag Sinus Texture into a fresh workspace, along with the Image Viewer. Connect the two, then double-click Sinus Texture and tweak its parameters until something interesting comes out the other side. Now right-click its icon and choose Duplicate from the context menu. Do this twice so you've got three exact copies of your customized Sinus Texture. Disconnect the Image Viewer and drag the Compose element in from the palette. The Compose element itself has no options, but it does have four inputs (one for each channel); connect each of your Sinus elements to one of the R, G, or B input connectors on the Compose element, then connect the Compose element's output to the Image Viewer.

When you play this network … ah, shucks—the result looks exactly as it did when you had only one Sinus. This is because the red, green, and blue channels now overlay to re-create what appears to be another grayscale image. It's just an illusion, however; double-click one of the Sinus elements and change one of its parameters even the slightest bit. Amazingly, the output image will now appear in color, since the three color channels no longer overlay one another precisely.

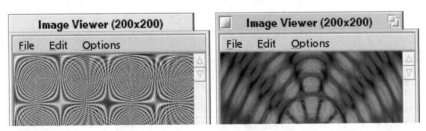

*Figure 13.14*

*The Compose and Decompose elements can be used to fuse grayscale images into RGB images or to deconstruct color images into their constituent color channels.*

Try making wider variances in the parameters associated with each Sinus element and you'll end up with some pretty strange results. The Decompose element, obviously, does the same thing but in the reverse direction.

 Equally (if not more) fascinating results can be derived from the Diffraction filter. While it offers many more image-generation options than Sinus, it's also far more mathematically intensive, so you'll lose the nearly real-time effects you get when working with Sinus.

 **You can combine Sinus or Diffraction textures with any existing network. Try integrating them into networks that already perform manipulations on text or images. You may want to tone down their effects by filtering them through the Image Operations element, described below.**

**Image Operations**   One of the more powerful elements is named Image Operations and lets you control exactly how two or more effects are combined. For example, you may be overlaying one image on top of another. Do you want it to be added to or subtracted from the first? If transparency is involved, do you want to respect or exclude the alpha channel? One of the best ways to familiarize yourself with the Image Operations element is to open the sample Text Effect 1 network, see how it plays, then double-click the Image Operations element and tweak its settings. Many of the options' purposes become clear only after seeing their repercussions in a simple environment.

 **It's very easy to create simple drop-shadow effects in ImageElements by using two identical Text elements, running one of them through the Displace element (to offset it by a few pixels) and the Blur element (to create a hazy shadow effect on the lower layer). For best results, send the results through the Image Operations Element with a setting of "Minimum" prior to output.**

 ImageElements works in real time by default. Any change you make in any preferences panel will take effect in the Image Viewer window immediately. For example, set an Image Operations element to Fade, and drag the slider left and right to see the impact on your entire image without first having to press the Apply button. If you have a slower machine or just don't particularly like the real-time effects, pull down File | Preferences, go to the Network tab, and disable the checkbox labeled "Network started when a parameter changes."

**Scripting**   Behind the scenes, ImageElements offers very extensive scripting support. Got 10,000 images to resize, flip, change to grayscale, and save in TIFF format? Grab a copy of Attila Mazzei's hey module and take a look at ImageElements' documentation, where you'll find detailed lists of scriptable properties and controls. Test some hey commands from the command line, then drop them into a shell script that loops through a directory of files.

# NetPBM

**www.qnx.com/~chrish/Be/software/**

As discussed in Chapter 9, *Preferences and Customization*, BeOS uses a system of Translators to give your applications the ability to read and write multiple file formats without the developer having to specifically code support for them into the application. The use of Translators comes up most often when dealing with various image file formats, since there are so many of them out there. The Translators system is fantastic, but what happens when you don't have a Translator installed for a file format you desperately need? If you're willing to work from the command line, a remarkable toolkit called NetPBM exists to help you translate between nearly any two image file formats in existence. In fact, NetPBM even supports a lot of old, exotic image formats that may never have corresponding BeOS Translators.

Because creating a separate converter to and from every known image file format would require thousands of separate tools, NetPBM gets around the problem by requiring you to convert an image first into a "lowest common denominator" format (.pbm, .pgm, or .ppm), and then from that format to the destination format. Even so, the NetPBM toolkit still consists of 180 conversion routines (though most of these are just symlinks pointing to a few actual binaries). Most of the routines are simple translation tools, but a handful of image generators and manipulation filters are also included.

**Installation** Download NetPBM for your platform into the root of your /boot volume and decompress the archive. It should create a netpbm subdirectory in /boot/home/config/bin. Now open /boot/home/.profile in a text editor and add this line:

```
export PATH=/boot/home/config/bin/netpbm:$PATH
```

You'll be able to use all of the NetPBM tools from the next Terminal you launch.

**Usage** To convert a file from one format to another, start by figuring out which converters are available for the format your image is in now. For example, if you take a screenshot in BeOS (by pressing the PrintScreen key on your keyboard), you end up with a Targa file in your home directory. Taking a quick look in ~/config/bin/netpbm, you see that the only converter that takes Targa files as input is called tgatoppm. That tells you that your intermediate format is going to be a .ppm file. Now you need to find out which formats can be created *from* a .ppm file. Looking in this directory again, you see that several common formats such as ppmtobmp, ppmtogif, and ppmtopict and several less common formats can be created from ppm files, so you know you'll be able to export your image in .bmp, .gif, or .pict formats.

Assuming you want to create a GIF image, and assuming your screenshot is called screen1.tga, you'll need to run two commands in sequence:

```
tgatoppm screen1.tga > screen1.ppm
ppmtogif screen1.ppm > screen1.gif
```

 **Since GIF images are limited to 256 colors by definition, you may need to "quantize" your image to a lower color depth before converting to GIF. (You'll know you need to do this if NetPBM yields an error message during conversion.) Use the command** ppmquant -fs 256 **to accomplish this. Here's a quick way to run the whole series from a single command, by using the pipe (Chapter 6,** *The Terminal***):**

```
tgatoppm screen1.tga | ppmquant -fs 256 | ppmtogif > screen1.gif
```

Bingo! You've got a GIF. But what happens when you need to convert between formats that don't offer an easy built-in path? Fortunately, NetPBM includes a converter capable of making educated guesses about file formats. For example, if you need to make a TIFF image out of your Targa, you'll find that the kit doesn't include any convenient built-in routines. The catch-all anytopnm converter gets the job done nicely:

```
anytopnm file.tga > file.pnm
pnmtotiff file.pnm > file.tif
```

In actual fact, the anytopnm converter is a script (rather than a binary) that runs tests against the file and then invokes a series of conversion binaries to get the job done. Speaking of scripts, you can easily write a quickie shell script to perform these two-step conversions in one step by using some of the techniques from **http://www.beosbible.com**. For example, here's a script you can use to convert a whole bunch of Targas to GIFs all at once. Save this as a file called tgatogif in ~/config/bin:

```
#! /bin/sh

# The next line takes a command-line argument as the filename
file="$*"

tgatoppm $file.tga > $file.ppm
ppmtogif $file.ppm > $file.gif

# Tell the user we've been successful
echo
echo Created $file.gif

# Remove the ppm file automatically. Who needs it?
rm $file.ppm

# Offer to remove the original tga as well, and do so
# if user enters "y"
```

```
echo Remove $file.tga?
    read yn
    if [ "$yn" = "y" ]; then
            rm $file.tga
    fi
```

Now, assuming you have a file called screen2.tga and you want to turn it into a GIF, all you have to do is type tgatogif screen2. A few seconds later you'll have a file called screen2.gif.

 **The NetPBM toolkit actually does much more than just convert between file formats. It's capable of all kinds of rotations, inversions, color depth and resizing operations, and so on. We don't cover those here because you'll probably be better served by one of the many GUI graphics applications available, but you may find them useful if you want to create a script that generates a series of images, all slightly different from one another. Study NetPBM's documentation for details.**

NetPBM has been ported to BeOS by our own Chris Herborth.

## roDesign's roColour
**www.rodesign.com**

No platform for digital content creators would be complete without an excellent color mixing tool, and roColour is the best we've seen on any platform. Unlike other color mixers, roColour doesn't just translate RGB values into hex values for use on your Web pages—it can communicate with any BeOS application that knows how to accept color values encoded in BMessages. For example, if you drag a color swatch from roColour to your Desktop, your Desktop will take on that color. Drag a color into StyledEdit or Pe, and you'll get the hex value of that color for use in your Web pages. Drag a color onto SoundPlay, and SoundPlay's interface will accept that hue. Any developer can configure an application to accept dragged color values. In other words, roColour isn't meant for any *particular* purpose, since it can interface with any application with color needs, and can output color data in all of the most common formats, notably those used by Web developers and programmers.

**Buckets of Colour** When you launch roColour, you'll see a large color field to the right, representing the current active color, and a row of dots along the bottom. Those dots are called "color buckets," and can be used to store a dozen of your most frequently used colors. You can drag a swatch of color from the active cell to any bucket, or from any bucket to any compatible application. This is the simplest use of roColour, but it gets better.

Since Web designers are one of the groups most likely to find roColour useful, the middle row of buckets function as a "mirror" of the arguments in the

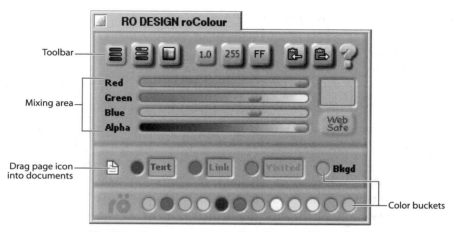

*Toolbar*

*Mixing area*

*Drag page icon into documents*

*Color buckets*

*Figure 13.15*

*Frequently used colors can be stored in "buckets" and dragged into compatible applications. Color messages can be copied to the clipboard in common color-encoding formats.*

<BODY> tag of an HTML document. Preview windows are provided so you can see how your current color choice will look as a text or link color. Look for the tiny icon that looks like a piece of paper and drag it into your HTML document; you'll have inserted an entire <BODY> tag, ready to go.

***Go Web Safe***  **Amazing as it may seem, huge numbers of users still have their displays set to render in 256 colors, rather than in the full spectrum of colors to which you've probably got your monitor set. Unfortunately, if you choose an HTML color value that lies outside the 256-color palette this audience is using, it may appear dithered on their screens. To limit the impact of this problem, browser vendors recognize a common palette of 216 colors that are shared between MacOS and Windows browsers when working in 256-color mode. To ensure that your colors look as good as possible on everyone's machine, click the Web Safe button before dragging or copying your colors to another document. This will cause roColour to use the closest match it can find, which may turn out just fine, or may truly suck. If the latter condition pertains, try working backwards, starting from a Web-safe color you like and building your site's palette around that.**

Use the three buttons at the top left of roColour's interface to toggle among three color-selection interfaces: the traditional RGB model, the hue/saturation/value model often favored by artists, and a unified spectrum palette without sliders.

**Output Modes**  The three buttons in the middle of the top row marked 1.0, 255, and FF let you specify which color-encoding system to use when converting chosen colors into alphanumeric representations. Programmers often represent color values as a mathematical "float" between zero and one. Color slider panels in many applications represent colors as red, green, blue, and alpha values, where each value is a number between 0 and 255. Finally, Web designers often represent colors with hexadecimal values. Click the appropriate button, and a corresponding value will be displayed for each slider when you click the word to its left.

**Enter Color Values Manually**  roColour is highly keyboardable (see the roColour documentation for details), and even lets you type the numerical equivalents of colors directly into its interface if you know them already (for example, you may be trying to match a color you've created in a paint program that also has an RGB readout). To make a given slider match a known color value, just click in the slider and type in the color value. This, by the way, is a great way to get a nice medium gray—assuming you've used the toolbar to establish 255 as the value range, just type 128, Tab, 128, Tab, 128, Tab (pressing the Tab key will cycle you through all elements of the roColour interface). On the other hand, if you want to learn the numerical equivalent of the color in one of your sliders, just click on the word to the left of the slider (Red, Green, or Blue/Hue, Saturation, or Value).

**Other roDesign Products**  While we were not able to evaluate them in time for publication, roDesign makes other sophisticated graphics tools as well. Backrow specializes in creating tiled backgrounds for Web pages and desktops, while Showboat lets you create interactive shows and scrapbooks for your digital photos. Both products should be available in early 1999.

# Thumbnail
**www.itap.physik.uni-stuttgart.de/~thorsten/Be**

Artists who use imaging applications on MacOS have long enjoyed the fact that icons for image files can display tiny versions of the images themselves. In other words, a folder full of image files doubles as a thumbnail database for quick visual reference. Depending on the clarity of the icons at that teensy-weensy size, this can make it much easier to determine at a glance which files are which, since humans are better at gathering information pictorially than at reading lists of filenames.

While BeOS won't create thumbnail versions of your icons on its own, you can get the same effect with Thorsten Seitz's Thumbnail. As described in Chapter 5, *Files and the Tracker*, BeOS icons are either inherited from attributes in the FileTypes database or stored in the attributes of individual files (if you've attached custom icons to them). Chances are, the icons for your image files are all the same right now, since they're being inherited from their filetypes. But when you drag an image file onto an open Thumbnail window, several interesting things happen.

anxiety.jpg        anxiic.gif        crowpct.gif

mainsgic.gif       maincic.gif       iMac-MedRes.jpg

**Figure 13.16**

*When an image is run through Thumbnail, large and small icon attributes are written to its file as scaled-down versions of the actual image.*

First, Thumbnail looks to see whether your system has an installed Translator for that image format. If it does, Thumbnail examines the image and determines whether its height or its width is its longer edge. It then shrinks that longer edge down to 96 pixels, letting the other dimension scale proportionally. The resulting thumbnail is written to an attribute attached to that file. Next, it scales the thumbnail itself down to ⅓ size, which results in a 32×32 pixel image which, as you know, is the size of the standard, large-format BeOS icon. The large icon is written to an attribute, and then *that* image is scaled down to a 16×16 image that is written to another attribute to create the mini-format icon. Finally, the height and width of the original file are written to height and width attributes in the same file. Amazingly, all of this happens in a just second or two (for most images). The result, as shown in the figures here, is simultaneous iconic excellence and enhanced Tracker functionality.

 If you've given up trying to create good-looking custom icons in Icon-o-Matic, think of Thumbnail as a great way to create photo-quality BeOS icons. Create any perfectly square icon in any imaging application, then run it through Thumbnail. You can then use the resulting icon system-wide, if you like, by dragging it to one of the icon wells in your FileTypes database.

**Easy Access**  If you're staring at a generic image icon and want to Thumbnail it, you don't even have to launch the Thumbnail application—just right-click the image and select Add-Ons | MakeThumbnail from the context menu. This add-on will launch Thumbnail automatically, passing the selected image to it as an argument. If the MakeThumbnail add-on does not appear in your context menu, look for it in the Thumbnail distribution folder and move it to /boot/home/config/add-ons/Tracker.

**Batch Processing**  If you'd like to create hundreds of thumbnails at once, you don't have to drag one file at a time onto the Thumbnail application window. If you have just a few images in a folder, select them all at once and run the Thumbnail add-on. If you've

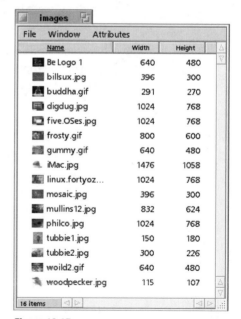

| Name | Width | Height |
|------|-------|--------|
| Be Logo 1 | 640 | 480 |
| billsux.jpg | 396 | 300 |
| buddha.gif | 291 | 270 |
| digdug.jpg | 1024 | 768 |
| five.OSes.jpg | 1024 | 768 |
| frosty.gif | 800 | 600 |
| gummy.gif | 640 | 480 |
| iMac.jpg | 1476 | 1058 |
| linux.fortyoz... | 1024 | 768 |
| mosaic.jpg | 396 | 300 |
| mullins12.jpg | 832 | 624 |
| philco.jpg | 1024 | 768 |
| tubbie1.jpg | 150 | 180 |
| tubbie2.jpg | 300 | 226 |
| woild2.gif | 640 | 480 |
| woodpecker.jpg | 115 | 107 |

16 items

**Figure 13.17**

*Thumbnail also writes image height and width data to attributes, so you can use the Tracker as an image database.*

got larger groups of files to be Thumbnailed—especially if they're living in nested subdirectories—just drag the entire parent folder onto Thumbnail (but see the tip below).

 **When dragging entire folders onto Thumbnail, you'll get an error message for every file encountered that isn't an image file, or for which you don't have a valid Translator installed. Rather than clicking OK to the error message over and over again, open up Thumbnail's preferences panel and select the Suppress Alerts checkbox.**

**The Big One**    Remember how the first attribute created was a large, 96×96 thumbnail? Where did it go, and what's it used for? As far as display in the Tracker goes, the answer is … nothing. It's simply there for the benefit of other applications. For example, a paint application could include a "contact sheet" that lets you view larger-size Thumbnails of your images together in a nicely labeled grid, and it could use the thumbnails already created by Thumbnail as its source data. The large thumbnail is an open-ended opportunity for which there were no applications at this writing, though you can probably expect to see some cropping up soon.

 **If you're sure you have no use for those large thumbnails and don't want your disk space being nibbled at by hidden image attributes, open up Thumbnail's preferences panel and tell it to stop creating them by deselecting the "Create large icons" checkbox. If you find you need them later, just turn it back on and reprocess your files.**

 Stay tuned for Seitz's next project, graFX (www.itap.physik.uni-stuttgart.de/ ~thorsten/Be/graFX/), a layering paint program that lets you apply any available effect with any available tool. graFX may be available by the time you read this.

## Pierre Raynaud-Richard
### Director of Graphics
*Interviewed by Henry Bortman*

**HB:** *When did you start working at Be?*

**PRR:** I first came for an internship in September–October '94. So I didn't know Be at all at that time. I was doing another internship. I was still at school in Paris, at the same school as Cyril [Meurillon]. I had a seven-month internship, and part of it had to be done in a non-French-speaking country. I had an internship in a game company in Bordeaux, and through a relationship with Jean-Louis they got me to come here to port the game. That was my first contact with Be.

I came back in September '95. I had a visa problem, like everybody around here, so I had to go back to Paris. There was snow in Paris, it was very cold, there was also a strike. That was one of the worst winters in Paris. I had to stay there and do some work from there up to the end of the year.

**HB:** *Were you working for Be from Paris?*

**PRR:** I was trying. I helped Benoit [Schillings] add 32-bit support to the App Server. I did some basic stuff, I worked on a couple of demos, like Flight. All the comments are still in French—shame on me! It was written in Paris. At that time my English was not very good.

So I came back on December 13 '95 and started officially on January 2. I was supposed to help Benoit on whatever he needed some help with. The first thing was writing graphics drivers. I did that for six months and at the same time I started helping Benoit on a small part of the App Server.

I love 3D, and I'd been working on 3D for games before, so I tried to push some 3D projects. At that time, a good way to push the project was to write a good demo, because the company needed some good demos to sell the product.

So I did the first very small version of the 3D Kit and then switched over, worked on the font engine, and then I started developing some sections of the Game Kit. So, I was working on various components of the graphics system. And that continued up to May '97. At that time the graphics team was composed of Benoit, who was the leader, George Hoffman, who was an intern and is now a full-time employee here, Scott Bronson, who has left us since, and me.

Benoit wanted to resign. Something totally unexpected that happened was that Erich [Ringwold] came in and proposed to me that I take over the graphics team. At that time my team was essentially me and George Hoffman. Only two people to deal with a lot of things: App Server, Game Kit, 3D Kit, printing, to come—still to come.

Now I have five engineers. One on 3D full time, one on the core of App Server full time, one on the new graphics architecture and drivers, another one only on drivers, and the last one is working on whatever small things need to be done.

**HB:** *Tell me a little bit about 3D. What were your goals for 3D and BeOS, and how do you think it is different from 3D capability on other systems?*

**PRR:** At the beginning when I arrived, it was not clear where the BeOS was going. I was just like probably millions of people wanting to poke around to find ideas, trying to find a way to be

## Pierre Raynaud-Richard (continued)

different and sell something. And also 3D hardware acceleration was not something common yet. So, I investigated some easy ways to introduce 3D into BeOS. That was the 3D Kit.

We never had enough time to push it hard enough and to polish it enough to make it really usable. That's a lot of work to develop a fully usable, high-level 3D API. Now 3D hardware acceleration is becoming really common. You can't really expect that on the 3D rendering side you are going to do much better than any other operating system when you use the same hardware. Like, an operating system like Windows is going to have drivers for all the latest new cards because manufacturers are going to write them; they are probably going to optimize them. And they are probably not going to help us write our own driver, so we cannot hope to beat them on that. So it seemed that the only reasonable thing was to integrate 3D so that using the overall capabilities of the BeOS could be more interesting.

So, we chose to go with OpenGL because, as you know, it's a well-defined standard. It's probably the most recognized one, it's reasonably efficient, it's totally portable, and so on. And at the same time that we are implementing and optimizing OpenGL based on 3D acceleration, we will also release a low-level 3D API for people like game developers who just want to access the raw power of the card and don't care about anything else.

We would like to support chipsets like the Riva 128 and the new 3D Live chipset. We will probably have to support a less impressive chipset that's more common, like ATI Rage Pro, perhaps Intel 740. But it mainly depends on the good will of the manufacturers, because without the proper documentation or help it's very difficult. It's a bad idea to reverse-engineer other drivers to get this information. The goal is to get it fully usable with a reasonable set of drivers in R5.

**HB:** *Tell me about the Game Kit.*

**PRR:** My point of view on the Game Kit—I've been working with game companies for years—was that basically what the game developer wants is easy access to the raw power of the machine, easy access to the driver API, then perhaps a simple and efficient way to handle the input issues, like keyboard command configuration, joystick, mouse, that sort of thing. I don't believe they want anything else. Basically, [they say] get rid of the OS, let me do my work, and give me a lot of power and an easy way to talk with the user.

So that's what we've been trying to do. That model fits very well with the overall BeOS design, which is to do things simply, but efficiently.

**HB:** *Do you expect it to be a gaming machine?*

**PRR:** An especially good gaming machine? I think it's going to be a decent gaming machine. Some big companies have shown some interest just because of the fact that as I told you, what they want is raw access to the hardware and not having the OS get in the way. And now that we are running on the Intel platform, we start to become a reasonable choice for them because, talking with some of the engineers, they just complain they have too much trouble with the OS. Like from time to time the OS will freeze because it's doing something else that depends on Windows. Then the user complains that, "Your game sucks," but you can't do anything about it.

So if we are able to run on the same hardware and we have a reasonable business model for allowing them to distribute or even launch their game from Windows, which would bootstrap BeOS and launch the game under BeOS, that sort of solution—then we would have an easy way to get an efficient platform for them to run their games based on Intel.

**HB:** *You're in the midst of a massive rewrite of the graphics system. What kinds of changes are you making?*

**PRR:** Probably the strongest point of the graphics system under BeOS is multithreading. It's very, very, very multithreaded—way more than any other commercial graphics system available. This is a critical difference between our graphics system and other graphics systems. So we have been working pretty hard on pushing that even further, and at the same time reworking the architecture of the whole graphics system to improve performance and modularity and expand-ability. That rework had to be done and at the same time we had to stay compatible with the existing API. That is a lot of work, so it has to be done slowly. We've been working on it for at least one year already, and I guess we'll need at least another year to get to something that we can say is close to the final architecture. But all the things we have been doing are pushing to an even more parallel model.

A good example is the BDirectWindow class. The idea of BDirectWindow, which is a big differ-ence with the old approach, is that the screen is no longer owned only by one part of the sys-tem, like the App Server. The App Server doesn't own the screen anymore. The App Server is giving away ownership of part of the screen to clients. So, for example, in the content area of a window in a DirectWindow, this part of the screen is given a dedicated client and the client is free to do whatever it wants with it. But this client is fully independent, fully parallel, and can do its stuff without any synchronization issues.

BDirect Window was released at the end of last year. We used it for the old video technology for DMA. Now that's the direction in which we are going for the whole system. What we are try-ing to get is to have every client be an independent client that owns some part of the graphic device and works on it. And as long as you don't move a window, resize a window, or change the position of the window, they are just working completely independent of one another. So it's a model that scales very, very well. And when you do move a window, there is a synchronization issue, but we have been learning about how to deal with it. It's much better to deal with those things only when, from time to time, a window moves or the another window changes, which is a very uncommon event, rather than having to go through a sharing protocol that you will have to use every single time you draw anywhere on the screen.

**HB:** *Fonts?*

**PRR:** As you know, we are using the Bitstream engine. It's probably not the best engine in the world, but it's doing a reasonable job. We have been improving the performance by a factor of three recently, just by improving access to the file, the font file itself. So, I think the performance of the font engine is starting to be pretty reasonable. When we have more time, I will be happy to have somebody rework the font architecture to be able to support a modular model so that you can plug in whatever font engine you want to use. But for now it's not the case, so we'll stay with that for some time.

### *Pierre Raynaud-Richard* (continued)

On the other side of the font system, on the API side where you get matrix information and so on, we have been extending the API for R4 and we will continue to try to give more freedom. For now, it's pretty closed. You can't do too much. You can do the basic services, but if you want to extract more subtle information, or go and do linear transformations on the glyphs before they are rendered, you can't do that. In R3, you have to basically write your own font engine completely from scratch if you want to do very special effects with fonts.

R4, the next rev, is going to improve things quite a bit, because the main application developers working on text processing have been complaining quite a lot about a couple of critical features that we are missing. And they should be supported in R4, so that should help quite a bit. But there is still more to come when we have time.

**HB:** *And those features have to do with being able to get at the glyph?*

**PRR:** Yeah, being able to get at the glyph and eventually use the glyph to do some special effects. Now we have a new concept, called a BShape, that is basically the equivalent of a path for PostScript. You define any shape based on lines and Bézier curves and you can use it to draw a mask or something. You can extract shapes from glyphs, so that's a good beginning.

**HB:** *What about transparency?*

**PRR:** The alpha channel has been put there "for future expansion"—very long time future expansion. It's so difficult to implement in a general way. Usually, when you want to do transparency, you want to do something special, so I would say it's better for the application to do it. If we try to make it general, it's going to be slow. And the second problem is that it is not supported by graphics accelerators, so whatever we do is going to be fully in software. It's really something you want to preprocess in memory first. And when it's done, you put it on the graphics card.

So, if you do that, then you're very close to just doing it in your own application. If you know what you want to do, just do it, because a general solution is not going to work for you. We could give developers something, but that would be a lot of work, and then people would say, "It sucks—I can write some code doing what I want three times faster than yours." And it's true, because an application developer's code would be dedicated and ours would be some general solution that can't be as good. We'd probably get a couple of good demos out of it, but I don't think it would be very efficient or used too much. And it's a lot of work.

**HB:** *I have to ask this. What about printing?*

**PRR:** Printing? We need to work on it—more. It's a difficult subject. I think we really need to get somebody on the team who really knows printing, knows the problems, and knows the solutions used by other companies, who can add a vision of where we should move printing to get something, as usual, simple and efficient and working well. We don't have that person. I'm working on it.

For now, we are doing our best to improve it. In R4 we are going to get better drivers. We have been working a lot with an application developer who has a strong need for good printing, so that we can solve most of their problems, and they can print a reasonably good-quality document from what they are doing.

R4 is a big step in the right direction. But as for a global vision for printing, I'm still looking for somebody. That's what happens in this company. On any subject, somebody who is really dedicated and passionate about the subject takes a problem and makes it move in one clear direction. We still need to do that for printing. Until then, we just have a "reasonable" printing solution.

**HB:** *Any impressions you want to share about living in the United States?*

**PRR:** The food is OK. As you know, the French are picky about food. After a while you can find a lot of good things around here. You can survive.

Movies are great. Movies are totally different from French, good movies. Here you get something different. If you understand that, and you know what you're going to watch, it's great. Sometimes it's so funny, it's so ridiculous, you just laugh from the beginning to the end. One I was laughing to death at with other French friends was Starship Troopers. One of my friends told me before I went to see it that it was Beverly Hills in space. And it was exactly that. And we laughed from beginning to the end. It was so great. It's not a great movie, for sure, but as they say around here, you need some fun.

# 14

# Media Applications

After all this talk about the many ways in which BeOS is optimized for handling high-bandwidth audio and video streams, you might expect this chapter to form the heart of this book. In a sense, it does. The tools covered here are among the most exciting BeOS applications available, and they excel at what they do in comparison to similar tools on other platforms. But there's a caveat.

Be has put an incredible amount of energy into creating a superior architecture on which developers can create next-generation A/V applications. But the cornerstone of that architecture, the Media Kit, was finalized only with the advent of R4. As a result, at the time this book was written, developers had been presented with the new Media Kit, but had not yet had much time to actually work with it. The field of high-powered A/V applications is going to spread and mature far beyond the list of applications you see here. Consider this an introduction to the field, but don't forget to check BeWare and BeDepot for further offerings.

# Audio Applications

BeOS lets applications talk to audio hardware with exceptionally low lag times, or "latencies." An audio signal can be sent from an application, through the audio subsystem, and to the sound card in 6 milliseconds or less, whereas the exact same sound card in the exact same system can incur latencies of 25 to 30ms under Windows. In laboratory tests, Be has brought audio latency down to 2ms in some cases, so we may enjoy even tighter audio responsiveness in post-R4 versions of the system. Because of this fact, and because of the performance advantages that arise naturally from pervasive multithreading, it doesn't take much to get vendors excited about developing audio applications for BeOS. Indeed, BeOS audio applications began to appear long before BeOS video applications. With the arrival of the Media Kit and the conveniences it offers developers, expect this field to grow considerably well into the future.

## Adamation's AudioElements
`www.adamation.com`

If you've already read the section on Adamation's ImageElements in Chapter 13, *Graphics Applications*, you've got a leg up on understanding how AudioElements works, since the working concept is identical. Rather than using a standard audio-editing interface featuring graphical waveforms, knobs, buttons, and channel sliders, AudioElements breaks the process of manipulating audio signals into "elements," each of which represents a very specific operation. Much as one would build a custom command-line tool by "gluing together" individual components, these elements can be arranged in a workspace and wired up into a "network." Let's say you want to take the signal coming from your sound card's input jack, run it through a high-pass filter, sample and hold for two seconds, and run the result through a digital delay. Just drag these four elements from the Elements palette, connect the output of each element to the input of the next, and double-click any elements that require customization. Save the result as a network and you'll be able to apply the same series of controls to any incoming sound at any point in the future.

**Getting Started**    The best way to familiarize yourself with AudioElements is to study a few of the many prebuilt networks bundled with the product. As with ImageElements, just press the Play button at the top of any network window to set it in motion. Note that many elements don't depend on either incoming signal or a preexisting audio file for source input—a wide array of sound synthesis modules are offered as elements as well. For example, open the network called "Interesting," and you'll notice that source signal originates from a pair of sine-wave generators. Because overlapping sine waves with differing wavelengths will always enter phase relationships that create additional, synergetic waveforms, a wonderfully haunting "wah-wah" effect is created. Click any of the six small buttons on one of the Sine generators while the network is playing to choose among square, sawtooth, constant, and triangular waveforms.

Whether you're playing a keyboard-based synthesizer or tweaking waveforms in AudioElements or any other software-based synth, it's interesting to note that waveforms typically sound just like they look in their graphical representations: A sine wave appears with smooth, flowing curves (like water waves), and sounds likewise; a triangular wave appears jagged and sounds somewhat nasal; while a squaretooth wave looks and sounds like an extremely fast-paced stutter. Visual cues will thus go a long way in helping you to build custom sounds in software that works in waveforms.

After stopping the network, double-click a wave generator to access a panel from which you can tweak the wave's frequency, amplitude, and phase. Since a single wave generator is infinitely customizable, you can imagine how far you can go by creating networks consisting of multiple generators, file inputs, filters, and other gadgets. The process is like building a custom synthesizer from electronic parts lying around the garage.

**Synthesis**    You'll find a wide array of tone-generation possibilities in the FM Synthesis element, which lets you construct sounds by establishing frequency modulation parameters. To get a handle on FM Synthesis, launch the bundled "Clockworks" network, then double-click the FM element, drag some sliders around, and try playing the network again. You can make dramatic changes with very slight parametric variations. To create a "fatter" sound, right-click the FM element and choose Duplicate from the context menu. Change the parameters of the second FM Synthesis element, then connect its output to the input of the Exponential Decay element, which lets you describe the tone's decay (or "tapering") mathematically (see Figure 14.01).

Many of the sample networks shipping with AudioElements use various tone-generation elements to demonstrate effects because of their sonic purity. Try disconnecting the source-generation element in an existing network and replacing it with a File Input element. Then just drag any `.wav` or `.aiff` file out of the Tracker and onto the File Input to see how that network affects an actual sound file, as opposed to pure tone.

**Do the Math** Another aspect of the "Clockworks" network with fascinating possibilities is the relationship between its Multiplier and Delay elements. Because these two are additively coupled before being fed to the speaker (see Figure 14.01), they function together as a single element, though their parameters are independently customizable. For example, change the 1.5 second delay parameter to 2.5 seconds, and your church bells will peal much more slowly. The .98 multiplier causes the church bells to slowly fade into nothingness; change this parameter to 1.0, and the bells will ring evenly into infinity, never fading. Dial it up to 1.1, and the bells will slowly grow louder. Most elements in the palette can be combined to work together in this way, just by using the Adder element and grouping other elements together as a subelement of the Adder.

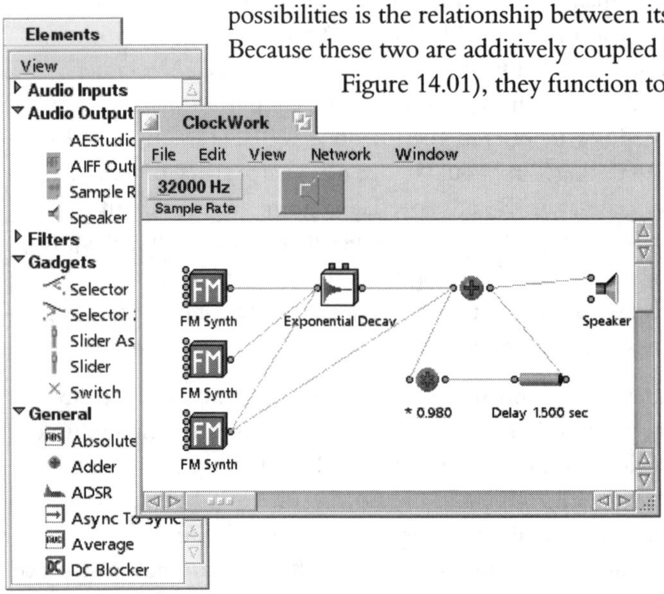

*Figure 14.01*

*Drag elements from the AudioElements palette onto a workspace and wire them up as desired. Pictured: the bundled "Clockworks" network modified with additional FM synthesis elements and corresponding connections for a "fatter" sound.*

Like ImageElements, AudioElements is totally scriptable, and ships with a copy of Attila Mezei's hey module. By studying the AudioElements scripting documentation, you'll find that you can easily drop a file onto an existing network, get or set all of an element's parameters, open and save networks, and more. This could make an otherwise time-consuming chore, such as adding an audio effect to each of 1,000 files and saving the results to a new directory with a new filetype, almost effortless—once you've built the initial shell script, of course.

**Bending the Waves**  Another very powerful element is the WaveShaper, which you can drop in between any two points in a network and use to take complete control over the waveform of the signal running through that node. Double-click on a WaveShaper element in an existing network and grab any point on the waveform in the resulting window. Drag it to another part of the window to deform the wave pattern visually, thereby altering its frequency or amplitude. Close the parameter window and play the network again to hear the results of your manipulations. Because the WaveShaper is excellent at giving you fine-grained control over sound forms, you'll probably want to reserve it for use in networks you've created that sound almost—but not quite—perfect.

## BamBam
**www.iae.nl/users/gertjan/be/**

BeOS includes a number of tools that make it easy to record and play audio tracks, but nothing that will let you edit or customize existing recordings. Gertjan van Ratingen's BamBam is 100% free and gives you all the standard tools you need for basic editing of stereo audio files.

If you've used stereo audio editors on other platforms, you'll find that BamBam operates in roughly the same way. Drag any .wav or .aiff audio file onto the BamBam icon (or into its application window) and it will be displayed graphically (see Figure 14.02). Press one of the play buttons at the left of the toolbar and the file will be played through the BeOS audio subsystem.

**Audio Editing 101**  In addition to standard cut, copy, and paste features, BamBam comes with a small collection of built-in audio-manipulation tools that you can use to alter the volume, direction, and channel placement of left and right audio tracks. Let's say you've got a file with several seconds of

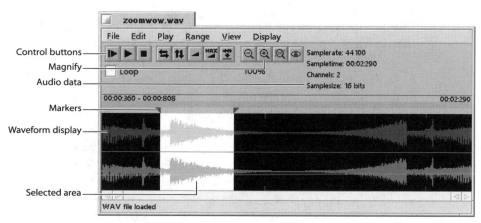

*Figure 14.02*

*Drag an audio file into BamBam and its waveform will be displayed graphically.*

silence at the beginning of the track that you want to crop out. Start by making sure you have a clear view of the track's beginning section. If the track is longer than around 30 seconds, you'll probably want to zoom in for a closer look so you can see what you're doing more clearly. Click the magnifying glass icon on the toolbar once or twice to zoom in, then use the horizontal scrollbar to glide toward the beginning of the file. Select the area represented by the nearly flat waveform—this represents the silence at the track's beginning. When you click the Play button while a range is selected, only the selected range will be played. If the selection is too large or too small, you don't have to start your selection over; just drag the triangular marker just above the waveform to the left or right until you've got it right, then tap Alt+X to remove the selected area.

 When you open a file in BamBam, it will load the entire thing into memory. If you have a limited amount of memory installed in your machine, be aware that loading a huge audio file could cause much or most of it to be loaded into virtual memory (that is, your swap file), which will mean a lot of disk swapping and a corresponding impact on performance. You almost certainly won't appreciate the effects of opening a 64MB audio file on a machine with 32MB of RAM, for example.

When you're ready to get a little more experimental, try copying and pasting selected data from one section of the file into another, just as you would do with a text editor. Hit Play again, and dig on your new gig as an audio collage artist. Of course, you can also copy and paste selected ranges from one file to another.

 **To open two BamBam windows at once, don't use File | Open or drag the new file into the BamBam window, as these methods will open the new file while closing the current one. Instead, drag the new file onto BamBam's application icon.**

**Number Nine, Number Nine ...** One of the easiest ways to get wild effects with BamBam is to reverse the direction of a selected range. Select an arbitrary range within your file and pull down Range | Reverse (or click the horizontal arrows icon on BamBam's toolbar). Press Play again and you'll find that the file plays forward, then backward for a few seconds, and then forward again—quite a trip. For an interesting symmetrical looping effect, try this: Starting with a brief (several seconds) source file, select the entire waveform, copy it to the clipboard, then reverse it. The version on the system clipboard will be stored in the normal direction, while the version in the BamBam Edit window will be backwards. Now, click your cursor at the very start of the file and paste from the clipboard. Select all, click the Loop checkbox, and click Play. The file will play forward, backward, forward, backward, and so on in an endless loop. If your surreal creation has a good beat (and just about any sound takes on a good beat when tweaked this way), dance to it.

**Ramp It**  You can create very professional-sounding fade-ins and fade-outs by using BamBam's "ramp" feature. If a file begins very suddenly and you'd like its volume to grow gradually from zero to full, select a few seconds at the beginning of your file, click the ramp icon (the triangular wedge on the toolbar), and a pair of sliders marked Start and End will appear at the upper right of the BamBam interface. Slide the Start control to 0% and leave the End control at 100%, then click the Ramp It button. BamBam will create an even fade from silence to full volume, covering the selected area. Deselect and click Play again to hear your fade. You can, of course, use values other than 0% and 100%, and can even amplify the signal all the way up to 200% if necessary. By the way, you can control signal amplification for the entire file in this way. If your file is too quiet, for example, select the entire file (Alt+A is the easiest way to do this), click the ramp icon, and use the sliders to change volume over the entire range from 100% to, say, 150%.

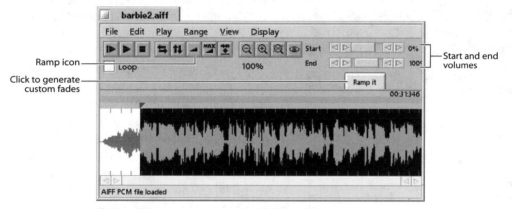

Ramp icon

Click to generate
custom fades

Start and end
volumes

*Figure 14.03*

*To create a fade-in effect, select a range and click the ramp icon. Adjust the Start and End sliders as necessary, then click the Ramp It button.*

***Perfect Levels***  In BamBam, as in all audio applications, it's important that your signal levels be optimum. In Figures 14.02–04, note that the highest points of the waveform come close to the top and bottom of the window without touching it too often. If the signal is so loud that the peaks exceed the window height consistently, you'll get clipping and distortion of certain frequency ranges in the final product. If the peaks are too far away from the window edges (that is, your signal is too low), you'll hear too much background noise and hiss in the final product. In addition, you probably want all of the audio files on your system to be stored at a fairly consistent amplitude so you're not constantly having to reach for your volume controls. BamBam makes it easy to adjust the amplitude of files on your system that are under- or over-recorded. Still, there's no substitute for making sure levels are optimized during the recording process, rather than after the fact.

**Recording** All of that is well and good for working with preexisting audio files, but BamBam is also an excellent tool for recording new audio files, whether from microphone, an incoming audio line from your stereo or VCR, your computer's CD player, or an external digital-to-analog converter. BamBam can record to a file on hard disk or directly into system RAM.

Recording directly into RAM has the advantage of being incredibly fast and accurate (you avoid the possibility of a really busy hard disk skipping a beat, for example), but be aware that you'll chew up a lot of memory very quickly with this method—almost 10MB per minute. If your system has 32MB or less of RAM installed, you're probably best off not using this option at all. In addition, the RAM recording option is limited to recordings of 60 seconds or less, so you'll have to be working with short clips.

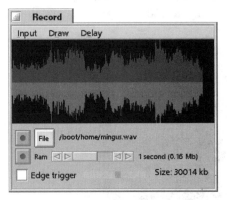

**Figure 14.04**

*Pull down File | Record and a window similar to this one will appear. Adjust recording levels with the system's Sound preferences panel, and click the File button to select an output location.*

Pull down File | Record and a new window similar to the one in Figure 14.04 will appear. Select a signal source from the Input menu (CD, Mic, Line, or DAC), and click the File button to select an output location for the file you're about to create. As soon as signal starts flowing through the chosen source (for example, as soon as a CD begins to play, if CD is chosen in the Input menu), the window will fill with a waveform representing the amplitude of that source. When ready, click the red record button. The Size indicator in the Record window will tell you how large the file you're creating has grown, in case that's a concern. When you're finished, click the record button again to stop. You can now close the Record window and open your new file in BamBam for fine-tuning, if necessary.

***Setting Recording Levels*** As described above, it's important that amplitude levels be optimized, and there's no better time to do that than when you're recording. However, you'll notice that there are no amplitude controls in the Record window. If the waveform displayed looks too high or too low, launch the BeOS Audio preferences panel and adjust the Input slider while watching your levels in BamBam. You'll get a better-quality end product by perfecting your levels at the time of recording, rather than adjusting them later.

By the time you read this, BamBam should have a sophisticated, multitrack successor called Pebbles. Keep an eye on BeWare or BeDepot for updates.

# FinalScratch
`www.n2it.net`

In the land of hip-hop, scratch, dub, and jungle music, thoroughly modern DJs create aural landscapes by using analog and digital equipment simultaneously: analog for its superior sound quality, the tangibility of the medium, and the vast vaults of source material it provides, and digital for the incredible elasticity offered by digital editing tools. One of the most fascinating fusions of analog and digital technologies in recent memory comes in the form of N2IT's FinalScratch, a combination hardware-software solution that lets DJs control digital software tools from the intuitive, hands-on interface offered by the traditional turntable and vinyl LP. Since a system like this involves controlling software tools from physical controls outside the computer, it requires extremely low audio latencies like those possible in BeOS. Consequently, FinalScratch is available only for BeOS.

FinalScratch is ordered as a kit, which includes a hardware controller box, a power supply, two special FinalScratch vinyl records, a set of audio cables, and the FinalScratch software for both x86 and PowerPC versions of BeOS. You supply the turntables, a full-duplex sound card, and the creativity.

The FinalScratch vinyl records are the heart of the system and contain 22 minutes per side of inaudible positioning signals, spaced at four clicks per millisecond. Timing signals from the playing record are pumped into the controller box, which routes them to the FinalScratch software. By "scratching" the records, you can manually alter the timing frequency being piped to the software with more precision than you would get by dragging a mouse around in a software interface. The FinalScratch software, in turn, feeds that timing signal to digital sequencers or audio players. Thus, you can "scratch" multiple simultaneous MP3 files being played through SoundPlay (covered in this chapter), or even use BeOS scripting controls to manipulate digital video streams in other applications. The possibilities offered by FinalScratch are impressive, and DJs are already using the system in live club events around the world. We were not able to test FinalScratch for this book, however.

FinalScratch was presented with a BeOS Masters' Award in 1998.

## MusicWeaver   *with Pete Goodeve*
`jwgibbs.cchem.berkeley.edu/~pete/beos`

In some respects, MusicWeaver works similarly to Adamation's AudioElements: Audio data streams can be manipulated by arranging input/output modules and filters graphically to create a flowchart-like diagram of an audio-processing sequence. Unlike AudioElements, which works with internally generated signals or audio data in .aiff or .wav format, MusicWeaver operates on MIDI data, which has very different requirements and offers very different output possibilities. To create a MusicWeaver diagram, you simply drag operational modules (called elements) out of the "drawer" and onto the workspace, connect them in sequences, and give the diagram a source signal on which to operate. Modules can be connected either in sequence or in parallel, and most modules offer associated control panels from which you can specify custom parameters. Anything in a MusicWeaver diagram can be altered at any time, even while music is flowing.

Because MIDI data can be fed into the system either from a file on disk or from a keyboard, you can use a diagram to apply effects to either stream type, or mix your own keyboard skills in with a currently playing MIDI file.

**Building Diagrams**    The process of dragging in elements and creating connections is quite simple, but there are some rules and guidelines you'll want to observe. Most MusicWeaver elements have small connection points on their right sides, representing that element's outputs; these points are known as "pips" in MusicWeaver parlance. Note that unlike Adamation's AudioElements, MusicWeaver elements do not have input pips. While only one path can emanate directly from any given output pip, you can create a branch from any path by dragging out from any intermediate point along a connection path to another element. If you want to do the reverse, and explicitly merge paths, use the JoinPaths element or attach them to a filter that accepts multiple inputs.

Once you have a path between any two elements, you can add a new element to the path without breaking it or interrupting its data flow by dropping the new element squarely onto the path itself (though you can't drag a Source element onto a path). Right-click any element (Mac users: Ctrl+Click), and select Panel from the context menu to tweak a given element's parameters. Items can be named and deleted from the same context menu. If an element has exactly one input and one output, you can remove it from its path by choosing Elide.

Most elements are simple filters—they perform some operation on the input stream and pass the signal to the output. Multiconnector elements usually display two output pips. Notably, all of their input and output connections have distinct functions; for example, incoming events might appear on one or the other output, depending on some criterion. Assigning specific roles to the connections on a multiconnector has a couple of consequences. First, because different types of input are allowed, you can't connect more than one stream to an input. You'll also need a way to associate the correct function with each connection. This is again done with a context menu: Right-click a connection point, and a menu of possibilities will appear.

 MusicWeaver lacks a menu bar and thus has no File menu. To save a diagram-in-progress, just right-click any blank area in the diagram and choose Save or Save As... from the context menu.

If you drag a diagram file into an open diagram window, its configuration will be re-created there if possible; any collisions with existing elements will abort the load.

**The Modules** The MusicWeaver modules fall into a few broad groups. Sources are origin points from which MIDI events enter the system, either from an external stream or having been generated by the element itself. Filters accept an input stream on one side, perform some operation on it, and pass it on to another element. Output points send MIDI events to the external world, and are really just special filters. Finally, multiconnector modules process events in more elaborate ways.

Filters can be grouped into subcategories. In addition to the output filters mentioned above, other filters actually transform some or all of the events passing through them (much as a filter in an imaging application transforms image data). For example, the Transpose filter shifts all note events up or down in pitch by a selected amount.

The very powerful filters known as markers do not actually alter MIDI events, but may tag them with marks if they meet some criterion. Some examples of Marker filters are ChanFilter, which marks all events on selected channels; MsgFilter, which marks selected types of MIDI events; KeyMarker, which marks selected notes of the scale; and KeyRange, which tags a range of the whole keyboard. Once marked, an event can be custom-processed by the Splitter element, which seeks out and responds to marked events. The Splitter's two output connectors (Through and Diverted) decide how to route a given event depending on its marks. For example, you can set up a Splitter so that an event is diverted down a given path in the diagram, duplicated into a new and parallel path, or blocked entirely. Once set, a mark remains attached to the event until it is cleared by the ClearMarks filter.

You'll also find a mixed bag of modules used for manipulating the timing of MIDI streams. For example, some modules let you add delays and echoes to streams (not to be confused with the "reverb" type of echo you can apply to audio signals in some software synths). Two modules used together are needed for this. MIDIDelay adds an increment of time to a MIDI event's timestamp. To actually implement the delay, you use the TimeSort element, which takes the events from the input stream, sorts them by timestamp, and emits them to its output at the specified time. Since TimeSort is a multi-connector element, its input stream can be passed on as well by playing the original along with an echo (for example). You can also feed a single TimeSort with several input streams (you'll usually need a JoinPaths to do this), and they'll all end up properly sorted in the output stream.

A synth expects a correct note-on/note-off sequence, but combining streams with different timing will likely destroy this regularity, resulting in very unpleasant early cutoffs and stuttering notes. The DeGlitch module is provided to cure this nastiness. This unique filter actually adds and removes note-off events for each note in each channel as necessary, thus maintaining a correct sequence. DeGlitch should be placed after (or even as) the final merge point of the streams concerned, before the actual output point.

**Putting the System to Work**  To get a handle on how all of this fits together, let's build a MusicWeaver diagram that diverts selected MIDI channels to a Transpose element, which will shift all incoming notes by an octave.

In Figure 14.05, the MidiPlay element on the far left reads MIDI files from hard disk. The MIDI event stream flows from this to the WvrSynth element at the far right, which turns the MIDI stream into an audible signal. Between the two lie a chain of elements that do the actual processing. Beneath the diagram are panels corresponding to each of the elements.

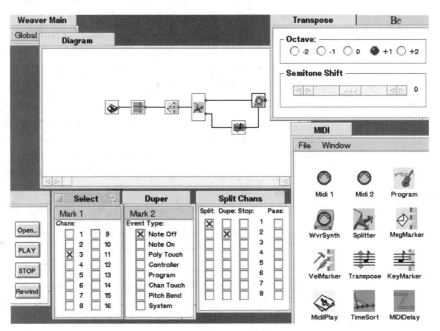

***Figure 14.05***

*A simple MusicWeaver diagram that will transpose notes in selected channels by an octave.*

First is a ChanMarker element and its corresponding Select panel. It's established Mark 1 on Channel 3. Following this is a MsgMarker (corresponding to the panel labeled Duper) that marks all note-off events with Mark 2. The stream then reaches a Splitter element (Split Chans) set (as default) to divert events tagged with Mark 1 and duplicate those with Mark 2. Diverted events are run through the Transpose element, which is set to raise notes by an octave.

The Transpose element offers tight control over the degree of transposition to perform; a slider control even lets you generate semi-tone alterations.

 Be sure and check out Goodeve's StreamWeaver toolkit, which applies similar concepts and principles to assembling shell commands in graphical diagrams.

## Objekt's ObjektSynth   *with Eric Iverson*
www.objektsynth.com

ObjektSynth is a real-time, multitimbral, modular, industrial-strength software synthesizer that works and sounds much like a traditional analog synth. It can be played via an external MIDI controller, through BeOS sequencers, or by controller software like Grabbo (discussed in this chapter) or MIDIKeys (see BeWare). Of course, ObjektSynth can play standard MIDI files as well. ObjektSynth ships with a variety of premade patches that can be used as is or edited. Patches can be used either singly or in groups. You can also create patches from scratch by assembling and connecting modules. Groups of patches can be saved and recalled as a single "project."

**Synth Programming**   The topic of synthesizer programming could easily fill a book (in fact, it fills many). If you already have experience with programming analog synthesizers, you can put your knowledge to work right away, as ObjektSynth will feel very familiar. If you've never programmed a synth before, the most practical way to learn is simple trial and error. Try making adjustments to premade patches, observing how the sound is affected with

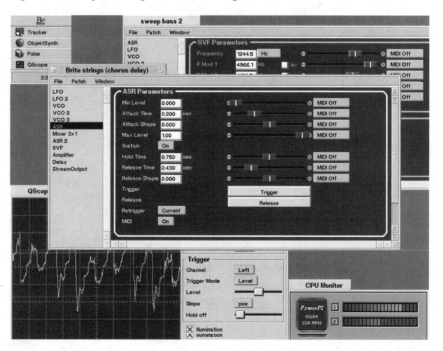

*Figure 14.06*

Two ObjektSynth patches running together with Pulse and QScope.

each tweak. Many modules' parameters use real-world values such as Hertz, decibels, and seconds. Current values are displayed in a text box with floating-point precision. Values are always updated onscreen as you drag sliders around. You can also type directly into a text box if you like.

 ObjektSynth plans to begin offering basic synthesizer programming tutorials on its Web site by the time you read this to help new users get up to speed with synth concepts in general. Stay tuned to `www.objektsynth.com`.

**Getting Started** To open a patch, drag it onto ObjektSynth's icon. Edit the patch by selecting a module from the list on the left side of the Patch window and adjusting its parameters with the mouse, by typing, or by sending MIDI control signals to the application. To replace an open patch, drop a new patch onto an open Patch window. Dropping several patches at once onto ObjektSynth's icon will open each patch in a separate window.

**Get MIDI-fied** If you're serious about making music with ObjektSynth, you'll probably want to play it by hooking up a MIDI controller or some kind of sequencing software. Since you'll often have several patches open at once, patches can be set to respond to MIDI signals on a specific MIDI port or channel, or from within a range of notes. Establish these parameters by selecting Patch Settings from the Window menu.

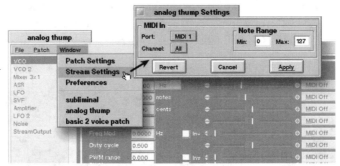

*Figure 14.07*

*The patch "analog thump" is set to respond to incoming MIDI signals on port 1, all channels, and the full range of notes.*

If you have a MIDI fader box connected to your machine, you can adjust several parameters at once; their corresponding onscreen controls and knobs will adjust themselves accordingly in real time. To do this, use the MIDI pop-up menus along the right side of the Patch window to assign continuous controllers to a module's parameters. Since there are no modes in ObjektSynth, you're always free to play and edit patches at any time. Any properly written BeOS application that sends MIDI signals through the MIDI OUT port can also control ObjektSynth—all you have to do is loop the MIDI OUT signal back to the MIDI IN port (this can be accomplished with a standard MIDI cable). Learn more about this procedure on the ObjektSynth Web site.

**Setting Buffer Sizes**   If you want to play ObjektSynth with an external MIDI controller, you may need to adjust the buffer stream settings to avoid any noticeable response delay. To adjust buffers, select Stream Settings from the Window menu to open the Stream Settings window. This displays the buffer size and buffer count, which reflect the settings currently specified by BeOS or by other applications. The following settings are suggested (but you can experiment with these controls to obtain optimal results for your machine):

- Sample rate: 44.1 KHz
- Buffer size: 512KB
- Buffer count: 2

If you have a fairly powerful machine, you could try a buffer size of 256KB or lower for very snappy response. Lower buffer sizes result in faster response times but consume more of CPU cycles, which means you could end up limiting the number of voices you can play simultaneously if you set the buffer size too low. Again, you'll need to experiment with this parameter to best accommodate your own synthesis needs and available horsepower.

**Editing Patches**   Select a module from the list on the left side of the Patch window and that module's controls will appear in the Patch window. Adjust the parameters and/or inputs for that module with the mouse (or by typing into a parameter's text field). To add modules to a patch, drag them from the Modules folder onto the module list. To delete modules, select the module you want to delete and choose Delete Module from the Patch menu.

**Working with Projects**   One very handy feature of ObjektSynth is its ability to save and recall entire groups of patches. "Projects" consist one or more patches and can have their own stream settings. To create a project that contains the currently open patches, simply select Save Project… from the File menu. To load a project, drop a project file onto the ObjektSynth icon, or choose Open Project… from the File menu, and ObjektSynth will close any currently open patches and replace them with the patches in that project.

# SoundPlay
www.xs4all.nl/~marcone/be.html

PlaySound, the default sound player shipping with BeOS (see Chapter 2, *Meet the System*), gets the job done, but that's about it. If you're seriously into messing with audio, there are a number of extra tools you'll want on your system, and Marco Nelissen's SoundPlay is among the coolest. For $12 you get an audio player that can handle any media format for which a decoder is available in BeOS's Media Kit (which includes the ever-popular .wav and .aiff formats, in addition to a few more obscure ones), plus excellent handling of MPEG Layer 2 and Layer 3 files. SoundPlay also happens to be the fastest MP3 player available for BeOS, and is (as far as Nelissen can determine) the only MPEG player in the world that can play MPEG files backwards. SoundPlay will also let you play a whole stack of audio files simultaneously, with some of them flowing forward and some backward, some at quarter speed and some at triple speed.

 How many files are in a "stack"? About a dozen at once seems to be the upper limit. Playing 12 .wav or .MP3 files at once utilizes only around 15% of a fast machine's CPU cycles, so processor power isn't the issue—SoundPlay is incredibly efficient. However, doing so requires so many simultaneous read/write operations scattered across the hard disk platter that most machines tend to get sluggish at this point. Limited RAM can also be a problem, and can result in data being swapped in and out of virtual memory, which will impact performance significantly. No matter how efficient BeOS may be, you'll be happier with 64MB or more of system memory if you're going to be doing much work with data-intensive media. Professional users will, of course, want much more memory than that.

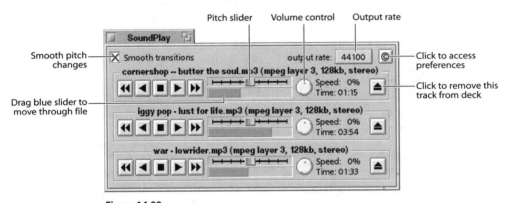

*Figure 14.08*

*SoundPlay can play almost as many simultaneous audio files as you like, each of them with independent pitch, direction, and volume controls.*

 If you like SoundPlay and want it to replace PlaySound as your system's default audio handler, use the FileTypes preferences panel (Chapter 5, *Files and the Tracker*) to associate common audio file formats with SoundPlay.

**Basic Operation** SoundPlay operation is pretty straightforward. Drag any standard audio file onto the SoundPlay interface and off it goes. To move forward or backward through the current file, grab the right edge of the blue progress indicator and drag. To change the speed, use the slider above the progress indicator—100% speed is normal, while anything below 0% will play backwards. You can adjust any file's speed from –400% to +400%, for some very wild effects. The round dial to the right of the sliders is a volume control, and you can "eject" (or stop) a file by clicking the rightmost button.

***Scratch Like a DJ*** If you select the "Smooth pitch changes" checkbox and then quickly manipulate the stop, reverse, and forward buttons, the pitch will rapidly "bend" into its new position after each click. The resulting sound is much like a DJ scratching on turntables. If you want to seriously "scratch" your MP3 files, SoundPlay can interface with the FinalScratch kit (covered in this chapter).

Things get really fun when you start playing multiple files simultaneously. Just launch any other audio file on your system that's associated with SoundPlay and it will be added as another "deck," or copy of SoundPlay attached to the already running copies (see Figure 14.08). All open decks play their respective audio files simultaneously, though you can start and stop each deck independently of the others by manipulating its controls. If you time everything carefully, you can use this multiple-deck capability as a sort of mixer, treating each deck as if it were an audio track, and even capture the output stream to hard disk with the Scope application (see below).

 Dragging another file onto SoundPlay will cause that file to play *instead of* the current file. If you want to play multiple files, files after the first must be launched from the Tracker, which means that either their filetype must be associated with SoundPlay, or you'll need to use the Open With… option in the Tracker's context menu. If you want to queue up another file to be played only after the current file is finished, hold down the Shift key as you drop the file onto SoundPlay.

**Figure 14.09**

*Create a SoundPlay playlist by dragging audio files in from the Tracker.*

**Managing Playlists** Since you'll usually want to play entire collections of music in sequence rather than simultaneously, SoundPlay lets you create playlists, so you can launch groups of files at once, organize your collections by category (such as jazz, hip-hop, or grunge), and create music collections that span multiple directories. To create a new playlist, click the copyright circle at the top right of SoundPlay's interface and choose New Playlist Editor… (or just hit Alt+E). Drag your favorite audio files from the Tracker into the Playlist Editor window, and rearrange them by dragging filenames up or down in the list. Arrange files alphabetically with the Sort button, or randomize their order with the Randomize button. When you've got your list dialed in, click Save As… to store your playlist. From now on, you can drag the playlist file itself into SoundPlay, rather than individual files.

To edit a playlist while it's playing, click on a song's title in the SoundPlay window and choose Playlist from the pop-up menu.

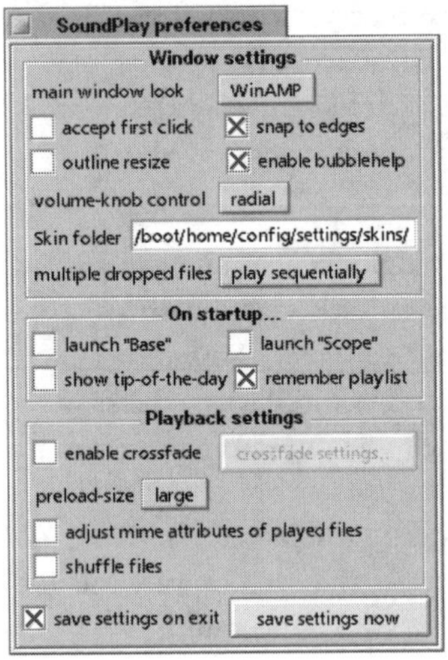

**Figure 14.10**

SoundPlay's Preferences panel lets you change the behavior of the window, define a location for WinAmp "skins," launch related items on startup, and change parameters related to playback.

**Preferences** There are a number of interesting customizations available in SoundPlay's Preferences panel, which you can access by clicking the copyright symbol in the main window.

One of the more interesting options here is the "accept first click" checkbox. When this is enabled, SoundPlay controls will react immediately when clicked, even when SoundPlay is not the frontmost window in BeOS (many Windows users wonder why this isn't the default behavior throughout BeOS—a very good question). "Snap to edges" will cause the SoundPlay window to align itself flush with any edge or corner of your screen when dragged to within a few pixels of the edge. If you leave the "remember playlist" box checked, when SoundPlay starts it will be playing the same song it was playing when you last quit the program. If you find the circular volume control knobs difficult to manipulate, change the volume knob preferences from radial to linear—the knob won't change in appearance, but you'll be able to control it by dragging across the top of it, rather than trying to twist it with your mouse. If you'd like the audio files in your playlist to fade smoothly from one to the next, select the "enable crossfade" box and click the Settings button, which will let you specify the number of seconds before a song's ending that it should start to fade out and the next song to fade in. If you regularly bring audio files onto your BeOS partition from other operating systems or from the Internet, you may want to leave the "adjust MIME attributes of played files" checkbox enabled. This will ensure that once a file has been played through SoundPlay, it will be associated with SoundPlay in the future.

SoundPlay also happens to be one of the slickest Replicants available for BeOS (at this writing). Turn on Show Replicants from the Be menu, then drag SoundPlay out of its application window and onto the Desktop, and its interface will disappear, leaving its controls to apparently float in thin air. Note, however, that this effect is partially lost if you use background bitmaps on your Desktop rather than solid colors; SoundPlay will take on the Desktop's solid color, and thus won't blend in with bitmapped backgrounds.

**Figure 14.11**

Embed SoundPlay in your Desktop as a Replicant, and its interface adopts the color of the Desktop behind it.

Got a copy of roColour (Chapter 13, *Graphics Applications*)? Try dragging colors out of roColour and onto SoundPlay's interface—SoundPlay will adopt and keep the new color, until you change it again.

**Interface Wild** By far the most popular MP3 player in the Windows world is a tool called WinAmp. One of the reasons for WinAmp's popularity is its uniquely customizable interface. Rather than sticking users with a single, boring Windows interface, WinAmp lets users create or download "skins,"

which are collections of bitmapped images with specific names and dimensions. Changing the entire look and feel of WinAmp is as simple as swapping its current skin for another, which can be done on the fly. Happily, SoundPlay can wear any of the hundreds of WinAmp skins out there (download skin collections from **www.winamp.com/skins/**). Create a subdirectory of /boot/home/config/settings called skins, then drop your skin folders into this directory. Click the copyright symbol in SoundPlay's interface and scroll over to the Skins submenu, where you'll find one entry for each subdirectory of ~/config/settings/skins. To return SoundPlay to its standard interface, select BeOS from the Skins submenu.

*Figure 14.12*

*SoundPlay wearing WinAmp "skins."*

**SoundPlay's Companion Apps** You'll find a couple of extra goodies in SoundPlay's folder: companion applications called Scope and Base. Scope monitors the ADC (analog to digital) and DAC (digital to analog) streams running through BeOS with a simple oscilloscope. But more importantly, it includes a Save to Disk button, so you can save everything that's currently

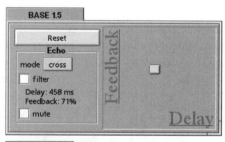

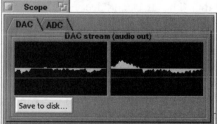

*Figure 14.13*

*SoundPlay's companions Scope and Base monitor the BeOS audio stream, and let you apply limited digital sound effects and/or record the stream to disk for later use.*

swimming through the BeOS audio stream to a .wav file on your hard drive for further editing in another application. Thus, by taking advantage of SoundPlay's ability to play multiple files simultaneously, you can use the program as a simple mixer, combining multiple files into a single file. It may not give you the control you'd get from a true mixing application, but it's cheap and simple to use.

Base also monitors the BeOS audio stream but lets you apply

real-time effects to it. Base's simple interface presents a draggable slider on a Feedback/Delay grid. Choose an audio effect from the Echo drop-down list (your choices are stereo, cross, ping-pong, spatial, and mono), then drag the slider around on the open field until you find an effect you like.

 **SoundPlay includes a full suite of scripting hooks. If you find yourself in the mood to create an automated audio show, use the hey techniques outlined at http://www.beosbible.com to control SoundPlay from a script written in bash, Python, or any other language enabled for BeOS scripting.**

## Q
www1.linkclub.or.jp/~sugiura/bjtalk-eye/tani/q.html

One of the easiest ways to create spontaneous digital music in BeOS is with Masaaki Tani's Q, a simple, three-channel analog sequencer similar in function to the antique synthesizers of the early to mid-1960s. With its huge array of tweakable buttons, dials, and picklists, Q is a geek's paradise and can easily consume hours of the free time you don't have if you're not careful.

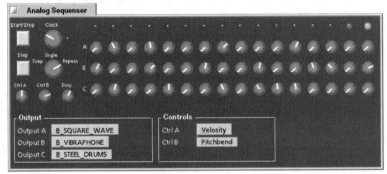

**Figure 14.14**

*Q lets you conduct a three-instrument MIDI orchestra by tweaking parameter dials.*

Q's three rows of dials (see Figure 14.14) correspond to three output channels. You can choose the instrument associated with each output channel from a list of more than 100 MIDI instruments. When you press Q's start/stop button, each column of dials will be visited in sequence, at a rate determined by the Clock dial. The red LED above each column will be illuminated as the sequence passes over that column. If any dials in that column are set to a nonzero value, that instrument will play one note, its pitch being determined by the setting of the dial. The attack and decay of each note is specified by the dial marked "Duty." In effect, you're in control of a three-instrument MIDI orchestra, and control the tempo, pitch, and decay of each note being played. You'll find actual operation much simpler than it may sound here.

Because there are 16 columns of dials, you will by default be playing 16-beat measures. However, you can easily control this too—just click any of the LEDs in the top row and the sequence will immediately begin terminating at that point instead, so you can change to (for example) 16-, 8-, or 4-note measures on the fly, while your tune is playing.

If you'd rather your sequence didn't loop into infinity, toggle the Repeat knob to Step, then click the Step button repeatedly. This will let you hear your composition one note at a time, which can be very useful when trying to perfect a given time slice. Toggling to Single mode will cause Q to play the entire measure through once and then stop, without repeating.

Q won't make you into a maestro, nor will it teach you even the most basic principles of music. It will, however, let you create surprisingly complex synthesizer grooves with amazing ease, which you can then record to hard disk with another utility (such as the Scope application that comes with SoundPlay) and use as background music for your next multimedia presentation or digital home video.

## nanodot

www.meadgroup.com/~eamoon/beos/

Eric Moon's nanodot is similar in principle to Q but is organized differently. Rather than letting you control the instrumentation for each channel separately, nanodot assigns the same instrument to each of four channels, then lets you choose the note for each channel separately by way of a picklist. However, the fact that nanodot won't let you choose a separate instrument for each channel should not be seen as a strike against it, because you can launch as many instances of nanodot as you like and set each instance to play a different instrument, thereby gaining almost unlimited control over your MIDI creations. However, nanodot recognizes only the basic 16 General MIDI channels, rather than the 100-plus available in Q.

*Figure 14.15*

*Though nanodot can play only one instrument at a time, you can launch many instances of the application at once to create multi-voice rhythmic sequences.*

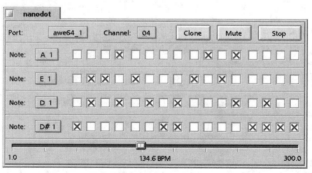

Also unlike Q, nanodot does not constrain you to using the software synthesizer built into BeOS. By using the Port picklist at the top of the nanodot window, you can choose MIDI input being piped into BeOS via your sound card, so you can attach external MIDI devices to your machine and use those as a source signal instead. Because nanodot uses on/off checkboxes rather than dials, you may also find it easier to achieve precision control over the tracks you create.

 If you can't seem to get a sound out of nanodot, it may be because the MIDI source picklist at the top of the application window is looking for MIDI signals coming from your sound card. Change this option to patch the name of your sound card to correct this.

## Rack Om 1.0
www.zog.net.au/dak/rack/

For those wild mixmasters who hark back to the old school, David Karla's Rack Om 1.0 virtually recreates a rack of classic Roland 303 Bassline monophonic synthesizers, complete with a dizzying array of attack, decay, sustain, release, filter, and modulation controls. If you're using an earlier version of Rack, be sure to upgrade to the latest version available on Karla's site—much has changed over time, and the guidelines here may not apply to old versions.

**Getting Started**  Launch Rack once, and a default patch will be loaded (a patch is a particular configuration of controls), and will appear at the bottom of Rack's window with a pair of start and stop buttons. To launch additional synthesizers, just launch Rack again; you won't see additional application windows, but additional pairs of start/stop buttons will appear in the bottom of the main application window. Each loaded synthesizer is associated with its own 16-note sequencer and 4-part drum module.

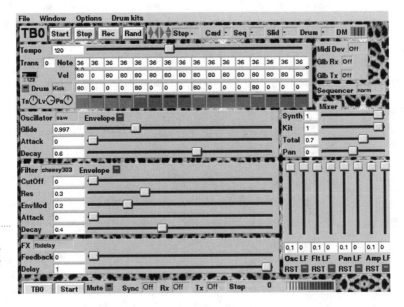

*Figure 14.16*

*Rack Om 1.0 emulates an entire rack of Roland 303 Bassline monophonic synths.*

Don't confuse the start/stop buttons associated with each loaded synthesizer with the program-wide start/stop buttons appearing at the top of the application window, which control all loaded synthesizers in unison.

 **While messing around in the Rack interface, be aware that many aspects of the UI that don't appear to be configurable controls actually are. Pay particular attention to the Step, Sequence, and Drum elements at the top of the application window. Click and hold on any of these to access a picklist for that control. Drum mutes can be particularly handy for pulling particular drum notes in and out of a sequence, as opposed to loading a whole new set of drums, sliders, and sequence bits.**

**Experimenting with Controls**  While some of the controls you'll find in Rack Om 1.0's interface serve an obvious purpose, you'll also find hundreds of controls with more mysterious purposes, especially if you launch any of the various Bank Sequence or Config editors from the main application's Window menu. Fortunately, Rack's own documentation details the purposes of these controls. Unfortunately, it doesn't document everything that you need to know about synthesizers to work with these controls effectively; consult a reference on the intricacies of synthesizer configuration for more details.

Particularly useful is the Mix window, which lets you set the main levels of all currently running Racks, and cross-fade them with a set of central controls.

 **Because it can take some time to perfect a Rack patch, save your work frequently. Saving a patch in Rack Om 1.0 is equivalent to saving a file in another application (a patch is simply a dump of the entire memory as it stands, including every bank that has been changed from its preset and all running synths). Karla has attempted to minimize the size of patch files as much as possible so that patches can be loaded spontaneously during performance. Note that saving a patch is not the same as saving music—a patch is just a particular configuration of controls. To actually save your music to disk with the demo version, you'll need to use an external converter such as the Scope application that ships with SoundPlay (covered in this chapter). The full, registered version will let you export audio directly to disk.**

**Working with Sequences**  A sequence is a pattern of 16 notes, and is displayed in Rack's upper window. Every sequence has an associated set of loop points that let you specify that a given sequence be shorter than 16 notes, if desired, and set a tempo. Typically, a sequence is equated with a single bar or measure of music. A sequence usually also has an associated drum pattern, which is a set of four drum parts (think of it as having four separate drummers at your disposal, and of their drum kits as having a nearly unlimited range of possible sounds). A drum part includes the attack velocity, mutes, pan controls, and levels of the drum notes in that sequence. You'll find controls for each of these parameters laid out cleanly in the sequencing section of Rack's interface.

**The Future**   If you think Rack Om 1.0 is amazing, Karla has an even more ambitious project up his sleeve in the form of a sequencer called Qua, which will act as a manager for Rack. Among other things, Qua will let you control Rack with a joystick and set its sliders via graphical envelopes (see the section on Adamation's studioA, later in this chapter, for more on envelopes). Qua will include its own sequence-generation language. According to Karla, "Think MAX+CuBase+emacs, all on acid." Qua should be available soon after this book's publication.

The "half-tab" version of Rack ships with a few features missing and an inability to save recordings to disk. "Full-tab" versions will include a host of additional features, including add-ons such as Twang (a guitar emulator with tube distortion) and Oasis (a standalone DJ console). Oasis will be a sample player/cross-fader capable of playing audio CDs and MP3 files. Oasis output can be pumped back into Rack and locked into its sequencer, transforming Rack into a full instrumental sampler.

## The Media Art of Douglas Irving Repetto
`shoko.calarts.edu/~glmrboy/bestuff.html`

When people talk about a computing platform for creativity, the usual implication is that the applications running on it enable creativity on behalf of the users. But who says that programs themselves can't be works of art? While there are a few applications out there that have unusually creative interfaces, it's rare to find an application that exists as a creative work in and of itself. The works of Douglas Irving Repetto are unusual in that they show that the paintbrush of a *fin-de-siecle artiste* can be lines of C++. You'll find the following works at the URL above, as well as on BeWare.

**SineClock**   As described earlier in this chapter, any time two or more sine waves run simultaneously, phase relationships arise spontaneously and synergetically. The result is a haunting, floating chorus of overtones, soothing to the soul. Rhythmic patterns arise as frequencies interlock with one another, then slowly slide out of sync. SineClock does nothing but sit in the corner of your Desktop generating interlocking sine-wave patterns. Since it can run as a Replicant, you can easily set it up to run automatically whenever your machine is turned on. It's like having a little piece of nature breathing and bubbling away beneath your daily workload.

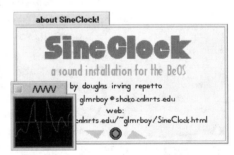

**Figure 14.17**

*SineClock runs in the background, generating a continuous chorus of interlocking sine waves.*

**Figure 14.18**

*All Possible Images will, given enough time, display all possible configurations of on and off bits in an 8-by-8 grid.*

**All Possible Images** If you find SineClock more distracting than soothing, you may prefer its visual analog, All Possible Images, or API. A simple 8-by-8 square hosts tiny blue LEDs blinking on and off in a seemingly random pattern. In fact, the blink sequence isn't random at all. Rather, it's generated by a mathematical algorithm that will, given enough time, cause *every possible combination* of lights to be displayed. Since each combination of on and off lights represents an image of some sort, API really will generate all possible images in this confined pixel space, given enough time. If that sounds like a simple task, think again: To run through all possible images in a 64-bit grid could take your machine thousands of years. (See the RC5DES contest described in Chapter 15, *Other Goodies*. Thousands of machines have been crunching away at that 64-bit puzzle for a year at this writing, and have barely investigated 1% of the possibilities.) If you fall in love with API and would like to make it a part of your living room, Repetto also makes a hardware version—a sort of digital kinetic sculpture for the home rather than the BeOS Desktop. See the URL above for details.

**American Thighs** While SineClock and API are soothing, American Thighs is the opposite. This is probably *not* something you'll want to keep running in the background while you work. American Thighs is loud and obnoxious in the extreme. In fact, you'd be well advised to turn your speaker volume way down before launching American Thighs, to save your eardrums and those of your neighbors. And if a wallop of scrambulated white noise doesn't yield enough pain for your taste, double your pleasure by launching it again—a second icon will float over your desktop, welded to the first, as the amount of noise doubles.

**Figure 14.19**

*In contrast to SineClock and API, American Thighs erects a wall of tangled white noise— excruciatingly ~~awful~~ artful.*

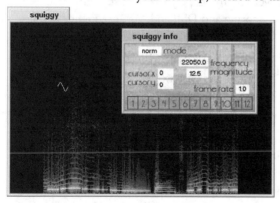

**Figure 14.20**

*Squiqqy lets you create images from manipulable sound sources.*

Launch the program as many times as you like—you can create a wall of American Thighs icons, all howling at top pitch. Consider it a form of primal therapy.

**Squiqqy** If you thought sonograms were of interest primarily to expectant mothers, you were correct. But there's no law that says a sonogram has to be a sound-picture of a little bubba—with Squiqqy, you can use any sound as the basis for a sonogram. Squiqqy is a spectral manipulation tool that lets you create, record, manipulate, and play back sound images, and it's intended as a tool for live performances. Its keyboard-centric interface means it has a bit of a learning curve, but you can keep the accompanying keyboard guide open in a small StyledEdit window for quick reference.

## Coming Soon

At this writing, a number of sophisticated audio applications and components had just been announced for BeOS. While we weren't able to get our hands on any of these products in time for publication, brief summaries are provided here. These products should be on the scene by mid-1999.

**EMU Systems' Audio Production Studio (APS)**   More than just an audio application, APS is a complete hardware/software solution for studio musicians interested in using the personal computer as the heart of a home recording system. An input/output module is installed in one of your computer's free drive bays, which lets you plug guitars, microphones, keyboards, and other instruments directly into the front of your PC. This I/O module connects internally to a dedicated PCI card inside the machine, sporting EMU's dedicated EMU10K1 DSP (digital signal processing) chip. The hardware kit interfaces with a suite of software including a MIDI and audio sequencer, a sample preset editor, mixer/effects control software, and hundreds of sounds on CD-ROM. According to EMU Systems, the system "gives users 64 voices of sampling, multitrack hard disk recording, and professional real-time DSP effects," and "records and plays full duplex, studio-quality audio directly onto hard drives while playing and recording MIDI sequences simultaneously." See **www.emu.com** for more information.

**Emagic's Logic Audio Series**   Germany's Emagic offers hardware/software audio recording solutions at four price and skill levels, covering ground all the way from casual enthusiast to hardcore recording professional. Logic Audio gives you integrated control over recording, playback, and real-time manipulation of digital audio, including scoring and DSP and MIDI sequencing. The company expects to see significant performance advantages in BeOS thanks to its extremely low audio latency levels and pervasive multithreading.

The system consists of a PCI recording card with two analog input and eight output jacks, plus stereo digital input/output ports. It also includes a pair of 18-bit digital-to-analog and analog-to-digital converters. See **www.emagic.de** for more information.

**Steinberg's NUENDO**   If the name Steinberg sounds familiar, it may be because of the company's longstanding reputation as leaders in the field of digital audio. NUENDO is an audio tool "aimed at music production, audio for film, video, and interactive media markets." NUENDO employs Steinberg's Virtual Studio Technology (VST) to offer real-time audio effects, an open plug-in architecture, and up to 256 tracks of digital audio and MIDI recording and editing. All audio processing in NUENDO is performed entirely with floating-point calculations for the highest possible dynamic range. NUENDO, by the way, is the same Steinberg technology used in many of Hollywood's SGI workstations to create audio soundtracks for film and video productions. NUENDO for BeOS promises to bring us one step closer to fulfilling the prophecy of BeOS as "the poor man's SGI." See `www.steinberg.de` for more information.

# Video Applications

Manipulating multiple streams of live video is one of the most resource-intensive tasks anyone can do with a computer, which is one reason why high-end video editing has historically remained in the realm of high-end hardware, outside the reach of the general consumer. As you know, one of the goals of the MediaOS is to change all that, and bring Hollywood-style video capabilities to consumer hardware. Even with BeOS behind them, however, vendors still see two distinct classes of users (with corresponding budgets to spend on video software): the general-purpose home or small-business video market, and the high-end video effects and rendering market. The applications covered in this section are split between the two categories (we'll let you know which are which).

Because the Media Kit appeared only with the advent of R4, we were not able to personally test a number of the coming BeOS video-editing applications, though we will include preview summaries.

## Adamation's personalStudio and studioA
`www.adamation.com`

Without question, Adamation has been way ahead of the game when it comes to using BeOS as a media-creation workstation. These folks were running high-profile demonstrations of their studioA video-editing software long before the competition. In fact, Intel's Andy Grove even opened the Agenda '98 conference with a demonstration of studioA running on BeOS for Intel Architecture, helping bring BeOS further into the public limelight. Unfortunately, directional shifts have resulted in release delays for Adamation's products, so we weren't able to test completed versions in time for publication.

The same core video-compositing and rendering engine lies beneath the surface of both personalStudio and studioA. The difference lies in the interfaces and overall capabilities of the two versions. studioA is the high-end, do-it-all

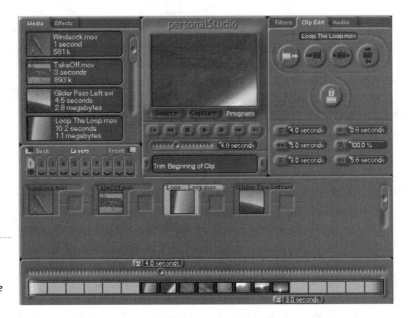

*Figure 14.21*

*personalStudio's unique interface helps make video editing an intuitive process.*

video suite for multimedia professionals, while personalStudio is a slimmed-down version aimed at video editing for the home and small-business markets. We were able to test a beta version of studioA and glimpse screenshots of personalStudio. Since both applications use similar editing principles and toolsets, the instructions here are general, rather than specific. Users should have no problem moving between the two applications if necessary.

**Both studioA and personalStudio also ship with the studioPlayer, a stand-alone media player that handles a wide array of audio, video, and image formats. Because studioPlayer ships with Translators for many file formats not supported by default in BeOS, purchasing one of Adamation's media products may end up extending the reach of your entire BeOS installation!**

All Adamation presentations and effects are rendered in real time, which means that performance factors are tightly connected to the resolution at which the presentation is displayed, the frame rate of the presentation, and the speed of your hardware. It's important to remember that when you're creating a presentation, all frames are being composited on the fly. When you export your presentation to a final movie format (such as QuickTime or AVI), it will be displayed frame by frame, not rendered. As a result, it may appear very differently on different machines running different operating systems. Be sure to test your movies on other machines and platforms before distributing them to the public.

**Getting Started** The easiest way to get familiar with Adamation's video-editing controls is to open one of the sample movies bundled with the distribution, then study its construction. To jump to any point in an existing presentation, click somewhere in the timeline. To preview a given subsection of a presentation, drag left and right over the timeline (this technique is known as scrubbing). Notice in particular the way in which horizontal rows of media stretch out and overlap one another as the timeline progresses. In contrast to traditional video-editing software, Adamation's software renders a unique thumbnail for each frame of video, rather than presenting the entire stretch of content with a single thumbnail repeated hundreds of times. Interestingly, any frame or collection of frames can be described as the amalgamation of another row (or "layer") of content. In other words, some of the layers you see spread out under the timeline may in fact be "children" of frames above them. After digging into a layer and its children for a closer look, return to viewing the overall presentation by selecting the parent layer and pulling down Layer | Root Layer. To reposition any layer in time, just grab its title bar and drag it left or right. Use the Zoom menu to get a closer look at any section of the timeline, or zoom back for a bird's-eye view.

 **To adjust the start and end points of any clip, select it in the main workspace, then pull down Worksheets | Edit Clip. You can then enter start and end points in precise numerical values.**

The currently selected frame will always be displayed in the Preview window, under which is a standard collection of play, pause, rewind, and fast-forward buttons. Right-click anywhere in the Preview window (Mac users: Ctrl+Command+Click) to access a context menu that will let you establish the preview size, render size, and output size independently of one another. Keep in mind that enlarging the preview size will have a corresponding impact on playback performance.

At the left side of the application window is the Media Bag, which stores bitmapped images, audio files, and existing animations or movies. To place a media object in the bag, just drag it out of the Tracker. To add that element to your presentation, just drag it from either the Media Bag or the Tracker into the workspace at the desired insertion point.

**Applying Filters**   On the right side of the application window you'll find a panel holding a collection of filters and effects. Filters are applied by dragging them from this panel and into the filters workspace, which is situated just below the main workspace. For a quick demonstration of the speed with which filters can be applied to presentations in Adamation products, drag the Rotate filter into the bottom of the application window. It will be applied to all of the frames currently displayed in the main workspace, and will rotate that portion of the presentation through 360 degrees. You can then press the play button immediately to see how the filter has affected the movie. To apply an effect like this to a presentation in a video editor on another platform could require minutes—or even hours—of rendering time, depending on the length and resolution of the presentation.

**Working with Key Frames and Envelopes** In most instances, you'll want to tightly control the segment of your presentation to which some effect is going to be applied. This is done by defining start and end points in specific locations. Such points are called key frames, and work in concert with another video-editing concept called envelopes, which are collections of settings applied to a given segment. Thus, the stretch of a presentation between any two key frames has an associated envelope, which in turn contains the settings specific to that segment. For example, sound envelopes control the volume and stereo balance for that segment, while video and still media elements have envelopes to control settings such as scaling, location, rotation, and transparency. In most cases, an envelope will cause the settings it defines to be applied evenly over the space between two key frames, using a process called linear interpolation.

To establish key frames and edit envelopes, right-click an element, select Envelope, scroll over to the Envelope submenu, and choose the envelope you want to define. The layer will now display a graph-like element, rather than a series of thumbnails. It may be easier at this point to use the Zoom menu to increase the vertical height of the layer so you can more clearly see what you're doing. Use your mouse to drag graph lines up and down, creating curves, cliffs, or whatever you like. Since envelopes function differently depending on the type of media being edited, it's impossible to make blanket statements here, but in general you'll be adjusting the depth or intensity of that effect as applied over time. For example, if you're editing the envelope for the layer itself and manipulate its graph lines so that they start and end at zero but peak in the

*Figure 14.22*

*Right-click any element and choose an option from the Envelopes submenu, then drag key-frame points around on the resulting graph.*

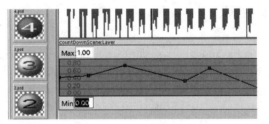

middle at 100%, that layer will slowly fade into full visibility as the presentation runs, then slowly disappear again. By default, one key frame is present at either end of the segment, but you can easily create more by clicking anywhere within the graph. You'll need to create more than two key frames if you want to do anything fancier than a simple linear fade.

**To make sure you retain control over all aspects of your presentation, always store it in Adamation's native presentation file format. When you're ready to share your presentation with the world, use the File | Export menu option to specify a movie format and codec details such as compression ratios, color depth, and resolution parameters. At this writing, studioA was capable of exporting movies in CinePak and QuickTime formats only, though other codecs were expected to become available soon.**

## Tebo Software's Grabbo  *with Bill Thibault*
`www.idiom.com/~tebo/`

Grabbo is an utterly unique application that analyzes live video information and transforms it into data that can be used to control other applications interactively, or to generate MIDI sequences. If that process seems difficult to visualize, just think of it as a sort of "video joystick." The source of control can thus be anything at which you can point a camera: your hand, your head, your pet iguana, the sky, television shows, or anything else. Possible applications include head tracking for 3D audio, gestural control of musical parameters (for instance, you wave your hand and the music rises to a crescendo), and adaptive interfaces for the handicapped. Grabbo does this by analyzing video streams and trying to match the current video frame with a set of stored images called keyframes, then reporting its findings as MIDI data or BMessages. The results of the analysis can control the internal synthesizer, be sent out a MIDI port to an external synthesizer, or be sent to another BeOS application using BMessages. Grabbo is a very powerful tool with some fascinating possibilities, but because it employs unusual working methods, it may take some study to get the most out of it.

Grabbo 0.9.2 ships with a companion app called 3dReceiver. At this writing, 3dReceiver was the only application to which Grabbo would send BMessages (or, more accurately, Grabbo 0.9.2 only sent messages to the application signature `application/x-vnd.stc-3dReceiver`). Future versions will allow the user to specify the application signature of the receiving application.

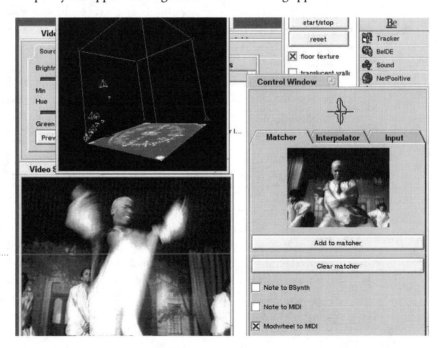

**Figure 14.23**

*Tebo's Grabbo analyzes video information and transforms it into BMessages or MIDI data.*

**Theory of Operation**   The technique Grabbo uses in image analysis is based on orientation histograms, which are formed by counting the number of edges visible in the image. The numbers of edges present for each of 36 or so different edge directions is the orientation histogram. The histogram is a global measure of the image as a whole, so that, for example, the same hand gesture will be recognized at any location in the frame. This technique also handles changes in lighting conditions fairly well.

For example, an image of square ceiling or floor tiles will have large numbers of edges at 90-degree angles: the orientation histogram will look like an X.

Grabbo's Matcher module maintains a list of keyframe images, numbered starting from zero. To add the current video frame to the list of keyframes, click the "add image to matcher" button. The index number of the keyframe that most closely matches the current video input is output as a message and/or a sequence of MIDI notes that can then be received and processed by another application.

The Interpolator module associates each of eight keyframes with a corner of a cube. Incoming video frames are compared to the keyframes to compute their similarity, and used to project, or interpolate, a position in the cube corresponding to the current video frame. For example, an image exactly matching a particular keyframe will be positioned directly at that keyframe's corner. Now consider two corners along an edge of the cube. If the left corner's keyframe image is of your head looking left, and the right corner's image is your head looking right, then when you look straight ahead, the interpolated position should be along the edge between the two corners. In 3D, with eight corners, and the right set of keyframes, you can learn to move around in a 3D environment using only your head. The 3D display is handled by the companion app, 3dReceiver. The three coordinates can also be output as MIDI "polypressure" messages or notes (where X=pitch, Y=velocity, and Z=channel). Notes are played at a constant rhythm independent of the frame rate of the analysis.

**Video Sources**   Grabbo works well with either black-and-white or color video sources. Since the analysis is based on edges, cluttered backgrounds are problematic. You'll probably find that pointing the camera at a blank wall or ceiling works well for hand gestures. Noisy sources, such as poorly received TV signals, are not handled very well due to the difficulty of detecting edges within the signal. Ideally, the input signal should be *slightly* blurred (this will reduce some of the jitter in the analysis output). You may want to slightly defocus your lens, or smear it with Vaseline, though as a practical matter, you may not have to worry about it much. Enabling "output smoothing" in the Interpolator can help. Future versions of Grabbo may include a feature to perform blurring in software.

**Input Settings**   The Input Settings window is from Steve Sakoman's BT848 driver (**www.sakoman.com**) and lets you configure your video tuner card for your locale, select an input connector, etc. (this should be replaced by the Media Kit in future versions). The Input tab in the Control window lets you establish the threshold at which edges should be detected. Edges with magnitudes lower than the established threshold are not counted in the histogram. The histogram of the current video input is displayed at the top of the Control window.

**The Matcher**   The Matcher, which displays the closest matching keyframe image, maintains a "private" list of keyframes and lets you add the current image as a new keyframe or completely clear the set of keyframes. Various MIDI output options can also be enabled from the Matcher. This module can be very useful when working with video from talk shows, soap operas, and similar material characterized by a small number of distinct camera angles. By grabbing a handful of nearly identical frames from each camera angle, you'll see the Matcher display one of the handful of keyframes for that angle. When a cut to a new camera occurs, the Matcher will immediately respond.

 **MIDI output generated in Grabbo can be sent to some software-based synthesizers, such as ObjektSynth (discussed earlier in this chapter). That means you should be able to play synthesizer compositions in ObjektSynth by standing in front of a video camera hooked to Grabbo and waving your arms around. The live performance possibilities are inspiring.**

**The Interpolator**   The Interpolator can be used to control a 3D cursor via incoming video signal. The 3dReceiver app displays the current position: Enable "draw labels" in 3dReceiver's 3D Controls window to see the order in which keyframes are assigned to corners. The first time you add an image to the Interpolator's (private) list of keyframes, it will be associated with the corner labeled 1, the next keyframe at corner 2, and so on.

While preparing to grab each keyframe, watch the orientation histogram display at the top of the Control window. For best results, each keyframe's histogram should be as different from the others as possible. Grabbo will work, however, with small differences in keyframes, at the cost of accuracy. Start off by assigning just two keyframes (1 and 2), then moving to 4 keyframes (1 through 4), then 8.

**Future Directions**   Future versions of Grabbo will work in the Media Kit framework, which should allow for easier input of both live and recorded video to Grabbo, enhanced MIDI routing options, and more. Other planned features include raising the number of dimensions in the Interpolator to six or more, supporting interactive modification of keyframe positions in 3D, output to arbitrary MIDI messages, user-configurable BMessage targets, and saving and loading of keyframes.

**Hardware Requirements**  At this writing, Grabbo required a video input card based on the BT848, BT878, or BT879 chip, and a video display card with DirectWindow support. Certain PCI Macs and clones (like the PowerCenter 150) have "insufficient PCI implementations" and will not work with the BT848. Future versions of Grabbo will have different requirements, and should support any devices supported by the BeOS Media Kit.

## Video Capture and Other Goodies

While most of the applications covered in this section are capable of working with common video cards, capture cards, and TV tuner modules, you'll find a collection of small, dedicated applications you can use to test the functionality of your video board at **www.sakoman.com**. Run by Be's own Steve Sakoman, this site offers downloadable tools that will let you display output from any television, VCR, or camcorder in a BeOS window, as well as save video data to disk. While many of these tools may eventually make their way into official distribution with BeOS itself or as downloadable extras from BeWare or BeDepot, Sakoman's site offers a great place to get your hands on alpha and beta versions of the latest video utilities in development by the man behind the curtain. Developers and users will also find a video-capture message board on the site for discussion of issues related to video capture and playback in general.

# Coming Soon

Though we weren't able to get our hands on the following applications in time for publication, each was the subject of press statements released during Comdex 1998 and should be available sometime in 1999. Brief summaries are provided here.

**Mediapede's UltraDV**  Like many of the audio/video tools covered in this chapter, Mediapede's UltraDV is not a port to BeOS of an application born on another operating system, but a fully native BeOS app designed to take maximum advantage of the system's media-optimized architecture. According to Mediapede, UltraDV employs a unique interface that breaks free from some of the limitations imposed by traditional video-editing applications, "enabling a faster and more creative workflow." UltraDV will let you create an unlimited number of tracks, and each track will be capable of storing any combination of audio, video, or bitmap data. You'll be able to expand, collapse, move, or resize tracks, and to drag components directly from the built-in Browser, which is UltraDV's media storage system. The Browser will also store transition effects, which can then be dragged onto "cues," which mark key points in a given production. Because UltraDV will take full advantage of the BeOS Media Kit, it will be able to output projects in any number of frame rates, sizes, color spaces, or formats.

**Figure 14.24**

UltraDV's intuitive digital video-editing interface is fully drag-and-drop aware.

Even before its release, UltraDV was garnering great reviews from early testers. One of CNN's chief engineers raved, "I have found UltraDV to be the easiest, fastest, most exciting new video product to be introduced in a long time." UltraDV is aimed at a wide target market, including video professionals, videographers, multimedia authors, and Web developers. See **www.mediapede.com** for more information.

**MGI's VideoWave**    Having already established a foothold as a capable video-editing package for the home market on the Microsoft Windows platform, VideoWave is heading to BeOS. VideoWave replaces the traditional timeline metaphor found in most video-editing suites with a nonlinear "Story Line," designed to let users concentrate on the essence of video authoring— telling a story. VideoWave supports media capture from common devices and features a wide array of transition and text-animation effects (52 different effects, total), a built-in MPEG encoder, chromakeying capabilities, and a standard collection of special effects such as twirls, wipes, fades, and ripples.

Designed for the home and business user, VideoWave for BeOS will include an introductory video and interactive tour to quickly familiarize new users with all aspects of video editing. VideoWave has won numerous awards from various industry magazines and institutions. See **www.mgisoft.com** for more information.

### Jon Watte
**Director of Application Engineering**
**Current reponsibilities: working on the Media Kit.**
*Interviewed by Henry Bortman*

**HB:** *Tell me about the new Media Kit.*

**JW:** Well, we are the MediaOS, and while we think that we have had for a long time the under-pinnings that make it possible to create good media applications, we don't really have the higher-level support that makes it easier for application developers. So, we're working hard on a new Kit to provide—as much as we can manage in time for R4—all the higher-level functionality that developers want. Like, Here's a file, please play it for me no matter what format it is.

**HB:** *How does the new Media Kit compare to QuickTime or ActiveMovie?*

**JW:** Well, it doesn't suck, that's how it compares to Windows. QuickTime is both an API and a file format and a technology and everything under the sun. We prefer to only be an API and then we deal with industry-standard file formats and industry-standard codecs by writing add-ons.

**HB:** *To an end user, what does that mean?*

**JW:** Suppose you're editing audio. The Media Kit provides a natural foundation for someone writing an audio editor, it gives them a plug-in architecture and kind of a flow, if you will, of how audio goes through the system. So, the user who buys an audio add-on for the BeOS can use that in any audio editing application, because they all use the Media Kit.

On the Mac, there are like three or four different audio plug-ins and they are all proprietary. There's the Steinberg format, and there's the DigiDesign format, and there's the Premiere format for audio effects plug-ins, and whatnot. The synchronization between these is interesting. You can do it, supposedly, but it's kind of hard.

We hope that the API we design is going to be flexible and powerful enough that there's only going to be one standard, so there's no confusion. And we have a well-defined synchronization mechanism that permeates the entire media system. So you should be able to have a MIDI file, and an audio file, and a video clip, and just tell all three of them to sync to one time source and go, and they should stay in sync. Now, depending on what hardware you have in your machine, it may or may not work perfectly, but we're seeing pretty good performance, even on standard cheapo PC hardware.

**HB:** *Does the BeOS enable real-time video effects without requiring dedicated hardware?*

**JW:** We don't do 640×480, 30 frames per second, because the PCI bus cannot sustain that. We do 320×240, at 30 frames per second, doing real-time effects. Now I'm talking about page flipping and chromakey, and effects that you would actually see on TV any night when you watch the news shows. 320×240 is actually about the same performance that you get from your VCR if you're a video hobbyist and you use VHS. And we can do that with an $80 video capture card, which does not compress. The DMA just dumps the data into memory. And even more interest-ing if you have regular $200 DMA IDE hard drive, our filesystem can sustain the 5 megabytes a second required to record this 30 frames per second video stream live, so you don't even need to compress. Of course, you need a real big hard drive if you want to do an hour of video, but hard drives are cheap.

**HB:** *So how did you end up at Be?*

**JW:** Interesting story. We have to zoom back in time. There is something that the U.S. Immigration and Naturalization Service sponsors called the Diversity of Immigration Lottery. In some countries, the INS holds a lottery every year. You send in an entry and some people, depending on how underrepresented that country is, are randomly drawn, and if they qualify—like they've gone through high school, they have no bad diseases, and things like that—they can receive a green card almost for free with no extra qualifications. So my wife entered and she won, and being immediate family to her, I was also eligible for the green card. This was in '94.

I was in Stockholm, Sweden. I'd been doing a lot of things. Most interestingly, I was in newspaper publishing for a long time and we did a workflow system called Scoop. It's still for sale. I worked on some accounting software. (Who hasn't done that sometime in their life?) Some client/server relational database consulting that went with the newspaper publishing thing. Then, as I worked my way through school, it was more like, set up some PC, or fix someone's crashed database from work, admin tasks like that. We also developed some porting tools to convert programs when Symantec changed their Think C class library from version 1.1 to version 2.0.

Anyway, so, sitting here with a wife who wants to move to the States and seeing that the only requirement that we so far didn't fulfill was having an offer of employment from the U.S., I just started calling all my friends that I met at various developers conferences, and emailing them, and saying, "Hey, I need a job." Thirty minutes later, I kid you not, Greg Galanos from Metrowerks calls me back and says, "You know, I was just thinking about you because of this porting kit that you did. We have some people who need a C++ guy for a secret project and we were thinking of whether you could consult with us." Thirty minutes and then it was done and I got an offer of employment at Metrowerks to head up this secret project for some secret client in Silicon Valley.

**HB:** *And is it still a secret?*

**JW:** No, it's not a secret. That was Be.

So I moved to the States in early '95 and landed in Austin, Texas. We just took our stuff, our two cats and that was fun. And I really liked Austin. It was a nice city. Nice university. I stayed there for two and a half years or so and then ties grew closer and closer to Be, and some internal politics at Metrowerks started to make me feel uncomfortable about what may or may not happen there. So, we mutually agreed that I would be an even better asset to Be working for Be directly rather than heading up the tools effort at Metrowerks.

**HB:** *And did you start working on the Media Kit right away?*

**JW:** No, I started working on something called Latitude, which was a technology that Metrowerks acquired that ports the Mac toolbox API or some subset of it to other platforms. The idea was to see what we could do with Latitude to move the new generation of Metrowerks tools based on the Mac toolbox to BeOS. But after a couple of months, I realized that it was just not ever going to be good. The Be programming model and the Mac programming model are like night and day.

## *Jon Watte* (continued)

They are so different, you just cannot take an application written with the assumption that this is a Mac and make it run well on BeOS without modification. And the whole idea behind Latitude was that you wouldn't need to modify your application code.

Anyway, so I worked on Latitude for a couple of months and we decided that it just would not be in our best interest to make it work. We could make it work, but the apps that would be ported by Latitude would suck. And that's not what we really want to show off with an OS that's supposed to be a clean start and provide good performance.

Meanwhile, the old Media Kit was really starting to show its limitations. It was good for the time, but as technology moves on and there are new horizons to exploit, if you will, we needed more. So, being a warm body with design experience—and also as a hobby, I've been an audio, MIDI-type buff for a long time—it made sense that I started doing that.

That brings us to the modern day.

**HB:** *What do you like about working here?*

**JW:** It's the people. The people and the work. I find that people here at Be are very opinionated and that's OK, because they actually think through their opinions before they voice them. So, when we have a shouting match, it's usually a shouting match between two very well-reasoned opinions and not just somebody being stubborn, right? And typically, it ends in one or the other person realizing that the other opinion was even more well thought out or even better suited to our common goal. Everybody takes the best idea and runs with it. And everybody here is good at what they do, so you don't get a lot of people who get in the way by not being able to keep up. That's a very stimulating environment.

And also the job. You know, we're creating a whole new OS that has the chance of sitting on the tables of a million people as a niche media OS doing fun things. You know, it's video, it moves, it makes noise, it makes music.

It's not fixing the Y2K problem.

# 15

# Other Goodies

· · · · · · · · · · · · · · · · · · · · · · · · · · · · · · · · · · · · · · · · ·

The applications and utilities in this chapter are wonderful to have on your system if you have a certain type of problem to solve, but few of them can be considered essential for most BeOS users. These tools won't help you become a better speller, create amazing graphics, back up your hard drive, or mix digital videos. They will, however, help you analyze your Web site's traffic logs, view Adobe Acrobat files, encrypt private documents, change your BeOS window colors, overthrow the government, and launder your socks. In other words, this is the stuff that wouldn't fit anywhere else in the book. Except where noted, everything in this chapter can be found on BeWare.

# The Kitchen Sink

Because this chapter is more or less a grab-bag of random goodies, there's no way to organize these tools by category so we've listed them alphabetically instead. Happy sifting!

**Don't Forget GeekGadgets!** In addition to all the goodies described in this chapter, you'll also find hundreds of Unix tools and utilities that have been ported to (or can be compiled for) BeOS in the GeekGadgets collection, available at **www.ninemoons.com/gg**. Installing GeekGadgets is covered in Chapter 6, *The Terminal*.

## Analog

If you run a Web site, you undoubtedly want to know how well it's doing. Who's visiting? How many pages are being "consumed" per visit? Which countries are your users coming from? How many pages have been served this week? On which day is traffic usually heaviest? While some service providers will provide this information to you in one form or another, chances are you have some very specific questions about your site's traffic patterns that your ISP-provided logs can't answer. For example, you might want to see statistics relating only to a few specific pages, or access totals for a single directory.

As discussed in Chapter 8, *Networking*, Web servers record incoming requests in a text file, adding a new line to the file for each request. While the exact format of these logs varies from one server to the next, each line typically includes the address of the user requesting the page, the time and date of the request, the path of the requested file, and whether or not the request was successfully served to the user. Some servers also log the type of browser being used by the visitor. In order to turn traffic logs into meaningful information, you have to either import them into a database for further study or run them through a log parsing tool that can analyze their data and spit out a report (usually in HTML format). The only log parser available for BeOS at this writing was Analog, which is a port of a Unix tool by Stephen Turner.

In order to run Analog, you must have access to your Web server's raw logs. If you don't know where to find these, ask your service provider—in some cases, raw logs are only available on request. If your ISP doesn't provide access to raw logs at all and you have a need for them, you might want to consider a different provider.

***Do It Yourself*** **If setting up Analog seems like too much work, or if you just need to quickly extract simple answers from your logs, remember that you can always use a simple** grep **command combined with** wc**'s line count feature to count the number of accesses to any single page. For example, if you need to know how many requests were made on a file called** beos/software.html **and your log file is called** 110798.log**, you can simply type**

```
grep beos/software.html 110798.log | wc -l
```

**You can easily drop a series of commands like this into a shell script to be used again in the future. You can even generate your own HTML or text-based reports this way!**

**Reporting with Analog** Analog's reports aren't exactly gorgeous, but they are incredibly customizable. If you're willing to spend some time with the voluminous documentation, there are probably very few statistical questions Analog can't answer. However, you'll need to be prepared to spend some preparation time configuring Analog to generate the exact reports you need. Since Analog is a command-line tool with no user interface, you'll need to configure its behavior by modifying text files and issuing command-line arguments.

Analog is fast. Really, really fast. How fast? Consider this: I use a shell script that runs the same log file against three separate Analog configuration files, generating three separate HTML reports. On a dual 300 Pentium II, a 7.2-MB log file can be parsed three times, generating three separate reports, in exactly four seconds. You can barely even open a file of that size in a text editor in that time!

If you find that the version of Analog distributed on BeWare has not been compiled for your platform, don't worry—it ships along with source code and compiles easily for any version of BeOS. Just type make in the program directory to create an application binary (see Appendix D for more on compiling source code). Move the analog binary to ~/config/bin, then return to the directory created when you unpacked the original archive. Look for a file called analog.cfg, which is the configuration file you'll be using to control how your log files are analyzed, what goes into the generated report file, and what gets left out. For now, leave this file as is and use the included logfile.log for testing.

To test your Analog installation, open a Terminal window in the Analog directory and type `analog`. When you issue the `analog` command with no arguments, it will assume that it should use arguments specified in `analog.cfg`. Once you get the hang of working with Analog, you can use any configuration file you like, which you'll probably want to store in a `config` subdirectory along with your log files.

A new HTML file will be created in the same directory; it will be an analysis of `logfile.log`, constructed as specified by the parameters in `analog.cfg`. If you want to use a different configuration file, you can specify its name at the command line:

```
analog +g"config/beos.cfg"
```

Note the lack of a space between the +g flag and the path to the configuration file, which is in quotes. The configuration file can store hundreds of different parameters (we'll get to a few of those in a minute), but a few of them are essential, starting with the input and output filenames:

```
LOGFILE logfilename.log
OUTFILE outputfile.html
```

**Establishing Log Formats** Because different Web servers generate logs in different formats, Analog needs to know which part of each line represents what kind of data. While Analog is capable of making educated guesses about some of the most popular formats, you'll need to describe your log format precisely if your logs differ even slightly from the standards. You do this by adding to your configuration file a `DEFAULTLOGFORMAT` line that consists of a series of arguments representing every element in one line of your logs. A complete list of arguments can be found in Analog's documentation, but for the sake of argument, let's say a line of your logs is formatted like this:

```
jay.bird.com - fred [14/Mar/1996:17:45:35 +0000] "GET /~sret1/ HTTP/1.0" 200 1243
```

You'll then need to add a line like this to your configuration file:

```
DEFAULTLOGFORMAT (%S - %u [%d/%M/%Y:%h:%n:%j] "%j %r %j" %c %b)
```

It looks hairy, but it's very logical. By studying the chart in Analog's documentation, you'll be able to determine that %S represents the server, %u represents the user, and so on. Note that every last punctuation mark and space needs to be represented specifically. Setting the log format can be a little tedious, but you only need to do it once. The nice thing about this system is that Analog can be made to work with nonstandard log formats, such as those generated by PoorMan.

Because PoorMan's log format is destined to change at some time after this writing, we'll publish the Analog DEFAULTLOGFORMAT for PoorMan on this book's Web site: **www.beosbible.com.**

**Building Reports** Once you've got your log file format established, the rest is a matter of fine-tuning the report format. Analog can run any of dozens of built-in reports, such as daily summaries, failed requests, user reports, browser reports, and so on. Include as many or as few reports in a single output file as you like. Each report is represented by a one-letter code, such as:

```
x General Summary
d Daily Summary
H Hourly Report
```

Use the chart in Analog's documentation to learn the code letters for the reports you want to run, then add a REPORTORDER line to your configuration file. The order in which you set the report codes in the configuration file is reflected in the final report. A very detailed REPORTORDER line might look like this:

```
REPORTORDER ixWDdHh45rEItSofskKBbvuJzcm
```

While there are reasonable default settings for each report, each one is also individually customizable, to varying degrees. You can specify things like upper and lower thresholds (so that your report doesn't include any page for which there were less than 10 requests, for example), depth levels (so you can specify that directory reports only go two levels deep), and file includes (so you can make sure Analog reports on specific files even if they don't fall within your upper and lower thresholds). You can establish a base URL, so that filenames in the report can be linked to the actual pages online. You can specify which filetypes are reported on and which are excluded, and you can tell Analog about equivalencies, to eliminate split reporting (for example, ~/words/ and ~/words/index.html are literally the same page, so you want to ensure they get consolidated into a single count).

***Redesigning Analog's Output*** The HTML pages output by Analog are functional, not beautiful. You won't find any parameters for configuring page background colors, for example. However, you may be able to dig around in the .c files that accompany the distribution, looking for HTML elements and editing them. You'll then need to recompile the program and run a report to test your changes. This technique is not for the squeamish!

Analog's documentation is extensive and detailed—it's all there; you just have to be willing to dig in and experiment.

It's easy to write shell scripts that invoke Analog reports. You might, for example, want to create multiple configuration files that look at the same log file from several different angles, create multiple output files in a given directory, and then link to these reports from a central index page for the convenience of the big cheese in your company. Look for the command-line options in Analog's documentation, test them, and drop them into your shell scripts for even more control. You could even have your script run automatically at a certain time every day by using a tool like Scheduler (Chapter 10, *System Tools and Utilities*).

# Behaviour
`www.student.nada.kth.se/~d96-ja/`

One of the harder problems in the realm of 3D animation lies in making objects move *convincingly*. It's not enough for a ball to bounce—it has to bounce differently depending on the elasticity and weight of the ball, taking into account the speed at which it was thrown and the hardness of the wall into which it collides. In other words, the computer must incorporate the laws of physics into its renderings to emulate the behavior of actual objects in the physical world.

**What Is Behaviour?** Johan Jansson has developed Behaviour for BeOS with this very intention. The project follows naturally from his involvement with POV-Ray (Chapter 13, *Graphics Applications*), which seeks to accurately emulate the behavior of light as it encounters objects with varying degrees of opacity, reflectivity, etcetera. Behaviour shares many traits with POV-Ray, but extends its principles to the moving world. Behaviour is not itself a raytracer, but it can export frames to the POV-Ray format that can then be used to texturize objects and batch-render them to digital movies.

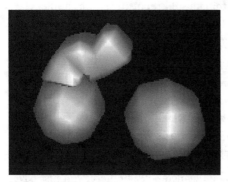

*Figure 15.01*

*Behaviour emulates the laws of the physical world, so that animated objects behave realistically regardless of what they're doing.*

Behaviour employs a unique description language to specify the shapes and physical properties of objects, then runs those parameters through a multithreaded mechanics engine that incorporates some of the laws of physics. Behaviour calculates the concepts of position, velocity, force, mass, radius, friction, damping, and tolerance, all of which can interact with objects. Thus, rather than animating a bouncing ball frame by frame, Behaviour lets you describe the ball and the wall and then lets physics take care of the rest. All rendering in Behaviour is accomplished via OpenGL.

Beyond its value as a fascinating toy, Behaviour can be used as an animation tool, a virtual laboratory, a vector/rational number calculator and plotter, or the basis for a virtual reality system. Spend enough time with your nose in the description files, and you could probably model the result of dropping an Edsel from the Empire State Building.

**Using Behaviour**   To install Behaviour, just double-click on the application binary to create a new MIME type on your system, associating Behaviour data files with the Behaviour application. Open the `datafiles` subdirectory and double-click one of the many provided samples. Included are examples of giant balls slamming into elastic nets, jointed pendula wrapping themselves around obstacles, gravitationally orbiting satellites, rigid blocks being smashed open by falling weights … you get the picture.

Some Behaviour scenes can be navigated through (depending on how they were constructed), using one of two navigational modes. In Orbital mode, drag your mouse to revolve your point of view left, right, or up and down. Zoom in by pressing 1; zoom out by pressing 3. In Lookat mode, click on an object and your point of view will begin to shift as the object moves, so that you're always facing it directly. The data file itself controls whether you're in Orbital or Lookat mode, not you. At this writing, the only way to determine the file's navigational mode was by trying both methods.

**Generating Behaviours**   Once you've viewed the sample data files, try opening one in a text editor and modifying some of its parameters. Tweak, save, and reload to see how, for example, changing the mass of an object affects an entire scene. Behaviour data files aren't exactly child's play, but they're not C++, either. By reading Behaviour's documentation and hacking away at the included demo files, you should be able to get a pretty good handle on the description language.

## BeStripper and Other Text Converters
www.kagi.com/ajlloyd/

One of the most frustrating things about plain text is that it's almost—but not quite—handled and displayed identically across operating systems. While the basic character set is the same whether you're on a MacOS, Windows, or Unix computer, line endings are handled differently on each.

- MacOS files end lines with a carriage return (CR).
- Windows files end lines with a carriage return and a line feed (CR/LF).
- Unix files end lines with a line feed (LF).

This means that text files transported between these platforms can end up with extra space between lines, missing space between lines, or nonprinting characters at the end of lines. BeOS uses Unix-style line feeds and can exchange text documents with Linux and other Unix operating systems without difficulty. If you bring text documents to your BeOS machine from

MacOS or Windows, however, you're going to get some funky display arti-facts. There are a number of ways to rectify the situation, either with third-party tools or with the `tr` command.

**BeStripper**    The easiest to use of the available text-format converters is Adam Lloyd's BeStripper. Just set the conversion you need (Mac-to-BeOS or Windows-to-BeOS) and drag a file onto BeStripper's open window. You won't receive any feedback from the program, but the conversion will be done instantly; double-click your text file in the Tracker and it should now display normally.

## Other Text-Format Converters

If you'd like a little more control than BeStripper has to offer, you can convert your text files between formats from the command line, using the `tr` (translate) tool that ships with your system, or with a third-party command-line tool like `ascii`, which simplifies the conversion process somewhat.

While the shell's translate tool has many options, all you need to know for now is that `tr` will perform a substitution between any two parameters, or a deletion if given the `-d` flag and a single parameter. Thus, you can use `tr` either to run quick search-and-replace operations or to delete a given string from any text file. Additionally, `tr` recognizes certain special characters, such as the three unique line endings listed above.

To convert a Mac text file into Unix text format, replace its carriage returns with new lines like this:

```
tr '\r' '\n'
```

For this to actually be useful, you'll need to use `tr` in combination with a pair of redirects:

```
tr '\r' '\n' < original_file > new_file
```

To fix DOS/Windows text files, just delete the carriage returns, leaving the line feeds intact:

```
tr -d '\r' < original_file > new_file
```

If you want the convenience of translating files from the command line but would rather not mess with tr's syntax, download `ascii`, drop it in ~/config/bin, and just type

```
ascii -to_unix input.txt output.txt
```

You can also use `ascii` to convert in the other direction, by simply replacing `-to_unix` with `-to_dos` or `-to_mac`.

# Ghostscript (PostScript and PDF Viewer)
absinthe.lightside.net/~jehamby/Code/

As of R4.0, there was no Adobe Acrobat reader for BeOS. While that may change in the future, it doesn't mean viewing those increasingly ubiquitous PDF (Portable Document Format) files is impossible. Fortunately, PDF is a nonproprietary file format—Adobe makes their money by selling the Acrobat PDF creation software so they give away the viewer to encourage the wide-spread use of PDF. In this spirit, PDF documents can be viewed and printed with non-Adobe tools, such as Jake Hamby's Ghostscript viewer for BeOS.

Ghostscript is an interpreter for the ages-old PostScript file format (the trade-mark to which is also owned by Adobe), which describes text, fonts, graphics, and page layouts by means of a rather arcane markup language. Ghostscript is a freeware utility from the Unix world capable of rendering the PostScript language. Because the PDF format is related to PostScript, Ghostscript is also capable of reading PDF (Acrobat) documents.

**Using Ghostscript**  The Ghostscript viewer for BeOS (as of this writing) is launched from the command line even though it displays documents in a GUI window. To Ghostscript-enable your system, download the viewer from BeWare (you may want to follow the link to the author's Web site to make sure you have the most recent version). You'll also need the accompanying archive of special Ghostscript fonts to make it work.

 Ghostscript fonts don't go in /boot/home/config/fonts, as you might expect. Instead, the Ghostscript fonts folder must be a subdirectory of the Ghostscript folder, which must, in turn, live in /boot/apps (though you can use a different location if you make the corresponding change to the environment variable in your .profile, below). Within the Ghostscript folder you'll find a handful of directories, of which only a couple are noteworthy. The docs folder contains a pile of informational text files that will introduce you to Ghostscript and brief you on licensing and usage issues. You'll want to read the file use.txt if you need more information than what's provided here. The examples folder holds a few sample PostScript documents (but no PDF samples you can use to test your installation). In the root of the folder are the gs executables and a readme file in HTML format.

To test your installation, open a Terminal window and invoke the gs command and an example filename, both with full paths:

```
/boot/apps/Ghostscript/gs /boot/apps/Ghostscript/examples/tiger.ps
```

If everything is installed correctly, this will cause the demo PostScript file shown in Figure 15.02 to be launched into the Ghostscript viewer.

*Figure 15.02*

*A demo PostScript file displayed in Ghostscript.*

You'll also see a smaller message window in which you can directly type Ghostscript commands. The Ghostscript documentation will tell you how to export the file to another format or send it to a printer, for example. Press Enter to page down when prompted, or close the window normally to quit. Now to test your font installation, type

`/boot/apps/Ghostscript/gs /boot/apps/Ghostscript/examples/alphabet.ps`

You should get a window full of letters. If so, you're in business. If not, check to make sure that you downloaded the Ghostscript fonts and placed them in a subdirectory of the Ghostscript folder.

Everything working properly? Then the only remaining step is to make the `gs` command easy to access. Open up `/boot/home/.profile` (or create it if you don't have one) and add this line:

`export PATH=${PATH}:/boot/apps/Ghostscript`

This will add the Ghostscript directory to your system path (see Chapter 6 for more on paths) so the `gs` command and all of the support files needed by it can be found by the shell without you having to specify them each time. To test your change, close *all* Terminal windows and reopen one, then type

`gs /boot/apps/Ghostscript/examples/tiger.ps`

If PostScript works for you, PDF will too. Grab any Acrobat file from one of your other partitions (or search the Web for "sample PDF" to download one) and give it a whirl.

# liblayout and PrefServer
www.xs4all.nl/~marcone/be.html

These two binaries, by developer Marco Nelissen, exist as a replacement or improvement to certain BeOS-provided services. Yes, it's true—BeOS isn't perfect. For example, you may have noticed that many dialog boxes, buttons, and picklists in BeOS will not resize themselves properly if you set your system fonts to be larger than the default size. Of course, Be recognizes this is as a problem and intends to rectify it in a future release. In the meantime, developers who invoke Nelissen's shared library, called liblayout, will end up with applications capable of scaling to accommodate outsize fonts. liblayout offers more than just font flexibility, however. Recall Figure 2.35 in Chapter 2, *Meet the System*—programs based on liblayout automatically gain the ability to be sent to an alternate workspace with a right-click, to accept dropped colors from mixers like roColour's, and to have application font sizes changed on the fly, without quitting the app first.

As a user, you don't have to do anything but drop the liblayout.so file into /boot/home/config/lib. Because some programs available on BeWare depend on liblayout.so to function properly, you'll be prepared should you ever happen to download one. Some examples of BeOS programs based on liblayout are SoundPlay, fontselector, SetPerms, TheClock, and SysInfo.

PrefServer, on the other hand, takes the client/server architecture of BeOS and extends it to the domain of application preference and settings files as well. The idea is that if a server monitors and manages settings files, it becomes trivial for programmers to do things like exchanging data with settings repositories via BMessages. PrefServer also offers the user system-wide control over the way preferences are stored and managed.

*Figure 15.03*

*Once PrefServer is installed, you'll have system-wide control over the way preferences are stored and managed (for applications that use PrefServer).*

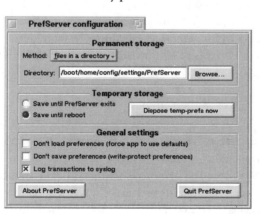

Chances are, you won't have much cause to fiddle with the PrefServer configuration panel shown in Figure 15.03, but it's not a bad idea to install it on your system so you'll be ready for any applications that depends on its presence.

# Perl

Practical Extraction and Report Language, or Perl, is a heavy-duty, ultra-flexible scripting language specializing in (but not limited to) text parsing. Perl scripts drive many online banks, search engines, discussion boards, random poetry generators, stores, catalogs, auctions, medical databases … you name it. If it's interactive, someone out there somewhere has gotten it running in Perl. The language isn't just for running dynamic Internet sites, either; Perl has many uses when installed locally on your own hard drive, or on network servers. In fact, Perl is so capable and so trusted that it's been found running parts of power plants, air traffic control towers, security systems, and other mission-critical environments.

You can easily install Perl for BeOS. Even if you don't speak Perl and have no desire to learn, there are hundreds of Perl scripts floating around out there that you can download and make immediate use of, much as you would a compiled command-line tool. In addition, it's possible that the BeOS implementation of Perl will at some point gain the ability to interact with BeOS's messaging architecture, meaning that you'll be able to automate BeOS applications from Perl scripts (though other languages, such as Python, are easier to learn and arguably better candidates for BeOS-native scripting needs).

If you're a Webmaster running a site from a BeOS machine, you'll find that most of the third-party Web servers described in Chapter 11, *Network Applications*, are capable of running CGI programs written in Perl.

To install Perl on your BeOS machine, download the port from BeWare for your platform (PowerPC or x86), place it in your /boot directory, and decompress it. A handful of tools will be added to ~/config/bin, and a new perl directory will be created under ~/config/lib. If you didn't unpack the archive from within /boot, you'll be looking at a new home directory with these directories contained within. You can easily move these folders into the proper locations. To test your new Perl installation, launch StyledEdit and enter the following lines:

```
#! /boot/home/config/bin/perl
print ("Hello, Dolly!\n");
```

Save the file as test.pl, open a Terminal window, cd to the same location as your new script, and type chmod +x test.pl to notify the system that the file is executable. Next, type the script's name: test.pl. The shell should report back Hello, Dolly! and return your prompt. If it worked, congrats—Perl is installed and properly working on your system. If you received any kind of error message, make sure you downloaded the correct version (for example,. you're not trying to run Perl for R3/x86 under R4/x86), and that you installed to the paths described earlier. Also make sure that you typed in the two-line script exactly as shown above (though it may also work without the parentheses).

You should have no difficulty working with Perl scripts written under other operating systems—Perl is Perl. However, the first line of each script must point to your system's Perl interpreter. Chances are, any script you download from a non-BeOS site will have a different path specified, such as /usr/local/bin/perl or /bin/env/perl. Make sure the first line always reads:

```
#! /boot/home/config/bin/perl
```

**Remember that most BeOS Web servers use MIME types in the filesystem to determine filetypes, rather than using an external extension-mapping table as do servers on other operating systems. This means that if you want your BeOS Web server to recognize CGI scripts (such as those written in Perl), you must give them the type** text/cgi**.**

# Python
www.python.org

While Perl is extremely powerful, it's also a somewhat terse language, often difficult to read and write for users who aren't already Perl savvy. More significantly for BeOS users, however, is the fact that (at this writing) Perl is not integrated with BeOS's native scripting environment. That means you can run Perl scripts on BeOS just fine, but you can't use a Perl script to control other BeOS GUI applications. Python, along with an accompanying hey module, is the first scripting language available for BeOS to make good on the promises offered by the language-neutral BeOS scripting environment, which theoretically lets you script any application from any language.

**What is Python?**  Like Perl, Python is "interpreted," meaning that you don't compile Python programs into binary format before running them. Rather, a separate "interpreter" parses the program at run-time. Python, which is fully object-oriented, is known for the elegance and clarity (but not over-simplification) of its syntax. Users should be able to get up to speed with Python quickly. The language is capable of interfacing with system calls specific to the platform on which it's running. The BeOS port of Python takes full advantage of BeOS's multithreading capabilities and is capable of dynamically loading "extension modules" from BeOS shared libraries (such as the "time" module in the example below). Python and its accompanying hey module has been brought to BeOS by our own Chris Herborth.

**Installing Python**    Installation is simple:

1.  Grab the current BeOS Python port from BeWare.

2.  If you downloaded the SoftwareValet package, double-click its icon and make sure you install the distribution to your /boot disk. Otherwise, Python won't be able to find all of its shared libraries (unless you perform additional surgery; advanced users will know what to do). Once the files have been installed, a simple script will be run automatically. If all went well, you'll see:

    ```
    ==============================
    If you can read this, Python is installed properly!
    Press Enter to close this window.
    ==============================
    ```

3.  If you downloaded the ZIP archive, unzip it in /boot:

    ```
    unzip archive_name.zip -d /boot
    ```

4.  To test Python manually, open a Terminal and type python. You should see something like:

    ```
    Python 1.5.1 (#22, May  8 1998, 07:25:39) [C] on beos1
    Copyright 1991-1995 Stichting Mathematisch Centrum, Amsterdam
    >>>
    ```

>>> is Python's prompt; you can type Python statements here and get immediate feedback:

```
>>> 1+2
3
```

A simple way to test your installation is to see if any of the included "dynamically loaded modules" work by importing one:

```
>>> import time
>>> time.ctime( time.time() )
'Sat Dec  5 10:21:20 1998'
```

If that works, you're in business! If you get an ImportError exception message, there's a problem with your installation; make sure there's a python* directory in ~/config/lib (at this writing, the directory should be named python1.5). The ImportError traceback will look something like this:

```
>>> import bozo
Traceback (innermost last):
File "<stdin>", line 1, in ?
ImportError: No module named bozo
```

Once you're satisfied everything is up and running properly, it's time to dig and start learning the language itself. You'll find the Python tutorial at **www.python.org/doc/** a great place to start.

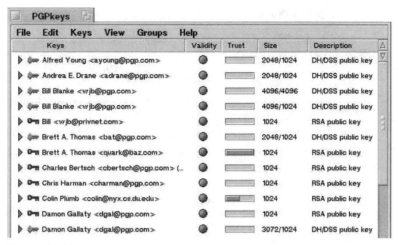

**Figure 15.04**

*The PGPkeys application helps you store and manage the public keys belonging to people with whom you need to exchange secure documents.*

## Pretty Good Privacy (PGP)
**www.killerbe.com**

If you have a need to keep your data secure from prying eyes, you'll want to use some sort of private encryption system, and you've no doubt heard that Pretty Good Privacy is the de facto standard. At this writing, developer Mark Elrod was bringing PGP to BeOS, and the product should be available by the time you read this (we were not able to test PGP for BeOS in time for publication).

PGP is based on a system of "keys"—each user has both a public and a private key. You issue your public key to people with whom you need to exchange secure documents. Meanwhile, your private key is stored safely on your own hard drive, and is used to open encrypted files or email messages addressed to you. Because both keys are needed to decrypt any document, it's almost impossible for a person to view a file not meant for their eyes (unless of course someone cracks into your system and learns your password somehow, but that's another story).

PGP can also be used to digitally sign files or the text of email messages. A digital signature is a very powerful means of ensuring that the data has not been modified in any way after the signature was applied to the data.

# RC5DES
**www.beoscentral.com/beosc/rc5/**

How would you like to use BeOS to help prove to the governments of the world that commonly endorsed encryption standards are insufficient to guarantee citizens the privacy they deserve? Various governments regard strong data encryption in different lights. At this writing, the U.S. government classified any encryption stronger than 56 bits as a "munition," making it a felony to transport outside of the United States (as one might via the Internet) any message encoded with a key length longer than 56 bits. In some countries, any encryption at all is completely illegal.

Encryption techniques usually involve a digital *key* that can be used to descramble a given message. The longer the key, the more difficult the message is to decrypt. While proponents of 56-bit encryption point out that it would take a typical computer thousands of years to simply try every possible key by brute force, its critics note that it isn't all that difficult to wire up thousands of computers to work on the problem in parallel. A group called **distributed.net** exists to prove that it's possible. In October 1997, the group finished cracking a 56-bit cipher after working on it for less than a year; it is now working on a far more complex 64-bit cipher.

 A 57-bit cipher would be twice as difficult to crack as a 56-bit cipher. The 64-bit challenge is thus 256 times more difficult than was the 56-bit version.

According to **distributed.net**, "The goal of the contests … is to quantify the security offered by the government-endorsed data encryption standard (DES) and other secret-key ciphers with keys of various sizes." **distributed.net** participants use their computers' idle time to test keys one at a time. These computers periodically log in to a central database responsible for doling out potential keys in blocks and keeping track of which keys have been tested and which have not. In effect, **distributed.net** is running a massive supercomputer with thousands of individual processors, all working at their own pace. RSA Laboratories currently offers a reward of US $10,000 to any individual or group who can crack the 64-bit cipher. The reward will be distributed as follows:

- $1,000 to the winner
- $1,000 to the winner's team
- $6,000 to a nonprofit organization
- $2,000 to **distributed.net**

Rather than working alone, RC5 crackers typically band together in teams. This brings a sense of camaraderie and friendly competition to the contest, as teams vie to climb the rankings. Team BeOS Central has been climbing through the ranks steadily. A high RC5 ranking, some believe, can help bring attention to the platform. Actually cracking the secret cipher, we all know, would result in tremendous press attention for BeOS.

**The Multiproc Advantage** For users with more than one processor in their machines, BeOS has an ace up its sleeve due to its excellent symmetric multiprocessing (SMP) capabilities. The same code running on the same dual-processor machine will run almost twice as fast under BeOS as under Windows 98, simply because Windows 98 ignores that second CPU. The same is true for a dual-processor PowerPC machine running both MacOS and BeOS.

To participate in the contest, head over to **www.beoscentral.com/beosc/rc5/**, read the instructions, and download and install the client. When you first configure the client, you'll give it an email address under which to register your processed keys. After your first submission of cracked blocks, you'll receive a password. Return to **distributed.net**, log in with your email address and password, and designate that all of your cracked blocks should be attributed to Team BeOS Central.

Even though RC5DES will run at full tilt every microsecond your computer has cycles to spare, don't worry about the client slowing your machine down;

## In Search of Heavenly Bodies

'Member that movie *Contact*, where, like, that lady from SETI was checking out the universe with those monstro radio dishes, and, like, she tapped into signals from intelligent beings on some planet and, like, nobody believed her and then that other dude flew in his mind to another dimension and everything was, like, all tripped out? That was cool, huh? Heh heh.

Breaking the 64-bit key would be a boon for BeOS, but pinning down final proof that intelligent life exists somewhere "out there" would be huge. The problem with searching the heavens for intelligent transmissions is that there's just so much data out there. Scanning the background radiation for patterns in the millions of possible frequency channels thus becomes a supercomputing problem. A group of SETI (Search for Extraterrestrial Intelligence) researchers has developed a mechanism by which radio astronomy data gathered from the Arecibo telescope in Puerto Rico can be parceled out in chunks to individual machines, who will scan the data for patterns and log their results back into a central database, similar to the way the RC5DES effort operates.

Sometime in early 1999, the project (to be known as SETI at Home) will go online. A BeOS client is scheduled to be made available at that time. To participate in the SETI at Home project, head over to **setiathome.ssl.berkeley.edu**, download the BeOS client, and start putting all of that idle horsepower to work! But if Earth ends up being destroyed by aliens as a result of your having found their secret hideout in the Alpha Centauri system, don't come running to me.

it runs at a very low priority, so that all of your horsepower is available to other applications. You can also configure the level of "niceness" at which RC5DES should run, though the default settings work quite nicely.

As **distributed.net** says, "... go forth and multiply, divide, rotate, invert, and conquer." And keep your computer on at night (but turn off that monitor to save energy!).

# X-Windows Server
**ftp.ninemoons.com/gg**

As described earlier, BeOS is (for the most part) POSIX-compliant. As a result, it's often possible to recompile Unix/Linux software for BeOS with minimal effort. POSIX compliance gives us the vast majority of command-line tools found in /boot/beos/bin, as well as the immense collection of additional tools available through the GeekGadgets collection, covered in Chapter 6. Interestingly, one of the applications available through GeekGadgets is an X-Windows server, which lets you run the X desktop familiar to Unix and Linux users.

Similar to the way in which BeOS uses a client/server model to distribute system resources from a centralized location, the Unix/Linux model uses the X server to allow applications to run in a windowed mode. By recompiling the X server and running it as a BeOS application, you can run windowed Unix/Linux programs that require the X server. In other words, you can run a Unix-style desktop and recompiled Unix applications from within BeOS. And since the X server is capable of running as a distributed application over TCP/IP networks, you can run the X server on BeOS and view applications it's running remotely, from another machine. Note, however, that this has nothing to do with emulation—you're just running a BeOS port of a Unix desktop, along with BeOS ports of Unix applications. If you have both BeOS and Linux installed on your machine, you'll have to store duplicate copies of applications you want to run under both systems: one copy compiled for Linux and living in a Linux partition, and another copy compiled for BeOS and living in a BeOS partition. Still, this system can offer some convenience if you'd rather not boot into Linux to run a particular program.

 In theory, it should also be possible to write a Linux application loader for BeOS/x86, since both systems use the ELF binary format. No such loader exists for BeOS at this time, but never say never...

If these applications need to be recompiled to run under BeOS anyway, why is the X-Windows server necessary at all? The answer is that Linux programs running in GUI mode often *depend* on the presence of a running X server, which is why we see so many more Unix/Linux CLI tools ported to BeOS than we do GUI applications. For example, a photo/paint application called The GIMP is popular among Linux users, but has not (as of this writing) been ported to BeOS in such a way that it can be run without the X server. The GIMP's dependence on X is said to be heavy enough that such a port would be more trouble than it's worth, and that it would be easier to rip the code apart and start fresh. However, since the X server will let you view and operate X applications running on remote systems, you may find it useful to install the BeOS X server if you work in a shared environment with Unix/Linux machines.

My honest opinion is that X for BeOS just isn't worth the effort for most users. Oh, did we mention that the X server tarball (`tar.gz` file) is almost 40MB and decompresses to more than 100MB?

If you choose to run X under BeOS, you'll find the latest version available with the rest of the GeekGadgets collection at **`ftp.ninemoons.com/gg`**. At this writing, there was no binary version available and it was necessary to compile the X server manually from source code. A precompiled binary version should be available by the time you read this. (See Appendix C for more on compiling software from source code.)

## Tim Martin
### User Interaction Designer
*Interviewed by Henry Bortman*

**HB:** *Your title is interesting. Explain the difference between a user interaction designer and a user interface designer.*

**TM:** There doesn't have to be a difference at all. It's just that a lot of times when people say "interface designer" they will assume that is merely the person who draws the graphics for the system or for the application or for whatever it is you're talking about. But I get much more into the lower levels of how the system works, what functions have to be there and what functions don't have to be there, and how the product works as the user is actually working through the different features.

Like, for instance, the dial-up networking, which we've massively changed in R4. There of course needed to be the layouts for the buttons and the text controls, and all the things that you needed to interact with, but you also needed to know where can the user access a method for dialing a connection. And where do they access a method to stop a connection that has already been dialed? What kind of feedback do they get, and where is the feedback that they get to tell them that the connection is currently up or that it's down or that the computer doesn't have a connection at all? Figuring out where the information is displayed and how the user can get to other information, the paths that they take.

**HB:** *And was that information missing before?*

**TM:** In the case of dial-up networking? Yeah, it wasn't there at all before. The system worked in a somewhat obfuscated manner. Whenever the computer thought that the dial-up connection needed to exist, it would make it on its own. The only interface that existed was that it would pop open a window and would allow you to stop it in process if you thought it was making the wrong decision. There was no method for you to have multiple profiles, and phone numbers, and people's addresses, and stuff like that. So, we had to bring all that into the system. We also needed to create a method to easily connect and disconnect at will.

**HB:** *When you're looking at reengineering user interaction for a particular part of the system, what's the process you go through?*

**TM:** Well, the first thing is that I have to make sure that I'm aware of who that particular part of the system is for. We have a general idea, sometimes too general, of who the user is of the operating system, who is using BeOS, or more importantly, who will be using the next version that we're selling, which can be someone different from who's currently using it. But then, for each part of the system, you have different kinds of people who are using it. The people who are using the Terminal are different than people who have to use dial-up networking on a daily basis. There's a lot of overlap for all the parts of the system, but you can't make an assumption that this person is going to know every part of the system equally well.

When you come to something like dial-up networking, we're talking about everyone who is at home using a computer that doesn't have a direct connection to the Internet, which is almost everyone. So that means it has to work for the people who totally know how PPP works as well as for the people who don't know anything about the Internet—who just know that they use the telephone line to connect and that they do some things, and then when they're done they have to disconnect if they want to use the telephone to talk.

Once I have some kind of profile for who the user is, very often I try to make a rigid persona, almost of an individual person. I say, OK, well, here's a person at home, and all they have is a phone line and they have a modem that's of this type. And that way when I come to decisions I say, Well, is it going to work for this person? So, if you have many of these—I have an engineer that works at home, I have a mother who checks for recipes online, and stuff like that—then every time I come to a decision, I can make sure that it works for all these different people.

Then I just look at the system as we have it and figure out what's missing, what needs to be added, and what needs to be taken away. From there I just start building concepts and ideas for how the system can work and simultaneously what part of that system can look like. I start showing it to other people and try to get a couple of them—although usually one—to implement it so we can play with it and try it. And if it works, then we continue in that direction. If it doesn't work, then we try another direction.

**HB:** *Do you do user testing, other than on the folks in the office?*

**TM:** I do, kind of. I have friends I use as guinea pigs, and I am in the constant process of trying to get the company as a whole to start pulling in people from outside and do some kind of official user testing, which I would either like to orchestrate or be highly instrumental in. We haven't up till now, and we're still kind of in the end of a rocky phase where all of our current users aren't what our future users will be. So I think probably between R4 and R5, or the next significant release after that, I will want to get real users that fit [the profile of] what marketing and sales believe to be our new users that will be paying us money for the product. Get a handful of them in a room, see what I can actually get through some user testing and protocol analysis on how they use the system and how they accomplish certain tasks, and what they think. But up till this point, we have not.

**HB:** *Were you hired specifically to work on user interaction?*

**TM:** Yeah. The story is a little more twisty than that. I knew about the company beforehand. I had read about them in magazines. I had never actually played with a BeBox, but I had heard about them and thought they were really cool and wished I had had one. So I kind of checked their Web site every now and then. So when from my previous job I was moving on to a new job, I was looking around and I happened to cross the Web site again and it was like, Hey, I'll look at their job listings again. Why not? And when I looked at their job listings, there was one that said, "graphics designer." Now, my educational training is in industrial design and product design, but of course, I worked alongside graphic designers all along. So, I looked at it, and I read the description, and it was like someone to do the graphics and visuals for the operating system and applications that are developed in-house.

That's very often part of what I do. And it had been totally what I had been doing at my last job. So I talked to the HR representative, and showed her my resume and everything, and she's like, "Oh, you've done this stuff in the past." And that got me far enough to talk to Peter

## Tim Martin *(continued)*

[Potrebic]. Once I was talking to Peter, I was like, Yeah I can do all that stuff, but this is what I really like to do. What I really like to do is figure out how the system is supposed to work and lay out the information and profile the users, and test to see if the system is working right. I like to do all that stuff, and that's what all my training is in, and that's what I'm really good at. And I was able to sell myself as that. And then he said, "OK, but you can still do the other stuff too?"

**HB:** *So you do occasionally draw icons?*

**TM:** Yeah, when they need to be done. But it doesn't take up nearly as much time as analyzing the system and trying to figure out what other things need to change. And there are things like laying out panels. You could look at it from one perspective and say it's graphical—you want to lay things out so that they look better. But usually it has a lot more to do with how the information is presented and cognitively what the person needs to understand and how they need to manipulate information once they are presented with it. So even though it might start out as, "We just need this to look better 'cause it's kind of confusing and people don't get it," when you start working on it, you're like, "Well, we don't even need a button that does this because the system should just do it automatically." Like, there shouldn't be a Save button, it should save when you're actually changing things and stuff like that. So, it might start off visual, but it's very often much deeper than that.

**HB:** *When you analyzed user interaction in BeOS, what did you feel it was good at and where did you think it needed work?*

**TM:** The things that I saw that were really cool were that it had laid the proper groundwork to do a bunch of things better than other operating systems, and even better than it was doing them now. Right away I saw the way that they dealt with filetypes. It's kind of a difficult system to get used to, a little bit difficult to understand at first, but once you get to the point of understanding how it works, it's really powerful and really cool.

**HB:** *What's cool about it?*

**TM:** It's almost easier to describe it by the deficits of other systems. For instance, in Windows, the type of file is defined by its extension, which isn't in itself bad, but that means that the name is actually part of the descriptor for the object itself. So when an application installs itself, it can claim other objects by their extensions. It can say, Well all of your .doc files and all your .txt files are now mine.

So every time I double-click on a file, it's dependent on what application I last installed. The order that you install applications suddenly becomes important. And on the Mac, they kind of have the other extreme, in that the file itself stores this information and it stores both the application that made it and the type of file, and it gives a lot of preferential treatment to the application that made it. So, I might have files of the same type that when I double-click on them load different applications. It's kind of like the application that last touched me—the thing I was last saved from.

In the BeOS, every file just has in it the information about what type of file it is—you know, I'm a graphics file that is a JPEG, I'm a graphics file that is a GIF, or I'm a text file that is a styled document—and there is a single preference panel that allows you to say, OK, I want to open all my graphics files with this program. There's one centralized location for me to set those things. And then furthermore, I can say, OK, HTML documents I usually want to view with NetPositive; but then when I'm looking at a particular HTML document, I can say, this one I want to open in Pe, or this one, I want to open in something else. You can set a system-wide preference and then very easily override it on a per-file basis. You don't change the type of file it is, it's still exactly what it was before, but this particular file has a different preferred application.

So, immediately, the problem is that when you put that kind of power in there, you suddenly have settings that are here and settings that are over there, and you're trying to figure out a good way to explain to the people what's going to happen when they double-click on an icon and where it is that they set which applications, or what kinds of files prefer which types of applications. But the system is clean enough and strong enough that I think it has a lot of potential.

**HB:** *And what was the biggest shortcoming?*

**TM:** It's really hard to see some of the deficiencies when you're looking at the system itself and not at applications. The biggest deficiency is that there aren't enough applications yet. You can't see how well or how poorly it does video editing if no application exists that will allow you to do video editing. But if you started playing around with the stuff, it seemed to me that the problem that showed itself was that things weren't all at a common level. Some things were really advanced and some things have kind of been left by the wayside for a while. There were inconsistencies where there didn't need to be inconsistencies. Like, we had drag-and-drop, but it worked here but not there.

Our operating system is presented as being very new and being non-legacy, but we have our own little legacy even though it's shorter than everybody else's. Even though Windows and Macintoshes go back into the '80s and before with their legacy, ours still exists. There are things that we ship with our product that haven't changed for a long time, and when it comes down to the interaction and the visuals, it jumps out at you sometimes. Like you'll launch an application and it doesn't have Quit in the menu. The way that things looked kind of needed to be cleaned up and brought up to a common level, I thought.

**HB:** *So that's happening in R4?*

**TM:** Yeah, we've gone through and cleaned up a lot of things. We've developed UI guidelines and are in the process of publishing them so that our developers do the same thing. We went through all of the applications and preference panels that we ship and tried to clean them all up to be of equal visual quality and also to have consistent layouts and consistent interaction, in that they all have Close boxes and they all have Revert buttons, but they don't have Save buttons—so everything, all the panels and stuff that come with the system and install with the system, all work in the same manner and all feel the same. And then we're also going through and trying to publish the documents so that third-party applications also follow the same rules that we follow.

*(continued)*

## Tim Martin (continued)

**HB:** *Do you have pet projects that you'd really like a chance to implement?*

**TM:** There's two. One of them is kind of a personal thing. The thing that I hear a lot of other people say is that we have a look, a décor for the BeOS, and it hasn't changed in a while. I think that we have an appearance and we have a look and we have a branding and it carries through, but I think that we need to update it a little bit in the same way that I think Microsoft makes little incremental updates with how the standard buttons work and how the standard widgets operate and things like that. Just kind of a visual thing, just a décor. Some people complain that our stuff looks childish. I don't agree that it looks childish in a bad way. I think that we have a fun appearance, and I think that we have a very colorful and bright appearance, and I think that our UI looks very simple.

But at the same time, I'd kind of like to tighten it up a little bit. You know, kind of things a little cleaner, a little tighter and then just for change, to kind of make it a little newer. To say, OK, we've had this UI for a couple of years and sure, things have changed about our window borders and this, that, and the other thing, but it would be nice to just kind of go once through and clean up the whole thing and make things a little tighter. I have certain pet peeves about things that are really granular, like the button that we have, the standard appearance is really heavy and it's really thick. It's OK when there's one or two, but if you put a row of them, it looks really dense. I'd like to change the visual of the buttons so it looks a little cleaner and a little simpler, so you can have a row of them and it wouldn't visually detract from your application.

**HB:** *Do you have a position on the yellow tabs?*

**TM:** Yes. I have a position on the yellow tabs. I don't dislike the yellow at all. I like the yellow. I like the fact that it's attention-getting. As far as the tabs go, it makes it difficult to manage windows at times. There are some very simple changes that we are in the process of making that make it possible to arrange the windows in a different way, so that the tabs become more useful than they are now. But I think they give us an incredible image for branding. I think that it is my goal now and it will continue to be my goal that if someone took a screenshot of BeOS and mailed it to someone else, it wouldn't matter if the word "Be" was anywhere on the screen. They should be able to look at it and just say that this is definitely BeOS. Windows has that and Mac has that, but I think we have even more distinctive features than they do.

**HB:** *The changes you're talking about with the tabs and window management, is that something for R4?*

**TM:** Yes. One of the things that people complained about was that when you have a tab, you have this inclination to stack windows on top of each other. You want to have the tabs all visible so that you can just flip through them, kind of like tabs are in a panel. The thing that stops you from doing that is that the tabs are always in the upper left-hand corner. Even though they stick up and they're short, they're all overlapping each other. So I've heard people ask for the capability to move the tabs left and right along the top of the windows. That's what we've been working on, making it so you can slide it back and forth so you can stack your windows on top of each other and arrange them so that you can just flip between the windows, which is kind of cool. It's a level of configurability that we didn't have before. It makes the tabs—which were before simply something we did to be different—it makes them different for a reason

So then my other direction is that I'd really like to work on systems that don't use windows and folders and files as the method to manipulate your information. And this of course is much longer-term, much larger in scope, and much more radical. But, I think there are specific applications where the metaphor either doesn't work or is unnecessary and I'd really like to investigate BeOS without the Tracker, or Tracker replacements that use entirely different methods of presenting information to people.

**HB:** *OK. Let's say you've got $10 million. You can do whatever you want.*

**TM:** I don't have any one direction that I favor, but I guess the things that I'd like to explore would be using forms in space. I know 3D is something that a lot of people throw around. Some people say it's a good idea, some say it's a bad idea, that it's only good for visualizations of particular types.

Of course, there are problems with representing information in three dimensions. So that kind of representation for me is limited to very specific presentations, like a machine that is playing computer games for instance. When you have a machine that only has computer games on it, it's very easy to forget about files because it's not important to you how many files there are or what they're called or where they exist. It's merely important what games you have installed. Each game can be represented as a single form. It can be represented two-dimensionally or three-dimensionally, it doesn't really matter. But you don't have to concern yourself with overlapping windows, and you don't care about drag-and-drop, and you don't care about all these things that make a multipurpose or general operating system easier to use or quicker to use or more efficient. That's not important for a very specific use, like games. So your representation can be completely different.

You could just have a form to represent each individual game that you have on your system. If you want to organize your games by group, then you can have forms that contain other forms. These forms don't have to be two-dimensional rectangles that have little icons in them. They can be 3D spheres or cubes that have other spheres and cubes and such inside of them. Or each game can have its own 3D shape. So one game maker might say, well our game is about a helicopter so our form is a 3D helicopter that's floating in space. The shapes don't have to be the traditional ones that you'd expect. That's a really simple example since the objects themselves don't have to necessarily interact very much. Picking an example where there's not a lot to worry about would probably be the best direction to take if you were going to do something totally different.

**HB:** *Do you think that the demands of a multipurpose operating system make it difficult to go in new directions for user interaction?*

**TM:** Yeah. If you're going to make a general operating system, then there are a lot of good reasons to not do anything totally radically different. If you don't have a good reason to move out of the folder and file and window arena of design, then why do it? If it doesn't make it easier to use and it doesn't make it better, then we shouldn't do it. And when you're talking about a general operating system, if we want to sit alongside other operating systems, and we want people to migrate, or to be able to use both systems, we wouldn't want to be confusingly different. If in our explorations

## Tim Martin (continued)

we could find different visuals and different representation methods that worked as well or better and were very different, then I would think that it would be a direction that we would want to explore, that we would want to think about, that we would want to show people and say, Does this let you work more like how you want to work, is this a better way of organizing your information?

**HB:** *Tell me about some of your other interests.*

**TM:** My real training is in product design so I actually like to do things at home that are more product-design related. I make my own furniture, I build things, I make models. I have models of products that I've designed. I have plastic models and toys. I collect toys, I collect electric toy trains and stuff like that. I guess being a product designer or being an industrial designer I already had in me the desire to have a lot of really nice objects, but then after being trained, I'm even more particular about the things that I own. I like to own lots of nice things. It's not like I go out and spend a lot of money on things, but if I'm looking for a TV stand and I can't find one that I like, I just make one.

   I have paintings and photographs, mostly black-and-white photography and oil paintings and acrylic paintings.

**HB:** *Do you have a darkroom?*

**TM:** No, and I wish I did. But that's OK, because I just take that energy and put it into painting, which I can do at my home, or I put it into making furniture, which I can do. So then if I move into a new place that has a room that I can turn into a darkroom, then I'll just kind of re-juggle all of my interests and start doing that for awhile.

**HB:** *What do you paint?*

**TM:** I paint just images that come into my mind. I don't paint photorealistically. I don't paint still lives or scenes. Usually, the way that I paint is more based on me not painting for long periods of time but having ideas and images just kind of drift in and out of my head. I don't have this image and say, OK, I'm going to paint this thing and when I'm done, this is what I'm going to have. What I think about is, I have these kinds of fragments of images in my head and I have ideas and emotions about what I want to be thinking and feeling when I see the finished prod-uct. And then when it actually comes to me sitting down and painting, I'll start putting the dif-ferent imagery and the different colors and whatnot on the canvas and never really trying to have a particular finished product in mind.

   I'm done at the point at which I look at it and I'm feeling the things that I wanted to feel or I'm feeling the things that I thought about it. So, when I'm done I'm always like, "Is this done? I think it's done. OK, I think it's done." It's not like if you were painting a still life, you're like, yes, I've painted the apple and I've painted the orange, and there's the bowl and there's the shadow and it's done. It's always kind of like a couple of months later I might go, you know, it needs a little more of something else, so I'll add it. And I don't paint that often. It takes me a long time to get enough emotion or enough thoughts together to actually paint something.

# 16

# Troubleshooting and Maintenance

When Be examined the history of computing for valuable object lessons, they paid as much attention to how *not* to do things as to how to do them. One of the unsung corollaries of the "fresh start" design approach is the fact that BeOS has far fewer problems than other operating systems (just take a leisurely stroll through Microsoft's online "knowledge base" to see what I mean). By reducing complexity and legacy, Be has been rewarded with a remarkably trouble-free system. That fact notwithstanding, nobody is perfect: BeOS is young, and people do experience problems with BeOS from time to time. This chapter covers the causes of, and cures for the most common BeOS problems, explains how to recover your system in the unlikely event of a disaster, and includes tips on overall system maintenance.

# General Troubleshooting

Problems with BeOS generally stem from one of a few main sources: incompatible hardware, failure to read instructions and FAQs, and system or application bugs. The first step in dealing with any kind of problem is being able to accurately isolate and reproduce it. In other words, if there are several possible causes of a problem, you need to narrow the list down to one candidate. Part and parcel of that process is the need to make sure the problem is reproducible—did UltraSuperPaint crash once on you, does it crash at random intervals, or can it be made to crash every time you launch the paint palette and hit Ctrl+Z?

 While the bulk of this chapter includes BeOS troubleshooting information that will be of interest to all users, some portions of this chapter deal exclusively with x86-related hardware issues. We're not ignoring PowerPC users here; there just isn't as much to say. Where Mac-specific comments are relevant, you'll find them noted.

## Narrow It Down

Effective troubleshooting often means taking it upon yourself to employ the scientific method: hypothesizing, experimenting, and documenting until you've got something concrete to work with. It's especially important to go through this process to get all the information you can before attempting to seek help from other sources. Let's look at isolation techniques for a hypothetical hardware problem, then do the same for software.

**Isolating Hardware Problems**   Let's say you're having trouble booting your machine after installing BeOS for the first time—every time the process begins, it hangs right after the boot screen says "Found boot record." A problem like this could be related to an incompatible video card or CD-ROM drive, or conflicting IRQs allocated to your sound and network cards. The best way to determine what is at fault in a scenario like this is to eliminate as many contenders as possible, then add them back in one at a time until the problem repeats itself. Of course, you can't do anything without a video card, so you'll have to leave that in. Thus, you'll want to start by removing your CD-ROM drive and network and sound cards. Does BeOS boot now? Good—then you know that your motherboard and video card are BeOS-compatible. Now try plugging your CD-ROM drive back in. If BeOS will no longer boot, you know that's the problem; either it's an unsupported device, or it's located at an improper location on your IDE chain.

 BeOS should simply ignore any devices it does not recognize; theoretically, no unsupported device should ever affect the boot process. However, in certain instances, this scheme does not work properly. Release 4 is even better about this than was R3, but the ISA architecture in x86 machines can make circumventing this quirk difficult in some cases. In rare instances, you may still need to take steps like the ones outlined in this section.

If BeOS still boots, add either your sound or network card back in. If you can boot with either of them but not both, you have successfully isolated the problem to a conflict between these two cards, and can take steps as necessary to resolve the situation (typically by juggling IRQs or disabling Plug-and-Play). Again, remove all possible problem points, then add them back in one at a time until the problem repeats itself.

The same basic principles apply to a system that's been working properly but suddenly goes wacky. The only things that can lead to this state of affairs are changes that you've made to the system—the system does not suddenly and arbitrarily rearrange itself. The cause-and-effect chain is usually pretty obvious here. If you've just swapped out your old network card for a new one and your sound card stops working, then clearly these two devices are in conflict and competing for resources. Because of the way BeOS manages resources, this is highly unlikely, but if this happens to you, the first thing to ask yourself is, "What changed recently? What have I added to or subtracted from the system?" Once you've answered this question, you have a starting point to begin your troubleshooting.

Mac users: It's even more unlikely that you'll experience hardware conflicts with BeOS—everything either just works, or is not supported by BeOS. Your keyboard and mouse only work on the ADB port and only PCI I/O cards are supported, so possible problem points are reduced. If you suspect issues with external SCSI disks or peripherals, try disconnecting them, then adding them back in one at a time.

 Problems do not occur randomly, even if they might seem that way. Except in the instance of something physically nebulous like a loose connector or a slowly failing hard drive, computer problems *always* happen for a reason. That reason may bedevil you in its elusiveness, but there's always a logical reason why things go wrong.

**Isolating Software Problems**   As of this writing, software conflicts on BeOS are virtually unheard of. The software conflicts endured by MacOS and Windows users have spawned entire cottage industries for which there is no analog in the BeOS world (a "conflict catcher" for BeOS would suffocate from lack of sales). That's not to say that BeOS applications never crash— some do—but those crashes are not due to conflicting DLLs or system extensions. The architectural simplicity and logic of BeOS pretty much prevents software conflicts completely, but a badly written application or driver can still crash due to its own internal errors. The process of isolating the cause of a problem can be helpful when you're trying to determine what's going wrong in a specific situation. Let's take a look at another hypothetical example.

Say you're working in an imaging application called UltraSuperPaint, and you're using it to save JPEG images. You create your masterpiece, pull down File | Save As, and save to your home directory. Later, you double-click the icon of one of your new files, and … it loads up in UltraSuperPaint. But hey, UltraSuperPaint isn't your preferred JPEG viewer, so why is it doing that? You examine the file's FileType and find out that, sure enough, the file isn't of type image/jpeg, like it should be. Is there a bug in the application that's giving the wrong filetype to your JPEG files? It might be worth thinking about this a bit before sending a bug report to the program's author.

Looking more closely at the image in UltraSuperPaint, you realize that your image still includes handles and grabbers around key objects. But JPEG is a raw image format and doesn't support handles and grabbers, which are features specific to UltraSuperPaint. Going on a hunch, you remove these and save again. This time, the image is saved correctly as image/jpeg, and comes up in NetPositive when double-clicked, as you want it to. Apparently, any time non-image data is part of your creation, UltraSuperPaint defaults to saving files in its native format, and only lets you save into "open" file formats when you're working with raw images. While this may not be an optimally designed program (and a note to the developer may still be in order), you've just solved your own problem with a little bit of sleuthing.

The process of isolating problems—whether hardware or software related—always boils down to the same steps:

1.  Try to imagine what factors could possibly contribute to the problem.

2.  Eliminate as many of those factors as possible, until the problem goes away.

3.  Start adding factors back in one at a time until the problem reappears.

Only after running through these steps should you proceed to look for outside assistance. This process will also make you a more savvy user, and you'll learn something every time—guaranteed.

## Looking for Help

Once you've determined that you can't solve a problem yourself, the next step is to seek help elsewhere, which usually means using one of the many online resources available to you. These break down into two basic categories: those offered by Be itself and those offered by the community of Be users and developers via mailing lists, newsgroups, and public Web sites.

**Read before Asking**  Hundreds of thousands of users are out there running BeOS on a daily basis so the chances are likely that your problem has been encountered before. Thus, you can reasonably conclude that someone out there somewhere knows the answer to your problem. In fact, you may even find the answer published, either in official documentation or on a user-support Web site. The trick, then, is knowing where to look.

If your problem relates to BeOS itself (rather than to a specific application), the first, best place to look is in Be's collection of FAQs (frequently asked questions) at **www.be.com/support/qandas/**. You'll also find the entire FAQ collection on your hard drive at /boot/beos/documentation/The_Be_FAQs. However, the version maintained online is regularly updated, and may include answers you won't find in your local copy.

Because a common source of problems is incompatible hardware, it's a good idea to study the BeOS ready lists maintained on Be's site as well. There are separate ready lists for PowerPC and Intel versions of BeOS, both accessible from **www.be.com/products/beosreadylist.html**.

While these pages record only officially supported hardware, Be maintains an additional page for Intel users called The Probably Compatible List. Since Be frequently hears from customers who have discovered that some piece of hardware works fine despite its not being officially supported, these reports can be a useful additional resource. You'll find The Probably Compatible List at **www.be.com/support/guides/probably_compatible_intel.html**.

You'll also find an excellent (and huge) database of unsupported hardware that happens to work with BeOS at **www.befunk.com**.

 It's important to understand the difference between supported and unsupported hardware. While unsupported hardware may or may not work with BeOS, Be can't help you if you run into problems with your unsupported hardware. That's what "supported" means: you have a right to Be's customer support and service channels if you can't get something working properly. It's important to make this distinction because some of the unofficial BeOS hardware sites out there do not offer support—they sometimes use the term supported loosely, applying it to anything that happens to work.

If you're looking for drivers for your peripheral devices or I/O cards, you'll find them in two locations: at **www.be.com/beware** and at the independently run BeOS Drivers site at **www.bebox.org/bedrivers**.

If you need assistance with a specific task, this book is probably the best place to look, followed by the BeOS documentation on your hard drive (/boot/beos/documentation/User's Guide). A large collection of specific tips and tricks for various tasks and applications can be found at the author's BeOS Tip Server (**www.birdhouse.org/beos/tips/**).

**Check the Database**    In addition to the plethora of FAQs and miscellaneous informational pages on Be's site, you'll also find a vast repository of all known BeOS bugs, which you can use to find out whether the behavior you're experiencing is unique to your machine or a known bug. Of course, the bug database only covers BeOS itself, not applications, but it can be very useful in some circumstances (not to mention interesting, if you're interested in such things). Point your browser to **www.be.com/developers/developer_library/bugs/**. Even though this database is contained within the developers' section of the site, it's perfectly accessible by mere mortals.

 The bug database lives a double life: You'll find feature requests in addition to bugs here, and thus also be able to determine whether Be plans to implement your dream function.

Always search the bug/feature database thoroughly before submitting a bug report or feature request of your own. This helps reduce needless work for the Be QA staff, which in turn means it has more time left to actually work on getting bugs fixed and features implemented.

By searching on keywords related to your problem, you'll be able to determine whether you're looking at an established problem. Each bug is labeled by a Be engineer according to criteria described in Table 16.1.

### Table 16.1  Bug classifications

| Classification | Description |
| --- | --- |
| Unclassified | Be hasn't yet had a chance to look at it; this is the default for newly submitted bugs. |
| Reviewing | It's been assigned to someone at Be to evaluate. |
| Declined Feature | The feature request was declined. |
| Not a Bug | The "bug" submitted isn't actually a bug or Be couldn't reproduce the bug. |
| User Error | It's the user's error, not the system's. |
| Duplicate Feature | The feature requested was submitted by someone else earlier. |
| Duplicate Bug | The bug was submitted by someone else earlier. |
| Acknowledged Feature | The feature was acknowledged as one which could possibly be added. |
| Acknowledged Bug | The bug was placed in the queue for fixing. |
| Implemented Feature | The feature will be implemented in an upcoming BeOS release. |
| Fixed Bug | The bug will be fixed in an upcoming BeOS release. |
| Unreproducible | Be couldn't reproduce the bug. |
| Will Not Fix | It won't be fixed. |

*The bug database at Be's Web site is searchable by the general public, and lives a double life as a repository for feature requests. Bugs and feature requests are classified by the above criteria.*

Finally, there are thousands of pages of miscellaneous information on Be's Web site, many of which include advice, suggestions, and useful clues on every Be-related topic under the sun. If you didn't find what you were looking for in the FAQs, try using the search function on the site, which is accessible from the navigation bar on every page. If you get too many responses to your initial query, you can significantly narrow the results by limiting your search to specific areas of the site, such as just the developers' sections, just the press releases, or just the user documentation.

**The Support Motherpage**  Always keep your eye on `www.be.com/support`, where you'll find the motherpage for all of Be's online support services, possibly including features that weren't available at this writing.

**Supply Good Data**  When you visit a foreign country, a universal rule of thumb is that the natives are much more willing to give you assistance if you at least attempt to speak some of their language. Showing that you care enough to learn a little of the local language demonstrates that you're willing to make an effort. Similarly, neither the members of the Be mailing lists and newsgroups nor Be customer support can help you if you don't give them useful information to go on. For example, here's an extremely poor (and unfortunately common) way to ask for help online:

"I just got a new computer and when I try to boot BeOS it hangs. What am I doing wrong? HELP!!!!"

A message like this will most likely be ignored by other users (or worse, could get you flamed). If you want assistance, no matter from whom, you should be prepared to describe all of your hardware, and the exact circumstances under which the problem occurs. The plea for help above leaves the following questions hanging, all of which are crucial to anyone who might want to lend a hand:

- Are you using the PowerPC or Intel version of BeOS?
- What motherboard and chipset are you running?
- What I/O cards (video, sound, network, other) are in the machine?
- What other operating systems are on the machine?
- What kind of CD-ROM drive is in the machine?
- At which point in the boot process does it hang?
- Did the problem always exist, or did it appear after you made some other change to your configuration?

Armed with this information, other readers have enough to go on and can venture an intelligent response to your query. Not all support questions require detailed system information, of course. If BeOS is running fine but you can't get a certain kind of system query to work, for instance, it's pretty clear that your motherboard isn't at fault. It *might*, however, be relevant to state whether you're running the PPC or Intel version of BeOS (of course, the PowerPC and Intel versions of BeOS should always be identical and this should not be an issue—but it can't hurt to supply this information). Remember to try to be selective when describing the problem and which subsystems could possibly be involved. On one hand, overwhelming other users with too much irrelevant information could result in your message being deleted without being read, while supplying insufficient information for other users to venture an intelligent diagnosis could also mean being ignored. The more concise and relevant the information you supply in your help requests, the more likely you are to receive free assistance.

# Where to Go for Help

Once you've narrowed down your problem as much as possible and are prepared to describe it accurately, it's time to send out your SOS. If you're pretty sure your problem can best be solved by other users, try to use one of the two primary online forums: the beusertalk mailing list and the `comp.sys.be.help` newsgroup. If you think your problem can best be solved by direct communication with Be, you'll want to use Be's customer support services.

**beusertalk** Be runs a series of mailing lists for users and developers. We strongly recommend that anyone interested in BeOS join the beusertalk mailing list by filling out the form at **www.be.com/aboutbe/mailinglists.html**. This list has the advantage of being highly focused and is administered by a Be employee with a strong sense of appropriateness; discussions that wander off-topic are killed regularly by the list administrator. While sometimes frustrating to users, this practice prevents your mailbox from being flooded by flame wars and digressions. Considering its ever-growing size, beusertalk is surprisingly low-traffic. Users do an excellent job of helping each other solve problems of all kinds, and freely dispense tips and tricks to those who ask.

**comp.sys.be.help** If, on the other hand, you're looking for unmoderated discussion and freewheeling flame wars about often-ridiculous minutiae, you'll want to frequent the `comp.sys.be` Usenet hierarchy, which consists of:

- `comp.sys.be.misc`
- `comp.sys.be.advocacy`
- `comp.sys.be.programming`
- `comp.sys.be.help`

It's important that you respect the breakdown of this hierarchy and post your support questions only to the last of these groups. Usenet may be unmoderated and freewheeling, but users don't appreciate cross-posting of questions to irrelevant groups. Do your part to keep the noise level to a minimum.

You'll find more readers for your question in `comp.sys.be.help` than in beusertalk, but you may also find poor advice. Because Be does not officially participate in these Usenet groups, it is not responsible for any advice doled out in them … and in our experience, a lot of the advice is downright wrong. Fish around for second opinions, but above all, read the existing posts before asking questions. Your question may have been asked dozens of times before.

At this writing, the only graphical newsreader available for BeOS is called BeInformed (Chapter 11, *Network Applications*), and is available from BeWare. For those who prefer a command-line interface, ports of UNIX newsreaders such as slrn and pine are also available. If your problem prevents you from using BeOS, newsreaders exist for every operating system—scan your favorite software library (such as **www.download.com** or **www.hotfiles.com**) for keywords "usenet" or "newsreader."

***Deja What?*** While your ISP's news server may expire messages every week or so (meaning that messages posted last week may no longer be available to you), you should know about a Web-based service called DejaNews (**www.dejanews.com**), which archives *huge* amounts of Usenet messages for posterity. As of January 1998, DejaNews was spooling around six gigabytes of Usenet data to tape every single day, and had archives reaching back several years. The service is an absolutely invaluable resource for research on any topic imaginable, not just BeOS. DejaNews also offers many advanced query options to help you fine-tune your searches; look for the Power Search link on the pages.

If you don't have a newsreader, you can post new messages from within DejaNews's interface. Keep in mind that if you respond to DejaNews messages, you may be responding to a long-dead thread—be sure and check the date of the message to which you're responding. This isn't necessarily a bad thing, but you should be aware that you could be rekindling a long-dead debate.

**Be Customer Support**  If you opt to contact Be for support directly, you should use their Web-based support form if at all possible. If there's absolutely no way to get Web access, you can always send a message to **custsupport@ be.com**. However, the Web-based support form includes a panel of picklists which ensure that Be is aware of your current hardware configuration, system version, and other important parameters. This enables Be to funnel your question to the most qualified support personnel in the shortest time possible.

When you submit a support question to Be, your correspondence is given an ID number, which will be reported in the subject line of an automatically generated email reply, confirming that your message has been received and is on queue. There's no need to respond to this initial message—Be support staff will get back to you soon with an actual response.

It's extremely important that you leave the subject line of your correspondences with customer support unchanged. The ID number on the subject line ensures that your correspondence is maintained with a person familiar with your problem. Removing or altering this ID number will result in response delays and possible backtracking of ground you've already covered, in addition to a loss of any relationship you may have built with the person who first responded to your message.

# Boot Problems

With the very first release of BeOS for Intel Architecture, it was quite common to be unable to boot BeOS on existing hardware. While huge strides have been made in this department with BeOS R4, there are still a few things that may cause the boot process to be somewhat sticky.

## The Chicken and Egg Video Dilemma

Early users of BeOS for Intel faced a logical paradox in some cases. Even if you were able to obtain an updated video driver, the installation CD didn't include a mechanism to let you install it. Potential users were thus locked out until they could obtain an installation CD that already included the required driver.

Release 3.1 offered a way out of this unfortunate loop by offering a "safe boot" mode, which is still present. If a driver is not found for the existing video card, a generic grayscale video driver is used instead. The system looks pretty ugly in safe boot mode, but it does offer a way out of the "chicken and egg" dilemma. Since the system is booted, a user in this situation can then load an appropriate driver for their card from a floppy, CD, or downloaded archive.

In addition, Release 3.0 was often intolerant of "holes" in the IDE chain. For example, if you had your boot drive configured as the master drive on the first IDE bus (IDE 0) and your CD-ROM drive configured as the slave on the second bus (IDE 1), BeOS would often fail to recognize the CD-ROM until it was moved to the first bus, still as the slave. This problem has been rectified. If for some reason you're attempting to install BeOS from an old 3.0 CD, it's strongly recommended that you obtain the latest CD from Be—for many more reasons than this.

Boot problems with BeOS pretty much boil down to two possibilities. In order of likelihood, these are:

1.  Unsupported or misconfigured hardware
2.  Inability to find the boot partition

# Unsupported and Misconfigured Hardware

With R4, BeOS gained a lot more grace when it comes to the boot sequence. If something critical isn't working properly, you should no longer be facing an uninformative black screen, and most unsupported hardware should simply have no impact on the boot sequence—BeOS will just ignore devices it doesn't recognize and move along if it can. Aside from errors in the boot manager configuration, the most common cause of an unsuccessful boot attempt is that no drivers can be found to communicate with some critical hardware installed in your system—most likely the video card, which is one component BeOS can't ignore. The solution to this problem is simple: check the BeOS ready lists and either acquire hardware that is supported, or look around for drivers that have been released since the version of BeOS you have was released. To install drivers that are not on the CD, boot into safe mode (if necessary) and drop them into the appropriate folders (as described in their documentation). In the case of video drivers, you'll need to reboot—all other drivers should become available to the system immediately.

The second most common cause of unsuccessful boot attempts is physically misconfigured hardware. Even if drivers are present for both your network and sound cards, for example, the system could lock up at boot time if both of them are trying to use the same IRQ. Theoretically, this should not happen, as BeOS does some very clever juggling of IRQ resources on its own. Most problems here arise from Plug-and-Play issues and IRQ conflicts, which can arise if you're using any ISA cards in your system.

**IRQ Conflicts**    In cases where you're attempting to add new hardware to a system that's already booting properly, the case is pretty clear-cut. If the system boots but the new hardware is not recognized, then either the new hardware is not supported, or a suitable driver could not be found. In either case, the system should still boot properly. If the system suddenly refuses to boot, however, you're almost certainly facing an IRQ conflict.

The vast majority of IRQ conflicts can be resolved by disabling your cards' Plug-and-Play features and by purchasing PCI rather than ISA cards whenever possible. In addition, you can use the Device preferences panel to manually configure some cards' addresses. Usage of Device preferences is covered in Chapter 9, *Preferences and Customization*.

 Mac users: Your machine is not affected by IRQ issues, and boot problems almost certainly boil down to unsupported hardware.

## *The IRQ Dilemma*

IRQ stands for Interrupt Request Queue and represents a sort of communications channel from the I/O device to the motherboard to the operating system. x86 motherboards have 15 available IRQs, and these funnel messages from your mouse, system timer, video card, network card, IDE bus, SCSI adapter, and so forth, to the rest of the system. 15 may sound like a lot of IRQs, but modern computers use them up very quickly, as many of them are reserved for critical system functions that are not user-configurable. Unfortunately, this number is "locked in" to the x86 motherboard architecture; if the industry could raise this number, they would have done it long ago. Additionally, the older ISA bus still present on most motherboards for backward compatibility will not let any two devices share a single interrupt (though PCI devices can and often do share IRQs). (This issue is finally being addressed by the new USB and FireWire specifications described at **www.beosbible.com**.)

PCI stands for Peripheral Component Interconnect and is a bus standard originally developed by Intel to circumvent some of the limitations of the older ISA bus (anyone remember VLB?). PCI can run at either 33 or 66 MHz, for compatibility with older and newer motherboards alike. While PCI is technically a 64-bit bus, it's usually implemented as a 32-bit bus, and is capable of 133 megabits per second of raw throughput when running at 33 MHz in a 32-bit configuration.

IRQs for devices such as sound and network cards are traditionally set by manipulating physical "jumpers" on the cards themselves—small bridges that connect two or more tiny electronic posts. By connecting these posts in various configurations as specified in each card's documentation, you can set an IRQ manually (configuration charts are also often printed on stickers attached to cards in case you lose the documentation). The trick is to get all of your devices operating on separate IRQs, though again, PCI devices can and do share interrupts.

The situation is further complicated by the advent of Microsoft's Plug-and-Play specification, a well-meaning but badly implemented means of having cards auto-configure themselves at boot time. Plug-and-Play I/O cards are typically jumperless. This saves the user the hassle of trying to manipulate tiny jumpers, but causes all kinds of problems for non-Microsoft operating systems. Why? Because if IRQs need to be specifically declared by the user for any reason, it's done by means of software that usually runs only under DOS or Windows.

In essence, the jumperless card is one big kowtow to Microsoft by the hardware industry, and annoys BeOS, BSD, OS/2, QNX, and Linux users and developers to no end. While these cards have simplified life for many Windows users in many instances, they don't always work as advertised, and have further complicated an already messy situation. Now we have jumpered and jumperless cards side by side in many machines, in addition to cards that can't be configured easily on a Microsoft-free machine.

To put it another way, Plug-and-Play is a kludgy workaround for a process (automatic hardware detection) that BeOS handles well on its own.

***Keep a DOS Boot Floppy Handy***  Most Plug-and-Play configuration software runs under DOS, which means that you can simply boot from a DOS boot floppy, then insert a second floppy containing the configuration software, make your changes, and reboot into BeOS. Thus, you don't have to have a Windows partition on your machine if you don't want to—if you have Windows installed on another machine, make a DOS boot floppy by clicking Start | Settings | Control Panel | Add/Remove Programs | Startup Disk. Store the disk alongside the floppies that came with your hardware devices.

***Don't Confuse Jumperless with Plug-and-Play***  While it's getting harder and harder to find jumpered cards these days, don't automatically assume that all cards without jumpers are necessarily Plug-and-Play. Many card vendors have moved to jumperless cards simply because people find them easier to configure. In fact, most modern PCI cards are jumperless, even if they aren't Plug-and-Play. You'll typically have a better experience in a multi-boot environment with non-PnP cards, while there should be no functional difference between jumpered and jumperless cards … except for the fact that jumperless cards need to be configured from DOS, while jumpered cards don't.

***Keep Windows out of This***  For convenience, Be allows Windows 95/98 users to keep a shortcut on their desktop that will shut down Windows and start BeOS. Starting BeOS this way does not shut the system down all the way, however, so when BeOS comes up, your Plug-and-Play cards have already been programmed to an IRQ that worked for Windows, but that may not for BeOS. This is one of the reasons why PnP is considered a pain in the neck by users of alternative operating systems. In fact, when purchasing a new network or sound card, it's advisable to steer clear of Plug-and-Play whenever possible. Many cards make it possible to disable all Plug-and-Play functionality, effectively returning them to the state of a "normal" card. If you're comfortable configuring IRQs (either via jumpers or from configuration utility software), you'll probably have the most luck by disabling or avoiding PnP altogether.

Many modern motherboards will also let you disable PnP at the BIOS level. To enter your system's BIOS, watch carefully as your machine boots for an onscreen message reading "Press Del (or F1) to enter Setup" or something similar. Doing so lets you configure many low-level aspects of your system's operation. Every BIOS is different, so I can't give exact advice here, but dig around in the BIOS menus and screens for a setting labeled something like "Disable Plug-and-Play OS." Of course, if you do this you'll have to manually configure all of your cards, but you'll be happier in the long run.

## *Unsupported Hardware*

As mentioned earlier in this chapter, BeOS should be smart enough to ignore any nonessential hardware that it doesn't recognize, or for which it can't find a suitable driver. In other words, unsupported hardware (whether internal I/O cards or external peripheral devices) should be transparent to the system and should thus have no effect on the boot process. Of course, the logical qualifier to this blanket statement is the term nonessential. Obviously, BeOS needs to find a few pieces of hardware that are essential to operating *any* computer, such as a motherboard and its chipset/glue logic (hardware engineers sometimes call anything used to connect circuit blocks together the "glue logic"—when you hear people talking about LX versus BX motherboards, for example, they're talking about different chipsets, or glue logic sets), a bootable disk partition, a minimum amount of RAM, and a video card. While the absence of a keyboard and/or mouse won't prevent BeOS from booting, it is of course essential to have some kind of input device.

A notable exception to the need for an input device is the case of a BeOS machine functioning as a server. In this instance, it's conceivable that you might want to remove a machine's keyboard and mouse to keep people (like kids) from tampering with it (or simply to save money by not attaching a keyboard you'll never use). You could then access and operate the machine remotely via telnet. Of course, this kind of operation is restricted to tasks that can be performed from the shell. Note also that this technique does not make a machine secure, because anyone can plug in a keyboard and mouse and have at it.

If you've just added new hardware and BeOS suddenly loses the ability to boot properly, your problem is one of misconfigured hardware, not one of unsupported hardware, since BeOS ignores devices it doesn't recognize. Boot problems due to unsupported hardware are encountered when installing BeOS, not thereafter (unless you're updating your system software, and some weird new bug has been introduced). Installation is covered in depth in Chapter 3, *Installation*, but in a nutshell, the trick is to check the ready lists on Be's site *before* attempting to install the system.

 When working in your system's BIOS, change only one setting at a time, test to see if it's fixed your problem, then return to make more changes if necessary. The BIOS is complex, and many settings can affect one another. Don't change anything in the BIOS that you don't understand, and keep a written record of original settings and changes made so you can restore things to how they were if necessary.

If you don't want to disable PnP on your system, and you're having problems getting your network or sound cards to work, try booting BeOS directly (from a boot manager or floppy) rather than from the Windows shortcut. Preventing Windows from configuring your PnP card may clear up your problem. If this turns out to be the case, you'll want to configure your system to provide a boot menu at startup. (See Chapter 3 for details.)

# Inablity to Find the Boot Partition

On a computer hosting more than one operating system, an interesting battle is waged for a tiny piece of prime real estate—the venerable master boot record (MBR). This is a small chunk of disk space marked as the first to be accessed after the system comes out of POST (Power-On Self-Test). When you first power on your computer, the system inspects itself, making sure all of its ducks are in a row. "How much RAM do I have? What kind of hardware is attached to me? What kind of special operational instructions are in my BIOS?" After this process is complete, disk drives specified in the BIOS as bootable drives are inspected for the presence of the MBR, which in turn sends back information on how the system should be booted. If you have only Windows on your system, the MBR simply boots Windows; but if more than one operating system is present, the MBR is often occupied by a special boot

## *Building a Boot Floppy*

BeOS boot floppies are not formatted with BFS and can't be mounted from the Tracker. Instead, the disk is filled to the brim with boot code in the form of raw data. The single file that occupies a boot floppy is called an image file, and must be installed on the floppy by using the dd utility, a tool used for transferring data between raw (unformatted) storage devices.

If you purchased BeOS on CD-ROM but later upgraded to a later version via download (probably through BeDepot), it's important that you follow Be's recommendation and create a new boot floppy commensurate with the new OS version—booting a later version of the operating system from a boot floppy created for an earlier version can have unpredictable results. The converse is not true, however; later boot floppies can always boot earlier versions of the operating system. In addition, floppies are by far the most unreliable of all storage media, so it's a good idea to make an extra boot floppy or two anyway, just to be safe.

You'll always be able to download the current boot image from **www.bedepot.com**, where you'll find instructions similar to these. After downloading and decompressing the .zip archive, you'll have a new file with a name something like intel_boot_floppy_r3.2.img. Open a Terminal window and cd to the same directory. Insert a floppy disk in your drive (keeping in mind that you'll lose any data currently on this disk). There's no need to delete its files or format it first—dd will overwrite the entire disk.

To transfer the image, type:

```
dd if=intel_boot_floppy_r3.2.img of=/dev/disk/floppy/raw
```

Naturally, you'll need to replace the filename (the part directly following if=) in this example with the name of the one you've downloaded. dd will complain if you get the filename wrong, so watch the punctuation. In the command above, if stands for input file and of stands for output file. The process takes longer than you might expect—your floppy drive will spin for a few loader, such as LILO, the BeOS boot loader, System Commander, or NT's native boot loader.

Unfortunately, the installation routines of some operating systems don't play nice with the MBR. Obnoxiously operating as if they're the only system you'll ever want to run, they don't even bother to recognize what's currently inhabiting the MBR, and insert their own instructions there. For example, if you already have a working BeOS installation and then decide to add Windows to your machine later, Windows will stomp all over your MBR; the next time you boot your system, you'll find it booting straight into Windows. Yes, Virginia, there are some rather insidious operating systems in this world.

One of the most common ways to step in this ugly puddle is to upgrade Windows 95 to Windows 98 on a system already multi-booting with BeOS. Fortunately, the DOS MBR always makes a backup, which you can restore

minutes. To speed up the process, you can optionally insert the argument bs=9k just after the dd, which will cause dd to create one track at a time, thereby finishing faster. When the command prompt returns, take the extra measure of caution and flush the data manually by typing sync. Remember that if you've upgraded your version of BeOS, you'll need to mark this as your new boot floppy for future reference.

While downloading a boot image from BeDepot or Be's Web site guarantees that you'll always get the latest version, you can also create a perfectly functional boot floppy by applying the dd command to the boot image already resident on your system—you'll find this file at /boot/beos/system/zbeos.

### BeOS Boot Floppies from Linux and Windows

If for any reason you're not able to boot into BeOS to create a boot floppy, it's possible to create one from other operating systems as well. Linux users also use the dd command for this purpose, but they'll need to reference the floppy device differently:

```
dd bs=9k if=intel_boot_floppy_r3.2.img of=/dev/fd0
```

Windows users need to use the rawrite tool, rather than dd. You can download rawrite from many Linux and FreeBSD Web and FTP sites; **ftp://ftp.freebsd.org/.25/FreeBSD/tools/** is a good one. If you're downloading the BeOS boot image or rawrite via FTP, make sure your FTP client is in binary mode—ASCII transfers render all binary files unusable.

Once you've got both rawrite.exe and the image file, place them in the same directory, open a DOS window, and type rawrite. When asked for the source file, type intel_boot_floppy_r3.2.img. When asked for a destination, enter your floppy drive's letter, such as a: or b:.

Boot floppies created under BeOS, Windows, and Linux are identical—there is no disadvantage to any of these methods.

via an undocumented option. After Windows has had its way with your boot record, boot to a DOS prompt and type

```
fdisk /mbr
```

This will restore the version of the MBR that was in use prior to the upgrade. For example, if you had System Commander in the boot record previously, System Commander will be restored. If Bootman occupied the MBR, Bootman will be restored. Depending on the particular boot loader, you may have to specify the new version of Windows now present; however, it will still remember and properly boot BeOS, Linux, or whatever else is running on your system.

 It's important to distinguish between the operating systems recognized by the master boot record and those that actually reside on your disk volume(s). Even though the first boot after installing another operating system may make it appear that your other OSs have vanished, this is almost certainly not the case. Unless you've done something rash with a disk partitioning or formatting utility along the way, your other systems are there—you just need to indicate their presence once again to your boot loader, whatever that may be. Don't panic, don't reformat your hard drive, and don't dive for the phone. Just try the fdisk /mbr trick. If for some reason that doesn't work, try reinstalling the boot loader software (if you're using a third-party utility like System Commander) or the operating system that you were using for a boot loader (if, for instance, you were using Windows NT's boot loader).

More information on multiple partitions and boot loaders can be found in Chapter 3.

 ***Garbage Onscreen at Boot Time*** **If you're attempting to boot from hard disk or floppy and you get nothing but strings of 1s and 0s or ASCII garbage, the cause is most likely a corrupt boot loader. If this is happening with a boot floppy, just trash the floppy and make a new one (from Windows or Linux if necessary). Use a brand new floppy disk to eliminate the possibility of another bad floppy, especially if most of yours are old and have been sitting around for a long time (which is increasingly true for many of us as the floppy disk fades into obsolescence). If this is happening from the hard disk, reinstall your boot loader. See Chapter 3.**

# Trapping Debug Information

Be takes bugs so seriously that they built a debug_server right into the system, the sole responsibility of which is to "listen in" on communications between software, hardware, and the operating system. The output of the debug_server is plain text, but Shakespeare it's not. For the most part, only programmers and hardcore silicon jocks can make heads or tails of it. However, if you ever get into a jam and end up in correspondence with Be's support staff, they may ask you for a copy of your debug output, which will help them determine exactly what's going on in your machine. On the other hand, you may just be insatiably curious and want to see a log of your system's communications with itself.

Debug output takes two basic forms, the one related to software and one to hardware. Even if most of it reads like Greek, it's worth knowing how to trap debug output so it'll be easier to work with support staffs (either application vendors' or Be's). Not to mention the fact that it makes for great cocktail party conversation and gets you in good with geeks.

## The Application Debugger

To enable application (software) debugging on your machine, open up the file /boot/home/config/boot/UserSetupEnvironment (if you only have a file called UserSetupEnvironment.sample, duplicate it and rename the duplicate without .sample on the end), and look for a line reading

```
# export BEDEBUG=true
```

Uncomment this line by deleting the # symbol in front of it. If your file doesn't have this line, you can type it in anywhere. Save the script and restart your machine. The next time one of your applications misbehaves, you'll know all about it, because a Terminal window will pop up in your face, offering a series of mysterious messages from the kernel. You can close these debug windows when they appear without ill effect. One of the most interesting things about having debugging turned on is that you may suddenly realize that some applications you thought were nicely behaved have been running on buggy code all along.

 The debug window that appears here, by the way, is the same window that appears when an application crashes and you click the Details button instead of OK.

While it's possible to type into a debug Terminal window, there's not much that an end-user can enter here to get useful or interesting information. However, if you need to send a bug report to an application developer, type sc (to get a "stack trace") into the window, then copy and paste the result into an email message to the developer. You can then close the debug window.

## Hardware Debug Output

As your system boots and goes through the process of initializing hardware, running its scripts, starting up servers, and so forth, it keeps a detailed account every step of the way. And if you press the magic key (see below) during the boot process, it sends all of this information straight to one of your serial ports. Interested in a glimpse of the world as seen through BeOS as it's waking up? You'll need a second computer, a crossed serial cable (also known as a null modem cable), and a generic communications program. BeOS includes the SerialConnect application, which is well-suited to the task. Windows has the built-in HyperTerm, and Mac users will need to use a standard serial cable (you can borrow one from a serial printer) and a third-party communications utility such as ProTerm, ProComm, or WhiteKnight.

Standard x86 hardware runs serial communications through serial port 1 (/dev/ports/serial1), Macs run them through the modem port (/dev/modem under BeOS/PPC), and the BeBox utilizes serial port 4 (/dev/ports/serial4). Once you've hooked up your cables, launch some communications software on the receiving machine and set it to 19,200 baud, 8 bits, no parity, 1 stop bit (you'll find these settings somewhere in its preferences menu). Now turn on the BeOS machine and keep your finger poised above the F1 key. When you see the first BeOS boot screen, press F1. If everything is set up properly and your F1 timing was good, debug output from the BeOS kernel will start to scroll by in your communications program. From there, you should be able to save it to a buffer or file for posterity (or technical support).

```
/boot/beos/system/add-ons/app_server/iridium refuse the job
Try to hire add-on /boot/beos/system/add-ons/app_server/s3 as graphic driver...
S3 B_OPEN_GRAPHICS_CARD isa_IO is 0x12152000
theMem: 2048, spaces: 0x00008c0f
Setting mode: 800x600x32@68.036293
/boot/beos/system/add-ons/app_server/s3 is the new graphic driver...
No changes in dir : /boot/beos/etc/fonts/ttfonts
Yikes! not ser-mouse motion data (0x8 0x0 0x1)!
Registering Floppy Motor off Daemon.
ether: probing at port 300, mem 000c8000 (irq 5).
ne2000 ethernet card found - 00:40:33:91:5a:9f
rvn: 48: inode @ 0x57f400 (270360) has bad magic 0x1
```

*Figure 16.01*

*A heavily edited excerpt from a BeBox's debug output during the system boot sequence. The top two lines show one video driver "refusing" the job of working with the video card, and the next accepting the position. Further down, you can see video modes being set, acknowledgement of the floppy drive unit, and network cards being probed. Not exactly scintillating beach reading.*

***Debug on Shutdown*** If you keep the receiving machine up and running for the duration of your BeOS session, more debug output will be spewed out during the shutdown process, which may prove useful if you're experiencing any kind of ongoing problems during shutdown.

# Application Problems

In general, unpredictable applications are the fault of the application developer, not of BeOS itself. If a particular application crashes regularly or os otherwise erratic, a polite email message to the developer or vendor is in order (you can almost always find an appropriate email address in the application's documentation or on the site from which you downloaded it). There are, however, a few places where applications and BeOS intersect.

## Walk of the Undead (Applications That Refuse to Die)

The BeOS User Interface Guidelines declare that when the last window of an application is closed, the application should quit entirely and clean up after itself. This means that its entry should disappear from the Deskbar and all hold on system memory should be erased. On occasion, however, a buggy app won't let go, and will cling to life desperately with its last remaining thread, a ghost of its former self.

Fortunately, there are a number of ways to permanently remove faulty apps. The first and easiest thing to try is to hold down Alt+Ctrl+Shift on the *right* side of your keyboard (Mac users: Shift+Option+Command on either side) while simultaneously clicking the application's entry in the Deskbar. Most of the time, this will put the poor bugger to sleep for good. If that doesn't work, it's time for Plan B: manual thread management.

There are two ways to manage threads yourself: via special GUI applications and via the Terminal.

**GUI Thread Management** There are a number of freeware and shareware thread managers available for download from BeWare, and I recommend that you keep at least one of them on your system. Not only do these allow for simplified thread assassination, but many of them also report interesting tidbits on system memory and CPU utilization. Two of the best such utilities available at this writing are TManager and TeamKiller, both available on BeWare. TeamKiller is lighter and faster to load, while TManager provides much more detailed information. You can kill a thread in either by selecting it and hitting Alt+K.

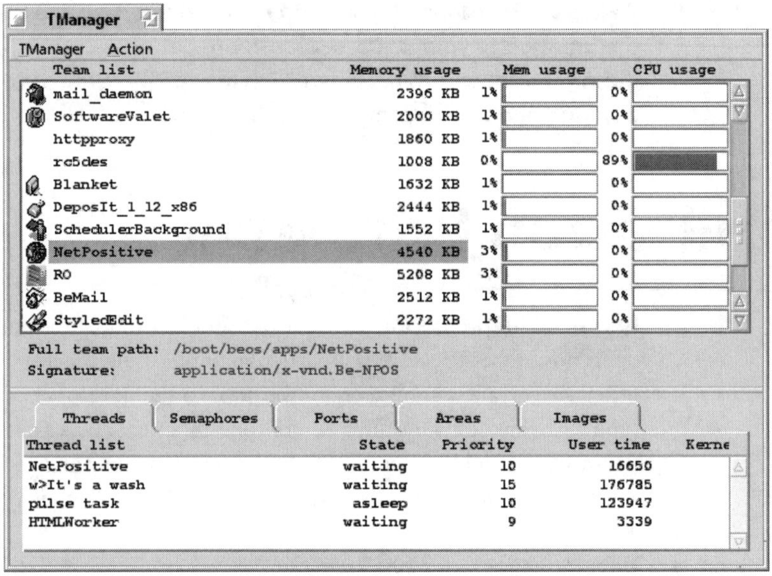

**Figure 16.02**

*TManager displays all running teams in its upper pane, along with histograms reporting memory and CPU utilization. Select a team, and its threads appear in the lower window. Kill a thread or team by selecting it and hitting Alt+K.*

**Terminal Thread Management** If you don't have a GUI thread manager already installed on your system, or if you simply prefer working at the command line, you can kill threads manually. Every running thread is assigned an ID number, and you can learn these IDs by typing ps into the Terminal. The output of ps is long and unwieldy, so you'll want to run its output through grep to find just the teams and threads containing keywords related to the task you want dead. Alternatively, use the less command to move through the output of ps one page at a time. See Chapter 6, *The Terminal*, for details on using grep and less.

Try this: Open two Terminal windows. In one of them, type yes and hit Enter. An endless stream of "y"s will start to flow. In the other Terminal window, type ps | grep yes. You'll see output something like this:

```
/bin/yes (team 69)
    207                    yes rdy 10   14801   69326
/bin/grep yes (team 79)
```

Note that the last line is reporting on the activity of the grep command itself, which is irrelevant to our task. What matters is the ID number of the yes command, which in this instance was 207. Now type kill 207 and the stream of "y"s in the first Terminal window will come to an abrupt halt. You can use this technique on any running thread, whether it relates to a Terminal command or a GUI application. Note, however, that many applications operate with more than one thread at a time so you'll need to kill them all separately to ensure the application in question is really dead.

An easy way to do this is to download the utility `killteam` from BeWare, and install it in `/boot/home/config/bin`. You'll be able to use its keyword feature to reduce all of this to a single command, such as `killteam -s yes` (the `-s` flag means that `killteam` should search on keywords).

Finally, if you installed the `hey` utility you can use `hey`'s simple syntax:

```
hey yes quit
```

 If the purpose of a thread isn't clear to you from reading its name, don't kill it! There are tons of threads running behind the scenes at any one time that are essential to BeOS's health and sanity. Kill the wrong thread and you could cut off critical system processes or lock up the system.

## Recover Application Settings

On occasion, applications can get into a funk and refuse to behave properly when they once functioned perfectly. While this is by no means common, when it does happen it's usually the result of a corrupt settings file. Applications typically store their settings in a file (or a folder full of files) in the `/boot/home/config/settings` hierarchy. For instance, NetPositive's settings file is at `/boot/home/config/settings/NetPositive/settings`. If NetPositive suddenly refuses to launch, a probable cause is that this file has been improperly written to or otherwise tampered with.

Fortunately, any well-written application that requires a settings file is capable of generating one if it doesn't find one at launch time. Thus, renaming the existing settings file and restarting the application is a good way to get a brand new one. Since you only renamed the settings file rather than deleting it, you've still got a backup copy, which you can try and open in a text editor later on to retrieve old settings if necessary. When you rename the file, give it a name similar to the original so you'll be able to find it easily in the future, if need be.

 Not all settings files are text files—some are stored as binary data (or as zero-byte files with settings stored in attributes) and are not user-editable. You can generally tell these apart at a glance by looking at their icons in the Tracker; binary settings files just get the generic blue icon, rather than a text icon. Binary settings files cannot be launched by double-clicking.

 Deleting an application's settings file will cause the application to launch in the same state that it did when you first installed it. For example, deleting NetPositive's settings file would cause it to forget your preferred fonts, home page, and cache configuration. It would not, however, affect your bookmark collection because this is stored in the `Bookmarks` subdirectory, not in the settings file itself.

***Multiple Personalities*** If, for some reason, you'd like to have a certain application configured to toggle settings (or if you want to share an application with another user on the same machine, before BeOS officially goes multi-user), you can always keep multiple settings files around and rename one of them to the name the application looks for as it's launching. In some cases, you can create two sets of settings that completely change the way an application looks and feels. You can even write scripts that find possible settings files and do the renaming for you; download TermSet from www.beosbible.com for a working example of this technique.

 ***Virgin Installations*** If a corrupt settings file is the problem, reinstalling the application will probably not fix whatever is wrong. This is because installation routines typically respect and preserve existing settings files. If you do need to reinstall an application and also want a new settings file, rename the settings file first, then reinstall.

# Video Problems

Video drivers for BeOS have been proven to be very stable; when they work, they work as advertised. The first rule of troubleshooting video conflicts is always to ensure that you're running the most recent available version of the video driver for your card. Check Be's driver updates page at **www.be.com/support/updates/**, or the card manufacturer's Web site, to see if an updated version has become available. Even if you don't have video problems, it's possible that an updated driver could improve performance or enable previously unavailable features, such as 3D OpenGL hardware acceleration.

Unlike Windows video drivers, BeOS video drivers always come in a single, neat file. If you want to install a new driver, use the Tracker to open up the folder /boot/home/config/add-ons/app_server, and install the driver there.

 As described in Chapter 5, *Files and the Tracker*, there are user-level and system-level add-ons directories. Drivers installed with BeOS live in /boot/beos/system/add-ons/app_server, while any drivers you add to the system yourself go in /boot/home/config/add-ons/app_server. Because user-level directories will supersede system-level directories, the user-added driver will be used in cases where the same driver is found in both locations.

After installing the driver, restart your machine (due to the fact that it's one of the first things loaded at boot time, the app_server is one of very few BeOS functions that cannot be restarted without rebooting the machine).

*Determining Your Video Chipset*  You'll notice that the folder containing video drivers contains both driver files named for specific brands of cards and others bearing more generic names. For example, in BeOS for Intel you'll find files with `Matrox` in their names, and others with names like `cirrus`. The drivers with generic names refer not to specific cards, but to *any* card using the named chipset. The `s3` driver, for instance, will run most any card using the once-ubiquitous S3 video chipset. If you don't know what chipset is being used by your video card, there are three ways to find out:

- Watch your boot sequence at startup carefully—the video chipset is often the first or second item to appear onscreen.

- Open up your computer, carefully remove your video card, and examine it for large, square, flat chips. One or more of them will have a stamp, such as "S3" or "cirrus." For example, Diamond Multimedia doesn't make their own video chips—they usually purchase them from S3 instead.

- Check the control panel, setup utility, or configuration software for the card from within another operating system on the same machine.

## Screen Size Problems

**Within BeOS**  There have been bugs in a few of the BeOS video drivers that occasionally cause them to not snap back to previous settings after being reset for any reason. For example, the Matrox Millennium driver sometimes gets confused when coming out of Game Kit mode. After you play a Game Kit game, screen saver, or demo (such as Life), it's possible that the edges of your desktop may appear partially off the edge of your screen. There doesn't appear to be any rhyme or reason to this occurrence; it happens to some users randomly, and only occasionally. If this happens, the easiest fix is to open the Screen preferences panel and switch momentarily to a different resolution, then back again. For instance, if you're running at 1024×768, you might switch to 800×600 and then back again—this should clear it up. Alternatively, if you keep some workspaces set at different resolutions, just toggle.

**Between Other Operating Systems**  The width of your desktop relative to the frame (bezel) of your monitor is partially a function of the current refresh rate. Modern multisync monitors are able to memorize settings for a wide variety of resolution, color depth, and refresh rate configurations, which is why you're able to boot, say, into Windows at 800×600 and BeOS at 1024×768 and still have the edges of your desktop line up properly with the edges of your monitor in both systems. However, the memory in some monitors may get confused if the refresh rate is set differently between various operating systems. In the example above, if Windows is set to 67 Hz and BeOS is set to 70 Hz, you may find that the screen image lines up differently between the two operating systems. Setting these to identical rates should clear up the problem for good and result in no visible display quality differences. It's generally much easier to fine-tune these settings in BeOS than it is in Windows or Linux because Windows refresh controls vary from one video driver to the next, and Linux refresh settings have to be tweaked via text files. Mac refresh settings can be tweaked from the Monitors control panel, but often don't offer fine granularity without the assistance of third-party utilities. In general, you'll find it easier to make BeOS match the settings of your other operating systems rather than vice versa.

While most modern monitors are capable of handling very high refresh frequencies and have trip circuits built in to protect them from being driven too hard, the usual caveats about refresh rates apply: Setting your refresh rate higher than your monitor can handle is pretty much the only way to physically damage your hardware by tweaking software controls. Monitors have been known to go up in flames from injudicious refresh rate tweaking; consult your monitor's documentation to learn its maximum safe refresh frequency before adjusting these controls. See Chapter 9 for more on refresh rates.

## BeOS Appears in Grayscale

If you boot into BeOS and the desktop environment appears in grayscale rather than in color, then BeOS has started in "safe boot" mode. This happens any time a compatible driver for your installed video card cannot be found. Safe boot mode is not damaging in any way, but you don't want to stay in it for long—not only is it U-G-L-Y (you ain't got no alibi!), but it also consumes about 50% of your processor resources, making BeOS noticeably less responsive.

***Video Sanity*** **If your video display ever becomes unreadable as a result of over-tweaking, you can always return to a "sane" video mode by hitting Control+Alt+Shift+F12. This will immediately restore your settings to 640×480, 8-bit, 60 Hz—the factory defaults.**

The only fix available to is to obtain and install a compatible video driver. You can find updated drivers on Be's site at **www.be.com/support/updates/**, or one may be included on a floppy disk or CD that came with your video card. You may also want to check the card manufacturer's Web site for a more recent version.

***Fixed-Frequency Monitors*** **If you're having trouble getting the Screen preferences panel to behave in general, make sure you don't have a fixed-frequency monitor. These less expensive, less flexible monitors do work with BeOS, but barely. (See www.beosbible.com for more information on hardware and peripherals.)**

# Sound Problems

As with video, audio on BeOS is reliable, too. Once it's working, it keeps working. If you're reading this, though, there's a good chance you're having trouble getting sound out of BeOS. Only a few possible causes exist.

## No Sound at All

The easiest way to check for continuity in your audio subsystem is to invoke the system beep. Open a Terminal and hit Ctrl+G. If sound comes out of your internal speaker, then your audio card is either not installed or not recognized. If the sound card is in place and working, the beep will be routed to your speakers.

If you can't get a peep out of BeOS, the problem can only be one of two things: an incompatible sound card driver or misconfigured hardware. If you have a multi-boot system, check to make sure you've got sound under Windows, Linux, or any other operating system. If so, the problem is purely driver-related; check **www.be.com/support/updates/** for updates or contact your hardware vendor to ask for BeOS driver support.

 **When contacting hardware vendors and asking for BeOS support, always state that you're a customer who is considering using another vendor's products because they do offer BeOS support. Threatening (nicely) to take your business elsewhere will make certain that your comments get forwarded to the right people. Take advantage of all opportunities to "vote" for BeOS in the marketplace ...** *without* **slipping into obnoxious evangelism.**

BeOS audio drivers are self-contained in single files, stored in the subdirectories /boot/beos/system/add-ons/kernel/drivers or /boot/home/config/add-ons/kernel/drivers. As always, the system-level folder contains system-provided drivers, and user-added drivers should go in the user-level folder (see Chapter 5 for details on the difference). To install a new audio driver, just drag it into /boot/home/config/add-ons/kernel/drivers. You should not need to reboot your machine for the new driver to take effect.

If you're not getting sound under any operating system, check to make sure the line from your sound card to your speakers is connected to the right output on the card (it should be marked "line out"). Many sound cards also have a volume control on them—make sure that it isn't turned down all the way. Finally, many computer speaker setups have a volume control built into the cable between the speakers and the sound card or amplifier. Check this as well.

When dealing with "no sound" situations, carefully turn volume dials all the way down before plugging cords into jacks. You could end up with a blast of ear-splitting noise, or blown speakers, if sound emerges suddenly while the volume is turned all the way up.

 **Sample Audio Files**  Beyond the Ctrl+G trick above, one of the best ways to test for sound on a fresh installation is to head straight for the /optional/sound **folder (you'll find this on the installation CD if you opted out of the optional items during installation) and double-click one of the files there. If you want continuous sound in order to work through cabling and configuration problems, you'll need something that lasts for a long time—try putting an audio CD in your CD-ROM drive and playing it from the** /boot/apps/CDPlayer **application.**

## No Sound from Specific Applications

If you know sound is working on your BeOS system in general but you can't seem to get an audio signal from a particular application, the most likely cause is that input toggles aren't set properly, either in BeOS or in the application itself. As described in Chapter 9 the Input tab of the Audio preferences panel includes an Input Source picklist that lets you toggle between receiving audio signals from your CD-ROM drive and the Line In or Microphone jacks on your sound card. Make sure the appropriate source is selected. In addition, some audio applications include input toggles of their own that must be set appropriately as well.

**Figure 16.03**

*After checking the input radio buttons in the Audio preferences panel, check any application-specific input settings. For example, ObjektSynth (pictured) will operate on the ADC (incoming) or DAC (outgoing) streams. Look around in your application's settings or preferences menus for similar options, as an incorrect setting here could prevent you from hearing any sound at all from that application.*

## Sound Is Too Quiet

If the signal coming out of your sound card is barely audible, chances are likely you're dealing with a slightly different version of a sound card than the one for which your driver was originally written (see the sidebar *Keeping Up with Changing Hardware*). The only cure for this situation is to obtain and install an updated driver.

### *Keeping Up with Changing Hardware*

One of the more frustrating aspects of dealing with the chaotic world of Intel hardware is the fact that specifications and chipsets change so often. When manufacturers do this, they often do so with little or no warning. They may tell Microsoft right away, but there's a good chance that Be may not hear about the change until their customers complain. Thus, a driver written by Be that worked perfectly with off-the-shelf hardware last month may not work for new purchasers of supposedly identical hardware. Meanwhile, Be gets blamed for advertising that certain hardware is supported and then having it fail in the field. The only fix in a situation like this (which I've seen happen with sound, network, and video capture boards alike) is for Be to obtain a later version of the hardware and revise its drivers.

# Network Problems

Few things in computing are as frustrating as not being able to connect to the outside world. Fortunately, networking is easier to set up and configure on BeOS than it is on any other system, and once working, it's as trouble-free as any other system service. Whether you're having trouble connecting to the Internet via PPP or to a machine across the room through your network interface card, you need to first determine whether your problem is hardware- or software-related. If you can perform these functions just fine from another operating system on the same machine, you know the hardware is configured correctly and will need to take a closer look at the settings in your Network preferences panel.

 ***Ping? Pong!*** When you're testing any Internet or TCP/IP connection, the first step is to ensure that any connection at all is possible. "ping" is the most basic, most fundamental of all TCP/IP connections because it simply tests to see whether it's possible to reach an address "out there" somewhere. ping is typically easier to work with than other connection methods due to its simplicity. For example, if you go to test your new PPP connection by checking your email and the attempt fails, you'll find that it's not easy to get BeOS to stop trying to contact the server. It's much easier to open up a Terminal window and type ping address, as in:

```
ping 192.168.0.1
```

**or**

```
ping www.be.com
```

**A successful ping attempt will return something like this:**

```
/boot/home>ping www.be.com
32 bytes from 207.126.103.9    sequence  1 round-trip-time 673.5 msecs
32 bytes from 207.126.103.9    sequence  2 round-trip-time 62.9 msecs
32 bytes from 207.126.103.9    sequence  3 round-trip-time 88.2 msecs
```

**An unsuccessful attempt will return something like this:**

```
/boot/home>ping lj123409
ping: lj123409: unknown host
```

To stop ping from pinging, tap Ctrl+C. Alternatively, you can limit the number of pings with the -c flag, for "count": ping -c 10 host. Once you've successfully pinged an address, you've established that your network server (net_server) is running, your card or modem is configured correctly, and all systems are go. However, a successful ping does not guarantee that you'll be able to connect to Web sites (your DNS settings could be missing or wrong) or check your email (the settings in the E-mail preferences applet could be wrong).

Because ping guarantees the presence of basic network services, it's used throughout this section.

## PPP Problems

If, after going through all of the steps in Chapter 4, *Get Online Fast*, you're still unable to make a connection with your ISP, then check your standard and debug settings. A couple of other common PPP problems are also addressed at the end of this section.

**Standard Settings**  Reopen the Dial-Up Networking preferences panel and recheck all of your settings. Common problems here include mistyping the phone number, choosing the wrong serial port, and choosing the wrong server type.

Double-check to make sure you've selected the modem closest to your exact model number. See Chapter 4 for information on editing the modems.ppp file to add initialization strings for unusual modems—many people find that they're able to get modems working under BeOS by taking a closer look at their init strings, and comparing them to the strings being used by MacOS, Windows, or Linux, or to the init strings posted on the manufacturer's Web site.

If simply copying the initialization string over to BeOS from another operating system or from the manufacturer's documentation doesn't do the trick, you may need to tweak the string further (though this is rare). Try adding K0 (that's a zero) to the string. If the string already contains a K# setting, replace it with K0. This disables data compression and may correct your problem. If this doesn't work, add M0 (that's a zero) to the string. If there is already a K# setting, replace it with M0. This disables error correction and may also do the trick.

 If you have an ISDN connection, remember that in most cases you'll need to dial 1+ (area code)+phone number, even when you're dialing to a location within your own area code. This typically does not count as a long-distance call.

**Debug Settings**  If you absolutely cannot make a connection no matter what you try, it's time to contact Be's customer support department, who will in all likelihood ask you to log a quick session and send them the results. To do this, open the Dial-Up Networking panel, click the Modems button, and check the box marked "Log all bytes sent/received." Attempt to log on, then log off again. Open a Terminal window and type cd /boot/var/log, then ls. You should see two files, called ppp-read.log and ppp-write.log. Zip these up by typing zip ppplog ppp*, then move the zip file to your home directory with mv ppplog.zip ~/. Attach that zip file to your return response to Be.

 These log files are a combination of printable and unprintable characters, meaning that they're very difficult to read. Unless you really know what you're looking for, it's unlikely that you'll be able to discover any useful information by examining these logs yourself.

**PPP Won't Dial**  This problem usually results from a failure of BeOS to communicate with the serial port, which in turn is normally caused by the Plug-and-Play OS option in the BIOS. Having this option enabled can cause serial ports to hang around waiting for PnP instructions from the OS, which of course BeOS does never issues. Disabling Plug-and-Play OS options in the BIOS will cure this for most people.

**Connection Begins but Isn't Completed**  If PPP dials out and begins logging into your ISP but never finishes connecting (or fails to assign you an IP address), make sure your ISP supports the PAP protocol, also known as standard PPP. If they don't, find out what authentication protocol they do use and make sure you've chosen the same settings in Dial-Up Networking. The CHAP protocol is not supported in R4, but it may be in the future, and there's always a possibility of third parties writing CHAP software—keep your eye on BeWare. You might try changing the Server Type to Manual in DUN, which will bring up a window you can use to manually log in to your ISP. This may make it easier to identify problem areas (for instance, you may have forgotten that you changed your password, or that the server is case-sensitive and you've entered your username or password in the wrong case). Finally, find out if your ISP has different dialup numbers to which you can connect; some ISPs run multiple server types, and sometimes deploy them on different dialup lines. It's surprisingly common for PPP problems to be fixed by simply dialing into a different modem pool.

***Check Be's PPP Troubleshooting Guide*** **If you're still not able to initiate a PPP connection, use another machine (or another operating system on the same machine) to check out Be's excellent PPP Troubleshooting Guide at `www.be.com/support/guides/ppp.html`.**

## Network Interface Card Problems

There are two points at which you may discover that you have a misconfigured or unsupported network interface card (NIC): upon installation or when first trying to make a network connection.

**NIC Installation Problems** After physically installing a network card and then attempting to tell BeOS about it by adding it to the Network preferences panel, you may be greeted by a message reading "Failed to initialized device." This can indicate one of several problems.

If the card is Plug-and-Play, this message probably indicates that you do not have the correct driver for this card installed in /boot/beos/system/add-ons/ net_server or /boot/home/config/add-ons/net_server. Since the Network preferences panel only allows you to install cards for which drivers already exist, this should not be a problem. However, as noted above, hardware manufacturers sometimes change their chipsets without warning, and your card may have been manufactured after the BeOS driver was written. In this case, check **www.be.com/support/updates/** to see whether Be has released an updated driver.

If the card is a non-Plug-and-Play ISA device, then BeOS was not able to allocate an available IRQ for the card, and you will have to set it to one manually. Depending on whether your card is jumpered or jumperless, you may have to do this by physically moving jumpers on the card, or by using the software configuration utility that shipped with it (for BeOS-only systems, see the sidebar *Keep a DOS Boot Floppy Handy*, above).

The nice thing about software configuration utilities is that they usually include an auto-detect routine that will set your card to the best IRQ automatically. Many utilities also include a diagnostics routine that will help you determine that the card is physically OK and that it can talk to another machine on the network. After reconfiguring your card's IRQ and DMA, return to the Network preferences panel and try again.

In some cases, it may be that you have the right driver installed but BeOS is having trouble mapping IRQs properly. You *may* be able to rectify the situation by fiddling with settings in the Devices preferences panel. See Chapter 9.

**Ping Thyself!**  If the Network preferences panel gave you no complaints when you set up your card, the chances are excellent that you're good to go. If, however, you're still not able to make a connection to the outside world, the first thing to do is to open a Terminal window and ping your own card's IP address. If the ping session is successful, then you know that BeOS sees the card—the route between the operating system and the card is open and clear. If it's not successful, you've got more tweaking to do.

If you can ping yourself but can't get to any address outside your own machine, then the problem can only lie outside of your system—in bad cables, hubs, or routers, or dead/misconfigured machines elsewhere.

**Unable to Access Local Network**  If you can ping yourself but can't reach any of the other machines on your network, start by double-checking all of your network settings. If you're positive they're correct, it's possible that the driver you're trying to use for your NIC is almost, but not quite the right driver. It may also result from having Plug-and-Play enabled in the BIOS. Be sure this is disabled and that the card you have matches the driver you're using.

 When troubleshooting network problems, always start small and work your way up. Begin with two computers connected through a hub and see if you can get a ping response across the hub. Once this is reliable, move up to a larger network, and finish with your normal network. This process helps you to isolate problems and to make sure that everything is hunky-dory on your end before blaming the network at large.

## Email Problems

Once you've established a solid network connection, it's not likely that you'll have networking problems with any application that runs over TCP/IP. However, there are a few minor difficulties that can arise.

**Outgoing Mail Is Not Sent**  After writing your first few test messages, it's possible you may notice that they've never been sent. The easiest way to test

*Figure 16.04*

*To find out whether BeOS is actually sending out the messages you've queued for delivery, run a system query on all email messages with a status of Pending.*

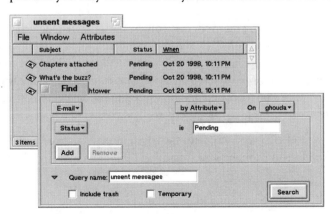

whether this is the case on your system (other than waiting to see if your friends think you're ignoring them) is to run an attribute query (see Chapter 7, *Working with Queries*) on all email messages with a status of "pending."

If you find that messages you thought you had sent are still pending, there's only one possible culprit: BeOS requires that you have *something* filled in in the Hostname field of the Network preferences panel. It doesn't matter what's filled in here, so long as it's not blank. The login name at your ISP is a good choice (if your ISP gave you a hostname separate from your login, use this). Fill in this field, restart networking, and your outgoing mail should go flying out the door next time you're connected.

## Web Problems

Again, if you're able to make any kind of Internet connection at all, you shouldn't have any difficulty accessing active Web sites. If all you get are "Failed to contact host" messages or something similar, the most likely culprit is an incorrect DNS setting in the Network preferences panel. Check with your ISP to obtain your DNS servers' IP addresses and make sure these match. Also make sure that "Disable DNS" is not checked.

*Figure 16.05*

*Without the correct DNS settings in the Network preferences dialog, BeOS has no way of knowing where to look to resolve* **www.be.com** *(for instance) into its "real" address, which is a numerical IP string. Check with your ISP to obtain your DNS servers' addresses, enter them here, and restart networking.*

## Telnet Problems

When telnetting into other machines, the Terminal identifies itself as "beterm." This happens behind the scenes so you won't be aware of it. Most of the time this won't cause any problems, but some host machines need to know they're talking to a more standard terminal type. This is especially true when telnetting into Linux boxes, where you may see the connection being initialized, but never be prompted for a username and password.

If telnet gives you any guff, the solution is to change your TERM type. To close the connection, type

```
export TERM=vt102
```

and try the connection again. If it works, add it to your .profile and you'll be set for life. If TERM=vt102 doesn't work, try TERM=vt100, TERM=ansi, or another common terminal type. (See Chapter 9 for more on tweaking .profile.)

# Disk Problems

BFS's robustness means that your disk volumes are about as safe from corruption and damage as possible; it's extremely rare for BeOS users to experience hard disk problems. However, no filesystem can protect your disk from hardware failure. Hard disks do wear out and fail from time to time. This is more true of IDE disks than of SCSI, but no moving parts in this world are immune from the forces of entropy. Your best hedge against losing data in the event of a disk failure is always to maintain regular backups.

In addition, it *is* possible to experience filesystem problems that are not hardware-related. BFS becomes more stable and robust with every release so problems become increasingly rare, but they do happen. In many cases, it's possible to resurrect a failed or corrupt volume with the tricks you'll learn in this section.

## Backups and BeOS

As with any operating system, the best defense against tragedy is to make regular system backups a part of your life. (See Chapter 10, *System Tools and Utilities*, to learn about BeB, a BeOS backup tool.) If you don't have a copy of BeB, zip has many capabilities that make the process easy. If you plan to store your backups on a non-BFS volume, it's crucial to use zip or another attribute-savvy format—otherwise if you ever need to restore a backup, you'll find many of your icons and file associations missing, in addition to any extra data associated with your files such as window position, color data, email header information, and everything else discussed in Chapter 5.

**Pre-Backup Considerations**  While you can certainly create backups by using the Tracker to copy files to another BFS-formatted partition (which will preserve your attributes), zip is easy to use and has a good compression ratio. Note that if you simply copy files from one volume to another, their modification dates will be changed, which is something you may or may not care about.

There are several ways to approach your backup, depending on how much time you want to spend on it and where you plan to store it. For example, some people put their backups on a Web or FTP server for safekeeping. This is a nice solution because you make your data safe even from catastrophic disasters like floods and fires and have the added security of the fact that your ISP probably makes regular system backups as well. The downside is the fact that your bandwidth may be limited, while your zip archives may be huge—and thus uploading the backup to the server may take a long time. In addition, your ISP may provide you with a limited amount of space.

In this case, your best bet may be to not make backups of your entire system, but just the data in your /boot/home directory tree. In the case of a restoration, you would still have to reinstall all of your applications, but you would know that all of your email, settings files, add-ons, and personal data are safe (presuming that you keep your personal data somewhere under /boot/home, as recommended elsewhere in this book). If, however, you also keep a lot of audio/visual data such as movies, audio files, and multimedia projects on your system, the resulting .zip file may be way too large to even contemplate uploading. In addition, many people storing large amounts of A/V data keep that stuff on separate disk volumes. You'll need to weigh the pros and cons of backing up that data—only you can place a value on your data.

Because BeOS does not maintain a registry similar to Windows's, and because the filesystem is simple and logical, it should be a simple matter to reinstall BeOS and then overwrite the directory tree with files extracted from your backup.

 When restoring files from a full-system backup, pay careful attention to the version of the operating system you're restoring. For example, if you last backed up your system under BeOS version 3.0, but have since upgraded to version 3.2, restoring the entire 3.0 backup over the top of a fresh 3.2 installation could potentially have unanticipated effects because certain portions of upgrades are designed to work only with each other, not with previous or future versions. While it's most likely that doing this would simply revert your system to version 3.0, play it safe and replace only your personal data, allowing the official system upgrade packages to handle versioning. In particular, refrain from overwriting the /boot/beos hierarchy when restoring, assuming you've done a fresh install to recover from your catastrophe.

Since zip files preserve your attributes, you can safely move or copy your backup files to any other filesystem, such as Mac, Windows, or Linux disk volumes, for storage (providing you have both read and write support for them).

***Save Archives Off-Site*** Remember that removable disks such as Jaz and Sparq cartridges have the added advantage of portability, so it's easier to store them off-site. Keeping your backups at a friend's house or in a secure location at the office may give you an extra layer of protection against floods, fires, and theft.

If you have a home network of two or more machines, a great solution to the storage question is to simply move your backup files from one machine to another. For example, I FTP my BeOS backups to an NTFS volume located on a machine across the room, and keep my NT backup files on a BeOS volume on the other machine. It goes without saying that it makes no sense at all to store backup files on the same physical hard disk as the system being backed up (even if that hard disk has multiple partitions and multiple operating systems). It can also be worth looking into external drive enclosures, which are inexpensive cases that allow you to turn a standard internal hard drive into a semi-portable external drive. Check online warehouses and auction sites for great deals on external enclosures.

On the other hand, if you have multiple hard disks in your machine, you'll be reasonably safe moving your backups between these disks, since it's extremely unlikely that two physical disks will crash at once. This solution isn't as optimal as getting the backup files off your machine entirely, but it's better than nothing.

**Backup Commands** Zip usage is covered in depth in Chapter 6. However, here's a quick summary of the most useful `zip` commands for creating backups. For easier identification of backup files later on, include the current date and possibly other descriptive content in each zip file's name. For example, we made weekly backups of the directory that contained this book while it was in progress and gave the backups names such as `biblebak.081398.zip`.

To back up everything in your home directory, type

```
zip -9ry HomeBak.date.zip /boot/home
```

where `HomeBak` is the name you give your backup and `date` is, obviously, the date. Remember: `-9` gives you maximum compression, `-r` means dig down through subdirectories, and `-y` means that links should be preserved but not followed. To back up your home directory but exclude files ending in `.zip`, `.tga`, `.tif`, `.tiff`, `.gif`, and `.jpg`, you'd use

```
zip -9ry HomeBak.date.zip /boot/home -x \*.zip \*.tga \*.tif* \.*gif \.*jpg
```

(this lets you create a lightweight backup of non-image files, while skipping any zip files hanging out in your `home` directory tree).

To create your backup on another volume on your system (so you don't have to move it there later) just use that volume's mount point in the path:

```
zip -9ry /fromage/backups/HomeBak.date.zip /boot/home
```

If you've already got a backup archive to which you want to add new or changed files, use the -u (only update changed files) and -g (add new files to the end of the archive) flags, like so:

```
zip -9ryug /path/to/archive.zip /boot/home
```

# Mouse Problems

If your mouse pointer won't move, there are three possible trouble spots on the Intel side, and one on the Mac side.

## x86 Mouse Problems

Mice do not work with IBM brand computers running BeOS. Be has yet to determine a reason for this behavior and is continuing to investigate. If this problem affects you, run a serial debug as described earlier in this chapter and send it to Be's customer support department.

Programmable and other advanced mice sometimes behave oddly. BeOS mouse drivers are compatible with vast majority of "typical" mice out there, but unusual models call for unusual drivers, which simply don't exist for BeOS at this writing. Advanced mice send the OS additional messages from their extra buttons, wheels, trackballs, touch pads, and so forth. While this situation may change in the future, your only solution may be to use a standard mouse while in BeOS.

If you have a serial (rather than PS/2) mouse, be sure the Plug-and-Play OS option is disabled in your BIOS—this usually clears serial mouse problems right up. Bus mice do not work, and probably never will.

## Macintosh Mouse Problems

On the Mac side, pretty much any ADB-compatible mouse in the universe should just work. Be does not maintain a list of known working mice, but they have tested some of the Kensington mice (in both 2- and 4-button mouse configurations) with success. If your mouse won't work with BeOS on a Macintosh or Mac clone, it simply isn't compatible.

# Disaster Recovery

There may come a day when you find yourself unable to boot your BeOS system normally for some reason. You may have accidentally made a change to an important boot script (you shouldn't be messing with scripts found under /boot/beos!), your hard drive's master boot record may have been damaged or overwritten somehow, or your hard drive mechanism could be on its last legs. Whatever the reason, don't panic, and remember: It's extremely unlikely that the actual data on your BeOS partition has been affected; it's probably just become hidden to the boot sequence for some reason. Regardless, rest assured that there's almost always a way to access that hidden data—you'll just have to go through the back door.

When you can't boot from your hard disk normally but still need to get into your system to either salvage files or repair whatever it is that's preventing a normal boot, you have two options. I'll summarize these options first, then we'll look more closely at each one.

- **Bypassing the bootloader:** Boot from your hard disk as usual, but bypass the normal bootloader (whether it be System Commander, LILO, or anything else) with the assistance of a BeOS boot floppy. BeOS will operate normally, and your usual /boot partition will still be your /boot partition. Use this method when something has gone wrong with your master boot record or your boot manager—any time you know that your BeOS partition is intact but you can't access it by booting from hard disk.

- **Bypassing both the bootloader and the hard disk:** Boot from the BeOS installation CD, bypassing both the bootloader and your normal boot drive. When you boot from CD, your system will not appear as it normally does because you've booted a copy of BeOS that lives on the CD ("virgin" BeOS). Once you've booted from the CD, you have two choices: You can either install (or reinstall) BeOS, or you can launch applications from the CD that will help you mount and work on your other partitions.

 Much of the emergency boot process described here is identical for PowerPC and x86 users, though it differs in some areas. Specifically, Mac users need not worry about boot floppies. See the sidebar *Emergency-Booting BeOS on the Mac* later in this section for Mac-specific details.

I strongly recommend that you practice some of the emergency procedures outlined in this section when your system is healthy, so you'll be well-prepared should your system ever become terminally ill. Knowing the Emergency Boot Drill can save your butt.

Both of the emergency boot methods outlined above involve using the BeOS boot floppy (although there is an alternative—we'll get to that in a bit). A boot floppy should have been in the package when you purchased BeOS; you probably used it to get your BeOS installation off the ground. If your floppy has been lost or damaged, or is outdated, it's very easy to create a new one (see the sidebar *Building a Boot Floppy* in this chapter). Because a boot floppy is a critical piece of software, it makes sense to create an extra just in case. Do it now, don't regret it later.

 The BeOS boot floppy contains 1.47MB of tightly compressed bootstrap code—just enough loader and kernel to negotiate the handoff of control from your system's hardware to the operating system. Unlike Windows boot floppies, BeOS boot floppies are not readable and writeable in the normal sense—you can't mount them from the Tracker, you can't edit startup files to accommodate special drivers, and so forth. This is a trait BeOS shares with Linux.

 It's important that your boot floppy not be older than the version of the operating system you're trying to boot. There's no guarantee that an earlier boot floppy will launch a later version of the operating system, though all BeOS boot floppies can launch earlier versions of the operating system, with one exception: Because the system's binary format changed between R3 and R4 (Intel only), an R3 boot floppy will find only R3 and earlier partitions, while R4 boot floppies will find only R4 partitions. In other words, you can't boot an R3 partition with an R4 boot floppy. However, an R3.2 floppy can boot R3.1 or R3.0, and so on.

## Bypassing the Bootloader

The first emergency boot option does not involve the installation CD—you'll be booting your system normally, but using the bootloader on the floppy rather than the one on your hard disk. One of the most common causes of non-functioning bootloaders is that some OS installation routines don't play nice. Windows, for example, is known for stomping all over the master boot record during installations and upgrades, requiring the reinstallation of the bootloader after the upgrade. A boot floppy can get you back into your BeOS system quickly in such a case. Remember that even if BeOS disappears from your boot menu, there's no reason to assume that its actual partition(s) were wiped out—they've just become temporarily hidden.

Insert the boot floppy and turn on your system. If there's a bootable BeOS partition on any of your hard drives, the boot floppy will find it. Note, however, that getting up and running this way doesn't fix your problem. You can keep booting from floppy for the rest of your life if you like, but what you really want to do is fix that boot record. You'll find suggestions on that in the section *Unable to Find Boot Partition*.

## Bypassing the Bootloader and the Hard Disk

The second emergency boot option is the key to disaster recovery. By booting from the BeOS installation CD instead of from your hard drive, you can get up and running on a system that might otherwise be unbootable. Once up and running, you can copy data to other partitions, edit scripts that might be trying to load something nasty, delete rogue Replicants that may have taken over your desktop, or run system tools to try and repair your damaged hard disk. Again, this is worth practicing now, while your system is healthy.

**Three Ways to Boot from CD**  There are three possible ways to boot the system from your installation CD.

- The first method assumes that your boot sector is intact and that you can still get to the "Booting BeOS" screen normally. With your installation CD inserted, boot to this screen and hold down the Spacebar. A menu will appear, asking which disk medium you want to boot from. Choose the CD volume by name, and you're on your way.

- As of R4, the BeOS installation CD became fully bootable. If your boot-loader has been trashed and you can't get to the "Booting BeOS" screen at all, you can try to boot the CD directly from your system's BIOS. Most modern x86 motherboards (though not all) support booting straight from CD. To find out whether your system is capable of this, enter your system's BIOS setup utility (usually by pressing F1 or Delete just after you turn on your machine) and look through the menus onscreen for something like "Boot options." If you find an entry like this, tell your BIOS to look for the CD as the first boot device, rather than the floppy drive, which it's proba-bly set to look for now. Save your changes as you exit the BIOS, insert the installation CD, restart your computer, and BeOS will take over. This tech-nique is very handy if you lose or damage your boot floppy!

- If your boot partition is damaged and your motherboard is not capable of booting from CDs, the final recourse is to use the BeOS boot floppy in conjunction with the CD. All x86 computers default to looking first for a boot record on a floppy drive at startup. When both the BeOS boot floppy and the BeOS installation CD are found in your machine, you'll boot from the CD automatically, rather than from the hard drive.

**Welcome to Limbo**  The result of all three of these techniques is identical: When you boot from CD, BeOS starts up in a different way. The system is running and the desktop is there, but the Tracker and the Deskbar have not yet been launched. The BeOS licensing agreement will appear onscreen. Click I Agree, and you'll be facing the main Installer dialog, giving you the option to install or reinstall BeOS. You can do that if you like (see Chapter 3), but that's not what we're here for—we're on a rescue mission.

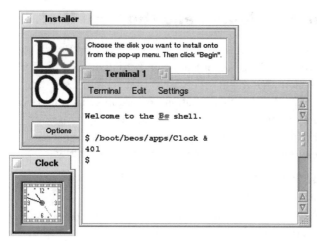

**Figure 16.06**

*After booting from the CD, you're in limbo mode—BeOS is fully functional, but it looks kind of funny because neither the Tracker nor the Deskbar is running yet. Open a Terminal as described above, and you can then launch any application from the CD by typing its path into the Terminal, followed by the & character.*

Instead of clicking any of Installer's buttons, hold down Ctrl+Alt+Shift+D on the left side of your keyboard—this will launch DriveSetup. Click again in the Installer dialog, and hit Ctrl+Alt+Shift+T to launch a Terminal window. At this point, you're in a sort of weird BeOS limbo—the system isn't fully booted in the way you're accustomed to seeing it and it's slow because it's running from CD, but at least you're in there. From here you can launch BeOS applications directly from the Terminal by typing in their paths followed by the & character. But enough about Quake—let's get back to work.

Note that the process of launching DriveSetup and the Terminal from the Installer screen may change by the time you read this. In other words, access to these tools may not always require the use of hidden keyboard shortcuts.

## Emergency-Booting BeOS on the Mac

Most of the emergency boot procedures outlined in this section apply equally to Macs and PCs, but there are some important differences. First of all, there is no such animal as a boot floppy for BeOS/PowerPC, since part of the MacOS system code always has to load before BeOS can enter the picture. Therefore, the only emergency boot option for Mac users running BeOS is to boot from the CD. Technically, you can't really boot from the CD either, for the same reason. However, once MacOS is running, you *can* force BeOS to load from CD rather than hard disk.

Start BeOS as you always do by using either the OS Chooser or BeOS Launcher. As soon as the Be logo appears, hold down the Shift key until a boot menu shows up. All bootable BeOS volumes attached to your system should be listed, and one of those should be your BeOS installation CD. If your CD is not listed, try scanning for boot volumes again by selecting that option from the list of available choices. Select this entry and you'll be off into limbo mode, and can use all of the disaster recovery techniques described in the rest of this section.

# Recovering Your Data

Now that we're here, it's all about trying to mount partitions so you can move your data to a safe place (assuming that you're here because your hard drive is on its last legs and about to give up the ghost).

**DriveSetup to the Rescue** Even though you weren't able to boot from your hard drive, it may still be possible to mount it. That, after all, is your only chance of recovering data if you do end up having to toss your hard drive. Because DriveSetup sees all physical disks attached to the system whether they have mounted partitions or not, your hard disk will almost certainly be visible in the main window.

Use the same technique covered in Chapter 9: Select your physical disk and expand the view of the partitions it contains by clicking the triangular latch to the left. Right-click in the selected area, select Mount, and look for your boot partition's name. With any luck, it won't be grayed out (which would indicate that DriveSetup thinks it's unmountable) and you can mount it now, making it available to the Terminal session waiting in the background. Even if it's grayed out and inaccessible, however, all is not necessarily lost.

DriveSetup is a powerful tool, and is capable of more than just partitioning and mounting your disk volumes. It also includes a Surface Test utility that examines every cluster on your physical disk for damage. The most likely scenario here is that your disk has sustained damage to a portion of the platter that just happened to also host your boot sector (the author has been down this road). As Surface Test does its thing, it not only marks bad blocks to prevent them from putting your data in jeopardy again, but it also moves data out of any blocks it sees as shady, and replaces it in stable disk territory. The test

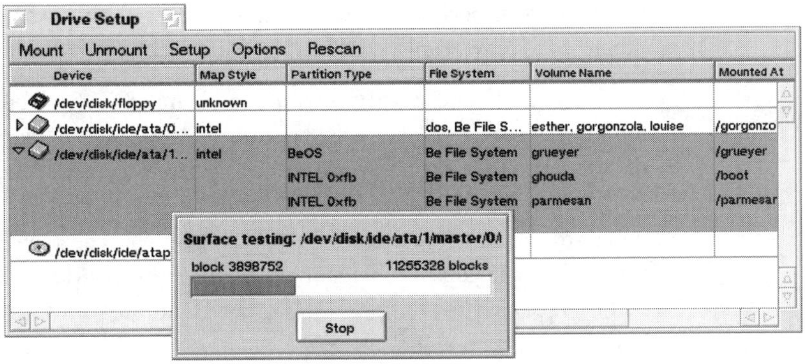

*Figure 16.07*

*It's not a bad idea to run DriveSetup's Surface Test from time to time, just to keep your volumes in optimum condition. Running it in times of emergency also may save you the drastic step of reinitializing your boot partition and starting over.*

will take a long time to run (as much as an hour, depending on the size and speed of your disk drive). When complete, it may or may not report errors. In my case, Surface Test did not report any errors … but when it was finished, my volume suddenly became mountable again, and the system resumed booting normally.

If these techniques are not successful, you have two final recourses. You can contact Be's customer support department, who may or may not be able to lead you through super-secret hacks—it's been known to happen. Or you can call it a day, hope that your backup is reasonably recent (you *do* have a backup, right?), and either reinitialize the partition (if DriveSetup will let you) or toss the hard drive in the nearest dumpster, head down to your local computer superstore, and take out a new lease on life with a brand new mega-drive.

 **Get Your Money Back**  Most drives fail within the life of their warranty if they're going to fail at all. Rather than tossing your drive, you might want to dig up that receipt and see if you're entitled to a refund or replacement.

**What Now?**  If you do manage to get your boot volume mounted, you have a decision to make: whether or not to try and boot from it now. On one hand, maybe your problem was a fluke, your system will normally, and you'll be all set. On the other hand, your problem could be a harbinger of impending failure, and you could be gambling with fate by trying to boot again. My advice is to jump into the Terminal and start trying to save your most important data.

**Terminal Emergency**  From within the Terminal, you have one last shot at trying to mount that stubborn volume. There are a few command-line tools on your system for mounting and unmounting disks, and these may be worth trying. However, I've never heard of a case where a volume could be mounted from the command line when DriveSetup had already failed. In any case, you may want to experiment with mount, unmount, and mountvolume, just to be confident that you've explored all the possibilities.

Of the three, the mountvolume command is most likely to be useful in a predicament, as it's as close as the Terminal comes to DriveSetup-like functionality. Rather than dealing with one volume at a time, mountvolume looks at all disks and partitions attached to the system. To display a chart of all volumes attached to your system (mounted or not), type mountvolume -lh. Interestingly, if you have an audio CD in your CD-ROM drive, mountvolume will even display every track as a separate volume. Not that that's useful. Your best shot at success here is to type mountvolume -all, which will cause the tool to try and mount everything it can. It's certainly worth a shot if you're in a bad way. Type mountvolume –help for a complete list of the tool's options.

The command mount uses the same syntax common on Unix systems to assign a raw storage device to a mount point in the filesystem: mount

[-t fstype] device directory. What you need to know in advance in order to use this command is that fstype (filesystem type) is bfs (though technically, you can leave this part out if you like, since the default is already bfs), and the directory is the raw "system name" for a given partition, as outlined in Chapter 5. Thus, to mount the third partition of a hard drive configured as master on your secondary IDE bus, you would use

```
mount -t bfs /dev/disk/ide/1/master/0_2 /plato
```

if you want the volume to be accessed as plato. Remember that numbering here starts from zero, so your primary IDE bus is 0 and your secondary bus is 1. Again, the easiest way to learn your system's raw device names is to mount all drives from the Tracker and then type df into the Terminal. Of course, df doesn't show you drives that aren't already mounted, so you may have to do some guessing if you don't know these already.

Unmounting is simpler: just type unmount mountpoint, as in unmount /plato.

**Saving Data from the Terminal**  Depending on your exact situation, it may or may not behoove you to save data from the Terminal. For example, if your physical disk is fine and you just have a glitch in your boot partition, then you have no way to save the data you need the most—a Catch-22. On the other hand, if you think your hard drive may be on its last legs, this would be a good time to grab what you can and head for the hills.

If you're running a multi-boot system, your Windows partitions should be writeable from within BeOS by the time you read this (Linux filesystem drivers are not on the R4 CD, but will probably be available in R5). Since that support is provided by drivers that also live on the installation CD from which you booted, those volumes should be accessible to you even when BeOS is in limbo mode. Therefore, you'll be able to zip up your most important directory structures straight to partitions belonging to other operating systems (see the zip briefing earlier in this chapter and also in Chapter 5.

Also available from the command line is a collection of utilities called mtools. Anyone who grew up on DOS will be comfortable with mtools, as they emulate the most common DOS file management commands, and even utilize drive letters rather than partition names. Crash course: just put an "m" in front of all your favorite DOS commands and do everything you would normally do. For instance, to get a directory listing from a Windows floppy, type mdir a: and hit Enter. To copy a file from BeOS to the floppy, use (for instance) mcopy /boot/home/filename a:/filename. While it's also possible to access hard disks with mtools, it takes a bit of setup, and it's really a moot point now that BeOS natively supports reading and writing to so many filesystems.

**Don't Worry** After all of that, you might be wondering if BFS is actually as stable as you thought. Don't worry—this information is here for emergency purposes, and those emergencies are pretty few and far between. Between the improved reliability of modern hard drives and BFS's journaling, most of us are far, far more likely to delete important data accidentally than we are to experience catastrophic hard disk scenarios. As always, there's no better preventive medicine than a good backup schedule.

# Tracker, Deskbar, and Replicant Problems

Considering that the Tracker is the single most complex application in BeOS, its stability and sophistication are marvels of engineering. Combined with the speed and flexibility of the underlying BFS filesystem, it's an unbeatable file management tool. People experience very few problems with the Tracker, and it undergoes constant revision and improvement.

## Killing and Restarting the Tracker

One of the Tracker's greatest vulnerabilities is the fact that it serves an umbrella function for many other parts of the operating system, and is thus connected with them for better and for worse. For example, the fact that Be has brought the notion of plug-ins to the OS itself (rather than just plug-ins for individual applications) means that the Tracker ends up getting connected to all kinds of software written by independent developers. Technically speaking, all Tracker add-ons run as threads inside the Tracker's memory space. If an add-on is badly written or unstable, it can end up bringing the Tracker down with it.

When the Tracker crashes, it usually doesn't just disappear, like a crashed application might. Instead, it sort of "hangs on by a thread," if you'll excuse the pun. It retains an entry in the Deskbar and its windows remain onscreen, though they become unresponsive. If the Tracker should crash on you, it's worth trying to kill it all the way off and then restart it again, rather than going for a full reboot. Make sure you have a Terminal window open and available, then hit it with the good ol' Vulcan Death Grip—Alt+Shift+Ctrl on the right side of your keyboard, while simultaneously left-clicking the Tracker's entry in the Deskbar. If you're lucky, all Tracker windows and all files and folders on your desktop will vanish at once. In your Terminal window, type:

```
/boot/beos/system/Tracker &
```

The Tracker should spring back to life in all its former glory, restoring your icons to the desktop and all Tracker windows to their former positions.

If the Tracker didn't die, you might want to try killing its threads and teams from the command line as described in Chapter 6, or launching one of the many graphical thread managers available. However, if the Vulcan Death Grip didn't do it, these tricks will probably fail too. Reboot time …

## Deskbar Problems

Though the Deskbar and Tracker are intimately related, they're still free-standing, independent applications. Occasionally, a Tracker crash will take the Deskbar with it, but more often, the Deskbar just keeps humming merrily along. If for some reason you do need to kill the Deskbar, you won't be able to do it with the Vulcan Death Grip. You'll need to kill off its threads and/or teams from the command line or with a graphical thread manager (see Chapter 6). To restart the Deskbar, type this into a Terminal:

```
/boot/beos/system/Deskbar &
```

## When Replicants Go Bad

While it's pretty rare, it is possible for a badly implemented Replicant to land on your screen in such a way that its handle is inaccessible, making it impossible to remove. If it's a large Replicant, it could cover up a significant portion of your desktop. While the bug that allows Replicants to do this should be fixed by the time you read this, it's still worth knowing that the Tracker stores its Replicants at /boot/home/config/settings/Tracker/tracker_shelf. Deleting this file should clear things right up.

 This trick will remove *all* Replicants from the Tracker, not just the offending one.

In very rare circumstances, it's possible for a rogue Replicant to "swell up"and take over the entire desktop, making it impossible for you to use your system (although this bug should not be present in BeOS R4). If this should happen, you'll need to boot from the BeOS installation CD (see *Disaster Recovery*, in this chapter), open up a Terminal, and delete the Tracker's shelf via the Terminal. Reboot and you should be all set.

**Zombie Replicants**   Every now and then, you may end up with a big question mark where one of your Replicants used to be. When you right-click on its handle, the context menu says "About <zombie>." This happens any time the application that's being replicated has been deleted, and there's nothing you can do to fix it but delete the Replicant, reinstall the application, and re-create the Replicant.

If you get a zombie but you know that the application hasn't been deleted, the most likely cause is a conflict of some kind with the application's signature and the way it's being seen by the Registrar. You might try deleting and re-creating the Replicant. If this doesn't work, a polite note to the developer is probably in order.

**Duplicate Files and Folders on Desktop**   As of BeOS R4, the desktop represents a unification of the desktop folders of all mounted volumes. That means that if you have multiple mounted BFS volumes on your system, you'll see files and folders from desktops on other partitions. This is a feature, not a bug, and can be very useful in some instances. If you don't like this behavior, there are two things you can do about it:

- If you like to always keep a folder on your desktop for, say, your most commonly accessed queries, don't create this folder on every desktop you boot into—just create it on one desktop, and it will automatically be accessible from all of them. Otherwise, you're going to end up with duplicate query folders on your desktop.

- If you don't like this behavior at all, you can turn it off by editing the Tracker's settings file, located at /boot/home/config/settings/Tracker/TrackerSettings. Open this file in a text editor and find the lines:

```
IntegrateNonBootBeOSDesktops on
IntegrateAllNonBootDesktops on
```

Change the on in each line to off. Save and close the settings file, then reboot your machine (or kill and restart the Tracker as described in Chapter 5.

**Unopenable Folders**   While it's very rare, it's possible to end up with folders that won't open when double-clicked. The *only* thing that can cause this to happen is that the folder has had its MIME type altered in some way—either by a sloppy script or by a slip of your own hand. If this happens on your system, right-click on the folder and select Add-Ons | FileType from the context menu. In the type field, enter:

```
application/x-vnd.Be-directory
```

Save and close the FileType panel and your folder will work again.

# Error Messages

BeOS has been called "a system without an hourglass." It would be great if we could say it were also "a system without any error messages," but it just ain't so. However, it would certainly be fair to say that you may use BeOS for a very long time without encountering anything as jarring as Windows's infamous "Blue Screen of Death" or MacOS's mysterious Type 11 or time bomb errors. Of course, we need to distinguish between two very different kinds of error messages: those that result from crashes and burns, and those that result from operator error.

## Crashing Messages

Since the advent of PR2, when BeOS crossed the stability threshold and joined other world-class operating systems in terms of uptime, it's been about as easy to crash BeOS as it is to find a decent cup of coffee in the midwest; that is to say, it's damn hard. When BeOS does crash, it usually just kind of grinds to a slow, silent halt. No error message, but it still counts as a system crash.

**Figure 16.08**

*In the vast majority of cases, crashing applications don't take the system down with them—you have memory protection to thank for that. Dismiss a dialog like this by clicking OK. If you're trouble-shooting with the application developer, they may ask you to click the Details button to launch the debugger and run a "stack trace" so you can send them the results.*

At this writing, crashing bugs were being aggressively steamrolled at Be HQ in preparation for R4. Nevertheless, bugs happen. It's a fact of life in software development, and nothing can change that. We can still take heart in BeOS's much lower crash rate compared to its Windows and Macintosh cousins. Not to mention the fact that we can reboot in a fraction of the time it takes them.

As far as genuine crash messages go, the most common one you'll see by far is the small dialog thrown onscreen by the debugger when an application crashes (Figure 16.08).

## Non-Crashing Messages

In reality, BeOS has dozens of error messages hidden away in its inner vaults—we just never get to see them. If you're feeling adventurous, open up the file /boot/develop/headers/be/support/Errors.h to peruse BeOS's general error base. This file doesn't include error messages per se, but it does give you a sense for the complex array of situations and eventualities an operating system vendor has to plan for. Many of these are clearly directed only toward programmers and are never seen by us mortals—messages for vexing situations like non-blocking semaphores whose ioctl pipes have gotten tangled around the device-seeking thread blockers from another team's POSIX linker. I hate when that happens.

Seriously though, there are a small handful of error messages you'll probably become friendly with before long. Some of the more common ones are discussed in the following sections.

**Not an Executable**    Occasionally you'll download an application, unpack it, double-click, and have a little dialog pop up in your face reading "Not an executable." This message can mean one of three things: A) you attempted to launch it on the wrong platform (it's a BeOS/PPC application that you're trying to run on BeOS/Intel or vice versa); B) you're trying to run an x86 R3 program on x86 R4 (remember—R3 and R4 use a different binary format on x86); or C) the application is dependent on a supporting library file which is not present on your system. If you're 100% positive you've downloaded the right version for your platform, then it's almost certainly a missing library problem. Have another read through the program's documentation and/or Web site. If extra libraries are required, that fact should be clearly advertised. If neither of the above is true, contact the software developer.

***Scan for Missing Libraries***    As described in Chapter 6 you can use the `strings` command to find text embedded in application binaries, then run the output through `grep` to find only the text strings that contain "lib." Try this:

```
strings ApplicationName | grep lib
```

The resulting list should tell you the names of the libraries the program depends on. Search your system for these libraries. If any turn up missing, take a closer look at the program's documentation—it may tell you where to find them. You may also want to have a look on BeWare.

Rest assured, however, that Be employees *do* test each and every upload to BeWare before making it publicly available. The software available on BeWare does work, providing it's appropriate for your system.

**No Preferred Application**    In Chapter 5 you became familiar with the process the Tracker and the Registrar use to establish a MIME type for files that arrive on your system without types. The set of rules used to make sure that alien files end up with an appropriate association get it right the vast majority of the time.

Thus, this error message almost never appears when you double-click files brought over from other operating systems—files with no MIME type aren't a problem. The difficulty comes with the occasional file that ends up on your system that *already has* a MIME type, but it's a weird one. Even then, this only presents a problem when the supertype is wrong. For example, if I send you a file with the type `text/x-sqxsyz`, it will still open in your favored text editor when double-clicked. The `text` supertype is enough to allow the Registrar to make an educated guess. However, if I send you a file with the type `x-zory/x-flipflop`, BeOS will not even be able to make an educated guess about an appropriate association because neither the type nor the supertype is registered in the system's MIME database. The situation may also arise with less common file formats from other systems, about which BeOS doesn't have a clue. For example, as of R3.2, BeOS has no idea what to do with a PDF (Acrobat) document when double-clicked, and presents the No Preferred Application dialog. BeOS will attempt to assign MIME types to files that don't have them, but it will never alter an existing type until you tell it to.

The easiest way to deal with this rare situation is to open up that file's FileType dialog and edit the type by hand. If you don't have a clue what type it should be either, try using the Same As... button in the dialog if you think it might be similar to another file on your system. Finally, simply wiping out (deleting) the MIME type, closing and saving the FileType panel, and double-clicking on the file will at least give the Tracker and Registrar the opportunity to use their own rules to attempt a determination.

 ***Help Out the Registrar*** Remember, the Registrar's internal rules specify that if an unknown file has an extension (like `.txt` or `.jpg`), and that extension is found in the MIME database, it'll use that to assign the MIME type first, rather than trying to examine the file and guess its type. You can help make this process smoother and more accurate by going into your system's global FileTypes preferences panel and adding extensions for the filetypes you transfer to BeOS on a regular basis.

**General OS Error** According to at least one Be employee, this catchall, generic message is only used by lazy programmers who haven't considered all the possible ways a clever user can muck with a good application. General OS Error is like a rare, elusive butterfly, appearing only briefly and in unpredictable places, usually in the nether recesses of the system. For example, we've encountered it when trying to mount a corrupt disk volume from the Terminal, and again months later when a beta application crashed suddenly. Well, at least it's better than a general protection fault (who's General Protection Fault, and what's he doing in my computer?).

**Permission Denied** As described in Chapter 5, BeOS is all geared up to go multiuser with a vengeance at some point in the future. In anticipation of that great day, the basic infrastructure of Unix-style permission settings is in place in the filesystem. As the primary user of your machine, you have "god" privileges and can change the permissions of any file you like (yes, even files in the /boot/beos hierarchy, even though you *must resist temptation* and leave them alone).

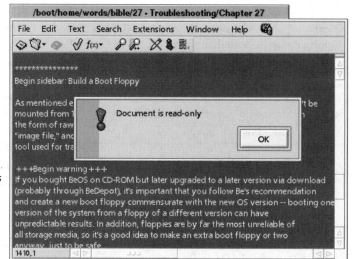

**Figure 16.09**

*Pe, the Programmer's Editor, complains when an attempt is made to alter even a single character of a write-protected document.*

 This may not always be true—Be may further write-protect the /boot/beos directory structure in an upcoming release, making these critical files and directories as secure from tampering as possible.

For now, though, you'll encounter this message when trying to edit a file that's been write-protected. If you're sure you want to edit the file in question after seeing this message, caveat emptor.

Full details on working with file permissions can be found in Chapter 6, but the short version is this: To make it possible to edit a protected file, fire up the Terminal, navigate to the file's directory, and type:

```
chmod +w filename
```

When you're done editing the file, turn write protection back on by typing `chmod -w filename`.

**Could Not Resolve Link**    Try this: Create a new folder on your desktop, create a link to it, then drag the original folder to the Trash. Double-click on the link, and you'll see an alert box like the one in Figure 16.10. BeOS is currently not very user-friendly when it comes to broken symlinks. There *are* good reasons for this, which have to do with the difficulty of maintaining links to and from other volumes, especially network volumes.

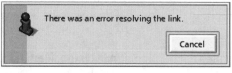

**Figure 16.10**

*Move the original file or folder to which a symlink points and the link will break. Moral of the story: Don't use symlinks for mission-critical situations where there's a chance of this happening.*

**Sorry, You Cannot Edit That Attribute!**  If you're using the Tracker to manage files and their attributes and get a message like this, it means that the attribute is set to be uneditable, either by the operating system or by the filetype itself. In some cases, such as file modification time/datestamps, there is nothing you can do about it—some attributes are permanently uneditable. In other cases, you can find the filetype's entry in your system's FileTypes preferences panel, double-click the attribute in question, and deselect the "uneditable" checkbox. Keep in mind, however, that application developers make attributes uneditable for a very good reason—do this only if you understand that there could be consequences (the application may stop working, for example).

**Insufficient Disk Space**  For the most part, this one needs no explanation—you've tried to move or copy data to a disk volume that's out of space. You'll need to delete some files, create some zip archives, or move some work to another volume.

One of the easiest ways to find any monster files you have that might be chewing up gobs of acreage is to use a query based on file size (see Chapter 7).

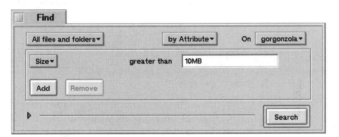

**Figure 16.11**

*To find huge files on your system, run an attribute query, change the type to Size | Greater Than, and type in a size, such as 10MB. You can conveniently delete or move files directly from the query results window.*

**B_LAUNCH_FAILED_APP_IN_TRASH**  The more you dig around in BeOS's system files, scripts, headers, and other documentation, the more you realize how unlike any other operating system company Be is. There are subtle bits of humor peppered throughout the system, but you have to dig around a fair bit to uncover the doozies. To be fair, this is a genuine error class (you'll get this message if you try to launch a file when its preferred handler is an application that you've moved to the Trash) … but I mean … c'mon!

# Appendices

# Appendix A:
# Keyboard Equivalencies and Shortcuts

BeOS's support for operation via keyboard still isn't quite what it could be. As of R4, there's still no way to run the system start to finish without an attached mouse, nor is there a way to minimize, zoom, move, or resize a window via the keyboard; and the all-important act of accessing pulldown menus via the keyboard is far too difficult if you don't have a 104-key "Windows" keyboard. Nevertheless, the system's keyboardability has improved steadily with every successive release, and we have confidence that it will one day become a keyboard junkie's dream. That said, here's a summary of all known keyboard shortcuts in BeOS R4.

## Standard Application Shortcuts

While almost every single BeOS application has a collection of hotkeys specific to itself, there are many functions commonly shared by almost all applications. Table A.01 shows the most common shortcut keys shared among most BeOS applications, but there's no guarantee that any particular application will implement them.

Hotkeys to send the cursor to end of line, start of line, end of document, and start of document are not clearly defined. Applications tend to implement these differently depending on whether the developer comes from a MacOS or Windows background. Hopefully the release of the new User Interface Guidelines will clear up this discrepancy. Note that all application hotkeys are implemented by vendors, so discrepancies are not the fault of Be or BeOS. This book strongly urges application vendors to seek community consensus on hotkey implementations.

**emacs Key Bindings** Many BeOS applications employ optional emacs-style key bindings for the convenience of those trained on this powerful Unix text-editor-cum-kitchen-sink. Notably, you'll find subsets of the most popular emacs key bindings in the bash shell, in BeMail, and in the third-party editors Pe and Eddie.

In addition to the standard hotkeys listed in Table A.01, almost every single BeOS application has a collection of hotkeys specific to itself. You'll find tables of application-specific hotkeys scattered throughout this book, and of course you can always learn any application's keyboard shortcuts by studying the triggers on its pulldown menus and by reading its own documentation.

### Table A.01  Standard Application Shortcuts

| Hotkey | Action |
| --- | --- |
| Alt+Q | Quit program |
| Alt+W | Close window (quit if only one window is open) |
| Alt+O | Open an existing document |
| Alt+N | Create a new document or window |
| Alt+S | Save |
| Alt+P | Print |
| Alt+A | Select all |
| Alt+F | Find/replace |
| Alt+G | Find again |
| Alt+I | Toggle italics |
| Alt+U | Toggle underline |
| Alt+B | Toggle bold |
| Shift | Select as cursor is moved (by mouse or navigation keys) |
| Alt+Z | Undo |
| Alt+X | Cut to clipboard |
| Alt+C | Copy to clipboard |
| Alt+V | Paste from clipboard |
| Escape | Cancel current operation |
| Spacebar | Page down in uneditable documents (such as received mail and Web pages) |
| Shift+Spacebar | Page up in uneditable documents |

*The most common hotkeys available in most BeOS applications.*

 **Reset Screen Preferences**  If your screen should become impossible to read due to settings beyond the monitor or video card's capabilities, or if the Screen preferences panel's controls are offscreen for some reason, pressing Ctrl+Alt+Shift+F12 will reset screen parameters to 640×480, 8-bit mode, 60 Hz refresh, returning things to a sane state.

## Keyboard Shortcuts in the Tracker

As described in Chapter 5, *Files and the Tracker*, there are many keyboard shortcuts that can be used for general file management. These are listed in Table A.02.

### *Table A.02  Keyboard Shortcuts in the Tracker*

| Hotkey | Function |
| --- | --- |
| Alt+A | Select All |
| Alt+E | Edit Name (rename a file or folder) |
| Alt+F | Start a system query |
| Alt+D | Duplicate the selected file or folder |
| Alt+I | Get Info on the selected item |
| Alt+N | Create a new folder |
| Alt+O | Open the selected item |
| Alt+T (or Delete) | Move the selected item to the Trash |
| Alt+W | Close this window |
| Alt+Y | Shrink the Tracker view to current icon layout |
| Alt+Up Arrow | Open the parent folder |
| Alt+Down Arrow | Launch the selected item |
| Alt+Right Ctrl+Up Arrow | Close the original window and open the parent |
| Alt+Right Ctrl+Down Arrow | Close the parent window and open the child |
| Menu Key+W, I | Icon View |
| Menu Key+W, M | Mini-icon View |
| Menu Key+W, L | List View |
| Right Ctrl+double-click file or folder | Close the Tracker window and launch a file or folder |
| Any letter | Jump to the first file beginning with that letter, or come as close as possible |
| Tab | Jump to the next file or folder in the current sort order |
| Esc | Stop renaming an item and restore name; pressing Esc twice deselects a selected block of files or folders |
| Shift+click | Select multiple nonadjacent items |
| Shift+drag | Select multiple adjacent items (note that you can select multiple blocks of nonadjacent items this way as well) |

 ***Another Way to Kill the Tracker*** As described at several points in this book, the Vulcan Death Grip can be used to kill practically any running application; hold down Ctrl+Alt+Shift (Mac users: Shift+Option+Command) on the right side of your keyboard and click the application's entry in the Deskbar. This works with the Tracker as well, but there's a second way to kill the Tracker: Ctrl+Alt+Shift+Z. Since the standard Vulcan Death Grip works in the Tracker as well, the only good reason to use this method is if for some reason the Deskbar isn't running or isn't responding. Note that a Tracker window must be frontmost (have focus) in order for this to work.

## Navigation

There are a number of ways to navigate around in BeOS via the keyboard.

**Confirmation Panels** If you close a document with Alt+W and the application presents a confirmation panel asking whether you want to Save, Close, or Cancel, you might be expecting to be able to choose one of these via keyboard as well … and you can, though you can't use the arrow keys, as you can in some operating systems. The trick is in the Tab key. Just as Tab lets you move between text fields, it will let you move between buttons such as these.

**Figure A.01**

*Simple button panels like these can be navigated with Tab or Shift+Tab. Enter presses the default button, while Spacebar presses the underlined button.*

The interesting thing to note about a panel such as this one is that there are actually two buttons that can be activated from the keyboard. The "default" button will always have a large ridge around it (see the Save button in Figure A.01); you can choose this button by pressing Enter on the keyboard. As you press the Tab key repeatedly, a blue underline appears beneath each button in turn. When you press the Spacebar, the currently underlined button will be pressed. To wheel through the buttons in reverse order, use Shift+Tab (just as you would use Shift+Tab in the Twitcher to reverse the direction of the "wheel").

**Dialog Boxes** In some cases, panels include buttons, checkboxes, picklists, and text fields all in the same dialog box. The same navigation principles described above still apply, but the Spacebar does even more work.

The E-mail preferences panel is a perfect example of a dialog like this. Tapping the Spacebar when one of the Mail Schedule picklists is highlighted will open that picklist. You can then use the arrow keys to choose an item from the list, then press the Spacebar again to choose that item. Tab your way down to a checkbox, and the Spacebar will function as a toggle switch, selecting and then deselecting that option.

**Figure A.02**

*The E-Mail Preferences panel, like all dialogs, is 100% keyboardable. A blue outline signifies the currently selected item, and tapping the Spacebar activates that item.*

Additionally, many dialog boxes break their controls

into groups. As you can see in Figure A.02, the E-Mail preferences panel is divided into four groups of controls. In a situation like this, Alt+Tab will move you around to the first control in each group, making it easy to navigate quickly in complex dialogs.

**Applications with Text Fields**   Some applications and dialogs include text fields wherein Tab is a perfectly legal character so it can't be used for navigation. For example, there's nothing stopping you from entering a Tab character into the body of a BeMail message. But if you want to move back up to the message's Subject line, Tab no longer does the trick. In a case like this, just use Alt+Tab instead of Tab alone (or Shift+Alt+Tab if you want to move backward through the fields).

**Switching Workspaces**   As described in Chapter 2, *Meet the System*, you can move among the first nine workspaces by holding down the Alt key and tapping a function key (F1 through F9). In addition, you can return to the last-used workspace with Alt+~ (that's a tilde character, which is positioned just to the left of the 1 key on most keyboards).

**Switching Applications**   As described in Chapter 2, the Twitcher functions somewhat like a keyboardable Deskbar, and lets you switch between running applications by using the keyboard alone (and in fact cannot be used with the mouse at all).

There are a couple of ways to operate the Twitcher. Tap Ctrl+Tab repeatedly to cycle through windows in the *current* workspace that are not minimzed. Press and hold Ctrl+Tab to invoke the Twitcher (Figure 2.01). Pressing Tab repeatedly while the Twitcher is open cycles through all running applications, regardless of workspace. Shift+Ctrl+Tab reverses the order of cycling. Releasing Ctrl+Tab when an application is selected brings that application to the front. When an application has more than one window open, the Up and Down Arrow keys navigate between them from within the Twitcher. To cycle through an application's open windows without bringing up the Twitcher, use Ctrl+Win+Tab (Mac users: Command+Option+Tab).

**File Panels**   When in any Open/Save file panel, you can easily jump to the root of the filesystem, that is, the desktop, by tapping Alt+D.

# Appendix B:
# Date/Time Formats
# Recognized by the Query Engine

As described in Chapter 7, *Working with Queries*, BeOS queries are capable of recognizing a very wide array of date and time formats.

Anything in the following list can be modified by attaching the modifiers before or after.

```
yesterday
last Friday
last June
day before yesterday
9 days before today
June 7, 1998
06/07/98
7 June '98
06071998
6-7-98
7 Jun. 1998
Mon, June 10th, 10:00:03 am 1993 GMT
Mon, June 10th, 1993 10:00:03 am GMT
Monday, June 10th, 1993 10:00 am GMT
Monday, June 5, 10:00 am 1993 GMT
Monday, 10 June ,1993 10:00 am GMT
Mon, 10 June, 1993 10:00:03 am GMT
Mon, 10 June, 10:00:03 am 1993 GMT
Monday, 10 June, 10:00 am 1993 GMT
10.10.93 10:20:00 am GMT
10.10.93 10:20 am GMT
Thursday 4/21/94 9:30 pm
Monday 4-21 4:30 pm
Tuesday 4-21 4 pm
Wednesday 4/21
Thursday, November 6, 1997
Sunday, 10:30 am
Sunday, 10 am
10:30 am, Sunday
10 am, Sunday
```

```
Fri Nov 19 16:14:55 1982
Fri Nov 19 16:14 1982
Fri 19 Nov 16:14:55 1982
Fri 19 Nov 16:14 1982
Friday, 19-Nov-82 16:59:30 EST
Friday, 19-Nov-82 16:59 EST
02 FEB 82 07:59:01 PST
02 FEB 82 07:59 PST
1994-01-27
1994-01-27 13:45:34
01-27-1994 1pm
01-27-1994 1pm
8/29/97 12:15:50 PM
3pm 11/17/97
2:45 11/27/97
2:45:30 11/27/97
Friday, 10:30:32 am GMT-0400
Friday, 10:30 am GMT-0400
10:30:32 am GMT-1
10:30 am GMT-1
Friday Jul 9
Friday 9 Jul
June 10, 1994 10 pm GMT
June 10, 10 pm
June 10 10:30 pm
10 June, 1994 11 am GMT+1
10 June 10:30 pm
June 10
10 June
3pm June 10th
1:30 June 10th
1 day 1 mon 1 year 4 hrs 2 mins 1 sec
next thursday 10:00:20
last monday 12:20 pm
next tuesday 4 pm
10:50 pm next thursday
4 pm next tuesday
3 pm
```

# Appendix C:
# Programming BeOS

BeOS is unlike the MacOS and Windows in the sense that it blurs the line between developers and end-users to a small degree by including a full and unlimited IDE (integrated development environment) with every copy of the OS. This means two things: First, if a downloaded application comes with its own source code, you're free to study it, make changes to it, recompile it, and share your improvements with the rest of the world. Second, any time you feel you're ready for and/or interested in programming BeOS applications, you have all the tools you need at your disposal; no need to spend extra money getting yourself equipped (you may, however, want to spring for additional "power" tools available through BeWare or BeDepot).

## Compiling Source Code

As mentioned elsewhere in this book, some BeOS applications are delivered not as ready-to-run binaries, but as raw source code. In some cases, you'll get both the source code and the compiled binary in the same package, and you can safely delete the source code if it doesn't interest you. At times, however, you may download applications that are delivered *only* as source code, and will need to compile them yourself.

There are two basic ways in which a project can be set up and managed prior to being compiled. The process of compiling source code will be different depending on which method the original developer used to set up the project.

**Working with .proj Files**  In one scenario, the developer uses the IDE that comes with the system. The IDE lets the developer create a sort of "umbrella file" defining all of the pieces that need to go into the final product. If you find a .proj file in one of the subdirectories of the downloaded archive, the project has been built in (and you'll need to compile it in) the IDE. The .proj file basically shepherds together all of the source code, header files, shared libraries, and other miscellaneous pieces it takes to build the final application. All you need to do is double-click the .proj file for your platform and pull down Project | Make. If everything goes well, the IDE will crunch along for a little while without spitting back errors. When it's finished, you'll have a new binary file ready to be run just as you would run any other program. (Remember: Generic binaries on BeOS have an icon that looks like a tiny pyramid, made of three cubes of different colors.)

If you double-click a .proj file and a window pops up reporting a series of errors, one of three things has happened:

- The program was written for another platform (that is, you may see errors when opening up a PowerPC BeOS project on an x86 BeOS machine; this is due to the different libraries—or different paths to the same libraries—needed for each architecture).

- The developer has used some custom paths in the files that aren't mirrored on your machine. Some developers even release source code with the names of their own disk volumes coded into the source files. Naturally, this should be considered an error on the developer's part. You may be able to fix the source files with a global search-and-replace operation in the IDE. Better yet, write the developer and tell them what they've done.

- The developer has not included all the components necessary to build a complete project on your machine (not without doing further programming or downloading extra libraries, anyway).

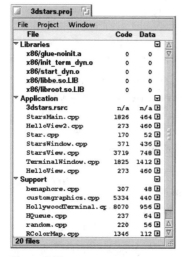

**Figure C.01**

*You don't have to be a programmer to compile downloaded source code, assuming that all your ducks are in a row. The BeIDE main window displays all of the component files that constitute a program prior to compilation.*

Thus, if the error window appears, you may as well close the IDE now, because the project isn't going to compile on your machine without further modification. If you have programming skills, you may be able to dig around in the source files and fix any lines that are causing errors, but there are simply too many variables and complexities for us to go into that here. If the project launched without reporting any errors, you'll be looking at a window something like the one shown in Figure C.01.

All you have to do now is to pull down Project | Make. The IDE's status bar (in the lower part of window) will begin to report the number of files it's processed. Depending on the size of the application and the speed of your machine, the process could take anywhere between a few seconds and several minutes. When it's finished, the status bar should report "18 files," or some such. Check again in the project directory, and you should find a binary file that didn't exist before, which you can launch in the usual way (remember that some tools and utilities can only be run from the Terminal, so they will not respond when double-clicked in the Tracker).

 **Poking at the Code**  Feeling geeky? Try double-clicking any of the filenames in the IDE project window. This will open them up in the IDE's editor, so you can study the code for yourself. If you're in an experimental mood, try tweaking parameters in the code, saving, and recompiling the project. See how far you can get without breaking the code entirely!

**Working with Makefiles** In the second scenario, the developer opts not to use the BeIDE and manages the project instead with a "makefile." A makefile is basically a long series of configuration parameters that does the same kind of work done by the IDE, but without the GUI interface or the same level of user-friendliness. Makefiles also offer extra levels of customization to the power user/developer. Because the makefile tradition comes to BeOS from Unix, you'll most often find makefiles when working with programs that have been ported to BeOS from Unix or Linux. However, this isn't always the case; some developers simply prefer working with makefiles because of the level of control they offer and because they're easier to move back and forth from one platform to another. You'll know when you've downloaded a program distributed in this format because A) you won't find a .proj file and B) you will find a file called Makefile.

Take a look around for a file called README, readme, readme.txt, INSTALL, or something similar. You'll be looking for a section of the README labeled something like Make Instructions. If you're lucky, the instructions will be easy to follow—most are. However, sometimes instructions are left over from the package's origin on a Unix platform and don't work properly on BeOS. Keep an eye out for a BeOS-specific README or directory with the package—it may have a name like readme.beos.

The first thing to try is to simply type make into the Terminal from within the program's directory. Hopefully, the shell will return a series of success messages, and a few seconds later you'll have a shiny new binary, ready to run.

However, sometimes the project needs to be preconfigured to deal with the specifics of the platform on which it will be running. It may need to know whether it's on PowerPC or Intel hardware, which version of the operating system is running, and the name and path to the compiler that will actually be crunching the code. Take a look around in the project directory for a shell script called configure. If you find one, you may be in luck. From the Terminal, run configure and let it do its thing; most of the time the configuration process runs quickly and reports no errors. When it's finished, try running make again; by rights, it should work this time.

If it still doesn't work, or if you didn't find a configuration utility, you may be able to help things along by hand-editing the Makefile itself. Open it in any text editor and look for a couple of lines up toward the top, specifying the operating system and the compiler. They'll look something like this:

```
CC=gcc
OS=BEOS
```

The CC= line refers to the compiler. If you're using BeOS for PowerPC, you'll need to change this line to read CC=mwcc. If the OS= line refers to another operating system, edit it to make sure it specifies BeOS (but use BEOS). Save the Makefile and try again.

If you still get nothing but errors after trying all of these things, chances are the package is still in development for BeOS, so it is not yet ready to "make" properly. In this case, you'll probably have no recourse other than to delete the download and wait for the author to offer a binary release. You may also want to send a nice note to the person doing the BeOS development, letting her know you're interested in her work and are looking forward to the completed version. Sometimes developers need a little assurance that people out there are actually interested in the work they're doing.

 In many cases, the compiler will spit back a lot of garbage that may seem unintelligible. This "garbage" doesn't necessarily mean anything bad is happening. You may be seeing a status report on how the process is going (which may be messy, but could in fact be reporting that everything is going fine), or you could be seeing warning messages. It's usually safe to ignore these warning messages; they could just be artifacts of the program not being fully tweaked for BeOS yet, or any of a dozen other things. As long as you don't see the message "halted" anywhere, and as long as you get a runnable application out the other end, you're fine.

## Getting Started with BeOS Programming

If you'd like to learn to create BeOS programs and applications, you'll need to learn C++, which is the object-oriented language in which all BeOS applications are written (though some low-level functions are written in straight C and even in assembly language). BeOS's clean and logical APIs make the system a great place to learn programming concepts in general. Rather than getting bogged down learning arcane methods and workarounds to cope with the baggage accumulated in other operating systems, you can get right down to business and achieve tangible results quickly.

If you already know C++, you've got a leg up, and will find BeOS easy to dive into. You'll want to start by reading the BeBook in its entirety (it's available on your hard drive at /boot/beos/documentation/BeBook, or online at **www.be.com/developers/**).

You'll also want to join the bedevtalk mailing list. If you're really, really serious about gettin' down in the dirt, you may also want to join becodetalk, which is very tightly focused on BeOS code-related issues. Details on all Be-run mailing lists can be found at **www.be.com/aboutbe/mailinglists.html**. Read and respect the mailing list posting guidelines; great efforts are made to keep discussions focused on topics that affect BeOS development exclusively. You'll also want to register as a BeOS developer, which is free at the Enthusiast level. More details on that later.

If you learn best by example, you'll find the source code to dozens of BeOS applications in the /optional directory of your BeOS installation CD. Some of the applications you'll find here are simple illustrations of common BeOS programming techniques, while others are full-featured applications. Feel free to use code you find in these sample apps in your own projects—that's what they're there for!

## Developers' Programs

Be runs a three-tiered developer-support program, offering varying levels of support and promotion for your development efforts. The first level is available for free to anyone interested in simply experimenting with BeOS software development; the other two offer more services and goodies, and are available at extra cost. Full details on the developer programs can be found at **www.be.com/developers/**.

## Further Reference

In addition to the services offered by Be at their own site, there are a number of development-oriented sites on the Web that may prove helpful.

- **BeGeek (www.begeek.com)**: General information of interest to developers including a number of essays, tutorials, and FAQs not available on Be's site.

- **B500 (www.b500.com/bepage/)**: A great collection of ready-to-use programmer's objects. Download them, modify them if necessary, and drop them into your own projects.

- **The bedevtalk Archives (www.abisoft.com/cgi-bin/bedev/)**: So much information flows through the bedevtalk mailing list, it's a good thing it's not all slipping away into the aether. Search through mailing list archives dating back to 1997.

- **The Neo-Programmers' Collective (home.beoscentral.com/npc)**. Because new programmers have to learn both C++ and the API of the operating system they're writing for at the same time, it can be problematic to take classes or read books geared toward systems other than BeOS. The NPC exists to help BeOS users interested in learning to program on BeOS find the assistance they need. NPC consists of a Web site and an accompanying mailing list.

# Appendix D:
# More Information on BeOS

If, after reading this book and studying Be's Web site, you're still hungry for more BeOS information, there are many more places to turn.

## Books

Amazingly, this book is currently the only BeOS book geared toward end-users, rather than programmers. You may, however, find books on general operating system design principles interesting for the sake of comparison. You'll find such books available at Be's online bookstore, at **www.be.com/purchase/bookstore.html**.

## Mailing List

Be, Inc. runs a mailing list just for end-users called beusertalk. Be takes care to make sure discussions stay focused and don't wander into general computing topics or flame wars. Traffic is generally moderate, and you can optionally subscribe in "digest mode," meaning you get one email per day consisting of all messages posted that day, rather than receiving them all individually. Subscribe at **www.be.com/aboutbe/mailinglists.html**.

## Usenet

If you're looking for general, freewheeling argument, discussion, and help on anything remotely related to BeOS, you'll want to check into the **comp.sys.be** Usenet hierarchy. Since Usenet is in no way controlled or monitored by Be, Inc., be wary of any information you find there. While there are many savvy BeOS users posting in these groups (and occasional posts from Be employees as well), there's also a very high proportion of rumor and idle speculation floating around, not to mention people trolling for fights, spreading poisonous innuendo, and in general peeing in the information pool. And, of course, the BeOS Usenet groups get their fair share of spam as well. If you can get past all of that, you'll also find a great deal of good information, useful tips, hints and leaks about actual upcoming products or OS features, and good camaraderie. As in the real world, it takes all types to create an online community.

There are five Usenet groups dedicated to BeOS discussion:

- `comp.sys.be.announce`
- `comp.sys.be.advocacy`
- `comp.sys.be.help`
- `comp.sys.be.programming`
- `comp.sys.be.misc`

You can download a Usenet reader for BeOS from BeWare. At this writing, the only graphical reader available was BeInformed, which is covered in detail in Chapter 11, *Network Applications*.

## Web Sites

There are tons of Web sites dedicated to exploring BeOS in all of its dimensions. Some of them are updated frequently, while others are more static. Because of the fluid nature of the Web, we can offer no guarantee that these sites will exist by the time you read this, or that newer sites won't have become available.

**Figure D.01**

*BeNews features a staff consisting of some of the world's most connected BeOS users and evangelists, and is updated throughout the day, every day.*

**News**  The following sites provide news and rumors related to BeOS on a daily basis, sometimes refreshing their top stories several times per day.

- **BeForever: `www.beforever.com`** (English)
- **BeNews: `www.benews.com`** (English)
- **BeOS Central: `www.beoscentral.com`** (English)
- **Administrator/BeOS: `www.administrator.de/beos/`** (German)
- **Be a Traveller: `web.jet.es/pong/principal.html`** (Spanish)
- **Just Be: `perso.club-internet.fr/mougel/beos/`** (French)

**Humor**  There's only one, but it's a great one. BeDope runs satirical BeOS news stories with a straight face. Half the fun can be trying to figure out whether the editor actually knows something you don't about Be's internal goings-on, or is making stuff up out of whole cloth.

- **BeDope: `www.bedope.com`**

## Primitive Volcanic Gods Choose BeOS over Windows
*by Mike Popovic, BeDope.*

On some isolated islands in the region of the world known as the Ring of Fire for its massive volcanic activity, time seems to stand still. Societies there often are at the same level of technology and culture as their great-great-grandparents. Not so for the Aletnu tribe, which has adopted advances in technology while retaining its cultural heritage.

"Yes, it is true in the past that our tribe, along with others, would throw young virgin girls into active volcanoes to appease the gods that live within them," said B'nila Varuna, Chief of the Aletnu tribe. "I am proud to say that the Aletnu tribe abandoned such outmoded thinking as far back as the 1950s."

A group of Aletnu researchers in the late 1940s begin experimenting with other objects in attempts to appease the Volcano Gods.

"It was groundbreaking work, but we were driven. More and more people resented throwing perfectly healthy nubile young women into the volcanoes, and a substitute had to be found," recalls one of the researchers. "There were of course many failures before any success. At one point, several gods seemed pleased with a mix of blenders, Playboy magazines, and cheese sandwiches, but Zamplatlu, stubborn god that he is, showed his displeasure by dousing a nearby village with a coating of toxic volcanic ash."

The breakthrough came in the 1950s after several televisions were thrown into a volcano on the verge of erupting and engulfing the town below in molten lava. Immediately, the volcanic activity subsided, indicating the gods' pleasure with the sacrifice.

Since then, a dedicated team of Aletnu tribespeople have followed technological trends and adapted them to appease their gods.

Eventually the gods would demand new sacrifices, which until recently, have mostly included personal computers running the Windows operating system.

"Windows was popular among people, and at first it seemed the gods were happy with the sacrifice," said Chief Varuna, recalling several incidents of hurling desktop and laptop systems into the fiery abyss.

However, the task of appeasing the Volcano Gods using Windows soon became a full-time hassle. It got to the point where tribal elders began collecting names of young virgins among the tribe, in case they had to return to the old ways of appeasing their vengeful gods of fire and destruction.

"In the old days, you would toss a virgin into the fire and not even have to think about a fiery rain of death from above for at least two weeks," said one tribesman. "Now, just days after tossing a Pentium 300 MHz system into a volcano, I find myself trudging back up the mountain to update the sacrifice."

Return visits on an almost daily basis involved the ritual sacrifice of additional memory, software, and peripherals.

"Sometimes you just had to give up and toss an entire new system in and hope it was configured correctly at the time," said one tribe member.

*Figure D.02*

Since the Web's only BeOS parody site is run by an actual Be employee, you never quite know whether its stories are fabricated from thin air or constitute subtle hints and leaks.

"The cost, both in terms of raw hardware and the lost time of my people, was becoming too much. Young virgin girls were beginning to seem like a small price to pay," Chief Varuna reported.

Then, the tribe discovered BeOS.

"We were impressed, and could only hope the gods would feel as we did," the Chief said.

Results were immediate and astounding. After several systems running BeOS were tossed into the volcanoes on a small test island, volcanic activity came to a standstill. BeOS was soon adopted on other islands and the result was the same.

"I tossed a BeOS system into a volcano two months ago, and I haven't had to return to offer another sacrifice since," one tribe member reported.

"I'm responsible for appeasing the gods who live in this chain of volcanoes, and now I simply sacrifice one BeOS computer, whereas it took three or four Windows machines to appease all the gods simultaneously," said another.

In a celebration last week, Chief Varuna named the entire Be team honorary tribe members.

"I would like to thank those responsible for bringing stability and order back to our way of life," Chief Varuna proclaimed. "It is a comfort to know our women will not once again be tossed to their fiery death, leaving them to their natural tasks of working in the fields, cooking our feasts, and bearing our children. Progress is wonderful!"

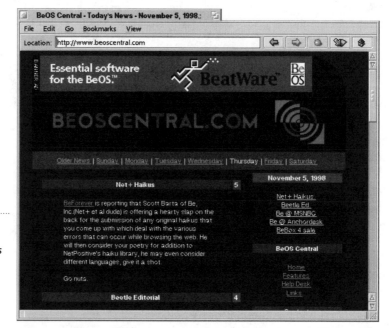

**Figure D.03**

Home of the
RC5DES effort,
BeOS Central offers
a large database
of BeOS informa-
tional resources in
addition to daily
news.

**General Information**    There are dozens of sites offering information
on hardware compatibility, BeOS gaming, and specific applications.
By following links from some of these sites, you'll find many, many more.

- **Beetle Magazine: `www.fortytwo.net/beetle/`** (editorials and
  discussions)

- **BeFunk: `www.befunk.com`** (hardware compatibility database)

- **Be Happy: `www.qnx.com/~chrish/Be/`** (includes a massive community list)

- **The BeOS Tip Server: `www.birdhouse.org/beos/tips/`**

- **The BeOS Web Ring: `www.planbe.com/beosring.html`**

- **BeTrieve: `www.betrieve.com`** (an independent alternative to BeWare)

- **ZDNet's BeHive: `www.behive.com`** (a portal to all BeOS coverage
  on ZDNet)

# Glossary

*If you don't find a term you're looking for here, you may find the PC Webopaedia an excellent additional resource (`www.pcwebopaedia.com`).*

## A

**Add-on** A module that can be added to an application or server to enhance its functionality. For example, the Tracker accepts add-ons that let users do things like zip a selected file or open a Terminal in the current directory; the filesystem accepts add-ons that let BeOS read from and/or write to filesystems from other operating systems; and the Application Server accepts add-ons that give BeOS support for video cards, and so on.

**Alpha channel** In 32-bit graphics mode, the part of a pixel reserved for transparency information. The alpha channel is encoded alongside red, green, and blue channels to specify the degree to which a graphical object is "see-through." See Chapter 13, *Graphics Applications*.

**Antialiasing** A technique used to make edges appear smoother onscreen. Without antialiasing, viewed up close, the edge of a font (for instance) appears to have black-and-white "stair steps" or "jaggies." By placing gray pixels in between the steps, antialiasing makes the edge appear smoother from a normal viewing distance.

**API** Short for application programming interface, an API is a library of objects and functions that programmers use to achieve a particular result. The term is used both in the big picture (as in "the BeOS API") and locally (as in "Here's the API for talking to sound card XYZ").

**Application signature** Also known as an app_sig, a unique string assigned to an application to distinguish it from all other applications on the system. While app_sigs are expressed in a form similar to that of MIME types (e.g. `application/x-vnd.company.application`), they are not in fact MIME types. The application signature can be used to launch an application, to maintain an internal roster of all running applications, or to send a message to another application.

**Argument** A parameter that accompanies a command, telling it exactly how to behave or what to act upon. In the `bash` command `ls J*`, for example, "J*" is the argument passed to the command `ls`.

**Asynchronous** When two or more data streams are not bound to one another in time, they are said to be "asynchronous." For example, an audio signal synchronized to match up with a video signal is said to be "isochronous," while two simultaneous but independent audio signals are asynchronous with one another.

**Attribute** A piece of data stored in the filesystem that is associated with a particular file but not a part of the file itself. For example, the *City* field of a *Person* file is an attribute, and does not live inside the file itself. Files can have as many attributes as necessary, and attributes can consist of any type of data (text, binary, integer, etc.). There is no limit to the size of an attribute. In geek speak, an attribute is "out of band" data.

## B

**bash** The Bourne Again Shell, one of several shells popular in the Unix world, and the only one that ships with BeOS. When you're using the Terminal application, you're using the bash shell—unless you've changed it, which is not recommended for the vast majority of users, since bash is easier to use than most other shells.

**BeBox** Built by Be, Inc. prior to the release of BeOS for PowerMacs, combines twin PowerPC processors (PowerPC 603 at 66 MHz or PowerPC 603e at 133 MHz), x86-standard I/O ports, keyboards, and mice, and a proprietary motherboard. The BeBox was distinguished by its dark blue case and vertical rows of green LEDs running up the front bezel indicating processor load. Only 2,000 BeBoxen are in existence. You can see images of the BeBox by searching Be's Web site on "bebox" or by visiting The Computer Museum in Boston.

**BDirectWindow** An API programmers can use to write video information directly to the heart of the video card, bypassing operating system overhead for maximum video and graphics performance. Not all BeOS video drivers support BDirectWindow, though most do.

**BFS** Short for Be Filesystem. An extremely robust and fast mechanism for managing files and folders at a low level in BeOS. The user does not experience BFS directly, only indirectly through the Tracker. BFS is covered in detail in Chapter 5, *Files and the Tracker*.

**Biff** A program that automatically checks an email server for new messages on a regular schedule. Allegedly named after the dog of the programmer who first created the Unix biff program. Biff the dog barked whenever anyone knocked at the door, just as the program alerts you whenever you have new mail. Schedules established in BeOS's Email preferences panel are the equivalent of biff for BeOS.

**Bit depth** In reference to monitor resolution, the number of bits of data assigned to each pixel. The higher the bit depth, the possible colors that can be assigned to each pixel and the greater the range of natural colors that can be displayed. Commonly expressed in bpp, or bits per pixel. 8bpp yields 256 colors from the BeOS palette; 16bpp (often called "high color"), yields about 65000 colors; and 32bpp (often called "true color"), yields about 16 million colors, plus alpha channel.

**BMessage** A parcel of information passed between threads, either within an application, between applications, or between applications and the operating system. A BMessage can store any amount of data and can consist of any datatype (text string, integer, binary, etc). BMessages are the cornerstone of the BeOS advanced messaging infrastructure, and enable you to do things like drop a color swatch from a color mixer onto the desktop or into a text editor.

**Bus** The path along which data moves on a printed circuit board such as the motherboard. The motherboard carries a main or "frontside" bus connecting CPU and memory, and separate PCI and ISA buses for the two different types of I/O cards.

# C

**Cache** A repository of information stored in a known memory location so the system or an application can retrieve it quickly, rather than going to disk if the information is needed again later. NetPositive caches the Web pages you visit so they'll appear more quickly on subsequent visits. A CPU caches instructions in case they need to be processed again later, and BeOS caches many fonts in memory so they can display quickly, without needing to be read in from disk.

**Child directory** A directory or folder that is inside of the current directory or folder; a subdirectory. Contrast with *parent directory*.

**Chipset** A collection of logic chips that live together on a motherboard or I/O card (such as on a network card). The chipset can determine any special features or properties of the board, such as its bus speed. Drivers are usually specific to a given chipset. Also called "glue logic" when referring to the chipset on a motherboard because it "glues" together the CPU, memory, and buses.

**CIFS** Short for Common Internet Filesystem, a file-access method based on the Windows SMB (Samba) protocol but extended to work over TCP/IP-based networks. CIFS differs from FTP in that it lets users actually work on files located on other computers, rather than requiring the files to be transferred to the client machine first, and then back to the remote machine later. BeOS achieves integration with Windows networks by way of CIFS.

**Class** A programming term referring to a collection of reusable objects sharing common properties. For example, a class called *vehicle* might contain objects called *car* and *truck*.

**CLI** Short for command-line interface. Any time you operate a computer by typing commands rather than using windows, icons, menus, and pointers, you are using a CLI. Contrast with *GUI*.

**Client** The object or application on the receiving end of a service provided by another object or application (a server). An email client receives mail from a mail server, a Web browser is a client receiving services provided by a Web server, and a BeOS application depends on services rendered by the app_server.

**Codec** From *co*mpressor/*de*compressor, a codec is a mathematical algorithm used to store audio, video, image, or other types of data. Codecs are built into file formats such as QuickTime, AVI, Indeo, AIFF, GIF, JPEG, and so on.

# D

**Daemon** Usually pronounced "day-mon," a software agent that "listens" in the background and snaps into action when requested. For example, a telnet daemon waits for and then handles incoming telnet requests, and the mail daemon lets you know when new messages arrive.

**Debug output** A detailed chronicle reporting on the internal state of a machine or application while in the midst of some activity. You can trap debug output from your computer by connecting its serial port to another machine with a terminal application open and listening. Debug output from applications can be seen by enabling the line export DEBUG=true in ~/config/boot/

UserSetupEnvironment. See Chapter 16, *Troubleshooting and Maintenance*, for details.

**DMA** Direct memory access, e.g. writing graphics information straight to the heart of an I/O card, bypassing much of the operating system's overhead. A good example of DMA in BeOS is the BDirectWindow API. Hard disk drivers also use DMA techniques to accelerate data transfer rates.

**Driver** A software component that mediates between the operating system and either a piece of hardware or a protocol. In BeOS, drivers take the form of add-ons that can be loaded dynamically (i.e. without rebooting the operating system). Sound card and filesystem drivers are examples of two such drivers/add-ons.

# E

**EGCS** Pronounced "eggs," the development toolchain (compiler, linker, and debugger) in use by BeOS for Intel architecture. EGCS has been developed by the free software community as a further step in the development of GCC, the GNU C Compiler. BeOS for PowerPC does not use the EGCS toolchain.

**Endian (big/little)** The order of bytes in a file or instruction, with big endian starting at th eleft an dlittle endian starting at the right. PowerPC systems can handle both big and little endians— although the Mac OS is big endian—and x86 systems use the little endian system. The term comes from *Gulliver's Travels*, where a group squabbled over whether to break eggs on the big end or the little end. From the machine's and end user's point of view, there is no advantage to either, although programmers may notice backward words in some compiler output.

**Environment variables** Operating system variables that are available outside of particular programs or applications. Established in SetupEnvironment and UserSetupEnvironment, environment variables include such things as the PATH statement and the location of the shell.

Environment variables established in .profile are available only to the current Terminal window.

**Ethernet**  A network protocol developed by Xerox, DEC, and Intel in 1976 and now the de facto local area network (LAN) standard used in homes, businesses, and institutional networks. Capable of 10 Mbps of throughput, or faster via extensions to the specification. See Chapter 8, *Networking*.

# F

**FFM**  Short for focus follows mouse: A configurable option found in the Mouse preferences panel. When this option is enabled, an end user can type directly into the window currently under the mouse pointer, even if it isn't the topmost window.

**Filesystem**  A low-level method of organizing and managing folders and files on a disk volume. Each operating system typically has its own filesystem. BeOS uses BFS, MacOS uses HFS and HFS+, Linux uses ext2fs, Windows uses FAT16, FAT32, and NTFS, and so on.

**Filetype**  A kind of file, such as a plain text document, a JPEG image, or a WAV sound file. Filetypes in BeOS are determined by MIME types using the form supertype/type; for example, text/plain, image/jpeg, or audio/wav.

# G

**GCC**  Short for the GNU C Compiler, a program that turns raw source code into runnable applications. GCC is available as free software and incorporated into BeOS R4 on the Intel side only. BeOS for PowerPC continues to use MWCC, a compiler by Metrowerks, Inc. (GCC for PowerPC targets is available as part of GeekGadgets, though it doesn't work with C++ at this writing).

**Geek Port**  A port on the back of the BeBox with no defined purpose of its own so that developers could create unique hardware devices to

work with BeOS applications. A 50-amp fuse protected the motherboard from Geek Port experiments gone haywire.

**GLUT**  The OpenGL Utility Toolkit, used by developers to write OpenGL programs. It includes a portability API so that programs can be made to run easily on other OpenGL operating systems. GLUT makes learning about and exploring OpenGL programming considerably easier.

**GNU**  Short for GNU's Not Unix: An organization, a philosophy, and a means of protecting the integrity of free software. The GNU philosophy allows developers to sell and profit from their software, but not at the expense of other developers' ability to continue development of that software or to profit from it themselves. Many of the command-line tools included with BeOS are protected by GNU's "copyleft" policy. See **www.gnu.org** for details.

**GUI**  Short for graphical user interface, the system of windows, icons, menus, and pointers (WIMP) that makes computers relatively easy to use, in contrast with the CLI (command-line interface) previously in use and still favored by some. Pioneered by Xerox/PARC, popularized by Apple, and now present in nearly every operating system.

# H

**Header**  A piece of source code that defines the API stored in the system libraries, or the classes used by a programmer for their application. BeOS includes many prefab headers developers can use to avoid having to write "basic plumbing." For example, if an application needs to be able to read and write files, it will include headers from the Storage Kit.

**Hobbit**  The processor around which the first BeBox was designed and built. It incorporated both CISC and RISC features, but AT&T preferred to call the Hobbit a RISC CPU. Though the Hobbit boasted many elegant design features, its failure to take significant hold in the market led AT&T to discontinue it, at which point Be moved to PowerPC CPUs.

**Hooks**  Points in an application that are open to other programs, enabling them to "hook onto" it and extend functionality. For example, BeOS applications have hooks that let other programs address them so that they can be automated via scripts.

**Host**  A computer that provides services to or makes itself accessible to other computers. An FTP site has a *hostname*, as does your computer when attached to a network.

# I

**Icon well**  The indentation in the FileTypes preferences panel and in each file's FileType dialog. Any BeOS icon can be placed in any icon well via drag and drop or via cut and paste.

**IDE**  This acronym has two meanings:

1. *Integrated development environment*: a graphical application developers can use to create other applications. Such an IDE includes project-management features that make it easier to tie together necessary headers, libraries, and source code files, to invoke the system's compiler, and to be notified of bugs in source code during the development process. Hardcore developers sometimes assemble projects via "makefiles," rather than using an IDE.

2. Depending on whom you talk to, either Integrated Drive Electronics or Intelligent Drive Electronics: a hard disk technology specification in which the drive controller is integrated into the device itself (though transfers are still ultimately controlled by the CPU). The preponderance of hard drives in the x86 world use IDE. Formerly bound by size and speed limitations, in recent years IDE drives have become much, much larger and faster.

**I/O**  Input/output. This can refer to any mechanism for moving data into or out of a computer, such as keyboards, serial and parallel ports, or video, sound, and network cards.

**IP address**  A unique numerical label that identifies a computer on a TCP/IP-based network. All computers attached to the Internet have IP addresses, which can be static (unchanging) or dynamic (different each time the computer connects).

**IRQ**  Short for interrupt request queue. In x86-based computers, an IRQ is a sort of channel along which data travels and is associated with a device in that computer. Some devices require their own to avoid IRQ conflicts. Other devices, notably PCI devices, are capable of sharing IRQs.

**Isochronous**  Refers to data streams that require strict adherence to timing. For example, when an audio stream must be synced to a video stream, the process must be isochronous. In contrast, asynchronous data streams can tolerate random delay intervals without impact on the application. Contrast with *asynchronous*.

# J

**Journal**  An aspect of the filesystem that keeps track of the location of data on the hard disk and ensures the filesystem's integrity in the event of a sudden crash or power failure.

# K

**Kits**  Collections of shared libraries that communicate with the system servers. Because they group classes of code along clean, logical lines, Kits make it easy for developers to build multimedia applications, for example.

# L

**LAN**  Short for Local Area Network, any network connecting multiple machines within a single organization. A LAN that operates across organizational boundaries, or that is spread across long distances, is called a WAN, for wide area networks.

**Latch** The triangular interface element often found in expandable/collapsible lists, or "outline views." Clicking a latch located next to a list entry causes the entry to expand and display its sub-elements. Clicking it again collapses the list, making it easier to see the entire list or "big picture" entries.

# M

**MIDI** Short for Musical Instrument Digital Interface, a specification that allows digital signals to trigger events (usually musical). The rendering of a MIDI signal is up to the receiving device or software, so the creator has no guarantee of how a MIDI composition will sound to the person playing it back. A subspecification called General MIDI defines a collection of sounds as being mapped to particular MIDI channels, so that this slippage can be minimized.

**MIME** Short for Multipurpose Internet Mail Extension, a specification originally used on the Internet to define how message attachments can be sent and received, and then extended to guarantee that Web browsers can correctly interpret datatypes sent by Web servers. BeOS extends the MIME system again to manage filetypes, in contrast to the Mac OS and Windows mechanisms, each of which suffer from limitations.

**Motherboard** The main system board in a computer, hosting the CPU(s) and RAM and providing sockets for all I/O cards.

**Mount point** The point in the filesystem at which a disk volume is mounted. Partitions are defined as devices under /dev/disk and its subdirectories but made accessible to the user as a directory entry in the root of the filesystem. This entry is the mount point. For example, a mounted volume named "Fred" will be accessible at the mount point /Fred.

# N

**Network interface** The point at which a computer connects to the outside world over a network. A network interface can take the form of a network interface card (NIC), a chipset built directly into the computer's motherboard, or a dial-up PPP connection working through a modem.

**NFS** Short for Network File System. Somewhere between a traditional filesystem and a network protocol, NFS lets computers running different operating systems mount each other's filesystems remotely over a TCP/IP network. NFS and CIFS are functionally similar, though NFS is much older, having been defined by Sun in the 1980s.

**NIC** Short for network interface card. An I/O card installed in a computer, connecting it to a LAN or WAN. Almost all NICs use the Ethernet communications standard and transfer data at rates of 10, 100, or 1,000 megabits per second.

# O

**Object** This term takes many forms but always refers to a discrete entity that is reusable and often shared. In object-oriented programming, for example, blocks of code can be moved around, shared between applications, and reused multiple times within the same program. At the OS level, object-oriented often refers to things like the relationship between system servers and the applications that share their services (services provided by the servers would be the objects in this scenario).

**OpenGL** A cross-platform API that can be used to create fast, sophisticated 2D and 3D graphics. Commonly used in CAD (computer-aided-design) and in games, OpenGL functions as a standard software interface to high-end geometry and rendering graphics hardware. BeOS is fully OpenGL-capable, though OpenGL hardware acceleration won't be supported until R5.

**Orthogonal**  In mathematics, this term means "mutually perpendicular." In computing, it can refer to an interface design wherein multiple tools behave with the same principles, even though they have different purposes. Becasso (Chapter 13) is an example of an application with an orthogonal interface because the artist uses the same tools in the same way whether she's painting or selecting objects.

# P

**Parent**  Usually used to refer to the parent directory, which is the directory that contains the current directory, the opposite of a subdirectory.

**Partition**  A section of a hard disk mapped out to contain something else and which acts like a separate disk. A partition can contain other partitions or volumes visible to the Tracker. Apple-mapped hard disks can contain 32 partitions, while Intel-mapped hard disks can contain four primary partitions. A primary partition, however, can contain extended partitions, which can in turn contain four logical partitions. Thus, it is possible to create 16 partitions on an Intel-mapped disk.

**Path**  The sequence of subdirectories leading to the current directory or file. If you're in your home directory and looking at a file called zoomer, then the path to zoomer is /boot/home/zoomer.

**PATH**  An environment variable telling the system where to look for commonly accessed files. A PATH statement (found in SetupEnvironment and UserSetupEnvironment) contains multiple paths separated by colons. Each directory in the PATH is searched in order when you type a command's name.

**PCI**  Short for Peripheral Component Interconnect, a bus type with a higher throughput rate than its precursor, ISA. I/O cards such as video, sound, and network cards fit into PCI slots and can share IRQs if necessary, enabling easier system configuration.

**Pervasive multithreading**  BeOS applications are multithreaded—they always have a minimum of two threads and often many more (with the

exception of non-GUI applications). Fine-grained threading of all processes provides maximum responsiveness even under heavy loads. "Pervasive" means that multithreading is present in every aspect of the operating system; even the filesystem itself is multithreaded. Pervasive multithreading is BeOS's key performance advantage and has profound implications for machines with more than one CPU. See also *thread*.

**POSIX**  In version 1003.1, POSIX is a cross-platform specification defining a core set of standard programming practices. Command-line programs written for one POSIX-compliant operating system can generally be recompiled to run on another with relative ease. In version 1003.2, POSIX is extended to define a common set of command-line tools and behaviors as well.

**PowerPC**  A computer architecture developed jointly by Apple Computer, IBM, and Motorola. PowerPC CPUs are based on the RISC (reduced instruction set computer) processor architecture and can provide excellent performance at low operating temperatures relative to comparable x86-based CPUs. The PowerPC architecture is known mostly for its implementation in the Apple Power Mac family and Mac OS clones.

**PPP**  Short for Point-to-Point Protocol, the standard protocol used for establishing dial-up Internet connections with Internet service providers (ISPs).

**Property**  In BeOS scripting, a property is an aspect of an application that can be scripted. For example, a window's title is one of its scriptable properties.

# R

**Refresh rate**  The number of cycles per second (Hz) at which the video information on a computer monitor is refreshed. The higher the refresh rate, the more rock solid the display. Higher refresh rates cause less eye and brain fatigue over long periods.

**Registrar**  An element of BeOS responsible for making sure that files have a MIME type. When they don't, the Registrar uses a set of rules to make a best guess. It almost always guesses accurately.

**Replicant** A portion of an application that can be exported and dropped into another application for further use, even after the original application has been closed or the machine restarted. Replicants are sometimes referred to as being freeze-dried applications. Named after the Replicants in Philip K. Dick's novel *Do Androids Dream of Electric Sheep?*, which later became the movie *Blade Runner* starring Harrison Ford.

**Resolution** The number of pixels squeezed into the area of the screen, measured as width×height. The resolution is a user option but is constrained by the capabilities of the monitor and the amount of memory in the video card.

# S

**Samba** A nickname for SMB, or Server Message Block, the protocol used in Microsoft networks; it also the name of a UNIX server that provides SMB networking services. BeOS can communicate with Samba networks through the CIFS client (see Chapter 8, *Networking*, for details).

**Scheduler** An element of multitasking operating systems that prioritizes threads so that background processes don't consume CPU cycles that would be better used by, for example, your Web browser. Programmers give their threads priority levels, which the scheduler recognizes while balancing those priorities against the needs of other running threads. The scheduler lets higher-priority threads run before lower-priority threads.

**Script** A series of commands stored in a text file and run as if it were a program. Unlike programs, however, the only job of scripts is to control the behavior of other programs (or command-line tools). See **www.beosbible.com** for details.

**SCSI** Pronounced "scuzzy," SCSI stands for Small Computer System Interface and is a specification for connecting devices (usually hard drives, CD-ROMs, and scanners) to a single interface, known

as a SCSI adapter. Up to seven devices can operate in a chain connected to a single adapter, which uses only a single IRQ. SCSI hard drives are traditionally much faster than IDE drives, though IDE technology has advanced significantly and is now fully capable of digital video throughput speeds. Many Macintosh computers come with a built-in SCSI port.

**Server** This term can mean many things but in BeOS it refers to a program running in the background and doling out system services to applications that need them. For example, the net_server dishes out network services and the media_server handles audio and video requests. Contrast with *client*.

**Shell** The command-line environment used to control an operating system without assistance from the GUI. Shells come in various flavors, including the bash shell, the korn shell, and tcsh. BeOS comes with the bash shell, though others can be used. The Terminal is a windowed application that hosts the running shell.

**Specifier** In BeOS scripting, the target of a command. For example, in the command get title of window 1 of NetPositive, the specifier is window 1 of NetPositive.

**SMP** Short for symmetric multiprocessing. In a computer with more than one CPU, tasks can be spread out evenly (symmetrically) over all available processors. While BeOS is not the only operating system that recognizes multiple processors, it is known for its extremely efficient SMP capabilities.

**Supertype** In a MIME type, the supertype is the larger class to which the exact MIME type belongs. All MIME types take the form supertype/type, so in the example text/plain, text is the supertype and plain is the type. There are a limited number of supertypes (application, audio, image, message, model, multipart, text, and video) and users *cannot* define new ones (though they can define new subtypes). Supertypes give applications a chance to deal with unfamiliar filetypes; for example, StyledEdit can attempt to load any kind of text/* file.

# T

**TCP/IP**  Short for Transfer Control Protocol/ Internet Protocol, it is the primary mechanism by which data is moved around on the Internet. Internet applications are built to speak TCP/IP, so that once a connection to the Internet has been established, they work over that connection automatically.

**Thread**  A portion of an application dedicated to handling a particular task, such as responding to mouse clicks, funneling audio data to the media_server, or crunching data in the background. All BeOS GUI applications have at least two threads, and more can easily be added for improved responsiveness.

**Trigger key**  A key that can be pressed (usually in combination with a modifier key) to access a menu function in an application. Trigger keys are denoted by light underscores beneath the trigger letter.

# U

**Unicode**  A 16-bit character encoding scheme agreed upon by the International Standards Organization and used to describe characters outside the standard ASCII character set. Unicode makes it possible display languages with complex characters, such as Japanese, Russian, or Hebrew.

**UTF-8**  An encoding of Unicode that uses only eight bits rather than 16, allowing the standard ASCII character set to fall under the umbrella of Unicode without wasting data space (16 bits is more data than is necessary to describe characters in the standard ASCII set). To retain ASCII compatibility, one or more 8-bit characters are used to encode each 16-bit Unicode value.

# V

**Virtual memory**  An extension of physical memory, stored on disk in a swap file. Pieces of running applications and the data they work with can be moved to virtual memory when something else needs the faster physical memory. If that application or data is needed again later, it can be retrieved more quickly from virtual memory than if it had to be read anew from a hard disk. Virtual memory becomes more important when less physical memory is available. See also *Cache*.

**Volume**  A portion of a hard disk roped off and mounted in the root of the filesystem. A physical hard disk can contain many volumes, and the Tracker sees each volume as a root object. In other operating systems, volumes are often called drives, though this term is easily confused with the physical disk drive.

# W

**Wildcards**  Symbols that can stand in for other symbols, often used in the shell to create filtered file listings. The wildcard symbol ★ stands in for one or more characters; thus, the command ls -l *.txt will list all files in the current directory ending with .txt. See Chapter 6, *The Terminal*, for details.

# X

**x86**  A generic description for the CPU architecture found in processors by Intel, Cyrix, AMD, and others. The term arises from the long lineage of Intel processors with names such as 286, 386, 486, and so on. The Pentium processor is not called "586" by Intel, though the "Pent" prefix implies the five.

# Index